Access 2003 Bible

Access 2003 Bible

Cary N. Prague, Michael R. Irwin, and Jennifer Reardon

Wiley Publishing, Inc.

Access 2003 Bible

Published by
Wiley Publishing, Inc.
111 River Street
Hoboken NJ 07030
www.wiley.com

Copyright © 2004 by Wiley Publishing, Inc., Indianapolis, Indiana

ISBN: 0-7645-3986-8

Manufactured in the United States of America

10 9 8 7 6 5 4 3

1B/RX/QZ/QT/IN

Published by Wiley Publishing, Inc., Indianapolis, Indiana
Published simultaneously in Canada

For general information on our other products and services or to obtain technical support, please contact our Customer Care Department within the U.S. at 800-762-2974, outside the U.S. at 317-572-3993 or fax 317-572-4002.

Wiley also publishes its books in a variety of electronic formats. Some content that appears in print may not be available in electronic books.

Library of Congress Control Number: 2003101923

About the Author

Cary N. Prague is an internationally best-selling author and lecturer in the database industry. He owns Database Creations, Inc., the world's largest Microsoft Access add-on company. Their products include a line of financial software; Business! for Microsoft Office, a mid-range accounting system, POSitively Business! Point of Sale software, the Inventory Barcode manager for mobile data collection, and the Check Writer and General Ledger. Database Creations also produces a line of developer tools including the appBuilder, an application generator for Microsoft Access, the EZ Access Developer Tools for building great user interfaces, appWatcher for maintaining code bases among several developers, and Surgical Strike, the only Patch Manager for Microsoft Access.

Cary also owns Database Creations Consulting, LLC., a successful consulting firm specializing in Microsoft Access and SQL Server applications. Local and national clients include many Fortune 100 companies including manufacturers, defense contractors, insurance, health-care, and software industry companies. His client list includes Microsoft, United Technologies, ABB, Smith & Wesson Firearms, Pratt and Whitney Aircraft, ProHealth, OfficeMax, Continental Airlines, and other Fortune 500 companies.

Formerly, he has held numerous management positions in corporate information systems, including Director of Managed Care Reporting for MetraHealth, Director of Corporate Finance and Software Productivity at Travelers Insurance where he was responsible for software support for 35,000 end users, and Manager of Information Systems support for Northeast Utilities.

He is one of the top best-selling authors in the computer database management market, having written over 40 books that have sold over one million copies on software including Microsoft Access, Borland (Ashton-Tate) dBASE, Paradox, R:Base, Framework, and graphics. Cary's books include 11 books in the *Access Bible* series (recently number one on the Ingram Bestselling Database Titles list and in the Amazon.com top 100), *Access 97 Secrets, dBASE for Windows Handbook, dBASE IV Programming* (winner of the Computer Press Association's Book of the Year award for Best Software Specific Book), and *Everyman's Database Primer Featuring dBASE IV.* He recently completed several books for Access 2003 including *Weekend Crash Course in Office Access 2003 Programming.* Cary recently sold a product line named eTools for Microsoft Access to MightyWords, a division of FatBrain.com and Barnes and Noble.

Cary is certified in Access as a Microsoft Certified Professional and has passed the MOUS test in Access and Word. He is a frequent speaker at seminars and conferences around the country. He is on the exclusive Microsoft Access Insider Advisory Board and makes frequent trips to Microsoft headquarters in Redmond, WA. He has been voted the best speaker by the attendees of several national conferences. Recently, he was a speaker for Microsoft sponsored conferences in New Orleans,

Hawaii, Phoenix, Chicago, Toronto, Palm Springs, Boston, and Orlando. He has also spoken at Borland's Database Conference, Digital Consulting's Database World, Microsoft's Developer Days, Computerland's Technomics Conference, COMDEX, and COMPAQ Computer's Innovate. He was a contributing editor to *Access Advisor* magazine and has written for the *Microsoft Office Developer's* journal.

He is active in local town politics serving on the South Windsor, Connecticut Board of Education, Parks and Recreation Commission, and the Board of Assessment Appeals.

Cary holds a master's degree in computer science from Rensselaer Polytechnic Institute, and an M.B.A and Bachelor of Accounting from the University of Connecticut. He is also a Certified Data Processor.

Michael R. Irwin is considered one of the leading authorities on automated database and Internet management systems today. He is a noted worldwide lecturer, a winner of national and international awards, best-selling author, and developer of client/server, Internet, Intranet, and PC-based database management systems.

Michael has extensive database knowledge, gained by working with the Metropolitan Police Department in Washington, D.C. as a developer and analyst for the Information Systems Division for over 20 years and assorted Federal Agencies of the United States Government. Since retiring in June 1992, he runs his own consulting firm, named The Irwin Group, and is principal partner in the company - IT in Asia, LLC, specializing in Internet database integration and emphasizing Client/Server and net solutions. With consulting offices in Cincinnati, Ohio, Bangkok, Thailand, and Manila, Philippines, his companies offer training and development of Internet and database applications. His company has the distinction of being one of the first Microsoft Solution's Providers (in 1992). His local, national, and international clients include many software companies, manufacturers, government agencies, and international companies.

His range of expertise includes database processing and integration between mainframe, minicomputer, and PC-based database systems, as well as B-2-B and B-2-C integration between back-end databases; he is a leading authority on PC-based databases.

He is one of the top best-selling authors in the computer database management market, having authored numerous database books, with several of them consistently on the best-sellers lists. His books, combined, have sold nearly a million copies worldwide. His most recent works include *The OOPs Primer* (Borland Press, *dBASE 5.5 for Windows Programming* (Prentice Hall), *Microsoft Access 2002 Bible, Microsoft Access 2002 Bible Gold Edition* (co-authored), and *Working with the Internet*. The *Access Bible* series have constantly been number one on the Ingram Best-selling Database Titles list and is consistently in the Amazon.com and Buy.com top 10. He has also written several books on customs and cultures of the countries of Asia (including China, Japan, Thailand, and India). Two of his books have won international acclaim. His books are published in over 24 languages worldwide. He has been a contributing editor and author to many well-known magazines and journals.

He is a frequent speaker at seminars and conferences around the world and has been voted the best speaker by the attendees of several international conferences.

Michael has developed and markets several add-on software products for the Internet and productivity related applications. Many of his productivity applications can be obtained from several of his Internet sites or on many common download sites. Many of his application and systems are distributed as freeware and careware. He has also developed and distributes several development tools and add-ins for a wide range of developer applications.

Jennifer Reardon is considered a leading developer of custom database applications. She has over ten years' experience developing client/server and PC-based applications. She has accumulated much of her application development experience working as lead developer for Database Creations. She has partnered with Cary Prague developing applications for many Fortune 500 companies.

Her most significant projects include a spare parts inventory control system for Pratt & Whitney's F22 program, an engineering specifications system for ABB-Combustion Engineering, and an emergency event tracking system for the State of Connecticut. She was also the lead developer of many of the Database Creations add-on software products including Business, Yes! I Can Run My Business, Check Writer, and the User Interface Construction Kit.

She has co-authored *Access 2003 Bible, Access 2002 Bible,* and *Access 2000 Weekend Crash Course*. She has also written chapters in other books on subjects including Data Access Pages, the Microsoft Database Engine, the VBA programming environment, creating help systems, and using Microsoft Office 2000 Developer. She has authored chapters in Microsoft Access 97 Bible and Access 97 Secrets.

Jennifer owns her own consulting firm, Advanced Software Concepts, providing custom applications to both the public and private sectors. She specializes in developing client information systems for state-managed and privately-held healthcare organizations. She has also developed a job costing and project management system for an international construction company. Her corporate experience includes seven years with The Travelers where she was an Associate Software Engineer serving on numerous mission-critical client/server software development projects using Easel, C, SQL Server, and DB2. She has contributed several chapters for books on dBase and Microsoft Access.

Jennifer holds a Bachelor of Science degree from the University of Massachusetts.

Credits

Acquisitions Editor
Greg Croy

Project Editor
Andrea C. Boucher

Technical Editor
Greg Guntle

Editorial Manager
Carol Sheehan

Vice President and Executive Group Publisher
Richard Swadley

Vice President and Executive Publisher
Bob Ipsen

Executive Editorial Director
Mary Bednarek

Project Coordinator
Regina Snyder

Graphics and Production Specialists
Beth Brooks, Amanda Carter, Jennifer Click, Joyce Haughey, Barry Offringa, Lynsey Osborn, Heather Pope

Quality Control Technicians
Carl William Pierce
Brian H. Walls

Senior Permissions Editor
Carmen Krikorian

Media Development Specialist
Angela Denny

Proofreading and Indexing
TECHBOOKS Production Services

This book is dedicated to some special people from South Windsor, Connecticut (in no particular order) who helped me in my quest of the last year to join the South Windsor Board of Education. Lincoln Streeter, Matt Streeter, Tim Moriarty, Tom Berstene, Teri Dickie-Gaignat, Carrie Momnie, Tom and Audrey Delnicki, Mayor Bill Aman, Town Manager Matt Galligan, John Mitchell, Barbara Barbour, Walter Mealy, Herb Asplund, Roy Normen, Jan Murtha, Bob Wilson, Hap Fitts, and many others in the South Windsor Republican Town Committee. Craig Zimmerman of the South Windsor Parks and Recreation Commission, Ray Favreau, Mike McCarty, and Elle Randazzo of the South Windsor Recreation Department, Joel Nadel of the Board of Assessment Appeals and Charlie Dana, Assessor, Anne Flint and Gabrielle Batz of the South Windsor Chamber of Commerce, and Dr. Joseph Wood, Superintendent of Schools. By allowing me to explore new opportunities and shamelessly promote myself, you have enriched my life and provided me with new friends and new challenges that I never knew existed.

— CNP

This book is dedicated to the people closest to me. First and foremost it is dedicated to my family—my wife, Dra. Arni Irwin, my sons Richard Rocco, Joseph Patrick, and David Joseph. While writing this book, they had to put up with my constantly telling them "Sorry, I have to do this first" in order for me to finish on deadline. It is also dedicated to my mother, Aurelia Irwin—74 years young and as strong as ever—who has continued to be my sounding board and example of strength. Finally, partner, Richard Mahonski, who passed away this year—I will truly miss him.

— MRI

This book is dedicated to my parents-in-law Tom and Arden Reardon. Way back during my college years, they provided me with the unique opportunity to be involved in the world of publishing as a part-time typesetter for their respective printing businesses. Together, we forged a method of setting type using my PC and modem and their Mergenthalers—this was 1983—much before the era of desktop publishing as we know it today. Now here I am enjoying being on the other side of the fence as an author. But, all the while that I am keyboarding my own work, I am always thinking back to the old days of how we used to have to keyboard all those crazy codes for font changes and em spaces and line spacing. Thanks for always being so supportive of me in the past 30 years that I have been part of your family.

— JR

Preface

Welcome to the *Access 2003 Bible* — your personal guide to a powerful, easy-to-use database management system. This book is in its ninth revision and has been totally re-written for Microsoft Office Access 2003 with new text, new pictures, and a completely new and improved set of example files..

This book examines Access 2003 with more examples than any other Access book ever written. We think that Microsoft Access is an excellent database manager and the best Windows database on the market today. Our goal with this book is to share what we know about Access and, in the process, to help make your work and your life easier.

This book contains everything you need in order to learn Microsoft Access to a mid-advanced level. You'll find that the book starts off with the basics and builds, chapter by chapter, on topics previously covered. In places where it is essential that you understand previously covered topics, we present the concepts again and review how to perform specific tasks before moving on. Although each chapter is an integral part of the book as a whole, each chapter can also stand on its own and has its own example files. You can read the book in any order you want, skipping from chapter to chapter and from topic to topic. (Note that this book's index is particularly thorough; you can refer to the index to find the location of a particular topic you're interested in.)

The examples in this book have been well thought out to simulate the types of tables, queries, forms, and reports most people need to create when performing common business activities. There are many notes, tips, and techniques (and even a few secrets) to help you better understand the product.

This book can easily substitute for the manuals included with Access. In fact, many users do not get manuals today, often relying on just the online help. This book will guide you through each task you might want to do in Access. We even created appendixes to be used as reference manuals for common Access specifications. This book follows a much more structured approach than the Microsoft Access manuals, going into more depth on almost every topic and showing many different types of examples.

Is This Book for You?

We wrote this book for beginning, intermediate, and even advanced users of Microsoft Access 2003. With any product, most users start at the beginning. If, however, you've already read through the Microsoft Access manuals and worked with the Northwinds sample files, you may want to start with the later parts of this book. Note, however, that starting at the beginning of a book is usually a good idea so you don't miss out on the secrets and tips in the early chapters.

We think this book covers Microsoft Access in detail better than any other book currently on the market. We hope you will find this book helpful while working with Access, and that you enjoy the innovative style of a Wiley book (formerly IDG Books, the people who make the *For Dummies* books).

Yes – If you have no database experience

If you're new to the world of database management, this book has everything you need to get started with Microsoft Access. It then offers advanced topics for reference and learning.

Yes – If you've used other database managers like dBASE or Filemaker

If you're abandoning another database (such as dBASE, Filemaker, Alpha, Paradox, FoxPro, R:Base) or even upgrading from Access 2.0, Access 95 or 97, or even Access 2000 or 2002 this book is for you. You'll have a head start because you're already familiar with database managers and how to use them. With Microsoft Access, you will be able to do all the tasks you've always performed with character-based databases — without programming or getting lost. This book will take you through each subject step by step.

Yes – If you want to learn the basics of Visual Basic Applications Edition (VBA) programming

VBA has replaced the Access Basic language. We know that an entire book is needed to properly cover VBA, but we took the time to put together many chapters that build on what you learn in the forms chapters of this book. The VBA programming chapters use the same examples you will be familiar with by the end of the book.

Conventions Used in This Book

✦ When you are instructed to press a key combination (press and hold down one key while pressing another key), the key combination is separated by a plus sign. Ctrl+Esc, for example, indicates that you must hold down the Ctrl key and press the Esc key; then release both keys.

✦ Point the mouse refers to moving the mouse so that the mouse pointer is on a specific item. Click refers to pressing the left mouse button once and releasing it. Double-click refers to pressing the left mouse button twice in rapid succession and then releasing it. Right-click refers to pressing the right mouse button once and releasing it. Drag refers to pressing and holding down the left mouse button while moving the mouse.

✦ When you are instructed to select a menu, you can use the keyboard or the mouse. To use the keyboard, press and hold down the Alt key (to activate the menu bar) and then press the underlined letter of the menu name; press Alt+E to select the Edit menu, for example. Or you can use the mouse to click on the word Edit on-screen. Then, from the menu that drops down, you can press the underlined letter of the command you want (or click on the command name) to select it.

✦ When you are instructed to select a command from a menu, you will often see the menu and command separated by an arrow symbol. Edit_Paste, for example, indicates that you need to select the Edit menu and then choose the Paste command from the menu.

✦ *Italic type* is used for new terms and for emphasis.

✦ **Bold type** is used for material you need to type directly into the computer.

✦ A `special typeface` is used for information you see on-screen — error messages, expressions, and formulas, for example.

Icons and Alerts

You'll notice special graphic symbols, or icons, used in the margins throughout this book. These icons are intended to alert you to points that are particularly important or noteworthy. The following icons are used in this book:

This icon highlights a special point of interest about the topic under discussion.

This icon points to a useful hint that may save you time or trouble.

This icon alerts you that the operation being described can cause problems if you're not careful.

This icon points to a more complete discussion in another chapter of the book.

This icon highlights information for readers who are following the examples and using the sample files included on the disk accompanying this book.

This icon calls attention to new features of Access 2003.

Sidebars

In addition to noticing the icons used throughout this book, you will also notice material placed in gray boxes. This material offers background information, an expanded discussion, or a deeper insight about the topic under discussion. Some sidebars offer nuts-and-bolts technical explanations, and others provide useful anecdotal material.

How This Book Is Organized

This book contains 39 chapters divided into four main parts and five sections. In addition, the book contains a fifth part containing four appendixes.

The main parts of the book include:

◆ Creating Desktop Applications

◆ Creating Enterprise Applications

◆ Creating Web Applications

◆ Advanced Topics

Part I: Creating Desktop Applications

Part I consists of three sections and for most Access users is all that you will ever need. The 26 chapters in this section (or about two-thirds of the book) cover everything you will need to do for your individual or workgroup applications including creating data tables, building forms and reports, and programming in VBA.

Working with Data Tables and Queries

The first section of the book contains seven chapters that will teach you all about data and conceptual designs of information.

Chapter 1 contains great conceptual material on understanding the basic elements of data, introduces you to the buzzwords of database management, teaches you how to plan a table and will show you the different data types. Chapter 2 teaches you how to create a table. You learn how to properly name fields and assign data types. You will learn how to rename fields and add fields to an already created table. Chapter 3 covers everything you need to know about entering data into forms and datasheets. You will learn how to add validation to fields, format fields and use various built in tools for making data entry easier. You will learn how to search for data and how to change and delete data values. In Chapter 4 you will learn more about creating tables and creating primary and foreign keys and relating them and using the Relationship builder tools in Access. In Chapter 5, you examine the concept of queries; then you create several queries to examine how data can be filtered, rearranged and displayed. Chapter 6 continues the query work started in the previous chapter, You will learn how to create more complex criteria to ask questions about your data. You will learn a little about SQL and WHERE clauses and how to use operators and expressions. Chapter 7 examines how to import, export, and attach external files, and how to copy Access objects to other Access databases.

Building Forms and Reports

The second section of the book contains ten of the most in-depth chapters ever written on forms and reports.

You'll begin in Chapter 8 with a visual tour of various types of forms and get a complete understanding of form controls. Chapter 9 teaches the basics of creating data-entry forms and using Wizards to simplify the creation process; using data-entry forms is also discussed. Chapter 10 examines the concepts of bound forms to table data sources and how to create unbound forms. Chapter 11 teaches how to add data validation to forms to prevent errors. It also teaches the basics for combo box controls. Chapter 12 teaches you how to professionalize the look for forms and reports through various formatting techniques and the use of color and special visual effects to create great-looking forms and reports that catch the eye and increase productivity Chapter 13 covers the basics of report creation and printing and introduces groups which allow reports to summarize data at many levels. Chapter 14 covers embedding subforms in forms and reports and how to link a parent form to a child form within a subform. Chapter 15 shows you how to create summaries and totals in reports and how to work with various group headers and footers. Chapter 16 discusses the various special reports types such as snaked column reports for directories, mail merge reports and labels. Chapter 17 explains the use of pictures, graphs, sound, video, and other OLE objects.

Automating Your Applications

The third section of the book covers VBA programming and how to use Visual Basic commands to control forms and reports and to build outstanding user interfaces.

Chapter 18 teaches the concepts of Visual Basic programming and how to edit a Visual Basic procedure. Chapter 19 covers the concept of event-driven programming and how Access uses commands to automate manual processes. Chapter 20 examines the built-in functions in Microsoft Access used for everything from manipulating strings to formatting dates. In Chapter 21 you learn about ADO and recordsets used to move data between forms and tables. This chapter is the most important chapter for programmers in understanding database management, Chapter 22 teaches you how to craft programming commands to find data. You will learn how to automate queries and link combo box selection to display data on a form. Chapter 23 teaches how to use subroutines to create reusable code modules for more efficient coding. Chapter 24 teaches you how to add error routines and proper debugging routines for programs. In Chapter 25, you learn how to create button menus known as switchboards, as well as traditional pull-down menus, and custom command bars used to build menus and toolbars. Chapter 26 teaches how to create a tab control and use continuous forms to display and switch between data views.

Part II: Creating Enterprise Applications

This fourth section of the book teaches how to build applications an entire enterprise can use.

Chapter 27 teaches the process of upsizing Access tables to SQL Server. You learn how to use the upsizing wizard and all the tasks you need to do to really make it work. While chapter 27 teaches how to upsize your data, chapter 28 teaches how to create an Access Data Project (ADP) to create a true client-server system. You learn how to upsize your programs and create ADO recordsets to work against SQL Server or the Microsoft Database Engine (MSDE). Chapter 29 delves further into the client server world teaching how to create stored procedures, triggers and pass-through queries to build true client server systems.

Part III: Creating Web Applications

The three chapters of section four cover building applications that work with data on the internet and with intranets. Chapter 30 covers building basic Data Access Pages (DAP) using many of the example you are already familiar with. Chapter 31 covers more advanced types of DAP's. Chapter 32 provides an overview of XML and schemas and also includes an overview of the new InfoPath product used to create forms with XML data.

Part IV: Advanced Access Database Topics

This part contains six chapters that present advanced topics on each of the basic tasks of Access. Chapter 33 examines how to exchange data with other Office products such as Word, Excel, Outlook and even PowerPoint. Chapter 34 covers security and protecting a database while chapter 35 shows you how to build and run help systems. Chapter 36 discuss advanced select query topics, including total, cross-tabulation, top-value, and union queries. Chapter 37 covers action queries, which change data rather than simply displaying records. Chapter 37 is also a compendium of advanced query topics that will leave you amazed at the power of Access. Chapter 38 shows you a multitude of techniques for increasing the speed of an application. Finally, Chapter 39 covers the new Access Developers Edition (ADE) and runtime.

Part V: Appendixes and Reference Material

The last part contains four appendixes. Appendix A presents a series of tables listing Access specifications, including maximum and minimum sizes of many of the controls in Access. Appendix B displays a database diagram of the many database tables used in this book so you can create your own system. Appendix C describes the CD-ROM. Appendix D is a discussion of standard naming conventions.

Guide to the Examples

The examples in *Access 2003 Bible* are specially designed to maximize your learning experience. Throughout this book you will see many examples of good business table design and implementation, form and report creation, and module coding in Visual Basic. You will see examples that use both Jet (the internal database of Microsoft Access) as well as examples that connect to SQLServer datbases. You will also see forms that work on the Web using Access's own Data Access Pages.

As every developer knows, it is important to understand what you are creating and programming from the application standpoint. This is sometimes called *the business of business*, and in this book we have chosen a simple example that any business or developer can hopefully relate to. More importantly, in this or any book you must relate to it successfully in order to learn. When developing systems you often find yourself analyzing applications that you don't have a lot of experience with. Obviously an aerospace engineer makes a better analyst when developing a system to track airplane engines, but any good developer can develop any system as long as they are willing to work with the business experts. In this book, the authors and their words will serve as the business experts.

The examples in this book will use a fictitious company named **Access Auto Auctions** or *AA Auctions* for short. AA Auctions buys and sells cars, trucks, and other vehicles. They directly sell these vehicles and also offer them for sale through auctions both at their equally fictitious showroom and on the Internet. The example database contains the necessary tables, queries, forms, reports and module code to facilitate their business needs.

Note　Within this guide we are going to use some terms that have not been thoroughly been explained yet. Feel free to skip over them and return to this guide often as you start new chapters that use these forms and reports.

Using the Example Files on Your CD

On your CD is a standard Windows setup program that will install the examples onto your hard drive. We have provided separate Microsoft Access database files for each chapter. They are arranged into subdirectories that are placed on your hard drive when you install the example files. The subdirectories are simply names Chapxx where xx is the chapter number. The database files are each named Chapxxyyyyyy.mdb where xx is the chapter number and yyyyyy is a description of the contents. For example, Chap07Start.mdb would be the database file you might open at the start of Chapter 7 and Chap07End.mdb would be how you would expect to find the database after you completed all of the exercises in the chapter . Some chapters will have no files while others may have many. Additionally, you may find other types of files with their own file extensions in each subdirectory. You will be instructed how to use each file throughout each chapter of the book.

Additionally, we have provided many fully working programs, demos, and trial versions of some of the best Microsoft Access tools for end-users and developers and provided links to these companies' websites so you can get the latest information from them.

In each chapter's database file, you will only see the objects that are needed for the chapter. We have also combined all the completed working forms and reports in two database files; **AccessAutoAuctions.mdb** contains all of the program objects (queries, forms, reports, and modules). The linked data file **AccessAutoAuctionsData.mdb** will contain only the tables used by the application. However, in the individual chapter files, you will see the program files (queries, forms, reports, and modules) in the same database file as the tables.

Tip While professional developers will always split program and data objects into two separate database files, it is acceptable during development to combine all of the objects into one database and split them when development is complete. When you are working in a program database and you are linked to your data file, you must load the data database file before you can make changes to the table design. You'll learn more about this throughout the book.

The Main Menu Switchboard

When you load the completed example file (Access Auto Auctions.mdb), you will see the main menu (known as a switchboard) shown in Figure FM-1. This switchboard contains buttons that display the main areas of the system.

Figure FM-1: The Access Auto Auctions main switchboard that allows the user to open various forms and reports.

These main areas include:

✦ **Contacts:** Buyers and Sellers of vehicles and parts that AA Auctions deal with. Rather than traditionally separate Customer and Supplier tables, the Contacts table provides a single access point to all people that AA Auctions needs to contact for any reason.

✦ **Sales:** This button displays an invoice form that lets AA Auctions enter information about the buyer (which comes from the Contacts information). It allows for an unlimited number of line items on the Invoice. Each item will be selected from information stored in the Products system.

✦ **Products:** Lists of everything that AA Auctions sells or offers for auctions These include vehicles, parts, and anything that needs to be tracked for sales or inventory purposes including descriptions, costs, selling prices, and even pictures of each vehicle or part.

✦ **Reports:** Any good application contains reports at many levels. This button actually does nothing. Normally, it would be used to display a generic report manager that displays reports while allowing specifications of the report name and parameters which will only show data between certain dates or for certain vehicle types. Though not specifically covered in this book, on the example CD of third party products, there is a generic report manager named the ez Report Manager you can use.

✦ **Company Setup:** This displays a form that contains information used by the entire system. This is used when you need global values such as your company name (Access Auto Auctions in this example) or other information that can be used by the entire application.

Understanding the Data Tables

Data is the most important part of any system and in Access (as well as every other database management system), data is arranged into logical groupings known as tables. Tables help define the structure of the data as well as hold the data itself. Tables are related to each other in order to pass data back and forth and to help assemble the chaos of data into well defined and formatted information.

The diagram in Figure FM-2 displays a representation of most of the data tables that make up the Access Auto Auctions example. As you will learn in Part 1 of this book, the lines, arrows, and symbols between the tables mean something important and communicates to the developer how the data interacts. You will learn terms like table, field, record, relationship, referential integrity, normalization, and primary and foreign keys as you begin to understand how tables work within a database.

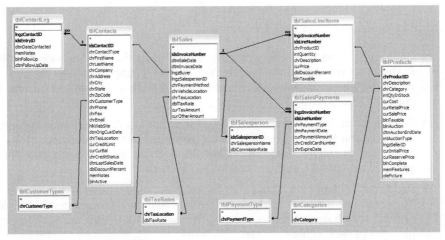

Figure FM-2: The Access Auto Auctions data relationship diagrams showing the example tables and their data fields.

Why There Are Prefixes in Front of Table Names and Data Fields in the Relationship Diagram

You might notice that each table name is prefixed with the letters *tbl*. You might also notice that each data field listed in Figure FM-2 is also prefixed with a variety of characters. These are *standard naming conventions,* prefixes assigned by developers to let other developers know the type of data these fields may contain when later used in Visual Basic programs. The characters tbl mean the object is a table. There are other prefixes for database objects such as qry (query), frm (form), rpt (report), and mod (module). Some of the common data field prefixes include chr (character), int (integer), dtm (date/time), and many others. You will see that we use standard naming conventions throughout this book.

Cross-Reference Naming conventions are more thoroughly discussed in Appendix D.

In the example database are approximately 11 tables as shown in Figure FM-2 that are used to create the Access Auto Auction applications. Many of the smaller tables are *lookup* tables whose sole purpose is to provide a list of valid selections. The larger tables hold the data used by the system itself. All of these tables include a number of data fields that are used as the definitions of the data. The lines between the tables show how tables how related by common data fields. If these terms are strange to you, don't worry. In the first few chapters, you will receive a full explanation of each of them. The tables include:

- ✦ tblSales

  - The **tblSales** table contains fields for the main part of the sale. This includes information that occurs once in the sale such as the Invoice Number, dates of the sale, the Buyer ID (which links to the tblcontacts table to retrieve information about the buyer including taxing information), the Salesperson ID (which links to the tblSalesperson table), the taxing location (which links to the tblTaxRates table), and various other financial information.

- ✦ tblSalesperson

  - The **tblSalesPerson** table contains a list of sales people that sell products for Access Auto Auctions along with their commission rates. It is linked to the Sales Invoice and is used when a Salesperson is selected in the Invoice form.

- ✦ tblTaxRates

  - The **tblTaxRates** table contains a list of taxing locations and tax rates and is used by the Sales Invoice when the buyer is selected in the form. The taxing location is retrieved from tblTaxRates and then the tax rate used by the Invoice to calculate taxes owed.

- ✦ tblSalesLineItems

  - The **tblSalesLineItems** table contains fields for the individual line items that will make up the sale. The sale may contain a variety of items. Several vehicles may be sold to a single buyer at one time. The buyer may buy parts, accessories, or services. You will see a form created later which allows for the data entry of an Invoice and an unlimited number of lineitems that will be stored in this table.

  - The data fields in the tblSalesLineItems table include the Invoice Number which is used to link the main Invoice table to the Invoice Lineitems table as well as the quantity purchased. The Product ID field (which links to the tblProducts table) is used to retrieve information about the product including the item description, price, and taxability status. A discount field allows a discount to be entered.

- The way this table will be used will violate true relational database theory. Rather than simply link from the tblSalesLineItems table to the tblProducts table by the common chrProductID field data values from the tblProducts table are copied to the tblSalesLineItems. This is often done with *time-dependent* data. If a customer bought a part today with a price of $10.00 and next week the price goes up to $15.00 as stored in the tblProducts table, it would be wrong if the Invoice then showed the price of $15.00.

Cross-Reference

You learn more about relational database theory and how to build tables in Section I of this book.

✦ tblSalesPayments

- The **tblSalesPayments** table contains fields for the individual payment lines. The invoice may be paid for by a variety of methods. The customer may make a deposit for the sale with a check, and then split the remaining amount owed with a variety of credit cards. By having unlimited payment lines in the Invoice form you can do this.

- The data fields in the tblSalesPayments table include the Invoice Number which is used to link the main Invoice table. There is a field for the payment type (which links to the tblPaymentType table) to only allow entry of valid payment types as well as the payment date, payment amount, and any check or credit card number and the credit card expiration date.

✦ tblPaymentType

- The table **tblPaymentType** is simply a lookup table with valid values for types of payments. Only valid payment types can be chosen for a payment.

✦ tblContacts

✦ The table **tblContacts** contains information about all the people and companies that Access Auto Auctions will have relationships with. This data includes customers, suppliers, buyers, and sellers. Names, physical addresses, phone and fax numbers, email addresses and Web sites and all the financial information about the contact is stored in this table. Unlike the tblSalesLineitems table information, this data is only linked from an Invoice form and with the exception of some changing financial data is never copied to any other table. This way if a customer changes their address or phone number, any Invoice which is related to the contact data, will instantly show the updated information.

✦ tblContactLog

- The **tblContactLog** table contains potentially multiple entries for each contact in the tblContacts table. This information includes the contact date, notes or items discussed, and follow up information. The contacts form will manage all of this information.

✦ tblCustomerTypes

- The **tblCustomerTypes** table simply contains a list of valid customer types that can be selected through the Contacts form. It is important in all applications that certain data be limited to valid values. In this example, each valid value will trigger certain business rules. Therefore, data entry must be limited to those values.

✦ tblProducts

- The **tblProducts** table contains information about each item that is sold or auctioned by Access Auto Auctions. This table contains information that is used by the Invoices line item section. The products table could also be used as an inventory table. However, since Access Auto Auctions will provide a wide variety of products and services, the term Products seemed to suit it better.

- The tblProducts table includes field data types of nearly every type available in Access. From a business viewpoint, there is a key field which will be user defined. The table contains a field for description and several types of costs, prices and quantity fields. There are also several fields that determine if a value is true or false including whether or not the item is being auctioned and whether it is taxable. A date field is used to display the auction end date. There are also a field for long text values (known as memo fields) for a list of features, and a field for a picture of each vehicle.

- The tblProducts table will be one of the main tables used in this book. The frmProducts form will be used to teach nearly all form development lessons in the book so you should pay particular attention to it.

✦ tblCategories

The **tblCategories** table is used to lookup a list of valid categories.

Understanding the Products Form

The **frmProducts** form shown in Figure FM-3 is the first form that will be used to teach you how to properly build forms. It is also one of the forms that you will use a lot of through the book. The Products form was developed with most of the form control types used in Microsoft Access to handle table data types such as text, currency, date, yes/no, memo, and OLE pictures. You will also learn how to use form control types such as labels and text boxes, command buttons, option group controls, check boxes, combo boxes, and toggle buttons. You will learn how to use lines and rectangles and all the special effects that go with them. There is also a tabbed dialog on the form which uses a subform control as well. There is even a popup calendar on the form. You will see several different form types and techniques to enter, search, filter, retrieve, and display data. The form includes techniques to hide controls, display them based on certain business rules and even update data in other tables. This form will be used to teach you how to work with long memo fields and pictures as well.

It is important to have a good understanding of the use of the form as well as the technical details of how to build it. The form will contain information about each product and is bound (tied to) the tblProducts table. As you enter information into the frmProducts form, it is stored in the tblProducts table. You learn more about that in Section II.

You will learn how to resize controls, how to align and space controls. You will learn how to copy and paste controls, secrets of moving controls as well as how to work with color, shading, text fonts, and even special effects. The frmProducts form can do all this and more. Later, after you master forms, you will learn how to add code behind this form and several others to make a truly powerful application. You will learn how to add code to the Invoice form to check to the quantity in stock before you can sell an item and then change the quantity in stock after you have sold it.

The top of the frmProducts form contains a control that allows you to quickly find a record. This *Quick Find* is programmed using VBA code behind a combo box selection. The bottom of the form contains a series of command buttons that will be used to demonstrate how to create new records, delete existing records, and display a custom search and custom print dialog.

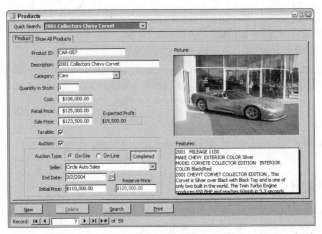

Figure FM-3: The Access Auto Auctions Products form which allows data entry for all vehicles and parts sold or auctioned.

Understanding the Product form subform

A form normally displays one screen of data. The frmProducts form contains a tab control. This lets you effectively use a form to display many screens of data. Each can use a different table or a different type of form. The frmProducts form displays a single record at a time. This is on the first tab named *Product*. The second tab named *Show All Products* displays many records at once as shown in Figure FM-4. This is actually a subform or a form (named **fsubProductsDisplayAll**) within the frmProducts form.

This form is another great example of how a form works. It displays many records at once but only selected fields. Each record contains a button to switch between the record in the second tab with the more detailed record in the first tab. There is also a button alongside each record to delete any records that are no longer needed. Each of the column headers are actually buttons with code behind them that can be clicked on to sort the records displayed by the form. One click and the data in that column is used to sort the records in ascending order. The next click into descending order.

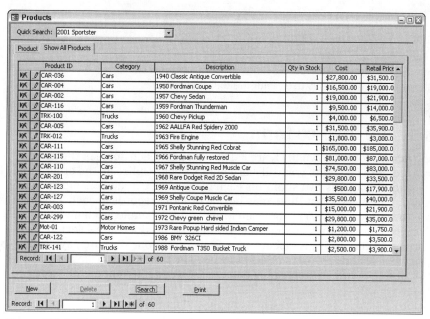

Figure FM-4: The Access Auto Auctions Products form's Show All Products tab that allows the user to display all of the products and go right to the details of any record.

Understanding the Contacts Form

The **frmContacts** form shown in Figure FM-5 is used to maintain information about the various contacts that Access Auto Auctions has relationships with. This includes the contacts name and address, whether they are a buyer, seller, or both. It includes information if the buyer or seller is a car dealer or parts store that they regularly do business with or someone who just once came to a auction, bid on a car, and won.

The Contact form like the Products form contains a tab control. This allows you to show several screens within one form. The Contacts form will be used in later chapters to teach how to display objects within a form based on certain conditions. It will show how to use a calendar to store and display data as well. Using information on the other tabs, you will also learn how to display other forms such as a Contact Log and how to synchronize information between two forms.

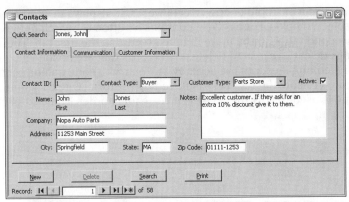

Figure FM-5: The Access Auto Auctions frmcontacts form showing a tabbed dialog and values used with the tblContacts table.

Using the Invoice form

The **frmSales** form shown in Figure FM-6 is used to teach some of the more advanced form concepts you will learn in this book. Unlike all the other forms, the Invoice form contains two subforms each of which use a relationship known as one-to-many. This means that there may be one or more records in each subform that relate (use the same key) as the main form. In this example, each invoice is used to sell one or more products to a buyer. After all the products are selected for the invoice and a total price is calculated, you can enter one or more payments to pay for the vehicle and any parts or accessories. The buyer may make a deposit with a check, and then pay the remaining balance with two different credit cards.

This form will also be used to teach simple and complex calculations. The calculation of the Amount column in the invoice line items is Qty x Price x (1-Discount%) for example. All of the amount records have to be totaled to calculate the subtotal field. Then a tax rate has to be retrieved and calculated to get the tax amount. This plus the other amount must be summed to get the total. All this is happening using fields in the Invoice Line items (**fsubSalesLineitems**) subform.

The second subform (**fsubSalesPayments**) will also be used to show how to calculate a total in one subform (the total of all payments) and then use that total with controls in other parts of the form. This is how the Amount Due control will be calculated. It will require data from the main form and both subforms to calculate its total.

These calculations will first be taught using nothing but properties of the controls themselves without any VBA code in the earlier chapters. You will learn many techniques for control referencing and calculating between forms. Later in the book, you will learn how to add more flexibility and power by using VBA code to replace the original techniques and then learn to use subroutines to really professionalize the application.

The Invoice form will also be used to teach several other important techniques including displaying values in other forms as you are taught how to display a product record by hiding a *double click* event in the product control of each lineitem. Each line item and payment can also be deleted by using a button and the code will be explained here as well. The bottom of the Invoice form will also contain buttons to create a new record a fill in any defaults as well as to delete an unneeded invoice and to display search and print dialogs.

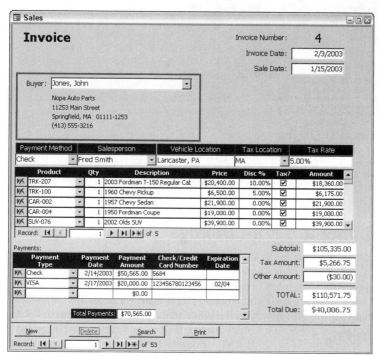

Figure FM-6: The Access Auto Auctions Sales Invoice form used to show multiple linked subforms and totals.

Understanding the Search Dialogs

Each of the main forms (Contacts, Products, Sales) can display a separate form known as a dialog (a form that is displayed on top of another). This allows you to choose from a variety of ways to search for a record. This is built using a standard Microsoft Access form. It contains an option group to allow the user to select a search type and then uses VBA code to assemble the desired records in a list box as shown in Figure FM-7. Once the user selects the desired record and presses the OK button, more VBA code is used to close the dialog box, and display the desired record in the Invoice form. There are separate search dialog forms for each of the major forms.

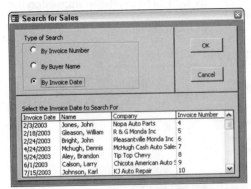

Figure FM-7: The Access Auto Auctions search dialog displaying a variety of searches for the Invoice form.

Understanding the Print Dialogs

Each of the main forms also use a separate form known as a dialog (a form that is displayed on top of another) to allow you to choose important print settings before printing the report that has been created to go with each form. In this example, you can see the Invoice's print dialog (**frmDialogSalesPrint**) as shown in Figure FM-8. This form allows you to print invoices for just the current Inviice record, for a selected date range, or even all invoices for a specific buyer. You will learn how to build this form and properly write the VBA code behind it. This form will also teach you how to filter data for reports, and to pass parameters to the Microsoft Access print routines. You will learn how to send preview a report to the screen or how to print any number of copies. You will also learn how to print multiple reports at once from this simple print dialog.

There are separate print dialogs for each of the major forms.

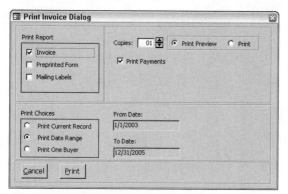

Figure FM-8: The Access Auto Auctions invoice
print dialog displaying a variety of reports for
the Invoice form.

As you go through each chapter, come back here to remember what you will learn
or where each form is. In each chapter's database file, you will only see the objects
that are needed for the chapter. The main databases, AccessAutoAuctions.mdb and
its linked data file AccessAutoAuctionsData.mdb will contain the finished example.
However, in the majority of all the chapter files, you will see the program files
(queries, forms, reports, and modules) in the same database file as the tables.

Acknowledgments

When we first saw Access in July of 1992, we were instantly sold on this new-generation database management and access tool. We have all spent the last eleven years using Access daily. In fact, we eat, breathe, live, and sleep Access! The fact that we can earn a living from our work on principally one product is a tribute to the designers of Microsoft Access. This product has changed the productivity of corporations and private citizens of the world. More people use this product to run their businesses, manage their affairs, track the most important things in their lives, and manage data in their work and play than any other product ever written. It is indeed a privilege to be part of this worldwide community. We have found readers in every county on the map and a few countries we never heard of. The global Internet age has allowed readers in emerging countries, in the Himalayan mountains, in Siberia, and even in Antarctica to contact us this year.

Now we have completely rewritten this book for Access 2003, with new examples and more in-depth coverage. We've covered every new feature we could think of for the beginning and intermediate users and especially enhanced our programming section. Over 500,000 copies of our Access Bibles have been sold for all versions of Microsoft Access; for this we thank all of our loyal readers.

Our first acknowledgment is to all the users of Access who have profited and benefited beyond everyone's wildest dreams.

There are many people who assisted us in writing this book. We'd like to recognize each of them.

To Greg Croy, whom we complain to each day. Thanks for listening, Pilgrim.

To all the people who really made this book possible. To Andy Cummings at Wiley Publishing, Inc., who pushes us beyond our limits. The word NO is not in his vocabulary! He challenges us daily with impossible tasks and deadlines (I don't care if the software doesn't work yet — write the book anyway, use your imagination — we must get this book out first). Cary thinks he wants us to get started on the Access 2006 Bible next month (July 2003), although the software won't be in beta for another two years.

Special acknowledgements go to our project and technical editors Andrea Boucher and Greg Guntle. We thank them for all their hard work on this book.

To the best literary agents in the business, Matt Wagner and Bill Gladstone, and all the folks at Waterside Productions for being our agents.

A special thank you to Bill Ramos, Tim Getsch, and the Microsoft Access Team

We would be remiss if we do not thank several people at Microsoft, especially Bill Ramos, Microsoft Access and Excel Product Manager. He was incredibly helpful in supplying us with beta builds and information not easily available. He kept us informed about last minute changes and sent us new CDs when our examples didn't work. When a few more things didn't work near the end of the beta, Tim Getsch worked with us to understand the last-minute changes. A special thank you goes to Sanjay Jacob, who supplied us with a copy of the Access Developers Edition and spent time teaching us the new features before beta release so that we could finish the last chapter of our book on time. To John Sigler, Group Product Manager, for his support through his people and his recognition of our ideas at a recent conference. While this is much appreciated, beating Cary at golf is unforgivable. Next time .....

Thanks to these wonderful people, we were able to deliver a quality book to our readers.

— Cary Prague, Michael R. Irwin, and Jennifer Reardon

To my family—Karen, David, Jeff (Tall man), and Alex (Turtle)—whom I ignore way too much. Finally, to the people of Database Creations who let me miss all of my deadlines while I worked on this book. To Kim, Larry, Diana, Julie, Phuc, Steve, Bill, Debbie, Radic, Karen, and especially Dick James for handling all my technical support calls.

— CNP

To all of our clients who let me get away and spend four months solely on re-writing this book. Although my telephone bills seem to reflect the opposite—I am so grateful to them for not insisting that I personally appear to solve their "critical" problems.

— MRI

To my clients who have been so understanding and patient with me while I have been juggling co-authoring two books simultaneously while trying to meet my many database project deadlines. Thanks for giving me "just a couple more days" when I most needed them. Thanks in advance also for permitting me to take some much-needed time off to catch my breath a little before the next big project gets underway.

— JR

Contents at a Glance

Contents

Part I: Creating Desktop Applications   299

Section II: Building Forms and Reports   299

Part I: Creating Desktop Applications   653

Section III: Automating Your Applications   653

Chatper 18: Understanding Visual Basic and the VBA Editor 655

Chapter 19: Introduction to Programming and Events 679

Chapter 20: Working with Expressions and Functions 713

Part IV: Advanced Access Database Topics   1081

Chapter 33: Exchanging Data with Office Applications 1083

Chapter 38: Increasing the Speed of an Application 1265

Chapter 39: Preparing Your Application for Distribution 1309

PART I
Creating Desktop Applications

SECTION I
Working with Data Tables and Queries

Understanding Data

In this chapter, you learn the concepts and terminology of databases and how to design the tables that will be used by your forms and reports. Finally, you build the actual tables used by the example, Access Auto Auctions, in this book.

Before you begin to use a database software package, you must understand several basic concepts. The most important concept is that the data is stored in a "black box" known as a *table,* and that by using the tools of the database system, you can retrieve, display, and report the data in any format you want.

After you understand the basic concepts and terminology, the next important lesson to learn is good database design. Without a good design, you constantly rework your tables, and you may not be able to extract the information you want from your database. Throughout this book, you learn how to use queries, forms, and reports and how to design each of these objects before you create one. The Access Auto Auctions case study provides invented examples, but the concepts are not fictitious.

This chapter is not easy to understand; some of its concepts are complex. If your goal is to get right into Access, you may want to skip to the section on building tables in this chapter. If you are fairly familiar with Access but new to designing and creating tables, you may want to read this chapter before starting to create tables.

Chapter 1 does not use the example CD. This is a chapter for you to read, view the screenshots, and learn many concepts you will use later in this book.

To jump right into using Access, skip to the section titled "Creating Database Tables" in Chapter 2.

The Database Terminology of Access

Before examining the actual table examples in this book, it's a good idea to have a firm understanding of the terminology that is used when working with databases — especially Access databases.

What is a database?

Generally, the word *database* is a computer term for a collection of information concerning a certain topic or business application. Databases help you organize this related information in a logical fashion for easy access and retrieval.

Databases aren't only for computers. There are also manual databases; we simply refer to these as *manual filing systems* or a manual database system. These filing systems usually consist of people, papers, folders, and filing cabinets — paper is the key to a manual database system. In a real manual database system, you probably have in/out baskets and some type of formal filing method. You access information manually by opening a file cabinet, taking out a file folder, and finding the correct piece of paper. You use paper forms for input, perhaps by using a typewriter. You find information by sorting the papers manually or by copying desired information from many papers to another piece of paper (or even into a computer spreadsheet). You may use a calculator or a computer spreadsheet to analyze the data further or to report it.

A computer database is nothing more than an automated version of the filing and retrieval functions of a manual paper filing system. Computer databases store information in a structured format that you define. They can store data in a variety of forms, from simple lines of text (such as name and address) to complex data structures that include pictures, sounds, or video images. Storing data in a precise, known format enables a database management system (DBMS) to turn the data into useful information through many types of output, such as queries and reports.

In an automated database management system such as Access, you use a computer to access the information or data stored in tables — entering data in the tables through data-entry forms and retrieving it by using a query. You can create and use queries to obtain a specific portion of data from the tables. Then a report outputs the data to the screen or a printer. Macros and modules allow you to automate this process and to create new menus and dialog boxes.

A relational database management system (RDBMS), such as Access, stores data in many related tables. Using queries, you can ask complex questions from one or more of these related tables, with the answers returning as forms and reports.

Using Multiple Databases

When using Access, you normally use only one database at a time. However, it can use more than one database simultaneously. As you build the example files in this book, you will ultimately separate the data (tables) from all the other objects (forms, reports, queries, and on and on) by placing the data tables in their own database and accessing the data by linking to them from another database containing all the other objects.

Databases, tables, records, fields, and values

Microsoft Access follows traditional database terminology. The terms *database*, *table*, *record*, *field*, and *value* indicate a hierarchy from largest to smallest.

Databases

In Access, a *database* is the overall container for the data and associated objects. It is more than the collection of tables, however — a database includes all objects. Database *objects* include tables, queries, forms, reports, data access pages, macros, and modules. In some computer software products, the database is the object that holds the actual data; in Access, this is called a *table*. Other products refer to the database as the collection of all tables related to the system.

Access can work with only one database at a time. Within a single Access database, however, you can have hundreds of tables, forms, queries, reports, pages, macros, and modules, all stored in a single file with the file extension .MDB (multiple database) or .ADP if you are using SQL Server Desktop Engine.

ADP file format is a special database format that is used by Access to act as a front end to access the underlying data stored in SQL Server (in MDF format). Chapter 28 covers Access Data Projects in detail.

Chapter 7 covers moving your tables to another database in detail.

Chapters 27 and 28 cover SQL server and Access projects in detail.

Tables

A table is just a container for raw information (called *data*), similar to a manila folder in a manual system that holds reports. When you enter data in Access, a table stores it in logical groupings of similar data (the tblProducts table, for example, contains data about items being sold) and the table's design organizes the information into rows and columns.

You create these tables after careful analysis of the type of information that you want to store, as discussed in the "Designing field names, types, and sizes" section later in this chapter. After you create a table, you can view the table in a spreadsheet-like form, called a *datasheet*, comprising rows (records) and columns (fields). Figure 1-1 shows a simple datasheet of the tblContacts table.

tblContacts : Table

Contact ID	Contact Type	First Name	Last Name	Company	Address	City	State	Zip Code
1	Buyer	John	Jones	Nopa Auto Part:	11253 Main Stre	Springfield	MA	01111-1253
2	Seller	Hank	Masters	Jiffy Auto Sales	623 Field Road	Springfield	MO	12345-
3	Both	Larry	Minkler	All Start Autos	971 E Main St	Detroit	MI	12345-6767
11	Both	Joe	Hammerman	Columbia Chevy	105 Main Street	Columbia	MA	12237-
12	Buyer	Cary	James	James Auto Pa	59 South Street	Portland	CT	06480-
13	Buyer	Mark	Uno	Fillion Sales An	8908 North Par	South Windsor	CT	06074-
14	Buyer	Brandon	Aley	Tip Top Chevy	1916 Erickson [	Fairbanks	MA	12333-
15	Both	Michael	Dennis	Newbury Auto	75 Main Street	Bedford	NY	10506-
16	Both	Mark	Martin	Peekskill Sales	51 Tolland Tnpk	Lake Peekskill	NY	10537-
17	Both	Karl	Johnson	KJ Auto Repair	350 Broadway S	Rye	NY	10580-
18	Both	William	Gleason	R & G Monda Ir	196 East Street	Derby	CT	06418-
19	Both	Alex	Tomaso	Tires National	46 School Stree	Oneco	CT	06373-
20	Both	Karla	Hayes	Hayes Auctions	54 E Center Str	Granby	CT	06035-
21	Seller	Teresa	Aikins	Middletown Aut	100 Northfield D	Middletown	CT	06457-
22	Both	John	Marino	Bill Thomas Sal	986 Buckinghar	Brewster	NY	10509-
23	Both	Donald	Peterson	Yantic Auto Par	8 Oak Street	Yantic	CT	06389-
24	Seller	Dennie	Parkson	ACC Car Sales	963 New Englar	Peekskill	NY	10566-
25	Buyer	Ann	Bond	A-1 Auto Sales	54 South Main	Colchester	CT	06415-
26	Seller	Joe	Crook	Main Street Use	61 North Main S	Windsor	CT	06095-
27	Both	Jeffrey	Lan	LAN Trucking	108 Thomas Ro	North Branch	NJ	08876-
28	Buyer	Matt	Smith	ABC Trucking	7 Depot Rd	Stratford	CT	06615-
29	Both	David	Smith	Fordman Coloni	123 Federal Str	Quincy	MA	12301-
30	Both	Cindy	Casey	Circle Auto Sale	123 South Stree	Newington	NH	12301-
31	Both	Karen	Bailey	Sammy Fordma	59 West Church	Westbourgh	MA	01581-
32	Both	Alvin	Schindler	Pine Plains BM	Rt 9	Pine Plains	NY	12567-
33	Both	John	Bright	Pleasantville Mc	46 Pleasantville	West Bridgewat	MA	02379-

Record: 1 of 58

Figure 1-1: A table displayed in a datasheet

Records and fields

As Figure 1-1 shows, the datasheet is divided into rows (horizontally from left to right) called *records* and columns called *fields*, with the first row (the heading on top of each column) containing the names of the fields in the database. Each row is a single record containing fields that are related to that record. In a manual system, the rows are individual forms (sheets of paper), and the fields are equivalent to the blank areas on a printed form that you fill in.

The data shown in the table has columns (vertically from top to bottom) of similar information, such as Contact ID, Contact Type, First Name, and Last Name; these columns of data items are fields. Each field is identified by a field name (the first row of the datasheet) that identifies its category of information. In addition, each field has a certain type of data (Text, Number, Date, and so on) in it and has a specified length.

The rows of data within a table are its records. Each row of information is considered a separate entity that can be accessed or sequenced as desired, and each record is made up of fields. Each record has all the fields (one each) of the database structure.

For example, looking at Figure 1-1, Row 1 has a Contact ID field with the value of "1," a Contact Type of "Buyer," a First Name of "John," and the remaining fields. Row 2 has a Contact ID field with the value of "2," a Contact Type of "Seller," a First Name of "Hank," and the other fields. Each row and record has all the fields of the database with a value in each (some of the values may be blank or empty, known as *null*). All the fields of information concerning a certain contact are contained within a specific record.

Values

At the intersection of a row (record) and a column (field) is a *value* — the actual data element. For example, John, the First Name in the first record, represents one data value. You may have a couple questions, such as:

✦ **How do you identify the first record?**

It's sitting in the first row of the datasheet and is the record with the buyer John Jones.

✦ **But what if you have more than one John Jones in your database?**

Whereas the fields of a record are known by the field name, records are usually identified by some unique characteristic or value within one or more of the fields of the record. This unique value makes each record different from all the other records. In the tblContacts table, the field that makes each record unique is the Contact ID; fields like the Contact Type, First Name, or Last Name are not unique because you may have two people named John Jones or more than one Buyer in the table.

Sometimes it takes more than one field to find a unique value. You can use Company and Contact Type, but it's possible for more than one customer to work for the same Company and all of them may be buyers or sellers. You can use the fields Company, Contact Type, and Last Name. Again, theoretically, you can have two different customers come in and both say, "Hi, my name's Jones — I work for Acme Company, and I am a seller." Creating a unique identifier (such as Contact ID) helps distinguish one record from another without having to look through all the values.

Using More Than One Table

A database, by definition, is a collection of tables. Just like a file cabinet usually contains many manila folders, a database contains one or more tables (that is, logical groupings of similar data). Most applications that are developed in Access have several related tables to present the information efficiently. An application that uses multiple tables can usually manipulate data more efficiently than it can with one large table.

Working with multiple tables

Multiple tables simplify data entry and reporting by decreasing the input of redundant data. By defining two tables for an application that uses customer information, for example, you don't need to store the customer's name and address every time the customer purchases an item.

After you've created the tables, they need to be related to each other. For example, if you have a Contacts table and a Sales table, you must relate the Contacts table to the Sales table in order to see all the sales records by the Contact. If you had only one table, you would have to repeat the Contact name and address for each sale record. Two tables let you look up information in the Contact table for each Sale by using the related fields Contact ID in Contacts and Buyer ID. This way, when a customer changes address (for example), it changes only in one record in the Contact table; when the Sales information is onscreen, the correct contact address is always visible.

Separating data into multiple tables within a database makes the system easier to maintain because all records of a given type are within the same table. By taking the time to segment data properly into multiple tables, you experience a significant reduction in design and work time. This process is known as *normalization*.

Tip   It's also a good idea to create a separate database for just your tables. By separating your design objects (queries, forms, reports, pages, macros, and modules) and the tables into two different databases, you can more easily maintain your application.

Later in this chapter, you have the opportunity to work through a case study for the Access Auto Auctions that consist of five tables.

Cross-Reference   For more information about the Access Application Splitter, see Chapter 7.

Why you should create multiple tables

The prospect of creating multiple tables always scares beginning database users. Normally, they want to create one simple table that contains information — in this case, a Customer table with all the sales performed by the customer and all the items sold or bought for each customer. So they create a single table containing all the fields, including fields for the personal information for customer (contact), Sales information (date of sale, sales person amount paid, any discount, and so on) and the products information (the quantity sold, the product information, individual prices, and so on) for each sale. Before you know it, the table has 50 fields or more. You add more fields as you think of more things that need to be captured.

As you can see, the table design begins to take on a life of its own. After you've created the single table, it becomes even more difficult to maintain. You begin to realize that you have to put in customer information for each sale a customer makes (repeating the information over and over). The same is true for the items purchased for each sale, which is usually more than one item sold for each sale (thus duplicating information again). This makes the system more inefficient and prone to data-entry mistakes. The information that is actually in the table becomes inefficiently maintained — many fields may not be appropriate for each record, and the table ends up with a lot of empty fields.

It's important to create tables that hold the minimum of information while still making the system easy to use and flexible enough to grow. To accomplish this, you need to consider making more than one table, with each table containing records with fields that are related only to the focus of that table. Then, after you create the tables, you can link them together by some means that will let you glean useful information from them. Although this sounds extremely complex, the actual implementation is relatively easy. Again, this process of creating multiple tables from a single table is known as *normalization* — or normalizing your tables.

Access Database Objects and Views

If you are new to databases (or even if you're an experienced database user), you need to understand some key Access concepts before starting to use the program. The Access database contains seven objects, which consist of the data and tools that you need to use Access:

- ✦ **Table.** Holds the actual data (uses a *datasheet* to display the raw data)

- ✦ **Query.** Lets you search, sort, and retrieve specific data

- ✦ **Form.** Lets you enter and display data in a customized format

- ✦ **Report.** Lets you display and print formatted data, including calculations and totals

- ✦ **Pages.** Lets you publish live forms to a corporate intranet

- ✦ **Macro.** Gives you easy-to-use commands to automate tasks without programming

- ✦ **Module.** Lets you create programs written in VBA (Visual Basic for Applications)

Datasheets

Datasheets are one of the many ways by which you can view data. Although not a database object, a datasheet displays a list of records from a table in a format commonly known as a *browse screen* or *table view*. A datasheet displays data as a series of rows and columns (comparable to a spreadsheet). A datasheet simply displays the information from a table in its raw form. This spreadsheet format is the default mode for displaying all fields for all records.

You can scroll through the datasheet using the directional keys on your keyboard. You can also display related records in other tables while in a datasheet. In addition, you can make changes to the displayed data.

Caution Use caution when making any changes or allowing a user to make any modifications in this format. When a datasheet record is changed, the data in the underlying table is the data actually being changed.

Queries and dynasets

You use a query to extract information from a database. A query can select and define a group of records that fulfill a certain condition. You can use queries before printing a report so that only the desired data is printed. You can also use a query with forms so that only certain records that meet the desired criteria appear onscreen. You can also use queries within procedures to change, add, or delete database records.

An example of a query is when a person at the Auto Sales office says, "Show me all customers, in alphabetical order by name, who live in Massachusetts and bought something over the past six months, and show them to me sorted by Customer name" or "Show me all customers who bought cars for a value of $35,000 or more for the past six months and show them to me sorted by customer name and then by value of the car." Instead of asking the question in actual English, the person uses a method known as *QBE*, which stands for *Query by Example*. When you enter instructions into the QBE Design window, the query translates the instructions into SQL (Structured Query Language) and retrieves the desired data. In the first example, the query first combines data from both the Sales and Contact tables, using the related field Contact ID (the common link between the tables). Then it retrieves the fields First Name, Last Name, and any others you want to see. Access then filters the records, selecting only those in which the value of Sales Date is equal to or less than six months from the current date. It then sorts the resulting records first by contact's Last and First names. Finally, the records appear onscreen in a datasheet. A similar action takes place for the second example — using Sales, Contacts, Invoice Items, and Products and the criteria being looked for is where the Description field has a car bought whose value in Price is greater than or equal to $35,000.

These selected records are known as a *dynaset* — a dynamic set of data that can change according to the raw data in the original tables.

After you run a query, the resulting dynaset can be used in a form that can be displayed onscreen in a specified format or printed on a report. In this way, user access can be limited to the data that meets the criteria in the dynaset.

Data-entry and display forms

Data-entry forms help users get information into a database table quickly, easily, and accurately. Data-entry and display forms provide a more structured view of the data than what a datasheet provides. From this structured view, database records can be viewed, added, changed, or deleted. Entering data through the data-entry forms is the most common way to get the data into the database table.

You can use data-entry forms to restrict access to certain fields within the table. You can also use these forms to check the validity of your data before you accept it into the database table.

Most users prefer to enter information into data-entry forms rather than datasheet tables; data-entry forms can be made to resemble familiar paper documents. Forms make data entry self-explanatory by guiding the user through the fields of the table being updated.

Display-only screens and forms are solely for inquiry purposes. These forms allow for the selective display of certain fields within a given table. Displaying some fields and not others means that you can limit a user's access to sensitive data while allowing inquiry into other fields.

Reports

Reports present your data in printed format. You can create several different types of reports within a database management system. For example, your report can list all records in a given table, such as a customer table. You can also create a report that lists only the customers who meet a given criterion, such as all those who live in the state of Washington. You do this by incorporating a query into your report design. The query creates a dynaset consisting of the records that contain the state code WA.

Your reports can combine multiple tables to present complex relationships among different sets of data. An example of this is printing an invoice. You access the customer table to obtain the customer's name and address (and other pertinent data) and the sales table to print the individual line-item information for the products ordered. You can then have Access calculate the totals and print them in a specific format on the form. Additionally, you can have Access output records into an *invoice report,* a table that summarizes the invoice.

Tip   When you design your database tables, keep in mind all the types of information that you want to print. Doing so ensures that the information you require in your various reports is available from within your database tables.

Cross-Reference   For descriptions of the remaining database objects (pages, macros, and modules), see the appropriate chapters.

Designing the system's objects

To create database objects, such as tables, forms, and reports, you first complete a series of tasks known as *design.* The better your design is, the better your application will be. The more you think through your design, the faster you can complete any system. Design is not some necessary evil, nor is its intent to produce voluminous amounts of documentation. The sole intent of design is to produce a clear-cut path to follow as you implement it.

The Seven-Step Design Method

Figure 1-2 is a version of the design method that is modified especially for use with Access. This is a top-down approach, starting with the Overall System Design and ending with the Menu Design, and consists of seven steps.

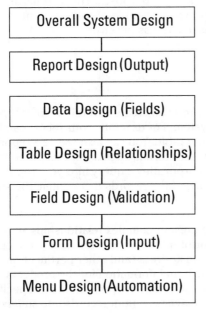

Figure 1-2: The seven-step design flowchart. This design methodology is one that has been modified specifically for use with Access databases.

These seven design steps, along with the database system illustrated by the examples in this book, teach a great deal about Access and provide a great foundation for creating database applications—including databases, tables, queries, forms, data pages, reports, macros, and simple VBA (Visual Basic for Applications) modules.

As you read through each step of the design process, *always* look at the design in terms of outputs and inputs. Although you see actual components of the system (customers, pets, visits, and visit details), remember that the focus of this chapter is how to design each step. As you watch the Access Auto Auctions system being designed, pay attention to the design process, not the actual system.

This process of looking at output/input is often referred to as performing a *needs analysis*.

Step 1: The overall design – From concept to reality

All software developers and end users face similar problems, the first of which is determining what will meet the needs of the end user (typically your client, your coworker, or yourself). It's important to understand the overall needs that the system must meet before you begin to zero in on the details.

The seven-step design method shown in Figure 1-2 helps you to create the system that you need, at a price (measured in time or dollars) that you can afford. The Access Auto Auctions database, for example, is a database system that allows the client to sell items (vehicles and parts) to customers. It can be ran individually or on the Internet, and needs to automate the following nine tasks:

✦ Entering and maintaining contact information (customers, sellers) — name, address, and financial history

✦ Entering and maintaining sales information — sales date, payment method, total amount (including tax), buyer ID, and other fields

✦ Entering and maintaining sales line items information — details of items actually purchased

✦ Viewing information from all the tables — Sales, Contacts, Sales Line Items purchased, and Payment Information

✦ Asking all types of questions about the information in the database

✦ Producing a current Contacts directory

✦ Producing a monthly invoice report

✦ Producing a Customer Sales History

✦ Producing mailing labels and mail-merge reports

Conceptual design

These nine tasks that the Access Auto Auctions needs to automate are conceptual at this point; they are the ones that you have been told about by the client. You may need to consider other tasks as you start the design process.

The design process is a repetitious procedure; as you finish each step, you need to look at all the previous steps again to make sure that nothing in the basic design has changed. For example, if you are creating a data-entry rule and decide that you need another field (that's not already in the table) to validate a field you've already defined, you have to go back and follow each previous step needed to add the field. You have to be sure to add the new field to each report in which you want to see it. You also have to make sure that the new field is on an input form that uses the table the field is in. Only then can you use this new field in your system.

Interviewing the user

Most of the information that is necessary to build the system comes from the people whom you are building the system for. This means that you need to sit down with them and learn about how the existing manual process works. To accomplish this you need to do a thorough *needs analysis* of the user or client's current system and how you anticipate automating it.

One way to accomplish this is to sit down and prepare a series of questions that can give you insight to how the client currently performs their business. For example, when considering automating an auto action system, you may consider asking these questions:

✦ What reports and forms are currently used?

✦ How are records currently kept on the sales?

✦ How are the manual records/charts filed of the contacts, their sales, or products they offer?

✦ What happens when a customer doesn't come back for a year or more?

✦ What do they do with the records after a year? Five years?

✦ How are billings processed?

As you ask these questions and others, the client will probably remember other things about their business that you should know.

A walk-through of the manual process is also necessary to get a "feel" for the business. You will probably have to go back several times to watch the manual process and how the employees work.

When you prepare to follow the remaining steps, keep the client involved — let them know what you are doing and ask for their input as to what you want to accomplish, making sure it is within the scope of their needs.

The process of prototyping

You may want to create a *prototype system* for the client to look at and play with to give you further input about what needs to be added to make the system functional for them.

In its simplest terms, a prototype is a working sample system. It comprises one or more tables that are used to demonstrate the forms and reports of the system. A prototype is made up of the visual parts of the system as opposed to the logical underlying structure of the system.

A prototype is only the visual representation of how the system will look and function after it's complete. Often you can build a prototype in a few days and give it to the client for their comments. This allows the user to see a working prototype demonstrating the data display and data access techniques through forms and reports.

Prototypes can be very stress-inducing. Essentially, they are an attempt to visualize the future and plan for change and are often undertaken without a clear vision of what the end result will be. Remember that a prototype is a working sample of the final system — it will need to be changed.

So why build one? Prototypes can help you visualize a strategy or direction, describe functionality or form, and demonstrate a proof of concept. You can use them to gauge customer reaction, explore system functionality, and test the system's concepts and directions.

Because of these reasons, prototyping offers a highly valuable tool in the overall building of your database system.

To build a prototype of the overall system, you have to quickly define the major components of your database from your specifications that you gathered during the initial meetings with the client. A prototype shouldn't become the final working system — it is only a sample system. Keeping this in mind, you shouldn't spend weeks and months on building one. Here's a good analogy to keep in mind: Think of a prototype system as the house fronts that are built for a street scene in a movie. They look great, but the moment you open the front door to the building, you find yourself in a vacant lot — it's all make-believe!

Basically, a good prototype saves time and significantly reduces the cost of the overall project.

Step 2: Report design — Placing your fields

After you've defined the Access Auto Auctions' overall systems in terms of what must be accomplished, you can begin report design.

Design work should be broken into the smallest level of detail, based on your knowledge of the current system. Start each new step by reviewing the overall design objectives. In the case of Access Auto Auctions, your objectives are to track customers (buyers and sellers), track sales, keep a record of all sales and items purchased, produce invoices, create a directory of contacts, and produce mailing labels. Figures 1-3 and 1-4 show two possible reports that the system may use.

Laying out fields in the report

When you see the reports that you will create in this section, you may wonder, "Which comes first — the chicken or the egg?" Does the report layout come first, or do you first determine the data items and text that make up the report? Actually, these items are conceived together.

It isn't important how you lay out the fields in this conception of a report. The more time you take now, however, the easier it will be when you actually create the report. Some people go so far as to place gridlines on the report so that they will know the exact location they want each field to occupy. In this example, you can just do it visually.

The reports in Figures 1-3 and 1-4 were created with two different purposes. The report in Figure 1-3 is used to display information about an individual contact (Buyer, Seller, or Both). In contrast, the report in Figure 1-4 is a typical invoice with billing and customer information. Both of these reports, although different purposes, were created based on the type of information that they will use. The actual layout was conceived simultaneous with determining what they need to have in them.

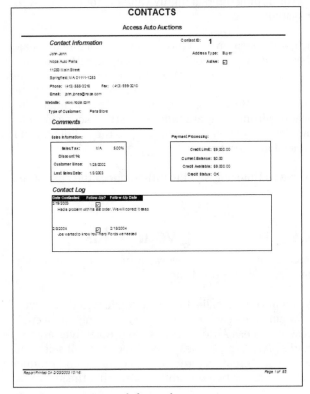

Figure 1-3: A contact information report

Tip   This process of creating any new reports should be done with pen and paper first. After you have reviewed any existing reports and the new ones you have created, you are ready to figure out what type of information you will need to put into your automated system.

Cross-Reference   If you want to learn more about the reports for the Access Auto Auctions system see Chapters 12 and 13.

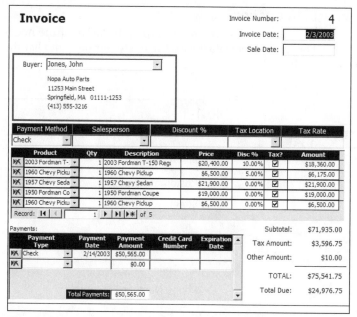

Figure 1-4: A sales invoice report sales information

Step 3: Data design — What fields do you have?

After you've decided what you want for output, it's time to think about how to organize your data into a system to make it available for the reports that you've already
defined (as well as for any ad hoc queries). The next step in the design phase is to
take an inventory of all the information or data fields that you need to create the
desired output (reports and forms). One of the best methods is to list the data items
in each report. As you do so, take careful note of items that are in more than one
report. Make sure that you keep the same name for a data item that is in more than
one report because the data item is really the same item.

Another method is to see whether you can separate the data items into some logical arrangement. Later, these data items are grouped into logical table structures
and then mapped on data-entry screens (forms) that make sense. You should enter
customer data (buyers and sellers), for example, as part of a contact table process,
not as part of a visit entry.

Tip   This process of grouping common information is known as one of the steps in the
process of *normalizing* your database. As you conceptually work with the data items
(or fields) you should group them together into logical groups (the customer-related
fields, the sales-related fields, and on and on).

Determining contact information

First, look at each report you have reviewed or attempted to make for the Access Auto Auctions system. For this system, start with the customer data and list the data items, as shown in Table 1-1.

Table 1-1
Customer-Related Data Items Found in the Reports

Contacts Report	Invoice Report
Customer Name	Customer Name
Street	Street
City	City
State	State
ZIP Code	ZIP Code
Phone Numbers	Phone Number
Type of Customer	
E-Mail Address	
Web Site Information	
Contact Log Information (4 fields)	
Discount Rate	
Customer Since	
Last Sales Date	
Sales Tax Rate	
Credit Information (4 fields)	

As you can see by comparing the type of contact (customer) information needed for each report, there are many common fields. Most of the data fields pertaining to the customer are found in both reports. Table 1-1 shows only some of the fields that are used in each report — those related to customer information. Fields appearing on both reports appear on the same lines in the table, which allows you to see more easily which items are in which reports. You can look across a row instead of looking for the same names in both reports. Because the related row and the field names are the same, it's easy to make sure that you have all the data items. Although locating items easily is not critical for this small database, it becomes very important when you have to deal with large tables.

Determining sales information

After extracting the customer data, you can move on to the sales data. In this case, you need to analyze only the Invoice report for data items that are specific to the Sales. Table 1-2 lists the fields in the report that contain information about the Sales.

Table 1-2
Sales Data Items Found in the Reports

Individual Invoice Report
Invoice Number
Sales Date
Invoice Date
Payment Method
Payment Salesperson
Discount (overall for sale)
Tax Location
Tax Rate
Product purchased (multiple lines)
Quantity purchased (multiple lines)
Description of Item purchased (multiple lines)
Price of Item (multiple lines)
Discount for each item (multiple lines)
Taxable? (multiple lines)
Payment Type (multiple lines)
Payment Date (multiple lines)
Payment Amount (multiple lines)
Credit card Number (multiple lines)
Expiration Date (multiple lines)

As you can see when you examine the type of sales information needed for the report, a couple of items (fields) are repeating; for example, the Product purchased, Number of items purchased, and Price of each item. Each invoice can have multiple items, and each of these items needs the same type of information — number ordered and price per item. Each Sales Invoice will probably have more than one item that is sold and being invoiced. Also, each invoice can have partial payments showing on it, and it is possible that this payment information will have multiple lines of payment information, so these repeating items can be put into their own grouping.

Determining line item information

You can take all the individual items that you found in the Sales information group above and extract them to their own group for the Invoice Report. Table 1-3 shows the information related to each line item.

Table 1-3 **Extracting Line Item Information**
Line Item Data Items
Product purchased
Quantity purchased
Description of item purchased
Price of item
Discount for each item
Taxable?

Looking back at the report in Figure 1-4, you can see that the above table doesn't list the calculated field amount, but you can recreate it easily in the report.

Tip   Unless a numeric field needs to be specifically stored in a table, simply recalculate it when you run the report (or form). You should avoid creating fields in your tables that can be created based on other fields — these calculation fields can be easily created and displayed in a form or report. Don't waste the storage space or your valuable time!

Combining the data

Now for the difficult part: You must determine what fields you need to create for the tables that make up the reports. When you examine the multitude of fields and calculations that make up the many documents you have, you begin to see which fields actually belong to the different tables. (You already did some preliminary work by arranging the fields into logical groups.) For now, include every field you extracted. You will need to add others later (for various reasons), although certain fields won't appear in any table.

After you have used each report to display all the data, it's time to consolidate the data by function (for example, grouped into logical groups) and then compare the data across those functions. To do this step, first you look at the contact information and combine all of its different fields to create one set of data items. Then you do the same thing for the Sales information and the Line Item information. Table 1-4 compares data items from these three groups of information.

Table 1-4 Comparing the Data Items from the Three Groups		
Contacts Data	**Invoice Data**	**Line Items Data Items**
Customer Name	Invoice Number	Product purchased
Street	Sales Date	Quantity purchased
City	Invoice Date	Description of item purchased
State	Payment Method	Price of item
ZIP Code	Payment Salesperson	Discount for each item
Phone Numbers (2 fields)	Discount (over all for this sale)	Taxable?
Type of Customer	Tax Location	
E-Mail Address	Tax Rate	
Web Site Information	Payment Type (multiple lines)	
Contact Log Information (4 fields)	Payment Date (multiple lines)	
Discount Rate	Payment Amount (multiple lines)	
Customer Since	Credit card Number (multiple lines)	
Last Sales Date	Expiration Date (multiple lines)	
Sales Tax Rate		
Credit Information (containing 4 fields)		

Consolidating and comparing data is a good way to start creating the individual table definitions for Access Auto Auctions, but you have much more to do.

As you learn more about how to perform a data design, you also learn that the information in the Contacts column must be split into two columns. Some of these items are used only once for the contact; other items can have multiple entries; for example, the Contact Log information. This is also true for the Sales column — the payment information can have multiple lines of information.

It is necessary to further break these types of information into their own columns, thus separating all related types of items into their own columns — an example of the *normalization* part of the design process. For example, one customer can have multiple contacts with the company. One customer can also have a sale in which he pays several payments to pay that sale off. Of course, we have already broken the data into three columns above: contacts, invoice of sales, and sales line items.

Keep in mind that one customer can have multiple invoices, and each invoice can have multiple line items on it. The contact (customer) group represents customer (buyer or seller) information, the invoice group contains information about individual sales, and the line items group contains information about each invoice. Notice that these three columns are all related; for example, one customer can have multiple invoices and each invoice may require multiple detail lines (line items). These relationships between tables can be different. For example, each Sales Invoice can only have one customer (thus a one-to-one relationship). In contrast, one customer can have multiple sales, forming a one-to-many relationship. A one-to-many relationship also exists between the sales invoice and the line items of the invoice.

Cross-Reference   Creating and understanding relationships is covered in Chapter 2.

At this point, you could continue to make additional columns for the things that have the potential of multiple lines, meaning contact log information and payment information. However, these three columns are the main groups of information (the three main tables) that will be needed for the Access Auto Auctions database. Other tables will be needed for the system and each of these groups, if made into a table, will require additional fields. But the fields in each column of Table 1-4 are many of the fields needed for each table used in the Access Auto Auctions database. You will make many more changes as the design is examined and enhanced.

Linking the groups/tables

Assuming that the three groupings represent the main three tables of your system, less additional fields, you will need to have some type of way to link these tables together. This means that you have to add one more identification number to each group. None of these groups/tables has a unique identifier (a way to make each record in the group unique and easy to find), which means that you will need to add at least one field to each group that can be used to link a specific record, or group of records, in one table to a specific record in another table. For example, you could create a contact ID number and put it in the Contacts table. Then add this same number into the Invoice table so that the Invoice table can look up that Contacts ID number in the Contacts table to get the information it needs about the customer. The same could be done for linking the Invoice and the Line Items table — create an invoice number that would be used in both of these tables. The linking of one group of data to another is done through special fields, known as *key* fields.

With an understanding of the need for linking one group to another, you can add some fields to each group. Table 1-5 shows two new groups and link fields created for each group/table. These link fields, known as *primary* or *foreign keys,* can be used to link these tables together.

		Table 1-5		
		System Tables with Keys		
Contacts Data	*Invoice Data*	*Line Items Data*	*Contact Log Data*	*Sales Payment Data*
Contact ID	Invoice ID	Invoice ID	Contact ID	Invoice ID
Customer Name	Contact ID	Line number	Contact Date	Payment Type
Street	Invoice Number	Product purchased	Contact Notes	Payment Date
City	Sales Date	Quantity purchased	Follow up?	Payment Amount
State	Invoice Date	Description of item purchased	Follow up date	Credit card Number
ZIP Code	Payment Method	Price of item		Expiration Date
Phone Numbers (2 fields)	Payment Salesperson	Discount for each item		
Type of Customer	Discount (over all for this sale)	Taxable?		
E-Mail Address	Tax Location			
Web Site Information	Tax Rate			
Discount Rate				
Customer Since				
Last Sales Date				
Sales Tax Rate				

With the link fields added to each table, you can now find a field in one table that can be used to link it to any table that needs to be related. For example, Table 1-5 shows a Contact ID field in both the Contacts table and the Invoice (Sales) table.

Creating specific types of links and understanding their importance is covered in more detail in Chapter 2 when discussing relationships. See Chapter 2 for a complete discussion of keys and relationships.

Step 4: Table design and relationships

You have identified the core of the three primary tables for your system, as reflected by the first three columns in Table 1-5. This is the general, or first, cut toward the final table designs. You have also created two additional tables (columns) from fields shown in Table 1-4.

Taking time to properly design your database and the tables contained within it is arguably the most important step in developing a database-oriented application. By designing your database efficiently, you maintain control of the data — eliminating costly data-entry mistakes and limiting your data entry to essential fields.

Although this book is not geared toward teaching database theory and all of its nuances, this is a good point to briefly describe the art of *database normalization*.

Database normalization

Database normalization can essentially be defined as the process of optimizing how you store and use the information in your tables. E. F. Codd, an employee of IBM, first proposed the normalization process back in 1972 (*Normalized Data Structure: A Brief Tutorial*, 1971, and *Relational Completeness of Data Base Sublanguages*, 1972). Codd proposed that a person should take each table and put it through a series of tests to "certify" whether or not it belonged to a certain *normal form*. He initially proposed three normal forms, which he named *first, second,* and *3rd normal form*.

Simply put, these "normal forms" are based on the functional dependencies of the fields within a table and how they interrelate with the other tables of the database system. Using normalization, you can ensure that the information in your tables is being utilized and stored efficiently.

Normalizing to 3rd Normal form

When possible, you should take your tables and try to normalize them to 3rd normal form. This simply means that you should separate your tables into the focused groups (the columns in Tables 1-4 and 1-5) that you've already started. After you separate the tables, you are ready to look at each table separately and determine if you can optimize them better. This is accomplished via a process known as normalizing to *Third Normal Form* (3NF). Third Normal Form requires three steps, as outlined in the following sections.

Often you perform these steps *after* you create all the fields that you need in your tables. You may want to jump back to this section after creating the actual tables for your Access Auto Auctions system.

The reasons you want to consider making your tables conform to 3NF is two-fold:

✦ **Eliminating Data Redundancy**. When typing data into tables, you may encounter two problems: First, typing the same data over and over consumes more space and resources than necessary. Second, entry of repetitive information is prone to typographical errors.

✦ **Unforeseen Scalability Issues**. The database tends to continue growing and takes on a life of its own after creation. If you fail to normalize your tables, you run the risk of "hard coding" in fields that later need to be expanded. For example, you may have two telephone fields in your system (one for home, one for business). Later, you may realize that you need to also capture cellular phone numbers and perhaps beeper numbers. Going back and changing the structure to accommodate this new information is problematic. You would need to move the telephone numbers to their own table and then have to change many forms and reports that refer to these fields in the new table. The system needs to be able to quickly adapt to these growth issues.

You can eliminate these types of problems by building your tables following the three basic steps of normalizing to Third Normal Form.

First normal form (1NF)

Converting a table to the first normal form is relatively simple. The first rule calls for the elimination of any repeating groups of data — moving repeating data into their own tables.

3rd Normal Form and the Access Auto Auctions

The tables used in the Example database, Access Auto Auctions, does not conform to 3rd Normal form. In many real business applications, you must sometimes sacrifice blind following of a rule for simple reality. For example, 1st normal form says that you will never have the same data in more than one place. The tblProducts table contains values for an item's Price. An invoice line item stored in the tblSalesLineItems table also contains a field for an item's Price. However, prices change. When you add an item to a sales invoice, you copy the current value of price. If you stored only the product's Item Number and looked up the price when printing the invoice at a point in time and the price has changed in the tblProducts table since the moment of purchase, you wouldn't agree to it (unless it went down). This is known as *time-dependent data* and is a reason to not technically follow 1st normal form at a database level. In fact, technically because one table records the price as it changes for an item and one records the price at a moment in time, they are different. Keep this in mind when reading this section. For clarity the two fields could be named differently for the distinction. To stick with 3rd normalized form you could create another linking table that contains the price of the item at time of sale and link this to the Line Items database – complicating the example in this book. For simplicity the book simply puts the field in both tables.

For example, looking at the Contacts table in Table 1-4, you see that you have a repeating group in the table of contact information fields. These contact related fields can be moved to their own table and then you can link the two tables by using a common field between them. Table 1-5 shows the fields moved into their own table and then linking the two tables together though the common field Contact ID.

There are also the City and State name fields in the contacts table. In reality, you should move these fields to another table and link it back to the Contacts table via the ZIP code (only if, in America, you use the nine-digit ZIP code instead of the traditional five-digit one). For this exercise, we acknowledge that it should be done. For simplicity, however, we will leave it in the database, allowing people to enter the five-digit code or other country codes.

Second normal form (2NF)

Converting a table to second normal form takes a bit more thought. It relies on each table having a defined primary key.

Simply explained, a *primary key* is a field or combination of fields in a table that makes each record in the table unique. Using this uniqueness, you can quickly find any record by searching for the unique (primary) key.

Cross-Reference   For more information on primary keys, see Chapter 2.

For example, in Table 1-5 you have both an Invoice ID field and a Line Number field in the Line Items Data table. If you combine these two fields together, they make a unique primary key. (Because each Invoice can contain more than one Line Item record, you need to link the Invoice table to the Line Item Table through the Invoice ID field; however, to make each record unique in the Line Items data table, you need to have another field that has a value for each line item number for each invoice — thus the Line Number field).

Looking at the Line Items Data table, you can see that there are two fields — Product Purchased and Description of Item Purchased. Because these data elements (fields) will probably be repeated over and over from one record to another, they should be moved to their own tables. Many customers may buy the same Product, with the same product on many different invoices. You should move these fields to another table by adding a Product ID code field in the Line Items Data table and creating a new Products table with the same field name (Product ID) to link the Product names and descriptions in the new Products table to the Line Items Data table.

Third Normal Form (3NF)

The final step in the 3NF model is a bit more difficult. It relies on each table having all the fields in the table *directly* related to the primary key field.

For example, using Table 1-5 as a guide, you see that the Invoice table has several fields unrelated to the Invoice table directly—Discount, Tax Rate, Payment Method, and Tax Location. These fields should also be moved to a more appropriate table or to their own tables and linked back to the Invoice table.

Cross-Reference For the purposes of this book, several of the fields in the final example will remain in this table and the other tables, not normalizing the actual system, even to 2NF.

In summary, when creating your tables, you should consider building them to 3NF. This greatly enhances both the accuracy and performance of your system.

Step 5: Field design data-entry rules and validation

The next step is to actually create your tables and define your fields for those tables. You also need to determine data-validation rules for each field and to define some new tables to help with data validation.

Designing field names, types, and sizes

First, you must name each field. The name should be easy to remember, as well as descriptive, so that you recognize the function of the field by its name. It should be just long enough to describe the field but not so short that it becomes cryptic. Access allows up to 64 characters (including spaces) for a field name.

You must also decide what type of data each of your fields will hold. In Access, you can choose any of several data types:

- ✦ **Text.** Alphanumeric characters; up to 255 characters
- ✦ **Memo.** Alphanumeric characters; long strings up to 65,538 (64K) characters
- ✦ **Number.** Numeric values of many types and formats
- ✦ **Date/Time.** Date and time data
- ✦ **Currency.** Monetary data
- ✦ **AutoNumber.** Automatically incremented numeric counter
- ✦ **Yes/No.** Logical values, Yes/No, True/False
- ✦ **OLE object.** Pictures, graphs, sound, video, word processing, and spreadsheet files
- ✦ **Hyperlink.** A field that links to a picture, graph, sound, video, word processing and spreadsheet files

One of these data types must be assigned to each of your fields. You must also specify the length of the text fields.

Cross-Reference   The section on "Creating the tblContacts table" in Chapter 2 covers this in more detail.

Designing data-entry rules

The last major design decision concerns data validation, which becomes important when you enter data. You want to make sure that only good data (data that passes certain defined tests) gets into your system. You have to deal with several types of data validation. You can test for known individual items, stipulating that the Gender field can accept only the values Male, Female, or Unknown, for example. Or you can test for ranges, specifying that the value of Weight must be between 0 and 1,500 pounds. Finally, you can test for compound conditions, such as whether the Type of Customer field indicates a seller, buyer, or both.

Designing lookup tables

Sometimes you need to design entire tables to perform data validation or just to make it easier to create your system; these are called *lookup tables*. For example, because Access Auto Auctions needs a field to determine the customer's tax rate, you decide to use a lookup table that contains the Tax location, and tax rate. Another example is when a customer pays an invoice using some specific method — cash, credit card, money order, and on and on. Because the tax rate can change, Access looks up the current tax rate whenever an invoice is created. The tax-rate value is stored in the Invoice/Sales table to capture the tax rate for each invoice because it is time-dependent data. Another purpose of a lookup table is to limit data entry in a field to a specific value. For example, you can use a table that contains Payment Methods. This payment methods table can be used as a lookup table to make sure only those methods in the table can be entered in the invoice table.

Tip   When you create a field in a table, you can use the data type "Lookup Wizard." It is not an actual data type, but is instead a way of storing a field one way and displaying it another way.

Although you can create a field on a data-entry form that limits the entry of valid Customer Types to seller, buyer, or both, you create a table with only one field — Type of Customer — and use the Type of Customer field in the Contacts table to link to this field in the Type of Customer lookup table.

Note   You create a lookup table in exactly the same way as you create any other table, and it behaves in the same way. The only difference is in the way you use the table.

In Figure 1-5, the actual tables for the Access Auto Auctions, several lookup tables have been added to the design.

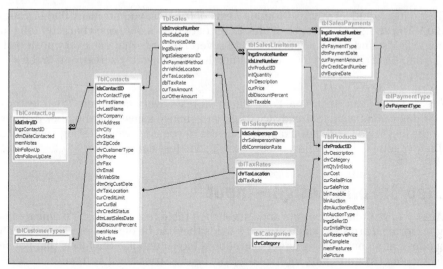

Figure 1-5: The tables of the Access Auto Auctions with several lookup tables

As Figure 1-5 shows, tblCustomerTypes, tblPaymentType, tblTaxRates, and tblCategories are all look up tables in the system.

Creating test data

After you define your data-entry rules and how the database should look, it's time to create test data. You should prepare this data scientifically (in order to test many possible conditions), and it should serve various purposes. For example, it should let you test the process of data entry: Do all the conditions that you created generate the proper acceptance or error messages? In addition, it may lead you to some conditions that you should test for that you hadn't considered. What happens, for example, when someone enters a blank into a field? How about numbers in a character field? Access automatically traps items such as bad dates or characters in Date and Numeric fields, but you must take care of the rest yourself.

The first type of test data you want to create is simply data that allows you to *populate*, or fill, the databases with meaningful data. This is the initial good data that should end up in the database and then be used to test output. Output consists mainly of your reports. The second type of test data you want to create is for testing data entry. This includes designing data with errors that display every one of your error conditions, along with good data that can test some of your acceptable conditions.

Test data should let you test routine items of the type you normally find in your data. You should also test for limits. Enter data that is only one character long for some fields, and use every field. Create several records that use every position in the database (and thereby every position in the data-entry screen and in the reports).

Create some "bad" test data. Enter data that tests every condition. Try to enter a customer number that already exists. Try to change a customer number that's not in the file. These are a few examples of what to consider when testing your system. Testing your system begins, of course, with the test data.

Step 6: Form design – Input

After you've created the data and established table relationships, it's time to design your forms. *Forms* are made up of the fields that can be entered or viewed in edit mode. If at all possible, your screens should look much like the forms that you use in a manual system. This setup makes for the user-friendliest system.

Designing data-entry screens

When you're designing forms, you need to place three types of objects onscreen:

✦ Labels and text box data-entry fields

✦ Special controls (multiple-line text boxes, option buttons, list boxes, check boxes, business graphs, and pictures)

✦ Graphical objects to visually enhance them (color, lines, rectangles, and three-dimensional effects)

When designing a form, place your fields (text boxes, check boxes, list boxes, and radio buttons) just where you want them on the form. Ideally, if the form is being developed from an existing printed form, the Access data entry form should resemble the printed form. The fields should be in the same relative place on the screen as they are in the printed counterpart.

After you have placed your fields on the form, you can check the order of the fields. In other words, when you fill in a field and tab to the next field, which field does the cursor move to next? The tab order for data entry normally moves from top to bottom and from left to right when you fill in the fields (text boxes and special controls). However, you can tell Access to use a different order for moving from one field to another. When placing the fields, be sure to leave as much space around them as is needed. A calculated field, such as a total that is used only for data display, can also be part of a data-entry form.

You can use labels to display messages, titles, or captions. Text boxes provide an area where you can type or display text or numbers that are contained in your database. Check boxes indicate a condition and are either unchecked or checked (selected). Other types of controls available with Access include list boxes, combo boxes, option buttons, toggle buttons, and option groups.

Cross-Reference

Chapters 8 through 10 cover the various types of controls available in Access. Access also provides a tool called *Microsoft Graph* that can be used to create a wide variety of graphs. Pictures can also be displayed using an OLE (Object Linking and Embedding) object stored in a database table, as you learn in Chapter 14.

In this book, you create several basic data-entry forms:

✦ Contact Log

✦ Contacts

✦ Sales

✦ Products

The Contact Log form

The Contact Log data-entry form shown in Figure 1-6 is the simplest of the data-entry forms that you create in this book. It is straightforward, simply listing the field descriptions on the left and the fields themselves on the right. The unique key field (primary key) is Entry ID. At the top of the form is the main header, a title that identifies this data-entry form by type: Contact Log.

Cross-Reference

You can create this simple form by using a Form Wizard. See Chapter 8 for details.

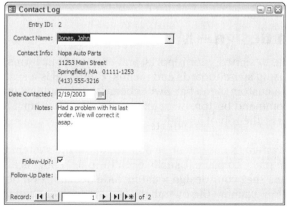

Figure 1-6: The Contact Log data-entry form.

The Contacts form

The Contacts data-entry form is a little more complex. It contains several types of controls, including a tab control, command buttons, and a check box. Figure 1-7 shows the Contacts form.

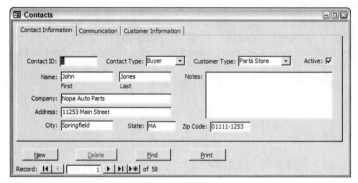

Figure 1-7: The Contacts data-entry form.

The Sales form

The next data-entry form combines data from several tables to provide general information about sales. This form contains information about customers, the sale, line items sold, any payments made on this sale; its primary purpose is to allow a user to enter this type of information into the database.

The Products form

The final form in this book is for adding the products that are sold in the system.

Step 7: Automation design — Menus

After you've created your data, designed your reports, and created your forms, it's time to tie them all together using switchboards and menus. Figure 1-8 is a switchboard form that also contains a custom menu bar. Switchboards are graphical menus, which are usually built with command buttons with text or pictures on them. Menus refer to the lists of commands at the top of a window.

Menus are the key to a good system. A user must be able to follow the system to understand how to move from place to place. Usually each form or report is also a choice on a menu, which means that your design must include decisions on how to group the commands. When you examine the overall design and look at all of your systems, you begin to see a distinct set of combinations.

Figure 1-8: A switchboard and menu for Access Auto Auctions.

You can use Access macros to create a menu on the top menu bar of the switchboard. This menu gives the user the choice of using pull-down menus or switchboard buttons.

Cross-Reference   You create this switchboard, along with the menus and a complicated dialog box, in Chapter 24.

✦   ✦   ✦

Creating and Building Tables

In this chapter, you learn how to start the process of creating a database and its tables. You will create the database container to hold your tables, forms, queries, reports, and code that you create as you learn Access. Finally, you will build the actual tables used by the example, Access Auto Auctions, in this book.

Before you begin to create the tables, you must create a container to store them in.

On the CD-ROM Chapter 2 does not use the example CD. In this chapter, you will create a blank database and begin to create your first tables.

Creating Database Tables

You create a database container to hold the tables, queries, forms, reports, and macros that you create as you learn Access. You also create the Sales and Contacts database tables, which stores data about the sales and customers of the Access Auto Auctions.

Before you can create the tables of the Access Auto Auctions, you must first create the actual database container to hold the tables.

Creating a Database

The Database window displays all the various object files from your database that you may create while using Access. Actually, a database is a single file. As you create new *object files*, they are stored within the database file. They are not separate files in themselves; rather, they are stored objects.

The database file starts at about 94,000 bytes (92K) and grows as you create new objects — tables, queries, forms, reports, macros, and modules. Adding data to an Access database also increases the size of the file.

There are many ways to create a new database file. When you start Microsoft Access, you see the Getting Started dialog box open in the Database window, as shown in Figure 2-1. You can also display this dialog box by selecting File ➪ New from the main Access menu — this opens the New File dialog box — and then clicking the Home icon at the top of the New File dialog box. (It looks like a sheet of paper with the right-top corner bent down.) Finally, you can click the New button (the first button in the toolbar) and select the Home icon.

Figure 2-1: The Getting Started dialog box opens along the right-hand side of the Access window, showing three general categories for creating a new database.

The Getting Started dialog box shows several groupings:

✦ **Open.** This lets you open an existing database file. The last four databases opened are displayed. Clicking the More choice opens the Open dialog box, which enables you to browse through your hard drive for the existing database you want to open.

✦ **Create a new file.** Clicking on this choice opens the New dialog box, which has two sections — New and Templates. The New section enables you to open a Blank Database, a Blank Data Access Page, a Project Using Existing Data, a Project Using New Data, or From Existing File. The Template section lets you search for new templates on Microsoft.com, go to the Templates Home page, and look for templates On My Computer.

Templates Section

In addition to using the New section to create a blank database, you can select the second section in the New File dialog box—Templates. This section has three choices: Search Office Online:, Templates Home page, and On My Computer.

Templates Home page

This choice activates your dialer program if you are not currently connected to the Internet. When connected to the Internet, your browser will be activated and display the Templates Home page of Microsoft Office Online. Here you can see a list of templates. The top figure in Figure 2-2 shows the Templates Home page after connecting to Microsoft.com.

The Templates home page displays many templates for all the Microsoft Office products. If you type Access in the search box located at the top-left corner and click on the right arrow button or press Enter, the Web site will display a series of online templates that can be used in Access.

Search Office Online:

Using the Search Office Online: choice of the Templates section, you can type a search criteria for a specific template. For instance, typing in the keyword "inventory," Access will go out to the Template section of the Web site and search for any templates for "inventory." In this case it reports the "Inventory Management Database" was found on the Microsoft.com site.

On My Computer

Clicking on this choice activates the Templates dialog box. When you open the Templates dialog box for the first time, it may look different than the one in Figure 2-2. Notice that the Templates dialog box has two tabs across the top—the General tab and Database tab. The first time you open this dialog box, the General tab may be active—clicking on the Database tab should show entries similar to Figure 2-2.

Notice that there are several database templates available in this window. Selecting one of them will create a new database with objects that can be used for that specific purpose. You can use any of these templates to build a specific database system. Once built you can modify any of the objects created for your particular need.

When you select a particular template, Access will activate the Database Wizard and ask you a series of questions about the fields to use for each table of the system and the look of your forms and reports. Finally it will ask you for the name of the system you are building and create the database and all its objects automatically.

Note   If you have the Templates dialog box open, close it at this time to continue with creating a new database.

Figure 2-2: The Templates Home page is activated by selecting Templates home page (top figure). The Templates dialog box with the Database tab active. This dialog box is activated by selecting the On My Computer choice in the Templates section of the New File menu (bottom figure).

Blank database

Creating a database is a very simple matter. Just follow the steps below:

1. Click Blank Database under the New category of the New File menu. If you are on the Getting Started menu, select Create a New File to go to the New File menu.

2. The File New Database dialog box opens. You can see any existing .MDB files in the file list part of the window. The New File Database dialog box may initially open to the My Documents folder. Navigate to the folder you want to place your new database file in — in the case of the author, it is a folder named "Access db Files."

3. A default name of *db1.mdb* will appear in the File Name text box at the bottom of the window. Simply type over this default name with the name **My Access Auto Auctions** or any other name you want to give the database. (Typing the extension *.mdb* is optional because Access automatically supplies it if you do not.)

4. Click the Create button.

When the new database is created, Access automatically opens it for you.

Note   As the database in Figure 2-3 shows, Access automatically creates the database file (container) using the Access 2000 format. This is for backward compatibility. If you want to use the newer format — Access 2002 — you will need to convert the database after it is created by selecting Tools ⇨ Database Utilities ⇨ Convert Database ⇨ To Access 2003.

Figure 2-3: The new database "My Access Auto Auctions" is created.

Tip

You can specify that Access 2003 uses the default database format of Access 2002 instead of version 2000. To change which format of the database Access uses when creating a new database, select Format⇨Options⇨Advanced Tab⇨Default File Format pull-down menu and choose Access 2002 format.

Cross-Reference

You learn more about file attaching in Chapter 7.

Caution

An Access 2002 database cannot be used by versions of Access from 2000 and earlier. However, Access can use previous formats of Access databases — 2.0, 95, 97, and 2000. Because the default version is 2000, you can use these files with Access 2000, Access 2002, or the current version. Of course you can change the default version to Access 2002 instead of 2000 (see tip above).

Understanding How Access Works with Data

There are many ways that Microsoft Access works with data. For simplicity, you will see the data stored in local tables in the examples of this book. A *local table* is a table stored within the Access .MDB file This is how you have seen examples so far.

In many professionally developed Microsoft Access applications, the actual tables are in their own database while the other interface objects (forms, reports, queries, pages, macros, and modules) are stored in another database. The reason for this is usually maintainability. By separating the data and their tables into another database you can easily do maintenance work on them (building new indexes, repairing the tables, and so on) without affecting the remainder of the system. In contrast, you may be working with a multi-user system and find a problem with a form or report object in the system. If you have all the data and interface objects in the same database, you would have to shut down the system while repairing the broken form or report — others could not be using the system while you repair one object. Instead, by separating the data from the other objects, you can fix the erring object while others are still working with the data. After you've fixed the problem, you can deliver the new changes to the others, and they can import it into their local database system. In addition, there is a more critical reason to separate your data from the interface objects — security. By maintaining the data separately in its own database, either locally or in a remote location, as in a multi-user environment, you can maintain better control over the information. Thus, the solution is to consider separating your tables, and their stored data, from the rest of the application.

While you may want to first develop your application with the tables within the .MDB database, later you can use the Database Splitter wizard to automatically move the tables in your .MDB file to a separate Access .MDB file and then attach the tables. You can also attach your tables to the Microsoft Database Engine or the larger SQL Server database. You can also attach to non-Microsoft servers such as Oracle, Informix, or Sybase.

Tip

You can save or convert an Access 2002 Database in Access 2000 or Access 97 format by selecting Tools ➪ Database Utilities ➪ Convert Database ➪ To Access 97 or Access 2000 File Format. The same is true for converting from Access 2000 to 2002 or 97.

Caution

If you enter a file extension other than MDB, Access saves the database file but does not display it when you open the database later. By default, Access searches for and displays only those files with an MDB file extension.

If you are following the examples in this book, note that we have chosen the name *My Access Auto Auctions* for the name of the database you create as you complete this chapter. This database is for our hypothetical business, Access Auto Auctions. After you enter the filename, Access creates the empty database.

On the CD-ROM

The CD-ROM that comes with your book contains multiple database files. The completed file containing all the data is named *Access Auto Auctions Data,* and the database with the completed objects is *Access Auto Auctions* (the completed application, including forms, queries, reports, macros, and modules).

The CD-ROM has database files for each chapter named CHAPxxStart.mdb and CHAPxxEnd.mdb, where xx is a chapter number; for example, 01, 02, and on and on. If a chapter uses files where the data is split off from the other objects, the names are CHAPxxPgmStart.mdb, CHAPxxDataStart.mdb, CHAPxxPgmEnd.mdb, and CHAPxxDataEnd.mdb. For this chapter, you will build only a single database: My Access Auto Auctions.

The Database Window

The Database window for the database CHAP01Start.mdb is shown in Figure 2-4. It comprises three basic parts. First is the Objects menu bar on the left side of the window and below it a Groups menu bar. Along the top of the window is the second part, the toolbar with the buttons Open, Design, and New. Finally, the third part is the open pane to the right and center that is used to show all the objects of the type selected (Tables, Queries, and so on).

The Database window can be thought of as a container that holds all the different objects that make up the database itself. When you click any of the object menu items (Tables, Forms, and so on), the open pane on the right of the menu bar displays the appropriate objects. For example, Figure 2-4 shows all the Tables objects because the Tables button is selected (it is also the default selection). If you click the Forms button, you will see all the forms that you have built in the open pane.

The menu bar comprises two different groups of menus: Objects types and Groups. The Objects type menu references all the object types that are used to make up the entire database. The Groups menu is used to store and retrieve different object types by use of a shortcut — it can contain any type of object.

Figure 2-4: The Database window. This window, or container, has three basic parts: the menu bars on the left side, the toolbar along the top, and the open pane.

Objects menu bar

The Database window contains seven buttons on the vertical Objects menu bar; using them, you can quickly select any of these objects that are available in Access:

- ✦ Tables
- ✦ Queries
- ✦ Forms
- ✦ Reports
- ✦ Pages
- ✦ Macros
- ✦ Modules

As you create new objects, the names of the files appear in the open pane of the Database window. You see only the files for the particular type of object selected. You can select an object type to view by clicking one of the object buttons.

In addition to the new objects that you create, the Database window shows several new object shortcuts for each object type selected. For example, in Figure 2-4 you see three new object shortcuts at the top of the object pane: Create Table In Design View, Create Table By Using Wizard, and Create Table By Entering Data.

Only the Tables, Queries, Forms, Reports, and Pages objects have new objects shortcuts. Queries, Forms, and Reports each have two, and the Tables and Pages have three. To see the two for Forms, simply click the Forms button, and the first two choices in the window pane are the new object shortcuts — Create Form In Design View and Create Form By Using Wizard.

Tip Inside the Object window pane are two or three create icons and their new object shortcut labels. These can help you get started and are provided for each type of object. You can turn off this new feature by choosing Tools ⇨ Options and de-selecting New Object Shortcuts.

There are four buttons on the right side of the toolbar that can change how you look at the objects in the database object pane — one to see Large Icons of objects, one for Small Icons, one for List Of Objects (default), and the last for Details Listing Of Objects.

Figure 2-4 shows the default (List) Database window view. In it you only see the object names; for example, table names such as tblContacts, tblSales, tblSalesLineItems, tblProducts, and more. You can switch to the Details view of the object files in the Database window by clicking the last button on the toolbar, a button that looks like a series of lines in a box. This shows information such as a description, the date modified, date created, and type of object. You can also view this detailed information by clicking View from your Access menu bar and then clicking Details.

Groups menu bar

The Groups menu has one default button under it: Favorites. Groups are used to store shortcuts to the different database objects so that they can be accessed quickly from one place. For example, you may want to add a shortcut for the Customer (tblContacts) table and the Customer (frmContacts) form or other different types of objects.

Tip When you place your database objects into a group, this creates a shortcut to that object. For example, assume you are working with a fairly large database with several hundred objects but that you are currently working with only three of those objects. Instead of switching between the seven database objects and browsing for the individual object names, you can store shortcuts to all the objects you use in a group you create.

The objects must already have been created to add them to a group. This figure uses objects that you create later and are not yet in this database.

You are not limited to the Favorites group. You can create your own groups menu choices under the Groups menu bar. To create a new group, right-click on the Favorites group and select New Group. This displays a dialog box where you can type in a group name. When you have typed in the group name, click OK and the group is created.

To display different database objects in your groups, click and drag the object into the desired group. The same toolbar buttons appear for the different objects as they normally do. The only command you can't perform when you are in a group is to create a new object (Table, Query, Form, Report, Pages, Macro, or Module). The toolbar buttons are described in the next section.

The Database window toolbar buttons

The toolbar buttons in the Database window enable you to "Open" an existing object that is highlighted (selected); display "Design" mode for the current highlighted object; create a "New" object; or "Delete" (the X button) the currently highlighted object. When a button is clicked, the appropriate action is taken. Before clicking Open or Design, you should select an object name by highlighting it. When you select New, the type of the new object that will be created depends on the object type button you have selected in the Objects menu bar (Form, Table, Query, or others). If you chose the Tables type, a new table is created. When you select some of the other object types, the toolbar buttons may change. When you select the Reports type, for example, the three available toolbar buttons are Preview, Design, and New.

The Access window toolbar

The toolbar shown in Figure 2-5 enables you to perform tasks quickly without using the menus. (Tools that are not available appear in light gray.)

If you place the cursor on a button without clicking and wait a short time (a second or two), a Help prompt known as a *Tool Tip* appears just below the button. If you want even more help, press Shift+F1, and then move the cursor to the object you want more information about and click it. You will see *What's This?* help: A small rectangle with a paragraph explaining the use of the selected object. Figure 2-5 shows the What's This? information box for the Tables button in the database container. Another way of getting Help is to select the Office Assistant button at the far right of the toolbar (it has a question mark inside a bubble), and then type a question in the Office Assistant box. Finally, you can type in your question directly in the new Help combo box along the right-most side of the menu bar of Access.

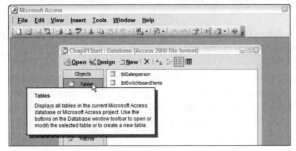

Figure 2-5: The Database window toolbar. Notice that it also shows the Shift-F1 information box that is displayed for the Tables Button in the database.

Starting from the left, you see the following toolbar buttons:

- ✦ **New (blank piece of paper):** Opens the New File menu
- ✦ **Open (open file folder):** Opens a database
- ✦ **Save (floppy disk):** Saves an object
- ✦ **File Search (Windows logo over a piece of paper with a magnifying glass):** Searches the disk for a file
- ✦ **Print (fax/printer name) (printer):** Prints an object to the printer
- ✦ **Print Preview (piece of paper with magnifying glass):** Views an object as it will look printed
- ✦ **Spelling (check mark below the letters *ABC*):** Checks the spelling
- ✦ **Cut (pair of scissors):** Removes the selection
- ✦ **Copy (two pieces of paper):** Copies the selection
- ✦ **Paste (clipboard with piece of paper):** Inserts from the clipboard
- ✦ **Undo (an arrow rotating counterclockwise and menu selection arrow):** Undoes the last action
- ✦ **OfficeLinks (icon of a large W with envelope and menu selection arrow):** Displays the links to Word and Excel
- ✦ **Analyze (table picture with two table icons and a menu selection arrow):** Displays the Analyze commands
- ✦ **Code (rectangle with red, blue, and yellow boxes on it):** Displays the Code window — optional and visible only if loaded
- ✦ **Microsoft Script Editor (an eight inside another eight on its side):** Displays the Script Editor window — optional and visible only if loaded. The editor is used to create VBScript or JScript for data access pages.
- ✦ **Properties (hand holding a piece of paper):** Displays the Properties window
- ✦ **Relationships (three tables with lines between them):** Displays the Relationships window
- ✦ **New Object: AutoForm (starburst over top-left corner of a table icon and a menu selection arrow):** Displays the New Object choices
- ✦ **Microsoft Access Help (cartoon caption bubble with a question mark inside):** Displays the Microsoft Access Help window
- ✦ **Toolbar Options (a menu selection arrow pointing down):** Allows you to add or remove toolbar buttons

Creating a New Table

After you design your table on paper, you need to create the table design in Access. Although you can create the table interactively without any forethought, carefully planning a database system is a good idea. You can make any changes later, but doing so wastes time; generally, the result is a system that is harder to maintain than one that is well planned from the beginning. Before you get started, you should understand the table design process.

 Cross-Reference   To refresh your knowledge on how to design your tables for this database, refer to the section titled "Step 3: Data Design – What Fields Do You Have?" in Chapter 1.

The table design process

Creating a table design is a multi-step process. By following the steps in order, your table design can be created readily and with minimal effort:

- ✦ Create a new table.
- ✦ Enter each field name, data type, and description.
- ✦ Enter properties for each defined field.
- ✦ Set a primary key.
- ✦ Create indexes for necessary fields.
- ✦ Save the design.

You can use any of these four methods to create a new table design:

- ✦ Click the New toolbar button in the Tables Object container of the Database window.
- ✦ Select Insert ➪ Table from the Access menu.
- ✦ Select New Table from the New Object button in the Access toolbar.
- ✦ Select Create table in Design view (first object in Tables pane of Database window) if the New object shortcuts option is turned on.

 Tip   If you create a new table by clicking the New button in the Database window, make sure that the Tables object button is selected first from the Objects menu bar.

With the "My Access Auto Auctions" database open, click the New button in the Database window to begin creating a new table.

The New Table dialog box

Figure 2-6 shows the New Table dialog box as Access displays it.

Figure 2-6: The New Table dialog box.

You use this dialog box to select one of these five ways to create a new table:

- ✦ **Datasheet View.** Enter data into a spreadsheet
- ✦ **Design View.** Create a table in Design view
- ✦ **Table Wizard.** Select a pre-built table that is complete with generic field definitions
- ✦ **Import Table.** Import external data formats into a new Access table
- ✦ **Link Table.** Link to an existing external data source

Access provides several ways to create a new table. You can design the structure of the table (such as field names, data types, and size) first, and then add data. Another method is to use the Table Wizard to choose from a list of predefined table designs. Access also gives you three new ways to easily create a new table. First, you can enter the data into a spreadsheet-like form known as Datasheet View; Access will create the table for you automatically. Second, you can use the Import Table Wizard to select an external data source and create a new table containing a copy of the data found in that source; the Wizard takes you through the import process. Third, you can use the Link Table Wizard, which is similar to the Import Table Wizard except that the data stays in the original location and Access links to it from the new table.

To create your first table, the Datasheet View is a great method for getting started; then you can use the table's Design View to make any final changes and adjustments.

Cross-Reference The Import Table and Link Table Wizards are covered in Chapter 6.

Select New from the Database window; then select Datasheet View and click the OK button to display a blank datasheet with which you can create a new table.

Using the Table Wizard

When you create a new table, you can type in every field name, data type, size, and other table property information, or you can use the Table Wizard (see Figure 2-7) to select from a long list of predefined tables and fields. Unlike the Database Wizard (which creates a complete application), the Table Wizard creates only a table and a simple form.

Wizards can save you a lot of work; they are meant to save you time and make complex tasks easier. Wizards work by taking you through a series of screens that ask what you want. You answer these questions by clicking buttons, selecting fields, entering text, and making yes/no decisions.

In the Table Wizard, first you choose between the lists of Business or Personal tables. Some of the Business tables are Mailing List, Contacts, Employees, Products, Orders, Suppliers, Payments, Invoices, Assets, and Students. The Personal list includes Guests, Recipes, Exercise Log, Plants, Wine List, Photographs, Video Collection, and more.

When you select a table, a list appears and shows you all the fields that you might want in the table. Select only the fields you want. Although they are all predefined for data type and size, you can rename a field after it's selected. When you've chosen your fields, another screen uses input from you to create a primary key automatically. Other screens help you to automatically link the primary key to another table and establish relationships. Finally, the Wizard can display the table, enable you to enter records into a datasheet, or even create an automatic form for you. The entire process of creating a simple table and form can take less than one minute! Whenever you need to create a table for an application on the Wizard's list, you can save a lot of time by using the Wizard.

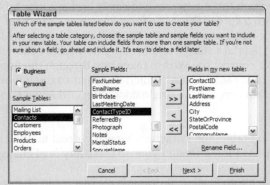

Figure 2-7: This is the first screen of the Table Wizard. It enables you to select an example type table (Contacts in this figure) then select fields to add to the table to be created.

Creating a new table with a Datasheet View

The empty datasheet appears, ready for you to enter data and create a new record. You begin by entering a few records into the datasheet. Each column will become a field, and each row will become a record in the table. (You learn more about these terms later in this chapter.) For now, all you have to do is add data. The more records you add, the more accurately Access can tell what type of data you want for each field and the approximate size of each data item.

When you first see the datasheet, it's empty. The column headers that will become field names for the table are labeled *Field1, Field2, Field3*, and so on. You can change the column header names if you want; they become the field names for the table design. You can always change the field names after you have finished creating the table. The table datasheet is initially named *Table* followed by a number. If there are no other tables named Table with a number, Access uses the name *Table1*; the next table is named *Table2*, and so forth. You can always change this name when you save the table.

Add the five records shown in Figure 2-8, and then change the column headers to the names shown by double-clicking on the field name (Field1, Field2, and so on).

Note
You can change a column name by double-clicking the column name and editing the value. When you're done, press Enter to save the new column header. If you enter a column header name that is wider than the default column width, adjust the column width by placing the cursor on the line between the column names and dragging the line to the right to make it wider or to the left to make it narrower.

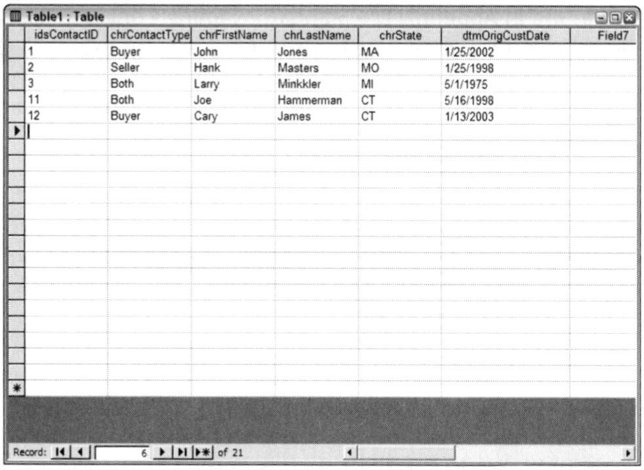

idsContactID	chrContactType	chrFirstName	chrLastName	chrState	dtmOrigCustDate	Field7
1	Buyer	John	Jones	MA	1/25/2002	
2	Seller	Hank	Masters	MO	1/25/1998	
3	Both	Larry	Minkkler	MI	5/1/1975	
11	Both	Joe	Hammerman	CT	5/16/1998	
12	Buyer	Cary	James	CT	1/13/2003	

Record: 6 of 21

Figure 2-8: A partially completed Datasheet view of the data used to create a new table. Notice that the first six fields have had their field names changed, and that each column holds the same type of data.

Tip

The Access and Microsoft Excel spreadsheet Datasheet windows work similarly. Many techniques are the same for both products; even many menus and toolbar buttons are the same.

Cross-Reference

When naming tables, fields, and other objects in this book, a naming convention is used. You can read more on this naming convention in Appendix D – Standard Naming Conventions.

When you have finished entering the data, save the table and give it the name *tblContacts*. To close the table and save the data entered, choose either Close from the File menu or click the Close button in the upper-right corner of the Table window (the button with the X on it). You can also click the Save button on the toolbar, but this only saves the table; you still have to close it.

Clicking the Close button in the window will activate a dialog box that asks whether you want to save changes to Table1. You have three choices – "Yes" to save the table and give it a name, "No" to forget everything, or "Cancel" to return to the table to enter more data.

For this example, select "Yes" to continue the process to save the table. The Save As dialog box appears, prompting you for a new name for the table. It shows you the default table name of Table1.

Enter **tblContacts** and click OK to continue to save the table. Yet another dialog box appears, asking whether you want to create a *primary key* — a unique identifier for each record, which you learn about later in the chapter. For now, just select No.

Tip

The tables, fields, and other objects (forms, reports, queries, and others) follow a convention that can be found in Appendix D – Standard Naming Conventions. The purpose of this "standard" method of naming is for clarification; for example, the prefix *tbl* stands for table and Contacts is the primary name of the table. When you look at system some time in the future, you will automatically know that *tbl* stands for table.

Access saves the table and returns you to the Database window. Notice that the table name "tblContacts" now appears in the table object list. If you did everything correctly, you have successfully created a table named tblContacts that has six fields and five records. The next step is to edit the table design and create the final table design you saw in Figure 1-5 of Chapter 1.

To open the tblContacts table in Design View, select it and then click the Design button. Figure 2-9 shows the tblContacts Table Design window with the design that was automatically created by the data you entered in the Datasheet View. Notice the field names that you created by entering their names in the first row of each column. Also notice the data types that Access automatically assigned to each field.

It looked at the information that you typed into each column and attempted to determine the type of data you entered. For example, it figured out that you wanted a Date/Time type field for the dtmOrigCustDate (Original Customer Date) column, and a Number type for the idsContactID field. In the next part of this chapter, you learn about these field types.

Caution The field idsContactID was automatically identified as a number by Access. In reality, we will use this as an AutoNumber field. This will be discussed later in this chapter.

Figure 2-9: The Table Design window contains the Field Names and Data types in the top pane and Field Properties for the current field in the bottom pane — in this case, the properties for the idsContactID field.

The Table Design Window

The Table Design window consists of two areas:

✦ The field entry area

✦ The field properties area

The *field entry area* is for entering each field's name and data type; you can also enter an optional description. The *property area* is for entering more options, called *properties,* for each field. These properties include field size, format, input mask, alternate caption for forms, default value, validation rules, validation text, required, zero length for null checking, index specifications, and unicode compression. The actual properties displayed depend upon the data type of the field. You learn more about these properties later in the book.

Tip   You can switch between areas (also referred to as panes) by clicking the mouse when the pointer is in the desired pane or by pressing F6.

Using the Table Design window toolbar

The Table Design window toolbar, shown in Figure 2-10, contains many buttons that assist in creating a new table definition.

Figure 2-10: The Table Design window toolbar.

Working with fields

Fields are created by entering a *field name* and a *field data type* in each row of the field entry area of the Table Design window. The *field description* is an option to identify the field's purpose; it appears in the status bar during data entry. After you enter each field's name and data type, you can further specify how each field is used by entering properties in the property area. Before you enter any properties, however, you should enter all your field names and data types for this example. You have already created some of the fields you will need.

Naming a field

A *field name* should be clear enough to identify the field to you, the user of the system, and to Access. Field names should be long enough to quickly identify the purpose of the field, but not overly long. (Later, as you enter validation rules or use the field name in a calculation, you'll want to save yourself from typing long field names.)

Cross-Reference   This book uses a naming standard for all objects. To learn more about the naming conventions used in this book, please refer to Appendix D — Standard Naming Conventions.

To enter a field name, position the pointer in the first row of the Table Design window under the Field Name column. Then type a valid field name, observing these rules:

✦ Field names can be from 1 to 64 characters.

✦ Field names can include letters, numbers, and many special characters.

✦ Field names cannot include a period (.), exclamation point (!), brackets ([ ]), or accent grave (`).

✦ You can't use low-order ASCII characters, for example Ctrl-J or Ctrl-L (ASCII values 0 to 31).

✦ You can't start with a blank space.

✦ You can't use a double quotation mark (") in the name of a Microsoft Access project file.

You can enter field names in upper-, lower-, or mixed case. If you make a mistake while typing the field name, position the cursor where you want to make a correction and type the change. You can change a field name at any time — even if it's in a table and the field contains data — for any reason.

Caution

After your table is saved, however, if you change a field name that is also used in queries, forms, or reports, you have to change it in those objects as well.

Specifying a data type

After you name a field, you must decide what type of data the field will hold. Before you begin entering data, you should have a good grasp of the data types that your system will use. Ten basic types of data are shown in Table 2-1; some data types (such as numbers) have several options.

Table 2-1
Data Types Available in Microsoft Access

Data Type	Type of Data Stored	Storage Size
Text	Alphanumeric characters	0–255 characters
Memo	Alphanumeric characters	0–65,536 characters
Number	Numeric values	1, 2, 4, or 8 bytes, 16 bytes for Replication ID (GUID)
Date/Time	Date and time data	8 bytes
Currency	Monetary data	8 bytes
AutoNumber	Automatic number increments	4 bytes, 16 bytes for Replication ID (GUID)
Yes/No	Logical values: Yes/No, True/False	1 bit (0 or −1)
OLE Object	Pictures, graphs, sound, video	Up to 1GB (disk space limitation)
Hyperlink	Link to an Internet resource	0–64,000 characters
Lookup Wizard	Displays data from another table	Generally 4 bytes

Figure 2-11 shows the Data Type drop-down list. It is used to select the choice for the type of data you want to save in the field you just created. When you move the pointer into the Data Type column, a down arrow (↓) appears in the text-entry box. To open this drop-down list, move the cursor into the Data Type column and click the down arrow (↓).

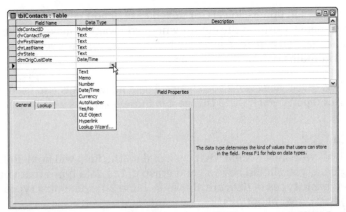

Figure 2-11: The Data Type drop-down list. You can quickly select the type of data you want to store in a field by clicking the list and selecting from it. You can also type in the name of the data type.

Text data is any type of data that is simply characters. These characters comprise alphanumeric characters, meaning numbers (0 through 9) and characters (A to Z, a to z). Names, addresses, and descriptions are all text data, as are numeric data that are not used in a calculation (such as telephone numbers, Social Security numbers, and ZIP codes). Although you specify the size of each text field in the property area, you can enter no more than 255 characters of data in any text field. Access uses variable length fields to store its data. If you designate a field to be 25 characters wide and you use only 5 characters for each record, then that is all the space you will actually use in your database container. You will find that the .MDB database file can get large quickly but text fields are not the cause. However, rather than allow Access to create every text field with the default 50 characters or the maximum 255 characters, it is good practice to limit text field widths to the maximum you believe they will be used for. Names are tricky because some cultures have long names. However, it is a safe bet that a postal code might be less than 12 characters wide while a U.S. state abbreviation is always 2 characters wide. By limiting the size of the text width, you also limit the number of characters the user can type when the field is used in a form.

The *Memo* data type holds a variable amount of data from 0 to 65,536 characters for each record. Therefore, if one record uses 100 characters, another requires only 10, and yet another needs 3,000, you use only as much space as each record requires.

The *Number* data type enables you to enter *numeric* data; that is, numbers that will be used in mathematical calculations. (If you have data that will be used in monetary calculations, you should use the *Currency* data type, which enables you to specify many different currency types.)

The *Date/Time* data type can store dates, times, or both types of data at once. Thus, you can enter a date, a time, or a date/time combination. You can specify many types of formats in the property entry area and then display date and time data as you prefer.

The *Currency* data type enables you to enter *numeric* data; that is, numbers that will be used with only two decimal places and can be used for mathematical calculations. You can specify many different currency formats with this data type. (If you have data that will be used for non-Currency, numeric calculations, you should use the *Number* data type.)

The *AutoNumber* data type stores an integer that Access increments (adds to) automatically as you add new records. You can use the AutoNumber data type as a unique record identification for tables having no other unique value. If, for example, you have no unique identifier for a list of names, you can use an AutoNumber field to identify one John Smith from another.

The *Yes/No* data type holds data that has one of two values and that can, therefore, be expressed as a binary state. Data is actually stored as –1 for yes and 0 for no. You can, however, adjust the format setting to display Yes/No, True/False, or On/Off. When you use a Yes/No data type, you can use many of the form controls that are especially designed for it.

The *OLE Object* data type provides access for data that can be linked to an OLE server. This type of data includes bitmaps (such as Windows Paint files), audio files (such as WAV files), business graphics (such as those found in Access and Excel), and even full-motion video files. Of course, you can play the video files only if you have the hardware and necessary OLE server software.

The *Hyperlink* data type field holds combinations of text and numbers stored as text and used as a hyperlink address. It can have up to three parts: (1) the visual text that appears in a field (usually underlined); (2) the Internet address — the path to a file (UNC, or Universal Naming Convention, path) or page (URL or Uniform Resource Locator); and (3) any sub-address within the file or page. An example of a sub-address is the name of an Access 2000 form or report. Each part is separated by the pound symbol (#).

The *Lookup Wizard* data type creates a field that enables you to use a combo box to choose a value from another table or from a list of values. This is especially useful when you are storing key fields from another table in order to link to data from that table. Choosing this option in the Data Type list starts the Lookup Wizard, with which you define the data type and perform the link to another table. You learn more about this field type later.

Entering a field description

The *field description* is completely optional; you use it only to help you remember a field's uses or to let another user know its purpose. Often you don't use the description column at all, or you use it only for fields whose purpose is not readily recognizable. If you enter a field description, it appears in the status bar whenever you use that field in Access — in the datasheet or in a form. The field description can help clarify a field whose purpose is ambiguous or give the user a fuller explanation of the values valid for the field during data entry.

Creating the tblContacts Table

Working with these nine different data types (plus the Lookup Wizard), you should be ready to create the final working copy of the tblContacts Table. When creating the table, you will have to create a field that can be used to link this table to two other tables, specifically the tblSales and tblContactLog tables. This link field will be defined as an AutoNumber field, which will prove problematic for the currently created tblContacts table.

AutoNumber fields and Access

Access gives special considerations to AutoNumber fields and assigning values to AutoNumber fields. You cannot change a previously defined field from another type to AutoNumber. If you try to change a previously defined field to an AutoNumber field type, Access reports an error, as shown in Figure 2-12. The dialog box points out that after you create a table and have added any records, you can't change the field type to AutoNumber from any other type.

Microsoft Access

Once you enter data in a table, you can't change the data type of any field to AutoNumber, even if you haven't yet added data to that field.

Add a new field to the table, and define its data type as AutoNumber. Microsoft Office Access then enters data in the AutoNumber field automatically, numbering the records consecutively starting with 1.

OK

Figure 2-12: The warning dialog box states that you may not change the field type of a table that already has records in it to AutoNumber.

When you created the table tblContacts by adding data in the datasheet view, Access automatically assigned a datatype of Number to the idsContactID field. This needs to be changed to AutoNumber. Because Access does not allow you to automatically change it when there are records in it, you will have to either delete the records in the table or delete the field.

To change the idsContactID field from number to AutoNumber, you need to return to the Datasheet View by clicking View, the left-most button under the word File. While in Datasheet View, click on the first column of the record. Notice that when you move your cursor over any row of this column, it changes to a small, right-pointing arrow. While you have a pointing arrow, click on the first field to highlight the entire record; once highlighted you can simply press the Delete key to delete the record. Figure 2-13 shows the record highlighted and the cursor turned to a right-pointing arrow. Access will display a confirmation dialog box confirming you want to delete this record. Answer yes. When this is done, you can go back and highlight the remaining records and delete them.

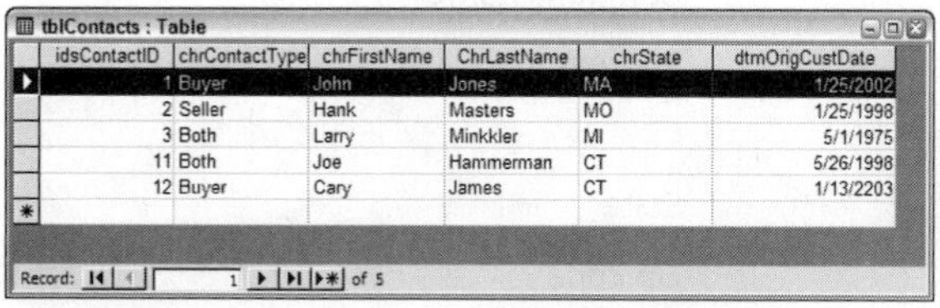

idsContactID	chrContactType	chrFirstName	ChrLastName	chrState	dtmOrigCustDate
1	Buyer	John	Jones	MA	1/25/2002
2	Seller	Hank	Masters	MO	1/25/1998
3	Both	Larry	Minkkler	MI	5/1/1975
11	Both	Joe	Hammerman	CT	5/26/1998
12	Buyer	Cary	James	CT	1/13/2203

Figure 2-13: Deleting a record in datasheet view.

With the records deleted you can now click the Design button (same button as the view, simply changed to design now) and return to the Design window.

Completing the tblContacts Table

With the tblContacts Table in Design View you are now ready to create or modify all the fields of the tblContacts Table. Table 2-2 shows the completed field entries for the tblContacts table. If you are following the examples, you should modify the table design now for these additional fields. Enter the field names and data types exactly as shown. You also need to rearrange some of the fields and delete the Value field you created. You may want to study the next few pages to understand how to change existing fields (which includes rearranging the field order, changing a field name, and deleting a field).

The steps for modifying the idsContactID field's data type from Number to AutoNumber is

1. Place the cursor in the Data Type column in the row of the idsContactID field.
2. Click the down arrow and select the data type of AutoNumber.

Tip You can also type in the name of the data type or the first unique letters. The type is validated automatically to make sure it's on the drop-down list. A warning message appears for an invalid type.

Table 2-2
Structure of the tblContacts Table

Field Name	Data Type	Description
idsContactID	AutoNumber	Used to link to tblSales and tblContact Log
chrContactType	Text	Buyer, Seller, or Both
chrFirstName	Text	First name
chrLastName	Text	Last name
chrCompany	Text	Company name
chrAddress	Text	Address
chrCity	Text	City
chrState	Text	State
chrZipCode	Text	Zip code
chrCustomerType	Text	Holds info like Parts Store, Dealer, Auctioneer, and so on
chrPhone	Text	Phone number
chrFax	Text	Fax number
chrEmail	Text	E-mail address
hlkWebSite	Text	Web site
dtmOrigCustDate	Date/Time	First date became customer
chrTaxLocation	Text	State for taxing information
curCreditLimit	Currency	Credit limit
curCurBal	Currency	Current balance
chrCreditStatus	Text	OK, HOLD, New
dtmLastSalesDate	Date/Time	Date of last sale
dblDiscountPercent	Number	Start discount percent authorized for contact
memNotes	Memo	Any miscellaneous notes
blnActive	Yes/No	Active contact

The steps for adding fields to a table structure are

1. Place the cursor in the Field Name column in the row where you want the field to appear.

2. Enter the field name and press Enter or Tab.

3. In the Data Type column, click the down arrow and select the data type.

4. Place the pointer in the Description column and type a description (optional).

Repeat each of these steps to create each of the data entry fields for the tblContacts table. You can press the down-arrow (↓) key to move between rows, or simply use the mouse and click on any row.

Changing a Table Design

As you create your table, you should be following a well-planned design. Yet changes are sometimes necessary, even with a plan — as in the case of changing the data type from Number to AutoNumber for the idsContactID field previously. You may find that you want to add another field, remove a field, change a field name or data type, or simply rearrange the order of the field names. You can make these changes to your table at any time. After you enter data into your table, however, things get a little more complicated. You have to make sure that any changes made don't affect the data entered previously.

In older versions of Access (versions 95 and earlier), changes to the table design could be made only in the Table Design window. Since Access 97, including Access 2002, you can make changes to the table design in a datasheet, including adding fields, deleting fields, and changing field names.

New Feature

In previous versions of Access, changing a field name usually meant that any queries, forms, reports, macros, or modules that referenced that field name would no longer work and had to be manually found and changed. Since Access 2002, it automatically seeks out most occurrences of the name and changes it for you.

Inserting a new field

To insert a new field, in the Table Design window, place your cursor on an existing field and select Insert ➪ Rows or click the Insert Rows button in the toolbar. A new row is added to the table, and any existing fields are pushed down. You can then enter a new field definition. Inserting a field does not disturb other fields or existing data. If you have queries, forms, or reports that use the table, you may need to add the field to those objects as well.

Deleting a field

There are three ways to delete a field:

✦ Select the field by clicking the row selector and pressing Delete.

✦ Select the field and choose Edit ➪ Delete Rows.

✦ Select the field and click the Delete Rows button on the toolbar.

When you delete a field containing data, a warning that you will lose any data in the table for this field displays. If the table is empty, you won't care. If your table contains data, however, make sure that you want to eliminate the data for that field (column). You will also have to delete the same field from queries, forms, and reports that use the field name.

Tip   When you delete a field, you can immediately select the Undo button and return the field to the table. But you must do this step before you save the changed table's definition.

Tip   If you attempt to delete a field that is part of a relationship (primary or secondary key field), Access will inform you that you cannot delete it until you delete the reference in the Relationships window.

If you delete a field, you must also delete all references to that field throughout Access. Because you can use a field name in forms, queries, reports, and even table-data validation, you must examine your system carefully to find any instances where you may have used the specific field name.

Changing a field location

One of the easiest changes to make is to move a field's location. The order of your fields, as entered, determines the initial display sequence in the datasheet that displays your data. If you decide that your fields should be rearranged, click on a field selector twice and drag the field to a new location.

Changing a field name

You can change a field name by selecting an existing field name in the Table Design screen and entering a new name; Access updates the table design automatically. As long as you are creating a new table, this process is easy.

Caution   If you used the field name in any forms, queries, or reports, however, you must also go to each object that references the field name and change it in them. (Remember that you can also use a field name in validation rules and calculated fields in queries, as well as in macros and module expressions — all of which must be changed.) As you can see, it's a good idea not to change a field name; it creates more work.

Changing a field size

Making a field size larger is simple in a table design. However, only text and number fields can be increased in size. You simply increase the Field Size property for text fields or specify a different field size for number fields. You must pay attention to the decimal-point property in number fields to make sure that you don't select a new size that supports fewer decimal places than you currently have.

When you want to make a field size smaller, make sure that none of the data in the table is larger than the new field width. (If it is, the existing data will be truncated.) Text data types should be made as small as possible to take up less storage space.

Tip   Remember that each text field uses only the number of characters actually entered in the field. You should still try to make your fields only as large as the largest value so that Access can stop someone from entering a value that may not fit on a form or report.

Changing a field data type

You must be very careful when changing a field's data type if you want to preserve your existing data. Such a change is rare; most data types limit (by definition) what kind of data you can input. Normally, for example, you cannot input a letter into a Number field or a Date/Time field.

Some data types do, however, convert readily to others. For example, a Number field can be converted to a Text data type, but you lose the understanding of mathematics in the value because you can no longer perform mathematical calculations with the values. Sometimes you might accidentally create a phone number or ZIP code as a Number and want to redefine the data type correctly as Text. Of course, you also have to remember the other places where you've used the field name (for example, queries, forms, or reports).

Caution   The OLE data type cannot be converted to any other format. Any field cannot be converted to an AutoNumber field if there is any data in the table already.

You need to understand four basic conversion types as you change from one data type to another. The paragraphs that follow describe each of these types.

To Text from other data types

Converting to Text is easiest; you can convert practically any other data type to Text with no problems. Number or Currency data can be converted with no special formatting (dollar signs or commas) if you use the General Number format; the decimal point remains intact. Yes/No data converts as is; Date/Time data also converts as is if you use the General Date format (mm/dd/yy hh:mm:ss AM/PM). Hyperlink data easily converts to Text. The displayed text loses its underline but the remaining Internet resource link information is visible.

From Text to Number, Currency, Date/Time, Yes/No, or Hyperlink

Only data stored as numeric characters (0, 1, 2, 3, 4, 5, 6, 7, 8, 9) or as periods, commas, and dollar signs can be converted to Number or Currency data from the Text data type. You must also make sure that the maximum length of the text string is not larger than the field size for the type of number or currency field you use in the conversion.

Text data being converted to Date data types must be in a correct date or time format. You can use any legal date or time format (such as 10/12/2001, 12-Oct-00, or October 1999), or any of the other date/time formats.

You can convert text fields to either a Yes or No value, depending on the specification in the field. Access recognizes Yes, True, or On as Yes values, and No, False, or Off as No values.

 Tip   Access can also convert Number data types to Yes/No values. Access interprets Null values as Null, 0 as No, and any nonzero value as Yes.

A text field that contains correctly formatted hyperlink text converts directly to hyperlink format — displaying text and address.

From Currency to Number

You can convert data from Currency to Number data types as long as the receiving field can handle the size and number of decimal places. Remember that the Field Size property in numeric fields determines the size (in bytes) of the storage space and the maximum number of decimal places. Anything can be converted to Double, which holds 8 bytes and 15 decimals, whereas Single holds only 4 bytes and 7 decimal places. (For more information, refer to "Entering field-size properties" later in this chapter and to Table 2-2.)

From Text to Memo

You can always convert from Text to Memo data types because the maximum length of a text field is 255 characters, whereas a memo field can hold up to 65,536 characters. You can convert from Memo to Text, however, only if every value in the memo fields is less than the text field size — that is, no more than 255 characters. Values longer than the field size are truncated.

Understanding Field Properties

After you enter the field names, data types, and field descriptions, you may want to go back and further define each field. Every field has properties, and these are different for each data type. In the tblContacts table, you must enter properties for several data types. Figure 2-14 shows the property area for the field named curCreditLimit; 10 options are available in the General section of the property area. Notice that there are two tabs on the property box — General and Lookup. Lookup is discussed later in this chapter.

 Tip   Figure 2-14 shows 10 property options available for the Currency field named curCreditLimit. Other types, such as Number and Date/Time (11), Text (14), or Yes/No (7) will show more or fewer options.

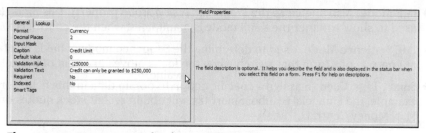

Figure 2-14: Property area for the Currency field named curCreditLimit.

Pressing F6 switches between the field entry pane and the property pane. You can also move between panes by clicking the desired pane. Some properties display a list of possible values, along with a downward-pointing arrow, when you move the pointer into the field. When you click the arrow, the values appear in a drop-down list.

Here is a list of all the general properties (note that they may not all be displayed, depending on which data type you chose):

✦ **Field Size.** Text: limits size of the field to the specified number of characters (1–255); default is 50.

✦ **New Values.** Allows specification of increment or random type.

✦ **Format.** Changes the way data appears after you enter it (uppercase, dates, and so on).

✦ **Input Mask.** Used for data entry into a predefined and validated format (Phone numbers, ZIP codes, Social Security numbers, Dates, Custom IDs).

✦ **Decimal Places.** Specifies number of decimal places (Numeric/Currency only).

✦ **Caption.** Optional label for form and report fields (replacing the field name).

✦ **Default Value.** The value filled in automatically for new data entry into the field.

✦ **Validation Rule.** Validates data based on rules created through expressions or macros.

✦ **Validation Text.** Displays a message when data fails validation.

✦ **Required.** Specifies whether you must enter a value into a field.

✦ **Allow Zero Length.** Determines whether you may enter the value " " into a text field type to distinguish it from a null value.

✦ **Indexed.** Speeds up data access and (if desired) limits data to unique values.

✦ **Unicode Compression.** Used for multi-language applications. Requires about twice the data storage but enables Office documents including Access reports to be displayed correctly no matter what language or symbols are used.

✦ **IME Mode.** Also known as the *Kanji Conversion Mode* property, this mode is used to show whether the Kanji mode is maintained when the control is lost.

✦ **IME Sentence Mode.** Used to determine the Sequence mode of fields of a table or controls of a form that switch when the focus moves in or out of the field.

✦ **Smart Tags**. Used to assign a specific action to obtain data in this field. For example, the Financial Symbol Smart tag will obtain recent stock quotes on MSN Money Central.

Note   IME Mode and IME Sequence Mode are available only if international support for Simplified Chinese, Traditional Chinese, or Japanese is enabled through Microsoft Office Language Settings. *IME* stands for Input Method Editor.

Entering field-size properties

Field size has two purposes. For text fields, it simply specifies the storage and display size. For example, the field size for the chrEmail field is 100 bytes. You should enter the size for each field with a Text data type. If you don't change the default field size, Access uses a 50-byte size for each text field in every record. You should limit the size to the value equal to the largest number of characters.

For numeric data types (Number, Currency and AutoNumber), the field size enables you to further define the type of number, which in turn determines the storage size. There are seven possible settings in the Numeric Field Size property, as described in Table 2-3.

You should make the field size the smallest one possible; Access runs faster with smaller field sizes. Note that the first three settings don't use decimal points but allow increasingly larger positive or negative numbers. Single and Double permit even larger numbers: Single gives you 7 decimal places, and Double allows 15. Use the Double setting when you need many decimal places or very large numbers.

Table 2-3
Numeric Field Settings

Field Size Setting	Range	Decimal Places	Storage Size
Byte	0 to 255	None	1 byte
Integer	-32,768 to 32,767	None	2 bytes
Long Integer	-2,147,483,648 to 2,147,483,647	None	4 bytes
Double	-1.797×10^{308} to 1.797×10^{308}	15	8 bytes
Single	-3.4×10^{38} to 3.4×10^{38}	7	4 bytes
Replication ID	N/A	N/A	16 bytes
Decimal	1 – 28 precision	15	8 bytes

Tip

Use the Currency data type to define data that stores monetary amounts.

Tip

The Replication ID (field size property) data type should be used for AutoNumber fields that are used in databases that will be replicated, and more than 100 records are routinely added. This is also true for any numeric field where the field is the primary key. When two copies of a table are synchronized, it is possible to get duplicate fields in the numeric values *unless* the field type is set to Replication ID. This will produce a 128-bit value that will require more disk space.

Using formats

Formats enable you to display your data in a form that differs from the actual keystrokes used to enter the data originally. Formats vary, depending on the data type you use. Some data types have predefined formats; others have only user-defined formats, and some data types have both. Formats affect only the way your data appears, not how it is actually stored in the table or how it should be entered.

Text and Memo data-type formats

Access uses four user-defined format symbols in Text and Memo data types:

@	Required text character (character or space)
&	Text character not required
<	Forces all characters to lowercase
>	Forces all characters to uppercase

The symbols @ and & work with individual characters that you input, but the < and > characters affect the whole entry. If you want to make sure that a name is always displayed as uppercase, for example, you enter > in the Format property. If you want to enter a phone number and allow entry of only the numbers, yet display the data with parentheses and a dash, you enter the following into the Format property: (@@@)@@@-@@@@. You can then enter 2035551234 and have the data displayed as (203) 555-1234.

You can also specify your own Custom Format for Text and Memo fields. To specify a custom format, you create a format specific for the field that you want to show. The example above for telephone numbers is a type of Custom Format; however, you have a bit more flexibility than suggested by the telephone example.

When creating a custom format, you can specify two sections for the format, separated by a semicolon (;). The first section is the format for the fields with text; the second is the format for fields with a *zero-length* value and a *null* value. To specify a custom format, you can use the @ (required), & (optional), < (convert to lowercase for display), or >(convert to all uppercase for display) symbols for the first part of the format and any text you wish to specify for the second part (surrounded by quotation marks). For example, the format: "**@@@-@@;"Unknown"[Red]** displays the data with a dash without you having to type a dash, and it will display the word *Unknown* (colored Red) if the field is left blank.

Number and Currency data type formats

You can choose from six predefined formats for Numeric or Currency formats and many symbols for creating your own custom formats. The predefined formats are as shown in Table 2-4, along with a column that shows how to define custom formats.

Table 2-4
Numeric Format Examples

Format Type	Number As Entered	Number As Displayed	Format Defined
General	987654.321	987654.3	######.#
Currency	987654.321	$987,654.32	$###,##0.00
Euro	987654.321	987,654.32	###,##0.00
Fixed	987654.321	987654.32	######.##
Standard	987654.321	987,654.32	###,###.##
Percent	.987	98.7%	###.##%
Scientific	987654.321	9.88E+05	###E+00
Euro	987654.321	987,654.32	###,###.##

All the formats above are the default formats based on setting the Decimal places property to AUTO.

Table 2-4 also shows the default format that would be built internally when selecting any of the built-in format definitions. However, you can also specify your own custom format in this field by typing your example data. Numeric custom formats have four parts that can be specified: (1) for positive numbers, (2) for negative numbers, (3) for zero values, and (4) for null values. You can even specify a specific color to display for each section. For example, you could create a custom format for Currency that may look like this: **$#,##0.00[Green]; ($#,##0.00)[Red]; "zero";"Null"** this format uses all four sections. It will display all values that are positive in green, values that are negative in red; any field that contains a 0 with the word *zero*, and any field that has not had a value entered with the word *Null*.

The symbols you can use in a numeric field custom format are period (.), comma (,), 0 (digit place holder that shows a digit or 0), # (digit place holder that shows the digit or nothing), $ (show the literal $), % (show % sign), E- or e- (minus sign next to scientific notation), and E+ or e+ (displays a minus sign next to negative numbers and a plus sign next to positive numbers). A final Currency example could be #,##0.00; (#,##0.00);;"Null". This will show the numbers displaying negatives in parentheses, a minimum of 0.00, and the word *Null* in fields with a null value. Note that the 0 section was not used because the minimum valued displayed was already 0.00.

Date/Time data-type formats

The Date/Time data formats are the most extensive of all, providing these seven predefined options:

✦ **General Date.** (Default) Display depends on the value entered; entering only a date will display only a date; entering only time will result in no date displayed; standard format for date and time is 2/10/03 10:32 PM

✦ **Long Date.** Taken from Windows Regional Settings Section Long Date setting; example: Wednesday, February 10, 2003

✦ **Medium Date.** Example: 10-Feb-03

✦ **Short Date.** Taken from Windows Regional Settings Section Short Date setting; example: 2/10/03

Tip

For the best Year 2000 compliancy, define all of your dates as Short Dates. When the Windows Regional Settings are changed to display four digit years, so will all of your date fields.

Note

Office 2003 automatically treats all two-digit dates before 30 as 2000–2029. Other dates are treated as 1930–1999.

✦ **Long Time.** Taken from Windows Regional Settings Section Time setting; example: 10:32:15 PM

✦ **Medium Time.** Example: 10:32 PM

✦ **Short Time.** Example: 22:32

You can also use a multitude of user-defined date and time settings, including these:

: (colon)	Time separator; taken from Windows Regional Settings Section Separator setting
/	Date separator
c	Same as General Date format

d, dd	Day of the month — one or two numerical digits (1–31)
ddd	First three letters of the weekday (Sun–Sat)
dddd	Full name of the weekday (Sunday–Saturday)
ddddd	Same as Short Date format
dddddd	Same as Long Date format
w	Day of the week (1–7)
ww	Week of the year (1–53)
m, mm	Month of the year — one or two digits (1–12)
mmm	First three letters of the month (Jan–Dec)
mmmm	Full name of the month (January–December)
q	Date displayed as quarter of the year (1–4)
y	Number of the day of the year (1–366)
yy	Last two digits of the year (01–99)
yyyy	Full year (0100–9999)
h, hh	Hour — one or two digits (0–23)
n, nn	Minute — one or two digits (0–59)
s, ss	Seconds — one or two digits (0–59)
ttttt	Same as Long Time format
AM/PM or A/P	Twelve-hour clock with AM/PM in uppercase as appropriate
am/pm or a/p	Twelve-hour clock with am/pm in lowercase as appropriate
AMPM	Twelve-hour clock with forenoon/afternoon designator, as defined in the Windows Regional Settings Section forenoon/afternoon setting

You can also specify custom formats for Data/Time types; however, they will be displayed based on the settings specified in the Regional Settings Properties dialog box in the Windows Control Panel. You can add a comma or other separator to your custom format, but you must enclose the separator in quotation marks. For example, the following format using the comma will display February 04, 2003 for the date 02/04/03: mmm dd", " yyyy.

Yes/No data-type formats

Access stores Yes/No data in a manner different from what you might expect. The Yes data is stored as a –1, whereas No data is stored as a 0. You'd expect it to be stored as a 0 for No and 1 for Yes, but this isn't the case. Without a format setting, you must enter –1 or 0, and it will be stored and displayed that way. With formats, you can store Yes/No data types in a more recognizable manner. The three predefined format settings for Yes/No data types are

✦ **Yes/No.** (Default) Displays –1 as Yes, 0 as No

✦ **True/False.** Stores –1 as True, 0 as False

✦ **On/Off.** Stores –1 as On, 0 as Off

You can also enter user-defined custom formats. User-defined Yes/No formats can contain up to three sections. The first section has no effect on the Yes/No data type but must always be a semicolon (;). The second section is used to display a value for the On or True values (literally stored as a –1). The third section is used to specify a value for the Off or False values (literally stored as a 0). If, for example, you want to use the values *Yep* for Yes and *Nope* for No, you enter **;"Yep"; "Nope"**. You can also specify a color to display different values. To display the Yep value in green and the Nope value in red, you enter **;"Yep" [Green]; "Nope" [Red]**.

> **Caution**
>
> There are two problems when changing the table level format property of a logical, Yes/No, field. First, if you enter a custom format like in the above example, you need to also change the default Lookup Display Control property from check box to Text box to see the new format. Second, after the format is assigned and the text box is the display method, the user will only be able to enter a 0 for –1. The format property affects only how the value is displayed, not how it is entered into the table.

Hyperlink data-type format

Access also displays and stores Hyperlink data in a manner different from what you would expect. The format of this type is composed of up to three parts:

✦ **Display Text.** The visual text that is displayed in the field or control

✦ **Address.** The path to a file (UNC) or page (URL) on the Internet

✦ **Sub-Address.** A specific location within a file or page

The parts are separated by pound signs. The Display Text is visible in the field or control, while the address and subaddress are hidden. For example, **Microsoft Net Home Page#http://www.msn.com.**

Entering formats

The tblContacts table uses several formats. The chrState text field has a > in the Format property to display the data entry in uppercase. The dtmOrigCustDate field has an mmm dd yyyy format to display the date of birth as the short month name, a space, the day and a four-digit year (Feb 04 2003). The blnActive field has a format of Yes/No with lookup Display Control property set to Text box.

Numeric custom formats can vary, based on the value. You can enter a four-part format into the Format property. The first part is for positive numbers, the second for negatives, the third if the value is 0, and the last if the value is null; for example, #,##0; (#,##0);"- -";"None".

Table 2-5 shows several formats.

Table 2-5 Format Examples		
Format Specified	**Data as Entered**	**Formatted Data as Displayed**
>	Adam Smith	ADAM SMITH
#,##0;(#,##0);"-0-";"None"	15 -15 0 No Data	15 (15) -0- None
Currency	12345.67	$12,345.67
"Acct No." 0000	3271	Acct No. 3271
mmm yy	9/11/03	Sep 03
Long Date	9/11/03	Friday, September 11, 2003

Entering input masks

Input masks enable you to have more control over data entry by defining data-validation placeholders for each character that you enter into a field. Another way of thinking about this is that the Input mask property lets you design a pattern that will be used to *input* information into the field. This pattern, or input mask, is what the users will see when they begin to enter the data. This pattern or mask is *not* saved in the underlying data. This is different from how the field will be displayed — controlled by the format property.

For example, if you set the input mask property to (999)000-0000, parentheses and hyphens appear as shown when entering data and an underscore (_)appears in place of each 9 or 0 of this phone number template. You would see (_) in your data entry field. Access will automatically add a \ character before each placeholder; for example, \(999\)000\-0000. You can also enter a multi-part input mask, such as !(999)000-0000;0;" ". The input mask can contain up to three parts separated by semicolons.

The first section of a multi-part mask defines the input mask itself (for example, !(999)000-0000). The ! is used to fill the input mask from right to left when optional characters are on the left side. The second section specifies whether Access stores the literal display characters in the table when you enter data. If you enter a 0 for this part, all literal display characters (for example, the parentheses and hyphen) are stored with the value; if you enter 1 or leave this part blank, only characters typed into the text box are stored. The third part specifies the character that Microsoft Access displays for spaces in the input mask. You can use any character; the default is an underscore. If you want to display a space, use a space enclosed in quotation marks (" ").

Note When you have defined an input mask and set the Format property for the same data, the Format property takes precedence when Access displays the data. This means that even if you've saved an input mask with data, it is ignored when data is formatted.

Some of the characters that can be used are shown in Table 2-6.

Table 2-6
Input Mask Characters

Character	Description
0	Digits only (0–9; entry is required; can't use plus [+] and minus [–] signs).
9	Only Digit or space (entry not required; can't use [+] and [–]).
#	Digit or space and sign (entry not required; blanks converted to spaces; the [+] and [-] signs are allowed).
L	Alphabetic Letters only (A–Z, a-z; no spaces allowed; entry is required).
?	Alphabetic Letters only (A–Z, a-z; no spaces allowed; entry is optional).
A	Alphanumeric Letters or digits (A-Z, a-z, 0-9; no spaces allowed; entry is required).
a	Alphanumeric Letters or digits (A-Z, a-z, 0-9; no spaces allowed; entry is optional).
&	Any character or a space (A-z, 0-9; entry is required).
C	Any character or a space (A-z, 0-9; entry is optional).
<	Converts all characters that follow the symbol to lowercase.
>	Converts all characters that follow the symbol to uppercase.
!	Causes input mask to fill from right to left, rather than from left to right, when characters on the left side of the input mask are optional. You can include the exclamation point anywhere in the input mask.
\	Displays the character that follows as the literal character (for example, appears as just A).
. , : ; - /	Decimal placeholder, thousands, and date time separator determined by Regional Settings section of the Control Panel.

Tip   Setting the Input Mask property to the word *Password* creates a password entry text box. Any character typed in the text box is stored as the character, but appears as an asterisk (*).

The Input Mask Wizard

Although you can enter an Input Mask manually, you can easily create an input mask for text or date type fields by using the Input Mask Wizard. When you click the Input Mask property, the builder button (three periods) appears. You can click the Build button to start the Wizard. Figure 2-15 shows the first screen of the Input Mask Wizard.

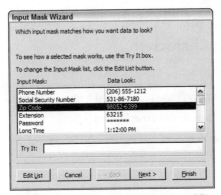

Figure 2-15: The Input Mask Wizard for creating input masks for text and date field types.

The Input Mask Wizard shows not only the name of each predefined input mask, but also an example for each name. You can choose from the list of predefined masks; click the Try It text box to see how data entry will look. After you choose an input mask, the next Wizard screen enables you to customize it and determine the placeholder symbol. Another Wizard screen enables you to decide whether to store any special characters with the data. When you complete the Wizard, Access places the actual input mask characters in the property sheet.

Tip   You can create your own input masks for text and date/time fields by simply clicking the Edit List button and entering a Descriptive name, Input Mask, place holder character, and a sample data content. Once created, the new mask will be available the next time you use the Input Mask Wizard.

You can enter as many custom masks as you need. You can also determine the international settings so that you can work with multiple country masks.

Entering decimal places

Decimal places are valid only for Number or Currency data. The number of decimal places can be from 0 to 15, depending on the field size of the numeric or currency field. If the field size is Byte, Integer, or Long Integer, you can have 0 decimal places. If the field size is Single, you can enter from 0 to 7 for the Decimal Places property. If the field size is Double, you can enter from 0 to 15 for the Decimal Places property. If you define a field as Currency (or use one of the predefined formats, such as General, Fixed, or Standard), Access sets the number of decimal places to 2 automatically. You can override this setting by entering a different value into the Decimal Places property.

Creating a caption

You use *captions* when you want to display an alternative to the field name on forms and reports. Normally, the label used to describe a field in a form or a report is the field name. Sometimes, however, you want to call the field name one thing while displaying a more (or less) descriptive label. You should keep field names as short as possible to make them easier to use in calculations. You may then want a longer name to be used for a label in forms or reports. For example, you may use the field name Length but want the label *Length (in)* on all forms.

Tip　Many of the fields in the tables of the Access Auto Auctions system use captions for the fields. It is a good idea to use a caption for your field names that will be displayed on the screen. For example, changing the name of the chrFirstName field to First Name (with a space between the words) makes the name more understandable to the user.

Setting a default value

A *default value* is the value Access automatically displays for the field when you add a new record to the table. This value can be any value that matches the data type of the field. A default is no more than an initial value; you can change it during data entry. To enter a default value, simply enter the desired value into the Default Value property setting. A default value can be an expression, as well as a number or a text string. Chapter 11 explains how to create expressions.

Note　Number and Currency data types are set automatically to 0 when you add a new record.

Working with validation

Data validation enables you to limit the values that are accepted in a field. Validation may be automatic, such as the checking of a numeric field for text or a valid date.

Validation can also be user-defined. User-defined validation can be as simple as a range of values (such as those found in the Length or Weight fields), or it can be an expression like the one found in the Gender field.

Figure 2-14 (shown earlier) displays the property area for the curCreditLimit field. Notice the validation options for the curCreditLimit field. The Validation Rule <250000 specifies that the number entered must be less than 250,000. The Validation Text message "Credit can only be granted to $250,000" appears in a warning dialog box (see Figure 2-16) if a user tries to enter a value greater than 250,000.

Figure 2-16: A data-validation warning box. This appears when the user enters a value in the field that does not match the rule specified in the design of the table.

Caution

The dialog box shown in Figure 2-16 will not display if you have the Show Office Assistant value turned on for Help. Rather, the message will be displayed in a message box shown by the Assistant, as shown in Figure 2-17.

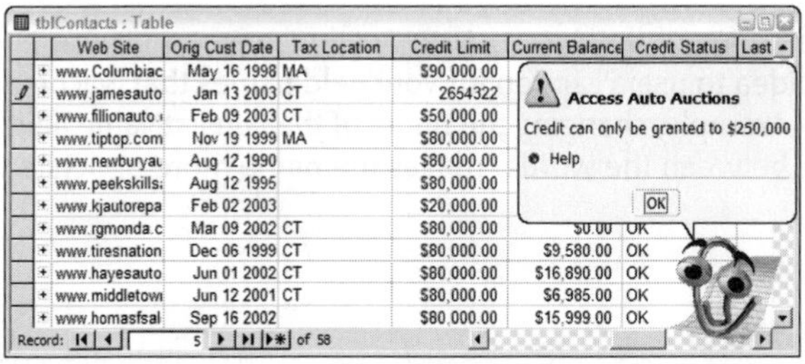

Figure 2-17: The warning displayed by the Assistant that a value was entered outside of the range of the accepted values.

You can also use Date values with Date/Time data types in range validation. Dates are surrounded, or *delimited*, by pound signs when used in data-validation expressions. If you want to limit the dtmLastSalesDate data entry to dates between January 1, 2000, and December 31, 2005, you enter Between #1/1/00# and #12/31/05#.

Tip

If you want to limit the upper end to the current date, you can enter a different set of dates, such as Between #1/1/00# and Date( ).

Following the design in Table 2-7, you can now complete all the property settings in the tblContacts table. Note that the design shows only the critical fields that must have their properties defined. You can also find this table (and the others in this book) in the Access Auto Auctions databases on the CD-ROM that accompanies this book.

Table 2-7 Properties for the tblContacts Table	
Field Name	**Properties**
idsContactID:	Caption – a Contact ID, Indexed – **Yes (No Duplicates) [Set when you make this field the primary key field]**.
chrContactType:	Caption – Contact Type.
chrFirstName:	Caption – First Name.
chrLastName:	Caption – Last Name.
chrCompany:	Caption – Company
chrAddress:	Caption – Address
chrCity:	Caption – City
chrState:	Format > , Caption – State
chrZipCode:	Input Mask – 00000\-9999;0;_ , Caption – Zip Code, Indexed Yes (Duplicates OK)
chrCustomerType:	Caption – Customer Type, Indexed Yes (Duplicates OK)
chrPhone:	Input Mask – !\(999") "000\-0000;0;_, Caption – Phone
chrFax:	Input Mask – !\(999") "000\-0000;0;_, Caption – Fax
chrEmail:	Field Size – 100 , Caption – Email
hlkWebSite:	Field Size – 100 , Caption – Web Site
dtmOrigCustDate:	Format – mmm dd yyyy, Caption – Orig Cust Date
chrTaxLocation:	Field Size – 2, Format - >, Caption – Tax Location, Indexed Yes (Duplicates OK)
curCreditLimit:	Format – Currency, Decimal Places – 2, Caption – Credit Limit, Validation Rule - < 250000
curCurBal:	Caption – Current Balance
chrCreditStatus:	Caption – Credit Status
dtmLastSalesDate:	Caption – Last Sales Date
dblDiscountPercent:	Caption – Discount Percent
memNotes:	Caption – Notes
blnActive:	Format – Yes/No, Caption – Active, Display Control (Lookup) – Text Box

Understanding the Lookup Property window

The Field Properties pane of the Table Design window has a second tab: the Lookup tab. After clicking this tab, you may see a single property, the Display Control property. This property is used for Text, Number, and Logical fields.

Figure 2-18 shows the Lookup Property window for the blnActive Yes/No field where Display Control is the only property. This property has three choices: Check Box, Text Box, and Combo Box. Choosing one of these determines which control type is used when a particular field is added to a form. Generally, all controls are created as text boxes except Yes/No fields, which are created as a check box by default. For Yes/No data types, however, you may want to use the Text Box setting to display Yes/No, True/False, or another choice that you specifically put in the format property box.

If you are working with text fields instead of a Yes/No field and know a certain text field can only be one of a few combinations, select the combo box choice for the display control. When you select the Combo Box control type as a default, the properties change so that you can define a combo box.

Cross-Reference   You learn about combo boxes in Chapter 10.

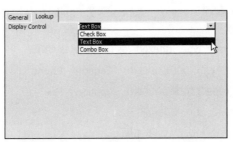

Figure 2-18: The Lookup property Display Control for a Yes/No field.

Note   The properties for a Lookup field are different for each data type. The Yes/No data type fields differ from text fields or numeric fields. Because a Lookup field is really a combo box (you learn more about these later), the standard properties for a combo box are displayed when you select a Lookup field data type.

Determining the Primary Key

Every table should have a *primary key* — one or more fields with a unique value for each record. (This principle is called *entity integrity* in the world of database management.) In the tblContacts table, the idsContactID field is the primary key. Each contact has a different idsContactID value so that you can identify one from the other. If you don't specify a primary key (unique value field), Access can create one for you.

Creating a unique key

Without the idsContactID field, you'd have to rely on another field for uniqueness. You couldn't use the chrLastName field because two customers could have the same last name. In fact, you couldn't even use the chrLastName and chrFirstName fields together (multi-field key), for the same reason — two people could be named James Williamson. You need to come up with a field that makes every record unique. Looking at the table, you may think that you could use the chrLastName and chrFirstName and chrCompany fields, but theoretically, it's possible that two people work at the same company with the same name. The easiest way to solve this problem is to create a single field with a unique value for each record — for example, the idsContactID field.

Cross-Reference Multiple-field primary keys are discussed in Chapter 3.

If you don't designate a field as a primary key, Access can create an AutoNumber field and add it to the beginning of the table. This field contains a unique number for each record in the table, and Access maintains it automatically. For several reasons, however, you may want to create and maintain your own primary key:

   ✦ A primary key is an index.

   ✦ Indexes maintain a presorted order of one or more fields that greatly speeds up queries, searches, and sort requests.

   ✦ When you add new records to your table, Access checks for duplicate data and doesn't allow any duplicates for the primary key field.

   ✦ Access displays your data in the order of the primary key.

By designating a field such as idsContactID as the unique primary key, you can see your data in an understandable order. In our example, the idsContactID field is assigned automatically by Access in the order that a record is put into the system.

Tip When creating a unique primary key, many developers believe that you should create it based on some method. For example, if it is a customer name, you may want to use the first four letters of their last name, the first initial, and then a three-digit unique number. Bill Jones could be JONESB001, Adam Jones could be JONESA002, and on and on.

Creating the primary key

The primary key can be created in any of four ways:

✦ Select the field to be used as the primary key and choose Edit ➪ Primary Key.

✦ Select the field to be used as the primary key and select the Primary Key button (the key icon) in the toolbar.

✦ Right-click the mouse to display the shortcut menu and select Primary Key.

✦ Save the table without creating a primary key, and Access automatically creates an AutoNumber field.

Before you click the Primary Key button or select the menu choice, you must click the gray area in the far-left side of the field that you want as the primary key. A right-pointing triangle appears. After you select the primary key, a key appears in the gray area to indicate that the primary key has been created.

Because a primary key must contain a unique value and that value cannot be a blank, you need to make sure that the table tblContacts is still empty in the My Access Auto Auctions database and then assign the primary key. Follow these steps to empty the table and create a primary key:

1. Select and open the table named tblContacts in the Database window.

2. Select all the fields by clicking in the first (selector) field and while holding the mouse button drag across all records. The records should be highlighted.

3. Press the Delete key and answer Yes to the dialog box that appears and says "You are about to delete **X** record(s)."

4. Click the Design button to move to the design window.

5. Select the idsContactID field.

6. Click the Primary Key button to make the idsContactID field the primary key.

7. Save the file.

The Indexes window

A primary key is really an *index*. In the table Design View, the key icon beside the idsContactID field indicates that this field is the primary key for the table. You can also see the primary key by looking at the Indexes window. (Figure 2-19 shows a primary key in the Indexes window.) You can display or hide this window by toggling the Indexes button on the toolbar or selecting View ➪ Indexes from the menu bar.

Using the Indexes window, you can determine whether an index is a primary key, whether or not it is unique, and whether null values should be ignored. Notice that the window in Figure 2-19 shows four indexes. All four indexes are built on a single field (idsContactID, chrZipCode, chrCustomerType, and chrTaxLocation) and in Ascending Order. Each index has an Index name — the idsContactID field is the Primary Key index; notice the key symbol in the first column. Looking at the primary properties pane of the window in Figure 2-19, you can see that it says this key is the Primary key and that the Unique property is set to Yes and Nulls are not ignored.

Index Name	Field Name	Sort Order
PrimaryKey	idsContactID	Ascending
chrZipCode	chrZipCode	Ascending
chrCustomerType	chrCustomerType	Ascending
chrTaxLocation	chrTaxLocation	Ascending

Indexes: tblContacts

Index Properties

Primary	Yes	
Unique	Yes	The name for this index. Each index can use
Ignore Nulls	No	up to 10 fields.

Figure 2-19: The Indexes window that shows all the indexes built for the tblContacts table. You can add more indexes directly into this window.

Note   If you create the tblContacts table as described in Table 2-7 you should have created these four indexes.

The Table Properties window

Just as each field has a property area, the overall table has one, too. While in the Table Design window, right-click while the cursor is inside the design area and choose Properties or click the Properties button (hand with a piece of paper) on the Table Design toolbar to display the Table Properties window.

Cross-Reference   Figure 2-20 shows the Table Properties window. Here you can enter the validation rule and message that are to be applied to the overall record that will be enforced when you save a record. You can assign a Description name for the table that will be displayed in datasheet mode. You can set up a default sorting order (other than by primary key) and even a default filter to show only a subset of the data. This is also where you can set up your sub-datasheets.

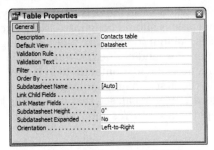

Figure 2-20: Setting general Table properties.

Printing a Table Design

You can print a table design by using Tools ⇨ Analyze ⇨ Documenter. The *Database Documenter* is an Access tool that makes it easy to document your database objects. When you select this command, Access shows you a dialog box that lets you select objects to print. In Figure 2-21, there is only one object, the tblContact table, under the Tables tab. You can select it by clicking the check box next to the table name.

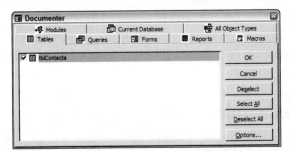

Figure 2-21: The Access Documenter dialog box.

You can also set various options for printing. When you click the Options button, a dialog box appears that enables you to select which information from the Table Design to print. You can print the various field names, all of their properties, the indexes, and even network permissions.

After you select which data you want to view, Access generates a report; you can view it in a Print Preview window or send the output to a printer.

Tip   The Database Documenter creates a table of all the objects and object properties you specify. You can use this utility to document such database objects as forms, queries, reports, macros, and modules.

Saving the Completed Table

You can save the completed table design by choosing File ➪ Save or by clicking the Save button on the toolbar. If you are saving the table for the first time, Access asks for the name of the table; enter it and click OK. Table names can be up to 64 characters long and follow standard Access field-naming conventions. If you have saved this table before and want to save it with a different name, choose File ➪ Save As and enter a different table name. This creates a new table design and leaves the original table with its original name untouched. If you want to delete the old table, select it in the Database window and press Delete. You can also save the table when you close it.

Manipulating Tables in a Database Window

As you create many tables in your database, you may want to use them in other databases or copy them for use as a history file. You may want to copy only the table structure. You can perform many operations on tables in the Database window, including

✦ Renaming tables

✦ Deleting tables

✦ Copying tables in a database

✦ Copying a table from another database

You can perform these tasks by direct manipulation or by using menu items.

Renaming tables

You can rename a table with these steps:

1. Select the table name in the Database window.

2. Click once on the table name.

3. Type the name of the new table and press Enter.

You can also rename the table by selecting Edit ➪ Rename or by right-clicking a table and selecting Rename from the shortcut menu. After you change the table name, it appears in the Tables list, which re-sorts the tables in alphabetical order.

Caution   If you rename a table, you must change the table name in any objects where it was previously referenced, including queries, forms, and reports.

Deleting tables

You can delete a table by selecting the table name and pressing the Delete key. Another method is to select the table name and select Edit ➪ Delete or by right-clicking a table and selecting Delete from the shortcut menu. Like most delete operations, you have to confirm the delete by selecting Yes in a Delete Table dialog box.

Copying tables in a database

By using the Copy and Paste options from the Edit menu or the toolbar buttons, you can copy any table in the database. When you paste the table back into the database, you can choose from three option buttons:

✦ Structure Only

✦ Structure and Data

✦ Append Data to Existing Table

Selecting the Structure Only button creates a new table design with no data. This enables you to create an empty table with all the same field names and properties as the original table. This option is typically used to create a temporary table or a history structure to which you can copy old records.

When you select Structure and Data, a complete copy of the table design and all of its data is created.

Selecting the button Append Data to Existing Table adds the data of one table to the bottom of another. This option is useful for combining tables, such as when you want to add data from a monthly transaction table to a yearly history table.

Follow these steps to copy a table:

1. Select the table name in the Database window.

2. Select Edit ➪ Copy.

3. Select Edit ➪ Paste.

4. Type the name of the new table.

5. Choose one of the Paste options.

6. Click OK to complete the operation.

Figure 2-22 shows the Paste Table As dialog box, where you make these decisions. To paste the data, you have to select the type of paste operation and type the name of the new table. When you are appending data to an existing table, you must type the name of an existing table.

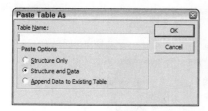

Figure 2-22: Pasting a table activates this dialog box. You can paste only the structure, the data and structure, or the data to an existing table.

Copying a table to another database

Just as you can copy a table within a database, you can copy a table to another database. There are many reasons why you may want to do this. Possibly you share a common table among multiple systems, or you may need to create a backup copy of your important tables within the system.

When you copy tables to another database, the relationships between tables are not copied; Access copies only the table design and the data. The method for copying a table to another database is essentially the same as for copying a table within a database. To copy a table to another database, follow these steps:

1. Select the table name in the Database window.

2. Select Edit ➪ Copy.

3. Open another database.

4. Select Edit ➪ Paste.

5. Type the name of the new table.

6. Choose one of the Paste options.

7. Click OK to complete the operation.

Adding Records to a Database Table

So far you have only created one table in the My Access Auto Auctions database: tblContacts.

Adding records is as simple as selecting the table name in the database container and clicking on its name to bring up the table in datasheet view. Once opened, you can type in values for each field. Figure 2-23 shows adding records in datasheet mode to the table.

You can enter information into all fields except the Contact ID field (idsContactID). AutoNumber fields will enter a number automatically for you.

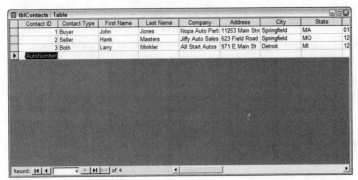

Figure 2-23: Adding records to a table using the table datasheet.

Although you can add records directly into the table through the datasheet view, it is not the most efficient way. It is better to add records through use of forms.

Chapter 4 covers adding records to tables using forms.

✦   ✦   ✦

Entering Data into Tables and Forms

In Chapter 2, you created a database container named My Access Auto Auctions to hold the tables, queries, forms, reports, and macros that you will create as you learn Access. You also created a table named tblContacts in datasheet mode and in the Design surface. In this chapter, you will use a datasheet to enter data into an Access table. Then you will work with displaying the data in the datasheet in many different ways. Using a datasheet to view and work with your data enables you to see many records at once. Using the tblContacts and tblProducts tables, you will learn to add, change, and delete data, as well as learn about the features available in Access for displaying data in a datasheet.

On the
CD-ROM
This chapter uses the database named CHAP03Start.mdb. If you have not already copied it onto your machine from the CD, you will need to do so now.

Understanding Datasheets

Using a datasheet is one of the many ways that you can view data in Access. Datasheets display a list of records in a format commonly known as a *browse screen,* in dBASE, a table view in Paradox, and a spreadsheet in Excel or Lotus 1-2-3. The format is also referred to as a *browse table* or *table view.*

A datasheet is like a table or spreadsheet because data is displayed as a series of rows and columns. Figure 3-1 is a typical datasheet view of data. Like a table or spreadsheet, a datasheet displays data as a series of rows and columns. Each row represents a single record, and each column represents a single field in the table. By scrolling up or down in the datasheet, you can see records that don't fit onscreen at that moment, and by scrolling left or right, you can see more columns or fields.

Datasheets are completely customizable, so you can view your data in many ways. By changing the font size, you can see more or less of your table onscreen. You can rearrange the order of the records or the fields. You can hide columns, change the displayed column width or row height, and lock several columns in position so that they continue to be displayed as you scroll around other parts of your datasheet.

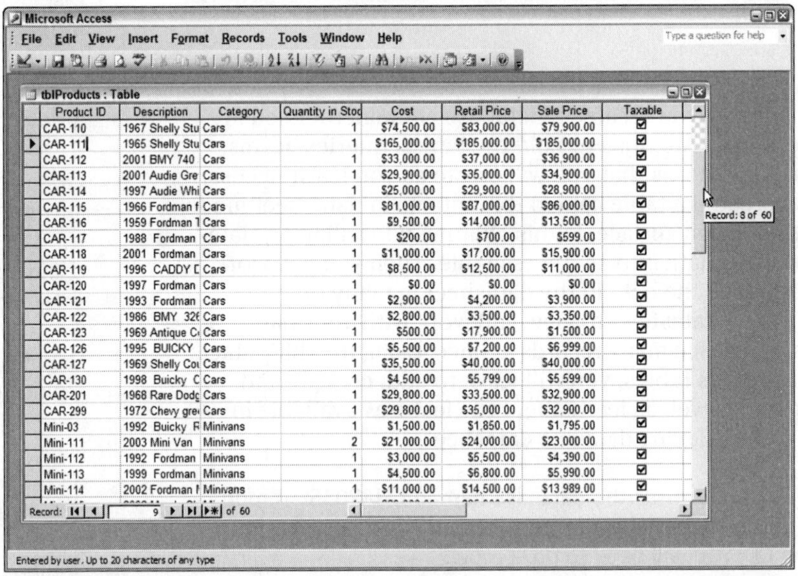

Figure 3-1: A typical datasheet view of data. Each column holds the common information that is found in a single field (like the Description or Retail Price). Each row represents a single record in the table.

You can sort the datasheet quickly into any order by using one toolbar button. You can filter the datasheet for specific records—making other records invisible. You can also import records directly to the datasheet or export formatted records from the datasheet directly to Word, Excel, or other applications that support *OLE* (Object Linking and Embedding) 2.x.

The Datasheet Window

The Datasheet window is similar to other object windows in Access. The actual Datasheet window is open within the Access window. At the top of the Access window, you see the title bar (displaying Microsoft Access), the menu bar, and the toolbars.

Quick Review of Records and Fields

As you recall, a *table* is a container for entering related information — patient records, a card list (Birthday/Xmas/Holiday), birthday reminders, payroll information, and on and on. Each table has a formal structure comprised of fields. Each field, when displayed in a *datasheet* (a two-dimensional sheet of information) can be found in each column, going from top to bottom. Each field has a specific type of data — text, numeric, date type, and so on. Each field has a unique name that is used to categorize the information stored in it. The table is composed of records, where each record stores information about a single entity (like a single customer or single product) in the fields of the table. One record is made up of information stored in all the fields of the table structure. For example, if a table has three fields — name, address, and phone number — then record one has one name, one address, and one phone number in it. Record two also has only one name, one address, and one phone number in it. All three fields can be found in each record — only the contents of those fields change. That is why a datasheet is an ideal way of looking at the contents of a table all at once — you can see the individual field contents by looking down any column (field). You can also review a single record's values by finding the row (record) that holds the information that you want to review and simply looking across the row to see all values for that specific record.

At the bottom of the Access window, you see the status bar. The status bar displays assorted information in the datasheet; for example, it may contain field description information (like in Figure 3-1, "Up to 100 character description of the product"), error messages, and warnings. If the field was given a description when it was created, the Field Description that you enter for each field is displayed here. If a specific field doesn't have a Field Description, Access displays the words *Datasheet View*. Generally, error messages and warnings appear in dialog boxes in the center of the screen rather than in the status bar. If you need help understanding the meaning of a button in the toolbar, move the mouse over the button, hovering over it, and a tooltip appears with a one- or two-word explanation.

In the center of the Access window in Figure 3-1 is another window — the actual Datasheet window. This Datasheet window displays the data in rows and columns. Each record occupies one row, and each column — headed by a field name in the first row or field title area of the browse window — contains that field's values. The display arranges the records initially by primary key and the fields by the order of their creation in the table design.

The right side of the window contains a scrollbar for moving quickly between records (up and down). As you scroll between records, a Scroll Tip (shown in Figure 3-1) tells you precisely where the scrollbar takes you. In Access 2003, the size of the scrollbar thumb gives you a proportional look at how many of the total number of records are being displayed. In Figure 3-1, the scrollbar thumb takes up about 12 percent of the scroll area, and 28 of 60 records are shown onscreen. You also have a proportional scrollbar at the bottom of the window for moving among fields (left to right and back). Also located at the bottom of the Datasheet window are the Navigation buttons (along the left side of the bottom of the frame). You can also use these buttons to move between records.

Moving within a datasheet

You can move easily in the Datasheet window by using the mouse pointer to indicate where you want to change or add to your data—just click a field and record location. In addition, the menus, toolbars, scrollbars, and navigation buttons make it easy to move among fields and records. You can think of a datasheet as a spreadsheet without the row numbers and column letters. Instead, your columns have field names, and your rows are unique records that have identifiable values in each cell.

Table 3-1 lists the navigational keys that you can use for moving within a datasheet.

Table 3-1 Navigating in a Datasheet	
Navigational Direction	*Keystrokes*
Next field	Tab
Previous field	Shift+Tab
First field of current record	Home
Last field of current record	End
Next record	Down arrow (↓)
Previous record	Up arrow (↑)
First field of first record	Ctrl+Home
Last field of last record	Ctrl+End
Scroll up one page	PgUp
Scroll down one page	PgDn
Go to record number box	F5

The Navigation buttons

The *Navigation buttons* (shown in Figure 3-2) are the six controls located at the bottom of the Datasheet window, which you click to move between records. The two leftmost controls move you to the first record or the previous record in the datasheet (table). The three rightmost controls position you on the next record, last record, or new record in the datasheet (table). If you know the record number (the row number of a specific record), you can click the record number box, enter a record number, and press Enter.

Figure 3-2: The Navigation buttons of a datasheet.

Note If you enter a record number greater than the number of records in the table, an error message appears stating that you can't go to the specified record.

The Datasheet toolbar

The Datasheet toolbar (shown in Figure 3-3) provides a way to work with the datasheet. The toolbar has many familiar objects on it, as well as some new ones.

Figure 3-3: The Datasheet toolbar.

The first icon is the View button, which allows you to switch between Table Design View, Datasheet View, PivotTable View, and PivotChart View. You can see all four choices by clicking the button's down-arrow (triangle pointing down). Clicking Design View permits you to make changes to the design of your table. You can then click the Datasheet View to return to the datasheet.

Note If you originally displayed a data-entry form, this icon has three primary choices: Table Design View, Datasheet View, and Form View, as well as the PivotTable and PivotChart Views.

The next icon, Save, looks like a floppy disk. Click this icon to save any layout changes to the datasheet.

Caution Save does not allow you to roll back changes to the data. As you move from record to record, the data is forever changed.

You can use the next icon, File Search, to activate the Basic Search dialog box (default), as shown in Figure 3-4. You can use this Search Box to search for specific files on your hard drive or network drive. You can switch to the Advance Search by selecting it at the bottom of the Basic File Search box.

Figure 3-4: The dialog box of the new toolbar button, File Search. This new tool lets you search for a specific file on your hard drive.

The next set of three icons includes Print (which looks like a printer and sends the datasheet information to your printer in a quick, two-dimensional table report) and Print Preview (which looks like a printed page with a magnifying glass and shows onscreen how your datasheet looks when printed). The third icon lets you spell-check your data using the standard Microsoft Office spell-checking feature.

Following the printer and spelling grouping are the editing buttons — Cut, Copy, and Paste — that are represented by these icons, respectively: scissors, two sheets of paper, and a clipboard. These three buttons allow you to remove a value, copy a value, and paste a value to the table. The objects that can be copied, removed, or pasted include a single value, a datasheet row, a column, or a range of values. You can copy and paste objects to and from other programs (such as Microsoft Word or Excel), but the Format Painter is not available in a datasheet.

The next icon, which looks like an arrow pointing counterclockwise, lets you Undo a change to a record, or, more globally, undo formatting.

The next icon is the Internet icon that enables you to insert a hyperlink.

The next two icons are the QuickSort icons. They are easy to identify — one is the letter A on top of the letter Z with the arrow pointing down (to represent alphabetical sort order), and the other icon is the reverse, Z to A (representing reverse sort order). You can select one or more columns and click one of these buttons to sort the data instantly, in ascending or descending order, using the selected columns as the sorting criteria.

The next three icons in this toolbar look like funnels. They let you determine and display only selected records. The first icon, Filter By Selection, lets you filter records to match a specific highlighted value in a given field. Each time you highlight a value, you add the selection to the filter. This additive process continues until the filter is cleared. (See the detailed discussion of this filter later in this chapter.)

The second icon, Filter By Form, turns each column of data into a combo box where you can select a single value from the datasheet and filter for matching records. Figure 3-5 illustrates how this works. A special window appears with the name of the table, which is tblProducts, and the Filter By Form title. Once open, you can click on a field, like in Figure 3-5, and select which choice you want to filter by. In Figure 3-5 you could select from "Cars, Minivans, Motor Homes, SUV, Trucks." Once selected, Access display only records that match your choice.

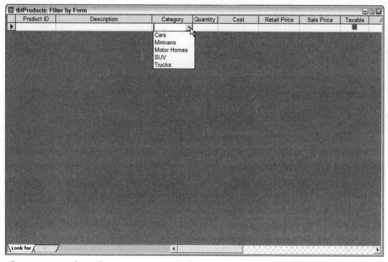

Figure 3-5: The Filter By Form window for filtering records via a series of field values. You simply select the value that you want from one or more columns and click the Filter By Form button.

You use the last icon in the group to turn any filter on or off; it is a toggle button. The first time you press it, you activate the search specified in the Filter By Form or Filter By Selection.

The Find icon is a pair of binoculars; clicking it displays a dialog box that lets you search for a specific value in a specific field.

The next two icons allow you to add a new record or delete an existing record. To create a new record, click the icon with the arrow and asterisk, and a new record row is added at the bottom of the datasheet. To delete an existing record, click anywhere in the record row that you want to delete and then click the icon with the arrow and X. A message displays, warning you that you are about to delete a record and that you won't be able to undo your change; select Yes to continue or No to save the record.

The next icon is the Database Window icon, which displays the Database window. Next is the New Object: AutoForm icon, which contains a pull-down menu that gives you choices so that you can create new objects, such as tables, queries, forms, reports, macros, and modules. Two interesting choices are the first two — AutoForm and AutoReport. When you click either of these, you immediately create a single record form or report that can be used without any further formatting.

The last icon is the Microsoft Access Help icon. When you click it, the Microsoft Access Help Window appears; here you can access help locally or through Office online at microsoft.com.

Opening a Datasheet

To open a datasheet from the Database window, follow these steps:

1. Using the CHAP03Start.mdb database from the CD, click the Tables button on the Objects menu bar of the Database window (in this case, CHAP03Start).

2. Click the table name that you want to open. (In this example, tblProducts.)

3. Click Open.

An alternative method for opening the datasheet is to double-click on the tblProducts table name.

 Tip   If you are in any of the design windows, you can click on the Datasheet button and view your data in a datasheet.

Entering New Data

When you open a datasheet, all the records in your table are visible; if you just created your table design, however, the new datasheet doesn't yet contain any data. Figure 3-6 is an empty datasheet. When the datasheet is empty, the record pointer on the first record is displayed as a right-pointing triangle.

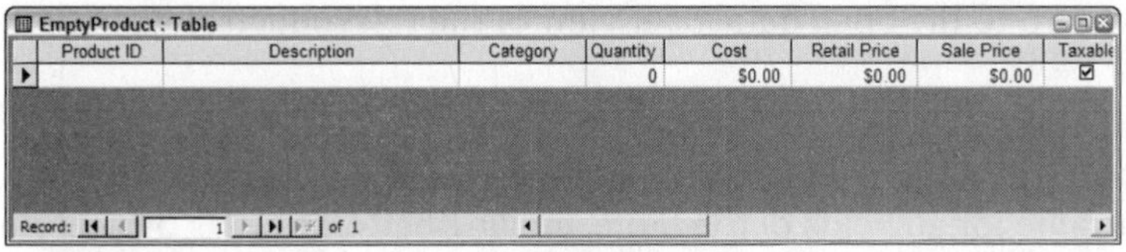

	Product ID	Description	Category	Quantity	Cost	Retail Price	Sale Price	Taxable
▶				0	$0.00	$0.00	$0.00	☑

Figure 3-6: An empty datasheet. Notice that the first record is blank and the record pointer, a right-pointing triangle, is shown in the left-most column.

If the datasheet already contains records, you enter information into a new record by clicking either the New Record button on the toolbar or the New Record button on the datasheet navigation bar. Access moves the pointer to the first field of the new record row, just below the last entered record. With the cursor is in the first field of the new record, you type in the value you want to enter, and then moving to the next field, enter a value, and so on. As you begin entering the record, the record pointer turns into a pencil, indicating that the record is being edited. A second row also appears as you begin to enter the first record; this row contains an asterisk in the record-pointer position, which indicates the next new record. The new-record pointer always appears in the last row of the datasheet; after you enter a record, it is inserted at the bottom of the table, immediately before the last row (a new blank record). Figure 3-7 shows adding a new record into the tblProducts table and the next new blank record below it.

The cursor generally starts in the first field of the table for data entry.

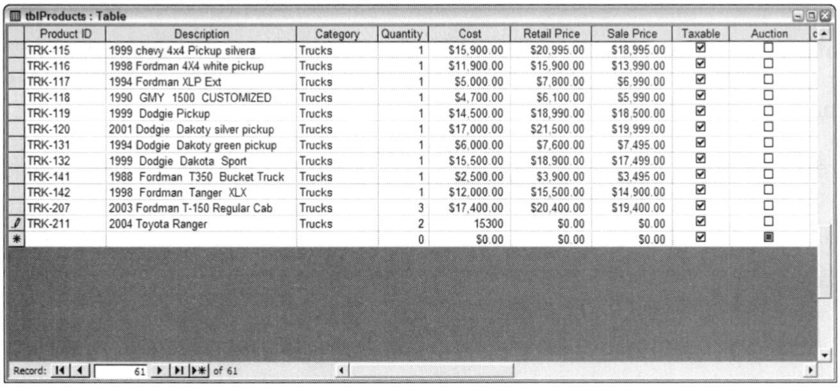

	Product ID	Description	Category	Quantity	Cost	Retail Price	Sale Price	Taxable	Auction
	TRK-115	1999 chevy 4x4 Pickup silvera	Trucks	1	$15,900.00	$20,995.00	$18,995.00	☑	☐
	TRK-116	1998 Fordman 4X4 white pickup	Trucks	1	$11,900.00	$15,900.00	$13,990.00	☑	☐
	TRK-117	1994 Fordman XLP Ext	Trucks	1	$5,000.00	$7,800.00	$6,990.00	☑	☐
	TRK-118	1990 GMY 1500 CUSTOMIZED	Trucks	1	$4,700.00	$6,100.00	$5,990.00	☑	☐
	TRK-119	1999 Dodgie Pickup	Trucks	1	$14,500.00	$18,990.00	$18,500.00	☑	☐
	TRK-120	2001 Dodgie Dakoty silver pickup	Trucks	1	$17,000.00	$21,500.00	$19,999.00	☑	☐
	TRK-131	1994 Dodgie Dakoty green pickup	Trucks	1	$6,000.00	$7,600.00	$7,495.00	☑	☐
	TRK-132	1999 Dodgie Dakota Sport	Trucks	1	$15,500.00	$18,900.00	$17,499.00	☑	☐
	TRK-141	1988 Fordman T350 Bucket Truck	Trucks	1	$2,500.00	$3,900.00	$3,495.00	☑	☐
	TRK-142	1998 Fordman Tanger XLX	Trucks	1	$12,000.00	$15,500.00	$14,900.00	☑	☐
	TRK-207	2003 Fordman T-150 Regular Cab	Trucks	3	$17,400.00	$20,400.00	$19,400.00	☑	☐
✎	TRK-211	2004 Toyota Ranger	Trucks	2	15300	$0.00	$0.00	☑	☐
*				0	$0.00	$0.00	$0.00	☑	■

Figure 3-7: Entering a record into the datasheet of the tblProducts table of the Chap03Start.mdb Database.

To add a new record to the open datasheet view of the tblProducts, follow these steps:

1. Click the New Record button.

2. Type in a value for all fields of the table, moving between fields by pressing the Enter key or the Tab key.

When adding or editing records, you may see four different record pointers:

✦ Current record

✦ Record being edited

✦ Record is locked (multi-user systems)

✦ New record

Caution   If the record contains an AutoNumber field, Access shows the name (AutoNumber) in the field. You cannot enter a value in this type of field; rather, simply press the Tab or Enter key to skip this field. Access automatically puts the number in for you when entering data.

Saving the record

After you have entered all the values in the record, you normally move to the next record. This action saves the record. Any time you move to a different record or close the table, the last record you worked on is written to the database and the record pointer changes from a pencil to a right-pointing triangle.

To save a record, you must enter a valid value (unique) into the primary key field. The primary key is validated for data type, uniqueness, and any validation rules that you have entered into the Validation Rule property. If you enter a duplicate value or do not enter a value, Access reports an error when you attempt to save the record. Figure 3-8 shows the error message Access shows when a duplicate field value is entered in the primary key field.

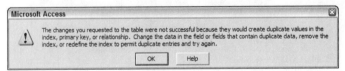

Figure 3-8: The error message Access displays when attempting to save a record with a duplicate primary key value entered into the new record.

Tip The Undo Current Field/Record icon in the toolbar can undo changes only to the current record. After you move to the next record, you must use the regular Undo icon. This works for a single record only. After you change a second record, you cannot undo the first record.

Tip You can save the record to disk without leaving the record by selecting Records ⇨ Save Record or by pressing Shift+Enter.

After you've entered a record, you understand what happens as you enter the first record. Next you learn how Access validates your data as you make entries into the fields.

Understanding automatic data-type validation

Access validates certain types of data automatically. Therefore, you don't have to enter any data-validation rules for these data types when you specify table properties. The data types that Access validates automatically include

- ✦ Number/Currency
- ✦ Date/Time
- ✦ Yes/No

Number or Currency fields allow only valid numbers to be entered into the field. Initially, Access lets you enter a letter into a Number field. When you move off the field, however, a dialog box appears with this message: `The value you entered isn't valid for this field`. The same is true of any other inappropriate characters. If you try to enter more than one decimal point, you get the same message. If you enter a number too large for a certain Number data type, you also get this message.

Date and Time fields are validated for valid date or time values. If you try to enter a date such as 14/45/05, a time such as 37:39:12, or a single letter in a Date/Time field, a dialog box appears with this error message: `The value you entered isn't valid for this field`.

Yes/No fields require that you enter one of these defined values: Yes, True, –1, or a number other than 0 (it displays as a –1) for Yes; or No, False, Off, or 0 for No. Of course, you can also define your own acceptable values in the Format property for the field, but generally these are the only acceptable values. If you try to enter an invalid value, the dialog box appears with the usual message to indicate an inappropriate value.

Understanding how properties affect data entry

Because field types vary, you use different data-entry techniques for each type. Previously in this chapter, you learned that some data-type validation is automatic. Designing the tblContacts table, however, means entering certain user-defined format and data-validation rules. The following sections examine the types of data entry.

Standard text data entry

The first field in the tblContacts table is an AutoNumber field; the next 13 fields are Text fields. After skipping the first field Contact ID, you simply enter a value in each field and move on. The Zip Code field uses an input mask (00000\-9999;0;) for data entry. The Phone and Fax fields also use an input mask (!\(999") "000\-0000;0;). These are the only fields that use any special formatting via the input mask. If you enter a value in lowercase in the State or Tax Location fields, they display in uppercase. This is done by specifying upper case (>) in the format property. You can validate text for specific values, and you can display it with format properties.

Tip   Sometimes you want to enter a Text field on multiple lines. You can press Ctrl+Enter to add a new line. This is useful, for example, in large text strings for formatting a multiple-line address field. It is also useful in Memo fields for formatting multiple-line entries.

Date/Time data entry

The Orig Cust Date and Last Sales Date fields in the tblContacts table are Date/Time data types, which both use a format value of Short date. However, they could have been defined as having a format of medium date (16-Mar-03) or long date (Sunday, March 16, 2003). Using either of these formats simply means that no matter how you type in the birth date — using month and year, day month year, or month day year, it always displays as the format specified — short date (03/16/03), medium date (16-Mar-03), or long date (Sunday, March 16, 2003). So if you type 4/8/05 or 8 Apr 05, Access displays the value in the correct format when you leave the field. The value 4/8/2005 is really stored in the table.

Tip   Formats affect only the display of the data. They do not change storage of data in the table.

Number/Currency data entry with data validation

The Credit Limit field in the tblContacts table has a validation rule assigned to it. It has a Validation Rule property to limit the amount of credit to $250,000. If the rule is violated, a dialog box appears with the validation text entered for the field. If a contact is allowed to have more than $250,000 credit, the validation rule can simply be changed in the table design.

OLE object data entry

You can enter the OLE (Object Linking and Embedding) data-type Picture field into a datasheet, even though you don't see the picture. An OLE field can hold many different item types, including

✦ Bitmap pictures

✦ Sound files

✦ Business graphs

✦ Word or Excel files

✦ Web page or Hyperlink

Any object that an OLE server supports can be stored in an Access OLE field. OLE objects are generally entered into a form so you can see, hear, or use the value. When OLE objects appear in datasheets, you see text that tells what the object is (for example, you may see Paintbrush Picture in the OLE field). You can enter OLE objects into a field in two ways:

✦ Pasting from the Clipboard

✦ Inserting into the field from the Insert ➪ Object menu dialog box

For thorough coverage of using and displaying OLE objects, see Chapter 12.

Memo field data entry

The last field in the table is memNotes, which is a Memo data type. This type of field allows up to 65,536 characters of text for each field. Recall that you entered a long string (about 260 characters) into the Memo field. As you entered the string, however, you saw only a few characters at a time. The rest of the string scrolled out of sight. By pressing Shift+F2, you can display a Zoom box with a scrollbar (see Figure 3-9) that lets you see about 1,000 characters at a time.

Figure 3-9: The Zoom box for a memo field. Notice that you can now see a lot more of the note in the memo field — not all 65,536 characters, but still quite a lot.

Note When you first display text in a zoomed window, all the text is selected and high-lighted in reverse video. You can de-select the text by pressing the Home key.

New Feature In the Zoom box, you see a Font button at the bottom. When you press this button, a dialog box appears, allowing you to determine the type of font to be used to display the memo in the memo Zoom box.

Note When you change the font for the text in a memo field, all the text is affected. You can't change the format of a single word or sentence.

Navigating Records in a Datasheet

It's not unusual to want to make changes to records after you've entered them. You may want to change records for several reasons:

✦ You receive new information that changes existing values

✦ You discover errors that change existing values

✦ You need to add new records

When you decide to edit data in a table, the first step is to open the table — if it isn't already open. From the Database window, open the tblProducts datasheet by double-clicking tblProducts in the list of tables.

Note If you are in any of the Design windows, you can click the Datasheet button to make changes to the information within the table.

Tip When you open a datasheet in Access that has related tables, a column with a plus sign (+) is added to access the related records, or sub-datasheets, and is displayed as the first column. Figure 3-10 shows the tblSales datasheet with the plus sign in the first column; clicking this opens a sub-datasheet of the line items for that sale. Sub-datasheets are thoroughly explained in Chapter 6.

Moving between records

You can move to any record by scrolling through the records and positioning your cursor on the desired record. When your table is large, however, you want to get to a specific record as quickly as possible.

▦ tblSales : Table								
Invoice Number	Sale Date	Invoice Date	Buyer ID	SalespersonID	Payment Metho	Vehicle Locatio	Tax Locatior ▲	
▶ + 4	1/15/2003	2/3/2003	1	1	Check	Lancaster, PA	MA	
+ 5	2/27/2003	2/18/2003	18	3	Check		CT	
+ 6	2/24/2003	2/24/2003	33	1	Check		MA	
+ 7	4/24/2003	4/24/2003	53	1	Cash		TX	
+ 8	5/24/2003	5/24/2003	14	2	Mastercard		MA	
+ 9	6/1/2003	6/1/2003	59	1	Cash		TX	
+ 10	7/15/2003	7/15/2003	17	3	Check		NY-ST	
+ 11	8/25/2003	8/25/2003	41	1	Visa		NY	
+ 12	8/26/2003	8/26/2003	56	3	Visa		AZ	
+ 13	9/25/2003	9/25/2003	52	1	Check		KY	
+ 14	9/30/2003	9/30/2003	55	2	Cash		GA	
+ 15	12/13/2003	12/13/2003	37	1	COD		NY	
+ 16	12/12/2003	12/12/2003	1	3			MA	
+ 17	2/25/2004	2/25/2004	33	1	Discover		MA	
+ 18	2/25/2004	2/25/2004	20	0			CT	
+ 19	9/1/2003	9/1/2003	14	1	Other		MA	
+ 20	9/6/2003	9/6/2003	37	3			NY ▼	
Record: I◄ ◄ 1 ► ►I ►✱ of 53				◄			►	

Figure 3-10: The Sales datasheet with the plus sign in the first
column for expanding each record to show related line items.

You can use the vertical scrollbar to move between records. The scrollbar arrows,
however, move the record pointer only one record at a time. To move through many
records at a time, you must use the scrollbar elevator (known as a *scroll box* in
Windows 95/98/NT) or click the area between the scrollbar elevator and the scrollbar arrows.

The Edit ➪ Go To menu, shown open in Figure 3-11, has several choices to help you
quickly move around the worksheet.

You can also use the five Navigation buttons, located along the bottom of the
Datasheet window (also shown in Figure 3-11), for moving between records. You
simply click these buttons to move to the desired record. If you know the record
number (row number of a specific record), you can click the record number box,
enter a record number, and press Enter. You can also press F5 to move to the record
number box.

Tip   Watch the Scroll Tips when you use scrollbars to move to another area of the
datasheet. Access does not update the record number box until you click a field.

Finding a specific value

Although you can move to a specific record (if you know the record number) or to a
specific field in the current record, usually what you really want to find is a certain
value in a record. You can use one of three methods for locating a value in a field:

✦ Select Edit ➪ Find

✦ Select the Find button in the toolbar (a pair of binoculars)

✦ Press Ctrl+F

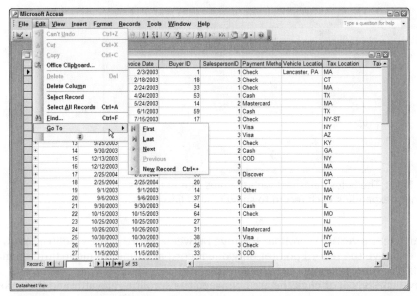

Figure 3-11: Moving between records using the Go To menu. You can do the same thing by using the Navigation buttons along the bottom of the window.

Choosing any of these methods displays the Find and Replace dialog box (shown in Figure 3-12). To limit the search to a specific field, make sure your cursor is on the field that you want to use in the search before you open the dialog box. You can also choose to search the entire table for the specified record by clicking the Look In combo box and selecting the table.

Figure 3-12: The Find and Replace dialog box. The fastest way to activate it is to simply press the Ctrl+F key combination.

Tip   If you highlight the entire record by clicking the record selector (the small gray box next to the record), Access automatically searches through all fields.

The Find and Replace dialog box lets you control many aspects of the search. In the Find What text box, you enter the value to be searched for. You can also display and choose from a list of items that you have previously searched for in this database. You can enter the value just as it appears in the field, or you can use three types of wildcards:

> * (any number of characters)

> ? (any one character)

> # (any one number)

To look at how these wildcards work, first suppose that you want to find any value in the Description field of the tblProducts table beginning with 2001; for this, you type **2001***. Then suppose that you want to search for values ending with Sedan, so you type ***Sedan**. If you want to search for any value that begins with 2001, ends with Sedan, and contains any number of characters in between, you type **2001*Sedan**.

The Match drop-down list contains three choices:

> ✦ Any Part of Field

> ✦ Whole Field

> ✦ Start of Field

The default is Whole Field. This option finds only the whole value you enter. For example, the Whole Field option finds the value FORD only if the value in the field being searched is exactly FORD. If you select Any Part of Field, Access searches to see whether the value is contained anywhere in the field; this search finds the value FORD in the field values FORDMAN and FORD. A search for FORM using the Start of Field option searches from the beginning of the field, returning no values because the field always begins with a year (1999, 2003, and so on). You can choose one of three search direction choices (Up, Down, All) in the Search combo box.

In addition to these combo boxes, you can use two check boxes at the bottom of the Find and Replace dialog box — Match Case and Search Fields As Formatted. Match Case determines whether the search is case-sensitive. The default is not case-sensitive (not checked). A search for SMITH finds smith, SMITH, or Smith. If you check the Match Case check box, you must then enter the search string in the exact case of the field value. (The data types Number, Currency, and Date/Time do not have any case attributes.)

If you have checked Match Case, Access does not use the value Search Fields as Formatted (the second check box), which limits the search to the actual values displayed in the table. (If you format a field for display in the datasheet, you should check the box.)

The Search Fields as Formatted check box, the selected default, finds only text that has the same pattern of uppercase and lowercase letters as the text you specified in the Find What box. Clear this box to find text regardless of case.

Caution Using Search Fields as Formatted may slow the search process.

When you click the Find Next button, the search begins. If Access finds the value, the cursor highlights it in the datasheet. To find the next occurrence of the value, you must click the Find Next button again. You can also select the Find Next button to find the first occurrence. The dialog box remains open so that you can find multiple occurrences. When you find the value that you want, select the Close command button to close the dialog box.

Changing Values in a Datasheet

If the field that you are in has no value, you can type a new value into the field. When you enter new values into a field, follow the same rules as for a new-record entry.

Note Usually, you change values by moving to the value that you want to change or edit and making the change.

Replacing an existing value manually

Generally, you enter a field with either no characters selected or the entire value selected. If you use the keyboard to enter a field, normally you select the entire value. (You know that the entire value is selected when it is displayed in reverse video.) When you begin to type, the new content replaces the selected value automatically.

To select the entire value with the mouse, use any of these methods:

✦ Click just to the left of the value when the cursor is shown as a large plus sign.

✦ Select any part of the value and double-click the mouse button. (This usually works unless the text contains a space.)

✦ Click to the left of the value, hold down the left mouse button, and drag the mouse to select the whole value.

✦ Select any part of the value and press F2.

Tip You may want to replace an existing value with the default from the Default Value table property. To do so, select the value and press Ctrl+Alt+Spacebar. If you want to replace an existing value with that of the same field from the preceding record, you can press Ctrl+' (single quote mark). You can press Ctrl+; (semicolon) to place the current date in a field as well.

Caution   Pressing Ctrl+– (hyphen) deletes the current record.

Changing an existing value

If you want to change an existing value instead of replacing the entire value, you can use the mouse and click in front of any character in the field. When you position the mouse pointer in front of an individual character, you activate Insert mode; the existing value moves to the right as you type the new value. If you press the Insert key, your entry changes to Overstrike mode; you replace one character at a time as you type. You can use the arrow keys to move between characters without disturbing them. Erase characters to the left by pressing Backspace, or to the right of the cursor by pressing Delete.

Table 3-2 lists editing techniques.

<table>
<tr><th colspan="2">Table 3-2
Editing Techniques</th></tr>
<tr><th>Editing Operation</th><th>Keystrokes</th></tr>
<tr><td>Move the insertion point within a field</td><td>Press the right- (→) and left-arrow (←) keys</td></tr>
<tr><td>Insert a value within a field</td><td>Select the insertion point and type new data</td></tr>
<tr><td>Select the entire field</td><td>Press F2 or double-click the mouse button</td></tr>
<tr><td>Replace an existing value with a new value</td><td>Select the entire field and type a new value</td></tr>
<tr><td>Replace a value with the value of the previous field</td><td>Press Ctrl+' (single quote mark)</td></tr>
<tr><td>Replace the current value with the default value</td><td>Press Ctrl+Alt+Spacebar</td></tr>
<tr><td>Insert a line break in a Text or Memo field</td><td>Press Ctrl+Enter</td></tr>
<tr><td>Save the current record</td><td>Press Shift+Enter or move to another record</td></tr>
<tr><td>Insert the current date</td><td>Ctrl+; (semicolon)</td></tr>
<tr><td>Insert the current time</td><td>Ctrl+: (colon)</td></tr>
<tr><td>Add a new record</td><td>Ctrl++ (plus sign)</td></tr>
<tr><td>Delete the current record</td><td>Ctrl+– (minus sign)</td></tr>
<tr><td>Toggle values in a check box or option button</td><td>Spacebar</td></tr>
<tr><td>Undo a change to the current record</td><td>Press Esc or click the Undo button</td></tr>
</table>

Fields that you can't edit

Some fields can't be edited, such as:

✦ **AutoNumber fields.** Access maintains AutoNumber fields automatically, calculating the values as you create each new record. AutoNumber fields can be used as the primary key.

✦ **Calculated fields.** Access creates calculated fields in forms or queries; these values are not actually stored in your table.

✦ **Locked or disabled fields.** You can set certain properties in a form to disallow entry for a specific field. You can lock or disable a field when you designate Form properties.

✦ **Fields in multi-user locked records.** If another user locks the record, you can't edit any fields in that record.

Using the Undo Feature

The Undo button is often dimmed in Access so that it can't be used. As soon as you begin editing a record, however, you can use this button to undo the typing in the current field. You can also undo a change with the Esc key; pressing Esc cancels either a changed value or the previously changed field. Pressing Esc twice undoes changes to the entire current record.

Several Undo menu commands and variations are available to undo your work. The following list explains how you can undo your work at various stages of completion:

✦ **Edit ⇨ Can't Undo.** Undo is not available.

✦ **Edit ⇨ Undo Typing.** Cancels the most recent change to your data.

✦ **Edit ⇨ Undo Current Field/Record.** Cancels the most recent change to the current field. Cancels all changes to the current record.

✦ **Edit ⇨ Undo Saved Record.** Cancels all changes to last saved record.

As you type a value into a field, you can select Edit ⇨ Undo or use the toolbar Undo button to undo changes to that value. After you move to another field, you can undo the change to the preceding field's value by selecting Edit ⇨ Undo Current Field/Record or by using the Undo button. You can also undo all the changes to an unsaved current record by selecting Edit ⇨ Undo Current Field/Record. After you save a record, you can still undo the changes by selecting Edit ⇨ Undo Saved Record. However, after the next record is edited, changes are permanent.

Copying and Pasting Values

Copying or cutting data to the Clipboard is a Microsoft Windows task; it is not actually a specific function of Access. After you cut or copy a value, you can paste into another field or record by using Edit ➪ Paste or the Paste button in the toolbar. You can cut, copy, or paste data from any Windows application or from one task to another in Access. Using this technique, you can copy entire records between tables or databases, and you can copy datasheet values to and from Microsoft Word and Excel.

Replacing Values

To replace an existing value in a field, you can manually find the record to update or you can use the Find and Replace dialog box. You can display the Find and Replace dialog in four ways:

✦ Select Edit ➪ Find

✦ Select the Find button in the toolbar (a pair of binoculars)

✦ Press Ctrl+F

✦ Select Edit ➪ Replace

This dialog box allows you to do a find and replace in the current field or in the entire datasheet. You can find a certain value and replace it with a new value in every place in the table that you are in.

After the Find and Replace dialog box is active, you should first click the Replace tab and type in the value that you want to find in the Find What text box, as shown in Figure 3-12. After you have selected all the remaining search options (turn off Search Fields As Formatted for example), click the Find Next button. You are taken to the first occurrence of what you want to find. After you get there, if you want to change the value of the current found item (under the cursor), click the Replace button, and it replaces the selected value. For example, Figure 3-13 shows that you want to find the value *Motor Homes* in the Category field of the tblProducts table and change it to the value *Camper*.

You can select your search options in the Find tab and then click the Replace tab to continue the process. However, it is far easier to simply do the entire process using the Replace tab. Enter what you want to find and the value that you want to use to replace the existing value. After you have completed the dialog box with all the correct information, select one of the command buttons on the side.

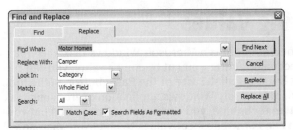

Figure 3-13: Find and Replace dialog box with the Replace tab showing. In this case you want to replace the value *Motor Homes* with *Camper*.

> ✦ **Find Next.** Finds the next field that has the value in the Find What field.
>
> ✦ **Cancel.** Closes the form and performs no find and replace.
>
> ✦ **Replace.** Replaces the value in the current field only. (***Note:*** You must use the Find Next button first.).
>
> ✦ **Replace All.** Finds all the fields with the Find What value and automatically replaces them with the Replace value.

Tip   Use the Find Next and Replace commands if you aren't sure about changing all the fields with the Find What value. When you use this command, you can pick the fields that you want to replace and the fields that you want to leave with the same value.

Adding New Records

You can add records to the datasheet by positioning the cursor on the datasheet's last line (where the record pointer is an asterisk) and entering the new record. You can go to a new record in many ways: You can select Insert ➪ New Record, or you can go directly to a new record by using the New Record button in the toolbar, the navigation button area, or the menu selection Edit ➪ Go To ➪ New Record. Another way to move quickly to the new record is to go to the last record and press the down-arrow (↓) key.

Sometimes you want to add several new records and make all existing records temporarily invisible. The menu item Records ➪ Data Entry clears the screen temporarily of all records while you are editing new records. When you want to restore all records, select Records ➪ Remove Filter/Sort.

Deleting Records

You can delete any number of records by selecting the record(s) and pressing the Delete key. You can also select the records and choose Edit ➪ Delete or place your cursor in a record and select Edit ➪ Delete Record. When you press Delete or choose the menu selection, a dialog box asks you to confirm the deletion (see Figure 3-14). If you select Yes, the records are deleted. If you select Cancel, no changes are made.

 Caution The Default value for this dialog box is Yes. Pressing the Enter key automatically deletes the records. If you accidentally erase records using this method, the action can't be reversed.

Figure 3-14: The Delete Record dialog box warns you that you are about to delete x number of records — the default response is YES (OK to delete) so be careful when deleting records.

 Caution If you have relations set between tables and *Enforce Referential Integrity* is checked — for example, the tblContacts (Customer) table is related to the tblSales table — then you can't delete a record unless the Cascade Delete check box is also checked and you are attempting to delete from the lowest child in the relationship builder (tblSales versus tblContacts). Otherwise, you receive an error message dialog box that reports that the record can't be deleted or changed because the table '<tablename>' includes related records.

You can select multiple contiguous records. To do so, click the record selector of the first record that you want to select and drag the record-pointer icon (right-pointing arrow) to the last record that you want to select.

Adding, Changing, and Deleting Columns

A very dangerous feature in Access 2003 is the capability to add, delete, and rename columns in a datasheet. This feature actually changes the data design. When you go to the Table Design screen and make changes, you know that you are changing the underlying structure of the data because you can see yourself do it. Within a datasheet, however, you may not realize the consequences of the changes that you are making. Any field name that is changed may cause any query, form, report, macro, or module that uses that name to no longer function. If you are creating applications for others, you should not allow users to use a datasheet to make the changes described in this part of the book.

Deleting a column from a datasheet

You can delete columns from a datasheet by selecting one column at a time and selecting Edit ⇨ Delete Column. When you take this action, a dialog box warns that you will be deleting all the data in this column, as well as the field itself, from the table design. More importantly, if you have used this field in a data-entry form or a report, you get an error message the next time you use any object that references this field name. You can't delete more than one column at a time.

Adding a column to a datasheet

You can add new columns to a datasheet by selecting Insert ⇨ Column, which creates a new column to the left of the column that your insertion point was in. The new column is labeled Field1. You can then add data to the records for the column.

Adding a new column also adds the field to the table design. When you save the datasheet, Access writes the field into the table design, using the characteristics of the data for the field properties.

Changing a field name (column header)

When you add a new field, you want to change the column name before you save the datasheet. You can change a column header by double-clicking the column header and editing the text in the column header. When you save the datasheet, this column header text is used as a field name for the table design.

Caution   When you change a column header, you are changing the field name in the table. If you have used this field name in forms, reports, queries, macros, or modules, they no longer work until you change them in the other objects. This is a dangerous way to change a field name; only experienced users should use it.

Displaying Records

A number of mouse techniques and menu items can increase your productivity when you add or change records. Either by selecting from the Format menu or by using the mouse, you can change the field order, hide and freeze columns, change row height or column width, change display fonts, and change the display or remove gridlines.

Changing the field order

By default, Access displays the fields in a datasheet in the same order that they appear in a table or query. Sometimes, however, you need to see certain fields next to each other in order to better analyze your data. To rearrange your fields, select a column (as shown in Figure 3-15) and drag the column to its new location.

Product ID	Description	Category	Quantity in Stock	Cost	Retail Price	Sale Price
CAR-001	20 Sportster	Cars	1	$32,656.00	$38,995.00	$36,999.00
CAR-002	1957 Chevy Sedan	Cars	1	$19,000.00	$21,900.00	$21,900.00
CAR-003	1971 Pontanic Red Converible	Cars	1	$15,000.00	$21,900.00	$20,900.00
CAR-004	1950 Fordman Coupe	Cars	1	$16,500.00	$19,000.00	$18,995.00
CAR-005	1962 AALLFA Red Spidery 2000	Cars	1	$31,500.00	$35,900.00	$35,900.00
CAR-036	1940 Classic Antique Convertible	Cars	1	$27,800.00	$31,500.00	$29,500.00
CAR-057	2001 Collectors Chevy Corvet	Cars	1	$108,000.00	$125,000.00	$123,500.00
CAR-110	1967 Shelly Stunning Red Muscle Car	Cars	1	$74,500.00	$83,000.00	$79,900.00
CAR-111	1965 Shelly Stunning Red Cobrat	Cars	1	$165,000.00	$185,000.00	$185,000.00
CAR-112	2001 BMY 740 Sedan	Cars	1	$33,000.00	$37,000.00	$36,900.00
CAR-113	2001 Audie Grey Stationwagon	Cars	1	$29,900.00	$35,000.00	$34,900.00
CAR-114	1997 Audie White Sedan	Cars	1	$25,000.00	$29,900.00	$28,900.00
CAR-115	1966 Fordman fully restored	Cars	1	$81,000.00	$87,000.00	$86,000.00
CAR-116	1959 Fordman Thunderman	Cars	1	$9,500.00	$14,000.00	$13,500.00
CAR-117	1988 Fordman Temto LRX	Cars	1	$200.00	$700.00	$599.00
CAR-118	2001 Fordman Ptaurus XES	Cars	1	$11,000.00	$17,000.00	$15,900.00
CAR-119	1996 CADDY DEVILLE SLX	Cars	1	$8,500.00	$12,500.00	$11,000.00
CAR-120	1997 Fordman Nustang GTX	Cars	1	$0.00	$0.00	$0.00
CAR-121	1993 Fordman Trobe SE	Cars	1	$2,900.00	$4,200.00	$3,900.00
CAR-122	1986 BMY 326CI	Cars	1	$2,800.00	$3,500.00	$3,350.00
CAR-123	1969 Antique Coupe	Cars	1	$500.00	$17,900.00	$1,500.00
CAR-126	1995 BUICKY RIV	Cars	1	$5,500.00	$7,200.00	$6,999.00
CAR-127	1969 Shelly Coupe Muscle Car	Cars	1	$35,500.00	$40,000.00	$40,000.00
CAR-130	1998 Buicky Centrum Custom	Cars	1	$4,500.00	$5,799.00	$5,599.00
CAR-201	1968 Rare Dodget Red 2D Sedan	Cars	1	$29,800.00	$33,500.00	$32,900.00
CAR-299	1972 Chevy green chevel	Cars	1	$29,800.00	$35,000.00	$32,900.00

Record: 1 of 60

Figure 3-15: Selecting a column to change the field order.

You can select and drag columns one at a time, or you can select multiple columns to drag. Suppose you want the field Quantity in Stock to appear before the field Description in the datasheet of the tblProducts. Use the following steps to make this change:

1. Position the mouse pointer on the Quantity field (column) name. The cursor changes to a down arrow.

2. Click to select the column and hold down the mouse button. The entire Quantity column is now highlighted. Release the mouse button.

3. Click the mouse button again; the pointer changes to an arrow with a box under it.

4. Drag the column to the left edge of the datasheet between the Product ID and Description field. A thin black column will appear between them (as in Figure 3-15).

5. Release the mouse button; the column is now moved to in front of the Description field of the datasheet.

With this method, you can move any individual field or contiguous field selection. You can move the fields left or right or past the right or left boundary of the window.

Note Moving fields in a datasheet does not affect the field order in the table design.

Changing the field display width

You can change the *field display width* (column width) either by specifying the width in a dialog box (in number of characters) or by dragging the column border. When you drag a column border, the cursor changes to the double-arrow symbol.

To widen a column or to make it narrower, follow these two steps:

1. Place the mouse pointer between two column names on the field separator line. The mouse pointer turns into a small line with arrows pointing to the left and right — if you have it in the correct location.

2. Drag the column border to the left to make the column smaller or to the right to make it larger.

Tip You can resize a column instantly to the best fit (based on the longest data value) by double-clicking the right column border after the cursor changes to the double arrow.

Note Resizing the column doesn't change the number of characters allowed in the table's field size. You are simply changing the amount of viewing space for the data contained in the column.

Alternatively, you can resize a column by choosing Format ➪ Column Width or by right-clicking the column header and selecting Column Width from the menu. When you click Column Width, the dialog box in which you enter column width in number of characters displays, as shown in Figure 3-16. You can also return the column to its default size by checking the Standard Width check box.

You can create an icon on your toolbar for Column Width. To do this, click the down arrow next to the Help button on the toolbar and select Add or Remove Buttons. Then select the Table Datasheet choice, and finally select the Column Width button. This button becomes the last button on that toolbar. To remove it, just repeat the process.

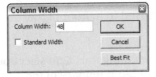

Figure 3-16: The Column Width dialog box.

Caution You can hide a column if you drag the column gridline to the gridline of the next column to the left. This also happens if you set the column width to 0 in the Column Width dialog box. If you do this, you must use Format ➪ Unhide Columns to redisplay the columns.

Changing the record display height

You can change the record (that is, row) height of all rows by dragging a row's border to make the row height larger or smaller, or you can select Format ➪ Row Height. Sometimes you may need to increase the row height to accommodate larger fonts or text data displays of multiple lines.

You can also create an icon on your toolbar for Row Height. To do this, click the down arrow next to the Help button and select Add or Remove Buttons. Then select the Table Datasheet choice, and finally select the Row Height button. This button becomes the last button on that toolbar. To remove it, just repeat the process.

When you drag a record's border, the cursor changes to the vertical two-headed arrow that you see at the left edge of Figure 3-17.

Product ID	Quantity in Stock	Description	Category	Cost	Retail Price	Sale P
CAR-001	1	2001 Sportster	Cars	$32,656.00	$38,995.00	$36.9
CAR-002	1	1957 Chevy Sedan	Cars	$19,000.00	$21,900.00	$21.9
CAR-003	1	1971 Pontanic Red Converible	Cars	$15,000.00	$21,900.00	$20.9
CAR-004	1	1950 Fordman Coupe	Cars	$16,500.00	$19,000.00	$18.9
CAR-005	1	1962 AALLFA Red Spidery 2000	Cars	$31,500.00	$35,900.00	$35.9
CAR-036	1	1940 Classic Antique Convertible	Cars	$27,800.00	$31,500.00	$29.5
CAR-057	1	2001 Collectors Chevy Corvet	Cars	$108,000.00	$125,000.00	$123.5
CAR-110	1	1967 Shelly Stunning Red Muscle Car	Cars	$74,500.00	$83,000.00	$79.9
CAR-111	1	1965 Shelly Stunning Red Cobrat	Cars	$165,000.00	$185,000.00	$185.0
CAR-112	1	2001 BMY 740 Sedan	Cars	$33,000.00	$37,000.00	$36.9

Record: 14 ◄ 1 ► ►I ►* of 60

Figure 3-17: Changing a row's height. Simply put the mouse pointer between two rows. When the mouse pointer changes to arrows pointing up and down, drag the height to what you want.

To increase or decrease a row's height, follow these steps:

1. Place the mouse pointer between two rows on the gray record selector. The cursor changes to the double pointing arrow (up and down).

2. Drag the row border upward to shrink all row heights. Drag the border downward to increase all row heights.

Note   The procedure for changing row height changes the row size for all rows in the datasheet.

You can also resize rows by choosing Format ➪ Row Height. A dialog box appears so that you can enter the row height in point size. You can also return the rows to their default point size by checking the Standard Height check box.

Caution   If you drag a record's gridline up to meet the gridline immediately above it in the previous record, all rows are hidden. This also occurs if you set the row height close to 0 (for example, a height of 0.1) in the Row Height dialog box. In that case, you must select Format ➪ Row Height and reset the row height to a larger number to redisplay the rows.

Displaying cell gridlines

Normally gridlines appear between fields (columns) and between records (rows). By selecting Format ➪ Datasheet, you can determine whether to display gridlines and how they look. Figure 3-18 shows the Datasheet Formatting dialog box that you use.

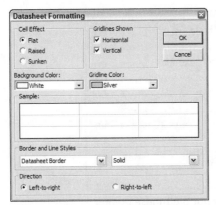

Figure 3-18: Changing cell gridlines

The Datasheet Formatting dialog box gives you complete control over gridlines. Using the Gridlines Shown check boxes, you can eliminate both Horizontal and Vertical gridlines. If you choose to keep the gridlines, you can change both the Gridline Color and the Background Color. A sample shows you what the effect you have chosen looks like. You can also determine whether the gridlines are Flat (default white background with silver gridlines), Raised (default silver background with gray gridlines), or Sunken (default silver background with white gridlines).

Caution

You can also determine the Border and Line Styles for each of the different datasheet borders. You can determine a different border for the Datasheet Border, Horizontal Gridline, Vertical Gridline, and Column Header Underline. To select a different border style for each border in the datasheet, first select the Border that you want to update from the left combo box and then the Line Style from the combo box on the right. Repeat the process for each border. Each border in Figure 3-19 has a different line style.

The different line styles that you can use for the different datasheet borders include

Transparent Border	Short Dashes	Dash-Dot
Solid	Dots	Dash-Dot-Dot
Dashes	Sparse Dots	Double Solid

tblProducts : Table							
Product ID	Quantity in Stock	Description	Category	Cost	Retail Price	Sale P
CAR-001	1	2001 Sportster	Cars	$32,656.00	$38,995.00	$36,9
CAR-002	1	1957 Chevy Sedan	Cars	$19,000.00	$21,900.00	$21,9
CAR-003	1	1971 Pontanic Red Converible	Cars	$15,000.00	$21,900.00	$20,9
CAR-004	1	1950 Fordman Coupe	Cars	$16,500.00	$19,000.00	$18,9
CAR-005	1	1962 AALLFA Red Spidery 2000	Cars	$31,500.00	$35,900.00	$35,9
CAR-036	1	1940 Classic Antique Convertible	Cars	$27,800.00	$31,500.00	$29,5
CAR-057	1	2001 Collectors Chevy Corvet	Cars	$108,000.00	$125,000.00	$123,5
CAR-110	1	1967 Shelly Stunning Red Muscle Car	Cars	$74,500.00	$83,000.00	$79,9
CAR-111	1	1965 Shelly Stunning Red Cobrat	Cars	$165,000.00	$185,000.00	$185,0
CAR-112	1	2001 BMY 740 Sedan	Cars	$33,000.00	$37,000.00	$36,9
CAR-113	1	2001 Audie Grey Stationwagon	Cars	$29,900.00	$35,000.00	$34,9
CAR-114	1	1997 Audie White Sedan	Cars	$25,000.00	$29,900.00	$28,9
CAR-115	1	1966 Fordman fully restored	Cars	$81,000.00	$87,000.00	$86,0
CAR-116	1	1959 Fordman Thunderman	Cars	$9,500.00	$14,000.00	$13,5
CAR-117	1	1988 Fordman Temto LRX	Cars	$200.00	$700.00	$5
CAR-118	1	2001 Fordman Ptaurus XES	Cars	$11,000.00	$17,000.00	$15,9
CAR-119	1	1996 CADDY DEVILLE SLX	Cars	$8,500.00	$12,500.00	$11,0
CAR-120	1	1997 Fordman Nustang GTX	Cars	$0.00	$0.00	
CAR-121	1	1993 Fordman Trobe SE	Cars	$2,900.00	$4,200.00	$3,9

Record: 14 ◄ 1 ► ►I ►* of 60 ◄

Figure 3-19: Different line styles are used for the different borders in the datasheet. In this case, the cell effect has been changed to change the Gridline Color (dark black) and change the Horizontal lines to dashes.

Changing display fonts

You can resize the row height and column width automatically by changing the display font. By default, Access displays all data in the datasheet in the MS Sans Serif 8-point Regular font. You may find that this font does not print correctly because MS Sans Serif is only a screen font. Arial 8-point Regular is a good match. Select Format ➪ Font to change the font type style, size, and style.

Setting the font display affects the entire datasheet. If you want to see more data on the screen, you can use a very small font. You can also switch to a higher-resolution display size if you have the necessary hardware. If you want to see larger characters, you can increase the font size.

To change the font to Courier 12-point bold, follow these steps:

1. Select Format ➪ Font. A dialog box appears.

2. Select Courier from the Font combo box, as shown in Figure 3-20.

3. Select Bold from the Font style combo box.

4. Enter **12** into the text box area of the Size combo box.

5. Click OK.

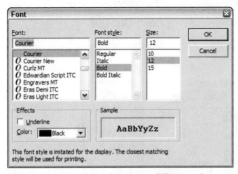

Figure 3-20: Changing to a different font and font size in the datasheet.

As you change font attributes, a sample appears in the Sample area. This way, you can see the changes that you are making before you make them. You can also change the font color if you want.

Hiding and unhiding columns

You can hide columns by dragging the column gridline to the preceding field or by setting the column size to 0. You can also use the Hide Columns dialog box to hide one or more columns. To hide a single column, follow these steps:

1. Position the cursor anywhere within the column that you want to hide.

2. Select Format ➪ Hide Columns. The column disappears. Actually, the column width is simply set to 0. You can hide multiple columns by first selecting them and then selecting Format ➪ Hide Columns.

After you've hidden a column, you can redisplay it by selecting Format ➪ Unhide Columns. This action displays a dialog box that lets you hide or unhide columns selectively by checking off the desired status of each field. When you are finished, click Close; the datasheet appears, showing the desired fields.

Freezing columns

When you want to scroll among many fields but want to keep certain fields from scrolling out of view, you can use Format ➪ Freeze Columns. With this selection, for example, you can keep the Product ID and Description fields visible while you scroll through the datasheet to find the product's features. The columns that you want to keep visible remain frozen on the far-left side of the datasheet; other fields scroll out of sight horizontally. The fields must be contiguous if you want to freeze more than one at a time. (Of course, you can first move your fields to place them next to each other.) When you're ready to unfreeze the datasheet columns, simply select Format ➪ Unfreeze All Columns.

Tip   When you unfreeze columns, the column doesn't move back to its original position. You must move it manually.

Saving the changed layout

When you close the datasheet, you save all your data changes but you lose all your layout changes. As you make all of these display changes to your datasheet, you probably won't want to make them again the next time you open the same datasheet. By default, however, Access does not save the datasheet's layout changes. If you want your datasheet to look the same way the next time you open it, you can select File ➪ Save; this command saves your layout changes with the datasheet. You can also click the Save icon on your toolbar (the icon with the floppy disk on it).

Caution   If you are following the example, don't save the changes to the tblProducts table.

Saving a record

As you move off a record, Access saves it. You can press Shift+Enter to save a record without moving off it. A third way to save a record is to close the table. Yet another way to save a record is to select Records ➪ Save Record.

Sorting and Filtering Records in a Datasheet

Finding a value lets you display a specific record and work with that record. If you have multiple records that meet a find criteria, however, you may want to display just that specific set of records. Using the Filter and Sort toolbar icons (or the Records menu option Sort), you can display just the set of records that you want to work with. You can also sort selected records instantly into any order that you want: Use the two QuickSort buttons to sort the entire table, or use the three filter buttons to select only certain records.

Using the QuickSort feature

Sometimes you may simply want to sort your records into a desired order. The QuickSort buttons on the toolbar let you sort selected columns into either ascending or descending order. The toolbar contains a different button for each order. Before you can click either the Sort Ascending (A-Z) or Sort Descending (Z-A) QuickSort buttons, you must select the fields that you want to use for the sort.

You select a field to use in the sort by placing your cursor in the field in any record. After the cursor is in the column that you want to use in the sort, click the QuickSort button. The data redisplays instantly in the sorted order.

If you want to sort your data on the basis of values in multiple fields, you can highlight more than one column: Highlight a column (as previously discussed), hold down the Shift key, and drag the cursor to the right. These steps select multiple contiguous fields. When you select one of the QuickSort buttons, Access sorts the records into major order (by the first highlighted field) and then into orders within orders (based on subsequent fields). If you need to select multiple columns that aren't contiguous (next to each other), you can move them next to each other, as discussed earlier in this chapter.

Tip   If you want to re-display your records in their original order, use Records ➪ Remove Filter/Sort.

Cross-Reference   You learn more about sorting in Chapter 4.

Using Filter By Selection

Filter By Selection is a technology within Access that lets you select records instantly on the basis of the current value that you selected. For example, using the tblProducts table, move your cursor to the Category column and click the Sort Ascending (A to Z) button. Access sorts the data by type of vehicle. Now highlight any of the records with the value Minivans. When you press the Filter By Selection button, Access selects only the records where the Category is Minivans. The tblProducts table contains seven records. After you have selected Minivans and pressed the Filter By Selection button, only seven records are shown and all have the value Minivans in the Category field.

The navigation button area of the Datasheet window tells you whether the database is currently filtered; in addition, the Apply Filter/Remove Filter icon (third filter icon that looks like a large funnel) is depressed, indicating that a filter is in use. When you toggle this button, it removes all filters or sorts. The filter specification does not go away; it is simply turned off.

Filter By Selection is additive. You can continue to select values, each time pressing the Filter By Selection button.

Tip You can also right-click the field content that you want to filter by and then select Filter By Selection from the menu choices.

If you want to further specify a selection and then see everything that doesn't match that selection (for example, where Description not equal to 2003 Mini Van), move the cursor to the field (Description field where the value is 2003 Mini Van) that you want to say *doesn't match* and right-click on the datasheet and select Filter Excluding Selection. You are now left with six records. This selects all Minivans except the 2003 Mini Vans records.

Imagine using this technique to review sales by salespeople for specific time periods or products. Filter By Selection provides incredible opportunities to drill down into successive layers of data. As you add to Filter By Selection and Filter Excluding Selection, it continues to add to its own internal query manager (also known as *Query By Example*). Even when you click the Remove Filter icon to redisplay all the records, Access still stores the query specification in memory. Figure 3-21 shows this Filter By Selection screen in a Datasheet.

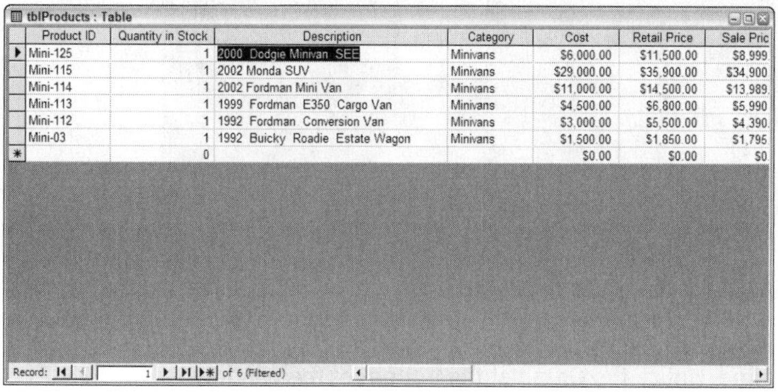

Figure 3-21: Using Filter By Selection. In this case you see all records for Minivans except 2003 Mini Van records.

Filter By Selection has some limitations. Most importantly, all the choices are added together (that is, Minivans and not 2003 Mini Van). This means that the only operation you can perform is a search for records that meet all the specified conditions. Another option, Filter By Form, lets you create more complex analyses.

If you want to use the Filter By Selection but can't find the selection that you want to use, but you know the value, right-click the field that you want to apply the filter to and select Filter For. This option allows you to type in the selection to filter for.

Using Filter By Form

Filter By Selection is just one way to filter data in Access. Another way is Filter By Form. Selecting the second filter icon changes the datasheet to a single record; every field becomes a combo box that enables you to select from a list of all values for that field. As Figure 3-22 shows, the bottom of the form lets you specify the *OR* conditions for each group of values that you specify.

In Figure 3-22, you can see two conditions created in the Filter By Selection example (described previously) in the single line of the Filter By Form screen. If you click the Or tab, you can enter a second set of conditions. Suppose you want to see SUV records also. You already have the specification for Minivans, except 2003 Mini Van. You would click on the Or tab (located at the bottom of the screen) and then select SUV from the now-empty Category combo box. When you click the Apply Filter button (the large funnel), 15 records display—SUVs and Minivans (except 2003 Mini Van).

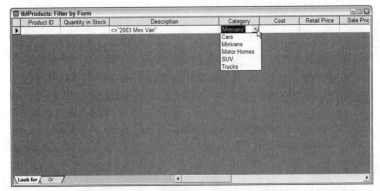

Figure 3-22: Using Filter By Form lets you set multiple conditions for filtering at one time. Notice the Or tab at the bottom of the window.

You can have as many conditions as you need. If you need even more advanced manipulation of your selections, you can choose Records ➪ Filter ➪ Advanced Filter/Sort and get an actual QBE (Query by Example) screen that you can use to enter more complex queries.

Cross-Reference   Later chapters explain more advanced concepts of queries.

Printing Records

You can print all the records in your datasheet in a simple row-and-column layout. Later you learn to produce formatted reports. For now, the simplest way to print is to select File ➪ Print or use the Print icon in the toolbar. This selection displays the standard Print dialog box, as shown in Figure 3-23.

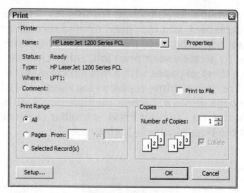

Figure 3-23: The Print dialog box.

Assuming that you set up a printer in Microsoft Windows, you can select OK to print your datasheet in the font that you selected for display (or the nearest printer equivalent). The printout reflects all layout options that are in effect when the datasheet is printed. Hidden columns don't print. Gridlines print only if the cell gridline properties are on. The printout also reflects the specified row height and column width.

Only so many columns and rows can fit on a page; the printout takes up as many pages as required to print all the data. Access breaks up the printout as necessary to fit on each page. For example, the tblProducts table printout is six pages. Three pages across are needed to print all the fields in the tblProducts table; each record requires three pages in length. Each record of the tblContacts table requires four pages in length.

Printing the datasheet

You can also control printing from the Print dialog box, selecting from several options:

- ✦ **Print Range.** Prints the entire datasheet or only selected pages or records.
- ✦ **Copies.** Determines the number of copies to be printed.
- ✦ **Collate.** Determines whether multiple copies are collated.

You can also click the Properties button and set options for the selected printer or select the printer itself to change the type of printer. The Setup button allows you to set margins and print headings.

Using the Print Preview window

Although you may have all the information in the datasheet ready to print, you may be unsure of whether to change the width or height of the columns or rows, or whether to adjust the fonts to improve your printed output. For that matter, you may not want to print out the entire datasheet; you may need printed records from only pages 3 and 4. Before making such adjustments to the datasheet properties, you should view the report onscreen. To preview your print job, either click the Print Preview button on the toolbar (a sheet of paper with a magnifying glass) or select File ➪ Print Preview. The Print Preview window appears (see Figure 3-24). The default view is the first page in single page preview. To view multiple pages, as in figure 3-24, select the multiple page button on the Print Preview toolbar (a square with four pages inside it), then select the type of view — in this case, 2 x 3.

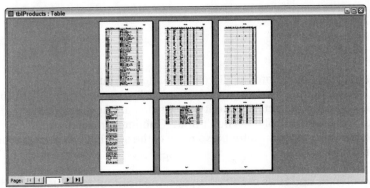

Figure 3-24: Print preview of a datasheet. You can specify up to 12 pages to view at one time through the View ➪ Pages menu.

After you select the Print Preview button, the screen changes to Print Preview mode. You see an image of your first printed page; a set of icons appears on the toolbar. You can use the Navigation buttons (in the lower-left section of the Print Preview window) to change pages, just as you use them to select records in a datasheet.

The toolbar buttons provide quick access to printing tasks:

- ✦ **Close Window.** Returns to Datasheet view
- ✦ **Print.** Displays the Print dialog box, which is accessible when you select File ➪ Print from the menu bar
- ✦ **One Page.** Toggles in and out to make the Print Preview show a single page
- ✦ **Two Pages.** Shows two pages in the Print Preview
- ✦ **Zoom Control.** Adjusts the Print Preview screen to show more or less detail

Tip You can view more than two pages by selecting View ➪ Pages and selecting One (1), Two (2), Four (4), Eight (8), or Twelve (12).

If you are satisfied with the datasheet after examining the preview, select the Print button on the toolbar to print the datasheet. If you are not satisfied, select the Close button to return to datasheet mode to make further changes to your data or layout.

✦   ✦   ✦

Creating and Understanding Relationships

So far, you have learned to create a simple table, to enter its data, and to display it in a datasheet. In the next chapter, you learn to use simple queries. All these techniques can be demonstrated using only a single table. However, as you learned in Chapters 1 and 2, most database systems are composed of many tables that are interrelated. The tblContacts table has been an excellent sample of a single table; it contains many different data types that lend themselves to productive examples.

It's time now to move into the real world of relational database management.

This chapter will use the database named CHAP04Start. mdb. If you have not already copied it onto your machine from the CD, you will need to do so now. If you're following the examples, you can use the tables already in this database or create these tables yourself in a database of your own naming.

If you want to create each of these tables, you can use Appendix B as a reference for each table's description; then use the steps you learned in Chapter 2 to create each table.

Tables Used in the Access Auto Auctions Database

Figure 4-1 diagrams the database of the Access Auto Auctions system. There are 11 tables in the figure, each of which requires its own table design, complete with field names, data types, descriptions, and properties.

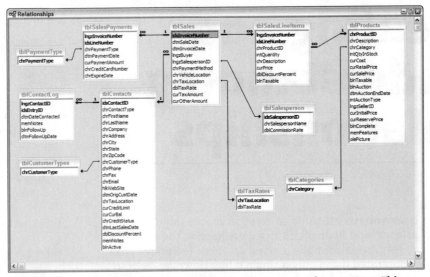

Figure 4-1: The database diagram for the Access Auto Auctions system. This diagram shows all the tables that are used in the system and how they relate to each other.

Cross-Reference

Figure 4-1 shows lines joining the tables. These are the relationship lines between the tables. Each line indicates a separate relationship between two tables; these are established either at the table level (using the Relationships window of Access) or by using a query. In this chapter, you learn to use the Relationships window to establish a relationship at the table level.

If you closely look at the lines between the tables in Figure 4-1, you will observe that some of the lines (relations) between the tables have writing above them.

For instance, the line between the tblSales and tblSalesLineItems tables shows a darkened, thicker line near both tables and a light line connecting them. The one near the tblSales table shows the number 1 above it, and the one near the tblSalesLineItems table shows the infinity symbol (∞) next to it. This simply means that there can be *many* line items (the infinity symbol) for every *one* sale. You can specifically tell Access that this is the case when you create the relationship diagram of all tables in your system. This will be discussed more, later in this chapter.

Of the 11 tables in the database diagram, 6 hold the main data about any sales in Access Auto Auctions and 5 are used for *lookups*.

A lookup table is simply a table that is used to hold secondary information that is related to the overall system. Lookup tables are good for holding common information that will be used over and over in a system. For example, the tblSalesPerson lookup table holds the actual name of the sales person, and the tblTaxRates table holds the correct tax rates for a specific tax location. These tables are used by the system to verify that the users enter an accurate Sales Person ID and Tax Location in the tblSales table. Other lookup tables are used to verify data being entered into other tables. For example, the Customer Type in Contacts is verified by the tblCustomerTypes table, and the Category field in the tblProducts table is verified by the tblCategories table. You can eliminate the lookup tables and still use the system if you want, although some of the value of the system may be lost. The six main tables are listed below:

✦ ***tbl*Contacts:** Contains information about each customer, such as purchaser or seller (one purchaser can have many sales).

✦ ***tbl*Sales:** Contains information about each sale (each sale can have many items purchased, but only one purchaser, contact).

✦ ***tbl*SalesLineItems:** Contains information about each item purchased during a sale (each line item will have one item detailed).

✦ ***tbl*Products:** Contains information about individual products that can be found in the tblSalesLineItems table (each line item will have a detail line in the Products table).

✦ ***tbl*SalesPayments:** Contains information about each payment made by the customer for a specific Sale (each sale can have more than one payment until it is paid in full).

✦ ***tbl*ContactLog:** Contains information about any contacts made with the Customer/Seller (each Customer/Seller may contact the Access Auto Auctions system more than one time for questions or problems).

The five lookup tables are listed below:

✦ ***tbl*PaymentType:** Used by the tblSalesPayments table to retrieve Payment type.

✦ ***tbl*CustomerTypes:** Used by the tblContacts table to retrieve a list of valid Customer types.

✦ ***tbl*TaxRates:** Used by the tblSales table to retrieve valid Tax Rates for each sale.

✦ ***tbl*SalesPerson:** Used by the tblSales table to retrieve valid SalesPerson information for each sale.

✦ ***tbl*Categories:** Used by the tblProducts table to retrieve valid category information for each item.

Note Technically, the tblContact table is a lookup to the tblSales table. This will be discussed more, later in this chapter.

To set relations between tables, you must first establish a link between fields, known as *key fields*, that contain some common information. The fields themselves do not need to have the same name (for example, the common link between the tblSales table and the tblContacts table — lngzBuyer versus idsContactID).

However, the contents in the linked fields must be of the same data type and length. Most importantly, the information contained within both fields (one value in each table) for any specific record must be the same in both tables for the link to work. Generally, a relationship is established by linking *key fields* between tables — the *primary* key in one table (the senior table, such as tblSales is primary to tblSalesLineItems and tblSalesLineItems is primary to tblProducts) to a *foreign* key in another table (the junior or secondary table — tlbSales is secondary to tblContacts). A table can have both a *primary* key and a *foreign* key in it — as is the case with the tblSales table, *idsInvoiceNumber* is a primary key (used to link to the tblSalesItems and tblSalesPayments tables) and *lngzBuyer* is a foreign key (used to link back to the tblContacts table).

A table can even have more than one primary or foreign key. It is easy to identify the primary key of any table when you look at its structure in the Relationships window or in the Query Design window — it will be in bold. It is more difficult to identify foreign keys, because they have no specific font formatting.

In Figure 4-1, each table has one or more fields in bold. These are the fields that define each table's primary key.

Understanding Keys

When you create your tables, as in those created in Chapter 2, you should assign each table a *primary key* — one or more fields whose contents are unique to each record. This key is a way to make sure that the table records contain only one unique value; for example, you may have several Contacts named Michael Irwin, and you may even have more than one living at the same address. So in a case like this, you have to decide on how you can create a record in the Customer database that will let you identify each Michael Irwin separately. That is what a primary key field can do for you. For example, the idsContactID field (a unique number that you assign to each Customer or Seller [Contact] that comes into your office) is the primary key in the tblContacts table — each record in the table has a different idsContactID number. (No two records have the same number.) This is important for several reasons: (1) you do not want to have two records in your database for the same customer, because this can make updating the customer's record virtually impossible; (2) you want to be assured that each record in the table is accurate, thus the information extracted from the table is accurate; and (3) you do not want to make the table (and its records) any bigger than necessary.

The capability to assign a single, unique value to each record makes the table "clean" and reliable. This is known as *entity integrity* in the world of database management. By having a different primary key value in each record (such as the idsContactID in the tblContacts table), you can tell two records (in this case, customers) apart. This is important because you can easily have two individual customers named Fred Smith in your table.

Theoretically, you could use the customer name and the customer's address, but two people named Fred D. Smith could live in the same town and state, or a father and son (Fred David Smith and Fred Daniel Smith) could live at the same address. The goal of setting primary keys is to create individual records in a table that will *guarantee* uniqueness.

If you don't specify a primary key when creating Access tables, Access asks whether you want one. If you say yes, Access creates a primary key for you as an AutoNumber data type. It places a new sequential number in the primary key field for each record automatically. Table 4-1 lists tables and their primary keys.

Note In Access, you can specify that a field be created that is an AutoNumber data type — a field that Access will automatically put a unique value in every time you add a new record to the table. It is important to note that you cannot use an AutoNumber data field in both tables to enforce referential integrity (more on this topic later) between tables. Therefore, it is important to specify another data type — such as Text or Numeric — for the primary key. (More about this topic later in this chapter.)

Table 4-1
Tables and Primary Keys

Table	Primary Key
tblContacts	idsContactID
tblSales	idsInvoiceNumber
tblSalesLineItems	lgzInvoiceNumber + idsLineNumber
tblProducts	chrProductID
tblContactLog	lngzContactID + idsEntryID
tblSalesPayments	lngzInvoiceNumber + idsLineNumber
tblSalesperson	idsSalespersonID
tblTaxRates	chrTaxLocation
tblCustomerTypes	chrCustomerType
tblPaymentType	chrPaymentType
tblCategories	chrCategory

Deciding on a primary key

As you learned previously, a table normally has a unique field (or combination of fields) — the primary key for that table — which makes each record unique. Often it's an ID field that uses the Text data type or Auto number. To determine the contents of this ID field, you specify a method for creating the value in the field. Your method can be as simple as letting Access automatically assign a value or using the first letter of the real value you are tracking along with a sequence number (such as A001, A002, A003, B001, B002, and so on). The method may rely on a random set of letters and numbers for the field content (as long as each field has a unique value) or a complicated calculation based on information from several fields in the table.

Table 4-2 lists the Access Auto Auctions tables and explains the plan for deriving the primary key values in each table.

As Table 4-2 shows, it doesn't take a great deal of work (or even much imagination) to derive a plan for key values. Any rudimentary scheme with a good sequence number always works. Access automatically tells you when you try to enter a duplicate key value. To avoid duplication, you can simply add the value of 1 to the sequence number. You may think that all these sequence numbers make it hard to look up information in your tables. Just remember that *normally* you never look up information by an ID field. Generally, you look up information according to the *purpose* of the table. In the tblContacts table, for example, you would look up information by Customer Name — last and first names. In some cases, the Customer Name is the same, so you can look at other fields in the table (ZIP code, phone number) to find the correct customer. Unless you just happen to know the Contact ID Number, you'll probably never use it in a search for information.

Table 4-2	
Deriving the Primary Key	
Table	**Derivation of Primary Key Value**
tblContacts	Individuals: AutoNumber field assigned by Access; incremented in sequence.
tblSales	Invoice Number: AutoNumber field assigned by Access; incremented in sequence.
tblSalesLineItems	Invoice Number (from Sales) and an AutoNumber set by Access; incremented in sequence.
tblProducts	Product Number, entered by the person putting in a new product.
tblSalesPayments	Invoice Number (from Sales) and an AutoNumber set by Access; incremented in sequence.

Table	Derivation of Primary Key Value
tblContactLog	Contact ID (from Contacts) and an AutoNumber set by Access; incremented in sequence.
tblPaymentType	Type of Payment - VISA, CASH, etc. used as lookup.
tblCustomerTypes	Type of Customer — Dealer, Auctioneer, Parts, etc. used as lookup.
tblSlaesperson	Sales Person ID: AutoNumber field assigned by Access.
tblTaxRates	Tax Location: entered by the person putting in a new record.
tblCategories	Category of Items: entered by the person putting in a new record.

Benefits of a primary key

Have you ever placed an order with a company for the first time and then decided the next day to increase your order? You call the people at the order desk. Sometimes they ask you for your customer number. You tell them that you don't know your customer number. This happens all the time. So they ask you for some other information — generally, your ZIP code or telephone area code. Then, as they narrow down the list of customers, they ask your name. Then they tell you your customer number. Some businesses use phone numbers as a unique starting point.

Database systems usually have more than one table, and these tend to be related in some manner. For example, the tblContacts table and tblSales table are related to each other via a link field called lngzBuyer in tblSales and idsContactID in tblContacts. The tblContacts table always has one record for each customer (buyer/seller), and the tblSales table has a record for Sales Invoice that the customer makes (every time he purchases something). Because each customer is *one* physical person, you only need one record for the customer in the tblContacts table. Each customer can make many purchases, however, which means you need to set up another table to hold information about each sale — thus the tblSales table. Again, each invoice is *one* physical sale (on a specific day at a specific time). Each sale has one record in the tblSales table. Of course, you need to have some way to relate the Buyer to the Sales they make in the tblSales table. This is accomplished by using a common field that is in both tables. In this case, the field lngzBuyer in tblSales and idsContactID in tblContacts (which has the identical type of information in both tables).

When linking tables, you link the primary key field from one table (the idsContactID in the tblContacts table) to a field in the second table that has the same structure and type of data in it (the lngzBuyer field in the tblSales table). If the link field in the second table is not the primary key field (and usually it isn't), it's known as a *foreign* key field (discussed later in this chapter).

Besides being a common link field between tables, a primary key field in Access has these advantages:

✦ A primary key field is one that is used to create an index for the table that greatly speeds up queries, searches, and sort requests.

✦ When you add new records, you must enter a value in primary key field(s). Access will not allow you to enter Null values, which guarantees that you'll have only valid records in your table.

✦ When you add new records to a table that has a primary key, Access checks for duplicate data and doesn't enable you to enter duplicates for the primary key field — thus it maintains its integrity.

✦ By default, Access displays your data in the order of the primary key.

Tip   An index is a special internal file that is created to put the records in a table in some specific order. For instance, the primary key field in the tblContacts table is an index that puts the records in order by idsContactID field. Using an indexed table, Access can display records in a specific manner and quickly find any record within the table using the index.

If you define a primary key based on part of the data in the record, you can have Access automatically place your data in an understandable order. In the example, the tblSalesLineItems database, the primary key is composed of two fields — lngzInvoiceNumber (which comes from the tblSales table) and a line number for a sequence (idsLineNumber field). This way, the tblSalesLineItems table places all related sales together in a sequential order displayed alphanumerically.

Tip   Primary key fields should be made as short as possible (built using as few characters and fields as possible), because they can affect the speed of operations in a database.

Creating a primary key

As discussed in Chapters 1 and 2, a primary key is created by selecting the field (or fields) that you want to use as a primary key and clicking on the Primary Key button on the toolbar (the button with the key on it). If you are specifying more than one field, you specify the fields that you want for the primary key and again click the Primary Key button. Selecting each field while holding down the Ctrl key specifies the fields.

When you're specifying multi-field primary keys, the selection order is important. Therefore, check your selection by clicking the Indexes button on the toolbar and looking at the field order. Figure 4-2 shows the two-field index for the tblSalesLineItems table. Notice that the lngzInvoiceNumber field is before the idsLineNumber field in the Indexes: tblSalesLineItems dialog box.

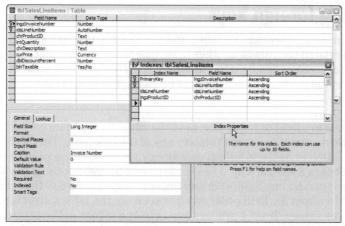

Figure 4-2: The Indexes: tblSalesLineItems dialog box showing a two-field primary key.

The Indexes: tblSalesLineItems dialog box shown in the center right-hand side of Figure 4-2 is opened when you open a table in Design View and select View ⇨ Indexes from the Access menu or click on the Indexes button (center of the toolbar with a series of parallel lines and a lighting bolt along side of them — to the right of the Key button). When the dialog box is open, it shows you all of the Indexes in that table — including primary keys, foreign keys, and other indexes for sorting. Notice that it shows the word PrimaryKey only in the ldgzInvoiceNumber field, although it still shows the graphical key (for primary key) to the left of both fields. This simply means that both fields together make up the primary key.

The order of these fields is critical; if you reverse them and make the idsLineNumber field the first part of the primary key, it will not work correctly — you may create a situation where you do not have a viable way to create unique records in the table.

Note   There are two additional index names in the Indexes: tblSalesLineItems dialog box. These are not keys, but indexes used to speed sorts used in these tables. If you regularly sort data in tables by the same field or fields, you should create an index for that field. An index is an internal table of values that maintains the order of the records. This way, when you need to sort data or find a piece of data instantly, Access can search through the index keys in a known order, rather than searching sequentially through the data.

Caution   Creating indexes slows data entry; each new record, deleted record, or change to the indexed field requires a change to the index. Use the index fields only when you actually need them — for example, when you need to speed sorting your application for later use. You will have to balance the display and reporting speed with the need of data-entry speed.

Understanding foreign keys

Primary keys guarantee uniqueness in a table, and you use the primary key field in one table to link to related records in another table (the Sales purchased by a specific Customer). The common link field in the other table (records that are associated with a record in the primary table) may not be (and usually isn't) the primary key in the other table.

The *common link field* is a field or fields that hold the same type of data (matching the content of the field exactly) as in the primary key of the link table. This common link field, or combination of fields, is known as a *foreign key* field. Like a primary key, which must be created in a special way, a *foreign key* must be created using the same structure; however, it can be any field(s) in any order of the structure of the table. You are not limited to a specific field order when you create the table's structure. By matching the same values (from a primary key field in a record in the primary key table to the values in a specific field of one or more records in a foreign key table) in both tables, you can relate records between tables.

In the relationship diagram of Figure 4-1, you saw a relationship between the tblContacts and tblSales tables. The primary key of tblContacts, idsContactID, is related to the lngzBuyer field in tblSales. In tblSales, lngzBuyer is the foreign key because it is the key of a related "foreign" table.

An example would be William Gleason in the tblContacts table with the idsContactID of 18. The one record in the Customer table with the idsContactID 18 is linked to two records in the tblSales table — one record of a sale on February 27, 2003 with an invoice number of 5and another for a sale on January 10, 2004 and invoice number of 32. Thus, there is one record in the tblContacts table with 18 in the idsContactID Field and two records in the tblSales table with lngzBuyer field having an 18 in it.

A relation also exists between the tblSales and tblSalesLineItems tables. The primary key of idsInvoiceNumber in tblSales is related to the lngzInvoiceNumber field (part of the complex primary key of tblSalesLineItems — comprises two fields) in the tblSalesLineItems table. In the tblSalesLineItems table, lngzInvoiceNumber is the foreign key because it is the key of a related foreign table.

Note   lngzInvoiceNumber is also the principal part of the complex primary key in the tblSalesLineItems table.

Understanding Relations between Tables

At the beginning of this chapter, you saw 11 tables in the Access Auto Auctions database and 10 relationships. Before you learn to create these relationships, it is important to understand them.

A review of relationships

First, you can create relationships between tables at two places: in the Relationships window that will relate them at a table level, and when you create queries to display information from those tables (known as the query level).

Relationships established at the table level take precedence over those established at the query level. If you specify a relationship between tables at the table level (in the Relationships window), Access will recognize it automatically when you create a multiple-table query that uses fields from more than one table.

Tip　　When you create a query and no Relationships are set, Access will automatically try to set relations between tables with similar field names.

With that said, it is now important to understand that there are four types of relationships that you can set between two tables:

✦ One-to-one

✦ One-to-many

✦ Many-to-one

✦ Many-to-many

Understanding the four types of table relationships

When you physically join two tables (by connecting fields with like information), you create a relationship that Access recognizes. Figure 4-3 shows the relationships between all the tables in the Access Auto Auctions system.

Notice that there are three one-to-many relationships between the primary tables (tblSales-to-tblSalesPayments, tblSales-to-tblSalesLineItems, and tblContacts-to-tblContactsLog), two one-to-many relationship between the primary tables (tblSalesLineItems-to-tblProducts and tblSales-to-tblContacts), and five one-to-many relations between the five lookup tables and the primary tables. The relationship that you specify between tables is important. It tells Access how to find and display information from fields in two or more tables. The program needs to know whether to look for only one record in a table or look for several records on the basis of the relationship. The tblSales table, for example, is related to the tblContacts table as a *many-to-one* relationship. This is because the focus of the Access Auto Auctions system is the Sales. This means that there will *always* be only one contact (buyer) related to every Sales record; that is, many sales can be associated with a single buyer (contact). In this case, the Access Auto Auctions system is actually using the tblContacts table like a lookup type.

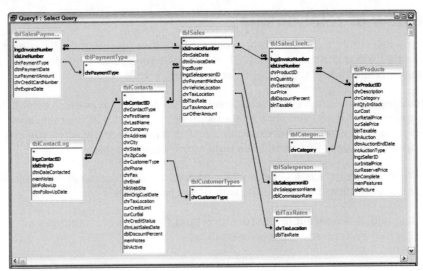

Figure 4-3: The Access Auto Auctions tables relationships.

Note   Relationships can be very confusing; it all depends upon the focus of the system. For instance, when working with the tblContacts and tblSales tables, you can always create a query that has a *one-to-many* relationship to the tblSales table, from the tblContacts. Although the system is concerned with sales (invoices), there are times that you will want to produce reports or views that are buyer-related instead of invoice-related. Because one buyer can have more than one sale, there will *always* be one record in the tblContacts table for *at least* one record in the tblSales table; there could be *many* related records in the tblSales table. So Access knows to find only one record in the Customer table and to look for any in the tblSales table (one or more) that have the same Customer Number.

The one-to-one relationship

The *one-to-one relationship*, though rarely used in database systems, can be a very useful way to link two tables together.

A good example of a one-to-one relationship occurs in most billing systems; a billing file is created to allow additional information necessary to invoice customers at a location other than their listed addresses. This file usually contains the customer number and another set of address fields.

Only a few customers would have a separate billing address, so you wouldn't add this information to the main customer table. A one-to-one relationship between a customer table and billing table may be established to retrieve the billing address for those customers who want to have a separate address for billing purposes and one for catalogs or other uses. Although all the information on one table could be added to the other, the tables are maintained separately for efficient use of space.

The one-to-many relationship

The *one-to-many relationship* is used to relate one record in a table with many records in another. Examples are one sale to many line items or one customer to many customer contacts. Both of these examples are one-to-many relationships. The tblSales-tblSalesLineItems relationship links the Invoice Number (the primary key of the tblSales table) to the Invoice Number in the tblSalesLineItems table (which becomes the foreign key of the tblSales table). There are only three one-to-many relations in the Access Auto Auctions system related to tblSales, there are five one-to-many relations in the entire system.

The many-to-one relationship

The *many-to-one relationship* (often called the *lookup table relationship*) tells Access that many records in the table are related to a single record in another table. Normally, many-to-one relationships are not based on a primary key field in either table. Access Auto Auctions has seven lookup tables (five primary lookup tables and two are primary tables of the system that are used as a "lookup" table – for example tblContacts can be a lookup table to tblSales), each having a many-to-one relationship with the primary table. The tblContacts table has a many-to-one relationship with the tblCustomerTypes table; each Customer Type record can be used for many buyers (contacts). Although (in theory) some consider this relationship a one-to-one, it is known as a many-to-one relationship because it does not use a primary key field for the link, and many records from the primary table link to a single record in the other table.

Some one-to-many relationships can be reversed and made into many-to-one relationships. If you set a relationship from tblSales to tblContacts, for example, the relationship becomes many-to-one; many Sales can have the same buyer (contact). So relationships depend on how the information in your tables is used and interpreted. Thus, one-to-many and many-to-one relationships can be considered the same — just viewed from opposite perspectives.

The many-to-many relationship

The *many-to-many relationship* is the hardest to understand. Think of it generally as a pair of *one-to-many relationships* between two tables, with a special table created (called a *junction* table) that is used to link them together. The junction table is composed of a minimum of two fields — the foreign keys from both tables it is linking together. These two fields are subsequently used to create the primary key in the junction table. This *junction* table could easily be created in the case of the tables, tblSales and tblSalesLineItems, in the Access Auto Auctions database by simply creating another table in between that contains both the invoice number and product number, making the primary key a combination of these two fields, and separating the Sales and LineItems with this new table.

For a true many-to-many relationship between these two tables, there has to be a junction table that is composed of a complex primary key created by joining the primary key from both tables in a single primary key in the junction table.

Understanding Referential Integrity

In addition to specifying relationships between tables in an Access database, you can also set up some rules that will help in maintaining a degree of accuracy, or *Referential Integrity,* between the tables. For example, you would not want to delete a contact (buyer or seller) record in your tblContacts table if there are related sales records in the tblSales table. If you did delete a customer record without first deleting the customer's sales (or a seller without first deleting any items sold to you by them), you would have a system that had sales without any buyers. This type of problem could be catastrophic.

Imagine being in charge of a bank that tracks loans in a database system. Now imagine that this system has *no* rules that say, "Before deleting a customer's record, make sure that there is no outstanding loan." It would be disastrous! So a database system needs to have rules that specify certain conditions between tables — rules to enforce the integrity of information between the tables. These rules are known as *referential integrity*; they keep the relationships between tables intact in a relational database management system. Referential integrity prohibits you from changing your data in ways that invalidate the links between tables.

Referential integrity operates strictly on the basis of the tables' key fields; it checks each time a key field, whether primary or foreign, is added, changed, or deleted. If a change to a value in a key field creates an invalid relationship, it is said to violate referential integrity. Tables can be set up so that referential integrity is enforced automatically.

When tables are linked, one table is usually called the *parent* and the other (the table it is linked to) is usually called the *child*. This is known as a *parent-child relationship* between tables. Referential integrity guarantees that there will never be an *orphan*, a child record without a parent record.

Cross-Reference If you connect to an SQL Server back end database or use the Microsoft Database Engine and create an Access Data Project, the Relationships window is different. This is discussed in Chapter 28.

Creating Relationships

Unless you have a reason for not wanting your relationships always to be active, create your table relationships at the table level using the *Relationships window*. The table relationships can be overridden later, in a query, if necessary. For normal data entry and reporting purposes, however, having your relationships defined at the table level makes it much easier to use your database system.

Access has a very powerful Relationships window. With it, you can add tables, use drag-and-drop methods to link tables, easily specify the type of link, and set any referential integrity between tables.

Using the Relationships window

You begin creating relationships in the Database window. From this window, you can select Tools⇨Relationships or click the Relationships button on the toolbar (usually the third button from the right side—three little squares, one on the left and two on the right, with blue tops and lines from the left one to the other two). The main Relationships window appears, which lets you add tables and create links between them.

Figure 4-4 shows the Relationships window with the 11 tables that you will add below and the Show Table window open to select those tables. Notice the toolbar associated with it (the arrow is pointing to the three icons). It has three options specific to the Relationships window—Show Direct Relationships, Show All Relationships, and Clear Layout (center right of toolbar). When first opened, the Relationships window is a blank surface. Tables are added to the window by using one of these methods:

✦ Add the tables before entering the Relationships window from the Show Table dialog box that's first displayed.

✦ Click the Show Table button on the toolbar.

✦ Click Relationships ⇨ Show Table from the menu bar.

✦ While in the Relationships window, click the right mouse button (which displays the shortcut menu) and select Show Table from the menu.

To start the Relationships window and add the Access Auto Auctions tables to the Relationships window, follow these steps:

1. Click the Relationships button on the toolbar. Access opens the Show Table dialog box.

2. Select all the tables (tblCategories, tblContactLog, tblContacts, tblCustomerTypes, tblPaymentType, tblProducts, tblSales, tblSalesLineItems, tblSalesPayments, tblSalesperson, tlbTaxRates) by clicking tblCategories, holding Shift, and clicking tblTaxRates. Then click Add.

3. Click the Close button on the Show Table dialog box. Your screen should look similar to the one in Figure 4-4 (minus the Show Table window). Notice that Access has placed each table in the Relationships window. Each table is in its own box; the title of the box is the name of the table. Inside the table box are the names of the fields for each table. Currently, there are no relationships, or lines, between the tables. Now you are ready to set relationships between them.

Note   If you select a table by mistake, it can be removed from the window by clicking in it and pressing the Delete key.

Tip   You may want to move and resize each table window to see all the fields, as shown in Figure 4-5.

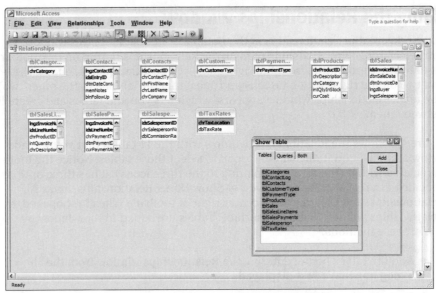

Figure 4-4: The Relationships window with 11 tables added.

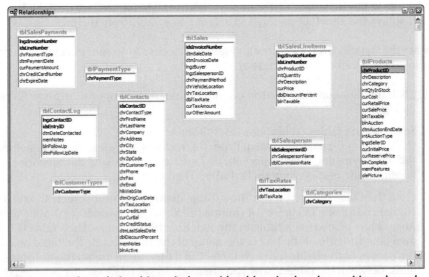

Figure 4-5: The Relationships window with tables sized and repositioned, ready to create the relationships between them.

Creating relationships between tables

With the tables positioned similar to those in Figure 4-5 in the Relationships window, you are ready to create relationships between the tables. To create a relationship between two tables, select the common field in one table, drag it to the field in the table you want to relate it to, and drop it on the common field.

Follow these steps to create a relationship between the tblSales and tblContacts tables:

1. Click the inqzBuyer field of the tblSales table.

Note If you select and begin to move a field in error, simply move the field icon to the window surface; it turns into the international No symbol. While it is displayed as this symbol, release the mouse button and field linking stops.

2. While holding down the mouse button, move the cursor to the tblContacts table. Notice that Access displays a field-select icon (a small rectangular box with lines inside of it) as you hold and drag the inqzBuyer field from the tblSales table.

3. Drag and drop the field-select icon to the idsContactID field of the tblContacts table. Access displays the Edit Relationships dialog box, as shown in Figure 4-6.

4. Click the Create button to create the relationship. Access closes the dialog box and places a join line between the tblSales and tblContacts tables.

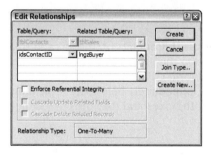

Figure 4-6: The Edit Relationships dialog box that is activated when you drag and drop the inqzBuyer field from the tblSales table onto the idsContactID field of the tblContacts table.

Note You can edit the relationship for any join by double-clicking the join line between the two tables. For example, double-clicking the join line between the tblSales and tblContacts tables reactivates the Edit Relationships dialog box for that link.

Tip Access automatically tries to determine the type of link between the two tables by looking at the data in the records of both tables and displays it at the bottom of the Relationships dialog box. Figure 4-6 shows that the type of relationship between the tblContacts and tblSales tables is a one-to-many type (or a many-to-one from the Sales to Contacts). However, it does not physically display the type of link between the tables in the Relationships window unless Enforce Referential Integrity is checked on.

Specifying relationship options in the Edit Relationships dialog box

The Edit Relationships dialog box has several options for the relationship between the Contacts and Sales tables. Figure 4-6 shows the dialog box and all the options. The Edit Relationships dialog box tells you which table is the primary table for the relationship (the one on the left side of the dialog box—in this case, tblContacts) and whether referential integrity is enforced (a check box below the names of the related fields on the left side). The dialog box also tells you the type of relationship (one-to-one or one-to-many—at the bottom of the dialog box) and lets you specify (after selecting Enforce Referential Integrity) whether *cascading* updates and *deletes* (automatically fix key changes or deletions in related records) between related tables are allowed.

Note For the following sections, activate the Edit Relationships dialog box for the link between the tblContacts and tblSales tables. To do so, double-click the join line between the tables.

Checking the primary table

The top of the dialog box has two table names—tblContacts on the left and tblSales on the right. The tblContacts table is considered the primary table for this relationship (because its primary index is being used for it). The dialog box shows the related fields for each table in a separate box immediately below the table names. Make sure that the correct table name is in both boxes and that the correct field is specified (idsContactID and indzBuyer).

Caution If you relate two tables incorrectly, simply click the Cancel button in the Edit Relationships dialog box. Access closes the dialog box and erases the join line, and you can begin again.

Tip If you relate two tables by the wrong field, simply select the correct field for each table by using the combo box under each table name.

Checking the Join Type between tables

The right side of the Edit Relations window has four buttons—OK, Cancel, Join Type, and Create New ... buttons. Pressing the OK button returns you to the

Relationships window with any changes specified. The Cancel button will cancel the current changes and also return you to the Relationships window. The Create New ... button will let you specify a new relation between two tables and fields.

The one button that you should also click after you first activate the Edit Relations dialog box is Join Type. This button will activate another window — the Join Properties dialog box. This dialog box lets you decide if you want to see records in both tables, see all records in one table or the other, or see only those that are related. For instance, to make sure that you have the correct join type between the tblSales and tblContacts tables, follow these steps:

1. Click the Join Type button to activate the Join Properties Dialog box.

2. Click the option that says "Include ALL records from 'tblSales' and only those records from 'tblContacts' where the joined fields are equal." (the third option on the authors system). The relationship between these tables should now look like the one in Figure 4-7.

3. Click the OK button to return to the Edit Relationships Dialog box.

4. Click the OK button of the Edit Relationships dialog box to return to the Relationships window.

Figure 4-7: A dialog box to set up the Join properties between the tblSales and tblContacts tables. Notice that it specifies ALL records from the tblSales table.

You have now specified that the relationship is from the tblSales table to the tblContacts table — meaning that many sales can be related to a single contact.

The Relationships window should now show an arrow going from the tblSales table to the tblContacts table. At this point, you are ready to set Referential Integrity between the two tables.

Tip Each relationship will be different, depending upon the focus of the tables. You should click on the Join Type button for each relationship to make sure that you have specified the correct data relationship between tables.

Enforcing referential integrity

After specifying the relationship, verifying the table and related fields, and specifying the type of join between the tables, you can set referential integrity between the tables by clicking the Enforce Referential Integrity check box below the table information. If you choose not to enforce referential integrity, you can add new records, change key fields, or delete related records without worrying about referential integrity—thus making it possible to change critical fields without being warned or prevented from doing so. With no integrity active, you can create tables that have orphans (Sales without a Contact) or parents without children (Contact without Sales). With normal operations (such as data entry or changing information), referential integrity rules should be enforced. By setting this option, you can specify several additional options.

Re-open the Edit Relationships dialog box for the relations between the tblSales and tblContacts tables by double-clicking on the join line.

Clicking the check box in front of the option Enforce Referential Integrity activates the two Cascading choices (Update and Delete) in the dialog box and enforces Referential Integrity. Figure 4-8 shows the Edit Relationships dialog box with Referential Integrity activated.

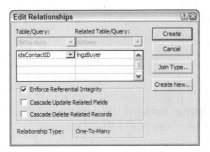

Figure 4-8: Referential Integrity set between the tblSales and tblContacts tables.

Note   You might find, when you specify Enforce Referential Integrity and click the Create button (or the OK button if you've reopened the Edit Relationships window to edit a relationship), that Access will not allow you to create a relationship and enforce referential integrity. The reason probably is that you are asking Access to create a relationship supporting referential integrity between two tables that have records that *violate* referential integrity rules, such as a child table with orphans in it. In such a case, Access warns you by displaying a dialog box similar to that shown in Figure 4-9. The warning happens in this example because there are some records in the tblSales database with no value in the lngzSalespersonID field of the record to correspond to a record in the tblSalesperson table. This means that Access cannot create referential integrity between this table and that you will have to go through the table and add values that will allow a corresponding relation between the two tables. Access returns you to the Relationships window after you click the OK button; you will need to de-select the Enforce Referential Integrity check box if it reports you cannot create it.

Figure 4-9: A dialog box warning that referential integrity cannot be created between two tables due to violations in some of the records between the two tables — one or more tblSales without a Salesperson ID is probably the problem.

Tip　To solve any conflicts between existing tables, you can create a Find Unmatched query by using the Query Wizard to find the records in the many-side table (in the case of the example in Figure 4-9, the tblSales table) that violate referential integrity. Then you can convert the Unmatched query to a Delete query to delete the offending records or add the appropriate value to the lngzSalespersonID field. You learn how to do this in Chapter 38.

Caution　When selecting Enforce Referential Integrity, Access does not check to see if you have Contacts without Sales. This is not an issue with referential integrity. You can have multiple Contacts that have no Sales, known as *widow* records. However, these records do not violate integrity; thus they are not checked for by Access. Even with enforcement on, you can still create a parent record without children (a Contact without any Sales). However, you can create a Find Unmatched query to delete these records. This will be covered in Chapter 38.

You could remove the offending records and return to the Relationships window and set referential integrity between the two tables. However, you should not do this, because Salesperson is not a critical field that requires Referential Integrity to be set between these tables.

Choosing the Cascade Update Related Fields option

If you specify Enforce Referential Integrity in the Edit Relationships dialog box, Access activates a check box option labeled Cascade Update Related Fields. This option tells Access that a user can change the contents of a related field (the primary key field in the primary table — idsContactID, for example).

When the user changes the contents of the primary key field in the primary table, Access verifies that the change is to a unique value (because there cannot be duplicate records in the primary table) and then goes through the related records in the many table and changes the foreign key value from the old value to the new value. Suppose you code your customers by the first two letters of their last names, and one of your customers gets married and changes the name that Access knows to look for. If the Primary Key depended up a scheme dependent upon the last name (like the first two letters of the last name), you could change the primary key, and all changes would ripple through other related records in the system.

If this option is not selected, you cannot change the primary key value in the primary table that is used in a relationship with another table.

Note If the primary key field in the primary table is a related field between several tables, this option must be selected for all related tables or it will not work.

Choosing the Cascade Delete Related Records option

Similarly, if you specify Enforce Referential Integrity in the Edit Relationships dialog box, Access activates the Cascade Delete Related Records check box. By selecting this option, you tell Access that if a user attempts to delete a record in a primary table that has child records, first it must delete all the related child records and then delete the primary record.

This can be very useful for deleting a series of related records. For example, if you have chosen Cascade Delete Related Records and you try to delete a particular customer (who moved away from the area), Access first deletes all the related records from the related tables—tblSales and tblSalesLineItems—and then deletes the customer record. In other words, Access deletes all the records in the sales line items for each sale for each customer—the detail items of the sales, the associated sales records, and the customer record—with one step.

If you do not specify this option, Access will not enable you to delete a record that has related records in another table. In cases like this, you must delete all related records in the tblSalesLineItems table first, then delete related records in the tblSales table, and finally delete the customer record in the tblContact table.

Tip To use this option, you must specify Cascade Delete Related Records for all of the table's relationships in the database. If you do not specify this option for all the tables in the chain of related tables, Access will not allow cascade deleting.

Caution Use this option with caution! Access does not warn that it is going to do a cascade delete when you build a Delete query. The program just does it. Later you may wonder where all your records went. However, if you delete a record in a form that has a subform with related records in it, Access will display a message saying it will delete "this record and all its related records."

Finishing the relationships between the tables of the Access Auto Auctions system

With the first relationship created for the system; between the tblSales and tblContacts, you can quickly create the remaining relations. Table 4-3 shows the table relationships (how each table relates or is linked to another), which fields are used to build the link, and the type of join line used between the tables.

Table 4-3
Table Relationships

From Table (field)	To Table (field)	Enforce Ref. Integrity	Type of Join Line
tblContacts idsContactID	tblSales lngzBuyer	YES	Include ALL records from tblSales and only those records from tblContacts where the join fields are equal
tblSales idsInvoiceNumber	tblSalesLineItems lngzInvoiceNumber	YES	Include ALL records from tblSales and only those records from tblSaleslineItems where the join fields are equal
tblSales idsInvoiceNumber	tblSalesPayments lngzInvoiceNumber	YES	Include ALL records from tblSales and only those records from tblSalesPayments where the join fields are equal
tblSales lngzSalespersonID	tblSalesperson idsSalespersonID	NO	Include ALL records from tblSales and only those records from tblSalesperson where the join fields are equal
tblSales chrTaxLocation	tblTaxRate chrTaxLocation	NO	Include ALL records from tblSales and only those records from tblTaxRates where the join fields are equal
tblSalesLineItems chrProductID	tblProducts chrProductID	YES	Include ALL records from tblSalesLineItems and only those records from tblProducts where the join fields are equal
tblProducts chrCategory	tblCategories chrCategory	NO	Include ALL records from tblProducts and only those records from tblCategories where the join fields are equal

Continued

Table 4-3 *(continued)*

From Table (field)	To Table (field)	Enforce Ref. Integrity	Type of Join Line
tblContacts idsContactID	*tblContactLog* lngzContactID	YES	*Include ALL records from tblContacts and only those records from tblContactLog where the join fields are equal*
TbContacts chrCustomerType	*tblCustomerTypes* chrCustomerType	NO	*Include ALL records from tblContacts and only those records from tblCustomerTypes where the join fields are equal*
tblSalesPayments chrPaymentType	*tblPaymentType* chrPaymentType	NO	*Include ALL records from tblSalesPayments and only those records from tblPaymentType where the join fields are equal*

After you have created all your relations, the final relationships window should look like the one shown in Figure 4-10. Notice that Access only shows the type of relationships (one-to-many or many-to-one) where you set Enforce Referential Integrity to YES. It also shows arrows between tables showing which table has precedence (which table will include ALL records). The table without the arrow pointing to it will include ALL records; the one with the arrow pointing to it will include only those records that match the other table.

Saving the relationships between tables

The easiest way to save the relationships you created between the tables is to click the Save button on the toolbar and then close the window. Another method is to close the window and answer *Yes* to the Save Relationships dialog box that appears.

Adding another relationship

After you specify all the tables, the fields, and their referential integrity status, you can add tables to the Relationships window by clicking the Relationships button on the toolbar and adding new tables.

Again, if there is data in a new table that violates referential integrity between it and a related table, you must fix the offending table by removing the records before you can set referential integrity between the tables.

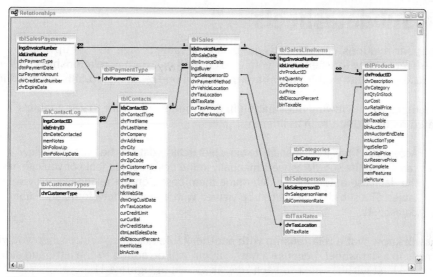

Figure 4-10: The final relationships created, showing the type of relations and demonstrating which tables have precedence.

Deleting an existing relationship

To delete an existing relationship, open the Relationships window, right-click the join line you want to delete, and select Delete from the Menu. Like in previous versions of Access, you could simply press the Delete key and answer Yes to the question *Are you sure you want to delete the selected relationship?*

Join lines in the Relationships window

When you create a relationship between two tables, Access automatically creates a thin join line from one table to another. Figure 4-10 shows a simple join line between several tables; for example, between tblSales and tblSalesperson or tblTaxRates, tblContacts and tblCustomerTypes, and on and on.

If you specify that you want to enforce referential integrity, however, Access changes the appearance of the join line. The join lines between tblSales and tblContacts or tblSalesLineItems and tblSalesPayments are examples where the join line changes. It becomes thicker at each end (alongside the table). It also has either a 1 or the infinity symbol (∞) over the thick bar of the line (on each side of the join line).

Printing a report of the relationships

When you have defined the relationships for your tables, you can create a graphical report of the relationships of the tables by selecting File ➪ Print Relationships from the Access menu while the Relationships window is open.

Using Subdatasheets

With your relationships set, you can revisit the table design and set up a sub-datasheet to view for the tables you have created one-to-may relationships between. Because some of the tables may have more than one relationship, this is a good idea.

Sometimes when viewing information in datasheets, you want to see a table's related records that are in a different table.

Note   Access 2003 has the capability to view hierarchical data in the Datasheet view. You can set up the sub-datasheets manually in the design of the table or you can have the database automatically determine them based on the relationships between tables. The sub-datasheets can be viewed with a table, query, form, and subform datasheets.

You will know that a relationship with another table has been set up when you view records in a datasheet, because a new column will be added to the left-hand side of the datasheet with a + next to each row, as shown in Figure 4-11.

	Invoice Number	Sale Date	Invoice Date	Buyer ID	SalespersonID	Payment Metho	Vehicle Locatio	Tax Location	Tax Rate
▶ +	4	1/15/2003	2/3/2003	1	1	Check	Lancaster, PA	MA	5.0000
+	5	2/27/2003	2/18/2003	18	3	Check		CT	6.0000
+	6	2/24/2003	2/24/2003	33	1	Check		MA	5.0000
+	7	4/24/2003	4/24/2003	53	1	Cash		TX	6.2500
+	8	5/24/2003	5/24/2003	14	2	Mastercard		MA	5.0000
+	9	6/1/2003	6/1/2003	59	1	Cash		TX	6.2500
+	10	7/15/2003	7/15/2003	17	3	Check		NY-ST	4.5000
+	11	8/25/2003	8/25/2003	41	1	Visa		NY	4.0000
+	12	8/26/2003	8/26/2003	56	3	Visa		AZ	5.6000
+	13	9/25/2003	9/25/2003	52	1	Check		KY	6.0000
+	14	9/30/2003	9/30/2003	55	2	Cash		GA	4.0000
+	15	12/13/2003	12/13/2003	37	1	COD		NY	4.0000
+	16	12/12/2003	12/12/2003	1	3			MA	5.0000
+	17	2/25/2004	2/25/2004	33	1	Discover		MA	5.0000
+	18	2/25/2004	2/25/2004	20	0			CT	6.0000
+	19	9/1/2003	9/1/2003	14	1	Other		MA	5.0000
+	20	9/6/2003	9/6/2003	37	3			NY	4.0000
+	21	9/30/2003	9/30/2003	54	1	Cash		IL	6.2500
+	22	10/15/2003	10/15/2003	64	1	Check		MO	4.5550
+	23	10/25/2003	10/25/2003	27	1			NJ	6.0000
+	24	10/26/2003	10/26/2003	31	1	Mastercard		MA	5.0000
+	25	10/30/2003	10/30/2003	38	1	Visa		NY	4.0000
+	26	11/1/2003	11/1/2003	25	3	Check		CT	6.0000
+	27	11/5/2003	11/5/2003	33	3	COD		MA	5.0000

Record: |◄| ◄| 1 |►| |►I| |►*| of 53

Figure 4-11: Displaying a datasheet that has related tables. Notice the plus sign field next to each Invoice Number (to the left). Clicking this will expand a new datasheet (sub-datasheet) of related records in the tlbSalesLineItems table.

When you click the + sign for a row, the related records in the sub-datasheet are shown. The tables that are set up to be sub-datasheets may have sub-datasheets for them, which allow the viewing of both related records for the main table that you are in and related records for the sub-datasheet.

Setting up sub-datasheets

You can set up sub-datasheets in the design view of a table by clicking View ➪ Properties from the Access menu bar, or by clicking the Properties button on your toolbar. This displays the Table Properties dialog box as shown in Figure 4-12.

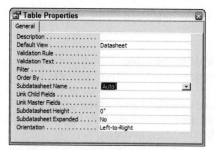

Figure 4-12: Table Properties.

Selecting a sub-datasheet name

If you are moving directly from Access 97 to Access 2003, you will notice that five new properties have been added to the Table Properties dialog box. All of these properties are related to sub-datasheets. Also notice the value entered for Subdatasheet Name — [Auto]. [Auto] automatically assigns the sub-datasheet name based on relationships set up in the database. To display a list of Tables and Queries in the database, click anywhere in the Subdatasheet Name field and a combo box displays, as shown in Figure 4-13.

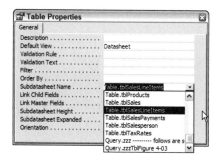

Figure 4-13: Displaying Table and Query names that may be linked to the tblSales table. In this case, it is selecting Table.tblSalesLineItems.

Entering the Link Child Fields and the Link Master Fields

The Link Child Fields and Link Master Fields property settings (immediately below the Subdatasheet Name property) must have the same number of fields and must represent data of the same type. For example, in this case, the tblSales (Master) table and the tblSalesLineItems (Child) table have different field names (one each) that contain the same type of data, Access will automatically pull the correct field name into these properties from the Relationship builder that you just created—lngzInvoiceNumber for Link Child Fields and idsInvoiceNumber for Link Master Fields. The subform will automatically display all the tblSalesLineItems found for each record identified in the main table's (tblSales) Invoice Number field.

Although the data must match, the names of the fields can differ, as in the example above.

If you change the name of either or both fields in the tables (which we don't recommend), you will have to enter these field names into the correct property.

Without the link fields entered, no records will be displayed when you try to display your sub-datasheet for the tblSales table because Access doesn't know what fields to automatically link (they would have to be the same name).

Caution   If you have not set the link between tables and you have created your relationship diagram, Access 2003 may still display the plus sign. If you click on the plus sign in datasheet mode, Access will display an Insert Subdatasheet dialog box like the one in Figure 4-14. Simply select the table you want to link (such as tblSalesLineItem), and Access will associate the correct property value in the sheet for you.

Figure 4-14: The Insert Subdatasheet dialog box.

Entering a Subdatasheet Height

The property for the Subdatasheet Height has a default value of 0 inches. This will show you the related records in a sheet that is up to 2 inches high. If the records don't fit in this space, scroll bars permit a view of all the records.

To change the height to a smaller or larger number, type in your preferred height in inches.

Expanding the Subdatasheet

The Subdatasheet Expanded field is a Yes/No field. If you have Yes entered in this field, the sub-datasheets are expanded, as shown in Figure 4-15.

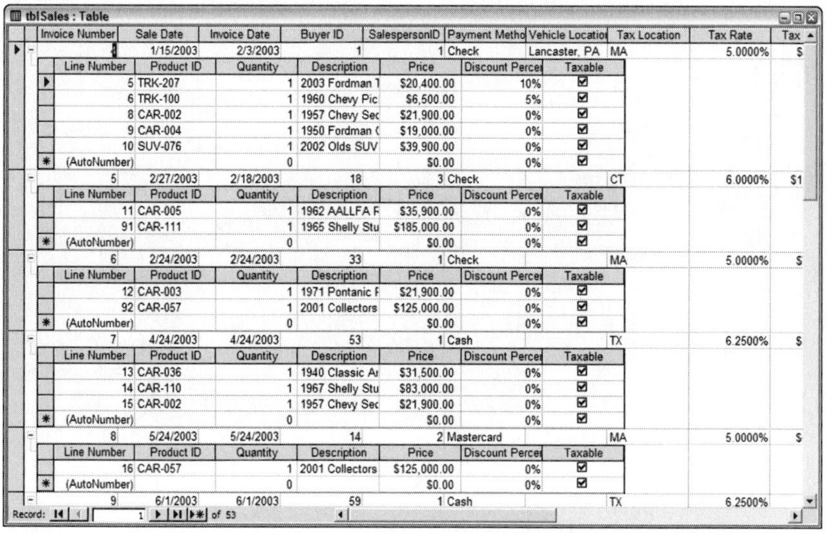

Figure 4-15: Viewing data in a datasheet with the Subdatasheet Expanded option set to Yes in the Table Properties from the Table Design window.

✦   ✦   ✦

Displaying Selected Data with Queries

In this chapter, you learn what a query is and you learn about the process of creating queries. Using the Sales (tblSales), Contacts (tblContacts), Sales Line Items (tblSalesLineItems), and Products (tblProducts) tables, you create several types of queries for the Access Auto Auctions database.

On the CD-ROM This chapter will use the database named CHAP05Start. mdb. If you have not already copied it onto your machine from the CD, you will need to do so now. After you have completed this chapter, your database should resemble the one in CHAP05End.mdb.

Understanding Queries

A database's primary purpose is to store and extract information. Information can be obtained from a database immediately after you enter the data or years later. Of course, obtaining information requires knowledge of how the database is set up.

For example, reports may be filed manually in a cabinet, arranged first by order of year and then by a *sequence number* that indicates when the report was written. To obtain a specific report, you must know its year and sequence number. In a good manual system, you may have a cross-reference book to help you find a specific report. This book may have all reports categorized alphabetically by type of report (rather than topic). Such a book can be helpful, but if you know only the report's topic and approximate date, you still may have to search through all sections of the book to find out where to obtain the report.

Unlike manual databases, computer-automated databases can easily obtain information to meet virtually any criteria you specify.

This is the real power of a database—the capacity to examine the data any way you want to look at it. Queries, by definition, ask questions about the data stored in the database. After you create a query, you can use its data for reports, forms, and graphs.

What is a query?

The word *query* is from the Latin word *quærere*, which means to ask or inquire. Over the years, the word *query* has become synonymous with *quiz*, *challenge*, *inquire*, or *question*. Therefore, you can think of a query as a question or inquiry posed to the database about information found in its tables.

A Microsoft Access query is a question that you ask about the information stored in your Access tables. The way you ask questions about this information is by using the query tools. Your query can be a simple question about information stored in a single table, or it can be a complex question about information stored in several tables. After you ask the question, Microsoft Access returns only the information you requested.

Using queries this way, you can ask the Access Auto Auctions database to show you only the trucks that were sold in the year 2003. To see the types of trucks sold for the year 2003, you need to retrieve information from three tables — tblSales, tblSalesLineItems, and tblProducts tables. Figure 5-1 is a typical Query Design window. Although it may look complex, it is actually very simple and easy to understand.

After you create and run a query, Microsoft Access will retrieve and display the set of records you asked for in a datasheet. This set of records is called a *dynaset*, which is the set of records selected by a query. As you've seen, a datasheet looks just like a spreadsheet, with its rows of records and columns of fields. The datasheet (of the dynaset) can display many records simultaneously.

You can easily query information from a single table using the Search and Filter capabilities of the datasheet view of a table (Filter by Selection and Filter by Form, as you did in Chapter 3). Using a query, you can view information from one table, or you can create a query and view common information from two or more tables at the same time (as in Figure 5-1). Many database queries will require information from several tables.

If you click the Datasheet View button on the toolbar, you will see that the query shows six records that match the query that was designed in Figure 5-1. This is a relatively easy query to design when you understand how the query design tool works. This query design has many of the elements present that show the power of the Access query engine — sorting a resulting dynaset, specifying multi-field criteria, and even using a complex Or condition in one of those fields.

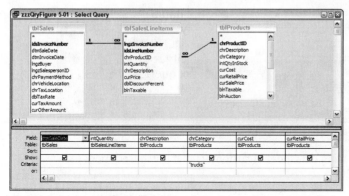

Figure 5-1: A typical three-table select query. This query will display the sales date, number of trucks, and type of truck for all trucks sold in the year 2003.

Access will let you build very complex queries using these same tools. Suppose, for example, that you want to send a notice to all previous buyers of more than one car in the past year that 11 new cars are up for auction. This type of query requires getting information from four tables: Contacts, Sales, Sales Line Items, and Products — although the main information you are looking for is in Contacts and Products.

Note   In this case, you want Access to show you a datasheet of all Contact names and addresses where they have met your specified criteria (two or more cars purchased in 2003). Access can retrieve customer names and cities from the Contacts table and then obtain the number of cars from the Products table and the year of sale from the Sales table. Figure 5-2 shows this complex query. Access then takes the information that's common to your criteria, combines it, and displays all the information in a single datasheet. This datasheet is the result of a query that draws from the tblContacts, tblSales, tblSalesLIneItems, and tblProducts tables. The database query performed the work of assembling all the information for you. Figure 5-3 shows the resulting datasheet.

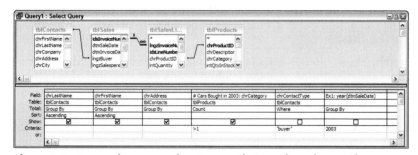

Figure 5-2: A complex query of customers that purchased more than one car in the year 2003.

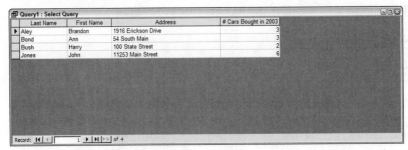

Figure 5-3: The resulting datasheet of customers that purchased more than one car in the year 2003.

Cross-Reference

As you learned in Chapter 3, you can use filters and filter by form to manipulate a single table. So, in this chapter, you will work with several tables — the tblContacts, tblSales, tblSalesLineItem, and tblProducts tables.

Types of queries

Access supports many different types of queries. They can be grouped into six basic categories:

✦ **Select.** These are the most common types of query. As its name implies, the select query selects information from one or more tables (based on specific criteria), creating a dynaset and displaying this information in a datasheet that you can use to view and analyze specific data; you can make changes to your data in the underlying tables.

✦ **Total.** These are special versions of select queries. Total queries provide the capability to sum or produce totals (such as count) in a select query. When you select this type of query, Access adds a Total row in the QBE (Query by Example) pane.

✦ **Action.** These queries enable you to create new tables (Make Tables) or change data (delete, update, and append) in existing tables. When you make changes to records in a select query, the changes must be made one record at a time. In action queries, changes can be made to many records during a single operation.

✦ **Crosstab.** These queries can display summary data in cross-tabular form like a spreadsheet, with the row and column headings based on fields in the table. By definition, the individual cells of the resultant dynaset are tabular — that is, computed or calculated.

✦ **SQL.** There are three SQL (Structured Query Language) query types — Union, Pass-Through, and Data Definition — which are used for advanced SQL database manipulation (for example, working with client/server SQL databases). You can create these queries only by writing specific SQL commands.

✦ **Top(n).** You can use this query limiter only in conjunction with the other five types of queries. It enables you to specify a number or percentage of the top records you want to see in any type of query.

Query capabilities

Queries are flexible. They provide the capability of looking at your data in virtually any way you can think of. Most database systems are continually evolving, developing more powerful and necessary tools. The original purpose they are designed for changes over time. You may decide that you want to look at the information stored in the database in a different way. Because information is stored in a database, you should be able to look at it in this new way. Looking at data in a way that's different from its intended manner is known as performing *ad hoc* queries. Querying tools are among the most powerful and flexible features of your Access database. Here is a sampling of what you can do:

✦ **Choose tables.** You can obtain information from a single table or from many tables that are related by some common data. Suppose you're interested in seeing the customer name along with the items purchased by each customer (from the tblContacts where type is a buyer or both). When using several tables, Access returns the data in a combined single datasheet.

✦ **Choose fields.** You can specify which fields from each table you want to see in the resultant dynaset. For example, you can look at the customer name, customer ZIP code, Sales date, and Invoice Number separated from all the other fields in the tblContacts or tblSales table.

✦ **Choose records.** You can select the records to display in the dynaset by specifying criteria. For example, you may want to see records for Sellers only in the tblContacts.

✦ **Sort records.** You may want to see the dynaset information sorted in a specific order. You may need, for example, to see customers in order by last name and first name.

✦ **Perform calculations.** You can use queries to perform calculations on your data. You may be interested in performing such calculations as averaging, totaling, or simply counting the fields.

✦ **Create tables.** You may need another database table formed from the combined data resulting from a query. The query can create this new table based on the dynaset.

✦ **Create forms and reports based on a query.** The dynaset you create from a query may have just the right fields and data that you need for a report or form. When you base your form or report on a query, every time you print the report or open the form, your query will retrieve the most current information from your tables.

✦ **Create graphs based on queries.** You can create graphs from the data in a query, which you can then use in a form or report.

✦ **Use a query as a source of data for other queries (subquery).** You can create additional queries based on a set of records that you selected in a previous query. This is very useful for performing ad hoc queries, where you may repeatedly make small changes to the criteria. The secondary query can be used to change the criteria while the primary query and its data remain intact.

✦ **Make changes to tables.** Access queries can obtain information from a wide range of sources. You can ask questions about data stored in dBASE, Paradox, Btrieve, and Microsoft SQL Server databases.

How dynasets work

Access takes the records that result from a query and displays them in a datasheet, in which the actual records are called a dynaset. Physically, a dynaset looks like a table; in fact, it is not a table. The dynaset is a *dynamic* (or virtual) set of records. *This dynamic set of records is not stored in the database.*

Note   When you close a query, the query dynaset is gone; it no longer exists. Even though the dynaset itself no longer exists, the data that formed the dynaset remains stored in the underlying tables.

When you run a query, Access places the resultant records in the dynaset. When you save the query, the information is not saved; only the structure of the query is saved—the tables, fields, sort order, record limitations, query type, and so forth. Consider these benefits of *not* saving the dynaset to a physical table:

✦ A smaller amount of space on a storage device (usually a hard disk) is needed.

✦ The query uses updated versions of any records changed since the query was last run.

Every time the query is executed, it reads the underlying tables and re-creates the dynaset. Because dynasets themselves are not stored, a query automatically reflects any changes to the underlying tables made since the last time the query was executed—even in a real-time, multi-user environment.

Creating a Query

After you create your tables and place data in them, you are ready to work with queries. To begin a query, follow these steps:

1. From the Database window, click the Queries Objects button.

2. Click the New button, which is the third button from the left.

The New Query dialog box appears, as shown in Figure 5-4. You select from the five choices. The first choice displays the Query Design window.

3. Select Design View and click the OK button.

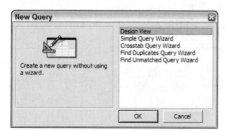

Figure 5-4: The New Query dialog box is activated by clicking the New button in the query container.

Figure 5-5 shows two windows. The underlying window is the Query Design window (titled Query1: Select Query). The accompanying Show Table dialog box is *nonmodal*, which means that you must do something in the dialog box before continuing with the query. Before you continue, you should add tables for the query to work with; in this case, the tblProducts table is highlighted to be added.

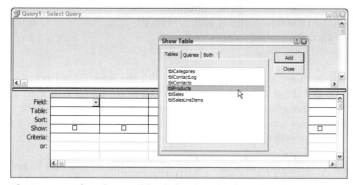

Figure 5-5: The Show Table dialog box in the Query Design window.

Selecting a table

The Show Table dialog box shown in Figure 5-5 displays all tables and queries in your database. You should see all the tables in the CHAP05Start database. You can add the tblProducts table to the query design with these steps:

1. Select the tblProducts table from the Show Table dialog box.

2. Click the Add button to add the tblProducts table to the Query Design window. Or you can double-click the table name instead of pressing the Add button.

3. Click the Close button.

Figure 5-6 shows the tblProducts table added to the query design surface, in the upper pane of the window.

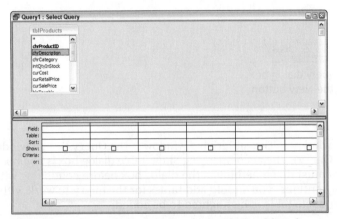

Figure 5-6: The Query Design window with the tblProducts table in the upper pane and the bottom pane currently empty. Notice that the bar between the two panes is dark: This is the pane-resizing bar that has been clicked to activate it.

Tip

When starting a new query, you can alternatively click the New Object button on the toolbar of the Database window (when the Query container is active) and choose Query. If you have already selected and opened a table or query before you start a new query, Access will assume you want to use the table or query already opened and load the selected table or query automatically.

While in Query Design mode, you can activate the Show Table dialog box to add more tables at any time; select Query ➪ Show Table or click the Show Table button (picture of table with plus sign).

Tip

You can also add tables by moving the mouse to any empty place in the top-half of the window (the Table/Query pane) and clicking the right mouse button to activate the shortcut menu. Then select Show Table.

When you want to delete a table from the Table/Query pane (top pane of the Query Design window), click the table name in the query/table entry pane (the upper portion of the window shown in Figure 5-6 — currently containing a single table, named tblProducts) and either click Delete or select Query ➪ Remove Table.

Tip You also can add a table to the Query/Table Pane by selecting the Database window and dragging and dropping a table name from the Tables window into the Query window.

Using the Query window

The Query window has two main views, the Design View and the Datasheet View. The difference between them is self-explanatory: The Design View is where you create the query, and the Datasheet View is where you display the query's dynaset.

The Query Design window should now look like Figure 5-6, with the tblProducts table displayed in the top half of the Query Design window.

The Query Design window is currently in the Design View; it consists of two panes:

✦ The table/query entry pane

✦ The Query by Example (QBE) design pane (also called the QBE grid)

The table/query entry pane, the upper pane, is where tables and/or queries and their design structures are displayed. The visual representation of the table is a small window inside the table/query entry pane. It shows the table name in the title bar of this small window and displays all the fields in the listbox of the window. This window can be resized by clicking on the edges and dragging it right or down to make it wider or longer.

The Query by Example (QBE) pane, the lower pane, is used for holding the field names that will be displayed and any criteria that will be used by the query. Each column in the QBE design pane contains information about a single field from a table or query in the upper pane.

Navigating the Query Design window

The title bar at the top of the Query Design window bears information about a particular window, the type of query, and the query name. Any new query is named Query1. Note that the title bar in Figure 5-6 displays the query type and name as Query1: Select Query.

The two windowpanes are separated horizontally by a pane-resizing bar. This bar, the dark line between the panes in Figure 5-6, is used to resize the panes. To enlarge the upper pane, click the bar and drag it down or drag the bar up to enlarge the lower pane. When you move the mouse pointer over the pane-resizing bar, the pointer turns into a small line with an arrow pointing up and another pointing down.

You switch between the upper and lower panes either by clicking the desired pane or by pressing F6 to move to the other pane. Each pane has scrollbars to help you move around.

Tip   If you make the tblProducts design structure longer, you can see more fields at one time. If you make it wider, you can see more of a field's name. To see more fields, first make the top pane larger; then size the tblProducts structure vertically.

You write the query by dragging fields from the upper pane to the lower pane of the Query window.

 Tip   After placing fields on the QBE pane (lower pane), you can set their display order by dragging a field from its current position to a new position in the pane.

Using the Query Design toolbar

The toolbar in the Query Design window contains several buttons specific to building and working with queries, as shown in Figure 5-7.

Figure 5-7: The default Query Design toolbar, with 21 buttons visible.

This toolbar has many buttons that can be helpful when designing your queries. Although they will be used and explained as they are used in the query chapters of this book, the primary buttons that will be used are listed below:

✦ **View (first button).** This button is used to switch between the Datasheet View and Design View of the query. It also enables you to display the underlying SQL statement that was created in the Query (more on this later).

✦ **Save (second button).** This button is used to save the query as you are working on it. It is a good idea to save your work often, especially when creating complex queries.

✦ **Query Type (twelfth button).** The button with two datasheets overlapping each other with a pull-down menu arrow is the Query type menu. It can be found underneath the Window menu item on the menu bar. It is used to specify the type of query you want to create.

✦ **Run (thirteenth button, an exclamation point).** This button is used to run a query. When working with Select Queries, as in this chapter, it simply displays the datasheet — serving the same function as the View button (first button). However, when working with action queries that will be covered in later chapters, it will actually run the series of actions specified by the user in the query.

✦ **Show Table (fourteenth button).** This button will activate the Show Table dialog box and enable you to add additional tables to the query.

The remaining buttons are used for more advanced queries, creating quick reports and forms, showing the database window, printing the contents of the query, or copy/paste actions.

Using the QBE pane of the Query Design window

As you saw earlier, Figure 5-6 displays an empty Query Design pane (QBE grid), which has six named rows:

✦ **Field.** This row is where field names are entered or added.

✦ **Table.** This row shows the table the field is from (useful in queries with multiple tables).

✦ **Sort.** This row enables you to enter sort directives for the query.

✦ **Show.** This check box determines whether to display the field in the resulting dynaset.

✦ **Criteria.** This row is where you enter the first line of criteria to limit the record selection.

✦ **Or.** This row is the first of a number of rows to which you can add multiple values to be used in criteria selection.

You learn more about these rows as you create queries in this chapter.

Selecting Fields

There are several ways to add fields to a query. You can add fields one at a time, select and add multiple fields, or select and add all fields. You can use your keyboard or mouse to add the fields.

Adding a single field

You can add a single field in several ways. One method is to double-click the field name in the field list (also called a table window); the field name will immediately appear in the first available column in the QEB pane. You can also add a field graphically to the QEB pane by following these steps:

1. Highlight the field name in the table window located in the table/query entry area — in this case, the chrDescription field.

2. Click the chrDescription field, and while holding the pointer down, drag the Field icon, which appears as you move the mouse, toward the QBE Design pane.

3. Drop the Field icon in the desired column of the QBE Design pane.

The Field icon looks like a small rectangle when it is inside the tblProducts table. As the mouse is dragged outside the tblProducts table, the icon changes to a circle-with-slash (the international symbol for "no"), which means that you cannot drop the Field icon in that location. When this icon enters any column in the QBE column, the field name appears in the Field: row.

Note If you drop the Field icon between two other fields, it appears between those fields and pushes all existing fields to the right.

Tip If you select a field accidentally, you can de-select it by releasing the mouse button while the icon is the No symbol.

Another way to add fields to the QBE Design pane is to click an empty Field: cell in the QBE Design pane and then type the field name in the field cell. Another method is to select the field you want from the drop-down list that appears when you click the down arrow button in the Field: cell of the QBE pane. Figure 5-8 shows selecting the chrDescription field from the drop-down list. Once selected, simply move to the next field cell and select your next field you wish to see in the query.

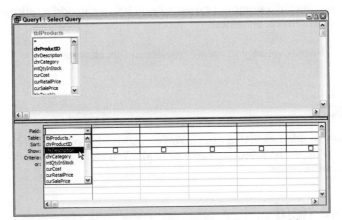

Figure 5-8: Adding fields in the QBE Design pane (grid). In the first column of the QBE pane, lower half, clicking the down arrow reveals a drop-down list from which you can select a field.

After you have selected your fields, you can run your query to see the results. To run the query, click the Datasheet button on the toolbar (the first icon from the left). When you are finished, click the Design button on the toolbar (the first one on the left) to return to design mode. You can also run the query by clicking the Run icon on your toolbar with the exclamation point on it, or by selecting Query ➪ Run. To return to the design window, click the Design View button on your toolbar (the first icon from the left).

Adding multiple fields

You can add more than one field at a time by selecting the fields you want to place in the query and then dragging and dropping the selection in the QBE pane. The selected fields do not have to be contiguous (one after the other). Figure 5-9 illustrates the process of adding multiple fields. Notice that three of the fields are contiguous and the fourth is further down in the table structure.

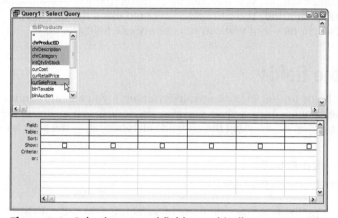

Figure 5-9: Selecting several fields graphically to move to the QBE Design pane. Notice that the field icon comprises three fields, which tells you that you are adding more than one field to the QBE pane.

To add *multiple contiguous fields*, follow these steps:

1. Remove any existing fields in the QBE pane by selecting Edit ⇨ Clear Grid from the menu.

2. Highlight in the table/query entry area the first field name that you want to add — in this case, chrDescription.

3. Hold the Shift key down and click the last field that you want to select — in this case, intQtyInStock. (All the fields in between will be selected as well.)

4. Click the selected fields and drag the Multiple Field icon, which appears as you move the mouse. The icon appears as a group of three field icons.

5. Drop the Multiple Field icon in the desired column of the QBE Design pane.

To add *multiple noncontiguous fields* to the query, follow these steps:

1. Remove any existing fields in the QBE pane by selecting Edit ⇨ Clear Grid from the menu.

2. Highlight in the table/query entry area the first field name that you want to add; for this example, click the chrDescription field.

3. Hold the Ctrl key down and click each field that you want to select. (Only the fields you select are highlighted.) For this example, click the chrCategory, intQtyInStock, and curSalePrice fields.

4. Click the selected fields and drag the Multiple Field icon, which appears as you move the mouse. The icon appears as a group of three field icons.

5. Drop the Multiple Field icon in the desired column of the QBE Design pane.

Notice that in the second example, you selected three fields that were contiguous — using the non-contiguous method. You can select any field using the Ctrl key — contiguous or non-contiguous — but you can select only one field at a time.

Adding all table fields

In addition to adding fields (either in groups or individually), you can move all the fields to the QBE pane at once. Access gives you two methods for choosing all fields: dragging all fields as a group or selecting the all-field reference tag — the asterisk (*).

Dragging all fields as a group

To select all the fields of a table, perform these steps:

1. Remove any existing fields in the QBE pane by selecting Edit ➪ Clear Grid from the menu.

2. Double-click the title bar of the table to select all the fields.

3. Point to any of the selected fields with the mouse.

4. Drag the Multiple Field icon to the QBE pane.

This method fills in each column of the QBE pane automatically. All the fields are added to the QBE pane from left to right, based on their field order in the tblProducts table. By default, Access displays only the fields that can fit in the window. You can change the column width of each field to display more or fewer columns.

Selecting the all-field reference tag

The first object (above the field names) in the tblProducts table is an asterisk, which appears at the top of the field list. When you select all fields by using the asterisk, you don't see the fields in the QBE Design pane; tblProducts.* in the Field: row indicates that all tblProducts table fields are selected. (This example assumes that the QBE Design pane is empty when you drag the asterisk from the tblProducts table to the QBE Design pane.)

The asterisk places the fields in a single Field: cell. Dragging multiple fields with the first technique added actual table field names to the Query Design window; each field is in a separate Field: cell across the QBE pane. If you change the table design later, you must change the design of the query, too. By using the asterisk for selecting all fields, you won't have to change the query later if you add, delete, or rename fields in the underlying table or query. (Access automatically adds or removes fields that change in the underlying table or query.)

To add the all-fields reference tag to the Query Design pane, follow these steps:

1. Remove any existing fields in the QBE pane by selecting Edit ⇨ Clear Grid from the menu.

2. Click the asterisk (*) in the tblProducts table to select this field.

3. Click the selected field and drag the Field icon to the first cell in the QBE Design pane.

The all-fields reference tag is in the QBE pane. This query displays the tblProducts fields.

Displaying the Dynaset

With the all fields reference tag (asterisks) selected, display the resultant dynaset by selecting either View ⇨ Datasheet View or the Datasheet button on the toolbar. The datasheet should look like the one shown in Figure 5-10. You can also display the dynaset by clicking the exclamation point icon or selecting Query ⇨ Run from your Access menu.

Product ID	Description	Category	Quantity in Stock	Cost	Retail Price	Sale Price
CAR-001	2001 Sportster	Cars	1	$32,656.00	$38,995.00	$36,999.00
CAR-002	1957 Chevy Sec	Cars	1	$19,000.00	$21,900.00	$21,900.00
CAR-003	1971 Pontanic F	Cars	1	$15,000.00	$21,900.00	$20,900.00
CAR-004	1950 Fordman C	Cars	1	$16,500.00	$19,000.00	$18,995.00
CAR-005	1962 AALLFA F	Cars	1	$31,500.00	$35,900.00	$35,900.00
CAR-036	1940 Classic A	Cars	1	$27,800.00	$31,500.00	$29,500.00
CAR-057	2001 Collectors	Cars	1	$108,000.00	$125,000.00	$123,500.00
CAR-110	1967 Shelly Stu	Cars	1	$74,500.00	$83,000.00	$79,900.00
CAR-111	1965 Shelly Stu	Cars	1	$165,000.00	$185,000.00	$185,000.00
CAR-112	2001 BMY 740	Cars	1	$33,000.00	$37,000.00	$36,900.00
CAR-113	2001 Audie Gre	Cars	1	$29,900.00	$35,000.00	$34,900.00
CAR-114	1997 Audie Whi	Cars	1	$25,000.00	$29,900.00	$28,900.00
CAR-115	1966 Fordman f	Cars	1	$81,000.00	$87,000.00	$86,000.00
CAR-116	1959 Fordman 1	Cars	1	$9,500.00	$14,000.00	$13,500.00
CAR-117	1988 Fordman	Cars	1	$200.00	$700.00	$599.00
CAR-118	2001 Fordman	Cars	1	$11,000.00	$17,000.00	$15,900.00
CAR-119	1996 CADDY D	Cars	1	$8,500.00	$12,500.00	$11,000.00
CAR-120	1997 Fordman	Cars	1	$0.00	$0.00	$0.00
CAR-121	1993 Fordman	Cars	1	$2,900.00	$4,200.00	$3,900.00
CAR-122	1986 BMY 326	Cars	1	$2,800.00	$3,500.00	$3,350.00
CAR-123	1969 Antique C	Cars	1	$500.00	$17,900.00	$1,500.00
CAR-126	1995 BUICKY	Cars	1	$5,500.00	$7,200.00	$6,999.00

Figure 5-10: The datasheet of the tblProducts table with all the fields selected for the query using the asterisks, or all-field reference tag (*).

Working with the datasheet

Access displays the dynaset (resulting view of records of the query) in a datasheet. The techniques for navigating a query datasheet, as well as for changing its field order and working with its columns and rows, are exactly the same as for the other datasheets you worked with in Chapter 3.

Access enables you to sort and filter the results of a datasheet created by a query. All data in Access is editable all the time.

Changing data in the query datasheet

The query datasheet offers you an easy and convenient way to change data quickly. You can add and change data in the dynaset, and it will be saved to the underlying tables.

When you're adding or changing data in the datasheet, all the table properties defined at the table level are in effect.

Returning to the query design

To return to the query design mode, select the Design View button on the toolbar (the first button on the left).

Tip　　　You can also toggle between the design and datasheet mode by selecting View ➪ Datasheet View or View ➪ Design View from the Query menu.

Caution　　Clear the query grid by selecting Edit ➪ Clear Grid. Next, add all the fields to the query grid by double-clicking the tblProducts data structure title bar and dragging all the selected fields to the query grid.

Working with Fields

There are times when you want to work with the fields you've already selected — rearranging their order, inserting a new field, or deleting an existing field. You may even want to add a field to the QBE pane without showing it in the datasheet.

Selecting a field

Before you can move a field's position, you must first select it. To select it, you will work with the *field selector row.*

The field selector row is the narrow gray row above the Field: row of each column. This row is approximately half the size of the others; it's important to identify this row because this is where you select columns, either single or multiple columns. Recall that each column represents a field. To select the chrCategory field, move the mouse pointer until a small selection arrow (in this case, a dark downward arrow) is visible in the selector row and then click the column. Figure 5-11 shows the selection arrow above the chrCategory column just before it is selected.

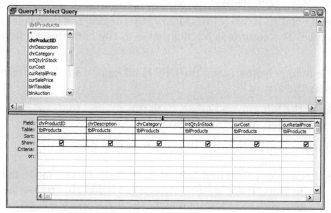

Figure 5-11: Selecting a column in the QBE pane. The pointer changes to a down-pointing arrow when you move over the selection row. After the arrow changes, you can click the selection row and the entire column will be highlighted.

Tip

You can select multiple contiguous fields by clicking the first field you wish to select and then dragging across the field selector bars of the other fields.

Caution

Extend mode will also enable you to chose more than one contiguous field in the QBE pane. If extend mode (F8) is on, you must first move the cursor into the column of the field that you wish to select (by clicking in any field) This moves the insertion point (I cursor) into the row whose column you want to select. If the insertion point is in an adjacent column and you select a column, you will select the adjacent column (containing the insertion point) as well. To deactivate extend mode (EXT), press the Esc key. You can see that EXT mode is active by looking at the bottom frame of Access—the letters EXT will be active on the right side of the frame (about a quarter of the way in).

Changing field order

After your fields are selected, you can move them. (Of course, you could delete all the fields and conditions and start the query over—although this method can be bothersome.) With the fields selected, you can move the fields on the QBE design by simply dragging them, as you have learned to move columns in a datasheet. Follow these steps to move a field:

1. Add several fields to the QBE pane.

2. Select the field you want to move (chrCategory) by clicking the field selector above the field name. The column is highlighted—as the chrCategory field is in Figure 5-12.

3. Click and hold the field selector again; the QBE Field icon, a small graphical box, appears under the arrow.

4. While holding down the left mouse button, drag the column to its new position (in this case, to the left of chrDescription).

5. Release the left mouse button to drop the field in its new position.

Figure 5-12 shows the chrCategory field highlighted (selected). As you move the selector field to the left, the column separator between the fields chrProduct and chrDescription changes (gets wider) to show you where chrCategory will go.

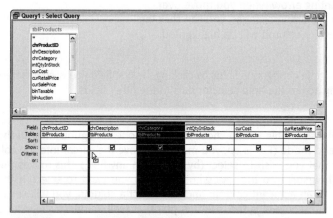

Figure 5-12: Moving the chrCategory field to between chrProduct and chrDescription. Notice the QBE field icon below the arrow near the chrDescription column.

Resizing columns in design mode

The QBE pane generally shows about five or six field columns in the viewable area of your screen—the remaining fields can be viewed by moving the horizontal scroll bar along the bottom of the window.

There are times that you may want to show more fields than those visible on the screen. You can resize the width of the field columns to make them smaller (or larger to show less) by moving the mouse pointer between the field selectors of the fields you want to adjust. After you have moved it between the two field selectors, the pointer turns into a thick vertical bar with arrows pointing to the left and right. With the sizing pointer, you can drag left or right to adjust the width of the column.

Removing a field

You can remove a field from the QBE Design pane. Select the field or fields to be deleted in the QBE Design pane, and then press Delete or select Edit ➪ Delete. To remove the curCost field from the QBE Design pane, follow these steps:

1. Select the curCost field (or any other field) by clicking the field selector above the field name.

2. Press Delete.

Tip   If the field is not selected but the insertion point is in it, you can select Edit ➪ Delete Columns. You can delete all the fields in the QBE Design pane in a single operation: Select Edit ➪ Clear Grid from the Query Design window's menu bar.

Inserting a field

You insert fields from the table/query entry pane in the QBE Design pane by selecting field(s) from the table/query entry pane and then dragging your selection to the QBE Design pane. These steps insert the Customer Number field:

1. Select the curCost field from the field list in the table/query entry pane (top pane).

2. Drag the field to the column where you want the field. If it is to go between two columns, put it to the left side of the column you want it to go before.

3. Drop the field by releasing the left mouse button.

Dragging a field to the QBE Design pane inserts it where you drop the field. If you drop it on another field, it is inserted before that field. Double-clicking the field in the table/query entry pane appends the field to the Field: list in the QBE Design pane.

Changing the field display name

To make the query datasheet easier to read, you can rename the fields in your query. The new names become the tag headings in the datasheet of the query. To follow along with this example, create a query using the fields from the tblProducts as shown in Figure 5-12. To rename the field chrProductID to Product ID and chrDescription to Description, follow these steps:

1. Click to the left of the 'c' of chrProductID in the Field: row of the QBE Design pane.

2. Type Product ID and a colon (:) between the new name and the old field name.

3. Click to the left of the 'c' in chrDescription and type in **Description:**.

The heading now is Product ID:chrProductID and Description:chrDescription. When the datasheet appears, you see *Product ID* and *Description*.

Note   Changing the datasheet caption changes *only* the name of the heading for that field in the datasheet. It does *not* change the field name in the underlying table.

Showing table names

Multiple tables can make it difficult to determine where a field has come. That's why the Table: row automatically shows where a field came from.

When you select a field for display in the QBE pane, the name of the source table is shown in the row directly below the field name. If you want to hide this row, click View ➪ Table Names as shown in Figure 5-13. The row with the table names disappears. To view the tables, follow the same procedure to turn it on. As Figure 5-13 shows, the table names are in the row immediately below the field name. Looking closely at the QBE pane, you can see the field name chrLastName and chrFirstName in the first row (Field:), and immediately below them is the name of the table tblContacts; moving to the rightmost field in view, dtmSalesDate, has the table tblSales in the Table: row.

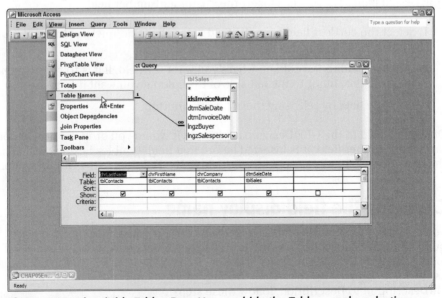

Figure 5-13: View/Hide Table: Row. You can hide the Table: row by selecting View ➪ Table Names from the Access Menu.

Showing a field

While performing queries, you may want to temporarily show only some of the fields. Suppose, for example, you use the tblContacts table and select several fields to display — chrContactType, chrLastName, chrFirstName, chrAddress, chrCity, and chrState. Then you decide that you want to temporarily look at the same data, less the chrContactType and chrAddress fields. You can start with a new query, deleting all the fields in the QBE pane, or you can simply indicate which fields you want to see in the datasheet by de-selecting the Show: box for the fields you do not want to see.

When you select fields, Access automatically makes every field a displayed field. Every Show: property is displayed with a check mark in the box.

To de-select a field's Show: property, simply click the field's Show: box, and the box clears. As you see in Figure 5-14, two fields have their Show: box de-selected. To re-select the field later, simply click the Show: box again.

Field:	chrContactType	chrLastName	chrFirstName	chrAddress	chrCity	chrState
Table:	tblContacts	tblContacts	tblContacts	tblContacts	tblContacts	tblContacts
Sort:						
Show:	☐	☑	☑	☐	☑	☑
Criteria:						
or:						

Figure 5-14: The Show: row is checked only for the fields chrLastName, chrFirstName, chrCity, and chrState. The other fields shown, chrContactType and chrAddress, have the Show: check box unchecked.

Caution   If you save a query that has an unused field (its Show: box is unchecked), Access eliminates the field from the query pane.

Changing the Sort Order

When viewing a dynaset, you may want to display the data in a sorted order. You may want to sort the dynaset to make it easier to analyze the data (for example, to look at all the tblProducts in order by Category).

Sorting places the records in alphabetical or numeric order. The sort order can be ascending (0 to 9 and A to Z) or descending (9 to 0 and Z to A). You can sort by a single field or sort using several fields.

Just as Access has a Show: property row for fields, there is a Sort: property row for fields in the QBE Design pane. In the following section, you learn to set this property.

Specifying a sort

To sort the records in the datasheet of Figure 5-14 by chrLastName and then by chrFirstName in ascending order, perform these steps:

1. Using the same query in Figure 5-14, click the Sort: cell for the chrLastName field. An arrow appears in the cell.

2. Click the down arrow at the right of the cell.

3. Select Ascending from the list.

4. Click in the Sort: cell for the chrFirstName field.

5. Select Ascending from the list.

Figure 5-15 shows the QBE pane with the two fields chrLastName and chrFirstName set to Ascending order. Notice that the chrFirstName field is still showing the sort options available. Also notice that the word Ascending is being selected in the field's Sort: cell.

Note   You *cannot* sort on a Memo or an OLE object field.

Figure 5-15: The chrLastName and chrFirstName fields have been selected to sort by Ascending order (0 to 9, A to Z).

Caution   If you sort on more than one field, the fields must be in order from left to right of the sort order you want. That is, in the example of Figure 5-15, the Last Name field must be to the left of the First Name field. Otherwise, Access will sort by first name and then last name.

Access always sorts the leftmost sort field first — this is known as *sort order precedence*. To make sure that Access understands how you want to sort your data, you must arrange the fields in order from left to right according to sort-order precedence. You can easily change the sort order by selecting a sort field and moving it relative to another sort field. Access corrects the sort order automatically.

If you click on the datasheet button to display the results of the sort of two fields, you will notice that the dynaset is arranged in order by two different fields. Figure 5-16 shows the multiple-field sort dynaset. The sort order is controlled by the order of the fields in the QBE pane (from left to right); therefore, this dynaset is displayed in order first by Last Name and then by First Name.

Last Name	First Name	City	State
Aikins	Teresa	Middletown	CT
Aley	Brandon	Fairbanks	MA
Bailey	Karen	Westbourgh	MA
Bond	Ann	Colchester	CT
Bright	John	West Bridgewater	MA
Bush	Harry	Mohegan Lake	NY
Calson	Larry	Chicota	TX
Casey	Cindy	Newington	NH
Casey	Debbie	Jackhorn	KY
Crook	Joe	Windsor	CT
Davis	Larry	Sherman Oaks	CA
Dennis	Michael	Bedford	NY
Gleason	William	Derby	CT
Grattie	Paul	Turon	KS

Record: ◄◄ ◄ 1 ► ►◄ ►* of 58

Figure 5-16: Multiple-field sort criteria. The order of the fields is critical. It will sort first by the left-most field and then sub-sort by the next field to the right.

Displaying Only Selected Records

So far, you've been working with all the records of the Contacts and Products tables. There are times when you may want to work only with selected records in these tables. For example, you may want to look only at records where the value of chrContactType is Buyer. Access makes it easy for you to specify a record's criteria.

Tip   If you are following along with the examples, start a new query using the tblProducts table and select all the fields before continuing.

Understanding record criteria

Record criteria are simply some rule or rules that you supply for Access to follow. These criteria tell Access which records you want to look at in the dynaset. A typical criterion could be "all Sellers," or "only those vehicles that are not Trucks," or "cars whose retail price is greater than $45,000."

In other words, with record criteria, you create limiting filters to tell Access which records to find and which to leave out of the dynaset.

You specify criteria starting in the Criteria: property row of the QBE pane. Here you designate criteria with an expression. The expression can be simple example data or can take the form of complex expressions using predefined functions.

As an example of a simple data criterion using the tblProducts table, you could type "TRUCKS" in the Criteria: cell of chrCategory and the datasheet displays only records for Trucks.

Entering simple character criteria

Character-type criteria are entered into fields that accommodate the Text data type. To use such criteria, type in an example of the data contained within the field. To limit the record display in the tblProducts table to CARS, follow these steps:

1. Select the tblProducts and add these fields to the QBE Design pane—chrDescription, chrCategory, and curCost.

2. Click the Criteria: cell in the chrCategory column in the QBE Design pane.

3. Type CARS in the cell.

4. Click the Datasheet button.

Only the cars are displayed—in this case, 26 records. Observe that you did not enter an equal sign or place quotes around the sample text, yet Access added double quotes around the value. Access, unlike many other applications, automatically makes assumptions about what you want. This is an illustration of its flexibility. You could enter the expression in any of these other ways:

✦ CARS

✦ = CARS

✦ "CARS"

✦ = "Cars"

Tip Access is NOT case sensitive, so you can type any of the following for CARS and it will only find cars—CaRs, CARS, cars, Cars, carS, or any other combination of uppercase and lowercase.

In Figure 5-17, the expression "CARS" is entered under chrCategory; the double quote marks were placed around the example "CARS" automatically by Access.

Figure 5-17 is an excellent example for demonstrating the options for various types of simple character criteria. You could just as well type Not Cars in the criteria column, to say the opposite. In this instance, you would be asking to see all records for vehicles that are not cars, adding only Not before the example text CARS.

Generally, when dealing with character data, you enter equalities, inequalities, or a list of values that are acceptable.

With either of these examples, Cars or Not Cars, you entered a simple expression in a Text-type field. Access took your example and interpreted it to show you all records that equal the example data you placed in the Criteria: cell.

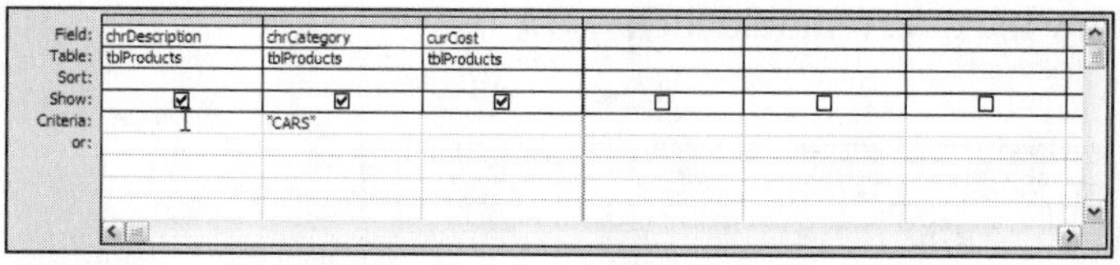

Figure 5-17: Specifying character criteria. You can type an example of the type of records you want to view. In this case, all CARS — so you type CARS in the criteria field of the chrCategory field.

This capability is a powerful tool. Consider that you have only to supply an example and Access not only interprets it but also uses it to create the query dynaset. This is exactly what Query by Example means: You enter an example and let the database build a query based on this data.

To erase the criteria in the cell, select the contents and press Delete, or select the contents and select Edit ⇨ Delete from the Query Design window's menu bar. You can also select Edit ⇨ Undo Cell Edit to revert to the previous content (in this case, a blank cell).

Entering other simple criteria

You can also specify criteria for Numeric, Date, and Yes/No fields. Simply enter the example data in the criteria field.

It is also possible to add more than one criteria to a query. For example, suppose that you want to look only at records from the tblContacts for Contacts who are both Sellers and Buyers (BOTH type in field chrContactType) and where these contacts have been customers since January 1, 2003 (where the value of dtmOrigCustDate is greater or equal to January 1, 2003). This would require placing example data in two different fields — the chrContactType field and the dtmOrigCustdate field. To do this, it is critical that you place both examples on the same line (Criteria: row). To create this query, follow these steps:

1. Create a new query starting with the tblContacts table.
2. Add the fields chrContactType, chrLastName, chrFirstName, chrState, and dtmOrigCustDate to the QBE grid.
3. Click the Criteria: cell in the chrContactType column in the QBE Design pane.
4. Type **BOTH** in the cell.
5. Click the Criteria: cell in the dtmOrigCustDate column in the QBE Design pane.
6. Type >= **01/01/03** in the cell.
7. Click the Datasheet button.

Figure 5-18 shows how the query should look.

Field:	chrContactType	chrLastName	chrFirstName	chrState	dtmOrigCustDate	
Table:	tblContacts	tblContacts	tblContacts	tblContacts	tblContacts	
Sort:					Ascending	
Show:	☑	☑	☑	☑	☑	☐
Criteria:	"both"				>=#1/1/2003#	
or:						

Figure 5-18: Specifying character and date criteria in the same query.

Access displays records of contacts that are both sellers and buyers that were customers from January 01, 2003 — in this example, it will display 17 records.

Cross-Reference   Multi-criteria queries are covered in depth in Chapter 6.

Access also compares Date fields to a value by using comparison operators, such as less than (<), greater than (>), equal to (=), or a combination thereof. Notice that Access automatically adds pound-sign (#) delimiters around the date value. Access recognizes these delimiters as differentiating a Date field from Text fields. It's the same as entering text data examples; however, you don't have to enter the pound signs. Access understands what you want (based on the type of data entered in the field), and it converts the entry format for you.

Caution   When adding comparison operators to a criteria and mixing greater than/less than with equals, the greater than sign must precede the equals sign, or Access will report an error.

Cross-Reference   Operators and Precedence are covered more in Chapters 6 and 20.

Printing a Query Dynaset

After you create your query, you can quickly print all the records in the dynaset. Although you can't specify a type of report, you can print a simple matrix-type report (rows and columns) of the dynaset that your query created.

You do have some flexibility when printing a dynaset. If you know that the datasheet is set up just as you want, you can specify some options as you follow these steps:

1. Use the datasheet you just created for both sellers and buyers that have been customers since 01/01/2003.

2. If you are not in the datasheet view, switch to the query datasheet mode by clicking the Datasheet button on the toolbar.

3. Select File ⇨ Print from the Query Datasheet window's menu bar.

4. Specify the print options that you want in the Print dialog box.

5. Click the OK button in the Print dialog box.

Tip In Step 3 above, you could have also pressed the Print button on the toolbar to immediately create a report of the datasheet and send it to the default Windows printer. If you print the datasheet this way, you will not have to do Steps 4 or 5.

Access now prints the dynaset for you if you have set up a default printer in Microsoft Windows. Your dataset prints out in the font selected for display or in the nearest equivalent your printer offers. The printout also reflects all layout options in effect when you print the dataset. Hidden columns do not print; gridlines print only if the Gridlines option is on. The printout does reflect the specified row height and column width.

Saving a Query

To save a query while working in design mode, follow this procedure:

1. Select File ⇨ Save from the Query Design window or click the Save button on the toolbar.

2. If this is the first time you're saving the query, enter a new query name in the Save As dialog box.

To save a query while working in datasheet mode, follow this procedure:

1. Select File ⇨ Save from the Datasheet File menu.

2. If this is the first time you're saving the query, enter a new query name in the Save As dialog box.

Tip The F12 key is the Save As key in Access. You can press F12 to save your work and continue working on your query.

Both of these methods save the query and return you to the mode you were working in. Occasionally, you will want to save and exit the query in a single operation. To do this, select File ⇨ Close from the query or the datasheet and answer Yes to the question Save changes to Query 'query name'? If this is your first time saving the query, Access prompts you to supply a query name and asks whether you want to save the query to the current database or to an external file or database.

You can leave the Query window at any time by any one of these ways:

✦ Select File ⇨ Close from the Query menu.

✦ Select Close from the Query window control box.

✦ Press Ctrl+F4 while inside the Query window.

All three of these methods activate an Access dialog box that asks, Save changes to Query 'Query1'?

Adding More than One Table to a Query

Using a query to obtain information from a single table is common; often, however, you need information from several related tables. For example, you may want to obtain a contact's (buyer's) name and the type of vehicles the contact has purchased. This requires use of four tables in a query.

There are four primary tables in the Example database—tblContacts, tblSales, tblSalesLineItems, and tblProducts. All four of these tables would be needed in the query to determine the type of vehicles each buyer purchased.

In Chapter 4, you learned about primary and foreign table keys and their importance for linking two tables together. You learned how to create relationships between two tables at the table level by using the Tools ➪ Relationships command from the Database window. Finally, you learned how referential integrity rules affect data in tables.

After you create the tables for your database and decide how the tables are related to one another, you are ready to begin creating multiple-table queries to obtain information from several tables at the same time.

By adding more than one table to a query and then selecting fields from the tables in the query, you can view information from your database just as though the information from the several tables was in one table.

The first step in creating a multiple-table query is to open each table in the Query window. The following steps show how to open the tblContacts, tblSales, tblSalesLineitems, and tblProducts tables in a single query:

1. Click the Queries object in the Database window.
2. Click the New toolbar button to create a new query.
3. Select Design View and click the OK button in the New Query dialog box.
4. Select the tblContacts table (in the Show Table dialog box) by double-clicking the table name.
5. Select the tblSales table by double-clicking the table name.
6. Select the tblSalesLineItems table by double-clicking the table name.
7. Select the tblProducts table by double-clicking the table name.
8. Click the Close button in the Show Table dialog box.

Note   You can also add each table by highlighting the table in the list separately and clicking Add.

Figure 5-19 shows the top pane of the Query Design window with the four tables you just added. Because the relationships were set at table level, the join lines are automatically added to the query.

Figure 5-19: The Query Design window with four tables added. Notice the join lines are already present.

Note   You can add more tables, at any time, by selecting Query ➪ Show Table from the Query Design window or by clicking the Show Table button.

Working with the Table/Query Pane

As Figure 5-19 shows, a single line is present between tables, going from the primary key field to the foreign key field, which signifies a connection between the tables.

Cross-Reference   These lines were pre-drawn because you already set the relationships between the tables earlier in Chapter 4.

The join line

When Access displays each set of related tables, it places a line between the two tables. This line is known as a join line. A *join line* is a graphical line that represents the relationship between two tables. In this example, the join line goes from the tblSales table to the tblContacts table to connect the two fields — idsContactID and lngzBuyer. Join lines also run from tblSales to tblSalesLineitems and tlbSalesLineItems to tblProducts, connecting these tables as well.

This line is created automatically because a relationship was set in the Relationship builder. If Access already knows what the relationship is, it automatically creates the line for you when the tables are added to a query. The relationship is displayed as a join line between two tables.

If Referential Integrity was set in the relationship between two tables, Access displays a thick portion of the line right at the table window similar to the line in Figure 5-19. The line starts heavy and becomes thin between tblSales and tblSalesLineItems (heavy on both ends). This line variation tells you that Referential Integrity has been set between the two tables in the Relationship Builder. If a one-to-many relationship exists, the many relationship is denoted by an infinity symbol (∞).

Note To resize the pane, simply click on the *pane resizing bar* and drag it down to enlarge the upper pane. After the pane has been resized, you can move the tables around to match those in Figure 5-2. Resizing the pane and moving tables are covered after this section.

Tip If you have not specified a relationship between two tables and the following conditions are true, Access 2003 automatically joins the tables:

1. Both tables have a field with the same name.

2. The field with the same name in both tables has the same data type (text, numeric, and so on).

3. The field is a *primary key* field in one of the tables.

Tip Access 2003 automatically attempts to join the tables if a relationship exists. It will not attempt to set the referential integrity — only the join. However, you can turn this property off by de-selecting the default Enable AutoJoin option from the global Access options tabbed dialog box. To display this option, select Tools ➪ Options, click the Tables/Queries tab in the options box, and de-select the Enable AutoJoin option (under the Query design section).

Resizing the Table/Query pane

When you place Field Lists on the Table/Query pane, they appear in a fixed size with little spacing between tables. When you add a table to the top pane, it initially shows five fields. If more fields are in the table, a scroll bar is added to the box (right side). The table window may show only part of a long field name, the rest being truncated by the window size. You can move the tables around the pane and resize them to show more field names or more of the field name. The first step, however, is to resize the pane itself. The Query Design window has two panes. The top pane displays your Field Lists, whereas the bottom QBE (Query by Example) pane below enables you to enter fields, sort orders, and define criteria. Often you will want the top pane to be larger than the bottom pane so that you can see more field names. The Query window's title bar tells you that you are creating a Select query (Query1: Select Query). If you change the query to another type of query (which you do in later chapters), the title bar changes to let you know what type of query you are creating.

You can resize the Table/Query pane by placing your mouse pointer on the thick line between the two panes. This is the *window split bar*, also known as the pane-resizing bar. The pointer changes to a small, thick bar with double vertical arrows (up and down), as shown in Figure 5-20, which enables you to drag the split bar up or down. To resize the panes, follow these steps:

1. Place the pointer on the window split bar.

2. Hold down the mouse button and drag the split bar down.

3. Release the bar when it is two lines below the QBE row "or."

The top pane is now much larger; the bottom pane is smaller but it still displays the entire QBE Design area. If the QBE Design area shows insufficient area, simply resize the entire window by selecting the bottom border of the window and then click and drag the window down — making it larger. You now have space to move the Field Lists around and properly view the Table/Query pane.

Note You can build a database diagram, as you did in Chapter 4, so that you view only the Field Lists by moving the split bar to the bottom of the screen and then positioning the Field Lists as you want within the full-screen area.

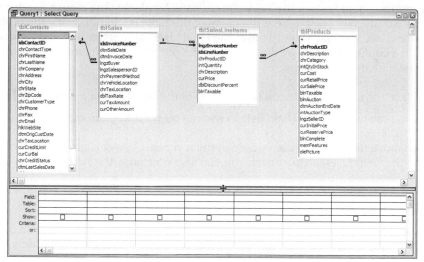

Figure 5-20: The Query Design window with the screen split arrow in the center on the window split bar and tables resized.

Looking at Figure 5-20, you see that the Query Design window has been resized and the pointer (changed to a line with arrows up and down) is on the window split bar. The table field lists have also been resized.

Manipulating the Field List window

Each Field List window begins at a fixed size, which shows approximately four fields and 12 characters for each field. Figure 5-19 shows how the initial field lists are displayed; Figure 5-20 shows them after they have been expanded. Each Field List window is a true window and behaves like one; it can be resized and moved. If you have more fields than will show in the Field List window, a scroll bar displays to enable you to scroll through the fields in the Field List window.

Note   After a relationship is created between tables, the join line remains between the two fields. As you move through a table selecting fields, the graphical line will move relative to the linked fields. For example, if the scroll box moves down (toward the bottom of the window) in the tblContacts table, the join line moves up with the customer number, eventually stopping at the top of the table window.

When you're working with many tables, these join lines can become visually confusing as they cross or overlap. If you move through the table, the line eventually becomes visible, and the field it is linked to becomes obvious.

Moving a table

You can move Field Lists in the Table/Query pane by placing the mouse pointer on the title bar of a Field List (where the name of the table is) and dragging the table to a new location. You may want to move the Field Lists for a better working view or to clean up a confusing database diagram (like the one shown in Figure 5-20). To move Field Lists, follow these steps:

1. Place the mouse pointer on the title bar of the table on the name of the Table.

2. Drag the table design (field list) to where you want to place it.

You can move the Field Lists anywhere in the top pane. You can spread them out by moving the Field Lists farther apart. You can also rearrange the Field Lists.

Removing a table

There are times when you need to remove tables from a query. Any table can be removed from the Query window. Follow these steps to delete the tblProducts table; remember, you can bring it back later:

1. Select the table you want to remove in the top pane of the Query window by clicking either the table or a field in the table.

2. Press the Delete key or select Edit ➪ Delete.

Note   Only one table can be removed at a time from the Query window. The menu choice Edit ➪ Clear Grid does not remove all tables; it removes all fields from the QBE pane. You can also remove a table by right-clicking a table and selecting Remove Table from the shortcut menu.

When you delete a table, any join lines to that table are deleted as well. When you delete a table, there is no warning or confirmation dialog box. The table is simply removed from the screen.

Adding more tables

You may decide to add more tables to a query or you may accidentally delete a table and need to add it back. You can accomplish this task by either selecting Query ⇨ Show Table or by clicking the *right* mouse button and selecting Show Table from the shortcut menu that appears. When you use either of these methods, the Show Table dialog box that appeared when you created the query is redisplayed.

Resizing a Field List window

You can also resize each of the Field Lists by placing the cursor on one of the Field List borders. The Field List is nothing but a window; thus, you can enlarge or reduce it vertically, horizontally, or diagonally by placing the cursor on the appropriate border. When you enlarge the Field List vertically, you can see more fields than the default number (five). By making the Field List larger horizontally, you can see the complete list of field names. Then, when you resize the Table/Query pane to take up the entire window, you can create a database diagram.

Adding Fields from More than One Table

You add fields from more than one table to the query in exactly the same way as when you're working with a single table. You can add fields one at a time, many fields grouped together, or all the fields from one or all tables.

Cross-Reference Adding fields from a single table was covered earlier in this chapter; this section covers the topic in less detail, but focuses on the differences between single- and multiple-table field selection.

Adding a single field

You can add a single field from any table to the QBE pane by several methods:

- ✦ Double-click a field name in the Table/Query pane.
- ✦ Click a field name in the Table/Query pane and drag it to the QBE pane.
- ✦ Click an empty Field cell in the QBE pane and type a field name.
- ✦ Click an empty Field cell and select the field from the drop-down list.

Caution If you type a field name in an empty Field cell that has the same name in two or more tables, Access enters the field name from the first table that it finds containing that field. Access searches the tables, starting from the left side in the top pane.

If you select the field from the drop-down list in the Field cell, you see the name of the table first, followed by a period and the field name. For example, the chrProductID in the tblSalesLineItems table is displayed as *tblSalesLineItems.chrProductID*. This helps you select the right field name. Using this method, you can select a common field name from a specific table.

The easiest way to select fields is still to double-click the field names while in the query/table design pane. To do so, you may have to resize the Field Lists to see the fields that you want to select.

Viewing the table names

When you're working with two or more tables, the field names in the QBE pane can become confusing. You may find yourself asking, for example, just which table the field chrDescription is from.

Access automatically maintains the table name that is associated with each field displayed in the QBE pane. The default is to display the table name below the name of the field. If you do not want to show the table name of each field in the QBE pane, select View ➪ Table Names and the toggle will be turned off (unchecked).

This command controls the display of table names immediately below the corresponding field name in the QBE pane. Figure 5-21 shows the QBE pane with the Table row below the Field row. It contains the name of the table for each field.

Field:	chrContactType	chrLastName	chrFirstName	dtmSaleDate	curPrice	intQuantity	chrDescription	
Table:	tblContacts	tblContacts	tblContacts	tblSales	tblSalesLineItems	tblSalesLineItems	tblProducts	
Sort:								
Show:	☑	☑	☑	☑	☑	☑	☑	
Criteria:								
or:								

Figure 5-21: The QBE pane with table names displayed. Notice that it shows all four table names.

After you add fields to a query, you can view your resultant data at any time. You can view all the data now by selecting the Datasheet icon. Figure 5-22 displays the data as currently selected. The fields have been resized to show all the data values.

The display of the table name is only for your information. Access always maintains the table name associated with the field names.

Adding multiple fields at the same time

The process of adding multiple fields at the same time is identical to adding multiple fields in a single table query. When you're adding multiple fields from several tables, you must add them from one table at a time. The easiest way to do this is to select multiple fields and drag them together down to the QBE pane.

Contact Type	Last Name	First Name	Sale Date	Price	Quantity	Description
Buyer	Jones	John	1/15/2003	$20,400.00	1	2003 Fordman T-150 Regular Cab
Buyer	Jones	John	1/15/2003	$6,500.00	1	1960 Chevy Pickup
Buyer	Jones	John	1/15/2003	$21,900.00	1	1957 Chevy Sedan
Buyer	Jones	John	1/15/2003	$19,000.00	1	1950 Fordman Coupe
Buyer	Jones	John	1/15/2003	$39,900.00	1	2002 Olds SUV
Both	Gleason	William	2/27/2003	$35,900.00	1	1962 AALLFA Red Spidery 2000
Both	Gleason	William	2/27/2003	$185,000.00	1	1965 Shelly Stunning Red Cobrat
Both	Bright	John	2/24/2003	$21,900.00	1	1971 Pontanic Red Converible
Both	Bright	John	2/24/2003	$125,000.00	1	2001 Collectors Chevy Corvet
Both	Mchugh	Dennis	4/24/2003	$31,500.00	1	1940 Classic Antique Convertible
Both	Mchugh	Dennis	4/24/2003	$83,000.00	1	1967 Shelly Stunning Red Muscle Car
Both	Mchugh	Dennis	4/24/2003	$21,900.00	1	1957 Chevy Sedan
Buyer	Aley	Brandon	5/24/2003	$125,000.00	1	2001 Collectors Chevy Corvet
Both	Calson	Larry	6/1/2003	$3,900.00	1	1988 Fordman T350 Bucket Truck
Both	Johnson	Karl	7/15/2003	$7,800.00	1	1994 Fordman XLP Ext
Both	Johnson	Karl	7/15/2003	$12,500.00	1	1998 Fordman Explorer XLP
Both	Smith	Joann	8/25/2003	$38,995.00	1	2001 Sportster
Both	Spindler	Peter	8/26/2003	$83,000.00	1	1967 Shelly Stunning Red Muscle Car
Both	Casey	Debbie	9/25/2003	$18,900.00	1	1999 Dodgie Dakota Sport
Both	Krammer	Casper	9/30/2003	$38,995.00	1	2001 Sportster
Buyer	Bush	Harry	12/13/2003	$1,750.00	1	1973 Rare Popup Hard sided Indian Camper
Buyer	Jones	John	12/12/2003	$12,500.00	1	1996 CADDY DEVILLE SLX
Both	Bright	John	2/25/2004	$35,900.00	1	1962 AALLFA Red Spidery 2000
Both	Hayes	Karla	2/25/2004	$31,500.00	1	1940 Classic Antique Convertible
Buyer	Aley	Brandon	9/1/2003	$21,900.00	1	1957 Chevy Sedan
Buyer	Bush	Harry	9/6/2003	$31,500.00	1	1940 Classic Antique Convertible
Both	Sakes	Matt	9/30/2003	$38,995.00	1	2001 Sportster
Both	Sakes	Matt	9/30/2003	$3,500.00	1	1986 BMY 326CI

Figure 5-22: Datasheet view of data from multiple tables. This resulting dynaset, from the query, contains 84 records.

You can select multiple contiguous fields by clicking the first field of the list and then clicking the last field while holding down the Shift key (as you click the last field that you want to add). You can also select non-contiguous fields in the list by holding down the Ctrl key while clicking individual fields with the mouse.

Adding all table fields

To add all table fields at the same time, select which table's fields you want to add, and then select the fields to be added. You can select all the fields by either double-clicking the title bar of the table name or by selecting the Asterisk (*) field. These two methods, however, produce very different results.

Selecting all fields using the title bar method

One method of selecting all the fields is to double-click the title bar of the table whose fields you want to select.

This method automatically selects all the fields (except the Asterisk). Once selected, all the fields can be dragged to the QBE pane. The fields are added in the order of their position in the table, from left to right (based on their field order in the table). By default, Access displays only the first five full fields in the QBE pane (lower pane). You can change the column width of each field to display more or fewer columns.

Selecting all fields using the Asterisk (*) method

The first object in each table is an asterisk (at the top of the field list), which is known as the *all-field reference tag*. When you select and drag the asterisk to the QBE pane, all fields in the table are added to the QBE pane, but there is a distinct difference between this method and the double-clicking method referred to previously: When you add the all-field reference tag (*), the QBE pane shows only one cell with the name of the table and an asterisk. For example, if you select the * in the tblProducts table, you see *tblProducts.* * displayed in one field row cell.

Unlike selecting all the fields, the asterisk places a reference to all the fields in a single column. When you drag multiple columns, as in the preceding example, you drag actual table field names to the query. If you later change the design of the table, you also have to change the design of the query. The advantage of using the asterisk for selecting all fields is that the query doesn't need to be changed if you add, delete, or rename fields in the underlying table or query. Changing fields in the underlying table or query automatically adds fields to or removes fields from the query.

Caution   Selecting the * does have one drawback: You cannot perform criteria conditions on the asterisk column itself. You have to add an individual field from the table and enter the criterion. If you add a field for a criterion (when using the *), the query displays the field twice — once for the * field and a second time for the criterion field. Therefore, you may want to de-select the Show cell of the criterion field.

Understanding the Limitations of Multiple-Table Queries

When you create a query with multiple files, there are limitations to what fields can be edited. Generally, you can change data in a query dynaset, and your changes are saved to the underlying tables. A primary key field normally cannot be edited if referential integrity is in effect and if the field is part of a relationship (unless Cascade Updates is set to Yes).

To update a table from a query, a value in a specific record in the query must represent a single record in the underlying table. This means that you cannot update fields in a Crosstab or Totals query because they both group records together to display grouped information. Instead of displaying the actual underlying table data, they display records of data that are calculated and stored in a virtual (nonreal) table called a *snapshot*.

Updating limitations

In Access, the records in your tables may not always be updateable. Table 5-1 shows when a field in a table is updateable. As Table 5-1 shows, queries based on one-to-many relationships are updateable in both tables (depending on how the query was designed). Any query that creates a *snapshot*, however, is not updateable.

Table 5-1 **Rules for Updating Queries**		
Type of Query or Field	*Updateable*	*Comments*
One Table	Yes	
One-to-One relationship	Yes	
Results contains Memo field	Yes	Memo field updateable
Results contain Hyperlink	Yes	Hyperlink updateable
Results contain an OLE object	Yes	OLE object updateable
One-to-Many relationship	Mostly	Restrictions based on design methodology (see text)
Many-to-One-to-Many	No	Can update data in a form or data access page if RecordType = Dynaset
Two or more tables with NO join line	No	Must have a join to determine updateability
Crosstab	No	Creates a snapshot of the data
Totals Query (Sum, Avg, etc.)	No	Works with Grouped data creating a snapshot
Unique Value property is Yes	No	Shows unique records only in a snapshot
SQL-specific queries	No	Union & Pass-through work with ODBC data
Calculated field	No	Will recalculate automatically
Read-only fields	No	If opened read-only or on read-only drive (CD-ROM)
Permissions denied	No	Insert, Replace, or Delete are not granted
ODBC Tables with no Primary Key	No	A primary key (unique index) must exist
Paradox Table with no Primary Key	No	A primary key file must exist
Locked by another user	No	Cannot be updated while a field is locked by another

Overcoming query limitations

Table 5-1 shows that there are times when queries and fields in tables are not update-able. As a general rule, any query that does aggregate calculations or is an ODBC (Open DataBase Connectivity)-based SQL (Structured Query Language) query (SQL-specific query) is not updateable. All others can be updated. When your query has more than one table and some of the tables have a one-to-many relationship, there may be fields that are not updateable (depending on the design of the query).

Updating a unique index (primary key)

If a query uses two tables that have a one-to-many relationship, the one side of the join must have a unique (primary key) index on the field that is used for the join. If not, the fields from the one side of the query cannot be updated.

Replacing existing data in a query with a one-to-many relationship

Normally, all the fields in the many-side table are updateable in a one-to-many query; the one-side table can update all the fields *except* the primary key (join) field. Normally, this is sufficient for most database application purposes. Also, the primary key field is rarely changed in the one-side table because it is the link to the records in the joined tables.

At times, however, you may need to change the link-field contents in both tables (make a new primary key in the one table and have the database program change the link field in all the related records from the *many* table). Access enables you to do this by defining a relationship between the two tables and using referential integrity. If you define a relationship and enforce referential integrity in the Relationship Builder, two selections are activated. If you want to enable changes (updates) to the primary key field, check the Cascade Update Related Fields box. By selecting this option, you can change the primary key field in a relationship; Access automatically updates the link field to the new value in all the other related tables.

 Cross-Reference   Chapter 4 covers the Relationship Builder in detail.

Design tips for updating fields in queries

✦ If you want to add records to both tables of a one-to-many relationship, include the join field from the *many-side* table and show the field in the datasheet. After doing this, records can be added starting with either table. The *one* side's join field is copied automatically to the *many* side's join field.

✦ If you do not want any fields to be updateable, set the Allow Edits property of the form to No.

✦ If you do not want to update some fields on a form, set the Tab Stop property for the control (field) to No for these fields.

✦ If you want to add records to multiple tables in a form (covered in later chapters), remember to include all (or most) of the fields from both tables. Otherwise, you will not have a complete record of data in your form.

Temporary inability to update in a one-to-many relationship

When updating records on the one side of a one-to-many query, you will *not* be able to change the many-side *join* field until you save changes to the one side. You can quickly save changes to the one side by pressing Shift+Enter or selecting File ➪ Save Record. After the one-side changes are saved, the join field in the *many*-side record can be changed.

Creating and Working with Query Joins

You can create joins between tables in these three ways:

✦ By creating relationships between the tables when you design the database. (Select Tools ➪ Relationships from the Database window or click the Relationships button on the toolbar.)

✦ By selecting two tables for the query that have a field that has the same data type and name in both tables and is a primary key field in one of the tables.

✦ By creating joins in the Query window at the time you create a query.

The first two methods are automatic in the Query design window. If you create relationships when designing the tables of your database, Access displays join lines based on those relationships automatically when you add the related tables to a query. It also creates an automatic join between two tables that have a common field, provided that field is a primary key in one of the tables and the Enable AutoJoin choice is selected (default) in the Options dialog box.

If relationships are set in the relationship builder, there may be times when you add a table to a query and it will not automatically be related to another table, as in these examples:

✦ The two tables have a common field, but it is not the same name.

✦ A table is not related and cannot be logically related to the other table (for example, the tblContacts table cannot directly join the Treatments table).

If you have two tables that are not automatically joined and you need to relate them, you join them in the Query Design window. Joining tables in the Query Design window does *not* create a permanent join between the tables. Rather, the join (relationship) will apply only to the tables for the query you are working on.

Caution All tables in a query should be joined to at least one other table. If, for example, you place two tables in a query and do not join them, Access creates a query based on a Cartesian product (also known as the cross product) of the two tables. This subject is discussed later in this chapter. For now, note that a Cartesian product means that if you have five records in table 1 and six records in table 2, the resulting query will have 30 records (5 x 6) that will probably be useless.

Joining tables

Figures 5-19 and 5-20 show the joined tblSales and tblContacts tables. They're joined automatically. Notice that there are join lines between the other tables also.

Note Tables are not joined automatically in a query if they are not already joined at the table level, if they do not have a common named field for a primary key, or if the AutoJoin option is off.

At this point, add the tblContactLog table to the query. To accomplish this, right-click and select Show Table ... from the menu, select tblContactLog, and close the dialog box. Notice that there is no join line between the new table and any other table in the query. It should be joined to the tblContacts table. To join the tblContacts and tblContactLog tables, follow the steps below:

1. Select the idsContactID field in the tblContacts Table in the Table/Query pane.

2. Drag the highlighted field to the tblContactLog table (as you drag the field, the Field icon appears).

3. Drop the Field icon on the lngzContactID field in the tblContactLog table (the Field icon disappears and a join line appears connecting the two tables via the fields specified).

Figure 5-23 shows the new join line between the two tables after it is created. When you perform this action (joining one field to another), the Field icon disappears immediately *before* the join line is displayed. As the Field icon moves between tables, it changes to the symbol that indicates that the icon cannot be dropped in the area between the tables. When it comes over the Field List of the tblContactLog, it changes back to the Field icon, indicating that it can be dropped on any field in that location. When you release the mouse button over the lngzContactID field of the table, the join line appears.

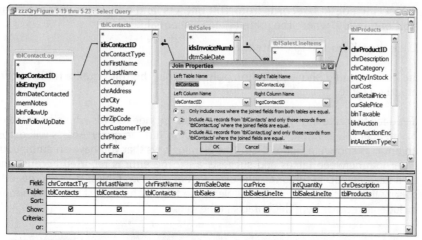

Figure 5-23: Joining tables in the Table/Query pane. Notice the join line is created between the tblContacts and tblContactlog tables. The figure also shows the Join Properties dialog box open to specify the type of join (which is opened by double-clicking on the join line).

Specify the type of join

With the join specified between two tables, you may need to specify the type of join you want — which records should show. The default action for creating a join in a query is to show only those records where the join fields from both tables are equal. Often this will not display all the records you need to see in the query datasheet. For instance, in this chapter, there is no relationship defined between the tblContacts and tblContactLog tables at the table level (relationship builder). As Figure 5-23 shows, the default join line between these tables has no arrow at either end of the join line, nor does it show the type of relationship between the tables (one-to-many, one-to-one, or many-to-one). The default join line between two tables is one where it will only include records where the join fields from both tables are equal. You can see this as choice one in Figure 5-23. Because tblContactLog will not have records for all records in tblContacts, you will need to change the type of link between the tables to include ALL records in tblContacts and only those from tblContactLog where the field value is equal. To activate the Join Properties dialog box and change the join type, follow the steps below:

1. Select the join line between the tblContacts and tblContactLog tables.

2. Double-click on the join line (or right-click and select Join Properties from the menu; alternately select View ➪ Join Properties from the menu). The Join Property dialog box appears (as shown in Figure 5-23).

3. Select "Include ALL records from 'tblContacts' and only those records from 'tblContactLog' where the joined fields are equal."

4. Click the OK button to create the join.

Now the query should show a join line pointing from the tblContacts table to the tblContactLog table.

Caution   If you fail to create this type of join, leaving it to include records where both tables have equal values in their fields, and attempt to run the query, Access will report an error, as shown in Figure 5-24. This warning says that you have an ambiguous outer join between tables and suggests a fix. The error is reported because the field idsContactID in tblContacts is used to join with two tables. Thus you need to specify the specific type of join between the tables. The easiest way is to simply include all records from tblContacts in the join.

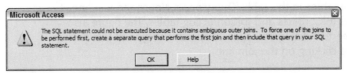

Figure 5-24: Running a query with an improper join type.

Of course, you can also create joins that make no sense, but when you view the data, you will get less-than-desirable results. If two joined fields have no values in common, you will have a datasheet in which no records are selected.

Caution   If you fail to create a join line between tables, the resulting dynaset, viewed in the datasheet, will be a Cartesian product in which each and every record is joined with each and every record in the second table. If one table has 100 records and the other has 200 records, the Cartesian join will create a table with 20,000 records and the results will make no sense.

Note   You can select either table first when you create a join.

You would never want to create a meaningless join. For example, you would not want to join the chrCity field from the tblContact table to the tbmSalesDate of the tblSales table. Although Access will enable you to create this join, the resulting dynaset will have no records in it.

Deleting joins

To delete a join line between two tables, you select the join line and press the Delete key. You can select the join line by placing the mouse pointer on any part of the line and clicking once.

Caution If you delete a join between two tables and the tables remain in the Query window unjoined to any other tables, the solution will have unexpected results because of the Cartesian product that Access creates from the two tables. The Cartesian product is effective for only this query. The underlying relationship remains intact.

Note Access enables you to create multiple-field joins between tables (more than one line can be drawn). The join must be between two fields that have the same data and data type; if not, the query will not find any records from the datasheet to display.

Understanding Types of Table Joins

In Chapter 4, you learned about table relationships and relating two tables by a common field. Access understands all types of table and query relations, including these:

✦ One-to-one

✦ One-to-many

✦ Many-to-one

✦ Many-to-many

When you specify a relationship between two tables, you establish rules for the type of relationship, not for viewing the data based on the relationship.

To view data in two tables, they must be joined through a link that is established via a common field (or group of fields) between the two tables. The method of linking the tables is known as *joining*. In a query, tables with established relationships are shown already joined. Within a query, you can create new joins or change existing joins; just as there are different types of relationships, there are different types of joins. In the following sections, you learn about these types of joins:

✦ Equi-joins (inner joins)

✦ Outer joins

✦ Self-joins

✦ Cross-product joins (Cartesian joins)

Inner joins (Equi-joins)

The default join in Access is known as an *inner join* or *equi-join*. It tells Access to select all records from both tables that have the same value in the fields that are joined.

Note   The Access manuals refer to the default join as both an equi-join and inner join (commonly referred to as an inner join in database relational theory). The Access Help system refers to it as an inner join. The terms equi-join and inner join are interchangeable; however, in the remainder of this chapter they shall be referred to as inner joins.

If records are found in either table that do not have matching records in the other table, they are excluded from the resultant dynaset and will not be shown in the datasheet. Thus, an inner join between tables is simply a join where records are selected when matching values exist in the joined field of both tables.

You can create an inner join between the tblContacts and tblSales tables by bringing these two tables into a new query and clicking on the join line to activate the Join Property dialog box and select the first choice — "Only include rows where the joined fields from both tables are equal." Remember that you are looking for all records from these two tables with matching fields. The idsContactID field and lngzBuyer contain the common field values, so the inner join will not show any records for Contacts that have no Sales or any Sales that do not relate to a valid ContactID number. The rules of referential integrity prevent Sales records that are not tied to a Contact number from being saved. Of course, it's possible to delete all Sales from a Contact or to create a new Contact record with no Sales records (possibly a Seller instead of a Buyer), but a Sale should always be related to a valid Contact (Buyer). Referential integrity should keep a Contact number from being deleted or changed if a Sale is related to it.

It's possible to have a buyer in the tblContacts table who has no sales. It's less likely, theoretically impossible, to have a Sale with no Buyer. If you create a query to show Contacts and their Sales, any record of a Contact without a Sale or a Sales record without a matching Contact record will not be shown in the resulting dynaset.

It can be important to find these lost records. One of the features of a query is to perform several types of joins.

Tip   Access can help find lost records between tables by using a Query Wizard to build a Find Unmatched Query (these are covered in Chapter 38).

Changing join properties

If you create join properties at table level, in the relationship builder they will be the default properties for your tables when working with queries. However, you can change these properties for a specific query at the query level.

With the tblContacts and tblSales tables joined, certain join behaviors (or *properties*) exist between the tables. The join property is a rule that says to display all records (for the fields you specify) that correspond to the characters found in the idsContactID field of the tblContacts table and in the corresponding lngzBuyer field of the tblSales table.

To translate this rule into a practical example, this is what happens in the tblContacts and tblSales tables:

✦ If a Buyer's record in the tblContacts table has an idsContactID (customer number) that is not found in any of the records of the tblSales table, that Buyer's record is not shown.

✦ If a record in the tblSales table has a number for a customer number that is not related to any number in the tblContacts table, that tblSales record is not shown.

This makes sense, at least most of the time. You don't want to see records for buyers without sales — *or do you?*

A join property is a rule that is enforced by Access. This rule tells Access how to interpret any exceptions (possible errors) between two tables. For example, as you saw earlier, should the non-corresponding records be shown?

Access has several types of joins, each with its own characteristics or behaviors. Access enables you to change the type of join quickly by changing its properties. You can change join properties by selecting the join line between tables and double-clicking the line or right-clicking and selecting Join Properties from the menu. When you do so, a Join Properties dialog box appears. If you double-click the join line between the tblContacts and tblSales tables, the dialog box in Figure 5-25 displays.

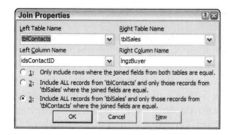

Figure 5-25: The Join Properties dialog box for the tblContacts and tblSales tables. Notice that the third option button is selected (for an outer join), because the join properties were set at table level.

As Figure 5-25 shows, the Join Properties dialog box has two parts: the four combo boxes and three option buttons. For now, you focus on the three options buttons:

1. Only include rows where the joined fields from both tables are equal. (This is the default.)

2. Include ALL records from "tblContacts" and only those records from "tblSales" where the joined fields are equal.

3. Include ALL records from "tblSales" and only those records from "tblContacts" where the joined fields are equal.

The first choice is commonly known as an *inner join,* and the other two are known as *outer joins.* These joins control the behavior of Access as it builds the dynaset from the query.

To create this query and change the value from the third option to the first, to create an inner join between the two tables, follow these steps:

1. Start a new query and select the tblContacts and tblSales tables. Select the chrContactType, chrLastName, and chrFirstName fields from the tblContacts table and dtmSaleDate from the tblSales table. (These fields will be displayed later.)

2. Double-click on the join line between the two tables.

3. Select the choice "1: Only include rows where the joined fields from both tables are equal." (This is normally the default.)

4. Click the OK button to return to the query design window.

Inner and outer joins

The Query Design window should now display two tables in the top pane of the Query window—tblContacts and tblSales, with four fields selected to display. If your query window does not have these two tables, create a new query and add them. The following sections use these tables as examples to explain how inner and outer joins operate.

Displaying an inner join

To display an inner join, follow this procedure: In the QBE pane, make sure you have selected the fields chrContactType, chrLastName, and chrFirstName from the tblContacts table and the field dtmSaleDate from the tblSales table. Then display the dynaset by selecting the Datasheet button on the toolbar. The datasheet should now look similar to the one shown in Figure 5-26, displaying each buyer's name and all buyers' sales dates. Scroll through the records until you reach the bottom of the datasheet. Notice that the value in the Contact Type column is either Both or Buyer for each record.

Notice that each of the 53 records has entries in all four fields. This means that every record displayed from the tblContacts table has a corresponding record or records in the tblSales table.

Return to query design mode by clicking the Design icon on the toolbar. When you double-click the join line between the tblContacts and tblSales tables, you see that the join property for these two tables becomes the first selection shown in the Join Properties dialog box. This is an inner join, or *equi-join,* the most common type. These joins show only the records that have a correspondence between tables.

Query1 : Select Query

Contact Type	Last Name	First Name	Sale Date
Buyer	Jones	John	1/15/2003
Buyer	Jones	John	12/12/2003
Buyer	Jones	John	2/26/2004
Both	Minkler	Larry	4/15/2004
Buyer	James	Cary	8/3/2004
Buyer	Aley	Brandon	5/24/2003
Buyer	Aley	Brandon	9/1/2003
Buyer	Aley	Brandon	12/15/2003
Buyer	Aley	Brandon	9/10/2004
Both	Dennis	Michael	8/28/2004
Both	Johnson	Karl	7/15/2003
Both	Johnson	Karl	12/2/2003
Both	Johnson	Karl	1/15/2004
Both	Johnson	Karl	6/13/2004
Both	Gleason	William	2/27/2003
Both	Gleason	William	1/10/2004
Both	Hayes	Karla	2/25/2004
Both	Hayes	Karla	5/1/2004
Both	Marino	John	7/20/2004
Buyer	Bond	Ann	11/1/2003
Buyer	Bond	Ann	11/2/2003

Record: 1 of 53

Figure 5-26: The datasheet for an inner join between the tblContacts and tblSales tables.

Creating a right outer join

Unlike inner joins (equi-joins), *outer joins* are used for showing all records in one table while showing common records in the other. The table or query that does not have a matching record will simply display empty cells in the datasheet when the dynaset is displayed.

When you have created an outer join, the join line will point graphically to one of the tables; as is the default action of the tblSales and tblContacts tables (being set at table level). If displaying the join property, it says to show all records from the main table (the one missing the arrow) while showing only matching records in the table being pointed to. For a further explanation, follow these instructions:

1. If you have left the Join Properties dialog box, double-click the join line between tblContacts and tblSales.
2. Select the second choice from the Join Properties dialog box, which includes *all* records from the tblContacts table and only those records from tblSales where the joined fields are equal. (This may be the third choice if you have the tblSales table to the left of the tblContacts table and no relationship built between the two tables.) Then click the OK button. Notice that the join line now has an arrow at one end, pointing rightward to the tblSales table, as in Figure 5-27. This is known in database terminology as a *right outer join*. (If the tblSales table is to the left of the tblContacts table, move it to the right and the arrow will point right — remember, the relationship here is that one Buyer can own many Sales.)
3. Click the Datasheet button to display this dynaset. Everything looks the same as before, except now there are 81 records instead of 53. Now move down the page and notice that everywhere there is a value of Seller in the Contact type

column, there is no corresponding Sale Date value (see Figure 5-28). These records result from selecting the join property that specifies "include all records from tblContacts table."

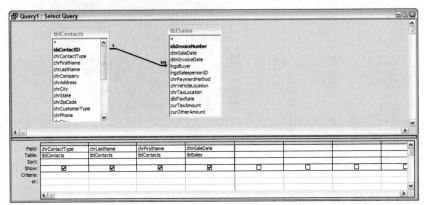

Figure 5-27: The join line for an outer join between the tblContacts and tblSales tables. The one and infinity signs are from the relationship set at table level with referential integrity.

Query1 : Select Query

Contact Type	Last Name	First Name	Sale Date
Buyer	Jones	John	1/15/2003
Buyer	Jones	John	12/12/2003
Buyer	Jones	John	2/26/2004
Seller	Masters	Hank	
Both	Minkler	Larry	4/15/2004
Both	Hammerman	Joe	
Buyer	James	Cary	8/3/2004
Buyer	Uno	Mark	
Buyer	Aley	Brandon	5/24/2003
Buyer	Aley	Brandon	9/1/2003
Buyer	Aley	Brandon	12/15/2003
Buyer	Aley	Brandon	9/10/2004
Both	Dennis	Michael	8/28/2004
Both	Martin	Mark	
Both	Johnson	Karl	7/15/2003
Both	Johnson	Karl	12/2/2003
Both	Johnson	Karl	1/15/2004
Both	Johnson	Karl	6/13/2004
Both	Gleason	William	2/27/2003
Both	Gleason	William	1/10/2004
Both	Tomaso	Alex	

Record: 1 of 81

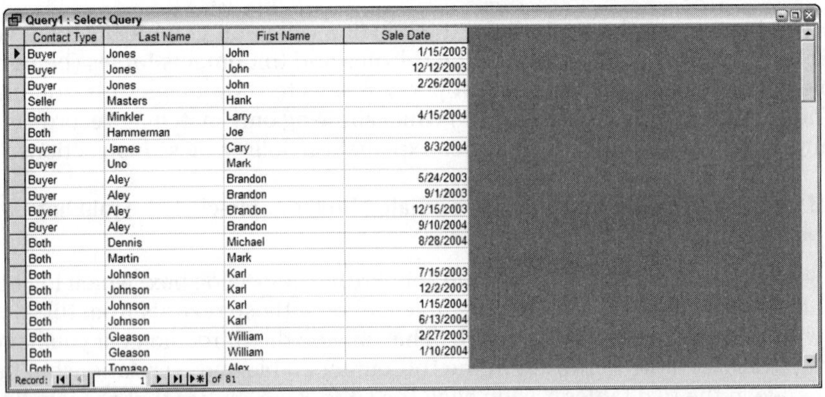

Figure 5-28: A datasheet with a right outer join. It shows all Contacts (buyers and sellers), including those with no Sales.

There are now 81 records, with the extra records being displayed in a record in the tblContacts table. There are many persons that do not have any corresponding records in the tblSales table (all of them are sellers). You can see one in the figure shown above . . . others are in the records not visible on the screen.

Unlike inner joins, outer joins show all corresponding records between two tables and records that do *not* have a corresponding record in the other table. In the preceding example, there were numerous records of Sellers but no corresponding record for any Sale where they are the buyer. Figure 5-28 shows four records in the window that do not have sales information — all of them have a value of Seller in the Contact Type column.

Caution   If you've changed the display order of the tables since adding them to the Query window, Access does not follow the new table order you set up; rather, it uses the original order in which you selected the tables. Because the information is normally the same in either table, it doesn't make a difference which field is selected first.

Tip   You may want to break the joins between tables that you have moved around and re-create the joins once you have put them in the order that you want. Now Access will accept your changes.

Creating a left outer join

Once in the query design, again double-click the join line between the tblContacts and tblSales tables. Select the third choice from the Join Properties dialog box, which asks to "include all records from tblSales." Then click the OK button. The join line now has an arrow pointing to the tblContacts table. This is known as a *left outer join*. (If the arrow points to the right in the top pane, the join is known as a right outer join; if the arrow points to the left, it's a left outer join.)

If you create this left-outer join query between the tables and select the Datasheet button to display the dynaset, you will see that you again have 53 records. This simply means that there are no records in the tblSales table (Sales without Buyers). If there were one or more sales without buyers, this query would show them. The Sales records, without Buyers, would result from selecting the join property to include all records from tblSales (a *left outer join* in database terminology).

Any Sales record without a Buyer is known as an *orphan* record. Referential integrity can't be set in the Relationships window if there is an orphan record. If you attempt to set Referential Integrity between tables and you cannot, simply remove any orphan records and then return to the Relationships window to set up referential integrity between the tables.

Cross-Reference   Removing unwanted, unrelated records is detailed in Chapter 38.

Creating a Cartesian product

If you add both the tblContacts and tblSales tables to a query but don't specify a join between the tables, Access combines the first tblContact record with all the tblSales records; then it takes the second record and combines it with all the tblSales records and continues until all the tblContacts records have been combined with all of the tblSales records. Combining each record in one table with each record in the other table results in a Cartesian product (cross-product) of both tables. Because the tblContacts table has 58 records and the tblSales table has 53, the resulting dynaset has 3074 records.

✦   ✦   ✦

Using Operators and Expressions in Multi-table Select Queries

I n previous chapters, you work with queries using criteria on a single field. You also get experience adding multiple tables to a query and joining the tables together. This chapter focuses on extracting information from multiple tables using multiple criteria in select queries.

Before working with queries, this chapter will focus on operators, functions, and expressions that are the fundamental building blocks for Access operations. You will often use them as criteria in queries to specify which records to display. They are also used to calculate fields in forms to show calculated information or to display data in a different format, and they are used in summary controls in reports to show totals and subtotals.

On the CD-ROM This chapter will use the database named CHAP06Start. mdb. If you have not already copied it onto your machine from the CD, you will need to do so now. When you have completed this chapter, your database should resemble the one in CHAP06End.mdb.

What Are Operators?

Operators let you add numbers, compare values, put text strings together, and create complex relational expressions. You use operators to inform Access that a specific operation is to be performed against one or more items.

Types of operators

The types of operators discussed in this chapter are listed below:

✦ Mathematical (arithmetic) operators

✦ Relational operators

✦ String operators

✦ Boolean (logical) operators

✦ Miscellaneous operators

When are operators used?

You find yourself using operators all the time. In fact, you use them every time you create an equation in Access. For example, operators specify data-validation rules in table properties, create calculated fields in forms, and specify criteria in queries.

Operators indicate that an operation needs to be performed on one or more items. Some common examples of operators are:

=

&

And

Like

+

Mathematical operators

There are seven basic mathematical operators. These are also known as arithmetic operators, because they are used for performing arithmetic calculations:

*	Multiply
+	Add
–	Subtract
/	Divide
\	Integer Divide
^	Exponentiation
Mod	Modulo

By definition, you use mathematical operators to work with numbers. When you work with mathematical operators, numbers can be any numeric data type. The number can be an actual number (constant value), or the value of a memory variable, or a field's contents. Furthermore, the numbers can be used individually or combined to create complex expressions. Some of the examples in this section are quite complex, but don't worry if you don't usually work with sophisticated mathematics. This chapter shows you how to work with mathematical formulas in Access.

The * (multiplication) operator

A simple example of when to use the *multiplication operator* is to calculate the total price of purchasing several items. You could design a query to display the number of items purchased and the price for each item. Then you could have a column containing the value of the number of items purchased times the price per item. In this case, you could get that information from the table tblSalesLineItems, and the formula would be [tblSalesLineItems.intQuantity] * [tblSalesLineItems.curPrice]. Another example could be a form for entering the number of items purchased and the per-item price. Then you could use a calculated field to calculate and display the total price for that number of items. In this case, the calculated field would contain a formula like [curPrice] * [intQuantity].

Note   The standard notation for dealing with field names in an expression is to enclose them in square brackets.

Tip   Notice that the name of the table is used before the field name in the above example. Because your tables only have one field named curPrice and intQuantity, you could have skipped the table names; however, it is good practice to specify the table name where the field comes from — separating the table name from the field name by a single period.

The + (addition) operator

If you want to create a calculated field in a query for adding the value of tax to the gross amount, you would use an expression similar to this: [Tax Amt]+ [tblSalesLineItems.curPrice]. To use this expression, you would have to create another calculated field in the query named [Tax Amt] that is created using the multiplication operator – Tax Amt: [tblSales.dblTaxRate] * [tblSalesLineItems. curPrice]. You could also create a form for adding the values in fields, such as Gross Amount and Tax, in which case you would use the expression [Gross Amount] + [Tax]. This simple formula uses the *addition operator* to add the contents of both fields and display the result in the object that contains the formula.

Besides adding two numbers, the *addition operator* can be used for concatenating two character strings — putting two text-based strings together forming a single text string. For example, you may want to combine the fields chrFirstName and chrLastName from the tblContacts table to display them as a single field. This expression is:

[tblContacts.chrFirstName] + [tblContacts.chrLastName]

Note   Notice that the name of the table is used before the field name. In this example, it isn't necessary because your tables only have one field named chrFirstName and chrLastName; however, it is good practice to specify the table name where the field comes from — separating the table name from the field name by a single period.

Cross-Reference   More can be found on concatenating strings later in this chapter.

Caution   Although you can concatenate (put two strings together) text strings by using the addition operator, you should use the ampersand (&). The reason for this appears in the section "String operators," later in this chapter.

The – (subtraction) operator

An example of using the *subtraction operator* on the same form is to calculate the final invoice amount minus a discount. The formula to determine the Net Invoice Amount of an item would be as follows:

[tblSalesLineItems.curPrice] -
([tblSalesLineItems.curPrice]*[tblSalesLineItems.dblDiscountPercent]).

Note   Although parentheses are not mathematical operators, they play an integral part in working with operators, as discussed later, in the section "Operator precedence."

The / (division) operator

You can use the *division operator* to divide two numbers and (as with the previous operators) display the result wherever you need it. Suppose, for example, that a pool of 212 people win the $1,000,000 lottery this week. The formula to determine each individual's payoff is 1,000,000 / 212, resulting in $4,716.98 per person.

Tip   Using Access's Immediate window that is built into the Visual Basic Window, you can determine the values of mathematical formulas. To activate the immediate window, press the Ctrl+G key combination. Once active, you can perform any calculation and have it display the results by placing a question mark in front of the calculation — for example, typing ? 1000000 / 212 and pressing Enter will result in an answer of 4716.9811. To close this window, close the Microsoft Visual Basic window.

The \ (integer division) operator

Should you ever need to take two numbers, round them both to integers, divide the two rounded integers, and receive a non-rounded integer, the *integer division operator* does it in one step. Here is an example:

Normal Division	Integer Conversion Division
100 / 6 = 16.667	100 \ 6 = 16
100.9 / 6.6 = 15.288	100.9 \ 6.6 = 14

Tip   Access has the round function for rounding fractional numbers to whole numbers. You can also use the integer division operator to round any number. Just integer-divide (\) the number you want to round by 1, as in 125.6 \ 1 = 126.

Note   Access rounds numbers based on the greater-than-.5 rule: Any number with a decimal value of x.5 or less rounds down; greater than x.5 rounds up to the next whole number. This means that 6.5 becomes 6, but 6.51 and 6.6 become 7.

What Are Integer Values?

Integers are whole numbers (numbers that have no decimal places), which in Access are the values between -32768 and +32767. They have no fractional part (meaning the part after the dot). (For example, 7.2 is not an integer, because it has a fractional part which is .2; 7 is the integer number!) Examples are 1; 722; 33; -5460; 0; and 22. They include all whole positive and negative numbers and 0. When you use the Int() function or the integer divide operator (\) to determine the integer part of any number, simply drop any decimal values. For example, the integer value of 45.123 is 45; for 2.987, the integer is 2; and so forth.

The integer divide operator can be a confusing operator until you understand just what it does. If you enter the following print statements in the Immediate window of Microsoft Visual Basic (accessed from Access), it should become clear:

? 101 / 6 results in 16.833.

? 101.9 / 6.6 results in 15.439.

? 102 / 7 results in 14.571.

? INT(102 / 7) results in 14.

? 101.9 \ 6.6 results in 14.

The last entry uses the integer divide sign (\) and is equivalent to rounding both numbers in the division operation (101.9 = 102 and 6.6 = 7), dividing 102 by 7, and converting the answer to an integer. In other words, it is equivalent to the following:

INT((101.9 \ 1) / (6.6 \ 1)) or INT(round(101.9)/ round(6.6))

The ^ (exponentiation) operator

The *exponentiation operator* (^) raises a number to the power of an exponent. Raising a number simply means indicating the number of times that you want to multiply a number by itself. For example, multiplying the value 4 x 4 x 4 (that is, 4-cubed) is the same as entering the formula 4^3.

The Mod (Modulo) operator

The *modulo operator* (mod), or remainder operator, takes any two numbers (number1 and number2) and divides the first by the second (number1 / number2), returning only the remainder. For example, if you type in the following examples in the Immediate window, it should become clear:

? 10 Mod 5 results in 0 (10 divided by 5 is 2 with a remainder of 0.)

? 10 Mod 4 results in 2. (10 divided by 4 is 2 with a remainder of 2.)

All numbers, if they are not integers, are first rounded to integers before the Mod operator is performed. For example:

? 22.24 Mod 4 results in 2. (22 divided by 4 is 5 with a remainder of 2.)

? 22.51 Mod 4 results in 3. (23 divided by 4 is 5 with a remainder of 3.)

? 21 Mod 5.49 results in 1. (21 divided by 5 is 4 with a remainder of 1.)

Relational operators

There are six basic relational operators (also known as comparison operators). They compare two values or expressions via an equation. The relational operators include the following:

=	Equal
<>,	Not equal
<	Less than
<=,	Less than or equal to
>	Greater than
>=,	Greater than or equal to

The expressions built from relational operators always return either a logical value or Null; the value they return says Yes (True), No (not True; that is, False), or Null (unknown/no value).

Note   Access actually returns a numeric value for relational operator equations. It returns a −1 (negative 1) for True and a 0 (zero) for False.

If either side of an equation is a Null value, the result will always be a Null.

The = (equal) operator

The *equal operator* returns a logical True if the two expressions being compared are the same. Here are two examples of the equal operator:

[tblProducts.chrCategory] = "Car"	Returns a True if the category is a car; False is returned for any other type.
[tblSales.dtmSaleDate] = Date()	Returns a True if the date in the dtmSaleDate field is today.

The <> (not-equal) operator

The *not-equal operator* is exactly the opposite of the equal operator. In this example, the car example is changed to not-equal:

[tblProducts.chrCategory] <> "Car"	Returns a True if Type of Category is anything but a car.
[tblProducts.chrCategory] != "SUV"	Returns a True if Type of Category is anything but an SUV.

Notice that you have two different ways to express not equal to: the <> or != symbols both mean exactly the same thing.

The < (less-than) operator

The *less-than operator* returns a logical True if the left side of the equation is less than the right side, as in this example:

[tblSalesLineItems.curPrice] < 1000	Returns a True if the Price field contains a value of less than 1000.

The <= (less-than-or-equal-to) operator

The *less-than-or-equal-to operator* returns a True if the left side of the equation is either less than or equal to the right side, as in this example:

[tblSalesLineItems.curPrice] <= 2500	Returns a True if the value of Price equals 2500 or is less than 2500.
[tblSalesLineItems.curPrice] !> 1500	Returns a True if the value of Price equals 1500 or is less than 1500.

Notice, in the second example, that you got the same results using the operator !> (not greater than). In other words, equal to or less than can be expressed using either operator, <= or !>.

Caution   Access 2003 is sensitive to the order of the operators. Access reports an error if you enter =<; the order is important. It must be less than or equal to (<=).

The > (greater-than) operator

The *greater-than operator* is the exact opposite of the less-than operator. This operator returns a True when the left side of the equation is greater than the right side, as in this example:

[tblSales.dblTaxRate] > 3.5 Returns True if the value of Tax rate is greater than 3.5.

The >= (greater-than-or-equal-to) operator

The *greater-than-or-equal-to operator* returns a True if the left side of the equation is either equal to or greater than the right side. For example:

[tblSales.dblTaxRate] >= 5   Returns a True if the field Tax rate contains a value equal to or greater than 5.

[tblSales.dblTaxRate] !< 5   Returns a True if the field Tax rate contains a value equal to or greater than 5.

Notice, in the second example, that you got the same results using the operator !< (not less than). In other words, equal to or greater than can be expressed using either operator, >= or !<.

Caution   Access 2003 is sensitive to the order of the operators. Access reports an error if you enter =>; the order is important. It must be greater than or equal to (>=).

String operators

Access has three *string operators*, also know as text operators. Unlike the other operators, these work specifically with the Text data type:

&	Concatenation
Like	Similar to...
NOT Like	Not similar to...

The & (concatenation) operator

The *concatenation operator* connects or links (concatenates) two or more objects into a resultant string. This operator works similarly to the addition operator.

Unlike the addition operator, however, the & operator always forces a string concatenation. For instance, this example produces a single string:

[chrFirstName] & [chrLastName]

However, in the resultant string, no spaces are automatically added. If [chrFirstName] equals "Fred" and [chrLastName] equals "Smith," concatenating the field contents yields FredSmith. To add a space between the strings, you must concatenate a space string between the two fields. To concatenate a space string between first and last name fields, you enter a formula such as this:

[chrFirstName] & " " & [chrLastName]

This operator can easily concatenate a string object with a number- or date-type object. Using the & eliminates the need for special functions to convert a number or date to a string.

Suppose, for example, that you have a Number field, which is House Number, and a Text field, which is Street Name, and that you want to build an expression for a report of both fields. For this, you can enter the following:

[House Number] & " " & [Street Name]

If House Number has a value of 1600 and Street Name is "Pennsylvania Avenue N.W.," the resultant concatenation of the number and string is as follows:

"1600 Pennsylvania Avenue N.W."

Perhaps you want to have a calculated field in a report that prints the operator's name and the date and time the report was run. This can be accomplished using syntax similar to the following:

"This report was printed " & Now() & " by " & [operator name]

If the date is March 21, 2003, and the time is 4:45 p.m., this concatenated line prints something like this:

This report was printed 3/21/03 4:45:40 PM by Michael R. Irwin

Notice the spaces at the end or the beginning of the strings. Knowing how this operator works makes maintenance of your database expressions easier. If you always use the concatenation operator for creating concatenated text strings, you won't have to be concerned with the data types of the concatenated objects. Any formula that uses the & operator converts all the objects being concatenated to a string data type for you.

Note Using the & with Nulls: If both objects are Null, the result is also a Null. If only one of the two objects is Null, Access converts the object that is Null to a string type with a length of 0 and builds the concatenation.

The Like (similar to) operator and NOT Like

The Like operator, and its opposite, the NOT Like operator, are used to compare two string objects by using wildcards. This operator determines whether one object matches, or doesn't match, the pattern of another object. The resultant value of the comparison is a True, False, or Null.

The Like operator uses the following basic syntax:

> *expression object* Like *pattern object*

Like looks for the *expression object* in the *pattern object*; if it is present, the operation returns a True. (The Like operator is discussed in more detail in Chapter 13.)

Note If either object in the Like formula is a Null, the result is a Null.

This operator provides a powerful and flexible tool for string comparisons. The pattern object can use wildcard characters to increase flexibility (see the sidebar "Using Wildcards").

Tip If you want to match one of the wildcard characters in the Like operation, the wildcard character must be enclosed in brackets in the pattern object. In the example

"AB*Co" Like "AB[*]C*"

the [*] in the third position of the pattern object will look for the asterisk as the third character of the string.

Following are some examples that use the Like operator:

[tblContacts.chrLastName] Like "M[Cc]*"	Returns a True for any last name that begins with "Mc" or "MC." "McDonald," "McJamison," "MCWilliams" are all True; "Irwin" and "Prague" are False.
[chrAnswer] Like "[!e-zE-Z]"	Returns a True if the Answer is A, B, C, D, a, b, c, or d. Any other letter is False.
"AB1989" Like "AB####"	Results in True because the string begins with the letters *AB* and is followed by any four numbers.

"#10 Circle Drive" Like "[#]*Drive"	Results in True because the first character is the pound sign (#) and the last part is the word *Drive*.
[Answer] NOT Like "[!e-zE-Z]"	Returns a False if the Answer is A, B, C, D, a, b, c, or d. Any other letter is TRUE.
[chrLastName] NOT Like "M[Cc]*"	Is True for any last name that DOES NOT begin with "Mc" or "MC." "McDonald," "McJamison," "MCWilliams" are all FALSE; "Irwin" and "Prague" are TRUE.

Boolean (logical) operators

Access uses six *Boolean operators*. Also referred to as *logical operators*, these are used for setting conditions in expressions. Boolean operators are used to create complex multiple-condition expressions. Like relational operators, these always return either a logical True or False or a Null. Boolean operators include the following:

And	Logical and
Or	Logical inclusive or
Eqv	Logical equivalence
Imp	Logical implication
Xor	Logical exclusive or
Not	Logical not

The And operator

You use the *And operator* to perform a logical conjunction of two objects; the operator returns the value True if both conditions are true. The general syntax of an And operation is:

   object expression 1 And *object expression 2*

Here is an example:

[tblContacts.chrState] = "MA" And [tblContacts.chrZipCode] = "02379-"	Is True only if both conditions are True.

Using Wildcards

Access lets you use these five wildcards with the Like operator:

Character	Matches
?	A single character (A to Z, 0 to 9)
*	Any number of characters (0 to n)
#	Any single digit (0 to 9)
[list]	Any single character in the list
[!list]	Any single character not in the list

Both [list] and [!list] can use the hyphen between two characters to signify a range.

If the conditions on both sides of the And operator are True, the result is a True value. Table 6-1 demonstrates the results.

Table 6-1
And Operator Resultants

Expression 1	Expression 2	Return Resultant
True	True	True
True	False	False
True	Null	Null
False	True	False
False	False	False
False	Null	False
Null	True	Null
Null	False	False
Null	Null	Null

The Or operator

The *Or operator* is used to perform a logical disjunction of two objects; the operator returns the value True if either condition is true. The general syntax of an Or operation is

> *object expression 1* Or *object expression 2*

The following two examples show how the Or operator works:

[chrLastName] = "Casey" Or [chrLastName] = "Gleason"	Is True if Last Name is either Casey or Gleason.
[chrTaxLocation] = "TX" Or [chrTaxLocation] = "CT"	Is True if the Tax location is either TX or CT.

If the condition of either side of the Or operator is True, a True value is returned. Table 6-2 demonstrates the results.

Table 6-2
Or Expression Resultants

Expression 1	Expression 2	Return Resultant
True	True	True
True	False	True
True	Null	True
False	True	True
False	False	False
False	Null	Null
Null	True	True
Null	False	Null
Null	Null	Null

The Not operator

The *Not operator* is used for negating a numeric object; the operator returns the value True if the condition is not true. This operator reverses the logical result of the expression.

The general syntax of a Not operation is:

Not *numeric object expression*

The following example shows how to use the Not operator:

Not [curPrice] <= 100000   Is true if Price is greater than 100000.

If the numeric object is Null, the resulting condition is Null. Table 6-3 demonstrates the results.

Table 6-3 **Not Operator Resultants**	
Expression	*Return Resultant*
True	False
False	True
Null	Null

Miscellaneous operators

Access has three very useful miscellaneous operators:

Between...And	Range
In	List comparison
Is	Reserved word

The Between...And operator

You can use the *Between...And operator* to determine whether an object is within a specific range of values. This is the general syntax:

object expression Between *value 1* And *value 2*

If the value of the object expression is between *value 1* and *value 2*, the result is True; otherwise, it is False.

The following is an example of the Between...And operator that uses the IIF function for a calculated field named Due 30 Days in a query to display current balance or nothing:

Due 30 Days: IIf([tblContacts.curCurBal] Between 0 And 4500,Null,curCurBal)

This displays the amount due in 30 days for values of greater than $4500.

The In operator

The *In operator* is used to determine whether an object is equal to any value in a specific list. This is the general syntax:

object expression In *(value1, value2, value3, ...)*

If the object expression is found in the list, the result is True; otherwise, the result is False.

The following example also uses the In operator as a criteria for a query:

In ('SUV','Minivans')

This displays only those vehicles that are SUVs or Minivans.

The Is (reserved word) operator

The *Is operator* is used only with the keyword *Null* to determine whether an object has nothing in it. This is the general syntax:

object expression Is Null, *value 1*

This example is a validation-check message in a data-entry form to force entry of a field:

IIF([chrLastName] Is Null, "a Last Name Must be Entered"," ")

Operator precedence

When you work with complex expressions that have many operators, Access must determine which operator to evaluate first, and then which is next, and so forth. To do this, Access has a built-in predetermined order, known as *operator precedence*. Access always follows this order unless you use parentheses to specify otherwise.

Parentheses are used to group parts of an expression and override the default order of precedence. Operations within parentheses are performed before any operations outside of them. Inside the parentheses, Access follows the predetermined operator precedence.

Precedence is determined first according to category of the operator. The operator rank by order of precedence is:

1. Mathematical
2. Comparison
3. Boolean

Each category contains its own order of precedence, which is explained next.

The mathematical precedence

Within the general category of mathematical operators, this order of precedence is in effect:

1. Exponentiation
2. Negation
3. Multiplication and/or division (left to right)
4. Integer division
5. Modulo
6. Addition and/or subtraction (left to right)
7. String concatenation

The comparison precedence

Comparison operators observe this order of precedence:

1. Equal
2. Not equal
3. Less than
4. Greater than
5. Less than or equal to
6. Greater than or equal to
7. Like

Precedence Order

Simple mathematics provides an example of order of precedence. Remember that Access performs operations within parentheses before operations that are not in parentheses. Also remember that multiplication and division operations are performed before addition or subtraction operations.

For example, what is the answer to this simple equation?

X=10+3*4

If your answer is 52, you need a better understanding of precedence in Access. If your answer is 22, you're right. If your answer is anything else, you need a calculator!

Multiplication is performed before addition by the rules of mathematical precedence. Therefore, the equation 10+3*4 is evaluated in this order:

3*4 is performed first, which yields an answer of 12. 12 is then added to 10, which yields 22.

Look at what happens when you add parentheses to the equation. What is the answer to this simple equation?

X=(10+3)*4

Now the answer is 52. Within parentheses, the values 10 and 3 are added first; then the result (13) is multiplied by 4, which yields 52.

The Boolean precedence

The Boolean category follows this order of precedence:

1. Not
2. And
3. Or
4. Xor
5. Eqv
6. Imp

Moving beyond Simple Queries

Select queries are the most common type of query used; they select information (based on a specific criterion) from one or more related tables. With these queries, you can ask questions and receive answers about information that's stored in your database tables. In previous chapters, you work with queries that use simple criteria on a single field in a table with operators, such as equal (=) and greater than (>).

Knowing how to specify criteria is critical to designing and writing effective queries. Although queries can be used against a single table for a single criterion, most queries extract information from several tables using more complex criteria.

Because of this complexity, your queries are able to retrieve only the data you need, in the order that you need it. You may, for example, want to select and display data from the Access Auto Auctions database to answer these questions:

✦ All buyers of Chevy cars or Ford trucks

✦ All buyers who have purchased something during the past 60 days

✦ All sales for items greater than $90,000.00 USD

✦ The number of customers from each state

✦ Any customers that have made comments or complaints

As your database system evolves, you will ask questions like these about the information stored in the system. Although the system was not originally developed specifically to answer these questions, you can find the information needed to answer them stored in the tables. Because the information is there, you find yourself performing ad hoc queries, which can be very simple or quite complex, against the database. You perform ad hoc queries by using select queries.

Select queries are the easiest way to obtain information from several tables without resorting to writing programs.

Using query comparison operators

When working with select queries, you may need to specify one or more *criteria* to limit the scope of information shown. You specify criteria by using *comparison operators* in equations and calculations. The categories of operators are mathematical, relational, logical, and string. In select queries, operators are used in either the Field: or Criteria: cell of the QBE (Query by Example) pane.

Here's a good rule of thumb to observe:

Use mathematical and string operators for creating calculated fields; use relational and logical operators for specifying scope criteria.

Cross-Reference We discuss calculated fields later in this chapter. You can find an in-depth explanation of operators earlier in this chapter.

Table 6-4 shows most of the common operators that are used with select queries.

Table 6-4
Common Operators Used in Select Queries

Mathematical	Relational	Logical	String	Miscellaneous
* (multiply)	= (equal)	And	& (concatenate)	Between...And
/ (divide)	<> (not equal)	Or	Like	In
+ (add)	> (greater than)	Not		Is Null / Not Null
– (subtract)	< (less than)			

Using these operators, you can ferret out groups of records like these:

✦ Product records that have a picture associated with them

✦ A range of records, such as all sales between November and January

✦ Records that meet both And *and* Or criteria, such as all records that are cars and are not either a Minivan or SUV

✦ All records that do *not* match a value, such as any category that is not a car

When you add a criterion to a query, you use the appropriate operator with an *example* of what you want. In Figure 6-1, the example is *CARS*. The operator is equal (=). Notice that the equal sign is *not* shown in the figure. The equal sign is the default operator for selection criteria.

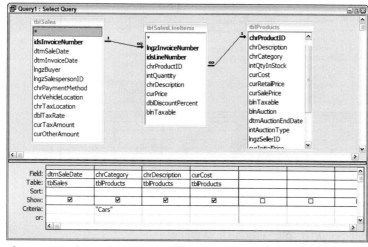

Figure 6-1: The QBE pane shows a simple criterion asking for all vehicles where the chrCategory is Cars.

Cross-
Reference   Chapter 5 gives an in-depth explanation of working with queries.

Understanding complex criteria selection

As Table 6-4 shows, you can use several operators to build complex criteria. To most people, complex criteria consist of a series of Ands and Ors, as in these examples:

✦ State must be Connecticut *or* Texas

✦ City must be Sunnyville *and* state must be Georgia

✦ State must be MA *or* MO *and* city must be Springfield

These examples demonstrate the use of both logical operators: *And/Or.* Many times, you can create complex criteria by entering example data in different cells of the QBE pane. Figure 6-2 demonstrates how to create complex And/Or criteria without entering the operator keywords And/Or at all. This example displays all the buyers and their sales that satisfy these criteria:

Live in either the state of Connecticut (CT) or the state of Massachusetts (MA) and whose type of vehicle purchase is not a car.

Note   You learn how to create this type of complex query later in this chapter.

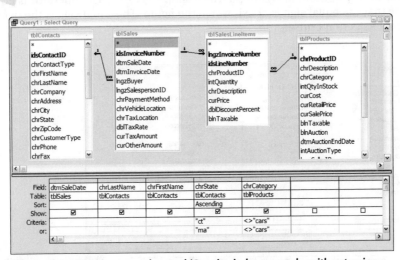

Figure 6-2: Creating complex And/Or criteria by example without using the And/Or operators. This Query uses both the Criteria row and the Or row to combine the And/Or criteria through example.

Access takes your graphical query and creates a single SQL SELECT statement to actually extract the information from your tables. You can see this SQL statement by selecting View ➪ SQL View from the Database menu. This action opens a new window named Query1: Select Query to display the actual SQL statement that was built. Figure 6-3 shows the statement that Access based on what you built with the example data in Figure 6-2. This is the same query in its written SQL format.

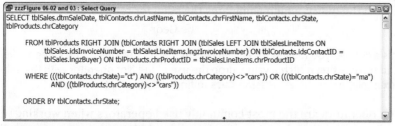

```
zzzFigure 06-02 and 03 : Select Query

SELECT tblSales.dtmSaleDate, tblContacts.chrLastName, tblContacts.chrFirstName, tblContacts.chrState,
tblProducts.chrCategory

    FROM tblProducts RIGHT JOIN (tblContacts RIGHT JOIN (tblSales LEFT JOIN tblSalesLineItems ON
        tblSales.idsInvoiceNumber = tblSalesLineItems.lngzInvoiceNumber) ON tblContacts.idsContactID =
        tblSales.lngzBuyer) ON tblProducts.chrProductID = tblSalesLineItems.chrProductID

    WHERE (((tblContacts.chrState)="ct") AND ((tblProducts.chrCategory)<>"cars")) OR (((tblContacts.chrState)="ma")
        AND ((tblProducts.chrCategory)<>"cars"))

    ORDER BY tblContacts.chrState;
```

Figure 6-3: The SQL window for the same query built in Figure 6-2. Notice that it contains a single OR statement and two AND statements (in the WHERE clause).

The SQL statement in Figure 6-3 has been separated by the author into a clearer way to read it. When you open your SQL window, you will see what appears to be one long multi-line statement with no breaks between it.

Cross-Reference

SQL statements in queries are covered in detail in Chapter 38.

Note

Sometimes you see a field name referred first by the table name and then by the field name, as shown in the SQL statement in Figure 6-3. When you see this kind of reference, it will have a dot (.) between the two names, such as Customer.[Customer Name]. This nomenclature tells you which table a field belongs to. This is especially critical when you're describing two fields that have the same name but are contained in different tables. In a multiple-table query, you see this format in the field list when you add a field to the QBE pane by clicking an empty column. You also see this format when you create a multiple table form by using the field list. The general format is Table Name.Field Name. If the field name or table name has spaces in it, you must surround the name with brackets [ ]; for example, tblSales.[Date of Sale] and tblContact.[Customer Last Name]. These two examples are for the purpose of demonstrating how you would enclose the field names with brackets.

Tip

We do not use spaces in table and field names; although many people do for better readability, it's really good idea to not use spaces at all. This way, you don't have to use brackets around your field or object names. For example, you can reference tblContact.[Customer Last Name] without a space between the names as tblContact.CustomerLastName—thus eliminating the need for using brackets. To do this, you need to create your table fields without using spaces.

If you build a mathematical formula for this query (not the SQL statement), it looks similar to this example:

(tblContacts.chrState = "CT" **AND** Not tblProducts. chrCategory = "Cars") **OR**
(tblContacts.chrState = "MA" **AND** Not tblProducts.chrCategory = "Cars")

You must enter the type of category (Not cars) example for each state line in the QBE pane, as shown in Figure 6-2. Later, you learn to use the And/Or operators in a Criteria: cell of the query, which eliminates the need for redundant entry of these fields.

Tip In this example, you looked for all vehicles that were not cars in the category field. To find records that match a value, drop the use of the Not operator with the value. For example, enter the expression **Cars** to find all types that are cars.

The And/Or operators are the most commonly used operators when working with complex criteria. The operators consider two different formulas (one on each side of the And/Or operators) and then determine individually whether they are True or False. Then the operators compare the results of the two formulas against each other for a logical True/False answer. For example, take the first And statement in the formula given in the preceding paragraph:

(tblContacts.chrState = "CT" **AND** Not tblProducts. chrCategory = "Cars")

The first half of the formula, tblContacts.chrState = "CT", converts to a True if the state is CT (False if a different state; Null if no state was entered in the field).

Then the second half of the formula, **Not** tblProducts. chrCategory = "Cars", is converted to a True if the Products Category is anything except Cars (False if Cars; Null if no Category was entered). Then the And compares the logical True/False from each side against the other side to give a resultant True/False answer.

Note A field has a Null value when it has no value at all; it is the lack of entry of information in a field. Null is neither True nor False; nor is it equivalent to all spaces or zero — it simply has no value. If you never enter a city name in the City field and just skip it, Access leaves the field empty. This state of emptiness is known as Null.

When the result of an And/Or is True, the overall condition is True, and the query displays those records meeting the True condition. Table 6-5 reviews the True and False conditions for each operator.

Notice that the And operator is True only when both sides of the formula are True, whereas the Or operator is True when either side of the formula is True. In fact, one side can be a Null value, and the Or operator will still be True if the other side is True. This is the difference between And/Or operators.

Table 6-5 Results of Logical Operators And/Or			
Left Side Is	Operator Is	Right Side Is	Resultant Answer Is
True	AND	True	True
True	AND	False	False
False	AND	True	False
False	AND	False	False
True	AND	Null	False
Null	AND	True	False
False	AND	Null	False
Null	AND	False	False
True	OR	True	True
True	OR	False	True
False	OR	True	True
True	OR	Null	True
Null	OR	True	True
False	OR	False	False
False	OR	Null	False
Null	OR	False	False

Using functions in select queries

When you work with queries, you may want to use built-in Access functions to display information. For example, you may want to display items such as:

✦ The day of the week (Sunday, Monday, and so forth) for Sales dates

✦ All customer names in uppercase

✦ The difference between two date fields

You can display all this information by creating calculated fields for the query. We discuss calculated fields in depth later in this chapter.

 Cross-Reference For more on Functions and their use in Forms, Reports, and Queries, refer to Chapter 20.

Referencing fields in select queries

When you work with a field name in queries, as you do with calculated fields or criteria values, you should enclose the field name in square brackets ([]). Access requires brackets around any field name that is in a criterion and around any field name that contains a space or punctuation. An example of a field name in brackets is the criterion [tblSales].[dtmSaleDate] + 30. You can find more examples like this later in the chapter.

 Caution If you omit the brackets ([]) around a field name in the criterion, Access may automatically places quotes around the field name and treat it as text instead of a field name.

Entering Single-Value Field Criteria

You'll encounter situations in which you want to limit the query records returned on the basis of a single field criterion, such as in these queries:

✦ Customer (buyer) information for customers living in the state of New York

✦ Sales of any motor homes

✦ Customers who bought anything in the month of January

Each of these queries requires a *single-value criterion*. Simply put, a single-value criterion is the entry of only one expression in a field. That expression can be example data, such as "NY," or a function, such as DatePart("m",[dtmSaleDate]) = 1. Criteria expressions can be specified for any data type: Text, Numeric, Date/Time, and so forth. Even OLE Object and Counter field types can have criteria specified.

 Cross-Reference For a full explanation of expressions, operators, identifiers, and literals, refer back to the earlier section of this chapter. For detailed explanation of functions, see Chapter 20.

 Note All the examples in this chapter rely on several tables: tblContacts, tblSales, tblSalesLineItems, and tblProducts. The CHAP06Start.mdb database contains the tables used in this chapter. The majority of these examples use only the tblContacts and tblSales tables.

Each series of steps in this chapter tells you which tables and fields make up the query. For most examples, you should clear all previous criteria. Each example focuses on the criteria line of the QBE pane. You can also view each figure to make sure you understand the correct placement of the criteria in each example. Only a few dynasets are shown, but you can follow along and view the data.

Entering character (Text or Memo) criteria

You use character criteria for Text or Memo data-type fields. These are either examples or data about the contents of the field. To create a text criterion to display customers who live in New York State, for example, follow these steps:

1. Open the tblContacts table in the Query design surface and add the First Name, Last Name, and State (chrFirstName, chrLastName, chrState) fields to the QBE pane.

2. Click the Criteria: cell for chrState field.

3. Type **NY** in the cell.

Your query should look similar to the query shown in Figure 6-4. Notice that only one table is open and only three fields are selected. You can click the Datasheet button to see the results of this query.

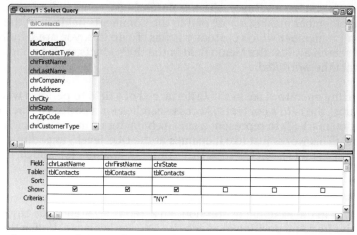

Figure 6-4: The Datasheet window showing the tblContacts table open. You see the example data NY in the Criteria row under the chrState field.

Tip   When specifying example-type criteria, it isn't necessary to match capitalization. Access defaults to case-insensitive when working with queries. Entering NY, ny, or nY provides the same results.

You don't have to enter an equal sign before the literal word *NY* because Access uses the equal operator as the default operator. To see all states except Ny, you must enter either the <> (not equal) or the Not operator before the word *NY*.

You also don't have to type quotes around the word *NY*. Access assumes that you are using an example literal *NY* and adds the quotes for you automatically.

Tip   If you type in quotation marks, you should use the double quotation mark to surround literals. Access normally uses the single quotation mark as a remark character in its programming language. However, when you use the single quotation mark in the Criteria: cell, Access interprets it as a double quotation mark.

The Like operator and wildcards

In previous sections, you worked with *literal* criteria. You specified the exact field contents for Access to find, which was "NY" in the previous example. Access used the literal to find the specific records. Sometimes, however, you know only a part of the field contents, or you may want to see a wider range of records on the basis of a pattern. For example, you may want to see all buyers information for those buyers who bought vehicles made in the 1950s (where descriptions begin with the characters *195*); so you need to check 1950, 1951, 1952, and so forth. Here's a more practical example: Suppose you have a Buyer who has purchased a couple of red cars in the last year. You remember making a note of it in the Comments field about the color, but you don't remember which customer it was. To do this, you are required to use a wildcard search against the Memo field in the tblProducts table to find any records that contain the word *Red*.

Access uses the string operator Like in the Criteria: cell of a field to perform wildcard searches against the field's contents. Access searches for a pattern in the field; you use the question mark (?) to represent a single character or the asterisk (*) for several characters. (This works just like filenames at the DOS level.) In addition to the two characters (?) and (*), Access uses three other characters for wildcard searches. Table 6-6 lists the wildcards that the Like operator can use.

The question mark (?) stands for any single character located in the same position as the question mark in the example expression. An asterisk (*) stands for any number of characters in the same position in which the asterisk is placed. Unlike the asterisk at DOS level, Access can use the asterisk any number of times in an example expression. The pound sign (#) stands for any single digit found in the same position as the pound sign. The brackets ([ ]) and the list they enclose stand for any single character that matches any one character of the list located within the brackets. Finally, the exclamation point (!) inside the brackets represents the Not word for the list — that is, any single character that does not match any character in the list within the brackets.

These wildcards can be used alone or in conjunction with each other. They can even be used several times within the same expression. The examples in Table 6-6 demonstrate how you can use the wildcards.

Table 6-6 Wildcards Used by the Like Operator	
Wildcard	**Purpose**
?	A single character (0-9, Aa-Zz)
*	Any number of characters (0 to n)
#	Any single digit (0-9)
[list]	Any single character in the list
[!list]	Any single character not in the list

To create an example using the Like operator, let's suppose that you want to find the record of a sports car with an exterior color of red. You know that the word *Red* is used in one of the records in the memFeatures field of the tblProducts table. To create the query, follow these steps:

1. Add the four tables: tblContacts, tblSales, tblSalesLineItems, and tblProducts.

2. Select the Last Name and First Name fields from the tblContacts table, and select the chrDescription and memFeatures fields from the tblProducts table to add the four fields to the QBE pane. (Although not necessary, you may want to set a sort order Ascending in the last name field and then first name field.)

3. Click the Criteria: cell of the memFeatures field.

4. Type *** red *** in the cell (be sure to put a space between the first asterisk and the 'R' and the last asterisk and the 'd', — in other words, asterisks before and after like this: [space]Red[space]).

Tip — In the above steps, you put a space before and after the word Red. If you did not, Access would find all words that have the word "red" in them, like aired, bored, credo, fired, geared, restored, and on and on. By placing a space before and after the word red, Access is being told to look for the word red only. Of course it would not find black/red or red/black with spaces around the word. If you need to find these, you could put them as additional criteria in the or cells.

When you click outside the Criteria: cell, Access automatically adds the operator Like and the quotation marks around the expression. Your query QBE pane should look similar to the one shown in Figure 6-5.

After creating this query, click on the datasheet button to look at the resultant dynaset. It should look similar to the one shown in Figure 6-6.

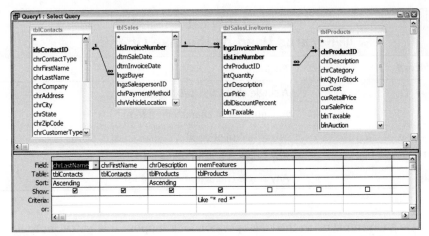

Figure 6-5: Using the Like operator with a select query in a Memo field. In this case, the query looks for the word *Red* in the memFeatures field.

Last Name	First Name	Description	Features
Bailey	Karen	1968 Rare Dodget Red 2D Sedan	MAKE DODGET EXTERIOR COLOR Silver MODEL CORONETE INTERIOR COLOR Red ENGINE 440
Bond	Ann	1965 Shelly Stunning Red Cobrat	1965 SHELLY-AMERICANA COBRAT. Completely restored. Stunning red with bl. flares. Side pipes, Halibrands, roll bar.
Bond	Ann	1968 Rare Dodget Red 2D Sedan	MAKE DODGET EXTERIOR COLOR Silver MODEL CORONETE INTERIOR COLOR Red ENGINE 440
Bright	John	1962 AALLFA Red Spidery 2000	1962 AALLFA 2000 "TOURING BODY" SPIDERY ID# AR1555555. A BEAUTIFUI WAS RESTORED AND FORMERLY OWNED BY NOTED COLLECTOR. Fire Er
Gleason	William	1962 AALLFA Red Spidery 2000	1962 AALLFA 2000 "TOURING BODY" SPIDERY ID# AR1555555. A BEAUTIFUI WAS RESTORED AND FORMERLY OWNED BY NOTED COLLECTOR. Fire Er
Gleason	William	1965 Shelly Stunning Red Cobrat	1965 SHELLY-AMERICANA COBRAT. Completely restored. Stunning red with bl. flares. Side pipes, Halibrands, roll bar.
Hayes	Karla	1965 Shelly Stunning Red Cobrat	1965 SHELLY-AMERICANA COBRAT. Completely restored. Stunning red with bl. flares. Side pipes, Halibrands, roll bar.
Mchugh	Dennis	1968 Rare Dodget Red 2D Sedan	MAKE DODGET EXTERIOR COLOR Silver MODEL CORONETE INTERIOR COLOR Red ENGINE 440

Record: 14 ◄ [1] ► ►I ►* of 8

Figure 6-6: The results of using the Like operator with a select query in a Memo field; the query looks for the word *Red* in the memFeatures field.

Tip

To make your query look like the one shown in Figure 6-6, you need to widen the Description and Features fields to see more of the contents and expand the number of lines to show for each record. To make each record more than one line, select the line between any two records in the record selector bar, as shown in Figure 6-6, between the first and second record. When the cursor becomes a small line with arrows pointing up and down, click and drag the field down to make each record show more lines.

Caution   The Like operator and its wildcards can be used only against three types of fields: Text, Memo, and Date. Using these with any other type can result in an error.

Clicking on the Datasheet button on the toolbar, you see that eight records match your query request — a red vehicle. Looking closer at the dynaset, you see that although there are eight records that match your criteria of the word red in the Features field, they do not all show red exterior color cars. In this case, you will have to physically examine each record to see if the exterior color of the vehicle is red (versus the interior). If you need to see records where the Features may show black/red or red/black, you will need to refine your search. These records are only those that have the standalone word red — [space]red[space]

Access automatically adds the Like operator and quotation marks if you meet these conditions:

✦ Your expression contains no spaces

✦ You use only the wildcards ?, *, and #

✦ You use brackets ([ ]) inside quotation marks " "

If you use the brackets without quotation marks, you must supply the operator Like and the quotation marks.

Using the Like operator with wildcards is the best way to perform pattern searches through Memo fields. It is just as useful in text and date fields as the examples in Table 6-7 demonstrate.

Table 6-7 shows several examples that can be used to search records in the tables of the Access Auto Auctions database.

Table 6-7
Using Wildcards with the Like Operator

Expression	Field Used In	Results of Criteria
Like "Ca*"	tblContacts.chrLastName	Finds all records of Contacts whose last name begin with 'Ca', examples: Calson and Casey
Like "* red *"	tblProducts.memFeatures	Finds all records with the word "red " anywhere within the Comments field
Like "C*"	tblSales.chrTaxLocation	Finds all records for Sales in states of a type that begin with the letter C

Continued

	Table 6-7 *(continued)*	
Expression	**Field Used In**	**Results of Criteria**
Like "9/*/2003"	tblSales.dtmSaleDate	Finds all records for the month of September 2003
Like "## South Main"	tblContacts.chrAddress	Finds all records for houses with house numbers between 10 and 99 inclusively; examples: 10, 22, 33, 51 on South Main
Like "[CDF]*"	tblContacts.chrCity	Finds all records for customers who live in any city with a name beginning with C, D, or F
Like "[!EFG]*"	tblContacts.chrCity	Finds all records for customers who do not live in any city that begins with the letters E, F, or G; all other city records are displayed

Specifying non-matching values

To specify a non-matching value, you simply use either the Not or the <> operator in front of the expression that you don't want to match. For example, you may want to see all Contacts (Buyers or Both buyers and sellers) and their sales for all states, but you want to exclude New York state. Follow these steps to see how to specify this non-matching value:

1. Open the tblContacts and tblSales tables.

Tip
If you only open the Contacts table, you will see both sellers and buyers. When you open both tables, only buyers are displayed because the tables are linked at a relationship level showing all sales records—thus eliminating the sellers.

2. Select the contacts chrLastName, chrFirstName, and chrState fields from the tblContacts table.

3. Click in the Criteria: cell of chrState.

4. Type **Not NY** in the cell. Access automatically places quotation marks around NY if you don't do so before you leave the field. You can also use <> instead of the word Not as in the figure.

The query should look similar to the one shown in Figure 6-7. The query selects all records *except* those for customers who live in the state of New York.

Note You can use the <> operator instead of Not in Step 4 of the previous instructions to exclude New York (NY). The resultant dynaset is the same with either operator. These two operators are interchangeable except with the use of the keyword Is. You cannot say Is <> Null. Rather, you must say Not Is Null or more accurately Is Not Null.

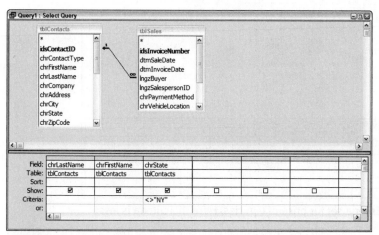

Figure 6-7: Using the Not operator in criteria. Entering **Not NY** in the State field displays all records except those where the State is NY (New York).

Entering numeric (Number, Currency, or Counter) criteria

You use numeric criteria with Number, Currency, or Counter data-type fields. You simply enter the numbers and the decimal symbol — if required — following the mathematical or comparison operator. For example, you may want to see all sales where the vehicle price was under USD $10,000 dollars. To create a query like this, follow these steps:

1. Start with a new query using the tblSalesLineItems and tblProducts tables.

2. Select the curPrice field from the tblSalesLineItems table, and chrDescription and chrCategory fields from the tblProducts table.

3. Click in the Sort: cell for curPrice.

4. Select Ascending from the pull-down menu.

5. Click in the Criteria: cell for curPrice.

6. Type **<10000** in the cell.

When you follow these steps, your query looks similar to the query shown in Figure 6-8. When working with numeric data, Access doesn't enclose the expression with quotes, as it does with string criteria.

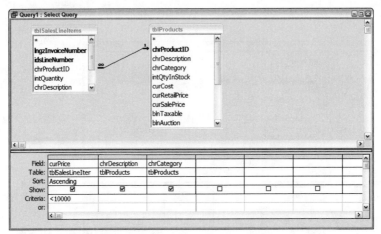

Figure 6-8: Criteria set for price of vehicles. Here the criteria is less than (<)10000.

If you run this query, the resulting dynaset should show 24 records under USD $10,000 sorted by price from USD $700.00 to $7,800.

Numeric fields are generally compared to a value string that uses comparison operators, such as less than (<), greater than (>), or equal to (=). If you want to specify a comparison other than equal, you must enter the operator as well as the value. Remember that Access defaults to equal when an operator is not specified in criteria. That is why you needed to specify less than (<) 10000 in the previous example query for vehicles under USD $10,000.

Working with Currency and Counter data in a query is exactly the same as working with Numeric data; you simply specify an operator and a numeric value.

Entering Yes/No (logic) criteria

Yes/No criteria are used with Yes/No type fields. The example data that you supply in the criteria can be for only Yes or No states. You can also use the Not and the <> operators to signify the opposite, but the Yes/No data also has a Null state that you may want to check for. Access recognizes several forms of Yes and No. Table 6-8 lists all the positive and negative values that you can use.

Thus, instead of typing Yes, you can type any of these in the Criteria: cell: On, True, Not No, <> No, <No, or -1.

Note A Yes/No field can have only three criteria states: Yes, No, and Null. Null only occurs when no default value was set in a table and the value has not yet been entered. Checking for "Is Null" displays only records with no value, and checking for "Is Not Null" always displays all Yes or No records. After a Yes/No field check box is checked (or checked and then de-selected), it can never be null. It must be either Yes or No (−1 or 0).

		Table 6-8				
		Positive and Negative Values Used in Yes/No Fields				
Yes	True	On	Not No	< > No	<No	−1
No	False	Off	Not Yes	< >Yes	>Yes	0

Entering a criterion for an OLE object

You can even specify a criterion for OLE objects: Is Not Null. For example, suppose you don't have pictures for all the vehicles and you want to view only those records that have a picture of the vehicle—that is, those in which the picture Is Not Null. You specify the Is Not Null criterion for the olePicture field of the tblProducts table. After you do this, Access limits the records to those that have a picture in them.

Although Is Not Null is the correct syntax, you can also type Not Null and Access supplies the Is operator for you.

Entering Multiple Criteria in One Field

In previous sections of this chapter, you worked with single-condition criteria on a single field. As you learned in those sections, you can specify single-condition criteria for any field type. In this section, you work with multiple criteria based on a single field. For example, you may be interested in seeing all records in which the Buyer comes from either New York, New Jersey, or Pennsylvania, or perhaps you want to view the records of all the vehicles that were sold during the first quarter of the year 2003.

The QBE pane has the flexibility to solve these types of problems. You can specify several criteria for one field or for several fields in a select query. Using multiple criteria, for example, you can determine which customers are from New York or New Jersey ("NY" or "NJ") or which vehicles were sold for the past 90 days (Between Date( ) And Date( ) - 90).

You use the And and the Or operators to specify several criteria for one field.

Understanding an Or operation

You use an Or operation in queries when you want a field to meet either of two conditions. For example, you may want to see all the records where the Customer lives in either NY or NJ. In other words, you want to see all records where a customer lives in New York, in New Jersey, or both (not physically possible—but assume a buyer could). The general formula for this operation is:

[chrState] = "NY" Or [chrState] = "NJ"

If either side of this formula is True, the resulting answer is also True. To clarify this point, consider these conditions:

✦ Customer 1 lives in NY—the formula is True.

✦ Customer 2 lives in NJ—the formula is True.

✦ Customer 3 lives in NY and NJ—the formula is True.

✦ Customer 4 lives in CT—the formula is False.

Specifying multiple values for a field using the Or operator

The Or operator is used to specify multiple values for a field. For example, you use the Or operator if you want to see all records of buyers who live in CT or NJ or NY. To do this, follow these steps:

1. Create a new query using the tblContacts and tblSales tables.

2. Select the Contact Name fields (First and Last Name) and State fields from the tblContact table and then select Sales date from the tblSales table.

3. Click in the Sort: cell of chrState.

4. Select Ascending from the pull-down menu.

5. Click in the Criteria: cell of chrState.

6. Type **CT Or NJ Or NY** in the cell.

Your QBE pane should resemble the one shown in Figure 6-9. Access automatically placed quotation marks around your example data—CT, NJ, and NY.

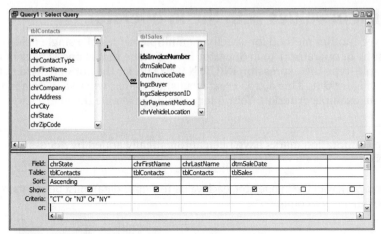

Figure 6-9: Using the Or operator. Notice the two Or operators under the chrState field—CT OR NJ OR NY.

Using the Or: cell of the QBE pane

Besides using the literal Or operator in a single statement on the Criteria row under the chrState field, you can supply individual criteria for the field on separate rows of the QBE pane. To do this, enter the first criterion example in the Criteria: cell of the field. Then enter the second criterion example in the Or: cell of the same field. Enter the next criterion in the cell directly beneath the Or: example; and continue entering examples vertically down the column. This is exactly equivalent to typing the Or operator between examples. Using the example in which you queried for state is NJ, NY, or CT, change your QBE pane to look like the one shown in Figure 6-10. Notice that each State abbreviation is on a separate row in the query.

Field:	chrState	chrFirstName	chrLastName	dtmSaleDate	
Table:	tblContacts	tblContacts	tblContacts	tblSales	
Sort:	Ascending				
Show:	☑	☑	☑	☑	☐
Criteria:	"CT"				
or:	"NJ"				
	"NY"				

Figure 6-10: Using the Or: cell of the QBE pane. You can place each bit of example data on its own row in the Or: cells.

Tip

Access allows up to nine Or: cells for each field. If you need to specify more Or conditions, use the Or operator between conditions (for example: CT Or NJ Or NY Or PA).

Using a list of values with the In operator

You can use yet another method for specifying multiple values of a single field. This method uses the In operator. The In operator finds a value that is one of a *list of values*. For example, type the expression **IN(CT, NJ, NY)** under the chrState field in the query used in Figure 6-10. This action creates a list of values, where any item in the list becomes an example criterion. Your query should resemble the query shown in Figure 6-11.

In this example, quotation marks have been automatically added by Access around CT, NJ, and NY.

Note   When you work with the In operator, each value (example data) must be separated from the others by a comma.

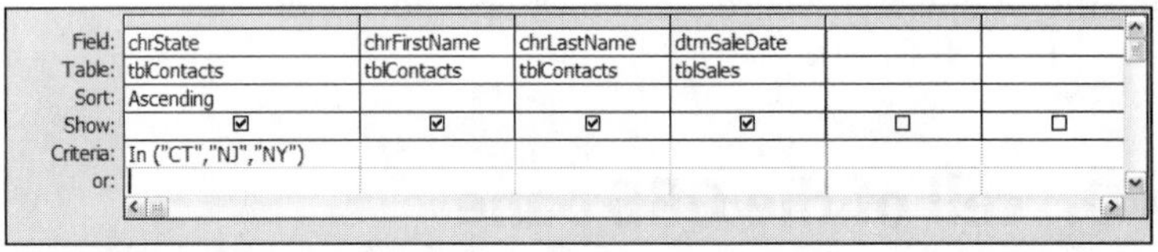

Field:	chrState	chrFirstName	chrLastName	dtmSaleDate		
Table:	tblContacts	tblContacts	tblContacts	tblSales		
Sort:	Ascending					
Show:	☑	☑	☑	☑	☐	☐
Criteria:	In ("CT","NJ","NY")					
or:						

Figure 6-11: Using the In operator to find all records for Buyer state being either CT, NJ, or NY.

Understanding an And query

You use And operators in queries when you want a field to meet both of two conditions that you specify. For example, you may want to see records of buyers that have purchased vehicles between October 1, 2003 and March 31, 2004. In other words, the sale had to have occurred during the last quarter of the year 2003 and first quarter of 2004. The general formula for this example is:

[dtmSaleDate] >= 10/1/2003 And [dtmSaleDate] <= 3/31/2004

Unlike the Or operator (which has several conditions under which it is True), the And operator is True only when both sides of the formula are True. When both sides are True, the resulting answer is also True. To clarify use of the And operator, consider these conditions:

✦ Sales date (9/22/2003) is not greater than 10/01/2003, but it is less than 3/31/2004 — the formula is False.

✦ Sales date (4/11/2004) is greater than 10/01/2003, but it is not less than 3/31/2004 — the formula is False.

✦ Sales date (11/22/2003) is greater than 10/01/2003, and it is less than 3/31/2004 — the formula is True.

Both sides of the operation must be True for the And operation to be True.

An And operation can be performed in several ways against a single field in Access.

Specifying a range using the And operator

The And operator is frequently used in fields that have Numeric or Date/Time data types. It is seldom used with Text data types, although it can be. For example, you may be interested in viewing all buyers whose names start with the letters *d*, *e*, or *f*. The And operator can be used here (>"Cz" and <"G"), although the Like operator is better (Like "[DEF]*"). Using an And operator with a single field sets a range of acceptable values in the field. Therefore, the key purpose of an And operator in a single field is to define a range of records to be viewed. For example, you can use the And operator to create a range criterion to display all buyers who have purchased vehicles between October 1, 2003 and March 31, 2004, inclusively. To create this query, follow these steps:

1. Create a new query using the tblContacts and tblSales tables.

2. Select the Contact Name fields (chrLastName and chrFirstName) from the tblContacts table, and select dtmSaleDate from the tblSales table.

3. Click in the Criteria: cell of dtmSaleDate.

4. Type **>= 10/1/2003 And <= 3/31/2004** in the cell.

The query should resemble the one shown in Figure 6-12. You can change the formula to >9/30/2003 And <4/1/2004 with identical results.

Field:	chrFirstName	chrLastName	dtmSaleDate		
Table:	tblContacts	tblContacts	tblSales		
Sort:					
Show:	☑	☑	☑	☐	☐
Criteria:			>=#10/1/2003# And <=#3/31/2004#		
or:					

Figure 6-12: Using the And operator with numeric fields. Notice that this query shows all records for sales during the last quarter of 2003 and the first quarter of 2004.

Using the Between...And operator

You can request a range of records from a single field by using another method — the Between...And operator. With the Between...And operator, you can find records that meet a range of values — for example, all Sales where the value of the vehicle was between USD $10,000 and USD $20,000. Using the example of sales between October 1, 2003 and March 31, 2004, create the query using the Between...And operator, as shown in Figure 6-13.

Field:	chrFirstName	chrLastName	dtmSaleDate		
Table:	tblContacts	tblContacts	tblSales		
Sort:					
Show:	☑	☑	☑	☐	☐
Criteria:			Between #10/1/2003# And #3/31/2004#		
or:					

Figure 6-13: Using the Between...And operator. The resulting datasheet will show the same 21 records as the query in Figure 6-12.

Caution   When you use the Between...And operator, the values entered in the Criteria field (in this example, 10/1/2003 and 3/31/2004) are (if they match) included in the resulting dynaset.

Searching for Null data

A field may have no contents for several reasons: For example, perhaps the value wasn't known at the time of data entry, or the person who did the data entry simply forgot to enter the information, or the field's information was removed. Access does nothing with this field; it simply remains an empty field. (A field is said to be *null* when it's empty.)

Logically, a Null is neither True nor False. A Null field is not equivalent to all spaces or to zero. A Null field simply has no value.

Access lets you work with Null value fields by means of two special operators:

   Is Null

   Is Not Null

You use these operators to limit criteria based on Null values of a field. Previously in this chapter, you learned that a Null value can be used to query for vehicles having a picture on file. In the next example, you look for Buyer records that don't specify Original Customer Date (dtmOrigCustDate). To create this query, follow these steps:

1. Create a new query using the tblContacts and tblSales tables.

2. Select the Buyer dtmOrigCustDate and Name fields from the tblContacts table, and select dtmSaleDate from the tblSales table.

3. Click in the Criteria: cell of dtmOrigCustDate.

4. Type **Is Null** in the cell.

Your query should look like the query shown in Figure 6-14. Select the Datasheet button to see that you have one record without a Customer Original Date — Larry Minkler. If you add a record in the database and don't enter a value in this field, that record shows in the resulting dynaset of this query as a null value.

Field:	dtmOrigCustDate	chrFirstName	chrLastName	dtmSaleDate		
Table:	tblContacts	tblContacts	tblContacts	tblSales		
Sort:						
Show:	☑	☑	☑	☑	☐	☐
Criteria:	Is Null					
or:						

Figure 6-14: Using the Is Null operator. If the database has any records with the dtmOrigCustDate field missing a value (the user clicked past the field), they will be shown as blanks in the dynaset when the datasheet button is pressed. Their actual value is defined as Null — or no value entered (versus a blank space).

Tip   When using the Is Null and Is Not Null operators, you can enter Null or Not Null and Access automatically adds the Is to the Criteria field.

Entering Criteria in Multiple Fields

Previously in this chapter, you worked with single and multiple criteria specified in single fields. In this section, you work with criteria across several fields. When you want to limit the records based on several field conditions, you do so by setting criteria in each of the fields that will be used for the scope. Suppose you want to search for all Sales of Cars in Kansas (KS). Or, suppose you want to search for SUVs in Massachusetts or Connecticut. Or, suppose you want to search for all SUVs in Massachusetts or Minivans in Connecticut. Each of these queries requires placing criteria in multiple fields and on multiple lines.

Using And and Or across fields in a query

To use the And operator and the Or operator across fields, place your example or pattern data in the Criteria: cells (for the And operator) and the Or: cells of one field relative to the placement in another field. When you want to use And between two fields, you place the example or pattern data across the same row. When you want to use Or between two fields, you place the example or pattern data on different rows in the QBE pane. Figure 6-15 shows the QBE pane and a conceptual representation of this placement.

Field:	Expr1: [Field 1]	Expr2: [Field 2]	Expr3: [Field 3]	Expr4: [Field 4]	Expr5: [Field 5]	
Table:						
Sort:						
Show:	☑	☑	☑	☑	☑	☐
Criteria:	"Ex1"	"Ex2"	"Ex3"			
or:				"Ex4"		
					"Ex5"	

Figure 6-15: The QBE pane with And/Or criteria between fields using the Criteria: and or: rows

Figure 6-15 shows that if the only criteria fields present were Ex1, Ex2, and Ex3 (with Ex4 and Ex5 removed), all three would be And-ing between the fields. If only the criteria fields Ex4 and Ex5 were present (with Ex1, Ex2, and Ex3 removed), the two would be Or-ing between fields. As it is, the selection for this example is (EX1 AND EX2 AND EX3) OR EX4 OR EX5. Therefore, this query is True if a value matches any of these criteria:

> EX1 AND EX2 AND EX3 (all must be True) or
>
> EX4 (this can be True and either/both of the other two lines can be False) or
>
> EX5 (this can be True and either/both of the other two lines can be False)

As long as one of these three criteria are True, the record is selected.

Specifying And criteria across fields of a query

The most common type of condition operator between fields is the And operator. You use the And operator to limit records on the basis of several field conditions. For example, you may want to view only the records of buyers who live in the state of Massachusetts and bought Chevys. To create this query, follow these steps:

1. Create a new query using the four tables, tblContacts, tblSales, tblSalesLineItems, and tblProducts.

2. Select the Contacts Names and State fields from the tblContacts table and then select the Description field from the tblProducts table.

3. Click the Criteria: cell of chrState.

4. Type **MA** in the cell.

5. Click the Criteria: cell for chrDescription.

6. Type **Like *chevy*** in the cell.

Your query should look like the query shown in Figure 6-16. Notice that both example data are in the same row. If you look at the datasheet, you will see seven records that match the criteria one truck and six cars.

Because you placed data for both criteria on the same row, Access interprets this as an And operation — where both conditions must be True. If you click on the Datasheet button, you see that you only have seven records in the resulting dynaset.

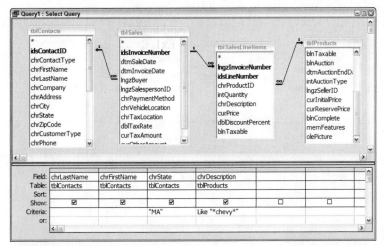

Figure 6-16: An And operator performing a mathematical operation based on two fields—MA in chrState and Like *chevy* in the chrDescription field.

Specifying Or criteria across fields of a query

Although the Or operator isn't used across fields as commonly as the And operator, occasionally Or is very useful. For example, you may want to see records of any vehicles bought by contacts in Connecticut or you may want to see records on SUVs, regardless of the state they live in. To create this query, follow these steps:

1. Use the query from the previous example, emptying the two criteria cells first.

2. Add the field chrCategory from the tblProducts table.

3. Click the Criteria: cell of chrState.

4. Type **CT** in the cell.

5. Click in the Or: cell for chrCategory (one line below the CT example).

6. Type **SUV** in the cell.

Your query should resemble the query shown in Figure 6-17. Notice that the criteria entered this time are not in the same row for both fields.

When you place the criterion for one field on a different line from the criterion for another field, Access interprets this as an Or between the fields. If you click on the Datasheet button, you see that you now have 28 records in the resulting dynaset. This is because you gave a criteria that stated "Show me all records where the State is CT," or the Category of vehicle is "SUV." Either condition is True—thus, more than one record meets the condition.

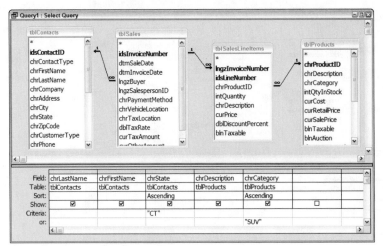

Figure 6-17: Using the Or operator between fields. Either condition must be True — either from the State of CT or the Type of vehicle is SUV.

Using And and Or together in different fields

After you've worked with And and Or separately, you're ready to create a query using And and Or in different fields. In the next example, you want to display information for all Buyers of SUVs in Connecticut and all Buyers of Trucks in New York. To create this query, follow these steps:

1. Use the query from the previous example, emptying the two criteria cells first.

2. Click the Criteria: cell of chrState.

3. Type **CT** in the cell.

4. Click the Or: cell of chrState.

5. Type **NY** in the cell.

6. Click the Criteria: cell for chrCategory.

7. Type **SUV** in the cell.

8. Click the Or: cell for chrCategory.

9. Type **TRUCKS** in the cell.

Figure 6-18 shows how the query should look. Notice that CT and SUV are in the same row; NY and TRUCKS are in another row. This query represents two Ands across fields, with an Or in each field.

Field:	chrLastName	chrFirstName	chrState	chrDescription	chrCategory		
Table:	tblContacts	tblContacts	tblContacts	tblProducts	tblProducts		
Sort:			Ascending		Ascending		
Show:	☑	☑	☑	☑	☑	☐	
Criteria:			"CT"		"SUV"		
or:			"NY"		"TRUCKS"		

Figure 6-18: Using Ands and Ors across fields to select all SUVs for Buyers that live in CT or all TRUCKs whose Buyers live in NY.

Clicking on the datasheet button should display eight records — four SUV records for CT and four truck records for NY.

A complex query on different lines

Suppose you want to view all records of Chevys that were bought in the first six months of 2003 where the buyer lives in MA, or any vehicle from buyers in California. In this example, you use three fields for setting criteria: tblContact.chrState, tblSales.dtmSaleDate, and tblProducts.chrDescription. Here's the formula for setting these criteria:

((tblSales.dtmSaledate Between #1/1/2003# And #6/30/2003#) AND (tblProducts.chrDescription = Like "*Chevy*") AND (tblContact.chrState = "MA")) OR (tblContact.chrState = "CA")

You can display this data by creating the query shown in Figure 6-19.

Field:	dtmSaleDate	chrLastName	chrFirstName	chrState	chrDescription	chrCategory		
Table:	tblSales	tblContacts	tblContacts	tblContacts	tblProducts	tblProducts		
Sort:				Ascending		Ascending		
Show:	☑	☑	☑	☑	☑	☑	☐	☐
Criteria:	Between #1/1/2(			"MA"	Like "*chevy*"			
or:				"CA"				

Figure 6-19: Using multiple Ands and Ors across fields. This is a rather complex Select query that can be built.

Note   You can enter the date 1/1/03 instead of 1/1/2003, and Access processes the query exactly the same. All Microsoft Office products process two-digit years from 00 to 30 as 2000 to 2030, while all two-digit dates between 31 and 99 are processed as 1931 to 1999.

Creating a New Calculated Field in a Query

Fields in a query are not limited to the fields from the tables in your database. You can also create *calculated fields* to use in a query. For example, you can create a calculated field named *Discount Amount* that displays the result of multiplying the value of the Discount Percent (dblDiscountPercent) times the Price (curPrice) in the tblSalesLineItem table.

To create this calculated field, follow these steps:

1. Create a new query using the tblContacts, tblSales, tblSalesLineItems, and tblProducts tables.

2. Select the Buyer Name fields (chrLastName and chrFirstName) from the tblContacts table; and the curPrice, dblDiscountPercent fields from the tblSalesLineItems table.

3. Click the first empty Field: cell.

4. Type the following **Discount Amt: tblSalesLineItems.curPrice * tblSalesLineItems.dblDiscountPercent** and click in another cell.

Your query should look like the one shown in Figure 6-20. The name of the calculated field is now "discount amount." If you didn't type the name in Step 4 above, Expr1: precedes the calculation. Notice that the Discount Amt formula does not completely show in Figure 6-20, however, it should match the formula entered in Step 4 above.

Note   For two reasons, a calculated field has a name (supplied either by the user or by an Access default). The name is needed as a label for the datasheet column, and the name is necessary for referencing the field in a form, a report, or another query.

Tip   To see the entire contents of the field cell, you can either drag the field until it is all visible or you can press the Shift+F2 keys to open the Zoom Window.

Notice that the general format for creating a calculated field is as follows:

Calculated Field Name: Expression to build calculated field

Field:	chrLastName	chrFirstName	chrDescription	curPrice	dblDiscountPercent	Discount Amt: tblSalesLineItems.curPr
Table:	tblContacts	tblContacts	tblProducts	tblSalesLineIte	tblSalesLineItems	
Sort:						
Show:	☑	☑	☑	☑	☑	☑
Criteria:						
or:						

Figure 6-20: A calculated field, Discount Amount, was created using two fields from the tblSalesLineItems table.

✦   ✦   ✦

Working with External Data

So far, you have worked with data in Access tables found in the database container that is open. In this chapter, you explore the use of data from other types of files. You learn to work with data from database, spreadsheet, HTML, and text-based files. After describing the general relationship between Access and external data, this chapter explains the major methods of working with external data: linking and importing/exporting.

This chapter will use the database named CHAP07Start. mdb as well as several other files (Chap07Link.mdb, CONTACTS.DBF, CONTACTS.DBT, Names.txt, SALES.DB, SALESLINEITEMS.TXT, CUSTOMERTYPES.HTML, Contacts Fixed.txt, and PRODUCTS.XLS) that you will use for linking. If you have not already copied these files onto your machine from the CD, you will need to do so now. After you have completed this chapter, your database should resemble the one in CHAP07End.mdb.

To use the final database, Chap07End.mdb, you will need to run the Linked Table Manager to reestablish valid links for all the tables. Using the Linked table manager is discussed later in this chapter in the "Viewing or changing information for linked tables" section.

Access and External Data

Exchanging information between Access and another program is an essential capability in today's database world. Information is usually stored in a wide variety of application programs and data formats. Access (like many other products) has its own native file format, designed to support referential integrity and provide support for rich data types, such as OLE objects.

Most of the time, this format is sufficient; occasionally, however, you need to move data from one Access database file to another, or even to or from a different software program's format.

Types of external data

Access has the capability to use and exchange data among a wide range of applications. For example, you may need to get data from other database files (such as FoxPro, dBASE, or Paradox files) or obtain information from an SQL Server, Oracle, or a text file. Access can move data among several categories of applications:

✦ Other Windows applications

✦ Macintosh applications (Foxbase, FoxPro, Excel)

✦ Spreadsheets

✦ PC database management systems

✦ Server-based database systems (SQL Server)

✦ Text and/or other mainframe files

Methods of working with external data

Often you will need to move data from another application or file into your Access database, or vice-versa. You may need to obtain information you already have in an external spreadsheet file. You can reenter all the information by hand — or have it imported into your database. Perhaps you need to put information from your Access tables into Paradox files. Again, you can reenter all the information into Paradox by hand or have the information exported to the Paradox table. Access has tools that enable you to move data from a database table to another table or file. It could be a table in Access, dBASE, or Paradox; it could be an Excel spreadsheet file. In fact, Access can exchange data with more than 15 different file types, including the following:

✦ Access database objects (all types, all versions)

✦ dBASE III+, IV, and 5

✦ FoxPro (all types using the ODBC drivers)

✦ Paradox 3.x, 4.x, 5.0, 7, and 8

✦ Text files (ANSI and ASCII; DOS or OS/2; delimited and fixed-length)

✦ Lotus WK1, WK3, and WJ2 (DOS)

✦ Excel 3, 4, 5-7, 97-2002

✦ ODBC databases (Microsoft SQL Server, Sybase Server, Oracle Server, and other ODBC 1.1-compliant databases)

✦ HTML tables, lists, documents

✦ XML documents

✦ Outlook and Outlook Express

✦ Exchange documents

✦ Microsoft IIS 1 and 2

✦ Sharepoint Team Services

✦ Microsoft Active Server Pages

✦ Microsoft Word Merge documents

✦ Rich Text Format documents

Access can work with these external data sources in several ways: linking, importing, and exporting. Table 7-1 lists and describes each method.

Table 7-1 Methods of Working with External Data	
Method	**Description**
Link	Creates a link to a table in another Access database or links to the data from a different database format
Import	Copies data from a text file, another Access database, or another application's format into an Access table
Export	Copies data from an Access table *to* a text file, another Access database, or another application's format

Note   Open Database Connectivity, or ODBC, is a standard method of sharing data between databases and programs. They use the Structured Query Language, or SQL, to manipulate the external data.

Should you link to or import data?

As Table 7-1 shows, you can work with data from other sources in two ways: linking or importing. Both methods enable you to work with the external data. There is a distinct difference between the two methods:

✦ Linking uses the data in its current file format (such as a dBASE, Paradox, or Excel file).

✦ Importing makes a copy of the external data and brings the copy into the Access table.

Each method has clear advantages and disadvantages.

When to link to external data

Linking in Access enables you to work with the data in another application's format — thus sharing the file with the existing application. If you leave data in another database format, Access can actually make changes to the table while the original application is still using it. This capability is useful when you want to work with data in Access that other programs also need to work with. For example, you might need to obtain updated personnel data from a dBASE file (maintained in an existing networked dBASE application) so that you can print a monthly report in Access. Another example is when you use Access as a front end for your SQL database — you can link to an SQL table and update the data directly to the server, without having to "batch upload" it later.

If you plan on using a table from another Microsoft Access database that is shared on a network, it is a good idea to simply link to it rather than import it. If another application will continue to be used to update and work with data in an external table (like in another format — dBASE or Paradox), it is best to link to it.

You can link to the following types of data in Access: another Access table (mdb, mda, mde), Excel spreadsheets, Exchange documents, Outlook documents, Paradox files, Text files, HTML Documents, dBASE files (III, 4 or 5), SharePoint Team Services, and ODBC databases.

Caution
Access 2003 has the capability to link to HTML tables and text tables for read-only access. You can use and look at tables in HTML or text format; however, the tables cannot be updated nor records added to them using Access. Also, if you are working with Paradox files and they do not have a primary key field defined (a .PX file associated with the .DB table), you will only be able to read the data — not change it.

The biggest disadvantage of working with linked tables is that you lose the internal capability of Access to enforce referential integrity between tables (unless you are linked to an Access database).

When to import external data

Access cannot link to certain file formats; these include Lotus 1-2-3 spreadsheet files. If you need to work with data from formats that cannot be linked to, you must import it.

Importing in Access enables you to physically bring an external table or data source into a new Access table. By doing this, Access will automatically convert data from the external format and copy it into Access. You can even import data objects into another Access database (rather than the one currently open) or Access project. If you know that you will use your data in Access only, you should import it. Generally, Access works faster with its own tables.

Of course, importing data means that you have significantly increased the storage space required for that particular data, because it now resides in two different files on the storage device.

Working with Other Access Databases

Access can open only one database at a time; therefore, you can't work directly with a table in a different database. Even so, if you need to work with tables or other Access objects (such as forms and queries) from another Access database, you don't have to close the current one. Instead, simply import or link the object in the other database to your current database. You'll be able to view or edit data directly in more than one database table.

Note   Because importing makes another copy of the data, you may want to erase the old file after you import the copy into Access. Sometimes, however, you won't want to erase it. For example, the data may be sales figures from a Lotus spreadsheet still in use. In cases such as this, simply maintain the duplicate data and accept that storing it will require more space.

One of the principal reasons to import data is to customize it to meet your needs. After a table has been imported, you can modify the structure and data types, and assign table-based rules for the table. You can specify a primary key, change field names (up to 64 characters), and set other field properties.

With linked tables, on the other hand, you are restricted to setting very limited field properties. For example, you cannot specify a primary key or assign a data entry rule (like only accept a date of birth less than today), which means that you can't enforce integrity against the linked table.

Note   When you link to a table in another Access database, you cannot do everything you can do with tables in the primary database from the currently open database. For instance, you cannot define a primary key or enforce referential integrity. However, if all the tables you want to work with are in an external Access database, you can open that database and specify all the table properties you wish to set: defining a primary key, defining relationships between tables, setting referential integrity between tables, changing a data type, specifying default values or validation rules, or even creating new indexes.

Data in unsupported programs

Although uncommon, there may be times that you need to work with data from a program that is not stored in the supported external database or file format. In cases such as this, the programs usually can export or convert their data in one of the formats recognized by Access. To use the data in these programs, export it to a format recognized by Access and then import it into Access. Most applications can export to dBASE file format. If the dBASE format is not available, most programs, even those on different operating systems, can export data to delimited or fixed-width text files, which you can then import into Access. When exporting to text files, you will lose any indexes associated with the tables.

Automating import operations

If you will be importing data from the same source frequently, you can automate the process by creating a macro or a Visual Basic for Applications procedure. This can be very helpful for those times when you have to import data from an external source on a regular schedule or you have complex requirements that must be met for importing the data.

Linking External Data

As the database market continues to grow, the need to obtain information from many different sources will escalate. If you have information captured in an ODBC SQL Server table or a Paradox table, you don't want to reenter the information from these tables into Access. Ideally, you want to open the table and use the information in its native format, without having to copy it or write a translation program to access it. For many companies today, this capability of accessing information from one database format while working in another is a primary goal.

Copying or translating data from one application format to another is both time-consuming and costly. The time it takes can mean the difference between success and failure. Therefore, you want a heterogeneous environment between your DBMSs and the data. Access provides this environment through linking tables.

Access can directly link to several database management system (DBMS) tables individually or simultaneously. After an external file is linked, Access builds and stores a link to the table. As pointed out previously, Access can link to other Access database tables; to non-Access database tables such as dBASE, FoxPro, and Paradox; and to non-database tables such as spreadsheets, HTML tables, and text tables. You can also split an Access database into separate databases, for easier use in a multi-user or client-server environment.

Types of database management systems

Access enables you to connect, or link, to several different DBMSs, directly accessing information stored in them. Access supports the following database systems:

- ✦ Other Access database tables
- ✦ dBASE (versions III, IV, and 5)
- ✦ FoxPro (via the FoxPro ODBC driver)
- ✦ Paradox (versions 3.0, 4.x, 5.x, and 7)
- ✦ Microsoft SQL Server, Sybase Server, Oracle, or any ODBC-aware database

You can link to any of these table types, individually or mixed together. If you link to an external file, Access displays the filename in the Database Tables window (just as it does for other Access tables), but the icon linked with the table will be different. It starts with an arrow pointing from left to right and points to an icon. An arrow pointing to a table icon tells you that it's an Access table, an arrow to a dB icon tells you that it's a dBASE table, and so on. Figure 7-1 shows several linked in the list, which are all external tables. These tables are linked to the current database. Notice that all the linked tables have an icon with an arrow. (The icon clues you in to the type of file that is linked.)

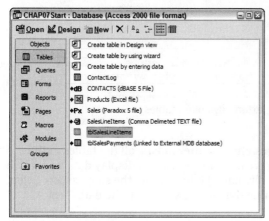

Figure 7-1: Linked tables in an Access database. Notice that each linked table has a graphic right arrow and another symbol for an icon.

In Figure 7-1, the arrows that appear to the left of some of the table names indicate linked tables. In addition to the link arrow indicator, you can tell by their icon which type of file they are linked to. For instance, Excel has the graphic X symbol in a box, Paradox has the Px symbol, dBASE tables have the dB symbol, and a Text file has a Notebook icon.

After you link a table to your Access database, you can use it as you would any other table. You can query against it, link another table to it, and so on. For example, Figure 7-2 shows a query designed using several linked tables: Contacts (from a dBase 5 table), Sales (from a Paradox table), SalesLineItems (from a comma-delimited text file), and Products (from an Excel file). Your application does not have to use Access tables at all; you can just as easily link to the Paradox and FoxPro tables.

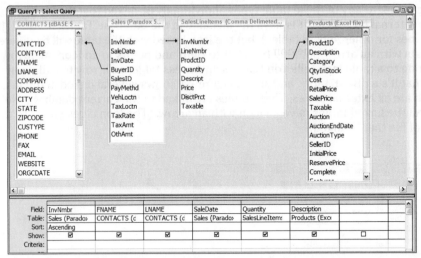

Figure 7-2: A query designed using externally linked tables.

This query will be built later in this chapter after linking all the tables in the CHAP07Start database. After it is created and run, it will display data from all the tables, both internally and externally linked information, the same as any Select query. Figure 7-3 shows the resulting dynaset as viewed in the datasheet.

Query1 : Select Query

InvNmbr	FNAME	LNAME	SaleDate	Quantity	Description
1	John	Jones	1/15/2003		
2	William	Gleason	2/27/2003		
3	John	Bright	2/24/2003		
4	Dennis	Mchugh	4/24/2003	1	1960 Chevy Pickup
4	Dennis	Mchugh	4/24/2003	1	1957 Chevy Sedan
4	Dennis	Mchugh	4/24/2003	1	1950 Fordman Coupe
4	Dennis	Mchugh	4/24/2003	1	2002 Olds SUV
4	Dennis	Mchugh	4/24/2003	1	2003 Fordman T-150 Regular Cab
5	Brandon	Aley	5/24/2003	1	1965 Shelly Stunning Red Cobrat
5	Brandon	Aley	5/24/2003	1	1962 AALLFA Red Spidery 2000
6	Larry	Calson	6/1/2003	1	1971 Pontanic Red Converible
6	Larry	Calson	6/1/2003	1	2001 Collectors Chevy Corvet
7	Karl	Johnson	7/15/2003	1	1940 Classic Antique Convertible
7	Karl	Johnson	7/15/2003	1	1967 Shelly Stunning Red Muscle Car
7	Karl	Johnson	7/15/2003	1	1957 Chevy Sedan
8	Joann	Smith	8/25/2003	1	2001 Collectors Chevy Corvet
9	Peter	Spindler	8/26/2003	1	1988 Fordman T350 Bucket Truck
10	Debbie	Casey	9/25/2003	1	1994 Fordman XLP Ext
10	Debbie	Casey	9/25/2003	1	1998 Fordman Explorer XLP
11	Casper	Krammer	9/30/2003	1	2001 Sportster
12	Harry	Bush	12/13/2003	1	1967 Shelly Stunning Red Muscle Car
13	John	Jones	12/12/2003	1	1999 Dodgie Dakota Sport
14	John	Bright	2/25/2004	1	2001 Sportster
15	Karla	Hayes	2/25/2004	1	1973 Rare Popup Hard sided Indian Camper
16	Brandon	Aley	9/1/2003	1	1996 CADDY DEVILLE SLX
17	Harry	Bush	9/6/2003	1	1962 AALLFA Red Spidery 2000
18	Matt	Sakes	9/30/2003	1	1940 Classic Antique Convertible
19	Paul	Grattie	10/15/2003	1	1957 Chevy Sedan

Record: 1 of 83

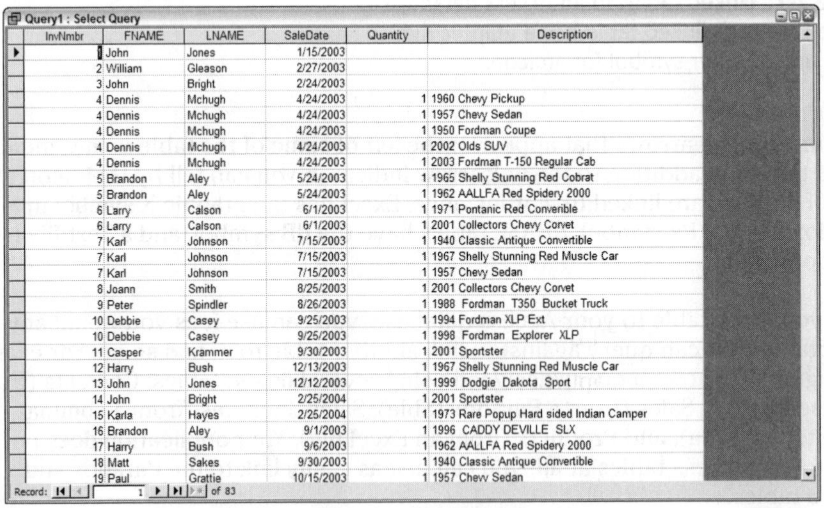

Figure 7-3: The datasheet view of externally linked data.

In Figure 7-3, the column heading names come from the field names in the underlying external tables. For instance, the second column and third column names, FNAME and LNAME, come from the underlying field name in the dBASE 5 table Contacts. The Description field name comes from the Excel table, and the first field, InvNumb, comes from the Paradox table named Sales. You can make the names more understandable by assigning a new name in the QBE pane of the query when you are designing it.

Note After you link an external table to an Access database, you cannot move the table to another drive or directory. Access does not actually bring the file into the MDB file; it maintains the link via the filename and the drive: path. If you move the external table, you have to update the link using the Linked Table Manager, explained in the "Viewing or changing information for linked tables" section later in this chapter.

Linking to other Access database tables

When you work with an Access database, normally you create every table you want to use in it. If the table exists in another Access database, however, you can link to the table in the other Access database (rather than re-creating it and duplicating its data). You may, for example, want to link to another Access table that is on a network or on the same computer.

After you link to another Access table, you use it just as you use another table in the open database. To link to the tblSalesPayments table in the Chap07Link database from the Chap07Start.mdb database file, follow these steps:

1. Open the Chap07Start.mdb database.

2. Select File ➪ Get External Data ➪ Link Tables... (or right-click anywhere in the Tables container and select Link Tables ... from the menu). Access opens the Link dialog box, as shown in Figure 7-4.

   Using the Link Tables dialog box, you can select the.MDB file you want to link to. You can also change the type of files displayed in the Link dialog box; it can link to any type of external data. Though the default is to show only Access files (.MDB), you can link to any of the supported file types.

3. Find and select the Chap07Link.MDB file in the dialog box. You may have to search for a different drive or directory.

4. Double-click the Chap07Link.MDB file (or select it and click the Link button). Access will close the dialog box and display the Link Tables dialog box.

   The Link Tables dialog box enables you to select one or more tables from the database selected (in this case, Chap07Link).

5. Select tblSalesPayments and click OK. Double-clicking the table name will not do anything—to select it, you must highlight it and then click OK.

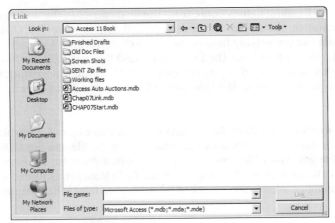

Figure 7-4: The Link dialog box opened for selecting which external table or .MDB to link to. The default file type is Microsoft Access.

After you link the tblSalesPayments table from the Chap07Link database, Access returns to the Database window and shows you that the table is now linked to your database. Figure 7-5 shows the tblSalesPayments table linked to the current database. Notice the arrow on the tblSalesPayements table's icon; it shows that the table has been linked from another source.

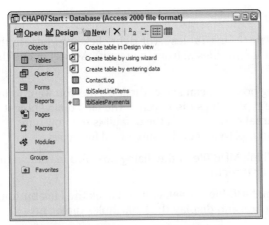

Figure 7-5: The Database window with the tblSalesPayments table added. Its table icon has a right-pointing arrow to the table.

Tip   You can link more than one table at a time by selecting each table before you click the OK button. You can also use the Select All button to select all the tables.

Linking to dBASE databases (tables)

You can link to DBF files. As with other Access database tables, after a dBASE file is linked, you can view and edit data in the DBF format.

dBASE (like FoxPro) saves tables in individual files with the extension DBF. In xBASE, these DBF files are called databases. In Access, however, a table is equivalent to an xBASE database. (Access considers a database a complete collection of all tables and other related objects.) To maintain consistency in terminology, this book considers xBASE databases to mean the same thing as dBASE or FoxPro tables.

Access and dBASE indexes

When you link a dBASE file, you can also tell Access to use one or more index files (NDX and MDX). The use of these indexes will improve performance of the link between dBASE and Access.

Caution

Microsoft has created dBASE ISAM drivers for Microsoft Jet 4.0 that do not require the installation of the Borland Database Engine (BDE), as in previous versions of Access, to provide full read/write access to dBASE files. The default ISAM drivers that ship with Microsoft Data Access Component (MDAC) 2.1 and later only enable read-only access to dBASE files unless the BDE is installed. To obtain these ISAM drivers that will give you full read/write access to dBASE files, you must contact Technical Support at Microsoft, and they will send them to you. You can also download the updated version of Microsoft Jet 4.0 from Microsoft's download center at www.microsoft.com/download/. At the site, select Keyword search, enter the words "Jet 4.0" in the keyword entry field, select your operating system, and click the Find It button to find the correct drivers. If you would prefer to use the BDE drivers, you can download them from http://info.borland.com/devsupport/. Then choose BDE (Borland Database Engine) to jump to the correct link (current version is 5.2) and click on the download link for version 5.2. If you are using BDE for linking to dBASE 5 (Visual dBASE) files, you should not use BDE version 5.x because it is not certified for use with dBASE 5 files. You will need to download two older versions onto your machine. You will have to download these files: the BDE 4.5x (which will only update an older version), and an older version (BDE 3.5), which is found via a hyperlink on the current version page at the bottom.

If you inform Access of the associated index files, Access will update the indexes every time it changes the DBF file. By linking a DBF file and its associated indexes, Access can link to DBFs in real time in a network environment. Access recognizes and enforces the automatic record-locking feature of dBASE as well as the file and record locks placed with xBASE commands and functions.

Caution

You should always tell Access about any indexes associated with the database. If you don't, it will not update them; dBASE or FoxPro will have unexpected problems if their associated index files are not updated.

When you tell Access to use one or more associated indexes (NDX, MDX) of a dBASE, Access maintains information about the fields used in the index tags in a special information file. This file has the same name as the dBASE file with an INF extension.

If you link a dBASE file and associated indexes, Access must have access to the index files in order to link the table. If you delete or move the index files or the Access INF file, you will not be able to open the linked DBF file.

Linking to an xBASE table

Linking to dBASE tables works the same. For example, to link the dBASE V table Contacts.DBF and its associated memo file (DBT), follow these steps:

1. Open the Chap07Start database and select File ⇨ Get External Data ⇨ Link Tables.

2. In the Link dialog box, select Files of type: dBASE 5. Access displays the dBASE 5 DBF files only.

3. Double-click Contacts.DBF in the Link Dialog box. (The associated memo file Contacts.DBT is linked automatically.)

4. Access activates the Select Index Files box and displays all NDX and MDX files if there are any index files present.

   There are no indexes for this table, so the Select Index Files dialog box will not display.

   If index files are present, you would select the appropriate .MDX or .NDX file and click the Select button.

   Access will display a dialog box that informs you that it has added the index .MDX.

   Then, if there is an index, you click the OK button to return to the Select Index Files dialog box.

 Note   If there are any other indexes to associate with this table, you select them here. If there were no indexes associated with this table, you would simply close this dialog box without selecting an index.

   When all indexes are selected, you click the Close button.

   If there is more than one index selected or a Multiple Index file (MDX) is selected with more than one index associated with the table, Access displays another, smaller, dialog box that is titled "Select Unique Record Identifier." This is talking about the primary key field. You would select this field and click the OK button.

5. Access then displays a dialog box that informs you that it has successfully linked 'Contacts.'

6. Click the OK button to return to the Link dialog box.

You are returned to this dialog box so that you can continue to select additional tables to link to.

7. Click the Close button to finish linking the Contacts dBASE file. Access displays the Database window with the file Contacts.dbf linked as shown in Figure 7-6.

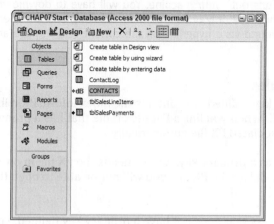

Figure 7-6: The dBASE table Contacts.dbf linked inside the Access database.

Note   You can cancel linking at any time by clicking the Cancel button in the Select File dialog box before you select a table.

When you add index files, Access automatically creates and updates an Access information file. This file contains information about the index and associated dBASE or FoxPro file, has the same name, and ends in the extension INF.

Linking to Paradox tables

You can link to Paradox .DB files in either Paradox 3.x, 4.x, 5.x, or 7 format. After a Paradox file is linked, you can view and edit data just like an Access database table.

Caution   Microsoft has created Paradox ISAM drivers for Microsoft Jet 4.0 that do not require the installation of the Borland Database Engine (BDE) as in previous versions of Access to provide full read/write access to Paradox files. The default ISAM drivers that ship with Microsoft Data Access Component (MDAC) 2.1 and later, only enable read-only access to dBASE files unless the BDE is installed. To obtain these ISAM drivers that will give you full read/write access to Paradox files, you must contact Technical Support at Microsoft and they will send them to you. You can also download the updated version of Microsoft Jet 4.0 from Microsoft's download center at www.microsoft.com/download. At the site, select Keyword search, enter the words "Jet 4.0" in the keyword entry field, select your operating system, and click the Find It button to find the correct drivers. If you would prefer to use the BDE drivers, you can download them from info.borland.com/devsupport. Then choose BDE (Borland Database Engine) to jump to the correct link (current version is 5.2) and click on the download link for version 5.2. If you are using BDE for linking to dBASE 5 (Visual dBASE) files, you should not use BDE version 5.x because it is not certified for use with dBASE 5 files. You will need to download two older versions onto your machine. You will have to download these files: the BDE 4.5x (which will only update an older version), and an older version (BDE 3.5), which is found via a hyperlink on the current version page at the bottom.

Access and Paradox index files

If a Paradox table has a primary key defined, it maintains the index information in a file that ends in the extension PX. When you link a Paradox table that has a primary key defined, Access links the associated PX file automatically.

If you link a Paradox table that has a primary key, Access needs the PX file in order to open the table. If you move or delete the PX file, you will not be able to open the linked table.

If you link a Paradox table to Access that does not have a primary key defined, you will not be able to use Access to update data in the table; you can only view it. This is true even if you have the BDE or new ISAM drivers loaded. You must have a primary key field defined in the Paradox table or it is not updateable when linked.

Like dBASE files, Access can link to DBs in real time in a network environment. Access recognizes and enforces the file- and record-locking features of Paradox.

To link to the Paradox 5 table Sales, follow these steps:

1. In the Chap07Start database, select File ➪ Get External Data ➪ Link Tables.
2. In the Link dialog box, select Files of type: Paradox. Access displays just the Paradox .DB files.
3. Select the Sales Paradox file and click the Link button.

   Access displays a dialog box that says "Successfully linked 'Sales.'"
4. Click OK to return to the Link dialog box.
5. Click Close to return to the database container.

Figure 7-7 shows that the Paradox table Sales has been linked to. It shows a right-pointing arrow and the letters 'Px' signifying a Paradox table. Notice that the dBASE Contacts table has a right-pointing arrow and the letters 'dB' signifying a linked dBASE table.

The Access Link Wizard

Unlike linking to dBASE or Paradox tables in the steps followed previously, when you link to an Excel spreadsheet, HTML table, or text file, Access automatically runs a Link Wizard to help you. In each case, you are asked whether the first line (record) contains the field names for the fields. If it does, click the check box to turn it on. If the first record does not hold the field names, you are given the option of specifying a name for each field or accepting the default names (field1, field2, field3, and so on).

Figure 7-7: The Paradox table is now linked into the database.

Linking to non-database tables

You can also link to non-database tables, such as Excel, HTML, and text tables. When you select one of these types of data sources, Access runs a Link Wizard that prompts you through the process.

If you link to an Excel table, you can update its records from within Access or any other application that can update Excel spreadsheets.

Follow these steps to link to the Excel Products spreadsheet:

1. In the Chap07Start database, select File ➪ Get External Data ➪ Link Tables.

2. In the Link dialog box, select Files of type: Microsoft Excel. Access displays the Excel files only.

3. Select the Products file and click the Link button.

   The Link Spreadsheet Wizard is activated, as shown in Figure 7-8. Here you will tell Access how to use the Spreadsheet. The first screen shows the table (Products) name in the top half and the sample data in the worksheet in the bottom half.

4. Click Next to continue through the Wizard.

   The next screen is displayed and shows a check box (First Row Contains Column Headings). The bottom of the screen has changed, showing the field headings above the contents and grayed out.

5. Make sure that the check box is checked and the field headings are correct. Then click the Next button to continue through the Wizard.

   Access displays the final screen of the Wizard and prompts for a table name to give the file Products.xls.

6. Accept the table name Products and click the Finish button.

   Access displays a dialog box that says "Finished linking table 'Products' to file Products.xls."

7. Click OK to return to the database container.

   Unlike linking to other Access, Paradox, and dBASE tables, Access immediately returns you to the database container, instead of to the Link dialog box to link to another table.

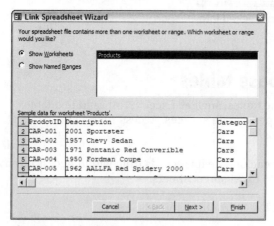

Figure 7-8: The first screen of the Link Spreadsheet Wizard.

With the Excel Products table linked, the database container should display four linked tables — Contacts (dBASE 5 type), Sales (Paradox 5 type), tblSalesPayments (Access table in the Chap07Link database), and Products (Excel file).

The other two types of non-database files that you can link to are HTML documents and text files. To link to these, Access also uses a Wizard to help you view and work with the contents. Linking to HTML and text tables will enable you to view and use tables in queries, forms, and reports. However, you cannot change the current record contents or add new records.

Follow these steps to link to the lookup table CustomerTypes.html, an HTML document:

1. Open the Chap07Start database and select File ➪ Get External Data ➪ Link Tables.

2. In the Link dialog box, select Files of type: HTML documents. Access displays the HTML files only.

3. Select the CustomerTypes file and click the Link button.

   Access starts the Link HTML Wizard and displays the first screen. It has a check box on the top half (First Row Contains Column Headings) and the bottom shows the contents of the HTML file.

4. Make sure that the check box First Row Contains Column Headings is not checked. Then click the Next button.

   Access displays the next screen where you can change the names of the fields and their data type. Figure 7-9 shows this screen. Notice that the bottom half shows the field contents and the single column heading—Field1. It also has an Advanced button that enables you to specify more advanced options. The top half has two entry fields—one for the Field Name, the other for the Data Type. It also has a check box that will enable you to skip importing the current field in the HTML table.

5. Change the field name for the first column from 'Field1' to CustomerType. The data type should remain Text.

   Access automatically changes the name of the field in the bottom screen as you type in the top entry field.

   If you have additional columns, you can change their field names by clicking on the column heading on the lower part of the screen.

Note   If you accidentally press the Enter key, when you need to change additional field names, Access displays the next screen. If this happens, simply click the Back button to return to the current screen.

6. Click the Next button.

   Access displays the final screen of the Wizard and prompts for a table name to give the file CustomerTypes.html.

7. Accept the table name CustomerTypes and click the Finish button.

   Access displays a dialog box that says "Finished linking table 'CustomerTypes' to file ... CustomerTypes.html."

8. Click the OK button to return to the database container.

Unlike linking to other Access, Paradox, and dBASE tables, Access immediately returns you to the database container, instead of to the Link dialog box to link to another table.

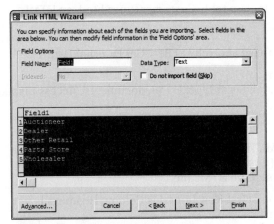

Figure 7-9: The HTML Wizard screen that is used to name the column headings (field names) for the linked table.

Finally, follow these steps to link to the table SalesLineItems, a text file:

1. Open the Chap07Start database and select File ➪ Get External Data ➪ Link Tables.

2. In the Link dialog box, select Text Files of type: Text. Access displays just the Text files.

3. Select the SalesLineItems file and click the Link button.

Access starts the Link Text Wizard and displays the first screen. It has two radio buttons in the top half (Delimited and Fixed Width), and the bottom shows the contents of the text file.

4. Select the first choice 'Delimited — Characters such as a comma or tab separate each field' and click the Next button.

Access displays the next screen, which will differ based on the choice you specified for the type of text file — fixed width or delimited. In this case, it displays a screen similar to the one shown in Figure 7-10. It asks which delimiter (field separator) the file uses for separating the fields in each row. Accept the default value of Comma. Looking at the example data, you should be able to determine that the field names are in the first column and that the data is being displayed correctly. The center of this screen has a check box that asks if the first row contains the field names. It also has a pull-down menu for Text Qualifier (what is used as the start and end of each field).

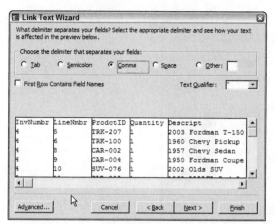

Figure 7-10: The Link Text Wizard's second screen that is used to specify the type of delimiter that is used to separate the fields, the Text Qualifier (used around each value), and whether the first row contains field names for the linked table.

5. Make sure the 'First Row Contains Field Names' check box is selected and the Text Qualifier is double quotations (") click the Next button.

   Access displays the screen where you can specify the field names for each column.

6. Here, you can change the field name for the columns from their default values and the data type.

   Check each of the field names and data types by clicking on the column heading in the lower portion of the window.

7. Moving to the Taxable column, highlight it by clicking on the column heading and then select Yes/No as the Data Type, as shown in Figure 7-11.

8. Click the Next button.

   Access displays the final screen of the Wizard and prompts for a table name to give the file SalesLineItems.txt.

8. Accept the table name SalesLineItems and click the Finish button.

   Access displays a dialog box that says "Finished linking table 'SalesLineItems' to file ... SalesLineItems.txt.

9. Click the OK button to return to the database container.

   Unlike linking to other Access, Paradox, and dBASE tables, Access immediately returns you to the database container, instead of to the Link dialog box to link to another table.

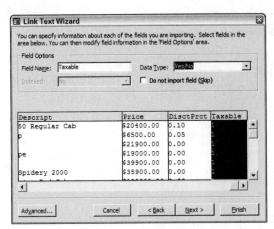

Figure 7-11: The Text Wizard's third screen that is used to name the column headings (field names) and data types for the linked table — in this case, the field Taxable has been changed to a Yes/No (logic) field.

At this point, all the tables have been linked into the database. The database container should now look like the one shown in Figure 7-12.

Figure 7-12: All the tables linked into the database system.

Splitting an Access database into two linked databases

Generally, you can split an Access application into two databases. One contains only your tables; the other contains all your queries, forms, reports, macros, and modules. This is extremely important when moving an application to a multi-user environment. The database with the queries, forms, reports, macros, and modules is installed on each client machine, while the database containing the source tables is installed on the server. This arrangement has several major benefits:

✦ Everyone on the network shares one common set of data.

✦ Many people can update data at the same time.

✦ When you want to update the forms, reports, macros, or modules, you don't have to interrupt processing or worry about data corruption.

When creating an application for a multi-user environment, you should consider designing the objects that will be in your database, anticipating putting them into two Access databases; it's easier to complete your application later. In General, it may prove more efficient to put all your data (tables) in their own database and all the visual objects and code in another. By separating these objects initially, you will find it easier to build the visual objects and associated code as you create the objects. There are some things you just can't do with a linked table without doing a little extra work; these tasks include finding records and importing data. By using different techniques with linked tables, however, you can do anything you can do with a single database.

If you're starting from scratch, you first create a database with just the tables for your application. You then create another new database and link the tables from the first database to the second, as explained in the section "Linking to other Access database tables" earlier in this chapter.

But if you have already built a system with all your objects (including the tables) in one database file, it's a little more difficult to split your tables. One method is to create a duplicate copy of your database. In one version, you delete all objects, leaving only the tables. In the other version, you delete only the tables. Then you use the database file without the tables as a starting point and then link to all the tables in the table database.

Access includes a Wizard called the Database Splitter that can do this for you automatically. Using the Access Auto Auctions database, for example, you can make a copy of the database and split all the tables (in the copy) into a separate database file. After the tables are separated from the other objects in the database, you can use the tables just as you did before; and you can always import all the tables back into the original database if you want.

Follow these steps to make a copy of the Access Auto Auctions database and split it:

1. Select File ➪ Open to display the Open database window.

2. Highlight the Access Auto Auctions database and press Ctrl-C to make a copy of the file in memory.

3. Press Ctrl-V to paste the Copy of the file in the same directory as the original file. Access will name it 'Copy of Access Auto Auctions.'

4. Highlight the new table "Copy of Access Auto Auctions" and open it.

   With the file copied and open, you are ready to start.

Note   The Database Splitter may *not* be installed if you selected the standard installation option when you installed Office 2003. If this is the case, have your Office 2003 CD handy when you choose the Database Splitter.

5. Start the Database Splitter Wizard by selecting Tools ➪ Database Utilities ➪ Database Splitter.

   This starts the Wizard to help you split a single database into two files. The first Wizard screen simply confirms that you want to split the database, as shown in Figure 7-13.

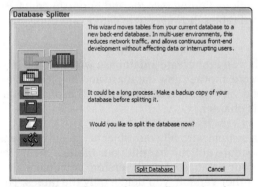

Figure 7-13: The Database Splitter Wizard. This is the first of two screens.

6. Click the Split Database button.

   The Wizard opens a Create Back-End Database dialog box and prompts you for the File name of the database to store all the tables in. The default name is Copy of Access Auto Auctions_be.mdb ("be" for back-end).

7. Accept the default name of the table for the back-end (same name with "be" added) and press the Split button.

The Wizard creates the new database and moves all the tables to it. Then it automatically creates links to those tables so that all the existing objects continue to work — forms, reports, and others. Finally, it displays an information dialog box that says "Database successfully split."

8. Press the OK key in the information dialog box that says "Database successfully split."

Access creates the new database, copies all the tables from the original database to the new database, and then links to them. When the process is done, a message tells you that the database was successfully split. Figure 7-14 shows the original database file (Copy of Access Auto Auctions) with all the tables linked to an external source (Copy of Access Auto Auctions_be).

Figure 7-14: The database named Copy of Access Auto Auctions with all the tables moved (split off) to another database (Copy of Access Auto Auctions_be) and linked to.

If you were to examine the tables and their relationships in the back-end database (Copy of Access Auto Auctions_be), you would see that all the relationships and referential integrity rules were also copied into the new database automatically.

Working with Linked Tables

After you link to an external table from another database, you can use it just as you would use another Access table. You can use it with forms, reports, and queries. When working with external tables, you can modify many of their features; for example, you can set view properties and relationships, set links between tables in queries, or rename the table.

Setting view properties

Although an external table can be used like another Access table, you cannot change the structure (delete, add, or rearrange fields) of an external table. You can, however, set several table properties for the fields in a linked table:

✦ Format

✦ Decimal Places

✦ Caption

✦ Input Mask

✦ Unicode Compressions

✦ IME Sequence Mode

✦ Display Control

Setting relationships

Tip   Access enables you to set permanent relations at the table level between non-Access external tables and Access tables through the Relationships builder, although it does not enable you to specify Referential Integrity between these external files and local tables. Access enables you to create forms and reports based on relationships set up in the Relationships builder — building an SQL statement that is stored in the Record Source property of the form or report. Of course, you can still build an external query and use that query for your form or report.

Note   If you link to tables from another Access database that already have relationships set between them, they will automatically inherit the relationship properties (referential integrity) set in the other database. These links cannot be deleted or changed.

Figure 7-15 shows the Relationships builder window active with all the tables in the Chap07Start database linked to each other at table level. To create these links, simply activate the Relationships window and build the relations between all the tables of the system. When building them, you notice that you can link the tables and Access will recognize the type of link (one-to-many or one-to-one), but you will not be able to Enforce Referential Integrity between tables.

Note   The tables that have been linked in this chapter do not have relationships set. You will need to link your tables using the Relationships builder if you want to permanently link them.

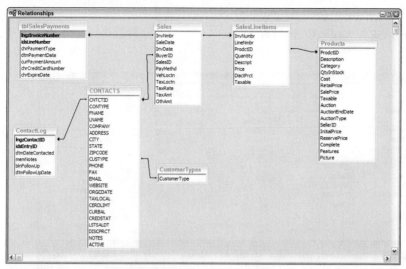

Figure 7-15: The relationships window with all the tables related together. All but two of these tables are external tables that are linked into the database.

Setting links between external tables

To set a link between an external table and another Access table, you can specify the link at the table level by using the Relationships builder tool or by simply creating a query and using the drag-and-drop method of setting links. After a link is set, you can change the join properties from inner join to external join by double-clicking the link.

> **Tip** If you set the relationships between the tables at the table level, the query will automatically bring the links in as you add the tables. The default link type is always an inner join. However, you will still have to specify an outer join if you wish to change to that type (left or right).

Using external tables in queries

When using a query, you can join the external table with another table, internal or external, as long as it is linked in the database. This gives you powerful flexibility when working with queries. Figure 7-16 shows a query using several different database sources:

- ✦ An Excel spreadsheet (Products)
- ✦ Access tables (both internal and linked) (ContactLog and tblSalesPayments)
- ✦ A Paradox table (Sales)

✦ A Text file table (SalesLineItems)

✦ A dBASE IV table (Contacts)

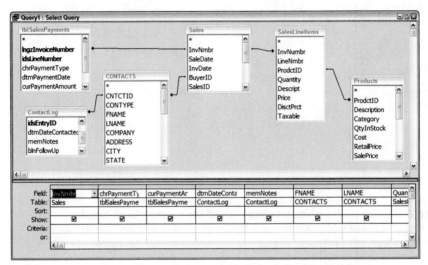

Figure 7-16: A query using several externally linked database tables.

Notice that the query in Figure 7-16 has joins between all tables. This query will obtain information from all the tables and display a datasheet similar to the one shown in Figure 7-17.

Query1 : Select Query

InvNmb	chrPaymentTyp	curPaymentAm	Date Contacte	Notes	FNAME	LNAME	Quantity	Description
1			2/4/2003	Had a problem witl	John	Jones		
2					William	Gleason		
3					John	Bright		
4	Check	$50,565.00			Dennis	Mchugh	1	1960 Chevy Pickup
4	VISA	$20,000.00			Dennis	Mchugh	1	1960 Chevy Pickup
4	Check	$50,565.00			Dennis	Mchugh	1	1957 Chevy Sedan
4	VISA	$20,000.00			Dennis	Mchugh	1	1957 Chevy Sedan
4	Check	$50,565.00			Dennis	Mchugh	1	1950 Fordman Coupe
4	VISA	$20,000.00			Dennis	Mchugh	1	1950 Fordman Coupe
4	Check	$50,565.00			Dennis	Mchugh	1	2002 Olds SUV
4	VISA	$20,000.00			Dennis	Mchugh	1	2002 Olds SUV
4	Check	$50,565.00			Dennis	Mchugh	1	2003 Fordman T-150 Regular Cab
4	VISA	$20,000.00			Dennis	Mchugh	1	2003 Fordman T-150 Regular Cab
5	Check	$1,000.00			Brandon	Aley	1	1962 AALLFA Red Spidery 2000
5	Check	$1,000.00			Brandon	Aley	1	1965 Shelly Stunning Red Cobrat
6	Check	$22,995.00			Larry	Calson	1	1971 Pontanic Red Converible
6	Check	$22,995.00			Larry	Calson	1	2001 Collectors Chevy Corvet
7	American Expre	$65,000.00			Karl	Johnson	1	1940 Classic Antique Convertible
7	American Expre	$20,000.00			Karl	Johnson	1	1940 Classic Antique Convertible
7	American Expre	$65,000.00			Karl	Johnson	1	1967 Shelly Stunning Red Muscle C
7	American Expre	$20,000.00			Karl	Johnson	1	1967 Shelly Stunning Red Muscle C
7	American Expre	$65,000.00			Karl	Johnson	1	1957 Chevy Sedan
7	American Expre	$20,000.00			Karl	Johnson	1	1957 Chevy Sedan
8	Cash	$5,000.00			Joann	Smith	1	2001 Collectors Chevy Corvet
9					Peter	Spindler	1	1988 Fordman T350 Bucket Truck
10	Cash	$1,000.00			Debbie	Casey	1	1994 Fordman XLP Ext
10	Cash	$1,000.00			Debbie	Casey	1	1998 Fordman Explorer XLP
11					Casper	Krammer	1	2001 Sportster

Record: 1 of 104

Figure 7-17: A datasheet display of the dynaset created by the query shown in Figure 7-16.

Renaming tables

You can rename a linked external table. Because Access enables you to name a table with as many as 64 characters (including spaces), you may want to rename a linked table to be more descriptive. For example, you may want to rename the dBASE table called Contacts to Contacts Table from dBASE.

To rename a file, you can select Edit ➪ Rename... from the Database menu. Another (quicker) method is to click the filename; after a pause, click it again, and enter a new name.

Note　When you rename an external file, Access does not rename the actual DOS filename or SQL Server table name. It uses the new name only in the Tables object list of the Access database.

Tip　If you rename a table that is being used in Access 2003 by queries, forms, or reports, Access will automatically adjust the table name in other objects (fix the file name automatically).

Optimizing linked tables

When working with linked tables, Access has to retrieve records from another file. This process takes time, especially when the table resides on a network or in an SQL database. When working with external data, you can optimize performance by observing these points:

　✦ **Avoid using functions in query criteria.** This is especially true for aggregate functions, such as DTotal or DCount, which retrieve all records from the linked table automatically and then perform the query.

　✦ **Limit the number of external records to view.** Create a query specifying a criterion that limits the number of records from an external table. This query can then be used by other queries, forms, or reports.

　✦ **Avoid excessive movement in datasheets.** View only the data you need to in a datasheet. Avoid paging up and down and jumping to the last or first record in very large tables. (The exception is when you're adding records to the external table.)

　✦ **If you add records to external linked tables, create a form to add records and set the DataEntry property to True.** This makes the form an entry form that starts with a blank record every time it's executed.

　✦ **When working with tables in a multi-user environment, minimize locking records.** This will free up records for other users.

Deleting a linked table reference

Deleting a linked table from the Database window is a simple matter of doing three things:

1. In the Database window, select the linked table you want to delete.

2. Press the Delete key or select Edit ⇨ Delete from the Database menu.

3. Click OK in the Access dialog box to delete the file.

Note   Deleting an external table deletes only its name from the database object list. The actual file is not deleted.

Viewing or changing information for linked tables

If you move, rename, or modify tables or indexes associated with a linked table, you can use the Linked Table Manager Wizard to update the links. (Otherwise, Access will not be able to find them.)

To use this tool, select Tools ⇨ Database Utilities ⇨ Linked Table Manager. Access will display a dialog box similar to the one shown in Figure 7-18. Select the linked table that needs the information changed, and click the OK button; Access will verify that the file cannot be found and will display a Select New Location of [table name] dialog box. Using this dialog box, you can find the missing file and reassign the information for the external link to Access. If all the files are already linked correctly, clicking the OK button will make Access go out and verify that all the selected tables are linked correctly and display an information box that says "All selected linked tables were successfully refreshed."

Tip   If you check the Always prompt for new location check box, it will prompt you for the tables that you select every time you run this Wizard—even if Access knows where the tables are located. It is best to leave this check box off.

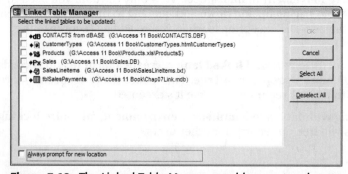

Figure 7-18: The Linked Table Manager enables you to relocate external tables that have been moved.

Note   If the Linked Table Manager Wizard is not present on your computer, Access will automatically prompt for you to enter the "original" Office CD into the CD-ROM to load it. If you did not instruct Office to install the Additional Wizards component during the Setup process, it will be loaded at this time.

Importing External Data

When you import a file (unlike when you link tables), you copy the contents from an external file into an Access table. You can import external file information from several different sources:

+ Microsoft Access (other unopened database objects: forms, tables, and so on)

+ dBASE III, IV, and 5

+ FoxPro (all versions using ODBC drivers)

+ Microsoft Excel (all versions)

+ Exchange documents

+ HTML Documents

+ Lotus 1-2-3 DOS and 1-2-3 for Windows (versions WKS, WK1, and WK3)

+ Outlook documents

+ Paradox 3.x, 4.x, 5.0, 7.0, and 8.0

+ SharePoint Team Services

+ Delimited text files (fields separated by a delimiter)

+ Fixed-width text files (specific widths for each field)

+ SQL databases (Microsoft SQL Server, Sybase Server, and Oracle Server)

+ XML Documents

+ Any other ODBC Databases

You can import information to either new tables or existing tables, depending on the type of data being imported. All data types can be imported to new tables, but only spreadsheet and text files can be imported to existing tables.

When Access imports data from an external file, it does not erase or destroy the external file. Therefore, you will have two copies of the data: the original file (in the original format) and the new Access table.

Note   If the filename of the importing file already exists in an Access table, Access adds a chronological number (1, 2, 3, and so on) to the filename until it has a unique table name. For example, if an importing spreadsheet name is Contacts.XLS and there is an Access table named Contacts, the imported table name becomes Contacts1. If Contacts and Contacts1 tables already exist, Access creates a table named Contacts2.

Importing other Access objects

You can import other Access database tables or any other object in another database. You can therefore import an existing table, query, form, report, macro, or module from another Access database. You can also import custom toolbars and menus.

As an example, use these steps to import the tblTaxRates table from the Chap07Link Access database:

1. In the Chap07Start database, click the Tables button to see the list of tables and then select File ➪ Get External Data ➪ Import. (An Import dialog box appears.)

2. In the Import dialog box, select Files of type: Microsoft Access.

3. Double-click Chap07Link.MDB.

   Access closes the Import select database dialog box and opens the Import Objects dialog box, as shown in Figure 7-19. At the bottom of this selection box, you can click the Options>> button; the dialog box expands to offer several additional import options.

4. In the box, select the tblTaxRates table by clicking tblTaxRates and then clicking the OK button.

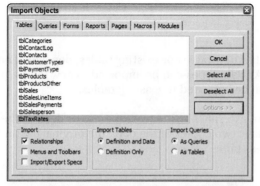

Figure 7-19: The Import Objects dialog box with the Options>> button pressed. You can expand Import window by clicking on the Options>> button to see additional choices.

Access imports the tblTaxRates table into the Chap07Start database and closes the Import Objects dialog box. You can select more than one item at a time, using the Select All and Deselect All buttons to select or de-select all the objects in a specific category or by control-clicking if you only desire a few.

The Options>> button enables you to further define how to import Access data. You can choose to import relationships, custom toolbars, and import/export specifications from an Access database. You can determine whether the tables you import come in with just the table design (definitions), or with the data as well. Finally, the last set of options enables you to decide whether queries you import come in as queries or run as make-table action queries to import a new table.

See Chapter 38 for details about make-table queries.

The tblTaxRates table appears in the Database window display without a link symbol in the icon. It has kept the name tblTaxRates because no other table in the database container has this name. Unlike linking the table, you have copied the tblTaxRate table and added it to the current database. Therefore, because it's not linked but instead an actual part of the database, it occupies space like the original Access table does.

Besides adding tables from other Access databases, you can also add other objects (including queries, forms, reports, macros, or modules) by clicking each of the tabs in the Import Objects dialog box. You can select objects from each and then import them all at one time.

Importing non-Access PC-based database tables

When importing data from PC-based databases, you can import two basic categories of database file types:

✦ dBASE

✦ Paradox

Each type of database can be imported directly into an Access table. The native data types are converted to Access data types during the conversion.

You can import any Paradox (3.0 through 8), dBASE III, dBASE IV, or dBASE 5 database table into Access. To import one of these, simply select the correct database type in the Files of type: box during the import process.

After selecting the type of PC-based database, select which file you want to import; Access imports the file for you automatically.

If you try to import a Paradox table that is encrypted, Access prompts you for the password after you select the table in the Select File dialog box. Enter the password and click the OK button to import an encrypted Paradox table.

When Access imports dBASE fields, it converts them from their current data type into an Access data type. Table 7-2 lists how the data types are converted.

Table 7-2 Conversion of Data Types from dBASE to Access	
xBASE Data Type	*Access Data Type*
Character	Text
Numeric	Number (property of Double)
Float	Number (property of Double)
Logical	Yes/No
Date	Date/Time
Memo	Memo

When importing any dBASE database file in a multi-user environment, you must have exclusive use of the file. If other people are using it, you will not be able to import it.

As with dBASE tables, when Access imports Paradox fields, the Paradox fields are converted from their current data type into an Access data type. Table 7-3 lists how the data types are converted.

Table 7-3 Conversion of Data Types from Paradox to Access	
Paradox Data Type	*Access Data Type*
Alphanumeric	Text
Number	Number (property of Double)
Short Number	Number (property of Integer)
Currency	Number (property of Double)
Date	Date/Time
Memo	Memo
Blob (Binary)	OLE

Importing spreadsheet data

You can import data from Excel or Lotus 1-2-3 spreadsheets to a new or existing table. The key to importing spreadsheet data is that it must be arranged in tabular (columnar) format. Each cell of data in a spreadsheet column must contain the same type of data. Table 7-4 demonstrates correct and incorrect columnar-format data.

> **Note**
>
> You can import or link all the data from a spreadsheet, or just the data from a named range of cells. Naming a range of cells in your spreadsheet can make importing into Access easier. Often a spreadsheet is formatted into groups of cells. One group of cells may contain a listing of sales by customer, for example. The section below the sales listing may include total sales for all customers, totals by product type, or totals by month purchased. By naming the range for each group of cells, you can limit the import to just one section of the spreadsheet.

Table 7-4 represents cells in a spreadsheet, in the range A1 through F7. Notice that the data in columns A, B, and C and rows 2 through 7 is the same type. Row 1 contains field names. These columns can be imported into an Access table. Column D is empty and cannot be used. Columns E and F do not have the same type of data in each of their cells; they may cause problems when you try to import them into an Access table.

Table 7-4 Spreadsheet Cells with Contents					
A	B	C	D	E	F
1	TYPE	WEIGHT	BDATE	JUNK	GARBAGE
2	DOG	122	12/02/92	123	YES
3	CAT	56	02/04/89	22	134.2
4	BIRD	55	05/30/90	01/01/91	DR SMITH
5	FROG	12	02/22/88	TEST	$345.35
6	FISH	21	01/04/93	═══	══
7	RAT	3	02/28/93	$555.00	<══ TOTAL

Figure 7-20 shows an Excel spreadsheet named PRODUCTS.XLS.

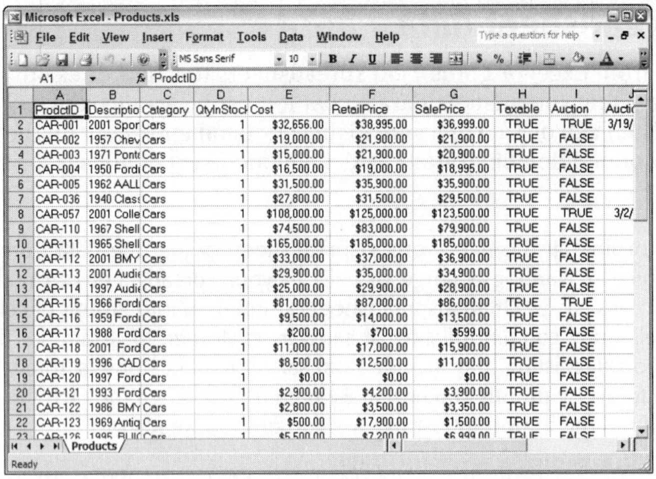

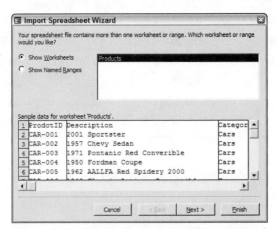

Figure 7-20: An Excel spreadsheet containing columns of information that could be imported easily into an Access table.

To import the Excel spreadsheet named PRODUCTS.XLS, follow these steps:

1. Open the Chap07Start database and select File ⇨ Get External Data ⇨ Import.

2. In the Import dialog box, select Files of type: Microsoft Excel.

3. Double-click PRODUCTS.XLS in the select box.

   Access closes the Import box and displays the first Import Spreadsheet Wizard screen; the screen resembles the one shown in Figure 7-21.

Figure 7-21: The first Import Spreadsheet Wizard screen.

This screen displays a sample of the first few rows and columns of the spread-sheet. You can scroll the display to see all the rows and columns if you want.

4. Click Next button to move to the second screen.

5. In this screen, click the check box to use the first row of the spreadsheet to name fields in the table.

The display changes to show the first row and column headings.

6. Click Next to display the third screen.

This screen enables you to determine where the data will go. You can create a new table (the default radio button) or add to an existing table.

7. Click Next to accept the default value of creating a new table and display the third screen.

This screen (shown in Figure 7-22) enables you to click each column of the spreadsheet to accept the field name, change it, and decide whether it will be indexed; the Wizard determines the data type automatically. You can also choose to skip each column if you want. You will specify the Primary Key field after this screen.

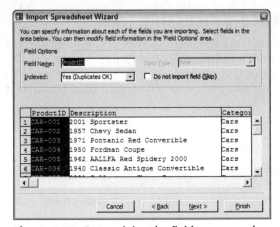

Figure 7-22: Determining the field names and data types.

8. Click Next to display the next Import Spreadsheet Wizard screen.

This screen enables you to choose a field for the primary key. You can let Access create a new AutoNumber field (by choosing Let Access Add Primary Key), enter your own (by selecting Choose My Own Primary Key and selecting one of the columns), or have no primary key.

9. Select Choose my own Primary Key and select the ProductID field.

10. Click Next to display the last Import Spreadsheet Wizard screen.

   The last screen enables you to enter the name for the imported table and (optionally) run the Table Analyzer Wizard.

11. Change the default Table name of Products to Products1 and click Finish to import the spreadsheet file. Access informs you that it imported the file successfully in an information box. Simply click OK to have Access return to the database.

The filename now appears in the Access database window. A standard Access table has been created from the original spreadsheet file.

Caution   If you import the Excel file that has the same name as the linked Excel file and that file is used in the Relationships builder, Access will overwrite the linked file with the imported file if you wish. It will warn you that it will overwrite the file when you attempt to save the file. If you do not wish to overwrite, press the NO button and give your imported file another name. In this case you used the name Products1, because you already have a linked table named Products.

Importing from word-processing files

Access does not offer a specific way to import data from word-processing files. If you need to import data from a word-processing file into Access, convert the word-processing file to a simple text file first and then import it as a text file. Most word processors have the capability to convert their formatted text-to-text files or ASCII files.

Importing text file data

Mainframe data is ordinarily output to a text file for use in desktop applications. You can import from two different types of text files: *delimited* and *fixed-width*. Access uses an *import/export specification* file as a guide in processing these types of files.

Access uses one Wizard for both types of text files. The Import Text Wizard assists you in identifying the fields for the import/export specification.

Delimited text files

Delimited text files are sometimes known as *comma-delimited* or *tab-delimited* files; each record is on a separate line in the text file. The fields on the line contain no trailing spaces, normally use commas as field separators, and require certain fields to be enclosed in a *delimiter* (such as single or double quotation marks). Usually the text fields are also enclosed in quotation marks or some other delimiter, as in these examples:

```
"Adams","Bryan","Williams Sports",02/04/2003
"Irwin","Michael",,,05/12/1992
"Johnson","Shirley","Johnson's Tailors",01/01/1999
"Lim","Arni","Audle, Lim, and Yoe, Surgeons",04/22/2000
"Prague","Cary","Cary Prague Books and Software",02/22/1986
"Zimmerman-Schneider","Audrie","Zimmer's Cafe",01/01/2001
```

Notice that the file has six records (rows of text) and four fields. A comma separates each field, and the text fields are delimited with double quotation marks. The starting position of each field, after the first one, is different. Each record has a different length because the field lengths are different.

> **Note**   You can import records from a delimited text file that has fields with no values. To specify a field with no value, place delimiters where the field value would be, and put no value between them (for example, "Irwin","Michael",,05/12/92). Notice that in the preceding example there are two commas after the field content "Michael" and before the field content 05/12/92. The field between these two has no value; it will be imported with no value into an Access file.

Fixed-width text files

Fixed-width text files also place each record on a separate line. However, the fields in each record are of a fixed length. If the field contents are not long enough, trailing spaces are added to the field, as shown in the following example:

```
Irwin        Michael      Michael Irwin Consulting        05/12/82
Prague       Cary         Cary Prague Books and Software   02/22/86
Zimmerman    Audrie       IBM                             01/01/59
```

Notice that the fields are not separated by delimiters. Rather, they start at exactly the same position in each record. Each record has exactly the same length. If a field is not long enough, trailing spaces are added to fill the field.

You can import either a delimited or a fixed-width text file to a new table or existing Access table. If you decide to append the imported file to an existing table, the file's structure must match that of the Access table you're importing to.

> **Note**   If the Access table being imported has a key field, the text file cannot have any duplicate key values or the import will report an error.

Importing delimited text files

To import a delimited text file named Names.TXT, follow these steps:

1. In the Chap07Start database, select File ➪ Get External Data ➪ Import.

2. In the Import dialog box, select Files of type: Text Files.

3. Double-click Names.TXT in the File Name list box.

Access displays the first screen of the Import Text Wizard dialog box for the table Names.TXT. The dialog box resembles the one shown in Figure 7-23.

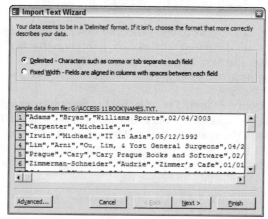

Figure 7-23: The first Import Text Wizard screen.

This screen displays the data in the text file and lets you choose between delimited or fixed-width. The default for the Wizard is delimited.

Note   Notice, at the bottom of the screen, the button marked Advanced. Click it to further define the import specifications. You will learn more about this option in the section "Importing fixed-width text files" following this section; generally, it's not needed for delimited files. Click the Cancel button to return to the Import Text Wizard.

4. Click the Next button to display the next Import Text Wizard screen.

As you can see in Figure 7-24, this screen enables you to determine which type of separator to use in the delimited text file. Generally, this separator is a comma, but you could use a tab, semicolon, space, or other character (such as an asterisk), which you enter in the box next to the Other option button. You can also decide whether to use text from the first row as field names for the imported table. It has correctly assigned the comma as the separator type and the Text Qualifier as quotation marks (").

Note   A *Separator* is the specific character that was placed between the fields in a delimited text file—often it is a comma or semicolon, although it can be any specific character. There can be a problem with the separator used—for example, in this case, the separator is a comma—if any of the fields have a comma in them. It could cause a problem when trying to import the data. (With the last name of IRWIN,

Michael versus the next name of PRAGUE, Sr., Cary, Cary's record has what appears to be an extra field in the last name — Sr.) This can cause all sorts of problems when importing the data. The *Text Qualifier*, for delimited text files refers to the marks that are often placed around text fields versus numeric and date fields. Often they are single quotation or double quotation marks.

Figure 7-24: The second Import Text Wizard screen.

5. Leave the First Row Contains Field Names check box unchecked because your data does not contain field names as the first field.

6. Click the Next button to display the next Import Text Wizard screen.

   This screen enables you to determine whether you're storing the imported data in a new table or an existing table. If you decide to use an existing table, you have to choose it from a list.

   The next few screens are exactly the same as the Import Spreadsheet Wizard screens shown in the "Importing spreadsheet data" section earlier in this chapter.

7. Click on each column of data and enter the following field names and data types: LastName - Text, FirstName - Text, CompanyName - Text, and CompanySince - Date/Time. Your screen should now look similar to the one shown in Figure 7-25.

   This screen enables you to select each column of the text import grid, accept or change the field name, decide whether it will be indexed, and set the data type (which is also automatically determined by the Wizard), or even skip adding the field to the final table. As with the Spreadsheet Import Wizard, you move from field to field by selecting the next field column — once selected, you can change its options also. You can choose to skip a column if you want.

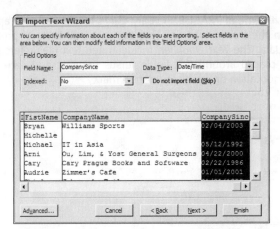

Figure 7-25:: The screen used to enter field names and data types for the Text Wizard. Notice that the field type has been changed to Date/Time for the field CompanySince.

8. Click Next to display the next Import Text Wizard screen.

   This screen enables you to choose a field for the primary key. You can enable Access to create a new AutoNumber field (by choosing Let Access Add Primary Key), enter your own (by selecting Choose My Own Primary Key and selecting one of the columns), or have no primary key.

9. Click the option button that says Let Access Add primary key.

10. Click Next to display the last Import Text Wizard screen.

    The last screen enables you to enter the name for the imported table and (optionally) run the Table Analyzer Wizard.

11. Accept the default name of Names and click Finish to import the delimited text file.

Access creates a new table, using the same name as the text file's name; then it displays an information box informing you that it created the table successfully. Clicking the OK button returns you to the database. The filename appears in the Access Database window, where Access has added the table Names.

Importing fixed-width text files

In fixed-width text files, each field in the file has a specific width and position. Files downloaded from mainframes are the most common fixed-width text files. As you import or export this type of file, you must specify an import/export setup specification. You create this setup file by using the Advanced options of the Import Table Wizard.

To import a fixed-width text file, follow these steps:

1. Open the Chap07Start database and select File ⇨ Get External Data ⇨ Import.

2. In the Import dialog box, select Files of type: Text Files.

3. Double-click CONTACTSFIXED.TXT in the File Name list box. Access opens the first screen of the Import Text Wizard dialog box for the table CONTACTS-FIXED.TXT.

   This screen displays the data in the text file and guesses whether the type of text file is delimited or fixed width. As you can see, the Wizard has correctly determined that it's a fixed-width file.

4. Click Next to display the next Import Text Wizard screen.

   This screen makes a guess about where columns begin and end in the file, basing the guess on the spaces in the file. Notice that it has missed the first field in the first column (combining the first and second fields together).

   Figure 7-26 shows that Access has done a pretty good job in this file. It has recognized several fields correctly, but missed the first field, combining it with the second field. You'll need to add a field break line in the structure.

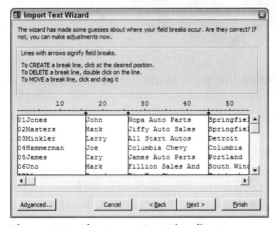

Figure 7-26: The Import Text Wizard's attempt to split the fields. Notice that two fields are merged together in the first column.

As you can see in Figure 7-26, you can drag a field break line, add one, or delete one to tell Access where the fields really are.

5. Move to position 3 (between the 01 and J of the first record named Jones).

6. When the pointer is in position on the lined bar in the center, create a break line by clicking at that position.

If you make a mistake and put the line in the wrong place, simply highlight the line and either move it by dragging it or double-click it to delete it.

Figure 7-27 shows the first and second fields now correctly designated.

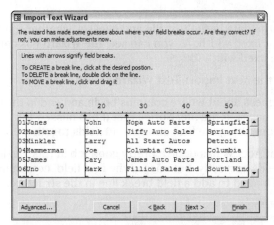

Figure 7-27: The field breaks now set correctly for the fields of the fixed-width table.

As you use these tools to define the field widths, you're completing an internal data table known as Import/Export Specifications.

7. Click the Advanced button to activate the Import Specification window for the ContactsFixed table.

Figure 7-28 shows the Import Specification screen active. This window is atop the Import Text Wizard window. This Import Specifications window is activated by clicking the Advanced button in the Import Text Wizard.

The section labeled Dates, Times, and Numbers describes how date, time, and numeric information is formatted in the import file.

8. Make sure that the Four Digit Years check box is on.

9. Click the Leading Zeros in Dates check box on.

The month and day in the data being imported includes a leading zero for numbers less than 10.

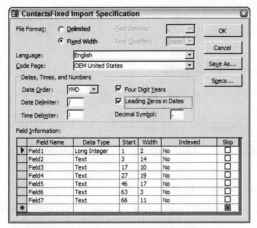

Figure 7-28: The Import Specification screen for fixed-width text files.

10. Click in the Date Order combo box and change the order from MDY (month day year) to YMD (year month date).

    In this example, the date field is formatted with the year first (four digit), then the month, followed by the day. The dialog box should look like the one shown in Figure 7-28.

    The bottom half of the Import Specifications dialog box has a section named the Field Information section. This section lists the name, data type, and position of each field in the import table. Although you can manually type the specifications for each field in this file, in this example you can accept the field information that Access has created for you and return to the Import Text Wizard.

11. Click the OK button to return to the Import Text Wizard.

12. After you return to the Wizard, press the Next button to move to the next screen.

    This screen enables you to determine whether the records should be added to a new table or an existing one.

13. Click the Next button again to move to the next screen.

    This screen enables you to specify the field names and any indexes for the fields.

14. With the first column highlighted, enter a field name of ContactID and Data Type of Long Integer.

15. Click the second field column named Field2.

16. With the Field2 highlighted, enter a field name of LastName and Data Type of Text.

17. Click the next field column named Field3.

18. With the Field3 highlighted, enter a field name of FirstName and Data Type of Text.

19. Click the next field column named Field4.

20. With the Field4 highlighted, enter a field name of Company and Data Type of Text.

21. Click the next field column named Field5.

22. With the Field5 highlighted, enter a field name of City and Data Type of Text.

23. Click the next field column named Field6.

24. With the Field6 highlighted, enter a field name of State and Data Type of Text.

25. Click the next field column named Field7.

26. With the Field7 highlighted, enter a field name of DateOfBirth and Data Type of Date/Time.

27. Click the Next button to move to the next screen.

This screen enables you to specify a primary key.

28. Click Choose My Own Primary Key and specify ContactID.

29. Click the Next button.

This step takes you to the last screen where you can name your file.

30. Accept the default name of ContactsFixed and click the Finished button.

Access again informs you that it has imported the file. Clicking the OK button will close the Wizard and return you to the database.

Caution   If you made a mistake and Access could not import the records correctly, perhaps you failed to specify the correct type of date conversion to get this type of error. Access will report a message like this: Finished importing file "XXX" to table "XXX". Not all your data was successfully imported. Error descriptions with associated row numbers of bad records can be found in Microsoft Access table "YYYErrors. NOTE that XXX and YYY will be actual names.

Using the Import Specification window

In earlier versions of Access, you had to specify the import/export specifications manually, specifying field lengths, delimited or fixed text, type of delimiter, how to export date fields, and so on. Although you can still specify this information by using the Import Specification window, as in Steps 7 through 11 above, it is easier to use the graphical tools (built into the Import Wizard) of Access.

Although the Import Text Wizard generally does a good job of importing your data correctly, at times you may need to specify field lengths and data types manually. If you use the Import Specification dialog box (shown in Figure 7-28), you can change or set all the options on one screen, which can be helpful.

One advantage of using this screen is the capability to specify the type of file to be imported from or exported to. The Language and Code Page fields determine the type of format. The default language is English. The Code Page combo box displays the code page types that are available for the language you select. Specifically, these choices are available for the English language:

✦ OEM United States

✦ Unicode

✦ Unicode (Big-Endian)

✦ Unicode (UTF-7)

✦ Unicode (UTF-8)

✦ Western European (DOS)

✦ Western European (ISO)

✦ Western European (Windows)

The default value is the Western European (Windows). Notice that in Figure 7-28 it has been changed to OEM United States. You may need to set this value if you are running a language that does not use the Roman character set used in English, French, German, etc. You can also specify the Field Delimiter option for delimited text files; the delimiter is used to separate the fields. You do this by using a special character such as a comma or semicolon. Four field-separator choices are available in this combo box:

;	Semicolon
{tab}	Tabulation mark
{space}	Single space
,	Comma

When working with delimited files, you can also specify your own field separator directly in this combo box.

Also, when working with delimited files, you can specify the Text Qualifier. It specifies the type of delimiter to be used when you're working with Text-type fields. Normally, the *text* fields in a delimited file are enclosed by specified delimiters (such as quotation marks). This is useful for specifying Number-type data (such as Social Security numbers) as Text type rather than Number type (it won't be used in a calculation). You have three list box choices:

{none}	No delimiter
"	Double quotation mark
'	Single quotation mark

The default value is a double quotation mark. This list box is actually a combo box; you can enter your own delimiter. If the one you want is not among these three choices, you can specify a different text delimiter by entering a new one directly in the combo box — for example, the caret symbol (^).

Note   If you use comma-delimited files, created by other PC-based databases, you should set the text qualifier to the double quotation mark (") and the field delimiter to a comma (,) if that is what they are in the text file being imported or linked.

Caution   If you specify your own delimiter, it must be the same on both sides of the text. For example, you can't use both of the curly braces ({ }) as user-specified delimiters; you can specify only one character. If you specify the left curly brace, Access looks for only the left curly brace as a delimiter — on both sides of the text:

{This is Text data enclosed in braces}

Notice that only the left brace is used.

When Access 2003 imports or exports data, it converts dates to a specific format (such as MMDDYY). In the example MMDDYY, Access converts all dates to two digits for each portion of the date (month, day, and year), separating each by a specified delimiter. Thus, January 19, 2004 would be converted to 1/19/04. You can specify how date fields are to be converted, using one of six choices in the Date Order combo box:

✦ DMY

✦ DYM

✦ MDY

✦ MYD

✦ YDM

✦ YMD

These choices specify the order for each portion of a date. The D is the day of the month (1-31), M is the calendar month (1-12), and Y is the year. The default date order is set to the American format of month, day, and year. When you work with European dates, the order must be changed to day, month, and year.

You use the Date Delimiter option to specify the date delimiter. This option tells Access which type of delimiter to use between the parts of date fields. The default is a forward slash (/), but this can be changed to any user-specified delimiter. In Europe, for example, date parts are separated by periods, as in 22.10.04.

Note When you import text files with Date-type data, you must have a separator between the month, day, and year or else Access reports an error if the field is specified as a Date/Time type. When you're exporting date fields, the separator is not needed.

With the Time Delimiter option, you can specify a separator between the segments of time values in a text file. The default value is the colon (:). In the example 12:55, the colon separates the hours from the minutes. To change the separator, simply enter another in the Time Delimiter box.

You use the Four Digit Years check box when you want to specify that the year value in date fields will be formatted with four digits. By checking this box, you can export dates that include the century (such as in 1881 or 2001). The default is to include the century.

The Leading Zeros in Dates option is a check box where you specify that date values include leading zeros. You can specify, for example, that date formats include leading zeros (as in 02/04/03). To specify leading zeros, check this box. The default is without leading zeros (as in 2/4/03).

Importing HTML tables

Access enables you to import HTML tables as easily as any other database, Excel spreadsheet, or text file. You simply select the HTML file you want to import and use the HTML Import Wizard. It works exactly like the link HTML Wizard described in detail earlier in this chapter.

Modifying imported table elements

After you import a file, you can refine the table in Design view. The following list itemizes and discusses some of the primary changes you may want to make to improve your table:

✦ **Add field names or descriptions.** You may want to change the names of the fields you specified when you imported the file. For example, xBASE databases enable no more than 10 characters in their names and no spaces.

✦ **Change data types.** Access may have guessed the wrong data type when it imported several of the fields. You can change these fields to reflect a more descriptive data type (such as Currency rather than Number, or Text rather than Number).

✦ **Set field properties.** You can set field properties to enhance the way your tables work. For example, you may want to specify a format or default value for the table.

✦ **Set the field size to something more realistic than the 255 bytes (characters) Access allocates for each imported text field.** Make the names descriptive enough without the need to make them too long—for example, "Last Name" versus "Last Name of the owner of pets coming from the merge table from Doctor Zervas's old practice." "Last Name" is sufficient to clarify what the contents of the field are.

✦ **Define a primary key.** Access works best with tables that have a primary key. You may want to set a primary key for the imported table.

Troubleshooting import errors

When you import an external file, Access may not be able to import one or more records, in which case it reports an error when it tries to import them. When Access encounters errors, it creates an Access table named Import Errors (with the user's name linked to the table name). The Import Errors table contains one record for each record that causes an error.

After errors have occurred and Access has created the Import Errors table, you can open the table to view the error descriptions.

Import errors for new tables

Access may not be able to import records into a new table for the following reasons:

✦ A row in a text file or spreadsheet may contain more fields than are present in the first row.

✦ Data in the field cannot be stored in the data type Access chose for the field. (This could be text in a numeric field—best case will import as 0s—or numeric trying to store in a date field.)

✦ On the basis of the first row's contents, Access automatically chose the incorrect data type for a field. The first row is OK, but the remaining rows are blank.

✦ The date order may be incorrect. The dates are in YMD order but the specification calls for MDY order. (When Access tries to import 991201 [YYMMDD], it will report an error because it should be in the format of 120199 [MMDDYY].)

Import errors for existing tables

Access may not be able to append records into an existing table for the following reasons:

✦ The data is not consistent between the text file and the existing Access table.

✦ Numeric data being entered is too large for the field size of the Access table.

✦ A row in a text file or spreadsheet may contain more fields than the Access table.

✦ The records being imported have duplicate primary key values.

The Import Errors table

When errors occur, Access creates an Import Errors table you can use to determine which data caused the errors.

Open the Import Errors table and try to determine why Access couldn't import all the records. If the problem is with the external data, edit it. If you're appending records to an existing table, the problem may be with the existing table; it may need modifications (such as changing the data types and rearranging the field locations). After you solve the problem, erase the Import Errors file and import the data again.

Note   Access attempts to import all records that do not cause an error. If you re-import the data, you may need to clean up the external table or the Access table before re-importing. If you don't, you may have duplicate data in your table.

If importing a text file seems to take an unexpectedly long time, it may be because of too many errors. You can cancel importing by pressing Ctrl+Break.

Exporting to External Formats

You can copy data from an Access table or query into a new external file. This process of copying Access tables to an external file is called exporting. You can export tables to several different sources:

✦ Microsoft Access (other unopened databases)

✦ dBASE III, dBASE IV, and dBASE 5

✦ FoxPro 2.x and Visual FoxPro 3.0 (through ODBC)

✦ Microsoft Excel (all versions 3, 4, 5 – 7 through 97-2002)

✦ HTML documents (as tables)

✦ Lotus 1-2-3 and 1-2-3 for Windows (versions WK1, WK3, and WJ2)

✦ Paradox 3.x, 4.x, 5.0, and 7-8

✦ SharePoint Team Services

✦ Delimited text files (fields separated by a delimiter)

✦ Fixed-width text files (specific widths for each field)

✦ Microsoft Active Server Pages

✦ Microsoft IIS 1-2

✦ XML document

✦ Text files

✦ Rich text formats (RTF)

✦ Microsoft Word Merge (.txt)

✦ ODBC Data Sources SQL databases (Microsoft SQL Server, Sybase Server, and Oracle Server)

When Access exports data from an Access table to an external file, the Access table isn't erased or destroyed. This means that you will have two copies of the data: the original Access file and the external data file.

Exporting objects to other Access databases

You can export objects from the current database to another, unopened Access database. The objects you export can be tables, queries, forms, reports, macros, or modules. To export an object to another Access database, follow these generic steps:

1. Open the database that has the object you want to export and select File ➪ Export from the Database menu.

2. Access opens the standard Save As dialog box (Export Table) — the same one that appears whenever you save an object to another name. The difference is that you can specify a different format (Save as type). When you open the combo box, a list of formats appears. Select the one you want; Access will save the data to that format.

When this process is complete, Access copies to the other database the object you specified and immediately returns you to the Database window in Access.

Note   If you attempt to export an object to another Access database that has an object of the same type and name, Access warns you before copying. You then have the option to cancel or overwrite.

Exporting objects to other external databases or to Excel, HTML, or text files

You can also export objects to databases (such as ODBC, dBASE, Paradox, and FoxPro) and text files (delimited and fixed width). To export any of these objects, simply follow these generic steps:

1. Select File ➪ Export from the Database menu.

2. Select the type of file you want the object to be saved to and specify a name.

3. Click the Save button.

Note

If you save a table to an HTML table, Access will create the HTML document, and if you check the Save formatted and the Autostart check boxes in the Export to dialog box, you can have Access start your browser to show you the form it created. Figure 7-29 shows the Contacts table exported as a formatted HTML table and displayed automatically in the Browser.

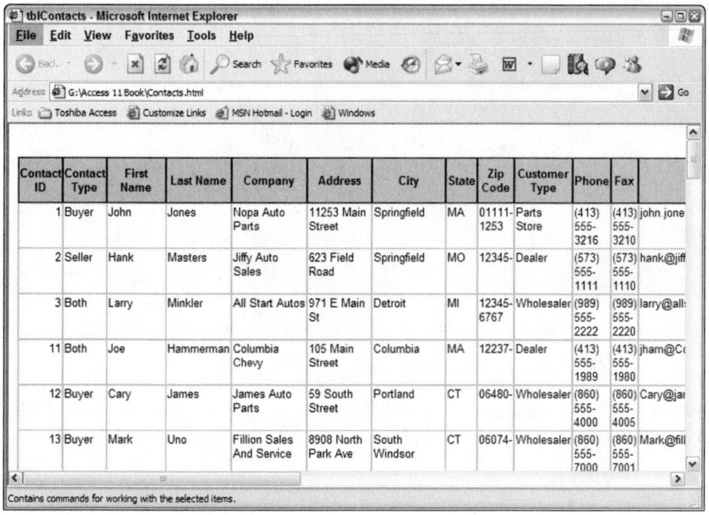
tblContacts - Microsoft Internet Explorer
File Edit View Favorites Tools Help
Search Favorites Media
Address G:\Access 11 Book\Contacts.html
Go
Links Toshiba Access Customize Links MSN Hotmail - Login Windows
Contact ID | Contact Type | First Name | Last Name | Company | Address | City | State | Zip Code | Customer Type | Phone | Fax
1 Buyer John Jones Nopa Auto Parts 11253 Main Street Springfield MA 01111-1253 Parts Store (413) 555-3216 (413) 555-3210 john.jone
2 Seller Hank Masters Jiffy Auto Sales 623 Field Road Springfield MO 12345- Dealer (573) 555-1111 (573) 555-1110 hank@jiff
3 Both Larry Minkler All Start Autos 971 E Main St Detroit MI 12345-6767 Wholesaler (989) 555-2222 (989) 555-2220 larry@all:
11 Both Joe Hammerman Columbia Chevy 105 Main Street Columbia MA 12237- Dealer (413) 555-1989 (413) 555-1980 jham@C
12 Buyer Cary James James Auto Parts 59 South Street Portland CT 06480- Wholesaler (860) 555-4000 (860) 555-4005 Cary@jai
13 Buyer Mark Uno Fillion Sales And Service 8908 North Park Ave South Windsor CT 06074- Wholesaler (860) 555-7000 (860) 555-7001 Mark@fill
Contains commands for working with the selected items.

Figure 7-29: Internet Explorer browser displaying the Customer's table exported to an HTML file.

✦ ✦ ✦

If you save a table to an HTML table, Access will create the HTML document and if you check the Auto Published and Link Figures check box stays, an Export to use log box you can keep Access start on a browser, showing the form it creates. Figure 7-25 shows the Contacts table exported as Administrator HTML table and displayed automatically in the browser.

Figure 7-25: Internet Explorer browser displaying the Customers table exported to an HTML file.

PART I

Creating Desktop Applications

SECTION II

Building Forms and Reports

Understanding the Many Uses of Forms and Controls

◆ ◆ ◆ ◆

In This Chapter

Understanding the types of forms that you can create

Looking at the difference between a form and a datasheet

Creating a form with the AutoForm Wizard

Understanding controls

Learning standards for using controls

◆ ◆ ◆ ◆

On the CD-ROM In this chapter, you will use the database file Chap08Start. mdb. The forms displayed in this chapter are found in the database file in the forms tab.

Forms provide the most flexible way for viewing, adding, editing, and deleting your data. They are also used for switchboards (forms with buttons that provide navigation), dialogs that control the flow of the system, and displaying messages. Controls are the objects on forms such as labels, text boxes, buttons, and many others. In this chapter, you learn about different types of forms and get an understanding about the types of controls that are used on a form.

Understanding Forms

Although you can view your data in many ways, a form provides the most flexibility for viewing and entering data. A form lets you view one or more records at a time while viewing all of the fields. A datasheet also lets you view several records at once, but each record is displayed as a row, so you can see only a limited number of fields at a time.

When you use a form, you can see all your fields at once, or at least as many as you can fit on a screen. By rearranging your fields in a form, you can easily get 20, 50, or even 100 fields on one screen. You can also use forms to create tabbed dialog boxes or main (graphical button) menus known as *switchboards*. Forms are useful for viewing data in a formatted display, as well as for entering, changing, or deleting data. You can also print forms with the visual effects that you create.

What are the basic types of forms?

These are the several basic types of forms:

- ✦ Columnar (also known as full-screen) forms, which are used for data entry, switchboards (used for navigation), dialogs, and message boxes

- ✦ Datasheets, which display many records at a time, like a spreadsheet, in rows and columns

- ✦ Tabular forms, which display more than one formatted record at a time

- ✦ Main/subforms, which display data that include parent/child relationships

- ✦ Pivot table forms (like those found in Microsoft Excel), which display cross-tabulation views of data

- ✦ Graphs, including bar charts, pie charts, line graphs, and other chart types

Figure 8-1 shows a *columnar form*; the fields are arranged in a columnar fashion with as many fields placed in the first column as will fit and then more placed in the second column, etc. The form can occupy one or more screen pages. Generally, this type of form simulates the hard-copy entry of data like a paper form. The fields can be arranged any way that you want. The form shown in Figure 8-1 is the form named frmProducts in the example database.

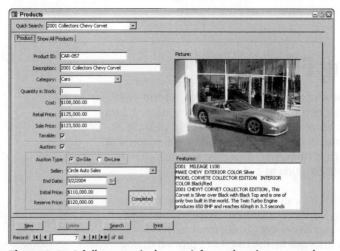

Figure 8-1: A full-screen (columnar) form showing a sample data record.

Most standard Windows controls are available when using Microsoft Access forms to simplify data entry. Lines, boxes, colors, and special effects (such as shadows or three-dimensional looks) enable you to make great looking, easy-to-use forms. Later in this chapter, you will learn about the various control types used in Microsoft Access forms.

Note In a columnar type form, you will generally see one record at a time.

Figure 8-2 shows a tabular form that displays many records at one time. The form in Figure 8-2 is found on the second tab of the frmProducts form. It is actually a *subform* (a form within a form). Notice that the form shows selected fields from the form shown in Figure 8-1. Both of these forms show data from the tblProducts table. While the columnar form provides a window to one record, the tabular or continuous form provides a link to many records.

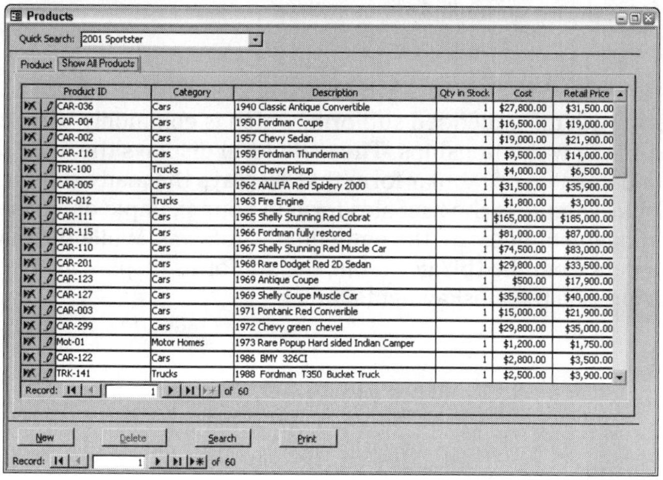

Product ID	Category	Description	Qty in Stock	Cost	Retail Price
CAR-036	Cars	1940 Classic Antique Convertible	1	$27,800.00	$31,500.00
CAR-004	Cars	1950 Fordman Coupe	1	$16,500.00	$19,000.00
CAR-002	Cars	1957 Chevy Sedan	1	$19,000.00	$21,900.00
CAR-116	Cars	1959 Fordman Thunderman	1	$9,500.00	$14,000.00
TRK-100	Trucks	1960 Chevy Pickup	1	$4,000.00	$6,500.00
CAR-005	Cars	1962 AALLFA Red Spidery 2000	1	$31,500.00	$35,900.00
TRK-012	Trucks	1963 Fire Engine	1	$1,800.00	$3,000.00
CAR-111	Cars	1965 Shelly Stunning Red Cobrat	1	$165,000.00	$185,000.00
CAR-115	Cars	1966 Fordman fully restored	1	$81,000.00	$87,000.00
CAR-110	Cars	1967 Shelly Stunning Red Muscle Car	1	$74,500.00	$83,000.00
CAR-201	Cars	1968 Rare Dodget Red 2D Sedan	1	$29,800.00	$33,500.00
CAR-123	Cars	1969 Antique Coupe	1	$500.00	$17,900.00
CAR-127	Cars	1969 Shelly Coupe Muscle Car	1	$35,500.00	$40,000.00
CAR-003	Cars	1971 Pontanic Red Converible	1	$15,000.00	$21,900.00
CAR-299	Cars	1972 Chevy green chevel	1	$29,800.00	$35,000.00
Mot-01	Motor Homes	1973 Rare Popup Hard sided Indian Camper	1	$1,200.00	$1,750.00
CAR-122	Cars	1986 BMY 326CI	1	$2,800.00	$3,500.00
TRK-141	Trucks	1988 Fordman T350 Bucket Truck	1	$2,500.00	$3,900.00

Figure 8-2: A tabular form.

Tabular forms do not have to have just basic data or single lines. The tabular form shown in Figure 8-3 combines the best of each of the forms shown in this chapter. You can format any part of a tabular form; your column headers can span lines and be formatted separately from the records (datasheets don't allow you to customize the column headers). Tabular forms can have multiple rows per record, as in Figure 8-3. You can add special effects (such as shadows) to the fields. Field controls can be option buttons, command buttons, and text boxes. There is no limit to the complexity of the forms you can create with tabular type forms.

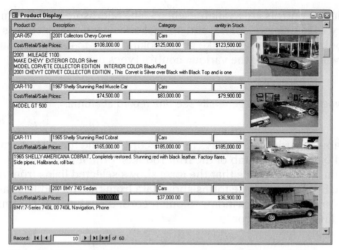

Figure 8-3: A tabular form shown on multiple lines with various controls.

Figure 8-4 shows a form with an embedded subform, which is commonly used to display data with one-to-many relationships. The main form displays the main table; the subform is often a datasheet or tabular form that displays the many side tables of the relationship. This example is the frmSales form in your example database. The product lines and payment lines are the embedded subforms. While the main invoice form displays data from the tblSales table, the subforms display data from the tblSalesLineItems and the tblSalesPayments tables.

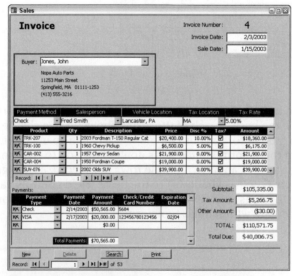

Figure 8-4: A main/subform form with multiple subforms.

In Figure 8-4, information for each invoice appears once, while the first subform shows many line item detail records. The second subform shows many payment line items. This type of form combines the benefits of forms and datasheets. A subform can show one record or more, each on multiple lines.

How do forms differ from datasheets?

If you display a table, you get an automatic datasheet view of your data. This is not a form object but simply a view of your data in a temporary datasheet. You can also create a form with a datasheet view and save the form. With a datasheet type form shown in Figure 8-5, you have very little control over the display of data. Although you can change the type and size of the display font, and rearrange, resize, or hide columns, you can't significantly alter the appearance of the data. By using form objects, you can place each field in an exact specified location, add color or shading to each field, and add text controls to make data entry more efficient.

A form has more flexibility in data entry than a datasheet. You can input data to multiple tables at the same time, and add calculated fields as well as enhanced data-validation and editing controls (such as option buttons, check boxes, and pop-up list boxes) to a form. Adding lines, boxes, colors, and static bitmaps enhances the look of your data, makes your form easier to use, and improves productivity.

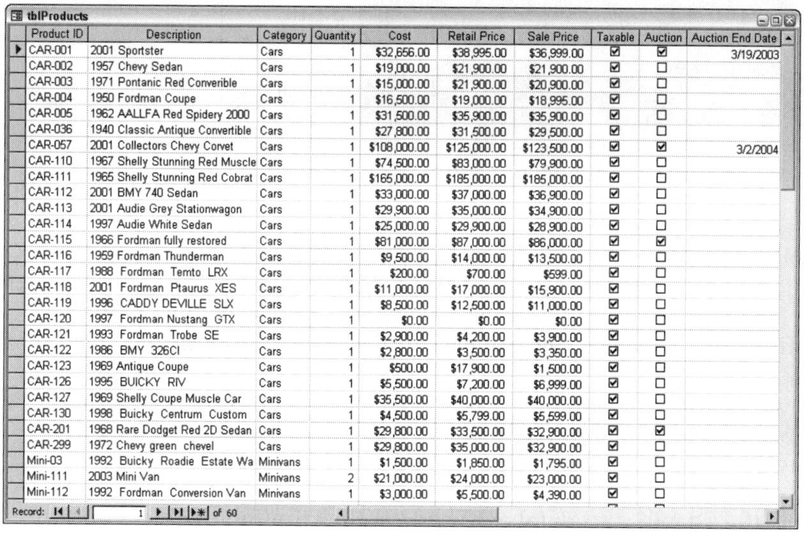

tblProducts

Product ID	Description	Category	Quantity	Cost	Retail Price	Sale Price	Taxable	Auction	Auction End Date
CAR-001	2001 Sportster	Cars	1	$32,656.00	$38,995.00	$36,999.00	☑	☑	3/19/2003
CAR-002	1957 Chevy Sedan	Cars	1	$19,000.00	$21,900.00	$21,900.00	☑	☐	
CAR-003	1971 Pontanic Red Converible	Cars	1	$15,000.00	$21,900.00	$20,900.00	☑	☐	
CAR-004	1950 Fordman Coupe	Cars	1	$16,500.00	$19,000.00	$18,995.00	☑	☐	
CAR-005	1962 AALLFA Red Spidery 2000	Cars	1	$31,500.00	$35,900.00	$35,900.00	☑	☐	
CAR-036	1940 Classic Antique Convertible	Cars	1	$27,800.00	$31,500.00	$29,500.00	☑	☐	
CAR-057	2001 Collectors Chevy Corvet	Cars	1	$108,000.00	$125,000.00	$123,500.00	☑	☑	3/2/2004
CAR-110	1967 Shelly Stunning Red Muscle	Cars	1	$74,500.00	$83,000.00	$79,900.00	☑	☐	
CAR-111	1965 Shelly Stunning Red Cobrat	Cars	1	$165,000.00	$185,000.00	$185,000.00	☑	☐	
CAR-112	2001 BMY 740 Sedan	Cars	1	$33,000.00	$37,000.00	$36,900.00	☑	☐	
CAR-113	2001 Audie Grey Stationwagon	Cars	1	$29,900.00	$35,000.00	$34,900.00	☑	☐	
CAR-114	1997 Audie White Sedan	Cars	1	$25,000.00	$29,900.00	$28,900.00	☑	☐	
CAR-115	1966 Fordman fully restored	Cars	1	$81,000.00	$87,000.00	$86,000.00	☑	☑	
CAR-116	1959 Fordman Thunderman	Cars	1	$9,500.00	$14,000.00	$13,500.00	☑	☐	
CAR-117	1988 Fordman Temto LRX	Cars	1	$200.00	$700.00	$599.00	☑	☐	
CAR-118	2001 Fordman Ptaurus XES	Cars	1	$11,000.00	$17,000.00	$15,900.00	☑	☐	
CAR-119	1996 CADDY DEVILLE SLX	Cars	1	$8,500.00	$12,500.00	$11,000.00	☑	☐	
CAR-120	1997 Fordman Nustang GTX	Cars	1	$0.00	$0.00	$0.00	☑	☐	
CAR-121	1993 Fordman Trobe SE	Cars	1	$2,900.00	$4,200.00	$3,900.00	☑	☐	
CAR-122	1986 BMY 326CI	Cars	1	$2,800.00	$3,500.00	$3,350.00	☑	☐	
CAR-123	1969 Antique Coupe	Cars	1	$500.00	$17,900.00	$1,500.00	☑	☐	
CAR-126	1995 BUICKY RIV	Cars	1	$5,500.00	$7,200.00	$6,999.00	☑	☐	
CAR-127	1969 Shelly Coupe Muscle Car	Cars	1	$35,500.00	$40,000.00	$40,000.00	☑	☐	
CAR-130	1998 Buicky Centrum Custom	Cars	1	$4,500.00	$5,799.00	$5,599.00	☑	☐	
CAR-201	1968 Rare Dodget Red 2D Sedan	Cars	1	$29,800.00	$33,500.00	$32,900.00	☑	☑	
CAR-299	1972 Chevy green chevel	Cars	1	$29,800.00	$35,000.00	$32,900.00	☑	☐	
Mini-03	1992 Buicky Roadie Estate Wa	Minivans	1	$1,500.00	$1,850.00	$1,795.00	☑	☐	
Mini-111	2003 Mini Van	Minivans	2	$21,000.00	$24,000.00	$23,000.00	☑	☐	
Mini-112	1992 Fordman Conversion Van	Minivans	1	$3,000.00	$5,500.00	$4,390.00	☑	☐	

Record: 1 of 60

Figure 8-5: A datasheet view of a form.

In addition, OLE objects (such as pictures or graphs) are visible *only* in a form or report. Although you can increase a datasheet's row size to see more of a Memo field displaying long text, using a form makes it easier to display large amounts of text in a scrollable text box, pictures, or any other object.

Tip

After you create a form with editing or enhanced data validation controls, you can still switch into Datasheet View, which lets you use data-validation rules and controls, such as combo boxes, in the datasheet.

Cross-Reference

If you are new to Microsoft Access and do not know how to start Microsoft Access or use the database window to create new objects, you should review the Introduction of this book.

Creating a form with AutoForm

From the Tables or Queries object in the Database window, a datasheet, or most design screens in Access, you can create a columnar form instantly with just a few mouse clicks by clicking the New Object drop-down button on the toolbar (an icon with a lightning bolt through it), as shown in Figure 8-6. After you click on the drop-down button next to the icon, you can then choose the AutoForm selection on the drop-down menu. The form will be created using whatever table or query was last selected.

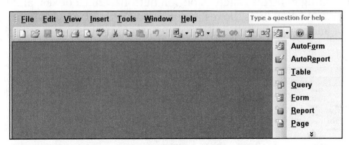

Figure 8-6: The New Object toolbar menu.

When you use AutoForm, you automatically get a Columnar form. If you want another form type, there are other ways to quickly create a form. Another method is to use Insert ➪ Form from the Access main menu and select one of the AutoForm choices from the dialog box that appears. You will see this in the next chapter.

With the AutoForm selection on the New Object toolbar button, the form can be created with no additional work. To create a columnar AutoForm using the tblProducts table, follow these steps:

1. From the Chap08Start database window, click the Tables object button

2. Select tblProducts.

3. Click the New Object button icon drop down arrow on the main Microsoft Access toolbar (not the Database window toolbar).

4. Select AutoForm.

The form instantly appears, as shown in Figure 8-7. Your screen resolution and the size of your monitor may show more or less of the form than in this figure.

5. Close the form and don't save it after you read the rest of this section in this chapter.

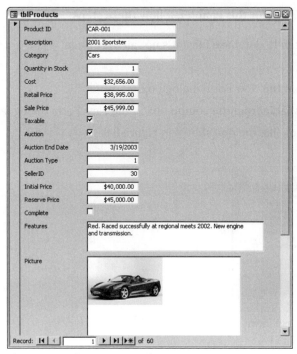

Figure 8-7: The AutoForm form.

The first record is displayed. Some values, however, are not properly displayed in different areas of the form. For example, if you look at the picture of the car in the first record, you can see a lot of white space around the value and it doesn't fit the area. Later in this chapter, you learn how to fix this, as well as how to customize the form.

Using AutoForm is the quickest way to create a form. Generally, however, you want more control over your form creation. Other Form Wizards can help you create a more customized form from the outset. In the next chapter, you will learn how to create other forms with wizards. Next, it is important to learn what goes on a form.

If you haven't closed the form you created in Figure 8-7, you can close it now without saving it.

The next part of this chapter will explain and demonstrate the various control types available in Access. Before you learn about controls, you should learn how to create a blank form and to display the list of fields available and also how to display the form's toolbox that you use to select various types of controls.

To create a blank form you need for this chapter, follow these steps:

1. Open the Chap08Start.mdb database file if it's not already open.

2. Select Insert ➪ Form.

3. Select Design View from the New Form dialog box.

4. Select the tblProducts table from the combo box in the New Form dialog box.

   Your screen should look like the one shown in Figure 8-8.

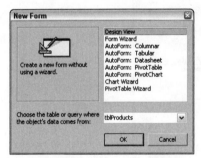

Figure 8-8: Creating a new form with the New Form dialog box.

5. Click OK to display the Form Design window.

6. Maximize the form by clicking the maximize button in the top-right corner of the window.

7. Expand the light gray area of the form to the full-window size by dragging the bottom-right corner of the light gray area to the bottom-right corner of the window. Figure 8-9 shows this blank form design.

8. If the Field list is not displayed, click on the Field List icon in the toolbar. If the form Toolbox is not displayed as shown in Figure 8-9, click on the Toolbox icon next to the field list icon.

Before continuing with this form, it is important to understand the basic concepts of controls.

Understanding Form Controls

Controls and properties form the basis of forms and reports. It is critical to understand the fundamental concepts of controls and properties before you begin to apply them to custom forms and reports.

Note While this chapter is about forms, you will learn that forms and reports share many common characteristics including controls and what you can do with them. As you learn about controls in this chapter, you will be able to apply nearly everything you learn when you create reports.

What Is a Control?

A *control* has many definitions in Access. Generally, a control is any object on a form or report, such as a label or text box. These are the same controls that you use in any Windows application, such as Access, Excel, or Web-based HTML forms, or those that are used in any language, such as .Net, Visual Basic, C++, or even C#. Although each language or product has different file formats and different properties, a text box in Access is the same as a text box in any other Windows product.

You enter data into controls and display data using controls. A control can be bound to a field in a table (when the value is entered in the control it is also saved in some underlying table field), or it can be unbound and displayed in the form but not saved when the form is closed. A control can also be an object, such as a line or rectangle. Calculated fields are also controls, as are pictures, graphs, option buttons, check boxes, and objects. Some controls that aren't part of Access are developed separately — these are ActiveX controls. ActiveX controls extend the base feature set of Access 2003 and are available from a variety of vendors. Many ActiveX controls are shipped with Access 2003.

Cross-Reference ActiveXcontrols are covered in Chapter 14.

Whether you're working with forms or reports, essentially the same process is followed to create and use controls. In this chapter, we explain controls from the perspective of a form.

Note The View menu contains many options to display the options of the form design window. In the figure above (and in the author's computer, the Grid (a series of horizontal and vertical lines) is turned off while the rulers at the top and left side are turned on.

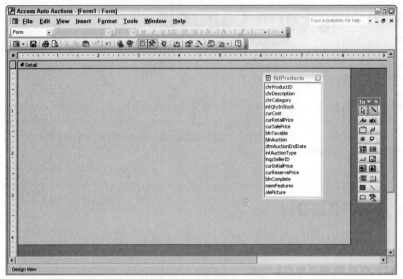

Figure 8-9: A new blank form showing the field list and form toolbox.

The different control types

Forms and reports contain many different control types. You can add some of these controls to forms by using the Toolbox shown in Figure 8-9. In this book, you learn to add and use the controls that are used most often (these are listed in Table 8-1). In this part of this chapter, you learn when to use each control and you also learn how these controls work.

Table 8-1
Controls You Can Create in Access Forms and Reports

Basic Controls

Label	Literal text is displayed in a label control.
Text Box	Data is typed into a text box.

Enhanced Data Entry and Data Validation Controls

Option Group	This group holds multiple option buttons, check boxes, or toggle buttons.
Toggle Button	This is a two-state button, up or down, which usually uses pictures or icons instead of text to display different states.

Enhanced Data Entry and Data Validation Controls

Option Button	Also called a radio button, this button is displayed as a circle with a dot when the option is on.
Check Box	This is another two-state control, shown as a square that contains a check mark if it's on and an empty square if it's off.
Combo Box	This box is a pop-up list of values that allows entries not on the list.
List Box	This is a list of values that is always displayed on the form or report.
Command Button	Also called a push button, this button is used to call a macro or run a Basic program to initiate an action.
Subform/Subreport	This control displays another form or report within the original form or report.
Tab Control	This control can display multiple pages in a file folder type interface.

Graphic and Picture Controls

Image	Displays a bitmap picture with very little overhead.
Unbound Object Frame	This frame holds an OLE object or embedded picture that is not tied to a table field and can include graphs, pictures, sound files, and video.
Bound Object Frame	This frame holds an OLE object or embedded picture that is tied to a table field.
Line	This is a single line of variable thickness and color, which is used for separation.
Rectangle	A rectangle can be any color or size or can be filled in or blank; the rectangle is used for emphasis.
Page Break	This is usually used for reports and denotes a physical page break.

Note   If the toolbox isn't displayed, you can display it by selecting View ⇨ Toolbox or by clicking the toolbox icon.

Figure 8-10 shows the toolbox with a new blank form. This is the design grid where you place the controls you will want on the form. You can also see the Field List window on the form ready for you to select the fields from the tblProducts table to use in your form.

Figure 8-10: The form toolbox with definitions of each control type.

Tip

You can move, resize, and anchor the toolbox on the window. You can anchor it to any border, grab it, and resize it in the middle of the window. The toolbox can be dragged anywhere on the form and you can additionally change the shape of the toolbox. It can be more square or be oriented horizontally instead of vertically across the screen.

The Control Wizard icon, located in the upper-right corner of the toolbox, does not add a control to a form; rather, it determines whether a Wizard is automatically activated when you add certain controls. The Option Group, Combo Box, List Box, Subform/Subreport, Bound and Unbound Object Frame, and Command Button controls all have Wizards that Access starts when you add a new control. You can use the More Controls icon (found in the bottom-right corner of the toolbox) to display a list of ActiveX controls, which you can add to Access 2003.

Standards for Using Controls

Most of you reading this book have used Microsoft Windows. You have probably used other applications in Windows as well, such as Word, Excel, and other Office applications. Using a Windows application and designing a Windows application, however, are two different tasks.

The controls in Access 2003 have specific purposes. The uses of these controls, however, are not decided by whim or intuition — a scientific method determines which control should be used for each specific situation. Experience shows you that correct screen and report designs lead to more usable applications.

Tip

In fact, you may learn that Office developers use the fonts and colors that Microsoft Office uses. Some of the simplest guidelines include using the Tahoma font for all form controls that are 12 points or smaller and the Verdana font for all font sizes above 12 point. Other Office standards include using only etched line rectangles (never sunken or raised), gray form backgrounds, flat label controls, and sunken text box controls with white backgrounds for data entry. The only item that should be raised on a form is a button that you can click. Finally, no control text is bolded except for an occasional label at the top of the form. Use of multiple colors may be attractive to you but, for professional designers, is reserved for circus applications.

On the CD-ROM

In the file Chap08Start.mdb are a series of forms that correspond to the examples in the remainder of the chapter. You may want to open each of them in design view or run them as you learn about the various control types. The form names are zzfrmFigure8-11 through zzfrmFigure8-17.

Label controls

You use a *label control* to display descriptive text (such as a title, a caption, or instructions) on a form or report. Labels can be separate controls, which is common when they are used for titles or data-entry instructions. When labels are used for field captions, they are often attached to the control that they describe.

You can display labels on a single line or on multiple lines. Labels are unbound controls that accept no input; you use them strictly for one-way communication (they are read-only). You can use them on many types of controls. Figure 8-11 shows many uses of labels, including titles, captions, button text, and captions for buttons and boxes. You can use different font styles and sizes for your labels, and you can boldface, italicize, and underline them.

You should capitalize the first letter of each word in a label, except for articles and conjunctions, such as *the, an, and, or,* and so on. You should follow several guidelines when you use label controls with other controls. The following list explains some of these placement guidelines, which are shown in Figure 8-11:

  ✦ **Command buttons.** Inside the button.

  ✦ **Checkboxes.** To the right of the check box.

  ✦ **Option buttons.** To the right of the option button.

  ✦ **Text box.** Above or to the left of the text box.

  ✦ **List or combo box.** Above or to the left of the box.

  ✦ **Group box.** On top of and replacing part of the top frame line.

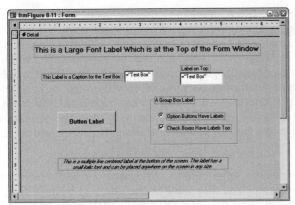

Figure 8-11: Sample label controls alone and with other controls.

Text box controls

Text boxes are controls that display data or allow the user to enter or edit information. In a text box, you can accept the current text, edit it, delete it, or replace it. You can use text boxes with most data types, including Text, Number, Date/Time, Yes/No, and Memo — and they can also be used as bound or unbound controls. You can use text box fields from tables or queries, or the text box can contain calculated expressions. A text box is the most-used control because editing and displaying data are the main purposes of any database system.

Every text box needs an associated label to identify its purpose. Text boxes can contain multiple lines of data and often do (you use one to display Memo field data, for example). Data that is too long for the width of the text field wraps automatically within the field boundaries. Figure 8-12 shows several different text boxes in Form view. Notice how the different data types vary in their alignment within the text boxes. The Features text box displays multiple lines in the resized text box, which also has a scrollbar.

Toggle buttons, option buttons, and check boxes

Button or *check box* controls allow the user to select a choice. Three types of buttons act in the same way, but their visual displays are very different:

✦ Toggle buttons

✦ Option buttons (also known as *radio buttons*)

✦ Check boxes

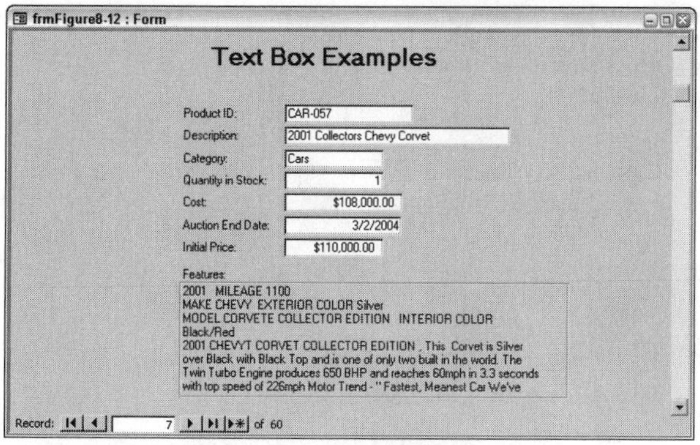

Figure 8-12: Sample text box controls.

These controls are used with Yes/No data types. You can use each control individually to represent one of two states: Yes or No, On or Off, or True or False. Table 8-2 describes the appearance of these controls in both states.

Toggle buttons, option buttons, and check boxes return a value of –1 to the bound table field if the button value is Yes, On, or True; they return a value of 0 if the button is No, Off, or False. You can enter a default value to display a specific state. The control is initially displayed in a Null state if no default is entered and no state is selected. The Null state's visual appearance is the same as that of the No state.

Although you can place Yes/No data types in a text box, it's better to use one of these controls. The values that are returned to a text box (–1 and 0) are very confusing, especially because Yes is represented by –1 and No is represented by 0.

| | Table 8-2 | |
| | **Button Control Visual Displays** | |
Button Type	**State**	**Visual Description**
Toggle button	True	Button is sunken
Toggle button	False	Button is raised
Option button	True	Circle with a large solid dot inside
Option button	False	Hollow circle
Check box	True	Square with a check in the middle
Check box	False	Empty square

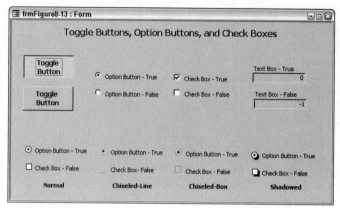

Figure 8-13 Sample toggle buttons, option buttons, and check boxes.

Note   As Figure 8-13 shows, using the special effects options from the Formatting tool-bar can change the look of the option button or check box. See Chapter 13 for more details.

Tip   You can format the display of the Yes/No values in Datasheet or Form view by set-ting the Format property of the text box control to Yes/No, On/Off, or True/False. If you don't use the Format property, the datasheet displays –1 or 0. Using a default value also speeds data entry, especially if the default is the value selected most often.

Option groups

An *option group* can contain multiple toggle buttons, option buttons, or check boxes. When these controls are inside an option group box, they work together rather than individually. Instead of representing a two-state Yes/No data type, controls within an option group return a number based on the position in the group. You can select only one control within an option group at a time; the maximum number of buttons in such a group should be four. If you need to exceed that number, switch to a drop-down list box (unless you have plenty of room on your screen).

An option group is generally bound to a single field or expression. Each button inside it passes a different value back to the option group, which in turn passes the single choice to the bound field or expression. The buttons themselves are not bound to any field; instead, they are bound to the option group box.

Figure 8-14 shows three types of buttons; two of these types are shown in option group boxes. In the Toggle Buttons option group, the second choice is selected; the same is true of the Option Buttons option group. Notice, however, that the first and third choices are selected in the Check Boxes rectangle; the check boxes are independent and are not part of an option group. When you make a new selection in an option group, the current selection is de-selected. For example, if you click on Option Button 3 in the option group box in the middle of Figure 8-14, the solid dot appears to move to the third circle, and the second circle becomes hollow.

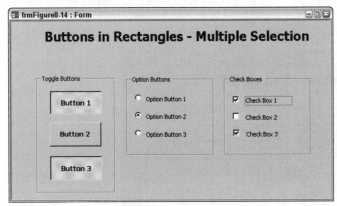

Figure 8-14: Three types of option groups.

Tip   You may want to create groups of buttons that look like option groups but have multiple selections. Rather than use an option button, simply enclose the group of buttons in a rectangle. Each button remains an individual entity instead of becoming part of a group.

List boxes

A *list box* control displays a list of data on-screen just like a pull-down menu, but the list box is always open. You can highlight an item in the list by moving the cursor to your desired choice and then pressing Enter (or clicking the mouse) to complete the selection. You can also type the first letter of the selection to highlight the desired entry. After you select an item, the item's value is passed back to the bound field.

List boxes can display any number of fields and any number of records. By sizing the list box, you can make it display more or fewer records.

Note   List boxes have a feature called Multi Select property that allows you to select more than one item at a time. The results are stored in a type of array and must be used with the VBA programming language.

List boxes are generally used when you have plenty of room on-screen and you want the operator to see the choices without having to click on a drop-down arrow.

A vertical — and horizontal — scrollbar is used to display any records and fields not visible when the list box is in its default size. The highlighted entry is the one that is currently selected. If no entries are highlighted, either a selection has not been made or the selected item is not currently in view. You can select only the items in the list.

You also have a choice of whether to display the column headings in list boxes. Figure 8-15 displays list boxes with three layout schemes.

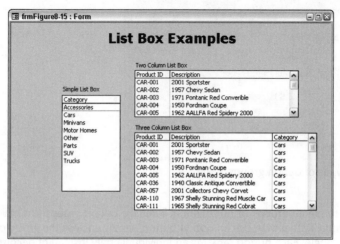

Figure 8-15: Sample list boxes.

Combo boxes

In Access, *combo boxes* differ from list boxes in two ways:

✦ The combo box is initially displayed as a single row with an arrow that opens the box to the normal size.

✦ As an option, the combo box lets you enter a value that is not on the list.

You see a list box and a combo box (shown both open and closed) in Figure 8-16.

Tab controls

The *tab control* is one of the most important controls because it allows you to create completely new interfaces by using the tabbed dialog box look and feel.

Most serious Windows applications now contain tabbed dialog boxes. Tabbed dialog boxes look very professional. They allow you to have many screens of data in a small area by grouping similar types of data and using tabs to navigate between the areas.

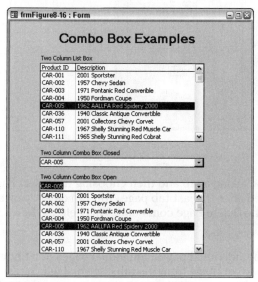

Figure 8-16: An example of the differences between combo boxes and list boxes.

The tab control gets its name from the fact that it looks like the tab on a file folder when you use it. Figure 8-17 shows the Access 2003 tab control icon and a tab control under construction on the design screen. As you can see, the tab control looks like the tabs seen in Form View.

You create a new Tab Control in the same way that you create any Access control. You select the tab control, as shown in Figure 8-17, and then you draw a rectangle to indicate the size of the control. When the tab control is initially shown, it is displayed with two tab pages. The tab control contains pages. Each tab that you define creates a separate page. As you choose each tab in Design View, you see a different page. You can place other controls on each page of the tab control. The control can have many pages; in fact, you can have multiple rows of tabs, each having its own page. You can place new controls on a page or copy and paste them from other forms or other pages. You can't drag and drop between pages of a tab control. To change the active page for the tab control, click the page that you want and it becomes active (even in design mode).

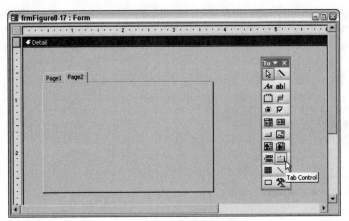

Figure 8-17: Designing a tab control

You can insert new pages by right-clicking a tab and then choosing the Insert Page command. The new page is inserted after the last tab page. You can delete pages by right-clicking a tab and choosing the Delete Page command. This deletes the active page and all the controls on it.

You can size the tab control but not individual pages. Individual pages don't have visual appearance properties — they get these from the tab control itself. You select the border of the tab control by clicking it — clicking directly on a page selects that page. As with an Access detail section, you can't size the tab control smaller than the control in the rightmost part of the page. You must move controls before resizing.

✦   ✦   ✦

Building and Manipulating Forms and Controls

On the CD-ROM   In this chapter, you will use the tblProducts tables in the chap09start.mdb database to provide the data necessary to create the examples used in this chapter.

Creating a Form with Form Wizards

Form Wizards simplify the layout process for your fields. A Form Wizard visually walks you through a series of questions about the form that you want to create and then creates it for you automatically. This chapter creates single-column forms with a Form Wizard, using the columnar form to create a full-screen form.

Creating a new form

You have several methods to create a new form using the Form Wizard:

> ✦ Select Insert ➪ Form from the Access window menu.
>
> ✦ Select the Forms object button and click the New button from the Database window.
>
> ✦ Select the New Object button combo box from the Access window, the datasheet, or the Query toolbar, and choose Form.

To start the Form Wizard, follow the next steps:

1. With the Forms object selected in the Database window, click New. From the New Form dialog box, choose the Form Wizard option.

2. Select the tblProducts table in the Choose the Table or Query ... combo box at the bottom of the New Form window.

Whichever method you used (hopefully you will follow the steps), the New Form dialog box appears, as shown in Figure 9-1. If you begin to create the new form with a table highlighted (or from a datasheet or query), the table or query that you are using appears in the text box labeled *Choose the table or query where the object's data comes from*. You can enter the name of a valid table or query (if you are not already using one) before continuing. You can choose from a list of tables and queries by clicking the combo box's selection arrow.

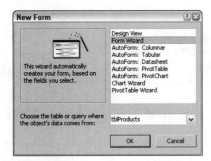

Figure 9-1: The New Form dialog box.

Selecting the New Form type and data source

The New Form dialog box provides nine choices for creating a form:

✦ **Design View.** Displays a completely blank form to start with in Form design.

✦ **Form Wizard.** Creates a form with one of four default layouts: columnar, tabular, datasheet, or justified using data fields that you specify in a step-by-step process that lets you customize the form creation process.

✦ **AutoForm: Columnar.** Instantly creates a columnar form.

✦ **AutoForm: Tabular.** Instantly creates a tabular form.

✦ **AutoForm: Datasheet.** Instantly creates a datasheet form.

✦ **AutoForm: PivotTable.** Instantly creates a pivot table form.

✦ **AutoForm: PivotChart.** Instantly creates a pivot chart form.

✦ **Chart Wizard.** Creates a form with a business graph.

✦ **PivotTable Wizard.** Creates an Excel Pivot Table form.

Choosing the fields

After you have selected the data for the form, you can press the OK button to move to the next New Form wizard dialog.

To continue with the Form Wizard, press OK.

After you press OK, the field-selection window appears. The field-selection dialog box has three work areas. The first area lets you choose multiple tables or queries, so you can create many types of forms, including those with subforms. As you select each table or query, the list box beneath Available Fields displays the possible fields, and below Selected Fields displays the selected fields. You can see in Figure 9-2 that three fields have just been selected.

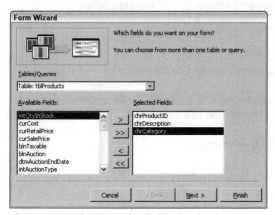

Figure 9-2: Choosing the fields for the form.

The field-selection area consists of two list boxes and four buttons. The Available Fields: list box on the left displays all fields from the selected table/query that was used to create the form. The Selected Fields: list box on the right displays the fields that you have selected for this form. You can select one field, all the fields, or any combination of fields. The order in which you add the fields to the list box on the right is the order in which the fields appear in the form. You can use the buttons to place or remove fields in the Selected Fields: box. Here is a description of these buttons:

>	Add selected field.
>>	Add all fields.
<	Remove selected field.
<<	Remove all fields.

When you highlight a field in the Available Fields: list box and click >, the field name appears in the Selected Fields: list box. You can add each field that you want to the list box. If you add a field by mistake, you can select the field in the Selected Fields: list box and click < to remove it from the selection. If you decide that you want to change the order in which your fields appear in the form, you must remove any fields that are out of order and reselect them in the proper order.

> **Note**   You can also double-click any field in the Available Fields: list box to add it to the Selected Fields: list box.

At the bottom of the form, you can see a series of buttons to use when the field selection is completed. The types of buttons available here are common to most Wizard dialog boxes:

✦ **Cancel.** Cancel form creation and return to the starting point.

✦ **Back.** Return to the preceding dialog box.

✦ **Next.** Go to the next dialog box.

✦ **Finish.** Go to the last dialog box (usually the form title).

> **Note**   If you click Next> or Finish without selecting any fields, Access tells you that you must select fields for the form before you can continue.

Here's how to select the Fields for this example:

1. Select all of the fields by clicking the >> button.

2. Click the Next button to display the dialog box from which to choose a form layout.

After you select all of the fields from the Available Fields list box, they all will appear to jump from the left list box to the right one.

Choosing the form layout

After you have chosen the fields, you must choose the type of layout. As Figure 9-3 shows, you can choose from six types of layouts:

✦ Columnar

✦ Tabular

✦ Datasheet

✦ Justified

✦ PivotTable

✦ PivotChart

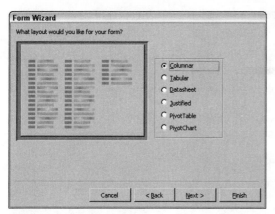

Figure 9-3: Choosing the type of layout for the form.

As you click through the button choices, the display on the left changes to show how the form will look if you use that choice.

1. Select the Columnar layout.

2. After you choose the type of layout, you can click the Next button to display the choices for style of the form, as shown in Figure 9-4.

Choosing the style of the form

You have many choices, which you can access by clicking the desired name in the list box. When you select a style, the display on the left changes to illustrate the special effect used to create the look.

The default look uses the Standard style, which creates a dark gray background and sunken controls. Figure 9-4 shows the Expedition style selected.

1. Select Expedition for the first form that you create in this chapter.

2. Click Next.

After you select the form's style, you are ready to create a title and view the form. The style that you select is used as the default the next time you use the Wizard.

Tip   You can customize the style by changing a form and then using the AutoFormat function in the Form design screen.

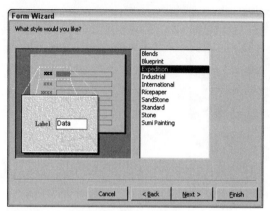

Figure 9-4: Choosing the style of your form.

Creating a form title

The form title dialog box is usually the last dialog box in a Form Wizard. It always has a checkered flag that lets you know you've reached the finish line. By default, the text box for the form title contains the name of the table or query used for the form's data. You can accept the entry for the form title, enter your own, or erase it and have no title. The title in Figure 9-5 is tblProducts, which is the name of the table as long as you don't already have another form named tblProducts. If you do, a number is added to the end of the name.

Change the form name to frmProductsWizard as shown in Figure 9-5.

Cross-Reference

The frm prefix is a naming convention that is used by professional developers. While tbl is the prefix for table objects, frm is the prefix for most forms. See Appendix D for a complete guide to Microsoft Access naming conventions.

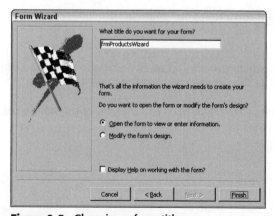

Figure 9-5: Choosing a form title.

Completing the form

After you complete all the steps to design your form, you open the new form by selecting one of these two options:

✦ Open the form to view or enter information.

✦ Modify the form's design.

1. Select Open the form to view or enter information.

2. Click the Finish button.

After you click the Finish button, the form appears in the Form View window (as shown in Figure 9-6).

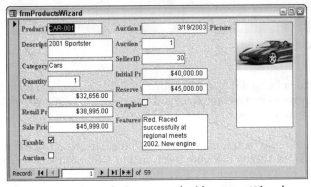

Figure 9-6: A form design created with a Form Wizard.

Changing the Design

To demonstrate how easy it is to manipulate the field controls, in this section you learn how to change the way the Picture field appears. Figure 9-6 shows a lovely view of the front half of the car — it would be nicer to see the whole car. To fix this, follow these steps:

1. Click the Design button (the button on the far left side of the toolbar with a little picture of a pencil, triangle, and ruler) to open the form in the Form Design window.

2. Click the Picture field (the large, empty rectangle next to the Picture label).

3. Click the Property icon in the toolbar (picture of a hand and a sheet of paper, the fifth icon from the right).

4. Click the Size Mode property and change it from Clip to Stretch (as shown in Figure 9-7).

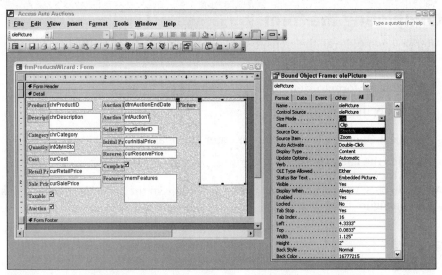

Figure 9-7: Changing a control property.

Tip   If you don't like the Ruler being displayed (as shown in Figure 9-7), or you want to turn on the grid for more precise control alignment, you can turn them on or off by selecting View ⇨ Ruler and/or View ⇨ Grid.

After you complete the property change, click the Form button to redisplay the form. The whole car is displayed, as shown in Figure 9-8. It may not be pretty as you have stretched it, but you can always resize the Picture box size (more about that later in this chapter) or use one of the other choices (like the Zoom Picture property) to correct it.

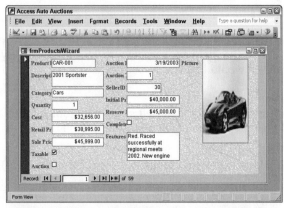

Figure 9-8: The form redisplayed to show the full picture of the car.

Chapters 10 through 13 teach you how to completely customize a form. In these chapters, you learn how to use all the controls in the toolbox, add special effects to forms, create forms with graphs and calculated fields, and add complex data validation to your forms.

Using the Form Window

The window shown in Figure 9-8 is very similar to the Datasheet window. At the top of the screen, you see the title bar, menu bar, and toolbars. The center of the screen displays your data, one record at a time, in the Form window (unless you have the Form window maximized). If the form contains more fields than can fit onscreen at one time, Access 2003 automatically displays a horizontal and/or vertical scrollbar that can be used to see the remainder of the record. You can also see the rest of the record by pressing the PgDn key. The status bar, at the bottom of the window, displays the active field's Field Description that you defined when you created the table. If no Field Description exists for a specific field, Access displays the words Form View. Generally, error messages and warnings appear in dialog boxes in the center of the screen (rather than in the status bar). The navigation buttons are found at the bottom of the screen. This feature lets you move quickly from record to record.

The Form toolbar

The Form toolbar — the lower toolbar, as shown in Figure 9-8 and Figure 9-9 — is almost identical to the datasheet toolbar you see when you display data from a table. The only difference is that if you click on the first icon, you will see it contains five selections: Design View, Form View, Datasheet View, PivotTable View, and PivotChart View.

Figure 9-9: The Form toolbar.

The form toolbar contains common tools that you can click on to save the form, spell check the contents of a field's value, cut, copy, paste, and filter your data.

Navigating between fields

Navigating a form is nearly identical to navigating a datasheet. You can easily move around the form window by clicking the field that you want and making changes or additions to your data. Because the form window displays only as many fields as can fit onscreen, you need to use various navigational aids to move within your form or between records.

Table 9-1 displays the navigational keys used to move between fields within a form.

Table 9-1 Navigating in a Form	
Navigational Direction	*Keystrokes*
Next field	Tab, right-arrow (→) or down-arrow (↓) key, or Enter
Previous field	Shift+Tab, left-arrow (←), or up-arrow (↑)
First field of current record	Home or Ctrl+Home
Last field of current record	End or Ctrl+End
Next page	PgDn or Next Record
Previous page	PgUp or Previous Record

If you have a form with more than one page, a vertical scrollbar displays. You can use the scrollbar to move to different pages on the form. You can also use the PgUp and PgDn keys to move between form pages. You can move up or down one field at a time by clicking the scrollbar arrows. With the scrollbar button, you can move past many fields at once.

Moving between records in a form

Although you generally use a form to display one record at a time, you still need to move between records. The easiest way to do this is to use the navigation buttons, as shown in Figure 9-10. The navigation buttons let you move to the desired record.

 Tip You can also press Ctrl+PgDn to move to the current field in the next record, or Ctrl+PgUp to move to the current field in the preceding record.

Record: I◄ ◄ | 1 | ► ►I ►✳ of 59

Figure 9-10: The form's record navigation buttons.

The record number between the navigation buttons is a *virtual record number*. The number is not attached to any specific record but just an indicator as to the record number you are on given the current filter or sort. It will change with each time you refilter or sort the records. The number to the right of the New Record icon displays the number of records in the current view. The current view is the records based on any filter applied to all the records in the table or query you are viewing.

Tip

Pressing F5 moves you instantly to the record number box. You can change the record number and press Enter and that record will be displayed.

Displaying Your Data with a Form

Earlier in the book, you learned techniques to add, change, and delete data within a table by using a datasheet. These techniques are the same ones you use within a form. Table 9-2 summarizes these techniques.

Table 9-2 Editing Techniques	
Editing Technique	*Keystrokes*
Move insertion point within a field	Press the right (→)- and left-arrow (←) keys
Insert a value within a field	Move the insertion point and type the new data
Select the entire field	Press F2 or double-click the mouse button
Replace an existing value with a new value	Select the entire field and type a new value
Replace value with value of preceding field	Press Ctrl+' (single quotation mark)
Replace current value with default value	Press Ctrl+Alt+Spacebar
Insert current date into a field	Press Ctrl+; (semicolon)
Insert current time into a field	Press Ctrl+: (colon)
Insert a line break in a Text or Memo field	Press Ctrl+Enter
Insert new record	Press Ctrl++ (plus sign)
Delete current record	Press Ctrl+− (minus sign)
Save current record	Press Shift+Enter or move to another record
Undo a change to the current record	Press Esc or click the Undo button

Working with pictures and OLE objects

OLE objects (Object Linking and Embedding) are objects not part of an Access database. Commonly these include pictures. An OLE field can also contain links to objects such as Word documents, Excel spreadsheets, and audio files such as .MP3, .WAV, or .WMV files. You can also include video files such as .MPE or .AVI files.

In a datasheet, you can't view a picture or any OLE object without accessing the OLE server (such as Word, Excel, or the Microsoft Media Player). In a form, however, you can size the OLE control area to be large enough to display a picture, business graph, or any visual OLE object. You can also size Memo text box controls on forms so that you can see the data within the field — you don't have to zoom in on the value, as you do with a datasheet field. Figure 9-8 shows both the picture and the Memo data displayed in the form. Each of these controls can be resized.

Any object supported by an OLE server can be stored in an Access OLE field. OLE objects are entered into a form so that you can see, hear, or use the value. As with a datasheet, you have two ways to enter OLE fields into a form:

✦ Paste them in from the Clipboard from the Edit menu.

✦ Insert them into the field from the Insert ⇨ Object menu.

 Chapter 14 covers using and displaying OLE objects in forms in more detail.

Memo field data entry

The Features field in the form shown in Figure 9-11 is a Memo data type. This type of field allows up to 65,536 bytes of text for each field. You can see the first two sentences of data in the Memo field. When you move the cursor (also known as the *insertion point*) into the Memo field, a vertical scrollbar appears, as you can see in Figure 9-11. Using this scrollbar, you can view the rest of the data in the field.

Better yet, you can resize the Memo control in the Form Design window if you want to make it larger to see more data. You can also press Shift+F2 and display a zoom dialog box, as shown in Figure 9-11, which lets you view about 17 lines at a time.

Switching to a datasheet

While in the form, you can display a Datasheet view of your data by using one of two methods:

✦ Click the Datasheet View button in the toolbar.

✦ Select View ⇨ Datasheet View.

The datasheet is displayed with the cursor on the same field and record that it occupied in the form. If you move to another record and field and then redisplay the form, the form appears with the cursor on the field and with the record it last occupied in the datasheet.

To return to the form from a datasheet, you can use either of these two methods:

✦ Click the Form button in the toolbar.

✦ Select View ⇨ Form View.

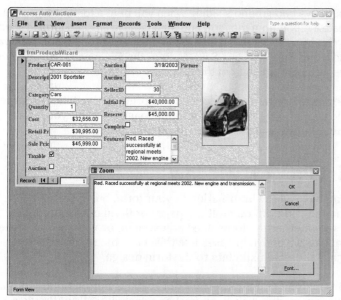

Figure 9-11: A memo field zoom dialog.

Saving a Record and the Form

As you move off each record, Access automatically saves any changes to the record. You can also press Shift+Enter to save a record without moving off of it. Another way to save a record is to close the form. You can save any changes to the current record by selecting Records ➪ Save Record. This action saves any changes and keeps the form open. When you are ready to close a form and return to the Database window (or to your query or datasheet), you can select File ➪ Close. If you made any changes to the form design, you are asked whether you want to save the design.

Printing a Form

You can print one or more records in your form exactly as they appear onscreen. (You learn how to produce formatted reports in Chapters 12, 13, and 15 to 17, later in the book.) The simplest way to print is to use the File ➪ Print selection or the Print toolbar button. Selecting File ➪ Print displays the Print dialog box.

Assuming that you have set up a printer in Microsoft Windows, you can select OK to print your form. Access then prints your form, using the font that you selected for display or using the nearest printer equivalent. The printout contains any formatting that you specified in the form (including lines, boxes, and shading), and converts colors to grayscale if you are using a monochrome printer.

Tip

Because you may have background shading when you print a form, it is generally preferred to create a report from the form and then remove any background shading. You can do this by selecting the open form in design view or unopened in the Database Window and then selecting Save As from the File menu. You can then choose the Save As report option from the displayed dialog box.

The printout includes as many pages as necessary to print all the data. If your form is wider than a single printer page, you need multiple pages to print your form. Access breaks up the printout as necessary to fit on each page.

Using the Print Preview window

You may find that you have all the information in your form, but you aren't sure whether that information will print on multiple pages or fit on one printed page. Maybe you want to see whether the fonts need adjustment, or you need only the printed records from pages 3 and 4. In cases like this, view the report onscreen before printing to make these adjustments to the form design.

To preview your printout, you either click the Print Preview button on the toolbar (a sheet of paper with a magnifying glass on top) or select File ➪ Print Preview. Figure 9-12 shows the Print Preview window.

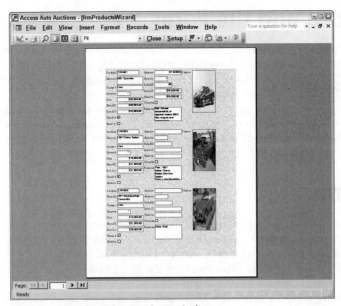

Figure 9-12: The Print Preview window.

If you are satisfied with the form after examining the preview, select the Print button on the toolbar to print the form. If you are not satisfied, click the Close button to return to the form in order to make changes to the data or design.

Close the form before continuing. You can save it if you want. You will not use this example form again in this chapter. In the next part of this chapter, you will create a new form without using a wizard.

Creating New Controls

Although the Form Wizard can quickly place your controls in the design window, you still may need to add more controls to a form, or start with a form design that is different from what the wizard can create.

You will now learn how to add controls to a form and how to manipulate them in the form design window without using the wizard.

To create a new form for this example, follow these steps:

1. Select the Forms object type from the database window.

2. Click on the New icon in the database window.

3. Select Design View in the top portion of the New Form window and select tblProducts from the bottom portion of the New Form window.

4. Press OK to create the blank form.

If the Field List window is not displayed, press the Field List icon on the toolbar. You screen should like Figure 9-13.

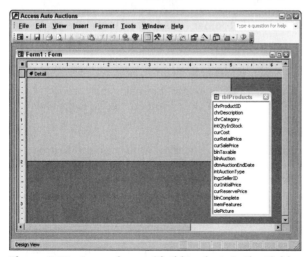

Figure 9-13: A new form with tblProducts in the Field List window.

Resizing the form area

The dark gray area of the form is where you can work. This is the size of the form when it is displayed. You can resize the dark gray area of the form by placing the cursor on any of the area borders and dragging the border of the area to make it larger or smaller.

The two ways to add a control

You add a control to a form in either of two ways:

✦ Drag a field from the Field List window to add a bound control.

✦ Click a button in the toolbox and then add new unbound control to the screen.

A bound control is one that is linked to a table field, while an unbound field is one that is not bound to a table field. A control bound to a table places the data directly into the table by using the form.

Using the Field List window

The Field List window shown in Figure 9-13 displays all the fields in the open table/ query that you used to create a form. This window is movable and resizable and displays a vertical scrollbar if it contains more fields than can fit in the window.

When you first create a new form in Design View, the Field List window is open and available to use. Later on, however, it may be closed. If it's closed, you can display it in the Field List window by using one of two methods:

✦ Click the Field List button on the toolbar (this button looks like an Access table).

✦ Select View ➪ Field List from the Form menu bar.

> **Note** After you resize or move the Field List window, it remains that size for all forms, even if toggled off or if the form is closed. Only if you exit Access is the window set to its default size.

Generally, dragging a field from the Field List window adds a bound text box to the Form Design window. If you drag a Yes/No field from the Field List window, you add a check box. If you drag a field that has a Lookup property, you add a list or combo box control. If you drag an OLE field from the Field List window, you create a bound object frame. Optionally, you can select the type of control by selecting a control from the toolbox and dragging the field to the Form Design window.

> **Caution** When you drag fields from the Field List window, the first control is placed where you release the mouse button. Make sure that you have enough space to the left of the control for the labels. If you don't have sufficient space, the labels slide under the controls.

You gain several distinct advantages by dragging a field from the Field List window:

✦ The control is bound automatically to the field that you dragged it to.

✦ Field properties inherit table-level formats, status-bar text, and data-validation rules and messages.

✦ The label control and label text are created with the field name as the caption.

✦ The label control is attached to the field control, so they move together.

Using the toolbox

By using the *toolbox buttons* to add a control, you can decide which type of control to use for each field. If you don't create the control by dragging it from the Field List window, the field is *unbound* (or, not attached to the data in a table field) and has a default label name like Field3 or Option11. After you create the control, you can decide what field to bind the control to, enter text for the label, and set any properties.

The deciding factor of whether to use the field list or the toolbox is this: Does the field exist in the table/query or do you want to create an unbound or calculated expression? By using the Field List window and the toolbox together, you can create bound controls of nearly any type. You will find, however, that some data types don't allow all the control types found in the toolbox. For example, if you select the Chart control type from the toolbox and drag a single field to the form, a text box control is added instead of a chart control.

Tip　In Access, you can change the type of control after you create it; then you can set all the properties for the control. For example, suppose that you add a field as a text box control and you want to change it to a list box. You can use Format⇔ Change To and change the control type. However, you can change only from some types of controls to others. You can change anything to a text box control; option buttons, toggle buttons, and check boxes are interchangeable, as are list and combo boxes.

Dragging a field name from the Field List window

The easiest way to create a text box control is to drag a field from the Field List window. When the Field List window is open, you can click an individual field and drag it to the Form Design window. This window works in exactly the same way as a Table/Query window in QBE. You can also select multiple fields and then drag them to the screen together by using these techniques:

✦ Select multiple contiguous fields by holding down the Shift key and clicking the first and last fields that you want.

✦ Select multiple noncontiguous fields by holding down the Ctrl key and clicking each field that you want.

✦ Double-click the table/query name in the window's title bar to select all the fields.

After selecting one or more fields, drag the selection to the screen.

Drag the chrDescription, chrCategory, curRetailPrice, and dtmAuctionEndDate fields from the Field List window to the form. If you haven't created a new form, create one first and resize the form as instructed at the beginning of this section. When you complete these steps successfully, your screen should look like the one shown in Figure 9-14.

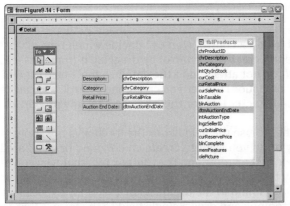

Figure 9-14: Fields dragged from the Field List window.

You can see four controls in the Form Design window — each one consists of a label control and a text box control (Access attaches the label control to the text box automatically). You can work with these controls as a group or independently, and you can select, move, resize, or delete them. Notice that each control has a label with a caption matching the field name, and the text box control displays the bound field name used in the text box. If you want to resize just the control and not the label, you must work with the two controls separately.

You can close the Field List window by clicking the Field List button on the toolbar or the close button on the Field List window.

Creating unbound controls with the toolbox

You can add one control at a time by using the toolbox. You can add any of the controls listed in the toolbox. Each control becomes an unbound control that has a default label and a name.

To create three different unbound controls, perform these steps:

1. Click the Text Box button (ab|) on the toolbox (the selected button appears with a colored background when it is selected).

2. Place the mouse pointer in the Form Design window (the cursor changes to the Text Box button).

3. Click and hold down the mouse button where you want the control to begin, and drag the mouse to size the control.

4. Click the Option Button on the toolbox (this button appears sunken).

5. Place the mouse pointer in the Form Design window (the cursor changes to an Option button).

6. Click and hold down the mouse button where you want the control to begin, and drag the mouse to size the control.

7. Click the Check Box button on the toolbox (the button appears sunken).

8. Place the mouse pointer in the Form Design window (the cursor changes to a check box).

9. Click and hold down the mouse button where you want the control to begin, and drag the mouse to size the control.

When you are done, your screen should resemble the one shown in Figure 9-15.

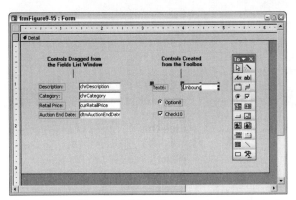

Figure 9-15: Three additional new unbound controls added by using the toolbox.

Tip   If you just click the Form Design window, Access creates a default-sized control.

In Figure 9-15, notice the difference between the controls that were dragged from the Field List window and the controls that were created from the toolbox. The Field List window controls are bound to a field in the tblProducts table and are appropriately labeled and named. The controls created from the toolbox are unbound and have default names. The default names are automatically assigned a number according to the type of control.

Later, you learn how to change the control names, captions, and properties. Using properties speeds the process of naming controls and binding them to specific fields. If you want to see the differences between bound and unbound controls, display the form in Form view by pressing the Form button in the toolbar or by selecting View ➪ Form View. You can see that the chrDescription, chrCategory, curRetailPrice, and dtmAuctionEndDate bound controls display data. The other three controls don't display data because they aren't bound to any data source. After you view the data, display the form in Design view again.

Selecting Controls

After a control is on the Form Design window, you can work with it; for example, you can resize it, move it, or copy it. The first step is to select one or more controls. Depending on its size, a selected control may show from four to eight *handles* (small squares called *moving and sizing handles*) around the control — at the corners and midway along the sides. The handle in the upper-left corner is larger than the other handles and you use it to move the control. You use the other handles to size the control. Figure 9-16 displays some selecting controls and their moving and sizing handles.

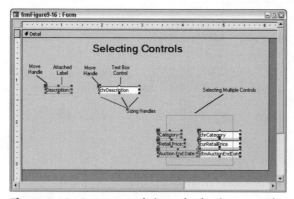

Figure 9-16: A conceptual view of selecting controls and their moving and sizing handles.

The Select Objects tool (top left-most icon) on the toolbox must be on for you to select a control. The pointer always appears as an arrow pointing diagonally toward the upper-left corner. If you use the toolbox to create a single control, Access automatically reselects the pointer as the default.

Deselecting selected controls

It's a good practice to de-select any selected controls before you select another control. You can de-select a control by clicking an unselected area of the screen that doesn't contain a control. When you do so, the handles disappear from any selected control.

Selecting a single control

You can select any single control by clicking anywhere on the control. When you click a control, all the handles appear. If the control has an attached label, the handle for moving the label also appears. If you select a label control that is part of an attached control, all the handles for the label control are displayed, and only the *Move handle* (the largest handle) is displayed in the attached control.

Selecting multiple controls

You can select multiple controls in these two ways:

✦ Click each desired control while holding down the Shift key.

✦ Drag the pointer through or around the controls that you want to select.

Figure 9-16 shows selecting the multiple bound controls graphically. When you select multiple controls by dragging the mouse, a light gray rectangle appears as the mouse is dragged. When you select multiple controls by dragging the pointer through the controls, be careful to select only the controls that you want to select. Any control that is touched by the line or enclosed within it is selected. If you want to select labels only, you must make sure that the selection rectangle encloses only the labels.

Tip   When you click on a ruler, an arrow appears and a line is displayed across the screen. You can drag the mouse to widen the line. Each control that the line touches is selected.

Tip   If you find that controls are not selected when the rectangle passes through the control, you may have the Selection behavior global property set to fully enclosed. This means that a control is selected only if the selection rectangle completely encloses the entire control. The normal default for this option is partially enclosed. You can change this option by first selecting Tools ⇨ Options and then selecting the Forms/Reports tab in the Options dialog box. The option Selection behavior should be set to partially enclosed.

By holding down the Shift key, you can select several noncontiguous controls. This lets you select controls on totally different parts of the screen, cut them, and then paste them together somewhere else onscreen.

Manipulating Controls

Creating a form is a multi-step process. The next step is to make sure that your controls are properly sized and moved to their correct positions.

Resizing a control

You can *resize* controls by using any of the smaller handles on the control. The handles in the control corners let you make the field larger or smaller in both width and height — and at the same time. You use the handles in the middle of the control sides to size the control larger or smaller in one direction only. The top and bottom handles control the height of the control; the handles in the middle change the control's width.

When the mouse pointer touches a corner handle of a selected control, the pointer becomes a diagonal double arrow. You can then drag the sizing handle until the control is the desired size. If the mouse pointer touches a side handle in a selected control, the pointer changes to a horizontal or vertical double-headed arrow. Figure 9-17 shows the chrDescription control after being resized. Notice the double-headed arrow in the corner of the chrDescriptioncontrol.

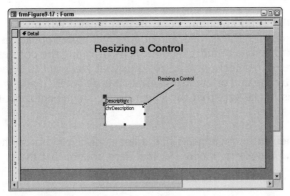

Figure 9-17: Resizing a control.

Tip   You can resize a control in very small increments by pressing the Shift key and pressing the arrow keys. This also works with multiple controls selected. Using this technique, a control changes by only 1 pixel at a time (or moves to the nearest grid line if Snap to Grid is selected in the Format menu).

Moving a control

After you select a control, you can easily move it, using either one of these methods:

✦ Select the control and, with the hand icon displayed, drag it to a new location.

✦ Select the control and place your mouse on the move handle in the upper-left corner of the control. With the index finger icon displayed, drag it to a new location.

If the control has an attached label, you can move both label and control with either method. It doesn't matter whether you click the control or the label; they move together.

You can move a control separately from an attached label by pointing to the move handle of the control and then dragging it. You can also move the label control separately from the other control by pointing to the move handle of the label control and dragging it separately.

Figure 9-18 shows a label control that has been separately moved to the top of the text box control. The hand icon indicates that the controls are ready to be moved together. To see the hand, the control(s) must already be selected.

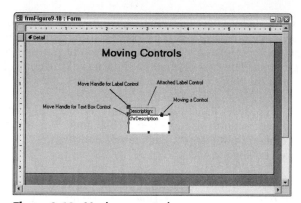

Figure 9-18: Moving a control.

Tip

You can move a control in small increments with the keyboard by pressing the Ctrl key and pressing the arrow keys after you select a control or group of controls.

You can restrict the direction in which a control is moved so that it maintains alignment within a specific row or column by holding down the Shift key as you press and holding down the mouse button to select and move the control. The control moves only in the direction that you first move it, either horizontally or vertically.

You can cancel a move or a resizing operation by pressing Esc before you release the mouse button. After a move or resizing operation is complete, you can click the Undo button or select Edit ➪ Undo Move or Edit ➪ Undo Sizing to undo the changes.

Aligning controls

You may want to move several controls so that they are all *aligned* (lined up). The Format ➪ Align menu has several options, as shown in Figure 9-19, which are described in the following list:

✦ **Left.** Aligns the left edge of the selected controls with that of the left-most selected control.

✦ **Right.** Aligns the right edge of the selected controls with that of the right-most selected control.

✦ **Top.** Aligns the top edge of the selected controls with that of the top-most selected control.

✦ **Bottom.** Aligns the bottom edge of the selected controls with that of the bottom-most selected control.

✦ **To Grid.** Aligns the top-left corners of the selected controls to the nearest grid point.

You can align any number of controls by selecting from this menu. When you choose one of the options, Access uses the control that is the closest to the desired selection as the model for the alignment. For example, suppose that you have three controls and you want to left-align them. They are aligned on the basis of the control farthest to the left in the group of the three controls.

Figure 9-19 shows several sets of controls. The first set of controls is not aligned. The label controls in the second set of controls have been left-aligned. The text box controls in the second set have been right-aligned. Each label, along with its attached text box, has been bottom-aligned.

Each type of alignment must be done separately. In this example, you can left-align all the labels or right-align all the text boxes at once. However, you must align each label and its text control separately (three separate alignments).

The series of dots in the background of Figure 9-19 is the *grid*. The grid can assist you in aligning controls. You can display the grid by selecting View ➪ Grid.

You can use the Format ➪ Snap to Grid option to align new controls to the grid as you draw or place them on a form. It also aligns existing controls when you move or resize them.

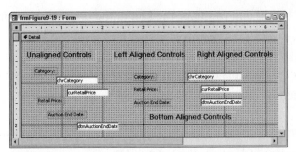

Figure 9-19: An example of unaligned and aligned controls on the grid.

When Snap to Grid is on from the Format menu, and you draw a new control by clicking on the form and dragging to size the control, Access aligns the four corners of the control to points on the grid. When you place a new control by clicking the control in the field list and then dragging it to the form, only the upper-left corner is aligned.

As you move or resize existing controls, Access 2003 lets you move only from grid point to grid point. When Snap to Grid is off, Access 2003 ignores the grid and lets you place a control anywhere on the form or report.

Tip

You can turn Snap to Grid off temporarily by pressing the Ctrl key before you create a control (or while creating or moving it).

You can change the grid's *fineness* (number of dots) from form to form by using the Grid X and Grid Y Form properties. The grid is invisible if its fineness is greater than 16 units per inch horizontally or vertically. (Higher numbers indicate greater fineness.)

Another pair of alignment commands can make a big difference when you have to align the space between multiple controls. The Format ➪ Horizontal Spacing and Vertical Spacing commands change the space between controls on the basis of the space between the first two selected controls. If the controls are across the screen, use horizontal spacing. If they are down the screen, use vertical spacing.

Tip

Aligning controls aligns the control boxes only. If you want to align the text itself within the controls (also known as *justifying the text*), you must use the form's formatting toolbar and select the Left, Right, or Center icons.

Sizing controls

The Size command on the Format menu has several options that help size controls based on the value of the data, the grid, or other controls. The Size menu options are:

✦ **To Fit.** Adjusts control height and width for the font of the text they contain.

✦ **To Grid.** Moves all sides of selected controls in or out to meet the nearest points on the grid.

✦ **To Tallest.** Makes selected controls the height of the tallest selected control.

✦ **To Shortest.** Makes selected controls the height of the shortest selected control.

✦ **To Widest.** Makes selected controls the width of the widest selected control.

✦ **To Narrowest.** Makes selected controls the height of the narrowest selected control.

Tip

You can access most of the Format commands by right-clicking after selecting multiple controls. When you right-click on multiple controls, a shortcut menu displays — this is similar to the Format menu on the Access menu bar. This is a quick way to resize or align your controls.

Grouping controls

Tip

Access 2003 can group controls. When controls are grouped, you can select and format many controls at once. While you can select multiple controls and format them, grouping is like a permanent selection. When you click on any of the grouped controls, they all are instantly selected and can then be formatted.

To group multiple controls, select the controls by holding down the Shift key and clicking them. After the desired controls are selected, select Format ➪ Group from the Access menu bar, as shown in Figure 9-20.

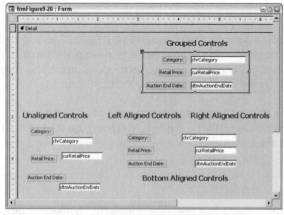

Figure 9-20: Grouping multiple controls together.

After you have grouped the objects together, whenever you click any of the fields inside the group, the entire group is selected. If you click again, just the field is selected. To resize the entire group, put your mouse on the side you want to resize. After the double arrow is displayed, click and drag until you reach the desired size.

To remove a group, select the group by clicking any field inside the group and then select Format ➪ UnGroup from the Access menu bar. This ungroups the controls.

Deleting a control

No longer want a specific control on the Form Design window? Delete it by selecting the control and pressing Delete. You can also select Edit ➪ Delete to delete a selected control or Edit ➪ Cut to cut the control to the Clipboard.

You can delete more than one control at a time by selecting multiple controls and pressing one of the Delete key sequences. You can delete an entire group of controls by selecting the group and pressing Delete or by selecting Edit ➪ Delete. If you have a control with an attached label, you can delete only the label by clicking the label itself and then selecting one of the delete methods. If you select the control, both the control and the label are deleted. To delete only the label of the chrDescription control, follow the next set of steps (this example assumes that you have the chrDescription text box control in your Form Design window):

1. Select the chrDescription label control only.

2. Press Delete.

The label control is removed from the window.

Attaching a label to a control

If you accidentally delete a label from a control, you can reattach it. To create and then reattach a label to a control, follow these steps:

1. Click the Label button on the toolbox.

2. Place the mouse pointer in the Form Design window (the mouse pointer becomes the Text Box button).

3. Click and hold down the mouse button where you want the control to begin; drag the mouse to size the control.

4. Type **Description:** and click outside the control.

5. Select the Description label control.

6. Select Edit ⇨ Cut to cut the label control to the Clipboard.

7. Select the chrDescription text box control.

8. Select Edit ⇨ Paste to attach the label control to the text box control.

Copying a control

You can create copies of any control by duplicating it or by copying it to the Clipboard and then pasting the copies where you want them. If you have a control for which you have entered many properties or specified a certain format, you can copy it and revise only the properties (such as the control name and bound field name) to make it a different control. This capability is useful with a multiple-page form when you want to display the same values on different pages and in different locations.

✦　　✦　　✦

Creating Bound Forms and Placing Controls

I n Chapter 9, you learned about the tools necessary to create and display a form — design view, bound and unbound
controls, the field list window, and the toolbox. In Chapters 8
and 9, you learned a lot about forms and what goes on them.
In this chapter, you'll begin to practice more and begin to
create the frmProducts form and the form that will later be
used for its subform. In this chapter, you will also learn about
properties.

On the CD-ROM You will use the tblProducts tables in the chap10start.mdb
database to provide the data necessary to begin to create
several types of simple forms. Each table is explained in
more depth as you are adding the fields to the forms.

Creating a Data-Entry Form without a Wizard

The first form you will create is a data-entry form that uses
a single table as shown in Figure 10-1. You will begin this in
Chapter 10 and complete it in Chapter 13 after a slight detour
in Chapter 12 to create reports using the same techniques you
will learn in Chapters 10 and 11. Later in this chapter, you will
create a continuous form that will later become a subform on
the second page of the tab dialog.

Generally, the more features you add to a form, the easier it is
to use for the end user. This form will demonstrate the use of
the majority of control types. These include label and text box
controls as well as data validation controls and formatting. It
also features a tab dialog and embedded pictures. You will

continue to modify this form in the next several chapters, adding more complex controls and features, making the form increasingly more powerful and functional.

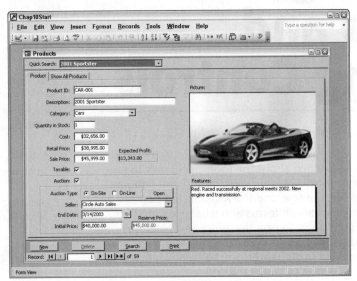

Figure 10-1: A professional looking data-entry form.

Creating a new blank form

You will start by creating a new blank form without first specifying a table to use. You will then bind it to the tblProducts table. Later you will add the controls. Follow these steps to create a new blank form:

1. Click the Forms object in the database window.

2. Click the New button to start a new form.

3. Select Design View in the New Form dialog box.

4. Do not choose any table or query in the bottom portion of this dialog.

5. Click the OK button to create the new form.

6. Maximize the Form window.

Resizing the form's workspace

Next, you must resize the form's workspace. In Figure 10-2 (shown after resizing), the light gray background is the *workspace*. If you place controls in the dark gray area surrounding it, the workspace expands automatically until it is large enough to hold the controls you placed there. The workspace size you need depends on the design of your form. If you want the form to fill the screen, make it the size of your screen; however, that depends on your screen resolution. More data can fit onscreen if you are using a higher resolution. Because many users may use a form you create, you should stay with the smallest size of any anticipated user.

Tip   To properly design this form, you should set your screen resolution at 1024 x 768. This is the most common screen resolution today. It provides the optimum size for viewing the various windows. The form you are designing will fit into a resolution set at 800 x 600 but it is easier to have multiple windows around the screen in 1024 x 768 video mode.

Note   The height of your form includes all sections, including the detail section and header form or page headers and footers.

Tip   There is software available that will resize a form to any size depending on your screen resolution and additionally let you change the window size of a form and automatically adjust all the controls on the form. One of the best is the EZ Form Resizer which is part of the EZ Access Developer Tools ($99-$495) from Database Creations, Inc. (www.databasecreations.com). You simply add the library to your modules and add one line of code behind your form to call it on the On Resize event of your form (you'll learn about events later).

Designing the Size of Your Form

Although the default form size is 5" wide x 2" down, you can easily adjust it by grabbing the borders of the form and changing the form size. However, you must carefully consider the minimum screen resolution your users will be using. Office 2003 requires Windows 2000 or Windows XP. That generally means that the users have a fairly new machine and are probably running their screens in at least 1024 x 768 resolution or a minimum of 800 x 600 resolution. You should no longer design screens to fit into 640 x 480. If someone is going to use an Access 2003 application, the memory requirements and speed alone dictate a newer computer. If users have a flat panel monitor, they simply don't work well below 1024 x 768. Most laptops today only run at 1024 x 768 or 800 x 600.

It is a good idea to assume that some people will be using 800 x 600, and you should design your screens to a maximum size of 6" x 4". This fits nicely in 800 x 600. You can go as large as 7½" x 4½" (as this example will be), but it begins to take over the whole screen at the lower resolutions. Anything larger than that and scroll bars appear in your form. You should be able to design a form to fit in the screen without the controls appearing crowded. When you need more space, you should consider tabs or multiple forms.

The easiest way to set the form size is to grab the border of the light gray area with your mouse and drag it to the size that you want. If you grab either the top or bottom borders, your mouse pointer becomes a double-arrow. If you grab the corner, the mouse pointer becomes a four-headed arrow (as shown in Figure 10-2), and you can size both sides at the same time. Next, you will set the form size to 7½" x 4½" inches, using Figure 10-2 as a guide. At this size, form scrollbars should not appear.

Follow these steps to change the form size:

1. Make sure that the ruler is displayed; if needed, select it from the View menu.

2. Place the mouse pointer at the bottom-right corner of the light gray workspace.

3. When the mouse pointer changes to a four-headed arrow, drag the workspace until the size is exactly 7½" x 4 ½".

4. Release the mouse button to accept the new size.

If controls are added beyond the right border, you have to scroll the form using a horizontal scroll bar to see these controls. This is generally not acceptable in a form. If controls are added beyond the bottom border, you have to use a vertical scroll bar to see these controls as well; this is acceptable because the form becomes a multiple-page form. Later in this chapter, you learn to control multiple-page forms.

Note   If you change to Form View and see a horizontal scroll bar along the bottom, either resize the right margin or turn the Record Selector property off for the form. This topic is covered later.

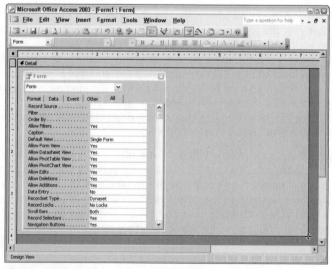

Figure 10-2: The blank form Design View window.

Understanding the design windows

The form uses a series of design windows to allow you to manipulate the form. You can determine everything about the form including the look of the form and each of the controls, how the form appears under certain conditions, and what data tables and fields each form and control uses. Figure 10-3 shows the major windows open on the form design screen. These include the following:

✦ Property Sheet

✦ Field List

✦ Toolbox

The Property Sheet window

In a form or report, each field (called a *control* in Access) has *properties* that further define the characteristics of the control. The form or report and sections of the form or report also have properties. In Figure 10-3, you see a Property window displaying some of the properties for a form. Usually, a Property window displays only a portion of the properties available for a specific control. The tabbed dialog box is used to display specific types of properties and the vertical scrollbar in the window lets you scroll through the complete list when you select All or size the window smaller than the number of displayed properties. You can also resize a Property window and move it around the screen.

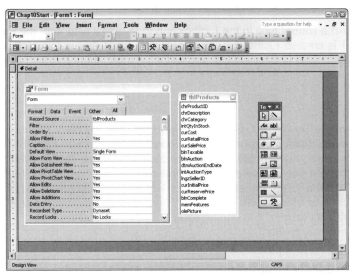

Figure 10-3: The blank form Design showing various windows.

Having many windows open at once and resizing and rearranging them onscreen helps you use information productively as you create objects (such as forms and reports) and use Access's features. Each of the windows is described in detail in their appropriate chapters in this book.

Each type of object has its own property window and properties. These include the form itself, each of the form sections, and each of the form's controls. You display each of the property windows by clicking on the object first. The property window will instantly change to show the properties for the selected object.

> **Tip**   To display the Form property window, click on the area between the rulers so that a small black square appears, as shown in Figure 10-3.

The Field List window

The *Field List* window (titled tblProducts and located next to the property window in Figure 10-3) displays a list of fields from the currently open table or query dynaset. You use Field List windows in Query Design, Form Design, and Report Design windows. You select fields from this window by clicking on them and then dragging the fields onto a query, form, or report. You can select fields individually, or you can select ranges or groups of fields to drag onto the form by using the Ctrl key or Shift key.

> **Note**   If you have not selected a valid Record Source, you will not see a Field List window.

> **Tip**   If you first select a control type in the Toolbox and then drag a field from the Field List, a control is created (using the selected control type) that is automatically bound to the data field in the Field List. You will learn more about this later in the chapter.

The Toolbox

Figure 10-3 displays the Toolbox in the top-right portion of the screen. You can use the Toolbox to design a form or report. The Toolbox is similar to a toolbar, but the Toolbox is initially arranged vertically and can be moved around. The Toolbox contains toggle buttons that you can select to add objects to a form or report, such as labels, text boxes, option group boxes, and so on — as shown in Figure 10-3. You can move the Toolbox or close it when you don't need it. You can also resize it by clicking and dragging its border. You can also anchor it with other toolbars by dragging it to an edge of the screen.

Displaying the Property window

The Property window is shown in Figure 10-3. If it is not displayed, choose View Properties from the form design menu or press the Properties icon (a hand holding a sheet of paper).

If Record Source is not displayed in the Property Window, it may be because you have not selected the Form properties. To select the Forms property window, click on the area in the upper-left corner of the form where the rulers meet.

Creating a bound form

A bound form is one that places data into a table when the record is saved. Forms can be bound or unbound. To create a bound form you must specify a data source in the form's Record Source property. In Figure 10-3, you can see the form's property window. If the form itself is selected, the very first property is Record Source. If you want your form bound to a data source, this is where the name of the data source goes. Figure 10-3 shows the Record Source property selected and the table tblProducts selected.

The data source can be on of three choices:

✦ **Table.** The name of a table from the current database file. The table can be a local table (stored in the database itself) or it can be linked to another Access database or an outside data source such as SQL Server.

✦ **Query.** The name of a query that references one or more tables from the current database file.

✦ **SQL Statement.** A SQL SELECT Statement that contains the name of a table or query.

In this example, you will select the tblProducts table as your Record Source. When you have selected the form's Record Source, it is time to start adding controls.

Understanding bound, unbound, and calculated controls

These are the three basic types of controls:

✦ Bound controls

✦ Unbound controls

✦ Calculated controls

Bound controls are controls that are bound to a table field. When you enter a value into a bound control, Access automatically updates the table field in the current record. Most of the controls that let you enter information can be bound; these include OLE (Object Linking and Embedding) fields. Controls can be bound to most data types, including text, dates, numbers, Yes/No, pictures, and memo fields.

Unbound controls retain the entered value, but they don't update any table fields. You can use these controls for text label display, for controls such as lines and rectangles, or for holding unbound OLE objects (such as bitmap pictures or your logo) that aren't stored in a table but on the form itself. Unbound controls are also known as *variables* or *memory variables*.

Calculated controls are based on expressions, such as functions or calculations. Calculated controls are also unbound because they don't update table fields. An example of a calculated control is =[curSalePrice] – [curCost]. This control calculates the total of two table fields for display on a form but is not bound to any table field.

Figure 10-1 shows examples of all these three control types. All of the labels, the line, the rectangles, and several other controls are all unbound. Most of the sunken data fields with white backgrounds are bound controls. The Expected Profit control is calculated.

Understanding properties

Properties are named attributes of controls, fields, or database objects that are used to modify the characteristics of a control, field, or object. Examples of these attributes are the size, color, appearance, or name of an object. A property can also modify the behavior of a control, determining, for example, whether the control is read-only or editable and visible or not visible.

Properties are used extensively in forms and reports to change the characteristics of controls. Each control on the form has properties. The form itself also has properties, as does each of its sections. The same is true for reports; the report itself has properties, as does each report section and individual control. The label control also has its own properties, even if it is attached to another control.

Properties are displayed in a Property sheet (also called a Property window because it is an actual window).

To display the Property sheet for the Description text box control, follow the steps below. You will be creating a new blank form.

1. Drag the first five fields, chrProductID through curCost, from the Field List window to the Form Design window.

2. Click the chrDescription text box control to select it.

3. Click the Properties button on the toolbar if the Property window is not displayed.

The screen should look like the one shown in Figure 10-4.

Saving the form

You can save the form at any time by pressing the Save icon (second icon from the left—looks like a floppy disk) or by choosing Save from the form's File menu.

When you are asked for a name for the form, accept the default name of **Form1** for now.

If you don't specify a name, each new form will have the name of *Form* followed by the next available sequential number.

When you close a form, it will ask you to save it. If you don't save a form, all changes since you opened the form (or the last time you pressed Enter) are lost. You should frequently save the form while you work if you are satisfied with the results.

To save the form and give it a name, click the Save icon in the toolbar. This saves the form with the name Form1. Later, you will enter a better name for the form.

Tip

If you are going to make extensive changes to a form, you might want to make a copy of the form. If you want to work on the form frmProducts, you can copy and then paste the form in the database window, giving it a name like frmProductsOriginal. Later, when you have completed your changes and tested them, you can delete the original copy.

Working with control properties

In Figure 10-4, the Property window has been sized to be larger than it normally displays. By widening the property sheet, you can see more of its values; by increasing the length, you can see more controls at one time. The vertical scrollbar lets you move between various properties.

Because the Property window is a true window, it can be moved anywhere onscreen and resized. It does not, however, have Maximize or Minimize buttons.

There are several ways to display a control's Property sheet:

✦ Select a control and click View ↪ Properties from the menu bar.

✦ Select a control and click the Properties button on the toolbar.

✦ Double-click any control.

✦ Right-click any control and select Properties from the menu.

Figure 10-4 shows the Property sheet for the Description text box. The first column lists the property names; the second column is where you enter or select property settings or options.

The Property window has an All tab that lets you see all the properties for a control. Or you can choose another tab to limit the view to a specific group of properties. The specific tabs and groups of properties are:

✦ **Format.** These properties determine how a label or value looks: font, size, color, special effects, borders, and scrollbars.

✦ **Data.** These properties affect how a value is displayed and the data source it is bound to: control source, input masks, validation, default value, and other data type properties.

✦ **Event.** Event properties are named events, such as clicking a mouse button, adding a record, pressing a key for which you can define a response (in the form of a call to a macro or a VBA procedure), and so on.

✦ **Other.** Other properties show additional characteristics of the control, such as the name of the control or the description that displays in the status bar.

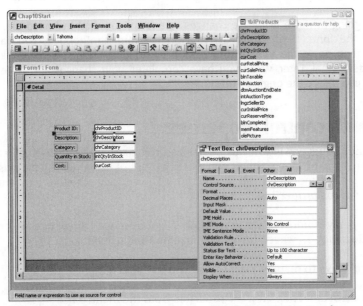

Figure 10-4: The Property window for the chrDescription text box.

Cross-Reference

The number of properties available in Access has increased greatly since early versions of Access. The most important new properties are described in various chapters of this book. For a discussion of new Event properties and Event procedures, see Section III: Automating Your Applications.

Naming control labels and their captions

You might notice that each of the data fields have a label control and a text box control. The label controls have the caption indicating the reason for the control. Normally, the label control has the same caption as the text box control name. The text box control name usually has the same name as the table field name.

In this example, the label control captions are different. This is because a Caption name was entered into the Caption property for each table field. It is a good idea when you are using standard naming conventions to enter a more English (or non-computer) type of name into the Caption property in each table field.

Table 10-1 shows the naming conventions for form and report controls. You can see a complete list in Appendix D.

Table 10-1 Form/Report Control Naming Conventions	
Prefix	**Object**
frb	Bound Object frame
cht	Chart (Graph)
chk	Check Box
cbo	Combo Box
cmd	Command Button
ocx	ActiveX Custom Control
det	Detail (section)
gft[n]	Footer (group section)
fft	Form footer section
fhd	Form header section
ghd[n]	Header (group section)
hlk	Hyperlink
img	Image
lbl	Label
lin	Line
lst	List Box
opt	Option Button
grp	Option Group
pge	Page (tab)
brk	Page break
pft	Page Footer (section)
phd	Page Header (section)

Continued

Table 10-1 *(continued)*	
Prefix	**Object**
shp	Rectangle
rft	Report Footer (section)
rhd	Report Header (section)
sec	Section
sub	Subform/Subreport
tab	Tab Control
txt	Text Box
tgl	Toggle Button
fru	Unbound Object Frame

The properties displayed in Figure 10-4 are the specific properties for Description text box. The first two properties, Name and Control Source, show the field name chrDescription.

The Name is simply the name of the field itself. When a control is bound to a field, Access automatically assigns it the bound field name. Unbound controls are given names such as Field11 or Button13. However, you can give the control any name you want.

With bound controls, the Control Source's setting is the name of the table field to which the control is bound. In this example, chrDescription refers to the field with the same name in the tblProducts table. An unbound control has no control source, whereas the control source of a calculated control is the actual expression for the calculation, as in the example =[curSalePrice] – [curCost].

The following properties always inherit their settings from the field's table definition. Figure 10-4 shows some of these properties and the settings that have been inherited from the tblProducts table:

- ✦ Format
- ✦ Decimal Places
- ✦ Status Bar Text (from the field Description)
- ✦ Input Mask
- ✦ Default Value
- ✦ Validation Rule
- ✦ Validation Text

Changing Default Settings for Attached Labels

Attached label controls are called compound controls because the two controls are attached. You can disable this feature by changing the Auto Label default setting. When Auto Label is set to Yes, a label control is automatically created that bears the name of the field to which the text control is bound. With Auto Label in effect, a label is created automatically every time you drag a field onto a form. Follow these steps to change the Auto Label default:

1. Display the Toolbox if it is not already displayed.
2. Display the Property window if it is not already displayed.
3. Click the Text Box button on the Toolbar. The title of the Property window should be Default Text Box.
4. Under the Format tab, scroll down until you see the Auto Label property.
5. Click the Auto Label text box.
6. Change the property setting to No.

The next property, Auto Colon, is related because if it is set to Yes, a colon automatically follows any text in a new label. Two other properties control where the attached label appears relative to the control itself. These are the Label X and Label Y properties. Label X controls the horizontal position of the label control relative to the text box control. The default setting is –1 (to the left of the text box control). As you make the value a smaller negative number, for example –0.5, you decrease the space from the attached label to the control. If you want the label to the right of the control (as you may for an option button), set the Label X property to a positive number, such as 1.5.

Label Y controls the vertical position of the label control relative to the text box control. The default setting is 0, which places the label on the same line as the text box control. If you want to place the label above the control, change the Label Y setting to –1 or a larger negative number.

The Label Align property lets you control the alignment of the text within the label.

If you changed the Auto Label property setting to No and you now drag fields from the Field List window to the form, no labels will be attached. The Auto Label property setting is in effect only for this form. Because you don't need to add further labeled fields to this form, you can leave Auto Label set to No.

Note   Changes made to a control's properties don't affect the field properties in the source table.

Each type of control has a different set of properties, as do objects such as forms, reports, and sections within forms or reports. In the next few chapters, you learn about many of these properties as you use each of the control types to create more complex forms and reports.

Changing a control's property setting

There are many different methods for changing property settings, including the following:

✦ Entering or selecting the desired value in a Property window.

✦ Changing a property directly by changing the control itself, such as changing its size.

✦ Using inherited properties from the bound field or the control's default properties.

✦ Entering color selections for the control by using the toolbar options.

✦ Changing label text style, size, color, and alignment by using the toolbar buttons.

You can change a control's properties by clicking a property and typing the desired value.

In Figure 10-4, you can see a down-arrow and a button with three dots to the right of the Control Source property-entry area. Some properties display the arrow in the property-entry area when you click in the area. This tells you that Access has a list of values from which you can choose. If you click the down-arrow in the Control Source property, you find that the choices are a list of all fields in the data source (the tblProducts table).

Some properties have a list of standard values such as Yes or No; others display varying lists of fields, forms, reports, or macros. The properties of each object are determined by the object itself and what the object is used for.

A feature in Access 2003 is the capability of cycling through property choices by repeatedly double-clicking on the choice. For example, double-clicking on the Display When property alternately selects Always, Print Only, and Screen Only.

When you see three dots on a button, you are looking at the Builder button, which opens one of the many Builders in Access. This includes the Macro Builder, the Expression Builder, and the Module Builder. When you open a builder and make some selections, the property will be filled in for you. You will learn about them later in this book.

Working with form properties

You use form properties to change the way the entire form is displayed. This includes properties such as the form's background color or picture, the form's width, and so on. Table 10-2 (in "Eliminating the record selector bar" later in this chapter) discusses some of the most important properties. Changing default properties is relatively easy: You select the property in the Property window and set a new value. Following are some of the more important form properties that you may want to be aware of and may want to set.

Changing the title bar text with the Caption property

Normally, the title bar displays the name of the form after it is saved. By changing the Caption property, you can display a different title on the title bar when the form is run. To change the title bar text, follow these steps. First close the current form and don't save it. You will be creating a new blank form.

1. Make sure the Form itself is selected. (Click the area where the rulers meet.)

2. Display the Form's Property window if it is not already displayed, and click the Format tab to show the Format properties. (Make sure the Property Window's Title Bar is Form.)

3. Click the Caption property in the Format area of the Property window.

4. Type **Products**.

5. Click any other property or press Enter.

You can display the form by clicking the Form View button on the toolbar to check the result. The caption you enter here overrides the name of the saved form.

Specifying how to view the form

Access 2003 uses several properties to determine how a form is viewed. The most common one is the Default View. The Default View property determines how the data is displayed when the form is first run. There are five choices:

✦ Single Form (displays one record at a time)

✦ Continuous Forms (showing more than one record at a time)

✦ Datasheet (row and column view like a spreadsheet or the standard query datasheet view)

✦ PivotTable (a datasheet with movable columns that can be swapped with rows)

✦ PivotChart (a graph made from a PivotTable)

Single Form is the default and displays one record per form page, regardless of the form's size. Continuous Forms tells Access to display as many detail records as will fit onscreen. Normally, you would use this setting to define the height of a very small form and to display many records at one time. Figure 10-5 shows such a continuous form with many records. The records have a small enough height that you can see a number of them at once.

In Figure 10-5, you can see the form's property window with the choices for the Default View property.

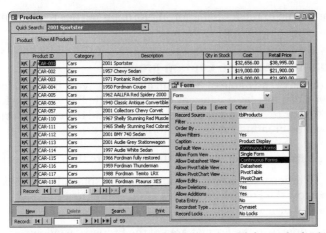

Figure 10-5: The Continuous Forms setting of the Default View property showing the frmProducts form's Show All Products tab and a continuous form.

A PivotTable form can display a field's values horizontally or vertically and then calculate the total of the row or column. Similar to this is the PivotChart, which displays a graphical analysis of data stored in a table, query, or form.

The Default View for this example will remain as a Single Form.

There are four separate properties to allow the developer to determine if the user can change the default view. These include Allow Form View, Allow Datasheet View, Allow PivotTable View, and Allow PivotChart View. The default settings are Yes to all of these properties, which lets you switch between Form and Datasheet view, as well as PivotTable and PivotChart view. If you set the Allow Datasheet View property to No, the Datasheet button and the View ➪ Datasheet menu selections cannot be selected; the data can be viewed only as a form. If you set the Allow Form View property to No, the Form button and the View ➪ Form menu selections cannot be selected; the data can be viewed only as a datasheet.

Eliminating the record selector bar

The Record Selectors property determines whether the Record Selector bar (the vertical bar on the left side of a form with a right pointing triangle indicating the selected record) is displayed. The Record Selector bar is very important in multiple-record forms or datasheets because a right-pointing triangle indicates the current record and a Pencil indicates that the record is being edited. Though the Record Selector bar is important for datasheets, you probably won't want it for a single record form. To eliminate it, simply change the form's Record Selectors property from Yes to No.

Set the Record Selectors property to No for your form.

Table 10-2 lists the most commonly used form properties and offers brief descriptions of each. You will learn more about many of these when they are used in examples throughout the chapters.

	Table 10-2 **Form Properties**	
Property	*Description and Options*	*Option Definition*
Format properties		
Caption	Displayed on the title bar of the displayed form.	
Default View	Determines the type of view when the form is run.	
	Single Form.	One record per page.
	Continuous Forms.	As many records per page as will fit (Default).
	Datasheet.	Standard row and column datasheet view.
	PivotTable.	Displays a field's values horizontally or vertically; then calculates the total of the row or column.
	PivotChart.	Graphical analysis of data.
Allow Form View	Form view allowed (Yes/No).	
Allow Datasheet View	Datasheet view allowed Yes/No).	
Allow PivotTable View	PivotTable view allowed (Yes/No).	
Allow PivotChart View	PivotChart allowed (Yes/No).	
Scroll Bars	Determines whether any scroll bars are displayed.	
	Neither.	No scrollbars are displayed.
	Horizontal Only.	Displays only horizontal scrollbar.
	Vertical Only.	Displays only vertical scrollbar.
	Both.	Displays both horizontal and vertical scrollbars.

Continued

Table 10-2 *(continued)*

Property	Description and Options	Option Definition
Record Selectors	Determines whether vertical record selector bar is displayed (Yes/No).	
Navigation Buttons	Determines whether navigation buttons are visible (Yes/No).	
Dividing Lines	Determines whether lines between form sections are visible (Yes/No).	
Auto Resize	Form is opened to display a complete record (Yes/No).	
Auto Center	Centers form onscreen when it's opened (Yes/No).	
Border Style	Determines form's border style.	
	None.	No border or border elements (scrollbars, navigation buttons).
	Thin.	Thin border, not resizable.
	Sizable.	Normal form settings.
	Dialog.	Thick border, title bar only, cannot be sized; use for dialog boxes.
Control Box	Determines whether control menu (Restore, Move Size) is available (Yes/No).	
Min Max Buttons		
	None.	No buttons displayed in upper-right corner of form.
	Min Enabled.	Minimize button only is displayed.
	Max Enabled.	Maximize button only is displayed.
	Both Enabled.	Minimize and Maximize buttons are displayed.

Property	Description and Options	Option Definition
Close Button	Determines whether to display Close button in upper-right corner and a close menu item on the control menu (Yes/No).	
What's This Button	Determines whether Screen Tips appear when user presses Shift+F1 for Help.	
Width	Displays the value of the width of the form; can be entered or Access fills it in as you adjust the width of the work area.	
Picture	Enter the name of a bitmap file for the background of the entire form.	
Picture Type	Determines whether picture is embedded or linked.	
	Embedded.	Picture is embedded in the form and becomes a part of the database file.
	Linked.	Picture is linked to the form. Access stores the location of the picture and retrieves it every time the form is opened.
Picture Size Mode	Determines how picture is displayed.	
	Clip.	Displays the picture at its actual size.
	Stretch.	Fits picture to form size (non-proportional).
	Zoom.	Fits picture to form size (proportional); this may result in the picture not fitting in one dimension (height or width).

Continued

Table 10-2 *(continued)*

Property	Description and Options	Option Definition
Picture Alignment	Determines picture alignment.	
	Top Left.	The picture is displayed in the top-left corner of the form, report window, or image control.
	Top Right.	The picture is displayed in the top-right corner of the form, report window, or image control.
	Center.	(Default) The picture is centered in the form, report window, or image control.
	Bottom Left.	The picture is displayed in the bottom-left corner of the form, report window, or image control.
	Bottom Right.	The picture is displayed in the bottom-right corner of the form, report window, or image control.
	Form Center.	The form's picture is centered horizontally in relation to the width of the form and vertically in relation to the topmost and bottommost controls on the form.
Picture Tiling	Used when you want to overlay multiple copies of a small bitmap; for example, a single brick can become a wall (Yes/No).	
Grid X	Displays setting for number of points per inch when X grid is displayed.	
Grid Y	Displays setting for number of points per inch when Y grid is displayed.	

Property	Description and Options	Option Definition
Layout for Print	Determines whether form uses screen fonts or printer fonts.	
	Yes.	Printer Fonts.
	No.	Screen Fonts.
Subdatasheet Height	Determines the height of a sub-datasheet when expanded.	
Subdatasheet Expanded	Determines the saved state of all sub-datasheets in a table or query.	Yes – The saved state of sub-datasheets is expanded.
		No – The saved state of sub-datasheets is closed.
Palette Source	The palette for a form or report.	(Default) indicates the default Access color palette. You can also specify other Windows palette files (.pal), .ico, .bmp, .db, and .wmf files.
Orientation	Determines the View Orientation.	
	Right-to-Left.	Appearance and functionality move from right to left.
	Left-to-Right.	Appearance and functionality move from left to right.
Moveable	Determines whether the form can be moved (Yes/No).	
Data properties		
Record Source	Determines where the data to be displayed in the form is coming from, or where the data is going when you create a new record. Can be a table or a query.	
Filter	Used to specify a subset of records to be displayed when a filter is applied to a form. Can be set in the form properties, a macro, or in Visual Basic.	

Continued

	Table 10-2 *(continued)*	
Property	*Description and Options*	*Option Definition*
Order By	Specifies the field or fields used to order the data in the view.	
Allow Filters	Determines whether a user will be able to display a filtered form (Yes/No).	
Allow Edits	Prevents or allows editing of data, making the form read-only for saved records.	
	Yes/No.	You can/cannot edit saved records.
Allow Deletions	Used to prevent records from being deleted.	
	Yes/No.	You can/cannot delete saved records.
Allow Additions	Used to determine whether new records can be added.	
	Yes/No.	You can/cannot add new records.
Data Entry	Used to determine whether form displays saved records.	
	Yes/No.	Only new records are displayed/ All records are displayed.
Recordset Type	Used to determine whether multi-table forms can be updated; replaces Access 2.0's Allow Updating property.	
	Dynaset.	Only default table field controls can be edited.
	Dynaset (Inconsistent Updates).	All tables and fields are editable.
	Snapshot.	No fields are editable (Read Only in effect).

Property	*Description and Options*	*Option Definition*
Record Locks	Used to determine multi-user record locking.	
	No Locks.	Record is locked only as it is saved.
	All Records.	Locks entire form records while using the form.
	Edited Record.	Locks only current record being edited.
Other properties		
Pop Up	Form is a pop-up that floats above all other objects (Yes/No).	
Modal	For use when you must close the form before doing anything else. Disables other windows; when Pop Up set to Yes, Modal disables menus and toolbar, creating a dialog box (Yes/No).	
Cycle	Determines how Tab works in the last field of a record.	
	All Records.	Tabbing from the last field of a record moves to the next record.
	Current Record.	Tabbing from the last field of a record moves to the first field of that record.
	Current Page.	Tabbing from the last field of a record moves to the first field of the current page.
Menu Bar	Used to specify an alternate menu bar.	
Toolbar	Use this property to specify the toolbar to use for the form. You can create a toolbar for your form by selecting the Customize option under the Toolbar command in the View menu.	

Continued

Table 10-2 *(continued)*		
Property	*Description and Options*	*Option Definition*
Shortcut Menu	Determines whether shortcut menus are active.	
Shortcut Menu Bar	Used to specify an alternate shortcut menu bar.	
Fast Laser Printing	Prints rules instead of lines and rectangles (Yes/No).	
Help File	Name of compiled Help file to assign custom help to the form.	
Help Context Id	ID of context-sensitive entry point in the help file to display.	
Tag	Use this property to store extra information about your form.	
Has Module	Use this property to show if your form has a class module. Setting this property to No can improve the performance and decrease the size of your database.	
Allow Design Changes	Determines when design edits can be made.	
	Design View Only.	Allows design edits in design view of the form only.
	All Views.	Allows design edits in all views.

Placing Bound Fields on a Form

The next step is to place the necessary fields on the form. You should already have the Product ID, Description, Category, Quantity in Stock, and Cost fields on the form. When you place a field on a form, it is called a *control* and it is bound to another field (its *control source*). Therefore, the terms *control* and *field* are used interchangeably in this chapter.

As you've learned, if you don't use a wizard to initially bind a table or query to a form and place your fields, the process of creating controls on your form consists of three basic tasks:

✦ Display the Field List window by clicking the Field List button on the toolbar.

✦ Click the desired Toolbox control to determine the type of control that is created.

✦ Select each of the fields that you want on your form and drag them to the form Design window.

Displaying the field list

Remember, to display the Field List window, click the Field List button on the toolbar (the icon that looks like a list sheet) or choose View ⇨ Field List from the main menu. The Field List window can be resized and moved around. The enlarged Field List window (shown in Figure 10-6) displays all the fields in the tblProducts table.

You can move the Field List window by clicking its title bar and dragging it to a new location.

Selecting the fields for your form

The method for selecting a field in the Field List window is the same as selecting a field from a query field list. The easiest way to select a field is to click it, which highlights it; then you can drag it to the Form window.

To highlight *contiguous* (adjacent) fields in the list, click the first field you want in the field list and move the mouse pointer to the last field you want; hold down the Shift key as you click the last field. The block of fields between the first and last fields is displayed in reverse video as you select it. Drag the block to the Form window.

Tip

You can highlight noncontiguous fields in the list by clicking each field while holding down the Ctrl key. Each field is then displayed in reverse video and can be dragged (as part of the group) to the form design window. One way this method differs from using the query field list is that you cannot double-click a field to add it to the Form window.

You will begin by moving the already placed controls closer to the top of the form and then selecting the remaining fields except the memFeatures and the olePicture fields.

To move the already created controls and select the fields you need for the Products form, follow these steps:

1. Draw an imaginary rectangle around the five already placed controls.

Make sure the first icon in the toolbox (the select arrow) is highlighted. Don't select the Rectangle option from the toolbox. This will select the five controls.

2. Drag the controls toward the top of the form as shown in Figure 10-6.

You should now have moved the five controls into position, as shown in Figure 10-6. Make sure the control block begins near the upper-left corner of the form.

3. Click on the curRetailPrice field.

4. Hold the Shift key down and click on the blnComplete field. Release the Shift key.

All the fields between curRetailPrice and blnComplete should be highlighted.

5. Click on the selected fields and drag the cursor icon that appears to just below the curCost control. Release your mouse button. Depending on where you release the mouse, you may have to move the controls around to line them up better.

The controls should appear as shown in Figure 10-6 after a little cleanup. Notice that the Yes/No fields are automatically created as check boxes.

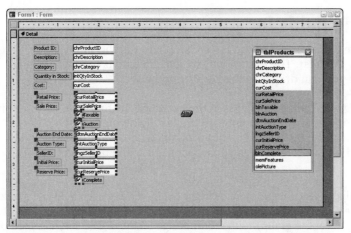

Figure 10-6: Bound fields from the tblProducts table after they have been dragged to the form. (The field icon is also shown that is displayed when dragging a group of fields.)

The next step is to move the last two fields into position. There should be enough room for the last two fields to the right of the controls already on the form.

1. Click on the memFeatures field.

2. Hold the Shift key down and click on the olePicture field. Release the Shift key.

Only the memFeatures field and the olePicture field should be highlighted.

3. Click on the selected fields and drag the cursor icon to the right of the chrProductID control near the top of the screen. Release your mouse button.

The controls should appear as shown in Figure 10-7. Notice the memo and picture fields are automatically created as larger text boxes.

4. Close the Field List window by clicking the Field List button on the toolbar.

Notice that there are two controls for each field that you dragged onto the form. When you use the drag-and-drop method for placing fields, Access automatically creates a label control that displays the name of the field; it's attached to the text control that the field is bound to.

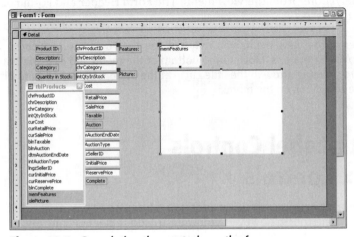

Figure 10-7: Completing the controls on the form.

Adding a Form Header or Footer

Although the form's Detail section usually contains the majority of the controls that display data, there are other optional sections in a form that you can add. These include a Page Header and Page Footer and a Form Header and Form Footer.

✦ **Form Header.** Displayed at the top of each page when viewed and at the top when the form is printed.

✦ **Page Header.** Displayed only when the form is printed; prints after the form header.

✦ **Page Footer.** Appears only when the form is printed; prints before the form footer.

✦ **Form Footer.** Displayed at the bottom of each page when viewed and at the bottom of the form when the form is printed.

A header goes before the detail section and a footer after it. A Form Header appears at the top of the form, while a Form Footer appears at the bottom. The Form headers and footers remain on the screen, while any controls in the Detail section can scroll up and down.

Note Page Headers and Page Footers are displayed only if the form is printed. They do not appear when the form is displayed.

You can create a Form Header or Form Footer by using the View menu. Near the bottom of the View menu is the Form Header/Footer option. This option will place a Form Header and Form Footer onto the form.

Select Form Header/Footer from the View menu. The Form Header and Form Footer should appear in the form.

Tip When you select the View menu, you may not see the Form Header/Footer or Page Header/Footer options. Move to the bottom of the menu and click the double downward pointing arrow in the little circle at the bottom of the menu to display all of the selections on the menu.

Working with Label Controls and Text Box Controls

Attached label controls are automatically added to a form when you drag a field from the Field List. Sometimes, however, you want to add text label controls by themselves to create headings or titles for the form.

Creating unattached labels

To create a new, unattached label control, you must use the Toolbox unless you copy an existing label. The next task in the example is to add the text header Products to your form in the Form Header. This task is divided into segments to demonstrate adding and editing text. To create an unattached label control, follow these steps:

1. Display the Toolbox.

2. Click the Label button on the Toolbox.

3. Click in the Form Header and drag the pointer to make a small rectangle about 1 inch long and ¼-inch high. When you place the cursor in the Form Header, it becomes a + sign with a capital A below and to the right.

4. Type **Products**.

5. Press Enter.

Your screen should look like the one shown in Figure 10-8. The cursor is shown as a label icon. This lets you know you can create another label if you want. Notice the Form headers and footers on the form. As you place controls within a header or footer, it will expand to the size of the control you are creating.

Tip
If you are not using one of the Form headers or footers and there are no controls on it, you can make it invisible by dragging the bottom border to meet the top border. If there are controls in the header or footer, you can change the header's or footer's Visible property to No to hide its contents.

Tip
To create a multiple-line label, press Ctrl+Enter to force a line break in the text.

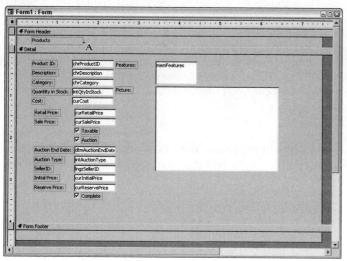

Figure 10-8: Adding an unattached label to the Form Header.

Modifying the text in a label or text control

To modify the text in a control, click inside the label and the mouse pointer changes to the standard Windows insertion point, an I-beam. You can now edit the text. Also notice that the Formatting toolbar icons become grayed out and cannot be selected. This is because you cannot apply specific formatting to individual characters. You can only apply formatting to the control (all of the text).

If you drag across the entire selection so that it is highlighted, anything new you type replaces the selected text. Another way to modify the text is to edit it from the control's Property window. One of the properties in a label's Property window is Caption. In the Caption property, you can edit the contents of a label control by clicking the value box and typing new text. If you want to edit or enter a caption that is longer than the space in the Property window, the contents will scroll as you type. Or you can press Shift+F2 to open a zoom box with more space to type.

The Formatting Toolbar

Access features a second toolbar known as the Formatting toolbar, shown in Figure 10-9 (which is described more fully in Chapter 13). Toolbars are really windows. You can move any toolbar by dragging it from its normal location to the middle of a form, and you can change its size and shape. Most toolbars can be docked to any edge of the screen (such as the left, right, or bottom).

The Formatting toolbar contains objects found in most Office toolbars. The first area of the Formatting toolbar (on the left side) selects a control or Form section, such as the Form or Page headers or footers, Detail, or the form itself. When you have many controls and you want (for example) to select a control that's behind another control, this selection combo box makes it easy. The next few objects on the Formatting toolbar change text properties. Two more combo boxes let you change the font style and size. (Remember, you may have fonts others do not have. Do not use an exotic font if the user of your form does not have the font.) After the font style and size combo boxes are icons for making a text control bold, italic, and underlined. Beyond those are alignment icons for left, center, and right text alignment. The last five pull-down icons change color properties, line types and styles, and special effects. See Chapter 13 for more complete descriptions.

In the next exercise, you will edit the text in the label control itself, and not in the control's Caption Property window. To edit the label so that it contains different text, follow these steps:

1. Click after the **s** in Products, the label control.
2. Type a space and then the text **Example**.
3. Press Enter.

The form title would also look better if it were larger.

Modifying the format of text in a control

To modify the formatting of text within a control, select the control by clicking its border (not in it). Then select a formatting style to apply to the label. Just click the appropriate button on the toolbar. To add visual emphasis to the title, follow these steps:

1. Click anywhere on the newly created form header label border. Little squares should appear around the control's borders.
2. Click on the Bold button on the Formatting toolbar.
3. Click on the drop-down arrow of the Font-Size list box.
4. Select 14 from the Font Size drop-down list.

You probably can only see a portion of the label. The label control now needs to be resized to display all the text.

Sizing a text box control or label control

When you select a control, from three to seven sizing handles appear depending on the size. One appears on each corner except the upper left (which contains the move handle and is slightly bigger), and one appears on each side. When the pointer moves over one of the sizing handles, the mouse pointer changes into a double-headed arrow. When this happens, click and drag the control to the size you want. As you drag, a dotted outline appears, indicating how large the label will be when the mouse button is released.

When you double-click on any of the sizing handles, Access usually resizes a control to a *best fit* for the text in the control. This is especially handy if you increase the font size and then notice that the text is cut off either at the bottom or to the right. For label controls, note that this *best-fit* sizing adjusts the size vertically and horizontally, though text controls are resized only vertically. This is because when Access is in form-design mode, it can't predict how much of a field to display — the field name and field contents can be radically different. Sometimes, however, label controls are not resized correctly and must be manually adjusted.

In the example, the text no longer fits within the label control, but you can resize the text control to fit the enhanced font size. To do this, follow these steps:

1. Click the *Products Example* label control.
2. Move the mouse pointer over the control. Notice that the mouse pointer changes shape as it moves over the sizing handles.
3. Double-click one of the sizing handles.

The label should resize itself along with adding depth to the Form Header section.

The label control size may still need readjustment. If so, place the mouse pointer in the bottom-right corner of the control so that the diagonal arrow appears and drag the control until it is the correct size. You also need to move some of the controls down to make room to center the label over the form. You can select all the controls and move them down using the techniques you learned in the previous chapter.

 Tip   You can also select Format ➪ Size ➪ To Fit to change the size of the label control text automatically.

As you create your form, you should test it frequently by selecting the form's View button on the toolbar. Click on the View Form icon to see the completed form so far. Figure 10-10 shows the form in its current state of completion.

Switch back to design view by again clicking on the form design view icon.

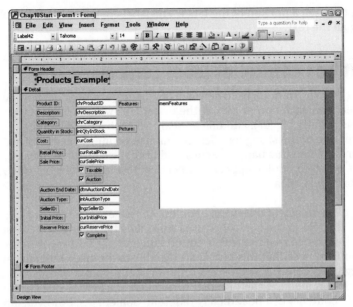

Figure 10-9: Formatting the new label.

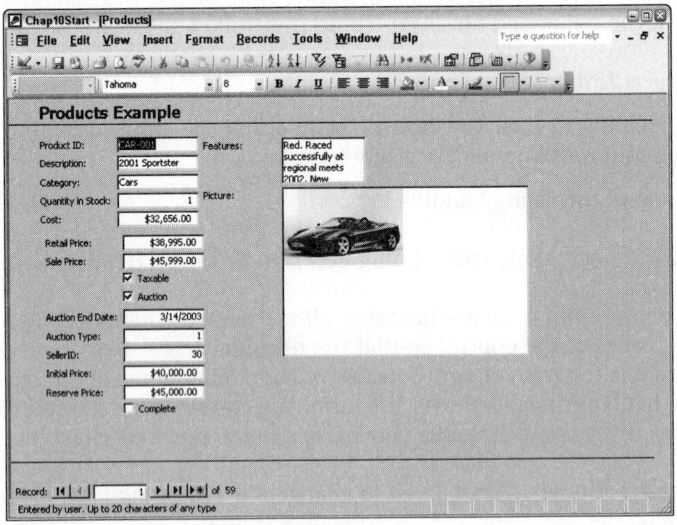

Figure 10-10: Viewing the form.

Now that you've dragged the fields to the form design and added a form title, you can move the text box controls into their correct position. You then will need to size each control to display the information properly within each field.

Deleting a control

You can delete a control by simply clicking on it in form design view and then pressing the delete key on your keyboard. The control and any attached labels should disappear.

You can bring them back by immediately selecting Undo from the form design Edit menu.

Select the Auction Type control and press the Delete key on your keyboard. This control displays a number 1. This field will be used later to demonstrate the use of an option group. You will see it again in Chapter 11.

Moving label and text controls

Before you move the label and text controls, it is important that you are reminded of a few differences between attached and unattached controls. When an attached label is created automatically with a text control, it is called a *compound control*— that is, whenever one control in the set is moved, the other control in the set is also moved.

To move both controls in a compound control, select one of the controls (either the label control or the data control) by clicking anywhere on it. Move the mouse pointer over either of the objects. When the pointer turns into a hand, you can click the controls and drag them to their new location.

You may notice that in a compound control, there are two move handles. One move handle is actually on the label control and one is on the data control. To move the label control separately from the data control, click on the label control's move handle (the cursor should change into a hand with the first finger raised). You can now move the label control only. To move only the data control, click on the data control's move handle (the cursor should change into a hand with the first finger raised) and move the data control separately from the label control.

Now go ahead and place the controls in their proper position to complete the form layout, using Figure 10-11 as a guide. You may notice that the check box control's label and date control positions have been reversed. The Reserve Price, Picture, and Features labels have also been moved above the controls instead of to the left of them. The Picture and Features controls have also been reversed and Picture is now on top and Features on the bottom of the form. You may also notice that the AuctionType field was removed.

You may also want to adjust the length of the various data fields as indicated by the Figure 10-11. Remember, you change the size of a control by selecting it and choosing one of the sizing handles as you learned in Chapter 9.

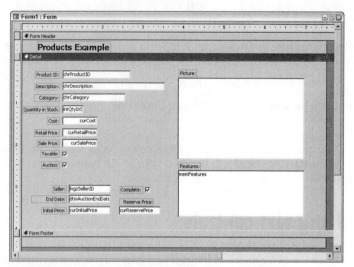

Figure 10-11: Repositioned text box and label controls in the Detail section.

Modifying the appearance of multiple controls

The text within the currency fields should all be right-aligned because the fields will appear below one another and the numbers inside the text boxes should align on the decimals. Make sure you have already aligned (both left- and right-aligned) the text box controls themselves. The following steps guide you through the process of changing the text alignment for the currency controls:

1. Select the curCost, curRetailPrice, and curSalePrice controls by clicking on them individually while holding down the Shift key.

2. Click the Align Right button on the toolbar (the right-most alignment icon between the underline and the background paint can icons).

You could have selected the label controls by using the drag-and-surround method.

Cross-Reference

Remember that you can select multiple controls and first use the Format ⇨ Align ⇨ Left or Format ⇨ Align ⇨ Right menu choices to line up one side of the controls. You can also change the Width property for a group of controls to make sure that when they are aligned together, they are the same width as well. See Chapter 9 for more details.

If you change to Form View now, the curCost, curRetailPrice, and curSalePrice data items are all right-aligned within the text controls. These are shown in design view in Figure 10-12.

Changing the control type

In Figure 10-11, the Complete control is a check box. Although there are times you may want to use a check box to display Boolean (Yes/No) type data, there are other ways to display one or the other type choices. One of those ways is a toggle button. A toggle button is raised if it's true and depressed (or at least very unhappy) if it's false.

Use these steps to turn the check box into a toggle button:

1. Select the Complete label control (just the label control, not the check box).

2. Press the Delete key to delete the label control because it is not needed.

3. Select the Complete check box.

4. Select Format ⇨ Change To ⇨ Toggle Button to change the control type.

The toggle button should now be displayed on the form. However, it needs to be placed into position and it needs some serious resizing. It will also need a caption for the face of the button.

1. Drag the toggle button slightly higher on the form so that the upper-left corner is just above the top of the lngzSellerID control.

2. Resize the toggle button control so that it is about ½-inch wide. Use Figure 10-12 as a guide.

3. Display the property window and enter Completed? in the Caption property of the toggle button.

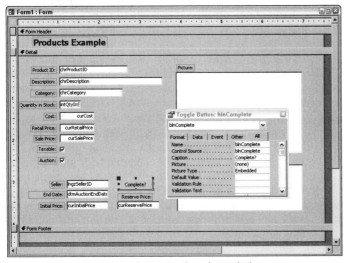

Figure 10-12: Finishing the Completed toggle button.

Setting the Tab Order

Now that you've completed moving all your controls into position, you should test the form again. If you change to Form View and press Tab to move from field to field, the cursor does not move from field to field in the order you expect. It starts out in the first field, *Product ID*, and then continues vertically from field to field, skipping some fields and moving fairly randomly around the screen. This route may seem strange, but that is the original order in which the fields were added to the form.

This is called the *Tab Order* of the form. The form's *default tab order* is always the order in which the fields were added to the form. If you don't plan to move the fields around, this is all right. If you do move the fields around or even delete one field and re-add it for any reason, you probably will need to change the order. After all, although you may make heavy use of the mouse when designing your forms, the average data-entry person still uses the keyboard to move from field to field.

When you need to change the tab order of a form, you can do so in one of two ways. In Design View, you may select the View ➪ Tab Order menu option or you may right-click any control and select Tab Order to change the order to match your layout. To change the tab order of the form, follow the next set of steps (make sure that you are back in Design View before continuing):

1. Select View ➪ Tab Order or right-click any control and select Tab Order.

2. Press the Auto Order button to place the controls in a roughly left to right, top to bottom order.

   The Tab Order dialog box is displayed as shown in Figure 10-13. When you press the Auto Order button, the controls are ordered beginning in the upper-left corner of the form and then continuing in a left to right order and top to bottom. Higher comes before lower and left comes before right.

Note   Notice the control names in the Custom Order list box. The control names in the Custom Order list box do not match the bound field names shown in the form design. It is a good idea to change your control names to use Standard Naming Conventions. The control names have been prefixed with standard naming conventions instead of the field data type. (See Appendix D.) When the controls are first dragged to the form's workspace, they will have the name of the bound field. You must manually change each control name from the table field prefix to the control prefix. For example, the field chrProductID is named txtProductID because it is a textbox. The control bound to the field blnTaxable has been named chkTaxable. While you don't have to do this (and many developers do not), it is nevertheless important to understand why you will see these prefixes in other developer's systems. You can see both the control name and the bound field name in the control's Property window.

3. Click the frbPicture Selection bar in the Tab Order dialog box (gray bar to the left of the field names).

4. Click again and drag the row to the bottom of the dialog box to a point below the txtReservePrice row.

5. Click the txtFeatures Selection bar in the Tab Order dialog box (gray bar to the left of the field names).

6. Click again and drag the row to the bottom of the dialog box to a point below the frbPicture row.

7. Click the OK button to complete the task.

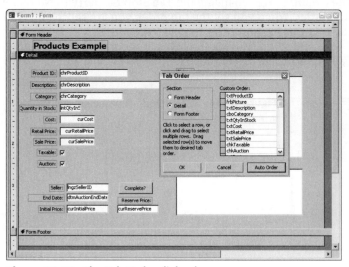

Figure 10-13: The Tab Order dialog box.

Navigating Your Application Through VBA

Professional developers frequently write hundreds or thousands of lines of VBA to control where the cursor moves when data entry occurs. System specifications often dictate automatically moving to other controls or even different forms based on the values entered in a control. For example, if a male gender check box is checked, a pop-up form may be necessary to capture some male-specific values. If an invoice amount exceeds the customers credit limit, a warning message may need to be displayed. Some applications have a specification that use of a mouse is optional by the customer. This often requires VBA code to handle alternative interface movement such as function keys or first letter selection instead of allowing mouse placement. Later in the book, you will learn how to develop mouse-optional interfaces.

The Tab Order dialog box lets you select either one row or multiple rows at a time. Multiple contiguous rows are selected by clicking the first Selection bar and dragging down to select multiple rows. After the rows are highlighted, the selected rows can be dragged to their new positions.

The Tab Order dialog box has several buttons at the bottom of the box. The Auto Order button places the fields in order from left to right and from top to bottom, according to their position in the form. This button is a good place to start when you have significantly rearranged the fields.

Each control has two properties that interact with this screen, as shown in Figure 10-14. The Tab Stop property determines whether pressing the Tab key lands you on the field. The default is Yes; changing the Tab Stop property to No removes the field from the tab order. When you set the tab order, you are setting the Tab Index property values. In this example, the control (*txtRetailPrice*) is set to 5, *chrProductID* is set to 1, and so on. Moving the fields around in the Tab Order dialog box changes the Tab Index properties of those (and other) fields.

Figure 10-14: Tab related properties in the Property window.

Using Multiple-Line Text Box Controls for Memo Fields

Multiple-line text box controls are used for Memo data types such as the memFeatures field. When adding a Memo field to a form, make sure that there is plenty of room in the text box control to enter a large amount of text. There are several ways to make certain that you've allowed enough space.

The first method is to resize the text box control until it's large enough to accommodate any text you may enter into the Memo field, but this is rarely possible. Usually the reason you create a Memo field is to hold a large amount of text; that text can easily take up more space than the entire form.

The default property for a text box control is to display a vertical scrollbar when it is not large enough for all the text. By allowing scrollbars on the Memo field's text box control, you can accommodate any amount of data. The *Features* control text box by default displays a vertical scrollbar if the text in the box is larger than the display area. If you do not want to display a scrollbar, you can set the Scroll Bars property in the Property window to None.

Working with Bound Object Frames on a Form

When you drag a field that uses the OLE data type to a form, Access creates a bound object frame automatically. This control can be resized and moved the same as any control. Pictures can be added in form view by clicking on the control and pasting a picture from the clipboard. You can also use the Insert Picture option from the menu.

Creating a Calculated Field

To understand creation of a calculated field, you will now create one. In Figure 10-1, you might have noticed a control with the label *Expected Profit*. This is actually a calculated field, which calculates the current sales price minus the current cost (curSalePrice-curCost).

The easiest way to do this is to create a new unbound control by clicking on the toolbox and dragging a text box control to the form design's workspace to the right of the Retail Price and Sale Price controls (see Figure 10-14).

To create this new calculated control, follow these steps:

1. Select the Text Box control in the Toolbox.

2. Drag the control to the right of the Retail Price and Sale Price controls.

   This will create a new unbound text box control along with a label control.

3. Select the new label control.

4. Display the Property window and change the label control's Caption property to Expected Profit.

5. Click on the new text box control and name it txtExpProfit by typing that in the Name property of the text box control. The txt prefix means it is a text box.

6. Place your cursor in the Control Source property of the txtExpProfit text box control.

7. In the Control Source property, type = **curSalePrice-curCost**.

8. Change the Format property to Currency.

9. Change the Decimal Places property to 2.

Your screen should look like the one shown in Figure 10-15.

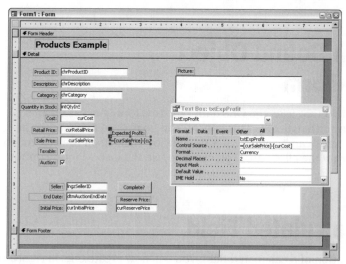

Figure 10-15: Creating a calculated field.

Fixing a Picture's Display

Before you complete the OLE bound object picture field, there is one more task to perform. The default value for the Size Mode property of a bound object frame is Clip. This means that a picture displayed within the frame is shown in its original size and truncated to fit within the frame. In this example, you need to display the picture so that it fits completely within the frame. When you're done, the design should look like the one shown in Figure 10-16. Two property settings let you do this:

✦ **Zoom.** Keeps picture in its original proportion but may result in extra white space.

✦ **Stretch.** Sizes picture to fit exactly between the frame borders.

Although the Zoom setting displays the picture more correctly, the Stretch setting looks better, unless the picture's proportions are important to viewing the data. To set the Size Mode property of a bound object frame, follow these steps:

1. Select the Picture bound object frame.

2. Display the Property window.

3. Select the Size Mode property.

4. Select Stretch.

Figure 10-16 shows the form in Form View. Notice the Property window for the bound object frame control. The Size Mode property is being set to Stretch.

When you complete this part of the design, you should save the form and then display it. You can now name this form frmProductsExample if you want. You will see it in its current completed state in Chapter 11. Figure 10-16 shows the form.

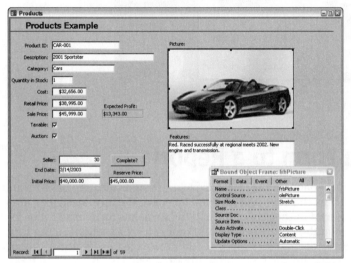

Figure 10-16: The completed form with a Memo and OLE field.

Printing a Form

You can print a form by selecting the File ➪ Print command and entering the desired information in the Print dialog box. Printing a form is like printing anything else; you are in a WYSIWYG ("What You See Is What You Get") environment, so what you see on the form is essentially what you get in the printed hard copy. If you added Page Headers or Page Footers, they are printed at the top or bottom of the page.

You can also preview the printout by clicking the File ➪ Print Preview menu command. This displays a preview of the printed page, as shown in Figure 10-17.

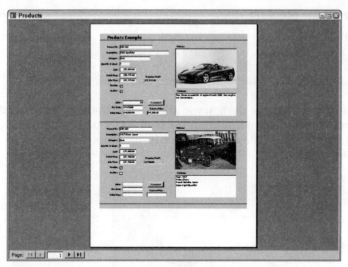

Figure 10-17: A preview of a form.

Converting a Form to a Report

By right-clicking a form name in the Database window and selecting Save As and then selecting Report as the Save As type, you can save the form design as a report. The entire form is placed in the report form. If the form has form headers or footers, these are placed in the report header and report footer sections. If the form has page headers or page footers, these are placed in the page header and footer sections in the report. After the design is in the Report Design window, it can be enhanced using the report design features. This allows you to add group sections and additional totaling in a report without having to re-create a great layout. You will learn more about this in later chapters.

✦   ✦   ✦

Adding Data-Validation Features to Forms

In the preceding three chapters, you learned to create a basic form. In this chapter, you learn techniques for creating several *data-validation* controls; these controls help ensure that the data being entered (and edited) in your forms is as correct as possible.

On the CD-ROM

In this chapter, you modify your form created in Chapter 10 to add the data-validation features shown in Figure 11-1. If you are following the examples, you should start with the form frmProductsExample in the Chap11Start.mdb database file on the CD-ROM that comes with this book. A few changes have been made for you from the form you created in Chapter 10.

You can see in Figure 11-1 that the Category and Seller controls have been changed to combo boxes. You can see the Auction Type field has been added and is an option group containing two option buttons. What you can't see is that other data validation has been added to various controls, including the Sale Price and Reserve Price controls.

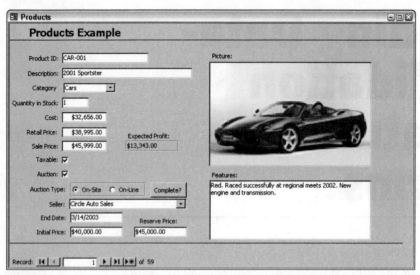

Figure 11-1: The frmProductsExample Data Entry form after adding validation controls.

Creating Data-Validation Expressions

There is an old expression: garbage in, garbage out. If bad data goes into a database, only bad data can come out when viewing the information from your forms and reports. If bad data was always easily recognizable, that would be great. But the reality is that people believe in what comes out of a computer system. A more correct expression is: garbage in, gospel out. Because a good application can make the worst data look good through complex analysis forms and wonderfully presented reports, it is even more important today to make sure the data is right.

Expressions can be entered into table design properties or a form control's Property window to limit input to specific values or ranges of values. The limit is effective when a specific control or form is used.

In addition, a status line message can be displayed that advises users how to enter the data properly when they move the insertion point into a particular control. You can also have a form show an error message if a user makes an invalid entry. These expressions can be entered in a table design or in a form's control. Expressions entered in a table design are automatically inherited or used by any form that uses the table. If the expression is entered only in a form, only that form will do the validation check.

Creating status line messages

Several types of validation text can be entered into a table design, as shown in Table 11-1. When the user of a form or datasheet moves the cursor into a control, messages can appear in the status line at the lower-left corner of the screen. In your table design, you enter these messages into the Description column, as shown in Figure 11-2. In this example, the status line message displays "Offering Price. Usually the highest price it is sold at" when the insertion point (cursor) is in the curRetailPrice field's control.

Table 11-1
Types of Validation Entered into a Table Design

Type of Validation	Stored in	Displayed in Form
Status line message	Description/Status Bar Text	Status bar
Validation expression	Validation Rule	Not displayed
Error message	Validation Text	Dialog box
Input mask	Input Mask	Control text box

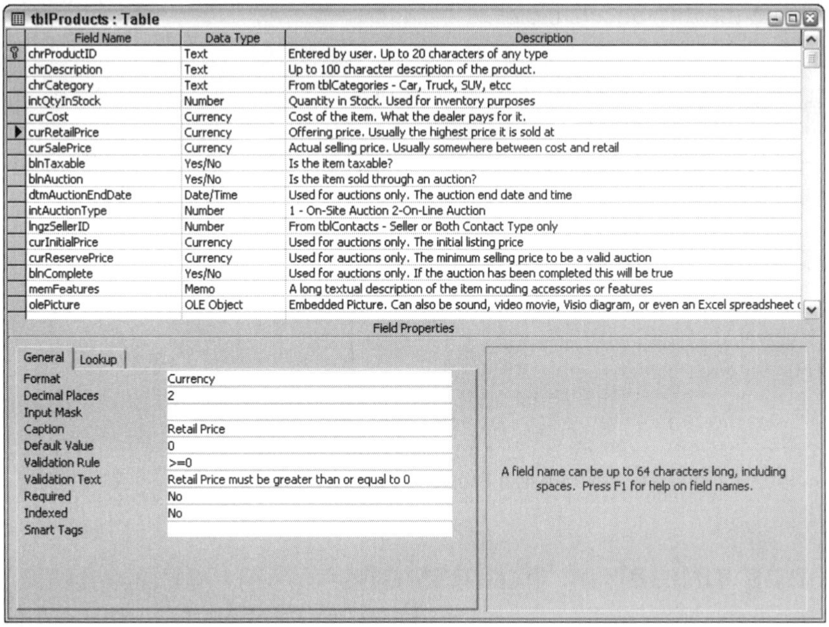

Figure 11-2: The field description and validation properties for the curRetailPrice field in the table design.

Entering table level validation expressions

Figure 11-2 shows a table design from the tblProducts table with the curRetailPrice field selected. The only properties that are displayed are for the highlighted field, although you can see all the descriptions in the upper part of the Table Design window. You enter validation expressions in the lower portion of the screen. *Validation expressions* are the rules the data must follow.

Any type of expression can be entered into the Validation Rule property box (found in the Field Properties pane of the Table Design window). In Figure 11-2, the expression >=**0** limits the entry to 0 or a positive number.

You can also display your own error message in a dialog box when data entry does not pass the validation rule. This text is entered into the Validation Text property box also found in the Field Properties pane of the table design. In this example, the dialog box will display "Retail Price must be greater than or equal to 0."

You can enter the same types of validation text into a form's property window if you want. When you create a form, the table validation properties are automatically known to each bound control on the form that uses any field with table level validation properties. They don't actually appear in the form controls properties but they do work. This way, if you enter validation expressions at the table level, you don't have to enter them again for each form. If you want to override them for a particular form, you can simply enter a new value for any of the properties in the form's control properties. Figure 11-3 shows the same properties in the form that were entered into the tblProducts table.

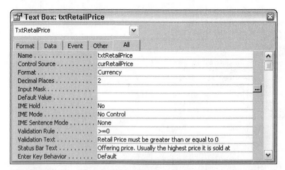

Figure 11-3: The form's Status Bar Text and Validation properties for the txtRetailPrice control bound to the curRetailPrice field in the form design Property window.

Entering validation expressions

You can enter a validation expression in a number of different ways for each field in your table or control in your form. For a number field, you can use standard mathematical expressions such as *less than*, *greater than*, *equal to*, or *not equal to* using the appropriate symbols (<, >, =, <>).

For example, if you want to limit a numerical field to numbers greater than 100, you enter the following validation expression in the appropriate property box:

> 100

To limit the numeric field to numbers not equal to 0, you enter:

<> 0

To limit a date field to dates before January 2005, you enter:

< #1/1/2005#

The # are known as delimiters and must surround any date expression where the date is an actual month, day, and year.

If you want to limit a numeric or date value to a range, you can enter:

Between 0 And 1500

or

Between #1/1/70# And Date( )

Note Date( ) is the current date (today).

Cross-Reference If you are not familiar with operators and delimiters in Microsoft Access, Chapter 5 covers various mathematical comparison operators and delimiters in queries. These expressions for entering query criteria are the same expressions you enter in form and table validation. These operators and various other functions are also described in Chapter 20.

Creating Choices with Option Groups and Buttons

Sometimes you don't want to enable a user to type anything at all. You want the user to pick a valid entry from a list. One of the ways to do this when you want to allow a single selection from a small group of choices is to use an option group. An *option* group is a control that contains other controls. You can limit input on your form in this way by using an *option button* control within the option group control. Option buttons were once known as *radio buttons*.

An option button by itself is a control that indicates whether a situation is True or False. The control consists of a string of text and a button that can be turned on or off by clicking the mouse. The Auction Type control shown in Figure 11-1 shows two option buttons. When you click the button, a black dot appears in its center, indicating that the situation is True; otherwise, the situation is False.

When you place more than one option button (or check box or toggle button) within an option group, only one can be true at a time. They work together and stop being independent. Only the option group is bound and therefore only one of the values within the group can be true. When the user clicks on one option to make it true, all other option buttons values are set to false. Each option button has a numeric value such as 1, 2, 3, etc. Each time a specific option button is set to true, its number is passed to the option group. As previously mentioned, only the option group is the only control bound to a table field. The option buttons themselves are unbound when part of an option group.

Generally, you use an option button when you want to limit data entry but more than two choices are available. You should limit the number of choices to four or five, however, when using option buttons. If you have more than four choices, use a list or combo box (described later in this chapter). If there is only one choice, true or false, you should use a check box.

Option buttons can increase flexibility in validating data input. For example, when an option group control is used for the intAuctionType field (as shown in Figure 11-1), it will pass a number: 1 represents On-Site and 2 represents On-Line. In Figure 11-1, you can see that label controls identify each option button's representation. Although you will see that a 1 has been assigned to the first option button labeled *On-Site* and a 2 has been assigned to the option button labeled *On-Line*, in reality you can assign any number to the option buttons. As long as each option button within the option group has a different value, the option group will work.

Only one of the option buttons can be made True for any given record. This approach also ensures that no other possible choices can be entered on the form. In an option group, the option group box itself is bound to a field or expression. In Figure 11-1 both option buttons and the surrounding box make up the option group. Each button passes a different value back to the option group box, which in turn passes a single value to the field or expression. Each option button is bound to the option group rectangle itself rather than to a field or expression. In this example, the option group control is bound to the intAuctionType field in the tblProducts table. If you look at the table itself, that field will contain a 0, 1, or 2 depending on if the option group is null (neither button has been selected for the specific record), 1 if On-Site was selected, and 2 if On-Line was selected.

Caution   Only fields with a Numeric data type (Integer, Single, Double) can be used for an option group in a form. In a report, you can transform nonnumeric data into numeric data types for display-only option buttons (see Chapters 12 and 13). You can also display an alternative value by using the Lookup Wizard in the Table design window and displaying a combo box.

To create an option group with option buttons, you must do two things:

✦ Create the option group box and bind it to a field.

✦ Create each option button and bind each one to the option group box.

Creating option groups

In Microsoft Access, the easiest and most efficient way to create option groups is with the Option Group Wizard. You can use it to create *option groups* with multiple option buttons, toggle buttons, or check boxes. When you're through, all your control's property settings are correctly set. This Wizard greatly simplifies the process and enables you to create an option group quickly, but you still need to understand the process.

Creating an option group box

When you create a new option group, the Option Group Wizard is triggered automatically. Clicking the Option Group tool on the Toolbox and drawing the control box rectangle starts the process. Another method is to click the Option Group button and then drag the appropriate field from the Field List window.

Caution

To start any of the Wizards that create controls, you must first have the Control Wizards button on the Toolbox selected.

Use the completed option group in Figure 11-1 as a guide. If the Toolbox and Field List are not open, open them now.

Create the option group box by following these steps:

1. Click the Option Group button on the Toolbox. When you release the mouse button, the Option Group button will remain depressed.

2. Select and drag the intAuctionType field from the Field List window to the space under the Customer Information box.

   The first screen of the Option Group Wizard should be displayed (as shown, completed, in Figure 11-4). You enter the label name for each option button, check box, or toggle button that will be in your option group on this screen. You enter each entry as you would in a datasheet. You can press the down-arrow ($\downarrow$) or tab key to move to the next row.

3. Enter On-Site and On-Line, pressing the down-arrow ($\downarrow$) key between choices.

   In Figure 11-4, you can see the intAuctionType field selected in the field list and the Option Group selected in the toolbox. You can also see the option group label and rectangle created just to the right and below the Auction checkbox on the form. Later, you will have to resize and move the controls within the completed option group.

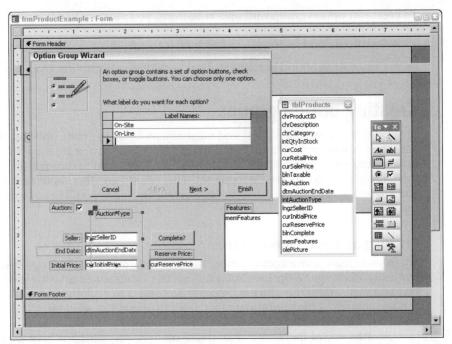

Figure 11-4: Entering the option group labels into the first Wizard screen for the Auction Type Control.

4. Click the Next button to move to the second Wizard screen.

You use the second screen to select which control will be the default selection. The Wizard starts with the first option as the default. If you want to make a different option button the default, select the Yes, the Default Choice Is option button and then select the default value from the combo box that lists your choices. In this example, you want the first option, On-Site, to be the default.

5. Click the Next button to move to the third Wizard screen used for assigning values.

This screen (shown in Figure 11-5) displays a default set of numbers that will be used to store the selected value in the bound option group field (in this example, the intAuctionType field) along with the actual values you entered. The screen looks like a datasheet with two columns. Your first choice, On-Site, is automatically assigned a 1, and On-Line is assigned a 2. This means that when On-Line is selected, a 2 is stored in the intAuctionType field.

In this example, the default values are acceptable. Sometimes, however, you may want to assign values other than 1, 2, 3, etc. You may want to use 100, 200, and 500 for some reason. As long as you use unique numbers, you can assign any values you want.

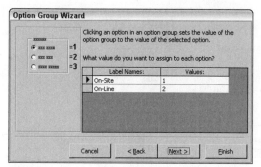

Figure 11-5: Assigning the value of each option button.

6. Click the Next button to move to the next Wizard screen.

   In this screen, you tell Access whether the option group itself is bound to a form field or unbound. The first choice in the Wizard—Save the Value for Later Use—creates an unbound field. You use this choice if you're going to put the option group in a dialog box and use the selected value to make a decision. However, you want to store the value in a table field, thus in this example you want the second value—Store the Value in This Field. The Wizard automatically selected it because you started with the Auction Type field. If you wanted to bind the option group value to a different table field, you could select from a list of all form fields. Again, in this example, the default is acceptable.

7. Click the Next button to move to the option group style Wizard screen.

   The upper half of this Wizard screen enables you to choose which type of buttons you want; the lower half enables you to choose the style for the option group box and the type of group control. The style affects the option group rectangle. If you choose one of the special effects (such as Etched, Shadowed, Raised, or Sunken), that value is applied to the Special Effect property of the option group. For this example (as shown in Figure 11-6), again you want to accept the default selections of Option buttons and Etched style. Notice that your actual values are used as a sample.

Note As you change your selections, the Sample changes to show how it will look.

8. Click the Next button to move to the final Option Group Wizard screen.

   This screen enables you to give the option group control itself a label that will appear in the option group border. Then you can add the control to your design and (optionally) display Help to additionally customize the control.

9. Change the caption to **Auction Type** from the default table field name as your caption for the Option Group.

   Click the Finish button to complete the Wizard.

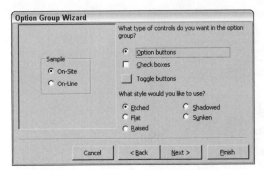

Figure 11-6: Selecting the type and look of your buttons.

You may want to switch to form view and test your option group by moving from one record to the next. Watch how the option button changes from one record to the next based on the data that is already in the table. If no value has been entered for the bound table field, neither option button will be selected as the bound field is null. When you are through, switch back to design view.

Your Wizard work is now complete. Six new controls appear on the design screen: the option group, its label, two option buttons, and their labels. However, you may still have some work to do. You may want to move the option buttons closer together, or change the shape of the option group box as shown in Figure 11-7, or change the Special Effect property of some controls. As you learned, you can do this using the property window for the controls.

Figure 11-7 shows the option group controls and the property window for the option group itself. Notice that the Default value is 1. Also notice that the Name property for the option group control is intAuctionType, the same name as the table field. You should change the option group control name to match standard naming conventions:

1. Rename the option group control optAuctionType by changing the Name property.

2. Leave the Control Source property unchanged.

You might also notice that the option group is vertical (option buttons above one another) and you want it to be horizontal. In order to do this, you first have to resize the option group rectangle so that it is large enough horizontally to hold the buttons across from each other. Then, move the buttons into position, and finally resize the option group rectangle into its final position:

1. Resize the option group rectangle wider by grabbing the right sizing handle and dragging it to the right.

2. Grab the On-Line control and its label and drag it to the right of the On-Site Control.

   You can use the Format ⇨ Align ⇨ Top menu option to align the two sets of controls if you want. Make sure the controls are aligned and the option buttons are vertically centered to their labels.

3. Resize the option group rectangle to fit around the option buttons by grabbing the right bottom corner sizing handle and dragging it up and to the right.

Remember, you can use the up, down, left, and right arrow keys to move your controls a little at a time. You can also press the Shift key first to resize the controls a little at a time. Make sure you have Format ⇨ Snap to Grid off if you want to move controls one pixel at a time.

Note

If you are using the keyboard to move or resize controls and Snap to Grid is off but the sizing or moving appears to move or resize your controls more than a little at a time, check that the form's Grid X and Grid Y property are set to at least 24 and more desirably 64. The higher the number is, the finer the grid divisions will be and the lesser the movement whether or not if the grid is visible.

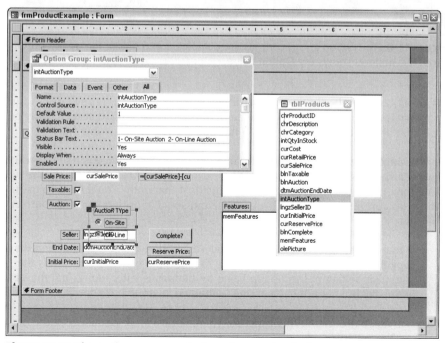

Figure 11-7: The option group controls and property window.

When you are through, the form should look like the one shown in Figure 11-8.

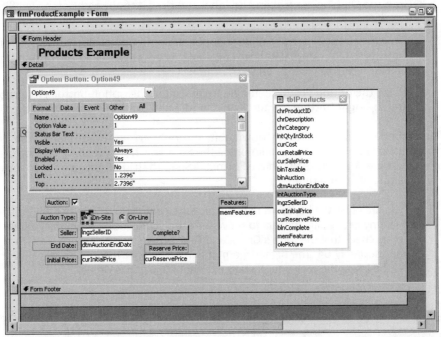

Figure 11-8: The option group controls are completed and one of the option button Property windows shows the Option Value.

Figure 11-8 shows the first option button selected. Notice that the Option Value property is set to 1, the value you accepted in the third Wizard screen. Only controls that are part of an option group have an Option Value property.

If you want to create an option group manually, the best advice is *don't*. If you must, however, the steps are the same as for creating any control. First create the option group box, and then create each button inside it manually. You'll have to manually set all data properties, palette properties, and specific option group or button controls.

Caution   If you create the option buttons outside the option group box and then drag or copy them into the option group box, they will not work. The reason is that the automatic setting of the Option Value for buttons is left undone, and the option button control has not been bound to the option group box control.

After you finish practicing this process, you can turn your attention to the next subject, Yes/No controls.

Creating Yes/No Options

There are many ways to show data properly from Yes/No data types:

✦ Display the values *Yes* or *No* in a text box control, using the Yes/No Format property to show –1 (True) or 0 (False), a Yes (True) or No (False), or True or False.

✦ Use a check box.

✦ Use an option button.

✦ Use a toggle button.

Although you can place values from Yes/No data types in a text box control and then format the control by using the Yes/No property, it's better to use one of the other controls. Yes/No data types require the values –1 or 0 to be entered into them. An unformatted text box control returns values (–1 and 0) that seem confusing, especially because –1 represents Yes and 0 represents No. Setting the Format property to Yes/No or True/False to display those values helps, but a user still needs to read the text *Yes/No* or *True/False*. A visual display is much better.

Toggle buttons, option buttons, and check boxes work with these values *behind the scenes* (returning –1 to the field if the button value is on and 0 if the button is off) but they display these values as a box or button, which is faster to read. You can even display a specific state by entering a default value in the Default property of the form control. The control is displayed initially in a Null state if no default is entered and no state is selected. The Null state appears visually the same as the No state.

The check box is the commonly accepted control for two-state selection. Toggle buttons are nice (they can use pictures rather than a text caption to represent the two states) but not always appropriate. It is hard to tell if a toggle button is shown True (depressed) or False (shown raised). Although you could also use option buttons, they would never be proper as a single Yes/No control.

Creating check boxes

A *check box* is a Yes/No control that acts the same as an option button but is displayed differently. A check box consists of a string of text (to describe the option) and a small square that indicates the answer. If the answer is True, a check mark is displayed in the box. If the answer is False, the box is empty. The user can toggle between the two allowable answers by clicking on the mouse with the pointer in the box.

Generally, any Yes/No field you create will automatically appear as a check box when you create a form. Sometimes, you want to create a check box to use with numeric or text type data fields.

The completed check boxes are shown in Figure 11-9 and the property window is visible for the chkAuction control. Notice some of the specific checkbox properties. The first is the Default Value. This value is No, indicating that initial value will be unchecked.

Another option for check boxes is Triple State. This option determines whether a check box can have three states: True, False, or Null. True appears as a checked box and False appears as a blank white box, but the Null value appears as a gray check box, indicating it has no value. If Triple State is No as it is in the example, there is no Null state. The checkbox is initially False (unless Default Value is set to True).

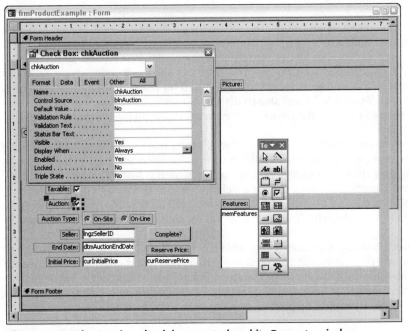

Figure 11-9: The Auction check box control and its Property window.

Tip   Although you can set the Display Control option of the Lookup tab in the Table Design to Check Box for any field with a Yes/No data type, you don't really need to. A check box is automatically created whenever you add a Yes/No field to a form. You can always change it to another type of control if you want.

Note   Before creating the check box controls, you could change the Default Check Box Label X property to a negative value; this would automatically place the check boxes to the right of the labels when they are created. The value to enter depends on the length of the labels. To save several steps when creating a group of similar-looking controls, change the Add Colon property to Yes to add a colon automatically and change the Special Effect property to Sunken.

Creating Visual Selections with Toggle Buttons

A *toggle button* is another type of True/False control. Toggle buttons act like option buttons and check boxes but are displayed differently. When a toggle button is set to True (in *pushed* mode), the button appears onscreen as depressed. When it is set to False, the button appears raised.

Toggle buttons provide a capability that the other button controls do not offer. That is you can set the size and shape of a toggle button, and you can display text or pictures on the face of the button to illustrate the choice a user can make. This additional capability provides great flexibility in making your form user-friendly.

In the last chapter, you learned how to create a toggle button. Later in the book, you will learn to use code to change the text caption on the toggle button face when it is depressed and again when it is false.

Adding a bitmapped image to the toggle button

As previously mentioned, you can display a picture on a toggle button rather than text. For example, you can modify the tglComplete toggle button you created in the last chapter, changing it to display a picture from the list that comes with Microsoft Access. Use the following steps to modify the button for the tglCompleter field:

1. Select the tglComplete toggle button.

2. Open the properties window and select the Picture property.

3. Click the Builder button (the button with three dots next to the property setting).

   The Picture Builder dialog box appears, which provides more than 100 predefined pictures. In this example, select the bitmap named Watch, as shown in Figure 11-10. The picture of the figure was actually taken *after* the picture was originally selected and saved to let you see both the process and the finished result.

4. Click the OK button to add the picture to the toggle button. The watch appears on the toggle button on the design screen. You may need to move it on the screen to make it fit between other controls.

In the property window, you can see the word (bitmap) appears in the Picture property.

Note   You could also have selected a picture from a ..bmp file or an .ico (icon) file by pressing the Browse button on the Picture Builder and by then selecting an external picture file. However, the button cannot size the picture. The picture must fit on the button, which means you generally need a very small picture of only 24 x 24 pixels for a large icon size picture or even smaller for a button on a toolbar.

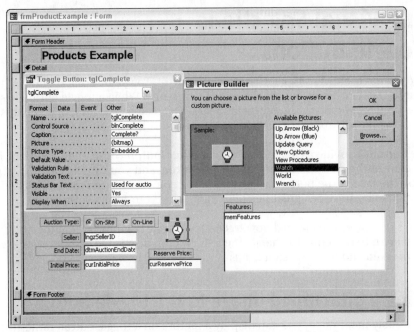

Figure 11-10: The Picture Builder dialog box used to create a picture on a toggle button.

Although you just changed the toggle button and added a picture, you will not be keeping it. To remove the picture from the toggle button, click on the Picture property, highlight the (bitmap) text, and erase it. After you confirm deleting the graphic, the Picture property will change to (none) and the text in the Caption property will again be displayed.

Although option buttons, check boxes, and toggle buttons are great for handling a few choices, they are not a good idea when many choices are possible. Access has other controls that make it easy to pick from a list of values.

Working with List Boxes and Combo Boxes

Access has two types of controls that enable you to show lists of data from which a user can select. These controls are *list boxes* and *combo boxes*.

The differences between list boxes and combo boxes

The basic difference between a list box and a combo box is that the list box is always open ready for selection, whereas the combo box has to be clicked to open the list for selection. Another difference is that the combo box enables you to enter a value that is not on the list. Finally, a combo box allows the user to enter success letters to find a value on the list. A list box only allows the first letter to be selected. If you enter the text SA into a *list box*, you will first go to the first value beginning with the letter S in a list, followed by the first value that begins with the letter A in the list. If you enter the text SA into a *combo box*, you will first go to the first value beginning with the letter S in the list followed by the first value that begins with the letters SA in the list. This is known as successive letter searching.

 Cross-Reference Chapter 8 contains details on these controls. Review Figures 8-15 and 8-16 if you are not familiar with list boxes and combo boxes.

A closed combo box appears as a single text box field with a downward-pointing arrow on its far right side. A list box, which is always open, can have one or more columns, from one to as many rows as will fit onscreen, and more than one item to be selected. An open combo box displays a single-column text box above the first row, followed by one or more columns and as many rows as you specify on the property window. Optionally, a list box or combo box can display column headers in the first row.

Settling real-estate issues

 Note You have to consider the amount of space that is available on the form before deciding between a list box and combo box. If only a few choices are allowed for a given field, a list box is sufficient. However, if there is not enough room on the form for the choices, use a combo box (a list box is always open, but a combo box is initially closed). When you use a list box, a user cannot type any new values, but instead must choose from the selection list.

When designing a list box, you must decide exactly which choices will be allowed for the given field and select an area of your form that has sufficient room for the open list box to display all selections.

For the examples in this chapter, you will learn to create combo boxes. Later, in Chapter 25, you will learn to create various types of list boxes.

Creating and Using Combo Boxes

As mentioned earlier, a *combo box* is a combination of a normal entry field and a list box. The operator can enter a value directly into the text area of the combo box or else click the directional arrow (in the right portion of the combo box) to display the list. In addition, the list remains hidden from view unless the arrow is activated, conserving valuable space on the form. A combo box is useful when there are many rows to display. A vertical scrollbar gives users access to the records that are out of sight.

In this next exercise, you will change the Category control from a text box to a combo box by using the Combo Box Wizard after first deleting the original text box.

Creating a single-column combo box

To create a single-column combo box using the Wizard, follow these steps:

1. Delete the existing Category text box field control and its label.

2. Click the Combo Box tool in the Toolbox. Make sure the Control Wizard toggle button (the top right icon in the toolbox) is depressed so the wizard will run in Step 3.

3. Display the field list and drag the chrCategory field to the area below Description.

   The Combo Box Wizard dialog is displayed. The first screen enables you to tell Access whether the values will come from a table/query, you will type a list of values, or Access will create a query-by-form list box to display all the unique values in the current table. Depending on your answer, you either select the number of columns (and type in the values) or select the fields to use from the selected table/query. In this example, the values come from a table.

4. Select the first option, I Want the Combo Box to Look Up the Values in a Table or Query; then click the Next button.

   As shown in Figure 11-11, the second Wizard screen enables you to choose the table from which to select the values. By using the row of option buttons under the list of tables, you can view all the Tables, Queries, or Both (tables and queries).

5. Select the tblCategories table and click the Next button.

   The third Wizard screen enables you to pick the fields you want to use to populate the combo box. You can pick any field in the table or query and select the fields in any order; Access creates the necessary SQL statement for you. The tblCategories table has only one field (chrCategory), a list of valid categories, so it is the only field in the Available Fields list.

6. Select the chrCategory field; click the right-pointing arrow to add it to the Selected Fields list and click the Next button to move to the next Wizard screen.

   This allows you to determine a sorting order for the records that will appear in the list.

7. Select chrCategory (the only field in the list) and click the Next button to move to the next Wizard screen.

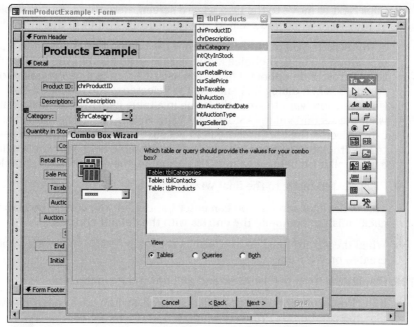

Figure 11-11: Selecting the table for the row source of the combo box.

In this screen, a list of the actual values in your selected field appears (as shown in Figure 11-12). Here you can adjust the width of any columns for their actual display. You can automatically adjust the columns to the largest value in the list by double-clicking on the line on the right on the column to be adjusted.

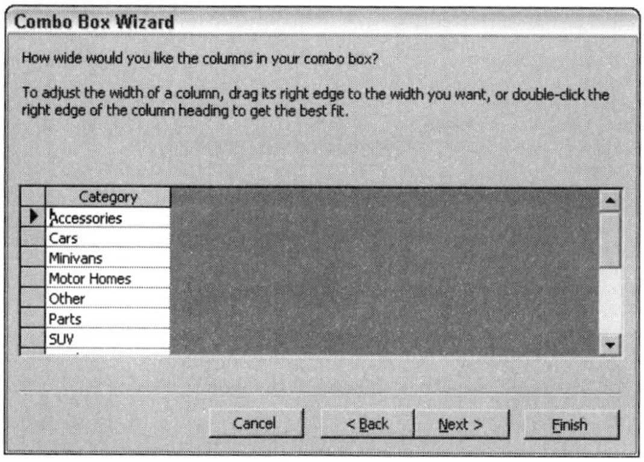

Figure 11-12: Adjusting the column width of the selection.

8. Click Next to move to the next wizard screen. Here there are two choices, just as they were when you created an option group earlier in this chapter.

   In this screen, you tell Access whether the combo box is bound to a form field or unbound. The first choice in the Wizard—Remember the Value for Later Use—creates an unbound field. You use this choice if you're going to put the combo box in a dialog box and use the selected value to make a decision. However, you want to store the value in a table field, thus in this example you want the second value—Store That Value in this Field. The Wizard automatically selected the chrCategory field because you started with it. If you wanted to bind the option group value to a different table field, you could select from a list of all form fields. Again, in this example, the default is acceptable.

9. Click Next to move to the final Wizard screen.

   This is the final screen. You can enter Caption for the combo box label and click Finish to complete the entries with the default choices.

   When the wizard finishes, the form is shown in design view with combo box created on the form.

10. Display the form in form view and pull down the combo box.

    If the Property window is not still displayed, switch back to form view and display the combo box Property window.

Figure 11-13 shows the combo box control in form view with the combo box open and the Property window displayed for the combo box. If you switch to form view and select the combo box, you can click on the down arrow and display the data as shown in Figure 11-13.

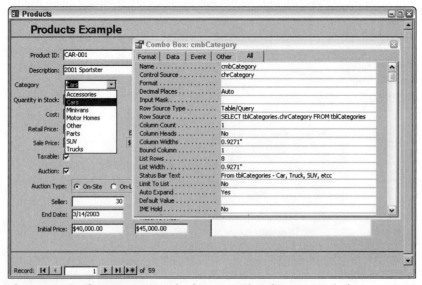

Figure 11-13: The Category combo box control and Property window.

Understanding combo box properties

As Figure 11-13 shows, several properties were set to define the combo box. The Wizard takes care of these for you, except for the Column Heads property, which adds the name of the column at the top of the combo box. You won't need this option for a single column list.

The Row Source Type and Row Source properties are used to specify what is displayed when the combo box is pulled down.

Row Source Type determines where the data comes from. The most common is Table/Query. Valid Row Source Type property options are listed in Table 11-2.

Table 11-2 Row Source Type Settings	
Row Source Type	**Source of the Data Type**
Table/Query	(Default setting) Data is from a table or is the result of a query or a SQL statement. The name of the table, query, or SQL statement is entered into the Row Source property.
Value List	List of items specified by the Row Source setting. You actually type in the values separated by commas.
Field List	List of field names from the Table/Query named by the Row Source setting.

The Row Source property settings depend on the source type specified by Row Source Type.

The method used to specify the Row Source property settings, as listed in Table 11-3, depends on the type of data source (which you specified by setting the Row Source Type).

Table 11-3 Row Source Property Settings	
Row Source Type	**Method of Setting the Row Source Property**
Table/Query	Enter the name of a table, a query, or an actual SQL statement.
Value List	Enter a list of items separated by semicolons.
Field List	Enter the name of a table or query.

In this exercise, you selected the tblCategories table and selected the only field within that table. Therefore, the Row Source Type was set to Table/Query, and the Row Source was set to a SQL statement: SELECT [tblCategories].[chrCategory] FROM [tblCategories] ORDER BY [chrCategory].

When Table/Query or Field List is specified as the Row Source Type, you can pick from a list of tables and queries for the Row Source. The table or query must already exist. This list box would display fields from the table or query according to the order they follow in their source. Other settings in the Property window determine the number of columns, their size, whether there are column headers, and which column is bound to the field's control source. You'll learn more about these in the next exercise.

The List Rows property was set to 8. It controls the number of rows that display when the combo box is opened, but the Wizard does not enable you to select this. You have to display the Property window to change this option.

The Limit To List property determines whether you can enter a value into the tblCategories table that is not in the list; this property is another one the Wizard does not enable you to set. You must set these directly in the Property window. The default No value for Limit To List says that you can enter new values because you are not limiting the entry to the list.

Tip Setting the Auto Expand property to Yes enables the user to select the combo box value by entering text into the combo box that matches a value in the list. This is also known as successive letter selection and is a great feature of combo boxes. As soon as the combo box finds a unique match, it displays the value without having to display the entire list. The default value is Yes for the Auto Expand property. To change it to No, you must do so in the Property window.

Creating a multiple-column combo box

Combo boxes can also display multiple columns of information. These columns are displayed in an order of your choosing. You can display selected columns from your data source and choose the sorting order of the records as well.

Figure 11-14 shows the combo box you will create next already completed. Notice that this combo box displays the Company Name and Customer Name in the order of the Company Name. You will use a query to help you accomplish this task. Also notice (in Figure 11-14) that the Company and Name column heads are displayed.

To understand the selection criteria of a multiple-column combo box, you will first change the current text box to a combo box by right-clicking on the control. Before you do that, move the Completed toggle button to the right of the Auction Type option group and make the Seller text box wider, as shown in Figure 11-15.

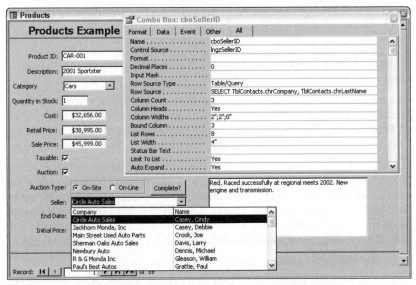

Figure 11-14: The Seller combo box control and Property window.

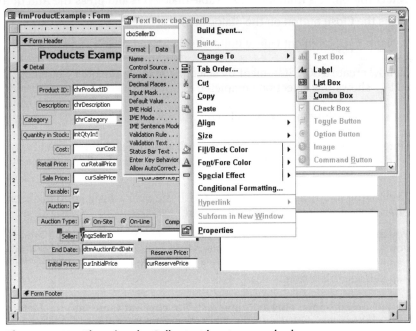

Figure 11-15: Changing the Seller text box to a combo box.

The first step is to change the text box into a combo box by following these steps:

1. Select the Seller text box.

2. Right click on the text box and select Change To⇨Combo Box, as shown in Figure 11-15.

   The text box changes to a combo box and the specific combo box properties are blank or display default settings. The Row Source Type property defaults to Table/Query. The first task is to create a Row Source for the combo box. This will require the tasks you learned in Chapter 5, because you have to create a Select query.

   If you look back at the Seller combo box in Figure 11-13, you can see it simply contained a number. This is the number of the Contact ID, which is the key field in the tblContacts table. This is the field that links from the tblProducts table to the tbContacts table. The combo box you are about to create will display meaningful contact information while still linking to this key field.

3. Click into the Seller combo box if it is not already selected.

4. Select the Row Source property and press the builder button (the little button on the right with three periods) to open the query design window.

5. Select tblContacts from the Show Table dialog box and press the Add button.

6. Press the Close button on the dialog box.

   A blank SQL Statement Query Builder is displayed.

You will now create a SQL Statement by selecting fields in the query builder. Figure 11-16 shows this selection completed.

The first step is to drag the three fields you will need:

1. Drag the chrCompany, chrLastName, idsContactID, and chrContactType fields in that order from the upper query design pane to the lower query design pane.

   Each of the first three columns dragged to the query design grid is checked off, indicating that they will be displayed.

   You are not going to display just the last name of the contact. You are actually going to display the last name followed by a comma followed by the first name. To do this, you have to create a concatenated string. In Figure 11-16, you can see this string.

2. Enter **ContactName: chrLastName & ", " & chrFirstName** into the Field area of the original chrLastName field, replacing the contents as shown in Figure 11-16.

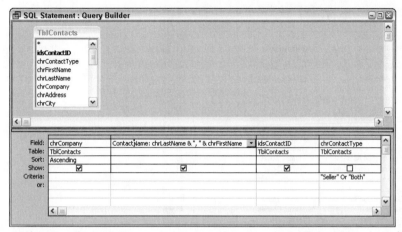

Figure 11-16: The Seller query window for the combo box row source.

This is a concatenated string because you place several text strings and fields together in a process known as *concatenation*. ContactName: means that the field will be known as the text ContactName if it is later used in code, and that is what the column header will be in the combo box for this column. The string chrLastName & ", " & chrFirstName takes the field chrLastName and joins it with a comma and space to the chrFirstName field. The & is the concatenation symbol and is used to join strings (text) and fields. Remember that any text must be in double quotes. There is a space after the comma and before the last double quote to add a space after the comma.

The next step is to tell the query how to sort the data.

3. Click into the *Sort:* row of the query design in the chrCompany column

4. Choose Ascending from the combo box list in this entry area, as shown in Figure 11-16.

   Finally, the last step is to limit the selection of contacts to those who are Sellers or Both buyers and sellers. You don't want to allow contacts who are only Buyers to be displayed in the Sellers combo box.

5. Click into the Criteria: row of the query design in the chrContactType column.

6. Enter **"Seller" or "Both"** in this entry area, as shown in Figure 11-16. Make sure you uncheck the Show: row check box because you don't want to display this row. You only want to filter the data.

   Before you close the query, you should verify that it works. Press the Run button (the exclamation point icon) on the toolbar. You should see a group of records similar to the ones shown in Figure 11-17.

7. Close the query and save the changes.

SQL Statement : Query Builder

Company	ContactName	Contact ID
ACC Car Sales	Parkson, Dennie	24
All Start Autos	Minkler, Larry	3
Allstate International Sales	Lieberham, Christopher	36
American Auto Sales	Mason, James	35
Bell Auto Sales	O'Hara, Robbie	50
Bill Thomas Sales, Inc	Marino, John	22
Chicota American Auto Sales	Calson, Larry	59
Circle Auto Sales	Casey, Cindy	30
Columbia Chevy	Hammerman, Joe	11
Corona Fordman Sales	Morris, Philp	47
El Pasco Auto Sales	Katzman, Joe	44
Elsa Honest Sales	Thamas, William	58
First Chance Auto	Tierney, Kevin	39
Fordman Colonial Times	Smith, David	29
Fordman Sales	Johnson, Meggie	38
Ghost Automobile Sales	Krammer, Casper	55
Greenleaf Car Sales	Verttie, Lou	61
Hatter Sales	Hatter, Charles	46

Record: 1 of 50

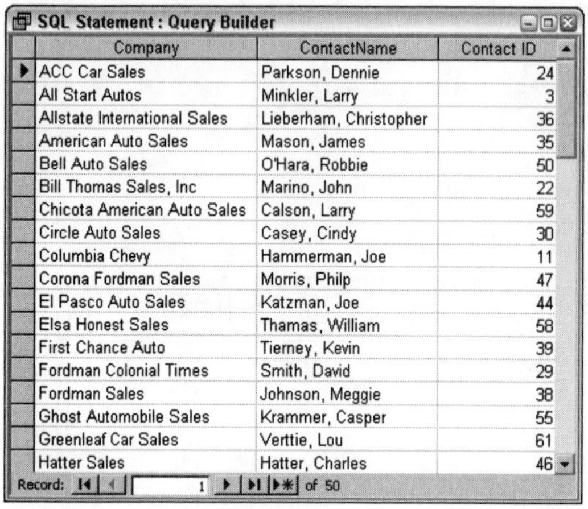

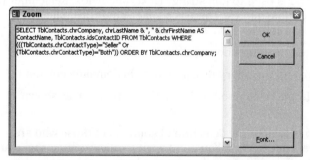

Figure 11-17: Checking the query results to verify that the combo box will work.

After you have closed the query, a SQL statement should appear in the Row Source of the combo box. You can more closely examine this SQL Statement by pressing Shift-F2 when your cursor is on the combo box Row Source property. This SQL Statement is shown in Figure 11-18.

Figure 11-18: The Seller combo box control and Property window.

Figure 11-18 shows the SQL equivalent of what was entered into the Query Design window. You will learn a lot more about SQL statements later in this book. The SELECT statement starts all queries that display data. The field names are listed, including the concatenated expression that uses the AS clause to display the new field name. The FROM clause indicates what table the fields come from. The WHERE clause lists any filters, and finally the ORDER BY specifies the sorting of the records.

Note

If the SQL Statement contains the keyword DISTINCTROW, the Wizard found more than one value that was the same in the list of data. For example, you may want to display a list of vehicle models from a list of active cars for sale. That set of records could have many items with Truck as one of the key values. DISTINCTROW would limit the displayed list to unique values.

Figure 11-19 shows the property window for the nearly completed combo box. The Row Source Type and Row Source are all set. However, you still have to change a few properties, including the following:

✦ **Column Count.** The number of columns to be displayed.

✦ **Column Heads.** Yes or No. Yes displays the field names as the first row. No just displays the data.

✦ **Column Widths.** The width of each column. Each value is separated by a semicolon.

✦ **Bound Column.** The column that passes the value back to the control source field.

✦ **List Rows.** The number of displayed rows in the combo box. Default is 8.

✦ **List Width.** The total width of the combo box when open. This should be at least the width of all the columns and optionally add plus .15 to allow for any scroll bar.

Make the following changes to complete the combo box:

1. Enter **3** in the Column Count property.

   You chose three columns that will be returned to the query. These include the Company, the concatenated contact name field, and the Seller ID from the tblContacts table.

2. Set the Column Heads property to Yes.

   Whenever you have two or more columns, you should display the column headers to identify each column.

3. Set the Column Widths property to 2";2";0".

   This allows 2 inches for the Company and Contact name fields and then hides the Seller ID. There is no need to see it because it is a number and means nothing except to link the values between the tblContacts table and the tblProducts table.

4. Set the Bound Column property to 3.

   The Bound Column indicates which column of the combo box is used to pass data back to the control's bound control source. In this example, the lngSellerID field will receive the value from the third column from the query, which was the idsContactID from the tblContacts table.

The List Rows property is set to 8 by default, and this is acceptable. Because the Seller combo box is near the bottom of the form, 8 is a good number. If there are more in the list that will fit below the combo box, the list may start above the combo box itself when it is opened.

5. Set the List Width property to 4".

This is one of the most misunderstood properties in combo boxes. This value should always be set to at least the sum of the Column Widths property, and probably a little bigger (.15 inches) to account for a scroll bar. If you don't set this property large enough, the combo box will contain a horizontal scroll bar and look very unprofessional.

6. Set the Limit to List property to Yes.

In order to protect good data, you must limit the data entry to valid sellers in the tblContacts table. The Limit to List property will prohibit entries not in the tblContacts table.

If you have followed the preceding steps properly, your Form design should resemble the one shown in Figure 11-19, and the Form view should look like the one shown in Figure 11-20.

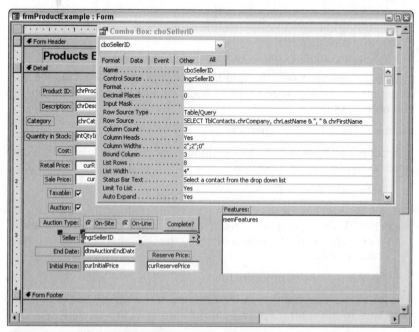

Figure 11-19: The Seller combo box control and Property window.

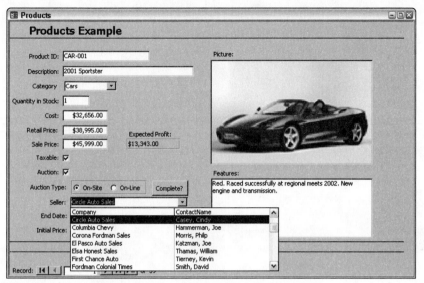

Figure 11-20: A multiple-column combo box in form view.

✦   ✦   ✦

Creating Professional-Looking Forms and Reports

In Chapters 10 and 11, you built a form that began with a blank Form Design. That form had no special formatting other than some label and text box controls. The most exciting objects on the form were the option group, check boxes, and toggle button. By using the various formatting windows and the Formatting toolbar, line and rectangle controls, background pictures, some limited color, and your own imagination, you can create professional-looking forms with a small amount of work.

In this chapter, you learn to format the data-entry form that you created in Chapter 11 to make it more readable and interesting to look at.

Making a Good Form Look Great

Just as you can use a desktop publishing package to enhance a word-processing document to make it more readable, you can use the tools in Form Design view to enhance a database form to make it more usable. One way that you can make your database form more usable is to draw attention to areas of the form that you want the reader to notice. Just as a headline in a newspaper calls your attention to the news, an enhanced section of a form makes the information that it contains stand out.

The Access form designer has a number of tools to make the form controls and sections more visually striking, such as the following:

✦ Fonts, Size, and Colors

✦ Lines and rectangles

✦ Color and background shading

✦ Three-dimensional effects (raised, sunken, etched, chiseled, shadowed)

✦ Background pictures

✦ Form headers and footers

In this chapter, you learn to use special formatting to verify fonts and add shading, shadows, lines, rectangles, and three-dimensional effects. Figure 12-1 shows the form as it appears after some special effects have been added.

On the CD-ROM   In this chapter, you modify your form created in Chapter 11 to add the formatting features shown in Figure 12-1. If you are following the examples, open either the form you created in Chapter 11 (frmProductExample) or the form frmProductExample in the Chap12Start.mdb database file on the CD-ROM that comes with this book.

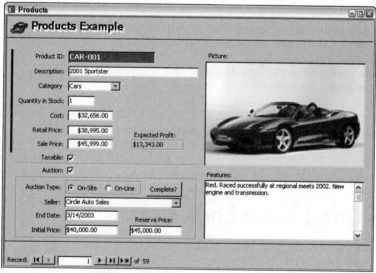

Figure 12-1: The enhanced form.

Understanding visual design

Access has a WYSIWYG (What You See Is What You Get) visual form designer. As you add controls onscreen, you see instantly what they look like in your form. If you want to see what the data looks like during the form design process, the onscreen preview mode lets you see the actual data in your form design without using a hard-copy device such as a printer.

The Access form designer lets you add color and shading to form text and controls. You can also display them in reverse video, which shows white letters on a black background. You can even color or shade the background of form sections. As you specify these effects, you see each change instantly on the Design screen.

Using the formatting windows and toolbar

The most important tools for enhancing a form are the formatting windows and the Formatting toolbar. You can choose from five formatting windows, including the following:

✦ Fill/Background color for shading

✦ Font/Foreground color for text

✦ Line/Border Color for lines, rectangles, and control borders

✦ Line/Border Width for lines, rectangles, and control borders

✦ Special Effect, such as raised, sunken, etched, chiseled, or shadowed

Note   You can display or remove the Formatting toolbar from the screen by selecting View ➪ Toolbars and selecting Formatting(Form/Report), or by right-clicking on the toolbar area and selecting Formatting(Form/Report). Figure 12-2 shows the five formatting windows pulled off of the toolbar and opened. You can use these windows to format the different controls in a form.

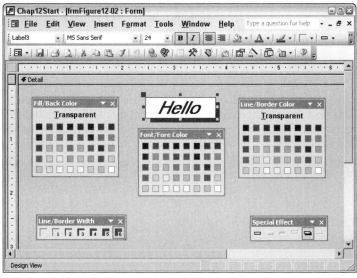

Figure 12-2: The five formatting windows.

Tip You can tell the selected color in the three color windows (Fill/Back Color, Font/Fore Color, and Line/Border Color) by looking at the small colored rectangle just below the three picture icons (Fill/Back Color, Font/Fore Color, Line/Border Color) in the toolbar.

A *formatting window* is a window similar to the toolbox or the Field List. You can move a formatting window around the screen, but you can't anchor it in the way that you can dock a toolbar to a window border. To open the window and place it on the surface, click the formatting tool icon's down-arrow and then click the title bar and drag it to where you want it. A formatting window can remain onscreen all the time; you can use it to change the options for one or more controls. To close a formatting window, click the Close button or reselect its icon on the Formatting toolbar.

You can modify the appearance of a control by using a formatting window. To modify the appearance of a control, select it by clicking it, and then click the formatting window that you need to change the control's appearance. (Refer to Figure 12-2 to see all five formatting windows.)

The Font/Fore Color (foreground text) and Fill/Back Color (background color) windows change the color of the text or background of a control. You can make a control's background transparent by selecting the Transparent button in the Fill/Back Color window. The Line/Border Color window changes the color of control's borders, lines, and rectangles. Clicking the Transparent button in the Line/Border Color window makes the border on any selected control invisible.

The Line/Border Width window changes the thickness of control borders, standalone lines, and rectangles. You can select the thickness of a line by using the thickness buttons. Available thicknesses (in points) are hairline, 1 point, 2 points, 3 points, 4 points, 5 points, and 6 points.

Note A point (approximately ½ inch) is a unit of measure for text and rule heights.

The Special Effect window lets you choose from Flat, Raised, Sunken, Etched, Shadowed, and Chiseled appearances for a control. The Special Effect window also provides a control property that lets you designate the border style. The border styles include the following:

   ✦ Transparent

   ✦ Solid

   ✦ Dashes

   ✦ Short Dashes

   ✦ Dots

   ✦ Sparse Dots

✦ Dash Dot

✦ Dash Dot Dot

After you have finished using a formatting window, you can close it by clicking the Close button in the upper-right corner.

Creating special effects

Figure 12-3 shows some of the special effects that can easily be created for controls with the Special Effect window. In the figure, you see that controls with gray as a background color display special effects much better than controls with white as a background color. In fact, a form background in gray or a dark color is almost mandatory to make certain special effects easy to see. The following sections describe each of these effects; you will use some of them later to modify the frmProductExample data entry form.

You can apply special effects to rectangles, label controls, text box controls, check boxes, option buttons, and option group boxes. Anything that has a box or circle around it can be raised, sunken, etched, chiseled, or shadowed.

By simply selecting the control and adding the special effect, you can make your forms look much better and draw attention to their most important areas.

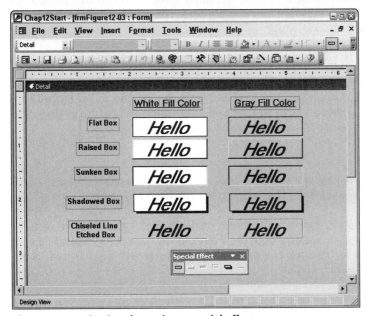

Figure 12-3: Viewing the various special effects.

Flat

In Figure 12-3, the first pair of labels exhibits the Flat special effect. The flat box stands out better when set against the gray background.

> **Tip**   You can also use the Border Width window to increase the width of the border lines, which makes the box more prominent. The Border Color window lets you change the color of the border. A thick white border also stands out.

Raised

The raised box is best used to set off a rectangle that surrounds other controls or for label controls. This box gives the best effect in a dark color against a dark background. As Figure 12-3 shows, the raised box is difficult to see with a white fill color. By increasing the width of the box, you can give the control the appearance of being higher than the surface of the onscreen background. You can achieve the raised three-dimensional effect by contrasting the white left and top borders with the black right and bottom borders.

Sunken

The sunken special effect is the most dramatic and most often used; it's the standard format for text box (data entry) controls in the Form Wizard. As Figure 12-3 shows, either the white or the gray fill color looks very good on a gray form background. You can also increase the width of the border to give the effect of a deeper impression. You achieve the sunken three-dimensional effect by using black left and top borders and white right and bottom borders. The effect works well with check boxes and option buttons.

Shadowed

The shadowed special effect places a solid, dark-colored rectangle behind the original control, which is slightly offset to give the shadowed effect. As Figure 12-3 shows, the black shadow works well behind a box filled with white or gray. You can change the border color to change the shadow color.

Etched

The etched effect is perhaps the most interesting of all the special looks. Essentially, it's a sunken rectangle with no sunken inside area.

> **Tip**   Current Microsoft Windows standards make heavy use of etched rectangles. Sunken rectangles around groups are a very old Windows 3.1 standard and should only be used for text box controls. Option groups or rectangles around controls should use the etched look.

Chiseled

The chiseled effect adds a chiseled line underneath a selected control.

Changing the forms background color

If your form is primarily intended for on-screen viewing (instead of print), it may be beneficial to color the background. A light gray background (the Microsoft Windows default) seems to be the best neutral color in all types of lighting and visual conditions. However, you may want to have a different color for the form's Header and Footer sections. To change the background for the form header or detail sections, select the desired section by clicking on the section's top border and then select the appropriate background color.

Tip   When you change the background color of form sections, also change the background of individual label controls for a more natural look. A label control generally doesn't look good if its background doesn't match the background of the form itself. Better yet, you can set the control's Transparent property to true or select Transparent from the Transparent button above the little squares of color in the Background color window.

Enhancing Text-Based Controls

Generally, you should ensure the accuracy of your label text and data before you start enhancing display items with shading or special effects. When your enhancements include label and text box control changes, begin with them.

Enhancing label and text box controls

You can enhance label and text box controls in several ways:

✦ Change the text font type (Arial, Times New Roman, Wingdings).

✦ Change the text font size (4–200).

✦ Change the text font style (bold, italic, underline).

✦ Change the text color (using a formatting window).

✦ Add a shadow (by duplicating the text and offsetting the copy).

Tip   The Windows standards call for text to be non-bold 8-point Tahoma font for all label and text controls and 12-point non-bold Verdana for large header labels.

Cross-Reference   In Chapter 10, you change the title's text in the label control in the form header. You then change the text's font size and font style. In the next section, you learn how to add a text shadow to the label control.

Creating a text shadow

Text shadows give text a three-dimensional look by making the text seem to float above the page while its shadow stays on the page. This effect uses the same basic principle as a shadowed box. Use this process to create text shadows:

1. Duplicate the text.
2. Offset the duplicate text from the original text.
3. Change the duplicate text to a different color (usually a lighter shade).
4. Place the duplicate text behind the original text.
5. Change the original text's background color to Clear.

To create a shadow for the title's text, follow these steps:

1. Select the Products Example label control in the Form Header.
2. Click Edit ⇨ Duplicate and select the duplicate label.
3. Click the Font/Fore Color window icon and choose white to change the duplicate text's color to white.
4. Drag the duplicate text up and to the right of the original text to create an offset from the text.
5. Click Format ⇨ Send to Back from the menu bar.

You may have to move the text or its shadow to be in the best position. You also may have to increase the Form Header section. The text now appears to have a shadow, as shown in Figure 12-4.

 Tip   To move the selected control a very small distance, press an arrow key; the control moves slightly in the direction of the arrow key that you use.

 Note   If you don't see the shadow, select the original text and then select the Transparent option on the Fill/Back Color Formatting toolbar.

 Tip   The box around the label control is not visible when the form is displayed because the Transparent button in the Border Color window is depressed.

When you duplicate the original text, the duplicate is automatically offset below the original text. When you place the duplicate text behind the original, it's hidden. You can redisplay it by placing the original text in front. If the offset (the distance from the other copy) is too large, the effect doesn't look like a shadow. You can perfect the shadowed appearance by moving one of the label controls slightly.

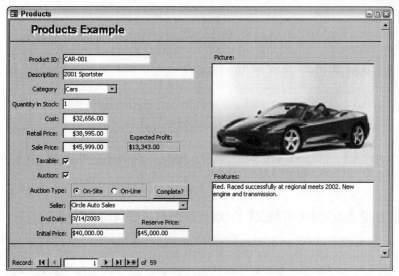

Figure 12-4: The text with a shadow and reverse video.

Caution

Although the shadow appears correct on-screen and looks great, it won't print correctly on most monochrome laser printers if you decide to save the form as a report or simply print the form. What you normally see is two lines of black text, which look horrible. If you plan to print your forms and don't have a printer that prints text in color (or prints many shades of gray by using graphics rather than text fonts), avoid using shadowed text on a form.

Changing text to a reverse video display and coloring it

Text really stands out when you create white text on a black background. This setup is called *reverse video*; it's the opposite of the usual black letters on white. You can convert text in a label control or text box to reverse video by changing the Back Color to black and the Fore Color to white. To change the Product ID text control to reverse video, follow these steps:

1. Select the Product ID text box control (not the label control).

2. Select Black from the Fill/Back Color formatting window.

3. Select White from the Font/Fore Color formatting window.

   To make it more dramatic, you may want to set the font to Bold and resize the control.

4. Press the Bold button on the toolbar to make the control bold.

5. Change the font size to 10 to make it a little larger.

6. Double-click the bottom right sizing handle to make the control fit the resized text.

As a key field, it should really stand out. Setting the background to red would do this.

7. Click on the Red square in the background color window.

The form should look like the one shown in Figure 12-5.

Caution   With some laser printers, you may not see reverse video if you print your form, because the printer's drivers can't print it.

Displaying label or text box control properties

As you change appearances of a label control or text box control using a formatting window, you are actually changing the control's properties. Figure 12-5 displays the Property window for the text box control that you just modified. As Figure 12-5 shows, a formatting window can affect many properties. Table 12-1 shows the various properties (and their possible values) for both label and text box controls.

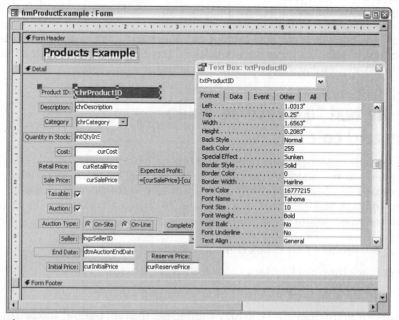

Figure 12-5: Text Box control properties.

Table 12-1
Label or Text Box Format Properties

Property	Options	Description
Format	Various Numeric and Date Formats	Determines how the data is displayed.
Decimal Places	Auto, 1-15	Determines how many decimal places, if any, you want to apply to this control.
Visible	Yes/No	Yes: Control is displayed normally No: Control is invisible when displayed.
Display When	Always, Print Only, Screen Only	Determines when the control is displayed.
Scroll Bars	None, Vertical, Horizontal, Both	Specifies when scrollbars are displayed.
Can Grow	Yes/No	If multiple lines of text are in the control, does the text box get larger?
Can Shrink	Yes/No	If fewer lines of text are in the control than in its initial size, does the text box height get smaller?
Left	Position of the left corner of the control in the current measure (include an indicator, such as centimeters or inches, if you use a different unit of measurement)	Specifies the position of an object on the horizontal axis.
Top	Position of the top corner of the control in the current measure	Specifies the position of an object on the vertical axis.
Width	The width of the control in the current unit of measure	Specifies the width of an object.
Height	The height of the control in the current unit of measure	Specifies the height of an object.
Back Style	Transparent, Normal	Determines whether a control's background is opaque or transparent.
Back Color	Any available background color	Specifies the color for the interior of the control or section.
Special Effect	Flat, Raised, Sunken, Shadowed, Etched, Chiseled	Determines whether a section or control appears flat, raised, sunken, shadowed, etched, or chiseled.

Continued

Table 12-1 *(continued)*

Property	Options	Description
Border Style	Transparent or Solid, Dashes, Dots (Lines/Boxes Only)	Determines whether a control's border is opaque or transparent.
Border Color	Any available border color	Specifies the color of a control's border.
Border Width	Hairline, 1pt, 2pt, 3pt, 4pt, 5pt, 6pt	Specifies the width of a control's border.
Fore Color	Any selection from a formatting window	Specifies the color for text in a control or the printing and drawing color.
Font Name	Any system font name that appears on the toolbar; depends on fonts installed	Specifies the name of the font used for text or a control.
Font Size	Any size available for a given font	Specifies the size of the font used for text or a control.
Font Weight	Extra Light, Light, Normal, Medium, Semi-Bold, Bold, Extra Bold, Heavy	Specifies the width of the line Windows uses to display and print characters.
Font Italic	Yes/No	Italicizes text in a control.
Font Underline	Yes/No	Underlines text in a control.
Text Align	General (default), Left, Center, Right	Sets the alignment for text in a control.
Reading Order	Context, Left-To-Right, Right-To-Left	Determines the reading order of the letters based on the language.
Keyboard Language	System, English	Determines the keyboard language for entry into the control.
Scroll Bar Align	System, Right, Left	Scroll bars can be placed on the left or right side of a control based on the language.
Numeral Shapes	System, Arabic, National, Context	Used for Arabic and Hindi languages for the shapes of numbers.
Left Margin		Used to set margins on a control. Enter in inches for the left margin. Can only be used for text box and label controls.
Top Margin		Used to set margins on a control. Enter in inches for the top margin. Can only be used for text box and label controls.

Property	Options	Description
Right Margin		Used to set margins on a control. Enter in inches for the right margin. Can only be used for text box and label controls.
Bottom Margin		Used to set margins on a control. Enter in inches for the bottom margin. Can only be used for text box and label controls.
Line Spacing		Used to specify line spacing for a control. Enter in inches for the amount of space between lines. Can only be used for text box and label controls.
Is Hyperlink	Yes, No	Used to specify if control is a hyperlink. If you select Yes, the text is blue and underlined. Can be used for a direct link to the Internet and for text box and label controls.

Although you can set many of these controls from the property sheet, it's much easier to drag the control to set the Top, Left, Width, and Height properties or to use a formatting window to set the other properties of the control.

Displaying Images in Forms

You can display a picture on a form by using an *image control*. This method is different from the way you use a bound OLE (Object Linking and Embedding) control. Normally, you store an OLE object (sound, video, Word, or Excel document) with a data record or with an unbound OLE object that is used specifically for storing OLE objects (those same sound, video, Word, or Excel documents) on a form.

Image controls in Access 2003 are used only for non-OLE objects, such as Paintbrush (.BMP), Icon file (.ico), or Web-like pictures (.jpg). Image controls offer a distinct advantage: Unlike OLE objects (which can be edited but use huge amounts of resources), the image control adds only the size of the bitmap picture to your computer's overhead. Using too many OLE objects in Access causes resource and performance problems. New and existing applications should use image controls only when you need to display pictures that don't change or don't need to be edited within Access.

Tip In previous versions of Access, you may have learned to select an unbound OLE object picture and then select Edit ⇨ Save As Picture. This technique broke the OLE connection but did not fix the resource problem.

You can add an image control to your form by either pasting a bitmap from the Clipboard or embedding a bitmap file. For example, you may want to add a picture of some cars to this form. Later you will add a large logo of Access Auto Auctions to create the main switchboard menu. On the CD that accompanies this book in the Chapter12 directory, you will find an icon file named cars.ico. In this section, you add this bitmap to the page header section of the form.

You can display an image object in one of three ways:

✦ **Clip.** Displays picture in its original size.

✦ **Stretch.** Fits the picture into the control regardless of size; often displayed out of proportion.

✦ **Zoom.** Fits the picture into the control (either vertically or horizontally) and maintains proportions; often results in white space on top or right side.

To add the logo to the form, follow these steps:

1. Select the Form Header section.

2. Select Insert ➪ Picture from the main menu.

On the CD or on your hard drive, find the directory in which the Access 2003 Bible example files have been placed. Find the directory for Chapter 12. You should see a list of the graphic files in the directory, as shown in Figure 12-6.

From this dialog box, you can select the type of picture object that you want to insert into your form. The dialog box supports many picture formats, including .BMP, .TIF, .WMF, .PCX, .ICO, .WPG, .JPG, .PCT, as well as any other picture format that your copy of Microsoft Windows supports.

Figure 12-6 shows the Preview of the AAAuctions.jpg file you will use later to create a background bitmap for the form and for the main switchboard.

If you don't see a preview of the picture, close the dialog and go back and select Insert Picture ➪ Views ➪ Preview. If you see a message that the Preview is not available, you will just have to select the picture to view it. You can always delete it if it is not what you expected. You can also choose the icon to the left of the Tools toolbar button in the dialog box and select the preview view.

3. Select cars.ico and click OK.

Notice that when you click on a file, it is first displayed in the Preview area on the right part of the dialog box before the picture is inserted.

If the file doesn't already exist and you want to create a new object (such as a Paintbrush picture), you must add an unbound OLE frame rather than an image control.

After you complete Step 3, Access returns you to the Form Design View window, where the picture is displayed.

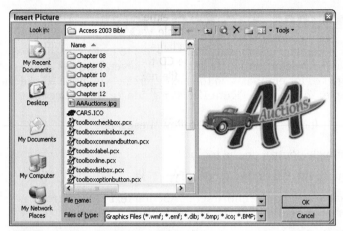

Figure 12-6: Previewing a picture.

The image control is complete and should look like the one shown in Figure 12-7.

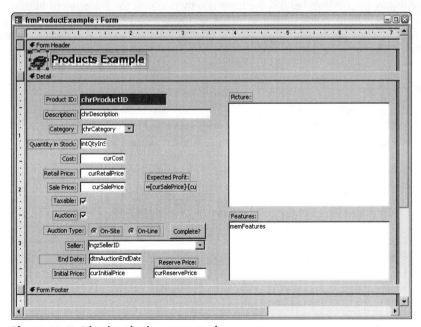

Figure 12-7: Viewing the image control.

Working with Lines and Rectangles

You can use lines or rectangles (commonly called *boxes*) to make certain areas of the form stand out and attract attention. In Figure 12-1, several groups of lines and rectangles are being used for emphasis. In the next exercise, you need to add the lines and the rectangle. You can use Figure 12-8 as a guide for this procedure.

To create the rectangle for the auction block, follow these steps:

1. Select the Rectangle control on the toolbox.

2. Click above and to the left of the Auction Type text.

3. Drag the rectangle around the entire set of Auction text box controls, as shown in Figure 12-8, and release the mouse button.

4. Select the etched effect in the Special Effect formatting window if it isn't already selected.

Tip

If the default rectangle is not transparent, Select Format ⇨ Send to Back or choose Fill/Back Color and select Transparent to redisplay the text boxes. You can also redisplay the controls behind the rectangle by checking the Transparent button of the Background Color option in a formatting window. This method, however, doesn't allow you to add other shading effects. For a rectangle, you should always select Format ⇨ Send to Back.

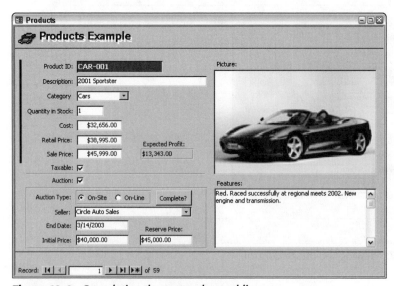

Figure 12-8: Completing the rectangles and lines.

You still need to add several lines to the form to learn about line placement. You need to add a single horizontal line between the Taxable and Auction checkboxes and a thicker vertical line down the left side of the form (beginning with the Product ID control and ending to the left of the Sales Price control). To add these lines, complete these steps (use Figure 12-8 as a guide):

1. Click the Line control in the toolbox.

2. Click to the left and below the Taxable control. Hold the Shift key down and drag the line icon to the right, releasing the mouse a little short of the Picture control, as shown in Figure 12-8.

   Holding the Shift key down keeps the line perfectly horizontal (Top Property does not change).

   The easiest way to make changes to display and formatting properties is to use the formatting icons in the form design toolbar. While you can always select a control and make changes or selections from the property window of each control, it is generally easier to simply select the control and change the desired properties by using the tool bar icons and their then displayed windows.

3. Select the chiseled special effect from the Special Effect icon in the formatting toolbar.

4. Create a new vertical line, starting just to the left of the Product ID field. To keep the line vertical, hold down the Shift key as you drag the line to just left of the bottom of the Sales Price control, as shown in Figure 12-8.

5. Select the 3 button in the Line/Border Width icon formatting window to make the line thicker.

6. Select the Blue color from the Line/Border Color window to make the line blue.

 Tip   If you hold down the Shift key while creating the line, the line remains perfectly straight, either horizontally or vertically, depending on the initial movement you make when drawing the line.

Before you do anything else, you might want to save the form. Everything you do for the rest of this chapter will not be saved. Currently, the form looks very professional. The tasks you are about to perform will not increase the professionalism of this form but are good ideas to know how to do.

Emphasizing Areas of the Form

If you really want to emphasize an area of the form, you can change a rectangle to raised or shadowed. In fact, you can add a shadow to any control. The most common types of controls to add a shadow to are rectangles and text boxes. You can create shadows with the Shadow special effect and a raised control with the Raised special effect.

Adding a shadow to a control

If the background is light or white, use a dark-colored rectangle. If the background is dark or black, use a light-colored or white rectangle. To create a shadow for the Description text box, follow these steps:

1. Select the Description control.

2. Select the Shadow special-effects button.

The Description control should have a shadow, as shown in Figure 12-9.

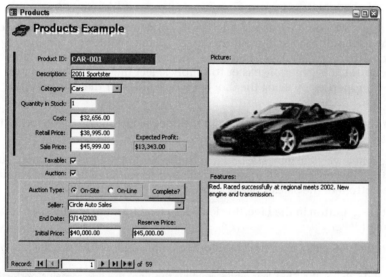

Figure 12-9: Adding shadows and a raised control.

Raising a group of controls

Raising a block of controls also can really make it stand out. The best way to do this is to add a rectangle around a group of controls and then change the rectangle property to raised. The current Microsoft Windows standard is to use etched rectangles, but raised can be used in special situations.

To create a raised rectangle, follow these steps:

1. Select the rectangle you recently created around the Auction controls.

2. Select the Raised special-effects button.

Your rectangle should be raised, as shown in Figure 12-9.

Changing the header dividing line

Form headers and footers are automatically separated from the Detail section by a solid black line. In Access 2003, you can remove this line by setting the Dividing Lines form property to No. This action removes the line and makes the form appear seamless. This is especially important if you have a background bitmap on the entire form, if you're using form headers or footers, and if you want a single look.

Adding a Background Bitmap

To add a really fun and sometimes important effect, you can add a background bitmap to any form, just as you added one control behind another. In Access 2003, you can do this by using the form's Picture properties. You have five properties to work with:

✦ **Picture.** The name of the bitmap picture; it can be any image-type file.

✦ **Picture Type.** Embedded or linked. You can save the picture in the database or you can just save the location (pointer) of the picture.

✦ **Picture Size Mode.** Clip, Stretch, or Zoom. Clip displays the picture only at its actual size starting at the Picture Alignment property. Stretch and Zoom fill the entire form from the upper-left corner of any header to the lower-right corner of any footer.

✦ **Picture Alignment.** Top-Left, Top-Right, Center, Bottom-Left, Bottom-Right, and so on. Use this property only when you use the Clip option in Picture Size mode.

✦ **Picture Tiling.** Yes/No. When you use a small bitmap with Clip mode, this repeats the bitmap across the entire form. For example, a brick becomes a brick wall.

For this example, you can add AAuctions.jpg to the background of the form. Use these steps to add a background bitmap:

1. Select the form itself by clicking in the upper-left corner of the intersection of the two design rulers or by selecting Form from the combo box at the left margin of the Formatting toolbar.

2. Display the Properties window; click the Picture property that's on the Format sheet of the Property window.

3. Enter **C:\access 2003 Bible\AAuctions.jpg** (or the path to where you have placed your bitmap on the disk). When you move to another property, the Access Auto Auctions logo (or your bitmap) appears in the upper-left corner of the form background.

4. Click the Picture Size Mode property and change it from Clip to Stretch. The picture now occupies the entire form background.

As Figure 12-10 shows, the white background of the picture (along with the thick, black lines) makes it difficult to see the fields.

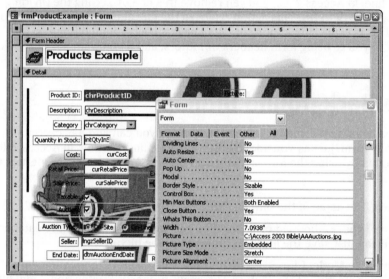

Figure 12-10: A bitmap picture behind a form.

Tip

Using background bitmaps adds some interesting capabilities to your form. For example, you can take this process a step further and incorporate the bitmap into your application. A bitmap can have buttons tied to macros (or Visual Basic for Applications code placed in the right locations). To help the office staff search for a patient, for example, you can create a form that has a map with three states behind it. By adding invisible buttons over each state, you can give the staff the choice of clicking a state to select the patient records from that state.

You can also scan a paper form into your computer and use that image as the form background. You do this by placing fields on top of the scanned form itself, which spares you from spending a great deal of time re-creating the form (which gives the phrase *filling out a form* a whole new meaning).

Using AutoFormat

You can change the format of an entire form by using the AutoFormat feature in Access 2003. This is the first menu option on the Format menu. AutoFormat lets you make global changes to all fonts, colors, borders, background bitmaps, and virtually all other properties on a control-by-control basis. This feature works instantly and completely and is totally customizable.

When you select Format ➪ AutoFormat, a dialog box appears, as shown in Figure 12-11. This window lets you select from the standard AutoFormats or any formats that you have created. The figure is shown after you click on the Options button. It lets you apply only fonts, colors, or border style properties separately.

In this example, you can choose the Blends AutoFormat type to change the style of the control fonts and colors and to change the background bitmap. As you select the different AutoFormats, you can see an example in the preview area to the right of the selections.

For example, you could click the Options button and deselect the check box for color (turn it off).

After you're finished, the controls appear, as shown in Figure 12-12. Notice that the title text size has changed and shadow boxes have appeared around most of the controls. Even the fonts are different. The reason is that the defaults for these controls are different from what you were using. This is probably not a format you will want to use often.

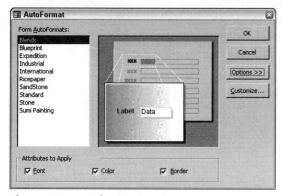

Figure 12-11: Selecting AutoFormat.

Customizing and adding new AutoFormats

You can modify existing AutoFormats — or define new ones — by creating a form, setting various form properties, and starting AutoFormat. Although AutoFormat changes the look of your form totally, it does its job on one control type at a time. This means that it can format a label differently from a text box and differently from a line or rectangle. This capability also lets you define your own formats for every control type, including the background bitmap.

After you have created a form that you want to use as a basis for an AutoFormat, select AutoFormat and click the Customize button. Another window appears, as shown in Figure 12-13. This window allows you to create a new format, update the selected format, or delete the selected format.

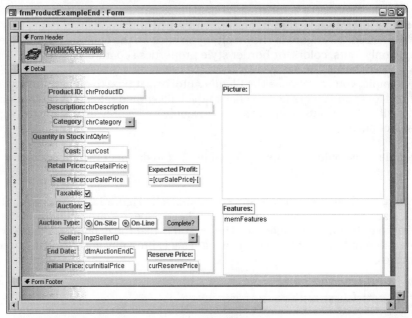

Figure 12-12: Data-entry form using the Blends format.

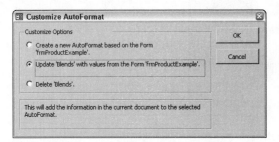

Figure 12-13: Creating your own AutoFormat.

Copying individual formats between controls

A subset of the AutoFormat technology is the Format Painter. This tool allows you to copy formatting properties from one individual control to another. To use the Format Painter, first select the control whose properties you want to use. Then click the Format Painter icon on the toolbar (the picture of a paintbrush, next to the Paste icon). Your mouse pointer changes to a paintbrush. Click the control that you want to update; Access copies the properties from the control that you first selected to the newly selected control.

✦   ✦   ✦

Understanding and Creating Reports

Reports provide the most flexible way for viewing and printing summarized information. Reports display information with the desired level of detail, while enabling you to view or print your information in almost any format. You can add multilevel totals, statistical comparisons, and pictures and graphics to a report. In this chapter, you learn to use Report Wizards as a starting point. You also learn how to create reports and what types of reports you can create with Access.

On the CD-ROM

In this chapter, you will create new reports using the report wizards and by creating a blank report without using a wizard. You will use tables created in previous chapters. If you are following the examples, open the Chap13Start.mdb database file on the CD-ROM that comes with this book and follow the instructions in each section of the chapter.

Understanding Reports

Reports are used for presenting a customized view of your data. Your report output can be viewed onscreen or printed to a hard copy device. Reports provide the capability to control summarization of the information. Data can be grouped and sorted in any order and then presented in the order of the groupings. You can create totals that add numbers, calculate averages or other statistics, and display your data graphically. You can print pictures and other graphics as well as memo fields in a report. If you can think of a report you want, Access can probably create it.

What types of reports can you create?

Four basic types of reports are used by businesses:

✦ **Tabular reports.** These print data in rows and columns with groupings and totals. Variations include summary and group/total reports.

✦ **Columnar reports.** These print data as a form and can include totals and graphs.

✦ **Mail-merge reports.** These create form letters.

✦ **Mailing labels.** These create multicolumn labels or snaked-column reports.

Tabular reports

Figure 13-1 is a typical tabular-type report in the Print Preview window. *Tabular reports* (also known as *groups/totals reports*) are generally similar to a table that displays data in neat rows and columns. Tabular reports, unlike forms or datasheets, usually group their data by one or more field values; they calculate and display subtotals or statistical information for numeric fields in each group. Some groups/totals reports also have page totals and grand totals. You can even have *snaked columns* so that you can create directories (such as telephone books). These types of reports can use page numbers, report dates, or lines and boxes to separate information. They can have color and shading and can display pictures, business graphs, and memo fields, like forms. A special type of tabular report, *summary reports,* can have all the features of a tabular report but not print the detail records.

Products Summary
Access Auto Auctions

Category	Product ID	Description	Qty in Stock	Cost	Retail Price	Sale Price	Profit
	CAR-130	1998 Buicky Centron Custom	1	$4,500.00	$5,799.00	$5,599.00	$1,099.00
	CAR-201	1968 Rare Dodget Red 2D Sedan	1	$29,800.00	$33,500.00	$32,900.00	$3,100.00
	CAR-299	1972 Chevy green chevel	1	$29,800.00	$35,000.00	$32,900.00	$3,100.00
			25	$799,356.00	$942,394.00	$916,441.00	$117,085.00
Minivans							
	Mini-03	1992 Buicky Roadie Estate Wago	1	$1,500.00	$1,850.00	$1,795.00	$295.00
	Mini-111	2003 Mini Van	2	$21,000.00	$24,000.00	$23,000.00	$2,000.00
	Mini-112	1992 Fordman Conversion Van	1	$3,000.00	$5,500.00	$4,390.00	$1,390.00
	Mini-113	1999 Fordman E350 Cargo Van	1	$4,500.00	$6,800.00	$5,990.00	$1,490.00
	Mini-114	2002 Fordman Mini Van	1	$11,000.00	$14,500.00	$13,989.00	$2,989.00
	Mini-115	2002 Monda SUV	1	$29,000.00	$35,900.00	$34,900.00	$5,900.00
	Mini-125	2000 Dodge Minivan SEE	1	$6,000.00	$11,500.00	$8,999.00	$2,999.00
			8	$76,000.00	$100,050.00	$93,063.00	$17,063.00
Motor Homes							
	Mot-01	1973 Rare Popup Hard sided Indian	1	$1,200.00	$1,750.00	$1,400.00	$200.00
			1	$1,200.00	$1,750.00	$1,400.00	$200.00
SUV							
	SUV-076	2002 Olds SUV	3	$35,900.00	$39,900.00	$38,900.00	$3,000.00
	SUV-111	1995 GMY JIMMIE SLE	1	$5,000.00	$7,500.00	$6,990.00	$1,990.00
	SUV-112	1995 Bjeep Laredot Red	1	$6,000.00	$8,900.00	$8,650.00	$2,650.00
	SUV-113	1998 Range Rover	1	$12,500.00	$0.00	$0.00	($12,500.00)
	SUV-114	1998 Fordman Explorer XLP	1	$9,000.00	$12,500.00	$11,950.00	$2,950.00
	SUV-121	1998 Isuzz Rodeo	1	$10,000.00	$15,100.00	$13,999.00	$3,999.00

3/30/2003 7:33:04 AM   Page 2 of 3

Figure 13-1: A tabular report in the Print Preview window of Access 2003.

Columnar reports

Columnar reports (also known as *form reports*) generally display one or more records per page, but do so vertically. Columnar reports display data very much as a data-entry form does, but the report is used strictly for viewing data and not for entering data. Figure 13-2 is part of a typical columnar report from the Access Auto Auctions database system in the Print Preview window.

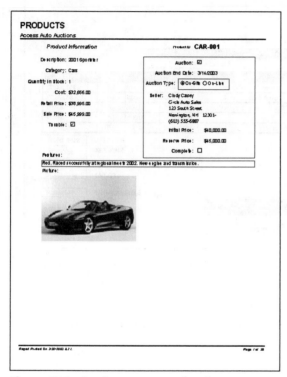

Figure 13-2: A columnar report showing report controls distributed throughout the entire page.

Another type of columnar report, known as a form/subform report, generally displays one main record per page (like a business form) but can show many records within embedded subforms. (You'll learn about subforms in Chapter 15.) An invoice is a typical example. This type of report can have sections that display only one record and at the same time have sections that display multiple records from the *many* side of a one-to-many relationship — and even include totals.

Figure 13-3 shows an invoice report from the Access Auto Auctions database system in the Print Preview window.

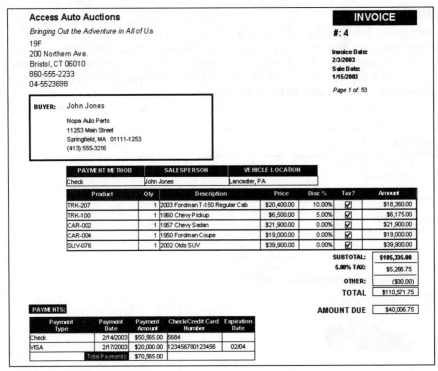

Figure 13-3: An invoice report.

Mailing labels

Mailing labels are also a type of report. You can easily create mailing labels, shown in Figure 13-4, using the Label Wizard to create a report in Access. The Label Wizard enables you to select from a long list of Avery label (and other vendors) paper styles, after which Access correctly creates a report design based on the data you specify to create your label. After the label is created, you can open the report in design mode and customize it as needed.

Cross-Reference

Mailing labels are covered in detail in Chapter 17.

The difference between reports and forms

The main difference between reports and forms is the purpose of the output. Whereas forms are primarily for data entry, reports are for viewing data (either onscreen or in hard copy form). Calculated fields can be used with forms and can calculate an amount based on the fields in the record. With reports, you calculate on the basis of a common group of records, a page of records, or all the records processed during the report. Anything you can do with a form—except data input—can be duplicated by a report. In fact, you can save a form as a report and then customize the form controls in the Report Design window.

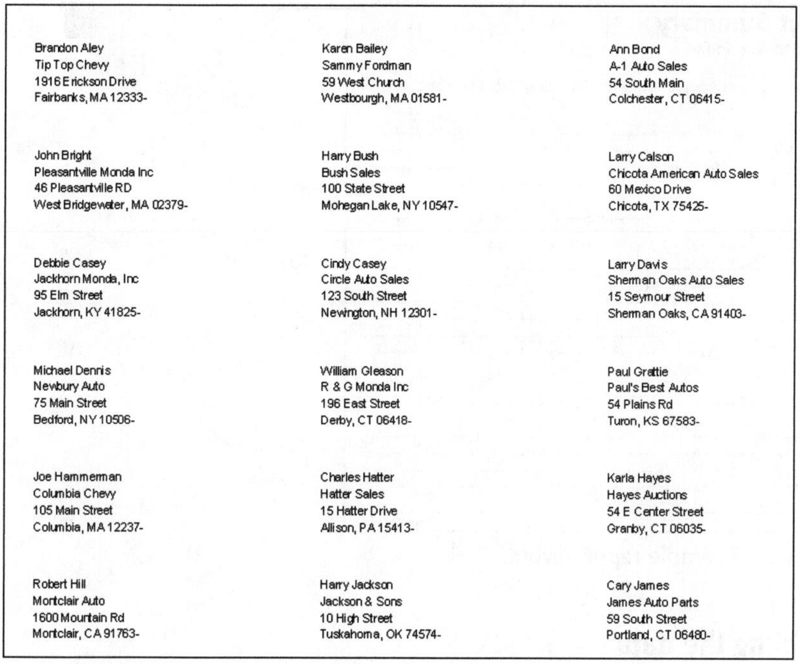

Brandon Aley Tip Top Chevy 1916 Erickson Drive Fairbanks, MA 12333-	Karen Bailey Sammy Fordman 59 West Church Westbourgh, MA 01581-	Ann Bond A-1 Auto Sales 54 South Main Colchester, CT 06415-
John Bright Pleasantville Monda Inc 46 Pleasantville RD West Bridgewater, MA 02379-	Harry Bush Bush Sales 100 State Street Mohegan Lake, NY 10547-	Larry Calson Chicota American Auto Sales 60 Mexico Drive Chicota, TX 75425-
Debbie Casey Jackhorn Monda, Inc 95 Elm Street Jackhorn, KY 41825-	Cindy Casey Circle Auto Sales 123 South Street Newington, NH 12301-	Larry Davis Sherman Oaks Auto Sales 15 Seymour Street Sherman Oaks, CA 91403-
Michael Dennis Newbury Auto 75 Main Street Bedford, NY 10506-	William Gleason R & G Monda Inc 196 East Street Derby, CT 06418-	Paul Grattie Paul's Best Autos 54 Plains Rd Turon, KS 67583-
Joe Hammerman Columbia Chevy 105 Main Street Columbia, MA 12237-	Charles Hatter Hatter Sales 15 Hatter Drive Allison, PA 15413-	Karla Hayes Hayes Auctions 54 E Center Street Granby, CT 06035-
Robert Hill Montclair Auto 1600 Mountain Rd Montclair, CA 91763-	Harry Jackson Jackson & Sons 10 High Street Tuskahoma, OK 74574-	Cary James James Auto Parts 59 South Street Portland, CT 06480-

Figure 13-4: A typical mailing-label report in the Print Preview window.

The process of creating a report

Planning a report begins long before you actually create the report design. The report process begins with your desire to view your data in a table, but in a way that differs from datasheet display. You begin with a design for this view; Access begins with raw data. The purpose of the report is to transform the raw data into a meaningful set of information. The process of creating a report involves several steps:

✦ Defining the report layout

✦ Assembling the data

✦ Creating the report design using the Access Report Design window

✦ Printing or viewing the report

Defining the report layout

You should begin by having a general idea of the layout of your report. You can define the layout in your mind, on paper, or interactively using the Access Report Design window. Figure 13-5 is a report layout created with Microsoft Word and served as a design from an analyst to a developer. This served as the basic design for the report shown in Figure 13-1. Good reports can first be laid out on paper, showing the fields needed and the placement of the fields.

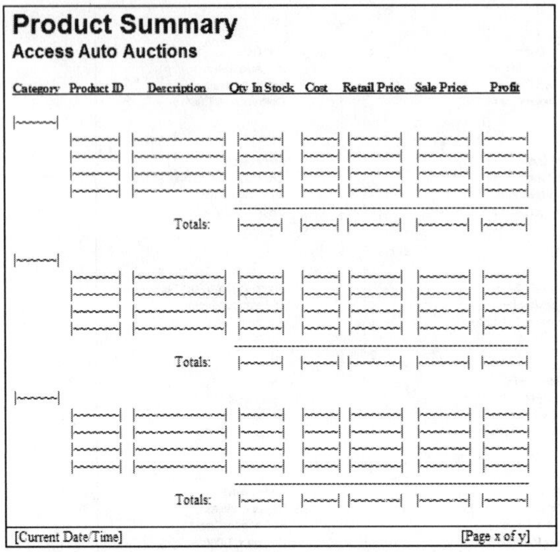
Product Summary
Access Auto Auctions
Category Product ID Description Qty In Stock Cost Retail Price Sale Price Profit
Totals:
Totals:
Totals:
[Current Date/Time]
[Page x of y]

Figure 13-5: A sample report layout.

Assembling the data

After you have a general idea of your report layout, you should assemble the data needed for the report. A report can use data from a single database table or from the results of a query dynaset. You can link many tables with a query and then use the result of the query (its dynaset) as the record source for your report. A dynaset appears in Access as if it were a single table. As you learned earlier in Section I of this book, you can select the fields, records, and sort order of the records in a query. Access treats this dynaset data as a single table (for processing purposes) in datasheets, forms, and reports. The dynaset becomes the source of data for the report and Access processes each record to create the report. The data for the report and the report *design* are entirely separate. In the report design, the field names to be used in the report are specified. Then, when the report is run, Access matches data from the dynaset or table against the fields used in the report and uses the data available at that moment to produce the report.

In this example, you will use data from only the tblProducts table.

Creating a Report with Report Wizards

With Access, you can create virtually any type of report. Some reports, however, are more easily created than others, when a Report Wizard is used as a starting point. Like Form Wizards, Report Wizards give you a basic layout for your report, which you can then customize.

Report Wizards simplify the layout process of your fields by visually stepping you through a series of questions about the type of report that you want to create and then automatically creating the report for you. In this chapter, you use Report Wizards to create both tabular and columnar reports.

Creating a new report

You can choose from many ways to create a new report, including the following:

✦ Select Insert ⇨ Report from the main menu when the Database window is selected.

✦ Select the Reports object button and press the New toolbar button on the Database window.

✦ From the Database window, the datasheet, or the query toolbar, click the New Object down arrow and select Report.

Regardless of how you start a new report, the New Report dialog box shown in Figure 13-6 appears. The dialog box in the figure is already filled in with the choices you are about to make.

Figure 13-6: The New Report dialog box.

The New Report dialog box enables you to choose from among six ways to create a report:

✦ **Design View.** Displays a completely blank Report Design window for you to start with.

✦ **Report Wizard.** Helps you create a tabular report by asking you many questions.

✦ **AutoReport: Columnar.** Creates an instant columnar report.

✦ **AutoReport: Tabular.** Creates an instant tabular report.

✦ **Chart Wizard.** Helps you create a business graph.

✦ **Label Wizard.** Helps you create a set of mailing labels.

To create a new report using a Report Wizard, follow these steps:

For the example below, use the tblProducts table:

1. Create a new report by first selecting the Reports object button and then pressing the New toolbar button.

2. In the New Report dialog box, select Report Wizard.

3. Select the table tblProducts and click OK. Figure 13-6 shows these choices selected.

4. Press the OK button to move to the next Report Wizard screen.

Choosing the data source

If you begin creating the report with a highlighted table or from a datasheet or query, the table or query you are using is displayed in the Choose the table or query box. Otherwise, you can enter the name of a valid table or query before continuing. You can also choose from a list of tables and queries by clicking the combo box selection arrow. In this example, you use the Hospital Report query you saw in Figure 10-5, which creates data for customer visits on the date 7/11/01.

Tip   If you begin creating a report in Design View, you don't need to specify a table or query in the New Report dialog box because you can select the Record Source later on from the Properties sheet.

Choosing the fields

After you select the Report Wizard and click the OK button, a *field selection box* appears. This box is virtually identical to the field selection box used in Form Wizards (see Chapter 9 for detailed information). In this example, select the fields from left to right (designed in Figure 13-5 and shown in Figure 13-7).

1. Select the chrCategory field and press the Select Field button (>) to place the field in the Selected Fields: area.

2. Repeat for the chrProductID, chrDescription, intQtyInStock, curCost, curRetailPrice, and curSalePrice fields and press the Select Field button (>) each time to place the field in the Selected Fields: area.

3. Click the Next button when you are through to move to the next wizard screen.

Tip   You can double-click any field in the Available Fields list box to add it to the Selected Fields list box. You can also double-click any field in the Selected Fields list box to remove it from the box. Access then redisplays the field in the Available Fields list box.

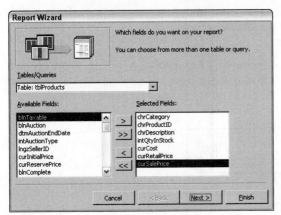

Figure 13-7: Selecting report fields.

You are limited to selecting fields from the original record source you started with. You can select fields from other tables or queries by using the Tables/Queries: combo box in this wizard screen. As long as you have specified valid relationships so that Access can link the data, these fields are added to your original selection and you can use them on the report. If you choose fields from tables that don't have a relationship, a dialog box will ask you to edit the relationship and join the tables. Or you can return to the Report Wizard and remove the fields.

After you have selected your data, click the Next button to go to the next wizard dialog box.

Selecting the grouping levels

The next dialog box enables you to choose which field(s) you want to use for a grouping. In this example, Figure 13-8 shows the chrCategory field selected as the only group field. This step designates the field(s) to be used to create group headers and footers. Groups are used to combine data with common values.

Using the Report Wizard, you can select up to four different group fields for your report; you can change their order by using the Priority buttons. The order you select for the group fields is the order of the grouping hierarchy.

Select the chrCategory field as the grouping field and click (>). Notice that the picture changes to graphically show chrCategory as a grouping field, as shown in Figure 13-8. This means that data will be grouped or separated by category and also totaled as well if the report chosen supports summarized footers.

After you select the group field(s), click the Grouping Options button at the bottom of the dialog box to display another dialog box, which enables you to further define how your report will use the group field.

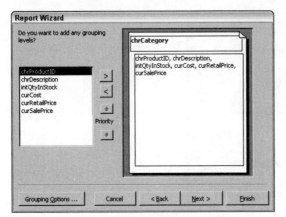

Figure 13-8: Selecting report group fields.

 Cross-Reference   You will learn more about groups, headers, and footers later in this chapter.

Defining the group data

The Grouping Options dialog box, which is displayed by pressing the Grouping Options ... button in the lower-left corner of the Report Wizard screen, enables you to further define the grouping. This selection can vary in importance, depending on the data type.

The list box displays different values for the various data types:

✦ **Text**. Normal, 1st Letter, 2 Initial Letters, 3 Initial Letters, 4 Initial Letters, 5 Initial letters

✦ **Numeric.** Normal, 10s, 50s, 100s, 500s, 1000s, 5000s, 10000s, 50000s, 100000s.

✦ **Date.** Normal, Year, Quarter, Month, Week, Day, Hour, Minute.

Normal means that the grouping is on the entire field. In this example, use the entire Customer Name field. By selecting different values of the grouping, you can limit the group values. For example, suppose you are grouping on the Product ID field. A typical Product ID value is CAR-01. The characters to the left of the – represent the category and the numbers to the right of the – are a sequential number. By choosing the Product ID field for the grouping and then selecting 3 Initial Letters as the grouping data, you can group the products by their category.

In this example, the default text-field grouping option of Normal is acceptable.

If you displayed the Grouping Options dialog box, click the OK button to return to the Grouping levels dialog box.

Click the Next button to move to the Sort order dialog box.

Selecting the sort order

Access sorts the Group record fields automatically in an order that helps the grouping make sense. The additional sorting fields specify fields to be sorted in the detail section. In this example, Access is already sorting the data by the chrCategory field in the group section. As Figure 13-9 shows, the data is also to be sorted by Product ID so that the products appear in alphabetical order in the detail section.

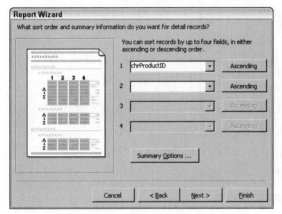

Figure 13-9: Selecting the field sorting order.

The sort fields are selected by the same method that is used for grouping fields in the report. You can select fields that you have not already chosen to group and use these as sorting fields. The fields chosen in this dialog box do not affect grouping; they affect only the sorting order in the detail section fields. You can determine whether the order is ascending or descending by clicking the button to the right of each sort field, which toggles between Ascending and Descending.

Selecting summary options

At the bottom of the sorting dialog box is a button named Summary Options. Clicking this button displays the dialog box shown in Figure 13-10. This dialog box provides additional options for numeric fields. As you can see in Figure 13-10, all of the numeric and currency fields are displayed and selected to be summed. Additionally, you can display averages, minimums, and maximums.

Sum should be checked. You can also decide whether to show or hide the data in the detail section. If you select Detail and Summary, the report shows the detail data; selecting Summary Only hides the detail section and shows only totals in the report.

Finally, checking the box labeled Calculate Percent of Total for Sums adds the percentage of the entire report that the total represents below the total in the group footer. If, for example, you had three products and their totals were 15, 25, and 10, respectively, they would show 30%, 50%, and 20% below their total (that is, 50) — indicating the percentage of the total sum (100%) represented by their sum.

Clicking the OK button in this dialog box returns you to the sorting dialog box. There you can click the Next button to move to the next wizard dialog box.

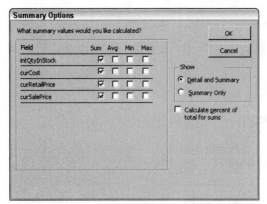

Figure 13-10: Selecting the summary options.

Selecting the layout

Two more dialog boxes affect the look of your report. The first (shown in Figure 13-11) enables you to determine the layout of the data. The Layout area provides six layout choices; these tell Access whether to repeat the column headers, whether to indent each grouping, and whether to add lines or boxes between the detail lines. As you select each option, the picture on the left changes to show the effect.

The Orientation area enables you to choose between a Portrait (up-and-down) and a Landscape (across-the-page) layout. This choice affects how it prints on the paper. Finally, the check mark next to Adjust the Field Width So All Fields Fit on a Page enables you to cram a lot of data into a little area. (Magnifying glasses may be necessary!)

For this example, choose Stepped and Landscape, as shown in Figure 13-11. Then click on the Next button to move to the next dialog box.

Choosing the style

After you choose the layout, you can choose the style of your report from the dialog box shown in Figure 13-12. Each style has different background shadings, font size, typeface, and other formatting. As each is selected, the picture on the left changes to show a preview. For this example, choose Casual (as shown in Figure 13-12). Finally, click the Next button to move to the last dialog box.

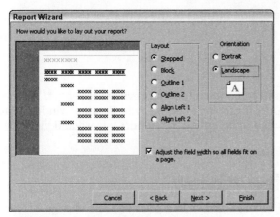

Figure 13-11: Selecting the page layout.

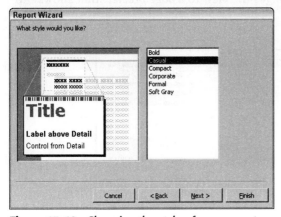

Figure 13-12: Choosing the style of your report.

Tip   You can customize the styles, or add your own, by using the AutoFormat option from the Format menu of the Report Design window and choosing Customize.

Opening the report design

The final Report Wizard dialog box contains a checkered flag, which lets you know that you're at the finish line. The first part of the dialog box enables you to enter a title for the report. This title will appear once at the beginning of the report, not at the top of each page. The default is the name of the table or query you used initially.

Change the report name to rptProductsCh13.

Next, you can choose one of the option buttons at the bottom of the dialog box:

✦ Preview the report

✦ Modify the report's design

For this example, leave the default selection intact to preview the report. When you click the Finish button, your report is displayed in the Print Preview window. Name the report rptProducts. Click Finish to complete the Report Wizard and view the report.

Using the Print Preview window

Figure 13-13 displays the Print Preview window in a zoomed view of page 2. This view displays your report with the actual fonts, shading, lines, boxes, and data that will be on the printed report. When the Print Preview mode is in a zoomed view, pressing the mouse button changes the view to a *page preview* that shows the entire page.

chrCategory	Product ID	Description	antity in Stock	Cost	etail Price	Sale Price
	CAR-123	1959 Antique Coupe	1	$500.00	7,900.00	1,500.00
	CAR-126	1995 BUICKY RIV	1	5,500.00	7,200.00	6,999.00
	CAR-127	1969 Shelly Coupe Muscle Car	1	5,500.00	0,000.00	0,000.00
	CAR-130	1998 Buicky Centrum Custom	1	4,500.00	5,799.00	5,599.00
	CAR-201	1968 Rare Dodget Red 2D Sedan	1	9,800.00	3,500.00	2,900.00
	CAR-299	1972 Chevy green chevel	1	9,800.00	5,000.00	2,900.00
Summary for 'chrCategory' = Cars (25 detail records)						
Sum			25	99,356.00	42,394.00	16,441.00
Minivans						
	Mini-03	1992 Buicky Roadie Estate Wagon	1	1,500.00	1,850.00	1,795.00
	Mini-111	2003 Mini Van	2	1,000.00	4,000.00	3,000.00
	Mini-112	1992 Fordman Conversion Van	1	3,000.00	5,500.00	4,390.00
	Mini-113	1999 Fordman E350 Cargo Van	1	4,500.00	6,800.00	5,990.00
	Mini-114	2002 Fordman Mini Van	1	1,000.00	4,500.00	3,989.00
	Mini-115	2002 Monda SUV	1	9,000.00	5,900.00	4,900.00
	Mini-125	2000 Dodgie Minivan SEE	1	6,000.00	1,500.00	8,999.00
Summary for 'chrCategory' = Minivans (7 detail records)						
Sum			8	76,000.00	00,050.00	33,063.00
Motor Homes						
	Mot-01	1973 Rare Popup Hard sided Indian Camper	1	1,200.00	1,750.00	1,400.00
Summary for 'chrCategory' = Motor Homes (1 detail record)						
Sum			1	$1,200.00	$1,750.00	$1,400.00
SUV						
	SUV-076	2002 Olds SUV	3	5,900.00	9,900.00	8,900.00
Sunday, March 30, 2003						Page 2 of 4

Figure 13-13: Displaying a report in the zoomed preview mode.

You can move around the page by using the horizontal and vertical scrollbars. Use the Page controls (at the bottom-left corner of the window) to move from page to page. These controls include VCR-like navigation buttons to move from page to page or to the first or last page of the report. You can also go to a specific page of the report by entering a value in the text box between the previous and next controls.

Figure 13-14 shows a view of the report in the multi-page preview mode of Print Preview. The sixth icon from the left displays up to six pages at a time. The magnifying glass mouse pointer selects part of the page to zoom in. In Figure 13-14, you can see a representation of the printed page. Use the navigation buttons (in the lower-left section of the Print Preview window) to move between pages, just as you would to move between records in a datasheet. The Print Preview window has a toolbar with commonly used printing commands.

If, after examining the preview, you are satisfied with the report, select the Printer button on the toolbar to print the report. If you are dissatisfied, select the Close button to return to the design window; Access takes you to the Report Design window to make further changes.

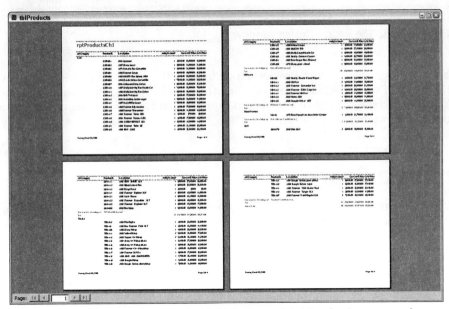

Figure 13-14: Displaying a report in Multiple Pages Print Preview's page preview mode.

Viewing the Report Design window

When you click Design View (the left-most button on the toolbar), Access takes you to the Report Design window, which is similar to the Form Design window. The major difference is in the sections that make up the report design. As shown in Figure 13-15, the report design reflects the choices you made using the Report Wizard.

Cross-Reference
You may also see the Toolbox, Sorting and Grouping dialog box, property sheet, and Field List window, depending on whether you pressed the toolbar buttons to see these tools. You learn to change the design of a report in this chapter as well as Chapters 14, 15, and 16.

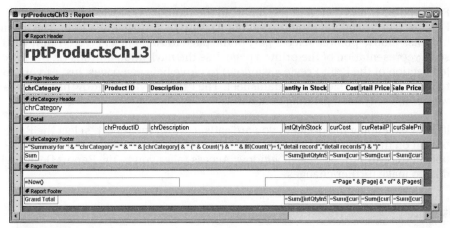

Figure 13-15: The Report Design window.

You can return to the Print Preview mode by selecting the Print Preview button on the Report Design toolbar or by selecting the Print Preview option on the File menu. You can also select Print or Page Setup from the File menu. This menu also provides options for saving your report.

Printing a Report

You can print one or more records in your report, exactly as they look onscreen, using one of these methods:

- ✦ Click File ➪ Print in the Report Design window.
- ✦ Click the Print button in the Preview window.
- ✦ Click File ➪ Print in the Database window (with a report highlighted).

If you select File ➪ Print, a standard Microsoft Windows Print dialog box appears. You can select the print range, number of copies, and print properties. If you click the Print button, the report goes immediately to the currently selected printer without displaying a Print dialog box.

Saving the Report

You can save the report design at any time by selecting File ➪ Save, or File ➪ Save As, or File ➪ Export from the Report Design window, or by clicking the Save button on the toolbar. The first time you save a report (or any time you select Save As or Export), a dialog box enables you to select or type a name.

Cross-Reference In Chapters 8 through 12, you learned to create a form and manipulate controls. Wizards are great for creating quick and simple reports, but they are fairly limited and give you little control over field type or placement. Although there are advantages to creating a report with a wizard and then modifying the report, the remainder of this chapter focuses on creating a report from a blank form without the help of the wizards. If you haven't read Chapters 8 through 12, now is a good time to read or review them, because the basic control and property concepts presented there are necessary to understand this chapter.

Starting with a Blank Form

Previous chapters about forms introduced you to all the tools available in the Report Design window. When you create reports, you use some of these tools in a slightly different manner from the way they are used to create forms. Therefore, it is important to review some of the unique report menus and toolbar buttons.

You can view a report in three different views: Design View, Layout Preview, and Print Preview. You can also print a report to the hard copy device defined for Microsoft Windows. You have already seen the preview windows in previous chapters. This chapter focuses on the Report Design window.

The Report Design window is where you create and modify reports. The empty Report Design window, shown in Figure 13-16, contains various tools, including the Toolbox.

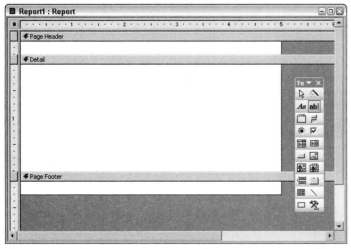

Figure 13-16: The Report Design window, showing the Toolbox.

The Design Window toolbar

The Report Design toolbar is shown in Figure 13-17. You click the button you want for quick access to such design tasks as displaying different windows and activating wizards and utilities. Table 13-1 summarizes what each item on the toolbar does. (The table defines each tool from left to right on the toolbar.)

Figure 13-17: The Report Design toolbar.

The Report Design toolbar is distinct from the Format toolbar. To make such changes as font selection and justification, you must first make sure that the Formatting (Form/Report) design toolbar is displayed.

Table 13-1	
The Design View Toolbar	

Toolbar Item	Description
Report View button	Drop-down box displays the three types of views available
Save button	Saves the current report design
File Search button	Finds text within a database or on your computer
Print button	Prints a form, table, query, or report
Print Preview button	Toggles to print preview mode
Cut button	Removes selection from the document and adds it to the Clipboard
Copy button	Copies the selection to the Clipboard
Paste button	Copies the Clipboard contents to the document
Format Painter button	Copies the style of one control to another
Undo/Redo button	Undoes/redoes previous commands
Insert Hyperlink button	Inserts hyperlink
Field List button	Displays or hides the Field List window
Toolbox button	Displays or hides the Toolbox
Sorting and Grouping button	Displays or hides the Sorting and Grouping box
AutoFormat button	Applies a predefined format to a form or report
Code button	Displays or hides the Module window
Properties button	Displays the properties sheet for the selected item

Toolbar Item	Description
Build button	Displays the Builder or Wizard for selected control or item
Database Window button	Displays the Database window
New Object button	Creates a new object
Microsoft Access Help button	Displays Access Help

Note The tools on the Report Design screen are virtually identical to the Form Design tools.

Banded Report Writer Concepts

In a report, your data is processed one record at a time. Depending on how you create your report design, each data item is processed differently. Reports are divided into sections, known as *bands* in most report-writing software packages. (In Access, these are simply called *sections*.) Access processes each data record from a table or dynaset, processing each section in order and deciding (for each record) whether to process fields or text in each section. For example, the report footer section is processed only after the last record is processed in the dynaset.

A report is made up of groups of *details* — for example, as shown in Figure 13-18, all the products sold by category. Each group must have an identifying *group header*, which for the first category in this example is Minivans. Each group also has a footer where you can calculate the total cost and profit for each category. For Minivans, the total profit is $17,063. The *page header* contains column descriptions; the *report header* contains the report title. Finally, the *report footer* contains grand totals for the report, and the *page footer* prints the page number.

The Access sections are listed below:

- ✦ **Report header.** Prints only at the beginning of the report; used for title page.
- ✦ **Page header.** Prints at the top of each page.
- ✦ **Group header.** Prints before the first record of a group is processed.
- ✦ **Detail.** Prints each record in the table or dynaset.
- ✦ **Group footer.** Prints after the last record of a group is processed.
- ✦ **Page footer.** Prints at the bottom of each page.
- ✦ **Report footer.** Prints only at the end of a report after all records are processed.

Figure 13-18 shows these sections superimposed on a report.

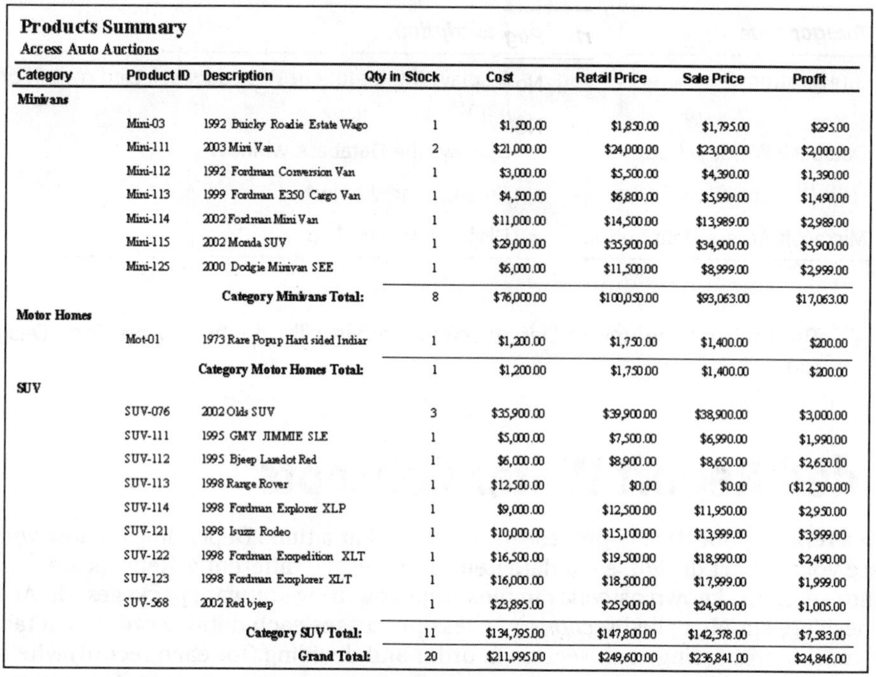

Products Summary
Access Auto Auctions

Category	Product ID	Description	Qty in Stock	Cost	Retail Price	Sale Price	Profit
Minivans							
	Mini-03	1992 Buicky Roadie Estate Wago	1	$1,500.00	$1,850.00	$1,795.00	$295.00
	Mini-111	2003 Mini Van	2	$21,000.00	$24,000.00	$23,000.00	$2,000.00
	Mini-112	1992 Fordman Conversion Van	1	$3,000.00	$5,500.00	$4,390.00	$1,390.00
	Mini-113	1999 Fordman E350 Cargo Van	1	$4,500.00	$6,800.00	$5,990.00	$1,490.00
	Mini-114	2002 Fordman Mini Van	1	$11,000.00	$14,500.00	$13,989.00	$2,989.00
	Mini-115	2002 Monda SUV	1	$29,000.00	$35,900.00	$34,900.00	$5,900.00
	Mini-125	2000 Dodgie Minivan SEE	1	$6,000.00	$11,500.00	$8,999.00	$2,999.00
		Category Minivans Total:	8	$76,000.00	$100,050.00	$93,063.00	$17,063.00
Motor Homes							
	Mot-01	1973 Rare Popup Hard sided Indiar	1	$1,200.00	$1,750.00	$1,400.00	$200.00
		Category Motor Homes Total:	1	$1,200.00	$1,750.00	$1,400.00	$200.00
SUV							
	SUV-076	2002 Olds SUV	3	$35,900.00	$39,900.00	$38,900.00	$3,000.00
	SUV-111	1995 GMY JIMMIE SLE	1	$5,000.00	$7,500.00	$6,990.00	$1,990.00
	SUV-112	1995 Bjeep Laredot Red	1	$6,000.00	$8,900.00	$8,650.00	$2,650.00
	SUV-113	1998 Range Rover	1	$12,500.00	$0.00	$0.00	($12,500.00)
	SUV-114	1998 Fordman Explorer XLP	1	$9,000.00	$12,500.00	$11,950.00	$2,950.00
	SUV-121	1998 Isuzz Rodeo	1	$10,000.00	$15,100.00	$13,999.00	$3,999.00
	SUV-122	1998 Fordman Exxpedition XLT	1	$16,500.00	$19,500.00	$18,990.00	$2,490.00
	SUV-123	1998 Fordman Exxplorer XLT	1	$16,000.00	$18,500.00	$17,999.00	$1,999.00
	SUV-568	2002 Red bjeep	1	$23,895.00	$25,900.00	$24,900.00	$1,005.00
		Category SUV Total:	11	$134,795.00	$147,800.00	$142,378.00	$7,583.00
		Grand Total:	20	$211,995.00	$249,600.00	$236,841.00	$24,846.00

Figure 13-18: Typical Report Writer sections.

How sections process data

Most sections are triggered by changes in the values of the data. Table 13-2 shows the records that make up the dynaset for the Products Summary Report (*Yes* indicates that a section is triggered by the data).

Table 13-2
Processing Report Sections

Category Name	*Product Name*	*Report Header*	*Page Header*	*Category Header*	*Detail*	*Category Footer*	*Page Footer*	*Report Footer*
Minivans	Mini-03	Yes	Yes	Yes	Yes	No	No	No
Minivans	Mini-111	No	No	No	Yes	No	No	No
Minivans	Mini-112	No	No	No	Yes	No	No	No
Minivans	Mini-113	No	No	No	Yes	No	No	No
Minivans	Mini-114	No	No	No	Yes	No	No	No
Minivans	Mini-115	No	No	No	Yes	No	No	No

Category	Product	Report	Page	Category	Detail	Category	Page	Report
Minivans	Mini-125	No	No	No	Yes	Yes	No	No
Motor Homes	Mot-01	No	No	Yes	Yes	Yes	No	No
SUV	SUV-076	No	No	Yes	Yes	No	No	No
SUV	SUV-111	No	No	No	Yes	No	No	No
SUV	SUV-112	No	No	No	Yes	No	No	No
SUV	SUV-113	No	No	No	Yes	No	No	No
SUV	SUV-114	No	No	No	Yes	No	No	No
SUV	SUV-121	No	No	No	Yes	No	No	No
SUV	SUV-122	No	No	No	Yes	No	No	No
SUV	SUV-123	No	No	No	Yes	No	No	No
SUV	SUV-568	No	No	No	Yes	Yes	Yes	No

As you can see, Table 13-2 shows 17 records. Three groups of records are grouped by the category. There are seven Minivans, one Motor Homes, and nine SUVs. Each record in the table has corresponding columns for each section in the report. "Yes" means that the record triggers processing in that section; "No" means that the section is not processed for that record. This report is only one page, so it is very simple.

The report header section is triggered by only the first record in the reports dynaset. This section is always processed first, regardless of the data. The report footer section is triggered only after the last record is processed, regardless of the data.

Access processes the page header section after the report header section for the first record and then every time a new page is started. The page footer section is processed at the bottom of each page and after the report footer section of the last page.

Group headers are triggered only by the first record in a group. Group footers are triggered only by the last record in a group. Notice that the Mot-01 Motor Homes record triggers both a group header and a group footer because it is the only record in a group. If three or more records are in a group, only the first or the last record can trigger a group header or footer; the middle records trigger only the detail section.

Access always processes each record in the detail section (which is always triggered, regardless of the value of a data item). Most reports with a large amount of data have many detail records and significantly fewer group header or footer records. This small report has as many group header and footer records as it has detail records.

The Report Writer sections

Figure 13-19 shows what a report design looks like in Access. It is the Report Design window for the Products Summary Report. As you can see, the report is divided into seven sections. The group section displays data grouped by Categories, so you see the sections chrCategory Header and chrCategory Footer. Each of the other sections is also named for the type of processing it performs.

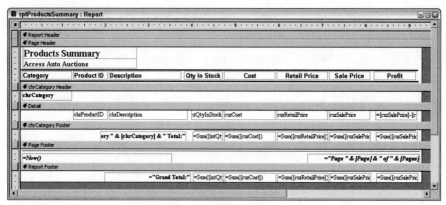

Figure 13-19: The Report Design window.

You can place any type of text or field controls in any section, but Access processes the data one record at a time. It also takes certain actions (based on the values of the group fields, the location of the page, or placement in the report) to make the bands or sections active. The example in Figure 13-19 is typical of a report with multiple sections. As you learned, each section in the report has a different purpose and different triggers.

Note   Page and report headers and footers must be added as pairs. To add one without the other, after the section is added, resize the section you don't want to a height of zero or set its Visible property to No.

Caution   If you remove a header or footer section, you also lose the controls in those sections.

Report header section

Controls in the *report header section* are printed only once at the beginning of the report. A common use of a report header section is as a cover page or a cover letter or for information that needs to be communicated only once to the user of the report.

You can also have controls in the report header section print on a separate page, which enables you to create a title page and include a graphic or picture in the section. There is a Force New Page property in the Report Header that can be set to *After Section* that will place the information in the Report Header into a separate page.

In Figure 13-18, the report header section is not used.

Note Only data from the first record can be placed in a report header.

Page header section

Text or field controls in the *page header section* normally print at the top of every page. If a report header on the first page is not on a page of its own, the information in the page header section prints just below the report header information. Typically, page headers serve as column headers in group/total reports; they can also contain a title for the report. In this example, placing the Products Summary report title in the Page Header section means that the title appears on every page.

The page header section shown in Figure 13-19 also has lines above and below the label controls. Each of the report's label controls is separate and each can be moved or sized individually. You can also change special effects (such as color, shading, borders, line thickness, font type, and font size) for each text control.

Both the page header and page footer sections can be set to one of four settings (this setting can be found in the Report's properties, not the section properties):

✦ **All Pages.** Both the page header and page footer print on every page.

✦ **Not with Report Header.** Neither the page header nor footer prints on a page with the report header.

✦ **Not with Report Footer.** The page header does not print with the report footer. The report footer prints on a new page.

✦ **Not with Report Header/Footer.** Neither the page header nor the footer prints on a page with the report header or footer.

Group header

Group headers sections normally display the name of the group. Access knows when all the records in a group have been displayed in a detail section when the group name changes. In this example, the detail records are about products and their costs and profits. The group header field control chrCategory tells you that these products are of a specific category type. Group header sections immediately precede detail sections.

It is possible to have multiple levels of group headers and footers. In this report, for example, the data is only for categories. However, in some reports you might have groups of information with date values. You could group your sections by year or month and year, and within those sections by another group such as category.

Note   To set group-level properties such as Group On, Group Interval, Keep Together, or something other than the default, you must first set the Group Header and Group Footer property (or both) to Yes for the selected field or expression. You will learn about these later in the chapter.

Detail section

The *detail section* processes *every* record in the data and is where each value is printed. The detail section frequently contains a calculated field such as profit that is the result of a mathematical expression. In this example, the detail section simply displays information from the tblProduct table except for the last control. The *profit* is calculated by subtracting the value of curCost from the value of curSalePrice.

Tip   You can tell Access whether you want to display a section in the report by changing the section's Visible property in the Report Design window. Turning off the display of the detail section (or by excluding selected group sections) displays a summary report with no detail or with only certain groups displayed.

Group footer

You use the *group footer section* to calculate summaries for all the detail records in a group. In the Products Summary report, the expression =Sum([curSalePrice] – [curCost]) adds all the calculations of Sale Price – Cost for a specific category. In the Minivans group, this expression sums the seven records. This type of field is automatically reset to 0 every time the group changes. (You learn more about expressions and summary fields in later chapters.)

Cross-Reference   You can change the way summaries are calculated by changing the Running Sum property of the field box in the Report Design window.

Page footer

The *page footer section* usually contains page numbers or control totals. In very large reports, you may want page totals as well as group totals (such as when you have multiple pages of detail records with no summaries). For the Products Summary Report, the page number is printed by combining the text Page, and built-in page number controls show Page x of y where x is the current page number and y is the total number of pages in the report. A text box control with the following expression in the Control Source property can be used to display page number information.

= "Page: " & [Page] & " of " & [Pages]

(which keeps track of the page number in the report).

You can also print the date and the time printed. Figures 13-19 and 13-20 show the date printed in the Page Footer section as well as the page numbers.

Report footer

The *report footer section* is printed once at the end of the report after all the detail records and group footer sections are printed. Report footers typically display grand totals or other statistics (such as averages or percentages) for the entire report. The report footer for the Products Summary report uses the expression =Sum with each of the numeric fields to sum the amounts.

Note　When there is a report footer, the page footer section is printed after the report footer.

The Report Writer in Access is a *two-pass report writer*, capable of preprocessing all records to calculate the totals (such as percentages) needed for statistical reporting. This capability enables you to create expressions that calculate percentages as Access processes those records that require foreknowledge of the grand total.

Cross-Reference　Chapter 15 covers calculating percentages.

Creating a New Report

Fundamental to all reports is the concept that a report is another way to view the records in one or more tables. It is important to understand that a report is bound to either a single table or a query that brings together data from one or more tables. When you create a report, you must select which fields from the query or table you want to see in your report. Unless you want to view all the records from a single table, bind your report to a query. Even if you are accessing data from a single table, using a query lets you create your report on the basis of a particular search criterion and sorting order. If you want to access data from multiple tables, you have almost no choice but to bind your report to a query. In the examples in this chapter, all the reports are bound to a query (even though it is possible to bind a report to a table).

Note　Access lets you create a report without first binding it to a table or query, but you will have no fields on the report. This capability can be used to work out page templates with common text headers or footers such as page numbering or the date and time, which can serve as models for other reports. You can add fields later by changing the underlying control source of the report.

Throughout this chapter and the next chapter, you learn the tasks necessary to create the Products Display Report (the partial first page is shown in Figure 13-20). In this chapter, you design the basic report, assemble the data, and place the data in the proper positions. In Chapter 14, you enhance the report by adding lines, boxes, and shading so that certain areas stand out.

As with almost every task in Access, there are many ways to create a report without wizards. It is important, however, to follow some type of methodology, because creating a good report involves a fairly scientific approach. You should create a checklist that is a set of tasks that will result in a good report every time. As you complete each task, check it off your list. When you are done, you will have a great-looking report. The following section outlines this approach.

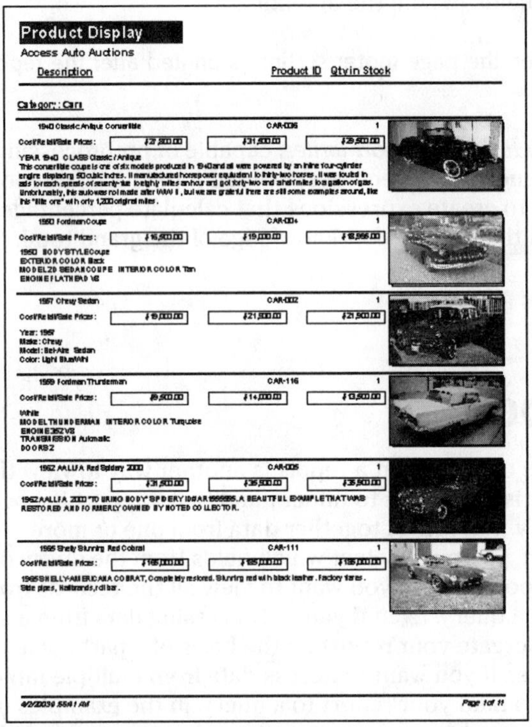

Figure 13-20: The Products Summary report.

Creating a new report and binding it to a query

The first step is to create a new report and bind it to the tblProducts table. Follow these steps to complete this process:

1. Press F11 to display the Database window if it is not already displayed.

2. Click the Reports object button.

3. Click the New toolbar button. The New Report dialog box appears.

4. Select Design View.

5. Click the combo box which label starts with Choose a table or query. A drop-down list of all tables and queries in the current database appears.

6. Select the tblProducts table.

7. Click OK.

8. Maximize the Report window.

A blank Report Design window appears (see Figure 13-21). Notice the three sections in the screen display: Page Header, Detail, and Page Footer. The report is bound to the table tblProducts. This means that the fields from the table are available for use in the report design and that they appear in the Field List window. It also means that the data from that table will be displayed when the report is viewed or printed.

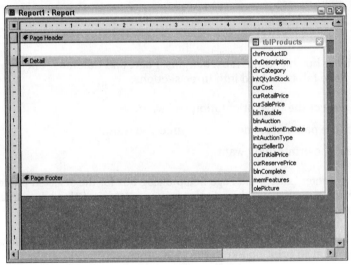

Figure 13-21: A blank Report Design window.

Defining the report page size and layout

As you plan your report, consider the page-layout characteristics as well as the kind of paper and printer you want to use for the output. If you use a dot-matrix printer with a wide-carriage feed, you design your report differently than for printing on a laser printer with 8½" x 11" paper. After you make these decisions, you use several dialog boxes and properties to make adjustments; these items work together to create the desired output. You learn to use these tools in the next several chapters.

First, you need to select the correct printer and page-layout characteristics by selecting File ➪ Page Setup. The Page Setup dialog box, shown in Figure 13-22 with the Page tab selected, enables you to select your printer and set printer options.

Figure 13-22: The Page Setup dialog box showing the Page tab.

The Page Setup dialog box has three tabs: Margins, Page, and Columns. The information under the Page tab is divided into three sections:

✦ **Orientation.** Select the page orientation you want.

✦ **Paper.** Select the paper size and paper source you want.

✦ **Printer.** Select the printer you want.

Note   If you click the Printer button, the Page Setup dialog box for the selected printer appears. Clicking Properties will then display a more extensive dialog box with all the applicable options.

The design for Product Summary report is to be a *portrait* report, which is taller than it is wide. You want to print on letter size paper that is 8½" x 11", and you want the left, right, top, and bottom margins all set to 0.250 or the minimum your printer will allow.

Follow these steps to create the proper report setup for the Products Summary report:

1. Open the Page Setup dialog box and select the Page tab.

2. Click the Portrait option button.

   Next to the Orientation buttons are two sheet-of-paper icons with the letter A pictured on them. The picture of the sheet is an indication of its setting.

3. Click the Margins tab.

4. Click the Top margin setting and change the setting to 0.250.

5. Click the Bottom margin setting and change the setting to 0.250.

6. Click the Left margin setting and change the setting to 0.250.

7. Click the Right margin setting and change the setting to 0.250.

Some printers may not allow margins as small as .250 for all four settings. If you receive a warning, you will need to use a different value.

8. Click OK to close the Page Setup dialog box.

Tip

Access displays your reports in Print Preview view by using the driver of the active printer. If you don't have a good-quality laser or inkjet printer available for printing, install the driver for one anyway so that you can view any graphics that you create (and see the report in a high-resolution display). Later, you can print to your inkjet or other available printer and get the actual hard copy in the best resolution your printer offers.

Caution

Figure 13-22 shows the option buttons in the bottom-left corner of the Page tab. If you are going to give your database or report to others, you should always select the first option, Default Printer. This way, if you have selected a printer the recipient doesn't have, the report will use their default printer. If you have selected the second option (Use Specific Printer), those who don't have that printer will get an error message and will not be able to use the report.

After you define your page layout in the Page Setup dialog box, you need to define the size of your report (which is not necessarily the same as the page definition).

To define the report size, place the mouse pointer on the right-most edge of the report (where the white page meets the gray background). The pointer changes to a double-headed arrow. Drag the pointer to change the width of the report. As you drag the edge, a vertical line appears in the ruler to let you know the exact width if you release the mouse at that point. Be careful not to exceed the width of the page you defined in the Page Setup dialog box.

When you position the mouse pointer at the bottom of the report, it changes to a double-headed arrow similar to the one for changing width. Dragging will change the height of the page footer section or other specified bottom section, not the height of the whole page. (Predefining a page length directly in the report section doesn't really make sense because the detail section will vary in length, based on your groupings.) Remember that the Report Design view shows only a representation of the various report sections, not the actual report.

To set the right border for the Product Display report to 7½", follow these steps:

1. Click the right-most edge of the report body (where the white page meets the gray background). The mouse pointer changes to a double-headed arrow.

2. Drag the edge to the 7½" mark.

3. Release the mouse button.

Note

You can also change the Width property in the property window for the report.

Tip

When you run your report and every other page is blank, it is a sign that the width of your report exceeds the width of your page. To fix this, decrease your left and right margin size or your report width. Sometimes, when you move controls around, you accidentally make the report width larger than your original design. For example, in a portrait report, if your left margin + report width + right margin is greater than 8½ , you will see blank pages.

Placing fields on the report

Access takes full advantage of Windows' drag-and-drop capabilities. The method for placing fields on a report is no exception. As with forms, when you place a field on a report, it is no longer called a field; it is called a *control*. A control has a *control source* (a specific table field) that it is bound to, so the terms *control* and *field* are used interchangeably in this chapter.

To place controls on your report:

1. Display the Field List window by clicking the Field List toolbar button.

2. Click the desired Toolbox control to determine the type of control that will be created if they are to be different from the default control types for the fields.

3. Select each of the fields that you want on your report and then drag them to the Report Design window.

Displaying the field list

To display the Field List window, click the Field List button on the toolbar. A small window with a list of all the fields from the underlying query appears. This window is called a *modeless* dialog box because it remains onscreen even while you continue with other work in Access. The Field List window can be resized and moved around the screen. The enlarged Field List window is illustrated in Figure 13-23, showing all the fields in the tblProducts table.

Tip

You can move the Field List window by simply clicking on the title bar and dragging it to a new location.

Selecting the fields for your report

Selecting a field in the Report field list is the same as selecting a field in the Query field list. The easiest way to select a field is simply to click it. When you click a field, it becomes highlighted. After a field is highlighted, you can drag it to the Report window.

You can highlight *contiguous* (adjacent) fields in the list by following these steps:

✦ Click the first field you want in the field list.

✦ Move the mouse pointer to the last field you want from the list.

✦ Hold down the Shift key and click the last field you want.

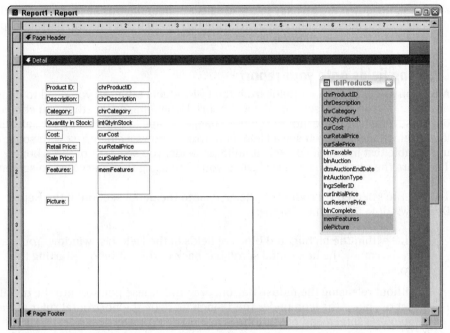

Figure 13-23: Dragging fields to the Design window.

The block of fields between the first and last field you selected is displayed in reverse video, indicating it is selected. You can then drag the block of fields to the Report window.

You can highlight noncontiguous fields in the list by clicking each field while holding down the Ctrl key. Each selected field will be displayed in reverse video; then you can drag the fields as a group to the Report Design window.

Note
Unlike the Query field list, you cannot also double-click a field to add it to the Report window.

You can begin by selecting the tblProducts fields for the detail section. To select the fields needed for the detail section of the Product Display report, follow these steps:

1. Click the chrProductID field.

2. Hold down the Shift key and click the curSalePrice field.

    The block of fields from chrProductID to curSalePrice should be highlighted in the Field List window, as shown in Figure 13-23.

3. Hold down the Ctrl key and click the memFeatures field and the olePicture field.

Holding down the Ctrl key lets you select noncontiguous fields. You should have two blocks of fields selected (the top seven fields and the bottom two fields), as shown in Figure 13-23.

Dragging fields onto your report

After you select the proper fields from the tblProducts table, all you need to do is drag them to the detail section of your report. Depending on whether you choose one or several fields, the mouse pointer changes shape to represent your selection. If you select one field, you see a Field icon, which shows a single box with some unreadable text inside. If you select multiple fields, you see a set of three boxes. These are the same icons you saw when you were using the Query Design screens.

To drag the selected tbProducts table fields into the detail section of the Report Design window, follow these steps:

1. Click within the highlighted block of fields in the Field List window. You may need to move the horizontal scroll bar back to the left before starting this process.

2. Without releasing the mouse button, drag the mouse pointer into the detail section; place the icon under the 1½-inch mark on the horizontal ruler at the top of the screen and next to the ½-inch mark of the vertical ruler along the left edge of the screen.

3. Release the mouse button.

The fields appear in the detail section of the report, as shown in Figure 13-23. Notice that for each field you dragged onto the report, there are two controls. When you use the drag-and-drop method for placing fields, Access automatically creates a label control with the field name attached to the text control to which the field is bound.

Note   Notice the Bound Object Frame control for the field named Picture. Access always creates a Bound Object Frame control for an OLE-type object found in a table. Also notice that the detail section automatically resizes itself to fit all the controls. Above the Bound Object Frame control is the control for the memo field Features.

You also need to place the desired field controls for the customer information you need in the page header section. Before you do this, however, you need to resize the page header frame to leave room for a title you will add later.

Resizing a section

To make room on the report for the title information in the page header, you must resize it. You can resize a section by placing the mouse pointer at the bottom of the section you want to resize. The pointer turns into a vertical double-headed arrow; drag the section border up or down to make the section smaller or larger.

Resize the page header section to make it larger by following these steps:

1. Move the mouse pointer between the bottom of the page header section and the top of the detail section.

2. When the pointer is displayed as a double-sided arrow, hold down the left mouse button.

3. Drag the page header section border down until it intersects the detail section's ruler at the ¾-inch mark.

4. Release the button to enlarge the page header section.

The page header section expanded to fit the fields that were dragged into the section. All the fields needed for the Product Display report are now placed in their appropriate sections.

Working with unattached label controls and text

When you drag a field from the Field List window to a report, Access creates not only a data control but also a label control that is attached to the data control. At times, you will want to add label controls by themselves to create headings or titles for the report.

Creating unattached labels

To create a new, unattached label control, you must use the Toolbox (unless you copy an existing label). The next task in the current example is to add the text headers *Product Display* and *Access Auto Auctions* to your report. This task demonstrates adding and editing text.

To begin creating an unattached label control, follow these steps:

1. Display the Toolbox.

2. Click the Label tool in the Toolbox.

3. Click near the top-left edge of the page header at about the ⅛-inch mark on the ruler; then drag the mouse pointer downward and to the right to make a small rectangle about 2½ inches wide and ½-inch high.

4. Type **Product Display**.

5. Press Enter.

Repeat the process for the label Access Auto Auctions and place it just below the Product Display label, as shown in Figure 13-24. As you create these label rectangles, it may make the Page Header section expand.

Tip
To create a multiple-line label entry, press Ctrl+Enter to force a line break where you want it in the control.

Tip If you want to edit or enter a caption that is longer than the space in the property window, the contents will scroll as you type. Otherwise, open a Zoom box that gives you more space to type by pressing Shift+F2.

Modifying the appearance of text in a control

To modify the appearance of the text in a control, select the control by clicking its border (not in the control itself). You can then select a formatting style to apply to the label by clicking the appropriate button on the Formatting toolbar.

To make the titles stand out, follow these steps to modify the appearance of label text:

1. Click the newly created report heading label Product Display.

2. Click the Bold button on the Formatting toolbar.

3. Click the arrow beside the FontSize drop-down box.

4. Select 18 from the FontSize drop-down list box.

5. Repeat for the Access Auto Auctions label, using a 12 pt font and Bold.

Figure 13-24 shows these labels added, resized, and formatted.

Currently, the label rectangles are much large than their displayed text. To tighten the display or to display all the text when a label rectangle isn't big enough, you can simply double-click the bottom left corner handle to resize it (which you will learn more about later in this chapter).

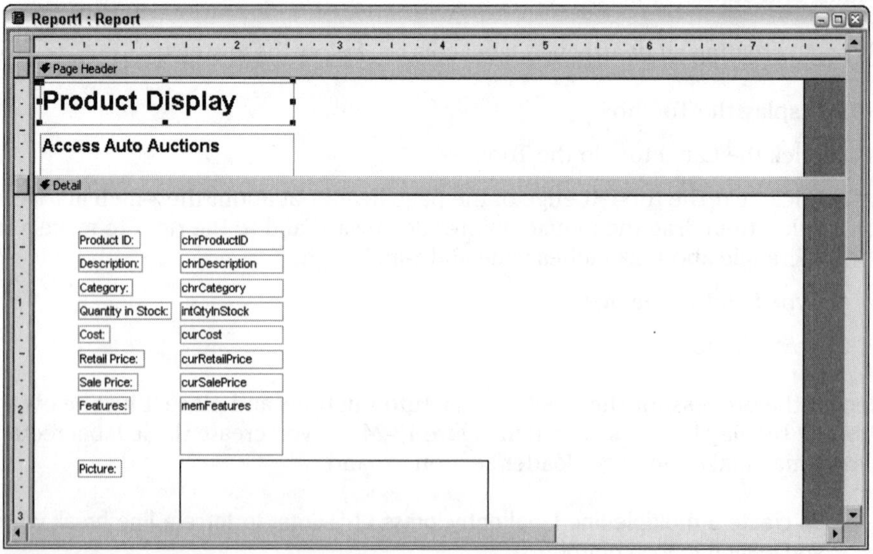

Figure 13-24: Adding unbound labels to the report.

Working with text boxes and their attached label controls

So far, you have added controls bound to fields in the tables and unbound label controls used to display titles in your report. There is another type of text box control that is typically added to a report: unbound text boxes that are used to hold expressions such as page numbers, dates, or a calculation.

Creating and using text box controls

In reports, text box controls serve two purposes. First, they enable you to display stored data from a particular field in a query or table. Second, they display the result of an expression. Expressions can be calculations that use other controls as their operands, calculations that use Access functions (either built-in or user-defined), or a combination of the two. You have learned how to use a text box control to display data from a field and how to create that control. Next, you learn how to create new text box controls that use expressions.

Entering an expression in a text control

Cross-Reference

Expressions enable you to create a value that is not already in a table or query. They can range from simple functions (such as a page number) to complex mathematical computations. Chapter 20 covers expressions in greater detail; for the example in this chapter, you use an expression that is necessary for the report.

A *function* is a small program that, when run, returns a single value. The function can be one of many built-in Access functions or it can be user-defined. For example, to facilitate page numbering in reports, Access has a function called Page that returns the value of the current report page. The following steps show you how to use an unbound text box to add a page number to your report:

1. Click in the middle of the page footer section, resize the page footer so that it is a ½ inch in height, and then create a text box about three-quarters of the height of the section and about ½-inch wide by resizing the default text box control.

2. Select the Text Box tool on the Toolbox.

3. Scroll down to the page footer section by using the vertical scroll bar.

4. Click the label control to select it. (It should say something similar to Text38.)

5. Click the beginning of the label control text, drag over the default text in the label control, and type Page: or double-click the text to highlight it and then replace it.

6. Click twice on the text box control (it says "Unbound"); type **=Page** and press Enter. (Notice that the Control Source property changes on the data sheet of the Property window to =[Page]. If the Property window is not open, you may want to open it to see the change.)

7. Click the Page label control's Move handle (upper-left corner); move the label closer to the =[Page] text box control until the right edge of the label control touches the left edge of the text box control.

Although this is a good exercise for creating labels and text boxes, a better way to add a page number in the Page Footer section is to use the automatic Page numbers dialog box. To do this, follow the steps below:

1. Delete the text box you created in the last example from the Page Footer section.

2. Select Insert ➪ Page Numbers... from the main menu.

The Page Numbers dialog box is displayed, as shown in Figure 13-25. You can also see the expression that will be created below in the Page Footer section.

3. Change the Format to Page N of M.

4. Change the Position to Bottom of Page [Footer].

5. Change Alignment to Right.

Format lets you choose between the final text Page N, where N is the page number, or Page N of M, where N is the current page number and M is the total number of pages in the report. It is recommended to always use Page N of M to make sure the report isn't missing any pages (or the last page). *Position* lets you determine if the page number expression is created in the Page Header or Page Footer. *Alignment* lets you determine if the text will be left, right, or centered aligned. Because this text expression is going to be placed at the bottom right corner of the report, the Right alignment is preferred. There is also a check box that can be unchecked and lets you eliminate the page number from the first page (if it were to be used as a cover page).

You can see in Figure 13-25 the completed text box expression:

="Page " & [Page] & " of " [Pages]

This would display Page 5 of 25 if page 5 was the current page and there were 25 pages in the report.

The = sign begins an expression. The & symbol (known as *concatenation*) joins keywords, fields, or other expressions to a text string. Text strings are surrounded by double quotes. [Page] and [Pages] are keywords and are surrounded (known as delimited) by braces ([ ]). Notice the "Page " text contains a trailing space. This is done so that there will be a space between the text Page and the current page number. Notice that there are both leading and trailing spaces in the text string " of ." Again, this separates the page numbers by a space from the word "of."

Tip You can always check your result by clicking the Print Preview button on the toolbar and zooming in on the page footer section to check the page number.

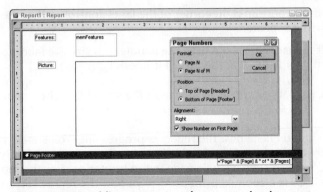

Figure 13-25: Adding a page-number expression in a text box control.

Sizing a text box control or label control

You can select a control by simply clicking it. Depending on the size of the control, from three to seven sizing handles will appear — one on each corner except the upper-left corner and one on each side. When you move the mouse pointer over one of the sizing handles, the pointer changes into a double-headed arrow. When the pointer changes, click the control and drag it to the size you want. Notice that, as you drag, an outline appears; it indicates the new size that the label control will be when you release the mouse button.

If you double-click any of the sizing handles, Access resizes a control to the best fit for the text in the control. This feature is especially handy if you increase the font size and then notice that the text is cut off, either on the bottom or to the right. Note that for label controls, this *best-fit sizing* resizes both vertically and horizontally, though text controls can resize only vertically. The reason for this difference is that in the report design mode, Access doesn't know how much of a field you want to display; the field name and field contents might be radically different. Sometimes label controls are not resized correctly, however, and have to be adjusted manually.

Changing the size of a label control

Earlier in this chapter (in the steps that modified the appearance of label text), you changed the characteristics of the Product Display label; the text changed, but the label itself did not adjust. The text no longer fits well within the label control. You can resize the label control, however, to fit the enhanced font size by following these steps:

1. Click the Product Display label control.

2. Move your mouse pointer over the control. Notice how the pointer changes shape over the sizing handles.

3. To size the control automatically, double-click one of the sizing handles. The label control size may still need to be readjusted.

4. Place the pointer in the bottom-right corner of the label control so that the diagonal double-arrow appears.

5. Hold down the left mouse button and drag the handle to resize the label control until it correctly displays all of the text (if it doesn't already).

Tip   You can also select Format ⇨ Size ⇨ To Fit to change the size of the label control text automatically.

Before continuing, you should check how the report is progressing. You should do this frequently as you create a report. You should also save the report frequently as you make changes to it. You can send a single page to the printer or view the report in print preview. Figure 13-26 is a zoomed print preview of how the report currently looks. The customer information is at the top of the page; the pet information is below that and offset to the left.

Notice the title at the top of the page. You can see the page number at the bottom if you click the magnifying glass button to zoom out and see the entire page. Only one record per page appears on the report because of the vertical layout. In the next section, you move the fields around and create a more horizontal layout.

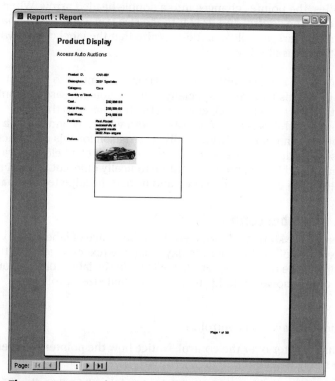

Figure 13-26: A print preview of the report.

Deleting and Cutting attached labels from text controls

In order to create the report shown in Figure 13-20, you must remove the label controls from several of the text box controls and place the label controls in the page header section.

It's very easy to delete one or more attached controls in a report. Simply select the desired controls and press Delete. However, if you want to move the label to the page header section, you can cut the label instead of deleting it. When removing attached controls, there are two choices:

✦ Delete only the label control.

✦ Cut the label control to the clipboard.

✦ Delete or cut both the label control and the field control.

If you select the label control and press Cut (Ctrl-X) or the Delete key, only the label control is removed. If you select the field control and press Cut or Delete, both the label control and the field control are removed. To cut an attached label control (in this case, the Product ID controls and their attached label), follow these steps:

1. Click the Close button on the toolbar to exit print preview mode. Select the Product ID label control only in the detail section.

2. Press Ctrl-X (Cut).

    After you have cut the label, you may want to place it somewhere else. In this example, you will want to place it into the Page Header section.

Pasting labels into a report section

It is probably just as easy to cut labels from controls placed in the detail section and paste them into the Page Header as it is to just delete the labels and create new ones in the Page Header. Regardless, you will now paste the label you have cut in the previous steps:

1. Click anywhere in or on the Page Header section.

2. Press Ctrl-V (Paste).

    The Product ID label appears in the Page Header.

3. Repeat for the Description, Category, and Quantity in Stock labels.

4. Delete the remaining label controls in the detail section, leaving all of the text box controls.

If you accidentally selected the data field control and both controls are cut or deleted, press the Undo toolbar button to undo the action.

Tip If you want to delete only the field control and keep the attached label control, first select the label control and then select Edit ⇨ Copy. Next, to delete both the field control and the label control, select the field control and press Delete. Finally, select Edit ⇨ Paste to paste only the copied label control to the report.

Moving label and text controls

Before discussing how to move label and text controls, it is important to review a few differences between attached and unattached controls. When an attached label is created automatically with a text control, it is called a *compound control*. In a compound control, whenever one control in the set is moved, the other control moves as well. With a text control and a label control, whenever the text control is moved, the attached label is also moved. Likewise, whenever the label control is moved, the text control is also moved.

To move both controls in a compound control, select one of the pair by clicking the control. Move the mouse pointer over either of the objects. When the pointer turns into a hand, click the controls and drag them to their new location. As you drag, an outline for the compound control moves with your pointer.

To move only one of the controls in a compound control, drag the desired control by its *Move handle* (the large square in the upper-left corner of the control). When you click a compound control, it looks like both controls are selected, but if you look closely, you see that only one of the two controls is selected (as indicated by the presence of both moving and sizing handles). The unselected control displays only a moving handle. A pointing finger indicates that you have selected the Move handles and can now move only one control. To move either control individually, select the control's Move handle and drag it to its new location.

Cross-Reference To move a label that is not attached, simply click any border (except where there is a handle) and drag it. You can also move groups of controls with the selection techniques you learned in Chapters 9 through 12.

To make a group selection, click with the mouse pointer anywhere outside a starting point and drag the pointer through (or around) the controls you want to select. A gray, outlined rectangle is displayed that shows the extent of the selection. When you release the mouse button, all the controls that the rectangle surrounds are selected. You can then drag the group of controls to a new location.

Tip The global option Tools ⇨ Options – Forms/Reports tab – Selection Behavior is a property that controls the enclosure of selections. You can enclose them fully (the rectangle must completely surround the selection) or partially (the rectangle must only touch the control), which is the default.

Make sure you also resize all of the controls as shown in the figure. The memo field memFeatures and the OLE picture field olePicture must also be changed in both size and shape.

Place all of the controls in their proper position to complete the report layout. You want this first pass at rearranging the controls to look like the example shown in Figure 13-27. You will make a series of block moves by selecting several controls and then positioning them close to where you want them. Then, if needed, you fine-tune their position. This is the way most reports are done.

Follow Figure 13-27 to begin placing the controls where they should be. You may want to notice that the control labels in the Page Header section have been underlined. Also notice the new label Cost/Retail/Sale Prices in the Detail section.

At this point, you are about halfway done. The screen should look like the one shown in Figure 13-27. (If it doesn't, adjust your controls until your screen matches the figure.) Remember that these screen pictures are taken with the Windows screen driver set at 1024 x 768. If you are using 800 x 600, 640 x 480, or large fonts, you'll have to scroll the screen to see the entire report.

These steps complete the rough design for this report. There are still properties, fonts, and sizes to change. When you make these changes, you'll have to move fields around again. Use the designs in Figure 13-20 only as a guideline. How it looks to *you*, as you refine the look of the report in the Report window, determines the real design.

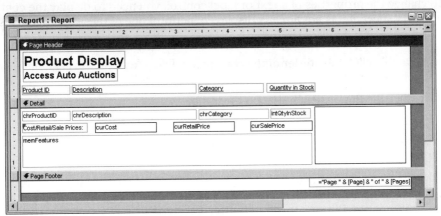

Figure 13-27: Rearranging the controls on the report.

Modifying the appearance of multiple controls

The next step is to format all the label controls in the Page Header section directly above the section separator to be underlined. The following steps guide you through modifying the appearance of text in multiple label controls:

1. Select all label controls in the bottom of the Page Header section by individually clicking them while holding down the Shift key. There are four label controls to select, as shown in Figure 13-27.

You could also have placed your cursor in the vertical ruler at about 1.25 inches and, when it changed to a right-pointing bold arrow, clicked the mouse to select all the controls in that horizontal area of the report.

2. Click the Underline button on the toolbar.

Note   You could also have selected all the label controls in the preceding steps by using the drag-and-surround method.

After you make the final modifications, you are finished, except for fixing the picture control. To do this, you need to change properties, which you do in the next section. This may seem to be an enormous number of steps because the procedures were designed to show you how laying out a report design can be a slow process. Remember, however, that when you click away with the mouse, you don't realize how many steps you are doing as you design the report layout visually. With a WYSIWYG (What You See Is What You Get) layout like that of the Access report designer, you may need to perform many tasks, but it's still easier and faster than programming. Figure 13-27 shows the final version of the design layout as seen in this chapter. In the next chapter, you continue to improve this report layout.

Changing label and text box control properties

To change the properties of a text or label control, you need to display the control's property sheet. If it is not already displayed, perform one of these actions to display it:

✦ Double-click the border of the control (anywhere except a sizing handle or Move handle).

✦ Click the Properties button on the toolbar.

✦ Select View ⇨ Properties.

✦ Right-click the mouse and select Properties.

The *property sheet* enables you to look at a control's property settings and provides an easy way to edit the settings. Using tools such as the formatting windows and text-formatting buttons on the Formatting toolbar also changes the property settings of a control. Clicking the Bold button, for example, really sets the Font Weight property to Bold. It is usually much more intuitive to use the toolbar (or even the menus), but some properties are not accessible this way. In addition, sometimes objects have more options available through the property sheet.

The Size Mode property of an OLE object (bound object frame), with its options of Clip, Stretch, and Zoom, is a good example of a property that is available only through the property sheet.

The Image control, which is a bound object frame, presently has its Size Mode property set to Clip, which is the default. With Clip, the picture is displayed in its original size and may be too large to fit in the frame. In this exercise, you will change the setting to Stretch so that the picture is sized automatically to fit the picture frame.

Cross-Reference Chapter 14 covers the use of pictures, OLE objects, and graphs.

To change the property for the bound object frame control that contains the picture, follow these steps:

1. Click the frame control of the picture bound object.

2. Click the Size Mode property.

3. Click the arrow to display the drop-down list box.

4. Select Stretch.

These steps complete the changes so far to your report. A print preview of the first few records appears in Figure 13-28. If you look at the pictures, notice how the picture is properly displayed and the Features field now appears across the bottom of the detail section. The labels are all underlined.

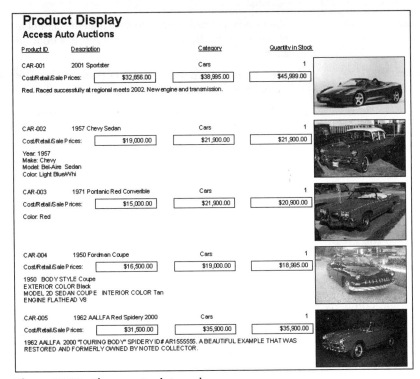

Figure 13-28: The report print preview.

Growing and shrinking text box controls

When you print or print-preview fields that can have variable text lengths, Access provides options for enabling a control to grow or shrink vertically, depending on the exact contents of a record. The option Can Grow determines whether a text control adds lines to fit additional text if the record contains more lines of text than the control can display. The option Can Shrink determines whether a control deletes blank lines if the record's contents use fewer lines than the control can display. Although these properties are usable for any text field, they are especially helpful for memo field controls like the Features control.

Table 13-3 explains the acceptable values for these two properties.

Table 13-3		
Text Control Values for Can Grow and Can Shrink		
Property	*Value*	*Description*
Can Grow	Yes	If the data in a record uses more lines than the control is defined to display, the control resizes to accommodate additional lines.
Can Grow	No	If the data in a record uses more lines than the control is defined to display, the control does not resize; it truncates the data display.
Can Shrink	Yes	If the data in a record uses fewer lines than the control is defined to display, the control resizes to eliminate blank lines.
Can Shrink	No	If the data in a record uses fewer lines than the control is defined to display, the control does not resize to eliminate blank lines.

To change the Can Grow settings for a text control, follow these steps:

1. Select the Features text box control.

2. Display the Property window.

3. Click the Can Grow property; then click the arrow and select Yes.

Note   The Can Grow and Can Shrink properties are also available for report sections. Use a section's property sheet to modify these values.

The report is starting to look good, but you may want to see groups of like data together and determine specific orders of data. In order to do this, you will use sorting and grouping.

Sorting and grouping data

Sorting enables you to determine the order in which the records are viewed in a datasheet, form, or report, based on the values in one or more fields. This order is important when you want to view the data in your tables in a sequence other than that of your input. For example, new products are added to the tblProducts table as they are needed on an invoice. The physical order of the database reflects the date and time a product is added. Yet, when you think of the product list, you probably expect it to be in *alphabetical* order by Product ID, and you want to sort it by Description of the cost of the product. By sorting in the report itself, you don't have to worry about the order of the data. Although you can sort the data in the table by the primary key or in a query by any field you want, it is more advantageous to do it in the report. This way, if you change the query or table, the report is still in the correct order.

You can take this report concept even further by *grouping*—that is, breaking related records into groups. Suppose that you want to list your products first by Category and then by Description within each Category group. To do this, you must use the Category and Description fields to sort the data. Groupings that can create group headers and footers are sometimes called *control breaks* because changes in data trigger the report groups.

Before you can add a grouping, however, you must first define a *sort order* for at least one field in the report using the Sorting and Grouping dialog box, which is shown completed in Figure 13-29. In this example, you use the Category field to sort on first and then the Description field as the secondary sort.

To define a sort order based on Category and Description, follow these steps:

1. Click the Sorting and Grouping button on the toolbar to display the Sorting and Grouping box.

2. Click in the first row of the Field/Expression column of the Sorting and Grouping box. A downward-pointing arrow appears.

3. Click the arrow to display a list of fields in the tblProduct table.

4. Select chrCategory in the field list. Notice that Sort Order defaults to Ascending.

5. Click in the second row of the Field/Expression column.

6. Click the arrow to display a list of fields in the tblProduct table.

7. Select chrDescription in the field list. Notice that Sort Order defaults to Ascending.

 Tip　To see more of the Field/Expression column, drag the border between the Field/Expression and Sort Order columns to the right.

Note   You can also drag a field from the Field List window into the Sorting and Grouping box Field/Expression column rather than enter a field or choose one from the field list in the Sorting and Grouping box Field/Expression column.

Although in this example you used a field, you can alternatively sort (and group) by using an expression. To enter an expression, click in the desired row of the Field/Expression column and enter any valid Access expression, making sure that it begins with an equal sign, as in =[curRetailPrice]-[curCost].

To change the sort order for fields in the Field/Expression column, simply click the Sort Order column and click the down arrow to display the Sort Order list; then select Descending.

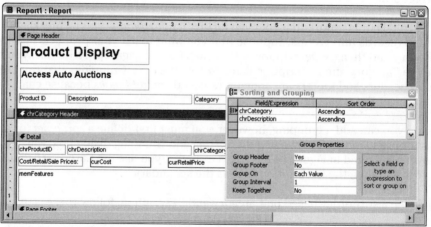

Figure 13-29: The Sorting and Grouping box completed.

Creating a group header or footer

Now that you have added instructions to sort by the Category and Description, you will also need to create a group header for Category to group all of the products by category. You don't need a group footer in this example because there are no totals by category or other reasons to use a group footer.

To create a group header that enables you to sort and group by the chrCategory field, follow these steps:

1. Click the Sorting and Grouping button on the toolbar if the Sorting and Grouping box is not displayed. The field chrCategory should be displayed in the first row of the Sorting and Grouping box; it should indicate that it is being used as a sort in Ascending order.

2. Click on the chrCategory row in the Field/Expression column.

3. Click the Group Header property in the bottom pane; an arrow appears.

4. Click the arrow on the right side of the text box; a drop-down list appears.

5. Select Yes from the list. (A header section bar appears on the report.)

After you define a header or footer, the row selection bar changes to the grouping symbol shown in Figure 13-29. This is the same symbol as in the Sorting and Grouping button on the toolbar. Figure 13-29 shows both the grouping row symbol and the newly created report section. The chrCategory header section appears between the page header and detail sections. If you define a group footer, it appears below the detail section. If a report has multiple groupings, each subsequent group becomes the one closest to the detail section. The groups defined first are farthest from the detail section.

The Group Properties pane (displayed at the bottom of the Sorting and Grouping box) contains these properties:

✦ **Group Header.** Yes creates a group header. No removes the group header.

✦ **Group Footer.** Yes creates a group footer. No removes the group footer.

✦ **Group On.** Specifies how you want the values grouped. The options you see in the drop-down list box depend on the data type of the field on which you're grouping. If you group on an expression, you see all the options. Group On has more choices to make.

For Text data types, there are two choices:

✦ **Each Value.** The same value in the field or expression.

✦ **Prefix Characters.** The same first *n* number of characters in the field.

For Date/Time data types, there are additional options:

✦ **Each Value.** The same value in the field or expression.

✦ **Year.** Dates in the same calendar year.

✦ **Qtr.** Dates in the same calendar quarter.

✦ **Month.** Dates in the same month.

✦ **Week.** Dates in the same week.

✦ **Day.** Dates on the same date.

✦ **Hour.** Times in the same hour.

✦ **Minute.** Times in the same minute.

Currency, or Number data types provide three options:

✦ **Each Value.** The same value in the field or expression.

✦ **Interval.** Values falling within the interval you specify.

✦ **Group Interval.** Specifies any interval that is valid for the values in the field or expression you're grouping on.

  • The Group Interval has its own options which include:

  • **Keep Together.** This option controls what's known as widows and orphans in the word processing world so that you don't have a header at the bottom of a page with no detail until the next page.

  • **Whole Group.** Prints header detail and group footer on one page.

  • **With First Detail.** Prevents the contents of the group header from printing without any following data or records on a page.

  • **No.** Do not keep together.

On the CD-ROM

After you create the Category group header, you are done with the Sorting and Grouping box for this report. You may need to make additional changes to groupings as you change the way a report looks; the following three sections detail how to make these changes. You should not make any of these changes, however, if you are following the examples or you should press the Save icon now to save the form in the current state and then discard the changes done to this form after this point.

Changing the group order

Access enables you to easily change the Sorting and Grouping order without moving all the individual controls in the associated headers and footers. Here are the general steps to change the sorting and grouping order:

1. Click the selector bar of the field or expression you want to move in the Sorting and Grouping window.

2. Click the selector again and hold down the left mouse button.

3. Drag the row to a new location.

4. Release the mouse button.

Removing a group header or footer

To remove a page or report header/footer section, use the View ➪ Page Header/Footer and View ➪ Report Header/Footer toggles. To remove a group header or footer while leaving the sorting intact, follow these steps:

1. In the Sorting and Grouping window, click the selector bar of the field or expression that you want to remove from the grouping.

2. Click the Group Header text box.

3. Change the value to No.

4. Press Enter.

To remove a group footer, follow the same steps, but click Group Footer in Step 2.

To permanently remove both the sorting and grouping for a particular field (and thereby remove the group header and footer sections), follow these steps:

1. Click the selector of the field or expression you want to delete.

2. Press Delete. A dialog box appears asking you to confirm the deletion.

3. Click OK.

Hiding a section

Access also enables you to hide headers and footers so that you can break data into groups without having to view information about the group itself. You can also hide the detail section so that you see only a summary report. To hide a section, follow these steps:

1. Click the section you want to hide.

2. Display the section property sheet.

3. Click the Visible property's text box.

4. Click the drop-down list arrow on the right side of the text box.

5. Select No from the drop-down list box.

Note Sections are not the only objects in a report that can be hidden; controls also have a Visible property. This property can be useful for expressions that trigger other expressions.

Sizing a section

Now that you have created the group header, you might want to put some controls in the section, move some controls around, or even move controls between sections. Before you start manipulating controls within a section, you should make sure the section is the proper height.

To modify the height of a section, drag the border of the section below it. If, for example, you have a report with a page header, detail section, and page footer, change the height of the detail section by dragging the top of the page footer section's border. You can make a section larger or smaller by dragging the bottom border of the section. For this example, change the height of the group header section to ⅜" with these steps:

1. Move your mouse pointer to the bottom of the chrCategory section. The pointer changes to a horizontal line split by two vertical arrows.

2. Select the top of the detail section (which is also the bottom of the chrCategory Header section).

3. Drag the selected band lower until three dots appear in the vertical ruler (⌘"). The gray line indicates where the top of the border will be when you release the mouse button.

4. Release the mouse button.

Moving controls between sections

You now want to move the chrCategory control from the Detail section to the chrCategory Header section. You can move one or more controls between sections by simply dragging the control with your mouse from one section to another or by cutting it from one section and pasting it to another section. Follow the instructions below to move the chrCategory control from the Detail section to the chrCategory section:

1. Select the chrCategory control in the Detail section.

2. Drag the chrCategory control up to the chrCategory Header section and drop it close to the vertical ruler, as shown in Figure 13-30.

3. Release the mouse button.

4. Press the Underline button to underline the chrCategory control to further highlight it as a group header. Sometimes, you might want to bold it or even increase the font size.

You should now do the following steps to complete the report design:

1. Delete the Category label from the Page Header.

2. Move the chrProductID control and its associated label after the chrDescription control and its associated label, as shown in Figure 13-30.

3. Move the chrDescription control and its associated label to the left so that it starts just to the right of the start of the chrCategory control in the chrCategory Header control.

   By offsetting the first control in the Detail section slightly to the right of the start of the control in the Group Header section, you show the hierarchy of the data presented in the report. It now will show that each group of products is for the category listed in the group header.

4. Lengthen the chrDescription control so that it approaches the chrProduct ID control.

   When you are done, the report design should look like the one shown in Figure 13-30.

Figure 13-30 shows this property window and the completed report design.

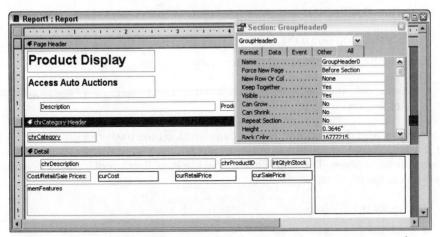

Figure 13-30: Completing the Group Header section and setting a Page Break.

Adding page breaks

Access enables you to add page breaks based on group breaks; you can also insert forced breaks within sections, except in page header and footer sections.

In some report designs, it's best to have each new group begin on a different page. You can achieve this effect easily by using the Force New Page property of a group section, which enables you to force a page break every time the group value changes.

The four Force New Page property settings are listed below:

✦ **None.** No forced page break (the default).

✦ **Before Section.** Starts printing the current section at the top of a new page every time there is a new group.

✦ **After Section.** Starts printing the next section at the top of a new page every time there is a new group.

✦ **Before & After.** Combines the effects of Before Section and After Section.

To create the report you want, you will force a page break before the chrCategory group by using the Force New Page property in the chrCategory header. To change the Force New Page property on the basis of groupings, follow these steps:

1. Click anywhere in the chrCategory header.

2. Display the Property window.

3. Select the Force New Page property.

4. Click the drop-down list arrow on the right side of the edit box.

5. Select Before Section from the drop-down list box.

Tip Alternatively, you can create a Group footer and set its Force New Page property to After Section.

Sometimes, you don't want to force a page break on the basis of a grouping, but you still want to force a page break. For example, you may want to split a report title across several pages. The solution is to use the Page Break tool from the Toolbox; just follow these steps:

1. Display the Toolbox.

2. Click the Page Break tool.

3. Click in the section where you want the page break to occur.

Note Be careful not to split the data in a control. Place page breaks above or below controls; do not overlap them.

Making the Report Presentation Quality

As you near completion of testing your report design, you should also test the printing of your report. Figure 13-31 shows a print preview of the first page of the Product Display report. You can see six records displayed. There are a number of things still to do to complete the report.

Obviously, the Picture needs to be changed so that it displays all of each car. Currently, the default Clip view is set. You will need to change that. But that is not the major problem. The report is very boring, plain, and not something you want to give to anyone else. If your goal is to just look at the data, this report is done. However, you need to do more before you are really done.

Although the report has good data that is well organized, it is not of professional quality. To make a report more visually appealing, you generally add some lines and rectangles, possibly some special effects such as shadows or sunken areas if you have a background on the report. You want to make sure sections have distinct areas separate from each other using lines or color. Make sure controls aren't touching each other (because text may eventually touch if a value is long enough). Make sure text is aligned with other text above or below and to the right or left.

In Figure 13-31, you can see some opportunities for professionalism.

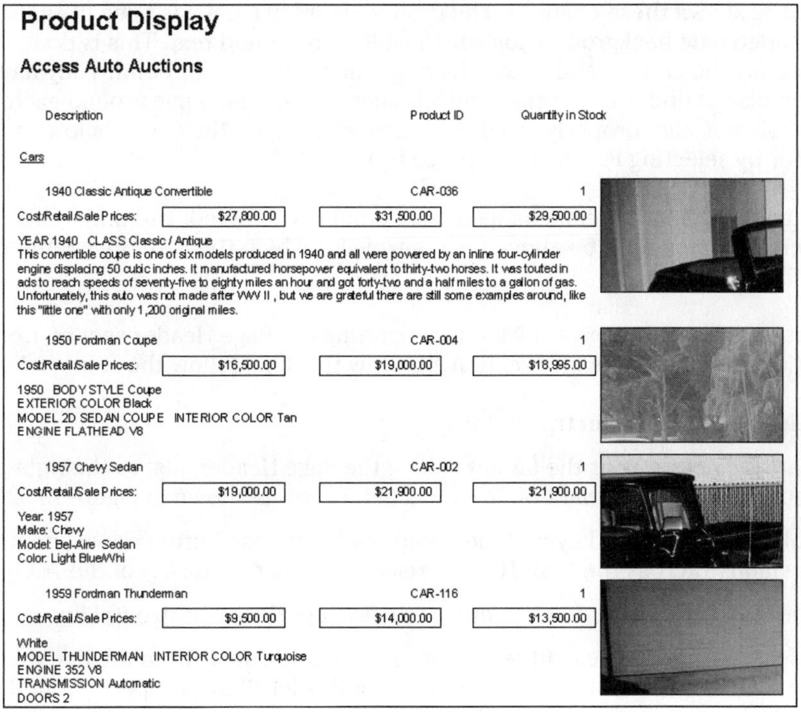

Product Display

Access Auto Auctions

Description	Product ID	Quantity in Stock

Cars

1940 Classic Antique Convertible | CAR-036 | 1

Cost/Retail/Sale Prices: [$27,800.00] [$31,500.00] [$29,500.00]

YEAR 1940 CLASS Classic / Antique
This convertible coupe is one of six models produced in 1940 and all were powered by an inline four-cylinder engine displacing 50 cubic inches. It manufactured horsepower equivalent to thirty-two horses. It was touted in ads to reach speeds of seventy-five to eighty miles an hour and got forty-two and a half miles to a gallon of gas. Unfortunately, this auto was not made after WW II, but we are grateful there are still some examples around, like this "little one" with only 1,200 original miles.

1950 Fordman Coupe | CAR-004 | 1

Cost/Retail/Sale Prices: [$16,500.00] [$19,000.00] [$18,995.00]

1950 BODY STYLE Coupe
EXTERIOR COLOR Black
MODEL 2D SEDAN COUPE INTERIOR COLOR Tan
ENGINE FLATHEAD V8

1957 Chevy Sedan | CAR-002 | 1

Cost/Retail/Sale Prices: [$19,000.00] [$21,900.00] [$21,900.00]

Year: 1957
Make: Chevy
Model: Bel-Aire Sedan
Color: Light Blue/Whi

1959 Fordman Thunderman | CAR-116 | 1

Cost/Retail/Sale Prices: [$9,500.00] [$14,000.00] [$13,500.00]

White
MODEL THUNDERMAN INTERIOR COLOR Turquoise
ENGINE 352 V8
TRANSMISSION Automatic
DOORS 2

Figure 13-31: Print previewing the data.

Adjusting the Page Header

In the Page Header are several large labels. They are too far apart. The column headers are too small and just hanging there. They could be underlined and made one font size larger. Access generally creates controls with 8 point fonts. These are great for screens but awful for people to view in a hard copy report. When you create a Word document, the default font size is 10 point. Most people change their default font size to 12 point because it is more easily readable. You should look at your hard copy report and decide if you need to issue magnifying glasses to people over 40. If so, you might want to enlarge some of your fonts.

Column headers should also be underlined and the entire Page Header should be separated from the Detail section by a line.

If you wanted to add some color to your report, you could make the report name a different color. Be careful not to use too many colors unless you have a specific theme in mind. Most serious business reports use one or two colors, and rarely more than three with the exception of graphs and charts.

Figure 13-32 shows these changes. The Product Display label has been changed to a reverse video blue background color with white foreground text. This is done by first selecting the control and then selecting Blue for the background. They have also been placed under each other and left aligned. The rectangle around each of the controls was also properly sized by double-clicking on the controls lower-right corner (or by selecting Format ⇨ Size ⇨ To Fit).

The column labels have been changed to 11 point text, bolded, and underlined. They were also moved to be above the controls for which they are the column headers.

The next step is to add a nice thick line separating the Page Header section from the chrCategory Group Header section. To draw this line, follow the steps below:

1. Select the Line tool in the toolbox.

2. Start the cursor near the far left side of the Page Header, just to the right and above of the 1 inch mark on the vertical toolbar, as shown in Figure 13-32.

3. Hold down the Shift key and then hold the left mouse button down and drag the mouse across the Page Header, releasing it just to the left of the 7½" mark.

   The Shift key is held down in order to draw a perfectly horizontal line.

4. Select the line and select the number 2 pt line thickness from the line thickness icon on the toolbar, or select the 2 pt Border Width property from the line's Property window.

   The line thickness icon should be next to the Border icon on the formatting toolbar.

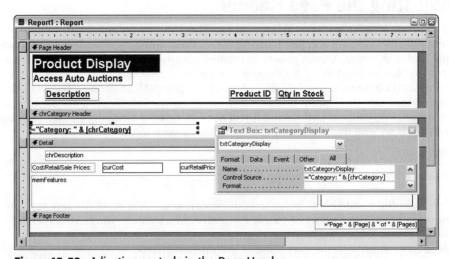

Figure 13-32: Adjusting controls in the Page Header.

Creating an expression in the Group Header

Figure 13-32 also shows that the chrCategory field has been replaced by an expression. If you just place the value of the category in the Group Header section, it looks out of place and may not be readily identifiable. Most data values should have some type of labels to identify what they are.

The expression =“Category: ” & [chrCategory] will display the text Category: followed by a space and then followed by the data value of the chrCategory field. The & symbol (known as the concatenation symbol) joins a string to a data field. Make sure you leave a space after the colon or the value will not be separated from the label. The text control has been bolded, underlined, and the font point size increased as well.

There is one more very important task to complete. If you simply changed the chrCategory text box to the expression and displayed the report, you would have seen an error in the Group Header where the category expression would be. You must rename the control to something other than the original name of the data field. The original control name was chrCategory and that was also the control name. Under standard naming conventions, the control should have been renamed txtCategory, but this may not have been done. When you create an expression using the original text box control and you use the field name in the control, you will cause an error. You cannot name a control the same name as any data field used within the expression itself. This is a limitation of Access. See the Caution below for more information.

Caution When you create a bound control, it often uses the name of the data field as the control name. If you then change the control to an expression using the data field in the expression without changing the name of your control, you will get a #Name or #Error when you display the control on a form or report. You must rename the control to something other than the original field name.

Follow the steps below to complete the expression and rename the control:

1. Select the chrCategory control in the chrCategory Group Header section.
2. Display the Property window for the control.
3. Change the Control Source property to =“Category: ” & [chrCategory].
4. Change the Name property to txtCategoryDisplay.

Changing the picture properties and the Detail section

The Detail section is in fairly good shape. Make sure the Description control is slightly indented from the Category expression in the Group Header. A label should be created, as shown in Figure 13-33, that identifies the values in the Cost, Retail Price, and Sale Price controls.

A line is also good to add to this Detail section to separate one record from another. This is often done when there are multiple lines of a record displayed.

The next step is to add a nice thick line separating each record. Because you don't want two lines at the bottom of each page (you'll be adding a line to the Page Footer next), you will put this line at the top of the Detail section. To draw this line, follow the steps below:

1. Select the Line tool in the toolbox.

2. Start the cursor near the far left side of the Detail section, just to the right and above the ⅛ inch mark on the vertical toolbar, as shown in Figure 13-33.

   You may have to first move all of the controls down in the Detail section to do this.

3. Hold down the Shift key and then hold the left mouse button down and drag the mouse across the Page Header, releasing it just to the left of the 7½ inch mark.

   The Shift key is held down in order to draw a perfectly horizontal line.

4. Select the line and select the number 2 pt line thickness from the line thickness icon on the toolbar or select the 2 pt Border Width property from the line's Property window.

Normally, numeric fields are right aligned. Because they are next to each other horizontally and not above each other vertically, they can be left aligned. Though the repeating groups of records are above each other, they are separated by a wide space and left alignment is okay

One task to complete is to change the Picture control to make the picture fit within the control and to add a shadow to *dress up* the picture and give it some depth. Follow the steps below to complete these tasks:

1. Select the olePicture control in the Detail section.

2. Display the Property window for the control.

3. Change the Size Mode property to Stretch.

4. Select Shadowed from the Special Effect window.

Creating a standard page footer

The Page Footer currently contains a page number control that you created earlier in this chapter. A standard page footer is one that contains things you place at the bottom of all your reports and that your users come to expect.

Although a *Page n of m* control is at the bottom, a date and time control would be nice as well. Many times, you print off a copy of a report and then discover some bad data. You correct the values, print off another copy, and discover you can't tell them apart. Having a print date and time solves this problem.

To create a date/time control, follow the steps below:

1. Select the TextBox control in the Toolbox.

2. Select the Page Footer section and create a text box control near the left edge.

   A text box control should appear with an attached label.

3. Delete the attached label.

4. Display the property window for the control.

5. Enter =**Now()** into the text box's Control Source property.

   This displays the current date and time when the report is run. If you use the Date() keyword, you would only get the current date and not the current time.

6. Select General Date from the control's Format property.

7. Select *Align Left* text from the formatting toolbar for this control.

   This control should have its text left aligned, but make sure the page number control contains right-aligned text.

The last step is to move the controls down a little from the Page Footer section band and add a line between the Page Header section band and these controls:

1. Select both the date and page number controls and move them down ⅛ inch.

2. While they are selected, press the Italic icon on the formatting toolbar.

   An italicized page footer looks more professional.

3. Select the Line tool in the toolbox.

4. Start the cursor near the far-left side of the Page Footer, just to the right and above the ⅛-inch mark on the vertical toolbar, as shown in Figure 13-33.

5. Hold down the Shift key and then hold the left mouse button down and drag the mouse across the Page Header, releasing it just to the left of the 7½" mark.

   The Shift key is held down in order to draw a perfectly horizontal line.

6. Select the line and select the number 2 pt line thickness from the line thickness icon on the toolbar or select the 2 pt Border Width property from the line's Property window.

   Your screen should look like the one shown in Figure 13-33. The Print Preview for this report is shown in Figure 13-34.

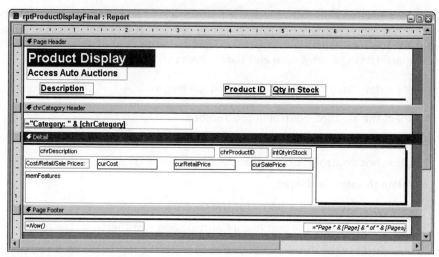

Figure 13-33: Adjusting controls in the Detail and Page Footer sections.

If every even-numbered page is blank, you accidentally widened the report past the 8-inch mark. If you move a control to brush up against the right page-margin border or exceed it, the right page margin increases automatically. When it is past the 8-inch mark, it can't display the entire page on one physical piece of paper. The blank page you get is actually the right side of the preceding page. To correct this, make sure that all your controls are within the 8-inch right margin; then drag the right page margin back to 8 inches.

Saving your report

After all the time you spent creating your report, you'll want to save it. It is good practice to save your reports frequently, starting as soon as you create them. This prevents the frustration that can occur when you lose your work because of a power failure or human error. Save the report as follows:

1. Select File ⇨ Save. If this is the first time you have saved the report, the Save As dialog box appears.

2. Type a valid Access object name. For this example, type **rptProductDisplayFinal**.

3. Click OK.

If you already saved your report, Access saves your file with no message about what it is up to.

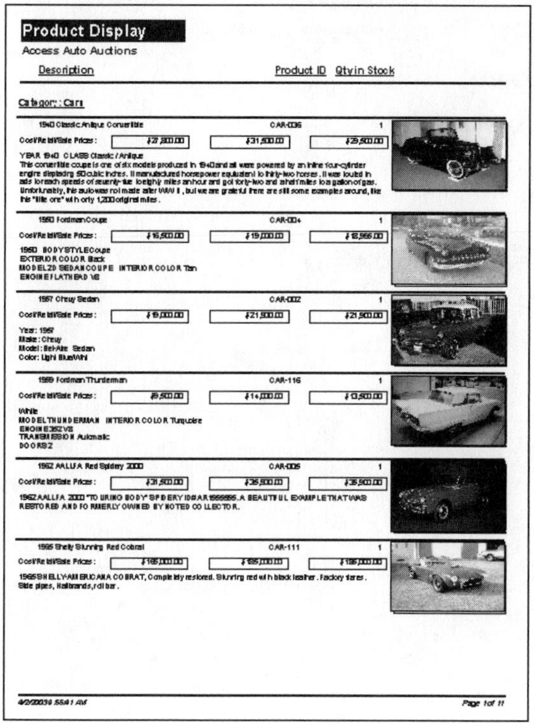

Figure 13-34: Print Preview of the Final Products Summary Report.

✦　　✦　　✦

Working with Subforms

On the
CD-ROM

This may be one of the most important chapters in this book. You will learn more in this chapter about creating the types of forms developed in serious Access applications than in any other chapter. You will learn how to create a complex form type report integrating multiple subforms and data from many different tables. You will also learn how to create totals within subforms and then how to use these totals in the main form. This chapter will use a sales invoice to teach you these concepts.

If you are following the examples, open the Chap14Start. mdb database file on the CD-ROM that comes with this book and follow the instructions in each section of the chapter.

Subforms and subreports give you great flexibility in displaying and entering data with multiple tables. By using parent-child form properties, you can still edit all the fields without worrying about data integrity problems. With a subform, you can even enter and edit data into a one-to-many form relationship. Subforms are important because they let you create forms that bring data together from multiple tables or even multiple records within a single table.

What Is a Subform?

A subform is simply a form within another form. It enables you to use data from more than one table in a form; you can display data from one table in one format while using a different format for data from the other table. You can, for example, display one contact record on a form while displaying other contact records on a datasheet or continuous format subform.

Although you can edit multiple tables in a typical form, using a subform gives you the flexibility to display data from several tables or queries at one time.

As you may recall, you can display data on a form in several ways:

✦ **Form.** Display one record on a form.

✦ **Continuous.** Display multiple records on a form.

✦ **Datasheet.** Display multiple records using one line per record.

Including a subform on your form enables you to display your data in multiple formats, or you can display data from multiple tables. Figure 14-1 shows the Sales Invoice form. There are two subforms in this form. The main form uses data from the tblSales table. The first subform in the middle of the parent (main) form lists the product selected for the sale. This data is copied using VBA code from the tblProducts table, although the data in the subform is actually bound to the tblSalesLineItems table. The second subform at the bottom of the form is used to enter payments for that invoice. The data is stored in the tblSalesPayments table. Notice that both the form (at the bottom) and the line item subform (in the middle of the form) have record selectors; each acts independently. One shows the number of invoices and the other shows the number of line items for the current form.

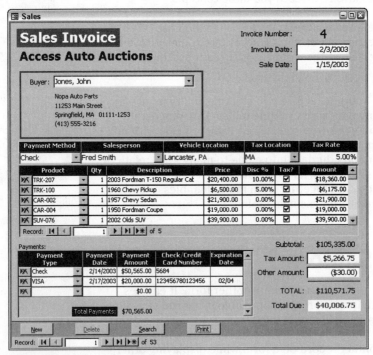

Figure 14-1: The Sales Invoice form.

When you create a subform, you link the main form to it by a common field of expression. The subform will then display only records that are related to the main form. The greatest advantage of subforms is their capability to show the one-to-many relationship. The main form represents the one part of the relationship; the subform represents the many side.

The data comes from a variety of tables. Some are the primary tables used on the form, while others are used as lookups to retrieve data to be copied to the primary tables.

Understand the data for the sales example

In Figure 14-2, you can see a database diagram. This data is used in various parts of the Sales Invoice form (frmSales).

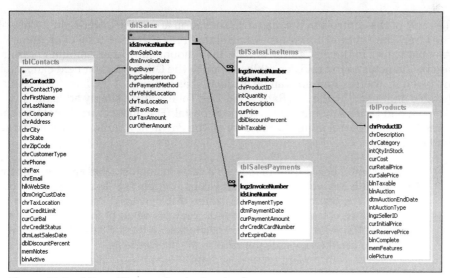

Figure 14-2: A Data Diagram for the Invoice form.

The tblSales table stores the data in the main part of the Sales Invoice form. This includes the Invoice Number, Invoice Date, and Sale Date (Invoice Date is the date you bill the customer, and Sale Date is the date the sale took place). The Buyer combo box control is used to look up name and address data in the tblContacts table. When a contact is selected in the combo box, the name and address information is displayed in the controls below. Only the ContactID information is stored in the tblSales table. Notice the relationship line between tblSales and tblContacts. The field in tblContacts is named idsContactID, while the value is stored in the lngzBuyer field in tblSales. As long as the data types are the same, a relationship can be made.

Note   Relationships do not have to be made using the Relationships window in Access. You can create temporary relationships using queries or implied relationships using controls, combo boxes, subform controls, or VBA code. You will see many examples of this throughout the book.

Five fields near the top of the Sales Invoice form just below the Buyer information display data stored in the tblSales table. The fields Payment Method, Salesperson, and Tax Location use values that are retrieved from tblPaymentType, tblSalesperson, and tblTaxRates, respectively. Although they are not shown on the diagram because there are no real relationships created or implied, the combo boxes do retrieve and place information into the tblSales fields when the Sales Invoice is created. The vehicle location field is simply typed in without any requirements for data validation. The Tax Rate field is automatically retrieved from the tblTaxRates table when the Tax Location is selected using the combo box. Because the data is copied from the tax rates table to the tblSales table, it can be changed. This process is known as *overriding* a value.

The rest of the controls in the main frmSales form are at the lower-right corner of the form. The Subtotal control is a control that references the total of all the Amount values in the first subform. The Tax Amount and Other Amount controls are bound fields to the tblSales table. Although the Other Amount field can simply be typed in, the Tax Amount can be calculated as the sum of the line items that are taxable multiplied by the Tax Rate value. The Total control simply adds the Tax Amount and Other Amount values to the Subtotal. The final control Total Due calculates the Total control minus the total of all the Payment Amount values in the second subform.

Note   When a combo box is used to look up a value in another table and the property *Limit to List* is Yes, you can only select values from the list. By using a combo box control for the tax location, you guarantee that only valid tax locations can be selected. Later, you will use VBA code to copy the value of the dblTaxRate field from the tblTaxRates table to the dblTaxRate field in the tblSales table. When you do this, you can then override the value in the tblSales table.

The sales line item subform is a separate form embedded in the frmSales form. This subform can be looked at in the database window and is the form named fSubSalesLineitems. The *fsub* prefix indicates the form is a subform. Notice that the name also includes the word *Sales.* This is part of good naming conventions. fSubSales indicates the subform is used in the main Sales form and the purpose is to show Lineitems.

The tblSalesLineItems table stores the many side of the one-to-many relationship between the sales and sales lineitems. Notice the common key field. The tblSales uses an autonumber data type primary key idsInvoiceNumber and links to the long integer field lngzInvoiceNumber in the tblSalesLineItems table. You will see how to create this relationship between the main sales form and sales lineitems subform.

If you look at the line item subform in the Sales Invoice form in Figure 14-1, you can see the Product column is a combo box. Each line in the sales lineitem subform contains values retrieved from the tblProducts table. When a product is selected in the lineitem subform, VBA code will be used to copy the product's description, price, and taxable status into the tblSalesLineItems table through the controls in the subform bound to the tblSalesLineItems table. The Qty and Disc % columns must be entered and the Amount control is calculated using the formula Qty * (Price * (1-Disc %)).

The Sales Lineitem subform actually would display all of the records in the tblSalesLineItems table for all of the Invoices if it weren't for two properties in the subform control itself. These properties allow you to automatically filter the sub-form records to display only the records where a value in the subform form matches a value in the main form. These control names will be entered into these subform control properties. The fields idsInvoiceNumber from the tblSales table and lngzInvoiceNumber from the tblSalesLineItems table will be used. You will see these properties later in the chapter.

The second subform is used to allow entry and display of the payments for the spe-cific invoice. The tblSalesPayments table stores the many side of the one-to-many relationship between the sales and payments. Notice the common key field in the tblSalesPayments table, which is exactly like the common key in tblSalesLineitems. You will see how to create this relationship separately between the main sales form and sales payments subform. You will look up the Payment Type on the Payments subform from the tblPaymentType table to allow only valid values in the payments.

You will learn how to create the referencing controls and the combo boxes that retrieve information. But before you learn this, you must learn the basics of subforms.

You can create a subform in several ways:

✦ Use the Form Wizard when you create a new form.

✦ Use the Subform Wizard in an existing form.

✦ Use the Subform button in the toolbox and modify control properties.

✦ Drag a form from the Database window to another form.

Creating Subforms with the Form Wizard

The Access Form Wizard can create a form with an embedded subform if you choose more than one table (or use a query with more than one table). If you don't use the Wizard, you have to create both the form and subform separately; then you embed the subform and link it to the main form.

Creating the form and selecting the Form Wizard

The Form Wizard creates both the form and the subform automatically when you specify more than one table in a one-to-many relationship. In this example, you create a form that displays information from the tblSales table on the main form; the subform shows information from the tblSalesLineitems table. To create the form, follow these steps:

1. Create a new form by selecting the Forms object button in the Database window and clicking the New toolbar button.

2. Select Form Wizard in the New Form dialog box and select the tblSales table from the tables/queries combo box, as shown in Figure 14-3.

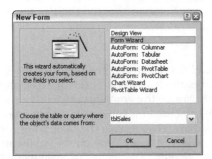

Figure 14-3: Selecting the Form Wizard.

After you select the Form Wizard and the table or query to use for the new form, you need to select the fields for the main part of the form.

Choosing the fields for the main form

You then select each of the fields you want on the main form. The tblSales table will be used for these fields. Figure 14-4 shows the completed field selection. To select the fields for this example, press the >> button to select all of the fields in the tblSales table.

Now you will change the table selected in the Tables/Queries to add the fields for the subform.

Selecting the table or query that will be the subform

Because a subform uses a data source separate from the form, you have to select the table or query to be used on the subform. You do this from the same wizard screen without pressing the Next button. To select another table/query for the form, select the tblSalesLineItems table from the combo box, as shown in Figure 14-5. This table will be used as the Record Source for the subform of the primary form.

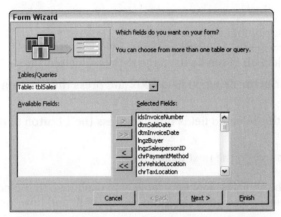

Figure 14-4: Selecting the fields for the main form.

You will notice after a few seconds that the field list below in the Available Fields list box changes to display fields in the tblSalesLineItems table. The fields already selected from the tblSales table in the Selected Fields list box remain.

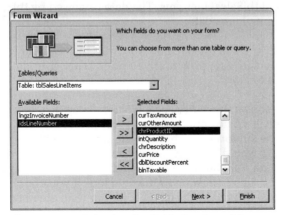

Figure 14-5: Selecting the fields for the subform.

Choosing the fields for the subform

Fields for the subform are selected in exactly the same way as fields for the main form. Those you select from the tblSalesLineItems table will be added to the list of fields already selected from the tblSales table. You want to select all the fields except the first two fields.

To select the fields for the subform, follow these steps:

1. Press the >> button to select all of the fields in the tblSalesLineItems table.

2. Select lngzInvoiceNumber in the Selected fields box and press the < button to de-select it.

3. Select idsLineNumber in the Selected fields box and press the < button to de-select it.

4. Click the Next button to move to the next dialog box.

After you select the fields for the tblSalesLineItems table, you can move to the next wizard screen to decide how the linkage between forms will be built and how the data on the form will look.

Selecting the form data layout

The next dialog box is shown as part of a conceptual diagram in Figure 14-6. A multitable relationship gives you many ways to lay out the data. The top part of the figure shows an automatic decision Access makes on the basis of the one-to-many relationship between tblSales and tblSalesLineItems. The data is viewed by tblSales, with a subform with the tblSalesLineItems data.

On the left side of the dialog box, you can choose how you want to view your form. Below the field view diagram, you can select whether you want to see your data as a Form with subform(s) or as Linked forms.

In the top part of the figure that shows the entire Form Wizard dialog box, you can see the form with a subform: tblSales fields are on the main form, and tblSalesLineItems fields are on the subform. The bottom-left part of the diagram shows conceptually what the data would look like if you viewed the data by tblSalesLineItems instead. The data from both tables would be placed on a single form. The bottom-right part of the figure shows how it would look if you chose to view the data by tblSales but chose Linked forms instead. Rather than creating a tblSales form with an embedded tblSalesLineItems subform, Access would create a tblSales form with a button to display the tblSalesLineItems form.

After you select the type of form you want (the data is viewed by tblSales, with a Form with subform(s) with the tblSalesLineItems data), as shown in the top half of Figure 14-6, you can click the Next button to move to the subform layout screen.

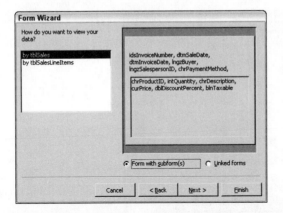

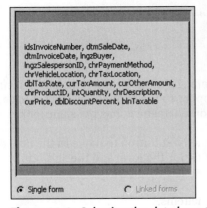

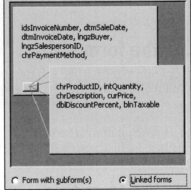

Figure 14-6: Selecting the data layout.

Selecting the subform layout

When you create a form with an embedded subform, you must decide which type of layout to use for the subform. The four possibilities are Tabular, Datasheet, PivotTable, and PivotChart. The datasheet is the easiest, but it may not be the choice you want to accept. Datasheets are rigid by nature; you cannot change certain characteristics (such as adding multiline column headers or precisely controlling the location of the fields below). You should choose a tabular layout for added flexibility. Whereas a datasheet combines the headers and data into a single control type (the datasheet itself), a tabular form places the column headers in a form header section, placing the field controls in the form's detail section. A tabular format creates a Continuous Form layout and also enables you to add any type of control to the subform where datasheets are limited to text boxes, check boxes, and combo boxes.

Select the Tabular layout, as shown in Figure 14-7.

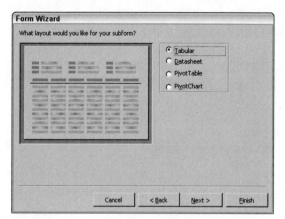

Figure 14-7: Selecting the subform tabular layout.

Selecting the form style

As with other Form Wizards, you can determine how the form will look by selecting one of the AutoFormat choices. The style applies to the main form. The subform, displayed as either a separate tabular form or a datasheet, has the same look.

You can select the Standard style and click the Next button to move to the final dialog box. This box enables you to select the title for the form and the subform.

Selecting the form title

You can accept the default titles (the table names that Access gives the main form and subform), or you can enter a custom title. The text you enter appears in the form header section of the main form. (See Figure 14-8.) Because the default names are the table names, you might want to change the tbl prefix to frm.

When you accept the names (or enter names of your choice), both the form and subform are saved as separate forms; they will appear in the Database window when you select Forms. You should try to name your forms and subforms something similar so that you can tell that they go together. After you complete this step, you can view your form or its design.

Displaying the form

After the forms are named, the screen displays either the form or its design, depending on the option button you choose. In this example, you see the form, as shown in Figure 14-9.

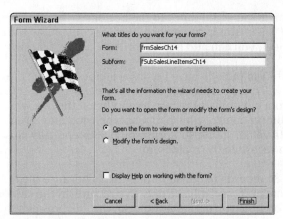

Figure 14-8: Selecting titles for the form and subform.

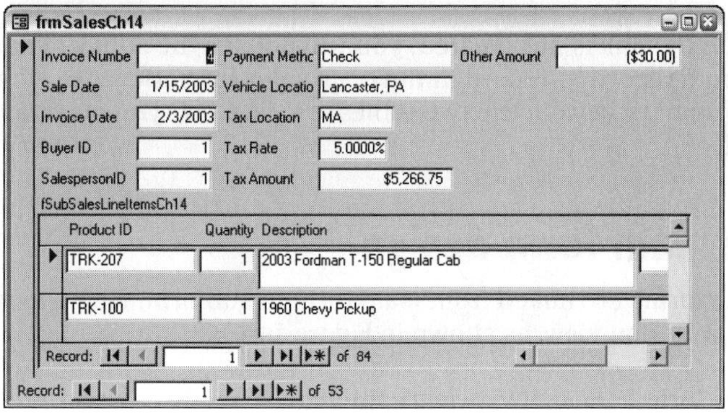

Figure 14-9: The frmSalesCh14 and fSubSalesLineItemsCh14 form.

The tabular form layout was chosen for the subform. Whether you create your sub-form through a wizard, by dragging an already created form to another form or by using the subform tool in the form toolbox, Access creates a datasheet, tabular (continuous) form, PivotTable, or PivotChart. You can change this by changing the Default View property of the subform form to Single Form, Continuous Forms (Tabular), Datasheet, PivotTable, or PivotChart.

As you can see in Figure 14-9, the subform only shows a portion of the fields. The controls need to be resized and rearranged. The main form controls also show data that is cut off (controls that are not wide enough to display the data). You can change the main form and subform all you need to. You can move fields around, adjust column widths, change the formatting, modify the distance between rows, and rearrange columns. When you make these changes, you'll see them in effect the next time you view the subform. If you scroll down to the bottom of the subform, you'll notice that the asterisk (*) appears in the record selector column. As with any continuous form or datasheet, you can add new records by using this row.

Both the main form and the subform initially have record selectors because they are separate forms. Later, you will change this. As you use the outer record selector on the main form, you move from one tblSales record to another. If the link was properly established in the subform control (this happens when common primary keys names are found), the data values in the subform would automatically change when you move from record to record in the main form.

If you notice, the figure shows 84 records in the subform. This is because the link is not yet established. After it is created, you will see only five records in the subform for this main form. Depending on how you create a subform, the link between the parent form and child subform may need to be created manually. You learn how to do this later in the chapter. If your link was automatically created, it is still important to learn how to create a link manually.

In this form right now, if the link is not created, you will not see the subform data change as you move from record to record in the main sales form. Because when the field names in the primary keys in the two tables are different, you may have to create the link manually.

Displaying the main form design

To understand how the forms are linked from main form to subform, view the main form you just created in Design view, as shown in Figure 14-10.

Figure 14-10 shows this form in design view with the link correctly completed. When you first open the form in design view, select the subform control, and display its properties window, the *Link Master Fields* property will be blank if the link is not established.

The design for the main form shows the fields from the tblSales table at the top and the subform control at the bottom. You should be able to see the actual controls from the subform form within the subform control.

Note   If you are used to using any older version of Microsoft Access, you previously saw only a gray box indicating the subform. You had to double-click the subform control to see the subform form itself.

Caution   If you do not use the wizard to create your forms and subforms, you must always first create the form you intend to use as a subform; the main form will not be usable until the subform form is created.

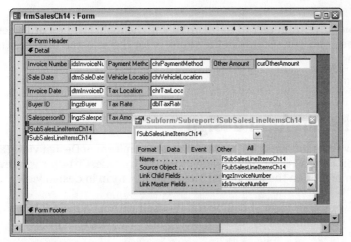

Figure 14-10: The frmSalesCh14 form in design view showing the subform control and its properties.

Linking a form and subform

The Subform control property sheet is also shown. Notice the two properties Link Child Fields and Link Master Fields; these properties determine the link between the main form and the subform. The field name from the main table/query is entered in the Link Master Fields property. The field name from the subform table/query is entered in the Link Child Fields property. When the form is run, the link determines which records from the child form are displayed on the subform.

Tip In previous versions of Microsoft Access before Access 2000, you could double-click the subform and instantly open the subform form. Access 2002 improves this by letting you work with the subform live in the main form. However, the subform control limits the space in which you have to work. You may find it easier to close the main form containing the subform control and open the subform form itself.

Note The subform control is used for both subforms and subreports.

You should now enter the name of the master field link from the tblSales table in the Link Master Fields property. The field to enter here, as shown in Figure 14-10, is idsInvoiceNumber, the name of the primary key field in the tblSales table.

1. Enter **idsInvoiceNumber** into the Link Master Fields property of the subform control.

   Display the form in form view after completing this step. Notice that the number of records in the subform record selector has decreased to only a few records. If you move from record to record using the main form record selector, you will see only the records in the subform for the selected invoice. The link is working!

2. Close the form.

Displaying the subform design

To understand how the subform is built, view the subform form in Design view (as shown completed in Figure 14-11). You should close the frmSalesCh14 (or whatever you named it) form and open the fSubSalesLineItemsCh14 form in design view.

A subform is simply another form; it can be run by itself without a main form. You should always test your subform by itself, in fact, before running it as part of another form.

In Figure 14-11, you can see that all the fields are from the tblSalesLineItems table. You can also create a subform design with fields from multiple tables by using a query as the data source.

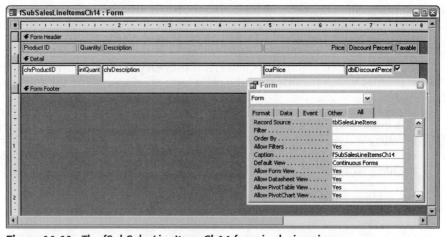

Figure 14-11: The fSubSalesLineItemsCh14 form in design view.

You need to resize the controls in this form to fit within this 5½-inch space including any scroll bars. You also want to move the controls closer to each other to save space and decrease the height of the Description field control. This natural restriction of space in a form is known as real-estate issues and is generally a user interface designer's biggest challenge, just as a home builder's challenge is designing a large home to fit on a small lot.

After rearranging the controls to fit in a smaller space, you also have to adjust the form width by selecting the area running vertically along the right edge of the form where the pointer will change to a double-headed horizontal arrow and move the border line to the left until it intersects the top ruler at a position slightly less than 5.5 inches. This way there is room for a scroll bar.

You also may want to center the labels on all of the controls to more evenly distribute them and change the special effects.

Notice that in the Form property sheet for the tblSalesLineItems subform, the Default View property is set to Continuous Forms. This will print the data in a tabular view, which gives you complete control over how the data looks and also over validation. For this example, you will use the Continuous Forms view. This means that the subform is displayed as a continuous form displaying multiple records, whether it is run by itself or used in a form. You can change it to a datasheet if you want or create a multiple-line form (which would then display its multiple lines on a subform).

 Tip   A subform that will be viewed as a datasheet needs only to have its fields added in the order you want them to appear in the datasheet. Remember that you can rearrange the fields in the datasheet.

 Tip   You can use the form footer of a subform to calculate totals or averages and then use the results on the main form. You learn how to do this later in this chapter.

The Form Wizard is a great place to start when creating a form with a subform. In the next section, however, you learn to create a subform without using a Form Wizard. Then you customize the subform to add combo box selections for some of the fields as well as calculate both row and column totals.

Close this subform, because you will not be using this form or subform again.

Creating the Sales Invoice Form

It is now time to learn how to create the frmSales form you saw in Figure 14-1. Figure 14-12 shows the form that has been created for you as a starting point.

 On the CD-ROM   The form in various amounts of completion will be given to you as a starting point. You will start by opening the form frmSalesExample1 found in the Ch14Start. mdb database file. This will be the starting point for your exercise.

In Figure 14-12 you can see that the main portion of the form without the subforms has been created for you. Actually, not only are both subforms missing (you'll create them later in the chapter), but all of the VBA code has been removed from the form. Additionally, the control references to the subforms in the Subtotal and Total Due along with the calculation in the Total controls have also been removed from the control's Control Source property.

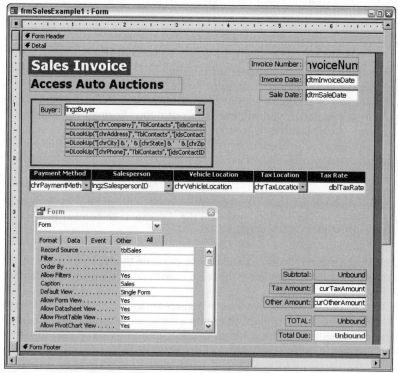

Figure 14-12: The Main frmSales form partially completed.

Creating a combo box that retrieves data

The Buyer combo box is a bound control that stores the value of the lngzBuyer field in the tblSales table. The value is retrieved from the tblContacts table when the combo box is used to display a buyer and his or her company. Figure 14-13 shows the form in its current state with the Buyer combo box control open on top of the form.

You can see in the figure that the combo box has two columns (Name and Company) — or does it? There must be at least three columns because one of the columns must store the value of the lngzBuyer field from the tblContacts table into the tblSales table as the bound field in the combo box. The reality is that there are 11 columns in the combo box. Six columns are actually returned to the combo box, three are on the query grid but not passed back to the combo box control as they are used for sorting, and two more chrContactType and blnActive are out of sight in the figure and are ignored by this example.

Figure 14-14 shows the query behind the Row Source property of the combo box. There are actually six columns in the query that are used in the combo box plus three additional columns used to sort the combo box data in the order of Last Name, First Name, and Company.

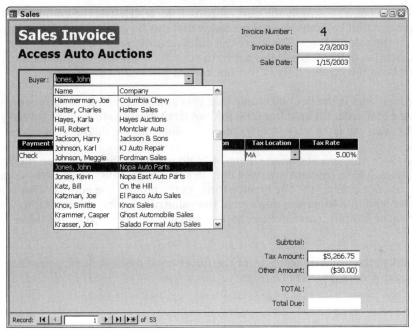

Figure 14-13: The buyer combo box, showing name and company.

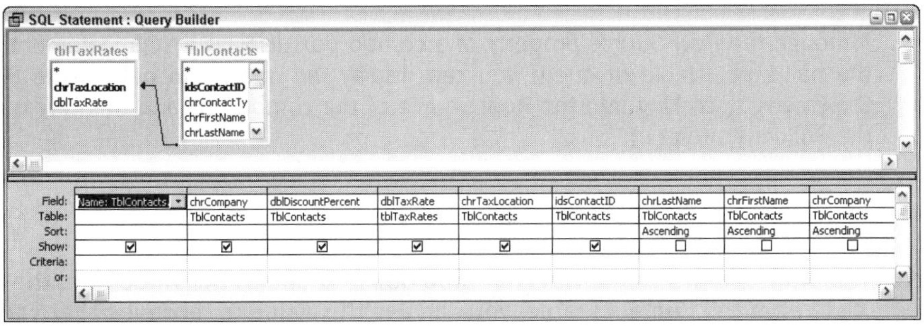

Figure 14-14: The buyer combo box Row Source query.

The first column is one of the visible columns and is a concatenation of the last and first name. The field uses the following expression:

Name: tblContacts.chrLastName & "," & tblContacts.chrFirstName

This concatenates the value of the Last Name field, a comma, a space, and the value of the first name field. The Name: also renamed the column to Name, so that appears at the top of the first column in the open combo box.

The second column is simply the chrCompany field, which lists the company. The third through fifth columns store three fields that can be used to populate control values on the sales invoice. These are the dblDiscountPercent, dblTaxRate, and chrTaxLocation fields. You will learn how to copy their values from the combo box to controls on the Invoice later in this book when you learn VBA coding.

The sixth column is the bound column that gets stored in the combo box control. This is the idsContactID field from the tblContacts table. By storing this primary key value, you can later retrieve any data you want from the tblContacts table.

The last three columns shown in Figure 14-14 do not have check marks in the Show: check boxes. These columns are used only to sort the data displayed in the combo box but are not available to the Invoice through the combo box control. This is a common technique when you don't need the value of the control but want to use it for sorting or filtering. Later in this chapter, you will see a reason to use these fields.

If you look at the property window for the Buyer combo box control, you will see the Column Widths property displays:

1.25";2";0";0"; 0";0"

This means that only the first two columns (Name and Company) are displayed. The other columns are hidden, although they are available to the form by referencing them with the Column method, as you will learn later in this chapter.

Tip   Although the Row Source property of a combo box displays a SQL Statement or the name of a table or query, you can display the query grid behind the SQL Statement by clicking into the Row Source of the combo box and then pressing the Builder button (...).

Displaying data from another table in a form

After you have completed the Buyer combo box that places the value from the Buyer field from the Contacts table, you can use this value to retrieve other values from the Contacts table. There are several ways to do this.

The first way is to use a function to retrieve the value and display it in the combo box. In this example, there are four text boxes that display the company, street address, city/state/zip, and phone number. All of these values can be looked up in the tblContacts table when the user has selected. Figure 14-12 showed these text boxes in design view, while Figure 14-15 shows these text boxes displayed on the form in form view.

> **Tip**
>
> Functions are built into Microsoft Access that let you perform a wide variety of tasks. Functions generally have options known as *parameters*. Functions are *called* by simply using their names and passing from 0 to unlimited parameters to the function. The function performs its calculations and generally returns a single value. A simple function could be Max(12,16), which would return the maximum value of 12 or 16. Obviously, the returned value would be 16.

Using a DLookup function

The DLookup function can be used to look up any one field value in a table. To look up the value of the Company field, you would enter the following expression in the first text box below the combo box control:

=DLookup("[chrCompany]", "tblContacts", "[idsContactID] = [lngzBuyer]")

DLookup is a function that contains three parameters. These parameters include:

✦ Field value to return from the specified table (can also be any valid expression)

✦ Table or Query name where the field is found

✦ String Expression with the criteria to use

The example above states to return the value of the chrCompany field from the tblContacts table where the value of the idsContactID field (from the tblContacts table) equals the value of the lngzBuyer field (which is stored in the cboBuyerID combo box control in the form).

As you can see in Figure 14-15, when the form is viewed, there are four text boxes with DLookup expressions (as shown in Figure 14-12). The third text box uses a compound expression that looks up several fields at one time.

=DLookUp("[chrCity] & ', ' & [chrState] & '   ' &
[chrZipCode] ","tblContacts","[idsContactID]=[lngzBuyer]")

This expression retrieves the values of the chrCity, chrState, and chrZipCode fields from the tblContacts table, concatenates them together, and produces the expression. Because all the fields come from one table and from one record criteria, a single DLookup could be used. Suppose you needed to get the chrState value from a fictitious table named States. The other two fields were in the tblContacts table. You could create an expression with three separate DLookups:

=DLookUp("[chrCity]","tblContacts","[idsContactID]=[lngzBuyer]")

 & "," &

DLookUp("[chrState]","tblStates","[idsContactID]=[lngzBuyer]")

 $ "" &

DLookUp("[chrZipCode]","tblContacts","[idsContactID]=[lngzBuyer]")

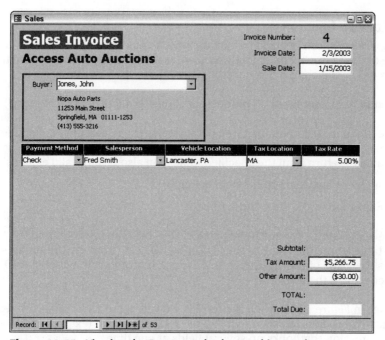

Figure 14-15: Viewing the Buyer combo box and its text boxes.

This concatenated expression joins the value of chrCity from the tblContacts table with a comma and space, and then concatenated with the value of chrState from the tblStates table (remember, this one doesn't actually exist) with a comma and space, and then concatenated with the value of chrZipCode from the tblContacts table.

The DLookup function is used extensively in Access applications, but it is not the best function to use. DLookup is known as a Domain Function. This means that it works against a set of data. When your data files are small, it is a great function. However, when there is a large number of records in the table from which you are retrieving data, the speed of the application could be abysmal. There are much better ways to retrieve data from a table than by using a DLookUp most of the time.

One such way, of course, is using VBA code, and you will learn how to do that in later chapters. Another way without programming is to use the Column method of a combo box. The cboBuyerID combo box control bound to the field lngzBuyer provides this opportunity.

Using the Column method of a combo box

To show you an example of this, consider the first text box below the combo box. This control currently uses a DLookup to retrieve the value of the chrCompany field from the tblContacts table. This means that when you select a value from the combo box control (that is already populated with values from the tblContacts table), the DLookup goes back out to the tblContacts table and retrieves the values again. This is very inefficient, and if there are a lot of records in the tblContacts table, it could be very time consuming.

Because the value of chrCompany is already in the combo box control in one of the columns, why not just retrieve it from the combo box? The Column method of the combo box enables this. The Column method allows you to reference one value in a control from another. To change the first text box from a DLookup to a Column method, follow the steps below:

1. Select the first text box under the combo box control.

2. Display the property window.

3. Replace the Control Source with =[cboBuyerID].Column(1).

Figure 14-16 shows this text box completed.

Note   Only combo boxes can be referenced with the Column method.

Make sure you use the name of the combo box, not its displayed Control Source. The combo box is named cboBuyerID. Even though the field name lngzBuyer is displayed in design view, that is the bound Control Source of the control, not its name.

The Column() method references a column in the combo box. The columns are numbered starting from 0. This is important. The numbering starts at 0. In this example, the first column (Column 0) is the First and Last name. The second column (Column 1) is the Company. Therefore, the column reference is to column(1). A period separates the control name from the Column() method.

Caution   Numbering starts at 0 when referencing a column of a combo box.

Later in this book, you will learn how to copy the value from one control or field in a table to another using VBA program code. This would keep the control editable because the Control Source would still be bound to a field in the form's Record Source, not a reference to another control.

Caution   When any control contains a reference to another control for a Control Source, it becomes read only; you can't change the value in the control.

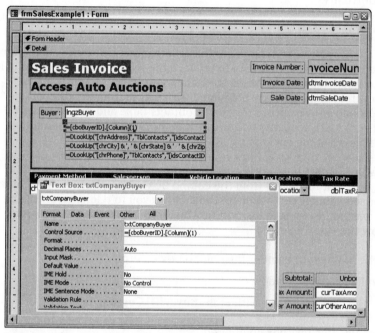

Figure 14-16: Using the column property in a text box.

Creating a Subform Without Wizards

As previously discussed, there are several ways to create a subform without wizards. You can drag an already created form from the Database window to a form, or you can use the Subform tool in the toolbox. The most desirable way is to drag the form from the Database window after you've already created it, because Access will try to create the links for you.

In this portion of the chapter, you'll work with only the frmSalesExample1 that you used in the last part of this chapter as a main form.

Working with Continuous Form subforms

You will use the form fsubSalesLineItemsExample1 as a subform. It has already been created for you as a starting point. You can see this subform in Figure 14-17.

As you can see in Figure 14-17, the subform is simply a form with a group of controls arranged horizontally. The property window is displayed. The Record Source of the form is the tblSalesLineItems table, which contains the line items for the Invoice form. Notice that the Default view is Continuous Forms. This means that the form will display multiple records when it is viewed. This is the setting you generally want in a subform that will display multiple records as the sales line item display needs to be.

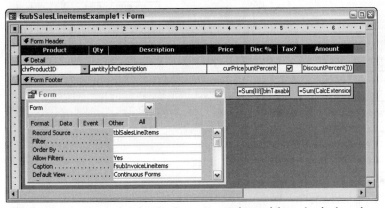

Figure 14-17: The fsubSalesLineitemsExample1 subform in design view.

Creating column labels in the form header

The Form Header of this form is created with a series of label controls. Each control's background color is set to black and the text color is set to white to give a nice highly contrasted look for the column headers. When creating this type of look, you need to be careful that your borders precisely overlap to create a clean thin look to the border lines.

Creating controls in the detail section

The detail section contains eight controls that provide the information needed for the invoice line items. The first control is a combo box that displays the Product ID, Description, Retail Price, Taxable status, and Quantity in Stock, as shown in Figure 14-18. The bound column of the cboProductID combo box control is the chrProductID field in the tblProducts table. You can see this information in the property window in Figure 14-18.

Tip

The width of an open combo box can be larger than the closed combo box control when you use the List Width property.

Figure 14-18 shows this subform being tested by simply viewing it in Form view. Before you worry about embedding the subform in a main form, you should run it by itself to test that it is correctly created. Although some complex forms with VBA code require the form to be embedded to test its visual look, this simple form can conveniently be looked at in Form view.

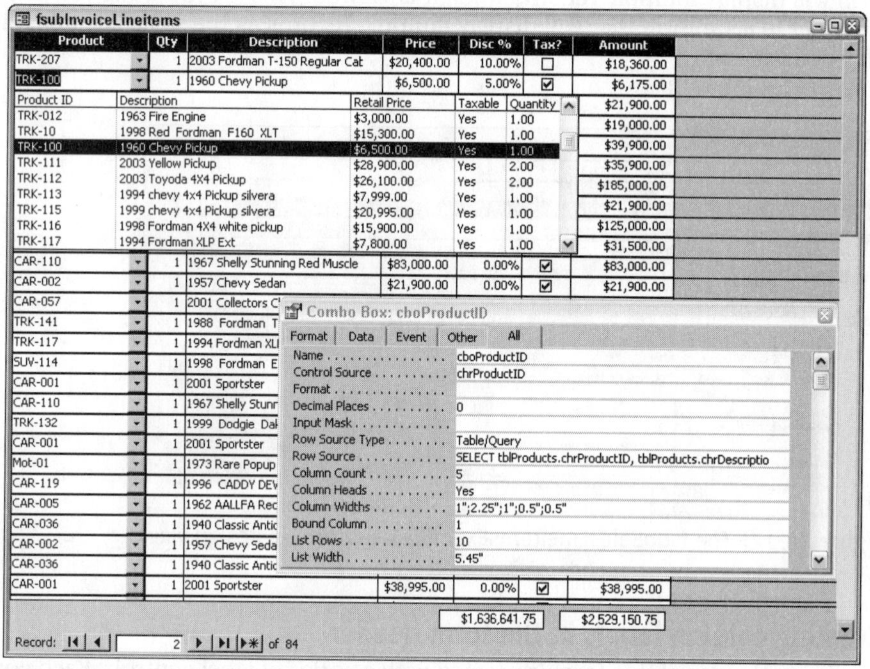

Figure 14-18: The fSubSalesLineitemsExample1 subform in form view.

The Qty control is used by the user to enter the quantity sold. The Description, Price and Tax? checkbox can be automatically filled in by using VBA code to copy the values from the combo box columns using the Column method, as you previously learned. You could simply place column method references in those three controls, but then they would be read only. In this example, you want to be able to make changes to the copied description, price, and tax status. However, because you want to copy the values to the controls for later updating, you must use VBA code. You will learn how to do this working with this example, later in the book in the programming section.

The Disc % column is another control that can be programmed. This value can come from the Buyer record in the tblContacts table. You will also see this later in the book.

One interesting visual task is the area behind the Tax? Check box. There is actually a rectangle with a white background placed behind the checkbox to continue the white look. You could also select a white background for the form's detail section.

Creating a calculated expression

The final control in the Detail section is shown in Figure 14-19. The txtAmount text box is a calculated expression that multiplies the quantity times the discounted price. The actual formula is shown in the property window in Figure 14-19. The calculation is:

=nz([intQuantity],0) * (nz([curPrice],0) * (1-nz([dblDiscountPercent],0)))

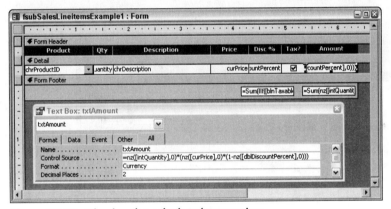

Figure 14-19: Viewing the calculated expression.

Tip

If any of the controls in a calculated expression are null, you might see a #Error or #Name instead of the calculated value. To fix this, you should use the nz (Null to Zero) function preceeding each control that could be 0. You can also set the Default Value of the control or table field to 0, but the 0 could be deleted. The nz precedes the control name, and the .0 comes after it. The .0 tells Access to substitute a 0 for the null value. You could use any number or even a character string in place of the value. Any time you are going to use any field in an expression that could possibly be null, you should use an nz function.

Creating a calculated summary expression

The txtAmount textbox control in the Detail section calculates the amount of a single line, but you can create a total of all the lines in the detail section with a summary expression. Summary expressions are created in the Form Footer section and use the Sum function to do this. If you look in the Form Footer as shown in Figure 14-20, you can see the control named txtItemsTotal. The expression in the control is:

=Sum(nz([intQuantity],0) * (nz([curPrice],0) * (1-nz([dblDiscountPercent],0))))

The =Sum function tells Access to sum all of the values in the continuous form using the expression within the parentheses. In this example, the expression from the detail section is used. Later in the Invoice form, you will create a control that will reference this total in order to show a total of all the line items.

> **Note**   Calculated summaries cannot simply use the name of the control in the Detail section if the control is a calculated expression itself. You must repeat the expression within the summary control.

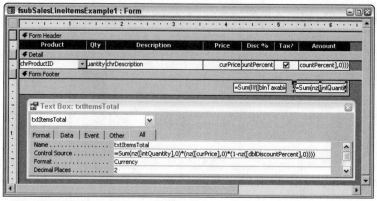

Figure 14-20: Viewing the calculated summary expression.

Creating a filtered calculated summary

The calculated summary expression placed in a footer section allows you to create totals from all records in a detail section. In this example, this allows you to create a subtotal for the sales invoice form. There may be times when you want to create a summary, but only for selected records. In this example, you can see in the invoice that there is a taxable indicator (checkbox) in each record. There is also a tax rate in the main part of the invoice, and below the subtotal control is a tax amount. In order to calculate the tax amount, you have to multiply the tax rate by the taxable amount.

The *taxable amount* is the subtotal of all taxable line items only. A taxable line item is a line item (record) where the tax checkbox is checked.

The control txtTaxableTotal, shown in Figure 14-21, totals all of the line items where the tax check box is true. This expression — albeit quite long — combines the Sum function and the expression you saw previously created with an IIF function (immediate IF).

The Immediate IF (IIF) function lets you make a binary (true false) decision within an expression. Suppose you want to evaluate whether an item is taxable; if it is taxable, you want to display the word "Yes" in a control, and if it is not taxable, you want to display the word "No." You could create the following simple expression:

=IIF([blnTaxable] = True,"Yes','"No")

The IIF function reads programmatically "If the field blnTaxable = True, Then return a value of "Yes" to the expression, Else return a value of "No." It is a way to introduce programming logic within an expression without using VBA coding. The IIF function is one of the most versatile functions used in Access.

In Figure 14-21, the expression is a little longer, but no more complicated. The following expression sums the quantity times discounted price, where the value of the blnTaxable field is true:

=Sum(IIF([blnTaxable = True,nz([intQuantity],0) * (nz([curPrice],0) *
    (1-nz([dblDiscountPercent],0))),0))

This calculates a taxable total (a total of the taxable items). This total can then be multiplied by the customer's tax rate to calculate the tax on the invoice. You will see this used later in the chapter.

> **Tip**
>
> You can combine multiple IIF statements in the same expression to create logic that is more than a single binary comparison. Two IF statements give you three comparisons, while three IIF statements together give you four comparisons. For example, suppose you have a field called chrCarModel that you want to display a different value in an expression based on three possibilities. You could code the expression like this:
>
> =IIF(chrCarModel="Mustang","Car",IIF(chrCarModel="Explorer","SUV","Minivan"))
>
> This would first check to see if the value was "Mustang", and if it were true, it would return the value "Car" to the expression. If it were false (not equal to Mustang), another comparison would be made to see if the value of chrCarModel was "Explorer." If this were true, the expression would be set to "SUV," and if it were not "SUV," no matter what the value of chrCarModel was, the expression would be set to "Minivan."

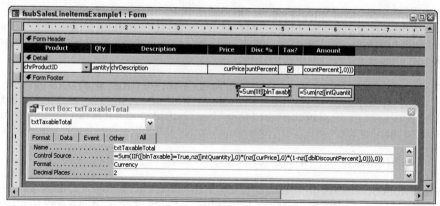

Figure 14-21: Viewing the filtered calculated summary expression.

Hiding a form section

If you display the form in form view as currently completed, you will notice that you can see the values in the form footer, as previously shown in Figure 14-18. Notice that the taxable total control on the left of the form footer is less than the subtotal control field. This is because not all of the line items are taxable.

Though this is good for testing to make sure the expressions are correct (you should hand calculate some of the line items and the totals to make sure they work as well), you do not want the totals visible on the form when it is used as a subform.

To hide the controls in the form footer, you could change each of the control's visible properties to No, but that would still leave the footer visible in the subform. To hide the form footer, you simply change the Visible property of the form to No. This will hide the form footer and the controls in it.

To hide the form's footer section:

1. Make sure the fSubSalesLineItemsExample1 form is open in Design view.

2. Display the Property window.

3. Select the Form Footer section.

4. Change the Visible property to No.

   This will hide the Form Footer section.

The form is now complete and ready to be integrated into the main form. In the next part of this chapter, you will place this form into the main form and create references to the subform form footer controls.

Adding the subform to the main form

After the subform is complete, you can add it to the main form. The easiest way is to display the main form in a window and then drag the subform to the main form. This action automatically creates the subform object control and potentially links the two forms.

To add fSubSalesLineItemsExample1 to the frmSalesExample1 form you're using as the main form, follow these steps:

1. Display the frmSalesExample1 form in a window in Design view so that you can also see the Database window.

2. Display the Form objects in the Database window.

3. Click the form name fSubSalesLineItemsExample1 and drag it to the frmSalesExample1 form, as shown in Figure 14-22. Let the cursor go just under the Payment Method control near the left border of the form. If you do that, it will fit perfectly on the form.

Tip   When you create a form that will be used for a subform, make sure the subform form will fit within the width of the main form.

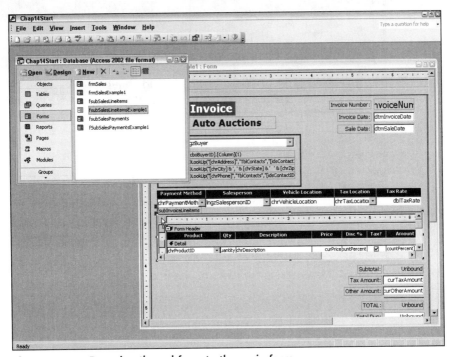

Figure 14-22: Dragging the subform to the main form.

4. Delete the label that is automatically added with the subform control (you can find this between the subform control and the Payment Method control above it on the far left of the screen).

You should switch to Form view to check the placement and size of the control. If you see four records in the subform, as shown in Figure 14-23, your control is sized properly.

You can also tell if your link has been automatically established. Notice the record counter just below the subform. If it contains a lot of records, the link is missing or incorrect. If there are only a few records, the link is working. If you change the main invoice record, you will see the records in the subform change if the link is correct.

5. If the subform control needs to be resized, make the changes to the subform control so that it fits onscreen as shown in Figure 14-23.

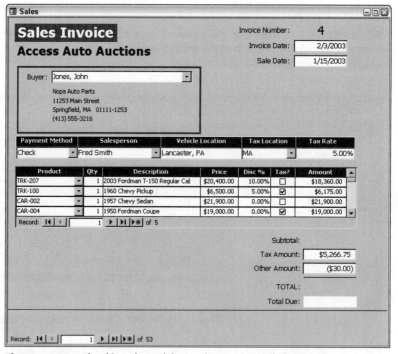

Figure 14-23: Checking the subform placement and size.

Tip

Sometimes, to resize a control properly, you must display it in form view, note the height or width to change, switch to design view, make your changes, and then start the process over again. You should not feel that this is design by trial and error; it's a perfectly normal development process.

The next step is to make sure that the subform correctly figured out the link between itself (the tblSalesLineItems table) and the main form (the tblSales table).

6. Display the property window for the subform control to see if there was an automatic link. If not, you will manually link the fields.

The property window form should look like the one shown in Figure 14-24. The Link Child Fields and Link Master Fields sections should be correctly filled in. You can see the field lngzInvoiceNumber in the Link Child Fields property (which is the primary key in the *tblSalesLineItems* table) and the field idsInvoiceNumber in the Link Master Fields property (which is the primary key in the *tblSales* table).

The main form (Master) and the subform (Child) are linked because the primary keys were compatible for both the tables (both were long integers, while the tblSales key was actually an AutoNumber, which is also a long integer). Sometimes Access cannot automatically link the primary keys. This is especially true when the link involves a multiple key field primary key. The next part of this chapter discusses manually linking these fields.

```
Subform/Subreport: fsubInvoiceLineItems                    ☒

fsubInvoiceLineItems              ⌄

Format  │ Data │ Event │ Other │  All

Name . . . . . . . . . . . . . . .  fsubInvoiceLineItems            ▲
Source Object . . . . . . . . .  fsubSalesLineItemsExample1
Link Child Fields . . . . . . . .  lngzInvoiceNumber          …
Link Master Fields . . . . . . .  idsInvoiceNumber
Status Bar Text . . . . . . . . .
Visible . . . . . . . . . . . . . .  Yes
Display When . . . . . . . . . .  Always
Enabled . . . . . . . . . . . . . .  Yes
Locked . . . . . . . . . . . . . .  No
Tab Stop . . . . . . . . . . . . .  Yes
Tab Index . . . . . . . . . . . .  18                              ▼
```

Figure 14-24: Checking the Master and Child fields link in the subform.

Linking the form and subform

When you drag a form from the Database window onto another form to create a subform, Access tries automatically to establish a link between the forms. This is also true when you drag a form or report onto a report. Figure 14-24 shows that the link was automatically made.

Access establishes a link under these conditions:

✦ Both the main form and subform are based on tables, and a relationship has been defined with the Relationships command.

✦ The main form and the subform contain fields with the same name and data type, and the field on the main form is the primary key of the underlying table.

If Access finds a relationship or a match, these properties show the field names that define the link. You should verify the validity of an automatic link. If the main form is based on a query, or if neither of the conditions just listed is true, Access cannot match the fields automatically to create a link.

The Link Child Fields and Link Master Fields property settings must have the same number of fields and must represent data of the same type. For example, if the tblSales table and the tblSalesLineItems table both have a single field primary fields (one each) that contain the same type of data, it doesn't matter what the field names are.

Although the data must match, the names of the fields can differ. For example, lngzInvoiceNumber is the primary key in the *tblSalesLineItems* table, and the field idsInvoiceNumber is the primary key in the *tblSales* table.

To create the link manually, simply enter the name of each linking field or fields in the Link Child Fields and Link Master Fields property areas. Remember that the master field is in the main form and the child field is in the subform form.

Without the link, if you display the form, you see all the records in the subform's record source in the subform. By linking the forms, you see only the line items for the specific invoice being displayed on the main form.

The last change to make to the form now is to reference the fields to display totals of all the line items in the subform and to calculate the total and subtotals.

Referencing controls in subforms

To create a total of the line items in the subform, you have to create an additional calculated field on the form you're using as a subform. Figure 14-19 showed several controls in the form footer on this form and was discussed previously in the chapter.

By using the form footer, the calculation occurs after all the detail records are processed. When the form is displayed in Single-form view, this total is always equal to the detail record. In Continuous Forms or Datasheet view, however, this calculation is the sum of the processed record.

As shown in Figure 14-25, these controls calculate the sum of the line items and a sum of the taxable line items.

Although the text box control containing the summary was created in the subform, it's displayed by a text box control (which refers to the subform control) placed in the main form. This control is shown in Figure 14-25.

Figure 14-25: Referring to a control in another form.

Because the field is in another form, it must be referred to with the fully qualified terminology. This is called control referencing and means that a control displays a value by referencing a value in another control and even in another form. This also makes that control read only.

```
Object type![Main Form name]![Subform control
name].Form![control name]
```

The object type is either Forms or Reports. In this example, it is a form and Forms will be used.

The main form is named frmSalesExample1 and the subform control name is fsubSalesLineitemsExample1. The control name of the control on the subform is txtItemsTotal.

The .Form means this control path points to another form.

Caution   If your form or subform control is named something different, use your names in place of these.

Although the subform control displays the name of the subform control's Source Object property (the name of the subform form) in design view, you must check the subform control's Name property setting for the actual control name.

To enter the reference to the subform control, enter the following into the Subtotal control's Control Source property. Make sure it looks like Figure 14-25.

As you can see in the property window, the Control Source property is as follows:

```
=[Forms]![frmSalesExample1]![fSubSalesLineItemsExample1]orm]![t
xtItemsTotal]
```

The first part of the reference specifies the name of the form; Forms tells Access that it's the name of a form. By using the ! character, you tell Access that the next part is a lower hierarchy. The dot is used before the Form to tell Access you are now going to another form specified in the subform control. The control name [txtItemsTotal] contains the value to be displayed on the subform. Remember that the reference begins with Forms (plural) and later uses .Form (without the *s*).

Previously in the chapter, you created two summary type controls. One calculated a sum of all line item amounts. The other calculated only the taxable amounts. In the main invoice form, you want to take this taxable amount value and multiply it by the tax rate to calculate the tax. You could do this by referencing the value on the subform (its control name is txtTaxableTotal). If you wanted to do this, you could create a calculated expression in the main invoice form and the txtTaxAmount control would be:

```
=[Forms]![frmSalesExample1]![fSubSalesLineItemsExample1].[Form]
![txtTaxableTotal]
      *   txtTaxRate
```

This multiplies the value of the txtTaxableTotal control by the txtTaxRate value. However, this would make the control read only because it would be a calculated expression. Instead, you can create this calculation in VBA code and then copy the calculated value into the txtTaxRate control. This would allow the customer to override the tax amount as needed. You will see this later in this book. For now, we will leave this field as a simple bound control that must be manually calculated.

Creating a simple calculated control

Sometimes you need to create a calculated control that contains references to controls on the current form only and not to any other forms. The TOTAL control on the invoice form calculates the sum of the Subtotal, Tax, and Other amounts, as shown in Figure 14-26. The txtTotal control needs to contain the following expression:

= [txtSubTotal] + [txtTaxAmount] + [txtOtherAmount]

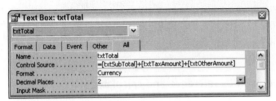

Figure 14-26: Displaying the totals.

As shown in Figure 14-26, enter the expression into the txtTotal control. When you display the form as shown in Figure 14-27, you can see the calculated total.

Caution

Never name the control the same as any controls or fields used in the calculation. If you do, you will receive a #Error or #Name in the control instead of its value when it is displayed.

The rest of this form will be completed in later chapters after you have learned some VBA programming commands.

In the next chapter, you will see how to create reports that display and summarize data including multilevel summaries, complex calculations and formatting, and even percentages.

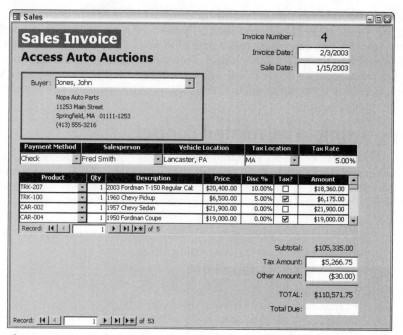

Figure 14-27: Displaying the linked subtotal reference and calculated expression.

✦　　✦　　✦

Creating Calculations and Summaries in Reports

♦ ♦ ♦ ♦

In This Chapter

Creating a full-page report using the sales invoice

Designing a report with multiple group totals

Creating several levels of sorting and grouping totals

Entering and using expressions and functions in text boxes

Using concatenation in text expressions

Calculating sums for each group

Calculating percentages based on group totals

Calculating running sums

Creating a report cover page

♦ ♦ ♦ ♦

In the preceding chapter, you learned to design and build the Invoice form with a series of subforms. You also learned how to create calculated expressions and summary expressions. In Chapter 13, you learned how to create basic reports. In this chapter, you learn to create several new reports using the techniques learned in the previous chapters.

On the CD-ROM

The starting points for both reports you will create in this chapter are included on your CD in Chap15Start.mdb. You will use these reports to complete the examples in this chapter.

Designing a Full-Page Report with Embedded Subforms and Totals

In the first part of this chapter, you create a report that displays information similar to the invoice form. This report displays data in an invoice format that lists the customer, invoice, line item, and payment information. The data is calculated for each line item and summarized for each invoice. The payments are separately summarized and used to determine an amount due.

Figure 15-1 is a sample printed page of the report. The page displays a single invoice record. Later in this chapter, you learn to create summary type reports that list data over time, including individual line-item percentages and cumulative running totals.

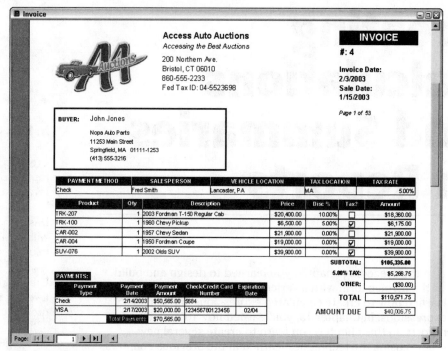

Figure 15-1: The sample Invoice Report page.

Designing and creating the query for the report

The Invoice Report uses fields from the tblSales, tblSalesLineItems, tblContacts, and tblSalesperson tables. Other tables used in the report but not in the report's Record Source include tblSalesPayments and tblCompanySetup.

Unlike the Invoice form, it does not matter if the data is read-only when joined together. This is why the Invoice form uses two subforms. The data in the main portion of the invoice form, the invoice line item subform, and the invoice payment subform are all fully editable. This is an important consideration for data entry forms, which is not important for reports. The report uses the detail section without a subform to display the invoice line items. The payments display will still use a subform because you cannot display two different sets of continuous (multiple line items) data in the Detail section. Because both the Invoice Lineitems and the Invoice Payments are in one-to-many relationships to the Invoice itself, one must be displayed in a subform.

The Record Source of the rptSales report shows the tables necessary for the report joined together. This query is a SQL statement (also saved as a query named qryInvoiceReport) behind the report's Record Source. The tables displayed in the top half of the query window have been resized and moved around to display the relationships properly, as shown in Figure 15-2.

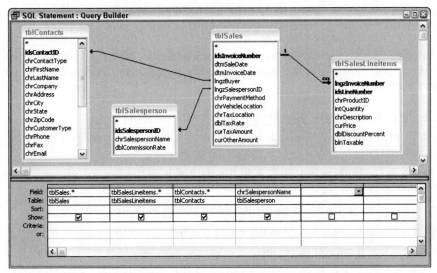

Figure 15-2: The Query Design window for the rptSales Record Source.

As you can see in Figure 15-2 and later in Figure 15-4, fields will be placed on the report from the tblSales table (to fill the top portion of the invoice and the tax and other amounts). Fields from the tblSalesLineItems table are used in the Detail section of the report. Contact information is also used in the top portion of the invoice (but only one contact for each invoice). The tblSalesperson table is used strictly as a lookup, so the salesperson name can be displayed instead of the ID stored in the tblSales table.

After your query is completed, you can create your report.

Cross-Reference Chapter 13 provides a detailed explanation of how to create a new report from a blank form; it also shows you how to set page size and layout properly. Chapter 14 teaches subforms and calculated and summary controls, which are also used in this chapter. If you are unfamiliar with these topics, read Chapter 13 and Chapter 14 before continuing. This chapter focuses on multiple-level groupings, calculated and summarized controls, and expressions in reports.

Designing test data

One of the biggest mistakes that you can make when designing and creating complex reports is to not check the results that the report displays. Because a report only displays the data you give it, you should look at the data created from a report's record source (table, query, or SQL statement).

Before creating a complete report, you should have a good understanding of your data. To check the results, you can simply display the query used for the report. If the report is based on a SQL Statement and not a saved query, you can click on the report's Record Source property and display the query that way.

For this example, you will use the report rptSalesExampleStart as a starting point for this report. To display the data used for the report's Record Source, follow the steps below:

1. Display the report rptSalesExampleStart in design view.

2. Display the Property window and place your cursor in the Record Source property.

3. Press the Builder Button (...) on the right side of the Record Source property area.

   The query grid should be displayed as shown in Figure 15-2.

4. Press the Run button (!) in the query toolbar to run the query.

   Your result should be displayed as shown in Figure 15-3.

   Figure 15-3 shows the query results to use for checking the first report that you create in this chapter. Notice for each repeating invoice group, the Invoice data is the same for the different line items. When joining tables with a one-to-many relationship, the fields on the one side (tblSales) will be the same for each of the many side records, because you are displaying the same record's fields over and over again. The many side (tblSalesLineItems) will be different for each record.

   Figure 15-3 shows the datasheet that's produced by this query; you can compare the results of each task in the report design to this datasheet. Some of the fields in the figure (most notably the line item data) were rearranged to show you the multiple line items for each invoice.

5. Close the query and return to the report design.

Invoice Num	Sale Date	Invoice Date	Buyer ID	SalespersonID	Product ID	Quantity	Description	Payment Method
4	1/15/2003	2/3/2003	1		1	TRK-207	1	2003 Fordman T-150 Regular Cab	Check
4	1/15/2003	2/3/2003	1		1	TRK-100	1	1960 Chevy Pickup	Check
4	1/15/2003	2/3/2003	1		1	CAR-002	1	1957 Chevy Sedan	Check
4	1/15/2003	2/3/2003	1		1	CAR-004	1	1950 Fordman Coupe	Check
4	1/15/2003	2/3/2003	1		1	SUV-076	1	2002 Olds SUV	Check
5	2/27/2003	2/18/2003	18		3	CAR-005	1	1962 AALLFA Red Spidery 2000	Check
5	2/27/2003	2/18/2003	18		3	CAR-111	1	1965 Shelly Stunning Red Cobrat	Check
6	2/24/2003	2/24/2003	33		1	CAR-003	1	1971 Pontanic Red Converible	Check
6	2/24/2003	2/24/2003	33		1	CAR-057	1	2001 Collectors Chevy Corvet	Check
7	4/24/2003	4/24/2003	53		1	CAR-036	1	1940 Classic Antique Convertible	Cash
7	4/24/2003	4/24/2003	53		1	CAR-110	1	1967 Shelly Stunning Red Muscle Ca	Cash
7	4/24/2003	4/24/2003	53		1	CAR-002	1	1957 Chevy Sedan	Cash
8	5/24/2003	5/24/2003	14		2	CAR-057	1	2001 Collectors Chevy Corvet	Mastercard
9	6/1/2003	6/1/2003	59		1	TRK-141	1	1988 Fordman T350 Bucket Truck	Cash
10	7/15/2003	7/15/2003	17		3	TRK-117	1	1994 Fordman XLP Ext	Check
10	7/15/2003	7/15/2003	17		3	SUV-114	1	1998 Fordman Explorer XLP	Check
11	8/25/2003	8/25/2003	41		1	CAR-001	1	2001 Sportster	Visa
12	8/26/2003	8/26/2003	56		3	CAR-110	1	1967 Shelly Stunning Red Muscle Ca	Visa
13	9/25/2003	9/25/2003	52		1	TRK-132	1	1999 Dodgie Dakota Sport	Check
14	9/30/2003	9/30/2003	55		2	CAR-001	1	2001 Sportster	Cash

Figure 15-3: A query for checking data results.

Examining the Invoice report design

Figure 15-4 shows the Invoice report design named rptSalesExampleStart. You should have opened this report in the preceding example. Because, in previous chapters, you have already worked with creating controls using simple expressions and summaries, much of this is already created for you.

Before you start changing this report, you will get an overview of how the report was created and how it differs from the Invoice form.

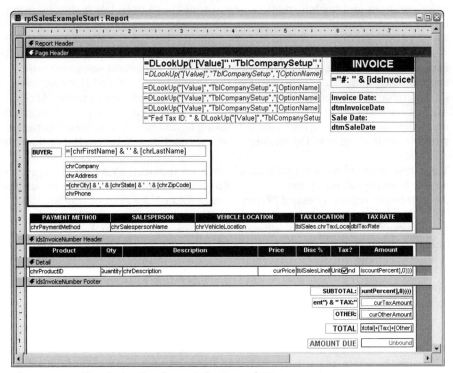

Figure 15-4: The design for the rptSalesExampleStart report.

Creating reports from existing forms

As you know, there are several ways to create a report. One way is to create the report from a blank report design, placing all of your fields as necessary. Another way, if you are creating a report that is based on a data entry form, is to simply right-click on the form in the database window and select Save As from the shortcut menu. You can then give it a name and save it as a Report.

To create this report, the authors actually did that as a starting point. Then many things were changed — some solely to discuss new techniques.

Changes to the Page Header section

The background of the form was changed from standard Windows gray to white. Most reports need to be printed or faxed and white is the best background color for printing or faxing.

The INVOICE label was moved to the upper-right corner of the report and the Invoice Number, Invoice Date, and Sale Date controls were altered slightly.

A block of DLookUp expressions were added to the top of the Page Header. These display your company name (Access Auto Auctions) in this example and the company's address and tax information. These could have been labels, but by using a table to store your information, you could use your system for several companies by simply duplicating your data and changing the Company Setup information stored in the tblCompanySetup table. The tblCompanySetup table follows an interesting format. There is a standard set of fields. The important ones are OptionName and Value. Option Name is the name of the option being entered (for example, CompanyName or Street). Value is the value of the option (for example, Access Auto Auctions or 200 Northern Avenue). By creating a table like this, you can add an endless number of options without having to add new fields. Your DLookUps can pass the desired value of OptionName and the function will return the options value.

The Buyer combo box and text boxes have been replaced by a series of text boxes. Rather than use DLookUp expressions, the control sources of the text boxes linked directly to the report's Record Source is used. DLookUps are notoriously slow because they require a lookup using the entire table. Directly displaying data from a record source is usually more efficient. In this query, the tblContacts table was linked in the query from the BuyerID field providing access to the data in the tblContacts table for the correct record.

The rest of the controls in the bottom of the Page Header section are all text boxes that come directly from the tblSales table.

By placing all of these controls in the Page Header section, they will be displayed at the top of each page of the Invoice if there are more line items than will fit on one page.

Understanding the Invoice Number Header section

The Invoice Number header contains labels for the detail section controls. They are displayed in reverse video (black background color, white foreground/text color). Because the labels are in the Invoice Number Header section, they will only print out once for each invoice, regardless of whether the invoice requires more than one page.

These labels could also have been in the Page Header section. If they are in the Page Header section, they are not repeated if the Invoice has multiple pages due to many line items. If you want the column headers on every page, move them to the Page Header section.

Working with controls in the Detail section

The Detail section contains the line items from the tblSalesLineItems table linked from the tblSales table. If you read previous chapters, you learned that the chrProductID field is selected in the frmSales form from the tblProducts table and the chrDescription, curPrice, and blnTaxable fields are copied from the tblProducts table to the tblSalesLineitems table. Here, they are displayed in the reports Detail section. The value of the dblDiscountPercent field is also displayed from the tblSalesLineItems table.

The Amount column uses the same expression found in the form:

=nz([intQuantity],0) * (nz([curPrice],0) * (1-nz([txtDiscountPercent],0)))

Remember that the nz function converts nulls to 0, so the calculation in the expression will work even if a quantity, price, or discount percent is missing.

Using calculations and expressions in the Invoice Number footer

The idsInvoiceNumber Footer section contains the subtotal of all the line items as well as the tax and other amounts, the grand total, and finally an amount due based on the total amount of payments from a subform you will be adding later in this chapter.

In the next section of this chapter, you will add the Access Auto Auctions logo to the report, add a subform to display and calculate the total payments, and create a new calculation to display the amount due.

Adding an unbound picture to the report

There are two types of unbound picture controls:

✦ **Unbound Object Frame:** An unbound object frame is a control that contains any type of object that is not bound to a table value. This includes pictures, sound files, video files, Word, Excel, or PowerPoint files, or any object that can be linked or embedded within another. Generally, when an unbound object frame is used, the embedded object can be double-clicked on and the source program is launched and the embedded item can be edited.

✦ **Image:** An image control displays pictures without any link to the source documents. You cannot edit the original image but only display it. If you don't need to edit the picture, you should use an image control because it takes less storage space.

Tip

You can create an unbound object control in order to edit the object and later change the unbound object control to an image control when you are through editing the object. This saves a tremendous amount of storage space and makes your database smaller. You change control types by right-clicking on an unbound object control and selecting Change To ⇨ Image from the shortcut menu.

To add an unbound picture, you use either the Unbound Object Frame control, the Image control from the toolbox, or the Insert Picture menu item:

1. Click on the Page Header section so that the control will be added to that section.

2. Select Insert ⇨ Picture from the report menu bar.

   This displays a dialog box that will allow you to select a directory where your picture is and then select the picture.

3. Select the Access 2003 Bible Directory and then the Chapter 15 directory.

4. Select the file AAAuctions.jpg.

   You should see the picture in the Insert Picture dialog box, as shown in Figure 15-5. If you don't see it, click on the Views button in the dialog box and select Preview. You can also select Thumbnails to get a preview.

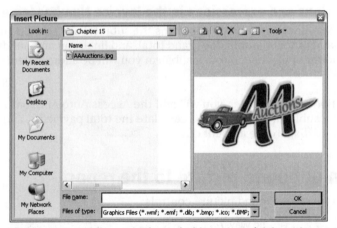

Figure 15-5: Adding an unbound object control (picture) to a report.

5. Click OK.

   The picture should appear and take up the majority of the Page Header section. You need to resize it.

6. Resize the picture by grabbing the bottom-right sizing handle of the control and making it fit in the area between the left ruler and the company information controls.

   Figure 15-6 shows the report after the image has been added.

7. Notice that the picture does not fit within the size of the control. The next step is to change the Size Mode property from Clip to Zoom.

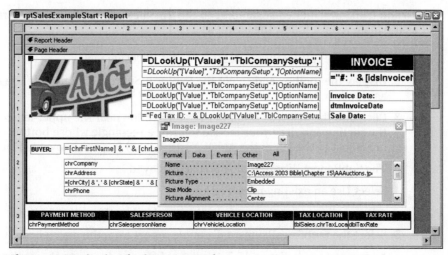

Figure 15-6: Viewing the image control.

8. Click on the image control and display the Property window.

9. Change the Size Mode property from Clip to Zoom.

You can resize the control rectangle to make the picture larger or smaller.

Adding the Payments subform

In this example, you will add the rsubSalesPaymentsExample subreport to the main report.

Note There is no real difference between a subform and a subreport. They both are just objects used in a specific way. A subform is just a form, and a subreport is just a report embedded in another form or report.

Tip You can embed a subform in a report.

You already learned how to drag a form or report from the database window to another form or report to create a subform or subreport. Another way to add a subreport to a main report is to create a subreport control in the correct place and then set the necessary properties. When you create the subreport control, if the subreport record source and the main report record source have a common key, it will potentially link the two reports automatically.

The Subreport wizard will also help you with this when you create a subreport control.

To add fSubSalesLineItemsExample1 to the frmSalesExample1 report you're using as the main report, follow these steps:

1. Display the rptSalesExampleStart report in Design view.

2. Display the toolbox and select the Subform/Subreport control in the toolbox, as shown in Figure 15-7.

3. Click into the idsInvoiceNumber Footer section near the upper-left corner of the section and drag your mouse to draw a rectangle whose bottom-right corner is just to the left of the AMOUNT DUE label (also as shown in Figure 15-7).

   The SubReport Wizard dialog box is displayed.

4. Select Use an existing report or form.

   A list of all forms and reports is displayed below the option button.

5. Select the rsubSalesPaymentsExample report from the dialog box.

   As you can see in Figure 15-7, the list of forms and reports shows the form or report name and the object type.

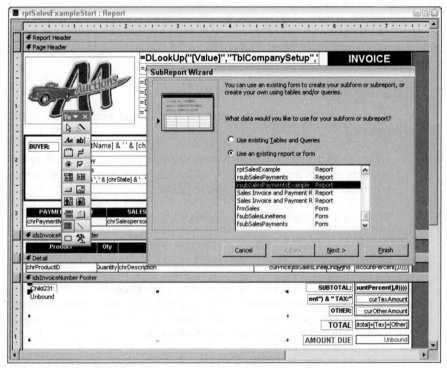

Figure 15-7: Adding the subreport control using the wizard.

6. Press the Next button to select a link between the main report and subreport.

7. Choose Define My Own and select idsInvoiceNumber from the left (Form/report fields) combo box and lngzInvoiceNumber from the right (Subform/subreport fields) combo box.

8. Press the Next button and then the Finish button to accept the default name and complete the subform creation.

   The payments subreport should appear on your report. You may need to resize the subreport and either change or eliminate the subreport label.

9. Resize the Payments subreport so that it looks like the one shown in Figure 15-8.

10. Change the subreport label caption to PAYMENTS and change the background color to black, change the foreground color to white, and make the text bold.

    Your screen should look like the one shown in Figure 15-8. Notice the link in the Property window between the report and the subreport.

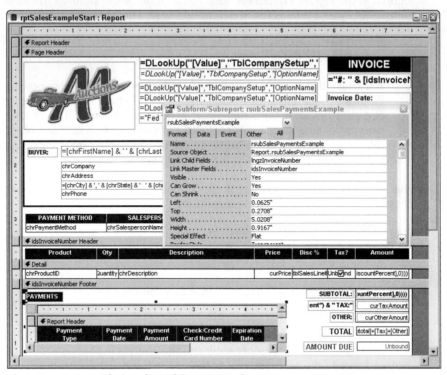

Figure 15-8: Completing the subform control.

Display your report by clicking the Preview button in the toolbar to show that the subreport is in proper size and relationship to the report. Also notice that the link should be working and two payments should be displayed if you are on the first record.

Tip   When you create a report that will be used for a subreport, make sure the subreport report will fit within the width of the main report.

The next step is to reference the control within the subreport to calculate the total payments and amount due of the entire invoice.

Creating a subreport reference to a summary control

You can see in Figure 15-8, in the bottom of the report's idsInvoiceNumber footer, a series of controls.

The SUBTOTAL control uses the Sum function to summarize all of the Amount records in the report's detail section. The formula is the same as the Amounts formula itself, except it uses the Sum function first. The expression is:

```
Sum(nz([intQuantity],0)*(nz([curPrice],0)*
(1-Nz([tblSalesLineitems].[dblDiscountPercent],0))))
```

Tip   You could also have used simply =Sum([txtAmount2]) to reference the control. Which way you reference controls depends on if there are any references where one value has to be calculated before another. Sometimes, when processing large amounts of data, Access gets confused and you will see a zero or a blank where a calculation would normally be. When you use the entire expression for a summary instead of referencing a control, this usually will not happen.

The Tax and Other amounts are simply bound controls from the tblSales table. They are simply listed as text box controls.

The Total control uses the expression =[txtSubtotal] + [txtTax] + [txtOther] to sum the three control values.

The last tax is to create an expression that references the total payments control (named txtTotalPayments) in the Payments subform control (named rsubPaymentsExample).

Figure 15-9 shows this expression in the property window for the txtTotalPayments control. Notice, in the Payments subform, the control in the Report Footer. This control, named txtTotalPayments, contains the following expression:

=Sum(curPaymentAmount)

This can then be referenced as shown in Figure 15-9. The reference is:

=[txtSubtotal]+[txtTax]+[txtOther]–[rsubSalesPaymentsExample].[Report]![txtTotal Payments]

This expression adds the total amounts, tax, and other and then subtracts the total payments. To reference the total payments control in the subreport, you have to use the fully qualified reference to the subreport.

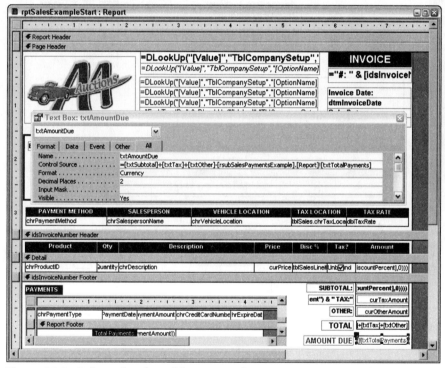

Figure 15-9: Referencing the subform control.

This reference includes:

    Subreportcontrolname.Report!controlnameinthesubreport

The .Report tells Access that it is looking for a report and not a form.

The expression:

[rsubSalesPaymentsExample].[Report]![txtTotalPayments]

references first the subform control named [rsubSalesPaymentsExample], then it uses the .Report to pass to the subreport, and finally it references the control named txtTotalPayments.

When you have completed this Invoice Report, you can view the final Invoice by displaying the report in Print Preview, as shown in Figure 15-10.

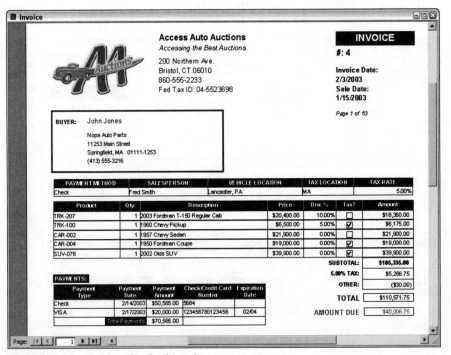

Figure 15-10: Viewing the final invoice report.

Creating a Multilevel Grouping Report with Totals

Besides a form type report, the most common type of report is a columnar report used to analyze data. This type of report can be as simple as a series of rows and columns with no summaries or totals, or a report can be very complex. Figure 15-11 shows a moderately complex report that you will create in the remainder of this chapter. You will learn how to create a complex record source as well as to format data and calculate various totals and percentages.

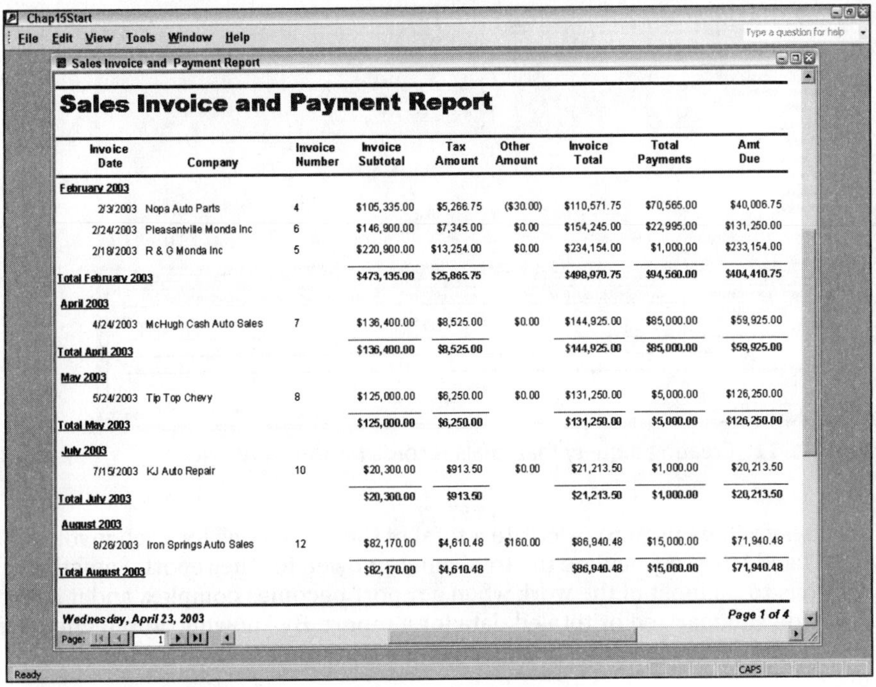

Sales Invoice and Payment Report

Invoice Date	Company	Invoice Number	Invoice Subtotal	Tax Amount	Other Amount	Invoice Total	Total Payments	Amt Due
February 2003								
2/3/2003	Nopa Auto Parts	4	$105,335.00	$5,266.75	($30.00)	$110,571.75	$70,565.00	$40,006.75
2/24/2003	Pleasantville Monda Inc	6	$146,900.00	$7,345.00	$0.00	$154,245.00	$22,995.00	$131,250.00
2/18/2003	R & G Monda Inc	5	$220,900.00	$13,254.00	$0.00	$234,154.00	$1,000.00	$233,154.00
Total February 2003			$473,135.00	$25,865.75		$498,970.75	$94,560.00	$404,410.75
April 2003								
4/24/2003	McHugh Cash Auto Sales	7	$136,400.00	$8,525.00	$0.00	$144,925.00	$85,000.00	$59,925.00
Total April 2003			$136,400.00	$8,525.00		$144,925.00	$85,000.00	$59,925.00
May 2003								
5/24/2003	Tip Top Chevy	8	$125,000.00	$6,250.00	$0.00	$131,250.00	$5,000.00	$126,250.00
Total May 2003			$125,000.00	$6,250.00		$131,250.00	$5,000.00	$126,250.00
July 2003								
7/15/2003	KJ Auto Repair	10	$20,300.00	$913.50	$0.00	$21,213.50	$1,000.00	$20,213.50
Total July 2003			$20,300.00	$913.50		$21,213.50	$1,000.00	$20,213.50
August 2003								
8/26/2003	Iron Springs Auto Sales	12	$82,170.00	$4,610.48	$160.00	$86,940.48	$15,000.00	$71,940.48
Total August 2003			$82,170.00	$4,610.48		$86,940.48	$15,000.00	$71,940.48

Wednesday, April 23, 2003 *Page 1 of 4*

Figure 15-11: Sample Sales Invoice and Payment Report.

You've learned how to create queries in previous chapters and how to create simple reports. You've been exposed to a variety of queries and expressions and learned to use them as record sources for reports. Now you are going to learn a new type of query and learn that a query can use another query (or several queries and tables) to create a record source for a form or report.

In the first example in this chapter, you created a query in the report's recordset (shown in Figure 15-2) that brought together all the fields from the tblSales, tblSalesLineItems, tblContacts, and tblSalesperson tables.

For the most part, the query and report used non-summarized data. The report calculated the amount total for each line item and the subtotal summed those amounts for an invoice total. In this example, the query needs to do all of that work.

Creating a total query

The first query you will need is found in your Chap15Start.mdb database file and is named qryCalculateTotalExtensionsbyInvoice. If you open it in design view, you will see that it looks like the query shown in Figure 15-12.

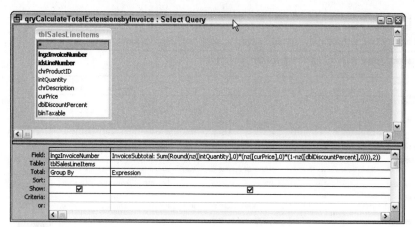

Figure 15-12: Creating a query that totals records for total amounts.

This query will be used to calculate a total of the extensions for each invoice. This will be used later to calculate the total amount owed for the report. Sometimes, the query has to do most of the work when a report becomes complex, and it is better to provide summarized or totaled data for a report. By knowing both techniques, you will be able to make the most productive decision.

The query uses only the tblSalesLineItems table. You might notice that two columns are used in the query. The first column displays a list of Invoice Numbers, and the second column calculates the extension and then summarizes the extensions for each invoice.

You might also notice a row in the query you have not seen before. This is the Total: row, which is a special type of Select query. This type of Select query summarizes data. It also can be used to create averages, minimums, maximums, and several other types of summaries.

A total query is created by first displaying the standard query design screen and then by pressing the total button on the toolbar (looks like an epsilon, Σ) or by using View ➪ Totals from the query menu.

A total query is generally used to summarize all data in a set of records or to summarize (or average) groups of data within a set of records. The Total: row is used to determine if a column is used to group a set of values (in this example, all records that are associated with each invoice number) or to aggregate a set of values (in this example, the total of the expression in the second column).

After the query is changed to a total query, the Total: row is displayed. Because this example only needs the Invoice Number and the total of all the extensions for each invoice number (similar to the subtotal in the last report you created), you only need two columns.

In the first column, the Invoice Number field from the tblSalesLineItems table is dropped on the query design grid. The Group By parameter is selected from the Total: row for that field. This tells the query to group the values by the field (Invoice Number) in the column. What is grouped depends on the other columns.

The second column is the expression:

Sum(Round(nz([intQuantity],0) * nz([curPrice],0) *
(1-nz([dblDiscountPrice],0))),2))

The expression rounds to two decimals the product of quantity x price x 1-discount. This gives the discounted price. The Sum parameter in the Total: row tells the query to sum the values.

Tip
The Round function is used to round a number when more decimals could be created than the field display will allow or is desired. If you have a simple addition or multiplication, you generally don't need to round the result. However, in this example, the discounted price is generally a decimal and this could create a fractional result that would be more than two decimals (pennies). The Round function will round the result back to two decimals.

To understand this better, suppose you didn't have a Total type query and you viewed the data with a simple Select query with just the Invoice Number and the expression above. You would see the total discounted price extension for each line item for each invoice. For example, Invoice Number 4 has five line items. You would see that the discounted price of each of the line items is 18360, 6175, 21900, 19000, and 39900, as shown in Figure 15-13.

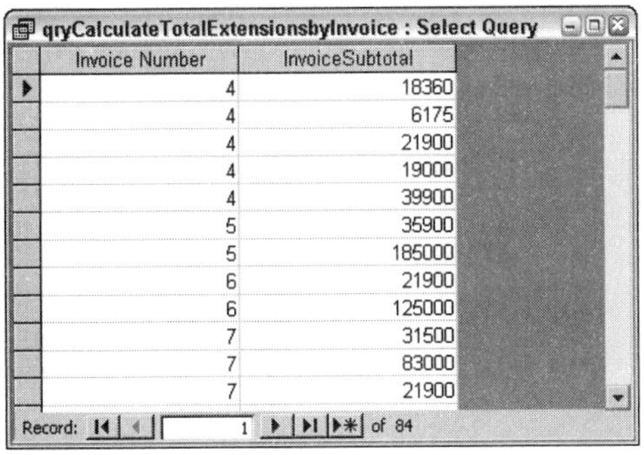

Invoice Number	InvoiceSubtotal
4	18360
4	6175
4	21900
4	19000
4	39900
5	35900
5	185000
6	21900
6	125000
7	31500
7	83000
7	21900

qryCalculateTotalExtensionsbyInvoice : Select Query

Record: 1 of 84

Figure 15-13: A Select query displaying Invoice Number and Extension Amount for each Lineitem.

When you run the total query, you see only one line for each invoice. The five line items for Invoice Number have been totaled, as shown in Figure 15-14.

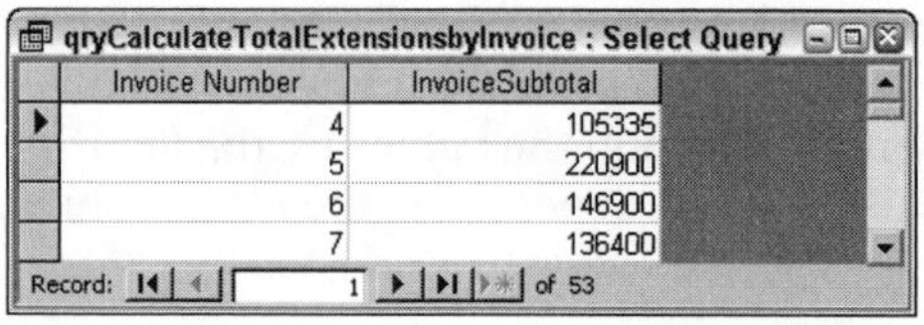

Figure 15-14: A Select query displaying totals or each Invoice.

The results from this query will be used along with the results from the following query, as shown in Figure 15-15. In order to calculate the amount due in the report you will create next, you need not only the total amount of the invoice (which will consist of the total extensions from the line items) but also you need to add the tax and other amounts, and then you will need to subtract the total payments. On the invoice form, you can have more than one payment. The total payments must be calculated for the report so that they can be subtracted from the total sale on each invoice to calculate the amount owed at the bottom of each invoice.

Figure 15-15 shows the total query named qryCalculateTotalPaymentsbyInvoice. The first column sets a Group By parameter on the lngzInvoiceNumber field. The second column sets a Sum parameter on the curPaymentAmount field. In this example, the total payment is simply a sum of the curPaymentAmount field and does not require an expression as does the total amount.

Note When you save a total query and look at it again, you may see the Sum parameter moved from the Total row to the field row and shown as a function Sum (the original field or expression). The Total row then displays the parameter *Expression* in place of the Sum.

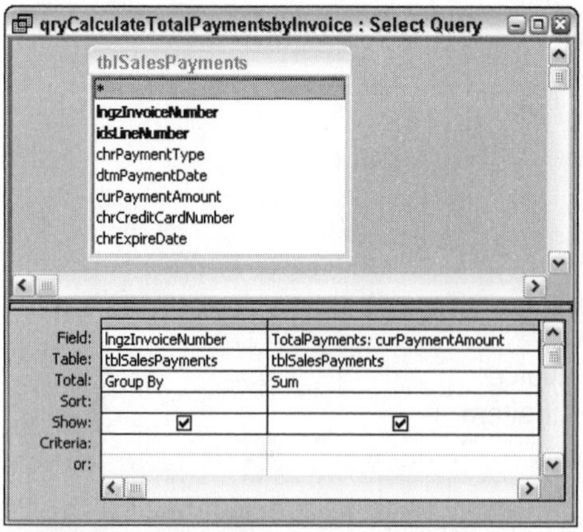

Figure 15-15: Creating a query that totals records for payments.

Now that you have seen how to create a Total query for the new Invoice report you are about to learn how to create, you need to learn how to bring these queries into another query to create the Record Source for the report.

Creating a query that uses a query

A query can display data from tables or even other queries. For this report, you will want to see a series of data that will include simple fields and complex calculations including summaries.

Figure 15-16 shows the qryInvoiceReport query that will become the record source for the new report shown in Figure 15-11.

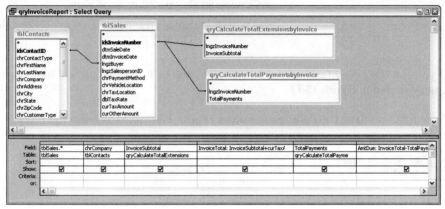

Figure 15-16: Creating a query that uses other queries and tables.

The query will bring together data from the following tables or queries:

- ✦ tblSales table (to identify the invoice number, invoice date, and contact, and also to retrieve the Tax and Other amounts)
- ✦ tblContacts table (to lookup the contact name)
- ✦ qryCalculateTotalExtensionsbyInvoice (total sale extensions)
- ✦ qryCalculateTotalPaymentsbyInvoice (total payments)

Notice that the tblSales table is linked to both of the queries through the idsInvoiceNumber link in the tblSales table to the lngzInvoiceNumber fields in both queries. The tblSales table is also linked to the tblContacts table from the lngzBuyer field to the idsContactID field.

The columns in the query are shown in Table 15-1.

Table 15-1
Columns in the qryInvoiceReport Query

tblSales.*	All of the fields in the tblSales table
chrCompany	The Company name used to identify the invoice customer
InvoiceSubtotal	The InvoiceSubtotal of all the extensions from the qryCalculateTotalExtensionsbyInvoice query
InvoiceTotal:	tableInvoiceSubtotal+curTaxAmount+curOtherAmount An expression that includes fields from the query qryCalculateTotalExtensionsbyInvoice and the tblSales table
TotalPayments	The Payment Total from the qryCalculateTotalPaymentsbyInvoice query
AmtDue:	InvoiceTotal – TotalPayments from the other query columns

If you run the query (and only show the columns in Table 15-1), it will look like the query shown in Figure 15-17.

Now that you have the data ready for the report, it is time to create the report.

Invoice Number	Invoice Date	Company	InvoiceSubtotal	Tax Amount	Other Amount	InvoiceTotal	TotalPayments	AmtDue
4	2/3/2003	Nopa Auto Parts	105335	$5,266.75	($30.00)	$110,571.75	$70,565.00	$40,006.75
5	2/18/2003	R & G Monda Inc	220900	$13,254.00	$0.00	$234,154.00	$1,000.00	$233,154.00
6	2/24/2003	Pleasantville Monda Inc	146900	$7,345.00	$0.00	$154,245.00	$22,995.00	$131,250.00
7	4/24/2003	McHugh Cash Auto Sales	136400	$8,525.00	$0.00	$144,925.00	$85,000.00	$59,925.00
8	5/24/2003	Tip Top Chevy	125000	$6,250.00	$0.00	$131,250.00	$5,000.00	$126,250.00
10	7/15/2003	KJ Auto Repair	20300	$913.50	$0.00	$21,213.50	$1,000.00	$20,213.50
12	8/26/2003	Iron Springs Auto Sales	82170	$4,610.48	$160.00	$86,940.48	$15,000.00	$71,940.48
14	9/30/2003	Ghost Automobile Sales	38995	$1,559.80	$0.00	$40,554.80	$40,554.80	$0.00
15	12/13/2003	Bush Sales	1750	$70.00	$0.00	$1,820.00	$1,820.00	$0.00
21	9/30/2003	Sakes American Autos	42495	$2,655.94	$0.00	$45,150.94	$25,000.00	$20,150.94
22	10/15/2003	Paul's Best Autos	18300	$833.57	$0.00	$19,133.57	$19,133.57	$0.00
24	10/26/2003	Sammy Fordman	33500	$1,675.00	$0.00	$35,175.00	$1,500.00	$33,675.00
25	10/30/2003	Fordman Sales	40000	$1,600.00	$0.00	$41,600.00	$100.00	$41,500.00
26	11/1/2003	A-1 Auto Sales	35000	$2,100.00	$0.00	$37,100.00	$25,100.00	$12,000.00
27	11/5/2003	Pleasantville Monda Inc	17000	$850.00	$0.00	$17,850.00	$17,850.00	$0.00
28	11/22/2003	A-1 Auto Sales	116500	$6,990.00	$0.00	$123,490.00	$100,000.00	$23,490.00
29	12/2/2003	KJ Auto Repair	12298	$553.41	$0.00	$12,851.41	$2,500.00	$10,351.41
30	12/15/2003	Tip Top Chevy	125000	$6,250.00	$0.00	$131,250.00	$20,000.00	$111,250.00
31	12/29/2003	Paul's Best Autos	19000	$877.98	$275.00	$20,152.98	$1,000.00	$19,152.98
33	1/15/2004	KJ Auto Repair	29500	$1,327.50	$0.00	$30,827.50	$5,000.00	$25,827.50

Figure 15-17: Displaying the data from the qryInvoiceReport.

Creating a new columnar report

You may want to refer back to Figure 15-11 to remind yourself of the report you are now going to create. Follow the steps below to create this new report:

1. Press F11 to display the Database window if it isn't already displayed.

2. Click the Reports object button.

3. Click the New toolbar button. The New Report dialog box appears.

4. Select Report Wizard from the list of choices.

5. Select the qryInvoiceReport query, as shown in Figure 15-18.

6. Click OK.

   The Report Wizard screen is displayed.

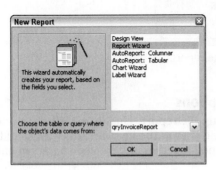

Figure 15-18: Starting a new report with the Report Wizard.

Selecting fields for the report

The next step is to select the fields that will be on the report. Because you assembled and summarized all of the data in the query you will need for the report, you simply have to select the fields in the correct order.

> **Tip** When you get proficient at creating reports, you may choose to not start with the wizard. You may want to create a blank report and just drag the fields you need from the field list, create your own groupings and summary fields, and format all of the data. In fact, many developers will not use wizards, stating that they are "toys for end users." Don't believe it. As preparation for this chapter, this author created this entire report from a blank report, doing everything manually. It took about 20 minutes. Then, this author used the wizard to accomplish the exact same steps, including the final formatting. It took about five minutes. Fifteen minutes may not seem like a lot of time saved, but when an application contains many forms and reports (sometimes in the hundreds), it adds up quickly. The best developers really do use wizards and every other tool the software provides for them.

First, select the dtmInvoiceDate field. Then, using Figure 15-19 as a guide, select the rest of the nine fields you will use for the report. (After you select all nine fields, the dtmInvoiceDate field is out of sight above the idsInvoiceNumber field.)

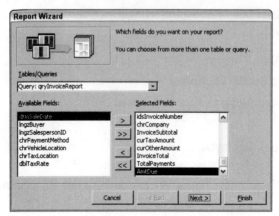

Figure 15-19: Selecting the fields for the report.

Selecting grouping fields and options

The next step is to select how to group the report. This report will have one group. The grouping will be by the month and year of the invoice. This way, all of the invoices for each month can be grouped together and totaled so that an analysis of each month can be performed.

1. Select the dtmInvoiceDate field and press the > button. Then, press the Next> button to accept the choice.

    Automatically, the field is grouped by Month, as shown in Figure 15-20. Access knows it is a date field and selects this automatically.

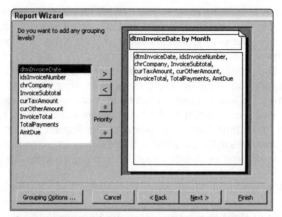

Figure 15-20: Selecting a group for the report.

You can press the Grouping Options...button and choose from a list for date field types that that include Normal, Year, Quarter, Month, Week, Day, and Hour or Minute for date fields including time. For other field types, there will be other options.

Because Month is the default option, you can just accept it.

2. Press the Next button to move to the next wizard screen.

Creating sorting options and calculations

Next, you need to select the sorting fields for the report. Because you selected the dtmInvoiceDate as a group field, the report is automatically sorted by the month of the date in the section header. You still may want to sort the data within the detail section beneath the header. For this example, there should be two sort directives:

1. Select dtmInvoiceDate as the first sort.

2. Select idsInvoice Number as the second sort.

   This way, beneath each month group, the detail data is sorted by date first; then for invoices on the same date, they are in the order of the Invoice Number.

   On the Sort Order and Summary Information wizard screen is a button labeled Summary Options. . . . When you press the button, you can determine what summary data you want to see with each field. Only numeric fields or expressions are listed here. Figure 15-21 shows this screen.

   The summaries on this data are for the InvoiceSubtotal, curTaxAmount, InvoiceTotal, TotalPayments, and AmtDue. These will appear in group, page, and report footers as calculated summary expressions.

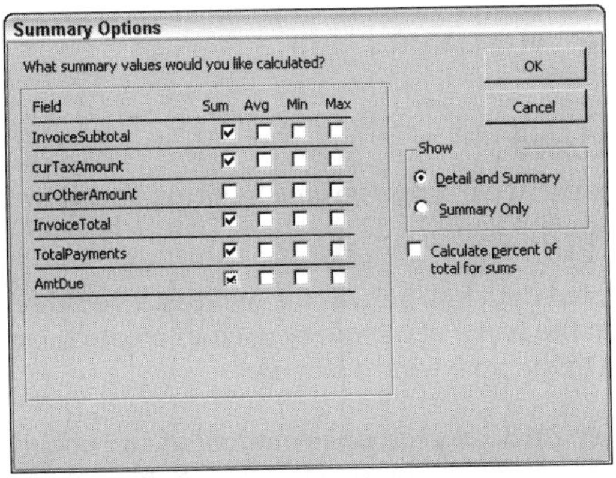

Figure 15-21: Selecting sorting options and calculations for the report.

Figure 15-21 shows that the Detail and Summary option is selected. If Summary Only was selected, there would be no fields in the detail section. Optionally, you can calculate percentages of each detail line or group totals of the report total by checking the Calculate Percent of Total for Sums check box.

3. Press the Next button to move to the next wizard screen.

Specifying the layout for the report

When the sorting and grouping options are completed, you are almost through. The next wizard screen lets you select the layout for the report, as shown in Figure 15-22.

In this example, the Layout of Stepped is selected as shown in the figure, the Orientation is Landscape, and the check box below the Layout option group is checked so that the width of the fields is small enough for all of the fields to fit on the report.

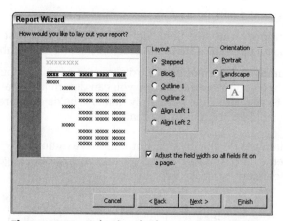

Figure 15-22: Selecting the layout of the report.

Completing the Report Wizard

After you complete this screen, you can pres the Finish button and view the report. Page one of the report is shown in Figure 15-23.

The report contains summarized data for each of the invoices. The title qryInvoiceReport comes from the name of the query used to create the report. You could have changed that in the final wizard screen.

Notice the first group February 2003. Each group is outdented and enclosed in a box. Notice that the labels in the Page Header don't fit well. Some are using the field names and encroach on another's space. You can shorten the labels or make them multiple line labels and take up less of a width. Each group footer contains several lines for identification and the actual values. The values are not well formatted. They need to be currency with two decimal places.

qryInvoiceReport

dtmInvoiceDate by	/oice Date	ice Number	Company	iceSubtotal x Amount		Other Amount	/oiceTotal	alPayments	AmtDue
February 2003									
	2/3/2003	4	Nopa Auto Parts	105335	$5,266.75	($30.00)	110,571.75	$70,565.00	40,006.75
	2/18/2003	5	R & G Monda Inc	220900	$13,254.00	$0.00	234,154.00	$1,000.00	33,154.00
	2/24/2003	6	Pleasantville Monda In	146900	$7,345.00	$0.00	154,245.00	$22,995.00	31,250.00
Summary for 'dtmInvoiceDate' = 2/24/2003 (3 detail records)									
Sum				473135	25865.75		498970.75	94560	404410.75
April 2003									
	4/24/2003	7	McHugh Cash Auto S	136400	$8,525.00	$0.00	144,925.00	$85,000.00	59,925.00
Summary for 'dtmInvoiceDate' = 4/24/2003 (1 detail record)									
Sum				136400	8525		144925	85000	59925
May 2003									
	5/24/2003	8	Tip Top Chevy	125000	$6,250.00	$0.00	131,250.00	$5,000.00	26,250.00
Summary for 'dtmInvoiceDate' = 5/24/2003 (1 detail record)									
Sum				125000	6250		131250	5000	126250
July 2003									
	7/15/2003	10	KJ Auto Repair	20300	$913.50	$0.00	$21,213.50	$1,000.00	20,213.50
Summary for 'dtmInvoiceDate' = 7/15/2003 (1 detail record)									
Sum				20300	913.5		21213.5	1000	20213.5
August 2003									
	8/26/2003	12	Iron Springs Auto Sale	82170	$4,610.48	$160.00	$86,940.48	$15,000.00	71,940.48
Summary for 'dtmInvoiceDate' = 8/26/2003 (1 detail record)									
Sum				82170	4610.48		86940.48	15000	71940.48
September 2003									

Sunday, April 27, 2003   Page 1 of 4

Figure 15-23: The report created by the wizard.

The page header has a date with no time and the page number. You will see many changes before this form is done.

Changing the report design

Before you can make changes you have to display the report in design view. If you did not follow the wizard in the previous example or you're not sure you have it correct, open the report named Sales Invoice and Payment Report Start, as shown in Figure 15-24.

It is important to understand various parts of the report and then to make the necessary changes to complete your report.

You can see in Figure 15-24 the various controls that make up the report. In previous chapters, you've already learned how to do everything this report requires. This includes creating and manipulating controls, and creating summary controls and reference controls in subforms. You've also learned how to create Page Headers and Footers and format controls within these sections.

The first thing to review is a group header and footer.

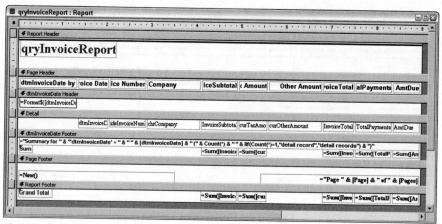

Figure 15-24: The report design created by the wizard.

Working with group headers and footers

The Group Header was created in the wizard. You can view the fields that are used for the group header and sorting in the detail section by pressing the Sorting and Grouping icon on the toolbar or by selecting View ➪ Sorting and Grouping from the report design menu.

Figure 15-25 shows the report design screen, along with both the Sorting and Grouping window and the Property window showing the text box used in the group header.

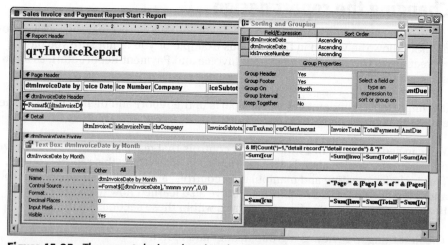

Figure 15-25: The report design showing the Group Header, Sorting and Grouping Option window, and Property window.

The first row in the Sorting and Grouping box lists the dtmInvoiceDate field. Notice the little icon on the gray area to the left of the first dtmInvoiceDate row. This lets you know that this field is used in either a group header or a group footer. You can see in the Sorting and Grouping window in Figure 15-25 that it is used in both. If you look at this window, you can see that the Group On type is Month, which was specified in the wizard.

You can see the format in the Property window for the text box that shows the expression:

=Format$([dtmInvoiceDate],"mmmm yyyy",0,0)

The Format function changes the display of the field value. The field is dtmInvoiceDate and the format is mmmm yyyy, which is the full spelling of the month (January, February, March ...) and the four-digit year with no day display.

The Keep Together option is set to No. The Keep Together option determines whether a new page is generated before the section header is printed. The choices for the Keep Together option are:

✦ **No:** The section header prints in the next available space without regard to what is in the detail section.

✦ **Whole Group:** The section header will start on a new page if it can get all of the detail records on the same page on the current page with the section header.

✦ **With First Detail:** The section header will print on the current page if at least one detail record fits on the current page, or if not, it will start on a new page.

The second dtmInvoiceDate field in the Sorting and Grouping window lets you sort data in the Detail section first by the actual invoice date within the month of the group header. The idsInvoiceNumber row allows the Detail section to sort the data first by invoice date and then by invoice number if there were multiple invoices on the same day.

Another important option is found in the section header properties themselves. If you click on any section header in a report header, you can see the Force New Page property, as shown in Figure 15-26.

Figure 15-26: Forcing a new page in the Group Header property window.

The Keep Together and Force New Page properties allow you to precisely control page breaks within each section, including Page and Report Headers and Footers, Group Headers and Footers, and even the Detail section.

Notice the four choices within the window:

✦ **None:** No page break with this section.

✦ **Before Section:** A page break occurs before this section prints.

✦ **After Section:** A page break occurs after this section prints.

✦ **Before & After:** A page break occurs both before and after this section.

Changing controls in the report

Before continuing to learn and review concepts of summary expressions, it is time to make a number of changes to improve the look and functionality of the report. Figure 15-27 shows all of these changes completed and should act as a roadmap for you to follow as you read the numbered instructions.

1. Change the label caption in the Report Header to Sales Invoice and Payment Report.

2. Change the label font to Arial Black font and use a 20-point font size.

3. Change all the labels in the Page Header section to be two line labels, as shown in Figure 15-27.

Note   Pressing Ctrl-Enter while on a text label will split the label where the cursor is. You can split labels into two, three, four, or as many lines as you need.

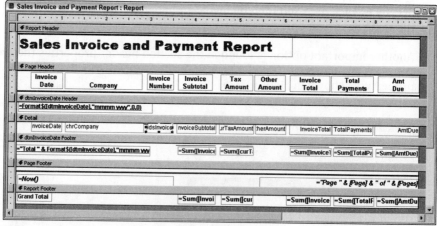

Figure 15-27: The Sales Invoice and Payment Report.

Tip

If you are creating multiline labels, you should make all labels the same height and make sure all the label controls are bottom aligned. If you have a two-line label and a one-line label in the any header section, you should still split the single line label so that there is a blank line on the top line and the text label on the bottom line. You create a blank line by placing your cursor in front of the text and pressing Ctrl-Enter in front of the single-line label.

4. Delete the dtmInvoiceDatebyMonth label at the beginning of the Page Header section.

5. Move all of the labels in the Page Header to the left so that the Invoice Date label is slightly to the right of the text box in the dtmInvoiceDate Header section, as shown in Figure 15-27. Move the Company label over one position as well.

6. Right-align all of the currency labels in the Page Header section with the text boxes and lines in the Detail section, dtmInvoiceDate Footer section, and Report Footer section.

7. In the dtmInvoiceDate Header section, make the border around the text box transparent.

8. In the dtmInvoiceDate Header section, change the font of the text box to Arial and make it **bold** and underlined. Also make the text box wider to accommodate the bold font.

You can change a label size by stretching the height of the control. You can change the label text from one line to two lines by positioning your cursor in the line where you want to break the line and then pressing the Enter key while holding down the Ctrl key.

9. Center align all of the labels.

10. Move all of the text boxes in the Detail section so that they are aligned under the labels in the Page Header section.

11. Change all the text boxes in the Detail section to Arial font.

12. Change all the numeric text boxes in the Detail section, group footer section, and report footer section to Currency format.

13. Delete the long Summary for text box in the dtmInvoiceDate Footer section.

14. Delete the Sum label at the far-left side of the dtmInvoiceDate Footer section.

15. Add some small lines above each of the summary text boxes in the dtmInvoiceDate Footer section.

16. Add a line across the Page Footer section.

17. Change the font in the Page Footer section to Italic.

18. Change the text from Grand Total to Report Total in the label in the Report Footer section.

19. In the Report Footer, change the font of the label to Arial Black.

20. Make the label wider so that it fits the full text.

You may have to make some of the fields wider and then realign the right side of the controls including the label controls in the Page Header section, the text boxes in the Detail section, the text boxes in the dtmInvoiceDate Footer section, and the text boxes in the Report Footer section.

When you have completed the changes, your screen should look like the one shown in Figure 15-27. If you don't want to make all these changes and simply want to start with the changed report, open the report named Sales Invoice and Payment Report Final on your example data file. There are a few other changes that have already been made, as shown in the rest of the chapter.

Using concatenation to join text and fields

It is good to review the concepts of concatenation. Concatenation operators can combine two strings, a string and an expression, or two or more expressions. An expression can consist of a string, a field, a function, or any combination. You can use several different operators for concatenation, including these:

+ Joins two Text data type strings

& Joins two strings; also converts non-Text data types to Text data

The + operator is standard in many languages, although it can easily be confused with the arithmetic operator used to add two numbers. The + operator requires that both strings being joined are Text data types.

The & operator is normally used and also converts non-string data types to string data types; therefore, it is used more than the + operator. If, for example, you enter the expression ="Today's Date Is:" & Date( ), Access converts the result of the date function into a string and adds it to the text Today's Date Is:. If the date is August 26, 2003, the result returned is a string with the value Today's Date Is:8/26/03. The lack of space between the colon and the 8 is not an error; if you want to add a space between two joined strings, you must add the space by pressing the spacebar on your keyboard after the : in Is and before the double quotes.

Access can join any data type to any other data type using this method. If you want to create the control for the dtmInvoiceDate footer concatenating the text "Total" with a Format function as shown in Figure 15-27, you enter the following expression:

="Total " & Format$([dtmInvoiceDate],"mmmm yyyy",0,0)

This appends the word Total and a space with the contents of the dtmInvoiceDate field formatted to Month and Year. No conversion occurs because the contents of the Format$ function and the text value Total are both already text. Notice the space between the last character in Total and the second double quotation mark.

Note If you use the + operator for concatenation, you must convert any non-string data types; an example is using the CStr( ) function to return a date with the Date( ) function to a string data type. If you want to display the system date with some text, you have to create a text control with the following contents:

="Today's Date Is: " +cstr(Date( ))

You can insert the contents of a field directly into a text expression by using the ampersand (&) character. The syntax is

="Text String "&[Field or Control Name]&" additional text string"

or

[Field or Control Name]&" Text String"

Calculating group summaries

Creating a sum of numeric data within a group is very simple. The following is the general procedure for summarizing group totals for bound text controls:

1. Create a new text control in the group footer (or header).

2. Enter the expression **=Sum([somecontrolname])** where *somecontrolname* is a valid field name in the underlying query or the name of a control in the report.

If, however, the control name is for a calculated control, you sometimes have to repeat the control expression depending on when it is calculated. In the dtmInvoiceDate footer, suppose that you want to enter the following expression into the text box control to display the total of the detail line:

=Sum([Invoice Total])

If you try this, it will work.

However, suppose you didn't create the calculation in the query. Suppose the detail section contained a control named InvoiceTotal, but its Control Source was:

=[InvoiceSubtotal] + [curTaxAmount] + [curOtherAmount]

You couldn't just enter =Sum([InvoiceTotal]). It wouldn't work. It is simply a limitation of Access. To create a sum for the InvoiceTotal in the detail section, you have to enter:

=Sum([InvoiceSubtotal] + [curTaxAmount] + [curOtherAmount])

This is one of the reasons it is easier to create expressions in the query. They can be more easily summed or other aggregate operations applied (minimum, maximum, average, etc.).

If you look at all of the summary controls in the dtmInvoice Number footer, the Page Footer, and the Report Footer, they all simply use the Sum function wrapped around the field name.

Before moving on and closing this chapter, you need to create a few more controls. Because Access features a two-pass report writer, you can create controls based on your knowledge of the final report. For example, you can create a control that displays the percentage of one total to a grand total or create a running sum total to display cumulative totals.

Changing the report margins and page setup

The report is currently 9 inches across and has margins of 1 inch on the top, bottom, left, and right. Because the paper used is standard 8½ inches in height and 11 inches across in landscape mode, it fits just perfectly.

In order to create the last example where you see running sums and percentages, you need to widen the report so that about 10 inches across can be used. Figure 15-28 shows the Page Setup window you see when you select File ⇨ Page Setup from the Report Design menu.

In the example shown in Figure 15-28, the value .25 was entered into all four Margin areas. The last one (Right) was automatically changed to .55 inches because the maximum width for the printer in landscape mode is apparently 11 inches — .80 inches or 10.2 inches.

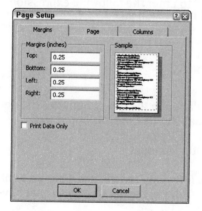

Figure 15-28: Viewing the Page Setup window.

If you are following along in the examples, try to set your margins all to 0.25 inches. Notice the left and right margins and subtract the total from 11 inches. This is what you will set your right margin to in the report.

Note The Page tab in the Page Setup window lets you choose between Portrait and Landscape printing. In Chapter 16, you will learn how to use these options to create multi-column reports.

Before you create new controls, you must change the margins of the current report to allow for more space in the width of the report.

Follow these steps to set the report width:

1. Click the right-most edge of the report body (where the white area meets the gray).

2. Drag the edge just to the left of the 10-inch mark on the ruler (or whatever you calculated as your maximum width).

3. Release the mouse button.

These steps complete the initial setup for the report. Next, you can create some new controls for the report.

Calculating percentages using totals

To determine what percent each line is of the total sales for a month, you will calculate a line percentage. By comparing the line item to the total, you can calculate the percentage of a particular item to the whole. To do this, you need to add a new control for the calculation. To create a new control that displays what percentage each line represents of the whole, follow these steps:

1. Duplicate the InvoiceTotal control in the Detail section, and name it InvoicePercent.

2. Position the duplicate to the right of the AmtDue control.

3. Change the Control Source to =[InvoiceTotal]/[Sum of InvoiceTotal].

4. Change the Format property to Percent.

5. Create a new label control with the caption "Total Percent" above it, as shown in Figure 15-29.

The calculation takes the individual line total control [InvoiceTotal]] in the detail section and divides it by the summary control [Sum of InvoiceTotal] in the dtmInvoiceDate Footer section. The Percent format automatically handles the conversion and displays a percentage.

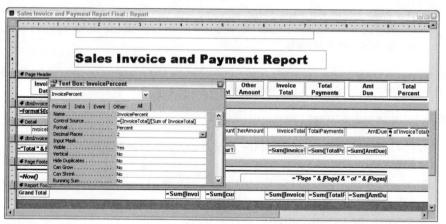

Figure 15-29: Creating a percentage control.

Calculating running sums

Access also lets you calculate running sums (also known as cumulative totals) easily—simply change the Running Sum property for a control. To create a running total of how much is spent as each pet's charges are totaled, follow these steps:

1. Duplicate the Invoice Subtotal control in the dtmInvoiceDate footer section.

2. Move it just under the original control, as shown in Figure 15-30.

3. Display the control's property sheet.

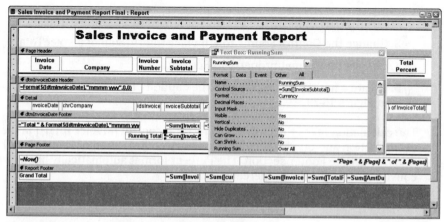

Figure 15-30: Creating a running sum control.

4. Change the Name to **Running Sum**.

5. Click the Running Sum property.

6. Select Over All from the drop-down list, as shown in Figure 15-30.

7. Create a label control and change the caption to **Running Total**.

Access now adds the current subtotal to all previous subtotals for each invoice. This is useful to present an overall summary in any group, page, or the report's Footer section. You can display the percentages and the running total by performing a print preview, as shown in Figure 15-31.

Invoice Date	Company	Invoice Number	Invoice Subtotal	Tax Amount	Other Amount	Invoice Total	Total Payments	Amt Due	Total Percent
February 2003									
2/3/2003	Nopa Auto Parts	4	$105,335.00	$5,266.75	($30.00)	$110,571.75	$70,565.00	$40,006.75	22.16%
2/24/2003	Pleasantville Monda Inc	6	$146,900.00	$7,345.00	$0.00	$154,245.00	$22,995.00	$131,250.00	30.91%
2/18/2003	R & G Monda Inc	5	$220,900.00	$13,254.00	$0.00	$234,154.00	$1,000.00	$233,154.00	46.93%
Total February 2003			$473,135.00	$25,865.75		$498,970.75	$94,560.00	$404,410.75	
		Running Total	$473,135.00						
April 2003									
4/24/2003	McHugh Cash Auto Sales	7	$136,400.00	$8,525.00	$0.00	$144,925.00	$85,000.00	$59,925.00	100.00%
Total April 2003			$136,400.00	$8,525.00		$144,925.00	$85,000.00	$59,925.00	
		Running Total	$609,535.00						
May 2003									
5/24/2003	Tip Top Chevy	8	$125,000.00	$6,250.00	$0.00	$131,250.00	$5,000.00	$126,250.00	100.00%
Total May 2003			$125,000.00	$6,250.00		$131,250.00	$5,000.00	$126,250.00	
		Running Total	$734,535.00						
July 2003									
7/15/2003	KJ Auto Repair	10	$20,300.00	$913.50	$0.00	$21,213.50	$1,000.00	$20,213.50	100.00%
Total July 2003			$20,300.00	$913.50		$21,213.50	$1,000.00	$20,213.50	
		Running Total	$754,835.00						

Figure 15-31: A print preview displaying percentages and running totals.

Creating a title page in a report header

The primary purpose of the report header is to provide a separate title page that only prints once in the report. The report header will contain the Access Auto Auctions logo and the report title.

In the sample Sales Invoice and Payment Report Start report, do the following to create this report header. They are shown completed in the Sales Invoice and Payment Report report and in Figure 15-32.

Follow these steps create the new report header:

1. Make the Report Header section much larger so that it is 4 inches in height.

2. Move the Sales Invoice and Payment Report to the bottom of the Report Header section.

3. Select Insert ➪ Picture … from the main menu and select the AAAuctions.jpg picture. Press OK to insert the picture and close the dialog box.

4. Position the picture and label as shown in Figure 15-32.

5. Change the Report Header section's Force New Page property to **After Section**.

   The After Section forces a new page after the report title prints.

Figure 15-32: Creating a report header for a title page.

✦   ✦   ✦

Presenting Data with Special Report Types

**On the
CD-ROM**
The starting points for both the reports you will create in
this chapter are included on your CD in Chap16Start.mdb.
You will use these reports to complete the examples in this
chapter.

For correspondence, you often need to create mailing labels
and form letters, commonly known as mail merges. The
Access Report Writer helps you create these types of reports
as well as the reports with multiple columns known as snaked-
column reports.

Creating Mailing Labels
Using the Label Wizard

You create mailing labels in Access by using a report. You can
create the basic label by starting from a blank form, or you
can use the Label Wizard. This wizard is much easier to use
and saves you a great deal of time and effort.

Access 2003 has no special report for creating mailing labels.
Like any other report, the report for a mailing label is made up
of controls; the secret to the mailing label is using the margin
settings and the Page Setup screen.

In previous chapters, you learned how to use the Page Setup
dialog box to change your margins. One of the tabs in the dialog box is Columns. When you select this tab, the Columns
dialog box expands to reveal additional choices you use to
control the number of labels across the report as well as how
the data is placed on the report. You learn how to use this dialog box later in this chapter.

The best way to create mailing labels is to use the Label Wizard. You create a new report to be used for a mailing label just as you create any other report (see Figure 16-1). To create a new report for a mailing label, follow these steps:

1. From the Database window, click the Reports object button.
2. Click the New toolbar button to create a new report.
3. Select Label Wizard.
4. Select tblContacts from the table/query combo box.
5. Click OK.

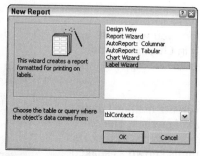

Figure 16-1: Choosing the Label Wizard.

The Label Size dialog box will now display.

Selecting the label size

The first wizard dialog box you see will ask you to select a label size. You can select the type of label stock you want to print to. Nearly a hundred Avery label stock forms are listed. (Avery is the world's largest producer of label paper.)

There are 40 other brands of labels that you can select from, including the following:

AE	Agipa	A-ONE	Boeder	CoStar
Durable	Ero	Formtec	Herlitz	Herma
HP	Inmac	Kokuyo	Leitz	Maco/Wilson Jones
NCR	Pimaco	RankXerox	Rotary Card	Unistat

To select a type of label other than Avery, click on the Filter by Manufacturer combo box to display the manufacturers available.

In these lists, you can find nearly every type of paper these manufacturers make. You can select from lists of English or Metric labels. You can also select sheet feed for laser printers or continuous feed for tractor-fed printers. Select between the two using the option buttons below the label sizes.

Tip If you do not see the Avery labels in the Label Wizard, click the Show custom label sizes check box to turn it off.

The list box shown in Figure 16-2 contains three columns:

✦ **Product number**. The model number on the Manufacturer label box.

✦ **Dimensions**. The height and width of the label in either inches or millimeters.

✦ **Number across**. The number of labels that are physically across the page.

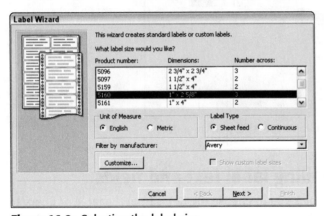

Figure 16-2: Selecting the label size.

When you select a label size, you're actually setting the Page Setup parameters, as you learn later in this chapter.

Select Avery number 5160, as shown in Figure 16-2. Notice that there are three labels across and that the size is shown as 1" x 2⅝". You'll see these values again when you examine the Page Setup dialog box. After you select the label size, you can again click on the Next button to go to the next dialog box.

Note You can also select the Customize button to create your own label specifications if the labels you're using are not standard labels.

Selecting the font and color

The next dialog box (shown in Figure 16-3) displays a set of combo boxes that enable you to select various attributes about the font and color of the text to use for the mailing label. For this example, click on the Italic check box to turn on the italic effect. Notice that the sample text changes to reflect the difference. Accept the remaining default choices of Arial, 8, Light, and black text. Click on the Next button to move to the next dialog box.

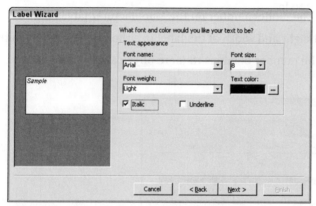

Figure 16-3: Selecting the font type, size, and color.

Creating the mailing label text and fields

The next dialog box enables you to choose the fields from the table or query to appear in the label. You can also add spaces, unbound text, blank lines, and even punctuation.

The dialog box is divided into two areas. The left area, titled Available fields, lists all the fields in the query or table. Figure 16-4, shown completed, displays the fields from the tblContacts table. The right area, titled Prototype label, shows the fields used for the label and displays a rough idea of how the mailing label will look when it's completed.

Note The fields or text you use in this dialog box serve only as a starting point for the label. You can make additional changes later in the Report Design window.

You can select a field either by double-clicking the field name in the Available fields area or by selecting the field name and then clicking on the > command button between the two areas. You can remove a field by highlighting it and then pressing Delete on your keyboard. You move to the next line by pressing the Tab key.

You may enter text at any point by simply placing your cursor where you want to insert the text and then typing the text, including spaces and punctuation marks.

If you add a new line to the label and leave it blank, it will appear only as a blank line on the label (provided you have also manually changed the Can Shrink property to No for the unbound text box control you created to display that blank line). The default property for this control is Yes; the blank line is not displayed, and the lines above and below the blank line appear together.

To create the label as shown completed in Figure 16-4, follow these steps:

1. Double-click the chrFirstName field in the Available fields list.

2. Press the space bar to leave a space after the chrFirstName field.

3. Double-click the chrLastName field in the Available fields list.

4. Press the Tab key to go to the next line.

5. Double-click the chrAddress field in the Available fields list.

6. Press the Tab key to go to the next line.

7. Double-click the chrCity field in the Available fields list.

8. With your cursor on the space after the chrCity field, type a comma (,) to add a comma to the label.

9. Press the spacebar to add a blank space to the label after the comma.

10. Double-click the chrState field in the Available fields list.

11. Press the spacebar to add a blank space to the label after the chrState field.

12. Double-click the chrZipCode field in the Available fields list.

13. Click the Next button to go to the next dialog box.

The completed label is displayed in Figure 16-4.

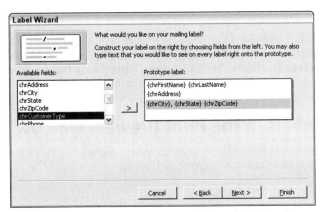

Figure 16-4: The completed label in the Label Wizard.

Sorting the mailing labels

The next dialog box will prompt you to select a field on which to sort, as shown in Figure 16-5. Depending on how you have your database set up (and on how you want to organize your information), you may sort it by one or more fields. The dialog box consists of two sections: one lists the Available fields; the other lists the selected Sort by fields. To select a field, double-click it (it will appear in the right-side column labeled Sort by:) or use the arrow buttons (> and >>). The single > means that only the highlighted field will be selected; the double > means that every field showing in the column will be selected. In this example, you will select chrLastName as the field to sort by. When you're done, click Next to bring up the final dialog box.

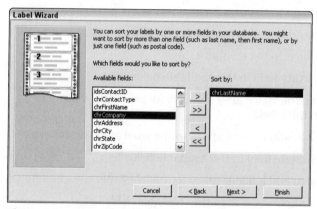

Figure 16-5: The Label Wizard's Sort By dialog box.

The order of fields in the Sort by column is their sort order, from the top down. If a database has first and last name, you can select the last name and then the first name.

The last dialog box of the Label Wizard names your report. The default name is Label, followed by the table name. In this example, that's Labels tblContacts. Make it a meaningful name, such as Customer Mailing Labels. This dialog box is shown in Figure 16-6. (Do not choose Finish; you use this dialog box in the next section.)

Displaying the labels in the Print Preview window

The final dialog box in the Label Wizard also enables you to decide whether to view the labels in the Print Preview window or to modify the report design in the Report Design window.

Make sure that "See the labels as they will look printed" is selected, and click the Finish button. You are taken directly to the Print Preview window (as shown in Figure 16-7). This is the normal Print Preview window for a report. By using the magnifying glass mouse pointer, you can switch to a page view to see an entire page of labels at one time, or you can zoom in to any quadrant of the report. By using the navigation buttons in the bottom-left corner of the window, you can display other pages of your mailing label report.

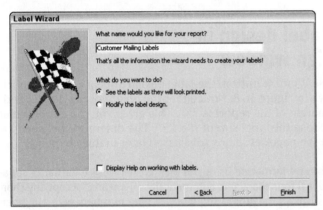

Figure 16-6: The final mailing Label Wizard dialog box.

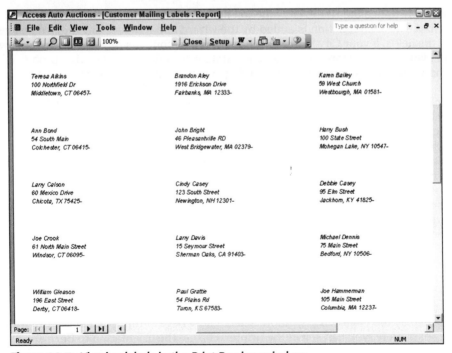

Figure 16-7: Viewing labels in the Print Preview window.

Note   Remember that a mailing label is simply a report; it behaves as a report normally behaves.

You can print the labels directly from the Print Preview window, or you can click the first button on the toolbar to display the Report Design window.

Modifying the label design in the Report Design window

When you click the Close Window button, the label design appears in the Report Design window, as shown in Figure 16-8. Notice that the height of the detail band is 1 inch and the right margin of the report is 2⅜". This gives you the measurement you defined when you chose the label size of 1" x 2⅜". The difference between 2⅜ and 2⅜ is the settings in the page setup box (discussed later in this chapter).

Note   The Zip Code field can be formatted using the @@@@@-@@@@ format to separate the first five and last four characters automatically. (@ means "accept any character".) This format displays the stored sequence of nine numbers with a hyphen placed where it properly goes. If there are only five numbers, that is all that is displayed.

You may notice that there is a function named Trim in front of the concatenated string. The Trim function is added by the wizard and removes any unused spaces in the fields. If your City field is 20 characters and contains New York, you don't want 12 blank spaces before the comma and state values. Trim handles that problem. The control source expression below (and shown in Figure 16-8) solves for the zip code.

Another change you could make is to the font size. In this example, Arial (the Helvetica TrueType font) with a point size of 8 is used. Suppose that you want to increase the text size to 10 points. You select all the controls and then click the Font Size drop-down list box and change the font size to 10 points. The text inside the controls becomes larger, but the control itself does not change size. As long as the text is not truncated or cut off on the bottom, you can make the font size larger.

You can also change the font style of any text. For example, if you want only the First Name and Last Name text to appear in italics, you will need to select the other two text box controls and de-select the Italics button on the toolbar. Earlier, you specified in the Wizard that all fields should be italic.

Now that you've changed your text like you want it, it's time to print the labels. Before you do, however, you should examine the Page Setup window.

To display the Page Setup window, select File ➪ Page Setup. The Page Setup window appears. Here, you can select the printer, change the orientation to Portrait or Landscape (have you ever seen landscape label paper?), change the Paper Size or Source settings, and set the margins. The margin setting controls the margins for the entire page. These affect the overall report itself, not just the individual labels.

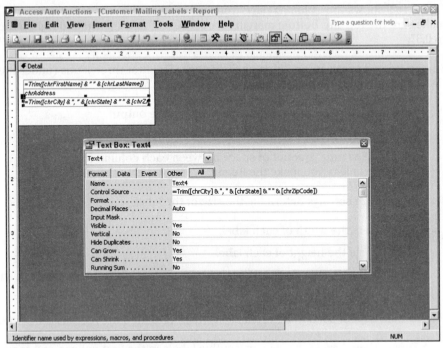

Figure 16-8: The Report Design window.

To view the settings of each label and determine the size and number of labels across the page, select the Columns tab. The window then displays additional options, as shown in Figure 16-9.

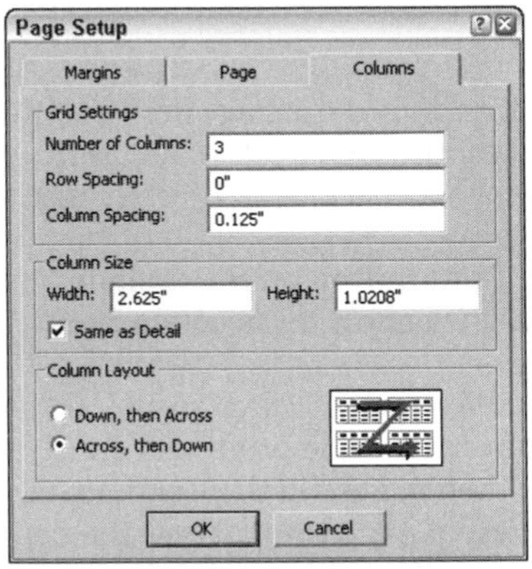

Figure 16-9: The Columns page from the Page Setup window.

Figure 16-9 shows the Columns page. You first need to click the Margins tab and make sure the top and bottom margins are set to 0.5" and the left and right margins to 0.3".

Several items appear in the Columns dialog box. The first three items (under the Grid Settings) determine the spacing of the labels on the page:

✦ **Number of Columns**. Number of columns in the output.

✦ **Row Spacing**. Space between the rows of output.

✦ **Column Spacing**. Amount of space between each column (this property is not available unless you make the Items Across property greater than 1).

The Column Size settings determine the size of the label:

✦ **Width**. Sets the width of each label.

✦ **Height**. Sets the height of each label.

✦ **Same as Detail**. Sets the Width and Height properties to the same width and height as the detail section of your report.

The Column Layout section determines in which direction the records are printed:

✦ **Down, then Across**. Prints consecutive labels in the first column and then starts in the second column when the first column is full.

✦ **Across, then Down**. Prints consecutive labels across the page and then moves down a row when there is no more room.

After the settings are completed, you can print the labels.

Printing labels

After you create the labels, change any controls, and view the Page Setup settings, you can print the labels. It's a good idea to preview the labels again. Figure 16-10 shows the final labels in the Print Preview window.

You can print the labels by simply selecting the Print button on the toolbar. You can also print the labels directly from the Report Design window by selecting File ➪ Print.

Of course, you must insert your label paper first. If you don't have any #5160 label paper, you can use regular paper. If you want the labels to be printed in consecutive format, like a telephone directory, select Down, then Across in the Columns tab shown in Figure 16-9. In fact, that's another feature of Access reports — the capability to create what is known as a snaked-column report.

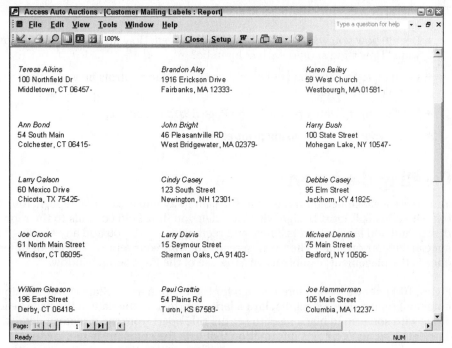

Figure 16-10: The final report print preview.

Creating Snaked-Column Reports

All the reports discussed in this book so far are either form-based (that is, free-form) or single-column lists. (Single-column means that each column for each field appears only once on each page.) Often this is not the best way to present your data. Access gives you another option: snaking columns. This option enables you to define the sections of a report so that they fit in an area that is less than half the width of the printed page. When the data reaches the bottom of the page, another column starts at the top of the page; when there is no more room on the page for another column, a new page starts.

The snaked-column technique is commonly used for text in telephone directories or newspapers and other periodicals. An example of a database use is a report that prints several addresses, side by side, for a page of adhesive mailing labels you feed through your laser printer. You just learned how to create labels for mailing. Now you will learn how to apply these same techniques in a report. Snaked-column reports have a major difference from mailing labels: They often have group sections, page headers, and footers; mailing labels have only data in the detail section.

The general process for creating a snaked-column report is as follows:

✦ Decide how you want your data to be displayed: How many columns do you want? How wide should each column be?

✦ Create a report that has detail and group section controls no wider than the width of one column.

✦ Set the appropriate options in the Page Setup dialog box.

✦ Verify your results by using print preview.

Creating the report

You create a snaked-column report in the same way you create any report. You start out with a blank Report Design window. Then you drag field controls to the report design and add label controls, lines, and rectangles. Next, you add any shading or special effects you want. Then you're ready to print your report. The major difference is the placement of controls and the use of the Page Setup window.

Figure 16-11 shows a completed design for the Customers by State (three snaking columns) report. The report displays a label control and the date in the page header, along with some solid black lines to set the title apart from the directory details. The detail section contains information that lists the company name, customer name, address, phone number, and e-mail. Then, within this section, you see three information fields about the customer's history with Access Auto Auctions. The page footer section contains another solid black line and a page number control.

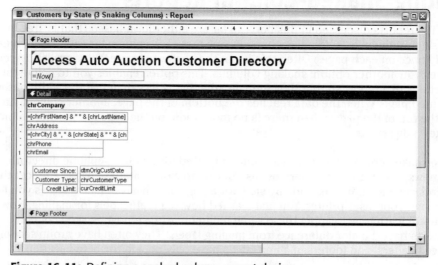

Figure 16-11: Defining a snaked-column report design.

What's important here is to make sure that the controls in the detail section use no more space for their height or width than you want for each occurrence of the information. Because you're going to be printing or displaying multiple detail records per page in a snaked-column fashion, you must note the size. In this example, you can see that the detail section data is about 1¾" high and about 2" wide. This is the size of the item you will define in the Columns dialog box.

Before continuing, you have to specify a sort order for the report. The report should be placed in order by State and then by Customer Number. You can do this by clicking the Sorting and Grouping button on the toolbar and typing the names of the fields in the dialog box.

Defining the page setup

Earlier in this chapter, in the "Creating Mailing Labels" section, you learned how to use Page Setup settings. Because you created the labels by using the Label Wizard, the values for the Page Setup were automatically adjusted for you. Next, you learn how to enter these values manually. Figure 16-12 shows the Page Setup dialog box and the settings used to produce the Customer Directory report. Again, it doesn't show you the settings for the margins. Before continuing, click on the Margins tab and set the left and right margins to 0.5" (the top and bottom should be 1 inch). Then click on the Columns tab to continue.

Figure 16-12: Defining the layout setup for a snaked-column report.

The first group of settings (Grid Settings) to change are the Number of Columns, Row Spacing, and Column Spacing. Notice that the Number of Columns setting is set to 3. This means that you want three customer listings across the page. This and the other two settings actually work together. As you learned in the section about mailing labels, these controls set the spacing between groups of data and how the data is to be shown (the number of columns). The Row Spacing should be set to 0.2" and the Column Spacing set to 0.4". This is one way to set up the multiple columns and allow enough space between both the rows and the columns.

The next grouping is the Column Size settings. In this example, the data is 1¾" high and about 2" wide in the detail section. You can define Width as 2.75 in and Height as 2.05 in. By adjusting the Grid Settings and Column Sizes, you control how your columned report will look.

Notice that the final grouping, Column Layout section, offers two settings: Down, then Across or Across, then down. The icon under Column Layout shows the columns going up and down. You saw in Figure 16-9 that when the setting is Across, then Down, the icon shows rows of labels going across. In this customer directory, you want to fill an entire column of names first before moving to the right to fill another column. Therefore, you select the Down, then Across setting. Click OK to save the Page Setup option changes and close the dialog box.

Printing the snaked-column report

After the expanded Page Setup dialog box settings are completed, you can print your report. Figure 16-13 shows the top half of the first page of the final snaked-column report in the Print Preview window. The data is sorted by state and customer number. Notice that the data snakes down the page. The first record is for Iron Springs Auto Sales, in Arizona. Below that is customer M&M Sales. There are four customers in the first column. After the fourth customer, the next customer (Montclair Auto) is found at the top of the middle column.

Access Auto Auction Customer Directory

Wednesday, April 16, 2003

Iron Springs Auto Sales	**Montclair Auto**	**ABC Trucking**
Peter Spindler	Robert Hill	Matt Smith
15 Mineral Drive	1600 Mountain Rd	7 Depot Rd
Iron Springs, AZ 86330-1230	Montclair, CA 91763-	Stratford, CT 06615-
(520) 555-8888	(909) 555-6666	(860) 555-3255
peter@ironsprings.com		mattsmith@abctrucking.com
Customer Since: 12/31/1996	Customer Since: 8/31/2001	Customer Since: 9/7/2001
Customer Type: Dealer	Customer Type: Dealer	Customer Type: Dealer
Credit Limit: $0.00	Credit Limit: $0.00	Credit Limit: $80,000.00

M&M Sales	**Sherman Oaks Auto Sales**	**Allstate International Sales**
Michael Moriety	Larry Davis	Christopher Lieberham
98 South Street	15 Seymour Street	6500 New London Rd
Green Valley, AZ 85614-	Sherman Oaks, CA 91403-	Milford, CT 06460-
(520) 555-6412	(818) 555-4456	(860) 555-9969
mmoriety@yahoo.com		lieberc@allstateinternational
Customer Since: 4/15/1999	Customer Since: 3/6/2001	Customer Since: 1/1/1990
Customer Type: Dealer	Customer Type: Dealer	Customer Type: Dealer
Credit Limit: $0.00	Credit Limit: $0.00	Credit Limit: $180,000.00

Figure 16-13: A snaked-column report.

Creating Mail Merge Reports

Now that you have learned how to create snaked-column reports and mailing labels (actually, they are the same thing), there is one more type of report to create — the mail merge report (also known as a form letter). A mail merge report is simply a report containing large amounts of text that have embedded database fields. For example, a letter may contain, within the body of the text, the amount a customer owes and the name of a pet.

The problem is how to control the word wrap. This means that the text may occupy more than one line, depending on the length of the text and the embedded field values. Different records may have different length values in their embedded fields. One record may use two lines in the report, another may use three, and another may require only one.

Access 2003 contains a Report Wizard that exports your data to Microsoft Word and launches the Word Print Merge feature. Why would you want to use a word processor, however, when you're working in a database? What happens if you don't use Word? Most word processors can perform mail merges using database data. Access itself does not have a specific capability to perform mail merging. Even so, as you see in this section, Access can indeed perform mail merge tasks with nearly the same precision as any Windows word processor!

In the first section of this chapter, you created mailing labels for customers that had placed an order. You can use these labels to address the envelopes for the mail merge letter you now create. Suppose that you need to send a letter to all your customers who have an order recently shipped. You want to let them know the shipment details such as the shipment date, method, and expected time of delivery.

Figure 16-14 shows a letter created with Access. Many of the data fields embedded in this letter come from an Access query. The letter was created entirely with the Access Report Writer, as were its embedded fields.

Assembling data for a mail merge report

You can use data from either a table or a query for a report. A mail merge report is no different from any other report. As long as you specify a table or query as the control source for the report, the report can be created. Figure 16-15 shows a typical query used for the letter. This query is the same query used in previous chapter examples, except that we have used the * to bring all fields from the tblSales and tblContacts tables into the query.

Access Auto Auctions
200 Northern Ave.
Bristol, CT 06010
860-555-2233

April 16, 2003

Nopa Auto Parts
11253 Main Street
Springfield, MA 01111-1253
(413) 555-3216

Copy by email: john.jones@nopa.com

Dear John Jones:

This letter is to inform you that the order you placed on January 15, 2003 has been shipped. You should expect to receive the order on or before January 29, 2003. Your order has been shipped by courier COD and you should have a money order ready in the amount of $40,006.75. This includes the invoice amount of $105,335.00 and tax and shipping of $5,236.75.

We appreciate your business. Since you became a customer in January 2002 we have enjoyed doing business with you. As a token of our appreciation, please take 10% off your next invoice as long as you have paid off your current balance of $0.00.

In advance, thank you very much and we look forward to doing business with you in the future.

Sincerely,

Patrick E. Thelic

Operations Manager
Access Auto Auctions

Figure 16-14: A letter created with the Access Report Writer.

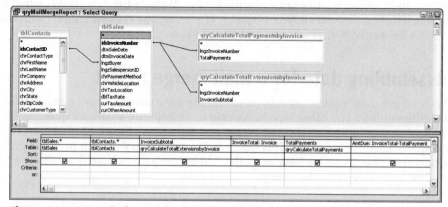

Figure 16-15: A typical query for a mail merge report.

Table 16-1 shows the fields or functions embedded in the text blocks used to create the letter. Compare the values in each line of the letter (shown in Figure 16-14) to the fields shown in the table. Later in this chapter, you'll see how each field or function is embedded in the text.

Table 16-1
Fields Used in the Mail Merge Report

Field Value or Name	Table	Usage in Report
Company Name	tblCompanySetup	Page header; displays the company name as entered in the table
Street	tblCompanySetup	Page header; displays the street address as entered in the table
City State Zip	tblCompanySetup	Page header; displays the City, State, and Zip Code as entered in the table
Phone Number	tblCompanySetup	Page header; displays the phone number as entered in the table
Date( )	Function	Page header; displays current date; formatted as mmmm dd, yyyy
chrCompany	tblContacts	Page header; displays Company Name
chrAddress	tblContacts	Page header; displays street in the address block
chrCity	tblContacts	Page header; part of city, state, ZIP code block
chrState	tblContacts	Page header; part of city, state, ZIP code block
chrZipCode	tblContacts	Page header; part of city, state, ZIP code block
chrPhone	tblContacts	Page header; displays phone number
chrEmail	tblContacts	Page header; displays email address
chrFirstName	tblContacts	Detail; part of salutation block
chrLastName	tblContacts	Detail; part of salutation block
dtmSaleDate	tblSales	Detail; first line of first paragraph; formatted as "mmmm dd"", """yyyy"
dtmSaleDate	tblSales	Detail; second line in first paragraph; formatted as "ww",2,[dtmSaleDate]), "mmmm dd"", """yyyy"

Continued

Table 16-1 *(continued)*

Field Value or Name	Table	Usage in Report
AmtDue	Query Expression	Detail; third line in first paragraph; formatted as $#,##0.00
InvoiceSubtotal	Query Expression	Detail; third line in first paragraph; formatted as $#,##0.00
curTaxAmount	Calculation	Detail; fourth line in first paragraph; used to calculate tax and shipping total; formatted as $#,##0.00
curOtherAmount	Calculation	Detail; fourth line in first paragraph; used to calculate tax and shipping total; formatted as $#,##0.00
dtmOrigCustDate	tblContacts	Detail; first line in second paragraph; formatted as mmmm yyyy
CurCurBal	Calculation	Detail; third line in second paragraph; formatted as $#,##0.00

Creating a mail merge report

After you assemble the data, you can create your report. Creating a mail merge report is much like creating other reports. Frequently a mail merge has only a page header and a detail section. You can use sorting and grouping sections, however, to enhance the mail merge report (although form letters normally are fairly consistent in their content).

Usually the best way to begin is with a blank report. Report Wizards don't really help you create a mail merge report. After you create a blank report, you can begin to add your controls to it.

Creating the page header area

A form letter generally has a top part that includes your company's name, address, and possibly a logo. You can print on preprinted forms that contain this information, or you can scan in the header and embed it in an unbound object frame. In our example, the Access Auto Auctions company name, address, and phone number are all displayed to the right of the logo. Each field contains a DLookUp Function with a value from the tblCompanySetup table. You can use the DLookup function to get the value of a particular field from a specified set of records — in our case, from the tblCompanySetup table.

The DLookUp function is entered as

=DLookUp("[Value]","TblCompanySetup","[OptionName]='Company Name'")

The function takes a value from the TblCompanySetup table where the Option Name is equal to Company Name, and populates the field on the report. When the report is printed, the company name as entered into the tblCompanySetup table will display in the page header section. Similar DLookUp functions are used for the address and phone number fields as well.

Usually, the top part of a form letter also contains the current date along with the name and address of the person or company to whom you're sending the letter. Figure 16-16 shows the page header section of the mail merge report. In this example, an unbound bitmap picture is inserted that contains the Access Auto Auctions logo. The DLookUp functions for the company information are partially displayed. As you can see in the top half of the page header section, the current date is also displayed along with a line to separate the top of the header from the body of the letter. You can see the calculated text box control's properties at the bottom of Figure 16-16. The Format( ) and Date( ) functions are used to display the date with the full text for month, followed by the day, a comma, a space, and the four-digit year.

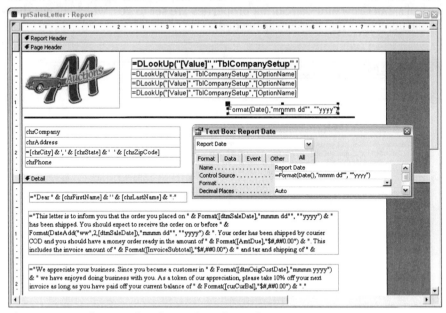

Figure 16-16: The page header section of a mail merge report.

The date expression is entered as

=Format(Date( ),"mmmm dd, yyyy")

and then automatically changed to

=Format(Date( ),"mmmm dd"",""yyyy")

This expression takes the system date of 4/16/2003 and formats the date as April 16, 2003.

The customer name and address fields are also displayed in the page header. The standard concatenated expression is used to display the city, state, and zip code fields:

=[chrCity] & "," & [chrState] & " " & [chripCode]

Working with embedded fields in text

The body of the letter is shown in Figure 16-17. Each paragraph is one large block of text. A standard text box control is used to display each paragraph. The text box control's Can Grow and Can Shrink properties are set to Yes, which allows the text to take up only as much space as needed.

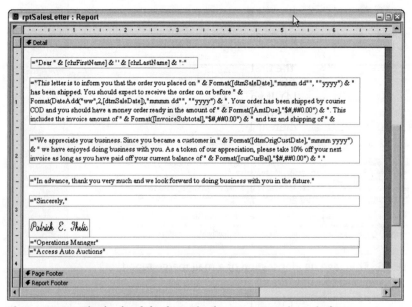

Figure 16-17: The body of the letter in the Report Design window.

Embedded in each text block are fields from the query or expressions that use the fields from the query. In the page header section, the & method is used to concatenate the city, state, and zip code. Although this method works for single concatenated lines, it does not enable word wrapping, which is critical to creating a mail merge report. If you use this method in large blocks of text, you get only a single, truncated line of text.

Note As you learned in Chapter 21, the & method of concatenation handles word wrap within the defined width of the text box. When the text reaches the right margin of a text box, it shifts down to the next line. Because the Can Grow property is turned on, the text box can have any number of lines. It's best to convert non-text data to text when you concatenate with the & method. Although this conversion isn't mandatory, the embedded fields are displayed more correctly when they are correctly converted and formatted.

The first text block is a single-line text box control that concatenates the text "Dear" with the fields chrFirstName and chrLastName. Notice the special symbols within the first text box control. Remember that each text box is made up of smaller groups of text and expressions. By using the & character, you can concatenate them.

The expression =“Dear” & [chrFirstName] & ‘ ’ & [chrLastName] & “:” begins with an equal sign and a double quote. Because the first item is text, it's surrounded by “ characters. [chrFirstName] and [chrLastName] need to be enclosed in brackets because they are field names; they should also be surrounded by & characters for concatenation. The two single quote marks in the center of the expression represent a space between the chrFirstName and chrLastName fields; also concatenated with the &. The colon at the end of the expression appears in the letter; it is text and must be surrounded by double quotes.

The next control produces the first paragraph of the letter. Notice that there are five lines in the text box control but only four lines in the first paragraph of the letter (as shown in Figure 16-14). If you compare the two figures carefully, however, you'll see that the text box for the second date field is on the third line of the paragraph in the text control, whereas it's in the second line of the paragraph in the printed letter. This is a good example of word wrap. The lines shrank to fit the data.

The first line of the text control displays a text string with the date field at the end of the line. Notice that the text string is both enclosed in double quotes and concatenated to the next expression by the & character. The end of the first line looks like this:

Format([dtmSaleDate],”mmmm dd””,”””yyyy”) & “

The expression displays the Sale Date and formats the field so that it shows a long date such as April 16, 2003. The second line of the paragraph is simply a text string ending with the & character to concatenate it to the next expression.

The third line begins with the Sale Date field; however, this field contains extra parameters to indicate a designated time in the future. The expression is

```
Format(DateAdd("ww",2,[dtmSaleDate]),"mmmm dd""," ""yyyy")
```

This expression is formatted in the same way as the last date field in the paragraph using the mmmm dd yyyy format. The DateAdd function in this example advances the original sale date by two weeks. In our example, the original shipment date was January 15. This expression adds two weeks to that date to display the expected delivery date of January 29.

The rest of the third line of the paragraph through most of the fourth is one long text string. It's simply enclosed in double quotes and concatenated by the & character. The end of the fourth line of the first paragraph contains an expression that formats a calculated currency field. The expression Format([AmtDue],"$#,##0.00") formats the dollar value to display in currency format with two decimal places.

The last line in the first paragraph contains the following expression:

```
Format([InvoiceSubtotal],"$#,##0.00")
```

The InvoiceSubtotal field is from the qryCalculateTotalExtensionsbyInvoice query. This is a calculated field that is formatted using a dollar sign, a comma (if the value is 1,000 or more), and two displayed decimal places. Without the format, the field would have simply displayed 105335 rather than $105,335.00 for this record.

The second paragraph contains two expressions; one on the first line to display the original customer date, and one on the last line for the current balance. Both fields are taken from the tblContacts table. The dtmOrigCustDate is formatted using the mmmm yyyy format. The curCurBal field is formatted using $#,##0.00" currency.

Tip   The maximum length of a single concatenated expression in Access is 254 characters between a single set of quotes. To get around this limitation, just end one expression, add an & character, and start another. The limit on the length of an expression in a single text box is 2,048 characters (almost 40 lines)!

The second paragraph also contains one long text string. The expression Format("ww",2,[dtmSaleDate]),"mmmm dd""","""yyyy") advances the dtmSaleDate by 2 weeks by using the part of the expression that is DateAdd("ww",2,[dtmSaleDate]). The bottom of the letter is produced using the label controls, as shown in Figure 16-17. These label controls display the closing, the signature, the owner's title, and the company name. The signature of Patrick E. Thetic is created here by using the Script font. Normally, you would scan in the signature and then use an unbound frame object control to display the bitmap picture that contains the signature.

One thing you must do is set the Force New Page property of the detail section to After Section so that a page break is always inserted after each letter.

Printing the mail merge report

You print a mail merge report in exactly the same way you would print any report. From the Print Preview window, you can simply click the Print button. From the Report Design window, you can select File ⇨ Print. The report is printed like any other report.

Using the Access Mail Merge Wizard for Microsoft Word

Another feature in Access 2003 is a Wizard to open Word automatically and start the Print Merge feature. The table or query you specify when you create the new report is used as the data source for Microsoft Word print merge.

To use the Mail Merge Wizard in Office Access 2003, you must have Microsoft Office Word 2003.

1. From the Database container window, click either the Tables or Queries object button.

2. Select the table or query you want to merge with Word.

3. Click the OfficeLinks drop-down button on the toolbar.

4. Select Merge It with Microsoft Word to start the Microsoft Word Mail Merge Wizard, as shown in Figure 16-18.

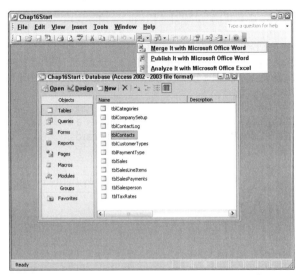

Figure 16-18: Selecting the Microsoft Word Mail Merge Wizard.

5. After you select Merge It with Microsoft Word, Access displays the Microsoft Word Mail Merge Wizard screen, as shown in Figure 16-19.

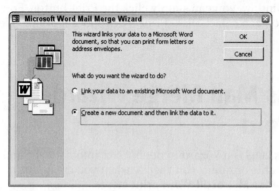

Figure 16-19: The Microsoft Word Mail Merge Wizard dialog box.

6. This screen enables you to decide whether to link your data to an existing Word document or to create a new document. If you select the option that says to Link your data to an existing Microsoft Word document, Access displays a standard Windows file-selection box that enables you to select an existing document. The document is retrieved, Word is displayed, and the Print Merge feature is active. You can then modify your existing document.

In this example, you start with a new document.

7. Select the option Create a new document and then link the data to it.

8. Click OK to launch Word and display the Print Merge toolbar.

Microsoft Word 2003 moves beyond wizards and embraces a new technology known as the task pane. As you can see in Figure 16-20, to the right of the standard Word window, the task pane combines traditional help and task-oriented wizards to attempt to simplify complex processes.

Note   If you used Microsoft Access 1.0-2.0, you might remember a technology known as *cue cards*. Task panes are the next generation of cue cards.

Tip   You can display a task pane in any Office XP application by right-clicking any toolbar and selecting Task Pane.

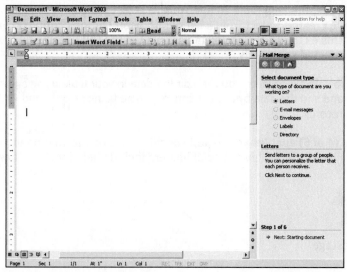

Figure 16-20: A blank Microsoft Word document with the Task Pane displayed.

Although you don't need to use the task pane to create a mail merge document, it is a good idea to understand how it can help you. As you can see in Figure 16-20, the first task pane asks you to select whether you want to create a letter, e-mail message, envelope, labels, or telephone-type directory. Based on your choices, different successive choices are available. For example, if you select Envelope, various envelope options are displayed in the later task panes. For this example, select the default choice of Letters.

Then click the Next button at the bottom of the pane. You are presented with the following choices:

✦ Use the current document.

✦ Start from a template.

✦ Start from existing document.

If you choose to start from an existing document or template, you can then select one to bring to the Word document area. Figure 16-21 shows a document that has been entered without any mail merge fields. You generally start with a document that has already been entered, or you can type one in.

Mail merge means that when the document is printed, data values from fields in a table are merged into the document. In this example, as you can see in Figure 16-21, placeholders in the form of xxx's have been entered where fields will be entered.

If you use the task pane, the next pane enables you to select recipients from an existing list you have created, select from a list of Microsoft Outlook contacts, or enter a new list. In this example, the recipients are part of the tblContacts table and do not have to be selected separately.

Note   If you choose to select recipients, you can edit the data in your table using a pop-up dialog box and sort the data by any column, eliminate blank records, and even select specific records.

The next task pane (4 of 6) enables you to add specific types of information to your letter, as shown in Figure 16-21. These special helpers include help for the following fields:

✦ Address blocks

✦ Greeting lines

✦ Electronic postage

✦ Postal bar code

✦ More items that enable you to insert the merge fields

Figure 16-21 also shows the Insert Merge Field dialog box, showing all of the fields in the tblContacts table that can be used within the letter.

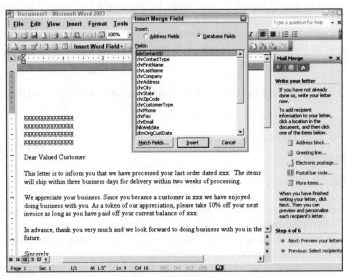

Figure 16-21: A Microsoft Word document ready for table fields to be entered.

After you decide where you want to include fields from your table in your letter, you can position your cursor in your letter and then select the field or fields you want in each position by simply double-clicking on them. Figure 16-22 shows the letter after the fields have been entered.

Tip You can also display the field list for the merge by pressing the Insert Merge Fields button located next to the Insert Word Field text on the Mail Merge toolbar.

Notice the name and address information at the top of the letter. This is made up of six separate fields. In the first sentence of the first paragraph, a field named dtmLastSalesDate has been added for the date of the customer's order. The second paragraph contains the field dtmOrigCustDate for the first time the customer made a purchase, as well as the curCurBal field for the customer's current balance.

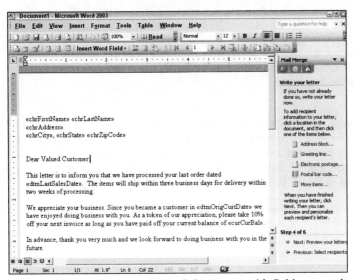

Figure 16-22: The Microsoft Word document with fields entered for the mail merge.

The next step automatically merges your date and displays the first record in your letter. As you can see, not only is the name and address of your customer displayed, but the dtmLastSalesDate value, the dtmOrigCustDate value, and curCurBal value are displayed.

The task pane displays some buttons that enable you to move between records and see how they are displayed, as shown in Figure 16-23. The task pane also enables you to exclude specific data records or edit the data while you are looking at the letter.

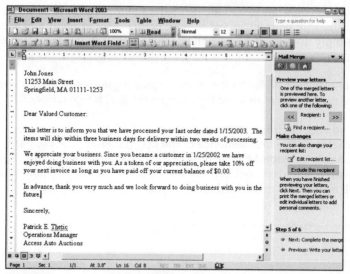

Figure 16-23: The Microsoft Word document displayed in preview mode with the data fields merged.

After you are through selecting the data you want, you can move to the last task pane and print all the letters or even edit individual letters before printing them. These are incredibly powerful new features and are only available with Microsoft Word 2003. By combining the database power of Access and the word processing and editing features of Word, you have a very powerful environment.

✦   ✦   ✦

Using OLE Objects, Graphs, Pivot Tables/ Charts, and ActiveX Controls

Access provides many powerful tools for enhancing your forms and reports. These tools let you add pictures, graphs, sound — even video — to your database application. Chart Wizards make it easy to build business graphs and add them to your forms and reports. ActiveX controls extend the power of Access 2003; new features borrowed from Microsoft Office 2003 make using Access forms more productive than ever. In this chapter, you learn about the different types of graphical and ActiveX objects you can add to your system. You also learn how to manipulate them to create professional, productive screen displays and reports. You will also learn how to use some of the new Office 2003 tools that work with Access 2003 forms.

Understanding Objects

Access 2003 gives you the capability of embedding pictures, video clips, sound files, business graphs, Excel spreadsheets, and Word documents; you can also link to any OLE (Object Linking and Embedding) object within forms and reports. Therefore, Access lets you not only use objects in your forms but also edit them directly from within your form.

Types of objects

As a general rule, Access can add any type of picture or graphic object to a form or report. You can interact with OLE objects with great flexibility. For example, you can link to an entire spreadsheet, a range of cells, or even an individual cell.

Access can embed and store any binary file within an object frame control, including even sound and full-motion video. As long as you have the software driver for the embedded object, you can play or view the contents of the frame.

These objects can be bound to a field in each record (*bound*) or to the form or report itself (*unbound*). Depending on how you want to process the OLE object, you may either place (*embed*) the copy directly in the Access database or tell Access where to find the object (*link*) and place it in the bound or unbound object frame in your form or report. The following sections describe the different ways to process and store both bound and unbound objects by using embedding and linking.

Using bound and unbound objects

A *bound object* is an object displayed (and potentially stored) within a field of a record in a table. Access can display the object on a form or print it on a report.

A bound object is bound to an OLE object data type field in the table. If you use a bound object in a form, you can add and edit pictures or documents record by record, the same way you can edit other data. To display a bound OLE object, you use a Bound Object Frame control. In Figure 17-1, the picture of the Corvette is a bound object. Each record stores a photograph of the car in the field named Picture in the tblProducts table. You can enter a different picture for each record.

An *unbound object* is not stored in a table; it is placed on the form or report. An unbound object control is the graphic equivalent of a label control. These are generally used for OLE objects in the form or report itself; they don't belong to any of the record's fields. Unbound objects don't change from record to record.

An *image control* that displays a picture is another example of an unbound object. Although an unbound OLE object frame allows you to edit an object by double-clicking on it and launching the source application (Paint, Word, Excel, a sound or video editor or recorder, and so on), an image control only displays a bitmap picture (usually in .BMP, .JPG, or .GIF format) that cannot be edited.

Tip   Always use an image control for unbound pictures; it uses far fewer computer resources than an OLE control and significantly increases performance.

In Figure 17-1, the Access Auto Auctions logo is an image control. The car is a bound OLE object; the graph is an unbound object. Though the graph is unbound, there is a data link from the graph template to the data on the form. This means the graph is updated each time data in the record changes.

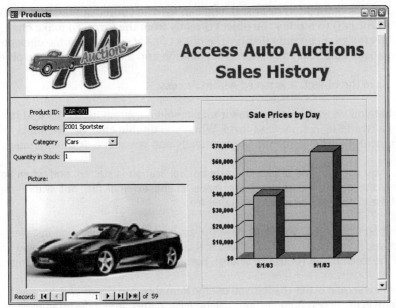

Figure 17-1: Bound and unbound objects.

Linking and embedding

The basic difference between linking and embedding objects within a form or report is that *embedding* the object stores a copy of it within your database. *Linking* an object from another application does not store the object in your database; instead, the external location of the object is stored.

Linking an object gives you two benefits:

✦ You can make changes to the object using the source application, without opening Access.

✦ The Access MDB database only uses space for the file path and filename to the external reference.

Caution   If the external file is moved to another directory (or if the file is renamed), the link to Access is broken. Therefore, opening the Access form that is linked to the object will result in an error message.

One benefit of embedding is that you don't have to worry about someone changing the location or name of the linked file. Because it is embedded, the file is part of the Access MDB database file. Embedding does have its costs, however. The first is that it takes up space in your database — sometimes a great deal of it (some pictures can take several megabytes). In fact, if you embed an .AVI video clip of just 30 seconds in your database for one record, it can use 10 or more megabytes of space. Imagine the space 100 records with video could use.

After the object is embedded or linked, you can use the source application (such as Excel or Paintbrush) to modify the object directly from the form. To make changes to these objects, you need only display the object in Access and double-click on it. This automatically launches the source application and lets you modify the object.

When you save the object, it is saved within Access.

Suppose that you've written a document management system in Access and have embedded a Word file in an Access form. When you double-click on the image of the Word document, Word is launched automatically and you can edit the document.

Note When you use a linked object, the external application is started, and when you modify the object the changes are made to the external file, not within your database as they are with an embedded file.

Note To edit an OLE object, you must have the associated OLE application installed in Windows. If you have embedded an Excel .XLS file but don't own Excel, you can view the spreadsheet (or use its values), but you won't be able to edit or change it.

On the CD-ROM In the next section of this chapter, you use the form shown in Figure 17-2. You can find the form in the Access Auto Auctions database file, named frmProductExampleStart.

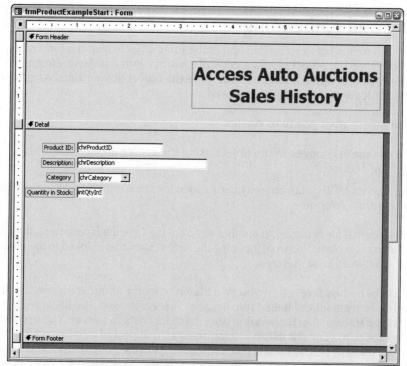

Figure 17-2: The frmProductExampleStart form.

Embedding Objects

You can embed objects in both unbound and bound object frames as well as in image frames. Embedding places the object in the Access database, where it is stored in the form, the report, or a record of a table.

Embedding an unbound object

Access provides two methods you can use to embed an unbound object in a form or report:

✦ You can simply paste an object on the form or report. Access adds an image or unbound object frame that contains the object.

✦ You can add an unbound object frame or image frame and then insert the object or picture into the frame.

Pasting an unbound object

If the object you want to insert is not an OLE object, you *must* first copy in the source application and then paste the object on the form. Generally today most applications include OLE technology and can be recognized by the Insert menu option. Sometimes, you may just want to select an image using Windows Explorer and copy and paste the object to an Access form. As an example, to cut or copy an object and then paste it into an image or unbound object frame, follow these steps:

1. Create or display any object by using any source application like Word, Excel, or Paint.

2. Select the object and choose Edit ➪ Cut or Edit ➪ Copy.

3. Display the Access form or report in Design View and click Edit ➪ Paste.

This process automatically adds an unbound object frame for an OLE object (such as Word or Excel) or an Image control for a Paint picture and then embeds the pasted object in it.

If the object you paste into a form is an OLE object and you have the OLE application loaded, you can still double-click on the object to edit it. For example, you can highlight a range of cells in an Excel worksheet and paste the highlighted selection into an Access form or report. You can use the same highlight-and-paste approach with a paragraph of text in Word and paste it on the Access form or report. You can paste both OLE and non-OLE objects on a form or report with this method, but you'll see that there are other ways to add an OLE object.

Inserting an image-type object

You can also use the second method to embed OLE objects or pictures into an unbound object frame or image frame like you did in Chapter 16. Suppose that you want to embed a file containing a Paint picture. In Figure 17-1, the picture of the Access Auto Auctions logo appears on the form in the form header in an *image control*. You can embed the picture by either pasting it into the image control or by inserting the object into the image frame (the rectangle that contains and displays the picture). Follow these steps to add an image control:

1. Open the form frmProductExampleStart in Design View.

2. Select the Image frame tool on the Toolbox.

3. Draw a rectangle in the Form Header, as shown in Figure 17-3, to add the image frame.

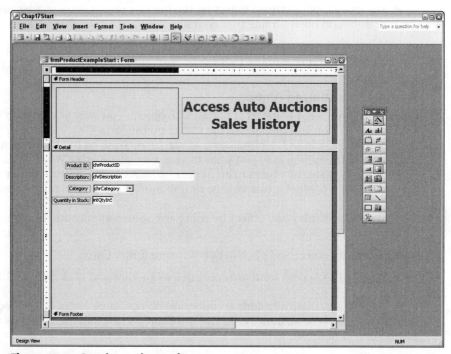

Figure 17-3: Creating an image frame.

When you add an image frame, the Insert Picture dialog box appears. This dialog box, shown in Figure 17-4, displays the image objects you have on your system. As you click on each file, a preview of the image appears to the right of the file selection list. If you don't see the preview, select Preview from the Views button in the Insert Picture toolbar.

To embed the existing Paint file AAAuctions.jpg in the image frame, follow these steps:

4. Using the standard file navigation dialog box, select AAAuctions.jpg from the folder in which your other database files reside. (This file was installed when you installed files from the *Access 2003 Bible* CD-ROM.)

5. Click on OK after the filename appears in the Insert Picture dialog box.

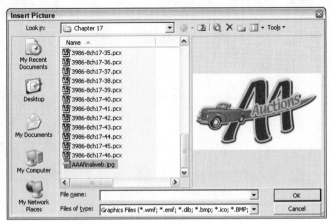

Figure 17-4: The Insert Picture dialog box.

Access embeds and displays the picture in the unbound object frame, as you can see in Figure 17-5. Notice that, in this figure, the picture of the auction logo does not seem to be displayed correctly. You can correct this by using the Size Mode property.

Figure 17-5 also shows some of the other properties of the Image control. The Picture property is set to the path and filename of the image you selected. The Picture Type property below has two choices. The default is Embedded and saves a copy of the bitmap picture in the database container in a compressed form. When you save the form and have chosen Embedded, the Picture property will change to (bitmap) rather than the name of the path and file for the original location of the picture. The other Picture Type option is Linked. This setting will maintain a link to the original picture. However, if you move the bitmap, the picture will no longer be displayed and the link will be broken.

Changing the display of an image

After you add an image to a form or a report, you may want to change the size of the object or the object frame. If you embed a small picture, you may want to adjust the size of the object frame to fit the picture. Similarly, you might want to reduce the size of the picture to fit a specific area on your form or report.

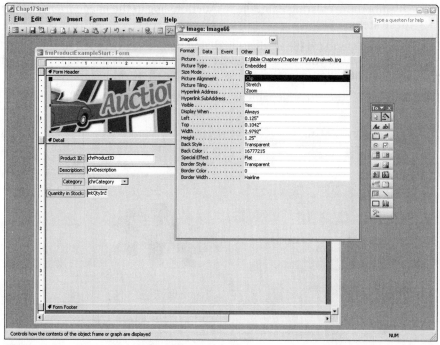

Figure 17-5: The image frame property sheet.

To change the appearance and proportions of the object you embedded, you must change the size of the image frame and set the Size Mode property. In Figure 17-6, you see the result of the three choices for the Size Mode property as well as the correct view of the picture:

✦ **Clip.** Shows the picture at its actual size, truncating both the right and bottom.

✦ **Stretch.** Fits the picture within the frame, distorting the picture's proportions.

✦ **Zoom.** Fits the picture proportionally within the frame, possibly resulting in extra white space.

You should use the Clip option only when the frame is the exact size of the picture or when you want to crop the picture. Stretch is useful when you can accept a slight amount of distortion in the picture. Although using Zoom fits the picture to the frame and maintains the original proportions, it may leave empty space in the frame. To change the Size Mode setting for the AAAFinalweb.jpg file on the frmProductExampleStart form, follow these steps:

1. Select the image frame in Design View.

2. Display the property sheet.

3. Change the Size Mode setting to Stretch.

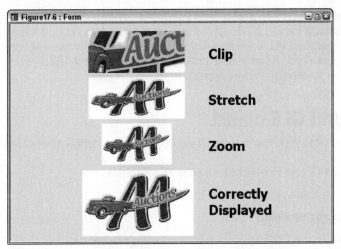

Figure 17-6: Results of using the various scaling options.

If you want to return the selected object to its original size, select it and choose Format ➪ Size ➪ To Fit.

When you have added a picture whose frame (border) is much larger than the picture itself and you have selected a Size Mode of Clip, the picture normally is centered within the frame. You can control this by using one of the Picture Alignment options, which are Center, Top Left, Top Right, Bottom Left, and Bottom Right. These options are also the same ones used when placing a picture in the background of a form using the form's Picture property. Using the Picture Tiling property, you can instruct Access to display many copies of a picture within a frame. For example, a stone wall is made up of many stones. You can specify one stone (Carved Stone.BMP) in your Windows directory and then set the Picture Tiling option to Yes to build a wall within your frame. Access copies the bitmap as many times as it needs to fit within the frame.

Embedding bound objects

You can store pictures, spreadsheets, word-processing documents, or other objects as data in a table. You can store (for example) a Paintbrush picture, an Excel worksheet, or an object created in any other OLE application, such as a sound clip, an HTML document, or even a video clip from a movie.

You store objects in a table by creating a field in your table that uses the OLE Object data type. After you create a blank bound object frame, you can bind its Control Source to the OLE Object field in the table. You can also drag the field to the form from the Field List window and it will automatically be bound.

You can then use the bound object frame to embed an object into each record of the table.

Note You can also insert objects into a table from the Datasheet view of a form, table, or query, but the objects cannot be displayed in a view other than Form. When you switch to Datasheet view, you'll see text describing the OLE class of the embedded object. For example, if you insert a .BMP picture into an OLE object field in a table, the text Picture or Paintbrush Picture appears in Datasheet view.

Adding a bound OLE object

To add an embedded OLE object in a new bound object frame, follow these steps:

1. Select the Bound Object Frame button from the Toolbox.

2. Drag and size the frame, as shown in Figure 17-7.

3. Display the properties sheet.

4. Type **olePicture** in the Control Source property. This is the name of the OLE field in the tblProducts table that contains pictures of the cars.

5. Set the Size Mode property to Zoom so that the picture will be zoomed proportionally within the area you define.

6. Select and delete only the bound object frame label (OLEBoundxx:).

7. Close and save the changes to this form.

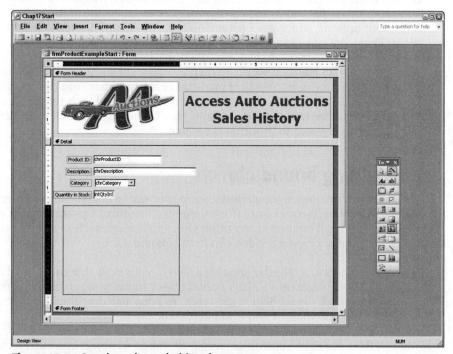

Figure 17-7: Creating a bound object frame.

Adding a picture to a bound object frame

After you define the bound object frame control and place it on a form, you can add pictures to it in several ways. You can paste a picture into a record or insert a file object into the frame. You insert the file object for a bound frame in nearly the same way you would insert an unbound object or image frame. The only difference is that, where an unbound image frame has a picture inserted in the design screen, a bound object frame contains a picture that is stored in a table, and therefore the picture is inserted in Form view like any other data.

To insert a picture or other object into a bound object frame, display the form in Form view, move to the correct record (each record can have a different picture or object), select the bound object frame, and then choose Insert ⇨ Object from the Form menu. The dialog box is a little different. Because you can insert any OLE object (in this example, a picture), you first have to select Create from File and then choose the first option, Bitmap Image. You can then select the actual picture. When you're through, the picture or object appears in the bound object frame in the form.

Note

If you create the object (rather than embed an existing file), some applications display a dialog box asking whether you want to close the connection and update the open object. If you choose Yes, Access embeds the object in the bound object frame or embeds the object in the datasheet field along with text (such as Paintbrush Picture) that describes the object.

After you embed an object, you can start its source application and edit it from your form or report. Simply select the object in Form view and double-click on it.

Editing an embedded object

After you have an embedded object, you may want to modify the object itself. You can edit an OLE object in several ways. Normally, you can just double-click on it and launch the source application; then you can edit the embedded OLE object. As an example, you could follow these steps to edit the picture of the car in Windows Paint or whatever your default application is for editing bitmaps:

1. Display the form frmProductExampleStart in Form view.

2. Move to record 2 (or whichever record contains blue car) and select the Picture bound object frame of the car.

3. Double-click on the picture. The screen changes to an image-editing environment with Windows Paint, Microsoft Photo Editor (or your default bitmap editor) menus and functions available. You may see the icon on the taskbar for the product (Microsoft Photo Editor) in Figure 17-8. Choose Maximize on the icon to edit the picture if in place editing is not allowed in Access.

Caution

If you get the message *The OLE object was changed to a picture or the link was broken*, it just means that our pictures may not be compatible with your system. Insert your own picture and try again.

Note Windows can support full in-place editing of OLE objects. Rather than launch a different program, it changes the look of the menus and screen to match Windows Paint, temporarily adding that functionality to Access.

4. Make any changes you want to the picture.

5. Click on any other control in the form to close Paint or Microsoft Photo Editor.

Figure 17-8: Editing the embedded object.

If you make any changes, you will be prompted to update the embedded object before continuing.

Caution In most cases, you can modify an OLE object by double-clicking on it. When you attempt to modify either a sound or video object, however, double-clicking on the object causes it to use the player instead of letting you modify it. For these objects, you must use the Edit menu; select the last option, which changes (according to the OLE object type) to let you edit or play the object. You can also convert some embedded OLE objects to static images, which breaks all OLE links and simply displays a picture of the object.

Linking Objects

Besides embedding objects, you can link them to external application files in much the same way as you would embed them. As you learned earlier, the difference is that the object itself is not stored in the form, the report, or the database table. Instead, Access stores the filename and path to the object, saving valuable space in the MDB file. This feature also allows you to edit the object in its source application without having to go through Access.

Linking a bound object

When you create a link from a file in another application (for example, Microsoft Excel) to a field in a table, the information is still stored in its original file.

Suppose that you decide to use the OLE Object field to store an Excel file containing additional information about the car's sales. If the Excel file contains history about the sales, you might want to link the information from the tblProducts record to this file.

Before linking information in a file to a field, however, you must first create and save the file in the source application.

On the CD-ROM On your CD-ROM should be a file named Car2.xls, which is an Excel 2003 worksheet. However, you can use any spreadsheet or word-processing file in this example.

To link information to a bound object, use the following steps showing you how to use the Picture bound object frame to link a tblProducts table record to an Excel worksheet:

1. Open Microsoft Excel or the source application, and load the document that contains the information you want to link to.

2. Select the information you want to link, as shown in Figure 17-9.

3. Click Edit ➪ Copy.

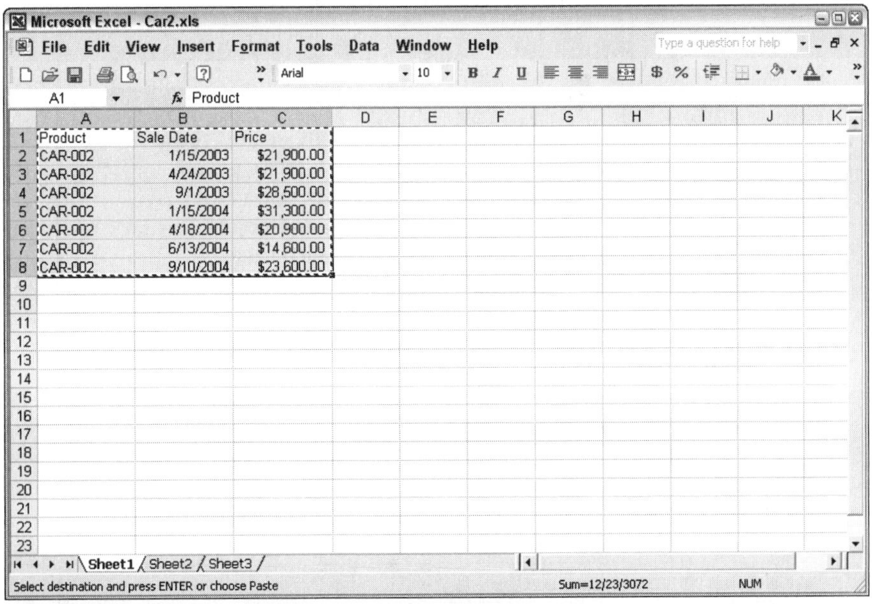

Figure 17-9: Copying a range from Microsoft Excel.

After you copy the range to the Clipboard, you can paste it into the bound object frame in the Access form by using the Paste Special option of the Edit menu.

4. Switch to Access and open the form frmProductExampleStart in Form view.

5. Go to record number 2 in the Access form or the record that contains blue car.

6. Select the bound object frame that you have been using at the lower-left part of the form.

7. Click Edit ⇨ Paste Special.

You may have to first click on the double down arrows at the bottom of the Edit menu to display Paste Special.

The Paste Special dialog box displays and asks you to choose whether you want to Paste or Paste Link the worksheet. The Paste option lets you embed the worksheet either as a static worksheet (the numbers never change until you double-click on the bound OLE frame to redisplay the worksheet), a picture, or a bitmap (you see the image of the numbers but it's just a picture and has no real data).

8. Select Paste Link and then choose Microsoft Excel Worksheet.

The linked Excel worksheet appears in the bound object frame, as shown in Figure 17-10. Access creates the link and displays the object in the bound object frame or it links the object to the datasheet field, displaying text (such as Microsoft Excel) that describes the object. When you double-click on the picture of the worksheet, Excel is launched and you can edit the data.

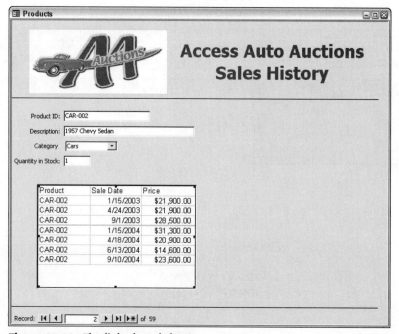

Figure 17-10: The linked worksheet.

Creating a Graph or Chart

You can use Microsoft Graph to chart data from any of your database tables or data stored within other applications (such as Microsoft Excel). You can create graphs in a wide variety of styles — bar graphs, pie charts, line charts, and others. Because Graph is an embedded OLE application, it does not work by itself; you have to run it from within Access.

Note   The terms Graph and Chart are used interchangeably in this chapter. Technically, you use Microsoft Graph to create a chart. There are many chart types that Microsoft Access cannot create. These have little to do with data, and include organization charts and flow charts. Because Microsoft Access creates data charts known as graphs, the term graph will be used throughout the chapter.

After you embed a graph, you can treat it as any other OLE object. You can modify it from the Design view of your form or report by double-clicking on the graph itself. You can edit it from the Form or Datasheet view of a form. The following sections describe how to build and process graphs that use data from within an Access table as well as from tables of other OLE applications.

The different ways to create a graph

Access provides several ways to create a graph and place it on a form or a report. Using the Graph form or Report Wizard, you can create a graph as a new form or report, add it to an existing form or report, or add it to an existing form and link it to a table data source. (To use this third method, in form Design View, click on the Unbound Object frame tool on the Toolbox and then choose Microsoft Graph 2003 Chart.) Unless you are already an experienced Graph user, familiar with it from previous versions of Access or Excel, you'll find it easier to create a new graph from the Toolbox. If you examine the Toolbox, however, you will not see a Chart Wizard icon. You must first customize the Toolbox so that you can add a graph to an existing form by using the Chart Wizard.

As a general rule (for both types of graph creation), before you enter a graph into a form or report that will be based on data from one or more of your tables, you must specify which table or query will supply the data for the graph. You should keep in mind several rules when setting up your query:

✦ Make sure that you've selected the fields containing the data to be graphed.

✦ Be sure to include the fields containing the labels that identify the data.

✦ Include any linking fields if you want the data to change from record to record.

Customizing the Toolbox

You may notice that the Chart Wizard button is missing from the Access Toolbox. This is an optional item, left for you to add. Fortunately, as with toolbars, the Toolbox can be customized.

The easiest way to customize the Toolbox is to right-click on it, display the shortcut menu, and choose Customize. The Customize Toolbars dialog box appears. Click on the Commands tab. You can select Toolbox from the list of toolbars and then (as shown in Figure 17-11) click on the Chart command and drag it to the Toolbox. This adds the missing icon permanently. You can rearrange Toolbox icons by clicking on an icon and dragging it to the desired location in the Toolbox.

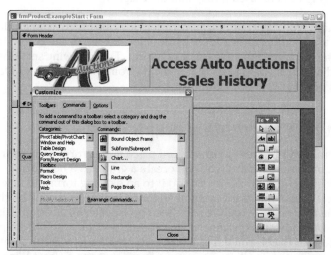

Figure 17-11: Customizing the Toolbox toolbar (shown after dragging the chart icon to the toolbox).

Embedding a Graph in a Form

As you learned earlier in this chapter, you can both link and embed objects in your Access tables, and you can create and display objects on your Access forms. Next you create and display a graph based on the Access Auto Auction data and then display it in a form.

This graph (which was shown in Figure 17-1) will show the dates a car was sold and the dollars received each time. When you move through the records in the tblProducts table, the form will display the data in graph format for each car's prices. You'll use a form that already exists but doesn't contain the graph: frmProductExample-NoGraph.

The form frmProductExample-NoGraph is in the Access Auto Auction.MDB database, along with the final version (called frmProductExampleEnd) that contains the completed graph.

Assembling the data

As a first step in embedding a graph, make sure that the query associated with the form provides the information you need for the graph. In this example, you need both the dtmSalesDate and the curPrice fields from the tblSalesLineItems table as the basis of the graph. You also need the idsInvoiceNumber field from the tblSales table to use as a link to the data on the form. This link allows the data in the graph to change from record to record.

Sometimes, you'll need to create a query when you need data items from more than one table. In this example, you can select all the data you need right from the Wizard; Access will build the query (actually an SQL statement) for you automatically.

Adding the graph to the form

The following steps detail how to create and place the new graph on the existing form (you should be in Design view of the form named frmProductExample-NoGraph):

1. Select the Insert Chart tool you added to the Toolbox, or select Chart from the Insert menu.

2. Position the cursor at about 4 inches in the upper-right side of the form.

3. Click the mouse button and hold it down while dragging the box to the desired size for the graph.

   Access 2003 displays the Chart Wizard dialog box you will use to embed a graph in the form. As shown in Figure 17-12, the first Chart Wizard screen lets you select the table or query with the data for the chart. By using the row of option buttons under the list of tables, you can view all the Tables, all the Queries, or Both.

   The following steps take you through the Wizard to create the desired graph and link it to your form:

4. Choose Query: qryChartExample as the data source for the graph as shown in Figure 17-12.

5. Click on Next to go to the next Wizard screen.

   The second screen of the Chart Wizard lets you select fields to include in your graph.

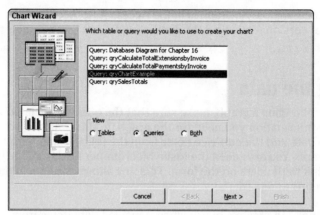

Figure 17-12: Selecting the query for the source of data for the graph.

6. You could select all the fields listed by double-clicking on them to move them to the Fields for Chart box or by clicking on the >> button to move the fields all at once. However, you want to add them in a specific order. Select the fields by double-clicking on them in the following specific order; dtmSaleDate, chrProductID, curPrice.

7. Click on Next to go to the next Wizard screen.

The third Chart Wizard screen (Figure 17-13) lets you choose the type of graph you want to create and determine whether the data series are in rows or columns. In this example, select a column chart; you'll customize it later using the graph options. As you click on each of the graph types, an explanation appears in the box in the lower-right corner of the screen.

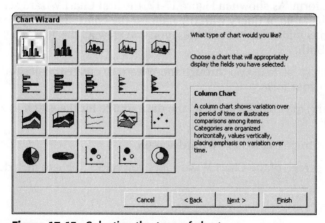

Figure 17-13: Selecting the type of chart.

8. Select the Column Chart (as shown in Figure 17-13), and then click on Next to go to the next Wizard screen. (The Column Chart is easiest to work with.)

The next Wizard screen, shown in Figure 17-14, shows the choices Access has made for you but lets you change the assumptions. The dtmSaleDate field has been used for the x-axis, and the InvoiceTotal field has been used in the y-axis to determine the height of the bars. If you want to change the assumptions, drag the field buttons on the right side of the screen to the simulated graph area.

Note   It is important to only choose the fields you will use for the graph if you want the wizard to figure out for you what to graph. Generally, a numeric field will become the y-axis variable as you generally graph amounts. A date/time field or text field is generally used for the x-axis.

For this example, the assumptions made by Access are fine. You may notice (in Figure 17-14) that each of the fields on the left side of the screen is actually a button. When you double-click on one, you can further define how the data is used in the graph.

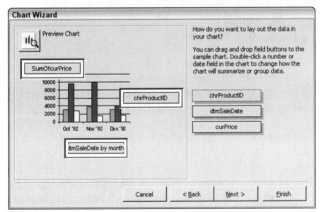

Figure 17-14: Laying out the chart's data elements.

Note   There is a button on the top-left corner of the Chart Wizard that lets you preview that chart at any time. This way, you can see the results of your selections.

Generally, the x-axis variable is either a date or a text field. The y-axis field is almost always a number (though it can be a count of values). Only numeric and date fields (such as the y-axis variable curPrice) can be further defined.

9. Double-click the SumofcurPrice field on the left side of the screen, and the dialog box shown in Figure 17-15 appears; it lets you define options for summarizing the field. Remember that there may be many records for a given summary; in this example, many cars may have been sold in the same month.

Tip

If you had several numeric fields, you could drag them (or any multiple fields) to the left side for a multiple series; these would appear in a legend and display more than one bar or lines in the graph. You can also drag the same field to both the x-axis and the Series indicator, as long as you're grouping differently. For example, you could group the dtmSalesDate by month and use it again in the Series grouped by year. Without using the dtmSalesDate field a second time as the series variable, you would have one bar for each month in sequential order — for example, Jan01, Feb01, Mar01... Dec01, Jan02, Feb02.... By adding the dtmSalesDate as a series variable and grouping it by year, you could get pairs of bars. Multiple bars can be created for each month, each a different color and representing a different year and a legend for each year.

Figure 17-15: Selecting options to summarize the y-axis numeric field.

10. As you can see in Figure 17-15, Sum has been chosen as the summarization type. You could change it to Average to graph the average amount of prices instead of summing all the price amounts. Click Cancel to accept Sum.

Caution

You must supply a numeric variable for all the selections except Count, which can be any data type.

11. Double-click dtmSaleDate by month, and the dialog box shown in Figure 17-16 appears to let you choose the date hierarchy from larger to smaller roll-ups. The choices include Year, Quarter, Month, Week, Day, Hour, and Minute. If you have data for many dates within a month and want to roll it up by month, you would choose Month. In this example, you want to see all the detail data. Because the data is in Sales by date (mm/dd/yy), you would select Day to view all the detail records. For this example, change the default selection from Month to Day and click OK.

12. After you change the group options from Month to Day for the dtmSaleDate field, click on Next to go to the next Wizard screen.

Figure 17-17 shows the field linking box. If you run the Chart Wizard from inside an existing form, you have the option to link a field in the form to a field in the chart. Even if you don't specify the field when you select the chart fields, you can make the link as long as the field exists in the selected table.

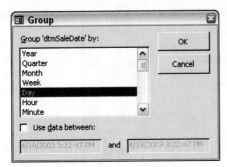

Figure 17-16: Choosing group options for a date field.

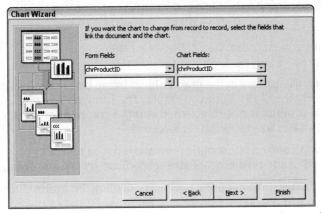

Figure 17-17: Linking fields between the form and the graph.

In this example, Access has correctly selected the chrProduct ID field from both the frmProductsExample form and the qryChartExample query. This way, as you move from record to record (keyed by chrProduct ID) in the frmProductExample form, the graph changes to display the data for that product.

13. Click Next to move to the last Wizard screen.

The last Chart Wizard screen, shown in Figure 17-18, lets you enter a title and determine whether a legend is needed. You won't need one for this example because you have only one data series.

14. Enter Sale Prices by Day for the graph title.

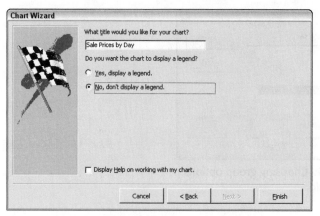

Figure 17-18: Specifying a chart title and legend.

15. Select the button next to No, Don't Display a Legend and click Finish to complete the Wizard.

    The sample chart appears in the graph object frame on the design screen (as shown in Figure 17-19). Until you display the form in Form view, the link to the individual product is not established and the graph is not recalculated to show the sale dates for a specific car's record.

    In fact, the graph shown is a sample preview; it doesn't use any of your data. If you were worried about where that strange-looking graph came from, don't be.

16. Click the Form View button on the toolbar to display the frmProductExample-NoGraph form and recalculate the graph. Figure 17-20 shows the final graph in Form view.

In Figure 17-19, you saw the graph and the property sheet. You display a graph by using a *graph frame*, which shows its data in either Form view or Design view. Now take a look at some properties in the property sheet. The Size Mode property is initially set to Stretch. You can change this to Zoom or Clip, although the graph should always be displayed proportionally. You can size and move the graph to fit on your form. When you work with the graph in the Graph window, the size of the graph you create is the same size it will be in the Design window.

The OLE Class property is set to Microsoft Graph Chart and the class itself is set to MSGraph.Chart.8. This is the same graph engine as in Access 97 and hasn't been changed in several Microsoft Access revisions. This is linked automatically by the Chart Wizard.

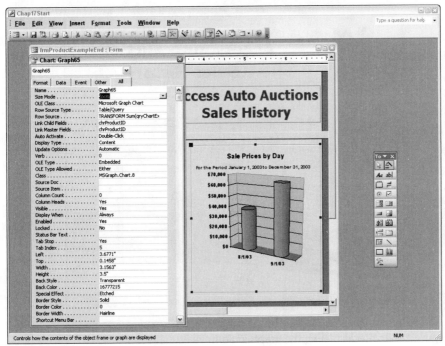

Figure 17-19: The graph in the Form Design window.

The Row Source property setting comes from the table or query you used with the graph, but it appears as an SQL statement that is passed to the Graph. The SQL statement (more on this later) created for this graph is

```
TRANSFORM Sum(qryChartExample.curPrice) AS SumOfcurPrice SELECT
(Format([dtmSaleDate],"Short Date")) AS Expr1 FROM
qryChartExample GROUP BY (Int([dtmSaleDate])),
(Format([dtmSaleDate],"Short Date")) PIVOT
qryChartExample.chrProductID;
```

The next two properties, Link Child Fields and Link Master Fields, control linking of the data to the form data itself. Using the link properties, you can link the graph's data to each record in the form. In this example, the chrProductID from the current Product record is linked to Sales records with the same chrProduct ID.

To change the appearance of the graph, you can double-click on the graph in Design view to open Microsoft Graph. After you make the changes you want, you can select File ➪ Exit, return to Microsoft Access, and go back to Design view.

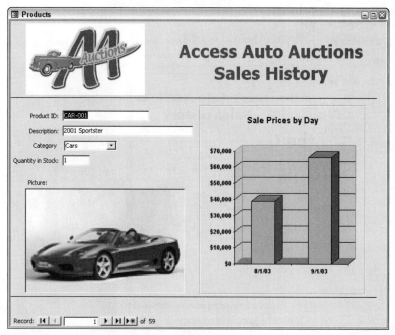

Figure 17-20: Recalculating the graph in Form view.

Customizing a Graph

After you create a graph within Access, you can enhance it by using the tools within Microsoft Graph. As demonstrated in the preceding section, just a few mouse clicks will create a basic graph. The following section describes a number of ways to make your graph a powerful presentation and reporting tool.

In many cases, the basic chart you create presents the idea you want to get across. In other cases, however, it may be necessary to create a more illustrative presentation. You can accomplish this by adding any of these enhancements:

✦ Entering free-form text to the graph to highlight specific areas of the graph

✦ Changing attached text for a better display of the data being presented

✦ Annotating the graph with lines and arrows

✦ Changing certain graphic objects with colors and patterns

✦ Moving and modifying the legend

✦ Adding gridlines to reflect the data better

✦ Manipulating the 3-D view to show your presentation more accurately

✦ Adding a bitmap to the graph for a more professional presentation

✦ Changing the graph type to show the data in a different graphic format, such as Bar, Line, or Pie

✦ Adding or modifying the data in the graph

After the graph appears in the Graph application, you can begin to modify it.

Understanding the Graph window

The Graph or Chart window, shown in Figure 17-21, lets you work with and customize the graph. As you can see, the *graph* itself is highlighted and each object of the graph is active including titles, axis labels, and even the bars themselves. The data last displayed is shown in the graph. A *datasheet* containing the data for the last record used is also displayed. In Figure 17-21, there are two price records for the graph.

✦ **Datasheet.** A spreadsheet of the data used in the graph.

✦ **Graph or Chart.** The displayed chart of the selected data.

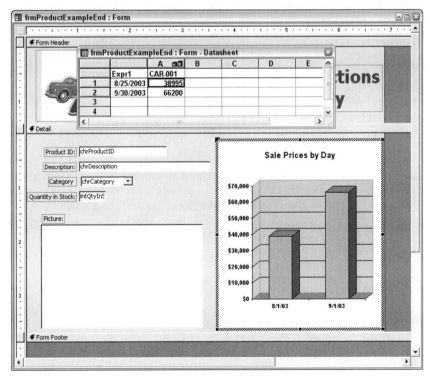

Figure 17-21: The Graph window.

In the datasheet, you can add, change, or delete data. Any data you modify this way is reflected immediately in the graph. After you change the datasheet in the Graph window, you can even tell Access whether to include each row or column when the graph is drawn.

Changing data in a linked record will change data in the graph for only as long as you are on that record. After you move off it, the changes are discarded.

More importantly, you can use the Chart portion of the Graph window to change the way the graph appears. By clicking on objects such as attached text (or on areas of the graph such as the columns), you can modify these objects. You can customize an object by double-clicking on an object to display a dialog box or by making selections from the menus at the top of the window.

Working with attached text

Text generated by the program is called attached text. These graph items are attached text:

- ✦ Graph title
- ✦ Value of y-axis
- ✦ Category of x-axis
- ✦ Data series and points
- ✦ Overlay value of y-axis
- ✦ Overlay value of x-axis

After the initial graph appears, you can change this text. Click on a text object to change the text itself, or double-click on any text item in the preceding list and then modify its properties.

You can choose from three categories of settings to modify an attached text object:

- ✦ **Patterns.** Background and foreground colors, borders, and shading.
- ✦ **Font.** Text font, size, style, and color.
- ✦ **Alignment.** Alignment and orientation.

Note   You can change attributes from the Format menu, too.

The Font options let you change the font assignment for the text within the text object, as shown in Figure 17-22.

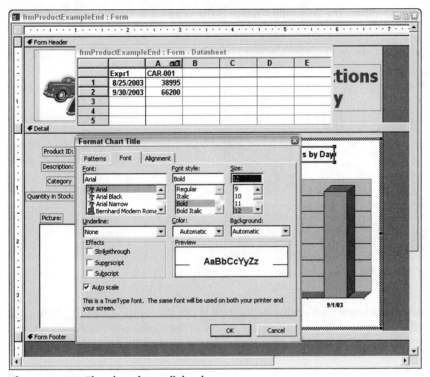

Figure 17-22: The chart fonts dialog box.

The chart fonts dialog box is a standard Windows font-selector box. Here you can select Font, Size, Font Style, Color, and Background effects. To change the text, follow these steps:

1. Double-click the chart title Sale Prices by Day.

2. Select the Font tab from the Format Chart Title dialog box.

3. Select Arial in the Font list box. (This is probably the default.)

4. Select Bold in the Font Style list box.

5. Select 12 in the Size list box.

6. Click on OK to complete the changes.

As you make the font changes, a sample of each change appears in the Preview box.

The Alignment tab in the dialog box lets you set the horizontal alignment (left, center, right, or justify), the vertical alignment (top, center, bottom, or justify), and the orientation (a control that lets you rotate your text on a compass).

Figure 17-23 shows the Alignment tab and the options available.

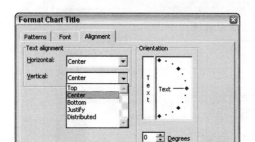

Figure 17-23: The Alignment tab.

The most important part of this dialog box is the Orientation setting. Although for some titles it is not important to change any of these settings, it becomes necessary to change them for titles that normally run vertically (such as axis titles).

Sometimes you may need to add text to your graph to present your data better. This text is called *free-form* (or *unattached*) text. You can place it anywhere on your graph and combine it with other objects to illustrate your data as you want. Figure 17-24 shows free-form text being entered on the graph, as well as the changes you previously made to the graph title.

In the next steps, you see how to add free-form text to the graph:

1. Type **For the Period Jan 1 2003 - Dec 31, 2003** anywhere on the graph, as shown in Figure 17-24.

   Microsoft Graph positions the text near the middle of the graph. The text is surrounded by handles so that you can size and position the text.

2. Drag the text to the upper-left corner of the graph.

3. Right-click on the text, select FormatText Box, and change the font to Arial, 10 point, italic.

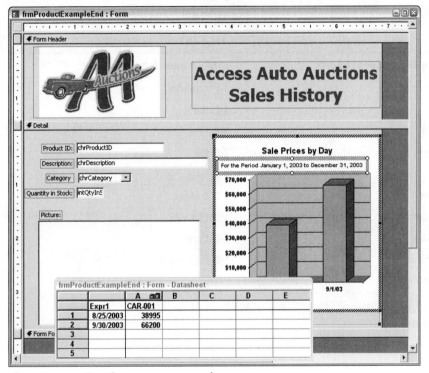

Figure 17-24: Free-form text on a graph.

Changing the graph type

After you create your initial graph, you can experiment with changing the graph type to make sure that you selected the type that best reflects your data. Microsoft Graph provides a wide range of graphs to select from; a few mouse clicks can change the type of graph.

Table 17-1 shows the different types of graphs you can select:

To select a different type of graph, select Chart ➪ Chart Type from the menu bar of the Chart window to display the various chart types. When you select any of the graph options, a window opens (as shown in Figure 17-25) to display all the different graphing options available within the selected graph type. Click on one of them to select your new graph type.

Table 17-1 Types of Charts	
Two-Dimensional Charts	**Three-Dimensional Charts**
Column	3-D Column
Bar	3-D Bar
Line	3-D Line
Pie	3-D Pie
XY (Scatter)	3-D Area
Area	3-D Surface
Doughnut	3-D Cylinder
Radar	3-D Cone
Surface	3-D Pyramid
Bubble	
Stock	
Cylinder	
Cone	
Pyramid	

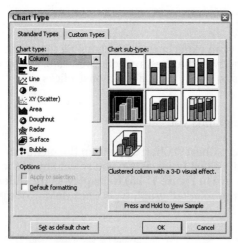

Figure 17-25: The chart types.

To display some different graph types, follow these steps:

1. Select Chart ➪ Chart Type, as shown in Figure 17-25.

2. Select Column from the Standard Types tab and select the 3-D Column type.

3. Click on OK to return to the Graph window.

Changing axis labels

You may want to change the text font of the x-axis so that you can see all the labels. Follow these steps to change axis labels:

1. Double-click on the x-axis (the bottom axis with the dates on it). You can see the Format Axis tabbed dialog box showing the Pattern tab in Figure 17-26.

2. Select the Font tab from the Format Axis dialog box.

3. Change the Size setting to 9 points by entering 9 in the Font Size box.

4. Click on OK to return to the chart.

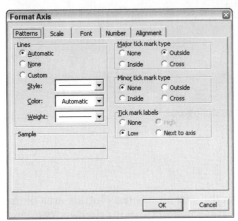

Figure 17-26: The Format Axis dialog box Pattern tab.

Changing a bar color, pattern, and shape

If you are going to print the graph in monochrome, you should always adjust the patterns so that they are not all solid colors. You can change the color or pattern of each bar by double-clicking on any bar in the category you want to select.

The Format Data Series dialog box is displayed. You can change the patterns and color of the bars from the first tab. If you press the Shape tab, as shown in Figure 17-27, you can select from cubes, pyramids, cylinders, or cones.

1. Double-click on any bar.

2. Click the Shape tab, select 4 – Cylinders for the bar shape and click OK.

3. Change to Form View and display the first record to see the graph change and view the cylinders better. If the graph doesn't change, press F5 to refresh the screen.

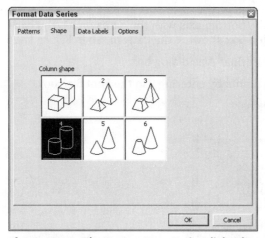

Figure 17-27: The Format Data Series dialog box showing the Shape tab.

Modifying gridlines

Gridlines are lines that extend from the axis across the plotting area of the graph to help you read the graph properly. You can add them for the x-axis and y-axis of your graph; if it's three-dimensional, an additional gridline is available for the z-axis. You can add gridlines for any axis on the graph. The *z-axis gridlines* appear along the back and side walls of the plotting area. The *x-* and *y-axis gridlines* appear across the base and up the walls of the graph.

1. Select the graph again, double-click and then click Chart ⇨ Chart Options to begin working with gridlines.

2. Click the Gridlines tab, as shown in Figure 17-28.

Here, you can define which gridlines are shown. The y-axis gridlines are shown on the left wall; the z-axis gridlines are shown on the back wall; and the x-axis gridlines are shown on the floor. You can change the line type by double-clicking on the grid-lines when you're in the normal Design view of the graph and working with the Format Gridlines dialog box to change the Patterns and Scale.

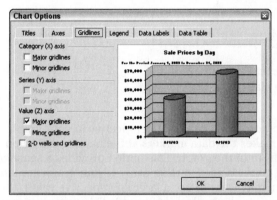

Figure 17-28: The Chart Options dialog box showing the Gridlines tab options.

Manipulating three-dimensional graphs

In any of the three-dimensional chart options, you can modify the following graph-display characteristics:

✦ Elevation

✦ Perspective (if the Right angle axes option is turned off)

✦ Rotation

✦ Scaling

✦ Angle and height of the axes

1. Click Chart ➪ 3-D View to change the 3-D View. The dialog box shown in Figure 17-29 appears. You can enter the values for the various settings or use the six buttons to rotate the icon of the graph in real time. When you see the view you like, click on OK and your chart will change to that perspective.

The Elevation buttons control the height at which you view the data. The elevation is measured in degrees; it can range from −90 to 90 degrees.

An elevation of zero displays the graph as if you were level with the center of the graph. An elevation of 90 degrees shows the graph as you would view it from above center. A −90-degree elevation shows the graph as you would view it from below its center.

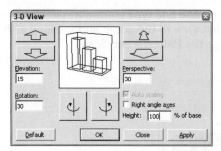

Figure 17-29: The 3-D View dialog box.

The Perspective buttons control the amount of perspective in your graph. Adding more perspective makes the data markers at the back of the graph smaller than those at the front of the graph. This option provides a sense of distance; the smaller data markers seem farther away. If your graph contains a large amount of data, you may want to use a larger perspective value (the ratio of the front of the graph to the back of the graph). This value can range from 0 to 100.

A perspective of 0 makes the back edge of the graph equal in width to the front edge. You can experiment with these settings until you get the effect you need.

The Rotation buttons control the rotation of the entire plotting area. The rotation is measured in degrees, from 0 to 360. A rotation of 0 displays your graph as you view it from directly in front. A rotation of 180 degrees displays the graph as if you were viewing it from the back. (This setting visually reverses the plotting order of your data series.) A rotation of 90 degrees displays your graph as if you were viewing it from the center of the side wall.

2. Change the rotation from 20 to 30 degrees by pressing the left rotation button once.

The Auto scaling check box lets you scale a three-dimensional graph so that its size is closer to that of the two-dimensional graph using the same data. To activate this option, click on the Auto scaling check box so that the X appears in the box. When this option is kept activated, Access will scale the graph automatically whenever you switch from a two-dimensional to a three-dimensional graph.

Two options within the 3-D View dialog box pertain specifically to display of the axes. The Right angle axes check box lets you control the orientation of the axes. If the check box is on, all axes are displayed at right angles to each other.

Caution If the Right Angle Axes check box is selected, you cannot specify the perspective for the three-dimensional view.

The Height box contains the height of the z-axis and walls relative to the width of the graph's base. The height is measured as a percentage of the x-axis length. A height of 100 percent makes the height equal to the x-axis. A height of 50 percent makes the height half the x-axis length. You can set this height percentage at more than 100 percent; by doing so, you can make the height of the z-axis greater than the length of the x-axis.

Caution   If you change the Height setting, your change will not be displayed in the sample graph shown in the 3-D View dialog box.

After you have made the desired changes, you can select OK which will bring you back to the Form Design screen. You may just see the buttons Close, or Apply, which will also do the same thing.

You might want to make one more change: A graph frame is really an unbound object frame, and you can change its border type and background (as you can for any unbound object frame). Figure 17-30 shows the final graph after the border has been changed to an etched special effect, and the background colored light gray or made transparent to match the background of the form. This allows the graph to stand out more than it would if you used a sunken white background. Figure 17-30 shows the first record in the database.

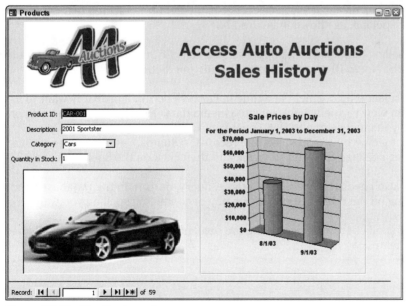

Figure 17-30: The final graph.

Integration with Microsoft Office

Access 2003 is not only integrated with Windows, it now shares many major components with Microsoft Office 2003. (If you are an Excel 2003 or Word 2003 user, you will be especially thrilled.) Access 2003 has an integrated Spell Checker that is used to make sure that the data stored in Access 2003 tables and database objects is spelled correctly. The dictionary is shared across all Office 2003 applications. There are also specific technical dictionaries for legal, medical, and foreign languages and also several custom dictionaries that you can maintain to store your own technical words. Access 2003 also shares the Office 2003 AutoCorrect features to fix errors while you type.

Checking the spelling of one or more fields and records

You can check the spelling of your data in either Form or Datasheet view. In Form view, you can spell-check only a single record—and field within the record—at a time. To check the spelling of data in Datasheet view, you would select the field or text containing spelling you want to check, and then click on the Spelling toolbar button (the icon with the check mark and the small letters ABC above it).

When you click on the icon, Access checks the field (or selected text within the field) for spelling, as shown in Figure 17-31.

In the Spelling dialog box that appears, you can click on Add if you want to add the word in the Not In Dictionary: box to the custom dictionary.

You can select only one field at a time in Form view. You'll probably want to use only Form view to spell-check selected memo data. To select multiple fields or records, you must switch to Datasheet view. To check the spelling of data in Datasheet view, you would select the records, columns, fields, or text within a field containing spelling you want to check and then click on the Spelling icon.

You can also check the spelling in a table, query, or form in the Database window by clicking on the table, query, or form object containing spelling you want to check.

You only spell-check the data inside the objects. Access 2003 cannot spell-check control names.

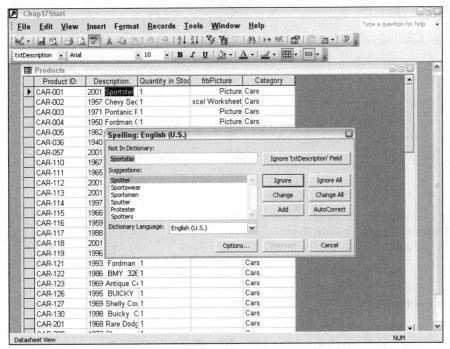

Figure 17-31: Spell-checking in Access.

Correcting your typing automatically when entering data

You can use the AutoCorrect feature to provide automatic corrections to text you frequently mistype and to replace abbreviations with the long names they stand for (also automatically). For example, you can create an entry "AAA" for Access Auto Auctions. Whenever you type AAA followed by a space or punctuation mark, Microsoft Access replaces *AAA* with the text *Access Auto Auctions*.

You can activate AutoCorrect by selecting Tools ➪ AutoCorrect Options. The dialog box shown in Figure 17-32 appears. You can select the Replace text as you type check box. In the Replace box, type the text you want corrected. In the With box, type the corrected text. When you click on Add, the word replacement combination will be added to the AutoCorrect dictionary.

Figure 17-32: Using AutoCorrect in
Access 2003.

AutoCorrect won't correct text that was typed before you selected the Replace text
as you type check box.

Using OLE automation with Office 2003

Access 2003 takes advantage of drag and drop; you can do it from a Datasheet view
across Excel and Word. You can instantly create a table in a Word document (or add
a table to an Excel spreadsheet) by simply copying and pasting (or dragging and
dropping) data from an Access datasheet to a Word document or an Excel spreadsheet. (Obviously, you must have Word or Excel to take advantage of these features.)

Creating an Excel type PivotTable

Access 2003 contains a PivotTable Wizard to create Excel PivotTables based on
Access tables or queries. A *PivotTable* is like a cross-tabulation of your data; you
can define the data values for rows, columns, pages, and summarization. Figure
17-33 shows a conceptual figure of a PivotTable.

A PivotTable can have multiple levels of rows, columns, and even pages. As you can
see in the conceptual figure, the center of the table contains numeric data; the rows
and columns form a hierarchy of unique data. In this figure, dates and employees
are the row hierarchies, along with multiple levels of subtotals. The column headers are types of products, and each page of the PivotTable is a different region.

**Cross-
Reference**   A PivotTable is like a cross-tab query (see Chapter 23) but much more powerful.

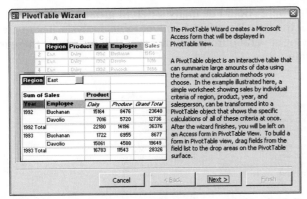

Figure 17-33: A conceptual view of a PivotTable displayed when you start the form PivotTable Wizard.

Before you begin creating a pivot table, you should make sure you can display a simple datasheet containing the data you want to analyze. Figure 17-34 shows a query using the tblContacts, tblSales, and tblSalesLineItems tables and the qryCalculateTotalPaymentsbyInvoice query in order to create an analysis of sales.

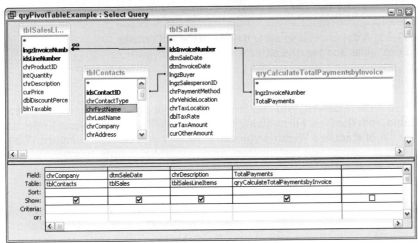

Figure 17-34: A query combining data from the tblContacts, tblSales, and tblSalesLineitems tables and the qryCalculateTotalPaymentsbyInvoice query.

After you have created your query, you should display the datasheet to make sure that the data you expect to see is displayed and that the type of data lends itself to PivotTable analysis. Because the idea of a pivot table is to manipulate or pivot various categorization data, there should be many different groupings of data. As you can see in Figure 17-35, the data is perfect for pivot table analysis. There are many customers, each having several purchases, on several dates where there is a total payment for each sale.

Sale Date	Company	Description	TotalPayments
1/15/2003	Nopa Auto Parts	2003 Fordman T-150 Regular Cab	$70,565.00
1/15/2003	Nopa Auto Parts	1960 Chevy Pickup	$70,565.00
1/15/2003	Nopa Auto Parts	1957 Chevy Sedan	$70,565.00
1/15/2003	Nopa Auto Parts	1950 Fordman Coupe	$70,565.00
1/15/2003	Nopa Auto Parts	2002 Olds SUV	$70,565.00
2/27/2003	R & G Monda Inc	1962 AALLFA Red Spidery 2000	$1,000.00
2/27/2003	R & G Monda Inc	1965 Shelly Stunning Red Cobrat	$1,000.00
2/24/2003	Pleasantville Monda Inc	1971 Pontanic Red Converible	$22,995.00
2/24/2003	Pleasantville Monda Inc	2001 Collectors Chevy Corvet	$22,995.00
4/24/2003	McHugh Cash Auto Sales	1940 Classic Antique Convertible	$85,000.00
4/24/2003	McHugh Cash Auto Sales	1967 Shelly Stunning Red Muscle Car	$85,000.00
4/24/2003	McHugh Cash Auto Sales	1957 Chevy Sedan	$85,000.00
5/24/2003	Tip Top Chevy	2001 Collectors Chevy Corvet	$5,000.00
7/15/2003	KJ Auto Repair	1994 Fordman XLP Ext	$1,000.00
7/15/2003	KJ Auto Repair	1998 Fordman Explorer XLP	$1,000.00
8/26/2003	Iron Springs Auto Sales	1967 Shelly Stunning Red Muscle Car	$15,000.00
9/30/2003	Ghost Automobile Sales	2001 Sportster	$40,554.80
12/13/2003	Bush Sales	1973 Rare Popup Hard sided Indian Camper	$1,820.00
9/30/2003	Sakes American Autos	2001 Sportster	$25,000.00
9/30/2003	Sakes American Autos	1986 BMY 326CI	$25,000.00
10/15/2003	Paul's Best Autos	1999 Fordman E350 Cargo Van	$19,133.57
10/15/2003	Paul's Best Autos	2000 Dodgie Minivan SEE	$19,133.57
10/26/2003	Sammy Fordman	1968 Rare Dodget Red 2D Sedan	$1,500.00
10/30/2003	Fordman Sales	1969 Shelly Coupe Muscle Car	$100.00
11/1/2003	A-1 Auto Sales	1972 Chevy green chevel	$25,100.00
11/5/2003	Pleasantville Monda Inc	2001 Fordman Ptaurus XES	$17,850.00

qryPivotTableExample : Select Query

Record: |◄| ◄| 1 |►|►I|►*| of 68

Figure 17-35: A datasheet displaying data from the tblContacts and tblSales tables and the qryCalculateTotalPaymentsbyInvoice query.

After the data is reviewed, you can create your pivot table. You start creating a PivotTable from the New Form dialog box, using the PivotTable Wizard selection from the list of standard Wizards you can select, as you can see in Figure 17-36. Notice that the query you just created, qryPivotTableExample, has been selected as the data source.

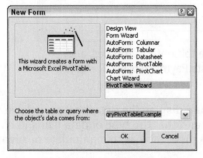

New Form

This wizard creates a form with a Microsoft Excel PivotTable.

Design View
Form Wizard
AutoForm: Columnar
AutoForm: Tabular
AutoForm: Datasheet
AutoForm: PivotTable
AutoForm: PivotChart
Chart Wizard
PivotTable Wizard

Choose the table or query where the object's data comes from: qryPivotTableExample

OK   Cancel

Figure 17-36: The New Form dialog box showing the PivotTable Wizard selected and the PivotTable Example query being used as the data source.

After you begin the PivotTable Wizard process, you will first see an introductory screen explaining how a PivotTable works (Figure 17-33). After you view this screen, press the Next button. Figure 17-37 displays the table/queries dialog box. You have already selected the query qryPivotTableExample. In this example, because the query only selected the four fields you want to use for the PivotTable, you can select all of the fields in the Available Fields list box, which moves them to the Fields Chosen for Pivoting list box.

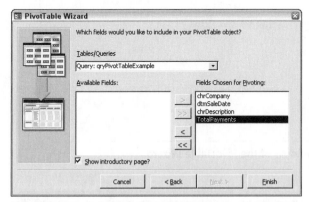

Figure 17-37: Selecting the Table/Query to supply data for the PivotTable and the fields to be used for pivoting.

Now that you have selected the data, you can press the Finish button to complete the process. The blank Pivot Table type form is displayed in Figure 17-38. If you were a user of the Access or Excel 2000 Pivot Tables, you will see a huge improvement. This layout screen now features live data links. The way it works is that you drag your fields for the Pivot Table onto the form from the Pivot Table field list shown at the bottom-right corner of the form. You can move the field list around and expand and collapse the data lists displayed. It will automatically group date type fields by week or month. You can also create your own calculated fields and summary fields at any level.

In this example, you are going to be using all of the fields for the pivot table. Starting in the upper-left corner of the form, which is where you drag and drop Filter Fields, you will drag the chrCompany name field. As you can see in Figures 17-39 and 17-40, this will create a combo box with the text chrCompany Name and initially displays all of the customers in the data sample. You can click on the combo box and filter the data for any or all of the customers. You can even select any number of customers using the check boxes you can see in Figure 17-40.

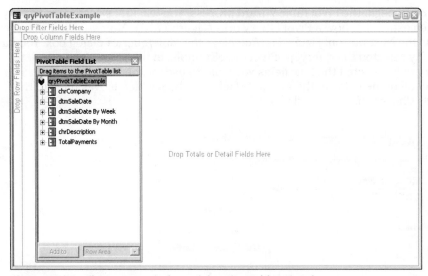

Figure 17-38: The Layout window of the PivotTable Wizard.

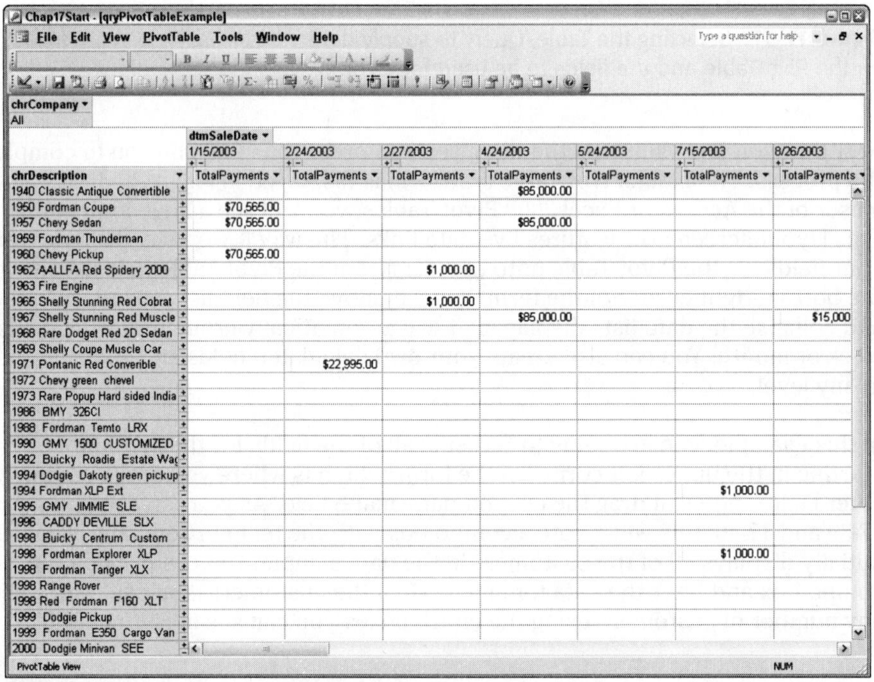

Figure 17-39: Data displayed in the PivotTable Wizard.

The chrDescription field will be used for the Row Field, and the dtmSalesDate field will be used for the Column Field. When you complete dragging and dropping these field names from the PivotTable Field List to the drop area, the live data appears along the top (Column Fields) or side (Row Fields). Instantly you can see your column headers, and the first row data appear like a data sheet. When you drag the TotalPayments field to the Total or Detail Fields area, data is filled in like a cross-tab query. Figure 17-39 shows this data after the fields are dragged to the form from the Field List.

The intersection of a row and a column displays a data value. For example, in Figure 17-39 you can see the value $70,565.00 where 1950 Fordman Coupe and 1/15/2003 intersect. This means that the 1950 Fordman Coupe was sold on 1/15/2003 and the total payment was $70,565.00. If you filtered the Company Name, you could see who owns the 1950 Fordman Coupe.

When your fields are dragged to the form and your data is displayed in the form, you can begin to manipulate the data. If you notice the data elements in either the rows or the column headers, you can see there are + and – signs on very small buttons next to each element. If you click on the – button, the data row or column is hidden. You can click on the + sign to redisplay the data from that column or row.

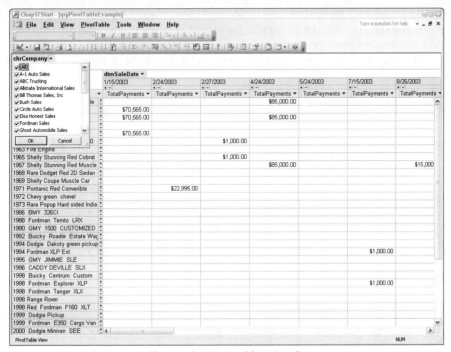

Figure 17-40: Changing a filter in the PivotTable Wizard.

Remember, the real value of a pivot table view is to pivot the data. You can also move row fields to the column area and column fields to the row area. You can filter by any of the selections. The three major filters chrDescription, dtmSaleDate, and chrCompanyName each have a downward-pointing arrow in the rectangle that contains the name. Figure 17-40 shows what happens when you press the down arrow on the chrCompany Name field.

A type of list box with a series of check boxes is displayed. If you click on the (All) selection, all of the customers below are either selected or de-selected. If you de-select all of the options, you will have no data displayed. You can then select the Companies you want to include in the selection. You can select 1, 2, 20, or as many as are displayed. When you press the OK button at the bottom of the list, the pivot table is filtered.

Pivot tables are very powerful. You can switch the row and columns by simply dragging the column or row designator to the other dimension. For example, you could move the dtmSaleDate from being a column field to being a row field. That could show you dates sold by product description. There is no limit to the number of ways you can manipulate the data.

Figure 17-41 shows the PivotTable menu. This helps you create subtotals, calculated fields, and totals, and helps you to do many things the individual buttons can do, such as expanding and collapsing levels and hiding or showing details. You can also Export the data directly to Microsoft Excel and create a PivotTable on a worksheet. Pivot Tables provide a great way to view hierarchical data in many ways. It can be much easier to use a pivot table than to create a multitude of reports.

Creating a PivotChart

Just as the PivotTable lets you display data, a PivotChart lets you represent data graphically. You begin by creating a new form and selecting the AutoForm: PivotChart. There is no specific PivotChart Wizard like there is a PivotTable Wizard. In Figure 17-42, you can see the New Form dialog box with the same query, qryPivotTableExample, selected that was used in the last example for the PivotTable Wizard.

After selecting the AutoForm: PivotChart and clicking OK, you will see a screen similar to the PivotTable design screen, except that an empty chart is shown (see Figure 17-43). The Chart Field List is identical to the Pivot Table Field list. You drag and drop fields to the chart areas in the same ways as the Pivot Table.

You can drag the chrCompany field as the overall Filter Field at the top of the screen. The Series would be what separates the various lines. The chrDescription would be appropriate for the Series. The Category field is usually time or dates, and the dtmSaleDate field can be dragged to the Category area. Finally, the TotalPayments can be dragged to the Data Field area.

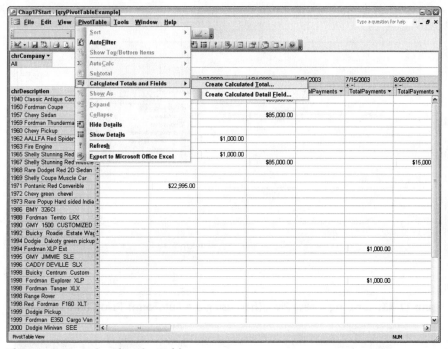

Figure 17-41: Using the PivotTable menu.

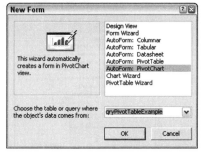

Figure 17-42: Creating a new PivotChart using the AutoForm: PivotChart selection.

After you drag these fields, the chart appears with data as shown in Figure 17-44. You can manipulate the data and change the look of the graph, chart type, axes lines, and any standard chart options.

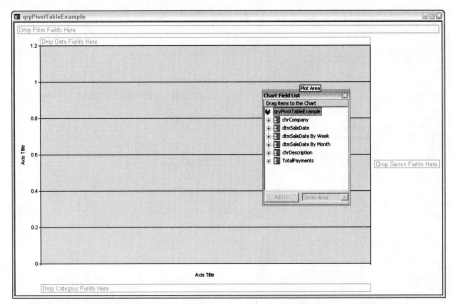

Figure 17-43: Creating a new PivotChart using the AutoForm: PivotChart selection.

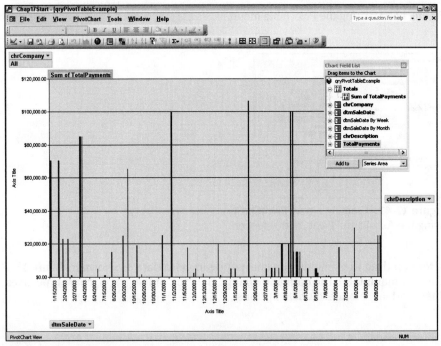

Figure 17-44: Viewing the selections on the PivotChart.

Using the Calendar ActiveX Control

ActiveX controls (also known as OCX controls) are not new to Access. Custom controls extend the number of controls already found in Access. Some of the more popular controls are Calendars, Tab Dialog box controls, Progress Meters, Spin Boxes, Sliders, and many others. Although they existed in early versions of Access, they were seldom used; they required separate sets of properties and were not totally stable. Access for Windows 95 introduced support for the new 32-bit controls, and Access 2003 continues their popularity. Access 2003 comes with several ActiveX controls. One of the most often used is the Calendar control. If you have Office 2003, you have many ActiveX controls from the new Microsoft Forms collection used to create Office forms without Access. There are many ActiveX controls from third parties for Access 2003. See the CD appendix for several demos of the best ActiveX controls that are compatible for Microsoft Access.

The Office Developers Edition is a separate product from Microsoft that allows you to create a run-time application that runs Microsoft Access applications without having Access on the computer. It also includes the Help compiler, a printed-language reference manual, the Windows Setup Wizard, many other ActiveX controls, and many new tools for Access 2003 and Office 2003 developers, including many Internet tools.

You can select Insert ➪ ActiveX Control or select the More Controls icon from the Toolbox to see a list of all your ActiveX controls.

If you don't have the Office Developer's Edition or the full Office 2003, you probably will see only the Calendar control. You add a custom control as you would to any unbound OLE control. To add a Calendar custom control to a new blank form, follow these steps:

1. Open a new form in Design view and display the Toolbox. Don't select any table in the New Form dialog box.

2. Select Insert ➪ ActiveX Control... or choose the More Controls icon from the Toolbox.

3. Select Calendar Control 11.0 and click on OK.

The Calendar control appears on the new form. The calendar can be resized like any unbound control, and (of course) it has properties. Figure 17-45 shows the Calendar control and its basic properties.

The Property window shows the properties specific to a Calendar control. These are the properties displayed by the Other tab. With these properties, you can change some of the display characteristics of the calendar, including the following:

✦ **DayLength.** System (Sunday, Monday, Tuesday), System (Medium) (Sun, Mon, Tue, . . .).

✦ **FirstDay.** First day of week displayed (Mon, Tue, Wed, Thu, etc., default is Sun).

✦ **GridCellEffect.** Flat, Raised, Sunken.

✦ **MonthLength.** System (January, February, . . .), System (Medium) (Jan, Feb, . . .).

✦ **ShowDateSelectors.** Display a combo box for month and year in Form view.

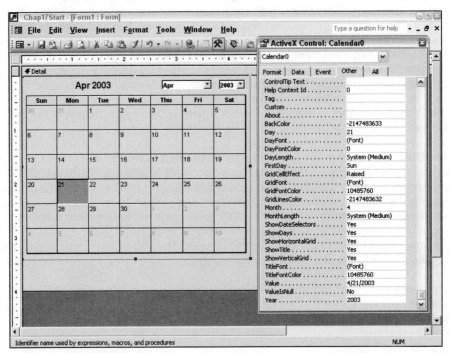

Figure 17-45: The Calendar control and the standard and additional Access properties.

Many other properties control the various colors and fonts of the calendar components. A number of value properties affect the display of the calendar and the selected date. Four properties change the display of the calendar data:

✦ **Day.** The day of the current month (21 in this example).

✦ **Month.** The month of the current date (4 in this example).

✦ **Year.** The year being displayed (2003 in this example).

✦ **Value.** The date displayed (4/21/2003 in this example).

Cross-Reference   The values can be changed in several ways. You can click on a date in the calendar in Form view, which changes the Value property. When the Value property changes, so do the Day, Month, and Year properties. You can also change these properties in the Property window or programmatically from a macro or Visual Basic for Applications.

Another way to change properties in a custom control is to display the Calendar Properties dialog box, as shown in Figure 17-46. This provides combo-box access to certain control properties. You can display this dialog box by selecting Edit ⇨ Calendar Object ⇨ Properties or by right-clicking on the Calendar control and selecting Calendar Object ⇨ Properties from the shortcut menu.

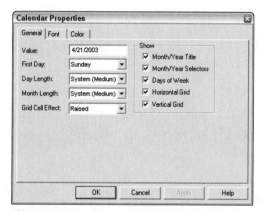

Figure 17-46: The Calendar Properties dialog box.

When you display the calendar in Form view, you can also display combo boxes (using the ShowDateSelectors property) to change the month or year, because you can only click on a day in the calendar. These are the Month/Year Selectors in the Property dialog box.

The calendar's real power is that you can link it to a field. When the calendar is changed, the field value changes. Likewise, if the field value changes, the calendar display changes. You can easily do this by linking the calendar to a field by using its Control Source property.

✦   ✦   ✦

PART I

Creating Desktop Applications

SECTION III

Automating Your Applications

Understanding Visual Basic and the VBA Editor

I f you have created or worked with a simple Access application, the operations of that application were most likely created using macros. Although macros provide a quick and simple method of automating an application, writing Visual Basic modules is the best way to create applications. Adding error routines, setting up repetitive looping, and adding procedures that macros simply can't perform give you more control of application development. In this chapter, you learn how to build an application framework and how to extend the power of an application using Visual Basic.

On the CD-ROM

In this chapter, you will use the database file Chap18start.mdb.

Migrating from Macros to Visual Basic

Should you now convert all of the macros in your applications to Visual Basic? The answer depends on what you are trying to accomplish. The fact that Access 2003 includes Visual Basic does not mean that Access macros are no longer useful; it simply means that Access developers will want to learn Visual Basic and add it to their arsenal of tools for creating Access applications.

Visual Basic is not always the answer. Some tasks, such as assigning global key assignments, can be accomplished only via macros. You can perform some actions more easily and effectively by using a macro.

A Visual Basic procedure may offer better performance. The opposite also is true: A Visual Basic procedure may run at the same speed as a macro counterpart, or even more slowly. If you code everything in your application using Visual Basic, you may find that the time needed to create an application actually increases.

When to use macros and when to use Visual Basic procedures

In Access, macros often offer an ideal way to take care of many details, such as running reports and forms. You can develop applications and assign actions faster using a macro because the arguments for the macro actions are displayed with the macro (in the bottom portion of the Macro window). You won't have to remember complex or difficult syntax.

Several actions you can accomplish via Visual Basic are better suited for macros. The following actions tend to be more efficient when they are run from macros:

✦ Using macros against an entire set of records — for example, to manipulate multiple records in a table or across tables (such as updating field values or deleting records)

✦ Opening and closing forms

✦ Running reports

Note

Visual Basic supplies a DoCmd object that you can use to accomplish most macro actions. This object actually runs the macro task. You could, for example, specify DoCmd.Close to run the close macro and close the current active form. Even this method has flaws. DoCmd cannot perform at least eight macro actions: AddMenu, MsgBox, RunApp, RunCode, SendKeys, SetValue, StopAllMacros, and StopMacro. Some of these actions have Visual Basic equivalents.

Although macros sometimes prove to be the solution of choice, Visual Basic is the tool of choice at other times. You probably will want to use Visual Basic rather than macros when you want to perform any of the following tasks:

✦ **Create and use your own functions.** In addition to using the built-in functions in Access, you can create and work with your own functions by using Visual Basic.

✦ **Create your own error routines and messages.** You can create error routines that detect an error and decide what action to take. These routines bypass the cryptic Access error messages.

✦ **Use Automation to communicate with other Windows applications or to run system-level actions.** You can write code to see whether a file exists before you take some action, or you can communicate with another Windows application (such as a spreadsheet), passing data back and forth.

✦ **Use existing functions in external Windows DLLs.** Macros don't enable you to call functions in other Windows Dynamic Link Libraries.

✦ **Work with records one at a time.** If you need to step through records or to move values from a record to variables for manipulation, code is the answer.

✦ **Maintain the application.** Unlike macros, code can be built into a form or report, making maintaining the code more efficient. Additionally, if you move a form or report from one database to another, the event procedures built into the form or report move with it.

✦ **Create or manipulate objects.** In most cases, you'll find that it's easiest to create and modify an object in that object's Design view. In some situations, however, you may want to manipulate the definition of an object in code. Using Visual Basic, you can manipulate all the objects in a database, including the database itself.

✦ **Pass arguments to your Visual Basic procedures.** You can set arguments for macro actions in the bottom part of the Macro window when you create the macro, but you can't change arguments when the macro is running. With Visual Basic, however, you can pass arguments to your code at the time it runs or use variables for arguments — something you can't do with macros. This capability gives you a great deal of flexibility in the way your Visual Basic procedures run.

✦ **Display a progress meter on the status bar.** If you need to display a progress meter to communicate progress to the user, Visual Basic code is the answer.

Tip

If you create a form or report that will be copied to other databases, create your event procedures for that form or report in Visual Basic instead of using macros. Because macros are stored as separate objects in the database, you have to remember which ones are associated with the form or report you are copying. On the other hand, because Visual Basic code can be attached to the form or report, copying the form automatically copies the Visual Basic event procedures associated with it.

Converting existing macros to Visual Basic

After you become comfortable with writing Visual Basic code, you may want to rewrite some of your application macros as Visual Basic procedures. As you begin this process, you quickly realize how mentally challenging the effort can be as you review every macro in your various macro libraries. You cannot merely cut the macro from the Macro window and paste it into a Module window. For each condition, action, and action argument for a macro, you must analyze the task it accomplishes and then write the equivalent statements of Visual Basic code in your procedure.

Fortunately, Access provides a feature that converts macros to Visual Basic code automatically. One of the options in the Save As dialog box is Save As Module. You can use this option when a macro file is highlighted in the Macros object window of the Database window. This option enables you to convert an entire macro group to a module in seconds.

To try the conversion process, convert the mcrOpenContacts macro in the Chapter18 database. Follow these steps to run the conversion process:

1. Click the Macros object button of the Database window.

2. Select the mcrOpenCustomers macro group.

3. Choose File ⇨ Save As. The Save As dialog box appears, as shown in Figure 18-1.

Figure 18-1: Saving a macro as a module.

4. Access assigns a default name for the new module as "Copy of" followed by the macro name. Enter a name for the new module and select module for the As option.

5. Choose OK. The Convert Macro dialog box appears, as shown in Figure 18-2.

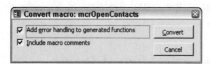

Figure 18-2: The Convert Macro dialog box.

5. Select the options that include error handling and comments, and click Convert.

   Access briefly displays each new procedure as it is converted. When the conversion process completes, the Conversion Finished! message box appears.

6. Click OK to remove the message box.

7. Access displays the new module in the Visual Basic Editor, as shown in Figure 18-3. Access names the new module Converted Macro- mcrOpenContacts.

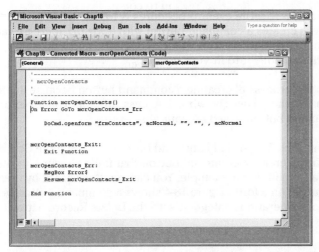

Figure 18-3: The newly converted module.

When you open the Visual Basic Editor for the new module, you can view the procedures created from the macros. Figure 18-3 shows the mcrOpenContacts function that Access created from the mcrOpenContacts macro.

At the top of each function, Access inserts four comment lines for the name of the function. The Function statement follows the comment lines. Access names the functions, using the macro library's name (mcrOpenContacts).

When you specify that you want Access to include error processing for the conversion, Access automatically inserts the On Error statement as the first command in the procedure. The On Error statement tells Access to branch to other statements that display an appropriate message and then exit the function.

 Cross-Reference Error processing is covered in more detail in Chapter 24.

The statement beginning with DoCmd is the actual code that Access created from the macro. The DoCmd methods run Access actions from Visual Basic. An action performs important tasks, such as closing windows, opening forms, and setting the value of controls.

 Tip You also can convert macros that are used in a form by opening the form in Design view and choosing Tools ⇨ Macro ⇨ Convert Form's Macros to Visual Basic in Forms Design view.

Using the Command Button Wizard
to create Visual Basic code

A good way to learn how to write event procedures is to use the Command Button Wizard. When Access creates a command button with a wizard, it creates an event procedure and attaches it to the button. You can open the event procedure to see how it works and then modify it to fit your needs.

The wizard speeds the process of creating a command button because it does all the basic work for you. When you use the wizard, Access prompts you for information and creates a command button based on your answers.

You can create more than 30 types of command buttons by using the Command Button Wizard. You can create a command button that finds a record, prints a record, or applies a form filter, for example. You can run this wizard by creating a new command button on a form. Figure 18-4 shows a command button being created in the Record Operations category, with the Delete Record action.

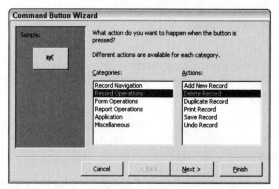

Figure 18-4: The Command Button Wizard.

Note   In the Access Auto Auctions database is a form named frmButton Wizard VBA Samples. This form, shown in Figure 18-5 in Design mode, contains the result of running the Command Button Wizard with several selections. The frmButton Wizard VBA Samples form contains a dozen command buttons created with the Command Button Wizard. You can review the procedures for each command button on the form to see how powerful Visual Basic code can be.

To view the sample code, follow these steps:

1. Display the frmButton Wizard VBA Samples form in Design view.

2. Display the Property window for the desired button.

3. Click the Builder button (. . .) for the On Click event property to display the command button's Module window, with the procedure.

Figure 18-5 shows the property sheet for the Delete Record command button, and Figure 18-6 shows the code for the Delete Record command button.

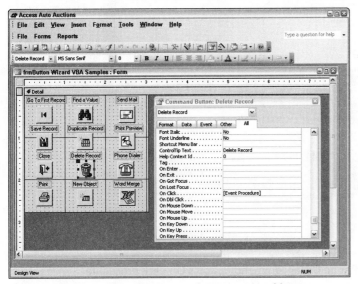

Figure 18-5: Examples of Command Button Wizard buttons.

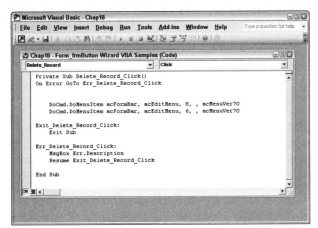

Figure 18-6: The Delete button's On Click procedure.

Figure 18-7 shows the code for a Dialer command button. The Phone_Dialer_Click procedure retrieves the text in the current field and then passes the text to a utility that dials the telephone.

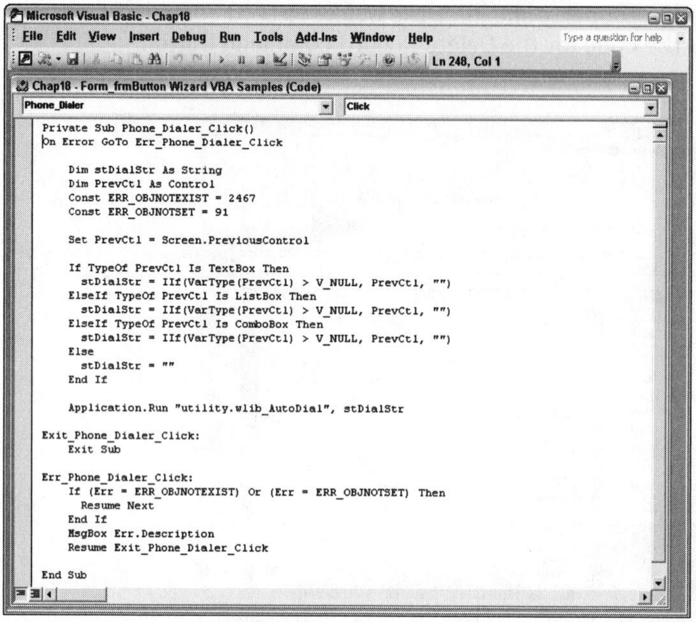

Figure 18-7: The Phone Dialer command button's On Click procedure.

After you become familiar with the code that the Command Button Wizard can create automatically, you are ready to begin creating some Visual Basic code of your own.

Creating Programs in Visual Basic for Applications

Access has an excellent variety of tools that enable you to work with databases and their tables, queries, forms, and reports without ever having to write a single line of code. At some point, you may begin building more sophisticated applications. You may want to make your applications more "bulletproof" by providing more intensive data-entry validation or implementing better error handling.

Some operations cannot be accomplished through the user interface, even with macros. You may find yourself saying, "I wish I had a function that would..." or "There just has to be a function that will let me...." At other times, you find that you are continually putting the same formula or expression in a query or filter. You may find yourself saying, "I'm tired of typing this formula into...." or "Doggone it, I typed the wrong formula in this...."

For situations such as these, you need the horsepower of a high-level programming language. Access provides a programming language called Visual Basic for Applications (VBA), which extends the capabilities of Access, offering power beyond the scope of macros.

Visual Basic has become the common language for all Microsoft applications. Visual Basic is in all Microsoft Office 2003 applications, including Access, Word, Excel, PowerPoint, and Outlook. It is available also in Project. Visual Basic is a modern, structured programming language that offers many of the programming structures programmers are accustomed to: If. . .Then. . .Else, Select Case, and so on. Visual Basic enables a programmer to work with functions and subroutines in an English-like language. The language also is extensible (capable of calling Windows API routines) and can interact through ADO (ActiveX Data Objects) and with any Access or Visual Basic data type.

Getting started with Visual Basic programming in Access requires an understanding of its event-driven environment.

Understanding events and event procedures

In Access, unlike early procedural programming environments, the user controls the actions and flow of the application. The user determines what to do and when to do it, such as changing information in a field or clicking a command button. They determine the flow of action and, through events, the application determines what action to take or ignore. In contrast, procedural-oriented programming languages require that the programmer determine the flow of what actions the user must follow. In fact, the programmer must program for all possibilities of user intervention — keystrokes a user may enter in error and actions to take based on the actions taken by the user.

Using macros and event procedures, you implement the responses to these actions. Access provides event properties for each of the controls you place on the form. When you attach a macro or event procedure to a control's event property, you do not have to worry about the order of actions a user may take on a particular form.

In an event-driven environment such as Access, the objects — forms, reports, and controls — respond to events. Basically, an event procedure is program code that executes when an event occurs. The code is directly attached to the form or report that contains the event being processed. An Exit command button, for example, exits the form when the user clicks that button. Clicking the command button triggers its On Click event. The event procedure is the program code (or macro) that you create and attach to the On Click event. Every time the user clicks the command button, the event procedure runs automatically.

Cross-Reference Programming for events is covered in more detail in Chapter 19.

There are two types of procedures:

✦ Sub

✦ Function

Sub and function procedures are grouped and stored in modules. The Modules object button in the Database window stores the common procedures that any of your forms can access. You can store all your procedures in a single module. Realistically, though, you'll probably want to group your procedures into separate modules, categorizing them by the nature of the operations they perform; for example, an Update module might include procedures for adding and deleting records from a table.

Sub procedures

A sub procedure is program code that does not return a value. Because it does not return a value, a sub procedure cannot be used in an expression or be called by assigning it to a variable. A sub procedure typically runs as a separate program called by an event in a form or report.

You can use a sub procedure to perform actions when you don't want to return a value. In fact, because you cannot assign a value to a control's event properties, you can only create sub procedures for an event.

You can call subs and pass a data value known as a parameter. Subs can call other subs. Subs also can call function procedures.

The code statements inside the sub procedure are lines of Visual Basic statements. These statements make up the code you want to run every time the procedure is executed. The following example shows the Exit command button's sub procedure:

```
Sub cmdExit_Click ()
   DoCmd.Close
End Sub
```

The cmdExit_Click () sub procedure is attached to the Exit command button's On Click event. When the user clicks the Exit command button, the command DoCmd Close executes to close the form.

Function procedures

A function procedure returns a value. You can use functions in expressions or assign a function to a variable.

Like sub procedures, function procedures can be called by other functions or by subs. You also can pass parameters to a function.

You assign the return value of a function to the procedure name itself. You then can use the value that is returned as part of a larger expression. The following function procedure calculates the square footage of a room:

```
Function nSquareFeet (dblHeight As Double, dblWidth As Double)
As Double
  nSquareFeet = dblHeight * dblWidth
End Function
```

This function receives two parameters for the height and width of the room. The function returns the results to the procedure that called it by assigning the result of the calculation to the procedure name (nSquareFeet).

To call this function, you could use code like this:

```
dblAnswer = nSquareFeet(xHeight, xWidth)
```

Understanding modules

Modules and their procedures are the principal objects of the Visual Basic programming environment. The programming code that you write is placed in procedures that are contained in a module. The procedures can be independent procedures, unrelated to a specific form or report, or they can be integral parts of specific forms and reports.

Two basic categories of modules can be stored in a database:

Form/Report	(CBF - Code Behind Form/CBR - Code Behind Report)
Standard Modules	(Stored in the Module Object)

As you create Visual Basic procedures for your Access applications, you use both types of modules.

Form and report modules

All forms and reports, and their controls, can associate event procedures with their events. These event procedures can be macros or Visual Basic code. Every form or report you create in your database contains a form module or report module. This form or report module is an integral part of the form or report, and is used as a container for the event procedures you create for the form or report. This method is a convenient way to place all of a form's event procedures in a single collection.

Creating Visual Basic event procedures in a form module can be very powerful and efficient. When an event procedure is attached to a form, it becomes part of the form. When you need to copy the form, the event procedures go with it. If you need to modify one of the form's events, you simply click the ellipsis button for the event, and the form module window for the procedure appears. Figure 18-8 illustrates accessing the event procedure of the First Record button's On Click event shown in the form named frmButton Wizard VBA Samples. Notice that in the On Click property is the text [Event Procedure]. When you click the Builder button next to [Event Procedure], you will see the module window for that form (and specifically the On Click event for that button control).

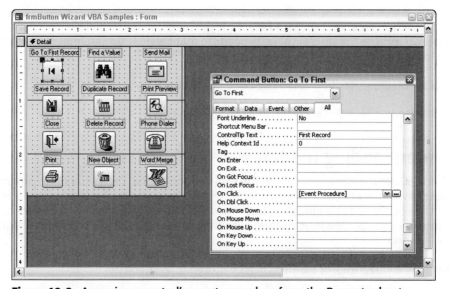

Figure 18-8: Accessing a control's event procedure from the Property sheet.

For more about the frmButton Wizard VBA Samples form, see the section "Using the Command Button Wizard to create Visual Basic code" earlier in this chapter (especially Figure 18-5).

Event procedures that work with a single form or report belong in the module of the form or report. A specific form's module should contain only the declarations and event procedures needed for that form and its controls (command buttons, check boxes, text labels, text boxes, combo boxes, and so on). Placing another form's or report's event procedures in this form's module doesn't make sense.

Standard modules

Standard modules are independent from form and report modules. These modules can be used to store code, in the form of procedures, that can be used from anywhere within your application. In early versions of Access (1.0 through 2.0), standard modules were known as global modules.

You can use standard procedures throughout your application for expressions, macros, event procedures, and even other procedures. To use a standard procedure, you simply call it from a control as a function or an event based on an event procedure, depending on the type of procedure that it is. Remember that two basic types of procedures are stored in modules:

✦ Subs, which perform actions without returning a value

✦ Functions, which always return a value

Tip Procedures run; modules contain. A procedure is executed; it performs some action. You create the procedures that your application will use. Modules, on the other hand, simply act like containers, grouping procedures and declarations together. A module cannot be run; rather, you run the procedures that are contained in the module. These procedures can respond to events or can be called from expressions, macros, and even other procedures.

You use the modules container of the database to store your standard procedures. The module container is the section of the database that has an object button labeled Modules.

Although you can place any type of procedure in any module, you should group your procedures into categories. Most modules contain procedures that are related in some way.

Creating a new module

Using the Modules tab, you can create and edit Visual Basic code or procedures. A procedure is simply some code, written in a programming language that follows a series of logical steps in performing some action. You could, for example, create a Beep procedure that makes the computer beep as a warning or notification that something has happened in your program. Each procedure is a series of code statements that performs an operation or calculation.

Modules are the containers used to organize your code. You can think of a module as being a library of procedures. You can create many modules for an Access database.

Cross-Reference Creating functions and procedures in modules is covered in more detail in Chapter 19.

For this example, you can use the Chap18 database, or you can open a new blank database. To create a new module, follow these steps:

1. Click the Modules object button in the Database window.

2. Click the New toolbar button.

Access opens Microsoft Visual Basic and creates a new module, named Module1, in a Code window. This new module should look like the one shown in Figure 18-9. In this figure, notice that Access places two lines of text in the first line in the window, beginning with Option Compare Database and then Option Explicit.

Note   If the new module you open does not show the first two lines of code, you will need to check to see if the Required Variable Declaration has been turned on (recommended). The Option Explicit statement appears if you turn on the option Require Variable Declaration. To check the status of this option, follow these steps:

1. Open an existing module, or create a new one. The Code window displays in Microsoft Visual Basic.

2. Select Tools ➪ Options... from the Code window toolbar. The Options dialog box displays.

3. In the Editor tab, check the box for Require Variable Declaration.

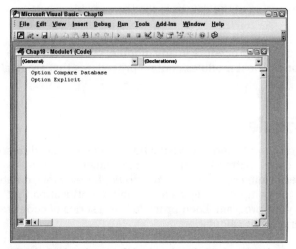

Figure 18-9: The newly opened code in the Visual Basic Editor.

Notice that the Code window in Figure 18-9 displays the tools for the Visual Basic Editor. Also notice the two combo boxes just below the toolbar. The right combo box displays Declarations, because you currently are in the declarations part of the module.

Each module includes two or more sections:

✦ A single declarations section

✦ A section for each procedure

Working in the Code Window

Whenever you create Visual Basic procedures for your Access applications, you write that code in a Code window. Although the Code window is confusing at first, it is easy to understand and use after you learn how each part is used.

When you enter Design mode of a module—whether it is via a form or report module or the modules object (Database window)—the Visual Basic Code window and its associated menu and toolbar open to enable you to create or edit your procedures.

When you open a module from the Modules object button of the Database window, the Code window has the same features as the Code window for a form or Report Design window. The only difference between the two is that for a form (or report) module, the Object and Procedure combo boxes on the toolbar list the form's objects and events. You can select these objects and events to create or edit event procedures for the form. The object combo box for a module you open from the Database window displays only one choice: General. The Procedure combo box contains only the names of existing procedures.

The Code window has four basic areas: the menu bar, the toolbar, the Code window, and the Immediate window.

The menu bar of the Code window has 10 menus: File, Edit, View, Insert, Debug, Run, Tools, Add-Ins, Window, and Help.

The Code window's toolbar (shown in Figure 18-9) helps you create new modules and their procedures quickly. The toolbar contains buttons for the most common actions you use to create, modify, and debug modules.

The Code window—the most important area of the Visual Basic Editor—is where you create and modify the Visual Basic code for your procedures. The Code window has the standard Windows features that enable you to resize, minimize, maximize, and move the window. You also can split the window into two areas. At times, you may want to edit two procedures at the same time; perhaps you need to copy part of one procedure to another. To work on two procedures simultaneously, choose Window ➪ Split from the Code window toolbar.

 Tip   You can resize the window by moving the split bar up and down. Now you can work with both procedures at the same time. To switch between windows, press the F6 key or click the other window.

The Immediate window enables you to try a procedure while you are still in the module. See the "Checking your results in the Immediate window" section in this chapter for an example.

The module is a convenient way to place a group of related event procedures in a single collection. Every form or report you create in your database contains a built-in form module or report module. This form or report module is an integral part of each form or report; it is used as a container for the event procedures you create for the form or report. Generally, if only a single form or report object will use the module, it should go behind the form or report. To view the module behind a form, follow these steps:

1. Open the form in Design view.

2. Select View ➪ Code from the Design window menu. The Visual Basic Editor displays the form's module in the Code window.

   If the module will be needed for several forms or reports, it should be placed in a standard module. Standard modules are stored in the Modules tab of the database container.

The declarations section

You can use the declarations section to declare (define) variables you want to use in procedures. A variable is a temporary storage location for some value and is given a name. You can declare variables that will be used only by the procedures in a module or by all procedures across all modules within a database. Examples of variables include:

✦ intCounter (an integer variable)

✦ curMySalary (a currency variable)

✦ dtmodaysDate (a date variable)

Caution   If you have the line of code Option Explicit in your module, which is the default in Access 2003 Visual Basic, you must explicitly declare your variables or you will get an error when you try to use them. This speeds up execution of Visual Basic modules. If you have a small application, you might want to remove the Option Explicit line of code, which will enable you to use variables without first defining their name and data type.

You are not required to declare variables in this section, because variables can also be declared in the individual procedures. In fact, if you remove the Option Explicit line from a procedure or function, you don't have to declare a variable at all. Access enables implicit variable declarations — that is, declarations created on the fly. If you enter a variable name in an expression and the variable hasn't been declared, Access accepts and declares it for you, giving it the data type consistent with its first use.

Tip   Entering the declaration statement Option Explicit forces you to declare any variables you will use when creating procedures for the module. Although this procedure involves a little more work, it speeds execution of module code by Access. For others who may need to work with your code later on, declaring variables provides assistance in documenting your code.

Creating a new procedure

After you complete any declarations for the module, you are ready to create a procedure. Follow these steps to create a procedure called BeepWarning:

1. Open the Module1 module you previously created as in Figure 18-9. Go to any empty line in the Code window.

2. Type **Sub BeepWarning** to name the module. The Code window should look similar to the one shown in Figure 18-10.

3. Press Enter.

If you enter the name of a function you previously created in this module (or in another module within the database), Access informs you that the function already exists. Access does not enable you to create another procedure with the same name.

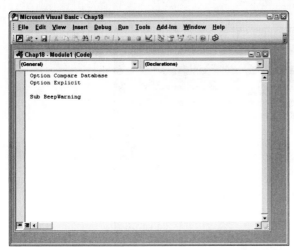

Figure 18-10: Entering a new procedure in the Code window.

Notice that when you pressed Enter, Access did three things automatically:

✦ Placed the procedure named BeepWarning in the Procedure combo box in the toolbar

✦ Placed parentheses at the end of the procedure name

✦ Added the End Sub statement to the procedure

The code window area has changed from the declarations section to the procedure code area.

Now you can enter the lines of code needed for your procedure. Enter the following lines of code into the module:

```
Dim xBeeps as Integer, nBeeps As Integer
nBeeps = 5
For xBeeps = 1 To nBeeps
   Beep
Next xBeeps
```

In this example, you are running the program five times. Don't worry about what the procedure does — you learn more about how to program specific tasks in Chapter 19.

Your completed function should look like the one shown in Figure 18-11.

When BeepWarning runs, it beeps for the number of times specified.

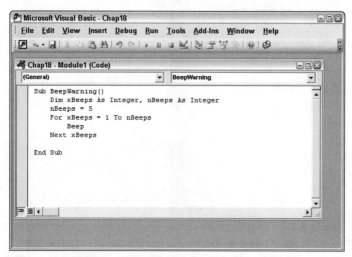

Figure 18-11: The BeepWarning procedure completed.

Using the Access 2003 Module Help

Suppose that you know you want to use a specific command but can't remember the syntax (syntax is computer grammar). Access 2003 features two types of module help, called Auto List Members and Auto Quick Info, to help you create each line of code.

Auto List Members is automatically displayed when you type the beginning of a command that has objects, properties, and methods following the main object. For example, if you enter DoCmd, a list of the possible commands is displayed, as shown in Figure 18-12. You can scroll through the list box and select the option you want.

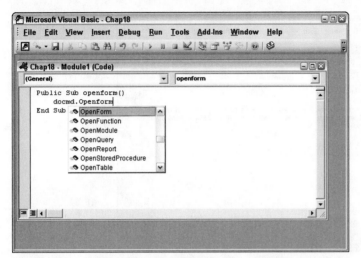

Figure 18-12: Access 2003 Auto List Members help in a module.

In this example, the OpenForm command is being selected. After you choose an option, either more Auto List Members help is displayed or, if the rest of the command options are parameters for the other type of module help, Auto Quick Info is displayed, as shown in Figure 18-13.

Auto Quick Info help guides you through all the options for the specific command. The bold word is the next parameter available for the command. Figure 18-13 shows that there are many parameters available for the OpenForm command. After you type the form name for the form name parameter, you type a comma to separate it from the next parameter section. As you enter each parameter or a comma to skip a parameter, the next parameter section in the help highlights as bold. You can remove the help by pressing Esc.

Compiling procedures

When you complete a procedure, you should compile it by choosing Debug ⇨ Compile from the Code window menu. The debug process checks your code for errors (a process known as syntax checking), and the compile process converts the programs to a format your computer can understand. If the compile operation is not successful, an error window appears.

Note   Access compiles all uncompiled procedures in the module, not just the current procedure.

Saving a module

When you finish creating a procedure, you should save it by saving the module. You can save the module by choosing File ⇨ Save, or simply close the Visual Basic window to save the module automatically.

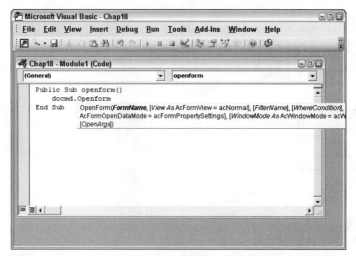

Figure 18-13: Access 2003 Auto Quick Info help in a module.

Creating procedures in the Form or Report Design window

All forms, reports, and their controls can have event procedures associated with their events. While you are in the Design window for the form or report, you can add an event procedure quickly in one of three ways:

✦ Choose Build Event from the shortcut menu (see Figure 18-14).

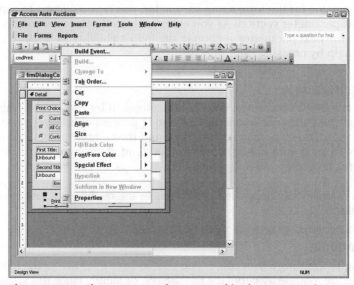

Figure 18-14: Shortcut menu for a control in the Form Design window.

✦ Choose Code Builder in the Choose Builder dialog box when you click the ellipsis button to the right of an event in the Property dialog box.

✦ Enter the text Event Procedure or select it from the top of the event combo box (see Figure 18-15).

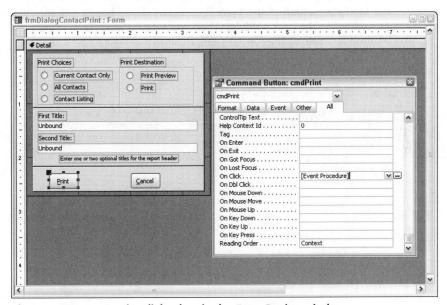

Figure 18-15: Properties dialog box in the Form Design window.

Whether you choose the Build Event from the shortcut menu choice or click the ellipsis button in the Property dialog box, the Choose Builder dialog box appears. Choosing the Code Builder item opens the Code window in Visual Basic, as shown in Figure 18-16. In Visual Basic, if you click the View Microsoft Access button, you can toggle back and forth between the Access form designer and the Visual Basic Module window.

Note If an event procedure is already attached to the control, the text [Event Procedure] is displayed in the event area. Clicking the Builder button instantly displays the procedure for the event in a Visual Basic Code window—hence the name Event Procedure.

Editing an existing procedure

To edit an existing procedure, follow these steps:

1. Click the Modules object button in the Database window.

2. Double-click the module name that contains the procedure. The declaration portion of the module appears.

3. Find the procedure you want and select it from the pull-down menu on the right of the module window.

Tip

After you are in a module, you can select any procedure in another module quickly by pressing F2 or choosing View ➪ Object Browser. Access displays the Object Browser dialog box, shown in Figure 18-17. Highlight a different module name in the Modules section of the View Procedures dialog box to see the names of all procedures in the new module. When you select a module, you then can select a method and display the function call, as shown in Figure 18-17.

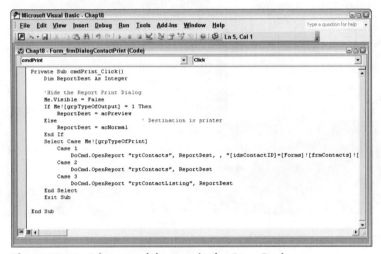

Figure 18-16: A form module open in the Form Designer.

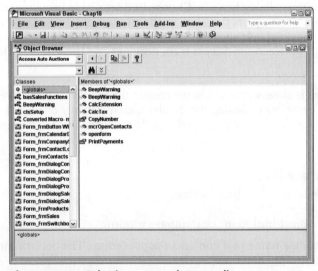

Figure 18-17: Selecting a procedure to edit.

Checking your results in the Immediate window

When you write code for a procedure, you may want to try the procedure while you are in the module, or you may need to check the results of an expression. The Immediate window enables you to try your procedures without leaving the module. You can run the module and check variables. You could, for example, type ? and the name of the variable.

To view the Immediate window, choose View ➪ Immediate Window. Figure 18-18 shows the Immediate window.

After you create a sub procedure, you can run it to see whether it works as expected. You can test it with supplied arguments.

Figure 18-18: The Immediate window.

To run the BeepWarning Sub procedure, follow these steps:

1. Activate the Immediate pane by selecting it from the View menu or clicking in it.

2. Type **BeepWarning** and press Enter. The BeepWarning sub runs.

You may have heard five beeps or (if you have a really fast machine) only a few beeps because the interval between beeps is short.

Figure 18-11, earlier in this section, shows the Visual Basic code for this sub procedure.

✦　　✦　　✦

Introduction to Programming and Events

When working with a database system, the same tasks may be performed repeatedly. Rather than doing the same steps each time, you can automate the process with VBA.

Database management systems continually grow as you add records in a form, add new queries, and print new reports. As the system grows, many of the objects are saved for later use—for a weekly report or monthly update query, for example. You tend to create and perform many tasks repetitively. Every time you add contact records, for example, you open the same form. Likewise, you print the same form letter for contacts that have purchased a vehicle in the past month.

You can create VBA code throughout your application to perform these tasks. The Visual Basic language offers a full array of powerful commands for manipulating records in a table, controls on a form, or just about anything else. This chapter continues Chapter 18's discussion of working with procedures in forms, reports, and standard modules.

On the CD-ROM

In this chapter, you will use the database file Chap19start.mdb.

Programming Events

An Access event is the result or consequence of some user action. An Access event can occur when a user moves from one record to another in a form, closes a report, or clicks on a command button on a form.

A Review of Events and Properties

Simply put, an *event* is some user action. The event can be an action such as opening a form or report, changing data in a record, selecting a button, or closing a form or report. Access recognizes approximately 60 events in forms and reports. To recognize an event, Access uses form or report *properties*. Each event has an associated form or report property. For example, the On Open property is associated with the event of opening a form or report.

You trigger an event procedure by selecting [Event Procedure] next to the desired property you want to respond to. The indicator [Event Procedure] specifies that the property has associated VBA code that will execute whenever this event is triggered. For example, if you want to run an event procedure for every record that displays in the frmProduct form, you select [Event Procedure] in the parameter field alongside the property On Current in the form named frmProducts.

Access applications are event-driven. Objects in Access respond to many types of events. Access responds to events with behaviors that are built in for each object. Access events can be recognized by specific object properties. For example, if a user checks or unchecks a check box using the mouse, the property OnMouseDown recognizes that the mouse button was clicked. You can have this property run an event procedure when the user clicks the mouse button.

Events in Access can be categorized into seven groups:

- ✦ **Windows (Form, Report) events:** Opening, closing, and resizing
- ✦ **Data events:** Making current, deleting, or updating
- ✦ **Focus events:** Activating, entering, and exiting
- ✦ **Keyboard events:** Pressing or releasing a key
- ✦ **Mouse events:** Clicking or pressing a mouse button down
- ✦ **Print events:** Formatting and printing
- ✦ **Error and timing events:** Happening after an error has occurred or some time has passed

In all, more than 50 events can be checked in forms and reports to specify some action after they take place.

How do events trigger actions?

You can create an event procedure that runs when a user performs any one of the 53 events that Access recognizes. Access can recognize an event through the use of special properties for forms, controls (fields), and reports.

For example, Figure 19-1 shows the property sheet for a form named frmProducts. This form has many properties, which may be used to respond to corresponding events. Forms aren't the only objects to have events; form sections (page header, form header, detail, page footer, form footer) and every control on the form (labels, text boxes, check boxes, and option buttons, for example) have events, too.

Where to trigger event procedures

In Access, you can run event procedures by using properties in forms and reports. There are no event properties for tables or queries.

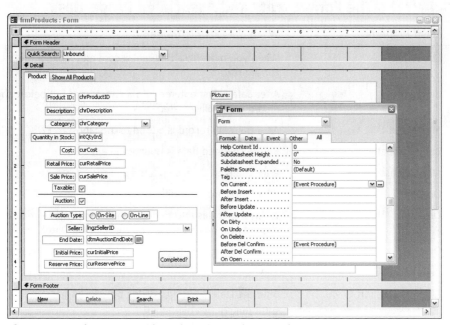

Figure 19-1: The property sheet for a form, showing the On Current property entered. This figure shows the form frmProducts in Design mode with the property sheet open.

Form Event Procedures

When you work with forms, you can create event procedures that execute based on events at the form level, the section level, or the control level. If you attach an event procedure to a form-level event, whenever the event occurs, the action takes effect against the form as a whole (such as when you move to another record or leave the form).

To have your form respond to an event, you write an event procedure and attach it to the event property in the form that recognizes the event. Many properties can be used to trigger event procedures at the form level. Table 19-1 shows each property, the event it recognizes, and how the property works.

When referring to form events, we are talking about events that happen to the form as a whole — not about an event that can be triggered by a specific control on a form. Form events execute when moving from one record to another or when a form is being opened or closed. Responding to control events is covered later in this chapter.

Table 19-1
The Form Events and Associated Properties

Event Property	When the Event Is Triggered
On Current	When you move to a different record and make it the current record
Before Insert	After data is first entered into a new record but before the record is actually created
After Insert	After the new record is added to the table
Before Update	Before changed data is updated in a record
After Update	After changed data is updated in a record
On Dirty	When a record is modified
On Undo	When a user has returned a form to clean state — record set back to unmodified state — opposite of On Dirty
On Delete	When a record is deleted but before the deletion takes place
Before Del Confirm	Just before Access displays the Delete Confirm dialog box
After Del Confirm	After the Delete Confirm dialog box closes and confirmation has happened
On Open	When a form is opened, but the first record is not displayed yet
On Load	When a form is loaded into memory but not yet opened
On Resize	When the size of a form changes
On Unload	When a form is closed and the records unload, and before the form is removed from the screen
On Close	When a form is closed and removed from the screen
On Activate	When an open form receives the focus, becoming the active window

Event Property	When the Event Is Triggered
On Deactivate	When a different window becomes the active window but before it loses focus
On Got Focus	When a form with no active or enabled controls receives the focus
On Lost Focus	When a form loses the focus
On Click	When you press and release (click) the left mouse button on a control in a form
On Dbl Click	When you press and release (click) the left mouse button twice on a control/label in a form
On Mouse Down	When you press the mouse button while the pointer is on a form
On Mouse Move	When you move the mouse pointer over an area of a form
On Mouse Up	When you release a pressed mouse button while the pointer is on a form
On Mouse Wheel	When you spin the mouse wheel
On Key Down	When you press any key on the keyboard when a form has focus; when you use a SendKeys macro
On Key Up	When you release a pressed key or immediately after the SendKeys macro
On Key Press	When you press and release a key on a form that has the focus; when you use the SendKeys macro
Key Preview	(YES or NO) Evoke keyboard macros for forms before keyboard events for macros
On Error	When a run-time error is produced
On Filter	When a filter has been specified but before it is applied
On Apply Filter	After a filter is applied to a form
On Timer	When a specified time interval passes
Timer Interval	Specify the Interval in milliseconds
Before Screen Tip	When the screen tip is activated
On Cmd Enabled	When a command has become enabled in a PivotChart or PivotTable
On Cmd Checked	When a PivotChart or PivotTable command has been checked (checked on the toolbar)
On Cmd Before Execute	When a PivotChart or PivotTable command has been selected from the toolbar, but not yet executed

Continued

Table 19-1 *(continued)*

Event Property	When the Event Is Triggered
On Cmd Execute	When a PivotTable or PivotChart command has been executed (after the execution)
On Data Change	When PivotTable or PivotChart data is changed or refreshed
On Data Set Change	When a new data set for the chart changes (for example when filtered)
On PivotTable Change	Whenever the list field, field set, or total is added or deleted in a PivotTable
On Selection Change	When a user makes a new selection; cannot be cancelled
On View Change	When a different PivotTable view of the current data is opened
On Connect	When a PivotTable connects to the underlying recordset
On Disconnect	When a PivotTable disconnects to the underlying recordset
Before Query	When a PivotTable is about to get a new data object
On Query	When the PivotTable receives a new data object
After Layout	When the PivotChart has already been laid out but before any rendering is done
Before Render	When the PivotChart is about to paint itself on the screen (before drawing begins)
After Render	When the object has been rendered in the PivotChart
After Final Render	When all the chart objects have been rendered
Begin Batch Edit	Fires when a user begins editing a batch in ADPs (form in batch edit mode)
Undo Batch Edit	Fires when a user undoes edits in a batch in ADPs (form in batch edit mode)
Before Begin Transaction	Before a batch transaction begins in ADPs (form in batch edit mode)
After Begin Transaction	After a batch transaction begins in ADPs (form in batch edit mode)
Before Commit Transaction	After you request a commit, but before the commit actually takes place in ADPs (form in batch edit mode)
After Commit Transaction	After a commit has been completed in ADPs (form in batch edit mode)
Rollback Transaction	Fires a batch transaction roll back in ADPs (form in batch edit mode)

Control Event Procedures

Controls can also trigger event procedures. For example, you can immediately verify complex data validation for a field (rather than when the record is exited) by using the field's Before Update property rather than the form's Before Update property.

Creating event procedures for a control event is done the same way you create procedures for form events. You select [Event Procedure] for the event to respond to; then you create the VBA code in the Visual Basic Editor that will execute when the event is triggered. Controls have many event properties. Table 19-2 shows each property, the event it recognizes, and how it works.

As Table 19-2 demonstrates, you can use any of the control events to trigger an event procedure. One of these, On Click, works only with command buttons.

Table 19-2 The Control Events and Associated Properties	
Event Property	*When the Event Is Triggered*
Before Update	Before changed data in the control is updated to the table
After Update	After changed data is updated in the control to the data
On Dirty	When the contents of a form or text of combo box or tab control changes
On Undo	When the form is returned to a clean state.
On Change	When the contents of a text box or combo box's text changes
On Updated	When an ActiveX object's data has been modified
On Not In List	When a value that isn't in the list is entered into a combo box
On Enter	Before a control receives the focus from another control
On Exit	Just before the control loses focus to another control
On Got Focus	When a non-active or enabled control receives the focus
On Lost Focus	When a control loses the focus
On Click	When the left mouse button is pressed and released (clicked) on a control
On Dbl Click	When the left mouse button is pressed and released (clicked) twice on a control/label
On Mouse Down	When a mouse button is pressed while the pointer is on a control

Continued

Table 19-2 *(continued)*	
Event Property	**When the Event Is Triggered**
On Mouse Move	When the mouse pointer is moved over a control
On Mouse Up	When a pressed mouse button is released while the pointer is on a control
On Key Down	When any key on the keyboard is pressed when a control has the focus or when the SendKeys macro is used
On Key Press	When a key is pressed and released on a control that has the focus or when the SendKeys macro is used
On Key Up	When a pressed key is released or immediately after the SendKeys macro is used

Opening a form with an event procedure

Most applications require multiple forms and reports to accomplish the application's business functions. Instead of requiring the users of the application to browse the database container to determine which forms and reports accomplish which tasks, an application generally provides a switchboard to assist users in navigating throughout the application. The switchboard provides a set of command buttons labeled appropriately to suggest the purpose of the form or report it opens. Figure 19-2 shows the switchboard for the Access Auto Auctions application.

Figure 19-2: Using a switchboard to navigate throughout the forms and reports of an application.

The Access Auto Auctions switchboard includes six command buttons. Each command button runs an event procedure when the command button is clicked. The Products command button, for example, runs the event procedure to open the Products form called frmProducts. Figure 19-3 shows the Properties window for the Product command button, called cmdProducts. Figure 19-4 shows the VBA code for the On Click event of the cmdProducts command button.

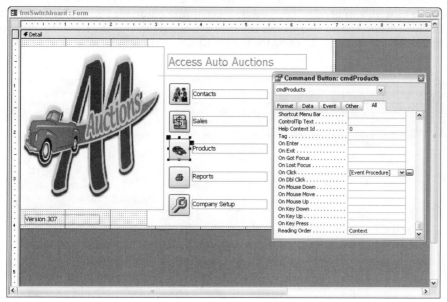

Figure 19-3: Specifying an event procedure for a control event.

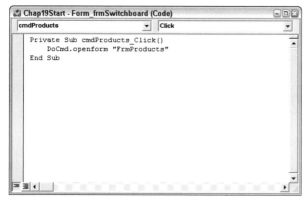

Figure 19-4: Using an event procedure to open a form.

Running an event procedure when closing a form

At times, you'll want to perform some action when you close or leave a form. For example, you may want Access to keep an automatic log of the names of everyone using the form, or you may want to close the form's print dialog box automatically every time a user closes the main form.

To close the frmDialogProductPrint form automatically every time the frmProducts form is closed, you need to create a new event procedure for the frmProducts form's On Close event. Figure 19-5 shows the Properties window for the frmProducts form. Figure 19-6 shows the VBA code for the On Close event of the frmProducts form.

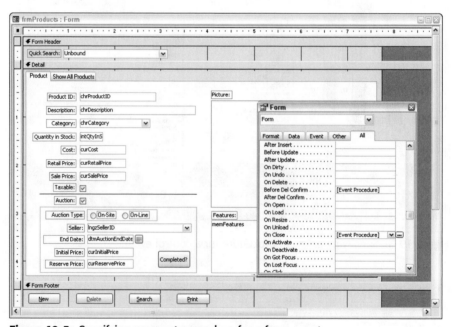

Figure 19-5: Specifying an event procedure for a form event.

The Form_Close event illustrated in Figure 19-6 first checks to see if the form frmDialogProductPrint is open. If it is open, the statement to close it executes.

Caution   Attempting to close a form that is not currently open will generate a run-time error.

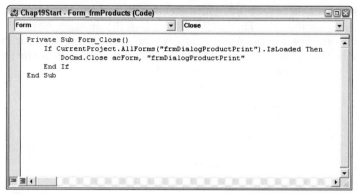

Figure 19-6: Running an event procedure when a form closes.

Using an event procedure to confirm a delete

Although it is possible to use the Access Form View toolbar to delete a record in a form, a better practice is to provide a Delete command button on the form. A Delete command button is a more user-friendly method because it provides a more obvious visual cue to the user as to how to delete a record. Additionally, the command button affords more control over the delete process because you can attach an event procedure that executes before actually deleting the record. In this event procedure, you can display a meaningful confirmation prompt to give the user a chance to cancel the deletion. Or, you may need to perform a referential integrity check to make sure that deleting the record does not cause a connection to the record from some other table in the database to be lost.

You can use the MsgBox() function in an event procedure to confirm a deletion. The event procedure for the cmdDelete button in the frmProducts form uses the MsgBox() function to confirm the deletion (as shown in Figure 19-7). For more information on using the MsgBox() function, see the sidebar "Using the MsgBox() function" later in this chapter.

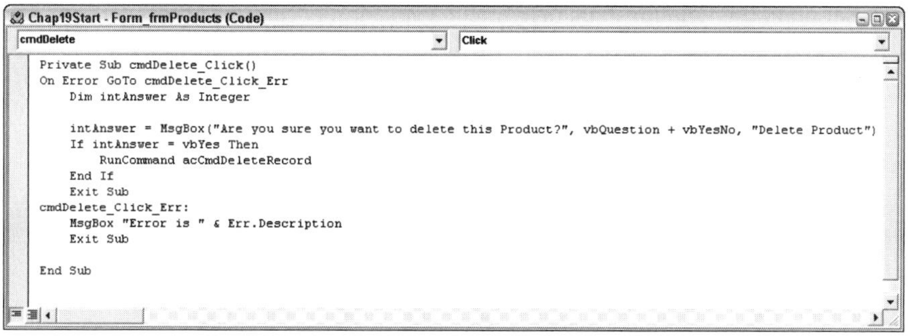

```
Private Sub cmdDelete_Click()
On Error GoTo cmdDelete_Click_Err
    Dim intAnswer As Integer

    intAnswer = MsgBox("Are you sure you want to delete this Product?", vbQuestion + vbYesNo, "Delete Product")
    If intAnswer = vbYes Then
        RunCommand acCmdDeleteRecord
    End If
    Exit Sub
cmdDelete_Click_Err:
    MsgBox "Error is " & Err.Description
    Exit Sub

End Sub
```

Figure 19-7: Using the MsgBox() function to confirm a deletion.

When the cmdDelete_Click() event procedure executes, Access displays a message box prompt like the one shown in Figure 19-8. Notice that the message box includes two command buttons: Yes and No. Access displays the prompt and waits for the user to make a selection. When the user selects the No command button, the event procedure simply exits and cancels the delete event.

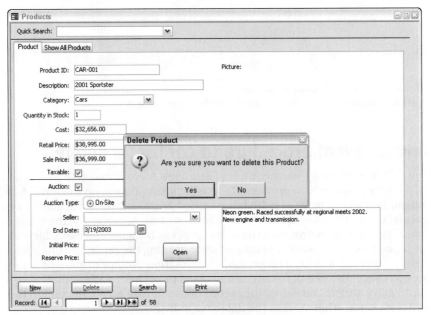

Figure 19-8: A confirmation prompt for deleting a record.

If the user selects the Yes button in the message box, the event procedure executes the statement RunCommand acCmdDeleteRecord to delete the record.

Caution   When the statement RunCommand acCmdDeleteRecord executes, it first checks to see if deleting the record will violate any Referential Integrity rules that you have set up in the Relationships diagram. If a violation occurs, an Access error message displays and the deletion is cancelled.

Cross-Reference   For more information on setting up referential integrity between tables in a database, see Chapter 2.

Using the MsgBox( ) Function

The MsgBox( ) function is a very powerful function that can be used to display a message in a dialog box, wait for a response by the user, and then return a value based on the user's selection. The function has five arguments:

```
MsgBox(prompt[, buttons] [, title] [, helpfile, context])
```

✦ The prompt argument is the text displayed as a question in the prompt.

✦ The buttons argument is the numeric expression controlling the buttons and icons to display in the dialog box.

✦ The title is the text displayed in the title bar of the prompt.

✦ helpfile and context are used to display helpful information when you also include a Help button in the message box.

 Cross-Reference   Adding context-sensitive help to an application is covered in Chapter 36.

Only the prompt argument is required. If you don't specify the buttons or title arguments, Access displays the default components: an OK button, no icon, and "Microsoft Access" as the title.

Access offers a wide range of button argument settings. The buttons argument is actually composed of four arguments that you concatenate together:

✦ Number and type of buttons

✦ Icon style

✦ Default button

✦ Modality of the message box, that is, if all applications or just Microsoft Access must suspend while waiting for user selection.

The value that you specify for each section of the argument is actually an integer value. But, Access provides some built-in values, called constants, that you can use so that you don't need to remember the integer values. The table below lists the MessageBox built-in values, the corresponding integer values, and the buttons each displays:

Constant	Value	Description
vbOKOnly	0	Display OK button only.
vbOKCancel	1	Display OK and Cancel buttons.
vbAbortRetryIgnore	2	Display Abort, Retry, and Ignore buttons.
vbYesNoCancel	3	Display Yes, No, and Cancel buttons.

Continued

Continued

Constant	Value	Description
vbYesNo	4	Display Yes and No buttons.
vbRetryCancel	5	Display Retry and Cancel buttons.
vbCritical	16	Display Critical Message icon.
vbQuestion	32	Display Warning Query icon.
vbExclamation	48	Display Warning Message icon.
vbInformation	64	Display Information Message icon.
vbDefaultButton1	0	First button is default.
vbDefaultButton2	256	Second button is default.
vbDefaultButton3	512	Third button is default.
vbDefaultButton4	768	Fourth button is default.
vbApplicationModal	0	Application modal; the user must respond to the message box before continuing work in the current application.
vbSystemModal	4096	System modal; all applications are suspended until the user responds to the message box.
vbMsgBoxHelpButton	16384	Adds Help button to the message box.
VbMsgBoxSetForeground	65536	Specifies the message box window as the foreground window.
vbMsgBoxRight	524288	Text is right-aligned.
vbMsgBoxRtlReading	1048576	Specifies text should appear as right-to-left reading on Hebrew and Arabic systems.

Using the preceding table, specify the buttons argument of the MsgBox( ) function by specifying one or more of the constants, separating each constant with a + sign. For example, to display the Yes and No buttons, with Yes as the default button, enter vbYesNo+ vbDefaultButton1.

In addition to displaying the message box with the options you specify, the MsgBox() function also returns a value that indicates which button the user selected. Each button that displays in the message box returns a unique value when the user selects it. The following table shows each button and the value that MsgBox() returns:

Constant	Value	Description
vbOK	1	OK
vbCancel	2	Cancel
vbAbort	3	Abort
vbRetry	4	Retry
vbIgnore	5	Ignore
vbYes	6	Yes
vbNo	7	No

If the dialog box displays a Cancel button, pressing the Esc key is the same as selecting the Cancel button.

Report Event Procedures

Just as with forms, reports can also use event procedures to respond to specific events. Reports respond to events for the overall report itself and at the section level. If you attach an event procedure to the overall report, it executes when the event occurs for the entire report, such as when you open or close the report. If you attach the event procedure at the section level, it executes when the event occurs within a section (such as when you format or print a report header section).

Several overall report event properties are available. Table 19-3 shows each property, the event that activates it, and how it works. As you can see, the list of report events is very similar to the form event list.

Table 19-3 **The Report Events and Associated Properties**	
Event Property	**When the Event Is Triggered**
On Open	When a report is opened but before it prints
On Close	When a report is closed and removed from the screen
On Activate	When a report receives the focus and becomes the active window
On Deactivate	When a different window becomes the active window
On No Data	When the report has no data passed to it from the active table or query
On Page	When the report changes pages
On Error	When a run-time error is produced in Access

Running an event procedure when a report opens

Opening a report that contains no data generally yields erroneous results. The report may display a title, if you included one, with no detail information. Or, it may display #error values for missing information. This type of situation can be a little scary for the user. To avoid this situation, you can use the On No Data event in a report to control what happens when there is no data for the report. You can attach an event procedure for the On No Data property to display an informational message box to the user and then cancel the opening of the report. Figure 19-9 shows the Properties window for the rptProducts report. Figure 19-10 shows the VBA code for the On No Data event of the rptProducts report.

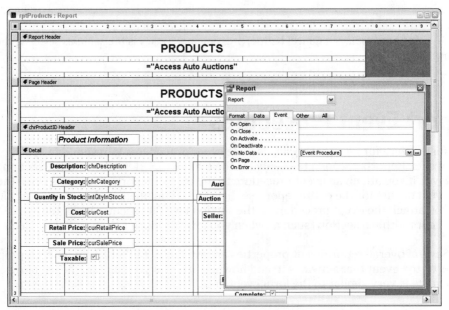

Figure 19-9: Specifying an event procedure for a report event.

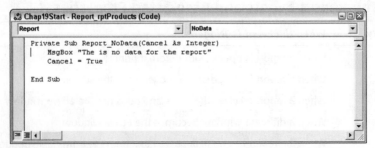

Figure 19-10: Running an event procedure when there is no data for a report.

The Report_No Data event illustrated in Figure 19-10 first displays a message box to advise the user that the report contains no data. Then the event procedure cancels the event by setting the variable Cancel to True.

Report Section Event Procedures

In addition to the event properties for the form itself, Access offers three event properties that you can use for report sections. Table 19-4 shows each property, the event it recognizes, and how it works.

| Table 19-4 | | |
| The Report Section Events and Associated Properties | | |
Event Property	Event	When the Event Is Triggered
On Format	Format	When Access knows what data goes in a section (but before laying out the data for printing)
On Print	Print	After Access lays out the data in a section for printing (but before printing the section)
On Retreat	Retreat	After the Format event but before the Print event; occurs when Access has to "back up" past other sections on a page to perform multiple formatting passes; this is in all sections except the Headers and Footers

Using On Format

You use the On Format property when the data to be displayed can affect page layout or when the report section contains calculations that use data from sections you don't intend to print. The event procedure will run before Access lays out the section (following your other property settings for the report, such as Keep Together, Visible, or Can Grow).

You can set the On Format and On Print properties for any section of the report. However, the On Retreat is not available for the page header or page footer sections.

For example, you may want to hide some data on the form, based on certain conditions. If the condition is met, the event procedure uses the Visible property of the control to hide or display the control. Figure 19-11 shows the Properties window for the On Format property of the detail section of the rptProducts report. Figure 19-12 shows the VBA code for the On Format event of the detail section.

Figure 19-11: Specifying an event procedure for formatting a report's detail section.

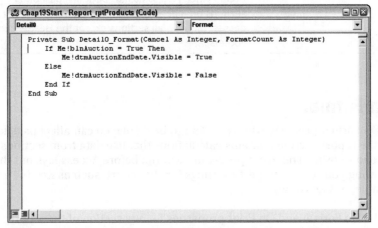

Figure 19-12: Running an event procedure to display or hide a control on a report.

The Detail0_Format event illustrated in Figure 19-12 first checks the value of the blnAuction control. If the value of blnAuction is True, the dtmAuctionEndDate control displays on the report. If the value of blnAuction is False, the dtmAuctionEndDate control is hidden.

The Visual Basic language offers a full array of powerful commands for manipulating records in a table, controls on a form, or just about anything else. To begin creating more sophisticated procedures with Visual Basic, you need to understand some of Visual Basic's fundamental programming elements. These basic elements include the following:

✦ Variables and how they interact with data

✦ Data types

✦ Programming syntax for logical constructs

The remainder of the chapter explains the concepts of the Visual Basic environment in Access and how you can use it to manipulate Access objects.

Using Variables

One of the most powerful concepts in programming is the variable. A variable is a temporary storage location for some value and is given a name. You can use a variable to store the result of a calculation, or you can create a variable to make the value of a control available to another procedure.

To refer to the result of an expression, you create a name to store the result. The named result is the variable. To assign an expression's result to a variable, you use the = operator. Following are some examples of calculations that create variables:

```
counter = 1
counter = counter + 1
today = Date()
```

Naming variables

Every programming language has its own rules for naming variables. In Visual Basic, a variable name must meet the following conditions:

✦ Must begin with an alphabetical character

✦ Must not contain an embedded period or type-declaration character

✦ Must have a unique name; the name cannot be used elsewhere in the procedure or in modules that use the variables

✦ Must be no longer than 255 characters

Although you can make up almost any name for a variable, most programmers adopt a standard convention for naming variables. Some common practices include the following:

✦ Using uppercase and lowercase characters, as in TotalCost

✦ Using all lowercase characters, as in counter

✦ Preceding the name with the data type of the value; a variable that stores a number might be called nCounter

Tip
When creating variables, you can use uppercase, lowercase, or mixed-case characters to specify the variable or call it later. Visual Basic variables are not case-sensitive. This fact means that you can use the TodayIs variable later without having to worry about the case that you used for the name when you created it; TODAYIS, todayis, and tOdAyIs all refer to the same variable. Visual Basic automatically changes any explicitly declared variables to the case that was used in the declaration statement (Dim statement).

When you need to see or use the contents of a variable, you simply use its name. When you specify the variable's name, the computer program goes into memory, finds the variable, and gets its contents for you. This procedure means, of course, that you need to be able to remember the name of the variable.

Visual Basic, like many other programming languages, allows you to create variables on the fly. In the Counter = 1 example, the Counter variable was not declared before the value 1 was assigned to it.

Declaring variables

When you declare a variable, Access sets up a location in the computer's memory for storing a value for the variable ahead of time. The amount of storage allocated for the variable depends on the type of data that you plan to store in the variable. More space is allocated for a variable that will hold a currency amount (such as $1,000,000) than for a variable that will never hold a value greater than, say, 255.

Even though Visual Basic does not require you to declare your variables before using them, it does provide various declaration commands. Getting into the habit of declaring your variables is good practice. Declaring a variable assures that you can assign only a certain type of value to it — always a number or always characters, for example. In addition, you can attain real performance gains by pre-declaring variables. A programming best practice is to declare variables at the top of the procedure. This practice makes the program easier for other programmers to work with later on.

Caution
Although Visual Basic does not require initial declaration of variables, you should avoid using undeclared variables. If you do not declare a variable, the code may expect one type of value in the variable when another is actually there. If, in your procedure, you set the variable TodayIs to Monday and later change the value for TodayIs to a number (such as TodayIs = 2), the program generates an error when it runs.

The Dim statement

To declare a variable, you use the Dim statement. When you use the Dim statement, you must supply the variable name that you assign to the variable. The format for the Dim statement is:

Dim [variable name] [As [type]]

The following statement declares the variable xBeeps.

Dim xBeeps As Integer

Notice that the variable name follows the Dim statement. In addition to naming the variable, you can use the optional As clause to specify a data type for the variable. The data type is the kind of information that will be stored in the variable: String, Integer, Currency, and so on. The default data type is known as variant. A variant data type can hold any type of data.

When you use the Dim statement to declare a variable in a procedure, you can refer to that variable only within that procedure. Other procedures, even if they are stored in the same module, do not know anything about the variable. This is known as a private variable because it was declared in a procedure and is only known in the procedure where it was declared and used.

Variables can also be declared in the declarations section of a module. Then, all the procedures in the module can access the variable. Procedures outside the module in which you declared the variable, however, cannot read or use the variable.

The Public statement

To make a variable available to all modules in the application, use the Public keyword when you declare the variable. Figure 19-13 illustrates declaring a public variable.

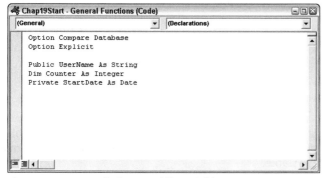

Figure 19-13: Declaring a public variable.

Notice that the statement is in the declarations section of the module. Public variables must be declared in the declarations section of the module.

Caution   You cannot declare a variable public within a procedure. It must be declared in the declarations section of a module. If you attempt to declare a variable public within a procedure, you receive an error message.

Although you can declare a public variable in any module, it seems logical to declare public variables only within the module that will use them the most. The exceptions to this rule are true global variables that you want to make available to all procedures across modules and that are not specifically related to a single module. You should declare global variables in a single standard module so that you can find them easily.

Tip   In a standard, report, or form module, you can refer to a public variable from a different form or report module. To access the value of a public variable from another module, you must qualify the variable reference, using the name of the form or report object. Employee_MainForm.MyVariable, for example, accesses a form named Employee_MainForm and obtains the value of the variable MyVariable.

The Private statement

The declarations section in Figure 19-13 shows the use of the Dim and Private statements to declare variables. Technically, there is no difference between Private and Dim, but using Private at the module level to declare variables that are available to only that module's procedures is a good idea. Declaring private variables does the following things:

✦ Contrasts with Dim, which must be used at the procedure level, distinguishing where the variable is declared and its scope (Module versus Procedure)

✦ Contrasts with Public, the other method of declaring variables in modules, making understanding your code easier

Tip   You can go to the declarations section of a module while you are creating an event procedure in a form by selecting declarations from the Procedure combo box. Another way to move to the declarations section is to select (general) in the Object combo box. Refer to the Module window combo boxes in Figure 19-13.

When you declare a variable, you use the AS clause to assign a data type to the variable. Data types for variables are similar to data types in a database table definition.

Working with Data Types

When you declare a variable, you also can specify the data type for the variable. All variables have a data type. The type of variable determines what kind of information can be stored in the variable.

A string variable — a variable with a data type of string — can hold any values ranging from A–Z, a–z, and 0–1, as well as formatting characters (#, -, !, and so on). Once created, a string variable can be used in many ways: comparing its contents with another string, pulling parts of information out of the string, and so on. If you have a variable defined as a string, however, you cannot use it to do mathematical calculations. Conversely, you cannot assign a number to a variable declared as a string.

Table 19-5 describes the 11 data types that Visual Basic supports.

Table 19-5
Data Types Used in Visual Basic

Type	Range	Description
Boolean	True or false	2 bytes
Byte	0 to 255	1-byte binary data
Currency	−922,337,203,685,477,5808 to 922,337,203,685,477,5807	8-byte number with fixed decimal point
Decimal	+/−79,228,162,514,264,337,593,543, 950,335 with no decimal point +/−7.9228162514264337593543950335 with 28 places to the right of the decimal; smallest non-zero number is +/0.0000000000000000000000000001	14 bytes
Date	01 Jan 100 to 31 Dec 9999	8-byte date/time value
Double	−1.79769313486231E308 to −4.94065645841247E−324 for negative values and 4.94065645841246544E−324 through 1.79769313486231570E+308 for positive values	8-byte floating-point number
Integer	−32,768 to 32,767	2-byte integer
Long	−2,147,483,648 to 2,147,483,647	4-byte integer
Object	Any object reference	4 bytes
Single	negative values: −3.402823E38 to −1.401298E − 45 positive values: 1.401298E −45 to 3.402823E38	4-byte floating-point number
String (variable-length)	0 to approximately 2,000,000,000	10 bytes plus length of string
String (fixed-length)	1 to approximately 65,400	Length of string

Continued

Table 19-5 *(continued)*

Type	Range	Description
Variant (with numbers)	Any numeric value up to the range of Double	16 bytes
Variant (with characters)	0 to approximately 2,000,000,000	22 bytes plus length of string
User-defined (using Type)	Same as Range of its data type	Number required by elements

Most of the time, you use the string, date, integer, and currency or double data types. If a variable always contains whole numbers between –32,768 and 32,767, you can save bytes of memory and gain speed in arithmetic operations if you declare the variable an integer type.

When you want to assign the value of an Access field to a variable, you need to make sure that the type of the variable can hold the data type of the field. Table 19-6 shows the corresponding Visual Basic data types for Access field types.

Table 19-6
Comparative Data Types of Access and Visual Basic

Access Field Data Type	Visual Basic Data Type
AutoNumber (Long Integer)	Long
AutoNumber (Replication ID)	—
Currency	Currency
Computed	—
Date/Time	Date
Memo	String
Number (Byte)	Byte
Number (Integer)	Integer
Number (Long Integer)	Long
Number (Single)	Single
Number (Double)	Double
Number (Replication ID)	—

Access Field Data Type	Visual Basic Data Type
OLE object	String
Text	String
Hyperlink	String
Yes/No	Boolean

Now that you understand variables and their data types, you're ready to learn how to use them in writing procedures.

Understanding Visual Basic Logical Constructs

One of the real powers of a programming language is the capability to have a program make a decision based on some condition. Visual Basic has this capability in two varieties: *conditional processing* and *repetitive looping*.

Conditional processing

Often, a program in Visual Basic performs different tasks based on some value. If the condition is True, the code performs one action. If the condition is False, the code performs a different action. An application's capability to look at a value and, based on that value, decide which code to run is known as conditional processing.

The procedure is similar to walking down a path and coming to a fork in the path; you can go to the left or to the right. If a sign at the fork points left for home and right for work, you can decide which way to go. If you need to go to work, you go to the right; if you need to go home, you go to the left. In the same way, a program looks at the value of some variable and decides which set of code should be processed.

Visual Basic offers two sets of conditional processing statements:

✦ If. . .Then. . .Else. . .End If

✦ Select Case

The If. . .Then. . .Else. . .End If statement

The If. . .Then and If. . .Then. . .Else statements allow you to check a condition and, based on the evaluation, perform a single action. The condition must evaluate to True or False. If the condition is True, the program moves to the next statement in the procedure. If the condition is False, the program skips to the statement following the Else statement, if present, or the End If statement if there is no Else clause.

In Figure 19-14, the Print Products Dialog box displays an option group, called Print Choices, that displays three options for printing Product reports. When you choose the option "Current Product Only," the report will print including data for the record currently displayed on the Products form. When you choose the "All Products" option, the report includes data for all of the products in the Products table. When you choose the "Product Listing" option, a report displays all of the products in a tabular format.

Figure 19-14: Choosing the option to print only the Current Product in the Print Products Dialog box.

Figure 19-15 illustrates the cmdPrint_Click() event procedure for the cmdPrint button in the frmDialogProductPrint If Statement form. The first If statement determines whether to view the report on the screen or send it to the printer. The next three If statements determine which report to print and whether to include all data or just the current record in the report.

```
Chap19Start - Form_frmDialogProductPrint If Statement (Code)
cmdPrint                                               ▼  Click                    ▼
Private Sub cmdPrint_Click()
    Dim ReportDest As Integer

    'Hide the Report Print Dialog
    Me.Visible = False
    If Me![grpTypeOfOutput] = 1 Then
        ReportDest = acPreview
    Else                         ' Destination is printer
        ReportDest = acNormal
    End If
    If Me![grpTypeOfPrint] = 1 Then
        DoCmd.OpenReport "rptProducts", ReportDest, , "[chrProductID]=[Forms]![frmProducts]![txtProductID]"
    End If
    If Me![grpTypeOfPrint] = 2 Then
        DoCmd.OpenReport "rptProducts", ReportDest
    End If
    If Me![grpTypeOfPrint] = 3 Then
        DoCmd.OpenReport "rptProductListing", ReportDest
    End If
    Exit Sub

End Sub
```

Figure 19-15: Using the If. . .Then. . .End If statement.

The Else statement is optional. You can use Else to test for a second condition when the If condition evaluates to False or just to perform an alternate set of actions when the If condition is false. When the If condition is True, the program executes the statements between the If condition and the Else condition. When the If condition evaluates to False, the program skips to the Else condition, if it is present. Then, if the Else condition is True, the program executes the following statement. If the Else condition is False, the program skips to the statement following the End If statement.

The ElseIf condition is also optional and works just like the Else condition. If the If condition is True, the program executes the following statement. If the If condition is False, and the program finds a following ElseIf condition, it checks the value of the ElseIf condition. If the ElseIf condition is True, the program executes the following statement. If the ElseIf condition is False, the program checks for an additional ElseIf condition or for an Else condition. An If...Then...End If statement can contain only one Else condition, whereas you can code as many ElseIf conditions as necessary. When using ElseIf conditions, the Else condition is optional. Figure 19-16 illustrates the cmdPrint_Click() event procedure for the cmdPrint button in the frmDialogProductPrint If Else Statement event procedure using ElseIf and Else conditions.

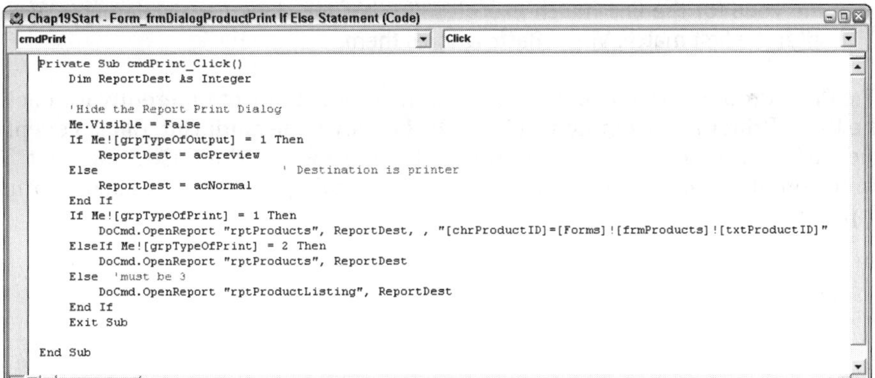

```
Chap19Start - Form_frmDialogProductPrint If Else Statement (Code)
cmdPrint                                          Click

Private Sub cmdPrint_Click()
    Dim ReportDest As Integer

    'Hide the Report Print Dialog
    Me.Visible = False
    If Me![grpTypeOfOutput] = 1 Then
        ReportDest = acPreview
    Else                    ' Destination is printer
        ReportDest = acNormal
    End If
    If Me![grpTypeOfPrint] = 1 Then
        DoCmd.OpenReport "rptProducts", ReportDest, , "[chrProductID]=[Forms]![frmProducts]![txtProductID]"
    ElseIf Me![grpTypeOfPrint] = 2 Then
        DoCmd.OpenReport "rptProducts", ReportDest
    Else   'must be 3
        DoCmd.OpenReport "rptProductListing", ReportDest
    End If
    Exit Sub

End Sub
```

Figure 19-16: Using the Elseif...Else conditions.

When you have many conditions to test, the If. . .Then. . .ElseIf...Else conditions can get rather unwieldy. A better approach is to use the Select Case construct.

The Select Case. . .End Select statement

Visual Basic also offers the Select Case statement to check for multiple conditions. Following is the general syntax of the statement:

```
Select Case test_expression
    Case expression value1
        code statements here (test expression = value1)
    Case expression value2
        code statements here (test expression = value2) ...
    Case Else
        code statements (test expression = none of the values)
End Select
```

Notice that the syntax is similar to that of the If. . .Then statement. Instead of a condition in the Select Case statement, however, Visual Basic uses a test expression. Then each Case statement inside the Select Case statement tests its value against the test expression's value. When a Case statement matches the test value, the program executes the next line or lines of code until it reaches another Case statement or the End Select statement. Visual Basic executes the code for only one matching Case statement.

Note   If more than one Case statement matches the value of the test expression, only the code for the first match executes. If other matching Case statements appear after the first match, Visual Basic ignores them.

The Print Products Dialog box processes the report to print differently for each of the three Print Choices options. Figure 19-17 shows the cmdPrint_Click() event procedure for the cmdPrint button in the frmDialogProductPrint Case Statement. The three condition statements determine which OpenReport action is used to print the appropriate report.

```
Private Sub cmdPrint_Click()
    Dim ReportDest As Integer

    'Hide the Report Print Dialog
    Me.Visible = False
    If Me![grpTypeOfOutput] = 1 Then
        ReportDest = acPreview
    Else                    ' Destination is printer
        ReportDest = acNormal
    End If
    Select Case Me![grpTypeOfPrint]
        Case 1
            DoCmd.OpenReport "rptProducts", ReportDest, , "[chrProductID]=[Forms]![frmProducts]![txtProductID]"
        Case 2
            DoCmd.OpenReport "rptProducts", ReportDest
        Case 3
            DoCmd.OpenReport "rptProductListing", ReportDest
    End Select
    Exit Sub

End Sub
```

Figure 19-17: Using the Select Case statement.

The cmdPrint_Click() event procedure, illustrated in Figure 19-17, performs the same actions as the previous two If...Then...EndIF examples. Notice how much easier to read the Select Case statement is as compared to the two previous examples.

The Select Case statement looks at the value of the control grpTypeOfPrint and then checks each Case condition. If the value of grpTypeOfPrint is 1 (Current Record Only), the Case 1 statement evaluates to True, and the Products report prints for the current Product record. If grpTypeOfPrint is not 1, Visual Basic goes to the next Case statement to see whether grpTypeOfPrint matches that value. Each Case statement is evaluated until a match occurs or the program reaches the End Select statement.

The Case Else statement is optional. The Case Else clause is always coded as the last Case statement of Select Case. You use this statement to perform some action when none of the Case values matches the test value of the Select Case statement.

In some procedures, you may want to execute a group of statements more than one time. Visual Basic provides some constructs for repeating a group of statements.

Repetitive looping

Another very powerful process that Visual Basic offers is repetitive looping — the capability to process a single statement or a group of statements over and over. The statement or group of statements is processed continually until some condition is met.

Visual Basic offers two types of repetitive-looping constructs:

✦ Do. . .Loop

✦ For. . .Next

The Do. . .Loop statement

The Do. . .Loop statement is used to repeat a group of statements while a condition is true or until a condition is true. This statement is one of the most common commands that can perform repetitive processes.

Following is the format of the Do. . .Loop statement:

```
DO [While | Until condition]
     code statements [for condition = TRUE]
     [Exit DO]
     code statements [for condition = TRUE]
LOOP [While | Until condition]
```

Notice that the Do. . .Loop statement has several optional clauses. The two While clauses tell the program to execute the code inside Do. . .Loop as long as the test condition is True. When the condition evaluates to False, the program skips to the next statement following the Loop statement. The two Until clauses work in just the opposite way; they execute the code within Do. . .Loop as long as the condition is False. Where you place the While or Until clause determines whether the code inside Do. . .Loop executes at least once. If you place the clause at the beginning of the statement and the condition is met (until) or not met (while), the statement will not execute at all. If you place the clause at the end of the statement, the statement will execute once before evaluating the condition for the first time.

The Exit Do clause is used to terminate the Do. . .Loop immediately. The program then skips to the next statement following the Loop statement.

The cmdPrint_Click() event procedure for the form frmDialogProductPrint Do Statement, illustrated in Figure 19-18, prints multiple copies of the report, based on the value of the Number of Copies control on the form. Notice that the procedure declares a variable named intCounter. The program increments the intCounter variable each time the report prints. When Counter is greater than Number of Copies, Do. . .Loop stops printing copies of the report.

```
Chap19Start - Form_frmDialogProductPrint Do Statement (Code)
cmdPrint                                              ▼   Click                    ▼
    Private Sub cmdPrint_Click()
        Dim ReportDest As Integer, intCounter As Integer

        'Hide the Report Print Dialog
        intCounter = 1
        Me.Visible = False
        If Me![grpTypeOfOutput] = 1 Then
            ReportDest = acPreview
        Else                         ' Destination is printer
            ReportDest = acNormal
        End If
        Select Case Me![grpTypeOfPrint]
            Case 1
                Do While intCounter <= Me!intCopies
                    DoCmd.OpenReport "rptProducts", ReportDest, , "[chrProductID]=[Forms]![frmProducts]![txtProductID]"
                    intCounter = intCounter + 1
                Loop
            Case 2
                Do While intCounter <= Me!intCopies
                    DoCmd.OpenReport "rptProducts", ReportDest
                    intCounter = intCounter + 1
                Loop
            Case 3
                Do While intCounter <= Me!intCopies
                    DoCmd.OpenReport "rptProductListing", ReportDest
                    intCounter = intCounter + 1
                Loop
        End Select
        Exit Sub
```

Figure 19-18: Using the Do. . .Loop statement.

The While clause causes the Do. . .Loop to exit when Counter reaches the limit. Using the While or Until clause is equivalent to using the Exit Do statement within the loop. The following is the same Do. . .Loop example using the Exit Do statement:

```
Do
        Docmd.OpenReport ...
        Counter = Counter + 1
        If Counter > .[Number of Copies] Then
                Exit Do
        End If
Loop
```

The While and Until clauses provide powerful flexibility for processing a Do. . .Loop in your code. Table 19-7 describes the various alternatives for using the While and Until clauses and how they affect the processing of code.

Table 19-7 **Repetitive Looping Using Do. . .Loop with the While and Until Clauses**	
Pseudo Code	*Purpose of Do. . .Loop*

Do	Code starts here
	If condition Then
	Exit Do
	End If

Loop	The code always runs. The code has some conditional statement
	(If. . .Then) that, if True, runs the Exit Do statement. The Exit Do statement allows the user to get out of Do. . .Loop. If that statement were missing, the code inside the loop would run forever.
Do	While condition code starts here for the condition on the Do While line being TRUE
Loop	The code inside the Do While loop runs only if the condition is True. The code runs down to the Loop statement and then goes back to the top to see whether the condition is still True. If the condition is initially False, Do. . .Loop is skipped; if the condition becomes False, the loop is exited when the code loops back to the Do While line. Exit Do is not needed for this purpose.
Do	Until condition code starts here for the condition on the Do Until line being FALSE
Loop	This code works the opposite way from Do While. If the condition is False (not True), the code begins and loops until the condition is True; then it leaves the loop. Again, the loop and its code are skipped if the Until condition is True
Do condition	Code starts here
Loop While	This code always runs at least one time. First, the code is executed and reaches the Loop While line. If the condition is True, the code loops back up to process the code again; if not, the code loop ends

Continued

	Table 19-7 *(continued)*
Pseudo Code	**Purpose of Do. . .Loop**
Do	Code starts here
Loop Until	This code works similarly to the preceding one. The code always runs at least one time. When the code reaches the Loop Until line, it checks to see whether the condition is True. If the condition is True, the code drops out of the loop. If the condition is False, the code loops back up to redo the code

The For. . .Next statement

For. . .Next is a shortcut method for the Do. . .Loop construct. You can use For. . .Next when you want to repeat a statement for a set number of times. The Step clause followed by an increment lets you process the loop in a specified step amount. For example, if start number was 10 and end number was 100 and you wanted to increment the counter by 10 each time, you would use Step 10. Though the loop would only be executed 10 times, the value of the counter would be 10, 20, 30, and so on, instead of 1, 2, 3, and so on.

Following is the general syntax of the For. . .Next statement:

```
For counter variable name  = start number  To end number
[Step increment]
code statements begin here and continue to Next If condition
code
[Exit For]
End If code can continue here after the Exit for
Next [counter]
```

You can code the previous example, illustrated in Figure 19-18, more efficiently using the For . . .Next construct. In Figure 19-19, notice that the For. . .Next statements replace the Do While. . .Loop statements used in the example. Notice also that the statement Counter = Counter + 1 is omitted. The For. . .Next construct is more efficient than the D While. . .Loop construct because you need to write fewer lines of code — the counter variable is incremented for you.

At the start of the For. . .Next loop, the program initializes intCounter to 1; then it moves on and executes the DoCmd statement. Whenever the program encounters the Next statement, it automatically increments intCounter and returns to the For statement. The program compares the value of intCounter with the value in the Number of Copies control. If intCounter is less than or equal to Number of Copies, the DoCmd executes again; otherwise, the program exits the loop.

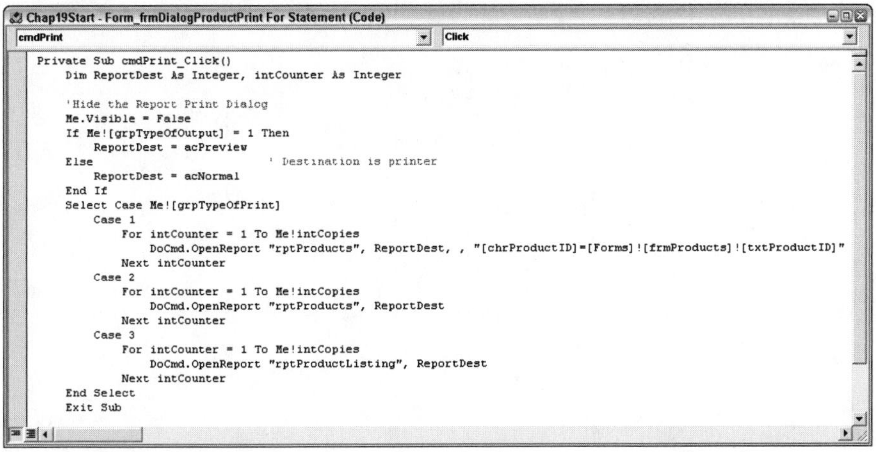

```
Chap19Start - Form_frmDialogProductPrint For Statement (Code)
cmdPrint                                              Click
Private Sub cmdPrint_Click()
    Dim ReportDest As Integer, intCounter As Integer

    'Hide the Report Print Dialog
    Me.Visible = False
    If Me![grpTypeOfOutput] = 1 Then
        ReportDest = acPreview
    Else                         ' Destination is printer
        ReportDest = acNormal
    End If
    Select Case Me![grpTypeOfPrint]
        Case 1
            For intCounter = 1 To Me!intCopies
                DoCmd.OpenReport "rptProducts", ReportDest, , "[chrProductID]=[Forms]![frmProducts]![txtProductID]"
            Next intCounter
        Case 2
            For intCounter = 1 To Me!intCopies
                DoCmd.OpenReport "rptProducts", ReportDest
            Next intCounter
        Case 3
            For intCounter = 1 To Me!intCopies
                DoCmd.OpenReport "rptProductListing", ReportDest
            Next intCounter
    End Select
    Exit Sub
```

Figure 19-19: Using the For. . .Next loop.

✦   ✦   ✦

Working with Expressions and Functions

In this chapter, you will gain a fuller understanding of expressions and functions. You have already used expressions and functions in some of your queries and forms in earlier chapters. Here you will focus on the parts of expressions, and you will also work with some of the most common built-in functions of Access. Built-in functions are very powerful in queries, forms, reports and the immediate window of Visual Basic.

On the CD-ROM This chapter will use the database named CHAP20Start.mdb. If you have not already copied it onto your machine from the CD, you will need to do so now. When you have completed this chapter, your database should resemble the one in CHAP20End.mdb.

What Are Expressions?

In general, an *expression* is the means used to explain or model something to someone or something. In computer terms, an expression is generally defined as a combination of a symbol, sign, figure, or set of symbols that presents or represents an algebraic fact as a quantity or operation. The expression is a representative object that Access can use to interpret something and, based on that interpretation, to obtain specific information. Simply put, an expression is a term or series of terms controlled by operators. Expressions are a fundamental part of Access operations. They are used to perform a calculation, manipulate characters, or test data.

You can use expressions in Access to accomplish a variety of tasks. You can use an expression as a property setting in SQL statements, in queries and filters, or in macros and actions. Expressions can set criteria for a query, filter, control macros, and perform as arguments in user-defined functions.

Access evaluates an expression each time it is used. If an expression is in a form or report, Access calculates the value every time the form refreshes (as with changing records and so forth). This ensures accuracy of the results. If an expression is used as a criterion in a query, Access evaluates the expression every time the query is executed, thereby ensuring that the criterion reflects any changes, additions, or deletions to records since the last execution of the query. If an expression is used in the table design as a validation rule, Access executes the evaluation each time the field is trespassed to determine whether the value is allowed in the field; this expression may be based on another field's value!

To give you a better understanding of expressions, consider the examples that follow—all of which are examples of expressions:

=rTrim(chrFirstName) & " " & rTrim(chrLastName)

=curPrice - (curPrice * tblSalesLineItems.dblDiscountPercent)<25000

blnTaxable=Yes

chrContactType="Buyer" And chrState="MA"

Sales.dtmSalesDate Between 6/2003 And 4/2004

Each is a valid expression. Access can use them as validation rules, query criteria, calculated controls, control sources, and control-source properties. Some expressions can use built-in functions like the first example, rTrim( ), which right trims all spaces from the field.

Figure 20-1 shows the use of an expression in the first field of the query. Notice that it has concatenated (joined) the two fields — chrFirstName &" "& chrLastName.

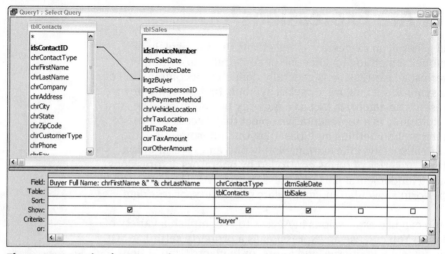

Figure 20-1: A simple query using an expression. Notice that the expression has a name attached to it: "Buyer Full Name" and the actual expression.

Note To see how this concatenated field was put together, you can find and open the query in the Chap20End.mdb; it is named zzz Figure20-01.

The parts of an expression

As the examples in the preceding section demonstrated, expressions can be simple or complex. They can include a combination of operators, object names, functions, literal values, and constants.

Remembering that expressions don't need to contain all these parts, you should understand each of the following uniquely identifiable portions of an expression:

Operators: >, =, *, And, Or, Not, Like, and so on.

Operators indicate what type of action (operation) will be performed on one or more elements of an expression.

Object names: Forms![frmContacts], chrLastName, curPrice, tblProducts.chrDescription

Object names, also known as *identifiers*, are the actual objects: tables, forms, reports, controls, or fields.

Functions: Date( ), DLookUp( ), DateDiff( )

Functions always return a value. The resultant value can be created by a calculation, a conversion of data, or an evaluation. You can use a built-in Access function or a user-defined function that you create.

Literal values: 100, Jan. 1, 2003, "Seller", "[A-D]*"

These are actual values that you supply to the expression. Literal values can be numbers, strings, or dates. Access uses the values exactly as they are entered.

Constants: Yes, No, Null, True, False

Constants represent values that do not change.

The following example illustrates the parts of an expression:

[dtmFollowUpDate] = Date( ) + 30 where:

[dtmFollowUpDate] is an object name or identifier.

= is an operator.

Date( ) is a function.

+ is an operator.

30 is a literal.

Figure 20-2 shows a simple form with two entry fields — Contacted On and Follow-up date. These fields are automatically filled in with today's date (Contacted On) and 30 days from now (Follow-up Date). If the user clicks into the memo field and starts to type a new record, when he leaves the field, the program checks to make sure that he put a Contacted on date in the field. If not, it adds today's date. If the user clicks on the follow-up field and the Contacted on date is not entered, it also adds today's date. Also, it automatically puts a value of today plus 30 in the Follow-Up date field.

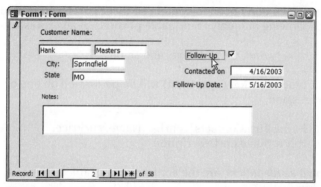

Figure 20-2: Using code that uses expressions to add field values to a record.

Note   To see how this concatenated form was put together, you can find and open the query in the Chap20End.mdb; it is named zzz Figure20-2 through 20-3. Figure 20-3 shows the code used in this form.

Figure 20-3 shows the code that contains the expressions to automatically check values in the fields in Figure 20-3.

Examining the code in Figure 20-3, you can see many expressions. A couple of them are Me.blnFollowUp, IsNull(Me.dtmDateContacted), and Me.dtmDateContacted = Date. Notice that all three of these use the word 'Me' with the field name. *Me* is a property, followed by a period, that is used to reference the current object (form, report, or class module). It is only used in Visual Basic code.

Creating an expression

Expressions are commonly entered in Property windows, action arguments, and criteria grids. As you create expressions, the area is scrolled so that you can continue to enter the expression. Although you can enter an expression in this manner, it is usually desirable to see the entire expression as you enter it. This is especially true when you are working with long, complex expressions. Access has a Zoom box that you can use to change how much of the expression you see as you enter it. Open this box by clicking where you want to enter your expression and pressing Shift+F2.

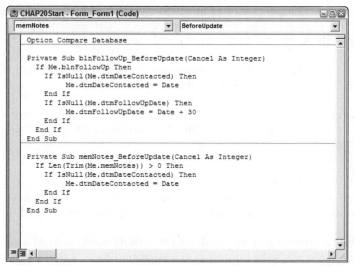

```
CHAP20Start - Form_Form1 (Code)

memNotes                          ▼   BeforeUpdate                ▼

  Option Compare Database

  Private Sub blnFollowUp_BeforeUpdate(Cancel As Integer)
     If Me.blnFollowUp Then
       If IsNull(Me.dtmDateContacted) Then
           Me.dtmDateContacted = Date
       End If
       If IsNull(Me.dtmFollowUpDate) Then
           Me.dtmFollowUpDate = Date + 30
       End If
     End If
  End Sub

  Private Sub memNotes_BeforeUpdate(Cancel As Integer)
     If Len(Trim(Me.memNotes)) > 0 Then
       If IsNull(Me.dtmDateContacted) Then
           Me.dtmDateContacted = Date
       End If
     End If
  End Sub
```

Figure 20-3: The code used for updating the fields in Figure 20-2.

As you enter expressions, Access may insert certain characters for you when you change focus. Access checks your syntax and automatically inserts these characters:

✦ Brackets ([]) around control names that have no spaces or punctuation in the name

✦ Pound signs (#) around dates it recognizes

✦ Quotation marks (" ") around text that contains no spaces or punctuation in the body

Note   The term *changing focus* refers to the movement of the insertion point out of the location where you are entering the expression, which is accomplished by pressing Tab or by moving the mouse and clicking another area of the screen.

Caution   Access reports an error when it changes focus when Access doesn't understand the date form entered, when the name of the control contains spaces, when a control is not placed in brackets, when an end parenthesis is missing in a function, and on and on.

Entering object names

Object names are identified by placing brackets ([]) around the element. Access requires the use of brackets when the object contains a space or punctuation in its name (like a dash). If these conditions are not present, you can ignore the brackets—Access inserts them automatically. The following expressions are syntactically identical:

lngzBuyer & [Sales Person ID]

[lngzBuyer] & [Sales Person ID]

Caution The field name IngzSalespersonID has been changed in the above example to Sales Person ID, placing spaces between the names to demonstrate how you would use brackets around the field name if it had spaces in it.

Notice that in both cases the brackets are placed around the lngzSales Person ID name because this object name contains spaces.

Although it isn't necessary to enter brackets around objects such as lngzBuyer in the second example, it is good programming practice to always surround object names with brackets for consistency in entry.

Entering text

Placing quotation marks around the text element of an expression identifies text. Access automatically places the quotation marks for you if you forget to add them.

As an example, you can type Buyer and Both into separate criteria cells of a query, and Access automatically adds the quotation marks around each of these two entries. Access recognizes these as objects and helps you.

Entering date/time values

Placing pound signs (#) around the date/time element identifies date/time data. Access will evaluate any valid date/time format automatically and place the pound signs around the element for you.

Expression Builder

Access has added an *Expression Builder* tool to help you build complex expressions. You can use it anywhere you can build an expression (such as creating a calculated field on a form or report). You can activate the builder tool in two ways:

✦ Press the Build button on the toolbar (the button with the ellipsis on it).

✦ Click the *right* mouse button and select Build from the shortcut menu.

Special identifier operators and expressions

Access has two special *identifier operators*: the dot (.) and the exclamation point (!). Access tables provide many ways to display any Access objects. You can use fields and their contents, and any field object can be reused repeatedly. You can display the field object in numerous forms and reports by using the same reference, the field object name, in every form and report.

For example, the field dtmSaleDate from the Sales table can be used in several different forms. When you want to use the dtmSaleDate field in an expression for a comparison, how do you tell Access which copy of the field dtmSaleDate it should use

A Few Words about Controls and Properties

When you create a form or report, you place many different objects on the form—fields in text boxes, text labels, buttons, check boxes, combo boxes, lines, rectangles, and so on.

As you select and place these objects on a form, each object is assigned a control name. Access supplies the control name according to predefined rules. For example, control names for fields default to a control-source name of the field name. The field name appears in the text box on the form. The label for the text box is assigned the control name Text, with a sequence number attached to it (for example, Text11 or Text12). The sequence number is added to make each control name unique.

After all objects are placed on the form, you can identify any object on the form (line, button, text box, and so on) by its unique control name. This control name is what you use to refer to a specific table field (or field on a form). You can change the name of the control that Access assigned to the object if you want. The only requirement for the new control name is that it must be unique to the form or report that contains it.

Every object on the form (including the form itself) has associated properties. These are the individual characteristics of each object; as such, they are accessible by a control name. Properties control the appearance of the object (color, size, sunken, alignment, and so forth). They also affect the structure, specifying format, default value, validation rules, and control name. In addition, properties designate the behavior of a control—for instance, whether the field can grow or shrink and whether you can edit it. Behaviors also affect actions specified for the event properties, such as On Enter and On Push.

for the expression? Because Access is a Windows database, it is possible to have several different forms open in the same session on the same computer. In fact, it is possible to have multiple copies of Access running the same data and forms.

With all this repetition, there must be a way to tell Access which dtmSaleDate field object you want the expression to use. That is the purpose of the dot and exclamation point as operator identifiers. These symbols clarify which field to use.

The ! (exclamation) identifier operator

The exclamation mark (!) is used in conjunction with several reserved words. One such reserved word is Forms. When this word is followed by !, Access is being told that the next object name is the form object name that you want to refer to.

Cross-Reference Additional keywords can be found in the next section, titled Special Keywords and Properties.

As an example, say that you have a Description field (chrDescription) that is in two forms—frmProducts and frmSales. (These two form names are objects; because there are no spaces in the names, you do not need to use square brackets to refer to them. However, it is a good idea to do so.) You want to refer to the Description field in the [frmProducts] form. The way to specify this form is by use of the ! and the *Forms* reserved word:

Forms![frmProducts]

Now that the form is specified, further refine the scope to add the field chrDescription.

Note   Although earlier chapters cover controls and properties, by this point you should have a partial understanding of what properties and controls are (for a refresher, see the preceding sidebar).

Actually, what you are specifying is a control on the form. That control will use the field you need, which is chrDescription. The control has the same name as the field. Therefore, you access this specific object by using the following expression:

Forms! [frmProducts]![chrDescription]

The second exclamation mark specifies a control on a form—one identified by the reserved word *Forms*.

By following the properties of each object, starting with the object Forms, you can trace the control source object back to a field in the original table.

In summary, the exclamation-point identifier is always followed by an object name. This object name is defined by using the name of a form, report, field, or other control name that was created in the database. If you don't use the existing name for the desired object, you can change the default value name of the source.

The . (dot) identifier operator

The . (dot) is also a key symbol that is used in conjunction with expression identification operators. Normally it is placed immediately after a user-defined object. Unlike the !, the . (dot) usually identifies a property of a specific object. Therefore, if you want to determine the value of the Visible property of the same control you worked with before, you specify it as follows:

Forms! [frmProducts]![chrDescription].Visible

This gives the value for the Visible property of the specific field on the specific form.

Note   Normally, the . (dot) identifier is used to obtain a value that corresponds to a property of an object. Sometimes, you can use it between a table name and a field name when you access a value associated with a specific field in a specific table, such as [tblSales].[lngzBuyer].

A thorough analysis of the two special identifier operators is beyond the scope of this book. Even so, you'll find that these identifiers enable you to find any object and the values associated with its properties.

Special keywords and properties

There are many special keywords and properties that Access uses to reference active objects. Two have already been referenced earlier in this chapter — the property Me used in Visual Basic to reference forms or reports and Forms used to reference the current active form. Although there are many keywords and properties, the following list are the most common keywords and properties you will use as references in your events and code for forms and reports:

Forms   The complete collection of forms in a database — used to specify a specific form. The Syntax is:

> Forms!frmContacts

Form   The current active form — used to access an object on a sub form within a specific form. The syntax is:

> Forms!frmMyForm.mySubFormObject.Form!theControlName

Reports   The complete collection of reports in a database — used to specify a specific report. The syntax is:

> Reports!rptContacts

Screen   The Screen object is used for the particular form, report, or control that has focus. It uses many properties to reference these objects. The syntax is:

> Screen.ActiveForm (used for active form)
>
> Screen.ActiveReport used for active report)
>
> Screen.ActiveDatasheet (used for active datasheet)
>
> Screen.ActiveControl (used for active control)

Me   Me is a special property that is used to reference the active form, report, or class module. It can only be used in Visual Basic code. The syntax is:

> Me!chrLastName (the same as Forms!frmContacts.chrLastName)
>
> Me!chrFirstName (the same as Screen.ActiveForm.chrFirstName)

As you work with your forms, report, and visual basic code, these special keywords and properties will be useful for writing efficient events.

A Quick Review of Events and Properties

Simply put, an *event* is some action. The event can be an action such as opening a form or report, changing data in a record, selecting a button, or closing a form or report. Access recognizes approximately 60 events in forms and reports.

To recognize one of these events, Access uses special form or report *properties*. Each event has an associated form or report property. For example, the OnOpen property is associated with the event of opening a form or report. These properties are known as event properties.

To perform some action when the event is triggered, you create either a macro or code and associate it with the property (in the above case, the OnOpen event property) by assigning the name of the macro or code function to that property as a parameter against the event property. When the user triggers the event, the code is executed, or run.

What Are Functions?

Functions are small programs that always, by definition, return a value based on some calculation, comparison, or evaluation that the function performs. The value returned can be string, logic, or numeric, depending on the type of function. Access provides hundreds of common functions that are used in tables, queries, forms, and reports. You can also create your own user-defined functions (UDFs) using the Access Visual Basic language.

Using functions in Access

Functions perform specialized operations that enhance the utility of Access. Many times, you find yourself using functions as an integral part of Access. The following are examples of the types of tasks that functions can accomplish:

✦ Define a default value in a table

✦ Place the current date and time on a report

✦ Convert data from one type to another

✦ Perform financial operations

✦ Display a field in a specific format

✦ Look up and return a value based on another

✦ Perform an action upon the triggering of an event

Access functions can perform financial, mathematical, comparative, and other operations. Therefore, functions are used just about everywhere — in queries, forms, reports, validation rules, and so forth.

Many Access functions evaluate or convert data from one type to another; others perform an action. Some Access functions require use of parameters; others operate without them.

> **Note**　A parameter is a value that you supply to the function when you run it. The value can be an object name, a constant, or a quantity.

Access functions can be quickly identified because they always end with parentheses. If a function uses parameters, the parameters are placed inside the parentheses immediately after the function name.

Examples of Access functions are as follows:

Now( )	Returns the current date and time
Rnd( )	Returns a random number
DateAdd( )	Returns a date based on an interval added
Ucase( )	Returns the uppercase of an object
Format( )	Returns a user-specified formatted expression

Types of functions

Access offers several types of functions. They can be placed in the following general categories:

✦ Conversion

✦ Date/Time

✦ Financial (SQL)

✦ Financial (monetary)

✦ Mathematical

✦ String manipulation

✦ Programming

✦ Domain

Immediate window

Microsoft Visual Basic has an *Immediate window* that you can use to test your code or functions. Figure 20-4 shows the Immediate window open in Visual Basic. It is located toward the bottom center of the figure. It has two lines of text in it — the print statement of LCase( ) function and the results answer.

The Immediate window is a nice tool to check on how a function works.

What Is a Program?

A program is a series of defined steps that specify one or more actions the computer should perform. A program can be created by the user or can already exist in Access; all Access functions are already created programs. For example, a Ucase() function is a small program. If you employ Ucase ( ) on a string, such as "Michael R. Irwin," Access creates a new string from the existing string, converting each letter to uppercase. The program starts at the leftmost letter, first converting M to M and then i to I, and so forth, until the entire string is converted. As it converts each letter, the program concatenates it to a new string.

You can activate Visual Basic from inside Access by simply pressing the hot key combination of Ctrl+G, by opening Visual Basic by clicking on the New button of the Modules container, or by clicking on the design button of an existing module. When you are in Visual Basic, select View ⇨ Immediate Window or press Ctrl+G. When you are active, you can use the print command (a question mark: ?) to display the results of any function.

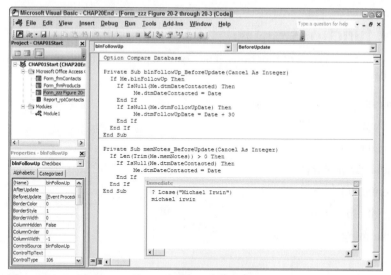

Figure 20-4: The Immediate window of Visual Basic with the LCase( ) function displayed.

Conversion

Conversion functions change the data type from one type to another. A few common functions are listed here:

Str( )   Returns a string, converted from a numeric. It always reserves (adds) a leading space for the plus sign:

Str(921.23) returns " 921.23" — A leading space is added.

Str(-123) returns "-123" — No leading space is added and the sign is shown.

LCase( )   Returns a string that is converted to lowercase:

LCase("Mike Irwin") returns "mike irwin" as in Figure 20-4.

UCase( )   Returns a string that is converted to uppercase:

LCase("Mike Irwin") returns "MIKE IRWIN".

Val( )   Returns a numeric value found in a string up to the first non-numeric character in the string:

Val("1234.56") returns 1234.56.

Val("10 Farmview 2 Ct") returns 10. The 2 is after the first non-numeric character 'F'.

CDate( )   Converts a string to a Date:

CDate("04 Feb 52") returns 02/04/1952.

CDate("February 4, 1952") returns 02/04/1952.

CSTR( )   Converts a numeric or Date to a string:

CSTR(#Feb 04, 52#) is converted to the string "02/04/1952" from date.

CSTR(12345) is converted to the string "12345" from number.

Format( )   Returns an expression according to the user-specified format:

Format("Next",">") returns NEXT.

Format("123456789","@@@-@@-@@@@") returns 123-45-6789.

Format(#12/25/03#,"d-mmmm-yyyy") returns 25-December-2003.

Format(Date( ), "Long Date") returns Wednesday, April 16, 2003 (or the current date)

Format(Now( ),"Long Time") returns 12:37:58 PM (or the current time)

The Format( ) function is one of the most powerful ways to display data in a specific format. You can specify a specific format by using keywords or a mask of symbols telling the Format( ) function how to display the data. Figure 20-5 shows a query using two Format( ) functions, both using a keyword—Long Date for the way the date is to be displayed and Percent for displaying the percent value instead of decimal.

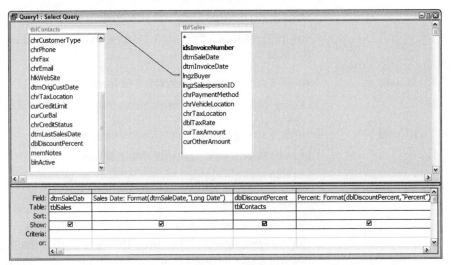

Figure 20-5: The Format( ) function being used in a query to display data in a specific manner.

Figure 20-6 shows the resulting datasheet using the format( ) function for the two fields. Notice that it shows the fields alongside each formatted field.

Sale Date	Sales Date	Discount Rate	Percent
1/15/2003	Wednesday, January 15, 2003	0.05	5.00%
2/27/2003	Thursday, February 27, 2003	0.11	11.00%
2/24/2003	Monday, February 24, 2003	0.025	2.50%
4/24/2003	Thursday, April 24, 2003	0.0325	3.25%
5/24/2003	Saturday, May 24, 2003	0	0.00%
6/1/2003	Sunday, June 01, 2003	0	0.00%
7/15/2003	Tuesday, July 15, 2003	0.055	5.50%
8/25/2003	Monday, August 25, 2003	0	0.00%
8/26/2003	Tuesday, August 26, 2003	0.0825	8.25%
9/25/2003	Thursday, September 25, 2003	0	0.00%
9/30/2003	Tuesday, September 30, 2003	0.075	7.50%
12/13/2003	Saturday, December 13, 2003	0.03	3.00%
12/12/2003	Friday, December 12, 2003	0.05	5.00%

Record: I◀ ◀ | 1 | ▶ ▶I ▶* | of 53

Figure 20-6: The datasheet from the format( ) function used in Figure 20-5.

Date/Time

Date/Time functions work with date and time expressions. The following are some common Date/Time functions:

Now( )	Returns the current date and time: 04/04/2003 12:22:34 PM.
Time( )	Returns the current time in 12-hour format: 12:22:34 PM.
Date( )	Returns the current date (vs. Now( ), which returns date and time): 04/04/2003.
Month( )	Returns a whole number that represents the month portion of a date. Month(Now( )) returns 04 (or today's month number).
Day( )	Returns a whole number that represents the day portion of a date. Day(Date( )) returns 16 (or today's day number of the month)
Weekday( )	Returns a whole number that represents the day of week for a specific date. Weekday(Date( )) returns 4 (for Wednesday or today's day of week number).
Year( )	Returns a whole number that represents the year portion of a date. Year(Date( )) returns 2003 (or today's year number).
DateDiff( )	Returns a number based on a specific time interval between two different dates. The time interval can be d (day), ww (weeks), m (months), q (quarters), yyyy (years). The syntax is: DateDiff("d", date( ), #02/04/52#) returns –18699 days if the date is 16 Apr 2003. DateDiff("y", date( ), #02/04/52#) returns –51 years if date is same. DateDiff("q", date( ), #02/04/52#) returns –205 quarters if date is same.

DateAdd( )   Returns a new date based on a specific time interval. The time interval can be d (day), ww (weeks), m (months), q (quarters), yyyy (years). The syntax is:

DateAdd("d",22, date( )) returns 5/8/2003 if the date is 16 Apr 2003.

DateAdd("ww",10, #01/01/2004#) returns 3/11/2004.

DatePart( )   Returns a number based on a specific time interval for a date. The time interval can be d (day), y (day of year), w (weekday), ww (weeks), m (months), q (quarters), yyyy (years). The syntax is:

DatePart("y", date( )) returns 106 if the date is 16 Apr 2003.

DatePart("ww", date( )) returns 16 if the date is 16 Apr 2003.

DatePart("q", date( )) returns 2 if the date is 16 Apr 2003.

Financial (SQL)

Financial (SQL) functions perform aggregate financial operations on a set of values. The set of values is contained in a field. The field can be in a form, report, or query. Two common SQL functions are listed below:

Avg( )   An example is Avg([Scores]).

Sum( )   An example is Sum([Gross Amount] + [Tax] + [Shipping]).

Financial (monetary)

Financial (monetary) functions perform financial operations. Several monetary functions are listed below:

DDB( )   Is the double-declining balance method of depreciation return. The syntax is:

DDB(initial cost, salvage value, life of product, period of asset depreciation)

NPV( )   Is the net present value, based on a series of payments and a discount rate. The syntax is:

NPV(discount rate, cash flow array( ))

FV( )   Is the Future Value of an annuity based on periodic, fixed payment and fixed interest rate. The syntax is:

FV(rate of percent - %/12, total number of payments, payment made each period, [OPTIONAL present value])

PV( )   Is the Present Value of an annuity based on periodic, fixed
                     payments to be paid in future and fixed interest rate. The syn-
                     tax is:

                         FV(rate of percent - %/12, total number of payments, pay-
                         ment made each period, [OPTIONAL future value])

SYD( )   Is the sum-of-years depreciation of an asset for a specific
                     period. The syntax is:

                         SYD(cost of asset, salvage value, length of useful life in
                         months, period given in months)

PMT( )   Is the payment for an annuity based on periodic, fixed pay-
                     ment and fixed interest rate. The syntax is:

                         PMT(rate per period - %/12, total number of payments, pre-
                         sent value of note)

                         PMT(.005, 360, -110000) returns payment amount of 659.51
                         for a 6% loan of 360 months for $110,000 USD.

Mathematical

Mathematical functions perform specific calculations. The following are some mathematical functions, with examples of how to use them.

Abs( )   Determines the absolute value of a number, the number with-
                     out a sign:

                         Abs(-14) results in 14.

                         Abs(14) results in 14.

Fix( )   Determines the correct integer for a negative number:

                         Fix(-1234.55) results in -1234.

Int( )   Determines the integer of a specific value:

                         Int(1234.55) results in 1234.

                         Int(-55.1) results in -56.

Round( )   Returns a number rounded to the specified number of
                     decimals:

                         Round(14.245, 2) results in 14.24 – rounding occurs over 5.

                         Round(17.1351, 2) results in 17.14 rounding up to .14.

Rnd( )   Returns a random number:

> Rnd( ) will return a random number – the next in the sequence.

> Rnd(-1) or any negative number will return the same random number every time, using the number as the seed (-1 in this case).

> Rnd(1) or any positive number will return a random number — the next in the sequence.

Sgn( )   Determines the correct sign of a number:

> Sgn(-14) results in -1 as will any negative number.

> Sgn(12) results in 1 as will any positive number.

> Sgn(0) results in 0.

Sqr( )   Determines the square root of a number:

> Sqr(9) returns 3.

> Sqr(14) returns 3.742.

There is another mathematical operator known as *MOD*, which lets a user determine the remainder between two numbers. That is, if you divide one number by another, the remaining digits are the Mod of the numbers. For example:

10 MOD 2 results in an answer of 0 (10 is evenly divisible by 2 with no remainder).

10 MOD 3 results in an answer of 1 (10 is divisible by 3, 3 times with a remainder of 1).

10 MOD 4 results in an answer of 2 (10 is divisible by 4, 2 times with a remainder of 2).

String manipulation

String functions manipulate text-based expressions. Here are some common uses of these functions:

InStr( )   Returns a number that represents the first position of one string in another string:

> Instr("abcd123efg234", "23") returns 6, the start position of '23'.

> Instr(7,"abcd123efg234","23") returns 11 — the 7 in the beginning tells the instr( ) function to start after position 7 of the string.

Left( )   Returns the leftmost characters of a string:

                   Left("abcdefg",4) returns "abcd."

Len( )   Returns the length of a string:

                   Len("abcdefgh") results in 8.

Lcase( )   Returns the lowercase of the string:

                   Lcase("Michael R. Irwin") Returns michael r. irwin.

LTrim( )   Removes leading spaces from a string:

                   LTrim("abcd") returns "abcd."

Mid( )   Returns characters from the middle of a string:

                   Mid("abcdefgh",3,4) returns "cdef.", starting at position 3
                   and reading 4 characters

Right( )   Returns the rightmost characters of a string:

                   Right("abcdefg",4) returns "defg."

RTrim( )   Removes trailing spaces from a string:

                   RTrim("abcd") returns "abcd."

Space( )   Inserts the specific number of spaces:

                   Space(6) returns "   " (six blank spaces).

Trim( )   Removes leading and trailing spaces from a string:

                   Trim("   abcd   ") returns "abcd."

Programming

Programming functions are those that don't fit in a specific category, yet are very useful in programming. The following are some programming functions, with examples of how to use them.

Choose( )   Returns a value based on an index parameter from a list.

                   Choose(2, "Slow", "Average", "Fast") returns "Average".

                   Choose(3, "A", "B", "C", "D") returns "C".

IsDate( )   Determines if an expression is a valid date.

                   IsDate("Feb 29, 2000") returns TRUE.

                   IsDate("Jup 4, 2003") returns FALSE.

IIF( )

Is used to return one of two parts based on the initial evaluation inside the function:

Function TestIt (TestNum as Integer)

TestIt = IIF(TestNum > 250, "Greater", "Smaller")

'

' if number passed is > than 250, returns the word "Greater"

' if number is less than 250, returns the word "Smaller"

'

End Function

IsMissing( )

Is used to check to see if a variable has been passed to the function:

Dim ReturnVal

ReturnVal = ReturnCheck( )

ReturnVal = ReturnCheck(4)

' Function ReturnCheck

Function ReturnCheck(Optional ABC)

If IsMissing(ABC) Then

   ReturnCheck = NULL

Else

   ReturnCheck = ABC * 2

End If

End Function

IsNull( )

Determines if an expression has no value (no data — Null), returning true or false:

IsNull([chrLastName]) returns false if there is a value in the field or true if no value is present.

NZ( )

Use this function to return a zero, a zero-length string, or another value when a variant is null. Default is zero-length string.

xName = "Mike"

? Nz(xName) results in "Mike"

? Nz(yName) results in ""

? Nz(yName,0) results in 0

Domain

A *domain* is a set of records contained in a table, a query, or an SQL expression. A query dynaset is an example of a domain. Domain aggregate functions determine specific statistics about a specific domain. If you need to perform statistical calculations in code, it must be done using domain aggregate functions. Domain aggregate functions can also be used to specify a criteria, update values, or even create calculated fields in a query expression.

Several examples of domain functions are listed below:

DAvg( )	Returns the arithmetic mean (average) of a set of values.
	DAvg("curCost","tblProducts") determines the average cost of vehicles sold. Figure 20-7 shows an example using DAvg( ) to show only vehicles where the cost is greater than or equal to the mean average.
DCount( )	Returns the number of records specified.
	DCount("chrProductID","tblProducts", "chrCategory = 'cars'") will go through the tblProducts table and count all records whose chrCategory value is 'cars'. Answer should be 25 for the table.
DFirst( )	Function returns a random record from a field in a table or query, when you need any value
	DFirst("chrFirstName", "tblContacts") will return a random name from the field chrFirstName. DLast( ) works the same.
DLookup( )	Returns the value of a specific field from the specified records.
	DLookUp("[Short Name]", "[tblPayType]", "[tblPayType].[chrPaymentType] = '"&[tblSales].[chrPaymentMethod]&"'") will find the correct short name for all payment types in the query. Figure 20-8 shows how the query field will look.
DMax( )	Function returns the highest value in a range of values.
	DMax("curCost","tblProducts") will return the highest price curCost from the tblProducts table. Should be $165,000.00 USD.
DMin( )	Function returns the lowest value in a range of values.
	DMin("curCost","tblProducts") will return the lowest price curCost from the tblProducts table. Should be $200.00 USD.
DSum( )	Returns the sum for a set of records specified.
	DSum("curCost","tblProducts", "chrCategory = 'cars'") will go through the tblProducts table and sum the chrCost of all record where the chrCategory is 'cars'. Answer should be $779,356.00 USD.

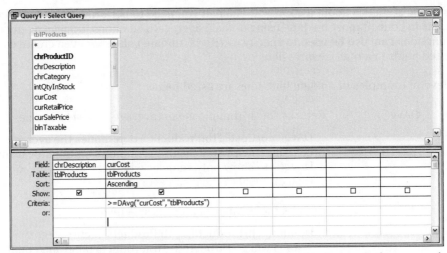

Figure 20-7: The DAvg( ) function being used in a query to show only those records that are valued greater than or equal to the mean average of all vehicles.

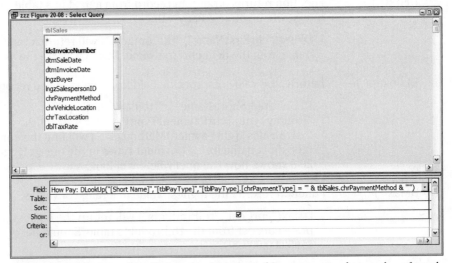

Figure 20-8: The DLookUp( ) function being used in a query to show values found in another table.

Using the DLookUp( ) Function for Lookup Tables

The DLookUp( ) function is rather difficult for people to understand. It is just a way to find a specific field value by looking up information based on a condition. DLookUp( ) finds information in a table that is not currently open. Although it can be easy to program and works well with small amounts of records, if your tables contain more than 5,000 records, you should do this with DAO code. This is the general syntax for the DLookUp( ) function:

```
DLookUp("[Field to display]", "[Lookup Table]", "<Criteria for
Search>")
```

"[Field to display]" in quotation marks is the field in the lookup table you want to find.

"[Lookup Table]" in quotation marks is the table containing the field you want to display.

"<Criteria for Search>" in quotation marks signifies criteria used by the lookup function.

Access suggests that Criteria for Search is not necessary, but if you want to use a different criterion for each record, it is essential. When you use DLookUp( ), the format of your criteria is critical. The syntax of Criteria for Search is as follows:

```
"[Field in Lookup Table] = '<Example Data>' "
```

You can replace the equal operator with any valid Access operator.

'<Example Data>' in single quotation marks is usually a literal, such as 'Cars' or 'AMEX'. If the data is a field in the current table, you must use the following syntax:

```
"& [Field in This Table] & "
```

Notice that the field is surrounded with double quotation marks (") and ampersands (&).

Although using the DLookUp( ) function to build a calculated field seems complex, it can be a simple way to create a query for use by a form or report. To create the query in Figure 20-8, follow these steps:

1. Select the tblSales table in the query design window.

2. Double-click the dtmSaleDate field in the table, and any other fields you want to look at.

3. In an empty field in the QBE pane, type: How Pay:DLookUp("[Short Name]", "[tblPayType]", "[tblPayType].[chrPaymentType] = '"&[tblSales].[chrPaymentMethod]&"'").

   Note: Before the &[tblSales] is a single quotation and then a double quotation mark.

   After [chrPaymentMethod]& is a double, then a single, then another double quotation mark.

   The current table value is specified second — '"&[tblSales].[chrPaymentMethod]&"'. The lookup table value is specified first — "[tblPayType].[chrPaymentType] =

When you enter the field name of the current table in the criteria for the DLookUp( ) function, you must not use spaces. After the equal sign, type the entry in this format:

```
single quote - double quote - ampersand - [field name] -
ampersand - double quote - single quote - double quote
```

No spaces can be entered between the quotation marks (single or double).

If you're having problems typing in Step 3, press Shift+F2 to activate the Zoom window. After activating the window, the entire contents will be highlighted; press F2 again to deselect the contents and move to the end of them.

If you now select the Datasheet option using the Query View button on the toolbar, you see a datasheet similar to the one in Figure 20-9. Notice that several records have no Payment method name, because these records have not been paid for.

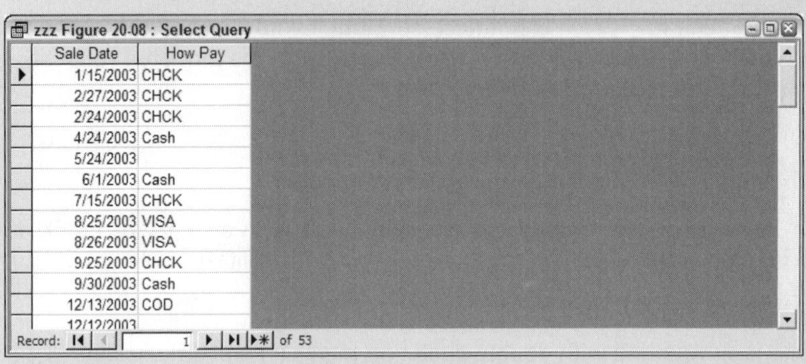

Sale Date	How Pay
1/15/2003	CHCK
2/27/2003	CHCK
2/24/2003	CHCK
4/24/2003	Cash
5/24/2003	
6/1/2003	Cash
7/15/2003	CHCK
8/25/2003	VISA
8/26/2003	VISA
9/25/2003	CHCK
9/30/2003	Cash
12/13/2003	COD
12/12/2003	

Record: 1 of 53

Figure 20-9: The datasheet using the DLookUp( ) function being used in a query to show values found in another table.

✦   ✦   ✦

Working with SQL, Recordsets, and ADO

The Visual Basic language offers a full array of powerful commands for manipulating records in a table, displaying data for controls on a form, or just about anything else. This chapter provides some in-depth examples of working with procedures that use SQL and ADO to manipulate database data.

Understanding SQL

Many of the procedures that you will write for working with Recordsets utilize Structured Query Language (SQL) statements to retrieve data from a database, add new data to a database, or update records in a database. When you use the graphical tools of the Query Design window to create a query, Access converts what you create into an SQL statement. This SQL statement is what Access actually executes when the query runs. SQL is a standardized language for querying and updating database tables, and it is used by many relational databases.

Although Recordsets do have the ability to work with the queries that are stored in the Access database container, many times you will find that creating the query on the fly in your code is quicker and easier than working with Access queries. SQL is relatively easy to understand and work with. This is a quick overview of SQL statements and how to create them in Access 2003.

On the CD-ROM   In this chapter, you will use the database file Chap21start.mdb.

Viewing SQL statements in queries

To view the SQL statement that Access creates while building a query, select View ➪ SQL View from the Query menu. Figure 21-1 shows a typical SQL statement that will display the product description, company name, and state for products purchased by contacts in Connecticut or New York.

Figure 21-1: An SQL statement in the SQL view window for an Access query

You can make changes to the query using either the Design window or the SQL window. As you are working with the query, you can alternately switch between view modes. If you are viewing in SQL view, you can return to the Design view by selecting View ➪ Design View. Any changes that you made to the query in SQL view are reflected in the Design view. When you make changes to the query in the Design view window, the changes are immediately updated in the SQL view window.

> **Tip**   If you are proficient in creating SQL queries on your own, you can even create a new query directly in the SQL window. To add new lines to the SQL statement, simply press Enter.

An SQL primer

As you can see, one way to learn how to create SQL statements is to build a query in Design view and then view the corresponding SQL statement in the SQL view window. The example in Figure 21-1 utilizes the four most common SQL commands. Table 21-1 shows each command and explains its purpose.

Using these four basic keywords, you can build very powerful SQL statements to use in your Access forms and reports.

Table 21-1 Four Common SQL Keywords	
Keyword	**Purpose in SQL Statement**
SELECT	This keyword starts an SQL statement. It is followed by the names of the fields that will be selected from the table or tables (if more than one is specified in the FROM clause/command). This is a required keyword.
FROM	This keyword specifies the name(s) of the table(s) containing the fields specified in the SELECT command. This is a required keyword. If more than one table is used you need to also specify a JOIN type, known as a Table Expression.
WHERE	This keyword specifies any condition used to filter (limit) the records that will be viewed. This keyword is used only when you want to limit the records to a specific group on the basis of the condition.
ORDER BY	This keyword specifies the order in which you want the resulting dataset (the selected records that were found and returned) to appear.

The SELECT keyword

The SELECT keyword is the first keyword used in two query types: in a select query or a make-table query. The SELECT keyword specifies the field(s) you want displayed in the result data.

After specifying the keyword SELECT, you need to specify the fields you want to display. The general syntax is:

```
SELECT Field_one, Field_two, Field_three ...
```

where *Field_one, Field_two*, and so on are replaced with the names of the table fields.

Notice that commas separate each field in the list from the others. For instance, if you want to specify Company Name and city using fields from a contacts table, you would specify the following:

```
SELECT [Company Name], City
```

Note   The field name Company Name needs brackets around it because it has a space in the name (see sidebar).

Using the Brackets around Field Names

Any field name that contains spaces requires the use of brackets. The brackets, [ ], let the SQL parser know you are referring to a specific field. If the field name does not contain spaces, you do not need to use the brackets.

If you need to view fields from more than one table, specify the name of the tables in which to find the fields. The SELECT statement would, for example, look like this to select fields from both the Contacts and Sales tables:

```
SELECT tblContacts.chrCompany, tblContacts.chrCity,
tblSales.dtmSaleDate, tblSales.idsInvoiceNumber
```

When you build a query in Access, it places the table name before the field name automatically. Actually, the table name is optional. You need only specify the table name if more than one table in the SQL statement has fields with the same name. For instance, a field named Invoice Number may appear in both a Sales table and a SalesLineItems table. If you want to SELECT an invoice number field in your SQL statement, you must specify which of these to use — the one in Sales or the one in SalesLineItems.

The following SQL SELECT Statement illustrates the syntax:

```
SELECT tblContacts.chrCompany, tblContacts.chrCity,
tblSales.dtmSaleDate, tblSales.idsInvoiceNumber,
tblSalesLineItems.chrProductID
```

 Tip   Although table names are not required for non-duplicate fields in an SQL statement, it's a good idea to use them for clarity.

You can use the asterisk wildcard (*) to specify that all fields should be selected. If you're going to select all fields from more than one table, specify the table, a period (.), and then the name of the field — in this case, the asterisk.

Specifying SELECT predicates

When you create an SQL SELECT statement, several predicates are available for the SELECT clause:

✦ ALL

✦ DISTINCT

✦ DISTINCTROW

✦ TOP

The predicates are used to restrict the number of records returned. They can work in conjunction with the WHERE clause (actually, in SQL terminology, the WHERE *condition*) of an SQL statement.

The ALL predicate selects all records that meet the WHERE condition specified in the SQL statement. If you do not specify the keyword ALL, all records are returned by default.

Use the DISTINCT predicate when you want to omit records that contain duplicate data in the fields specified in the SELECT statement. For instance, if you create a query and want to look at both the Company Name and the Products the customer purchased, without considering the number of products of a single Category, the SELECT statement would be as follows:

```
SELECT DISTINCT chrCompany, chrCategory
```

If a customer purchased two minivans — that is, has two minivan records (one 2002 Fordman Mini Van and one 1992 Fordman Conversion Van) in the tblSalesLineItems table — only one record will appear in the result set. The DISTINCT predicate tells Access to show only one record if the values in the selected fields are duplicates (that is, same company name and same product category). Even though two different records are in the tblSalesLineItems table for the customer, only one is shown. DISTINCT eliminates duplicates based on the fields selected to view.

The DISTINCTROW predicate is unique to Access. It works much like DISTINCT, with one big difference: It looks for duplicates on the basis of all fields in the table(s), not just the selected fields. For instance, if a customer has purchased two different product records in the tblSalesLineItems table, use the predicate DISTINCTROW in this SQL statement:

```
SELECT DISTINCTROW chrCompany, chrDescription
```

In this example, both product records are displayed. DISTINCTROW looks for duplicates across all of the fields selected for the query. If any field is different (in this case, the description), both records are displayed in the result set.

The TOP predicate is also unique to Access. It enables you to restrict the number of records returned to the TOP <number> of values. For instance, the following SELECT statement will display the first five contact records:

```
SELECT TOP 5 chrCompany FROM tblContacts
```

You can use the TOP predicate in conjunction with the ORDER BY clause to answer some practical business questions. This example uses the TOP predicate with the ORDER By clause:

```
SELECT TOP 5 chrCompany FROM tblContacts ORDER BY
dtmLastSalesDate DESC
```

This example returns a list of companies with the five highest last sales dates. In other words, the query lists all of the companies and orders them by their last sales date in descending order, and then it only picks the first five companies in the ordered list.

The TOP predicate has an optional keyword, PERCENT, that displays the top number of records on the basis of a percentage rather than a number. To see the top two percent of your contacts, you would use a SELECT statement like this one:

```
SELECT TOP 2 PERCENT chrCompany
```

The FROM clause of an SQL statement

As the name suggests, the FROM clause specifies the tables (or queries) that hold the fields named in the SELECT statement. This clause is required; it tells SQL where to find the records. If you fail to use the FROM portion of the SELECT statement, you will receive an error. Due to the required use of the FROM clause, some people refer to the SELECT statement as the SELECT ... FROM statement.

When you're working with one table, the FROM clause simply specifies the table name:

```
SELECT chrCompany, chrCity
FROM tblContacts
```

When you are working with more than one table, you can supply a table expression to the FROM clause to specify how to retrieve data from the multiple tables. The FROM clause is where you set the relationship between two or more tables for the SELECT statement. The table expression can be one of three types:

✦ INNER JOIN ... ON

✦ RIGHT JOIN ... ON

✦ LEFT JOIN ... ON

Use INNER JOIN ... ON to specify the traditional inner or equijoin of Access. To join two tables, you link them using a field that both tables have in common. For instance, the contacts and sales tables have a common contactID field. To join the sales and contacts tables, the table expression syntax is:

```
SELECT tblSalesLineItems.chrDescription, tblContacts.chrState,
tblContacts.chrCompany
FROM (tblContacts INNER JOIN tblSales ON
tblContacts.idsContactID=tblSales.lngzBuyer)
```

Notice that the FROM clause specifies the main table to use (tblContacts). Then the INNER JOIN portion of the FROM clause specifies the second table to use (tblSales). Finally, the ON portion of the FROM clause specifies which fields will be used to join the table.

The LEFT JOIN and RIGHT JOIN work exactly the same, except that they specify an outer join instead of an inner join, or equijoin. You use outer joins when you want to return records from a parent table even if the dependent table does not contain any records with matching values specified in the ON clause. The following example shows the same query coded as an outer join:

```
SELECT tblSalesLineItems.chrDescription, tblContacts.chrState,
tblContacts.chrCompany
FROM (tblContacts RIGHT JOIN tblSales ON
tblContacts.idsContactID=tblSales.lngzBuyer)
```

In this example, the query will include contacts that had no sales. If the query does not find a match in the sales table, the fields chrState and chrCompany will still display in the result set even if the sales table contains no records that match the idsContactID in the contacts table. The chrDescription field will simply be blank in the result set for any contacts that had no sales.

The WHERE clause of an SQL statement

Use the WHERE clause of the SQL statement only when you want to specify a condition. This clause is optional, unlike SELECT ... and FROM.

The SQL statement in Figure 21-1 specified the following WHERE clause:

```
WHERE (((tblContacts.chrState)="NY" Or (tblContacts.chrState)="CT"))
```

The WHERE condition can be any valid expression. It can be a test on a single field, as in the example above, or a complex expression based on several criteria.

Note   If you use the WHERE condition, it must follow the FROM clause of the SQL statement.

The ORDER BY clause

Use the ORDER BY clause to specify a sort order. It will sort the displayed data by the field(s) you specify after the clause, in ascending or descending order. Using the example in Figure 21-1, the query was sorted by all three of the fields in the SELECT clause:

```
ORDER BY tblSalesLineItems.chrDescription, tblContacts.chrState,
tblContacts.chrCompany;
```

The fields specified in the ORDER BY clause do not have to be the same fields specified in the SELECT clause. You can sort by any of the fields included in the tables you specify in the FROM clause.

Specifying the end of an SQL statement

Because an SQL statement can be as long as 64,000 characters, a way is needed to tell the database language that you've finished creating the statement. End an SQL statement with a semicolon (;).

Note   Access is very forgiving about the ending semicolon. If you forget to place one at the end of an SQL statement, Access will assume that it should be there and run the SQL statement as if it were there. On the other hand, if you place a semicolon inside an SQL statement accidentally, Access will report an error and attempt to tell you where it occurred.

When you become proficient at creating SQL statements, you can begin using them to create very powerful programs that retrieve and manipulate data in your applications.

Note   For a more in-depth introduction to SQL, get the book *SQL Bible,* by Alex Kriegel and Boris M. Trukhnov, published by Wiley Publishing, Inc.

Creating Programs to Update a Table

Updating data in a table by using a form is easy. You simply place controls on the form for the fields of the table that you want to update. For example, Figure 21-2 shows the Sales form. The name of the form is frmSales. The fields that you see on the form update the tblSales, tblSalesLineitems, and tblSalesPayments tables.

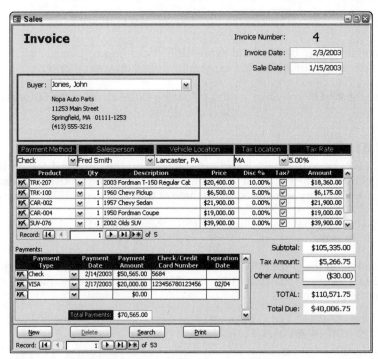

Figure 21-2: Using a form to update data in tables.

Sometimes, however, you want to update a field in a table that you do not want to display on the form. When information is entered in the Sales form, for example, the field for the last sales date (dtmLastSalesDate) in the tblContacts table should be updated to reflect the most recent date on which the Contact purchased a product. When you enter a new sale, the value for the dtmLastSalesDate field is the value of the field for Sale Date (dtmSaleDate)on the Sales form.

Because the contact's last sales date refers to the field labeled Sale Date on the Sales form, you do not want the user to have to enter it in two places. Theoretically, you could place the dtmLastSalesDate field as a calculated field that is updated after the user enters the Sale Date. Displaying this field, however, could be confusing and really does not pertain to the items for the current sale.

The best way to handle updating the dtmLastSalesDate field is to use a Visual Basic procedure. You can use Visual Basic procedures to update individual fields in a record, add new records, or delete records.

Updating fields in a record using ADO

To update the dtmLastSalesDate field by using a Visual Basic procedure, you use the After Update event for the Sales form. The After Update event runs a procedure to update the tblContacts table. The procedure is shown in Figure 21-3.

The Form_AfterUpdate procedure for the Sales form updates the dtmLastSalesDate field in the tblContacts table. This procedure uses special programming language to operate directly on a table in the Access Auto Auctions database.

```
Chap21Start - Form_frmSales (Code)
Form                                          AfterUpdate

    Private Sub Form_AfterUpdate()
On Error GoTo Form_AfterUpdate_Err
        Dim rsContacts As New ADODB.Recordset
        Dim SQLStmt As String

        If Not IsNull(Me!cboBuyerID) Then
            If Not IsNull(Me!txtSaleDate) Then
                SQLStmt = "SELECT * FROM tblContacts WHERE idsContactID = " & Me!cboBuyerID
                rsContacts.Open SQLStmt, CurrentProject.Connection, adOpenDynamic, adLockOptimistic
                If Not rsContacts.EOF Then
                    rsContacts!dtmLastSalesDate = Me!txtSaleDate
                    rsContacts.Update
                End If
                rsContacts.Close
                Set rsContacts = Nothing
            End If
        End If

        Exit Sub

    Form_AfterUpdate_Err:
        MsgBox "Error is " & Err.Description & " updating Sales form.", vbCritical, "System Error"

    End Sub
```

Figure 21-3: Using ADO to update a table.

The programming language used to access and manipulate the data in a database is called ActiveX Data Objects, or ADO. When you update data by using a form, Access itself uses an entire system of programs, written in ADO, to access and update the database.

ADO is a versatile means of accessing data from various locations. The Access Auto Auctions examples you have seen so far show you how you can use Access to update data in a local Access database. That is, all of the tables, queries, forms, and reports are stored in one Access database located either in a folder on your desktop or on a server. But Access, as a client-server development tool, can interact with all kinds of databases. You can develop forms and reports in one Access database that get their data from an entirely separate Access database that may be on your local desktop or on a remote server. You can even link to non-Access databases like Oracle and SQL Server just as easily as linking to an Access database.

As a data access interface, ADO allows you to write programs to manipulate data in local or remote databases. Using ADO, you can perform database functions including querying, updating, data-type conversion, indexing, locking, validation, and transaction management.

Earlier versions of Access included the Data Access Objects (or DAO) data access interface. Improvements in data access technology have taken Access to new levels as a client-server development tool. ADO, a refinement of DAO, represents these improvements and provides a simpler, more powerful array of data access tools.

Caution   Visual Basic currently supports DAO. However, Microsoft does not plan to provide any future DAO enhancements. All new features will be incorporated only into ADO. You should use ADO for any new development projects.

Writing An ADO Procedure

To use ADO functions and methods, you first declare ADO variables using the Dim statement. The Dim statements in this example declare ADO variables for the name of the recordset that the procedure wants to access (rsContacts), and a string variable (SQLStmt) to hold the SQL statement for retrieving the tblContacts record. A recordset is simply a set of records from a database table or the set of records that result from running a query.

Tip   DAO and ADO share some data types. Because both ADO and DAO have a Recordset type, you must precede the variable name with the appropriate class. When you are referring to a DAO recordset, you use the DAO.Recordset data type. ADO recordsets are referred to as type ADODB.Recordset.

The ADO Recordset object provides the Open method to retrieve data from a table or query. The Open method has four parameters: Source, ActiveConnection, CursorType, and LockType. The Source parameter is the name of the data source to open. The Source parameter in this example is the variable SQLStmt, which contains an SQL statement to retrieve the tblContacts record for the contact who made a purchase in the Sales form. The ActiveConnection parameter refers to a pre-defined connection to the database. A connection is a communication line into the database. You use CurrentProject.Connection to refer to the currently active Microsoft Access database connection—Access Auto Auctions in this example. The Open method runs the query specified in the SQLStmt variable and assigns the record or records resulting from running the query to the ADO recordset variable.

You can make a recordset updatable by using the CursorType and LockType parameters. The CursorType and LockType properties determine how ADO can access and modify the recordset.

Table 21-2 describes the recordset properties you can set.

Table 21-2 Recordset Properties		
ADO Cursor Type	**ADO Lock Type**	**Description**
adOpenForwardOnly	adLockReadOnly	You can only scroll forward through records. This improves performance in situations where you do not need to update, as in finding records and printing reports.
adOpenDynamic	adLockOptimistic	Additions, changes, and deletions by other users are visible, and all types of movement through the Recordset are allowed.
adOpenStatic	adLockReadOnly	A static copy of a set of records that you can use to find data or generate reports. Additions, changes, or deletions by other users are not visible.

If you don't specify a CursorType or LockType, ADO automatically creates the Recordset as an adOpenForwardOnly/adLockReadOnly type Recordset. This type of Recordset is not updatable. So if you will need to make changes to the data in the Recordset, you need an understanding of the various CursorType/LockType combinations and how they affect the capabilities of a Recordset.

When you use ActiveX Data Objects, you interact with data almost entirely by using Recordset objects. Recordset objects are composed of rows and columns, just like database tables. When the Recordset has been opened, you can begin working with the values in its rows and columns.

If the Recordset is opened as an updatable Recordset — that is, by using the adOpenDynamic cursortype and adLockOptimistic locktype — the Recordset opens in Edit mode automatically.

Before you change data in any of the Recordset's fields, however, you need to make sure that you are in the record you want to edit. When a Recordset opens and the Recordset contains a record or records, the current record is the first record. If the Recordset contains no records, the property EOF is true. Because the SQL statement in the example in this topic is based on the table's unique key, you know that the first record in the Recordset is the only record.

Caution If you attempt to manipulate data in a Recordset that contains no records, a run-time error occurs.

To update a field in the current record of the Recordset, you simply assign a new value to the name of the field. In Form_AfterUpdate procedure in Figure 21-3, you assign the value of the Sale Date field (txtSaleDate) on the frmSales form to the Last Sale Date field (dtmLastSalesDate) in the Recordset.

After you make the desired changes in the record, use ADO's Update method to save your changes. The Update method copies the data from the buffer to the Recordset, overwriting the original record.

In ADO, changes are automatically saved when you move to another record or close the recordset. In addition, the edited record is also saved if you close a recordset or end the procedure that declares the recordset or the parent Database. However, you should use the Update method for better code readability and maintainability.

To cancel pending changes to a recordset in either ADO, use the CancelUpdate method. In ADO, you must issue the CancelUpdate method before moving to another record.

The Close statement at the end of the Form_AfterUpdate procedure closes the Recordset. Closing recordsets when you finish using them is good practice.

Updating a calculated field for a record

In the Sales form example, the form's Tax Amount field displays the tax that must be collected at the time of the sale. The Tax Amount field is not a simple calculation. The Tax Amount is determined by the following items:

✦ The sum of the item amounts purchased that are taxable

✦ The customer's tax rate that is in effect on the sale date

✦ The Other Amount field and whether or not the Other Amount field is a taxable item

When the user changes information for the current sale, any one or all three of these factors can change the Tax Amount. The Tax Amount field must be recalculated whenever any of the following events occur in the form:

✦ Adding or updating a line item

✦ Deleting a line item

✦ Changing the buyer to another customer

✦ Changing the Tax Location

✦ Changing the Other Amount

To recalculate the tax amount when any of these events occur, you must create Visual Basic procedures.

Recalculating a field when updating or adding a record

Figure 21-4 shows the code for adding or updating a line item on the Sales form.

```
Chap21Start - Form_fsubSalesLineItems (Code)

Form                                           AfterUpdate

Private Sub Form_AfterUpdate()
    Dim dblTaxRate As Double, curTaxAmount As Currency

    dblTaxRate = CDbl(Nz(Forms!frmSales!txtTaxRate, 0))
    curTaxAmount = CalcTax(dblTaxRate, Me.lngzInvoiceNumber)
    If Forms!frmSales!chkOtherTaxable = True Then
        curTaxAmount = curTaxAmount + (Nz(Forms!frmSales!txtOtherAmount, 0) * dblTaxRate)
    End If
    Forms!frmSales!txtTaxAmount = curTaxAmount
End Sub
```

Figure 21-4: Recalculating a field after a form is updated.

A single event can handle recalculating the Tax Amount when new line items are added or when a line item is changed — when an item's price is changed, for example. For both of these events, you can use the subform's After Update event. The After Update event occurs when a new record is entered or when any value is changed for an existing record.

The Form_AfterUpdate procedure for the fsubSalesLineItems subform executes when a line item is added to the Sales form's subform, or when any information is changed in a line item. The Form_AfterUpdate procedure recalculates the Tax Amount field on the Sales form. The variable dblTaxRate is used to temporarily hold the customer's tax rate (the value of the control txtTaxRate on the frmSales form). The variable curTaxAmount is used to temporarily store the value returned by the CalcTax() function. The CalcTax() function is the code that actually calculates the tax amount. When the After_Update procedure calls the CalcTax() function, it passes two parameters: the value of dblTaxRate and the value of the current line item's invoice number (Me.lngzInvoiceNumber). Figure 21-5 shows the CalcTax() function.

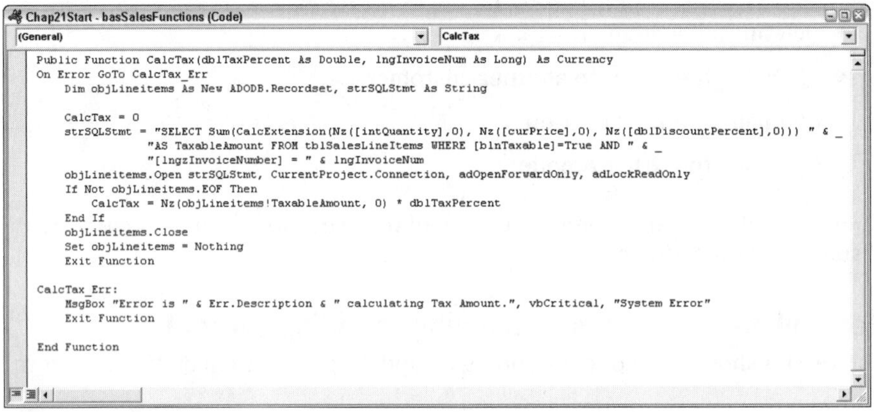

```
Chap21Start - basSalesFunctions (Code)
(General)                                              CalcTax

    Public Function CalcTax(dblTaxPercent As Double, lngInvoiceNum As Long) As Currency
    On Error GoTo CalcTax_Err
        Dim objLineitems As New ADODB.Recordset, strSQLStmt As String

        CalcTax = 0
        strSQLStmt = "SELECT Sum(CalcExtension(Nz([intQuantity],0), Nz([curPrice],0), Nz([dblDiscountPercent],0))) " & _
                     "AS TaxableAmount FROM tblSalesLineItems WHERE [blnTaxable]=True AND " & _
                     "[lngInvoiceNumber] = " & lngInvoiceNum
        objLineitems.Open strSQLStmt, CurrentProject.Connection, adOpenForwardOnly, adLockReadOnly
        If Not objLineitems.EOF Then
            CalcTax = Nz(objLineitems!TaxableAmount, 0) * dblTaxPercent
        End If
        objLineitems.Close
        Set objLineitems = Nothing
        Exit Function

    CalcTax_Err:
        MsgBox "Error is " & Err.Description & " calculating Tax Amount.", vbCritical, "System Error"
        Exit Function

    End Function
```

Figure 21-5: Using ADO to recalculate a total field.

The CalcTax function uses ADO to create a recordset that sums up the quantities and prices for the taxable items in the tblSalesLineItems table for the current sale. The function receives two parameters: the buyer's tax rate (dblTaxPercent) and the invoice number for the current sale (lngInvoiceNum). The function's return value is initially set to 0 at the top of the function. The ADO code checks to see if the recordset returned a record. If the recordset is at the end of the field (EOF), the recordset did not find any line items for the current sale — and CalcTax remains set to 0. If the recordset did return a record, the return value for CalcTax is set to the recordset's TaxableAmount field times the tax rate (dblTaxPercent).

When the Form_AfterUpdate procedure receives the result of the CalcTax() function, it continues to the next statement in the procedure. The next statement in the procedure checks to see if the Sales form's Other Taxable field (chkOtherTaxable) is True. If Other Taxable is true, the procedure must also calculate tax on the Other Amount field. The calculation for the tax on Other Amount simply multiplies the value of the Other Amount field (txtOtherAmount) times the tax rate (dblTaxRate). Then it must add this result to the curTaxAmount value returned by the CalcTax() function.

At the end of the procedure, the form's Tax Amount field is set to the value of the curTaxAmount variable.

When the Buyer, Tax Location, or Tax Rate fields are changed in the Sales form, you use the AfterUpdate event for the individual control to recalculate the Tax Amount. Figure 21-6 shows the code for the txtTaxRate_AfterUpdate event.

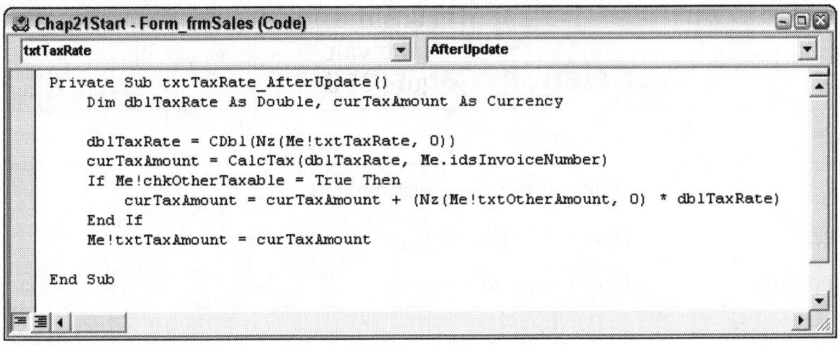

Figure 21-6: Recalculating a field after a control is updated.

The code for the txtTaxRate_AfterUpdate event is the same code used for the line items subform's AfterUpdate event. In fact, you can use the same code for the Buyer and Tax Location controls as well.

Checking the status of a record deletion

To recalculate the Tax Amount field when deleting a line item, you use the form's AfterDelConfirm event. The form's AfterDelConfirm event, shown in Figure 21-7, is similar to the code for the subform's AfterUpdate event.

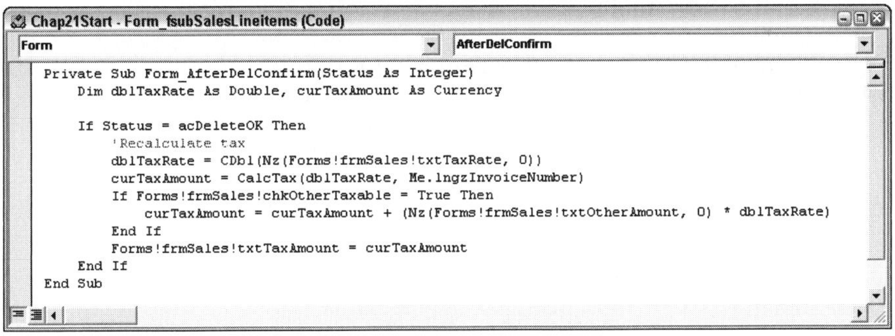

Figure 21-7: Recalculating a field after a record is deleted.

The AfterDelConfirm event occurs after a record is actually deleted or after a deletion is canceled. If the BeforeDelConfirm event isn't canceled, the AfterDelConfirm event occurs after the Delete Confirm dialog box is displayed. The AfterDelConfirm event occurs even if the BeforeDelConfirm event is canceled. The AfterDelConfirm event procedure returns status information about the deletion. Table 21-2 describes the deletion status values.

Table 21-2
Deletion Status Values

Status value	Description
acDeleteOK	Deletion occurred normally
acDeleteCancel	Deletion canceled programmatically
acDeleteUserCancel	User canceled deletion

The AfterDelConfirm procedure for the Sales form example checks to see if the deletion actually occurred (acDeleteOK). If the deletion occurred, the procedure runs the code to recalculate the Tax Amount.

Adding a new record

You can use ADO to add a record to a table just as easily as you can to update a record. To add a new record to a table, you use the AddNew method. The following shows the ADO procedure for adding a new customer to the Customer table:

```
Private Sub New_Contact_Click()
On Error GoTo New_Contact_Click_Err
Dim rst As New ADODB.Recordset

rst.Open "tblContacts", CurrentProject.Connection,
adOpenDynamic, adLockOptimistic
    With rst
        'Add new record to end of Recordset object
        .AddNew
        ![chrLastName] = "Townshend"    'Add data
        ![chrFirstName] = "Charles"
        .Update                         'Save changes
    End With
rst.Close
Set rst = Nothing
New_Contact_Click_Exit:
    Exit Sub
New_Contact_Click_Err:
    MsgBox Err.Description
    Resume New_Contact_Click_Err
End Sub
```

As you see in this example, using the AddNew method is very similar to using ADO to edit Recordset data. The AddNew method creates a buffer for a new record. After entering the AddNew command, you simply assign values to the fields. When you enter the Update command, the new record buffer is added to the end of the Recordset.

Deleting a record

To remove a record from a table, you use the ADO method Delete. The following code shows the ADO procedure for deleting a record from the tblContacts table.

Note Notice that you need to code only one statement to delete a record. You do not follow the Delete method with Update. As soon as the Delete method executes, the record is removed from the Recordset permanently.

```
Private Sub Delete_Contact_Click()
On Error GoTo Delete_Contact_Click_Err
Dim rst As New ADODB.Recordset, SQLStmt as string

SQLStmt = "SELECT * FROM tblContacts WHERE [idsContactID] = " &
_
        Me![txtContactID]
Rst.Open SQLStmt, CurrentProject.Connection, adOpenDynamic, & _
adLockOptimistic

With rst
If not .EOF Then
    'Delete the record
    .Delete
End If
End With
rst.Close
Set rst = Nothing
Delete_Contact_Click_Exit:
    Exit Sub
Delete_Contact_Click_Err:
    MsgBox Err.Description
    Resume Delete_Contact_Click_Exit
End Sub
```

Deleting related records in multiple tables

When you write ADO code to delete records, you need to be aware of the application's relationships. The table containing the record you are deleting may be participating in a one-to-many relationship with another table.

Take a look at the Relationships Diagram, shown in Figure 21-8, for the tables used in the Sales form example. The tblSales table has two dependent tables associated with it: tblSalesLineItems and tblSalesPayments.

The Edit Relationships dialog box shows how the relationship is set up between the tables tblSales and tblSalesLineItems. The relationship type is defined as a One-To-Many and Referential Integrity is Enforced. A One-To-Many relationship type indicates that the parent table (the One side), tblSales, has a dependent table (the Many side), tblSalesLineItems. While tblSales can contain only unique instances of the values in idsInvoiceNumber, tblSalesLineItems may contain several records with the same value as idsInvoiceNumber in tblSales. When you enforce referential integrity on a One-To-Many relationship, you are telling Access that a record in tblSales cannot be deleted if records with the same invoice number are in the table tblSalesLineItems. If Access encounters a delete request that violates referential integrity, Access will display an error message and the delete will be cancelled.

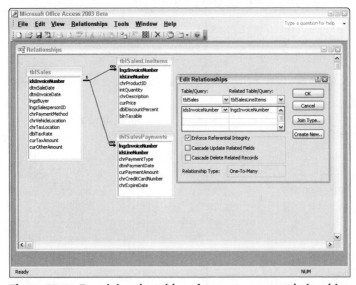

Figure 21-8: Examining the tables of a one-to-many relationship.

When you write ADO code to delete a record, you need to first check to see if there are any One-To-Many relationships between the table containing the record to delete and any other tables in the database. If there are dependent tables, the records in the dependent tables need to be deleted before Access will allow you to delete the record in the parent table.

Fortunately, you can write a single procedure using ADO code to delete records in both the dependent table or tables and the parent table. Figure 21-9 shows the code for the cmdDelete command button in the frmSales form.

The cmdDelete_Click procedure deletes the records in the tables tblSalesPayments, tblSalesLineItems, and tblSales that have an Invoice Number that matches the current Invoice Number displayed on the Sales form.

The first statement in the cmdDelete_Click procedure uses the NewRecord property to check to see if the current record displayed in the Sales form is a new record. If the record is a new record, the next statement, Me.Undo, simply undoes any changes that were made to the record. If the current record is not a new record, the procedure displays a message box to confirm that the user really wants to delete the record. If the user selects the Yes button, the procedure issues the commands to delete the records from the tables. The variable SQLStmt is used to hold the SQL statement for locating and deleting all of the records in the tblSalesPayments table that have an lngzInvoiceNumber that matches the idsInvoiceNumber on the Sales form. The SQLStmt variable is passed as a parameter to the Execute method of the current project's (CurrentProject) Connection. You can pass either the name of a query or an SQL statement as a parameter to the Execute method. The Execute method simply runs the specified query or SQL statement.

```
🗐 Chap21Start - Form_frmSales (Code)
cmdDelete                                        ▼   Click                                         ▼
    Private Sub cmdDelete_Click()
    On Error GoTo cmdDelete_Click_Err
        Dim intAnswer As Integer, SQLStmt As String

        If Me.NewRecord Then
            Me.Undo
        Else
            intAnswer = MsgBox("Are you sure you want to delete this Invoice?", vbQuestion + vbYesNo, "Delete Invoice")
            If intAnswer = vbYes Then
                'Delete all payments for this invoice
                SQLStmt = "DELETE * FROM tblSalesPayments WHERE lngzInvoiceNumber = " & Me.idsInvoiceNumber
                CurrentProject.Connection.Execute SQLStmt
                'Delete all line items for this invoice
                SQLStmt = "DELETE * FROM tblSalesLineItems WHERE lngzInvoiceNumber = " & Me.idsInvoiceNumber
                CurrentProject.Connection.Execute SQLStmt
                'Now delete the invoice record
                RunCommand acCmdSelectRecord
                RunCommand acCmdDeleteRecord
            End If
        End If
        Exit Sub
    cmdDelete_Click_Err:
        MsgBox "Error is " & Err.Description
        Exit Sub
```

Figure 21-9: Using ADO code to delete multiple records.

Note   If the query or SQL statement contains a WHERE clause and the Execute method does not find any records that meet the WHERE condition, no error occurs. If the query or SQL statement contains invalid syntax or an invalid field or table name, however, the Execute method will fail and an error situation will occur.

When the Execute command completes for deleting the tblSalesPayments records, the procedure changes the value of SQLstmt to the SQL statement required to delete the records in the tblSalesLineItems table. Then the new SQLstmt parameter is passed to run the Execute method for the tblSalesLineItems table.

After the tblSalesLineItems records are deleted, the tblSales record can then be deleted. The following statements in the cmdDelete_Click procedure, are used to select the current record and then delete the current record:

```
RunCommand acCmdSelectRecord
RunCommand acCmdDeleteRecord
```

In this example, the two RunCommand statements will select and delete the current record in the frmSales form.

✦   ✦   ✦

Automating, Searches, Filters, and Query Parameters

In the previous few chapters, you learned the basics of programming, reviewed some of the built-in functions, and experienced the various logical constructs. You've learned about ADO and how to access data in tables and queries through SQL recordsets. You have also learned a lot about forms and queries in previous chapters. In this chapter, you will use all of this knowledge and learn how to display selected data in forms or reports using a combination of techniques involving forms, visual basic code, and queries.

On the CD-ROM

In the Chap22Start.mdb database, you will find a number of forms to use as a starting point and other completed forms to compare to the forms you change in this example. All of the examples use a modified version of the frmProducts form and the tblProducts table.

Adding an Unbound Combo Box to Select One or More Records

When viewing a form, you often have to page through hundreds or thousands of records to find the record or set of records you want to work with. You can teach your user to press the Find (binoculars) button on the toolbox, explain how to first place their cursor in the field being searched, how to use wildcards, what to do to see other records, and so on, but this defeats the purpose of a programmed application. If you build an application, you want to make it easier for your users to become productive with your system, not teach them Microsoft Access.

Figure 22-1 shows the frmProducts form with an additional control at the top. This is a combo box that is not bound to any control source in the form. The unbound combo box is used to look up a record in the tblProducts table and then display that record in the form through some code. You will see several ways to do this in the chapter.

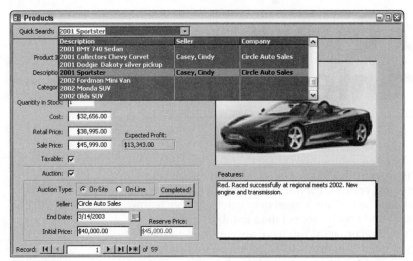

Figure 22-1: The frmProductsExample1Start form with an unbound combo box displaying the record description, seller, and company.

The design for the combo box is shown in Figure 22-2. Notice that the Control Source property is empty. This combo box is not bound to any field in a table. It is used only by the form. There are four columns that can be viewed in the query for the Row Source, as shown in Figure 22-3. The first is the Description from the tblProducts table. The second and third columns are taken from the tblContacts table. The second column is the seller from an auction's Last Name and First Name together. The third column is the seller's company. The last column is not displayed and is the chrProductID field in the tblProducts table.

This is also the Bound Column for the combo box and is what the value of the combo box will equal when a description record is selected in the combo box. Notice that the fourth column width is 0", which hides the displayed value when the combo box is pulled down.

The Column Heads property is set to Yes because whenever there are three or more displayed columns, you should display column heads as well.

This combo box will be used for all the examples in this chapter. Now you will learn how to find records in a variety of ways using the combo box and the code behind it.

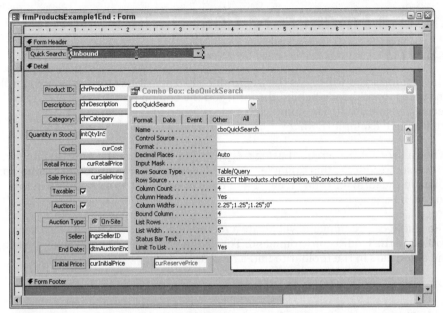

Figure 22-2: The frmProducts form in design view, showing the Property window for the unbound combo box control.

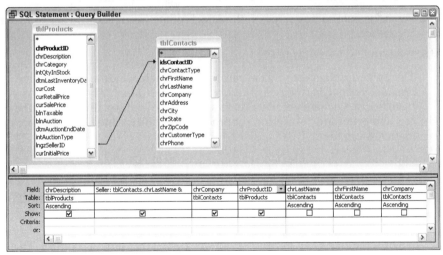

Figure 22-3: The query behind the Row Source property of the cboQuickSearch combo box.

Using the FindRecord Command to Locate a Record

The first form you will use is the frmProductsExample1Start form where you will enhance it to add code behind the form and the combo box that selects a specific record by going to it. The completed code is found in the form frmProductsExample1End.

When a user selects a record using a combo box, it triggers the AfterUpdate event to run some code. In this example, you are going to take the unbound combo box found in the form and add an event and code to find the record selected in the combo box.

The FindRecord command will locate a record in any field by specifying a value passed to the FindRecord command. This is the programmed equivalent of using the binoculars in the toolbar to find a record.

To create an event procedure behind the combo box, follow the steps below:

1. Display the frmProductsExample1Start form in design view.

2. Click on the cboQuickSearch combo box and display the Property window.

3. Select the Event tab and click on the After Update event.

4. Press the combo box arrow in the After Update event line and select Event Procedure.

5. Press the Builder button (...) that appears in the right side of the line.

   The procedure appears in a separate Visual Basic window. The first line, *Private Sub cboQuickSearch_AfterUpdate()*, is automatically created. As you have learned, whenever you create an event procedure, the name of the control and event are part of the subprocedure. The last line End Sub is also automatically created.

6. Enter the four lines of code exactly as shown in Figure 22-4.

The first line is:

```
Me.txtProductID.SetFocus
```

This line programmatically moves the cursor to the txtProductID control. This is the first step in using the FindRecord command. Just as you need to manually move the cursor to a control in order to use the Find icon in the toolbar, you programmatically must place the cursor in the control.

The next block of code is:

```
If Not IsNull(Me.cboQuickSearch) Then
    DoCmd.FindRecord Me.cboQuickSearch
End If
```

This block of code first checks to make sure that the value is filled in (is not null) before using the FindRecord command. If a value is found in the combo box, the FindRecord command is run using the selected value of the chrProductID (the bound column) from the combo box row source.

If the value is found in the current control on the form, the record is displayed as the current record in the form. If the value is not found, the current record continues to be displayed.

The first value found by the FindRecord command is determined by a series of parameters, including whether the case is matched and whether the search is forward, backward, or the first record found. When you enter DoCmd.FindRecord and press the spacebar, you will see all of the available options. Regardless, the FindRecord command only finds one record at a time while allowing all other records to be viewed.

Tip   Me. is always faster than using Forms!someformname in front of the control name. When you use Me, the program can instantly find the current form. When you use the syntax Forms!someformname, the program must search for the form alphabetically from the list of all forms in the database file. Forms starting with the letter A are found first and those with Z last.

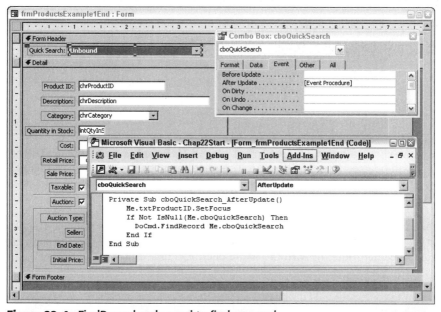

Figure 22-4: FindRecord code used to find a record.

Using the Bookmark to Locate a Record

The FindRecord command is a good way to search when the control you want to use to find a record is displayed on the form. It is also a good way if the value being searched for is a single value. However, many times the value being used in the search is a field or more than one field in the control source of the form, but not necessarily a control on the form. A bookmark is another way of finding a record.

You can use the form named frmProductsExample2Start to follow this example. The completed code is found in the form frmProductsExample2End.

Figure 22-5 shows code to use a bookmark that is added behind the AfterUpdate event of the combo box.

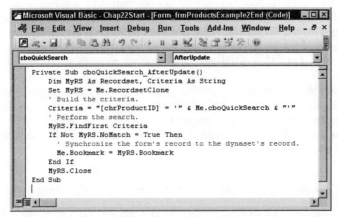

```
Private Sub cboQuickSearch_AfterUpdate()
    Dim MyRS As Recordset, Criteria As String
    Set MyRS = Me.RecordsetClone
    ' Build the criteria.
    Criteria = "[chrProductID] = '" & Me.cboQuickSearch & "'"
    ' Perform the search.
    MyRS.FindFirst Criteria
    If Not MyRS.NoMatch = True Then
        ' Synchronize the form's record to the dynaset's record.
        Me.Bookmark = MyRS.Bookmark
    End If
    MyRS.Close
End Sub
```

Figure 22-5: Bookmark code used to find a record.

The first two lines are:

```
Dim MyRs As Recordset, Criteria As String
Set MsRs = Me.RecordsetClone
```

These two lines dimension a recordset named MyRs and a string named Criteria. These will be used later in the code. The next line uses the recordset and sets it to a copy of the currently displayed data (known as the RecordsetClone). This is a key word that you can use in code.

The next line builds a SQL string that can be as complicated as you want. It also shows how to build a SQL statement in code. Thefollowing line concatenates the field name chrProductID with the value of cboQuickSearch:

```
Criteria = "[chrProductID] = '" & Me.cboQuickSearch & "'"
```

Notice that three parts of the criteria string are concatenated together.

The first part is a double quote, then the field name followed by an equal sign, and then a single quote followed by a double quote. This builds the following string:

```
[chrProductID] = '
```

The single quote at the end is the first delimiter for a string that will be built next. The value of Me. cboQuickSearch is then concatenated to the string. Assuming the value of cboQuickSearch is CAR-001, the string would now be:

```
[chrProductID] = 'CAR-001
```

Notice that the value is not properly delimited. It still needs another single quote at the end. The last part of the criteria concatenated is "'", which adds the needed single quote.

> **Tip**
>
> Creating criteria in code is sometimes complicated. Remember that the objective is to build a string that could be copied into a query SQL window and run as is. Often, the best way to create a criteria string is to create a query design, switch to SQL view, and then copy the SQL to a code window. Then, break up the code's WHERE clause into field names and control values, inserting concatenation symbols and delimiters. In this example, there is no WHERE clause but the idea is the same.

After the criteria string is completed, you can use the recordset to search for the record. The following line uses the FindFirst method of the recordset, passing the criteria string like a WHERE clause of a SQL statement:

```
MyRs.FindFirst Criteria
```

The FindFirst method attempts to find a record matching the criteria in the Criteria string.

> **Note**
>
> You don't have to create a Criteria variable and then set the criteria string to it. You can simply place the criteria after the MyRs,FindFirst method, like this:
>
> ```
> MyRs.FindFirst  "chrProductID = '" & Me.cboQuickSearch &
>   "'"
> ```
>
> However, when you have complex criteria, it may be easier to create the criteria separately from the command that will use the criteria string so you can debug the string separately.

The next lines are used to determine if the record pointer in the form should be moved.

```
If Not MyRs.NoMatch = True Then
  Me.Bookmark = MyRS.Bookmark
End If
```

When a bookmark is set, a value is also set to determine if the bookmark is valid (the record was found). The .NoMatch method is used to determine if the record was found. Unfortunately, this command requires the computer equivalent of a double negative. Essentially, it says if there is not a nomatch, then the bookmark is valid. Why the syntax is not If MyRs.Match is a mystery to everyone, but it simply isn't.

If the match is found, the forms bookmark (Me.Bookmark) is set to the recordset bookmark (MyRs.Bookmark) and the form repositions itself to the first matching record. This does not filter the records but merely finds the first record that matches the criteria. All of the other records are still visible in the form.

The last line of code simply closes the recordset.

Note Criteria can be as complex as you need them to be, even involving multiple fields of different data types. Remember that strings need to be delimited by single quotes, dates need to be delimited by pound signs, and numerics don't require any delimiters.

The bookmark method is preferable to the FindRecord method because it allows for more complex criteria and doesn't require the control being searched to be visible.

Filtering a Form Using Code

The form frmProductsExample3Start form can be used to add code behind the form and the combo box that selects a specific record by going to it. The completed code is found in the form frmProductsExample3End.

Although using the FindRecord method or a bookmark to locate a record allows you to quickly go to a record meeting the criteria you want, it still shows all the other records in a table or query recordset and doesn't necessarily keep all the records together. Filtering a form lets you view only the record or records you want, hiding all nonmatching records.

Filters are good when you have large recordsets and want to view only data matching your needs.

Figure 22-6 shows the two lines of code necessary to create and apply a filter to a recordset. Each form contains a filter behind the form. Usually it is blank and means the form is unfiltered (all of the records are displayed).

The first line of code sets the criteria to the Me.Filter property:

```
Me.Filter = "chrProductID = '" & Me.cboQuickSearch & "'"
```

The second line of code turns on the filter. You can put all the criteria that you want in a filter property, but unless you turn it on with the Me.FilterOn = True statement, the filter will not be active. By using a filter, you hide all the records that do not meet the criteria. You show only the records that meet the criteria. With a filter, you can page from record to record and only see the records matching the filter.

```
Me.FilterOn = True
```

The first line sets the filter using the same SQL string built in the previous example. The difference is that you don't have to create a criteria string. You just set the Me.Filter property to the criteria string itself.

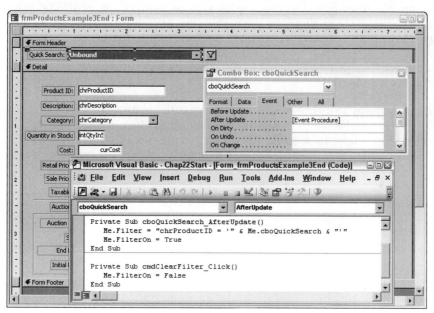

Figure 22-6: Code for filtering and clearing a filter behind a form.

Caution   If you create a form filter and then save the form design with the filter set, the filter is saved with the form. The next time the form is opened, the filter is active. Always clear the filter manually from the form's Filter property before saving the form.

Whenever you turn on a filter, you must create a way to turn it off. If you look at the top of Figure 22-6, you can see a small button next to the combo box. This button could be used to turn off the filter. The second procedure shown in Figure 22-6 in the Visual Basic code window is attached to the OnClick event of the button. The following line of code turns off the filter and displays all of the records in the form:

```
Me.FilterOn = False
```

Using a Query to Filter a Form Interactively

There may be times when you want to have one form control another. There may be times when you want a recordset to display selected data based on instant user decisions. For example, each time a report is run, a dialog box is displayed and the user can enter a set of dates or a specific product or customer. One way to do this is to use a parameter query.

Creating a parameter query

A parameter query is any query that contains one or more criteria that are based on a variable. Normally, you enter a value such as "SMITH", 26, or 6/15/04 in a criteria entry area. You can also enter a variable such as [Enter the Last Name] or a reference to a control on a form such as Forms!frmProducts![cboQuickFind].

You can see this query completed in your database with the name qryProductParameterQuery.

The simplest way to create a parameter query is to create a standard select query, add a criteria, and run it to make sure it works. Then change the criteria to Like [some string], where *some string* is the question you want to ask the user. Figure 22-7 shows a parameter query that asks the user whenever the query is run to enter the Product ID.

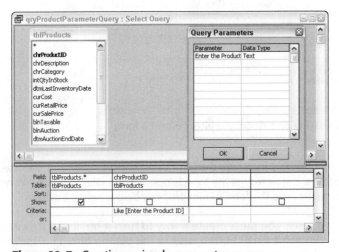

Figure 22-7: Creating a simple parameter query.

Any time the query is run, even if it is used as the record source for a form or report or the row source for a list or combo box, the parameter will be displayed — and depending on what is entered, the query criteria filters the query results.

You may remember learning that the Like operator allows for wildcard searches. For example, if you want to filter the query records for any Product ID that starts with the letters CAR, you would enter CAR* when the parameter dialog box displays the question *Enter the Product ID*. Without the parameter, you would have to enter Like "CAR*" in the criteria area of the query.

Also notice in Figure 22-7 that there is a dialog box with Query Parameters in the title bar. This is necessary only when a parameter query requires special formatting for the parameters. These would primarily include date/time entries or specially formatted numbers. One entry has been placed in the dialog box that is actually not necessary to show how it works. You enter the name of the parameter text and then choose the data type. The Text data type, in reality, would never do anything because anything can be treated as text.

Tip   The wildcards * (anything after this position) and ? (one character in this position) can be used with a Like operator in any query or SQL string.

Figure 22-8 shows this query running and the parameter dialog box being displayed. The text CAR* has been entered into the dialog box, meaning that any product whose Product ID begins with the characters CAR will be displayed.

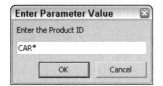

Figure 22-8: Running the parameter query.

Tip   If you want to add more complex parameters, such as a range of dates, you could enter **Between [Enter the Start Date] and [Enter the End Date]** as a criteria in a date field. This would display two separate parameter dialog boxes and then filter the date value appropriately.

Creating an interactive dialog box

The only problem with parameter queries is that they are great for simple things but not for complex situations. A better technique is to create a simple form and place controls in the form that can then be used to be passed to a query that uses the values from the dialog box to filter the query data.

Figure 22-9 shows the form frmFilterProductbyDescription, showing a combo box to be used to select a record. A combo box gives the user the choice of selecting a single record from a known set of records or entering a wildcard election (if the Limit to List property is False).

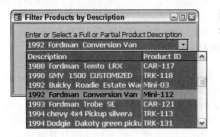

Figure 22-9: Creating a dialog box for selecting records.

The combo box shown in Figure 22-9 displays two columns — Description and Product ID. The dialog box contains only the combo box and some instructional text labels. The Description is the bound column and makes the chrDescription field available to a query that references the form control, as shown in Figure 22-10.

Figure 22-10 displays the query in your database named qryProductFormReferenceQuery. It selects all the fields from the tblProducts table and then creates a criteria line using the chrDescription field that references the form control. Notice the expression in the query criteria area:

```
Like [Forms]![frmFilterProductsbyDescription]![cboDescription]
```

This expression references the control named cboDescription (the combo box) in the form named frmFilterProductsbyDescription. The combo box returns the value of the selected Description or a wildcard selection like 1992*, which would show all of the vehicles starting with 1992.

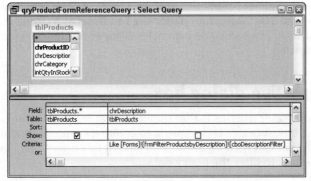

Figure 22-10: Creating a query that references a form control.

Using the With Command

The With command is used to save time by not referencing the controls on the form explicitly (which means directly): for example, Forms!frmProductsExample4Start.SetFocus. This requires Access to search alphabetically through the list of forms in the database container. If there were 500 forms (and some large systems have this many or more) and the form name started with z, this would take a measurable amount of time. Because there is more than one reference to the form, this would have to take place multiple times. The With command finds the exact location of the find and sets up an internal pointer to the form so that all subsequent uses of the form to reference a form control or property or to use a form method (like .Requery or .SetFocus) are much faster.

When you use the With command and reference the form name, you simply use a . or a ! and reference the control, property, or method just like the Forms!formname was first. You can see this in Figure 22-11.

For each With, you must have an End With.

Linking the dialog box to another form

The dialog box shown in Figure 22-10 does more than just create a value that can be referenced from a query. It actually contains code to open the form named frmProductsExample4Start, which contains the query named qryProductFormReferenceQuery as its record source.

Figure 22-11 shows the design of this dialog box and the Event Procedures behind the Cancel and OK buttons found on this form. When the OK button is pressed, the code in Figure 22-11 is run.

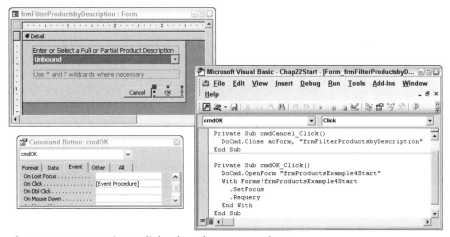

Figure 22-11: Creating a dialog box that opens a form.

The code opens the form, sets focus to it, and then requeries the form to make sure the latest selection is used within that form. The .SetFocus command is necessary to move focus to the form that is opened. The .Requery command requeries the form when it is opened. This actually isn't necessary because a form automatically requeries the form's Record Source the first time it is opened. However, if the form is already opened—for example, if you use the dialog box a second time to search for another record—the requery command must run to change the data.

✦   ✦   ✦

Calling Subprocedures and Functions

In this chapter, you will learn how to create reusable procedures and functions to make coding easier and allow multiple events or objects to use the same code. You will learn how to pass parameters to a function and how a function can return values as well. You have already seen how to create many different types of procedures, but you may not understand when to create each one. This chapter will teach you why and when to create each type of procedure.

On the CD-ROM

In the Chap23Start.mdb database, you will find the frmSales form and its accompanying subforms. You will also find all of the tables from the Access Auto Auctions application and several modules. You will use the frmSales form as a starting point as you learn how to create functions and procedures. The file Chap23End.mdb contains all of the code for the form that you will see in this chapter and some additional completed code as well.

Understanding the Difference Between a Subprocedure and a Function

Procedures and functions both contain lines of code that you can run. When you run a procedure or function, you call it. *Calling*, *running*, or *invoking* are all terms meaning to *execute* (or run) the statements (or lines of code) within the procedure or function. All of these terms can be used interchangeably (and they will be, by different developers). Although, technically, you call a program with the Call command, invoke a function by using its name as the first thing on a line, or run code with the Run command in the immediate window, they all do the same thing — which is to cause lines of code to be processed, run, executed, or whatever you want to call it.

The real and only difference between a procedure and a function is that functions return a value when called. *Returning a value* means that the function creates a variable and places a value into it when it is done running. You can ask the function to return a Boolean (yes/no) value to determine, for example, if the process being run was successful. You could see if a file exists, if a value was greater than another value, or anything you choose. A function can return a date, a number, or a string. In one of the examples, you will see a function that is used to calculate the tax amount for the invoice and then returns the value so that it can be placed into the tax control.

A procedure does not return a value. However, while a function directly returns a value to a variable created as part of the function call, there are other ways within a function or procedure to communicate values to form controls or declared variables in memory.

Understanding where to create a procedure

You can create a procedure in one of two places:

✦ In a module object

✦ Behind a form or report event

You create a subprocedure or function in a module when the procedure will be shared by events in more than one form or report or by an object other than a form or report (queries can use functions to handle very complex criteria).

If the code you are creating will only be called by a single procedure or form, the subprocedure or function should be created behind an event in the form or report.

 Note   A module is a container for multiple subprocedures and functions.

Calling procedures and functions

Procedures (actually subprocedures) can be called in a variety of ways and from a variety of places. They can be called from events behind forms and reports. They can be placed in module objects and called by simply using their name or by using the Call statement. Here are some examples:

```
someprocedurename

Call someprocedurename

Somevalue = somefunctioname
```

Only functions have equalities as they return values. Subprocedures are simply called, do their work, and close. Although functions return a single value, both subprocedures and functions can place values in tables, in form controls, or even in public variables available to any part of your program. You will see several examples of this in this chapter.

Creating a procedure

The first procedure you will create in this chapter will be used to retrieve several values from the cboBuyerID combo box columns and use them in the form. The RowSource of the cboBuyerID combo box contains six active columns, which are as follows:

Visual Basic Column Number	Value
0	Name: tblContacts.chrLastName & ", " & : tblContacts.chrFirstName
1	chrCompany (from tblContacts)
2	dblDiscountPercent (from tblTaxRates)
3	dblTaxRate (from tblTaxRates)
4	chrTaxLocation (from tblContacts)
5	idsContactID (from tblContacts) — the Bound Column

Note   Combo box row sources start with column 0, so column 2 is the third column in the row source.

The objective of this exercise is to learn about procedures, but it will also serve to teach you some additional Visual Basic commands. The code should be entered into the cboBuyerID AfterUpdate event.

To create an Event Procedure in a form, follow the steps below:

1. Select the cboBuyerID control in the frmSales design view.

2. Display the Property window for the control.

3. Select Event from the tabs in the Property window.

4. Click in the After Update event and select [Event Procedure] using the combo box arrow on the After Update line.

5. Press the builder button (...) to open the Visual Basic window.

6. Enter the lines of code below into the Visual Basic coding window, as shown in Figure 23-1.

7. Select Compile Chap23Start from the Debug menu to check your syntax.

8. Close the Visual Basic window and return to the frmSales form.

```
Me.Recalc
If Not IsNull(Me!cboBuyerID) Then
    If Not IsNull(Me!cboBuyerID.Column(2)) Then
        Me!txtDiscountRate =
Format(Me!cboBuyerID.Column(2),"Percent")
        Me!txtTaxLocation = nz(Me!cboBuyerID.Column(4))
        Me!txtTaxRate = nz(Me!cboBuyerID.Column(3),0)
    End If
  Else
    Me!txtDiscountRate = Null
    Me!txtTaxLocation = Null
    Me!txtTaxRate = Null
End If
```

The code first performs a Recalc on the form to update any values that may be in
an uncalculated state, like a buyer ID in the process of being selected or a line item
that was in the process of being selected when the combo box was used. Anytime
you are doing data entry and need code to run to perform some process, it is a
good idea to first run a Recalc command. The Me. refers to the current form and
substitutes in this example for Forms!frmSales!.

Note   Technically, there is no such thing as a procedure. In Access, a procedure begins
            with the Subprocedure command. However, it is still referred to as a procedure.

The first IF statement checks to make sure a buyer ID was selected by making sure
the current value of the bound column in the combo box was not null. If it is not (a
valid value was selected in the combo box), a second IF statement checks to make
sure that not only the value of cboBuyerID is valid but also that the value of the
third column (dblDiscountPercent) is not null.

If the discount field is valid, the values from that and other combo box columns can
be used to fill controls on the form.

Notice the nz function in front of the statements that retrieve the value from column 3 and column 4 of the combo box. The nz function (null to zero) is used to prevent null or zero length string errors. For example, in the following statement if the
value of Me!cboBuyerID.Column(4) was null, it would cause an error when
Me!txtTaxLocation was set to the null value:

```
Me!txtTaxLocation = nz(Me!cboBuyerID.Column(4))
```

The nz function around the right side of the equation sets it to a blank if the value
is null.

The following line uses an alternative value to the default blank:

```
Me!txtTaxRate = nz(Me!cboBuyerID.Column(3),0)
```

This line of code sets the value of the equality to 0 if the third column in null. This
is important that numeric variables are set to 0 instead of a blank.

Figure 23-1 shows the procedure created in the Visual Basic editing window after entering the commands described previously. After you complete entering them, press the Save button on the toolbar to save your code before closing the Visual Basic window.

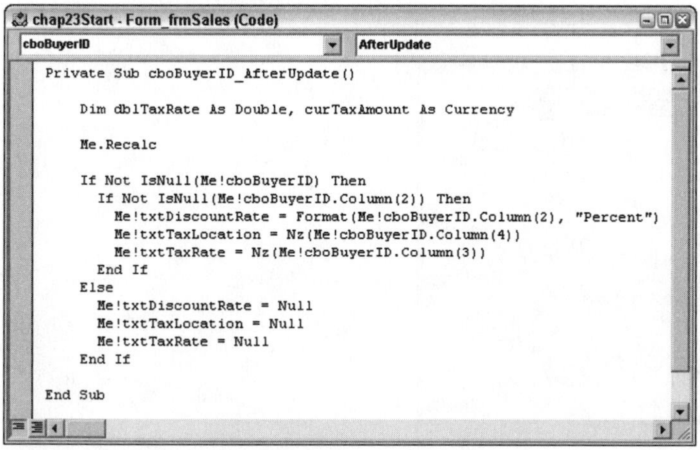

```
chap23Start - Form_frmSales (Code)
cboBuyerID                              AfterUpdate

    Private Sub cboBuyerID_AfterUpdate()

        Dim dblTaxRate As Double, curTaxAmount As Currency

        Me.Recalc

        If Not IsNull(Me!cboBuyerID) Then
            If Not IsNull(Me!cboBuyerID.Column(2)) Then
                Me!txtDiscountRate = Format(Me!cboBuyerID.Column(2), "Percent")
                Me!txtTaxLocation = Nz(Me!cboBuyerID.Column(4))
                Me!txtTaxRate = Nz(Me!cboBuyerID.Column(3))
            End If
        Else
            Me!txtDiscountRate = Null
            Me!txtTaxLocation = Null
            Me!txtTaxRate = Null
        End If

    End Sub
```

Figure 23-1: The frmSales cboBuyerID AfterUpdate event procedure in the Visual Basic editing window.

The procedure behind this form will be run each time the value of the cboBuyerID combo box is changed. When the value of the Buyer ID is changed, this will update the value of the tax location and tax rate. However, you must then change the value of the tax amount. This code can now be added to this procedure. Later, you will make a separate procedure from this new code.

Creating Functions

Functions differ from procedures in that you generally pass functions parameters, and most importantly, functions return a single value. In these examples, you will create functions to calculate the extension for a single line item, create a function to calculate the total of all the taxable line items, and then apply the current tax rate to that value.

Although functions can be created behind individual forms or reports, usually they are created in modules. This first function will be created in a new module that you will name basSalesFunctions. To do this, follow the steps below:

1. Display the Database window by pressing the F11 key.

2. Select the Modules tab.

3. Select the module named basSalesFunctions and press the Design icon in the database toolbar. This has already been provided for you.

4. The Visual Basic window is displayed with the title basSalesFunctions (Code) in the title bar. The next task is to create and name the first procedure or function.

Select Procedure... from the Insert menu.

The Add Procedure dialog box is displayed, as shown in Figure 23-2.

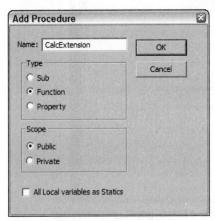

Figure 23-2: The Add Procedure dialog box.

5. Enter CalcExtension as the name of the procedure.

6. Select Function from the option group on the dialog box.

7. Press the OK button to complete the new function.

The empty function now appears in the Visual Basic editor. Notice that the top line begins with Public Function and the function name. Later, you will add the passed parameters to this first line.

Enter the statements below into the Visual Basic editor:

```
Dim curExtension As Currency
CalcExtension = 0
curExtension = intQuantity * curPrice
CalcExtension = curExtension -
(curExtension*dblDiscountPercent)
```

The first statement declares the variable curExtension as Currency. This will be used in an intermediate step. The next line of code sets the value of CalcExtension to 0. Notice that this variable is not declared with a Dim statement. You might also notice that it has the same name as the function. This is not by coincidence. The name of the variable used to return the value to the calling program is automatically declared by the name of the function itself. You will also learn how it gets its data type in the next section.

The next line of code creates a calculation setting the product of two variables, intQuantity and curPrice, to the previously declared variable, curExtension. You might notice that the two variables on the right side of the equation are not declared. You will also learn how it gets its data type in the next section.

Finally, the last line of code performs one more calculation to take the extension and apply any discount to it. By placing the calculated value into the CalcExtension variable, it is automatically passed back to the calling program.

Handling passed parameters

Now, the question you should be asking is this: Where are these variables coming from and how are they declared? The answer is simple. They are the passed parameters from the original function call.

The next step is to modify the Function statement at the top to handle the passed parameters and the returned data type.

Before you can create variables for the passed parameters, you must know what parameters are being passed. In this example, three parameters will be passed:

Parameter Name	Data Type
intQuantity	Integer
curPrice	Currency
dblDiscountPercent	Double

These parameter names can be anything you want them to be. Think of them as variables you would normally declare. All that is missing is the Dim statement. They do not have to be the same name as the variables used in the function call. Normally, you would use the names of fields in a table or controls on a form or even variables created in the calling procedure.

These variables are passed and their data types declared by placing them in parentheses after the function name with the syntax variable name as datatype.

For example:

Public Function somecame(varname1 as somedatatype, varname2 as somedatatype)

For this example, you will change the first line as described in the following steps:

1. Type the entire line over the original Public Function CalcExtension line using a single line.

```
Public Function CalcExtension(intQuantity As Integer,
curPrice As Currency, dblDiscountPercent As Double) As
Currency
```

2. Select Compile Chap23Start from the Debug menu to check your code.

Correct any errors you might find and then close the Visual Basic window.

3. Save the module basSalesFunctions if you are asked.

Each parameter is listed in the form *varname as somedatatype* separated by commas. In this example, there are three parameters. Each one corresponds to the table previously shown. After the parentheses, the data type declaration of the value is passed back to the calling program. CalcExtension is the name of the function and the variable, and its data type will be Currency.

Your screen should look like the one shown in Figure 23-3.

Figure 23-3: The completed CalcExtension function.

Calling a function and passing parameters

Now that you have completed the function it is time to test it.

Normally, a function call comes from a form or report event or from another procedure, and it passes variables or the controls on a form or report. However, the function call may not even use variables. For example, you can test this function by going to the immediate window and using hardcoded numbers or characters known as literals.

Follow the steps below to test the function:

1. Press Ctrl-G to display the Immediate Window.

2. Enter **? CalcExtension(5,3.50,.05)**.

This would pass the values as 5 to the intQuantity variable, 3.50 to the curPrice variable, and .05 (5%) to the dblDiscountPercent variable. This would calculate and return an extension of 16.625 using those numbers, as shown in Figure 23-4.

3. Close the Immediate window and the Visual Basic window and return to the Database window.

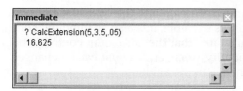

Figure 23-4: Testing the CalcExtension function in the Immediate window.

The next task is to use the function to calculate the extension. You can add a call to the function from the frmSales form's line item subform's Amount field. You can display the frmSales form in design view, then click into the fsubSalesLineitems subform, and finally click into the txtAmount control in the subform. Display the property window and enter the following into the Control Source property, as shown in Figure 23-5.

```
=CalcExtension(Nz([intQuantity],0),Nz([curPrice],0),Nz([dblDiscountPercent],0))
```

This function call passes the values from three controls in the subform to the CalcExtension function in the module and returns the value back to the control source of the txtAmount control each time the line is recalculated or any of the parameters change.

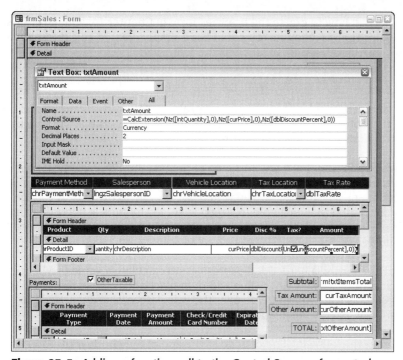

Figure 23-5: Adding a function call to the Control Source of a control.

Of course, entering a function call or any expression into the control source of a control makes the control read only. In this example, it is also an unbound control. There is no field in the tblSalesLineItems table that the txtAmount control is bound to. This is as designed. Because the quantity, price, or discount can be changed, all three places would need to trigger a change to the amount.

Our business rule is that this value should always be calculated, and the user can enter the quantity and item number, override the price retrieved from the inventory table, and override the discount retrieved from the contacts table, but the calculation of extended amount (quantity * price * discount) will always be used.

The CalcExtension function can be used in a variety of ways by other events within this form and by any form or report, because it *lives* in a module. If it were created behind the frmSales form, it would be accessible from only that form.

Creating a Function to Calculate Taxes

When you create a line item, you determine whether or not it is taxable. You can then add up all the extensions for all the taxable line items to determine the taxable total. This total can then be multiplied by the tax rate to determine the tax.

When you learned how to create the frmSales form in Chapter 14, you never created a calculation for the tax amount. You could have simply created an expression for the control named txtTaxAmount, such as the following:

```
=fSubSalesLineitems.Form!txtTaxableTotal * txtTaxRate
```

This expression would reference the sum control expression (txtTaxableTotal) created in the fSubSalesLineitems subform (fSubSalesLineitems) and multiply it by the tax rate (txtTaxRate) in the frmSales form.

However, while this would display the value of the tax, the expression entered into the txtTaxAmount control would also make the txtTaxAmount control read-only because it contains an expression. You would not be able to override the calculated amount if you wanted to. Being able to override some amounts is potentially important. Tax is one of the fields that needs to be changed once in a while for specific business purposes.

A better way than using a hardcoded expression to calculate a value of a control is to create a function to calculate a value and then place the value of the calculation in the control. This way, you can type over the calculated value if you need to or even determine when the calculation will occur.

You could enter the following line of code at the end of the cboBuyerID AfterUpdate event code you entered previously. This way, each time you chose a new contact on the sales form, after the contacts tax rate is retrieved on the frmSales form, the tax is recalculated.

```
Me.txtTaxAmount = Me.fSubSalesLineitems.Form!txtTaxableTotal * Me.txtTaxRate
```

You could also enter this line of code in the After Update events behind the intQuantity, curPrice, dblDiscountPercent, and even the chkTaxable controls. Each time one of those fields changes, the value of the tax needs to be updated as well. Actually, a better place would be to place the code in the AfterUpdate event of the fsubSalesLineitems. This way, the tax can be recalculated each time any of the values are updated in any form line.

Although you can use a simple expression that references controls on forms and subforms, this would only work behind the specific form. Suppose you also need to calculate tax in other forms or in reports. There is a better way than relying on a form.

This is an old developer's expression: "Forms and reports lie. Tables never lie." This means that the controls of a form or report often contain expressions, formats, and Visual Basic code that may make a value seem to be one thing when the table contains another. The table containing the data is where the real values are stored and from where calculations and reports should retrieve data.

Figure 23-6 shows this function created. You can go to the basSalesFunctions module in Chap23Start and enter this code into the CalcTax function header provided for you or you can see it in action in the Chap23End.mdb database file.

Figure 23-6: The CalcTax function.

The function will be called from the After Update events behind the intQuantity, curPrice, or dblDiscountPercent controls in the subform. The CalcExtension function is used to calculate the sum of the taxable line items from the tblSalesItems table. The SQLstatement combined with the ADO code creates the total. The calculated total amount is then multiplied by the passed parameter dblTaxPercent to calculate the tax. The tax is set to the variable CalcTax (the name of the expression).

Functions and subprocedures are important to the concepts of reusable code within an application. You should try to use functions and subprocedures and pass them parameters every time you can. A good rule is this: The first time you find yourself copying a group of code, it is time to create a procedure or function.

✦   ✦   ✦

Effective Debugging and Error Handling in VBA

Great systems have great error handling. Error handling is important for both the end user and the developer. A system must be able to handle expected errors as well as unforeseen ones. In this chapter, you will first learn the process of debugging an Access application. You will learn about the built-in error handling tools in Microsoft Access, including VBA Assistance, the VBA syntax checker, compiler, breakpoints, watchpoints, and the Immediate windows. You will then learn advanced techniques, including building a generic error handler and system information screen to give the user control over the errors and learn how to leave an audit trail for the developer. You will finally learn ways to handle errors remotely.

On the CD-ROM

This chapter is a departure from the other example files you have used in the book. When you load the sample database file named Chap24.mdb, you will see an interface, as shown in Figure 24-1. Match the chapter headers and the interface lines to go to the right code for each example.

Click on any item to display an explanation of the technique. Double-click on any of the items to display the module code in design view, and follow the instructions in the interface display or code window comments. Because the code window in Visual Basic is a separate physical window, it sometimes must be moved to display any dialog boxes. Comments start with a single quote. Much of the code in the examples also has single quotes in front of it because it is purposely typed incorrectly and causes errors (the purpose of this chapter). You may have to remove the single quote in front of some of the early examples to view the error or view the assistance already built into Microsoft Access.

There are many more examples in Chap24.mdb than are described in the text of this chapter. After you read the chapter, go back through all of the examples and try them. You will learn more about debugging than you probably ever want to know, but it will serve you well as you develop and debug your programs.

Tip   Good developers spend one-third of their time designing a program, one-third of their time programming, and one-third of their time testing and debugging. It is advisable to have someone other than the developer test the program.

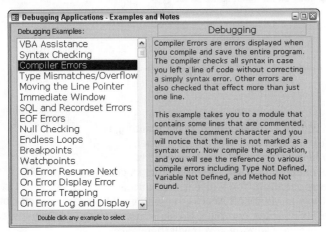

Figure 24-1: The Chap24Start.mdb example database.

Testing and Debugging Your Applications

Testing is the first step in a process that lets you insure that your application is working as designed. Each time you move from form or report design or the Visual Basic Editor to running those same forms, reports, and VBA code, you are testing your application. Each time you write a line of code and move to another line, you are testing your code. Each time you change a property in a form or report and move your cursor to another property, you are testing your form or report.

Testing is the time to see if your application runs the way you designed it, or even if it runs at all. When you run an application and it doesn't work, you have found a *bug*. Fixing the problem is known as *debugging*. This term dates back to the earliest electron tube computers. Legend has it that a moth shorted out a hardware circuit. Removing the moth was known as debugging the system and is attributed to the late Admiral Grace Hopper, an early pioneer in computing.

You may have already learned a lot about testing and debugging. When you run a report and no data appears, you probably have learned to check the report's Record Source property and to view the data in the query or table to see if the data source is the problem. If you run a form and you see #Name or #Error in individual controls, you have learned to check the Control Source of the Control. Perhaps you have an incorrect reference to a table field or you spelled something wrong.

Maybe you had too many parentheses or have used a control name in a formula that uses the control name. Each time you had this problem, you probably asked someone with more experience than you what the problem was, or perhaps you looked it up in a manual or researched the syntax of the formula.

When you run forms and reports, Access may report an error if it finds something seriously wrong. When you create VBA code, there are a wide variety of tools built into the editor to help you.

VBA Assistance: Auto Quick Info and Auto List Members

While you are learning VBA syntax, working in the code window can seem awkward compared to everything else you may have developed in your Access application. The Visual Basic Editor, however, has some built-in features to help you on your way to becoming a VBA expert.

As you type each line of code in your procedure, on-screen help — called Auto Quick Info and Auto List Members — guides you through the vast array of commands and options available for your procedure.

Auto Quick Info help displays the options for the command you entered. The next parameter to enter displays in bold. As you specify each parameter and press the spacebar between parameters or you enter the comma separator, the next parameter you would enter displays in bold. Figure 24-2 shows the Auto Quick Info help for all of the parameters of the MsgBox command.

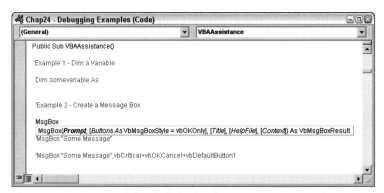

Figure 24-2: Auto Quick Info help for the MsgBox command.

Auto List Members automatically displays when you type the beginning of a command — for example, when you enter MsgBox and press the spacebar key to display a list of options. You can then enter the message and press the comma (,) key. Then, a list of possible commands displays, as shown in Figure 24-3. You can either select one of the commands in the list, or continue typing the command if you already know the one you want to use.

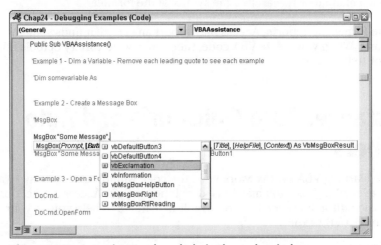

Figure 24-3: Auto List Members help in the code window.

Syntax checking — The first step

When you type a line of code in VBA, each character is being evaluated against the known but limited set of valid VBA commands. When you have completed entering each line of code, another built-in tool known as the syntax checker is used to make sure the line of code contains valid entries.

Syntax is the name given to computer grammar. Figure 24-4 shows a statement typed incorrectly and the error message that is displayed. You may also notice that the lines are different colors. Black indicates a valid line of code. Green is used for comments, and red is used when a line has been flagged by the syntax checker and not yet corrected.

Unlike some other languages, VBA will let you leave a line of code that has an error and fix it later. Sometimes, it is another line of code that needs to be added or changed in order to fix a subsequent line.

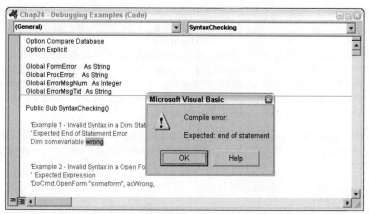

Figure 24-4: A Microsoft Access 2003 syntax error.

Compiling Procedures

After you create a subprocedure or function and want to make sure all of your syntax is correct, you should compile your procedures by choosing Debug ➪ Compile project name from the VBA menu. This action checks your code for errors and also converts the programs to a form your computer can understand. If the compile operation is not successful, an error window appears, as shown in Figure 24-5.

This level of checking is more stringent than the single-line syntax checker. Variables are checked for proper references and type. Each statement is checked for all proper parameters. All text strings are checked for proper delimiters such as "text string."

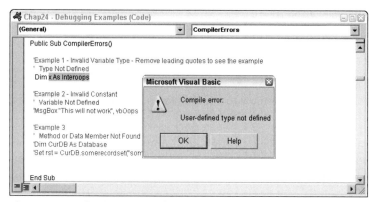

Figure 24-5: Viewing a compile error.

Handling Null Values

Null values require special handling when they can potentially exist. This is especially true when assigning the value of an unknown table field, combo box column, or memory variable to another. If an unexpected error occurs because the value being retrieved is not valid, your system will crash. The most common type of assignment errors are handling nulls, blanks, and zero-length strings as well as invalid data types.

The IsNull function handles null values. This is a value that has never been entered. A string is null until something is entered into it. Using the IsNull function is a great start but does not cover all possibilities.

    If IsNull(somevariable) Then dosomething

Suppose you enter a value into a variable and then, after saving it, you go back and delete the value. This creates a zero-length string. The IsNull function does not trap zero-length strings. This requires a check of the length of the value.

You could enter If Len(somevariable) = 0 to check for a zero-length string. If the statement evaluated to True, you would not place the zero-length string into the variable. However, suppose the value was Null; checking the length of it would cause an error. You can use a different function to convert null values to blanks and then combine the two functions to perform both checks. The command would be:

    If Len(Nz(somevariable)) = 0

The nz function (null to zero) converts a null to a blank for strings and to a zero for numerics or dates. The length of this can then be checked. There is, however, one more function that may need to be used. If the value was null and the nz function is used, the resulting blank value would return a value of 1 when the Len function is used to check the length. The Trim function can be used to remove trailing blanks (or all blanks if the string consists only of blanks) and will allow a value of 0 to be returned to the check. The final statement would then be:

    If Len(Trim(Nz(somevariable))) = 0

Access compiles all currently uncompiled procedures, not just the one you are currently viewing. If you receive a compile error, you should immediately modify the code to rectify the problem. Then try to compile the procedure again. If there are further compile errors, you will see the next error.

When your application is compiled, the Debug ⇨ Compile menu choice is disabled. Before implementing an application at the customer's site, you should make sure that your application is compiled.

Your database is named with a standard Windows name such as Chap24, but there is a separate project name that Microsoft Access uses internally. You will see this when you compile your database. When the database file is first created, the project name and the Windows filename will be the same. The project name is not changed when you change the Windows filename. You can change the project name by selecting Tools ➪ projectname Properties (where project name is the current internal project name).

Compiling your database only makes sure that you have no syntax errors. The compiler can only check for language problems by first recognizing the VBA statement and then checking to see that you specify the right number of options and in the right order.

After you compile your program, you should also compact your database. Each time you make a change to your program, it stores both the changes and the original version. When you compile your program, it may double in size as the compiled and uncompiled versions of your code are stored. When you compact the database, it will reduce the size of the database by as much as 80 percent as it eliminates all previous versions internally.

Handling Runtime Errors

You might create a line of code that references a certain form, and that form is expected to be opened by a previous module. If that form is not open when the program runs, you cannot determine that during the compile step, because the compiler evaluates each procedure separately and does not try to compare the logic between procedures or modules. When the program runs, however, you will get an error message.

When you get an error message, you can likely respond to it. However, some errors are harder to understand than others, and some require you to instantly recognize the problem. For example, Figure 24-6 shows a simple program that declares and creates a text string variable and a numeric variable and then tries to assign the numeric variable the value of the text string. You probably already know that you can't put letters in a numeric field.

The error message in Figure 24-6 reports a Runtime error '13:' — which happens to be a Type mismatch. Unless you know the problem, how does this message help you? Without a great deal of experience, how do you then fix this type of problem? In fact, how do you determine what the problem is?

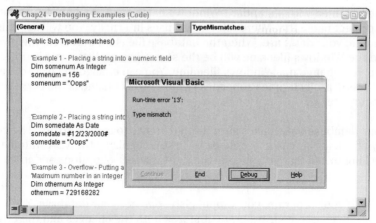

Figure 24-6: A runtime error message.

In the error dialog box in Figure 24-6, you can see a button labeled Debug. The Debug button will stop the program where it is running and place you on the offending statement. The program is in a state of limbo. All of the values of temporary variables are intact, and you can view them to help you solve the error. The End button will cause the program to stop running, and you cannot use any tools to check the problem.

Figure 24-7 shows this statement. It is highlighted by a yellow background, indicating that it is the offending statement, and there is an arrow in the left margin. There are several tools you can then use to find your problem.

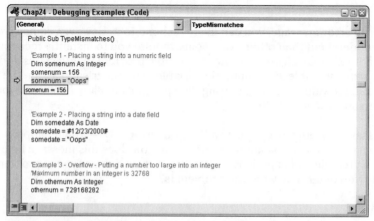

Figure 24-7: Displaying the value from a running variable.

If you place your cursor over any variable in the highlighted area, you can see the current value. If you examine Figure 24-7, you can see the arrow in the left margin, indicating that the highlighted line is the currently running line of code. You can also see the rectangle containing the text *somenum = 156*, the current value of the variable named somenum, which has been set to 156. You could also see that the value of somenum is currently 156.

Although you can place your cursor on the running variable and determine the values, you may want to see the value of other variables as well. Sometimes, depending on how the program is structured, you can do this, but you are usually limited to the latest values created.

Using the Immediate, Locals, and Watches Windows

There are several more tools that can help you debug a program. These include the Immediate, Locals, and Watches windows. Each can be displayed as part of the Visual Basic editor window by selecting View ➪ Immediate Window, View ➪ Locals Window, and View ➪ Watch Window. Each may be necessary depending on the severity of your problems and the mysteriousness of the error.

The Immediate window is an area where you can run procedures, check the value of variables, check an expression, or run a single line of VBA code. You can run a VBA subprocedure by using the syntax Call *procedurename* where *procedurename* is a subprocedure. You can also run a function by adding a ? in front of the call and adding a variable for the return value, such as ? x = functionname. You can check the value of any variable running in your program by adding a ? in front of the variable name.

You can see the values of the running variables in Figure 24-8. Here, in the Immediate window, you see that ? somenumber was entered and produced the value 200.

You can add watchpoints by using the Add Watch or Edit Watch options from the Debug menu.

The Locals window can be used to display all of the active memory items in your running program. These include forms, modules, and variables. In Figure 24-8, you can see the Locals window in the bottom-left corner of the figure. Because only a simple module is running, you only see the reference to that object. If you were also running a form, you would see a reference to the form object along with a tree diagram that could be exploded to show each control on the form and the value of each control for the current record. This is important when you are debugging a module behind a form or report.

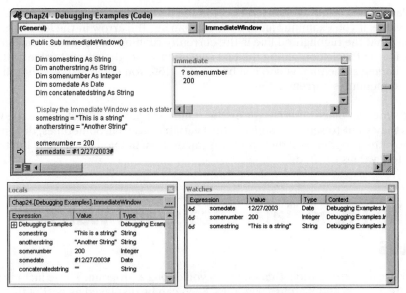

Figure 24-8: Using the Immediate, Locals, and Watches windows.

Generally, you start with just the module debugger and then, if necessary, move into the Immediate window. If you need to view more variables, you might display the Locals window. There is also an advanced window known as the Watches window. Although this is outside the scope of this book, the Watches window lets you set up specific values to watch for and then stop the program when a value is reached. For example, if you are expecting an incremental value to reach 500 by 1 and it never does, you might set a Watch variable to see if it hits 100, rather than randomly check the program when it runs. If the watchpoint (as it is called) hits 100, the program is stopped and the line of code that the program was on when the value reached 100 is highlighted. This is the same as a runtime error without the actual error.

When the program stops, there are some other tools you can use to step through the program one line at a time. You can also move to previously executed lines to check your program logic. Besides the watch window, you can stop your program at a specific point by using a breakpoint.

Creating a Breakpoint

There is one more code debugging tool that professional developers use, known as *breakpoints*. Whereas the watch window watches for a specific value, breakpoints simply watch for a specific line to be executed and stop the program at that statement.

A breakpoint is often used to stop a program from running before it causes an error. This way, all the variables and conditions of the objects can be checked before the error occurs.

To set a breakpoint, display your program in design view and press the F9 function key or press the Toggle Breakpoint menu item from the Debug menu. Figure 24-9 shows a breakpoint on the line that starts a loop. After you set the breakpoint, you can close the module and the breakpoint will be remembered until the database file is closed. When you run the program and that module is executed, the program will stop on that line and display the program at the breakpoint.

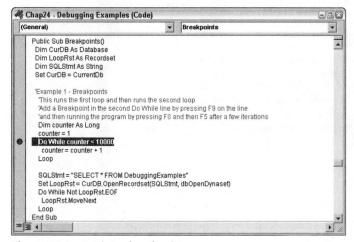

Figure 24-9: Setting a breakpoint.

When the program is run (by moving to the top line and pressing F5 or F8 to run one line at a time) and is stopped, you can use options on the Debug menu to control the execution. The Debug menu is shown in Figure 24-10 with the line stopped where the breakpoint is set. Notice the solid red circle and the yellow arrow in the margin. The red circle indicates the breakpoint, and the arrow indicates the current line.

You can set as many breakpoints as you want, but generally more than one may be confusing unless you are trying to determine if a block of code is being run at all.

The Debug menu is broken into five areas. The first area lets you compile the application. You generally don't do this while the program is running.

The next area lets you use different methods to continue running your program one or more statements at a time.

✦ **Step Into:** Run the next one line of code.

✦ **Step Over:** Run the next line of code and all the code in any called procedures.

✦ **Step Out:** Run the entire current procedure and then stop with the next line in the original called procedure.

✦ **Run To Cursor:** You can move your cursor to a later line and run all the statements between the current line and the line where the cursor is.

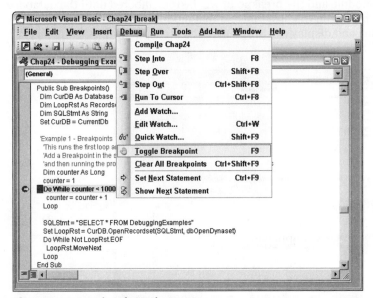

Figure 24-10: Using the Debug menu.

The next group lets you add or edit a watchpoint in the Watch window. You can also run a quick watch to just see the value of a variable, similar to entering ? *somevariablename* in the Immediate window.

The next group lets you toggle a breakpoint on or off or clear all breakpoints. When you close a database file, all breakpoints are automatically cleared.

The final menu choices are perhaps the most powerful. Set Next Statement lets you move the cursor to any line of code — forward or backward — and then run the program starting with that line. If you are trying to correct an error and keep getting it wrong, being able to go backward is very important. Show Next Statement simply highlights without running the next statement that will run.

There are also several options on the Run menu that will help you debug a program:

✦ **Continue:** Continues running the program without stopping, until it reaches the next error, breakpoint, or the program's conclusion.

✦ **Break:** Stops the program where it is running. You can also use Ctrl-Break to stop a running program and cause a manual break. If you accidentally create an endless loop, this will stop the program.

✦ **Reset:** Stops the error process and lets you restart the program from any desired line of code.

When you are debugging a running program and finally get a line of code corrected, make sure you press the Save icon, or your changes will not be saved when you close the procedure.

By using the wide variety of debugging tools, you will be able to diagnose your coding problems and quickly solve them. You can also use the Visual Basic Help system to help you understand the problem being reported, but generally errors will be yours to solve.

Errors

Assuming you get past the syntax checking using the VBA editor and you also get past the errors that Access will find when you compile your application, the only remaining errors that can occur will occur at runtime. Runtime errors occur for a multitude of reasons. When they do occur, the error will cause one of following four things to happen:

✦ A fatal error and the application crashes

✦ An untrapped error and the Access error dialog box appears

✦ A handled error and your code takes care of the problem

✦ An Unknown application error that will not cause an Access error

Types of errors

A *fatal error* is a non-recoverable error that will crash an application. These errors are generally a result of an operation outside the Access environment, so Access cannot handle it and your code will therefore not be able to handle it. These types of errors generally occur when a Windows API is called. Because you cannot do much about these fatal errors other than to fix them, you can concentrate on the types of errors you can control.

The Access Error dialog box will appear for *untrapped errors*, as shown in Figure 24-11. This can be good for development because problems can be traced to the specific line of code that caused the error. When you press the Debug button, the VBA window will open and highlight the guilty line of code. But this is not the kind of reaction you generally want with your applications and end users. For this reason, having an error handler and making it a *handled error* is much better. You can sometimes not just alert the user of a problem, but maybe prevent the user from even worrying about the problem by having the code take some action to either work around the error or correct the problem.

The last type of error is the unknown application error. This is a logic error in the code. No error is displayed because the program is working the way it was coded. For example, an endless loop can occur if you forget to advance a record pointer as you traverse a recordset or your Do Loop never ends. The problem is that the code is doing the wrong thing. This could be the hardest type of error to discover. There are several different ways to handle these errors:

✦ Check the results programmatically by redundantly checking the results.

✦ Use the Watch window or breakpoints to watch the code run line by line.

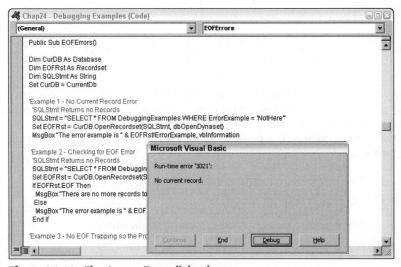

Figure 24-11: The Access Error dialog box.

The elements of error handling

Access 2003 provides several basic programming elements to work with for errors, including the following:

✦ VBA Error statements

✦ The Error event

✦ The Errors collection

✦ The Err object

When Access detects an error, most of the time an object is created for the error.

VBA error statements

There are two basic VBA statements for handling errors:

✦ On Error ...

✦ Resume ...

The On Error statement enables or disables error handling There are three forms of the On Error statement:

✦ On Error Resume Next

✦ On Error GoTo somelabelname

✦ On Error GoTo 0

The On Error GoTo somelabelname statement enables an error-handling routine. The label should be the label for the error-handling routine. When this statement is executed, error handling is immediately enabled. When an error then occurs, execution goes to the line specified by the label argument, which should be at the beginning of the error-handling routine.

To disable error handling, use the On Error GoTo 0 statement. This statement also resets the properties of the Err object.

The On Error Resume Next statement ignores the line that causes an error and continues execution with the line following the line that caused the error. No error-handling routine is called. This statement is useful if you want to ignore errors. Figure 24-12 shows a program that simply ignores a potential null or EOF error.

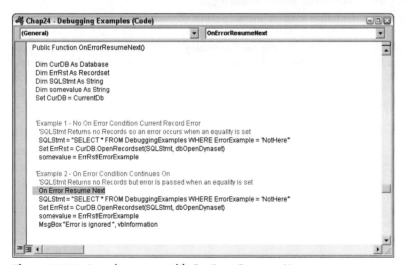

Figure 24-12: Ignoring errors with On Error Resume Next.

You return to the main procedure from an error handler using the Resume statement. If you do not want to resume execution in case of an error, the Resume statement is not necessary. All you need to do is exit the procedure.

As with the On Error statement, there are three forms of the Resume statement:

✦ Resume or Resume 0

✦ Resume Next

✦ Resume somelabelname

The Resume or Resume 0 statement returns execution to the line at which the error occurred. This statement is typically used when the user must make a correction. This might occur if you prompt the user for the name of a file to open and the user enters a filename that doesn't exist. You can then force the execution of the code back to the point where the filename is requested.

When your error handler corrects or works around the problem that caused the error, the Resume Next statement is used. It returns execution to the line immediately following the line at which the error occurred.

If you need to continue execution at some other place besides the line that caused the error or the line after the line that caused the error, the Resume Label statement should be used. It returns execution to the line specified by the label argument.

Handling an error with error messages

The On Error GoTo Label format allows you to trap an error and then display either a custom message box or generic display. Figure 24-13 shows a program with a simple recordset. Notice the On Error GoTo DisplayError command. When an error occurs, control is transferred to the DisplayError label, which displays a simple message box.

The message box uses the Err object to report the error number, description, and source.

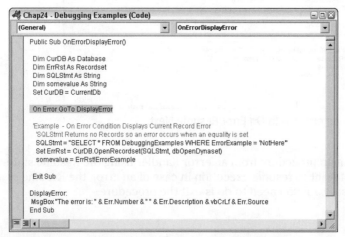

Figure 24-13: Handling errors with On Error GoToLabel.

The two types of error objects in Access are based on whether the error was detected by ADO or Access. The Errors collection is part of the ADO object model. The Err Object is part of the Access and DAO object model. In addition to these two elements, Access has an Error Event that gets triggered when an error occurs with a form or report.

The Err object

The err object is created by VBA. When an error occurs, information about that error is stored in the Err object. The Err object contains information about only one error at a time. When an error occurs, the Err object is cleared and updated to include information about that most recent error.

The Err object has several properties, including Number, Description, and Source. The Number is the internal number of the error, and the Description gives you a little more information about the error. The Err object also has two methods: Clear, to clear information from the Err object; and Raise, to simulate an error.

When an error occurs relative to the Jet database engine or ADO, you need to refer to the Errors collection to get more information.

The error event

Access also provides for an error event when running a form or report. This provides a nice way to trap an error when VBA code is not running. This event is triggered when an error occurs on a form or report. You need to create an event procedure for the On Error event to trap these errors. The procedure would look like one of the following, depending on whether it was a form or a report:

```
Private Sub Form_Error(DataErr As Integer, Response As Integer)
'Insert error handler here
End Sub

Private Sub Report_Error(DataErr As Integer, Response As Integer)
'Insert error handler here
End Sub
```

There are two arguments for these subroutines: DataErr and Response. DataErr is the error code returned by the Err object when an error occurs. Note that the Err object isn't populated with information after the event occurs. You need to use the DataErr argument to determine what error occurred. The second argument, Response, should contain either one of the following constants:

✦ **AcDataErrContinue:** Ignore the error and continue without displaying the default Access error message.

✦ **AcDataErrDisplay:** Display the default Access error message. (This is the default.)

When you use AcDataErrContinue, you can then supply a custom error message or handler in place of the default error message.

Error-handling procedures

There are obviously numerous ways to deal with errors within forms, reports, and code. Each form and report, as well as each function and subroutine, can and probably should have an error-handling routine. It is not unusual to see a good part of the development effort devoted to error handling. As you look through the various components in our example application, you will see numerous examples of error-handling routines.

Probably the most common routine is the following one:

```
Function SampleCode
'Dim statements here

    On Error goto ErrorHandler
    'insert functional code here
    Exit Function

ErrorHandler:
    'error handler code here
    Msgbox err.description
    'either enter a resume statement here or
' nothing and let the function end

End Function
```

The On Error statement enables the error handler, and if an error occurs, execution will continue on the line after the label ErrorHandler. This label could be any valid VBA label. The error-handler code would deal with the error and then either resume execution back in the body of the procedure or just exit the function or subroutine. The inclusion of the Msgbox statement in the error handler is a typical way of informing the user what happened.

When an error occurs in a called function or subroutine that doesn't have an enabled error handler, VBA will return to the calling procedure looking for an enabled error handler. This process will proceed up the calling tree until one is found — or if one is not found, execution will stop with an Access error message displayed.

The Errors collection

When an error occurs in an ADO object, an error object is created in the Errors collection of the Connection object. These are referred to as Data Access errors. When an error occurs, the collection is cleared and the new set of objects is put into the collection. Although the collection only exists for one error event, the event could generate several errors. Each of these errors is stored in the Errors collection. The Errors collection is an object of the Connection object, not ADO.

The Errors collection has one property, "Count," which contains the number of errors or error objects. It has a value of zero if there are no errors. There are a few properties of the Error object. These include Description, HelpContext, HelpFile, Number, and Source. When there are multiple errors, the lowest-level error is the first object in the collection, and the highest-level error is the last object in the collection.

When an ADO error occurs, the VBA Err object contains the error number for the first object in the Errors collection. You need to check the Errors collection to see whether additional ADO errors have occurred.

In the following code, you will find an error handler that can be used in a procedure that deals with an ADO connection. When an error occurs, the code following the label ErrorHandler runs and first checks to see if the Error object contains any items. If it does, it checks to see if the error is the same as the Err object. If it is the same, the error was an ADO error and the variable strMessage will contain the descriptions of all the errors in the Errors collection. If it is not an ADO error, the error is from VBA and the single Err.Description value will be displayed:

```
Dim cnn As New ADODB.Connection
Dim errX As ADODB.Error
Dim strMessage As String

    On Error goto ErrorHandler

    'insert code here

    GoTo Done

ErrorHandler:
    If cnn.Errors.Count > 0 Then
      If err.Number = cnn.Errors.Item(0).Number Then
        'error is an ADO Connection Error
        For Each errX In cnn.Errors
          strMessage = strMessage & err.Description & vbCrLf
        Next
        MsgBox strMessage, , "ADO Error Handler"
      End If
    Else
        'error is a VBA Error
        MsgBox err.Description, , "VBA Error Handler"
    End If
Done:
```

Logging Errors

An even better option is to trap errors and log them to a file for later use. The program shown in Figure 24-14 causes an error and runs a function called DispError.

Figure 24-14: Handling errors with a logging routine.

The DispError function is passed two parameters from the module that identifies the primary and secondary source of the error. This is entered by the developer to later determine the exact location of the error. Sometimes, an error occurs but you cannot pinpoint the procedure or function where it came from. Sometimes, it can be from a form module or report module, or sometimes the source is a procedure in a specific module.

Figure 24-15 shows the DispError function. The function uses the two passed parameters as well as the number and description from the error to open another form that gives a brief look at the problem.

The form shown in Figure 24-16 is named AppError on the example database. As you can see, the four parameters are passed from the error routine through the DispError function to the AppError form.

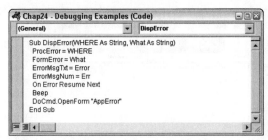

Figure 24-15: The DispError function.

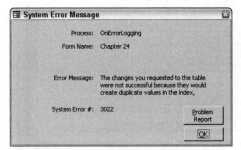

Figure 24-16: The AppError form.

On the AppError form is a button with the caption Problem Report. This opens a form named Problem Report Dialog, as shown in Figure 24-18. Before the form is opened, a set of code (as shown in Figure 24-17) is run to create a record in the Problem Report table. This allows errors to be recalled by the user and enhanced if necessary by allowing them to add more information about the error, including the steps to duplicate the error and comments about how the error occurred.

The Problem Report form can also be printed or e-mailed to a technician. The Problem Report form and logging system can be an invaluable debugging tool for the technical support person because it allows an end user to better communicate a problem without losing the details or miscommunicating the problem.

By using proper debugging techniques and using error handlers, you can create great crash-proof applications.

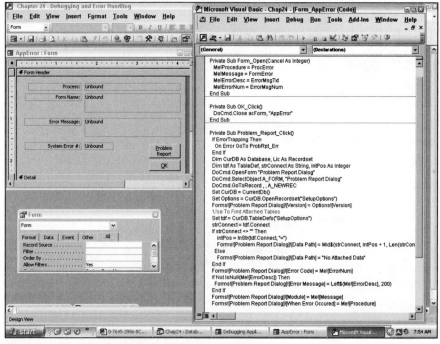

Figure 24-17: Opening the Problem Report form.

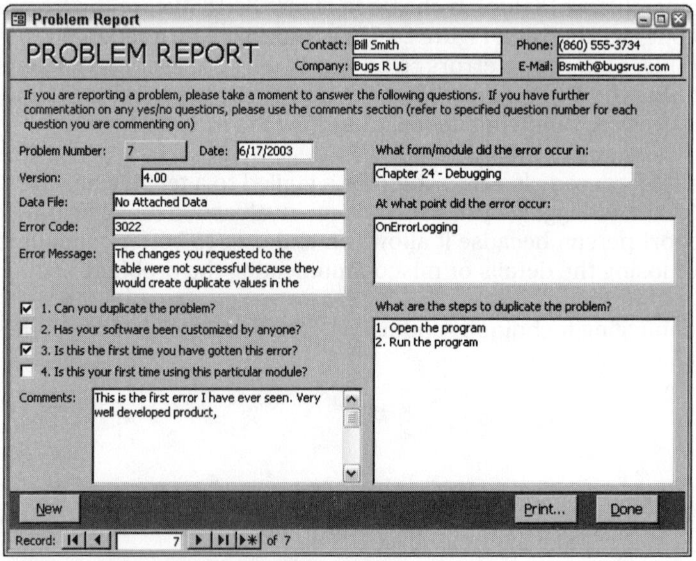

Figure 24-18: The Problem Report form.

✦   ✦   ✦

Creating Switchboards, Command Bars, Menus, Toolbars, and Dialog Boxes

I n previous chapters, you learned how to create individual Access objects, such as tables, queries, forms, reports, and macros. You worked with each object interactively in Access, selecting the Database window and using the assorted objects.

In this chapter, you tie these objects together into a single database application—without having to write or know how to use a complex database program. Rather, you automate the application through the use of switchboards, dialog boxes, and menus. These objects make your system easier to use, and they hide the Access interface from the final user.

On the CD-ROM This chapter will use the database named CHAP25Start.mdb. If you have not already copied it onto your machine from the CD, you will need to do so now. After you have completed this chapter, your database should resemble the one in CHAP25End.mdb.

Switchboards and Command Buttons

A *switchboard* is fundamentally a form. The switchboard form is a customized application menu that contains user-defined command buttons. With these command buttons, you can run macros that automatically select actions, such as opening forms or printing reports.

Using a switchboard button, you can replace many interactive user steps with a single button selection (or *click*). For example, if you want to interactively open the frmContacts and frmSales forms, you must perform three actions: Switch to the Database window, select the Forms tab, and open the two forms individually. If you use a switchboard button to perform the same task, you simply click the button. Figure 25-1 shows the switchboard window for the Access Auto Auctions system with several buttons. Each command button triggers a macro that performs a series of steps, such as opening the frmContacts form or running the rptCustomerMailingLabels Report.

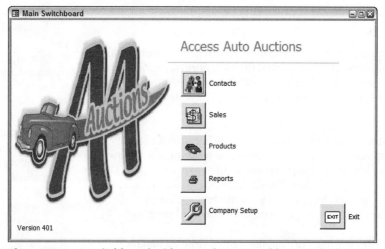

Figure 25-1: A switchboard with several command buttons for forms and reports.

By using a switchboard and other objects that we discuss in this chapter, you can tie your database objects together in a single database application. The application has a user interface that you create rather than the Access interactive interface. A primary component of that user-defined interface is the switchboard that you create.

Using a switchboard

A switchboard's primary use is as an application interface menu. The switchboard in Figure 25-1 is the application interface menu for the Access Auto Auctions database. As the figure shows, the switchboard contains several command buttons. When the user clicks on any switchboard button, a macro is triggered that performs some action or a series of actions.

Creating the basic form for a switchboard

You create a switchboard by adding command buttons to an existing Access form. The form in Figure 25-1 is a standard Access display form. Forms can have many uses, including data entry, data display, and switchboards.

Because switchboard forms are used as application menus, they tend to use a limited number of form controls. Typically, you find command buttons, labels, object frames (OLE objects, such as pictures), lines, and rectangles. Normally, switchboards lack the other types of form controls, such as text boxes (bound to fields), list and combo boxes, graphs, subforms, and page breaks.

To create a basic switchboard form, you place labels like titles and group headings on the form. In addition to the labels, you may also want to place lines, rectangles, and pictures on the form to make it aesthetically appealing. You create the basic switchboard form by using the techniques that you learn in the chapters that cover form objects.

Consider, for example, the switchboard in Figure 25-1. Apart from the command buttons, this is a typical Access application form. Its major components are a title, some other text controls, various colored rectangles, a line, and a picture (image control).

Tip   You can create a switchboard using a standard Access form or having Access create your menu for you using the Switchboard Manager under the Database Utilities choice of the Tools menu. Using the Switchboard Manager is covered later in this chapter.

To create the basic form for the Access Auto Auctions system, follow these steps:

1. Create a new form by clicking on the New button in the Forms Objects window.

2. Select Design View in the New Form dialog box and click the OK button.

3. Resize the form to be approximately 7 inches wide and 4 inches high by dragging the bottom-right corner of the detail section (after making the form design window large enough to resize it visually).

4. Double-click in the details section, or click on the properties button to open the property sheet for the form.

5. Select the Format tab and then click in the Back Color; then click on the Build button for the Back Color property. This will activate the Color dialog box. Your screen should resemble the one shown in Figure 25-2.

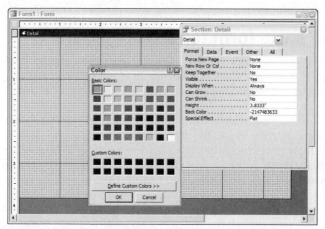

Figure 25-2: The new AAASwitchboard form with the property sheet open and the Color picker dialog box.

6. Select white from the choice of colors and click the OK button to change the Background color to white. You will be returned to the Property Sheet and the color will be changed to the number 16777215, which represents white.

7. Click in any other property area and the background color will be changed to white.

8. Select a label object from the Toolbox, place it on the form starting at about the 3 inch wide and ½ inch down location, and change the following properties — Caption: Access Auto Auctions; Font Size: 22; Fore Color: to a medium gray.

9. Select a line object from the Toolbox and place it immediately below the label object.

10. Select an image object from the Toolbox and place it on the left side of the form and size it to fit the blank area.

11. Select the AAAfinalweb.jpg filename in the Insert Picture dialog box that appears (you may have to go to the directory that has the file to find it), and press the OK button. Change the Size Mode property (under the Format tab) to Stretch.

    Your form should now resemble the one shown in Figure 25-3.

12. Save your form, naming it **frmAAASwitchboard**.

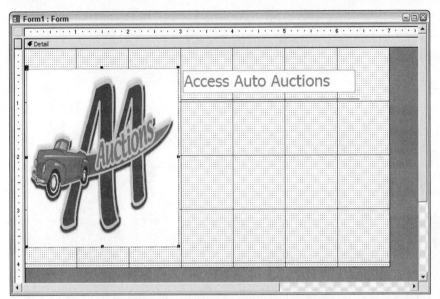

Figure 25-3: The basic frmAAASwitchboard before putting the command buttons on it.

With the basic form created, you are ready to work with command buttons.

Working with command buttons

Command buttons are the type of form control that you use to run macros or VBA routines. Command buttons are the simplest type of form controls, having the single purpose of executing a macro or VBA procedure that can exist behind a form or in a module procedure.

In this example, you create command buttons that run macros or VBA procedures. As you learned in previous chapters, macros or VBA procedures perform a multitude of tasks in Access, including:

- ✦ Opening and displaying other forms
- ✦ Opening a pop-up form or dialog box to collect additional information
- ✦ Opening and printing reports
- ✦ Activating a search or displaying a filter
- ✦ Exiting Access

Figure 25-4 shows a command button named *Command1* and its property sheet. This property sheet contains the event properties available for a command button.

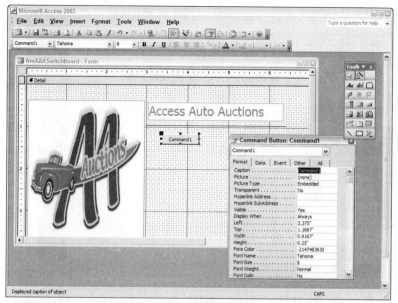

Figure 25-4: A single-button switchboard form with its open property sheet. Notice that it has a command button and a label added to it.

Each event property can trigger a macro or VBA procedure. For example, to trigger a macro named *mcrOpenSales* when the user clicks on the button, place the mcrOpenSales macro in the parameter box for the On Click property. The keyword *On* identifies an event property. The property identifies the user event that must occur to trigger an action.

Cross-Reference

Linking is covered in the section "Linking a command button to a macro," later in this chapter.

On Click and On Dbl Click are mutually compatible. If you activate both the On Click property (giving it a macro name) and the On Dbl Click property, Access follows this order of precedence for the mouse clicking and trapping:

1. On Click (single click)

2. On Dbl Click (double-click)

3. On Click (single click)

In other words, Access processes an On Click first and then an On Dbl Click and, finally, an On Click again. Access always processes the On Click if it is defined. To prevent the second On Click macro from running, place a CancelEvent action in the On Dbl Click macro.

What Is Focus?

To understand the terminology associated with command buttons, you need to know the term *focus*. The two command button properties On Enter and On Exit gain or lose focus. In other words, the focus represents the next item of input from the user. For example, if you tab from one button to another, you lose the focus on the first button as you leave it, and you gain the focus on the second as you enter it. In a form with several command buttons, you can tell which button has focus by the dotted box around the label of the button. Focus does not denote the state of input, such as when you press a button; rather, focus is the object that is currently active and awaiting some user action.

The focus for mouse input always coincides with the button down, or *pointer*, location. Because focus occurs at the moment of clicking a command button, the property On Enter is not triggered. The reason for this is that On Enter occurs just before the focus is gained; that state is not realized when you select a command button by using a mouse. The On Enter state never occurs. Rather, the focus and On Click occur simultaneously, bypassing the On Enter state.

In addition, if the macro you call from an On Click opens a dialog box (message box, pop-up form, and so forth), the second click is lost and the On Dbl Click is never reached. If you use On Click and On Dbl Click, the On Click should not open a dialog box if you need to capture the On Dbl Click.

Creating command buttons

A command button's primary purpose is to activate, or run, a macro or event procedure (VBA procedure). Access gives you two ways to create a command button:

✦ Click the Command Button icon in the Form toolbox.

✦ Drag a macro name from the database container to the form.

In this chapter, both of these methods are used at least once as you learn to create the six command buttons that are shown in Figure 25-1 (four buttons to display a form, one to display a report switchboard, and one to exit the application). In this first example, you learn to create the first form button using the Command Button Wizard.

When using the Command Button Wizard, in addition to creating a command button, you can also automatically display text or embed a picture on the button. More importantly, you can create VBA modules to perform tasks (even if you don't know a single command in VBA), including:

✦ Record Navigation (Next, Previous, First, Last, Find)

✦ Record Operations (Save, Delete, Print, Add, Duplicate)

✦ Form Operations (Open, Close, Print, Filter)

✦ Report Operations (Print, Preview, Mail)

✦ Application (Run Application, Quit, Notepad, Word, Excel)

✦ Miscellaneous (Print Table, Run Query, Run Macro, Auto Dialer)

 Cross-Reference In Chapters 18 and 19, you learn to create and edit Visual Basic code with the Command Button Wizard.

To create the Contact form button using the Command Button Wizard, follow these steps:

1. Open the frmAAASwitchboard form in Design mode.

2. Make sure that the Control Wizards icon is toggled on in the toolbox. Located at the top of the toolbox, it looks like a wand with three little blue circles below it in a triangle and three black dots on a line. It should look similar to the button shown in Figure 25-5.

Figure 25-5: The Control Wizards icon button toggled on in the toolbox.

3. Click the Command Button icon in the toolbox.

4. Place the mouse pointer on the form in the form design screen, below the line object and to the top right of the image object, and draw a small rectangle. It should be immediately below the word Access.

 Note Command buttons have no control source. If you try to create a button by dragging a field from the Field List, a text box control (not a command button) is created. You must draw the rectangle or drag a macro to create a command button.

The Command Button Wizard displays the dialog box shown in Figure 25-6. You can select from several categories of tasks. As you choose each category, the list of actions under the When Button Is Pressed header changes. In addition, the sample picture changes as you move from action to action. In Figure 25-6, the specified category is Record Navigation and the desired action is Find Next.

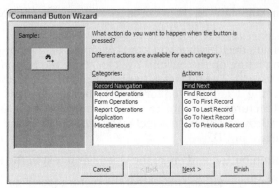

Figure 25-6: The Command Button Wizard's Categories and Actions dialog box.

5. Choose the Form Operations category and the Open Form action.

6. Click Next to move to the next screen.

The Wizard displays a list of the Access Auto Auctions database's forms.

7. Select the frmContacts form and click Next> to move to the next Wizard screen.

The next screen is a specific dialog box for this button. Because you chose the Open Form action, Access uses built-in logic to ask what you want to do now with this form. As Figure 25-7 shows, Access can automatically write a VBA program behind the button to open the form and show all records; if necessary, it can let you specify fields to search for specific values after you open the form.

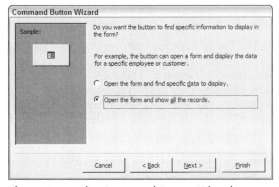

Figure 25-7: The Command Button Wizard open form with a specific data question.

8. Select Open the form and show all the records (default). Then click Next to move on.

The next screen lets you decide what you want to appear on the button. You can display text or a picture on the button. You can resize the button to accommodate any size text. The default is to place a picture on the button. You can choose from the default button for the selected action, or you can click in the Show All Pictures check box to select from over 100 pictures. You also can click on the Browse button to select an icon (.ICO) or bitmap (.BMP) file from your hard drive or CD.

9. Click on the Text option button and erase the Open Form text in the text box.

The sample button displays nothing instead of the picture (see Figure 25-8).

Figure 25-8: Selecting a picture or text for the button.

10. Click Next to move to the final Wizard screen, which lets you enter a name for the button and then displays the button on the form.

11. Enter **CommandContacts** as the name of the button and click Finish.

The button appears on the Form Design screen, as shown in Figure 25-9.

Notice the property sheet displayed in Figure 25-9. The On Click property displays *Event Procedure*, which means that a module is stored *behind* the form. You can see this VBA module library by pressing the Builder button (three dots) next to the [Event Procedure] text. Figure 25-10 shows the code created and associated with this command button.

When you click the CommandContacts button, the VBA program runs and the frmContacts form opens.

Note   A module window appears with the specific VBA program code necessary for opening the frmContacts form (see Figure 25-10). You don't need to look at this code unless you plan to change the program. To close this module window, press Alt+Q or select File ➪ Close and Return to Microsoft Access. This topic is discussed in Chapter 18.

Figure 25-9: Adding a button to the form design.

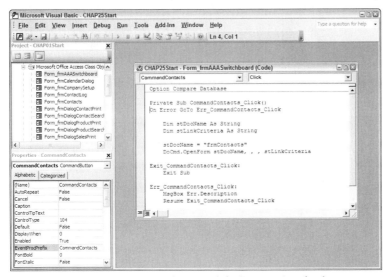

Figure 25-10: The event procedure module for opening the frmContacts form.

Note   You can create a command button and attach a macro very easily—or attach pictures—without using the wizard. However, if you want to dabble in Visual Basic, the Command Button Wizard is a great place to start.

Associate a text label with a command button

With the command button now linked to open the form frmContacts, you may want to create a label object and associate it with this button.

To associate a label with this command button, follow these steps:

1. Select the label object and place the label on the form alongside the command button you just created.

2. Change the Caption Property to **Open Contacts Form** or type this into the label object directly.

Note
Now your form should look similar to the one shown in Figure 25-11. Notice that the label has a small box to the left of it containing a yellow yield sign with an exclamation point. This lets you known that the label you have just created is not associated with a control object. If you deactivate the label control, the small yellow box will disappear until it is reactivated.

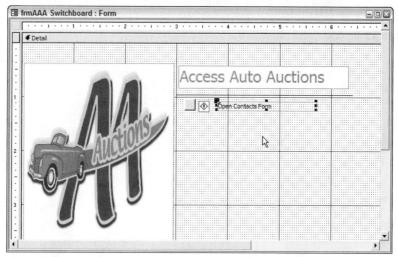

Figure 25-11: A label object added to the form to associate with the command button.

3. Select the small box with the yellow yield sign and select Associate Label with Control form the pull-down menu.

Access opens the Associate Label dialog box, similar to the one shown in Figure 25-12.

Figure 25-12: The Associate Label dialog box, open to associate a label with the command button.

4. Select the CommandContacts control object from the choices (currently the only choice) and click the OK button.

You are returned to the design surface and the label is now associated with the command button as shown in Figure 25-13.

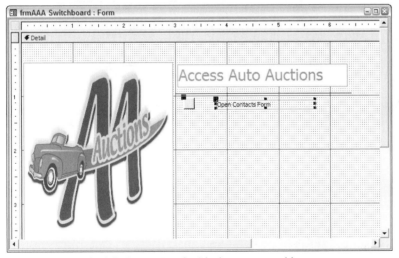

Figure 25-13: The label associated with the command button.

Copying existing command buttons and labels

You can use the Command Button Wizard, as shown on the previous page, to create the remaining buttons and their associated labels. However, it is just as easy to associate a macro or an event procedure to a command button after it is created.

For instance, you can click on the first button and choose Edit ⇨ Duplicate from the menu bar to duplicate the button. Doing this four times will place four new command buttons and their associated labels on the form under the first one—for a total of five buttons. The Exit button will be discussed later. You would then only need to change the text or graphic on each button and change the code or macro behind each button's On Click event.

Note   This only duplicates the button itself, not the code behind the button.

After you duplicate the Customer button for all the other text entries except the last one, your screen should look like the one shown in Figure 25-14. Notice that all the buttons have the same text associated with them—Open Contacts Form. However, only the first button has an actual procedure associated with it. The others have no macro or event procedure associated with them yet. You need to change the text associated with each button and assign either your own VBA procedure or a macro with them.

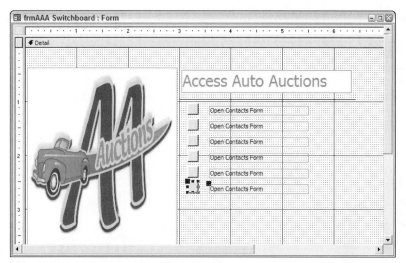

Figure 25-14: The switchboard with five buttons onscreen; all but the first one need to be modified.

Linking a command button to a macro

As soon as you create a command button in the Design window, it becomes active. You can click on it, although it doesn't perform any action unless you created it with the Wizard. Switching to the Form window by clicking on the Form button on the toolbar displays the switchboard. You can use any of the six buttons that you created in form design mode.

Each time you click on a button, it graphically pushes down, showing that it is selected. Except for the first Contacts button, however, nothing else occurs; only the button movement happens. By switching back to design mode and clicking on the Design button on the toolbar, you can link a macro to the button.

To link a command button to a macro, you enter the macro name into the property cell of one of the command button's event properties. To see the property sheet for a command button, follow these steps:

1. Select the second command button on the form. This will become the Open Sales command button.

2. If the Properties Sheet is not active, click the Properties button on the toolbar or select View ➪ Properties.

A property sheet similar to the one shown in Figure 25-15 should be visible on your screen. Notice that the event properties begin with the word *On* in the property sheet. The On Click pull-down has been selected, showing several macros available.

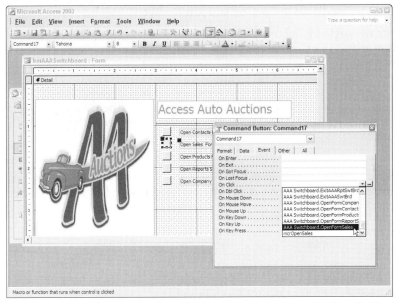

Figure 25-15: The property sheet for the second command button linking a macro to the On Click property.

The property most commonly used to link a command button to a macro is On Click. This property runs a macro whenever a user clicks the button. When the button is selected, the On Click property becomes True and the specified macro runs. To associate the OpenFormSales macro in the AAA Switchboard macro group, follow these steps:

1. Make sure the Open Sales command button is still selected.

2. In the property sheet for the command buttons, click the On Click property cell in the Event tab area.

3. Select AAA Switchboard.OpenFormSales from the list of macros in the cell and press Enter.

Make sure that both the macro group name and then the macro name separated by a period display in the On Click property.

Note   When you enter a macro name, the macro doesn't have to exist. You can enter the name of a macro that you want to create later. In this way, you can create the switchboard first and the macros later. If the macro name that you enter in the On Click cell doesn't exist when you open the form and click the button, Access displays an error message.

With the macro now assigned to the command button, you should change the text associated with it to reflect that it will open the Sales form. Follow these steps to change the text of the label:

1. While still in design mode with the property sheet open, select the second label (associated with the button you just changed).

2. Change the text of label by assigning the value Open Sales Form to the Caption property or by double-clicking on the label and changing it directly on the form.

By using these methods, you can now complete the properties for five of the form's buttons, assigning a macro for each button on the basis of the On Click property. Table 25-1 shows each button name and the procedure or macro that it calls.

Table 25-1
The Five Form Buttons and Their Procedure/Macro Names

In Rectangle	*Button Function*	*Macro Name.Macro for On Click*
Form	Contacts	Event Property (created by Button Wizard)
Form	Sales	AAA Switchboard.OpenFormSales
Form	Products	AAA Switchboard.OpenFormProducts
Form	Reports Switchboard	AAA Switchboard.OpenFormReportSwitchboard
Form	Company Setup	AAA Switchboard.OpenFormCompanySetUp

Note   The AAASwitchboard.OpenFormReportSwitchboard macro actually opens a second switchboard that has a series of reports for the system that can be selected and printed. This switchboard form will be created later in this chapter, using the switchboard manager.

The macros for the frmAAASwitchboard form

In this example, each command button opens a form by using the OpenForm macro actions. If you want to open a report, you can assign a command button a macro that uses the OpenReport macro action instead. The Exit button closes the form with the Quit macro action.

You can create each macro and its actions by following these general steps:

1. Enter a macro name in the Macro Name column. You may need to display this column if it is off.

2. Enter a macro action in the Action column (such as OpenForm, OpenReport, or Close) or select the macro action from the drop-down list box.

3. Enter a macro argument (name of the form or report) for each action.

4. Optionally, enter a remark (as a reminder) in the Comment Column.

Another way to add a macro action and argument is to drag the form or report from the Database window to the macro's Action column. Access automatically adds the correct action in the Action column, which is OpenForm or OpenReport. Access also adds the correct argument in the Name cell of the arguments.

There is a group macro already created for this chapter in the CHAP25Start.mdb database. However, if you want to create the group macro for this chapter from scratch, follow Table 25-2. This table shows each macro name, the action for each macro, and the form name. (These are shown in Figure 25-16.) The AAA Switchboard macro should already exist in the Macro Object list of the Database window.

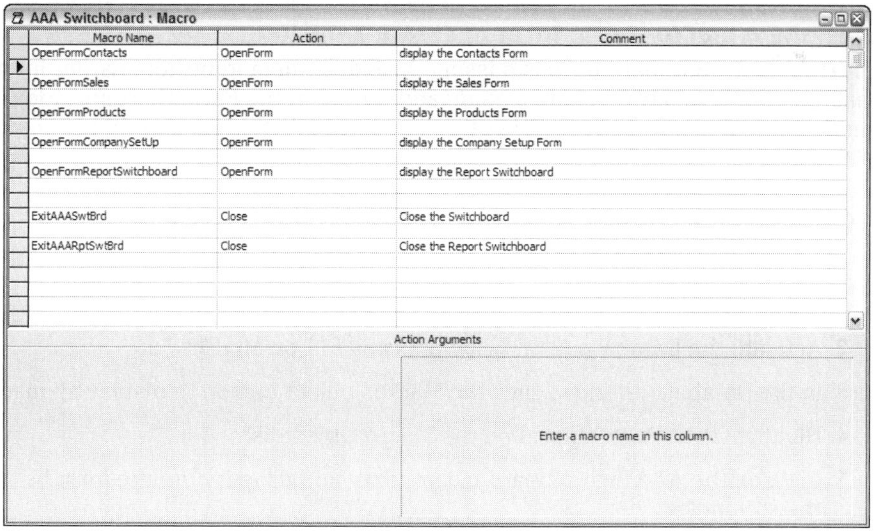

AAA Switchboard : Macro

Macro Name	Action	Comment
OpenFormContacts	OpenForm	display the Contacts Form
OpenFormSales	OpenForm	display the Sales Form
OpenFormProducts	OpenForm	display the Products Form
OpenFormCompanySetUp	OpenForm	display the Company Setup Form
OpenFormReportSwitchboard	OpenForm	display the Report Switchboard
ExitAAASwtBrd	Close	Close the Switchboard
ExitAAARptSwtBrd	Close	Close the Report Switchboard

Action Arguments

Enter a macro name in this column.

Figure 25-16: The macros used for the frmAAASwitchboard form.

Note The last macro, ExitAAARptSwtBrd, is not used by frmAAASwitchboard. However, it will be used later when you create the Report Switchboard, frmAAAReportSwitchboard, using the Switchboard Manager.

Table 25-2
Macros Used in the Group Macro

Macro Name	Action	Argument Name (Form, Report, Object)
OpenFormContacts	OpenForm	frmContacts
OpenFormSales	OpenForm	frmSales
OpenFormProducts	OpenForm	frmProducts
OpenFormCompanySetUp	OpenForm	frmCompanySetup
OpenFormRptSwitchboard	OpenForm	frmAAAReportSwitchboard
ExitAAASwtBrd	Close	frmAAASwitchboard
ExitAAARptSwtBrd	Close	frmAAAReportSwitchboard

Table 25-2 shows that the Close action, associated with the ExitAAASwtBrd macro, closes the frmAAASwitchboard form. The last macro created will be used later in this chapter when you create another switchboard using the Switchboard Manager. All, except the last macro, work with the actual frmAAASwitchboard form. You learn to create the Exit command button next.

Dragging a macro to the form to create a button

The frmAAASwitchboard form is missing the Exit command button. Earlier in this chapter, you learn a way to add a command button in the Form Design window. Another way that you can create a command button is to drag and drop a macro name from the macro Database window to a position on the switchboard.

For example, to create an Exit command button for the frmAAASwitchboard form by using the drag-and-drop method, follow these steps:

1. Enter the design mode for the frmAAASwitchboard form.

2. Activate the Database window by pressing F11 or Alt+F1.

3. In the Database window, click the Macros object button to display all macros.

4. Highlight AAA Switchboard on the Macro Object list.

5. Click on the AAA Switchboard macro; drag and drop it onto the form below the rectangles.

6. Click in the cell of the On Click property, which is under the Event tab, of the Exit button.

7. Move to the end of the macro group name and type **.ExtAAASwtBrd** or select AAA Switchboard.ExitAAASwtBrd from the pull-down menu.

8. Click on the button name and change it to **Exit**.

Your screen should now look similar to the screen shown in Figure 25-17. Notice that when you add the macro to the form using the drag-and-drop method, Access automatically creates a command button, names it the same as the macro, and places the macro name (in this case, a group name) in the On Click property of the button.

Figure 25-17: The new button that you created by dragging and dropping a macro onto the form.

When you add the macro name to the On Click property, you don't have to add the macro group name. Rather, you move to the end and place a period after the group name and then the macro name. Access automatically brings the group name into the On Click property for you.

Note   If you drag and drop a macro that is not a group macro, Access correctly places the macro name in the On Click property and names the button the same as the macro.

Caution   If you drag a macro group, as you did in this example, and do not add a macro name to the On Click property, Access runs the first macro in the macro group.

Adding a picture to a command button

The five command buttons that you create contain nothing in the Caption property of the button. The last button currently contains the text, Exit, in the Caption property of the command button. Instead of entering text in the caption property, you can have any button display a picture. For example, one of the files with the CHAP25Start.mdb is named *EXIT.BMP*, which is a bitmap of an exit sign. You can have the Exit command button show the picture EXIT.BMP rather than the word *Exit*.

To change a command button to a picture button, use one of these methods:

✦ Type the name of the bitmap (.BMP) containing the picture into the Picture property of the button.

✦ Use the Picture Builder to select from an icon list that comes with Access.

✦ Specify the name of an icon or bitmap file.

To change the Exit command button to the picture button EXIT.BMP, using the Picture Builder, follow these steps:

1. With the frmAAASwitchboard form in Design mode, click on the Exit command button.

2. Display the Property window.

3. Select the Picture property, which is under the Format tab, for the Exit button.

4. Click the Builder button (three dots on a little button).

   The Picture Builder dialog box appears. No picture initially appears in the left frame because the button that you are modifying has none. Because you are adding a picture for an Exit button, you may want to see if Access contains an Exit button. You can scroll down the list of Available Pictures, as shown in Figure 25-18. Access has an Exit picture, but it may not be what you want. You can select any bitmap or icon file on your disk.

Figure 25-18: The Picture Builder is active with the default exit button highlighted.

5. Click the Browse button.

   The Select Picture dialog box shows a standard Windows directory list. Select the directory that contains your EXIT.BMP file.

6. Select the EXIT.BMP file and click Open.

The Select Picture dialog box closes and you are returned to the Picture Builder dialog box. The new EXIT.BMP bitmap appears in the sample area. Although it doesn't fit in the sample, it should fit on the button when it is displayed. Figure 25-19 shows the EXIT.BMP in the sample area.

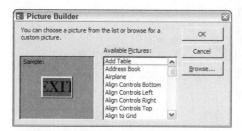

Figure 25-19: Viewing a sample bitmap in Picture Builder.

7. Click OK to accept the bitmap.

Note   Access places the path of the bitmap in the Picture property. After you save the application, however, the bitmap is no longer required to exist in the path because it is embedded in the database. You can remove the name of the path.

8. Resize the button so that the picture shows only the word *Exit*.

Your form should look like the one shown in Figure 25-20. Notice that the button has been resized and moved slightly closer to the right margin of the form in Figure 25-20. If you examine the Property Sheet in Figure 25-20, you can see that Access added the path and filename of the bitmap to the Picture property cell for the Exit button.

Tip   You also can type the filename directly into the Picture property. If Access can't find the picture file, it displays a dialog box stating that it can't find your file. If you know the drive and directory where the file is located, enter them in the Picture cell with the filename (for example, C:\Access Bible\Examples\EXIT.BMP).

This action completes frmAAASwitchboard. Save your switchboard. Your next task is to create frmAAAReportSwitchboard using the Switchboard Manager.

At this point, you could go back and add graphics to all the buttons as shown in the initial switchboard at the beginning of this chapter — Figure 25-1.

Note   You have several other bitmaps pictures with the chapter files that you can use to duplicate the Switchboard shown in Figure 25-1.

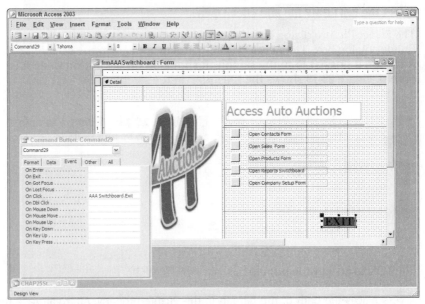

Figure 25-20: The final form with a Picture button added.

Working with the Switchboard Manager

Previously, you created a switchboard by placing all the command buttons on a new form. Access has a Wizard that allows you to create a switchboard; it is called the Switchboard Manager.

In the previous section, you created frmAAASwitchboard and placed a command button on it to open frmAAAReportSwitchboard. This form has not been created yet. You could create this switchboard the same way as you created the AAA Switchboard; however, you can also create it using the Switchboard Manager.

The Switchboard Manager lets you create a dynamic switchboard that can be modified, changed, and added to anytime during the life of your application. Figure 25-21 shows a Switchboard created with the Switchboard Manager. After it was created, the picture was embedded and a label was changed in the form design window.

Caution   The Switchboard Manager creates a special table, called *Switchboard Items*, which is used to maintain the information for the actions and choices on each switchboard. Although you can browse through and change the records in this table, you should never make changes to it unless you are thoroughly familiar with how it works.

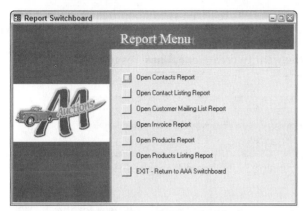

Figure 25-21: A Switchboard created with the Switchboard Manager.

Creating the Report Switchboard

Note You can skip this section unless you are interested in how the Switchboard Manager works.

To create frmAAAReportSwitchboard (as shown in Figure 25-21) using the Switchboard Manager, follow these steps:

1. Select Tools ➪ Database Utilities ➪ Switchboard Manager from the main menu as shown in Figure 25-22.

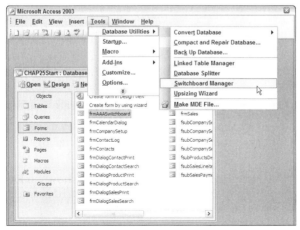

Figure 25-22: Starting the Switchboard Manager.

If this is the first time Access has created a switchboard in your application, it will show a dialog box similar to the one shown in Figure 25-23. It informs you that the Switchboard Manager could not find a valid switchboard for this database and asks if you want to create one. Click Yes to continue.

Figure 25-23: First time running Switchboard Manager dialog box.

Access will create the Switchboard Items table that it uses for the Switchboard and open the Switchboard Manager dialog box, as shown in Figure 25-24.

Caution If you have a form named Switchboard when you first run the Switchboard Manager, Access will report an error and tell you to either rename the form named Switchboard or delete it before it will begin.

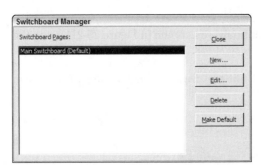

Figure 25-24: The Switchboard Manager dialog box.

The Switchboard Manager window will automatically create a default Switchboard named Main Switchboard (default).

2. With the Main Switchboard (default) switchboard name highlighted, press the Edit button.

Access opens the Edit Switchboard Page dialog box, as shown in Figure 25-25. Here you can change the name of the title bar (Switchboard Name) for the switchboard and add the individual switchboard items.

3. Click in the Switchboard Name entry field and change the name from Main Switchboard to **Report Switchboard**.

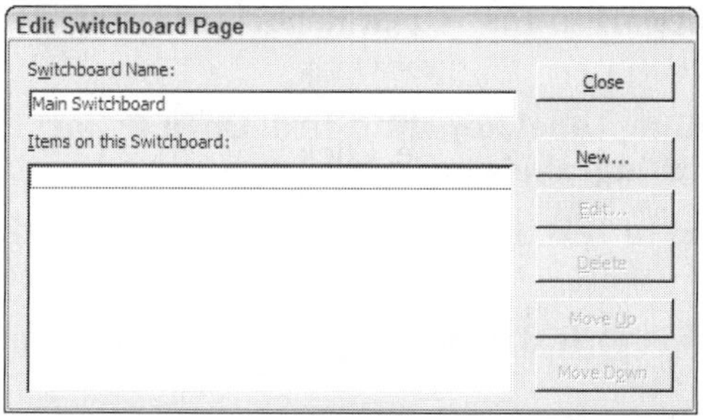

Figure 25-25: The Edit Switchboard Page
dialog box.

4. Click the New button to add the first command button to the report
   switchboard.

   Access opens the Edit Switchboard Item dialog box as shown in Figure 25-26.
   Here you can enter the text you want to associate with the command button,
   the command (or action), and Object name.

5. Change the Text entry field content from New Switchboard Command to **Open
   Contacts Report**.

6. Select Open Report from the Command entry field, as shown in Figure 25-26.

Figure 25-26: The Edit Switchboard item dialog
box with the Command pull-down menu open to
select Open Report.

7. Select rptContacts from the pull-down menu of the Report entry field.

8. Click the OK button to return to the Edit Switchboard Page.

   The first menu choice, Open Contacts Report, has now been added to your
   switchboard. Now you need to continue to add the other reports to the
   switchboard and, finally, click the Exit button.

   The remaining steps have been shortened to show the selections for each
   menu choice; simply click on the New button, add the selections as described,
   press the OK button to return, and add the next menu choice.

9. Enter **Open Contact List Report** to Text; **Open Report** to Command; **rptContactListing** to Report.

10. Enter **Open Customer Mailing Label Report** to Text; **Open Report** to Command; **rptCustomerMailingLabels** to Report.

11. Enter **Open Invoice Report** to Text; **Open Report** to Command; **rptInvoice** to Report.

12. Enter **Open Products Report** to Text; **Open Report** to Command; **rptProducts** to Report.

13. Enter **Exit – to AAA Switchboard** to Text; **Run Macro** to Command; **AAA Switchboard.ExitAAARptSwtBrd** to Macro.

At this point, the Edit Switchboard Page should look like the one shown in Figure 25-27.

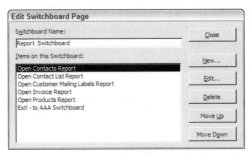

Figure 25-27: The finished Edit Switchboard Page dialog box with all seven menu items listed.

14. Click the Close Button to return to the Switchboard Manager main dialog box.

The Switchboard Manager main dialog box should now show the one Switchboard in the Switchboard pages, named Report Switchboard (default).

15. Click the Close Button to save your work and return to the database window.

Access creates two files — a table named Switchboard Items and a switchboard form with the name Switchboard.

Note   The table named Switchboard Items, as shown in Figure 25-28, is used by Access to build the switchboards that were initially created by the Switchboard Manager. You can use the Manager to create numerous switchboards that call each other or open forms and reports. All the switchboard information is stored in this table and used every time you create a switchboard or modify it. When you run the switchboard, Access uses this table to create command buttons dynamically.

Switchboard Items : Table

SwitchboardID	ItemNumber	ItemText	Command	Argument
1	0	Report Switchboard		Default
1	1	Open Contacts Report	4	rptContacts
1	2	Open Contact List Report	4	rptContactListing
1	3	Open Customer Mailing Labels Report	4	rptCustomerMailingLabels
1	4	Open Invoice Report	4	rptInvoice
1	5	Open Products Report	4	rptProducts
1	6	Exit - to AAA Switchboard	7	AAA Switchboard.ExitAAARptSwtBrd
	0			

Record: 1 of 7

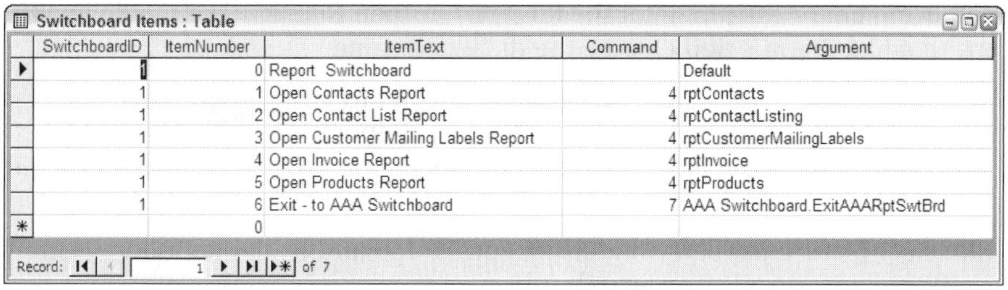

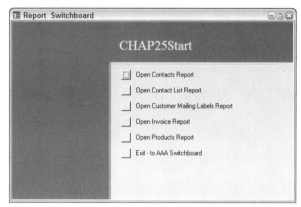

Figure 25-28: The Switchboard Items table open. This table was created by the Switchboard Manager.

With the Switchboard created, you can now run it and test the buttons. Figure 25-29 shows the Switchboard being run. If you try all the buttons, all of them should work, except the Exit button.

Figure 25-29: The Report Switchboard Items table created by the Switchboard Manager.

Modifying a switchboard in the form design window

Normally, any switchboard you create using the Switchboard Manager must have menu items edited, deleted, or added via the Manager. However, there are some cosmetic changes you can make to the switchboard form in the form designer.

Looking at the Report Switchboard form in Figure 25-29, you see that it automatically put the name of the database (CHAP25Start) in the form. It also places a picture holder to the left of the menu choices (not obvious in the figure) that you can change in the form design window. At this point, click on the Design button to add a graphic and change the label of the form. While in the design surface, follow these steps to add a graphic and change the database name:

1. Double-click anywhere in the left side of the Detail section.

   Access selects the picture object and opens the property sheet for the picture object.

2. Select Picture property under the Format tab and click the Builder button (three dots on a little button).

   Access opens the Insert Picture dialog box.

3. Select the picture file AAAfinalweb.jpg from the correct directory and press the OK button.

   Access brings the picture in and shows it in the picture object. However, the picture will appear stretched, as shown in Figure 25-30.

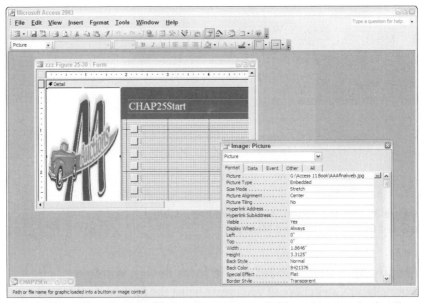

Figure 25-30: The picture added to the Report switchboard is stretched and the property sheet shows the picture name added to the Picture property.

4. Change the Size Mode property from Stretch to Zoom for the picture object.

5. Click on the label object with the Caption saying 'CHAP25Start'.

6. Change the Caption property to **Report Menu** and leave the field to make the change on the form.

Your Report Switchboard should look similar to the one shown in Figure 25-31.

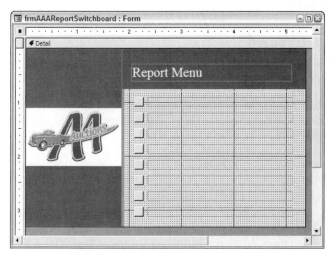

Figure 25-31: The new Report Switchboard with the label changed to Report Menu and a picture added.

Notice that the command buttons are there, but there is no text associated with them. Access fills them and their action automatically when the form is run, using the values in the Switchboard Items table.

Caution Do not attempt to add command buttons or make changes to the command buttons or their labels in a switchboard created using the Switchboard Manager. Access will ignore the changes and use those in the table.

At this time, you should save the changes you made to the switchboard and run it to verify that the changes took.

With the switchboard running, you will quickly determine that you still have not fixed the Edit button. To fix the Exit Button, you need to simply rename the name of the switchboard from Switchboard to **frmAAAReportSwitchboard**. When it is renamed, the Exit button works because the macro that is associated with the Exit command button is looking for the form named frmAAAReportSwitchboard. This macro was created earlier in this chapter when you created the macro named AAA Switchboard.

Running the form again, the Exit button works correctly; it closes the form. Because the form is supposed to be opened from the frmAAASwitchboard, it will return you to that form if it was called from it.

Now both switchboards should work correctly.

Tip   Renaming the switchboard will not affect the Switchboard Manager, because the form name of the switchboard is not used by the Manager. Rather, it uses an internal pointer to switchboard.

Editing an existing switchboard

With frmAAAReportSwitchboard created, you can add additional menu choices, change existing actions, and even delete menu choices.

To change any menu choices in the switchboard, you need to rerun the Switchboard Manager and make the changes there. For instance, to add another report (the rptProductListing report), follow these steps:

1. Open the Switchboard Manager by selecting Tools ⇨ Database Utilities ⇨ Switchboard Manager.

2. Click on the Edit button with the Report Switchboard (default) highlighted.

3. In the Edit Switchboard Page, click on the New button.

4. In the Edit Switchboard Item, enter the following values — **Text: Open Product Listings Report**; **Command: Open Report**; **Report: rptProductListing**.

5. Click the OK button to return to the Edit Switchboard Page.

6. Highlight the newest menu item — Open Product Listings Report — and press the Move Up button one time.

   Access will move the newest menu item above the Exit - to AAA Switchboard menu item. The Edit Switchboard Page dialog box should now look like the one shown in Figure 25-32.

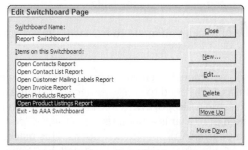

Figure 25-32: The Edit Switchboard Page dialog box with the newest menu item added and moved up one position.

7. Click the Close button to return to the main Switchboard Manager dialog box.

8. Click the Close button to return to the database container and save the changes you have made to the switchboard.

When you run frmAAAReportSwitchboard, the new report has been added, as shown in Figure 25-33.

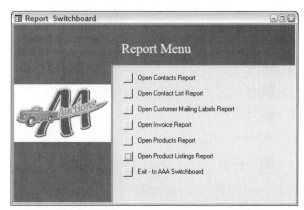

Figure 25-33: The final frmAAAReportSwitchboard with all the reports added.

In addition to adding new menu choices, you can use the Switchboard Manager to create new switchboards, delete menu items from an existing switchboard, or modify the action of a menu item in an existing switchboard.

This action completes frmAAAReportSwitchboard. Save your switchboard. Your next task is to customize the menu bar to correspond to the buttons on the switchboard so that you can make your choices from the menu or the buttons.

Creating Custom Menu Bars, Toolbars, and Shortcut Menus

Not only can you create switchboards with Access; you can also create a custom drop-down menu bar that adds functionality to your system. You can add commands to this menu that are appropriate for your application. These commands may be the actions specified in your switchboard command buttons. When you create a custom drop-down menu bar, the new bar replaces the Access menu bar.

Tip   Only a form references the menu bar; you can create a single menu bar and use it for several forms.

Figure 25-34 shows frmAAASwitchboard with a custom drop-down menu bar. Each choice on the bar menu (File, Forms, and Reports) has a drop-down menu associated with it.

Figure 25-34: The custom drop-down menu bar for frmAAASwitchboard.

You can create custom menus in Access in two ways:

✦ Use the Access Command Bar Object.

✦ Use macros (this was the only way to create menus in very early versions of Access — Access 95 and earlier).

Tip

If you previously created menus in Access 2.0 or Access 95, you can convert them to the new menu bar object by selecting the macro to be converted and then by choosing Tools ⇨ Macro ⇨ Create Menu from Macro. You also can use the other two options, Create Toolbar from Macro and Create Shortcut Menu from Macro, to create these objects.

If you have menus that you previously created in Access 97, Access 2000, or Access 2002 you don't need to convert them.

Understanding command bars

The Access Command Bar object lets you create three types of menus:

✦ **Menu Bars.** Menus that go along the top of your forms and that can have drop-down menus, too.

✦ **ToolBars.** Groups of icons generally found under the menu bars.

✦ **Shortcut Menus.** Pop-up menus that display when you right-click on an object.

Command Bars enable you to duplicate the Access user interface, including adding pictures to your menus.

Creating custom menu bars with command bars

You can create the custom menu bar that's shown in Figure 25-34 by first creating the top-level menu consisting of three elements — File, Forms, and Reports. You can create the top-level menu by selecting View ➪ Toolbars ➪ Customize, as shown in Figure 25-35.

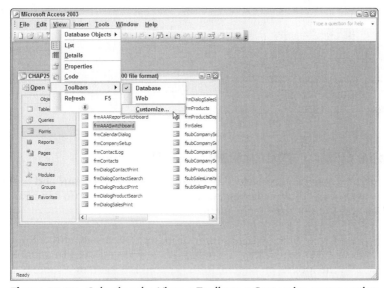

Figure 25-35: Selecting the View ➪ Toolbars ➪ Customize menu option.

If you've never really looked at an Access menu bar, Figure 25-35 is a good example because many of the menu bars have pictures in front of the text. Notice the separator lines on the View menu — you learn how to add these lines in this chapter. Also notice the check box on the toolbar's submenus. This option indicates whether the menu bar is displayed. In this example, only the Database menu bar is displayed. The Web menu bar is hidden.

Cross-Reference   You learn about Access and the Internet in Chapters 31 and 32.

Select Customize and the dialog box shown in Figure 25-36 appears.

Figure 25-36: The Customize dialog box for toolbars.

Changing existing menus and toolbars

From this dialog box, you can also select any of the pre-existing menus and toolbars and customize them by adding, removing, or moving menu items. You can also change pictures and the purpose of the menu.

To change the menu items, display the toolbar or menu that you want to change and then directly change it by clicking the menu items that you want to manipulate. If you click and hold the mouse on a menu item, a submenu item, or a toolbar icon, a little gray button appears over the top of the item. You can then move the icon to a different location by dragging it to the new location. To remove the menu item or icon, simply drag it to a place away from the toolbar. To add a new item, select the Commands tab in the Customize dialog box, find the category that contains the item you want, and then drag the item to the toolbar or menu.

You can create a whole new item by selecting All Macros or New Menu and dragging it to the menu or toolbar that you want it to be on. See the next section to learn how to add a new menu.

Creating a new menu bar

To create a new menu bar, click the New button from the Customize dialog box. A dialog box appears, asking you to name the custom toolbar. The default name is Custom 1. Name this new menu bar *AAA Custom Command Bar* and click OK.

The new menu bar is added at the bottom of the Customize dialog box and a small gray rectangle (the new menu bar) appears in the center of the screen, along side the Customize dialog box. The new toolbar name also appears in the list at the bottom of the Toolbars list, as shown in Figure 25-37.

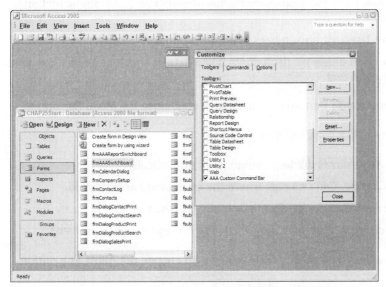

Figure 25-37: Creating a new menu bar in the Customize dialog box. Notice that the last entry in the Customize dialog box is the new toolbar you just created. The figure also shows the new toolbar to the top-left corner of the Customize dialog box.

Tip

You can move this menu to the top of the screen by dragging it so that it looks like a normal menu bar — however, it would have no items on it.

Before you begin to drag commands or text to the command bar, you must decide what type of command bar it is. Highlight the AAA Custom Command Bar under the Toolbars tab in the Customize dialog box and then click on the Properties button.

Figure 25-38 shows the Toolbar Properties dialog box. Here you can select each of the command bars in your system.

Figure 25-38: The Toolbar Properties dialog box for the AAA Custom Command Bar.

The important portion of this dialog box is the middle portion. The first option is Type. You have three Type choices:

✦ **Menu Bar.** Used for drop-down menus of commands containing text and, optionally, pictures.

✦ **Toolbar.** Used for button bars of pictures only.

✦ **Popup.** Used either for drop-down menu lists or shortcut menus; can contain pictures and text.

For this example, you want to create a menu, so choose the Menu Bar option.

The next option, Docking, has four options:

✦ **Allow Any.** Allows docking horizontally or vertically.

✦ **Can't Change.** Can't change where the command bar is docked.

✦ **No Vertical.** Can dock only horizontally (across the screen).

✦ **No Horizontal.** Can dock only vertically (up and down the screen).

For this example, you want to create a menu, so choose the Allow Any option.

The rest of the options are five check boxes:

✦ **Show on Toolbars Menu.** Displays the selected toolbar on the View ➪ Toolbars menu list.

✦ **Allow Customizing.** Allows the user to change this with the Customize menu.

✦ **Allow Resizing.** Allows you to resize a floating toolbar or menu bar.

✦ **Allow Moving.** Lets you move the menu or toolbar between floating or docking.

✦ **Allow Showing/Hiding.** Lets you show/hide the menu through the View ➪ Toolbars menu.

For this example, you can select all the choices to give the menu maximum flexibility. After you have made the selections, click the Close button to return to the Customize dialog box.

Tip   You may want to drag the new menu bar to the top of the Office window so that it shows on the toolbar menu to complete creating the AAA Custom Command Bar, as shown in Figure 25-39. Figure 25-39 shows the menu bar right below the Office toolbar on the toolbar menu.

Adding a submenu to a custom menu bar

Most menu commands are placed on submenus. It is rare for a top-level menu item to do anything but display a submenu. The submenu contains the actual menu item that — when clicked — runs the desired action, such as opening a form or printing a report.

To create a submenu menu bar, select New Menu from the Categories list box within the Commands tab section; then select the New Menu choice from the Commands list box, as shown in Figure 25-39, drag it to the AAA Custom Command Bar, and drop it. Figure 25-39 shows the New Menu command being dragged to the AAA Custom Command Bar. After it is dropped on the bar, the New Menu text appears on the menu bar. Click on the New Menu choice on the bar, and a gray rectangle appears immediately below it. This is the area where you place additional commands, under the New Menu choice. This New Menu is actually a submenu of the custom menu bar AAA Custom Command Bar.

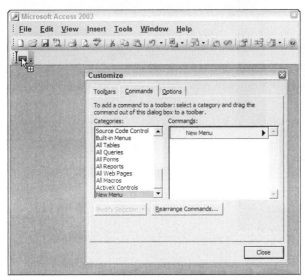

Figure 25-39: Creating a submenu using the Commands tab of the Customize dialog box.

To rename the menu name from New Menu to File, right-click on it, and then name it *File* by clicking in the Name area of the pop-up menu and changing the name from New Menu to File. Figure 25-40 shows the right-click menu with the name being changed to File. Repeat these steps to create two new submenus alongside the new File menu, and name them *Forms* and *Reports*.

After you have defined your three menus, you can add commands to the submenus. Again, you can drag the menu commands directly to the submenu area.

Dragging the New Menu item to another menu automatically links the main menu and the submenu and makes the original menu choices non-selectable. The main menu (AAA Custom Command Bar) is now permanently a menu bar. You can still change the defaults for the submenu items as you create them to display text, pictures, or both.

Caution   After you add submenus to a menu bar, you can't change it to a toolbar or pop-up menu.

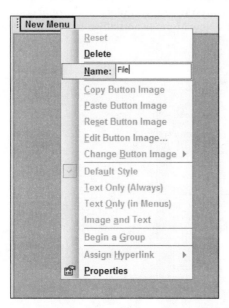

Figure 25-40: Changing the name of the submenu to File using the right-click menu.

Adding commands to a menu bar to create a submenu

You can add commands to a custom menu bar by dragging any of the preexisting commands to the menu bar, or you can add any of your tables, queries, forms, reports, or macros to the menu bar. You can add any of these items to preexisting menus as well.

Using a pre-existing command fills in all the options for you. Unless you are planning to use an action found on one of the Access built-in menus, however, you should create your own menus by first creating a new command bar and making it a menu bar, as discussed in the previous section.

After you have defined the blank submenus on the menu bar, you can drag commands to them. For this example, you may want to add the Forms menu items first.

Follow these steps to add an item to display the Contacts form when the first item is selected on the Forms menu:

1. If you are not in the Customize dialog box for toolbars, select View ⇨ Toolbars ⇨ Customize . . . to activate it. In the Customize dialog box, select the Commands tab.

2. Select All Forms from the Categories list.

3. Select frmContacts from the Commands list box on the right and drag it to the Forms menu bar. When you drop it, the text frmContacts appears on the menu bar; name it **Contacts**.

4. Repeat the process for the frmSales command; name it **Sales**.

5. Repeat the process for the frmProdocts form and name it **Products**.

Your Forms submenu commands should now look similar to the ones shown in Figure 25-41.

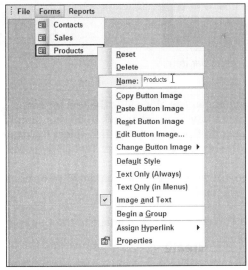

Figure 25-41: Creating command items for the submenu Forms.

Changing the look of the submenu items

When you click on the Forms menu, each of the items has a form icon along side the name of each form, as you can see in Figure 25-41. You can change how any menu item will appear in the menu. There are several options available. You can have each menu item display a graphic Image and text, Text only, or even change the graphic image along side the text.

If you right-click on any of the submenu items while the Customize dialog box is active, you can change the picture, or even change whether a picture is displayed at all. Figure 25-42 shows the Change Button Image selection of the View ⇨ Toolbars ⇨ Customize menu.

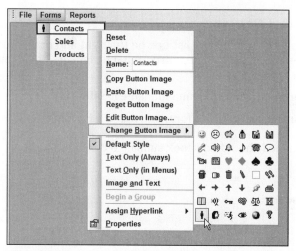

Figure 25-42: Changing the display of a menu bar item.

For the forms menu bar, you can change the image along side the text for each choice. Notice that all three button images have been changed; to do this, simply right-click each menu item, select Change Button Image, and then select the desired picture to add a new picture. To have the text only show, select Text Only (in Menus).

When working with the graphic image, the shortcut menu contains five options for changing pictures on menus or toolbar icons:

✦ **Copy Button Image.** Copies the current button face image to the Clipboard.

✦ **Paste Button Image.** Copies the current picture in the Clipboard to the button face.

✦ **Reset Button Image.** Changes the button face image to the default image.

✦ **Edit Button Image.** Uses the internal image editor to change an image.

✦ **Choose Button Image.** Changes the button face image from a list of images stored in Access.

You can change the button image in several ways. The easiest method is to select from a set of button images that Access stores internally, as shown in Figure 25-42. When you choose a picture and click OK, the button image changes.

As Figure 25-42 shows, you don't have many pictures to choose from. You can, however, create your own image and copy it to the Clipboard. After you have an image on the Clipboard, you can use the Paste Button Image option of the shortcut menu to add the image to the button. You must size the image to fit the button. You can also use the Edit Button Image to change the image after you've placed it on the button face. You can edit the button face by moving the image around and changing individual pixels of color.

As Figure 25-42 also shows, you can change the caption of the text and the way it's displayed. You have four additional options for displaying the menu or toolbar option:

✦ **Default Style.** Displays image and text for menu bars, pictures for toolbars, and both for pop-ups.

✦ **Text Only (Always).** Displays text only for menu bars and pop-ups.

✦ **Text Only (in Menus).** Displays text on menu bars, graphics on toolbars, and both on pop-ups.

✦ **Image and Text.** Displays pictures and text on menu bars and pop-ups.

Tip   To remove the images and display just text, select the Text Only choice for each submenu item.

Tip   The pop-up menu also has a Begin a Group choice. If you check the Begin a Group check box, Access places a horizontal separator line before the menu item.

You can further customize each item for your specific purpose. You can display the properties for any menu by clicking on the Properties button, as shown at the bottom of the pop-up menu in Figure 25-42. Figure 25-43 shows the properties for the Contacts Item that has been enhanced. Here, you set the rest of the actions for the menu item.

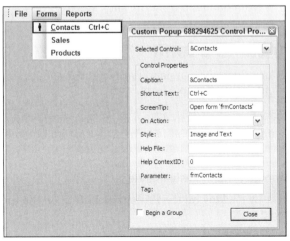

Figure 25-43: Changing the display of a menu bar item in the property dialog box.

Each menu item has a list of properties, as shown in Figure 25-43. After the Control Properties window displays, you can change the Selected Control to any of the menu items without returning to the previous menu. Changing the caption changes the text on the menu.

> **Tip** To define a hot key for the menu item, you can add an ampersand (&) in front of the hot key letter.

The caption property has been changed with the addition of an ampersand (&) in front of the letter *C*. This allows you to press the letter *C* after displaying the Forms menu in this example. Any letter can be used as a hot key by placing the ampersand before it. If you set up an AutoKeys macro list, you can also specify the shortcut text, as shown in Figure 25-43. Notice the Ctrl + C next to the Contacts menu item as well as in the shortcut text area.

You also can define the screen tip text for the control by entering text in the ScreenTip area.

The most important option is normally the On Action item. This option allows you to specify a VBA function or macro that should run when the menu item is selected. In this example, because you drag each form from the forms list to the menu, the action is already known in the Properties sheet for the item. In fact, the name of the form to open is stored in the Parameter option of the window.

The other options let you choose the Help File name and entry point if you click on Help while selecting the menu. The Parameter entry is used to specify optional parameters when calling a VBA function.

You can complete the Reports menu items by dragging the desired reports to the Reports menu item from the All Reports commands. You can add the Exit function to the File menu by dragging the Exit command from the File category.

Attaching the menu bar to a form

After you have completed the AAA Custom Command Bar menu bar and its sub-menus, you are ready to attach the menu bar to a form.

To attach a menu bar to a form, open the form in design mode and set the Menu Bar property of the form to the menu bar name. To attach the AAA Custom Command Bar menu bar to the frmAAASwitchboard - No Buttons form, follow these steps:

1. Open the frmAAASwitchboard form in design mode.

2. Display the property sheet by clicking on the Properties button on the toolbar if it is not already displayed.

3. Click on the small black box to the left of the ruler (immediately below the toolbar).

   Access displays the title *Form* for the property sheet.

4. Click on the Other tab in the property sheet and click in the Menu Bar property of the Property window.

5. Select the AAA Custom Command Bar from the pull-down menu (or type the menu bar name).

By following these steps, you attach the menu bar named AAA Custom Command Bar with its drop-down menus to the form. You should have a design screen similar to the one shown in Figure 25-44.

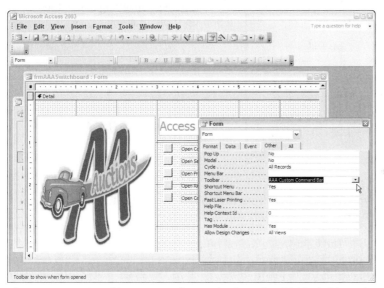

Figure 25-44: Attaching a menu bar to the form frmAAASwitchboard using the Menu Bar property.

Every time the form frmAAASwitchboard is opened, the new menu bar will automatically be displayed. Access will replace its default menu bar with the one you created. When the form is closed, the menu bar will also be closed and the Access default menu will be displayed.

Creating shortcut menus

Access allows you to create *custom shortcut menus* that open when you right-click them. These menus can replace the standard shortcut menus in Access. Shortcut menus can be defined for the form itself or for any control on the form. Each control can have a different shortcut menu.

A shortcut menu is simply another type of command bar. You can begin a shortcut menu by selecting View ➪ Toolbars ➪ Customize and then choosing the New button from the Toolbars tab of the Customize dialog box. In this example, you can name the new menu *Sales Shortcut*.

After you create the new command bar, you can select it and click on the Properties button in the Customize dialog box. The Toolbar Properties dialog box displays. Change the Type to Popup, as shown in Figure 25-45.

Figure 25-45: Creating a pop-up shortcut menu requires converting a new toolbar to a pop-up shortcut menu.

Changing the type of the toolbar from the default Menu Bar to Popup raises a message warning you that you must edit the menu items in the Shortcut Menus Custom section. Shortcut Menus is a standard Access toolbar that is found under the Toolbars tab in the Customize dialog box of toolbars, as shown in Figure 25-46. When you click on Shortcut Menus, a list of all menu bars appears on a command bar. By selecting any of these menu items, such as Database, Filter, or Form (which are shown on the left side of the menu bar in Figure 25-46), a submenu displays listing all of the shortcut menus available on the standard Access design screens. All of the shortcut menus, except the extreme right Custom submenu, are built-in pop-up menus for Access.

Looking at the Shortcut Menus toolbar, the last item on the command bar is Custom. When you click on this item, a list of all the shortcut (pop-up) menus that you have defined displays. The only shortcut menu defined prior to this point in the book is the Sales Shortcut. Notice the Sales Shortcut pop-up menu is displayed with a blank menu bar to the right of the Sales Shortcut menu. This is where you drag your selections, the same way you did for menus.

You add menu items to a shortcut menu in exactly the same way that you add any menu item. Although the empty Sales Shortcut menu rectangle displays, as shown in Figure 25-46, click on the Commands tab in the Customize dialog box and then select All Forms in the Categories list. You can then drag any command to the shortcut menu. For this example, add three forms (frmContacts, frmSales, and frmProducts) by dragging them to the menu.

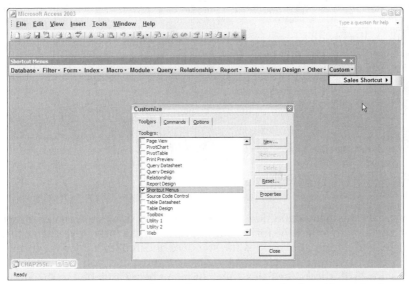

Figure 25-46: The activate list of shortcut menus is displayed by activating the Shortcut Menus toolbar.

As you add each of the forms, it appears on the shortcut menu. You can change their name and the image next to them, as you did with menus earlier. You display the menu to change the details of each of these menu items by clicking the item and then right-clicking. The shortcut menu in Figure 25-47 has been defined and each of the original form names has been changed to the more standard names for the example. It has also had a menu choice of DatabaseWindow and Access Help added from the Window and Help Categories: list box. Also notice the separator line between the forms and the last two choices. You can create this line by selecting the Begin a Group option while on the Database Window, as shown in Figure 25-47. If you want to, you can change the pictures for each of the icons next to the menu item by using the button image options.

Tip By clicking on Properties for any of the menu items, you can set the shortcut keys, ToolTips, actions, and Help file.

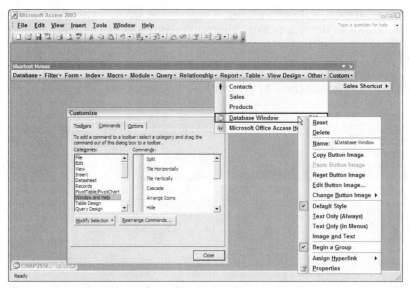

Figure 25-47: Creating and modifying the shortcut menu bar.

After you create the menu definition and save the shortcut menu, you can attach the shortcut menu to either the form or any control on the form. If you attach the shortcut menu to a form, it overrides the standard shortcut menu for the form. If you attach a shortcut menu to a control, it displays only after you right-click the control. Figure 25-48 shows the Sales shortcut menu being attached to the Shortcut Menu Bar property of the frmAAASwitchboard Buttons.

Figure 25-48: Adding the shortcut menu to the frmAAASwitchboard form.

You may also notice that the Shortcut Menu property is set to Yes. This is for either the default shortcut menus or the shortcut menus that you create. If it is set to No, you don't see any shortcut menus when you right-click.

Figure 25-49 shows the shortcut menu on the Access Auto Auctions Switchboard - No Buttons form. The menu displays to the right of wherever you clicked the mouse, even if it extends beyond the window. The actions listed in the menu macro run when you select the desired menu item.

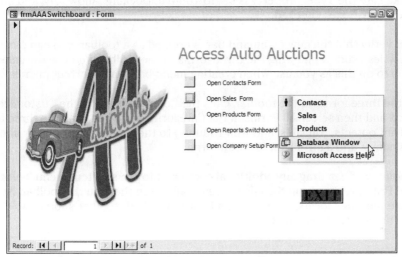

Figure 25-49: Viewing the frmAAASwitchboard with the shortcut menu active.

Note   If you want to delete a shortcut menu, you must first select the shortcut menu by displaying the list of toolbars in the View ⇨ Toolbars ⇨ Customize dialog box and then click on the Properties button. The Shortcut menus are visible only by opening the Selected Toolbar combo box at the top of the Toolbar Properties dialog box. You must change the type from Popup to Menu Bar. After you do this, you can return to the Toolbars tab, where you can now see the shortcut menu, and press the Delete button. Remember that when you change a command bar to a pop-up menu, it is visible only on the shortcut menu's Custom tab or in the Selected Toolbar list in the Toolbar Properties dialog box.

Creating and using custom toolbars

In addition to creating new menus and pop-up menus, Access lets you define new toolbars for your application and customize existing toolbars. Access also lets you customize the pictures on the buttons (known as *button faces*). For example, suppose that when you display frmAAASwitchboard, you want a toolbar that lets you open the various forms with one button push. You can create a new toolbar or even add some icons to the standard form toolbar. For this example, you create a new toolbar.

A toolbar is just another type of command bar. To create a custom toolbar, follow these steps:

1. Select View ➪ Toolbars ➪ Customize.

2. Click the New button from the Toolbars tab in the Customize dialog box.

3. Type **AAA Toolbar** in the New Toolbar dialog box and click OK.

4. Select Properties.

5. Make sure the Type: property is set to Toolbar, Docking: Allow Any, and all five check boxes checked.

After you verify that the new command bar is created as a toolbar, you can close the Properties window and drag the three forms to the toolbar. You use the same technique to do this as you use when creating menu bars and shortcut menus.

To drag the three forms to the toolbar, click the Commands tab in the Customize dialog box and then select All Forms in the Categories list. Then drag the three form names (frmContacts, frmSales, and frmProducts) to the toolbar. The toolbar shows the form names and a form icon for each form.

At this point, you can drag any additional command to the shortcut menu. Select Print and Print Preview from the File Category and drop them on the toolbar. Notice that unlike the three forms, they show an image only. Your toolbar should look similar to the one shown in Figure 25-50.

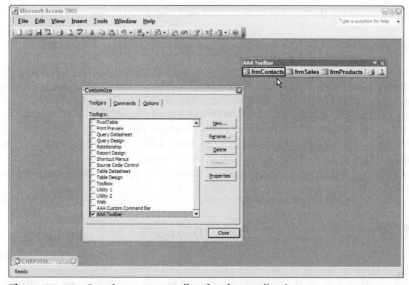

Figure 25-50: Creating a new toolbar for the application.

Tip   You can add a space and a separator line between icons by selecting Begin a Group on the icon that you want placed to the left of the line.

Note   To have a toolbar object only show the graphical image, select default style from the pop-up menu for each object.

Examining Figure 25-50, you notice that all the forms have both the graphic image and the form name on the toolbar. At this point, you can right-click on each toolbar object and change these properties. For instance, right-click on the frmContacts button; select the Change Button Image of a graphical figure and select default style. Changing these two items will make the toolbar button show the graphic of a graphical figure. You can do the same to the other two forms. To place a separator between the print button and products form, right-click on the print button and select Begin a Group.

Attaching the toolbar to a form

After you complete AAA Toolbar, you are ready to attach the toolbar to a form.

To attach a toolbar to a form, open the form in design view and set the Toolbar property of the form to the toolbar name. To attach AAA Toolbar to the frmAAASwitchboard form, follow these steps:

1. Open the frmAAASwitchboard form in design view.
2. Display the property sheet by clicking the Properties button on the toolbar if it is not already displayed.
3. Click the small blank box to the left of the ruler (immediately below the toolbar).

   Access displays the title *Form* for the property sheet.
4. Click the Toolbar property in the Property window.
5. Select the AAA Toolbar from the pull-down menu (or type the toolbar name).

By following these steps, you can attach the AAA Toolbar with its picture buttons to the form. You should end up with a design screen similar to the one shown in Figure 25-51.

When you set a form's menu bar or toolbar to a custom menu bar or toolbar, the menu bar and toolbar display automatically when you open the form. When the focus changes to another form, the custom menu bar and toolbar for the previous form are removed. The menu bar and toolbar are replaced with the newly displayed form's menu bar and toolbar if the form's properties specify them.

After you have made these changes, you display the frmAAASwitchboard, as shown in Figure 25-52. The AAA Toolbar, AAA Custom Command Bar menu, and the Sales Shortcut menu bar are all seen in the figure. A tool tip for each toolbar button will display when you hold the mouse pointer over one of the toolbar buttons.

Figure 25-51: Attaching a toolbar to the frmAAASwitchboard form using the Toolbar property.

Figure 25-52: Displaying a custom toolbar in a form.

Adding control tips to any form control

Although you must add screen tips to toolbars by using the toolbar customization windows, you can add a tool tip known as a *control tip* to any control using the form designer.

When users place their mouse pointer on a control, textual help resembling a tool tip can display with a cream-colored background. You can create a control tip by entering text into the ControlTip Text property of any control. Whatever you enter into this property displays when you place the mouse pointer on a control and pause it there for about a second.

Starting the switchboard automatically when you open the database

With the frmAAASwitchboard form created — along with the menu, toolbar, and pop-up menus associated with it — you may want to have the form automatically start up every time you open the database. There are two ways to automatically start the form every time the database is loaded: Create an AutoExec macro file, or specify the form name in the Startup options dialog box.

Running a macro automatically when you start Access

After you create the switchboard, a menu bar, and the associated submenus and toolbars, you may want Access to open the form automatically each time you open the database. One method to automatically load a form at startup is to write an AutoExec macro. When Access opens a database, it looks for a macro named AutoExec. If the macro exists, Access automatically runs it. To create an AutoExec macro to open the switchboard automatically, follow these steps:

1. Create a new macro (you name it *AutoExec* later).

2. Type **Minimize** (or select the action) in the next empty Action cell.

   This command will minimize the database window when it is first loaded.

3. Type **OpenForm** (or select the action) in the next empty Action cell.

4. Type **frmAAASwitchboard** (or select the switchboard form name) in the Form Name cell in the Action Arguments pane.

Save the macro with the name *AutoExec*. After you do this, Access runs the macro automatically each time you open the database.

The AutoExec macro shows two actions. The Minimize action minimizes the Database window, and the OpenForm action opens the switchboard.

This method has the advantage of assigning multiple actions to be performed when first starting a database. In this case, you minimized the database window before opening the switchboard form.

Tip To bypass an AutoExec macro, simply hold down the Shift key while you select the database name from the Access File menu.

Controlling options when starting Access

Rather than run a macro to open a form when Access starts, you can use the Access startup form to control many options when you start Access, including:

✦ Changing the text on the title bar

✦ Specifying an icon to use when Access is minimized

✦ Global custom menu bar

✦ Global custom shortcut menu bar

✦ Displaying a form on startup (for example, the application's switchboard)

✦ Controlling the display of default menus, toolbars, the Database window, and the status bar

Figure 25-53 shows the Access Startup dialog box. You can display this by selecting Tools ➪ Startup or by right-clicking the border of the Database window and selecting Startup.

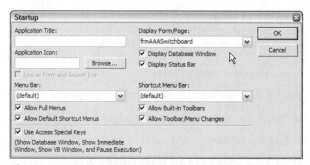

Figure 25-53: The Startup dialog box for the database.

Tip You can bypass the options in the Startup dialog box by holding the shift key while starting the database.

Note If you uncheck Display Database Window in the Startup dialog box, the database will not be displayed and when you leave the Switchboard program, it will still not be visible.

Creating a Print Report Dialog Box Form in Visual Basic

A dialog box is also a form, but it's different from a switchboard in that the dialog box usually displays information, captures a user entry, or lets the user interact with the system. In this section, you create a complex dialog box that prints reports.

By using a form and some event procedure code, you can create a dialog box that controls printing of your reports. For example, the products dialog box in Figure 25-54 displays a list of choices so that you can print only one product's record, all products, or a product listing.

Figure 25-54: A Products Print Reports dialog box.

Although this dialog box is more complex than a switchboard, it uses the same types of Access objects, which include the following:

✦ Forms

✦ Form controls and properties

✦ Event procedures

Creating a form for printing products

The form that you create in this example displays the various controls. The form contains three basic sections.

The upper-left corner of the form contains three option buttons, which are placed within an option group titled Print Choices. The option buttons let you select one of the three listed printing choices. If you select All Products, you can print or preview that report. If you select Current Product Only, as shown in Figure 25-54, you can print or preview only the current record.

The upper-right corner of the form contains two buttons. The first option button, Print Preview, can be passed to a simple event procedure as a value to open the report in Print Preview mode. The second option button, Print, will pass a value to the same event procedure to print the choice selected in the first section to the default printer. These values are passed when the user presses the Print button contained in the final section of the form.

To create a printer dialog form, first create a blank form and size it properly by following these steps:

1. Create a new blank form unbound to any table or query.

2. Resize the form to ½ inches x 3 inches.

3. Change the Back color to dark gray.

With the basic dimensions created, place three rectangles on the form to give it a distinctive look. You can create the three rectangles by following these steps:

1. Click on the Rectangle button in the toolbox.

2. Using Figure 25-54 as a guide, create three separate rectangles.

   The first two rectangles are approximately 1 inch high, and the third is about ¾-inch high.

Each rectangle in this example is shown with the Raised special effect. To create this effect, follow these steps:

1. Select a rectangle.

2. Change the Back color to light gray.

3. Click on the Raised special-effect button in the Special Effect window.

4. Click on the Transparent button in the Border Color window for the first two rectangles (leave the third one solid).

5. Change the Border Width to 2 pt for the first two rectangles. Leave the third rectangle's width set to hairline.

6. Repeat Steps 1 through 5 for the second and third rectangles.

7. Finally, to enhance the Raised special effect, drag each rectangle away from the adjacent rectangles so that the darker background of the form shows between the rectangle borders. You may need to resize one of the rectangles to line up the edges.

Creating the option group

After you create the form and the special effects, you can create the necessary controls.

The first set of controls is the option group. In Chapter 9, you learn to use the Option Group Wizard to create option buttons. To create the option group and option buttons, follow the steps given here and use Figure 24-54 as a guide. In this example, the option group buttons are not bound to a field; they are used to select the specific type of report to print — not to enter data:

1. Click the Option Group button in the toolbox, making sure that the Control Wizard icon is on.

2. Draw an option-group rectangle within the left side of the upper rectangle, as shown in Figure 25-54.

3. Enter Current Product Only, All Products, and Product Listing as three separate labels in the first Option Group Wizard.

4. Click the Finish button to exit the wizard screen.

   Your option buttons and the option group appear in the first rectangle. You may need to move or resize the option group's box to fit properly. You may also need to change the color and caption for the "Print Choices" label for the option group.

5. With the Option group selected, change the name of the control to grpTypeOfPrint in the Property Sheet.

   This name will be used in your event procedure.

With the first Option Group created, you can create the second object group alongside the first, in the right side of top rectangle. This group should have Print Preview and Print as the two separate labels in the second Option Group Wizard. Then change the name of the caption to "Print Destination." Name this option group grpTypeOfOutPut; this name will be used in your event procedure.

Creating two text boxes on the print report form

The next controls that you need in the dialog box are the two text boxes in the center rectangle. These text boxes are used to capture two title lines from the user for the report. To create the text boxes, using Figure 25-54 as a guide, follow these steps:

1. Click on the Text Box button in the toolbox.

2. Using Figure 25-54 as a guide, create the first text box in the middle rectangle.

3. Move the label control to a position above the text box if necessary.

4. Change the name of the control to txtFirstTitle to be used by the event procedure.

5. Change the caption of the associated label to First Title:.

6. Repeat Steps 1 through 5 for the second text box, placing it below the first and changing the name of the control to txtSecondTitle and its label to Second Title:.

Creating command buttons

After you complete the option group, the option buttons, and the text boxes, you can create the two command buttons. These pushbuttons trigger the actions for your dialog box. Figure 25-54 shows the two buttons:

✦ **Print.** Prints the selected report to the default print device.

✦ **Cancel.** Closes the dialog box without printing any report.

To create each command button, follow the next set of steps. Because each button is the same size, duplicate the second button from the first:

1. Turn the Wizard off; then Click the command button in the toolbox.

2. Create the first command button, as shown in Figure 25-55.

3. Select Edit ➪ Duplicate to duplicate the first command button.

4. Move the button to the right of the first.

   You now need to change the command button captions. The remaining steps show how to make these changes.

5. Select the first command button and change the Caption property to &Print.

6. Select the second command button and change the Caption property to &Cancel.

   You now need to change the name of each button.

7. Select the first command button and change the Name property to cmdPrint.

8. Select the second command button and change the Name property to cmdCancel.

Before continuing, you should save the form. Save the file but leave the form onscreen by selecting the menu option File ➪ Save. Name the form *frmDialogProductPrint*.

Note   This form already exists in the CHAP25Start database. You can assign a different name to the one you created—perhaps frmProductPrintDialog, to continue with this section.

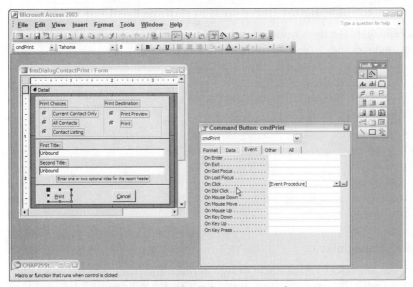

Figure 25-55: The dialog box with all the pieces in place.

When you have completed the form, you are halfway done. Your next task is to create the event procedures and attach them to the two command buttons. You can specify the event procedures to the correct event properties of the two command buttons on the form.

Creating the Print event procedures

Event procedures are attached to the events of controls or objects. These events include entering, exiting, updating, or selecting a control. In this example, the event procedures are attached to command buttons of the form.

In Chapter 23, you learned how to create subroutines using Visual Basic for Applications. The event procedures used for this dialog box are similar.

Creating the Print Event procedure

The Print command button, cmdPrint, simply calls an event procedure when the user presses the button.

To create the code, follow these steps:

1. While in design mode for the form frmDialogProductPrint, activate the Property Sheet.

2. Select the Print command button.

3. Click in the On Click event property under the Event tab.

4. Click on the build button (three dots) to start the Event Procedure.

Access displays the Choose Builder dialog box, like the one shown in Figure 25-56.

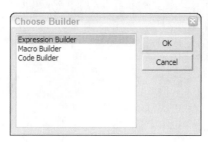

Figure 25-56: The dialog box to select which type of builder you want to work with.

5. Select Code Builder.

Access Microsoft Visual Basic design surface and place a skeleton on the screen with the name of the subroutine [Private Sub cmdPrint_Click() ... End Sub].

6. Type in the following code between the Private Sub .... End Sub:

```
Dim ReportDest As Integer
Me.Visible = False
If Me![grpTypeOfOutput] = 1 Then
    ReportDest = acPreview
Else                    ' Destination is printer
    ReportDest = acNormal
End If
Select Case Me![grpTypeOfPrint]
 Case 1
DoCmd.OpenReport "rptProducts", ReportDest, ,
"[chrProductID]=[Forms]![frmProducts]![txtProductID]"
 Case 2
  DoCmd.OpenReport "rptProducts", ReportDest
 Case 3
  DoCmd.OpenReport "rptProductListing", ReportDest
End Select
Exit Sub
```

This code is fairly easy to understand. The first line simply dimensions (or declares) the variable ReportDest as an integer.

The next line, Me.Visible = False, is used to hide the print dialog box.

The next few lines (If .... Else ... Endif) look at the value of the button option group to determine if it should print the report to the printer (value 2, or not 1) or display in print preview (value 1). It looks at the grpTypeOfOutput object you named for the button object grouping.

The next few lines (Select Case ... End Select) look at the value of the button option group for the Type of Choice to determine if it should print the current product only, print the entire list of products, or create a product list report. It looks at the grpTypeOfPrint object you named for the button object grouping. If the grpTypeOfPrint value is one, it will print only the current product. The code immediately after the Case 1 line should be on one continuous line (rather than two as shown above). The first two Cases use the rptProducts report and the last choice uses the rptProductListing report.

That is all there is to the code. The other fields in the frmDialogProductPrint form are picked up by the report program to print the headings.

Creating the Cancel Event procedure

The Cancel command button, cmdCancel, also calls an event procedure when the user presses the button.

To create the code, follow these steps:

1. Select the Cancel command button.

2. Click in the On Click event property under the Event tab.

3. Click on the build button (three dots) to start the Event procedure.

   Access displays the Choose Builder dialog box, like the one in Figure 25-56.

4. Select Code Builder.

   Access Microsoft Visual Basic design surface and place a skeleton on the screen with the name of the subroutine [Private Sub cmdCancel_Click() ... End Sub].

5. Type in the following code between the Private Sub ... End Sub:

   ```
   DoCmd.Close
   ```

That is all the code that is needed for the Cancel button. Simply close the form and return to whatever program called it.

Creating dialog boxes to obtain user input and then pass those values on is a relatively easy way to communicate between products. In this case, you built a dialog box that printed reports based on user input. Dialog boxes can be used as a way to let a user search for a specific record, find it, and return to the calling program. The Access Auto Auctions system has several dialog boxes that are used to search and print based on user input. They are already created for you with their underlying code in the forms container of the database. They all begin with frmDialog.

✦   ✦   ✦

Programming Continuous Forms, Tab Dialogs, and Command Buttons

CHAPTER

26

◆ ◆ ◆ ◆

In This Chapter

Creating a tab
control

Working with
continuous forms

Programming tab
controls

Creating and
programming
command buttons

◆ ◆ ◆ ◆

Up to this point, you have learned how to create professional forms and reports. In the last few chapters, you have learned how to add programmed routines to your forms. In this chapter, you will learn to automate some of the tasks that too often are left to the user to learn, and you will use the Access user interface. Although Access has a great user interface that allows a knowledgeable user to control nearly anything on a form, it is better to provide a simple set of buttons for your specific application that the user can consistently follow from task to task.

In this chapter, you will work with the frmProducts form that you created in Chapters 8 through 12. You will enhance it by adding a tab control to the form and moving all of the controls to the first tab in the tab control. You will view a continuous form that lists all of the products, and then you will embed the form on a subform that you create on the second page of the tab control. This continuous form will contain a button that you will program to change tabs and display the current record in the continuous form. Finally, you will add several buttons to the form footer and program them to do routine tasks such as create a new record, delete the current record, and display a search or print dialog box.

On the CD-ROM To begin this chapter, open the database file named Chap26Start.mdb. This file contains the frmProducts form and table, ready for you to add the tab control and already created continuous form named fsubProductsDisplayAll (without the necessary code you will add).

Working with Tab Controls

Tab controls (also known as tabbed dialog boxes) are one of the most used controls today, after the basic text box. They provide a seamless way to take advantage of precious screen real estate while allowing you to divide your form into logical sections. A tab control can have a nearly endless number of tabs in multiple rows. You can control the placement of each tab as well as the number of rows, the width of the tabs, and even how the tabs look and behave.

To begin this chapter, open the form frmProducts in design view.

As you can see in Figure 26-1, there are many controls on this form. These controls are in the Detail section of the form. You can think of a form itself as a foundation. The controls on a form can be thought of as the first story or layer. These controls sit on the form just as the first story of a building sits on the foundation. When you add a subform control to a form, it creates its own layer. The controls on a subform's form can be thought of as a second story. The same is true for a tab control and each of its pages. The tab control itself sits on the form, but the controls that are placed on each page make up a separate layer. However, unlike a subform whose controls must be referenced *through* the subform control name, controls on pages of a tab control can be referenced directly.

The next step will be to create the tab control and copy all of the controls currently in the Detail section to the first page you will create in the tab control. Before you create the tab control, you should cut the controls from the form, because it is more difficult to move them after you create the tab control.

1. Select all the controls in the form's detail section.

   The best way to do this is to place your cursor in the top left corner of the Detail section and then highlight all of the controls within the section. If you choose Select All from the Edit menu, you will get all of the controls in all of the sections.

2. Select Edit⇨Cut from the form design menu. (You can also press Ctrl-X to cut the controls to the clipboard.)

   Your controls in the Detail section should all disappear. They are held safely in the clipboard, including their control names, all of their relative placement information, and their formatting. Any code behind the controls remains with the form itself.

Caution When you paste the controls back onto the form after you create the tab control, any events behind these controls must be reconnected to the code behind the form by clicking into each event and selecting Event Procedure.

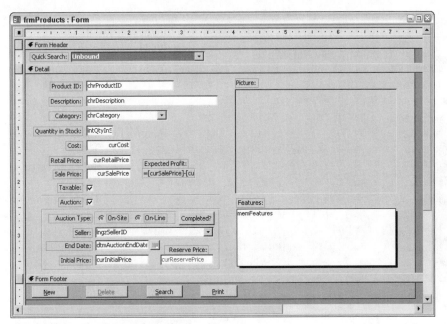

Figure 26-1: The frmProducts form

Tip   You can see a list of all your procedures by opening the Visual Basic code window and looking at the procedures using the General selection in the left combo box. Each of the orphaned event procedures are listed with the control name and event. This is also a good way to spot orphaned procedures that were created and later had the control to which they were connected, renamed, or deleted.

Creating a tab control

The Detail section of your form should be blank if you followed the previous steps. The controls from your Detail section should be safely stored in the clipboard. You can now create your tab control.

1. Display the form toolbox.

2. Select the tab control.

3. Use the tab control tool cursor to draw a rectangle from the top left to the bottom right of your Detail section, as shown in Figure 26-2.

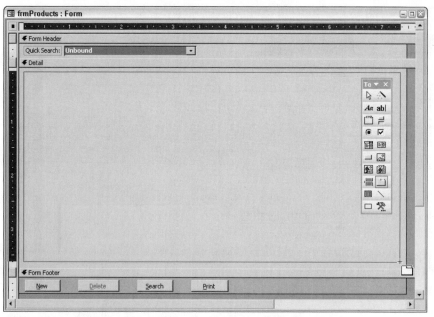

Figure 26-2: Adding a tab control

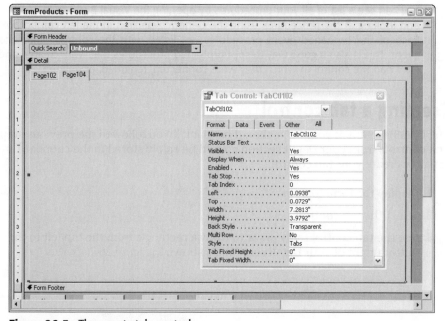

Figure 26-3: The empty tab control

When you release the mouse, your tab control appears as shown in Figure 26-3. Two tab control pages are shown. This is the default number of tabs. You can add as many tab pages as you need — and even create multiple rows of tabs. When the tab control is created with two default pages, there are actually three controls created: the tab control itself, page 1, and page 2. Each of these controls has its own name and other properties. The properties specific to the tab control are shown at the bottom of the property window in Figure 26-3.

The tab control itself is named TabCtlxxx. Each tab control page has a default name of Pagexxx, where xxx is a three digit number, dependent on a lot of things outside your control. You can change the Name property of each page and of the tab control itself.

You can set several properties for a tab control that change the look of the tab area of the control. See Table 26-1.

Table 26-1 Tab Control Properties	
Tab Control Property	**Explanation**
Back Style	Determines the color of the area below the tabs themselves. The tab area is standard windows gray and cannot be changed.
	Transparent: Shows the background through the area below the tabs.
	Normal: Displays the area below the tabs in the same gray color as the tabs themselves.
Multi Row	Determines if multiple rows are displayed when the number of tabs exceeds the width of the tab control. You can change the width of each tab by using the Tab Fixed Height option. You have little control over which tab is in which row. By changing the order of the tabs (by using each tab page's Page Index property), you can determine the order of the tabs, and by watching the width of the tab control itself and the width of the tabs, you can usually move tabs to desired rows.
	Yes: Multiple Rows are allowed.
	No: Only one row is allowed.

Continued

Table 26-1 *(continued)*	
Tab Control Property	*Explanation*
Style	Specifies the visual look of the tab area.
	Tabs: The default look. Shows the tabs as in Figure 26-3. Each tab looks like a file folder tab with the currently selected page appearing to be in front of the other tabs.
	Buttons: Appears as little raised rectangles sitting at the top of the tab control area. The selected tab button is depressed like a toggle button.
	None: The tabs are invisible and do not appear above the tab control area. The tab pages must be manipulated with code. This setting is used when you want to programmatically control what users see without giving them the ability to select each page. Can also be used when a large number of controls need to be viewed on a single form but in specific groups.
Tab Fixed Height	0" displays the tabs as normally viewed. Really small numbers (.001) can also hide the tabs, and large numbers (such as 2") can make them large.
Tab Fixed Width	0" displays the tabs based on the amount of text in each tab page's Name or Caption property. Any other number makes all the tabs the same width. Used to fill out the tabs across an entire area or to manipulate their location on one or more rows.

Changing the tab control page properties

If you click on a tab control page, you can see that it has some properties specific to that page. The most important properties are Caption, Picture, Picture Type, and Page Index. The Caption property lets you change the text in each tab.

1. Select the first tab and change the Caption to Product.

2. Select the second tab and change the Caption to Show All Products.

The Picture property allows you to add a picture or icon to the left side of each tab. The pictures are not resizable and must already be small enough to fit on the tab. You select the pictures the same way you select any picture, by clicking on the builder button in the property and selecting a built-in picture file from the Picture Builder or an external .bmp or .ico file from the available browse file dialog box.

The Picture Type property lets you embed a picture from an external source or link to an external picture to save space within the .mdb file.

The Page Index property lets you determine the order of the tabs. The tabs generally are numbered from 0 to the number of tabs –1. If you change the Page Index property to a different number, it can change the order of the tabs. You could change the first tab's Page Index property to 11 and the second to 6, which would switch the order of the tabs.

Tip   It is good to keep the tab pages in a sequential order. In order to programmatically change tabs, you can reference the Page Index property. It is a lot easier if the Page index numbers correspond to the visual order of the tabs.

Copying controls from a Detail section to a tab control page

Now that you have created the tab control on the form, you can paste the controls you previously cut to the clipboard back to the tab page you want. Follow the steps below to paste the controls on the first tab page:

1. Click on the first tab (which should be labeled Products).

   The property window should display the properties from the first page to show that you have successfully selected the first page of the tab control and not the tab control itself.

2. Select Paste from the Edit menu (or press Ctrl-V).

The controls cut from the form now appear on the first tab page. You may need to move the group of controls slightly to place them beginning in the upper left portion of the tab control's first page. You may also want to adjust the placement of the tab control itself and the space to the right and below the Detail section to give the control good visual placement. By adding space all around the control, you enhance the three-dimensional look of the control. A tab control should never be simply stuck up in the top left corner of a form.

Caution   Make sure you have selected the tab control page. If you have incorrectly selected the tab control itself, any controls pasted to the control will actually be pasted to the tab control and not to any of the pages. The controls will be displayed on all pages.

Tip   If you want to display a control such as a label that you want displayed on all tab pages, place the control on the tab control itself and not on any specific page.

Figure 26-4 shows these controls on the first tab page.

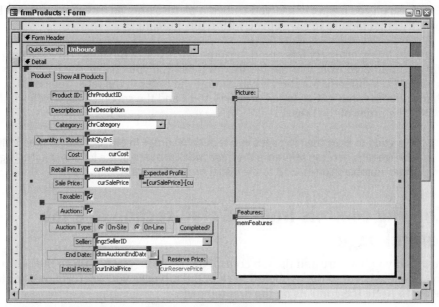

Figure 26-4: Placing the controls on the tab page

Programming Continuous Forms

In the example database Chap26Start.mdb, there is a form named fsubProductsDisplayAll, as shown in Figure 26-5. This form contains selected controls from the frmProducts form. The form Default View property is set to Continuous Forms so that all the records in the underlying tblProducts table can be viewed together. The important controls in this form are the two buttons at the beginning of the line.

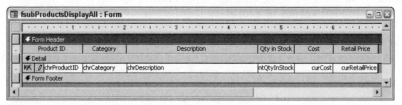

Figure 26-5: The fsubProductsDisplayAll subform in design view

The first button contains code to delete the current record. You will see this code later in this chapter. The second button contains code to display the entire record on the first page. Although the Quick Search combo box works well at the top of the frmProducts form, this is another way of viewing all your records and quickly selecting one record.

This subform also contains code to quickly re-sort the data by each of the columns in the subform. This code is linked to the OnClick event of each label in the Form Header section of the subform. All the code for the buttons and labels is already coded for you behind the subform. It will all be explained in the following pages.

This form will be used as a subform in the tab control, so the first task is to create a subform control on the tab control's second page and then select this subform in the subform control's Source Object property.

Embedding a subform in a tab control

You create a subform control in a tab control page the same way you create a subform control in any form's Detail section:

1. Select the second page of the tab control.

   Make sure you have selected the second tab itself, or the subform will be placed on the tab control itself and display on every page.

2. Select the Subform/Subreport control from the toolbox.

3. Draw a subform rectangle within the tab control page, as shown in Figure 26-6.

   Using the SubForm Wizard that is displayed, select Use an existing form, and choose the fsubProductsDisplayAll form.

   This automatically fills the Source Object property of the subform control with the fsubProductsDisplayAll form name.

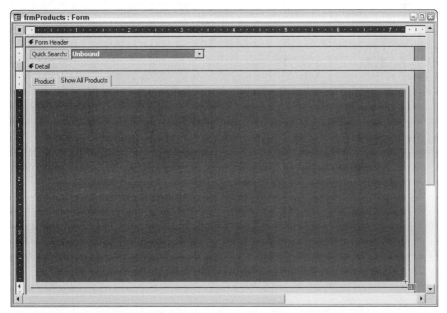

Figure 26-6: Creating a subform control

4. Press Next to move to the next wizard screen.

This screen displays only when you place a subform in the Detail section of a form. It is used to create a parent-child subform link to filter the data displayed in the subform to match the data in the main form. In this example, you do not want a link. You want to show all the records in a continuous form so that you can see all of the records.

5. Select Choose from a list, and then choose None from the list of links.

None will be the last selection in the list. When you choose None, you will see all of the records in the continuous form.

6. Press Finish.

The subform control is created with the fsubProductsDisplayAll form as the Source Object. You should see the actual form (fsubProductsDisplayAll) in the subform control, as shown in Figure 26-7. Sometimes, you only see a gray box and you have to leave the form and reopen it.

Before continuing and learning how to add code to the various buttons on the subform, view the form in form view by pressing the View button on the toolbar (the first button) and choosing Form View. Then select the second tab (Show All Products). Your form should look like the one shown in Figure 26-8.

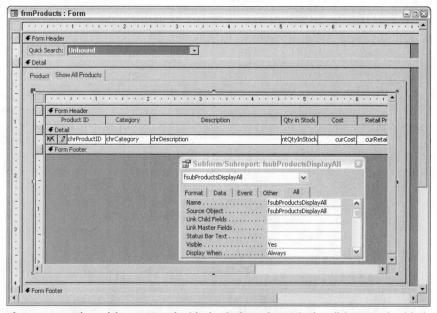

Figure 26-7: The subform control with the fsubProductsDisplayAll form embedded in it

Referencing Controls in a Tab Control and Subform

When you reference controls within a tab control, you can simply reference the controls as if they were on the form itself. When you reference a control within a subform, you must first reference the subform control itself. For example, to reference the control named txtProductID in the first tab, you would use the following reference:

```
Forms!frmProducts!txtProductID
```

However, if you want to reference the same control on the second tab, which contains the subform, you would have to use the following reference:

```
Forms!frmProducts!fSubProductsDisplayAll.Form!txtProductID
```

Referencing controls on any subform requires you to reference the control through the subform control and the .Form parameter, regardless of whether or not it is embedded in a tab control. Although the tab control is not a *container* type control, the subform control is.

If you don't see the tabs separated by space on all four sides, you should move the tab control away from the top or left borders. If there is too much space to the right or below the tab control, you should adjust the form borders so that there is equal space around the control. When you have the form exactly as you want it displayed, press the Save button (second from the right) on the form view toolbar, which will *lock in* the size of the form window.

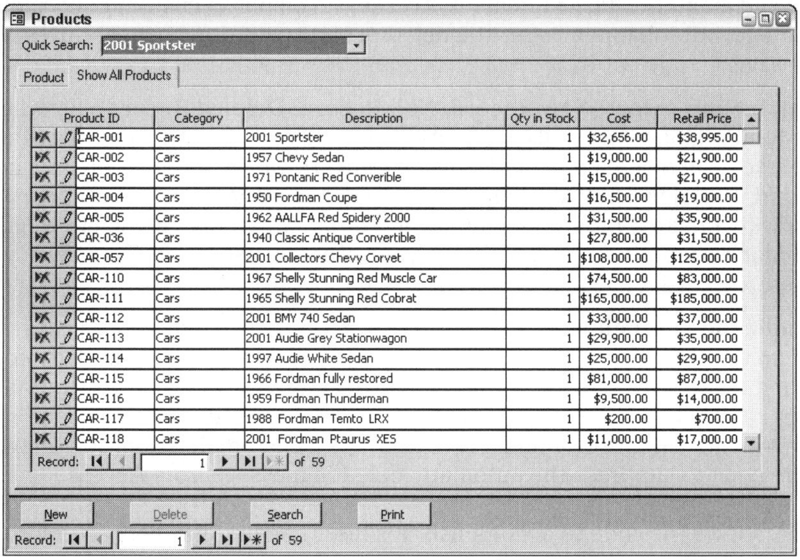

Figure 26-8: The frmProducts form's Show All Products tab

Creating code to delete a record from a continuous form

In the continuous form, there is a command button that has been created. Code will be entered behind the On Click event to confirm that the user really wants to delete the record and then the code will delete the record.

There are several ways to delete a record. Generally, you are going to use the following command:

```
RunCommand acCmdDeleteRecord
```

This command can be run as long as a single record is currently selected. Sometimes, you have to explicitly select a record by using the following command:

```
RunCommand acCmdSelectRecord
```

However, if you are sitting on a record (for example, when you press a Delete button on a continuous form's line), you can simply run the RunCommand acCmdDeleteRecord statement.

Good coding means that you always want to think about more than just the simple task at hand. When deleting a record, you always should do a few things first:

✦ **Confirm the delete:** This means that you want to ask users if they are sure that they want to delete the record. You can do this with a simple message box and an If-Then-Else statement. Access can display a custom confirmation message, but it happens after the deletion and is not the most user-friendly message.

✦ **Trap for any errors (New Record, Null Record, Deleted Record):** If you use the RunCommand acCmdDeleteRecord and the cursor is on a record with a valid key, the delete command will work fine. However, if the record is a new record, contains a null key value, is deleted, has a referential integrity problem with a related table value, or several other situations, the delete will fail. If you don't properly trap for an error, your program will crash. Whenever you delete a record, you must trap for a possible error.

✦ **Handle the post-delete message:** Whenever you delete a record, Access will automatically confirm the delete as it is happening. If you have already confirmed the delete before you run the delete code, you will want to stop Access from confirming the delete a second time. (This becomes user-interface harassment.) In this example, you will create a custom deletion, so you will write code to suppress the automatic deletion message from Access.

Figure 26-9 shows the code to accomplish this task. The first line sets an error trap in case there are any problems. The error trap would trigger the message box at the bottom of the code window. The Dim statement sets up a variable to use to confirm the delete.

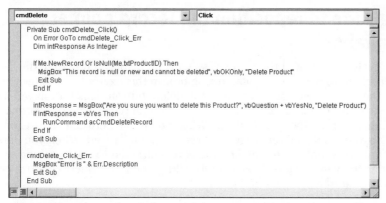

Figure 26-9: The code window to delete a record in the continuous form

The second block of code checks to make sure the line is not a new record or a null record. In this continuous form, because new records are not allowed to be created, this should be an impossible situation. But if the form property is ever changed, this code is ready. The code uses the NewRecord method of a form and the IsNull function to check both conditions. If either condition is True, a message box is displayed to let the user know the record cannot be deleted, and the program exits the procedure.

The program continues if the record can be deleted, and a message box is displayed to collect a response and set it to the variable previously dimensioned. The message box confirms if you want to delete the product and if the response is vbYes (the user clicks on the Yes button in the message box), the command is run to delete the record. There is no Else clause, so if the user presses the No button in the message box, the program just ends and nothing happens.

There is one more task for any delete procedure that uses a custom confirmation message. The code goes behind the form's BeforeDelConfirm property, as you can see in Figure 26-10. The code goes behind the BeforeDelConfirm property of the form because it is a form event. The simple two lines of code use built-in variables to stop the automatic delete message.

Figure 26-10: The code window to suppress Access's automatic confirmation message

Creating code to reposition the record pointer between tabs

The next task is to understand the many ways you can display a record in the same form in different views when using a tab dialog box. In this example (as shown in Figure 26-8), there is another button next to the delete button. This button will be used to change from the continuous form showing all the records on the second tab to the one complete record on the first tab. When you move between records on the second tab, the displayed record in the first tab is unchanged. When you press the button, the record pointer on the first tab is repositioned to the matching record by using the value of the chrProductID field in the txtProductID control on the form, as you can see in Figure 26-11.

Figure 26-11: The code window to reposition the record pointer on the main form

A variable named strProductID is set to capture the value of the txtProductID control on the continuous form. Focus is moved to the main form's txtProductID control. Rather than use Forms!frmProducts, the Parent method is used, which moves from the subform to the main form that contains the subform. This way, if you ever rename the main form, you do not have to change the code.

Tip
Any time you need to reference the main form from a subform, use the Parent method instead of the Forms!formname method. You cannot use Me because that would refer to the subform.

Now that focus is on the main form, the tab will automatically change. This works only when the controls are on the main form and are not embedded in a subform. In fact, sometimes you have to manually (programmatically) change the tab, as will see later in this chapter.

The final line of code uses the DoCmd.FindRecord method to reposition the pointer to the record. When the key field is displayed and the form uses a single field key, it is the easiest method to reposition the pointer.

Suppose you have a more complex situation, requiring you to change the tab manually and reposition the record pointer to a field. Additionally, you need to display a record that contains a multi field key or the primary key field is not on the form. You must use a more complex version of code. The following code shows this alternative:

```
Me.TabCtl02.Pages(0).SetFocus
Dim rstProducts As New ADODB.Recordset
Set rstProducts = Me.RecordsetClone
rstProducts.FindFirst "[chrProductID] = '" & txtProductID & "'"
If Not rstProducts.NoMatch = True Then
    Me.Bookmark = rstProducts.Bookmark
End If
rstProducts.Close
```

The first line allows you to manually change pages and set focus to the tab itself. Tabs are numbered by default from 0 to the number of tabs –1, so the first page usually will have an index of 0. You use the .Pages method of the tab control to set focus to the tab. However, you must check the Page Index property of the tab page you want to go to, because you can change this property to any number.

The next block of code creates a recordset and then uses the RecordsetClone method of the form (which is like creating a query to the Record Source of the form) to set what is known as a bookmark. A bookmark is a pointer to a record. When you use the FindFirst method to locate a record whose chrProductID table field matches the value of the txtProductID control, a bookmark on the form can be set to the recordset's bookmark, which repositions the form's record pointer to the matching record.

Creating code to sort data columns using labels

If you look at the fSubProductsDisplayAll form in design view, as shown in Figure 26-12, you can see the lblCategory label selected, code behind the On Click event of the label (yes, labels can be clicked on), and the code behind the event.

The code shown at the bottom of Figure 26-12 sorts the data in the chrCategory control alternatively in ascending or descending order. The OrderBy property of the form is used to sort the data by the field name listed in the code. You must use the underlying table field name and not the control name. By checking the current value of the property, you can tell if the data is currently sorted by the value and you can switch it from ascending to descending or descending to ascending.

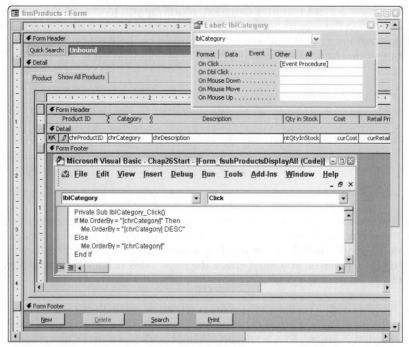

Figure 26-12: The code window to reposition the record pointer on the main form

Common Code for Common Functions

At the bottom of the frmProducts form is a series of four buttons to handle common functions that users need to do in every form. These include creating new records, deleting the current record, displaying a custom search dialog box, and displaying a custom print dialog box to print one or more records in one or more reports.

The command buttons use the On Click property to run the code behind the event. The code for the New button is very simple and consists of one line, as shown in Figure 26-13.

Deleting the current record can be a little more complicated, depending on error trapping, relationships, and any custom messages you want to display to the user. The code shown in Figure 26-14 is the code behind the Delete button at the bottom of the form.

In this example, there is a lot of code. After first setting a basic error trap, several variables and a recordset are dimensioned.

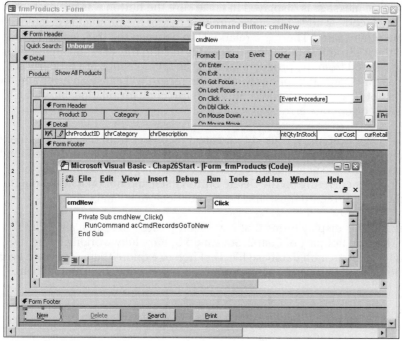

Figure 26-13: Code to go to a new record in a form

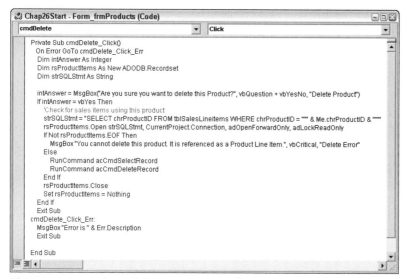

Figure 26-14: Code to delete a record in a form

Next, a custom message is displayed to make sure the button was not pressed accidentally. Then code is added to make sure that before the product is deleted, it is not used in other tables. There is a relationship between the tblSalesLineItems table and the tblProducts table. If the record is used in the sales line item table, it cannot be deleted from the products table. If the relationships are properly set in the database window, attempting to delete the record will cause an error and the record will not be deleted. However, it is better to code for relationships than to allow Access to generate errors.

To do this, a SQL statement is used to create a recordset from the tblSalesLineItems table using the current product ID in the WHERE clause. If any records are found, the product cannot be deleted. Otherwise, the record is selected and deleted. Because focus is currently on the Delete button itself and not on a field from the record, the current record must first be selected before it can be deleted.

The other buttons display forms that have been created to search and print records. They are not part of Chap26Start.mdb but are fully working in the AccessAutoAuctions.mdb database file. Feel free to explore them. They will be covered in more detail in later chapters, but now is a good time to examine them.

✦   ✦   ✦

PART II
Creating Enterprise Applications

SECTION IV
Upsizing to SQL Server and MSDE 2000

Upsizing Data to a SQL Server Database

SQL Server 2000 Desktop Engine, also called MSDE 2000, is a client/server data engine alternative to the Microsoft Jet database engine. In Access 2003, MSDE 2000 is built on SQL Server 2000 and is compatible with the full Microsoft SQL Server 2000 version. If you anticipate your small workgroup application to eventually accommodate 20 or more users — or even hundreds or thousands of users — you probably want to use MSDE 2000. In this chapter, you learn how to set up MSDE 2000 and how you can use it to build powerful client/server database applications.

On the CD-ROM   In this chapter, you will use the database file Chap27start.mdb.

Understanding MSDE 2000

MSDE 2000, also called SQL Server 2000 Desktop Engine, is a client/server database engine that is designed to be compatible with the SQL Server database engine. Think of MSDE 2000 as a scaled-down version of SQL Server. With some exceptions, it provides all of the power of SQL Server, yet it has been optimized to run on desktop computers running Windows 98, Windows ME, Windows XP, Windows NT 4.0, and Windows 2000 (or later).

Applications developed using MSDE 2000 can be run under SQL Server 2000 Standard Edition or SQL Server 2000 Enterprise Edition without modification. This capability is a great advantage to both application developers and their customers.

In the rapidly changing business environments of today, many software development projects begin targeting a handful of users. Within a relatively short span of time, the application needs to be available across the enterprise, consisting of possibly hundreds or thousands of users. In a typical scenario like this, the customer faces expensive development costs and lost time when the application needs to be modified to accommodate the larger environment. Or, in the worst-case scenario, the customer may be forced to abandon the smaller application and reengineer it with a client/server toolset. MSDE 2000 provides the scalability required by growing business environments.

Developers who don't have access to a network running SQL Server can build client/server applications using MSDE 2000 on a personal computer. Some simple changes to the connection information are all that is required when the time comes to connect the application to SQL Server.

Comparing MSDE 2000 and Jet

MSDE 2000 is a true client/server database engine. That is, the *interface objects* (forms, reports, and shortcuts to data access pages) are stored locally on the workstation in a Microsoft Access project. The data, however, is stored on a local or network server. Additionally, much of the processing of data (running queries and stored procedures) occurs on the server. This is very different from the Jet database because, regardless of where you have the data, all the records in a table are returned to the local workstation when processing a bound form or report. Client/server architecture minimizes the work of both the client and the server and cuts down on the amount of information traveling over the network.

Microsoft Jet is the default database engine included with Access 2002. MSDE 2000 is an alternative database engine to the Microsoft Jet database engine. If you have developed applications in previous versions of Microsoft Access, you should be familiar with Microsoft Jet.

Jet is the file/server data manager behind the Microsoft Access database. A Microsoft Access database can store all of an application's database objects, including the interface objects and the data. Jet moves the data back and forth between tables and forms and reports. Jet is described as a file server database engine because its job is merely to store and retrieve data. There is no distribution of processing between server and workstation as occurs in the client/server architecture.

Although MSDE 2000 provides the optimum in power and flexibility, Jet is the appropriate environment for many types of situations. Therefore, it's important to choose the right database engine for the job.

Choosing the right database engine

Designing a database application requires careful consideration of the business environment's current situation, as well as strategic planning for expansion — either in the number of users or in the volume of data to be stored and retrieved. Delivering an application that's unable to handle the growing needs of the business — or, worse, that can't handle even the initial needs of the business environment — can be a real career-buster. Although it's tempting to design every application with a "the sky's the limit" approach so that it can accommodate the full spectrum of business environments, you need to find the right balance between maximum flexibility and simplicity.

When selecting the database engine that is most appropriate for your application, consider these four criteria:

✦ Simplicity

✦ Data integrity

✦ Number of users

✦ Volume of data

In the simplicity category, Jet gets the score. As the default database in Access 2003, creating a Jet database is much easier than creating one for MSDE 2000. It is also the most compatible with previous versions of Access. Although Access provides built-in security administration, Jet databases don't require security (user IDs and passwords). MSDE 2000 does require security and uses the Windows NT security model. The memory and hard drive space requirements for Jet databases are low as compared to MSDE 2000.

Tip You can always upsize a Jet database to SQL Server later on using the Upsizing Wizard. You may need to make some modifications to the application, however.

When considering data integrity, MSDE 2000 is the most reliable choice. MSDE 2000 includes the same data integrity technology that is provided in SQL Server 2000. All changes that you make to the database are logged to a transaction file. In the event of a database disaster — a hardware failure or power interruption, for example — the database can repair itself using the log file. With Jet, however, this kind of disastrous event can permanently corrupt the database. As anyone who has ever tried to repair an Access database knows, a reliable backup strategy is a must. For some mission-critical applications, though, restoring from yesterday's backup can result in a major business interruption. For those types of applications, MSDE 2000 is the best option.

Note When addressing the limitations of MSDE 2000, remember that it is 100-percent compatible with SQL Server 2000.

Both Jet and SQL Server 2000 Desktop Engine are designed for the single workstation or small workgroup. Generally, MSDE 2000 can handle the same number of simultaneous users as Jet. MSDE 2000, however, has a limit of five active simultaneous query batches. That is, the database engine can process up to five queries at one time. The server will queue any subsequent queries until one or more of the previous five query batches completes. Despite this limitation, MSDE 2000, as a client/server database engine, has the performance advantage over Jet even in a small workgroup situation. MSDE 2000 processes queries on the server and moves only the resulting data to the client workstation. Jet, on the other hand, must move the data to the client so that the client workstation can process the query.

Both Jet and MSDE 2000 have a maximum database size of 2GB. For applications that accumulate a large volume of data over a long period of time, consider including an archive/purge utility in the application. For many business situations, only a relatively small volume of data needs to be active at any point in time.

If you have determined that MSDE 2000 is the right database engine to utilize in your database application, you are ready to begin working with this powerful feature of Access 2003.

Table 27-1 compares the capabilities of SQL Server and Jet. The table comes from the "Microsoft Access 2000 Data Engine Options" whitepaper and is reprinted with permission from Microsoft.

 Note   **Access msdn at** `http://msdn.microsoft.com/library/default.asp?url=/library/en-us/dnacc2k/html/acmsdeop.asp` **for more information on MSDE.**

Table 27-1
Comparison of SQL Server/MSDE 2000 and Jet

Requirement	SQL Server (use MSDE if these are future requirements)	Microsoft Access (Jet)
Scalability	SMP support	No SMP support
	Virtually unlimited number of concurrent users	Maximum of 255 users
	Terabyte levels of data	2 GB of data
	Transaction logging	No transaction logging
Business Critical	7X24 support and QFE	No 7X24 support
	Point-in-time recovery	Recoverable to last backup
	Guaranteed transaction integrity	No transaction logging
	Built-in fault tolerance	No built-in fault tolerance
	Security integrated with Windows NT	No integrated security with Windows NT
Rapid Application Prototyping	Access is UI for both engines and offers WYSIWYG database tools and built-in forms generation	

Installing MSDE 2000

MSDE 2000 doesn't install automatically when you install Office 2003. It is provided as a separate installation process included on the Microsoft Office 2003 CD-ROM.

Hardware requirements

Chances are, if you are successfully running Microsoft Office Access 2003 on your personal computer, your hardware meets the minimum requirements for MSDE 2000.

MSDE 2000 requires a computer with a Pentium 166-MHz or higher processor with 32MB of RAM, although 64MB or more is recommended. MSDE 2000 requires approximately 45MB of hard drive space for a typical installation—25MB for program files and 20MB for data files. Optionally, you can store the program files and data files on separate drives. Remember that you need additional space for your database files.

Tip   In reality, you should have a minimum of 128MB on any computer system running Microsoft business software purchased in 2001 or later.

Note   MSDE, Microsoft Data Engine, is the previous version of Microsoft SQL Server 2000 Desktop Engine. MSDE is compatible with SQL Server Version 7. Although MSDE 2000 provides some additional features, the two desktop versions are very similar. For the purposes of this discussion, any of the concepts that applied to MSDE certainly apply to SQL Server 2000 Desktop Engine.

Software requirements

MSDE 2000 requires one of the following operating systems: Windows 98, Windows Me, Windows NT Workstation 4.0 with Service Pack 5 or later, Windows NT Server 4.0 with Service Pack 5 (SP5) or later, Windows NT version 4.0 Server Enterprise Edition with SP5 or later, Windows 2000 Professional, Windows 2000 Server, Windows 2000 Advanced Server, or Windows 2000 Datacenter Server.

Running the SQL Server 2000 Desktop Engine Installation Program

To install MSDE 2000, insert the Office 2003 CD-ROM into your CD-ROM drive and select Run from the Start menu. In the Run box, type **D:\MSDE2000\MSDE2KS3. EXE** (or use whatever letter corresponds to the drive containing your installation CD-ROM). Click OK to begin the installation.

Caution   If you have installed MSDE, an older version of MSDE 2000, you should uninstall it before installing MSDE 2000.

Because some Windows programs interfere with the Setup program, the installation program may warn you to shut down any applications that are currently running. You can simply click on the Continue button to continue the setup, or you can click on the Cancel button to cancel the installation and run the installation later.

When you run MSDE2KS3.EXE, the License Agreement screen displays. Click the I Agree button to accept the terms of the license agreement and begin the installation process. Next, the installation program prompts for a folder name where it can unpack the MSDE installation files. The Installation Folder dialog box is shown in Figure 27-1.

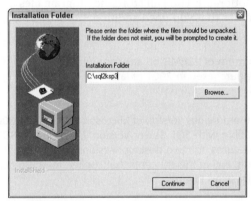

Figure 27-1: Choosing a folder for the installation files.

When the installation program finishes copying the files to the installation folder, you are ready to install MSDE 2000. In the Run box, type **C:\sql2ksp3\MSDE\setup.exe SAPWD=sa** (or use whatever drive letter and folder corresponds to the Installation Folder you specified. Click OK to begin the installation.

The installation program installs and configures MSDE 2000 automatically. A progress meter displays during the installation and configuration process, as shown in Figure 27-2.

Note   These installation instructions correspond to the installation procedure provided by Microsoft's beta-testing staff at the time this chapter was written. Actual installation instructions may be revised by the time the product is released.

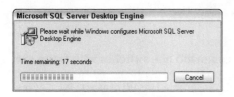

Figure 27-2: The SQL Server Desktop Engine installation progress meter.

When you have installed all of the MSDE 2000 files, the progress meter disappears. Depending on the installation operating system, the installation program may request that you restart the computer to complete the installation.

Note   It is a good idea to restart the computer after installing new software.

Customizing the installation of SQL Server 2000 Desktop Engine

The Setup program for MSDE 2000 comes with built-in setup parameters. It does not display any screens for customizing the setup for parameters, such as the target directory for the MSDE 2000 program files, the target directory for storing the SQL Server data files, or the default SQL Server name. To override these built-in settings, you must run Setup.exe using command line switches.

Table 27-2 displays the command line switches that you can use to customize the installation.

Table 27-2
Configuration Options for Installing MSDE 2000

Setting	Description
TARGETDIR	The name of the folder to install MSDE 2000. The default value is C:\Program Files\Microsoft SQL Server\.
DATADIR	The name of an optional folder for data files. The default value is the value of TARGETDIR.
COLLATION	The name of a collation sequence.
INSTANCENAME	The name of the SQL Server. The Default value is MSSQLSERVER.
USEDEFAULTSAPWD	Set the default password to NULL when the SA user logs in.
SAPWD="sa_password"	Assign the specified password to the SA login.
SECURITYMODE=SQL	Use Mixed-Mode SQL Server security instead of Windows Integrated Security.

Note   You must enter the setting options in uppercase.

The following is an example of entering command line switches with Setup.exe:

```
C:\sql2ksp3\MSDE\setup.exe TARGETDIR="C:\Program Files\Microsoft SQL Server\"
DATADIR="C:\Program Files\Microsoft SQL Server\MSSQL\Data\"
COLLATION="SQL_Latin1_General_CP1257_CS_AS" INSTANCENAME=myinstance SAPWD=sa
```

Starting the SQL Server 2000 Desktop Engine

When you have completed the setup, the SQL Server Service Manager displays on the Windows taskbar. To work with an MSDE 2000 database, you must first start the SQL Server Service Manager.

When you install MSDE 2000, SQL Server Service Manager starts automatically. You can run the SQL Server Service Manager any time by choosing it from your Windows taskbar.

The SQL Server Service Manager, shown in Figure 27-3, allows you to choose the type of service that you want to start. The Server box lists the names of the servers that SQL Server Service Manager has found. In this example, the JENXP server is the name of the desktop where MSDE 2000 was installed. The Services box lists the names of the SQL Server services that you can start. The services you can start include:

✦ SQL Server: Database server for SQL Server.

✦ Distributed Transaction Coordinator: Distributed transaction server.

✦ SQL Server Agent: Runs scheduled administrative tasks.

Figure 27-3: Using SQL Server Service Manager.

To open the SQL Server Service Manager dialog box, double-click on the SQL Server Service Manager icon in the Windows taskbar. To start MSDE 2000, select SQL Server in the Services box. Then click Start/Continue.

Tip   Selecting the option "Auto-Start service when OS starts" in the SQL Server Service Manager automatically starts the service when you boot up Windows.

When MSDE 2000 has started, an arrow displays next to the server in SQL Server Service Manager, as shown in Figure 27-4.

Figure 27-4: Starting MSDE 2000.

When MSDE 2000 starts, the Pause and Stop buttons in SQL Server Service Manager are enabled. When you are running SQL Server in a multi-user environment, you may need to stop the server at some point in order to perform an administrative task. Before stopping the server, select the Pause button to pause the server. Pausing the server prevents any additional users from logging into the server. Then you can alert any currently logged-in users to complete their work and log out of the server. When you are certain that all users have logged out, select the Stop button to stop the server.

Caution   Stopping SQL Server prevents anyone from connecting to the database and drops any currently connected users. Disconnecting a user unexpectedly could lead to data loss.

After you have successfully installed MSDE 2000 and started the server, it's time to get started working with a SQL Server database.

Using the Upsizing Wizard

Many organizations today are becoming more and more dependent on their database applications to manage everyday business operations, and these applications are growing both in volume of data and number of users. Applications that you may have developed using Microsoft Access — even in the past year or two — may be starting to strain the organization's network. At the same time, client/server databases like SQL Server 2000 are becoming more popular, even with smaller businesses, as these databases become easier to install, use, and maintain.

If any of your clients are among the Fortune 500 set, you may be among those who have been recently advised of a new mandate that all applications must conform to client/server technology only — no file-server database management allowed. Your business partner at one of these corporations has probably contacted you in a state of alarm. Having already invested a significant amount of their budget into the Access application that you developed for them, they are naturally concerned that they may have to invest at least the same amount, if not a substantially larger amount, to redesign it to fit the new architecture.

Fortunately, with Access 2003 and its Upsizing Wizard, you can provide a relatively simple and inexpensive solution that retains a significant amount of the original development effort while providing a database that conforms to client/server methodology.

You can convert the tables stored in an existing Microsoft Access database (.mdb) to a client/server database automatically using the Microsoft Access Upsizing Wizard. The Upsizing Wizard takes a Jet database and creates an equivalent SQL Server database with the same table structures, data, and many other attributes of the original database. The Upsizing Wizard re-creates table structures, indexes, validation rules, defaults, autonumbers, and relationships, and takes advantage of the latest SQL Server functionality wherever possible.

Before upsizing an application

You should perform these steps prior to converting an application using the Upsizing Wizard:

✦ **Back up your database:** Although the Upsizing Wizard doesn't remove any data or database objects from your Access database, it's a good idea to create a backup copy of your Access database before you upsize it.

✦ **Ensure that you have adequate hard drive space:** At a minimum, you must have enough hard drive space to store the new SQL Server database. Plan to allow at least twice the size of your Access database to allow room for future growth. If you expect to add a lot of data to the database, make the multiple larger.

✦ **Set a default printer:** You must have a default printer assigned, because the Upsizing Wizard creates a report snapshot as it completes the conversion.

✦ **Assign yourself appropriate permissions on the Access database:** You need read/design permission on all database objects to upsize them.

✦ **Start the SQL Server Service Manager:** It must be running for the Upsizing Wizard to create the new SQL Server database.

Starting the Upsizing Wizard

After you have completed the steps to prepare for the conversion, you are ready to upsize your application. First, open the Microsoft Access database that you want to convert. This example upsizes the Chapter 27 version of the Access Auto Auctions database (Chap27Start.mdb). Second, select Tools ⇨ Database Utilities ⇨ Upsizing Wizard from the Access menu. The first screen of the Upsizing Wizard displays, as shown in Figure 27-5.

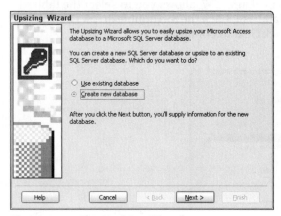

Figure 27-5: The Upsizing Wizard.

In the first Upsizing Wizard screen, you can choose to either copy your existing data to an already existing SQL Server database, or to create a new SQL Server database. For this example, choose Create new database. Then click Next. The second Upsizing Wizard screen displays, as shown in Figure 27-6.

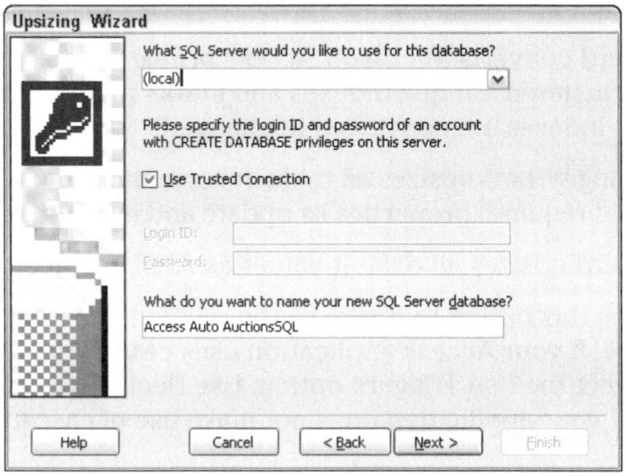

Figure 27-6: Setting up the new SQL Server database.

In this Wizard screen, you define the connection information for the new SQL Server database. For this example, type **(local)** as the name of the SQL Server. Check the Use Trusted Connection check box. Type Access Auto AuctionsSQL as the name of the new SQL Server database. Then click Next to continue.

Tip You use (local) when creating an MSDE database on a desktop computer. If you want to create the database on a server on your network, select the server name from the list.

The next Wizard screen, shown in Figure 27-7, allows you to select the tables to upsize to the new SQL Server database. Click the >> (double-arrow) button to export all of the tables. Then click Next to continue.

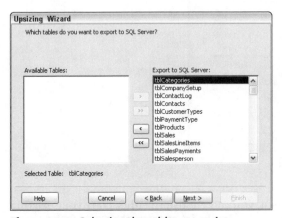

Figure 27-7: Selecting the tables to upsize.

In the next screen, which is shown in Figure 27-8, you can take advantage of many of the powerful database features available in SQL Server, including:

✦ **Indexes:** The Upsizing Wizard converts Microsoft Access primary keys to Microsoft SQL Server non-clustered, unique indexes and marks them as SQL Server primary keys. Other indexes are converted unchanged.

✦ **Validation rules:** The Upsizing Wizard upsizes all table, record, and field validation rules, and it upsizes field required properties as update and insert triggers.

✦ **Defaults:** The Upsizing Wizard upsizes all default values as ANSI defaults.

✦ **Table relationships:** Choose this option to preserve the relationships that you have defined for your tables. If your Access application uses cascading updates or deletes, also select the Use Triggers option. Use Declared Referential Integrity (DRI) if your application does not make use of cascading updates and deletes.

✦ **Timestamp fields:** Microsoft SQL Server uses a timestamp field to indicate that a record was changed (not *when* it was changed) by creating a unique value field and then updating this field whenever a record is updated. In general, a timestamp field provides the best performance and reliability. Without a timestamp field, SQL Server must check all the fields in the record to determine whether the record has changed, which slows performance. If you choose Yes, let wizard decide, timestamp fields are created only for tables that contain floating-point (Single or Double), memo, or OLE object fields.

✦ **Don't upsize any data:** Choose the option Only Create the Table Structure; Don't Upsize Any Data if you only want to create the SQL Server database structures using your existing database, but leave the new tables empty.

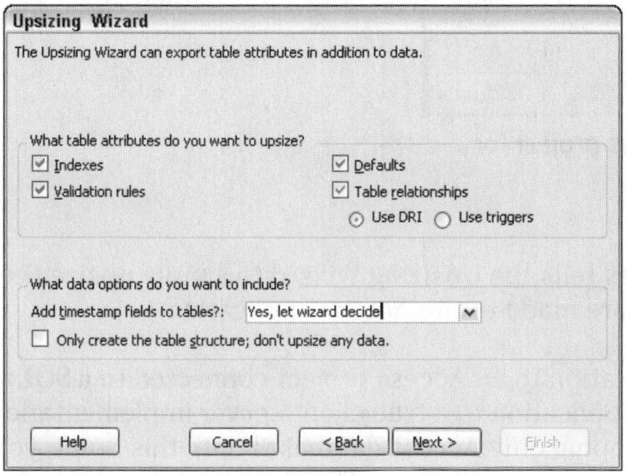

Figure 27-8: Selecting the table attributes.

After you have made all of your selections, click Next to continue.

Figure 27-9 shows the next Wizard screen. In this screen, you can tell the Upsizing Wizard to change the existing Access application so that it can work with the new SQL Server database. Or, you can tell the Upsizing Wizard to use the existing Access application to create a new Access project.

If you select Create New Access Client/Server Application, the Upsizing Wizard creates a new Access project. The File Name for the new project (.adp) is the Access application's file name followed by the "CS" suffix. The Upsizing Wizard converts all of the Access application's interface objects (forms, data access pages, reports, and code) into the new Access project and connects the project to tables and queries stored in the new SQL Server database.

The Link SQL Server Tables to Existing Application selection tells the Upsizing Wizard to modify your Access database to work with the new SQL Server database. Queries, forms, reports, and data access pages automatically connect to the data in the new Microsoft SQL Server database rather than the data in your Microsoft Access database. The Upsizing Wizard renames the Microsoft Access tables that you upsize with the suffix _local_. For example, if you upsize the Customers table, the table is renamed Customers_local in your Access database. Then, the Upsizing wizard creates a linked SQL Server table named Customers.

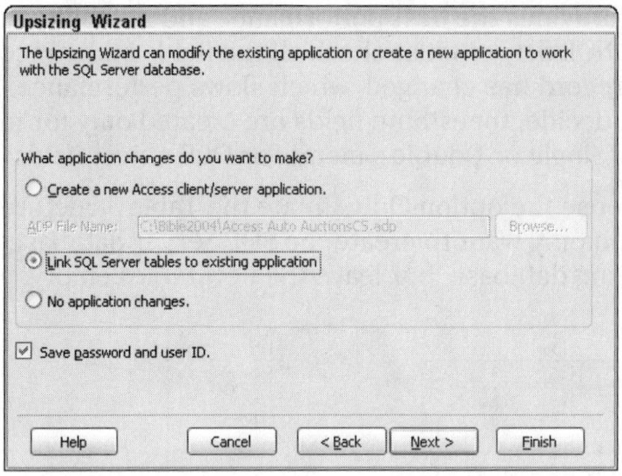

Figure 27-9: Creating a new Access project for the new SQL Server database.

Selecting No Application Changes tells the Upsizing Wizard to simply upsize the data to SQL Server. No changes are made to the Access application.

Upsizing the entire Access application to an Access project connected to a SQL Server database converts your application to a true client/server implementation. However, if you have been developing only Access databases until this point, you will find client/server development is very different. The Upsizing Wizard takes you only part of the way. The Upsizing Wizard doesn't make any changes to modules and macros. In Chapter 21, you learned that programming with recordsets in Access projects requires a different command set. You also need to make many changes to your tables and queries to reach full functionality in the new architecture.

For this example, choose the option Link SQL Server Tables to Existing Application. Although this option continues to use the Jet database engine to retrieve data from the database, it requires the least amount of application modification.

If you leave the Save Password and User ID option unchecked, users are prompted for the user ID (*SA* in our example) and password (*none* in our example) each time they try to open the SQL Server database.

After you have completed the information for this screen, click Next.

You have now reached the final Wizard screen, which is shown in Figure 27-10. The Upsizing Wizard now has all of the information that it needs to create the SQL Server database. Click Finish to begin the conversion.

The conversion process takes several minutes to complete. A message box displays the progress of the conversion, as shown in Figure 27-11.

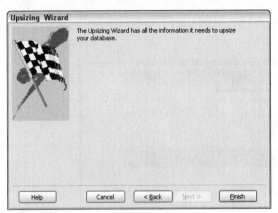

Figure 27-10: The final Upsizing Wizard screen.

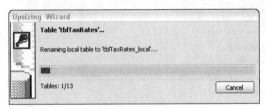

Figure 27-11: Waiting for the Upsizing Wizard to complete the conversion process.

Note   If the Upsizing Wizard encounters any referential integrity errors while converting your data to the new SQL Server database, an error message displays. If you encounter an error message, you can click Yes to proceed with the conversion. Any problem data is not converted to the new database. If you don't want to omit the problem data, you must click No to cancel the conversion process.

When the conversion process completes, the Upsizing Wizard automatically displays a report snapshot. An example of the report snapshot is shown in Figure 27-12. The report snapshot includes information about each step of the conversion process for your application. The Upsizing Wizard report contains information about the following:

✦ Database details, including database size.

✦ Upsizing parameters, including what table attributes you chose to upsize and how you upsized.

✦ Table information, including a comparison of Access and SQL Server values for names, data types, indexes, validation rules, defaults, triggers, and whether or not timestamps were added.

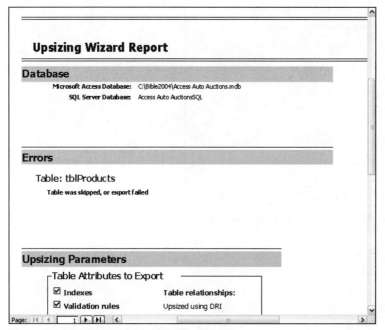

Figure 27-12: The Upsizing Wizard report.

✦ Any errors encountered, including database or transaction log full; inadequate permissions; device or database not created; table, default, or validation rule skipped; relationship not enforced; query skipped (because it can't be translated to SQL Server syntax); and control and record source conversion errors in forms and reports.

Tip   The report snapshot is stored in the same folder as your application so that you can refer to it later.

The Upsizing Wizard will successfully convert the data types used in Access to the corresponding data types used in SQL Server. Table 27-3 shows the equivalent SQL Server data type for each Access data type.

Table 27-3 Comparison of Access and SQL Server Data Types	
Microsoft Access Data Type	*SQL Server Data Type*
Yes/No	Bit
Number	Tinyint, smallint, int, real, bigint, float, decimal, numeric
Currency	Money, Smallmoney
Date/Time	Datetime, Smalldatetime

Microsoft Access Data Type	SQL Server Data Type
AutoNumber	int (with **Identity** property defined)
Text	Varchar(n), Nvarchar(n)
Memo	Text
OLE Object	Image
ReplicationID (GUID)	uniqueidentifier (SQL Server 7.0 or later)
Hyperlink	char, nvarchar (With the Hyperlink property set to Yes)
(no equivalent)	Nchar
(no equivalent)	varbinary
(no equivalent)	smallint
(no equivalent)	timestamp
(no equivalent)	Char, nchar
(no equivalent)	user-defined
(no equivalent)	sql_variant

Although the Upsizing Wizard can handle mapping Access data types to SQL Server datatypes, there are other conversion issues you will need to be aware of. If the Upsizing Wizard Report indicates that a table has been skipped, examine the field names in each of the Access tables to ensure that they adhere to the following constraints:

✦ The first character must be a letter or the "at" sign (@).

✦ The remaining characters may be numbers, letters, the dollar sign ($), the number sign (#), or the underscore (_).

✦ Spaces are allowed, but the Upsizing Wizard will insert brackets ([ ]) around the field name.

✦ The name must not be a Transact-SQL keyword. SQL Server reserves both the uppercase and lowercase versions of keywords.

On the CD-ROM For a list of SQL Server reserved keywords, open the database SQLKeywords.mdb on the companion CD.

If any field name in an Access table fails to follow these guidelines, the Upsizing Wizard will not be able to upsize the table. The Upsizing Wizard Report will inform you that it has skipped the table with the offending field name. However, the wizard does not always provide the reason the table was skipped. When you review the report, you can refer back to this section to review the field naming rules.

In addition to field name constraints, the Upsizing Wizard will also fail to upsize a table if it encounters any of these situations:

✦ If the field size between two fields participating in an Access relationship are not exactly the same for both fields.

✦ No unique index.

✦ A unique index on a field and Required property is set to **No**.

✦ More than two foreign keys defined on a single table.

✦ Invalid values for a date/time field—values must be >=1/1/1753.

Tip   There is a handy tool available called SSW Upsizing Pro! that you can use to analyze your Access database before upsizing it to SQL Server. Check their website at www.ssw.com.au/ssw/UpsizingPRO for more information.

After you are finished reviewing the report, close it. When you close the report, the Upsizing Wizard displays the modified Access application. As you can see in Figure 27-13, the tables tab of the Access database container has changed. Each of the original Access tables has been renamed with the suffix _local. An arrow and a world icon precede the SQL Server tables. The arrow indicates that the table is an attached table. The world icon indicates that the table is an ODBC-attached table.

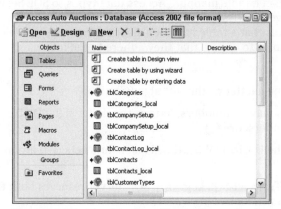

Figure 27-13: Viewing the tables in the upsized database.

✦   ✦   ✦

Working with Access Projects

The Access 2003 Upsizing Wizard provides a quick and easy way to upsize Access data to SQL Server 2000 Desktop Engine (MSDE 2000). The Upsizing Wizard automatically creates an *Access project* (an Access data file that allows you to work directly with the MSDE 2000 database). The simplest and quickest upsizing method simply links the new SQL Server data to the existing Access application. Although this option moves your data to a client/server architecture, it takes you only part of the way. Even though the data now resides in a client/server database, the linked tables in the existing *Access front end* (the forms, reports, and data access pages) continue to use the Microsoft Jet database engine to retrieve information from the database.

Cross-Reference For a comparison of Jet and SQL Server 2000 Desktop Engine, see Chapter 27.

On the CD-ROM In this chapter, you will use the database file Chap28Start.mdb.

Using linked SQL Server tables in an Access front end can be an acceptable solution for most small-workgroup environments. However, for environments with large numbers of users or where large volumes of data are processed, you need a solution that utilizes client/server architecture in both the front-end and back-end databases.

In addition to providing access to SQL Server data, Access projects can also contain *front-end objects,* such as forms, reports, data access pages, macros, and modules. The good news is that if you are moving from an existing Access front end to SQL Server, you don't have to build these objects from scratch. The Access Upsizing Wizard does most of the work for you.

Upsizing to an Access Project

In Chapter 27, you learn how to use the Access Upsizing Wizard to convert Access data to MSDE 2000. You can use the Access Upsizing Wizard to convert the Access front end, along with its data, to an Access project.

Caution   Back up your database before upsizing.

Starting the Upsizing Wizard

When you are ready to upsize, open the Access application. The following example shows you how to upsize the Access Auto Auctions database. For this chapter, use the Chap28Start.mdb. Select Tools ⇨ Database Utilities ⇨ Upsizing Wizard from the Access menu. The first screen of the Upsizing Wizard displays, as shown in Figure 28-1.

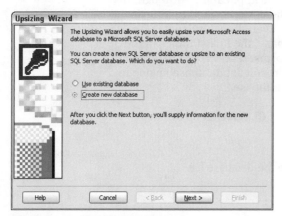

Figure 28-1: The Upsizing Wizard.

In the first Upsizing Wizard screen, you can choose to copy your existing data to an SQL Server database that already exists or to create a new SQL Server database. For this example, choose Create new database. Then click Next. The second Upsizing Wizard screen displays, as shown in Figure 28-2.

Caution   Be sure to start the SQL Server Service Manager before completing this wizard screen.

Cross-Reference   See Chapter 27 for more information on working with the SQL Server Service Manager.

Upsizing Wizard
What SQL Server would you like to use for this database?
(local)
Please specify the login ID and password of an account with CREATE DATABASE privileges on this server.
Use Trusted Connection
Login ID:
Jen
Password:
What do you want to name your new SQL Server database?
AccessAutoAuctionsSQL1
Help
Cancel
< Back
Next >
Finish

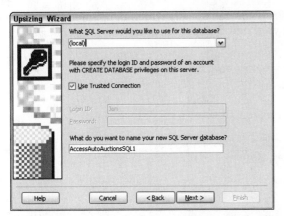

Figure 28-2: Setting up the new SQL Server database.

In this Wizard screen, you define the connection information for the new SQL Server database. For this example, type **(local)** as the name of the SQL Server. Select "Use Trusted Connection." You create the AccessAutoAuctionsSQL in Chapter 27, so for this database, use the name AccessAutoAuctionsSQL1. Then click Next to continue.

The next wizard screen, shown in Figure 28-3, allows you to select the tables to upsize to the new SQL Server database. Click the >> button to export all of the tables. Then click Next to continue.

Upsizing Wizard
Which tables do you want to export to SQL Server?
Available Tables:
Export to SQL Server:
tblCategories
tblCompanySetup
tblContactLog
tblContacts
tblCustomerTypes
tblPaymentType
tblProducts
tblSales
tblSalesLineItems
tblSalesPayments
tblSalesperson
Selected Table: tblCategories
Help
Cancel
< Back
Next >
Finish

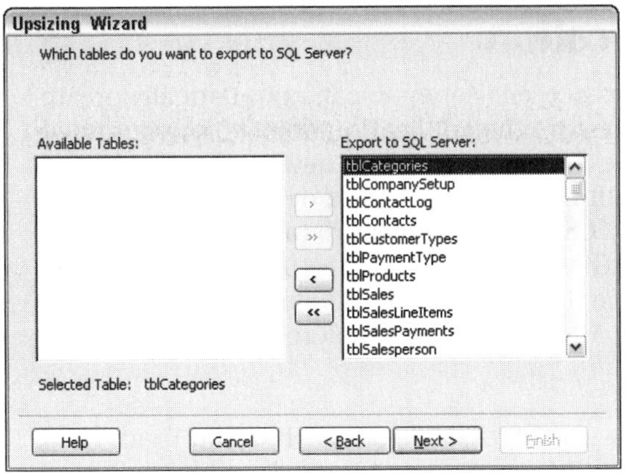

Figure 28-3: Selecting the tables to export.

In the screen shown in Figure 28-4, you can specify which of the many SQL Server features you want to enable in your new SQL Server database.

Figure 28-4: Selecting the SQL Server table attributes.

Cross-Reference Refer to Chapter 27 for more information on each of these SQL Server features.

When you have made all of your selections, click Next to continue.

Using the Upsizing Wizard to create a Client/Server Application

Figure 28-5 shows the next wizard screen. Here you can automatically create a Microsoft Access project file to store the application objects for your new client/server application. Choose the option Create a new Access client/server application. The wizard automatically assigns a default name for your new project by adding the suffix "CS" to your Access database file name. Type AccessAutoAuctionsCS for the ADP file name. Leave the Save password and user ID option unchecked to force the user to enter a logon ID and password whenever the project is opened. After you have completed the information for this screen, click Next.

You have now reached the final wizard screen, which is shown in Figure 28-6. The Upsizing Wizard now has all of the information that it needs to create both the SQL Server database and the Access project. Click Finish to begin the conversion.

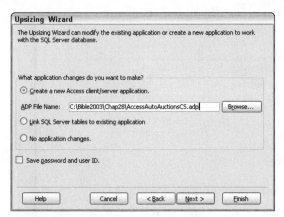

Figure 28-5: Automatically creating an Access project.

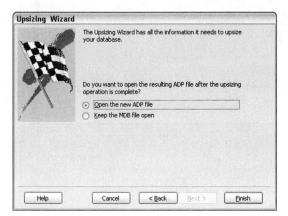

Figure 28-6: The final Upsizing Wizard screen.

The conversion process takes several minutes to complete.

When the conversion process completes, the Upsizing Wizard automatically displays a report snapshot. An example of an Upsizing Wizard report snapshot is shown in Figure 28-7. Browse the report snapshot to review the conversion details about each of the objects that the Upsizing Wizard converted.

After you are finished reviewing the report, close it. When you close the report, the Upsizing Wizard automatically loads the new Access project. Figure 28-8 shows the database container for the AccessAutoAuctionsCS project.

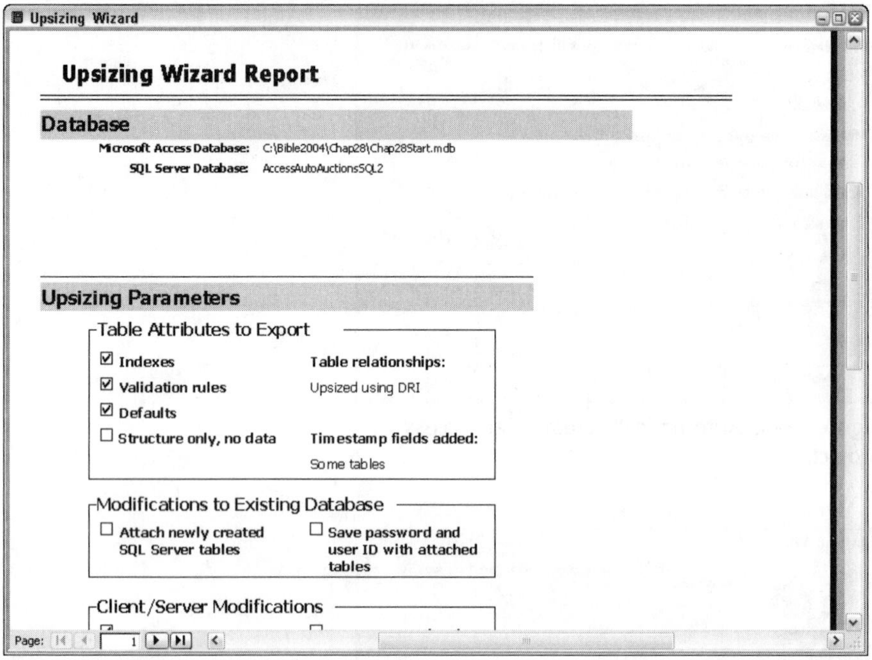

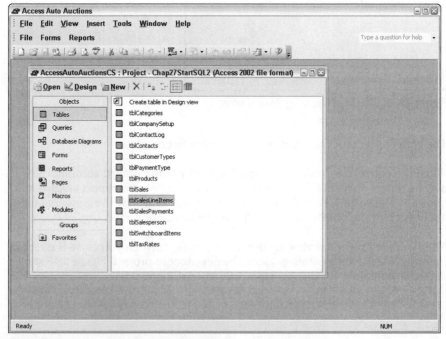

Figure 28-7: The Upsizing Wizard report.

Figure 28-8: The upsized Access project.

The Access Upsizing Wizard migrates the native Access objects into their corresponding objects in the new Access project. Although Access projects are organized into the same groupings of objects (tables, queries, forms, reports, and so on) as native Access databases, project objects differ significantly in how they work compared to native Access. The similarities and differences are outlined below.

✦ **Tables:** Individual tables are converted to SQL Server tables. Data types are converted to their corresponding SQL Server data types.

Cross-Reference

Refer to Chapter 27 for a listing of SQL Server data types and how they compare to native Access data types.

✦ **Queries:** Queries are converted into views, stored procedures, and functions according to the following rules:

- Select queries that don't have an ORDER BY clause or parameters are converted to views.

- Action queries are converted to stored procedure action queries. Access adds SET NOCOUNT ON after the parameter declaration code to make sure the stored procedure runs.

- Select queries that use either parameters or an ORDER BY clause are converted to user-defined functions. If necessary, the TOP 100 PERCENT clause is added to a query that contains an ORDER BY clause.

- Parameter queries that use named parameters maintain the original text name used in the Access database and are converted either to stored procedures or inline user-defined functions.

✦ **Forms and Reports:** Converted with no changes.

✦ **Data Access Pages:** The Upsizing Wizard changes the OLE DB connection and the data binding information in the Microsoft Office data source control to work with the new SQL Server database, and it copies the page's corresponding HTML file to the same location as the Access project, renaming the HTML file with a "_CS" suffix. The new pages in the Access project retain the original name, so that hyperlinks between the Access project Pages continue to work.

✦ **Command Bars:** Converted with no changes.

✦ **Macros and Modules:** Converted with no changes.

To take full advantage of SQL Server and an Access project, you need to make some fairly significant changes to your newly converted application. Although the Upsizing Wizard tries to make its best guess as to the most efficient conversion approach, you should review the table and query designs and revise them as necessary. Recordsources and Controlsources for forms and reports are converted without any changes. In an implementation with a large number of users, you don't want to bind forms and reports directly to a table or even a query.

Note

If you are converting an application created in an earlier version of Access, you may also need to manually convert code from Data Access Objects (DAO) to ActiveX Data Objects (ADO) in your modules.

Using Unbound Forms

Access projects allow you to bind a form's Recordsource directly to a table. A *bound form* is a form that's tied directly to a table or query, providing a constant open connection to all of the data in the table or query. Although this approach is a quick and easy way to present and update data on the form, this is not the most efficient way to work with data in the client/server world.

Bound forms maintain a constant connection between the server and the workstation. The server must maintain a record lock on the data displayed on the form — even if the user is simply viewing it. Open connections and record locks consume server resources. If you are operating in an environment with many users or where users are working with large volumes of data and transactions, you want to use unbound forms.

An *unbound form* is a form that doesn't maintain a constant open connection to a table or query. You retrieve data from a table or query one record at a time. The load on the server is significantly reduced because it doesn't need to maintain open connections or record locks.

Here are some common reasons to implement unbound forms:

✦ Improved performance due to retrieval of a minimal amount of data.

✦ Improved control of record-locking conflicts.

✦ Bypasses Access automatic record saving, providing ability to confirm saving or canceling record changes.

✦ Required for database security considerations.

VBA code is used to handle all of the data used in the form. You must write a procedure to handle searching for and displaying the data. You must write other procedures to handle updating the data. The following list covers most of the tasks that a typical unbound form needs to handle:

✦ Retrieving the set of data to be viewed or edited on the form.

✦ Loading the data into the form's controls.

✦ Searching for another record.

✦ Determining when data on the form has changed.

✦ Saving changed data.

✦ Undoing changes to data.

✦ Moving to other records in the set (first, last, next, previous).

✦ Creating a new record.

Creating the code for each of these tasks may seem like a lot of work. But if you want to build a true client/server application, this is the best approach.

Working with unbound forms

Creating the VBA functions to display and process data in an unbound form requires the use of the ActiveX Data Objects (ADO) programming model. ADO enables you to write an application to access and manipulate data in a database server through an OLE DB provider. ADO supports key features for building client/server and Web-based applications.

Cross-Reference
See Chapter 21 to review the basic concepts of the ADO programming model.

For an example of a working unbound form, we use the frmContactsUnbound form. Figure 28-9 shows the Customers Unbound form in Normal view.

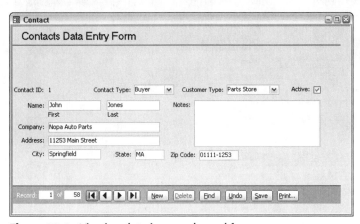

Figure 28-9: Viewing data in an unbound form.

The frmContactsUnbound form demonstrates virtually any function you need to add, edit, delete, and find records. The buttons in the form's footer section perform these functions. The Undo button allows the user to restore the original data for the record after changes have been made but before the Save button is selected. The Print button opens a print dialog box that provides several choices for printing the form's data. The Save button allows the user to immediately process changes made to the data.

Note
In bound forms, changes are saved automatically when the user closes the form or moves to another record. Because these automatic update features are disabled when using unbound forms, you must provide a way to actively save the data.

Because the unbound form doesn't have a record source, it doesn't contain any built-in record navigation buttons. The record navigation buttons included on the frmContactsUnbound form provide the same functionality provided by a bound Access form. The user is also provided with controls to show the current record number as well as the total number of records.

Creating an unbound form

In unbound forms, the form's Record Source is blank. Additionally, the Control Source for each of the form's controls is blank. The controls are named using the corresponding column names of the form's table. The Design view of the Customers Unbound form is shown in Figure 28-10.

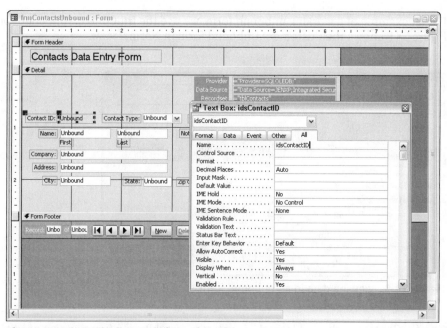

Figure 28-10: Designing an unbound form.

Tip   A quick and easy way to set up the controls for an unbound form is to initially bind the form to the table. Then, drag the table's fields to the form. This action reduces any errors in naming the fields to match the names of the fields in the table. Before completing the design of the form, remove the Control Source properties of the fields and the Record Source property for the form.

On the top right of the Customers Unbound form are four dark gray controls. You use these controls to connect the form to the database. The Visible property of these controls is set to False so that they can't be seen when the user is viewing the form. The names and Control Source properties for these special fields must be set according to the items listed in Table 28-1.

Table 28-1
Connecting an Unbound Form to a SQL Server Database

Control Name	Control Source
xProvider	="Provider=SQLOLEDB;"
xDataSource	="Data Source=(local);Integrated Security=SSPI;Initial Catalog=AccessAutoAuctionsSQL1"
xRecordset	="tblContacts"
xKey	="idsContactID"

The bottom right area of the unbound form also contains the following hidden controls:

✦ FlagEdited is checked when a field's data is updated.

✦ FlagFind is checked when searched criteria is selected.

✦ UpdateCtr is incremented each time the record is changed.

Displaying data on the form

The form actually contains only a minimal amount of code. The form's On Load event retrieves the data to display on the form. Figure 28-11 shows the On Load event procedure code.

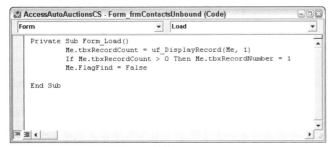

```
AccessAutoAuctionsCS - Form_frmContactsUnbound (Code)
Form                            Load

   Private Sub Form_Load()
        Me.tbxRecordCount = uf_DisplayRecord(Me, 1)
        If Me.tbxRecordCount > 0 Then Me.tbxRecordNumber = 1
        Me.FlagFind = False

   End Sub
```

Figure 28-11: The On Load event procedure for an unbound form.

The On Load event procedure calls the function uf_DisplayRecord. The code for the uf_DisplayRecord function is not stored with the form. In fact, most of the form's code is stored in the basUnboundFormUtilities module. By storing these functions in a module, you can use the same functions over and over for any other unbound forms that you want to include in your application. Figure 28-12 shows the basUnboundFormUtilities Module Window.

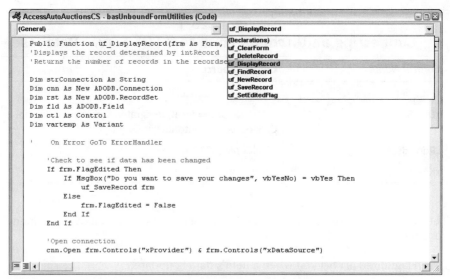

Figure 28-12: The functions of the basUnboundFormUtilities module.

The first task of the uf_DisplayRecord function is to retrieve the data to display on the form. The following code snippet shows the statements used to retrieve the form's data:

```
'Open connection
    cnn.Open frm.Controls("xProvider") &
frm.Controls("xDataSource")

    'Open recordset
    If Len(frm.Filter) = 0 Then
        rst.Open "Select * From " & frm.Controls("xRecordset")
& " Order by " & frm.Controls("xKey"), cnn, adOpenStatic
    Else
        rst.Open "Select * From " & frm.Controls("xRecordset")
& " WHERE " & frm.Filter & " Order by " & frm.Controls("xKey"),
cnn, adOpenStatic
    End If
```

The uf_DisplayRecord function establishes a connection to the database specified in the form's xProvider and xDataSource fields. Then, it checks the form's filter property. If a filter is not set, the function retrieves all of the rows in the table specified in the form's xRecordset field. If the form's filter is set, the function specifies a WHERE clause to include only some of the rows specified in the form's xRecordset field.

The second task of the uf_DisplayRecord function is to display the first row of retrieved data on the form. The following code snippet shows the statements used to load the data into the form's fields:

```
'Iterate through controls on form that match fields in
recordset
    For Each ctl In frm

        'if error the field is not on the form
        On Error Resume Next
        Err = 0
        vartemp = rst.Fields(ctl.Name).Name
        If Err = 0 Then
            On Error GoTo ErrorHandler
            'if control enables then set default value from tag
            '   and set focus if tab index 0
            If ctl.Enabled Then
                ctl.Value = rst.Fields(ctl.Name).Value
                If ctl.TabIndex = 0 Then ctl.SetFocus
            End If
        End If
    Next
```

Basically, this section of code steps through each of the controls on the form. This is the reason that you name the control to match the name in the database table. The value of the control is set to the value of the column name in the table that matches the control's name. Then, the focus is set to the field that is first in the tab order (TabIndex 0).

Along with the uf_DisplayRecord function, the basUnboundFormUtilities module contains all of the other functions that make an unbound form work, including:

✦ uf_NewRecord adds a new record.

✦ uf_SaveRecord saves the current data on the form to a new or existing record.

✦ uf_FindRecord finds a set of records meeting a specified criteria.

✦ uf_DisplayRecord retrieves and displays a selected record.

✦ uf_DeleteRecord deletes a record.

✦ uf_ClearForm clears all fields on the form.

✦ uf_SetEditedFlag is called by a field on the form when the field is updated.

On the CD-ROM

You can find both the frmContactsUnbound form and the basUnboundFormUtilities module in the AccessAutoAuctionsCS project file in the Examples folder of this book's CD-ROM.

You should take a few minutes to become familiar with the code for these functions. Each function, except for the uf_SetEditedFlag function, receives the name of the calling form as a parameter.

Updating data

You can use the functions in the basUnboundFormUtilities to add new records, delete records, and save edited records. To implement any of these functions in the unbound form, simply create an event procedure for the appropriate button on the form. Then call the function from the button's event procedure.

To add a new record, you create an event procedure for the New button's On Click event. The New button's On Click event calls the uf_NewRecord function. Figure 28-13 shows the On Click event procedure for the Customers Unbound form's New button.

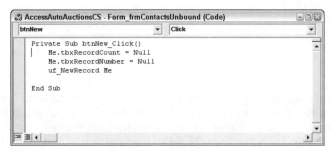

Figure 28-13: Using a button to call a basUnboundFormUtilities function.

The New button's On Click event procedure first updates the record number and record count fields in the form's navigation button section. These fields should be empty when creating a new record. Then the event procedure calls the uf_NewRecord function passing the name of the form as a parameter.

The uf_NewRecord function sets the form up to enter a new record. The following code snippet shows the statements used to clear the form's fields.

```
'Iterate through controls on form that match fields in
recordset
    For Each ctl In frm

        'if error the field is not on the form
        On Error Resume Next
        Err = 0
        vartemp = rst.Fields(ctl.Name).Name
        If Err = 0 Then
            On Error GoTo ErrorHandler
            'if control enables then set default value from tag
            '    and set focus if tab index 0
            If ctl.Enabled Then
                If IsNull(ctl.Tag) Then
                    ctl.Value = Null
                Else
                    ctl.Value = ctl.Tag
```

```
            End If
            If ctl.TabIndex = 0 Then ctl.SetFocus
        End If
    End If
Next
```

The code in the uf_NewRecord function loops through each field on the form. Each field's value property is set to Null. Then, the focus is set to the first field in the tab order.

Caution   Before clearing the fields on the form, check to see if the user changed any of the data. If the data has changed, prompt the user to save or undo the changes.

You can use the uf_SaveRecord function to save the data on the form. Use the Save button's On Click event to call the uf_SaveRecord function.

The first task of the uf_SaveRecord function is to locate the record in the table. This section of code is illustrated in the following code snippet:

```
'Check to see if data has been changed
If Not frm.FlagEdited Then
    MsgBox "Nothing to save"
    GoTo Done
End If

'Open connection
cnn.Open frm.Controls("xProvider") & frm.Controls("xDataSource")

'Open recordset to determine type of key field and setup Criteria
rst.Open "Select * From " & frm.Controls("xRecordset"), cnn, adOpenStatic
Select Case rst(frm.Controls("xKey").Value).Type
    Case adChar, adVarWChar, adLongVarWChar
        strCriteria = frm.Controls("xKey") & " = " & Chr(39) &
frm.Controls(frm.Controls("xKey")).Value & Chr(34)
    Case adDate
        strCriteria = frm.Controls("xKey") & " = " & "#" &
frm.Controls(frm.Controls("xKey")).Value & "#"
    Case Else    'assume numeric
        strCriteria = frm.Controls("xKey") & " = " &
str(frm.Controls(frm.Controls("xKey")).Value)
    End Select
    rst.Close

    'Determine if this is a new record or a changed record
    rst.Open "Select * From " & frm.Controls("xRecordset") & " WHERE " &
strCriteria, cnn, adOpenKeyset, adLockOptimistic
```

The function first checks to see if the form has been edited. If not, the function simply exits. Otherwise, it opens a connection to the recordset simply to determine the key field's data type so that a criteria string can be created. The criteria string is used to search the recordset for a record with the same key field. This is necessary so that the function can determine whether to update an existing record or create a new record.

If it is a new record, the function uses the AddNew method and iterates through the controls on the form that match the fields in the recordset to create a record with the new data. The UpdateCtr field is set to 1 for the new record.

If an existing record has the same key field, the code must check to make sure that the record has not been changed. The code to perform the check is shown below:

```
'Check to see if this record was already updated by another user
        If rst("UpdateCtr") <> frm.Controls("UpdateCtr").Value Then
            Response = MsgBox("This record was already updated by another user."
& vbCrLf & _
                "Do you want to overwrite the other user's changes?", _
                vbInformation + vbYesNo, "Data already changed")
            If Response = vbNo Then
                rst.Close
                Exit Function
            End If
        End If
```

The UpdateCtr field in the form is compared to the value of the UpdateCtr field in the table. If the two values are different, the record was updated in between the time that the record was displayed on the form and the time that the user pressed the Save button. A message prompts the user to go ahead and overwrite the record in the table with the user's changes or to cancel the user's update.

To update the existing record, the values in the form's fields are copied to the recordset's field and the recordset is updated. The code to update the recordset is shown below:

```
'Iterate through controls on form that match fields in recordset
        For Each ctl In frm
            'if error the field is not on the form
            On Error Resume Next
            Err = 0
            vartemp = rst.Fields(ctl.Name).Name
            If Err = 0 Then
                On Error GoTo ErrorHandler
                'if control enabled then
                '   if it is not an auto increment field
                '       if data is not null or an empty string
                If ctl.Enabled Then
                    If Not rst.Fields(ctl.Name).Properties("IsAutoIncrement")
Then
                        If Not IsNull(ctl.Value) And Not ctl.Value = "" Then
                            vartemp = ctl.Value
                            rst(ctl.Name).Value = vartemp
                        End If
                    End If
                End If
            End If
        Next
        'Increment the Update Counter
```

```
rst("UpdateCtr") = rst("UpdateCtr") + 1
'Update the recordset
rst.Update
rst.Close
```

The fields are also checked to see if the field is an Auto Increment type and whether it is enabled. If it is an Auto Increment type, the field value is not updated. The UpdateCtr is incremented by 1.

A message box displays if the record has been successfully saved, and the flagEdited field is reset.

Finding a record

You can find records with the function uf_FindRecord. This function can find a record based on criteria entered in any field on the form. The function checks the value of the FlagFind field on the form. If this flag is true, the form contains the criteria to do the find. If the flag is false, the form is cleared so that the user can enter the criteria. A message displays, telling the user to enter the criteria and to press the Find button again to retrieve the records.

You can set the default value of this flag to True so that when the form is opened, the user can start entering criteria right away. After the function completes, the resulting criteria is stored in the Form's filter property for later use. The function does a check to see if the current record has been saved before clearing the form out for the criteria.

The heart of the operation of this function is to create a criteria string. Criteria can be specified for any combination of fields on the form. The function creates a criteria string with an "AND" between all of the selected fields. For example, in our sample application, you can enter a state and all records for that state are retrieved. You can search for a customer number or a phone number as well. The code to create the criteria string is shown below:

```
'Iterate through controls on form that match fields in recordset
      strCriteria = ""
      For Each ctl In frm
        'if error the field is not on the form
        On Error Resume Next
        Err = 0
        vartemp = rst.Fields(ctl.Name).Name
        If Err = 0 Then
          On Error GoTo ErrorHandler
          If ctl.Enabled Then
            If Not IsNull(ctl.Value) And Not ctl.Value = "" Then
              If Len(strCriteria) > 0 Then strCriteria = strCriteria & " AND "
              Select Case rst(ctl.Name).Type
                Case adChar, adVarWChar, adLongVarWChar
                  strCriteria = strCriteria & ctl.Name & " = " & Chr(39) &
ctl.Value & Chr(39)
```

```
                    Case adDate
                        strCriteria = strCriteria & ctl.Name & " = " & "#" &
ctl.Value & "#"
                    Case Else    'assume numeric
                        strCriteria = strCriteria & ctl.Name & " = " &
str(ctl.Value)
                End Select
            End If
          End If
        End If
      Next
      rst.Close
```

The trick to making the criteria string is to find the fields on the form that the user has filled in and then look up the type of field in the recordset to determine how to format the criteria string. For text fields, we need to enclose the search value in single quotes, and for dates the search value needs to be enclosed with "#". For numbers, no delimiter is needed.

When all of the controls have been checked, the recordset is opened with the criteria. The code below shows how the criteria string is used to retrieve the data:

```
'Open recordset with criteria
      If Len(strCriteria) > 0 Then strCriteria = " WHERE " & strCriteria
      rst.Open "Select * From " & frm.Controls("xRecordset") & strCriteria & "
ORDER by " & frm.Controls("xKey"), cnn, adOpenStatic, adLockBatchOptimistic
      If rst.RecordCount = 0 Then
        MsgBox ("No records found")
        uf_FindRecord = 0
      Else
        uf_FindRecord = rst.RecordCount
        frm.Filter = Mid(strCriteria, 8)    'store the criteria for later
        frm.FlagFind = False
        frm.FlagEdited = False
        'Display first record
        uf_DisplayRecord frm, 1
      End If
```

If the record count is not zero, the criteria string is stored in the form's filter property and the first record is displayed on the form. The uf_FindRecord function calls the uf_DisplayRecord function to display the filtered data on the form.

Unbound forms can improve performance when you are developing an application for a client/server database. However, although bound forms in Access provide built-in processing for retrieving and updating data, you need to duplicate this functionality yourself using Visual Basic code and ADO. Hopefully, the basUnboundFormUtilities module and frmContactsUnbound form included with this book can get you well on your way.

✦   ✦   ✦

Working with Access Projects and SQL Server Tables and Queries

♦ ♦ ♦ ♦

In This Chapter

Checking a project's SQL Server connection

Working with tables in an Access project

Using views to query Data

Manipulating data with stored procedures

Using a user-defined function to perform a calculation

Automatically updating data with triggers

♦ ♦ ♦ ♦

You can use an Access project to create and maintain an MSDE 2000 database. You can also use an Access project to create the user-interface objects — forms, reports, data access pages, macros, and modules — that get their data from MSDE 2000. The database window for a project looks very similar to the Access database window you are already accustomed to. In fact, creating the user-interface objects is virtually the same as creating them in Access. Figure 29-1 shows the database window for the Access Auto Auctions project.

In this chapter, you will use the database file Chap29Start.adp.

Be sure to start the SQL Server Service Manager before opening the example project.

See Chapter 27 for more information on working with the SQL Server Service Manager.

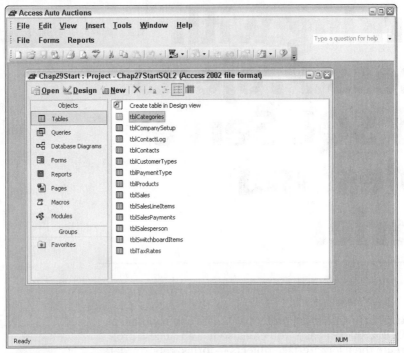

Figure 29-1: Viewing the database window for a project.

Even though you can create the data objects — tables, views, and stored procedures — in a project, the data objects are actually being stored in a separate MSDE 2000 database (.MDF) file. The MSDE 2000 file is created automatically when you upsize data from an Access .mdb file, or when you create a new project.

Determining a Project's Database Name

You can determine the name of the MSDE 2000 database that is connected to the current project by selecting File ➪ Connection from the Access menu. The File ➪ Connection menu option displays the Data Link Properties dialog box. The Data Link Properties dialog box, shown in Figure 29-2, shows the properties for the database connection for the current project.

The data link properties shown in Figure 29-2 are the properties for the connection to the Chap27StartSQL2 database.

Cross-Reference
The properties for creating an MSDE 2000 database connection are covered in Chapter 27.

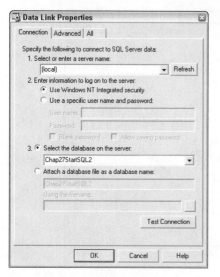

Figure 29-2: Determining a project's database connection.

Working with Tables

Working with a table in an Access project is very similar to working with a table in an Access database. Because the topics of creating tables, queries, forms, and reports are covered in detail in other chapters, this section focuses on the design tool methods that differ from Access database design tool methods.

To view the design of a table, first make sure that the Tables object is selected. Select the name of the table to view. Then select the Design button in the database container. The Table Design window displays.

Working with fields in the Table Design window

Figure 29-3 shows the Table Design window for the tblSales table. The table design tool is fairly similar to the Access database table design tool. The Table Design window consists of two areas:

- ✦ The field entry area
- ✦ The field properties area

The field entry area is where you enter each field's name and the data type and length for each field. The properties area is a tabbed dialog box containing the two tabs, Columns and Lookup. The Columns tab contains a list of properties for each field selected in the field entry area. Field properties are a set of characteristics that provide additional control over how the data in a field is stored, entered, or displayed. The Lookup tab allows you to specify the default control type to use for the field when it is placed on a form.

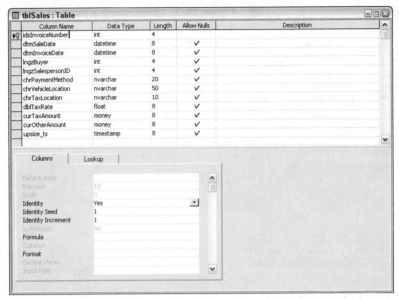

Figure 29-3: The Table Design window.

You can create fields by entering a field name and a field data type in each row of the field entry area of the Table Design window. You must enter a data type and length for each field name that you enter. You can further describe each field by completing any of the extended properties available for the data type that you selected. Table 29-1 describes some of the extended properties that you can set for each field.

Cross-Reference   Chapter 27 discusses the comparison of Access and SQL Server data types.

Table 29-1
Extended Properties

Field Property	Description
Default Value	The default value to set for this column whenever a new row is added to the table.
Precision	Maximum number of digits. Default value provided based on data type.
Scale	Maximum number of digits to the right of the decimal point. Default is 0.
Identity	Autonumbers the records in a table.
Identity Seed	The first number to assign to an identity record. Default is 1.
Identity Increment	The amount to increment each identity record.

Field Property	Description
Is RowGuid	Shows whether the column is used by SQL Server as a ROWGUID column. You can set this value to Yes only for a column that is an identity column.
Formula	Shows the formula for a computed column.
Collation	Shows the collating sequence that SQL Server applies by default to the column whenever the column values are used to sort rows of a query result. To use the default collating sequence for the database, choose <database default>.
Format	Shows the display format for the column.
Decimal Places	Shows the number of decimal places to be used for displaying values of this column. If you choose Auto, the number of decimal places is determined by the value you choose in Format.
Input Mask	Provides a default mask for inputting data into the field.
Caption	Shows the text label that appears by default in forms using this column.
Indexed	Shows whether an index exists on the column.
Hyperlink	Indicates whether the values in this column can be interpreted as hyperlinks.
IME Mode	Determines the IME (Input Method Editor) status of the column for entering international data into the values for the column.
IME Sentence Mode	Determines what additional IME conversion applies by default when users enter values into the column.
Furigana	Used with Japanese IME. Indicates a column into which the Furigana equivalent of the text entered by the user is stored. When the user enters a value into this column, that value is stored, and in addition, the Furigana equivalent of the entered text is stored in the column named in this control.
Postal Address	Specifies a control or field that displays either an address corresponding to an entered postal code or customer barcode data corresponding to an entered address.

The Table Properties window

Figure 29-4 shows the Table Properties window for the tblSales table. The Table Properties window includes five tabs. These five tabs allow you to specify properties for your table.

Figure 29-4: Setting the Table properties.

You can set the following properties using the Tables tab:

✦ **Selected table:** Shows the name of the table that you selected in the Database Container. You cannot update this property.

✦ **Owner:** The name of the user who created the table. The Owner is automatically assigned using the logon ID of the person who created the table, or using the Microsoft SQL Server role that the logon ID is a member of. You cannot update this property. Shows the name of the table's owner.

✦ **Table name:** Shows the name of the table that you selected in the Database Container.You can rename the table using this property.

✦ **Table Identity Column:** Identifies the column that will be auto-incremented. You can choose a column from the drop-down list, or leave the property blank if you do not want an auto-increment column for the table.

✦ **Table ROWGUID Column:** Identifies the column that will be used as a unique identifier for database replication. You can choose a column from the drop-down list, or leave the property blank if you do not want to use database replication.

✦ **Table Filegroup:** Identifies the file group where the table's data will be stored. If you have created file groups for your project, you can select a file group from the drop-down list. If you have not set up a file group for your project, Access assigns the table to the default file group called Primary.

✦ **Text Filegroup:** Identifies the file group where the table's text and image data will be stored. You can select a file group from the drop-down list. Access assigns the Primary file group if you have not set up a file group for the project.

✦ **Description:** Displays a description for the table. This field can be edited.

The Relationships tab, shown in Figure 29-5, shows the relationships properties for the tblSales table. You can use this tab to set up relationships between a table and one or more other tables in the database.

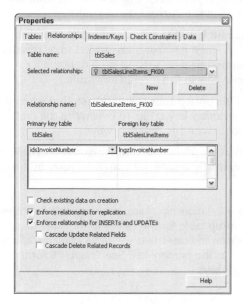

Figure 29-5: Setting the Relationships properties.

You can set up a relationship for the table using the following properties:

✦ **Table name:** Displayes the name of the table that you selected in the Database Container.

✦ **Selected relationship:** Displays the name of a relationship that has been defined for the table. You can view the properties for other relationships defined for this table using the drop-down list.

✦ **New:** Select this button to create a new relationship for the selected database table.

✦ **Delete:** Select this button to remove the selected relationship from the database.

✦ **Relationship name:** Displays the name of the relationship shown in the Selected relationship field. To rename the relationship, enter a new name in this field.

✦ **Primary key table:** Displays the name of the table that is the primary key table for the relationship. The column names listed below the Primary key table field are the primary key table's columns that are participating in the relationship.

✦ **Foreign key table:** Displays the name of the table that is the foreign key table for the relationship. The column names listed below the Foreign key table field are the foreign key table's columns that are participating in the relationship.

✦ **Check existing data on creation:** If you check this option after making changes to the Relationship properties, the database will check to make sure that the changes can be applied to data that already exists in the database.

✦ **Enforce relationship for replication:** If you check this option, the database will copy the relationship to replicas of the current database.

✦ **Enforce relationship for INSERTs and UPDATEs:** If you check this option, the database will apply the relationship when new rows are added to or rows are deleted from the database. This option prevents users from deleting a row in the primary key table if it matches a row in the foreign key table.

✦ **Cascade Update Related Fields:** This option tells the database that when the primary key value changes in the primary key table, to overwrite the matching key values in the foreign key table with the new key value.

✦ **Cascade Delete Related Fields:** Tells the database that when a row is deleted in the primary key table, to automatically delete the matching rows in the foreign key table.

Note

When a key icon displays next to the Relationship Name property, this indicates that the selected table acts as the lookup table for the values in the table named as the foreign-key table. An infinity icon indicates that the table contains values that are looked up in the table listed as the primary-key. See Chapter 6 for more information about primary and foreign keys.

The Indexes/Keys tab (see Figure 29-6) shows the primary key columns and other indexes created for the tblSales table. You can use the Indexes/Keys tab to specify primary keys, indexes, and unique constraints for the table.

Figure 29-6: Setting the Indexes/Keys properties.

Use the following properties to set up an index for the table:

✦ **Table name:** Displays the name of the table that you selected in the Database Container.

✦ **Selected index:** Displays the name of an index that has been defined for the table. You can view the properties for other indexes defined for this table using the drop-down list.

✦ **Type:** Displays the type of the index selected in the Selected index field. The type can be Index, Primary key, or Unique constraint. You cannot update this property.

Note   A constraint is a way to limit the values that a user can enter into a field in a table. A unique constraint ensures that no duplicate values are entered into specified columns that are not a table's primary key. For example, a Social Security Number column could be defined as a unique constraint, so a user cannot enter the same social security number for two different employees.

✦ **New:** Select this button to create a new Index or Key for the table.

✦ **Delete:** Select this button to remove the index selected in the Selected index field.

Note   If you try to delete a primary key that participates in relationships, a message appears asking you if you want to delete all the relationships, too. You cannot delete a primary key without first deleting the relationships that it participates in.

✦ **Index name:** Displays the name of the index in the Selected index field. You can rename the index by entering a new name in this field.

✦ **Column name/Order:** Lists one or more column names that are participating in the selected index. You can use the Order column to sort the column values in either ascending or descending order.

✦ **Index Filegroup:** If you have defined Filegroups, you can select one for the selected index here, or accept the default Primary Filegroup.

✦ **Create Unique:** When you check this option, the database will check all new rows added to the table to make sure the values for the index columns are unique. When you select this option, you also must specify whether you are creating an index or a constraint. When you select the Index button, you can also select the option Ignore Duplicate Key. The Ignore Duplicate Key options tells the database that it can allow duplicate values for the index columns for bulk inserts. If you leave Ignore Duplicate Key unchecked and perform a bulk insert, the entire bulk insert will be rejected if any values for this index are not unique.

✦ **Fill factor:** You can use this option to specify how full the database can fill each index page. If you leave this option as 0%, the database will use the default Fill factor. Use this option for fine-tuning database performance.

✦ **Pad Index:** If you specified a Fill Factor of more than zero percent, and you selected the option to create a unique index, you can use this option to tell the database to use the Fill Factor as the amount of space to leave open on each interior node of the index.

✦ **Create as CLUSTERED:** Use this option to create the index as a clustered index.

Note

Creating an index as clustered tells the database to keep the physical order of the rows in the table the same as the order of the index's key values. You can create only one clustered index for a table. A clustered index is a good idea for a table that will participate in queries that return large volumes of data. It is also a good idea for lookup-type tables that contain only a small number of rows that are fairly static. It can take a significant amount of time to modify a clustered index because the database must physically reorder the rows in the table.

✦ **Don't automatically re-compute statistics:** Use this option to tell the database to continue using previously created statistics. If you select this option, the index will be created much more quickly, but over time performance will degrade using outdated statistics.

✦ **Validation Text:** Use this field to enter an appropriate message to display when a user attempts an operation that violates the index.

When you want to define a non-unique constraint for a table, you can use the Check Constraints tab, shown in Figure 29-7. Constraints are similar to validation rules in an Access database.

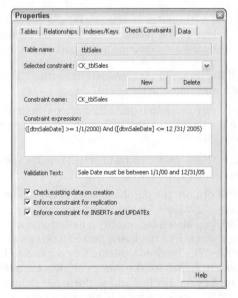

Figure 29-7: Viewing the Check Constraints page.

Use the following properties on the Check Constraints tab to set up a new constraint for a table:

✦ **Table name:** Displays the name of the table that you selected in the Database Container.

✦ **Selected Constraint:** Displays the name of a constraint that has been defined for the table. You can view the properties for other constraints defined for this table using the drop-down list.

✦ **New:** Select this button to create a new constraint for the selected database table.

✦ **Delete:** Select this button to remove the selected constraint from the database.

✦ **Constraint name:** Displays the name of the constraint in the Selected Constraint field. You can rename the constraint by entering a new name in this field.

✦ **Constraint expression:** Displays the SQL syntax of the constraint you selected in the Selected Constraint field. This field is required for new constraints.

✦ **Validation Text: :** Use this field to enter an appropriate message to display when a user attempts an operation that violates the constraint.

✦ **Check existing data on creation:** If you check this option after making changes to the Check Constraint properties, the database will check to make sure that the changes can be applied to data that already exists in the database.

✦ **Enforce constraint for replication:** If you check this option, the database will copy the check constraint to replicas of the current database.

✦ **Enforce constraint for INSERTs and UPDATEs: :** If you check this option, the database will apply the check constraint when new rows are added to or rows are deleted from the database. The Data tab allows you to set the sort order and subdatasheet for a table. Figure 29-8 shows the Data tab for the tblSales table.

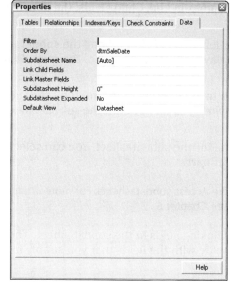

Figure 29-8: Setting the Data properties.

To set up a sort order or subdatasheet, use these properties in the Data tab:

✦ **Filter:** Displays the SQL syntax for the Filter to apply to the table.

✦ **Order By:** Displays the column name to sort the table on. To enter more than one column name, separate the column names with a comma.

Caution

Setting the Filter and/or Order By properties performs client-side operations. That is, the data is filtered and/or sorted by the client when the client receives the entire result set from the database.

Tip

If you want to sort records in descending order, type **DESC** at the end of the string expression.

✦ **Subdatasheet Name:** Displays the name of the table or query to bind to the subdatasheet. Accept the default, [Auto], to tell the database to use existing relationships to determine which table to bind to the subdatasheet.

✦ **Link Child Fields:** Displays the column or columns in the subdatasheet that match the column or columns in Link Master Fields. Although the column names do not have to be the same as the column names in Link Master Fields, the data in the columns must match.

✦ **Link Master Fields:** Displays the column or columns that coincide with the column or columns in Link Child Fields. Although the column names do not have to be the same as the column names in Link Child Fields, the data in the columns must match.

✦ **Subdatasheet Height:** Displays the default heightfor viewing the subdatasheet.. A vertical scrollbar will display automatically if all of the rows do not fit in the selected height.

✦ **Subdatasheet Expanded:** Select Yes to automatically expand the subdatasheet when the table opens. Select No if you do not want the subdatasheet to expand automatically.

✦ **Default View:** Displays the view type for the subdatasheet. You can select from Datasheet, PivotTable, or PivotChart.

Cross-Reference

Subdatasheets in a project work just like Access subdatasheets. For more information on working with subdatasheets, see Chapter 6.

✦ **Link Child Fields:** Shows the list of linking fields in the subdatasheet. The fields that you list here should coincide with the fields that you supply in the Link Master Fields control.

Understanding Project Queries

You use queries in an Access project the same way you use them in an Access database — to view, change, add, or delete data.

Projects provide three types of queries for working with data:

- ✦ Views
- ✦ Stored procedures
- ✦ User-defined functions

As Chapter 27 explains, project tables are not stored within the Access project. Neither are views, stored procedures, and user-defined functions. Instead, they are stored in the server database.

Note Access projects don't store any data or data-definition type objects. Only code-type objects, such as forms, reports, links to data access pages, macros, and modules are stored in the project. All data-related objects are stored directly in the server database.

Creating views

Of the three query types, the view is the type most similar to an Access query. You use a view when you need to retrieve one or more columns from one or more related tables in the database. The View Query Designer works just like the Access Query Designer. If you are comfortable using the Access Query Designer, you will find that the Query Designer for a View is just as easy to use.

To create a view, select the Queries object and then select Create view in designer. The Query Designer opens. You can add a table, another view, or a function to the new view by selecting from the list of tables, views, and functions shown in the Add Table window. The Add Table window displays, as shown in Figure 29-9.

When you have finished using the Add Table window, select the close button to close the Add Tables window. When the Add Tables window closes, you can begin working with the Query Designer window. You can select columns and enter criteria in the same way that you design queries in an Access database. Figure 29-10 shows the qryCustomerMailingLabels query in the Query Designer window.

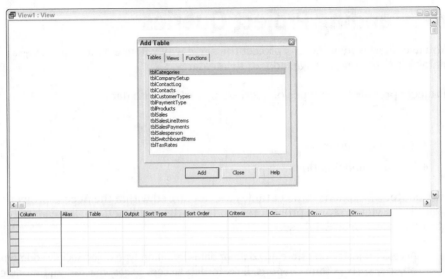

Figure 29-9: The Add Table window in the Query Designer window.

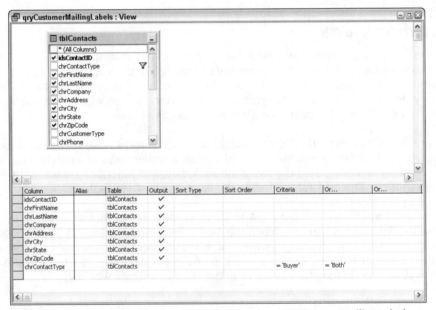

Figure 29-10: The Query Designer window for the qryCustomerMailingLabels query.

With views, you can retrieve information that is stored in tables or related tables from functions, or even from other views. You can retrieve all the rows and columns from a table, or select individual columns and specify criteria to filter the rows to retrieve. When you select columns and specify criteria, symbols display next to the table's column name to indicate the type of operation to be performed on the field. Figure 29-10 shows that criteria have been specified for the chrContactType column.

Views support only SELECT queries. If you need to use commands, such as UPDATE, INSERT, or APPEND, you must create a stored procedure.

Creating stored procedures

A *stored procedure* is a special type of query that allows you to use commands to manipulate data in the database. Creating a stored procedure is very similar to creating a view or an Access database query.

Stored procedures provide a handy container for storing all of the SQL statements that you use throughout your application. Instead of writing SQL statements in your code, you can store them here and call them from your code in much the same way that you call a function stored in a module. Some of the many benefits of stored procedures are as follows:

✦ Can contain multiple SQL statements.

✦ Can call another stored procedure name.

✦ Can receive parameters and return a value or a result set.

✦ Are stored in a compiled state on the server, so they execute faster than if they were embedded in your code.

✦ Are stored in a common container in your application so that others can maintain them more easily.

Using a stored procedure to sort data

To create a new stored procedure, first make sure that the Queries object is selected. Then select the item labeled Create stored procedure in designer. The Design window for the spCustomersAlphabetized stored procedure is shown in Figure 29-11.

The spCustomersAlphabetized stored procedure includes the same table, columns, and criteria as the qryCustomerMailingLabels view. The difference is that the spCustomersAlphabetized stored procedure specifies a Sort Order for the chrLastName and chrFirstName columns.

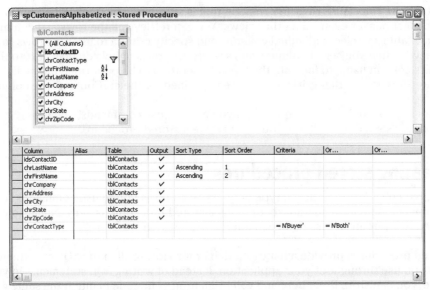

Figure 29-11: Creating a stored procedure.

You can specify a Sort Order for a column in a view. However, to sort a view requires the use of the TOP 100 PERCENT clause with the Select statement. When you add a Sort Order to a view, Access automatically adds the TOP 100 PERCENT clause to the Select statement.

Caution

The TOP clause degrades performance because it causes the sorting to be done on the client machine instead of on the server. The TOP clause is not required for sorting Select queries in a stored procedure. The server performs sorting of stored procedure data.

Tip

You can add a view to a stored procedure.

When you use the graphical tools of the Query Design window to create a stored procedure, Access converts what you create into Transact-SQL programming language. The Transact-SQL commands are what SQL Server actually executes when the query runs. You can view the Transact-SQL program for the stored procedure by selecting View ➪ SQL View from the Query menu. Figure 29-12 shows the SQL View for the spCustomersAlphabetized stored procedure.

You can make changes to the stored procedure using either the Design window or the SQL window. As you are working with the stored procedure, you can alternately switch between view modes. If you are viewing in SQL view, you can return to the Design view by selecting View ➪ Design View. Any changes that you made to the query in SQL view are reflected in the Design view. When you make changes to the query in the Design view window, the changes are immediately updated in the SQL view window.

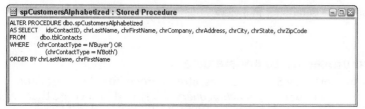

Figure 29-12: Viewing the SQL View of a stored procedure.

Tip

If you are proficient in creating stored procedures on your own, you can even create a new stored procedure directly in the SQL window.

Using parameters with a stored procedure

If you want to run a stored procedure with different criteria values every time you run it, you can add a parameter to the stored procedure's criteria. A *parameter* is a place-holder for the column's criteria. For example, you may want to retrieve all sales of a certain product category. But, you may want to retrieve all sales of SUV-types one time, or all sales of Minivans another time. The spSalesForCategory stored procedure uses the Enter_Category parameter, as shown in Figure 29-13.

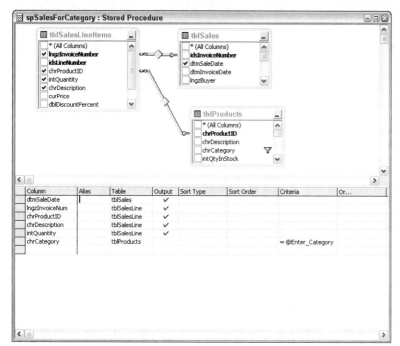

Figure 29-13: Creating a stored procedure with a parameter.

Note   You can't specify a parameter in a view.

Using a stored procedure to update data

Although views support only Select queries, stored procedures support action queries as well as Select queries. An *action query* is a stored procedure that inserts, modifies, or deletes data by using the SQL INSERT, UPDATE, and DELETE statements. The spUpdateProductPrice stored procedure, shown in Figure 29-14, is an example of an Update action query.

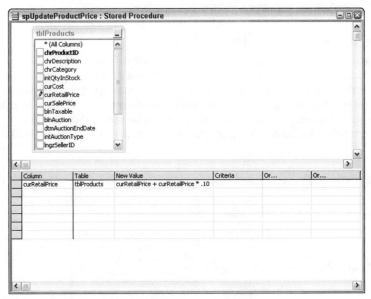

Figure 29-14: An Update action query.

The spUpdateProductPrice stored procedure increases each of the values in the curRetailPrice column in the tblProducts table by 10 percent. Notice that the Grid pane of the stored procedure contains different columns than the columns shown in the Select query examples. To create an action query using the Query Designer, select the Query menu item. Then choose the type of action query that you want to create: Make-Table, Update, Append, Append Values, or Delete.

Creating user-defined functions

User-defined functions combine the best features of views and stored procedures into a single query. You can pass parameters to user-defined functions. They can also include views, stored procedures, or other functions. User-defined functions can't be used to update, insert, or delete data in a database.

To create a function, select the Queries object and then select Create function in designer. The Query Designer opens. You can add a table, a view, or another function to the new function by selecting from the list of tables, views, and functions shown in the Add Table window.

The design for the fnSalesForCategory function, shown in Figure 29-15, looks just like the design for the spSalesForCategory stored procedure.

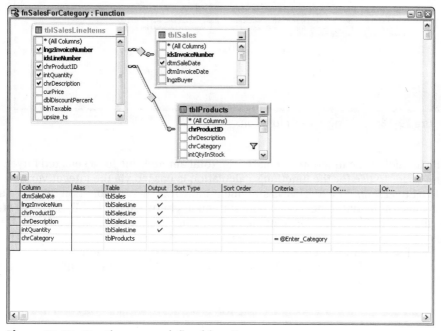

Figure 29-15: Creating a user-defined function.

Basically, the user-defined function is a simpler version of the stored procedure. If your query needs to accept one or more parameters and return a single value or a single table, you should use a user-defined function for the query rather than a stored procedure. Stored procedures are geared for performing more complex query operations, such as multiple Select statements, table updates, and returning multiple result sets.

You can create two types of user-defined functions:

✦ Scalar functions

✦ Table-valued functions

Creating a function to return a single value

Scalar functions return a single data value of the type defined in a RETURNS clause. Figure 29-16 shows the SQL View for the fnCalcBalDue function.

```
⚙ fnCalcBalDue : Function                                                  ⊟◻☒
ALTER FUNCTION dbo.fnCalcBalDue
       (@lngzBuyerNum as int)
RETURNS money
AS
      BEGIN

          RETURN (SELECT  Sum( fnCalcExtension.ExtendedAmount + dbo.tblSales.curTaxAmount + dbo.tblSales.curOtherAmount - fnCalcPayments.Payments)  AS TotAmt
          FROM      dbo.tblSales LEFT OUTER JOIN
          dbo.fnCalcPayments() fnCalcPayments ON dbo.tblSales.idsInvoiceNumber = fnCalcPayments.lngzInvoiceNumber LEFT OUTER JOIN
          dbo.fnCalcExtension() fnCalcExtension ON dbo.tblSales.idsInvoiceNumber = fnCalcExtension.lngzInvoiceNumber
          WHERE    (dbo.tblSales.lngzBuyer = @lngzBuyerNum) )

      END
```

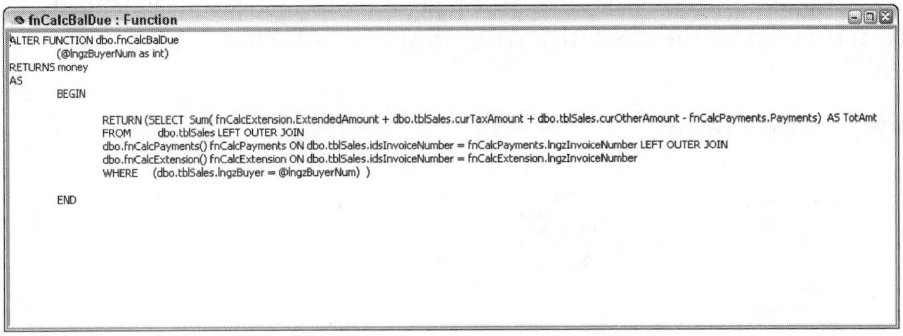

Figure 29-16: Creating a scalar function.

The fnCalcBalDue function calculates the total amount due for a selected buyer. The buyer to use for the function's calculation is passed via the integer variable @lngzBuyerNum. The RETURNS statement indicates that the function returns a single value of the datatype money. The statements between the BEGIN and END statements are the Transact-SQL statements that compute the return value. When the function executes, it performs the query specified in the SELECT statement. The SELECT statement retrieves the data from the database to compute the value of TotAmt. The value of TotAmt that results from the SELECT statement becomes the RETURN value for the function.

You can use a scalar user-defined function in a query the same way you use built-in functions in queries. To call the fnCalcBalDue function, you use a query like this one:

```
SELECT * FROM tblContacts WHERE dbo.fnCalcBalDue(tblContacts.idsContactID) >=
2000
```

When you call a user-defined function, you must use two-part syntax. Two-part syntax refers to prefixing an object reference with the object owner's name. In the example above, dbo refers to the owner of the function fnCalcBalDue. When you select a table, view, or function in the Query Designer, Access automatically inserts the object owner's name.

> **Note**   In SQL Server, the dbo is a special user who has permissions to perform all activities in the database. Any member of the sysadmin fixed server role who uses a database is automatically identified as a dbo. When a dbo user creates database objects, SQL Server assigns the ownership of those objects to the user dbo. Users who belong to server roles other than sysadmin are not identified as dbo users. When non-dbo users create database objects, their username is assigned as the object's owner.

Creating a function to return a table

Table-valued functions return a table of data. Figure 29-17 shows the SQL View for the fnSalesForCategory function.

```
fnSalesForCategory : Function
ALTER FUNCTION dbo.fnSalesForCategory
(@Enter_Category nvarchar(50))
RETURNS TABLE
AS
RETURN ( SELECT    dbo.tblSales.dtmSaleDate, dbo.tblSalesLineItems.lngzInvoiceNumber, dbo.tblSalesLineItems.chrProductID, dbo.tblSalesLineItems.chrDescription,
              dbo.tblSalesLineItems.intQuantity
FROM       dbo.tblSalesLineItems INNER JOIN
              dbo.tblSales ON dbo.tblSalesLineItems.lngzInvoiceNumber = dbo.tblSales.idsInvoiceNumber INNER JOIN
              dbo.tblProducts ON dbo.tblSalesLineItems.chrProductID = dbo.tblProducts.chrProductID
WHERE     (dbo.tblProducts.chrCategory = @Enter_Category) )
```

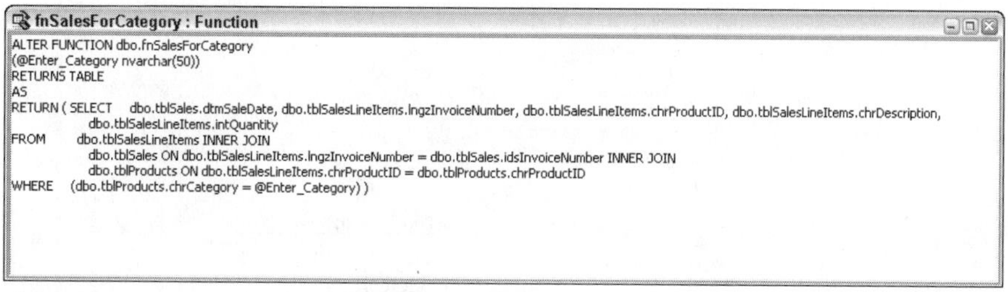

Figure 29-17: Creating an inline function.

The function shown in Figure 29-17 is the SQL View of the function shown in Figure 29-15. The fnSalesForCategory function returns the sales detail information for sales of a specified category. The nvarchar variable @Enter_Category contains the category parameter passed by the calling program. The RETURNS TABLE statement shows that the function will return a table of data containing one or more records. The RETURN statement contains a single SQL statement. When the function executes, it performs the query specified in the SELECT statement. The SELECT statement retrieves the row or rows of data from the database. The table that results from the SELECT statement becomes the RETURN value for the function.

Using functions in stored procedures

You can create a stored procedure that combines information from tables with tables and values that are returned from user-defined functions. Figure 29-18 shows the spCombined stored procedure.

The spCombined stored procedure calculates the total amount due for each invoice in the tblSales table. This stored procedure joins the tblSales table to the fnCalcPayments and fnCalcExtension functions.

When you add a function to the Query Designer, the Query Designer displays the function's columns just as if they were columns in a table. In the spCombined stored procedure, the ExtendedAmount value in the fnCalcExtension function is included as a column in the stored procedure's output. It is also included in the stored procedure's calculated column called TotalDue.

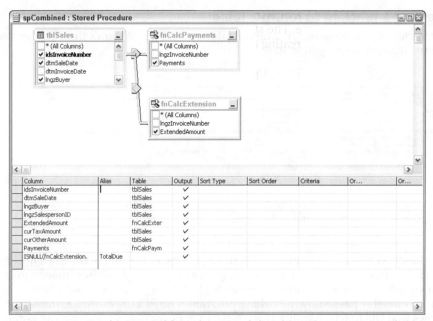

Figure 29-18: Combining a table with a user-defined function.

Using triggers to automatically update data

A trigger is a special type of stored procedure that you can implement that will execute automatically whenever a table is updated, records are deleted, or new records are added. Triggers can include complex SQL statements that can query or even update other tables the instant that a change occurs to the table associated with the trigger.

To create a trigger, select the Tables object and then select the table that you want to create the trigger on. Right-click the name of the table to display the shortcut menu. Choose Triggers . . . from the shortcut menu. The Triggers for Table dialog box displays. Select New to create a new trigger for the table. The SQL View window for the new trigger displays as shown in Figure 29-19.

```
tblSales_Trigger1 : Trigger
CREATE TRIGGER tblSales_Trigger1
ON dbo.tblSales
FOR /* INSERT, UPDATE, DELETE */
AS
        /* IF UPDATE (column_name) ...*/
```

Figure 29-19: Creating a trigger.

The SQL View window for a new trigger looks very similar to the SQL View window for a new stored procedure. The statements that automatically display serve as a template to assist you in creating the Transact-SQL statements for the new trigger.

Figure 29-20 shows the tblSales_UpdateContact trigger for the tblSales table.

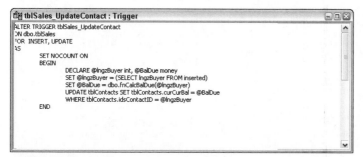

```
ALTER TRIGGER tblSales_UpdateContact
ON dbo.tblSales
FOR INSERT, UPDATE
AS
        SET NOCOUNT ON
        BEGIN
                DECLARE @lngzBuyer int, @BalDue money
                SET @lngzBuyer = (SELECT lngzBuyer FROM inserted)
                SET @BalDue = dbo.fnCalcBalDue(@lngzBuyer)
                UPDATE tblContacts SET tblContacts.curCurBal = @BalDue
                WHERE tblContacts.idsContactID = @lngzBuyer
        END
```

Figure 29-20: Using a trigger to update data in another table.

The trigger tblSales_UpdateContact executes whenever an insert or update occurs to the tblSales table. This trigger includes some complex Transact-SQL statements. It first declares two local variables: @lngzBuyer and @BalDue. The @lngzBuyer variable is used to retrieve the buyer ID (lngzBuyer) of the new or changed record.

Note   In SQL Server, when a new record is added to a table, it is first stored temporarily in a table called inserted. When the new record is saved, the record is moved from the inserted table to the target database table. When a record is changed, it is first stored temporarily in the inserted table. When the changed record is saved, the original record is deleted and the changed record is added from the inserted table to the target table.

Next, the trigger calls the function fnCalcBalDue to calculate the total of the invoice amounts and payments for this buyer and stores the function's result in the variable @BalDue. Then, the UPDATE SQL Statement updates the curCurBal field in the tblContacts record with the @BalDue value for the selected buyer.

The big advantage of implementing a stored procedure as a trigger is that a trigger will execute regardless of whether the change to the table's data has occurred in the table manually or through a form.

✦   ✦   ✦

PART III

Creating Web Applications

SECTION V

Creating Data Access Pages and Using XML and InfoPath

Using and Creating Access Objects for Intranets and the Internet

The Internet, and particularly the World Wide Web, has become an important part of all businesses today. Whether you simply use the Internet to search for information or whether you're part of a vast corporate intranet, you need to be able to use Microsoft Access to store and disseminate the data that is moved across the network wire.

Access contains many features that allow you to store data found on the Internet in your database container in standard Access tables. You can also create a table, form, or report in Access and save it as an HTML-based table, which you can then use on any Web site. In addition, Access offers a feature known as *data access pages*; these are a special type of Web page. They allow you to view and work with data by using Microsoft's Internet Explorer browser (version 5.x or better), which gives you access to dynamic (live) and static (non-updated) information across an intranet or the Internet. You can store this data in a Microsoft Access database or a Microsoft SQL Server database.

What Are Intranets?

An *intranet* is simply the use of Internet technologies within an organization (or company). Intranets help in cutting costs and offer fast and easy accessibility to day-to-day information. They offer some features that are often lacking in Internet technology — speed, security, and control. An intranet is a network (or networks) that works on a local or wide area network that uses TCP/IP, HTTP, and other Internet protocols and looks like a private version of the Internet. You can use an intranet in much the same way that you use the World Wide Web to store information on home pages and Web sites. One of the leading methods of creating World Wide Web pages is to use HyperText Markup Language (HTML). This is the de facto language of the Web. Web browsers (such as Amaya, Internet Explorer, Netscape, Opera, and others) read and interpret this HTML code to display the text and graphics on the screen.

On the CD-ROM

This chapter will use the database named CHAP30Start.mdb. It also requires two additional HTML files — New Customers.htm and MyTemplate01.htm. If you have not already copied them onto your machine from the CD, you will need to do so now. When you have completed this chapter, your database should resemble the one in CHAP30End.mdb and all the associated files with it.

Before you can use Chap30End.mdb, you will need to refresh the links for all the HTML files and Data Access Pages (DAP).

Types of Web Pages That Access Can Create

Microsoft Access can create many different types of Web pages. It can create Data Access Pages, up-to-date read-only data pages, or (static) snapshots of data from a table, query, form, or report.

If you need to manipulate the data from your databases directly in a Web page, you need to create data access pages. If you simply want to have up-to-date, read-only data displayed, you can create Active Server Pages (ASP) or IDC/HTX files used by Microsoft Internet Information Server. If you only want to display a snapshot of information from a specific point and time, you can create plain static HTML documents.

To make sure that your Web pages appear consistent, you can also use an HTML template file that you create.

Data access pages

Data access pages, or DAPs, were first introduced in Access 2000. In the simplest sense, data access pages are a combination of forms and reports for the Web.

Note DAPs are HTML pages that are attached directly to data in the database and can be used to display static or dynamic information. They can be attached to a single table or several tables via a query. They can be used like Access forms, except that data access pages are designed to run in the Internet Explorer 5.x Web browser. They are HTML pages that can be deployed to the Internet, deployed to an intranet, or used within Access.

Older versions of Access, like Access 97, didn't use or create data access pages; however, you had the ability to create a form or report and publish it to an HTML document viewable on the Web. These HTML documents, or pages, were static — the data was fixed, not updatable. Access still lets you create static data pages from your tables, queries, forms, and reports (discussed later in this chapter), but data access pages remove the interim step of exporting an object to an HTML page, because they are HTML documents from the start. As pointed out at the beginning of this section, data access pages were first introduced in Access 2000.

You can view active and dynamic data, update data, and print data access pages. You can apply filters, sort, or manipulate objects within the HTML document (like Pivot Tables, Charts, and Spreadsheets) in real-time.

New Feature Access 2003 extends the functionality of data access pages in several areas, including deployment, ability to directly create a data access page from other objects (tables, queries, forms, and reports), and more flexibility in designing and browsing DAPs. It also includes more robust support for eXtensible Markup Language (XML) — including it in your DAPs. This functionality is a result of the technologies that are built into Internet Explorer (version 5.5 is recommended) and the Office Web Components.

Unlike Access forms and reports, data access pages are stored in the Windows file system as HTML pages, rather than in the Access database or project.

After you create them, you can use data access pages directly in an Access program or within the Web browser. These files are specifically designed for Internet Explorer 5.0 (or greater) and make use of dynamic HTML and XML technology.

What Is HTML?

If you're unfamiliar with HTML, you should make this topic your next learning experience. Web pages are formatted by using a special language called HyperText Markup Language (HTML). With HTML, you can create a Web page containing text, pictures, or links to other Web pages. Each Web page is identified by its address, which is called a *Uniform Resource Locator* (URL): for example, `http://www.databasecreations.com` or `http://www.ItInAsia.com`. Using Access' Internet tools, you can translate Access objects and data into an HTML-compatible format.

Note At the time of this writing, data access pages (DAPs) work only with Microsoft's Internet Explorer 5.0 (or greater). To take advantage of many of the new features of DAPs in Access, you need to use IE 5.5 (or greater). Many of the features of DAPs also rely upon the Office XP Microsoft Web Components (MSOWC). Both of these applications need to be installed on your computer to take full advantage of the power of DAPs.

Data access pages are more than simple forms for the Internet. They offer a totally new way for the user to interact with live data. Using the browser, you can display summarized data, such as Sales By Product or Sales By Month. With a mouse click, you can also display the detail information for each summarized item — for example, individual sales by invoice. The tools to summarize, expand, sort, and filter the data are available in the browser itself. These pages let you work with dynamic information; that is, your browser can access live data from within your databases in an interactive fashion.

Tip To build a data access page, users work with the new Data Access Page designer; Access can open any existing HTML file in this feature. After you open a page in Access, you can add data-bound fields to the page easily and quickly. To build a data access page, users work with the Data Access Page designer.

Working with dynamic and static views of Web-based data

When working with data in Web-based files, you can access the data statically (data that never changes) or dynamically (data that can change). If the data doesn't change, the HTML file can display the information statically. Data access pages are not necessary to create stagnant data. However, if the data that is to be displayed in the HTML page changes often, you want to display the data dynamically, using a data access page.

Typically, an HTML page, created via the data access page, gets its data from an Access database or an Access project connected to a SQL Server database (version 6.5 or greater).

How Web applications use static HTML pages

Web applications — specifically browsers — use static HTML pages to display data that was originally in a database table or series of tables. It is static; after you create the HTML page, the data in the page doesn't change. The data is a physical part of the page; it is actually embedded in the page.

Access lets you create a static Web page from any table or query by exporting the datasheet results to an HTML page.

To create a static Web page from any table or query, simply select the table or query object that you want to export from within the correct database container (table or query object type). After you highlight the table or query object, select File ➪ Export from the menu. An alternate method is to right-click the object (table or query name) and select Export from the pop-up menu. This activates an Export As dialog box that allows you to specify a name for the new file and how you want to save it. Follow these steps to export the tblContacts table of the Chap30Start database to a static HTML page:

1. Select the tblContacts table in the Chap30Start database (only highlight it; you don't need to open it).

2. Select File ➪ Export from the menu, or right-click and select Export from the pop-up menu. Access displays the Export Table dialog box (and displays the Customer table name in the title bar).

3. Select "HTML Documents" from the Save as type text box.

4. Type **ContactsTable** in the File name text box.

5. Click Export to save the tblContacts table to the file named *ContactsTable.html*.

Figure 30-1 shows the exporting of the tblContacts table to an HTML page. It shows the active Export [table or query name] As dialog box.

As Figure 30-1 shows, you can choose a specific format for the HTML page to be created. To choose a specific format, simply click the Save formatted check box, and when you click the Export button, you are given another dialog box—the HTML Output Options, as shown in Figure 30-2. You can choose a specific HTML template format file by typing in a name or by clicking the Browse button and selecting from existing HTML templates.

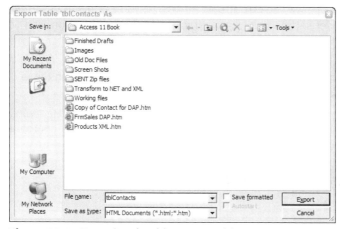

Figure 30-1: Exporting the tblContacts table to an HTML page.

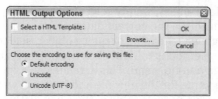

Figure 30-2: Specifying an HTML template format file for saving a table in HTML format.

How Web applications use dynamic HTML pages

In contrast to static pages, dynamic HTML pages support viewing and working with live, up-to-date data. A Web application can display and work with live data from databases in several ways. Traditionally, this was accomplished using server-side technology. Methods such as CGI (Common Gateway Interface) and Microsoft's ASP (Active Server Pages) do the job. These are programming methodologies that allow you to write code and store it at the server level where the database application resides. Then, when the user wants to look at live data, the user sends a CGI script or ASP query to the database sitting on the Web server. The server takes this request and processes it, returning the requested data to the end user.

Previously, the data being sent back was up-to-date, but not live, and it was stored in an HTML file that your browser displayed. This changed with Access 2000 and is enhanced in Access 2003, which uses ASP technology tied together with Microsoft's implementation of the Extensible Markup Language (XML).

What Are HTML Template Files?

An *HTML template file* is a file that you create in HTML that is used by Access to enhance the appearance and navigation of your HTML-generated files. You can use it to include a company logo in the header section, a background image in the body section, and your own navigation buttons in the footer section of an HTML report.

The template is a text file that includes HTML tags and tokens that are unique to Access. The tokens are used to tell Access where to insert output and other information in the generated HTML files.

If you specify an HTML template file in the dialog box, Access merges the HTML template file with the .html, .asp, and .htx output files, replacing the tokens with the appropriate items.

Cross-Reference For a more detailed explanation of HTML Template Files, see the "HTML Template Files" section later in this chapter.

Working with dynamic HTML

You use dynamic HTML when you need to access data that changes frequently and you or your users need to enter and retrieve live data from an Access database using a Web form.

Access lets you create dynamic HTML pages, or data access pages, from within Access and display them in Access or Microsoft's Internet Explorer 5.0 or greater. Figure 30-3 shows a data access page in Access. This page displays information about buyers and their purchases.

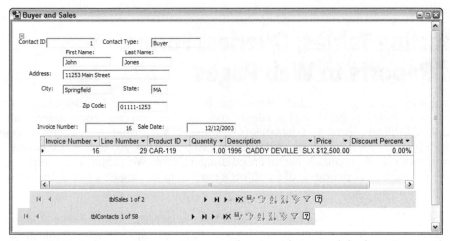

Figure 30-3: A data access page in Access showing a buyer and the buyer's purchases for each invoice.

You can create these pages to display and work with your data in either datasheet or form mode.

After you create them, you can add new records, modify existing information stored in the tables, or simply view records in the Access tables from the Web. You can even move between records in the table or from within the browser by using HTML-based controls located on the dynamic HTML Web form.

Note   Access 2003 uses HTML table tags for the navigational controls — thus improving performance of DAPs — and removes the ActiveX controls from the Office Web Components DLL file (as in previous versions). Finally, the Navigation control now uses styles and images, letting you customize the images and formatting of the Control.

What Is XML?

XML, or eXtensible Markup Language, is a standard language for describing how data, which is displayed on the Web in browsers, is delivered across the Web. It works in conjunction with HyperText Markup Language (HTML), which is the language that is used to create and display Web pages. HTML is an excellent tool for displaying text and image information in Web browsers, but it is very limited in the way it can handle data and data structures. This job is delegated to XML, which defines the data and how it should be structured, separating the data from the presentation.

Exporting Tables, Queries, Forms, and Reports to Web Pages

You may often want to output information from an Access table, query, form, or report to a Web page. Using the File ➪ Export option, you can export individual tables, forms, reports, and datasheets to static HTML format. Access creates one Web page for each report page, datasheet, and form that you export. Exporting objects to HTML format is useful for creating a simple Web application, verifying the format and appearance of an object's output, or adding files to existing Web applications.

When you export an object, you can also specify an HTML template file along with your output files. The HTML template contains HTML tags and special tokens unique to Access that enhance the appearance, consistency, and navigation of your Web pages.

Exporting an Access table to static HTML format

If you want to export a table to static HTML format, you simply click the table name in the database container and select File ➪ Export. For example, earlier in the chapter, you exported the tblContacts table to an HTML page named ContactsTable.html.

Cross-Reference   See the section titled "How Web applications use static HTML pages," earlier in this chapter.

The resulting HTML page is based on the entire table. Values from most fields (except OLE objects and hyperlink fields) are output as strings. Fields with a Hyperlink data type are output as HTML links using <A HREF> tags. All unformatted data types, except Text and Memo, are saved with right alignment as the default. Text and Memo fields are saved with left alignment by default. OLE objects are simply ignored and not included in the resulting HTML page.

Figure 30-4 shows the resulting HTML page that you can create by following the above steps. Notice that it doesn't include many items you may expect. For example, it doesn't include column headings for each of the columns. Also, the widths of several of the columns (for example, ZipCode and Telephone Number) appear randomly selected. It does include the name of the table centered across the top line (you may have to move the horizontal direction bar to see it). Also, the discount field has been converted from a percentage using the percent sign to a decimal value (5% is now 0.05) and some records appear to be missing values (have blank spaces like the notes and some of the discount amount records).

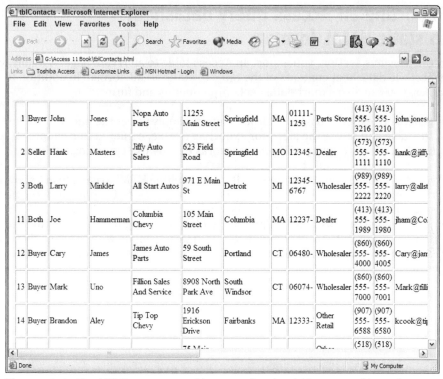

Figure 30-4: The HTML page created by exporting the tblContacts table to the ContactsTable.html file, shown in IE.

Caution   When exporting a table to an HTML file, Access doesn't save the heading column names, nor does it save data in the same format as it appears in the datasheet — unless you use an HTML template to export the file. It doesn't support the Format or Input Mask Properties of the table.

Tip   If you want Access to automatically display the HTML page after generating it, select Autostart in the Export dialog box and it displays immediately after you create it in Internet Explorer.

Although the layout of the HTML page doesn't simulate the formatting, headers, or even page orientation and margins that are set for the datasheet of the table, you can correct this by using an HTML template file that is covered later in this section.

After you have created your HTML pages, you can publish them to your Web site.

Exporting an Access query datasheet to static HTML format

In the previous section, you export an Access table to an HTML page. Actually, you export the datasheet contents of the table to static HTML format. In addition to tables, you can also export datasheets from queries and forms.

In general, to export a datasheet from a query, simply select the query name instead of the table and follow the steps for exporting a table, earlier in this chapter. If the query is a standard query, the process works exactly like exporting a table.

If you don't specify an HTML format file, the resulting HTML page doesn't show any formatting or input masks. However, it does support the Sort orders and the non-display of any fields that have their Show check box unchecked. Figure 30-5 shows a query named qryCustomers Alphabetized (representing the contacts that are either buyers or both [sellers and buyers]) in Design mode with three fields specified for a Sort — chrLastName, chrFirstName, and then chrCompany. By exporting this query to an HTML document, the HTML page sorts the items in the correct order. It also specifies a criteria of "Buyer" or "Both" (lacking all Sellers) in the chrContactType field. For instance, you can export this query to an HTML document named Customers Alphabetized HTML.htm.

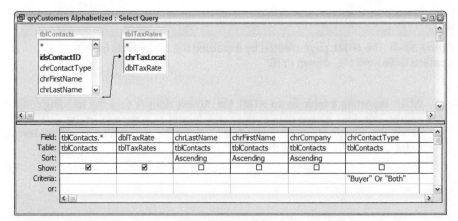

Figure 30-5: A query with three fields specified for sort order and criteria for another field.

Tip

A large datasheet produced from a query may take a long time to output and to display through a Web browser. Consider reducing the size of the datasheet, dividing the datasheet into smaller datasheets by using criteria (such as a date field), or using a report or form to view the data.

Caution

One important issue to keep in mind when exporting a query to an HTML page is working with *parameter queries* — queries that work interactively with the user at run-time. The resulting HTML document is created *after* the parameter query is run to obtain the parameter from the user.

Access creates the new HTML document with the user-specified parameter. If you compare this HTML page to the structure of the query in Figure 30-5, you can see that it is indeed in sort order by Last Name, then First Name, and finally by Company, as in the query. Figure 30-6 shows the Customers Alphabetized HTML html file in sorted order.

14	Buyer	Brandon	Aley	Tip Top Chevy	1916 Erickson Drive	Fairbanks	MA	12333-	Other Retail	(907) 555-6588	(907) 555-6580	kcook@ti
31	Both	Karen	Bailey	Sammy Fordman	59 West Church	Westbourgh	MA	01581-	Wholesaler	(413) 555-1212	(413) 555-1210	baileyk@s
25	Buyer	Ann	Bond	A-1 Auto Sales	54 South Main	Colchester	CT	06415-	Dealer	(860) 555-6152	(860) 555-6150	annbond@
33	Both	John	Bright	Pleasantville Monda Inc	46 Pleasantville RD	West Bridgewater	MA	02379-	Dealer	(781) 555-6388	(781) 555-6380	JohnB@pl
37	Buyer	Harry	Bush	Bush Sales	100 State Street	Mohegan Lake	NY	10547-	Dealer	(212) 555-9000	(212) 555-9001	Hbush@bi
59	Both	Larry	Calson	Chicota American Auto Sales	60 Mexico Drive	Chicota	TX	75425-	Dealer	(903) 555-8874	(903) 555-8874	

Figure 30-6: The resulting html file from the query in Figure 30-5.

After you create your HTML pages, you can publish them to your Web site.

Exporting an Access form datasheet to static HTML format

In the previous sections, you learn how to export an Access table and query to an HTML page. Actually, you export the datasheet contents of them to a static HTML format. In addition to tables and queries, you can also export the datasheet of forms.

Note   Exporting a form to an HTML document doesn't export the form's structure; rather it simply exports the field contents of the form, based on the underlying table or query of the form and the tab order. To see what is actually exported, you can click on the datasheet button on the toolbar when the form is open.

To better understand what actually occurs when you export the datasheet of a form, consider the Customer and Sales form (actual name—frmCustomer&Sales in the Access Auto Auctions.mdb), as shown in Figure 30-7.

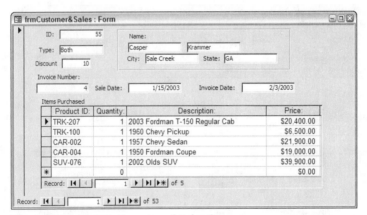

Figure 30-7: The Customer and Sales form.

Examining Figure 30-7, you can see that the form displays the Customer and Sales Invoice information in the upper portion of the form, one record at a time, while displaying the associated Sales line items records in a datasheet-like subform in the bottom half of the form. Actually, this form is a FORM that has a subform included within it.

To understand how Access exports the contents of this form to an HTML document, follow these steps:

1. In the Database window, click the Forms button to see the names of the forms.

2. Open the frmCustomer&Sales form. Access opens the form, and you can see the same form as shown in Figure 30-7.

3. Either select View ⇨ Datasheet View from the menu or select Datasheet view from the View button on the toolbar.

4. After the datasheet displays, you can scroll from left to right to see the fields being displayed in the datasheet of the form. Access shows 10 fields total, starting with (column headings) ID:, Type:, and Name:, and ending with Sale Date: and Invoice Date:. Figure 30-8 shows the Datasheet view of the form.

	ID:	Type:	Name:	chrLastName	City:	State:	Discount	Invoice	Sale Date:	Invoice Date:
+	55	Both	Casper	Krammer	Sale Creek	GA	10	4	1/15/2003	2/3/2003
+	18	Both	William	Gleason	Derby	CT	5	5	2/27/2003	2/18/2003
+	33	Both	John	Bright	West Bridgewater	MA	7.5	6	2/24/2003	2/24/2003
▶ +	53	Both	Dennis	Mchugh	Jefferson	TX	20	7	4/24/2003	4/24/2003
+	14	Buyer	Brandon	Aley	Fairbanks	MA	5	8	5/24/2003	5/24/2003
+	59	Both	Larry	Calson	Chicota	TX	5	9	6/1/2003	6/1/2003
+	17	Both	Karl	Johnson	Rye	NY	0	10	7/15/2003	7/15/2003
+	41	Both	Joann	Smith	New Town	NY	2.5	11	8/25/2003	8/25/2003
+	56	Both	Peter	Spindler	Iron Springs	AZ	8.75	12	8/26/2003	8/26/2003
+	52	Both	Debbie	Casey	Jackhorn	KY	0	13	9/25/2003	9/25/2003
+	55	Both	Casper	Krammer	Sale Creek	GA	10	14	9/30/2003	9/30/2003
+	37	Buyer	Harry	Bush	Mohegan Lake	NY	0	15	12/13/2003	12/13/2003
+	1	Buyer	John	Jones	Springfield	MA		16	12/12/2003	12/12/2003
+	33	Both	John	Bright	West Bridgewater	MA	7.5	17	2/25/2004	2/25/2004
+	20	Both	Karla	Hayes	Granby	CT	0	18	2/25/2004	2/25/2004
+	14	Buyer	Brandon	Aley	Fairbanks	MA	5	19	9/1/2003	9/1/2003

frmCustomer&Sales : Form
Record: ◄ ◄ 4 ► ►I ►* of 53

Figure 30-8: Datasheet of the form opened in Figure 30-7, showing the fields.

5. Select File ⇨ Export from the menu. Access displays the Export Form As dialog box.

6. In the Save As Type dialog box of the Export Form As dialog box, select HTML Documents. Access automatically assigns the default name of the HTML page as the same name of the form — replacing the ampersand with an underscore (frmCustomer_Sales). Keep this name for the example.

7. The Save formatted check box is checked and grayed out for the form. You can't change this check box.

8. Click the Export All or Export button, whichever is displayed. Access responds by activating an HTML Output Options dialog box, as shown in Figure 30-9. You use this box to select an HTML template to use for the exporting of the datasheet.

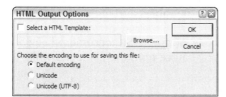

Figure 30-9: The HTML Output Options dialog box.

9. If the check box for Select a HTML Template is checked, you need to uncheck it at this time; otherwise, skip this step.

10. Click the OK button to start exporting the datasheet of the form.

Unlike exporting a table or query, forms require use of an HTML template file. If you don't specify one, Access automatically uses an internal default value for a format.

Figure 30-10 shows part of the resulting HTML page displayed in Internet Explorer. Your fields may show different values — for example most of the discount rate fields may show 0.

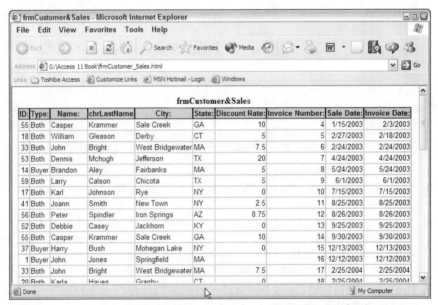

Figure 30-10: The HTML page created from the frmCustomer&Sales form.

As Figure 30-10 shows, this HTML page has some basic formatting added. It has the header row with field names above each column. The formatting specified for any fields is shown as formatted in the form (Discount Rate is still a percent instead of decimal). Comparing this form to the datasheet of Figure 30-8, you can see that it is a better match than the HTML pages for the tables and queries created earlier.

Note   You can view the HTML source code of any HTML document being viewed in Internet Explorer by selecting View ➪ Source from the file menu while the HTML document is active.

Tip   If you want Access to automatically display the HTML page after generating it, select Autostart in the Export dialog box, and it displays immediately after it is created in Internet Explorer.

Caution Access only creates an HTML document from the fields of the primary form, not the sub-form.

Comparing the HTML page in Figure 30-10 to the actual form in Figure 30-7, you can see that none of the Sales Line Item fields are added to the HTML page — only the Contact and Sales fields. When converting a form to an HTML document, only the principal form objects are converted — in this case, the Customer and Sales information. The Sales Line Item fields are actually in a separate form, named frmSubCustomer&Sales.

When converting forms, the values from most fields (except OLE objects and hyperlink fields) are output as strings. They are transferred to the HTML document, as shown in Figure 30-10. If you have an OLE object, it is simply ignored when outputting to the HTML page. The hyperlinks are copied over and stored in the HTML document as hyperlinks, using the <A href=...> tag.

After you create your HTML pages, you can publish them to your Web site.

Changing Page Setup properties for datasheets

When exporting a form, table, or query, objects are formatted similarly to the way they appear in the datasheet, including defined Format or Input Mask properties if you specify an HTML template. However, the column widths are automatically fitted to the display page properties of the datasheet (normally 8 inches wide). To change these settings, display the datasheet of the form and use the Page Setup command on the File menu before you export it.

Exporting a datasheet to dynamic HTML format

You can create dynamic HTML documents for datasheets that reside in Microsoft IIS 1-2 (IDC/HTX format) or Microsoft Active Server Pages (ASP format). These pages are created at run-time when the user requests the information — thus, they are dynamic.

When you export a datasheet to either of these formats, the generated HTML document queries the database for current data and sends that information back to the requesting browser.

You can also save forms as ASP files that emulate most of the functionality of the original form and display the data from your database on the Web server.

The process of exporting a dynamic HTML format is essentially the same as exporting a static format except that you choose the Microsoft IIS 1-2 or Microsoft Active Server Pages choice instead of the HTML Documents choice.

Note   Exporting to an Active Server or IIS 1-2 document is not the same as a data access page. These options create both an HTML document and an appropriate related file for access by the corresponding server (an IIS or an ASP server).

In general, to export a datasheet to dynamic HTML format, follow these steps:

1. In the Database window, click the name of the table, query, or form that you want to export, and then click Export on the File menu.

2. In the Export dialog box, in the Save As Type dialog box, click Microsoft IIS 1-2 or Microsoft Active Server Pages, depending on which dynamic HTML format you want to use.

3. If you want to save to a different drive or directory, click the down arrow at the right of the Save in combo box and select the drive or folder to export to.

4. In the File name box, enter the file name.

5. Click Export.

6. Enter the appropriate information in the HTX/IDC Output Options or Microsoft Active Server Pages Output Options dialog box, as shown in Figures 30-11 and 30-12.

7. For either Output Options box, enter the location of the HTML template (or let it use the default value) in the HTML Template text box.

8. In the Data Source Name text box, enter the name of the ODBC data source that you connect to when the server-generated HTML files are processed on the Web server.

Figure 30-11: The HTX/IDC Output Options dialog box for exporting to a dynamic datasheet.

Caution   You must specify the machine or file data source name that you use on the World Wide Web server and, if required, a username and password to open the database. If you are exporting to ASP file format, you must enter the full destination URL for the ASP file's directory (folder). For example, if you are storing the ASP files in the \SalesApp folder on the \\Pubweb server, type **http://pubweb//salesapp/**.

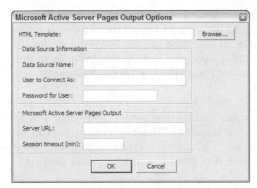

Figure 30-12: The Microsoft Active Server Pages Output Options dialog box for exporting to a dynamic datasheet.

After you finish, you are ready to publish your dynamic HTML document(s) to the Web.

Exporting a form to dynamic HTML format

You can design an Access form for use in a World Wide Web application and then save it to dynamic HTML format as ASP files. Several types of forms can be out-putted: view forms (to display records), switchboard forms (to act as the home page or to navigate to related pages, such as all reports), and data-entry forms (to add, update, and delete records). Most of the controls on your forms are saved as ActiveX controls that perform the same or similar functions as on the original forms.

Caution If you have any Visual Basic code behind your forms or controls, none of it is saved or run when you create or activate the ASP file.

In general, to export a form in dynamic HTML format, follow these steps:

1. In the Database window, click the name of the form that you want to export, and then click Export on the File menu.

2. In the Export dialog box, in the Save As Type dialog box, click Microsoft IIS 1-2 (*.htx; *.idc) or Microsoft Active Server Pages (*.asp), depending on which dynamic HTML format you want to use.

3. Change the drive or folder to Export to (if you want to) by clicking the Save in: combo box.

4. In the File name box, enter the file name.

5. Click Save.

You must specify the machine or file data source name that you use on the Web server, and , if required, a username and password to open the database. If you are exporting to ASP file format, you must enter the full destination URL for the ASP file's directory (folder). For example, if you are storing the ASP files in the \SalesApp folder on the \\Pubweb server, type **http://pubweb//salesapp/**.

Access outputs a continuous form as a single form. Access outputs most controls as ActiveX controls but ignores any Visual Basic code behind them. The output files simulate, as closely as possible, the appearance of the form by creating the appropriate HTML tags to retain attributes, such as color, font, and alignment. However, all data types are output unformatted, and all Format and InputMask properties are ignored.

If a form is in Datasheet view or its Default View property is set to Datasheet when you export to ASP file format, Access outputs the form as a datasheet. If the form is in Form or Design view, or its Default View property is set to Single Form or Continuous Forms, Access outputs the form as a form.

After you finish, you are ready to publish your dynamic HTML document(s) to the Web.

Processing an IDC/HTX file on the Web server

After you output a table, query, or form to an IDC/HTX file, Access creates two files: an HTML extension file (*.htx) and an Internet Database Connector file (*.idc). The .idc file contains a query in the form of an SQL statement. For example, exporting the qryCustomerSales query produced the .idc file, as shown in Figure 30-13.

```
qryCustomerSales.IDC - Notepad
File  Edit  Format  View  Help
Datasource:
Template:qryCustomerSales.htx
SQLStatement:SELECT tblContacts.chrContactType,
tblContacts.idsContactID, tblContacts.chrFirstName,
tblContacts.chrLastName, tblContacts.chrCity, tblContacts.chrState,
tblContacts.dblDiscountPercent, tblSales.idsInvoiceNumber,
tblSales.dtmSaleDate, tblSales.dtmInvoiceDate
+FROM tblContacts INNER JOIN tblSales ON
tblContacts.idsContactID=tblSales.lngzBuyer
+WHERE (((tblContacts.chrContactType)<>"Seller"));

Password:
Username:
```

Figure 30-13: The SQL statement created for an .idc file that was exported to Microsoft IIS 1-2 format.

The .htx file is an HTML file that contains the formatting information and placehold-ers for where to insert the values returned from the query in the .idc file. Using Microsoft FrontPage, you can examine the format skeleton for the qryCustomerSales query. Figure 30-14 shows the associated .htx file in Front Page.

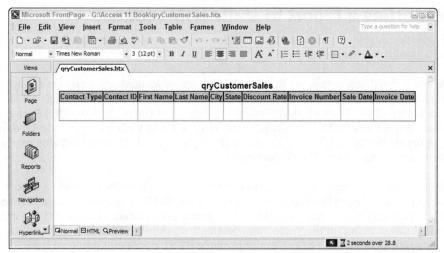

Figure 30-14: A portion of the associated .htx file that was exported to Microsoft IIS 1-2 format.

Figure 30-14 shows the left-most portion of the Preview view of the .htx file created. It is displayed in Microsoft's FrontPage.

After you publish the IDC/HTX files to a Web server, IIS can open the database (via an ODBC driver and the .idc file connection information), run the query in the .idc file, obtain the data, merge the results with the .htx file, and publish one .html file, sending it dynamically to the Web browser that requested the information.

Processing ASP files on the Web server

When you export a table, query, or form as an ASP file, Access creates a Microsoft Active Server Page (*.asp) file. Active Server is an integral part of Microsoft Internet Information Server 3.x or later.

The .asp file contains the HTML tags combined with one or more queries in the form of SQL statements, Visual Basic Scripting code (VBScript), and template directives. The .asp file also contains the ODBC connection information to connect to the source database—either an Access or SQL Server database. It includes the data source name and user name/password (can be prompted at run-time).

After you publish an .asp file to a Web server, IIS can do the following: Run the VBScript code located in the .asp file, call ActiveX controls, open the database, run the queries in the .asp file, obtain the results, merge them with the HTML tags, and send the resulting page back to the Web browser that requested the information.

Exporting a report to static HTML format

Reports can also be exported to HTML format. However, reports are always output to a static file format type.

When exporting a datasheet from a table, query, or form, Access creates a single HTML page. Every record that is in the datasheet is placed into the single HTML document. If you have a few thousand records, all of them are submitted to the same page. If the HTML document is too large, it takes a very long time to load in the browser. This is why you should limit the amount of information being exported from a datasheet to an HTML document.

In contrast, exporting Access reports is a bit smarter. When you export a report object, each page of the report is sent to its own HTML document. In other words, if a report has two pages, two HTML documents are created. The second and subsequent pages maintain the same name as the first, simply appending a chronological numeric value (2, 3, 4, etc.) after the primary HTML document name.

To export the rptContacts First 5 Only in the Access Auto Auctions database, follow these steps:

1. In the Database window, click the Reports button to show the names of the reports.

2. Select the rptContacts First 5 Only.

3. Click Export on the File menu (or right-click and select Export).

4. In the Export dialog box, in the Save As Type dialog box, click HTML Documents. Access supplies the default name of rptContacts First 5 Only in the File Name text box.

5. In the File name box, change the filename to Customer Report - 5 Records.

6. The Save formatted check box is checked and grayed out for the form. You can't change this check box.

7. Click the Export button. Access responds by activating an HTML Output Options dialog box. This box is used to select an HTML template to use for the exporting of the datasheet.

8. If the check box for Select a HTML Template is checked, you need to uncheck it at this time; otherwise, skip this step.

9. Click the OK button to start exporting the report to an HTML document.

Note

In the HTML Output Options dialog box, you can specify an HTML template to use. If you don't specify an HTML template file containing navigation tokens, Microsoft Access provides a default navigation scheme. The default scheme for Reports includes adding page numbers and several text navigation links (first, previous, next, and last) at the bottom of each page.

Tip

If you want Access to automatically display the first HTML page of the Report after generating it, select Autostart in the Export dialog box, and it is displayed immediately after it is created in Internet Explorer.

Figure 30-15 shows the resulting HTML report created by exporting the Access report.

Figure 30-15: The first page of an HTML document that was created by exporting an Access report.

Looking at the bottom of the HTML document, you can see several navigation controls similar to the ones shown in Figure 30-15. Looking closely at the bottom of the page, you see several things automatically added to the report. First is the date it was printed on. To the right of that is the Page counter (1 of 2), and at the very bottom-left corner are four navigation text hyperlinks — First, Previous, Next, and Last. If you click on the Next text, you are taken to the second page of the report.

The HTML file is based on the recordset behind the report, including any current Order By or Filter property settings. If the datasheet contains a parameter query, Access first prompts you for the parameter values and then exports the results that match the query. Most controls and features of a report, including subreports, are supported except for lines, rectangles, OLE objects, and subforms. However, you can use an HTML template file to include report header and footer images in your output files.

Note If the Access report contains more than one page, Access exports a different HTML document for each page.

The output files simulate, as closely as possible, the appearance of the report by creating the appropriate HTML tags to retain attributes, such as color, font, and alignment. Fields with a hyperlink data type are output as HTML links using <A HREF> tags. Access outputs a report, unlike a datasheet, as multiple HTML files, one file per printed page. The counting systems for multi-page reports follows the pattern of the filename with no number for the first page, then the filename with an incrementing number for every page after that: Customer Report - 5 Records.html, Customer Report - 5 Records 2.html, Customer Report - 5 Records 3.html, and so on. If you create an HTML document for the Customer Report - 5 Records report, Access will create five different pages for the report. The layout of the HTML pages simulates the page orientation and margins set for the report. To change these settings, display the report in Print or Layout Preview, and then use the File menu's Page Setup command before you export it. If you look at the query behind the report, you will see that it specifies the top five records only; if you remove the top 5 option, the report will print 54 records instead.

Note You can't output a report to dynamic HTML format.

HTML template files

When Exporting datasheets, forms, and reports to HTML documents, IIS 1 or 2 documents, and ASP documents, you can specify one or more HTML template files, which you can use to enhance the functionality of those pages. Typically, you want to enhance the navigational functionality of datasheets, add graphics or other appearance features, and maintain consistency between your HTML documents.

HTML template files let you add these types of enhancements to your static HTML pages or dynamic server-generated HTML files.

For example, you may want to add a company logo in the header of a report or at the top of all HTML static pages; or you may want to place navigational controls on your pages.

An HTML template file is a text file that you create by using HTML tags and tokens that are unique to Access. These tokens are used to input specific information into the final HTML document that is created when you export a table, query, form, or report.

Access recognizes seven specific template tokens:

✦ <!–AccessTemplate_Title–>, which is used to place the name of the object in the Browser title bar.

✦ <!–AcessTemplate_Body–>, which is used to designate where the output of the object is to be placed in the <body> of the HTML document.

✦ <!–AccessTemplate_FirstPage–>, which is used to create an HTML anchor tag (<a href= ...>) in the document to point to the first page of a multi-page document.

✦ <!–AccessTemplate_NextPage–>, which is used to create an HTML anchor tag (<a href= ...>) in the document to point to the next page, after the current page, of a multi-page document.

✦ <!–AccessTemplate_PreviousPage–>, which is used to create an HTML anchor tag (<a href= ...>) in the document to point to the previous page, after the current page, of a multi-page document.

✦ <!–AccessTemplate_LastPage–>, which is used to create an HTML anchor tag (<a href= ...>) in the document to point to the last page of a multi-page document.

✦ <!–AccessTemplate_PageNumber–>, which is used to display the current page number of the document.

Each of these tokens can be placed in an HTML document that can be used as a template to tell Access how to format or display the object being exported to HTML code. It lets you enhance the appearance and navigation of your static HTML documents. For instance, you can add images, add backgrounds, specify foreground and background colors, and so on to the document.

Figure 30-16 shows a simple HTML template file named MyTemplate01.htm.

As Figure 30-16 shows, several HTML Access tokens are placed in the HTML code of the template. It uses the token <!–AccessTemplate_Title–> to display the title of the table in the browser when the HTML document is created. It also uses two of the navigational tokens — <!–AccessTemplate_FirstPage–> and <!–AccessTemplate_LastPage–> — to place links for multi-page documents.

```
MyTemplate01.htm - WordPad
File   Edit   View   Insert   Format   Help

<html>
 <head>
  <Title><!--AccessTemplate_Title--></title>
 </head>
 <body bgcolor=cyan>
  <img src = "MyGLOBE.GIF" height="40" -50 width="43" -60>
     
  <a href = "<!--AccessTemplate_FirstPage-->">TopPage</a>
  <a href = "<!--AccessTemplate_LastPage-->">LastPage</a>
  <p>
  <!--AccessTemplate_Body-->
 </body>
 <p>
 <img src = "MyGLOBE.GIF" height="40" -50 width="43" -60>
    
 <a href = "<!--AccessTemplate_FirstPage-->">TopPage</a>
 <a href="<!--AccessTemplate_LastPage--%3E">LastPage</a>
</html>

For Help, press F1
```

Figure 30-16: An HTML template file named MyTemplate01.htm.

After you create the template file, you can use it by specifying it in the HTML Output options dialog box that appears when you specify Save Formatted in the Export dialog box. Figure 30-17 shows the top part of an HTML document that is running in Internet Explorer and that was exported from a query named qryCustomerMailingLabels. It used the HTML template file MyTemplate01.htm to create the HTML document.

Notice that the exported HTML code shows a graphic and two navigational links (TopPage and LastPage). It also shows the name of the query object (qryCustomerMailingLabels) that was used for the HTML export and column headings, and some basic color was added to the page.

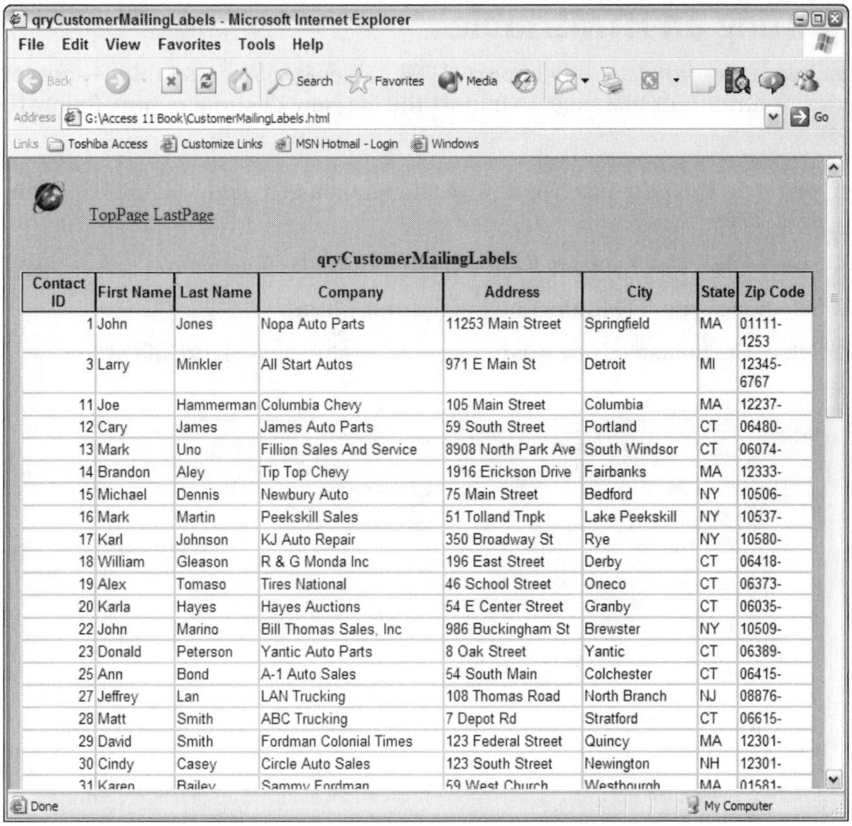

Contact ID	First Name	Last Name	Company	Address	City	State	Zip Code
1	John	Jones	Nopa Auto Parts	11253 Main Street	Springfield	MA	01111-1253
3	Larry	Minkler	All Start Autos	971 E Main St	Detroit	MI	12345-6767
11	Joe	Hammerman	Columbia Chevy	105 Main Street	Columbia	MA	12237-
12	Cary	James	James Auto Parts	59 South Street	Portland	CT	06480-
13	Mark	Uno	Fillion Sales And Service	8908 North Park Ave	South Windsor	CT	06074-
14	Brandon	Aley	Tip Top Chevy	1916 Erickson Drive	Fairbanks	MA	12333-
15	Michael	Dennis	Newbury Auto	75 Main Street	Bedford	NY	10506-
16	Mark	Martin	Peekskill Sales	51 Tolland Tnpk	Lake Peekskill	NY	10537-
17	Karl	Johnson	KJ Auto Repair	350 Broadway St	Rye	NY	10580-
18	William	Gleason	R & G Monda Inc	196 East Street	Derby	CT	06418-
19	Alex	Tomaso	Tires National	46 School Street	Oneco	CT	06373-
20	Karla	Hayes	Hayes Auctions	54 E Center Street	Granby	CT	06035-
22	John	Marino	Bill Thomas Sales, Inc	986 Buckingham St	Brewster	NY	10509-
23	Donald	Peterson	Yantic Auto Parts	8 Oak Street	Yantic	CT	06389-
25	Ann	Bond	A-1 Auto Sales	54 South Main	Colchester	CT	06415-
27	Jeffrey	Lan	LAN Trucking	108 Thomas Road	North Branch	NJ	08876-
28	Matt	Smith	ABC Trucking	7 Depot Rd	Stratford	CT	06615-
29	David	Smith	Fordman Colonial Times	123 Federal Street	Quincy	MA	12301-
30	Cindy	Casey	Circle Auto Sales	123 South Street	Newington	NH	12301-
31	Karen	Bailey	Sammy Fordman	59 West Church	Westborough	MA	01581-

Figure 30-17: The top part of an HTML document in IE that was created using the HTML template file.

Importing and Linking (Read-Only) HTML Tables and Lists

In addition to exporting an HTML table, query, form datasheet, or report, you can import or link to an HTML table directly. This process uses the standard Import or Linked Table Wizard shown and used in Chapter 7.

Importing an HTML table

When importing, you can only import HTML tables into Access tables—not into queries or forms. For instance, to import the file New Customers.htm, follow these steps:

1. Switch to the Database window for the database to show all tables in the database.

2. Select File ➪ Get External Data ➪ Import from the File menu.

3. Select file type HTML Documents (*.html;*.htm).

4. Select the filename New Customer.htm, as shown in Figure 30-18.

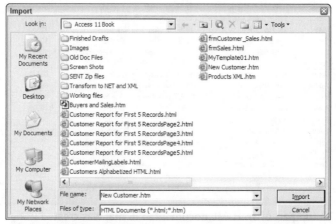

Figure 30-18: The Import dialog box—selecting the New Customer HTML page.

5. Click the Import button. Access starts the Import HTML Wizard.

6. Click the First Row Contains Column Headings check box.

7. Review the data and column headings to make sure the table imports correctly, and press the Next button. The next screen asks if you want to import to a New table (default) or to an existing table. Accept the default to import to a new table.

8. Click the Next button to accept the default values. The next screen lets you move through the fields and specify indexing or Skip the field.

9. Select an Indexed value of Yes (No Duplicates) for the Contact ID field, as shown in Figure 30-19.

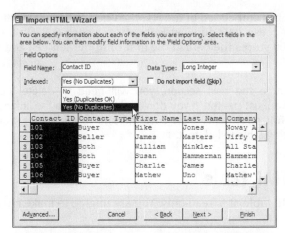

Figure 30-19: The Import HTML Wizard specifying an index field for the Contact ID field.

10. Click the Next button. Access moves to the Choose a primary key page. The default value is let Access add a primary key. It adds a new field to the left of the structure labeled ID.

11. Click the Choose my own primary key radio button. Access removes the ID field and selects the Contact ID field in the text box.

12. Click the Next button. Access then moves to the last page of the Wizard.

13. Type the name **New Customers** in the Import to Table text box.

14. Click the Finish button. Access imports the file and reports that it did so successfully by displaying a message box.

15. Click OK to return to the database container and see that the New Customers table has been imported.

If your HTML file contains more than one table or list, repeat the steps for each table or list that you want to import or link.

A table that is embedded within a table cell in an HTML file is treated as a separate table when you import or link. A list embedded in a table cell is treated as the contents of a cell, and each item in the list is delimited with the carriage return/line feed characters.

If the data being imported contains a URL link or file hyperlink, Access converts HTML links to a Hyperlink data-type column, but only if all values in a table column or list contain hyperlink addresses defined by an <A HREF> tag. You can change the data type when using the Import HTML Wizard or the Link HTML Wizard. Access ignores GIF and JPEG images embedded in the HTML tables or lists. For data that spans rows or columns, Access 2002 duplicates the data in each cell. On the other hand, Microsoft Excel 2000 stores the data in the first or upper-left cell and then leaves other cells blank.

Caution   Before continuing on to the next section, you will need to delete the New Customer table that you just created. If you don't delete it and do the linking to an HTML table (same HTML document — New Customers.htm), you will be prompted to overwrite the existing table to link to it.

Linking to an HTML table

When you link to an HTML table, it is read-only. You are unable to make changes to the table.

For instance, to link to the file New Customers.htm, follow these steps:

1. Switch to the Database window for the database to show all tables in the database.

2. Select File ⇨ Get External Data ⇨ Link Tables from the File menu.

3. Select file type HTML Documents (*.html;*.htm).

4. Select the filename New Customers.htm and either double-click or click the Link button after selecting it. Access starts the Link HTML Wizard.

5. Check the First Row Contains Column Headings checkbox to turn it on.

6. Click the Next button. Access takes you to the screen that allows you to skip any fields in the structure.

7. Click the Next button. Access takes you to the last page, which asks if you want to change the name of the Linked file.

8. Click the Finish button to accept the name given. Access displays a message box informing you that it linked to the table correctly.

9. Click OK to be returned to the database container.

The HTML table is now linked in the table section of the database container.

Using Hyperlinks to Connect Your Application to the Internet

Microsoft Access includes hyperlinks that help you connect your application to the Internet or to an intranet. A hyperlink can jump to a location on the Internet or on an intranet, to an object in your database or in another database, or to a document on your computer or on another computer connected by a network. Normally, you embed a hyperlink in a form. However, by storing hyperlinks in a table, you can programmatically move to Internet URLs or Office objects, such as a Word document by using a bookmark, an Excel spreadsheet using a sheet or range, a PowerPoint presentation using a slide, or an Access object, such as a table, form, or report.

Using the Hyperlink data type

Microsoft Access provides a Hyperlink data type that can contain a hyperlink address. You can define a table field with this data type in order to store hyperlinks as data in a table. Imagine, for a moment, the future where all customers have e-mail addresses — or even their own Web sites. You want to include a customer's e-mail address or Web site in a linkable file, much like an automatic phone dialer code is commonly added to a customer's phone number today.

Figure 30-20 shows the Hyperlink data type being assigned to the hlkWebSite field in the tblContacts table; changing from Text type to Hyperlink.

Note The field hlkWebSite should be left text type for the overall system. However, you can change it to hyperlink for this chapter.

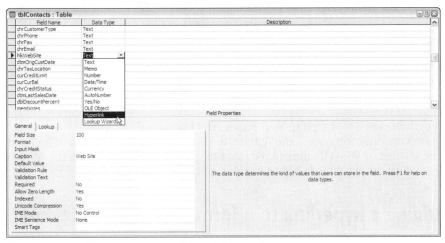

Figure 30-20: Creating a hyperlink in a table design.

Using the Hyperlink data type lets you input text or combinations of text and numbers stored as text and used as a hyperlink address. A hyperlink address can have as many as three parts:

✦ **Displaytext.** The text that appears in a field or control.

✦ **Address.** The path to a file (UNC path) or Web page (URL).

✦ **Subaddress.** A location within the file or page.

The easiest way to insert a hyperlink address in a field or control is to click on the Hyperlink menu choice on the Insert menu. The Insert Hyperlink dialog box appears, as shown in Figure 30-21.

The dialog box gives you many options. You can specify an existing file or Web page, choose an object in the database, create a new page, or specify an e-mail address.

The Hyperlink data type can contain as many as 2,048 characters.

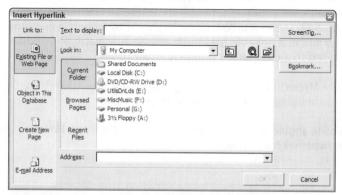

Figure 30-21: Inserting a hyperlink in the hyperlink field of a table is easy using the Hyperlink dialog box.

When you click on a hyperlink field, Access jumps to an object, document, Web page, or other destination.

Hyperlinks are not limited to Web pages. You can specify a hyperlink to forms, reports, or other objects in the database. You can even create a link to an Excel spreadsheet or Word document. For that matter, you can link to any file on your network or across your in-house intranet or the Internet.

Adding a hyperlink to a form, report, or datasheet

You can use hyperlinks in forms, reports, and datasheets to jump to objects in the same or another Access database; to documents created with Microsoft Word, Microsoft Excel, and Microsoft PowerPoint; and to documents on the global Internet or on a local intranet. You can also add hyperlinks to reports. Although hyperlinks in a report won't work when viewed in Access, the hyperlinks do work when you output the report to Word, Excel, or HTML.

You can store hyperlinks in fields in tables, just as you store phone numbers and fax numbers. For example, the Suppliers table in the Northwind sample database (that comes with Access) stores hyperlinks to home pages for some of the suppliers.

You can also create a label or picture on a form or report or a command button on a form that you can click to follow a hyperlink path.

Figure 30-22 shows the frmCustomer&SalesHyper Form open in the form designer and specifying a hyperlink. Notice that there are two hyperlinks in the figure: New Customers HTML file and Open Products Table. Both hyperlinks are built using label fields. The first link opens the html file New Customers.htm in the default browser when the label is clicked. The second opens the form frmProductsSimple in the current database.

To specify an external file, place the name of the file in the Hyperlink Address property, as shown in Figure 30-22. If you are going to specify a link to an object in the current database, leave the Hyperlink Address field blank and fill in the Hyperlink SubAddress with the object type and the object name.

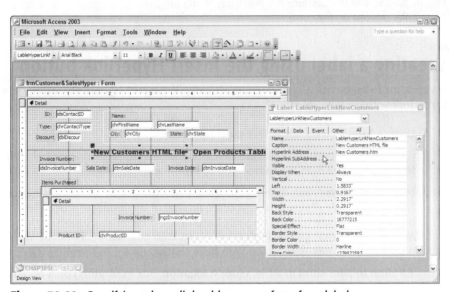

Figure 30-22: Specifying a hyperlink address on a form for a label.

To see how the hyperlink was created, open frmCustomer&SalesHyper in design mode and examine the Hyperlink and SubHyperlink properties of both labels. You can view it, and it should resemble the one shown in Figure 30-23.

Looking at Figure 30-23, you see the pointer has been changed to a pointing finger of a hand and it shows the help tip. If you pass your pointer over the link and hold it there for a second or two, Access will display the help tip with the link filename.

If you entered a valid hyperlink and you click on the link, Access takes you to that location on the Web, opens the new form, or performs whichever action is associated with the link.

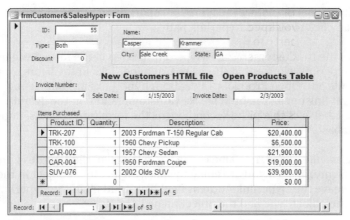

Figure 30-23: The frmCustomer&SalesHyper form with two hyperlinks created on the form.

Creating a label using the Insert Hyperlink button

If you want to automatically create a label using the Insert Hyperlink button on a form, follow these general steps:

1. Open a form or a report in Design view.

2. Click Insert Hyperlink (a picture of a globe with a single chain link below it — to the left of the field list button) on the toolbar.

3. In the Insert Hyperlink dialog box, specify a UNC path or a URL in the Link to File or Web Page dialog box. If you are unsure of the filename, click the File button to navigate to a file on your hard drive, on a local area network, or on an FTP server that you've registered. For a Web page name, click the Web page button to navigate to the Web page that you want to use.

   To jump to a location in a file, enter a location. For example, type a bookmark name for a Microsoft Word document or a slide number for a PowerPoint presentation.

   To jump to an Access object, enter the object type and object name (for example, Form Customer), or click the Browse button. The Browse button displays a list of the objects in the current database. Select the object that you want to open.

4. Click OK in the Insert Hyperlink dialog box.

Access adds a label to the form or report. To test the link, right-click the label, point to Hyperlink on the shortcut menu, and click Open.

When you create a label this way, Access sets the Hyperlink Address property of the label to the value that you specified in the Link to File or URL box, and the Hyperlink SubAddress property to the value (if any) that you specified in the Named Location in File box. Access uses the Caption property for the display text that you see in the label itself. You can change any of these properties to modify the hyperlink.

You can also add hyperlinks to a picture (Image Control) or command button control in the same way.

✦   ✦   ✦

Building and Working with Data Access Pages

✦ ✦ ✦ ✦

In This Chapter

Working with data
access pages

Creating data
access pages
using the Wizard

Creating and
working with
grouped pages

Exporting Access
objects to a data
access page

Importing an existing
data access page

✦ ✦ ✦ ✦

Using Access, you can create many different types of Web pages. In Chapter 30, you work with Access to create static and dynamic Web pages based on the different objects of Access — tables, queries, forms, and reports. You learn how to create snapshots of your data by creating HTML documents and even up-to-date, read-only data, created at the server side, by creating Active Server Pages (ASP). This chapter demonstrates the power of data access pages in Access.

Data access pages (DAPs) were first introduced in Access 2000. They are a special type of Web page connected directly to the data in your database. This data can be stored in a Microsoft Access database (*.mdb) or a Microsoft SQL Server database (accessed via an Access Data Project database — *.adp).

On the CD-ROM

This chapter will use the database named CHAP31Start.mdb. It also uses the external file named ContactsAccess2002.htm. If you have not already copied them onto your machine from the CD, you will need to do so now. After you have completed this chapter, your database should resemble the one in CHAP31End.mdb.

Caution

If you use CHAP31End.mdb, you will need to reestablish links to the external tables before they will work correctly.

Working with the Data Access Pages

You can use data access pages like any another Access object — select them from the Pages Object container. Unlike other Access objects, however, you can also use them independent of Access with Microsoft's Web browser.

It's easy to create a new data access page. You can build one from scratch, using the Page Designer, or you can use a wizard to create a new page.

What is a data access page?

In its simplest form, a data access page (DAP) is a Web page that is connected directly to the data in your Access database. The page allows you to display and sometimes edit the data in the underlying database.

The most exciting part about DAPs is the ability to drill down into grouped data. This ability lets you use DAPs to explore and analyze information stored in the underlying tables. The user can view summary information or drill into the data to learn more about the detail records associated with the summary information.

Figure 31-1 shows a data access page created to display Contacts and Sales information. Currently it shows only the customer (contact) information, and if you click on the next button of the navigation bar, it moves to the next Customer and shows that customer's information. The sales information is not visible at this time.

To show the Sales information, you simply click on the Expand/Collapse control button in the form to the left of the Customer ID (the mouse pointer in Figure 31-1 is pointing to it). Notice that the Expand/Collapse button (a small box with a visible plus or minus sign) next to the Contact ID is displaying a plus sign. By clicking this object, the information being displayed expands, as shown in Figure 31-2, displaying the sales information for that customer. This process is known as *drilling down* into the data.

Figure 31-1: A data access page for Customers (Contacts) and Sales in Access with the Expand/Collapse control closed (+) on the Customers.

Microsoft's Internet Explorer and data access pages

The DAP shown in Figure 31-1 is running in Access. However, you can also run the same data access page in Microsoft's Internet Explorer. Figure 31-2 shows the same form displayed in IE 6.0, with the sales detail area shown by expanding both the Contact ID Expand/Collapse control and the Invoice Number Expand/Collapse control. The Invoice Number Expand/Collapse control has actually been set to expand automatically — thus showing the details of each sale on the invoice.

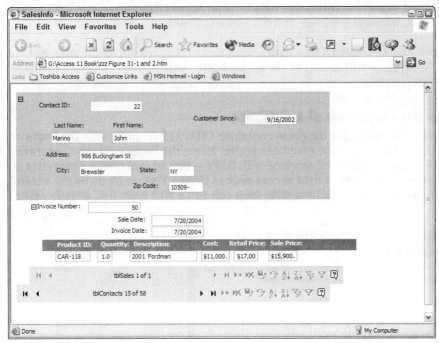

Figure 31-2: The same data access page for Customers and Sales in IE with the Expand/Collapse controls open (-).

To display data access pages, users need to have both Microsoft Internet Explorer 5.x or higher and the newest Microsoft Office 2003 Web Components (MSOWC) files installed on their machines. Internally, Access uses Internet Explorer and MSOWC (Office 2003 version) to actually display and work with the information in the data access page.

New Feature

In Access 2000, each person wanting to use data access pages was required to purchase a separate copy of Microsoft Office for their computer to obtain the MSOWC files, which IE 5.x or greater needed to access and display DAPs. In the current version of Access, this is no longer a requirement. The users must still have IE 5.x or greater and MSOWC, but they can obtain them from Microsoft's Web site.

Tip   You can go to Microsoft's Web site at www.microsoft.com and download the MSOWC (for Office XP) and the current version of IE from the site. You can find these files by searching the support section of Microsoft's site. Downloading these files takes an inordinate amount of time if you are downloading at 56K or slower. You can also contact Customer Support by telephone to have a copy sent for a small shipping charge.

The records in the page shown in Figure 31-1 and 31-2 can only be viewed; however, you could make the fields capable of being updated, edited, deleted, filtered — even grouped or sorted. This is live data from an Access database — the tblContacts, tblSales, tblSalesLineItems, and tblProducts tables.

When Access creates a new data access page, it utilizes Microsoft Internet Explorer technology (in edit mode) as the actual design environment to create the page within Access.

The Page container of a database

Figure 31-3 shows the database container, CHAP31Start.mdb, with the Pages object button selected and the container active. Inside the Pages container are three choices for creating and working with DAPs — two let you create a new data access page (you can create a data access page in Design View or by using the wizard), and one lets you edit an existing page (you can edit a Web page that already exists).

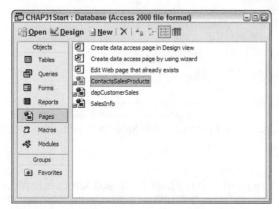

Figure 31-3: The Pages container of a database.

When you create a data access page within Access, you are actually creating two separate parts:

✦ The Data Access Page object, which is stored in the Pages container and maintains a link to the underlying HTML file

✦ The HTML document, which contains the HTML and XML code for the page

The HTML document, or file, is stored independently of the DAP object in the database. This allows the browser (IE 5.x or later) to use this file independently of Access. It also makes it easy for you to deploy the HTML documents for use in your intranet or across the Internet.

Cross-Reference The separation of the object and document can cause deployment problems that are covered later in this chapter.

Creating a data access page is very similar to creating a form or report in Access. You use the Data Access Page design mode, or the wizard, to create the page. After it's completed, the page becomes a fully functional HTML document.

When you create your pages, you need to decide if you are creating a page using a single table/query or multiple tables. If you use multiple tables, you create what is known as *grouped pages*.

Creating a single table data access page

You can create a single table data access page by using the wizard or building it yourself in Design view.

Cross-Reference You can also convert an existing table, query, form, or report to a data access page directly. This is covered later in this chapter.

Using the Page Wizard to create a single table data access page

The easiest way to create a single table data access page is to let the Data Access Page Wizard help you. For instance, to create a new data access page for the Customers table, follow these steps:

1. Select the Pages object button from the Objects bar of the CHAP31Start.mdb database.

2. Double-click Create Data Access Page by Using Wizard.

3. Select the tblContacts table from the Tables/Queries drop-down combo box on the first page of the wizard.

   Figure 31-4 shows the first page of the Page Wizard with the tblContacts table selected.

4. Select chrContactType, idsContactID, chrFirstName, chrLastName, chrAddress, chrCity, chrState, chrZipCode, and dtmOrigCustDate from the Available Fields list box. You can select them by highlighting each field and pressing the right arrow button (>) or by double-clicking the field name.

5. Click Next to move to the next page.

   Access displays the grouping levels page of the wizard.

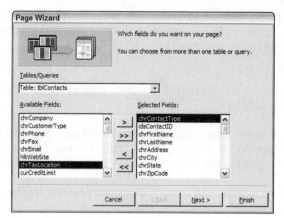

Figure 31-4: The first page of the Page Wizard.

6. Select chrContactType for a grouping level by double-clicking the field name. Figure 31-5 shows the grouping level set.

7. Click Next to move to the next page.

Access displays the sort order page of the wizard.

8. Specify chrLastName and chrFirstName (Ascending for both) for the sort order on this page.

9. Click Next to move to the next, and final, page.

10. Specify Contact Info by Type as the title for the new page.

11. While still on this page, choose the Open the page radio button.

12. Click the Finish button and be patient. The wizard performs many steps to create the new data access page.

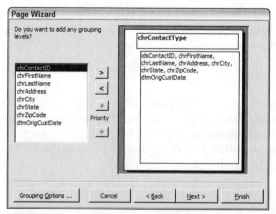

Figure 31-5: The grouping level set in the Page Wizard.

Access creates the new Web document, giving it a title name of Contact Info by Type (on the title bar when the HTML document is open).

Access has not saved the file to the hard drive yet; Access has only created and opened it as a virtual file.

Figure 31-6 shows the newly created Contacts Info by Type data access page running in Access. As this figure shows, only the Contact Type (chrContactType) field is initially displayed on the form. When the page is initially created (using the wizard), the expand button (plus [+] sign) displays next to Group of chrContactType. When you click the plus (+) sign, it is replaced by the collapse button (minus [–] sign), and the detail information for each contact displays below the Contact Type heading.

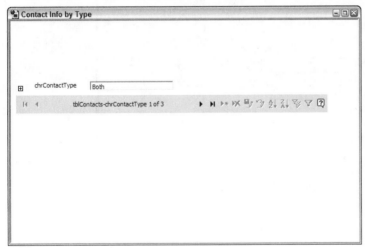

Figure 31-6: The new Contact Info data access page running in Access.

The form in Figure 31-6 also has a navigation bar, known as a *record management control* in Access, along the bottom of the page. It shows three records that can be viewed, based on "chrContactType." There are three contact types: Both, Buyer, and Seller. If you click the expand button alongside of the Contact Type, you see a second navigation bar (above the first one) also displayed — this one for all the records that match that contact Type (in this case "Both"). These are used to perform several functions, including the following:

✦ Moving between records in the page

✦ Adding new records to the underlying table(s)

✦ Deleting records

✦ Sorting records by a specific field

✦ Setting filter conditions for viewing records

In addition to these navigational controls, the page also has an expand control next to the chrContactType text (top-left corner). It is the small box that displays either a plus (+) sign or a negative (–) sign. It is used to expand and close a level of information in the page. In this case, it is used to display individual customer information (level 2) when the negative sign is showing (as in Figure 31-7), or only the Contact type information when the positive sign is showing (as in Figure 31-6). When you run the form, clicking the expand control toggles between expanded (+) and closed (–) modes.

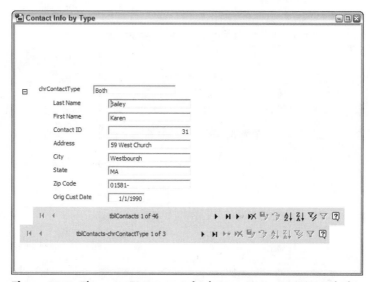

Figure 31-7: The new Customer Info data access page, expanded to show both levels of the page.

You can change the default action of this expand control before saving your new data access page by making a change to the page in the Design view window. Follow these steps to change the default behavior of the expand control:

1. Click the View button or select View ➪ Design View from the menu.

2. Open the Properties dialog box by selecting View ➪ Properties from the menu or by clicking the Property button on the toolbar.

3. With the property sheet open, right-click the gray Header: tblContacts-chrContactType band, as shown in Figure 31-8 (or anywhere in the page — on or below the Header band Header: tblContacts-chrContactType).

If you click in a different area, your menu looks slightly different from the one in Figure 31-8.

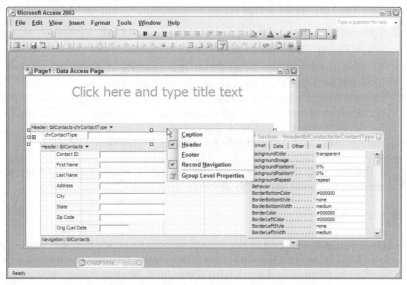

Figure 31-8: Activating the right-click menu. Notice that the Property sheet shows the Section: Header: tblContacts-chrContactType object active.

4. Select Group Level Properties from the menu.

   Access changes the property sheet focus to the properties of the Group level object, as shown in Figure 31-9.

5. Change the ExpandedByDefault property to True, as shown in Figure 31-9.

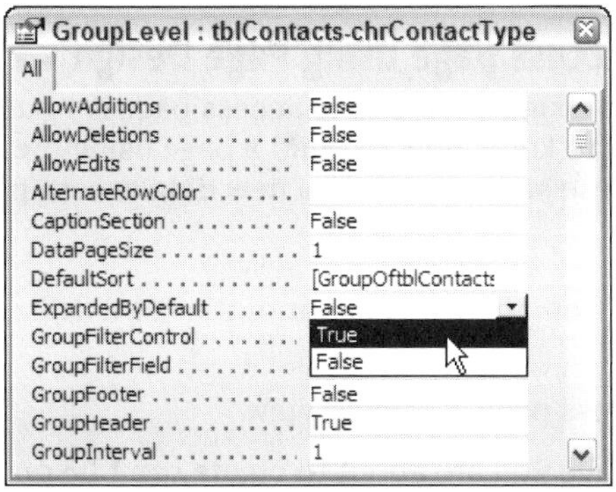

Figure 31-9: Changing the ExpandedByDefault property of the Group Level object to True.

6. Save your work by selecting File ➪ Save (or press Ctrl+S, or close the window and answer Yes to the Save Changes dialog box).

Access opens the Save As Data Access Page dialog box. This is where you save the DAP as an actual HTML document (*.html or *.htm).

7. You can accept the default name of the Contact Info by Type.html and click the Save button.

Access saves the page as an HTML document and displays a warning dialog box that tells you that the Connection string to this page specifies an absolute page. It lets you know that this page may not work on a network, unless the connection string of the page is changed to a network path (using Universal Naming Convention — UNC). This problem is covered later in this chapter in the section "Making your DAPs available to the Web."

Note If the Warning dialog box does not appear, it is because you have previously checked the Don't Show This Warning Again check box.

8. Click OK.

The HTML file is not stored in the database container. Rather, it is stored in the Windows file system in a subdirectory. Microsoft's Internet Explorer 5.x or higher can be used to display and work with these files. Access stores only a page object that points to the HTML file in the Pages container of the database window — not the actual file.

If you saved your page in Step 6 by pressing Ctrl+S or selecting File ➪ Save from the menu, close the page to return to the Pages container of the database.

Note In Access 2000, you had the option of accomplishing this same process by clicking on the Sorting and Grouping button (the seventh button from the right side of the toolbar) or by selecting View ➪ Sorting and Grouping on the menu. This method has been removed from Access 2002 and 2003.

Creating a single table data access page using Page Design View

Although the easiest way to create a single table data access page is to use the Data Access Page Wizard, it's also good to know how to build a page using the Design View tools. For example, follow these steps to create a new data access page for the Pets table:

1. Select the Pages object type from the Objects Bar of the CHAP31Start database.

2. Double-click Create data access page in Design View.

Access warns you that the page you are about to create can't be opened in Design view of Access 2000 or 2002. However, the page can be used in view mode in Access 2000 or 2002 if you have installed the newest Microsoft Office Web Components.

3. Click OK.

   Access takes you to the page's Design view. If the Property sheet is open, close it at this time.

4. Click in the area Click Here and Type Title Text (labeled in light gray), and then type **Products Info**.

5. Click in the area labeled "Drag fields from the Field List and drop them on the page" to select it. Notice that the area has been selected.

   Access highlights the unbound section of the page.

6. With the Unbound section selected in the Design View, select View ⇨ Field List from the menu (or click the Field List button) if the field list is not already open.

   Access opens the Field List, as shown in Figure 31-10.

Figure 31-10: The Page Design view with the Field List open.

7. The Tables folder should already be expanded—if it isn't, click it to show all the table names in the list.

8. Click the Products table to show all the fields from this table.

9. Select the chrProductID, chrDescription, chrCategory, intQtyInStock,curCost, curRetailPrice, curSalePrice, blnTaxable, and blnAuction fields and drag them to the section on the page labeled Drag Fields from the Field List. . . .

   Access opens a Layout Wizard, as shown in Figure 31-11. This wizard lets you select the method that Access should use to lay out the fields you have selected from the tblProducts table.

Figure 31-11: The Layout Wizard activated.

Note If the Layout Wizard does not activate, delete the field dropped onto the page and open the toolbox. When the toolbox is open, click on the Control Wizards button (on the top row, second button) to activate it.

10. Select the default value (Columnar) and click OK.

Access creates a simple bound span (Input Box) and a label for each field. It also changes the section heading by renaming it to "Header: tblProducts," and adds a Navigation: tblProducts section below the Header section for the Products table and places the Record management toolbar and its control objects in it.

11. Save your work and name it *Products Info.html*.

After you save your data, you can use it in Access or IE 5.x or later. This page can only be edited in Access 2003. It can be used and displayed in Access 2000 and 2002 if the user has installed both IE 5.x or later and the Office 2003 Web Components DLL on his or her computer.

New Feature Notice that all of the fields in Figure 31-12 are selected. Access, using Internet Explorer, lets you select more than one object at a time in the Page Design view. If your computer doesn't have IE5.5 or later, you are only capable of selecting one object at a time with IE 5.0.

Figure 31-13 shows the finished Products Info page that you just created. Notice that this page doesn't have an Expand/Collapse button. This page could have had additional control objects to make it more functional.

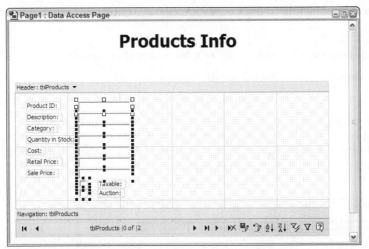

Figure 31-12: The resulting layout of control objects created by the Layout Wizard.

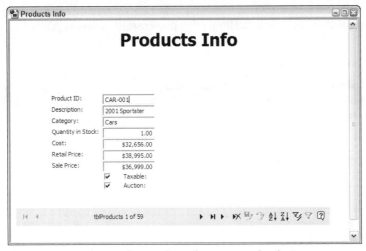

Figure 31-13: The Products Info Web page running in Access.

Editing a single table Web page that already exists

You can bring any preexisting HTML document into Access by selecting the third choice in the Pages object container — Edit Web page that already exists.

When you select this option, a Locate Web Page dialog box displays so that you can select and open the Web page (*.htm, *.html) file that you want to link to in Access.

For example, to open and link to the ContactsAccess2002.htm document, follow these steps:

1. In the Pages container, double-click Edit Web page that already exists.

   Access opens the Locate Web Page dialog box.

2. Select ContactsAccess2002.htm from the dialog box and click the Open button.

   Access displays a message box similar to the one shown in Figure 31-14, informing you that this html file was created in another version of Access and you must first convert it to the current version of Access. After it is converted, you cannot open it in a previous version of Access.

Figure 31-14: The Message box informing you that this html file was created in a previous version of Access.

> **Note**
>
> This message will not appear if the html page was created in Access 2003.

3. Click the Convert button.

   Access displays a second message box stating that it made a backup copy of your original page. It named it the same with the tag 'bak' added to the last part of the name.

4. Click the OK button.

   Another message box opens, informing you that the program cannot find the database or some of its objects and that you need to update the connection information on the page.

5. Click the OK button.

   Access now opens the HTML document in Page Design View, as shown in Figure 31-15. Notice that no tables are displayed in the Field List dialog box.

   At this point, you will need to link the Data Page to the correct table in the current database—tblContacts.

> **Note**
>
> If the form was created in Access 2003 and the connection string is recognized by the program, the document will be opened in the Page Design View and Access also opens the Field list to the appropriate table.

6. Click on the Page connection properties button on the Field List.

   The Page connection properties button is on the Field List dialog box toolbar (the first button under the title bar Field List—pointed to by the cursor in Figure 31-15).

Access opens the Data Links Properties dialog box and activates the Connection tab, highlighting the 1. Select or Enter a Database Name: entry field.

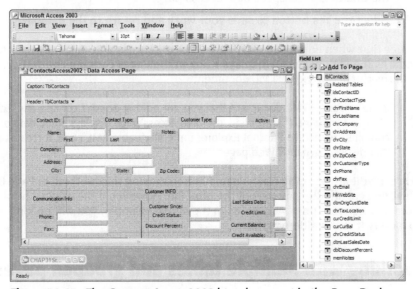

Figure 31-15: The ContactsAccess2002.htm document in the Page Design view of Access.

7. Click on the build button to the right of the 1. Select or Enter a Database Name: entry field.

   Access opens the Select Access Database dialog box.

8. Select CHAP31Start.mdb and press the Open button.

   Access returns to the Data Links Properties dialog box, placing the path and name of the database you have selected.

9. Click on the Test Connection button to verify that the connection has been set for this html file.

   Access displays the Microsoft Data Link message box, informing you that the Test completed successfully.

10. Click the OK button.

    Access returns to the Data Links Properties dialog box.

11. Click the OK button of the Data Links Properties dialog box.

    Access returns you to the ContactsAccess2002 data access page and opens and displays the tblContacts fields in the Field List dialog box.

12. Make any changes you want to the ContactsAccess2002 document.

13. Close your page.

Access activates a dialog box, asking you if you want to save changes made to the ContactsAccess2002 data access page.

14. Select the Yes button to save your work and return to the database.

Notice that when editing an existing Web page, Access automatically uses the same name as the Web page and displays a link in the Pages container with the same name as the underlying HTML document.

Note   If the existing HTML document that you are editing doesn't contain any Extended Markup Language (*.xml) code, the data access page displays static data only. If it contains Microsoft's Internet Explorer understandable XML code, it creates a table that displays dynamic Web pages.

You can edit any existing html file and link to it using this method. In Page Design View, you can modify any part of the html file. However, if the original html file is from another version of Access, as in the above example, you will no longer be able to modify it in the older version.

Working with multiple tables and grouped pages

Up to this point you have worked with single tables — Contact Info by Type, Products Info, or the tblContacts table in the ContactsAccess2002.htm document.

You have even worked with a simple grouped page in the Contact Info By Type document of Figures 31-6 and 31-7. You created this page by using the Page Wizard. The grouped page was based on the type of Contact in the top-most group and specific customer information in the inner group (detailed customer information).

Although this is one way you can use grouped pages, most of the time you work with multiple related tables, placing each in its own grouping.

Understanding grouped pages

Usually, grouped pages are data access pages that contain data from more than one database object. Most of the time, the database objects are tables, but they can also be multiple queries or a combination of tables and queries.

You group a page based on one or more fields from the selected database objects. Each page can contain multiple levels of groups.

You can create grouped data access pages by using the Page Wizard or in the Page Design view. When working with the Design view, you can create new groups by promoting fields or entire objects to a new group, or by dragging fields from other objects into a group section.

After a group is created, it can also be demoted.

When creating a grouped page, use the UniqueTable property to allow updates to the data in the various groups. Sometimes, this property is automatically set.

Creating a grouped data access page using the Page Wizard

By using the Page Wizard, you can create a grouped page for multiple tables. You can create a page using the wizard by selecting a single query with all the appropriate fields in it or by selecting multiple tables when you work with the wizard.

When creating a grouped page with the Page Wizard, the resulting page is based on one recordset and one or more grouping definitions behind the page. The recordset contains information from all tables used and the grouping definition for the fields used in the group. The Page Wizard doesn't prompt you for the Unique Table for the group field, making the page unable to be updated. You can manually set the Unique Table property to the appropriate table in the group properties if necessary.

Using a query to create a group data page with the Page Wizard

You can create a grouped page for contacts and their sales with line item and product information (type of vehicle and description) by using the qrySales Info for Buyers query. This query has fields from all four primary tables. In this case, you may want to show several fields from the related tables, and you need to group the information by the tblContacts.idsContactID field and then create a second grouping by tblSales.idsInvoiceNumber. The remaining fields remain in the third group.

To create this type of DAP, follow these steps:

1. With the CHAP31Start pages database open and the Pages object button selected, double-click the Create data access page by using wizard choice in the container.

   Access starts the Page Wizard.

2. Select the Query: qrySales Info for Buyers from the Tables/Query drop-down box on the first page.

3. After you select the query, press or click the > button to select and move all fields to the Selected Fields list box.

4. Click the Next button to move to the next screen.

5. Select idsContactID as a grouping level by highlighting it and pressing the > button. After you select idsContactID, select idsInvoiceNumber to create a second grouping level.

   At this point, the wizard screen should look similar to the screen shown in Figure 31-16.

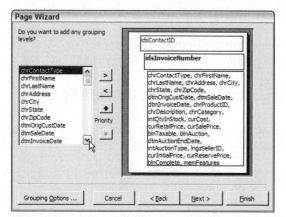

Figure 31-16: Page Wizard with two group levels set.

6. Click the Next button.

Access moves to the sort order screen.

7. Select the chrLastName field in the first combo box to sort by name first.

8. Select the chrFirstName field in the second combo box.

9. Click the Next button.

Access displays the last screen of the Page Wizard. Accept the default name of qrySales Info for Buyers.

10. Click the Open the page radio button.

11. Click the Finish button to complete the data access page.

Access creates the DAP with three grouping levels and opens it. If you click on the Expand/Collapse button for the idsContactID field group and then open the idsInvoiceNumber group by clicking on its Expand/Collapse button, your grouped page should look similar to the one shown in Figure 31-17.

As Figure 31-17 shows, this page contains three levels of group data. Each level has its own navigation controls. If you scroll down to the bottom of the page, you will see three navigation controls. If you click the Next button of either top-level group, the idsInvoiceNumber or idsContactID, the groups below collapse automatically. The default action for the Expand/Collapse control button is to collapse automatically. You can change this default action by setting a value of True for the ExpandByDefault property of each Group level.

Note At this point, the DAP isn't saved to an HTML file. You should save your work by clicking the Save button and saving the HTML file.

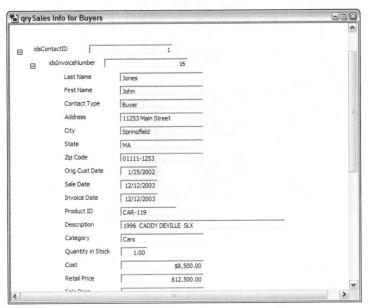

Figure 31-17: The top half of a grouped data access page with three levels of grouping.

The resulting group page is one recordset, and one grouping definition is set behind the page. This DAP is not updateable as created. You can tell this by looking at the New, Delete, Save, and Undo buttons of the navigation bar for each group. You can change the UniqueTable property manually to make the innermost group updateable for a specific table.

Cross-Reference You change the UniqueTable property in the next section when you create a multi-grouping page based on two tables.

At this point, you can take the page into the Design view and make any changes to it, such as leaving groups expanded by default, or changing background colors for the individual groups, or even moving fields around. Figure 31-18 shows the same data access page after being redesigned.

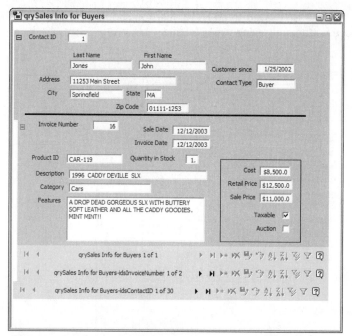

Figure 31-18: The same three-group data access page with modification made to the page and the Products fields of the innermost group updateable.

Creating a two level group data page in the wizard using three tables

You can create a grouped page for Contacts and their Sales by using the three tables — tblContacts, tblSales, and tblSalesLineItems. In this case, you may want to show several fields from the related tables, and you need to group the information by the Contact ID field and then further group by the Invoice Number. The remaining fields remain in the third group.

To create this type of DAP, follow these steps:

1. With the CHAP31Start database open and the Pages object button selected, double-click the Create data access page by using wizard choice in the container.

   Access starts the Page Wizard.

2. Select the Table: tblContacts from the Tables/Query drop-down box on the first page.

3. Move the idsContactID, chrFirstName, chrLastName, chrAddress, chrCity, chrState, chrZipCode, and dtmOrigCustDate fields to the Selected Fields list box.

4. Select the Table: tblSales from the Tables/Query drop-down box on the first page.

5. Move the idsInvoiceNumber, dtmSaleDate, and dtmInvoiceDate fields to the Selected Fields list box.

6. Select the Table: tblSalesLineItems from the Tables/Query drop-down box on the first page.

7. Move the intQuantity, chrDescription, and curPrice fields to the Selected Fields list box.

8. Click the Next button to move to the next screen.

   The Grouping levels screen of the Page Wizard is shown.

9. Select the idsContactID field as a grouping level field by highlighting it and pressing the > button or double-clicking on it. Next > button.

10. Select the idsInvoiceNumber field as a grouping level field by highlighting it and pressing the > button or double-clicking on it.

11. Click the Finish button.

    Access creates the DAP with three grouping levels and opens it in Design View.

12. Click in the Group section with the idsContactID field and make the section larger to accommodate several tblContacts fields.

13. Click in the inner section and select the fields labeled First Name, Last Name, Address, City, State, Zip Code, and Orig Cust Date. After you select them, cut them by pressing Ctrl+X or selecting Edit ➪ Cut from the menu.

14. Click in the top group section and paste the fields into this section by pressing Ctrl+V or selecting Edit ➪ Paste.

    You can now rearrange the fields to look more pleasing to the user.

15. Click in the center group section, containing the idsInvoiceNumber field, and expand it.

16. Click in the inner section and select the Sale Date and Invoice Date fields. After you select them, cut them by pressing Ctrl+X or selecting Edit ➪ Cut from the menu.

17. Click in the center group section and paste the fields into this section by pressing Ctrl+V or selecting Edit ➪ Paste.

    At this point, you should have three fields left in the inner grouping: Quantity, Description, and Price.

18. Select and move the three fields in the inner group section to the top of the section, placing the labels atop each text box as shown in Figure 31-19.

    Figure 31-19 shows all three groups with their left and right borders moved and all three made large enough to accommodate the fields within them.

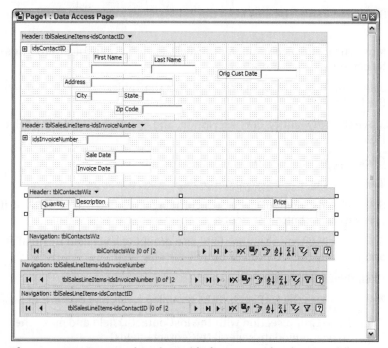

Figure 31-19: Page Design View with three group levels set and the inner group with the final three fields at the top of the group.

19. While at the inner group containing the three fields, right-click on the Header: of this section to select the header only of the section.

20. Select Caption from the menu.

Access opens a caption section for this inner group. Figure 31-20 shows the Caption section added to the inner group.

21. With the Caption Section open, move all three of the labels to the Caption section from each of the text boxes in the inner group. Make sure that they are still above the text boxes they are associated with. Then move the text boxes to the top of the inner group as shown in Figure 31-20. Then resize both the Caption and Inner Group sections to only show their contents.

22. Switch to Page View by clicking the View button.

After you are in View mode, you can expand the Expand/Collapse button for the idsContactID field group to see the Sales Invoice Number and Invoice and Sales Dates. You can further drill down into the line items by expanding the Expand/Collapse button for the idsInvoiceNumber to see the remaining fields in the page. It should look similar to the one shown in Figure 31-21.

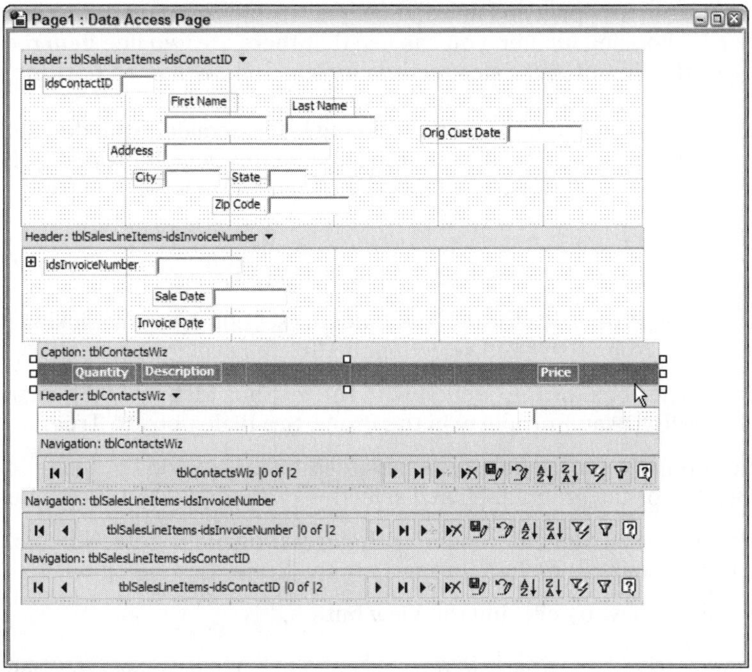

Figure 31-20: The Caption Section opened with the three labels from the fields placed inside the section.

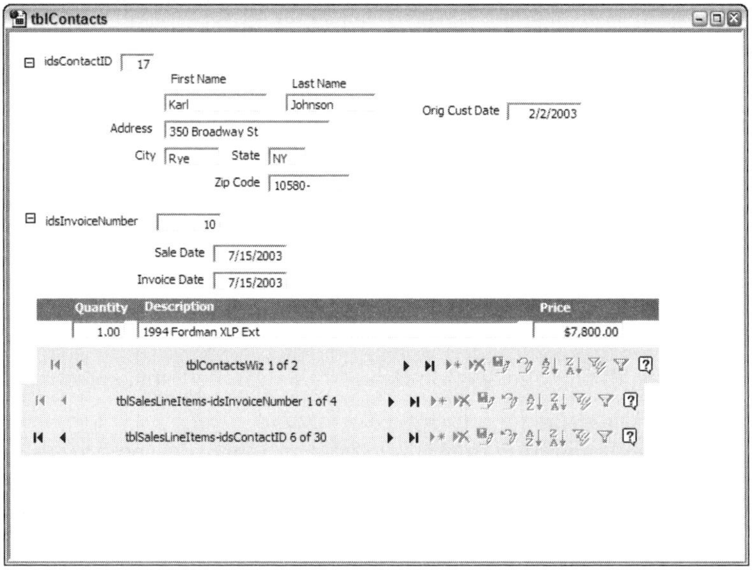

Figure 31-21: Three non-updateable tables, showing information by Contact, then by Invoice, and then by associate line items.

Looking at the data access page in Figure 31-21, you see it is sitting on Contact record number 17. Looking further, you can see that there are two line item records (inner group) for the first of four Sales records for the Contact named Karl Johnson.

At this point, you may want to make both grouping levels remain expanded at all times. To accomplish this, you need to set the ExpandedByDefault property of the Group Level to True. Follow these steps to set each group level to expand automatically:

1. Switch to Design View by clicking the View button.

2. View the Group Properties for the idsContactID section by right-clicking in the Header: or the group itself and selecting the Group Level Properties.

3. In the Properties box for the Section with the text box idsContactID, change the ExpandedByDefault property in the Properties dialog box to True.

4. View the Group Properties for the idsInvoiceNumber section by right-clicking in the Header: or the group itself and selecting the Group Level Properties.

5. In the Properties box for the Section with the text box idsInvoiceNumber, change the ExpandedByDefault property in the Properties dialog box to True.

6. Switch to Page View by clicking the View button.

Now the grouping sections will remain open as you move level to level through the pages.

You now have a data access page based on tblContacts, tblSales, and tblSalesLineItems grouped by Customer ID and Invoice Number. Notice that you can't update any data in any of the groups, as shown in Figure 31-21. This inability to update data is visibly apparent by the disabled New, Delete, Save, and Undo buttons on the Navigation bar.

To allow updates to the data in the Line Items fields of the group, you must set the UniqueTable property of the Section to the tblSalesLineItems table. To set the UniqueTable to tblSalesLineItems, follow these steps:

1. Switch to Design View by clicking the View button.

2. View the Sections Properties for the Header: tblSalesLineItems section (inner grouping). A quick way to open the Properties dialog box with this section active is to double-click the Header section.

3. In the Properties box for the Section HeadertblSalesLineItems, select the Data tab.

4. Select tblSalesLineItems from the UniqueTable property combo box, as shown in Figure 31-22.

5. Switch to Page View.

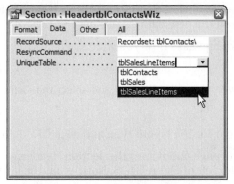

Figure 31-22: Selecting the tblSalesLineItems table for the UniqueTable property of the data access page.

If you wish, you can abandon or save this page to any filename you wish. It will not be used any more in this chapter.

Working with grouped data access pages in Design view

You can also create a grouped data access page in Design view.

New Feature

Access has several enhancements to creating grouped pages. These features include Lightweight Headers, automatic indenting, drop zones (used to easily create a new grouping), and selecting multiple objects in Design view (with IE 5.5 or later installed). These are covered in this section and the next.

Creating a Grouped Data Access Page manually

To manually create a grouped page of Contacts and Sales with two groups, follow these steps:

1. From the Pages object in the Database Window, click the New button.

2. In the New Data Access Page dialog box, accept the default of Design View and click OK.

   If you haven't turned off the warning dialog box, Access displays a message telling you that the page created can't be changed in Access 2000 or 2002. However, if you have loaded Microsoft Office 2003 Web Components, you are capable of viewing and working with it in Access 2000 or 2002.

3. If the field list is not open, open it by clicking the Field List button.

4. From the field list, expand the tblContacts table.

5. Highlight and select the idsContactID, chrFirstName, and chrLastName fields and drag them to the design grid on the new data access page.

Access displays the Layout Wizard and asks how you want the fields to be displayed in the section.

Note If the Layout Wizard does not activate, open the Toolbox and select the Control Wizards button at the top of the box.

6. Select the default value of Columnar for the layout type and click OK.

Access puts the three fields on the page and names the section Header: tblContacts, as shown in the center left of Figure 31-23. Notice that the labels and text boxes are a set size.

7. Drag the chrContactType field to the page. As it moves into the page, a *new* section called Create New Section above tblContacts appears. Drop the chrContactType field in this new section. It receives a bright highlighted border as you move the chrContactType field into it.

Figure 31-23 shows the new section header appearing where you drop the Type of Customer Field. This is called a *drop zone*. After you drop the field, Access automatically creates a new group based on the chrContactType (Contact Type).

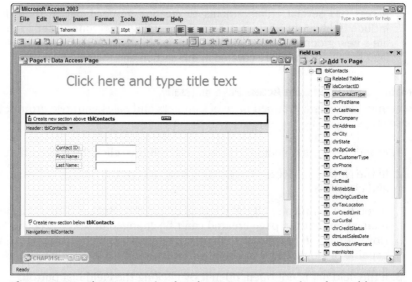

Figure 31-23: The new section header Create New Section above tblContacts is visible as the chrContactType field is dragged onto the work surface of the page.

8. Now you can remove the section at the top that says Click Here and Type Title Text. To remove it, click anywhere on the grayed text.

9. Press the Delete key three times to remove this section.

10. Go to the section with the customer fields (Header: tblContacts), rearrange the fields by moving them up, and then resize the labels to make them fully readable. Then resize the section so that only a little white space remains after the last field. Figure 31-24 shows how the screen may look after it is fixed.

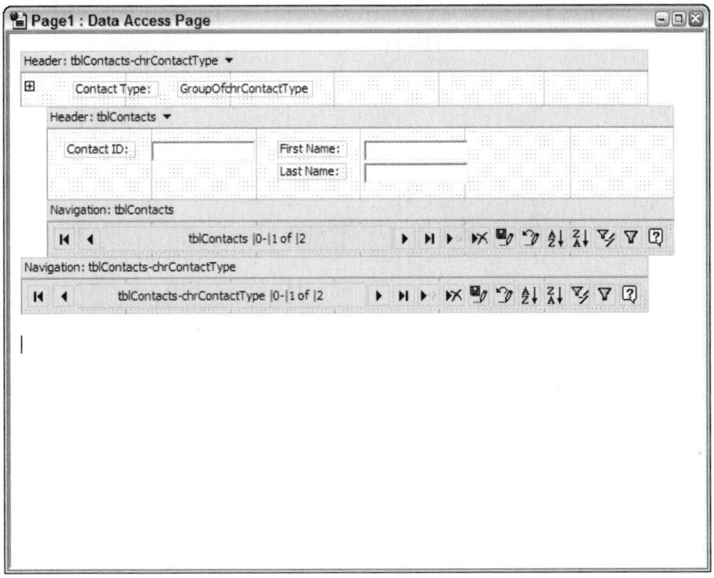

Figure 31-24: The new section header for Contact Type is visible, the section labeled Header: tblContacts has been resized, and the fields have been moved around.

Notice in Figure 31-24 that the groups are automatically indented by Access when it creates them.

11. Click the View button (datasheet icon on left) to see how the page looks so far.

Viewing the data access page, all three Types of Contact records are visible with an Expand/Collapse button to the left of them. When creating a grouping page in this manner, the default value for the DataPageSize property is 10. This means that the grouping shows 10 records at a time.

If you click on the Expand/Collapse button of the first Type of Customer, you see that it displays the first 10 (of 46) records for the next group as well. These can be changed later. Figure 31-25 shows the first several records where the Type of Contact is "both."

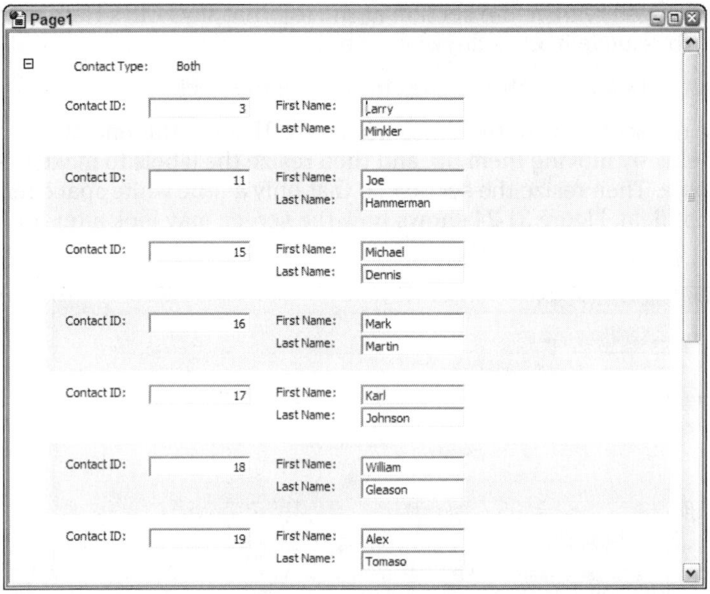

Figure 31-25: The new page with the first Type of Contact section expanded and showing several Contact records for the Type of Contact being "both."

Notice that, in Figure 31-25, you can update the fields in the tblContacts table section (not the Type of Contact or the Contact ID, but the other two fields). Access automatically updates the Section Header: tblContacts's UniqueTable property with the tblContacts table name. To verify this, while in Design View, double-click on the Header: tblContacts table section to activate the property sheet and display all the properties for Section: HeadertblContacts. Then select the Data tab, and the value tblContacts is placed in the UniqueTable text box.

12. Return to Design View by clicking the View button again if you haven't returned.

Now you can add the Sales table below the tblContacts group. If the Property sheet is active, close it.

13. Returning to the Field List, expand the Related Tables option under the tblContacts table. Then expand the Sales table under this option.

14. Select and drag the fields idsInvoiceNumber, dtmSaleDate, and dtmInvoiceDate on the new drop zone that appears at the bottom of the Header: tblContacts section (right above the Navigation bar for the tblContacts section). Figure 31-26 shows the new drop zone named Create New Section below tblContactgs. When this new drop zone becomes visible, drop the fields on the left-most side of the new section.

Access displays the Layout Wizard and asks how you want the fields to be displayed in the section.

15. Select the Tabular radio button and click OK.

Access automatically creates a Caption section and a Header section, putting the titles for each field in the Caption section and the three fields in tabular fashion under the field titles. The field names and titles section may need to be resized at this point.

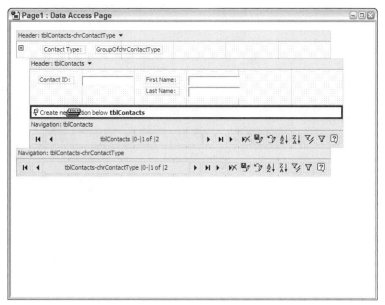

Figure 31-26: Another new drop zone below the tblContacts Section. This is where you drop the tblSales table fields. Notice that the multi-field pointer is on the left-most side of the drop zone.

At this point you can change the Group Level Property ExpandedByDefault to true for both groups, or leave it as is.

16. Switch to Page view to examine the data access page.

If you expanded both the chrContactType (1) and the idsContactID groups, your screen should look similar to the one shown in Figure 31-27. Notice that the page has been scrolled down to Contact Type: Buyer.

As Figure 31-27 shows, each group level is indented approximately ½ inch from its higher group. Access does this automatically when you create the page.

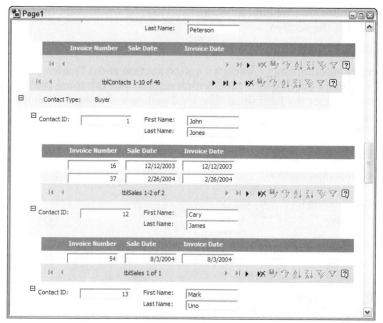

Figure 31-27: A data access page with three groups shown. The first two groups have been expanded.

Notice that the fields in the Sales table area (Invoice Number, Sale Date, and Invoice Date) are also updateable by default. This also indicates that the UniqueTable property for this section has been set to the tblSales table automatically.

Design Features Enabled by Internet Explorer 5.5 or Later

If you have installed Internet Explorer 5.5 or later in Access, several features have been added to the design surface of data access pages. The most important one is the ability to select multiple objects while in Design view. Access 2000 DAPs didn't allow you to select multiple controls to move, size, or apply common property settings. In Access 2003, you can select multiple controls and move them or resize them simultaneously. You can even activate the Property sheet, and if you select multiple controls, a Multiple Selection section appears, allowing you to change many format, data, and other properties universally to all the controls selected.

In addition, IE 5.5 or later has eliminated the alignment and sizing toolbar controls and has added them to the Format menu of the Page Design. If you use IE 5.0, in Access 2002 or 2003, the alignment and sizing work the same as in Access 2000 — using the alignment and sizing toolbar to align or size individually selected controls.

Before continuing, you should save this data access page and name it *Contacts and Sales Grouped*.

Creating a grouped page by promoting a field

You can also create a grouped page by promoting a field in an existing group. For instance, you can create a simple data access page of Contacts and promote the Type of Contact (chrContactType) field in the group to a group above it. To accomplish this, follow these steps:

1. Click Create data access page in Design View in the Pages container of the database window.

2. If the Field List is not active, activate it, and if the Properties dialog box is active, turn it off.

3. Expand the tblContacts Table.

4. Select the chrContactType, chrFirstName, and chrLastName fields, and drag them to the design grid on the new data access page.

    Access creates a Group titled Header: tblContacts and opens the Layout Wizard.

5. Accept the default value Columnar and click OK.

6. You may rearrange the fields to make the page more pleasing.

7. Select and right-click the Type of Contact (chrContactType) field in the Header: tblContacts group.

    Access opens a right-click menu.

8. Click the menu choice Promote, as shown in Figure 31-28.

    Access moves the field and adds a new group level.

9. Save this page and name it *Contacts with Sales Pivot Table*.

Access promotes the field Type of Contact to its own group above the remaining Contact fields. After it's saved, you can look at the data access page to verify that it promoted the group Type of Contact correctly. It shows all three Type of Contact records with an Expand/Collapse button along each one. Clicking this button shows you the Contact records for each type.

Note   This data access page is used in the next section.

Creating a multi-table page with a pivot table

When working with multiple tables in data access pages, you are not limited to putting fields from a linked table in their own grouping as you were above with the tblSales table in Figure 31-27. You can create a simpler page that displays the tblSales table in a pivot table.

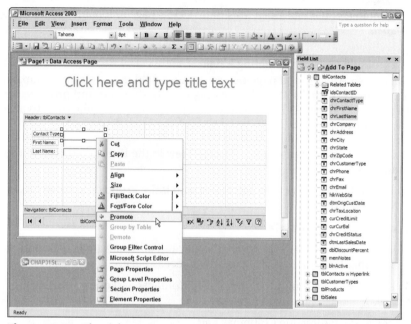

Figure 31-28: The right mouse menu that's used to promote a field to a higher group level.

Pivot tables were first introduced in Access 2000 and offer the ability to place an entire table or select fields from a table in a pivot table that is similar in appearance to a datasheet. This pivot table doesn't have to exist in its own group; rather, it can exist in the current group. For example, to add the tblSales table to the Contacts and Sales Pivot Table page that you just created in the previous section, follow these steps:

1. Open the Contacts and Sales Pivot Table page in Design view, if it isn't already open.

2. If the field list is not active, open it.

3. Expand the tblContacts table icon and click the Related Tables icon to expand it; finally, expand the tblSales table icon.

4. Select the idsInvoiceNumber, dtmSaleDate, dtmInvoiceDate, and lngzSalespersonID fields of the tblSales table, drag them to the Group Header: tblContacts section of the page (below the current fields), and drop them.

Access displays the Layout Wizard and asks how you want the fields to be displayed in the section.

5. Choose the PivotTable radio button and click OK.

Access drops the PivotTable in the group below the Contact fields.

6. Resize the pivot table to fit in the space while showing all the fields.

The page design should now look similar to the one shown in Figure 31-29.

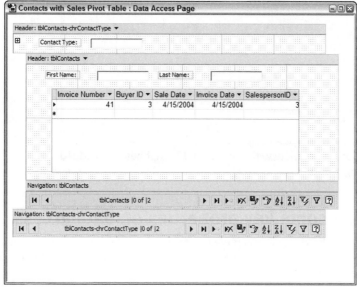

Figure 31-29: A pivot table that has been added to an existing group.

7. Switch to Page view to examine the data access page.

8. While in Page view, click the Expand button of the Type of Contact to see the tblContacts fields and tblSales fields (which are in the pivot table).

The page should now look similar to the one shown in Figure 31-30. Notice that both the Contact fields in the group and the Sales fields in the pivot table are all editable.

9. Save your data access page.

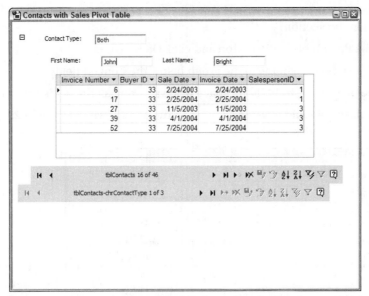

Figure 31-30: A Page view with the pivot table that has been added to an existing group.

Changing some key properties on data access pages

While creating the data access page Contacts and Sales grouped, Access automatically assigns values to several properties. This section discusses those properties and how to change them.

Working with group level properties

After you start working with more than one table, you probably put fields in different groups, as in the section "Working with Multiple Tables and Grouped Pages" earlier in this chapter. You may be interested in changing two properties—DataPageSize and ExpandedByDefault. The DataPageSize property value is set to 10 in many instances. This means that you automatically see up to 10 records for each group of records. The ExpandedByDefault property value is set to False in most instances. You may want to set it to True in some groups so that you automatically see the next level without having to expand the control.

To change these properties, you need to activate the Property sheet and show all the properties related to that group. The property sheet in the Page Design view is different than the one in the forms or Reports Design view; it is lacking the drop-down list field (in forms and reports) that lets you select any control object on the page.

New Feature

In Access 2000, you could change the properties by clicking on the sorting and grouping button or select View ➪ Sorting and Grouping in the Page Design View. After selecting this, you would then select the group whose properties you want to change. These choices have been eliminated from Access 2002 and 2003. In lieu of this method, Access has added what are called *lightweight headers*. These lightweight headers are designed to work with the changes that have been made to Office 2003 visuals — they are like a menu of choices for each header section. The properties of each section are more discoverable. To get to the properties of any section, you can right-click on the header or click on the drop-down arrow in the header as shown in Figure 31-31.

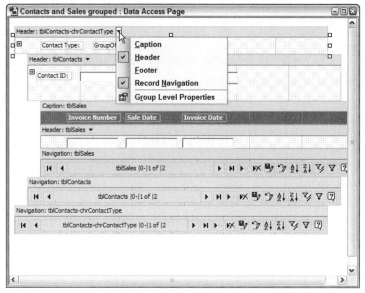

Figure 31-31: A new lightweight header in Page Design view.

As Figure 31-31 shows, the lightweight header has five choices — four are toggle switch types (caption, header, footer, and record navigation), and the fifth is the Show the Group Level Properties.

Figure 31-31 also shows that both the Header section and the Record Navigation section are active (check marked on). If you click-off the Record Navigation section, the corresponding Navigation control section is removed from the data access page.

Turning on the Caption section creates a new area for the group titled Caption, as in the Caption area for Sales in Figure 31-27, shown earlier in the chapter.

Turning on the Footer section also creates a new area for the group just above the Navigation section, titled Footer.

Caution If you uncheck the Header section to deactivate it, Access removes the entire section and all corresponding sections for that group — Caption, Footer, and Record Navigator.

Using the lightweight header menu, you can access the properties of the Group Level. For instance, you may want to access the Group Level properties for the Contact Type Group, in the Contacts and Sales grouped DAP, to change the ExpandedByDefault value to True and the DataPageSize property to 1. To accomplish this, follow these steps:

1. Open the Contacts and Sales grouped data access page in Design View.

2. Click the down arrow of the Contact Type Header bar (tblContacts-chrContactType) to activate the Lightweight Headers (or right-click it).

3. Select Group Level Properties from the menu.

   Access opens the property sheet (if it is closed) and displays all the properties for the Group Level tblContacts.

4. Select the DataPageSize property in the property box and set to 1.

5. Select the ExpandedByDefault property and select True.

6. Switch to Page view to examine the data access page.

   While in Page view, you can see that the Contact Type group is automatically expanded, showing the next group level (Contact information) — this is because ExpandedByDefault has been set to True.

7. Click on the Expand/Collapse button of the Contact Type to close the Customer records.

   Access is only showing one Contact Type group — this is because DataPageSize has been reset to 1.

8. Switch to Page view to examine the data access page.

9. Click the down arrow of the tblContacts Header bar to activate the Lightweight Headers (or right-click it).

10. Select Group Level Properties from the menu for this heading.

11. Select the DataPageSize property in the property box and set to 1.

12. Select the ExpandedByDefault property and also select True.

13. Switch to Page view to examine the data access page with both Expand/Collapse controls set to True.

While in Page view, you can see that the Contact Type group and the tblContacts group are automatically expanded showing the next group level (Sales information) — this is because ExpandedByDefault has been set to True for both. The data access page should look similar to the one shown in Figure 31-32.

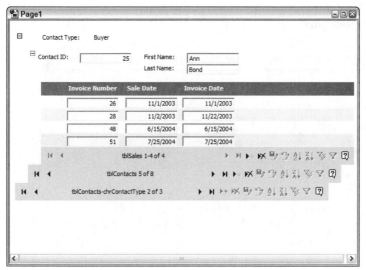

Figure 31-32: A three-group page in Page View with the ExpandByDefault and DataPageSize set.

14. Save your data access page.

Another Group level property, *RecordSelector*, lets you display a record selector when you have more than one record present on the page — when the DataPageSize property is set to a number greater than 1. The default value for this property is False. For example, you may want to display a record selector for the Sales table group in the same page you just worked with. To put a Record Selector alongside each record in the Sales Group (tblSales), follow these steps:

1. Open the Contacts and Sales grouped data access page in Design mode.

2. Click the down arrow of the tblSales Header bar to activate the lightweight headers (or right-click it).

3. Select Group Level Properties from the menu.

   Access opens the property sheet (if it is closed) and displays all the properties for the Group Level tblSales.

4. Select the RecordSelector property in the property box and set it to True. (It should be the last property of the GroupLevel: tblSales.)

5. Switch to page view to examine the data access page with a record selector alongside of each Sales record in the tblSales Group Section.

The new data access page should now look similar to the one shown in Figure 31-33.

6. Save your page.

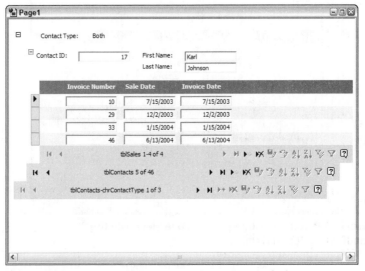

Figure 31-33: A three-group page in Page View with the RecordSelector set on the Sales records.

The DAP in Figure 31-33 shows record selectors alongside each record of the Sales table (in this case, four records). The mouse pointer is pointing to the first record selector. The user can quickly move to any record in the set by clicking the selector.

Changing the title of a page

Examining Figure 31-33, you see that the title of the DAP is currently Page1. You can change this by opening the Property sheet and following these steps:

1. Open the Contacts and Sales grouped data access page in Design mode.

2. Open the Property sheet and then click on the title bar of the DAP.

3. Select Other tab in the property sheet Page: Page1.

Access opens the Other section of the property sheet.

4. Select the Title property in the property box and set the value to Contacts and Sales Grouped. (It should be the second-to-last property of the Page: Page1.)

5. Switch to page view to examine the data access page with the new title in the title bar.

6. Save your page.

Changing the absolute path property of a page

If you have not turned the warning off, every time you save a data access page, Access pops up a warning box like the one shown in Figure 31-34.

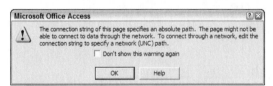

Figure 31-34: The Warning box that appears when saving a DAP.

As you can see in Figure 31-34, Access informs you that the connection string for the page is an absolute page (hard-coded to a specific drive and directory). When using this on a network, or when you copy the database and files, you need to let Access know where the database is moved. In a network environment, you need to change the connection string to specify a network path, called a Universal Naming Convention (UNC) path.

To change the absolute path for the data source of a data access page, you need to change the ConnectionString property of the page. To change the path for the Contacts with Sales Pivot Table page, follow these steps:

1. Open the Contacts with Sales Pivot Table page in Design view.

2. If the property sheet is not open, open it.

3. Click one time on the title bar of the Page window or in the white area above the top group.

   The Property sheet informs you that it is displaying the properties for the Page by the title, which has changed to Page: Contacts with Sales Pivot Table.

4. In the Data tab section, move the cursor to the ConnectionString property text box (second one from the top).

5. While the cursor is in the ConnectionString text box, press the Shift-F2 key combination to activate the Zoom window.

   The Zoom window appears with the entire connect string highlighted.

6. In the Zoom window, move the cursor to the right side of the first line where it says "Data Source=", positioning it just after the equals sign.

7. Select and remove the drive and path information all the way up to the name of the database (CHAP31Start.mdb) as shown in Figure 31-35. After the physical path is highlighted, simply press Delete to remove it.

Figure 31-35: The Zoom window with the cursor moved to the insertion point to correct the data source of this database and the physical path highlighted to be removed.

8. Click OK to save the changes and return to the property sheet.

9. Save your page.

With the absolute page reference gone, you can now use this database on a network drive and simply refer to the database as you do for other files in the network.

There is one other side issue — moving the database. If you move the database and the underlying HTML file, you also need to change the hard-coded path of where to find the HTML file from the page object in the Access Pages container. Follow these steps to remove the hard-coded path from the properties of the page object:

1. Select the Pages button of the database and then select (highlight) the Contacts with Sales Pivot Table object name.

2. Select View ➪ Properties from the menu or right-click and select Properties from the right-mouse button menu.

Access opens the Objects Property sheet for the page object Contacts with Sales Pivot Table. It should look similar to the one shown in Figure 31-36.

3. Click in the Path: text box.

4. Remove the path reference to the HTML filename, leaving only the HTML filename in the Path text box.

5. After you have removed the drive and path name, click on the Apply Button to store the filename without a path.

6. Click OK to save the newly set properties.

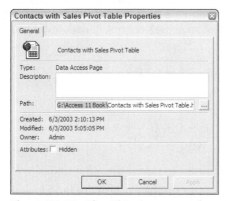

Figure 31-36: The Object property sheet for objects in a database.

With the path removed from the page object reference, the database and its associated HTML files can be moved to any drive or directory and will run as expected.

Changing properties of the Expand/Collapse control

New Feature

In Access 2000, the Expand/Collapse control was an ActiveX control. It has been changed to HTML code using graphic files in Access 2002 and 2003. It has several new properties that you can work with to change the physical appearance of the control.

Under the Format tab of the Control object (Expand/Collapse) property sheet, you can change the Cursor property to 25 different values — the default is a pointing hand. This property controls what is displayed when the user moves the cursor over the control. Also of interest is the Display property, which has seven different values — the default is inline. If you change this property, it controls how the control displays; for instance, if you select block, the control is displayed in an outlined solid block.

Under the Other tab, the *Src* property can be set to change the appearance, or picture, as displayed by the Expand/Collapse control. You have six choices — the default is a Black Plus/Minus sign. You can select a black arrow to have it show a right-pointing arrow when collapsed and a down-pointing arrow when expanded.

Changing properties of the Navigation control

New Feature

In Access 2000, the Navigation control was also an ActiveX control, and you were limited to the functionality of the ActiveX control. In Access 2002 and 2003, the Navigation control is an HTML table with styles and images associated with all the buttons. This feature lets you customize the images and formatting of the buttons. Also, by using HTML code instead of an ActiveX control, it loads faster and requires fewer resources to operate.

Figure 31-37 shows the Navigation control bar for data access pages.

Figure 31-37: The Navigation control for DAPs.

The look of the Control and all the buttons on the Control are built based on HTML styles. These styles are implemented as classes in the page's <STYLE> tag. Because they are based on styles, you can easily change the look of the Navigation control.

Removing buttons from the Navigation bar

Using HTML code makes it a simple matter to remove buttons on the navigation control. For instance, to remove the new, delete, save, undo, filters, sort, and help buttons from the tblContacts - chrContactType Navigation bar of the Contacts and Sales grouped page, follow these steps:

1. Open the Contacts and Sales group page in Design view.

2. Move to the bottom of the page in Design view to show the Navigation bar for tblContacts - chrContactType.

3. If you have IE 5.5 or later loaded on your machine, select all the buttons from the New button through the Help button, as shown in Figure 31-38. If you don't have IE 5.5 or later on your machine, you must select each one independently (repeating Steps 3 and 4 until they are all gone).

4. Press Delete to remove all the buttons at one time. If you don't have IE 5.5 or later on your machine, you must repeat Steps 3 and 4 until all the buttons are removed. At this point, the Navigation bar should look similar to the one shown in Figure 31-39.

5. With the buttons removed, you can now resize the Navigation bar by selecting the right side and moving it inward (toward the left) until it is resized to what you like.

6. Save your work.

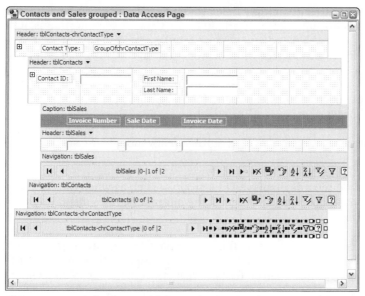

Figure 31-38: Selecting multiple Navigation bar buttons to delete them.

Figure 31-39: The Navigation bar with several buttons deleted.

Changing images on a button of the navigation bar

To change the image of any control on the Navigation bar, you simply follow these general steps:

1. With the data access page in Design view, click After on the Navigation control.

2. Click the image that you want to change.

3. View the property sheet and select the Other tab.

4. Replace the Src property with the path to the new image. It can be a file path or HTTP address.

Specifying default settings for new DAPs

When you add a Caption section to a header, the default background color of the Caption is set to blue, as in the Caption section of the Pets table shown in Figure 31-31 earlier in the chapter. This enables the user to visually see a contrast between the sections.

When you right-click to add multiple fields to the header section after adding a Caption, the labels are automatically added to the Caption section (that is, if the control wizards are enabled and you choose Tabular from the Layout Wizard, as you did previously in the chapter with the Pets table in the Customer and Pets Grouped page).

If you add a footer section to a header, the footer section puts a 1-point blue line across the top border.

When you create a new section, Access automatically indents the section a specific amount.

If you have multiple records displayed in a group — such as when the DataPageSize property is set to a number greater than 1, the alternating rows display a different color — for contrast.

All of these actions are controlled by the default page format properties of Access. Figure 31-40 shows the new options that you can set for data access pages. To access these options, simply select Tools ⇨ Options from the menu and select the Pages tab.

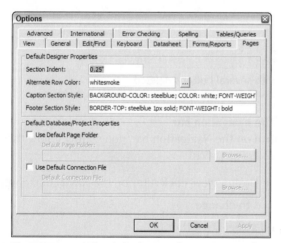

Figure 31-40: The default page format properties of Access.

As Figure 31-40 shows, you can change the default values of four properties — Section Indent, Alternate Row Color, Caption Section Style, and Footer Section Style.

Working with the Data Outline in Page Design view

Access has a data outline graphical tool for data access pages. The Data Outline displays a tree-like view of the data model of a data access page. Figure 31-41 shows the Data Outline window open with the data model of the Contacts and Sales grouped data access page.

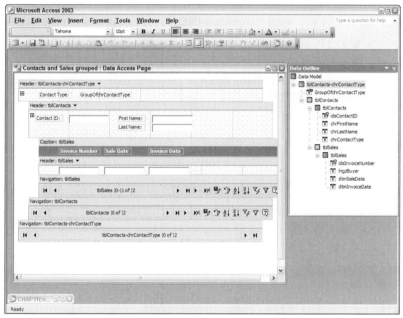

Figure 31-41: The data outline of a data access page.

As Figure 31-41 shows, the Data Outline window displays a tree view of the data model of the data access page. It shows the record sources, fields, and any calculated controls on the page. As you click on any object in the data model, it is automatically selected in the Design window.

You can use the data outline to review the structure of a page.

To activate the Data Outline tool, simply select View ➪ Data Outline from the Page Design view menu or click the Data Outline button.

Saving other Access objects as data access pages

You can convert any table, query, view, form, and report to a data access page. To do this, you simply need to select an object and save it as a data access page. The type of page that is created depends on the type of object being saved.

When you save an object to a data access page, Access uses XML Transform internally to create the data access page. This Transform, actually a Style sheet (named ReportML2DAP.xsl) containing XML code, is used to convert the objects into a data access page. However, this is not visible to the user.

To save any of these objects as a data access page, you simply follow these general steps:

1. Select the object you want to create a data access page from in the database.

2. After you select it, choose File ⇨ Save As (or right-click and select Save As . . .) from the menu.

   Access opens the Save As dialog box and puts a default name of "Copy of [Object Name]" in the text box, as shown in Figure 31-42.

Figure 31-42: The Save As dialog box is used to save any object to a data access page; in this case, it is saving a table.

3. Either accept the default Save to filename or enter a new name to save the data access page to.

4. Select Data Access Page in the AS: drop-down list box.

5. Click OK.

   Access opens the New Data Access Page dialog box and puts the default name in the text box.

6. Click OK to save the new Web page.

That is all there is to creating a DAP from any database object.

You need to be aware of some other issues when saving certain types of Access objects to a data access page. These issues are covered in the following sections.

Converting a table, query, or view to a data access page

When saving a table, query, or view to a data access page, the new page contains all the fields from the table in a tabular layout. The fields are outlined, record selectors are enabled, and the page size is set to display 10 records at a time.

The resulting DAP appears similar to a table datasheet. Figure 31-43 shows a data access page created from the tblContacts table.

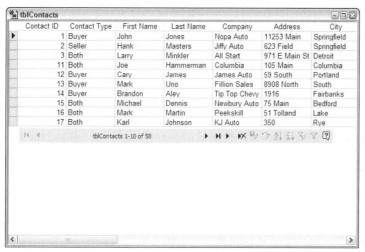

Figure 31-43: A data access page created from a table.

The data access page created in Figure 31-43 is updateable, as you can see from the active New and Delete buttons on the Navigation bar.

> **Caution** If the Default view of your object is set to PivotTable or PivotChart view, the page created contains the PivotTable or PivotChart representation of the object instead.

Converting a form to a data access page

When saving a form to a data access page, the new page contains *most* of the fields from the underlying table or query.

When converting a form to a DAP, the following objects are either ignored or changed, as follows:

✦ Any bound or unbound object frames are not supported and will not be converted — they are simply ignored.

✦ Toggle buttons and tab controls are not supported and will not be converted — they are simply ignored.

✦ Any diagonal lines will be converted to horizontal lines on the new data access page.

✦ Any subform in a form will not be converted to a data access page.

✦ Any value lists used as row sources will be placed as an unbound list type when converted.

✦ If a list box or combo box uses multiple columns as its data source and display, only the first visible column of the original control will be converted.

✦ Controls placed in the header section will be placed in unbound controls in the caption section of the outermost group level (top level).

✦ Controls placed in the footer section will be placed in unbound controls in the navigation section of the outermost group level (top level).

✦ Pictures in a form are converted to bitmaps and placed in a folder below the current location that is named "Images." These are not pictures in bound object frames — only those that are image types in forms.

✦ Expressions that refer to the properties of a form or subform are ignored.

✦ Any code that would not run in a data access page is imported into the page as a comment block at the end of the document. Any code behind the form or control events is not converted to a data access page.

✦ Hyperlinks associated with a label or command button control are not converted over to the data access page. They will not be active when the form is converted to a page.

✦ If the form contains ActiveX controls, only those controls that support the IpersistPropertyBag interface are implemented in the page.

Creating a DAP from a form with the default view of Single Form

Most forms have the Default View property set to Single Form. If you create a page from a form that has this value, the new data access page looks similar to the form you are creating it from. The fields and text are placed in the same relative position on the new Web document as they were in the form.

For example, follow these steps to create a data access page from the Pets table:

1. Open the form frmContactsAll from the Form container of the database.

   The frmContactsAll form should look similar to the one shown in Figure 31-44.

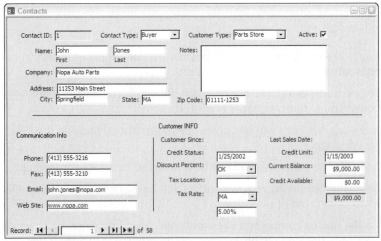

Figure 31-44: The frmContactsAll form has multiple pull-down combo boxes.

2. With the form still open, select File ➪ Save As . . . from the menu.

Access opens the Save As dialog box and puts a default name of "frmContactsAll" in the text box.

3. Accept the default "frmContactsAll" name and select Data Access Page in the AS: drop-down list box.

4. Click OK.

Access opens the New Data Access Page dialog box and puts the default name in the text box.

5. Click OK to save the new Web page.

Access attempts to create the new frmContactsAll data access form, and if there are no errors, it then opens it for you to examine. In this case, Access encountered errors and displays a message box that says "Microsoft Access is unable to create the data access page," as shown in Figure 31-45. The problem is that the drop-down combo boxes and the Tax Rate field use a lookup function (=Format([cboTaxLocation].[Column](1),"Percent")).

Figure 31-45: A message box reporting the form can't be converted to a DAP.

These combo boxes need to be converted to text boxes before you can create a data access page. To change the combo boxes to text boxes, follow these steps:

1. Click on the View button to go into the Design View with the frmContactsAll form.

2. With the form in Design view, you need to select any one of the four combo box fields — chrContactType, chrCustomerType, chrCreditStatus, and chrTaxLocation.

Although you can select all four simultaneously by holding the shift key and selecting each one, you will not be able to convert all of them at the same time. You must select one field at a time.

3. With one of the four fields selected, right-click to activate the menu and select Change To >> Text Box.

Access immediately changes the combo box to a text box.

4. Repeat Steps 2 and 3 until you have converted all four fields.

Access opens the New Data Access Page dialog box and puts the default name in the text box.

5. Click on the txtTaxRate field (labeled Tax Rate:) and press the delete key to remove it.

6. Click OK to save the changed form.

With the four fields changed to Text Boxes and the Tax Rate field removed, you can now save the form as a DAP. When it is saved as a DAP, it should look similar to the one shown in Figure 31-46.

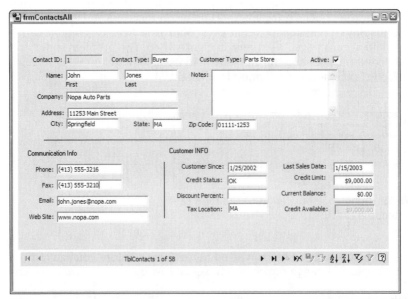

Figure 31-46: A new data access page created from the frmContactsAll form.

All of the other fields are on the page in the same relative positioning as the original frmContactAll form. It even has a Navigation control and a record selected bar added to the data access page.

Creating a DAP from a form with the default view of datasheet

If the form you are converting has the Default View property set to Datasheet, the resulting Datasheet is also a datasheet-like view. The data access page is very similar to the ones you created by saving a table or query.

For example, if you save the frmSubCustomer&Sales form to a data access page, the new page looks like the one shown in Figure 31-47. Because the form's Default View is set to Datasheet, the page created is also similar to a datasheet.

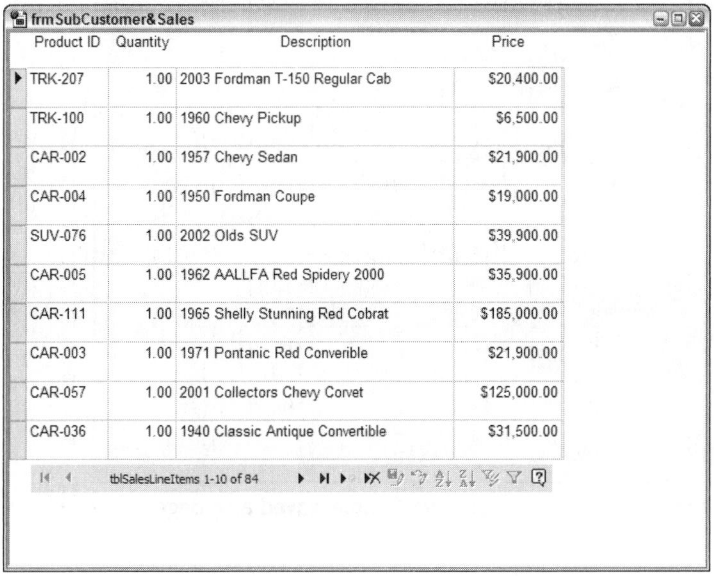

Product ID	Quantity	Description	Price
TRK-207	1.00	2003 Fordman T-150 Regular Cab	$20,400.00
TRK-100	1.00	1960 Chevy Pickup	$6,500.00
CAR-002	1.00	1957 Chevy Sedan	$21,900.00
CAR-004	1.00	1950 Fordman Coupe	$19,000.00
SUV-076	1.00	2002 Olds SUV	$39,900.00
CAR-005	1.00	1962 AALLFA Red Spidery 2000	$35,900.00
CAR-111	1.00	1965 Shelly Stunning Red Cobrat	$185,000.00
CAR-003	1.00	1971 Pontanic Red Converible	$21,900.00
CAR-057	1.00	2001 Collectors Chevy Corvet	$125,000.00
CAR-036	1.00	1940 Classic Antique Convertible	$31,500.00

Figure 31-47: A new data access page created from the frmSubCustomer&Sales form.

Creating a DAP from a form with the default view of continuous forms

If the form that you are converting has the Default View property set to Continuous Forms, the resulting Datasheet has the page size property set to All and the navigation control is present but not used for First Record, Previous, Next, or Last. However, the Navigation control is still present if the record selector is on in the form. If present, the buttons available are Add, Delete, Sort, Filter, and Help. For example, if you save the form frmContactsSimple to a data access page, they both look similar to those shown in Figure 31-48.

As Figure 31-48 shows, the Form (top left corner) has the navigational bar visible with the ability to step through the individual form pages. In contrast, the data access page (bottom right corner) created from this form, shows all 58 forms continuously, and at the bottom (not visible in the figure) the navigation bar has several buttons deactivated.

Creating a DAP from a form with the default view of PivotTable or PivotChart

If the form that you are converting has the Default View property set to PivotTable or PivotChart view, the resulting Datasheet uses the appropriate ActiveX control to represent the component.

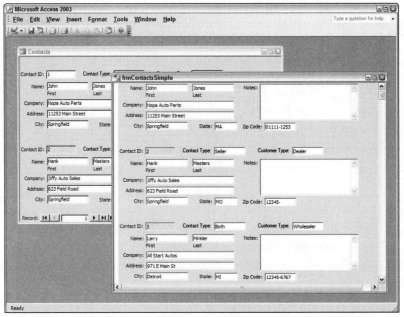

Figure 31-48: A continuous form, frmContactsSimple, saved as a page.

Creating a DAP from a form with a subform

If the form that you are converting has a subform in it, such as the frmCustomer&Sales form shown in Figure 31-49, the subform is not converted.

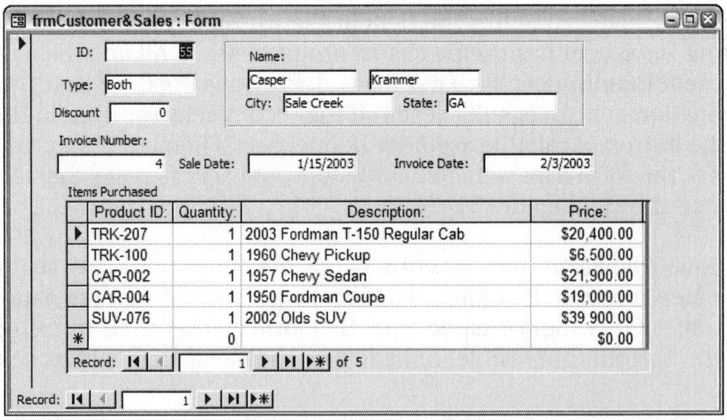

Figure 31-49: A form with a subform to be saved as a data access page.

When you convert this form to a data access page, the resulting page looks like the one in Figure 31-50. Notice that none of the Sales information from the subform was brought over to the page from the original form in Figure 31-49.

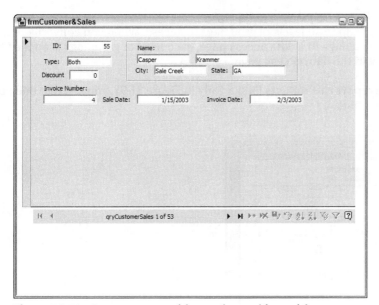

Figure 31-50: A page converted from a form with a subform.

Converting a report to a data access page

Reports in Access databases (both *.mdb and *.adp) can be saved as data access pages. The same objects that are ignored or changed in forms are ignored or changed in data access pages.

Cross-Reference See the section titled "Converting a form to a data access page" earlier in this chapter.

Unlike forms, a report is not interactive: Data in reports is saved as text boxes in data access pages with a style and appearance similar to what appears on the report.

Because reports only have two views, they are simpler to work with as compared to forms. However, reports support subreports, groupings, multiple columns, multiple headers and footers, ActiveX controls, and many summary functions. Understanding how a report is converted to a DAP is important.

Creating a DAP from a report with multiple columns

When you convert a report that contains multiple columns to a data access page, the resulting page is a single column wide.

Creating a DAP from a report with groupings

A report can have up to 10 levels of groupings in Access. When you convert a report that contains groupings to a data access page, each level of groupings is applied to a different level in the data access page.

Looking at the report rptProducts First 5 Only in Figure 31-51, you see that one page is displayed at a time.

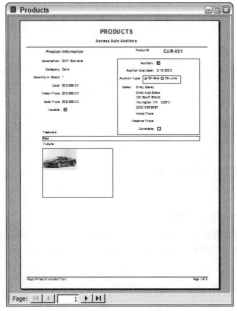

Figure 31-51: A report with groupings.

The DAP created from the report in Figure 31-1 does not display the same as the report. It has added an Expand/Collapse control to the innermost level with the vehicle information. Figure 31-52 shows the resulting DAP from the report. There are five records shown, each having an Expand/Collapse control.

It also has added a navigation bar for this level. You can expand the level to see the product information, which makes the data access page more functional. The DAP has eliminated the page footer formulas for the date on which the report was printed and the page numbers. You can go into Design view and modify the page to correct these problems.

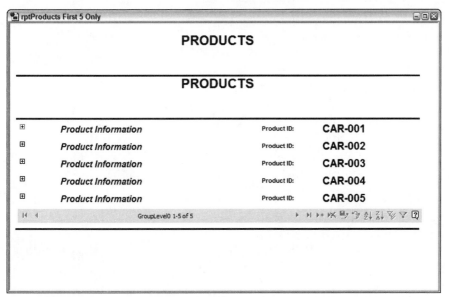

Figure 31-52: The DAP from a report with grouping.

Caution You can get unexpected results when converting multiple grouped reports to data access pages.

The resulting data access page has two titles for Products and the grouping title has been made Product Information. Also notice that none of the fields are linked to the text boxes in the Caption section of the Header Group Level 0. You can change these in Design View of the DAP.

Creating a DAP from a report with subreports

Like forms with subforms, if you convert a report with a subreport to a data access page, the subreport is not included in the page.

XML, Access, and InfoPath

I n this chapter, you work with XML inside Access. After completing this chapter, you should have a working knowledge of XML and how Access utilizes its power.

On the CD-ROM This chapter will use the database named CHAP32Start. mdb. It also uses several other files for importing that are included with the database (NewCustomersANDSales.xml, New Customers AND Student TWO FILES.xml, Binding-ReadingPrograms.html, Products.xml, and Products.xsd). If you have not already copied them onto your machine from the CD, you will need to do so now. When you have completed this chapter, your database should resemble the one in CHAP32End.mdb

XML Data and Access

Office 2003 has added system-wide support for eXtensible Markup Language (XML). It is one of the biggest changes offered in this version of Office. The biggest winners for enhancements are Excel and Word; however, Access has also added more support for XML data than in previous releases. Using Access, you can include XML in several ways:

✦ Use the built-in tools to import and export XML data (started in Access 2002), including related tables (new in 2003 release).

✦ Import XML files and information from SharePoint Team Services (also in XML format) directly to Access tables.

✦ Export XML forms and reports using an XML-based language called ReportML. It is also used to create HTML and DAP files.

✦ Link an HTML page to an XML data file by taking the page offline in Internet Explorer 5.x or later.

✦ Set Data Access Page properties inside Access to allow the page to bind to an external XML data file.

✦ Embed the XML data directly inside the page by setting page properties.

Using XML in Access, data from almost any external application can be transformed for use by Access.

New Feature Using Access, you can import and export XML data, including related tables.

Import XML data into Access (Jet, SQL Server or SQL Server Desktop Engine — formally known as MSDE) if it was a previously generated XSD file from Access. This gives you the data typing, relationships, keys, and indices.

Export Access objects (tables, queries, views, datasheets, forms, or reports) to XML data (as an XML file) and associated schema (as an XSD file). It can export to Jet, SQL Server, or SQL Server Desktop Engine databases. You can also export reports as XML/XSD with presentation, which creates the data, and XSL that formats the data, and an ASP or HTML wrapper to view the data/report in a browser capable of using XML. You can bind the exported report to an SQLS database and view live Access reports in the browser.

Using eXtensible Stylesheet Language Transformation (XSLT) files, you can even convert data into an Access data format.

Understanding XML

XML is the standards-based language protocol for describing and delivering data across the Web to a browser, just as HTML (HyperText Markup Language) code is the standard language for creating and displaying Web pages with graphics and text in them. The best part of XML in Access is that you can work with XML without ever writing a single line of XML code. However, knowing the basics of XML can help you visualize how it will help you in a business.

HTML describes how a Web page should look; in contrast, XML defines the data and describes how the data should be structured. XML separates the data from the presentation so that the same XML data can be presented in multiple ways by using different presentation methods. XML, like HTML, uses tags and attributes. However, XML uses these tags only to delimit pieces of data, leaving the interpretation of the data up to the application that receives and reads it.

By using XML, it is possible to use and move data across the Internet or intranet between dissimilar applications and systems. The XML protocol specifies the guidelines, rules, and formal conventions to be used for designing data formats and structures. By following these recommendations, the data files produced can be easily created and read by different computer systems. XML data structures are self-describing; thus, any platform that can interpret XML can use and display the data they contain.

XML and Internet Glossary

The many new terms associated with XML and the Internet can be confusing. Here are some of the basic XML terms you will see in this chapter and others on XML:

✦ **CSS (Cascading Style Sheet)** is a collection of formatting instructions to control the display of a document. Generally, they are stored separately from the data, but can be in the same document as the data.

✦ **DTD (Document Type Definition)** is a set of rules that store element names and attributes. It defines how these can be combined and in which order they will be applied.

✦ **Element** is any tag — the start and stop identifiers of an item defined in an XML document.

✦ **HTML (HyperText Markup Language)** is a set of rules that specify how a Web page is created and displayed.

✦ **Open (Open Standard)** is a technology that has been adapted for use and development by the public, without the need for paying licensing fees. It is owned by no single organization or company. This is in contrast to proprietary standards owned by a specific company or organization.

✦ **SGML (Standard Generalization Markup Language)** is a set of rules that specify how a Web document is created and displayed.

✦ **W3C (World Wide Web Consortium)** is an organization that creates standards for the Web. Its sole purpose is to create new technologies and standards for the Web.

✦ **XHTML (eXtensible HyperText Markup Language)** extends the use of traditional HTML.

✦ **XML (eXtensible Markup Language)** is a data interchange format. XML data is also referred to as XML document, the .xml file that contains the raw XML data, stored independently of how it is presented.

✦ **XML schema** is the document that defines the content, entities, and elements allowed in an XML document.

✦ **XSD (XML schema definition)** is the file containing the schema information for an XML file.

✦ **XSL (eXtensible Stylesheet Language)** is used to create style sheets that can be attached to XML documents for presenting data.

✦ **XSLT (XLS Transformations)** is used to transform the structure of an XML document for creating different views.

What is XML?

XML was developed by the W3C as a means of specifying an easy-to-use and easy-to-read standard that allows the exchange of data across different hardware, database, and other software platforms all over the world.

It is hard to specify a concise definition for XML. It is a specification, a format, and a standards-based language protocol. It is a subset of the SGML that is designed for Web documents. In its easiest concept, it is a format used to exchange data between applications.

Some people call XML a markup language, because that is what its name suggests. But XML is more than a language of tags. Users do not rely on a specific set of tags; rather, they can create their own markup language specific to their own data needs. They can specify rules to create their own tags and style sheets. This is because each individual tag describes the content and meaning of the data, rather than how it is formatted or displayed. The following code shows a simple example of an XML document containing information about new customers:

```
<NewCustomers>
 <NewCustomer>
  <CustomerID>DI001</CustomerID>
  <CustomerName>Dinbart, Duane</CustomerName>
  <CustomerCompany>Dingbats All Around</CustomerCompany>
  <CustomerTitle>Sales Representative</CustomerTitle>
 </NewCustomer>
<NewCustomer>
  <CustomerID>MC001</CustomerID>
  <CustomerName>McCormic, Michael</CustomerName>
  <CustomerCompany>Tiles R Us</CustomerCompany>
  <CustomerTitle>Vice President</CustomerTitle>
 </NewCustomer>
</NewCustomers>
```

As the code in shows, each element has an opening tag and a closing tag (for example, the Customer ID is enclosed with a beginning <CustomerID> and an ending </CustomerID> tag). The tagged elements are nested inside other tags: <CustomerID> and <CustomerName> are nested inside <NewCustomer>, </NewCustomer> tags. <NewCustomer> is nested in <NewCustomers>.

Working with XML, you use your own class information — <NewCustomer> — that can be easily converted into an Access database or any other database. Using an XML schema, you can make the XML data usable in different forms, reports, and tables.

All the tags in this example are defined by the person creating the XML document. The example above could have had the tag <NewCustomers> named <MyNewPeople> or anything else. The critical part is that it has an end tag by the same name. When importing the above file into an Access table, the tags <NewCustomer> and </NewCustomer> are used to delineate individual records in the table definition titled NewCustomer. The NewCustomers tag can have more than one table definition within it. In fact, NewCustomer can also have additional related tables embedded within it.

Cross-Reference

This is covered in more detail in the section "Creating your own XML Documents," later in this chapter.

By separating the data from the function of the data, you can add a new function for use of that data in another form. Because XML data is stored separately from how it is displayed, it can be used in a wide variety of formats.

What are XML schemas?

When working with XML, you need to describe the structure of the data in a format that Web browsers and other XML-enabled programs can recognize. The data needs some way to let the document that is using it know how to read and apply the data inside the document. The *XML schema* (*.xsd) is used to create that description. The XML schema file is a formal specification of the rules for an XML document, specifying a series of element names, as well as which elements are permissible in the document and in which combinations. It is a part of the XML standard, known as the XML Schema standard.

By using a schema, you can verify that any XML document that is used to import data into or export data from Access to another format contains the defined structure and specific data requirements needed by Access. After you create a schema, it can be given to your customers or other users to let them use it to structure any data they provide to you.

Using XSL to display XML data

XML uses syntax that describes the data in an XML document without describing how the data should be displayed. eXtensible Stylesheet Language (XSL) is what is used to actually tell the XML-enabled program how to display the XML data. Using XSL, you can direct which data should be selected and displayed, and the order of displaying. It uses a combination of XML-like and HTML tags to create a template for creating the output.

When Access creates a data access page using the Save As option, it uses an XML schema file internally and an XSL file named RPT2DAP.xsl to write the data access page telling the page how to display the data. The contents of that file are shown in Figure 32-1.

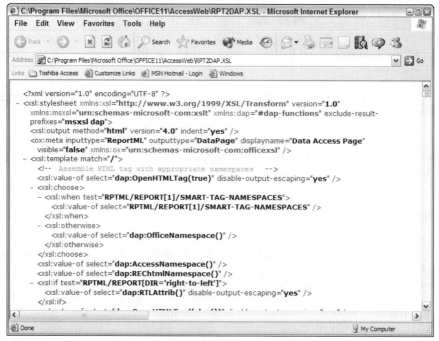

Figure 32-1: The top-most part of the RPT2DAP.xsl file.

If you open the file in Figure 32-1 and scroll through it, you see many new tags that are XML specific. After you became familiar with XML, schema, and XSL files, you can modify this one to add additional functionality to the capabilities of exporting an Access object to a data access page.

Access also uses an XML schema file, named RPT2HTML4.xsl, for creating HTML documents based on the W3C HTML 4.x standard.

Tip   XSL files do not have to be linked to XML documents for IE 5.x or greater to display the document correctly.

Using XSLT with XML data

XSLT (eXtensible Stylesheet Language for Transformations) lets you transform XML documents into a new form. This lets you bring legacy data, stored in proprietary format, into an XML form and transform it to fit your specific XML standards.

Creating Your Own XML Documents

When you export a table, query, form, or report to XML, Access automatically creates an XML file and any associated .xsd, .xsl, and .html file you specify.

However, you can create your own XML file (.xml) using any simple text editor. You do not need to create your own XML documents from scratch, but doing so will give you a firm understanding of what XML documents actually are.

The process of creating a simple XML document

The code shown in the "What is XML" section shows the contents of a simple XML document that stores several fields for each customer. This file can be created in Notepad or any other simple text editor. The XML document NewCustomers.xml is shown in Figure 32-2.

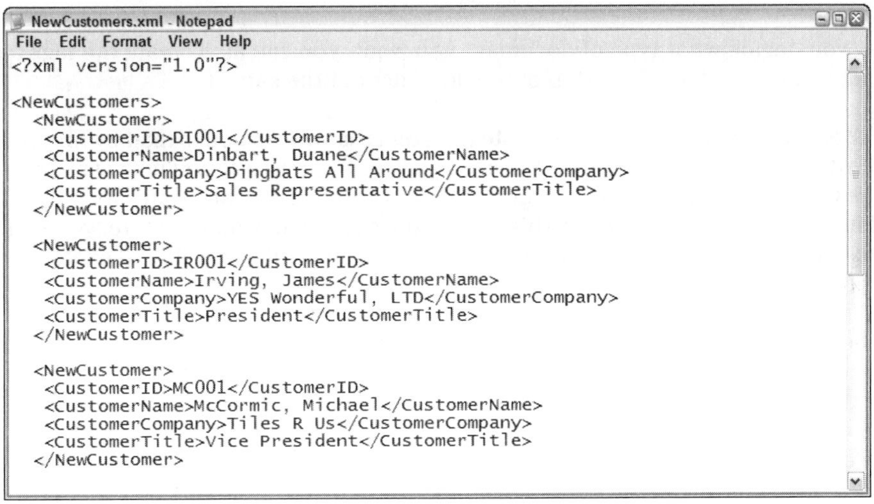

```
NewCustomers.xml - Notepad
File  Edit  Format  View  Help
<?xml version="1.0"?>

<NewCustomers>
  <NewCustomer>
    <CustomerID>DI001</CustomerID>
    <CustomerName>Dinbart, Duane</CustomerName>
    <CustomerCompany>Dingbats All Around</CustomerCompany>
    <CustomerTitle>Sales Representative</CustomerTitle>
  </NewCustomer>

  <NewCustomer>
    <CustomerID>IR001</CustomerID>
    <CustomerName>Irving, James</CustomerName>
    <CustomerCompany>YES Wonderful, LTD</CustomerCompany>
    <CustomerTitle>President</CustomerTitle>
  </NewCustomer>

  <NewCustomer>
    <CustomerID>MC001</CustomerID>
    <CustomerName>McCormic, Michael</CustomerName>
    <CustomerCompany>Tiles R Us</CustomerCompany>
    <CustomerTitle>Vice President</CustomerTitle>
  </NewCustomer>
```

Figure 32-2: The top-most part of the NewCustomers.xml file.

The NewCustomers.xml document in Figure 32-2 shows a typical single table XML document. It is simply a listing of tags and data.

To create a simple XML document, you need to follow these general steps:

1. Decide on what type of data you want to put in your XML document — a customer table, library system, inventory system, cookbook recipes, and on and on.

2. Decide on the name of the table or tables you want to create.

3. Decide on the fields you want to include in each record.

4. Specify a name for the general category (step 1), table (step 2), and fields (step 3), and use it for tags for each level.

5. Specify the field contents for each record in the XML document.

6. Create your XML document starting with a declaration line specifying that the document is the type XML. This uses the special tag <?xml version="x.x"?>. Currently, the version number is 1.0.

7. Enter the start tags, end tags, and all the contents for your XML document.

8. Save and name your XML document.

Deciding on the tags for an XML document

As the steps show above, you need to decide on what type of XML document you want to create and then decide on the table name and field names that you want in the XML document.

As you decide what type of document you want, you can also create the tags names that will be used for each step of the document at the same time.

For example, you may want to create a system that tracks books read by first through third graders in a table named SchoolBooks. In this system, you may want to track the book title, author name, student name, student grade, and date when the student read the book. Although this is the only table you want to create, you realize that the system will probably grow in time, so you want to be able to expand on it as necessary.

The first tag you will need to create goes at the beginning and end of the XML document and will be used to enclose all the other tags in it. Called the *root element*, this is the entity that you are describing in your document. You can think of it as an XML grouping tag. There can only be one root element in each XML document. Perhaps you want to make this system a reading program system. Therefore, you can use the names <ReadingProgram> and </ReadingProgram> as the first-level tag names — the root elements for the XML document.

Next, you create your *child nodes* inside the root element. These child nodes are the elements that make up your data. Think of these child nodes (first level of child nodes inside the root elements) as the tags you will use to name your tables. You can have more than one child node name or, using the database analogy, table in each grouping inside the root element of an XML document.

These child nodes will actually describe the contents of your data. Child nodes can be created inside child nodes. Thus, it is possible to have multiple levels of child nodes in a single XML document.

Assuming you want to create this table and have all these records to be in the same table, you now need to create a set of child node tags that will be used for the start and end for each record with a specific table. For instance, you may want to have a child node called <SchoolBooks>. This child node is the first level of child nodes under the root element <ReadingProgram>. Just think of this as the name of the individual table that you are creating. For this exercise, use the tags <SchoolBooks> and </SchoolBooks>. These tags will be used inside the root element, system-level (analogy) tags (<ReadingProgram>, </ReadingProgram>).

With the root element tags and the first-level child node tags (table analogy) identified, you are ready to decide on the tags to use for each field of each record inside each child node tag. Here you will create another level of child nodes; these child nodes will specify the database fields in the table. These child tags are actually nested within other child tags. These tags are used before and after every field of each record: <BookTitle>, <Author>, <Student>, <Grade>, and <DateRead> will be the start tags and </BookTitle>, </Author>, </Student>, </Grade>, and </DateRead> will be the end tags.

Tip   The difference between the start and end tag is simply using the slash in front of the end tag name. The end tag name is the same name you used for your start tag.

Deciding on the data for an XML document

With the tags specified, you are ready to move to the next step. Now you need to define the contents for each field of each record in the table. Using this information, you can create a simple XML document, using Notepad, which will hold the records. For instance, you will want to enter the following four records:

One:

```
Captain Pajamas, Defender of the Universe
Bruce Whatley
David Johnson
2
2003-07-14
```

Two:

```
The Cat in the Hat
Dr. Suess
David Johnson
2
2003-07-20
```

Three:

```
I ' m Not Going to Get Up Today
Dr. Suess
Kyle Stevens
3
2003-07-14
```

Four:

```
Julie B. Jones Has a Peep in Her Pocket
Barbara Park
Carmen Wilson
1
2003-08-16
```

Putting the tags and data together

With the four record contents defined and the structure defined, you are ready to create the actual XML document. Figure 32-3 shows the skeletal structure of your XML document.

```
Untitled - Notepad
File  Edit  Format  View  Help
<?xml version="1.0"?>

<ReadingProgram>

   <SchoolBooks>

      <BookTitle>    </BookTitle>
      <Author>       </Author>
      <Student>      </Student>
      <Grade>        </Grade>
      <DateRead>     </DateRead>

   </SchoolBooks>

   <SchoolBooks>

      <BookTitle>    </BookTitle>
      <Author>       </Author>
      <Student>      </Student>
      <Grade>        </Grade>
      <DateRead>     </DateRead>

   </SchoolBooks>

</ReadingProgram>
```

Figure 32-3: The skeletal structure of the XML document.

Notice in Figure 32-3 that all the tags (root element and child nodes) have already been placed in the text file and in their correct positions. None of the data has been entered yet. It is often a good idea to create skeletal structure first for your XML file and then fill in the data after you complete the structure. Notice that the child node tags <BookTitle>, </BookTitle> and <Author>, </Author> are nested within the child node tags <SchoolBooks> and </SchoolBooks>. Finally, these child nodes are nested within the root elements <ReadingProgram> and </ReadingProgram>.

Figure 32-3 shows the first line of the XML document with a special declaration tag that you must enter for any document to know how to work with your XML file. It is simply the text <?xml version="1.0"?>. This tells any program that will use this XML document that it is using xml version 1.0. As an XML document grows more sophisticated, you can include more information in this declaration. You can specify what tags are legal in your document and where the style sheet is on the computer.

Now that the skeleton is created, you can add the actual data to each field of each record by creating a record skeleton for each record and placing the data between the field tags you have created. Figure 32-4 shows two record skeletons, which are child nodes (beginning with the <SchoolBooks> tag and ending with the </SchoolBooks> tag).

Figure 32-4 shows the same XML document with the data added.

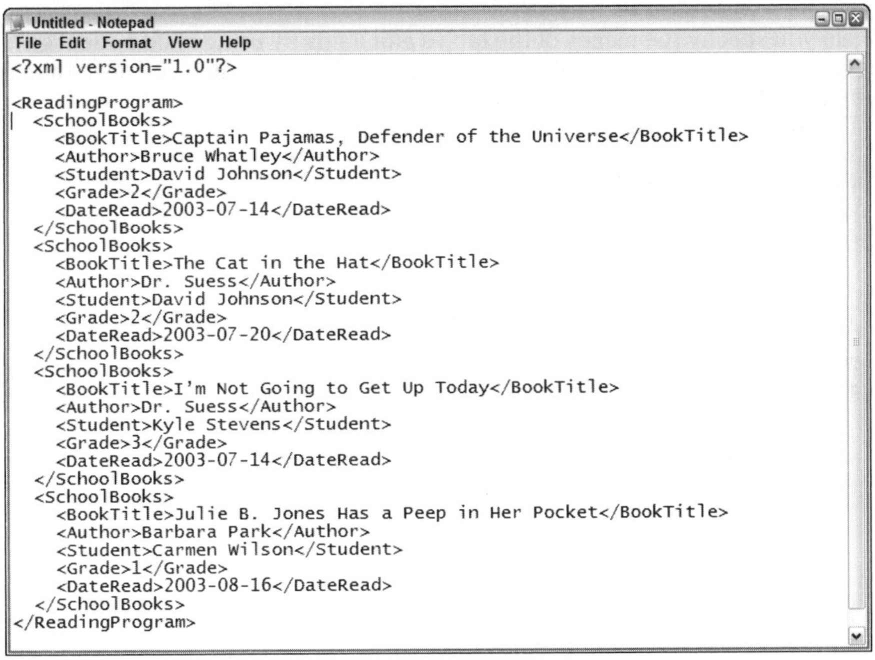

```
Untitled - Notepad
File  Edit  Format  View  Help
<?xml version="1.0"?>

<ReadingProgram>
  <SchoolBooks>
    <BookTitle>Captain Pajamas, Defender of the Universe</BookTitle>
    <Author>Bruce Whatley</Author>
    <Student>David Johnson</Student>
    <Grade>2</Grade>
    <DateRead>2003-07-14</DateRead>
  </SchoolBooks>
  <SchoolBooks>
    <BookTitle>The Cat in the Hat</BookTitle>
    <Author>Dr. Suess</Author>
    <Student>David Johnson</Student>
    <Grade>2</Grade>
    <DateRead>2003-07-20</DateRead>
  </SchoolBooks>
  <SchoolBooks>
    <BookTitle>I'm Not Going to Get Up Today</BookTitle>
    <Author>Dr. Suess</Author>
    <Student>Kyle Stevens</Student>
    <Grade>3</Grade>
    <DateRead>2003-07-14</DateRead>
  </SchoolBooks>
  <SchoolBooks>
    <BookTitle>Julie B. Jones Has a Peep in Her Pocket</BookTitle>
    <Author>Barbara Park</Author>
    <Student>Carmen Wilson</Student>
    <Grade>1</Grade>
    <DateRead>2003-08-16</DateRead>
  </SchoolBooks>
</ReadingProgram>
```

Figure 32-4: The completed XML document.

As Figure 32-4 shows, the actual XML document is only concerned with the data — its structure and data contents.

With the XML document now created, your last step is to save it, calling it Reading Program.xml.

 Cross-Reference You will use the Reading Program.xml file later when you import an XML table into Acess, in the section tltled "Importing XML Data."

Creating a multi-table XML document

Now that you have created a simple, single table XML document, you are ready to create a more complex XML document — one that contains two or more tables.

A multi-table XML document can import more than one table into Access at the same time.

When creating a multi-table document, you can create one that has independent tables or one that is composed of linked tables. Both series of tables are created the same way.

Again you specify the names of the tables and fields by using child node tags. To have Access utilize a multi-table XML document for importing, you need to make sure that all the tables being imported are within the system grouping start and end tags.

For example, Figure 32-5 shows a multi-table XML document, named NewCustomersANDSales.xml, displayed in the Microsoft Internet Explorer. This file is already created for you so that you can examine it more closely.

This is a much more complex, but simple to understand, XML document. It is made up of more than one table, each embedded within the other. Opening NewCustomersANDSales.xml in Internet Explorer, you can go through it and see that it has three tables specified:

> <NewCustomer> with customer information.
>
> <NewCarsBought> with a link field to customer, an invoice number, and sales date.
>
> <NewCarsBoughtLineItem> with a link field to the invoice table (NewCarsBought) and vehicle information.

Each tag has a dash next to it, making it easy to see where each table starts and ends. Only the beginning tag has a dash; the ending tag does not have one. This XML document has all three tables within the <NewCustomers> system grouping <NewCustomers>. You could have also created each table separately, as long as they were all within the <NewCustomers> grouping.

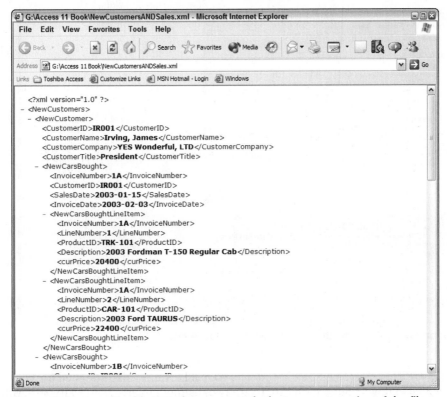

Figure 32-5: A multi-table XML document. Only the top-most portion of the file can be seen.

You must make sure that all the tables you want to have in your XML document are within the root element, the first set of tags you specify (<NewCustomers> and </NewCustomers> in this case). If you try to put them outside of the root element tags, Access will not process the file correctly.

Caution If you try to create two root element tags—two or more system-level tags using the database analogy—in a single XML document, Access will have problems trying to parse them and may crash. At a minimum, it will simply ignore the file. You must maintain only one root element in each XML document.

You do not need to embed another table and its child nodes (<NewCarsBought> is inside <NewCustomer>), within another as in the XML document shown in Figure 32-5. When working with related tables, it is usually easier to embed the linked tables under each table so that you are sure that you have placed the correct linking information for joining the table later.

If you have two independent tables in the same XML document you can place each table separate within the primary tags, as shown in Figure 32-6.

```
New Customers AND Student TWO FILES.xml - Notepad
File  Edit  Format  View  Help
<?xml version="1.0"?>

<NewCustomers>
  <NewCustomer>
    <CustomerID>IR001</CustomerID>
    <CustomerName>Irving, James</CustomerName>
    <CustomerCompany>YES Wonderful, LTD</CustomerCompany>
    <CustomerTitle>President</CustomerTitle>
  </NewCustomer>
  <NewCustomer>
    <CustomerID>MC001</CustomerID>
    <CustomerName>McCormic, Michael</CustomerName>
    <CustomerCompany>Tiles R Us</CustomerCompany>
    <CustomerTitle>Vice President</CustomerTitle>
  </NewCustomer>

  <NewStudents>
    <StudentID>WC011</StudentID>
    <StudentName>Williams, Clara</StudentName>
  </NewStudents>
  <NewStudents>
    <StudentID>WC021</StudentID>
    <StudentName>Wilson, Clark</StudentName>
  </NewStudents>
  <NewStudents>
    <StudentID>AW011</StudentID>
    <StudentName>Abels, William</StudentName>
  </NewStudents>

</NewCustomers>
```

Figure 32-6: A non-related multi-table XML document.

This file, New Customers AND Student TWO FILES.xml, is also supplied for you. Examining it, you can see that there are two distinct tables: <NewCustomer>, with two records (field contents) specified, and <NewStudents>, with three records (field contents) specified.

Displaying XML Documents in Internet Explorer

After you create an XML document, there are times you will probably want to display it in Internet Explorer (version 4.x or later).

You can create a relatively simple Dynamic HTML (DHTML) document to create an HTML table and display specific child nodes from the XML file you created. This Dynamic HTML file can use a Java applet that is found in IE 4.x or later to data bind the XML data saved in the XML file to the HTML table.

You can create a simple Web page with the code shown here:

```
<html>
<head>
  <title> XML Data binding </title>
</head>
<body>
 <! --Java Applet-->
  <APPLET code="com.ms.xml.dso.XMLDSO.class"
    MAYSCRIPT id=xmldatasource Width="75%" Height="20">
    <PARAM NAME="URL" VALUE=" Reading Program.xml ">
  </APPLET>
<p> Databinding of XML from file Reading Program </p>
<table id="table" border="1" width="100%"
      datasrc="#xmldatasource">
  <thead>
   <tr>
     <th> Student </th>
     <th> Grade </th>
     <th> Title of Book </th>
     <th> Author </th>
   </tr>
  </thead>
  <tr>
   <td><div datafld="Student"></td>
   <td><div datafld="Grade"></td>
   <td><div datafld="BookTitle"></td>
   <td><div datafld="Author"></td>
  </tr>
</table>
</body>
</html>
```

You can type the code shown here or modify it using the file named BindingReadingPrograms.html, included with this chapter.

This HTML code parses the XML document by using a Java applet that is a standard part of IE 4.x or later. You can also download this applet from Microsoft's Web site. Add the applet code as shown in Listing 32-2 to your HTML. You only need to change the PARAM NAME "URL" VALUE property to the location or URL of the XML document.

This DHTML code works by data binding with the datasrc="#xmldatasource" tag in the Table declaration where #xmldatasource is the same name of the Java applet ID object in your code. After you have linked the table to the datascr, you need to specify the field names of each field you want to see in the table to an XML child node name. To link the field name to the child node name, assign the correct child node name to each datafld property of the <div> tag.

After creating them, you can add additional records to the XML document and the Web page will automatically reflect the changes. Figure 32-7 shows the resulting Web page when you run the BindingReadingPrograms.html program in Internet Explorer (4.x or later).

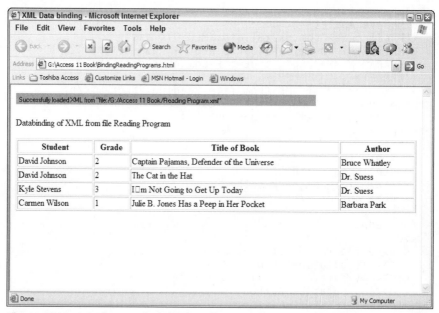

Figure 32-7: A Web page that displays the contents of specific fields from an XML document.

Exporting to XML

Exporting database data to an XML file is a great way to move and store your information in a format that can be used across the Web. You can export any of the following:

✦ Just the data from a table, query, datasheet, form, or report in an XML file.

✦ Just the schema (data structure=) of a table, query, datasheet, form, or report to an XML schema file (with the extension of xsd), including the primary key and index information.

✦ Both the data and schema into both XML and XSD files.

✦ Embed the schema in the XML document or create a separate schema file.

New Feature   Export the data in linked tables at the same time as the main table.

New Feature Select a transforms file to use after exporting.

✦ Save the structure of a table, query, datasheet, form, or report into a file that describes the presentation (*.xsl) of the structure and data.

✦ Access will create a custom display format (*.xsl) file and can create a Web document to run in either the browser (an *.html document) or server (an *.asp formatted file).

After an XML file is created, it can be bound to an HTTP query request, an SQL Server database, or SQL Server Desktop Edition to work with live Access reports in a browser.

Exporting a table or query to XML

To export a table or query to an XML document, follow these general steps:

1. Select the table or query object name in the database container.

2. Select File ➪ Export from the menu (or right-click and select Export... from the menu).

   Access opens the Export Table dialog box.

3. Select XML (*.xml) in the Save As Type drop-down list box. Then select the directory you want to save the files to.

4. Enter a new filename to save the XML document to.

5. Click the Export button.

   Access opens the Export XML dialog box, shown in Figure 32-8. It has already selected to export the data and schema.

Figure 32-8: The Export XML dialog box.

6. If you want to export only the data or only the schema, deselect the item that you don't want to export.

7. If you want to also have Access create an XSL file and an HTML document so that you can view the data in the Web browser, select the Presentation of your data (XSL) check box.

8. Click the More Options ... button to open the expanded Export XML dialog box (shown in Figure 32-9) and specify more options.

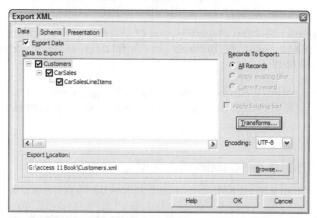

Figure 32-9: The Export XML dialog box that is opened when you press the More Options .... button on the standard Export XML dialog box.

New Feature

In the Data tab section, you can specify linked table records to be exported in the XML document. You can also specify a Transforms file to use to transform the data after exporting data by clicking on the Transforms ... button. Finally, you can specify a different filename and location for the .xml file in this section.

You can click on the Schema tab and specify to include primary key and index information as well as to embed the schema in the .xml file or save as another file.

Finally, if you click on the Presentation tab, you can specify the type of Export presentation you want to create and the name and location of the presentation file.

9. After you have completed these steps, Click OK.

Access automatically creates all specified files — XML, XSD, XSL (if requested), and HTML.

Figure 32-10 shows the contents of the xml file created by exporting the Customers table.

You could also export the table named Products, which has an OLE Object of pictures of vehicles in it. The field OLEPicture is encoded and exported.

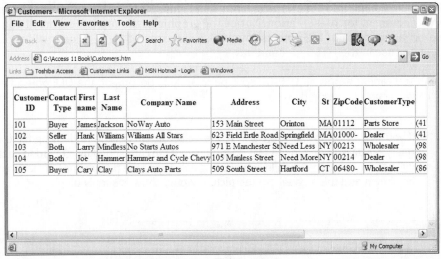

Figure 32-10: The Customers.xml file viewed in IE 6.x.

Caution   If your table or query has an OLE Object in it, the field contents will be exported to the XML document; however, the corresponding html document will not show it. In lieu of being able to see the picture, the field name will be there and the cell containing the OLE Object will display an ellipsis enclosed in brackets: [...].

Cross-Reference   If you import an XML document with the contents of an OLE Object, the OLE Object will be imported correctly. Refer to the section "Importing XML Data."

Exporting linked tables

If you export the Customers table in the CHAP32Start database and select the linked tables (CarSales and CarSalesLineItems) in the expanded Export XML dialog box, under the Data tab, Access will store the records from these tables in the XML document with the Customers records. However, the HTML document that is created when you select Export Presentation (HTML 4.0 Sample XSL) and select Client (HTML) will not show the linked table records. Access will create a simple HTML file that will display only the Customers records.

If you want to create an HTML document that displays all the records from all three tables, you will need to create it yourself.

Exporting a form to XML

When you export a form to an XML document, the resulting XML document will create a continuous form type HTML file that displays each record in a continuous form. This is true even when the Default View property is set to Datasheet or Single Form.

The form Mailing Info On Contacts, shown in Figure 32-11, can be exported to an XML document for presentation. Notice the graphic in the top left corner. If you export a form with image objects (pictures from external files), Access will export them for use in the HTML document.

Note   You cannot export an OLE Object type to an XML document; the OLE object field will simply be ignored.

Caution   If your form has an OLE Object in it, the field contents of the underlying table or query will be exported to the XML document, but the corresponding HTML document will not show it in the form. In lieu of being able to see the picture, the field label will be shown and the area where the picture would show is simply blank.

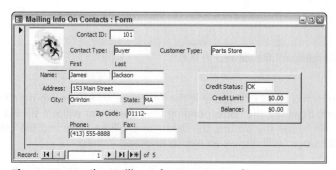

Figure 32-11: The Mailing Info On Contacts form.

For example, to export the form named Mailing Info On Contacts, follow these steps:

1. Select the form named Mailing Info On Contacts from the database container.

2. Select File ➪ Export ... from the menu (or right-click and select Export... from the menu).

   Access opens the Export Form dialog box.

3. Select XML in the Save As Type drop-down list box. Then select the directory you want to save the files to.

4. Enter a new filename to save the XML document to, or accept the default name of Mailing Info On Contacts.

5. Click the Export button.

   Access opens the Export XML dialog box. It only has Data (XML) choice checked.

6. If you only want to export the data or want to also export the schema, make the correct adjustments.

7. Click the Presentation of your data (XSL) button.

8. Click the More Options .... button and when the expanded Export XML dialog box opens, click on the Presentation tab.

9. Click Export Presentation (HTML 4.0 Sample XSL) to select export to presentation files.

Notice the section in the middle titled Include Report Images and the button Put Images In have been selected. The default directory that will be created is named Images. Keep this name. However, you can change the name and Access will create the new directory with the name you specify. This directory is used to store any embedded image files in the form. In this case, it will store the picture of people in the top left corner. This screen is shown in Figure 32-12.

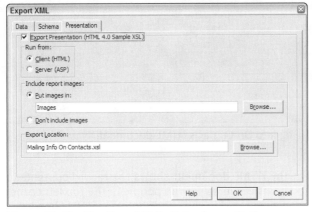

Figure 32-12: The Export XML dialog box with the Presentation tab selected. Notice the center with the Include report images information.

10. Click OK.

Access creates the XML document, an XSL file, and a corresponding HTML document that can be opened in IE 4.x or later to look at the data and new page. It also creates a subdirectory named Images below the current directory where the XML, XDS, XSL, and HTML files are located. Figure 32-13 shows the Mailing Info On Contacts HTML created from the XML, XDS, and XSL documents being viewed in IE 6.x.

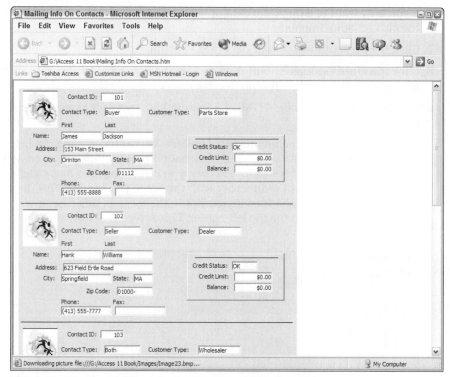

Figure 32-13: The Mailing Info On Contacts HTML document.

As Figure 32-13 shows, the HTML document shows the record contents in continuous form style. It also shows the image of the people in the top left corner of each record. This image has been stored in the subdirectory named \Images.

Note   When you move your XML files (XML, XSD, XSL, and HTML), you will also have to move the subdirectory named \Images and its contents.

Exporting a report to XML

To export a report to an XML document, you follow the same general steps you did for creating an XML document from a form.

If you export the Listing of Customer who purchased vehicles report, you are given the same options as when you exported a form when you click on the More Options choice in the Export XML dialog box. You can specify a directory name to hold any images that may be in the report. The resulting output of the HTML file will again display all the records in one continuous form.

Figure 32-14 shows the Listing of Customer who purchased vehicles report exported to an XML document and an associated HTML presentation file.

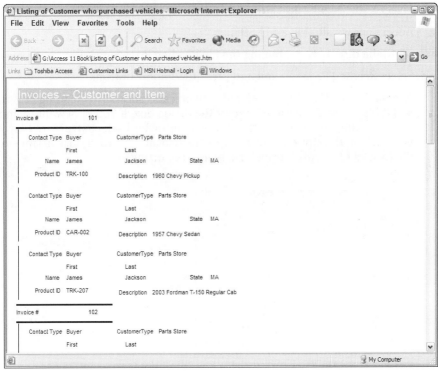

Figure 32-14: The Listing of Customer who purchased vehicles HTML document.

Importing XML Data

You can also import existing XML documents into Access. They will be imported into an Access table. The actual data that is being imported is stored in the XML file, and the schema information (structure, keys, and indices) is stored in the XSD file.

Importing simple, single table XML data

To import the XML file named Reading Program.xml (that you created in the section titled "Creating your own XML documents"), follow these steps:

1. With the database open, select File ➪ Get External Data ➪ Import from the menu or right-click in the Tables container of the database and select Import.

   Access opens the Import dialog box.

2. Select XML (*.xml; *.xsd) from the Files of type drop-down list box.

   Access shows all XML and XSD files.

3. Go to the directory containing the file Reading Program.xml.

4. Select Reading Program.xml and press the Import button.

   Access displays the Import XML dialog box and shows the Reading Program. xml table name. Figure 32-15 shows the dialog box. If you only want to import the structure, you can click the Options button and select structure only. If you click on the Options button, you are also allowed to choose a Transform file to select to apply a transform before importing.

Figure 32-15: The Import XML dialog box.

5. Click OK.

   Access imports the table Reading Program.xml and displays an information box that tells you that it imported the file.

6. Click OK.

The new table, Reading Program.xml, has been added to the database.

When Importing XML files, you can import the XML file or the XSD file. If you want to import the key or indices information (primary keys and secondary), you select the XSD file instead of the XML file.

Tip

If there is only an XSD file (no associated XML document), you can import the structure and key information, but there will be no data in the new database structure. The data is stored in the XML file.

Importing a single table with OLE Object from an XML document

You can also import an XML document that has OLE Objects embedded in it. For instance, you can import the Products.xml table and its associated Products.xsd file by following the same steps outlined above.

When it is imported, which will take some time because the file has encrypted information for the OLE field olePicture, you can link it to the form Products in the database and display the contents of the new imported Products table from the XML document.

Figure 32-16 shows the form named Products with the imported Products table linked to it and displaying the olePicture field (picture of the vehicle). This shows that you can store and import OLE type objects in an XML document.

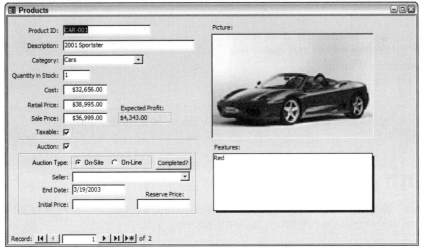

Figure 32-16: The imported Products table shown in the Products form with the olePicture field intact.

Note To link the Products table to the Products form, go into design mode of the Products form, open the Properties dialog box, and change the Record Source property under the Data tab to the Products table you just imported.

Importing multi-table XML data

In addition to importing data from a single file stored in an XML document, you can also import multiple tables from a single XML document.

You have two XML documents with the database: NewCustomersANDSales.xml and New Customers AND Student TWO FILES.xml. Both of these XML documents have more than one table in them.

If you import the two tables (NewCustomer and NewStudents) from the New Customers AND Student TWO FILES.xml file, you will see that the Import XML dialog box will show you two tables, as shown in Figure 32-17.

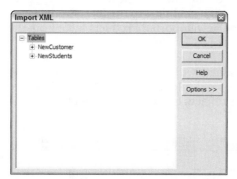

Figure 32-17: The Import XML dialog box with two tables shown.

When you click on the OK button, it will import two tables — NewCustomer and NewStudents — into your database from the single XML document.

InfoPath and Access

Although this book is about Access, this section offers a quick overview of InfoPath and how it can enhance or integrate with Access.

Most businesses do not live in a void, with branches running independently from each other. For instance, a software development company has several departments or branches that interact with each other daily or weekly. The Sales branch needs to know the amount of inventory available in the purchasing department at any given time. Management needs to know what the Research and Development office is working on. This interaction is typical in any company. The amount of information, or data, that is moving between branches of a business during the normal business process of any company is often done in a non-productive way.

Microsoft Office 2003 has added a new XML-specific product known as InfoPath 2003, which can assist many businesses in addressing their information needs efficiently and effectively. InfoPath 2003 is based entirely on XML technology, offering the end user a way to use dynamic forms that can be immediately placed in an XML document or linked to a database. Using XML as the underlying file format makes the document universally available within a business. Using InfoPath requires no special XML coding.

Figure 32-18 shows a simple form that is used to gather membership information.

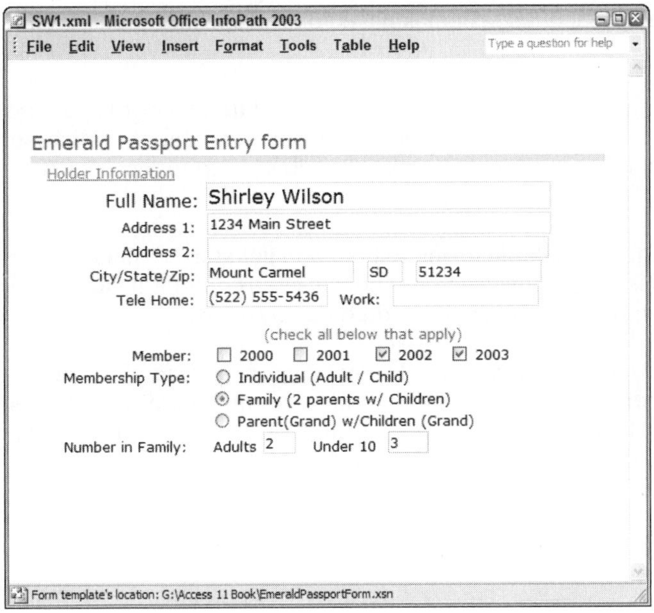

Figure 32-18: An InfoPath form that gathers membership information.

Figure 32-18 shows a typical form that you can create quickly in InfoPath. The form saves its data in native XML format.

Because InfoPath creates native XML files, the resulting XML file can be imported or attached to an existing Access table. InfoPath can also be used to create independent forms for data entry based on an existing Access table.

Quick overview of InfoPath

InfoPath lets you quickly create a form using a familiar Office design interface and forms-based controls and text-editing (data validation and conditional formatting) methods. After you create a form, it is then published as a template in a shared location for your users to enter data into. After a user enters data, he can save the data into a standard XML-formatted file. By using XML-formatted data, companies can make better use of the stored information across the organization.

Because InfoPath's file format is XML, information collected in InfoPath forms can easily be shared by other applications. It is a great tool that can be used by organizations and companies to gather data that is essential to their business. Using InfoPath, companies can quickly develop dynamic forms that can be used to gather that data, without needing a knowledge of XML or the capability to write XML code. InfoPath can also used predefined schemas based on the specific needs of the corporation.

When creating InfoPath forms, you can create them for data entry or for querying existing data. You can submit data to a database or query a database (Microsoft SQL Server or Microsoft Access) or even link to a web service to receive or submit data.

InfoPath includes numerous sample forms to help you get started quickly. These forms can be used as is or modified to your specific needs. InfoPath can also be used on a Tablet PC so that your users can add data anywhere.

InfoPath can be used to replace any manual form process. Instead of having users enter data from a paper form, they can enter it directly into InfoPath to be used across the company. The underlying schema of the XML form can control data entry and ensure that the data is stored immediately in the linked database or web service.

InfoPath can create an XML form that saves all data in XML format or a form that is bound to an underlying SQL Server or Access table. A form that is bound to a database table can have the records submitted (appended) to the underlying database table. Figure 32-19 shows an InfoPath form that is bound to a table named Customer for InfoPath in the CHAP32Start database.

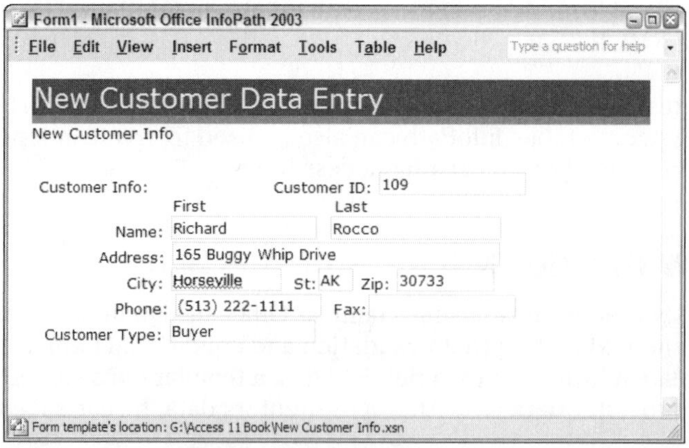

Figure 32-19: An InfoPath form that is bound to an Access table.

Creating an XML-Based InfoPath form

The simplest type of form to create in InfoPath is a standard XML-based form. The form in Figure 32-18, shown earlier in this section, is a simple XML form that was created in InfoPath.

After you start InfoPath, you can select File ➪ Design a Form... from the menu. This opens the Design a Form task pane along the right side of the screen. Figure 32-20 shows the Design a Form task pane.

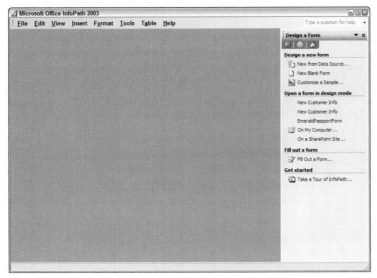

Figure 32-20: InfoPath open with the Design a Form task pane active.

Follow these steps to quickly create a simple XML form table with a title:

1. Select the New Blank Form choice from the menu.

   InfoPath creates a blank page with the Design Task's pane open.

2. Select Layout from the Design Task pane.

   InfoPath opens the Insert layout tables area.

3. Click on the choice Table with Title.

   InfoPath places the table object on the empty form, as shown in Figure 32-21.

4. Click in Click to add a Title.

5. Type in Mailing List Names.

6. Click on Data Source in the Task pane.

   InfoPath opens the Work with the data source: area, as shown in Figure 32-22.

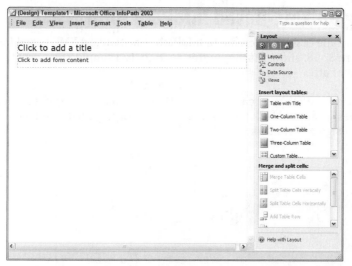

Figure 32-21: A table object with Title placed on the empty form.

Figure 32-22: The Work with the data source: area.

Now you are ready to add your data entry fields to the form. However, before adding fields, you need to add their labels first. Unlike Access, you can type directly on the form, using the spacebar and Enter key to move the visible text around.

7. Click in the area labeled Click to add form content.

   InfoPath removes the words Click to add form content.

8. In the top-left corner, press the Enter key three or four times to move the cursor down a few lines. Then press the spacebar four times to move the cursor four spaces.

9. Type **Address:** and press the Enter key to move to the next line.

10. On this line, type in **City:** **State:** **Zip:** with sufficient spaces between them. Then move the cursor in front of the word City: and press the spacebar until the colons line up for City: and Address:.

   Your form should now look similar to the one shown in Figure 32-23.

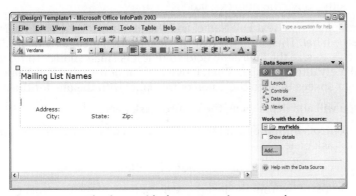

Figure 32-23: The form with the text portion entered.

You are now ready to create and enter the linked XML fields. You can add fields directly in the Data Source task pane or you can use the Controls task pane. First, you create and enter a Text field for name in the Data Source task pane.

11. Click the Add button in the Data Source task pane or right-click on the table name myFields and select Add from the popup menu.

   InfoPath opens the Add Field or Group dialog box, as shown in Figure 32-24. Initially, there are no values in the Name field.

12. Type in the value **FullName** with no spaces in the Name: box and check the Cannot be blank (*) check box, as shown in Figure 32-24.

13. Click the OK button

   InfoPath places the text field FullName under the table name myFields, with an asterisk next to it to show that it cannot be blank.

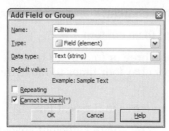

Figure 32-24: The Add Field or Group dialog box.

14. Drag the field FullName to the work surface of your form, dropping it on the line directly above the Address: label.

    InfoPath places the text Full Name: and the text box for the field FullName above the label. The FullName text box is placed immediately below the label Full Name. Resize the FullName field so that it is small enough to relocate immediately after the label. Then move in front of the label Full Name, and put sufficient spaces to align the colon of this label with the one for the Address.

    Now you will add fields using the Control task pane.

15. Select Controls from the menu in the Data Source task pane to open the Controls task pane.

16. Move the cursor in the form alongside of the Address: label.

17. Select the Text Box from the Insert controls: pane of the Controls task pane by clicking on it or dragging it to the insert position.

    If you simply click on the Text Box control in the Insert controls: pane, InfoPath places the Text Box control under the label Address:. This is also true if you drag it alongside the label. Again, you need to resize the Text Box control to align next to the label Address.

18. Select the Text Box label again for the remaining three fields (City, State, and Zip).

    At this point, your form should have all the fields and labels in positions similar to the form shown in Figure 32-25 (minus the check box field at the bottom).

    Finally, you can add a check box to the form for a field to determine whether the address is a work address. (If the check box is checked, the addresss is a work address; if it's not checked, the address is not a work address.)

19. The line under the last field label (State:) moves the cursor so that it is one line below and in front of the word State. Click on the check box control.

    The check box is added with a default label named Field xx.

20. Change the label Field xx to Is This a Work Address?. Your form should now look like the one shown in Figure 32-25.

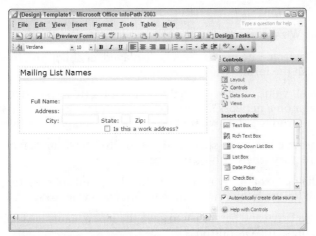

Figure 32-25: The new form with all text fields placed, including a check box field.

Now that your form is created, you need to publish it. Publishing a form is the act of saving it and making it available to all the users.

Note   The name of the default table, myFields, can be changed by displaying the Data Source Task pane, right-clicking on the table name, selecting properties, and then renaming the table name. When you created the fields that you entered on the form using the Insert Controls method above, the field names were simply named in chronological order—field1, field2, field3, and so on. You can also change these names to a more usable name by changing their name properties. You may want to rename the fields Address, City, State, Zip and WorkAddr for clarity.

To publish your form, follow these steps:

1. Select File ➪ Save to activate a Microsoft Office InfoPath dialog box with two choices—Publish... and Save....

Figure 32-26 shows this dialog box.

Figure 32-26: The dialog box activated the first time you save the form.

2. Click the Publish... button.

The Publishing Wizard is activated.

3. Click the Next button. The next screen is displayed, enabling you to select where to publish the form.

4. Select the default value of where to publish this form (to a shared folder on this computer or on a network). Click the Next button. The next screen is displayed, enabling you to select where to save the file and give the form a name.

5. Click on the Browse button to specify where to save the form. Make sure you save it to a directory where others can access it.

The Browse dialog box is activated. Select the drive and subdirectory, and specify a name for the InfoPath template file that you want to save.

6. After selecting a Drive and Directory to save the file to, name it Mailing List Template and press the OK button.

You are returned to the Publishing Wizard and the filename is entered in both fields — the actual filename and the name of the form.

7. You can keep the default values of the names and press the Next button.

8. Click on the Finish button of the next screen that simply re-checks to confirm that you have saved the file to a common directory for all users to access.

9. When you are on the last page, you are informed that the template has been saved and is ready for use. You can notify users that the template is available if you click on the Notify Users button. Your default e-mail program is activated with a notification message ready to send to users. All you have to do is add the e-mail addresses of the users that you want to advise.

10. Click on the Close button to return to InfoPath and save your work.

With the template file created, you can now close the InfoPath program.

Creating an InfoPath form attached to a database

The second type of form you can create is one that is attached to a database. For example, you can create an InfoPath template form to attach to the Customer for InfoPath table in the CHAP32Start database. After you create the form, you can save each record added to the form in InfoPath as an XML document or submit the record to be attached to the Access table.

Creating this form is similar to creating the non-attached form in the previous example. However, when you start, you specify that you want to create a New [form] from Data Source ... in the Design a Form task pane.

Using the Data Source Setup Wizard

Follow these steps to use the Data Source Setup Wizard to create a form based on the CHAP32Start.mdb table Customer for InfoPath:

1. Select File ➪ Design a Form ... from the menu.

2. Select New from Data Source ... from the Design a Form task pane.

   InfoPath opens the Data Source Setup Wizard, as shown in Figure 32-27.

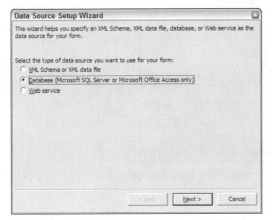

Figure 32-27: The Data Source Setup Wizard.

3. Select Database (Microsoft SQL Server or Microsoft Access only) on the first screen of the setup wizard. Click the Next button.

4. Click on the Select Database button on the second screen. When the Wizard opens the Select Data Source dialog box, find CHAP32Start.mdb.

5. With CHAP32Start.mdb highlighted, click the Open button.

6. In the Select Table dialog box (as shown in Figure 32-28), select the Customer for InfoPath table and press the OK button.

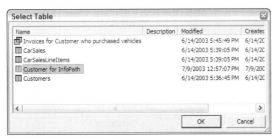

Figure 32-28: The Select Table dialog box.

InfoPath returns to page two of the Data Source Setup Wizard and displays the Data source structure in the bottom area of the screen.

7. Press the Next button to continue.

8. You are taken to the final screen, as shown in Figure 32-29.

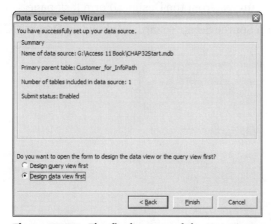

Figure 32-29: The final screen of the Data Source Setup Wizard.

This final screen shows pertinent information about linking the InfoPath form to the database table. Notice that the Submit status of this form is Enabled and that the Design data view first option has been selected.

9. Select Design data view first and press the Finish button.

Caution The Submit status is only Enable, meaning that you are able to save the record directly to the database table when the table has a primary index field. Otherwise, the form can only write XML documents, and you will have to import them into the database table within Access.

InfoPath returns you to the design window with a blank form visible. Using the Setup Wizard, InfoPath creates two views in your form: one for queries (which add the fields from the table to the view), and one for the data view (for entering data). The data view is just a blank form.

When you click on the Views choice in the Data Source task pane, the Select a View: area of the pane is displayed and you can see two choices: Data Entry (default) and Query. These are the two views of the form that InfoPath has created for you. Figure 32-30 shows the Views task pane open on the right side of the program and the two view names displayed in the Select a View area.

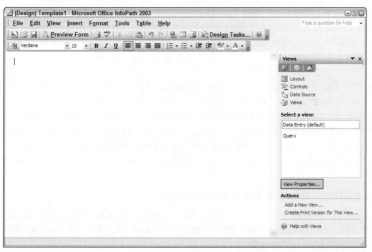

Figure 32-30: An InfoPath form with two views linked to a database.

At this point, you can create your Data Entry form (view) or you can click on the Query view to see the Query form that InfoPath created for you already. Figure 32-31 shows the Query view form created by the wizard.

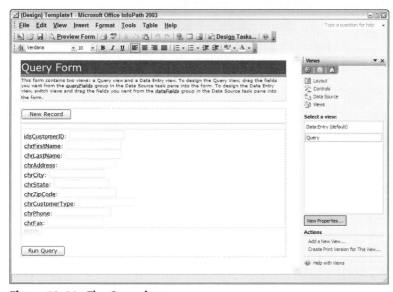

Figure 32-31: The Query form.

Notice that the Query form view has two buttons on it: Run Query and New Record. The appropriate code is already attached to each button. If you click on the Preview Form button or select File ⇨ Preview Form from the menu, you can see how this form will work.

When you click on the Preview Form, InfoPath activates a preview window and lets you enter a value in any field of the Query form. After you enter a value, click on the Run Query button to query against the table and find any record that matches your request. Activate the Data Entry view to display the results. In this case, it will display a blank Data Entry view because you have not placed any control objects on the form yet. Clicking on the Close Preview button returns you to the design window.

Placing field objects on the Data Entry view

Now you can start to add the fields and data validation rules to your Data Entry view. First, you need to redisplay the Data Entry (default) view by selecting it in the Select a view: portion of the pane.

When you have the Data Entry form view (blank form) displayed, select Data Source from the menu of the Views task pane. This displays the Work with the data source: area of the Data Source task pane. Figure 32-32 shows the Data Source Task pane opened. Notice that two sub-data sources are under the source myFields. The first sources (queryFields) are the fields used in the Query view form that you already visited. The second sources (dataFields) are the fields that you need to add to the form for adding and displaying data from the table.

Figure 32-32: The Data Source task pane with the dataFields sub-data source expanded.

With the sub-data source dataFields expanded, you can now add these fields to the form. You can add any title you want and then add each field to the form until your form resembles the one shown in Figure 32-33.

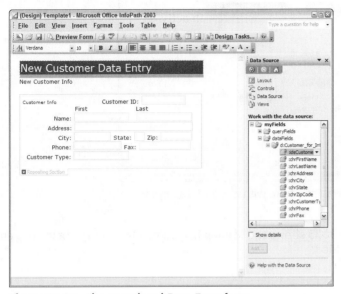

Figure 32-33: The completed Data Entry form.

Looking at the form in Figure 32-33, you can see that it has a title consistent with the one from the Query view and the fields entered on the form.

At this point, you may want to try your form to see whether the two views work correctly. Click on the Views choice in the pane to activate the Views Task pane and select the query view, and then select Preview From from the toolbar. With the Preview active, type **102** in the idsCustomerID field and press the Run Query button. InfoPath should now display a record for Hank Williams, as shown in Figure 32-34.

Now that you have verified that the form and views are working correctly, click the Close Preview button to return to the design window. Finally, you can save your work and name it New Customer Info Template.

Working with an InfoPath form

To use any InfoPath form, you simply need to find its location on your network and run it like any other Windows application.

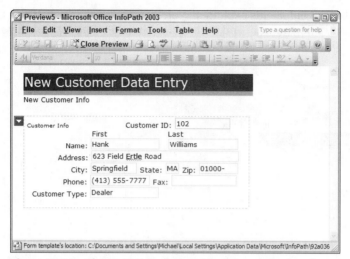

Figure 32-34: The Data Entry form with a record displayed.

For example, Figure 32-35 shows the Mailing List Template.xsn form being run and a new record being added.

Figure 32-35: The Mailing List form active with a record added.

Saving data to an XML document

When a form is active, you can save the record to an XML document for later use by simply selecting File ⇨ Save from the menu and specifying a name for the XML document.

Note Only one record can be saved at a time to an XML document using InfoPath. You cannot enter more than one record and have it save multiple records to one XML document.

For example, run the Mailing List Template form and add the values you see in Figure 32-36.

Figure 32-36: Data entered into the Mailing List Template form.

With the data entered, select File ➪ Save to save the file and name it MRI001.xml. Now the file has been saved to an XML document.

Querying an InfoPath form linked to Access

If you created a query form as you did earlier in the New Customer Info Template. xsn form, you can query for a single record or multiple records. For example, after activating the New Customer Info Template form, you can enter a value of **MD** in the chrState field and press the Run Query button. InfoPath finds any records where the state is Maryland in the table Customer for InfoPath within the CHAP32Start database; then it displays the results in the Data Entry form.

Figure 32-37 shows two records retrieved and displayed.

Tip To return to the query window, select View ➪ Query.

While displaying the resulting query against an Access table, you select either record and you cut, copy, and remove the record from the linked table.

Submitting new data to an Access table

Using the same form, New Customer Info Template, you can add a new record to the form and save it to an XML document as you did earlier with File ➪ Save, or you can Submit the new record to the Access table it is linked to by selecting File ➪ Submit.

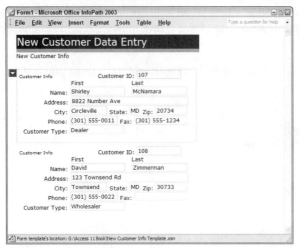

Figure 32-37: Displaying more than one record that matches a query.

If there are any problems, InfoPath does not save the record and it displays an error message box informing you of the problem.

Importing an InfoPath XML document into Access

After you have created your InfoPath templates and created XML documents, you can import them into Access just like you import any other XML document.

For example, you can import the MRI001.xml file that you saved earlier. To import this file, follow these steps:

1. Open the CHAP32Start database in Access if it isn't already open. Make sure the Tables object is selected and the Tables container is visible.

2. Select File ➪ Get External Data ➪ Import... from the menu.

3. Select XML (*.xml, *.xsd) as the file type.

4. Select the MRI001.xml file after locating it and click the Import button.

   Access displays the Import XML dialog box, as shown in Figure 32-38. Notice that it shows a table named myFields. When you expand it, you see the field names, as shown in the figure. This is the table you created when you made the template form earlier.

   The Options button in Figure 32-38 has also been pressed to show the three Import Options available: Structure Only, Structure and Data, and Append Data to Existing Table(s).

Figure 32-38: The Import XML dialog box.

5. Click the OK button to import the single record in the MRI001.XML document into a table named myFields.

If you have several XML documents that contain myFields records, you can select the Append Data to Existing Table(s) option to append each record individually to the table myFields. If you do not append each record, a new table will be created for each record, adding a number after the table name: myFields1, myFields2, and so on.

✦   ✦   ✦

Advanced Access Database Topics

✦ ✦ ✦ ✦

Exchanging Data with Office Applications

On the CD-ROM
This chapter will use the database named CHAP33Start. mdb. A word template file named Thanks.dot, is also included for use in this chapter. If you have not already copied them onto your machine from the CD, you will need to do so now. There is no CHAP33End.mdb. Because this chapter relies on the use of Visual Basic code, it and the forms that are driven by it have already been created for you.

As companies standardize their computer practices and software selections, it is becoming more and more important to develop *total* solutions: In other words, solutions that integrate the many procedures of an organization. Usually, various procedures are accomplished by using different software packages, such as Word for letter writing, Exchange and Outlook for mailing and faxing, Powerpoint for presentations, and Excel for financial functions. If the organization for which you are developing has standardized on the Microsoft Office suite, you can leverage your knowledge of Visual Basic for Applications to program for all of these products.

Note
Automation, formerly called *OLE Automation,* is a means by which an application can expose objects, each with its own methods and properties, that other applications can create instances of and control through code. Not all commercial applications support Automation, but more and more applications are adopting Automation to replace the outdated DDE interface. Consult with a specific application's vendor to find out if it supports or plans to support Automation in the program.

Using Automation to Integrate with Office

The Microsoft Office applications mentioned in the previous section all support Automation. Using Automation, you can create objects in your code that represent other applications. By manipulating these objects (setting properties and calling methods), you can control the referenced applications as though you were programming directly in them, thus allowing you to create seamless integrated applications by using Automation.

Creating Automation references

Applications that support Automation provide information about their objects in an *object library*. The object library contains information about an application's properties, methods, and *classes*. An application's class is its internal structure for objects; each class creates a specific type of object — a form, a report, and so on. To reference an application's objects, Visual Basic must determine which specific type of object is being referenced by an object's variable in your code. The process of determining the type of an object variable is called *binding*. You can use two methods for binding an object — *early binding* and *late binding*.

Early binding an object

Using the References dialog box in the Visual Basic window of Access, you can explicitly reference an object library. When you explicitly reference an object library, you are performing early binding. Automation code executes more quickly when you use early binding.

Note   To access the References dialog box of VBA, you need to activate the Visual Basic window by either creating a new module or displaying the design of an existing module.

To create a reference, first create a new module or open any existing module in your application database in the Visual Basic Design screen. After you have a module in Design view, a new command, References, is available from the Tools menu. Figure 33-1 shows the References selection on the Tools menu. Select Tools ➪ References to access the References dialog box. Figure 33-2 shows the References dialog box.

In the References dialog box, you specify all the references that your application needs for using Automation or for using other Access databases as library databases. To select or deselect a reference, click its check box.

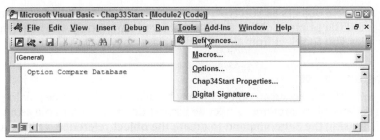

Figure 33-1: The Tools ➪ References menu item is available only after you have a module in Design or New view in Access. This menu item activates the VBA window.

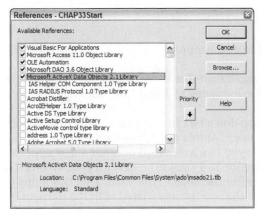

Figure 33-2: Early binding by setting references is the most efficient way to perform Automation.

Caution For this chapter, you will need to make sure that several reference libraries are active. You may not initially have the following four references available (checked):

```
Microsoft DAO 3.6 Object Library
Microsoft ActiveX Data Objects Recordset 2.7 Library
Microsoft Word 11.0 Object Library
Microsoft Office 11.0 Object Library
```

If these libraries aren't active (or, visible at the top of the list), find them in the selection list box by scrolling to them, and then check them on.

After you reference an application for Automation, you can explicitly dimension any object variable in that reference library. The New object coding help feature displays the available objects as you type, as shown in Figure 33-3. In addition, after you have selected the primary object and have entered a period (.), the help feature of Access enables you to select from the available class objects (see Figure 33-4).

Late binding an object

If you don't explicitly reference an object library by using the References dialog box, you can set an object's reference in code by first declaring a variable as an object and then using the Set command to create the object reference. This process is known as *late binding*.

To create an object to reference Microsoft Word, for example, you can use the following code:

```
Dim WordObj As Object
Set WordObj = New Word.Application
```

The Set command is discussed in the next section.

Tip   If you create an object for an application that is not referenced, no drop-down help box, such as the ones shown in Figures 33-3 and 33-4, will display.

Figure 33-3 shows the automatic drop-down box that appears immediately after you type the word **new** in the Dim statement. At this point, you can select one of the application object name types displayed (such as *word*) or enter a new application object name type that you define. Figure 33-4 shows the new drop-down box that appears when you type a period (.) after the object type *word*. This box helps you by displaying all known object types that can be associated with the particular primary object name. In this case, clicking the Application object type adds this to the *word.* portion of the object, thus *word.application*.

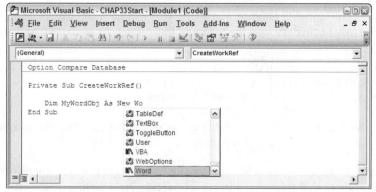

Figure 33-3: When an Automation Server is referenced, its objects are immediately known by Visual Basic.

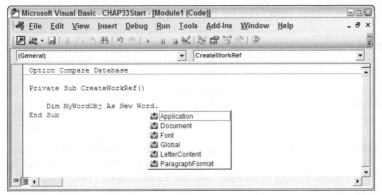

Figure 33-4: The new drop-down syntax help of Visual Basic makes using referenced Automation Servers easy.

Creating an instance of an Automation object

To perform an Automation operation, the operating system needs to start the application — if it isn't already started — and obtain a reference, or *handle*, to it. This reference will be used to access the application. Most applications that support Automation, called *Automation Servers,* expose an Application object. The Application object exists at the top of the object application's hierarchy and often contains many objects, as well.

Using the New keyword to create a new instance

The simplest (and most efficient) method to create any Automation object is to early bind the specific Automation Server reference library to the module by activating it, using the Tools ⇨ References menu. After you bind it, you can then create a new instance of the object by using the New keyword in Visual Basic. In the examples shown in Figure 33-3 and Figure 33-4, the variable MyWordObj is set to a new instance of Word's Application object. If you have not bound the Microsoft Word 11.0 Object Library, you will need to do so or you will receive an error.

> **Caution** If you don't create a reference to the Automation Server by using the References dialog box, Visual Basic doesn't recognize the object type and generates an error on compile.

Every time you create an instance of an Automation Server by using the New keyword, a new instance of the application is started. If you don't want to start a new instance of the application, use the GetObject function, which is discussed later in this chapter. Not all Automation Servers support the New keyword. Consult the specific Automation Server's documentation to determine whether it supports the New keyword. If the New keyword is not supported, you need to use the CreateObject function, which is discussed in the following section, to create an instance of the Automation Server.

Using the CreateObject function to create a new instance

In addition to creating an instance of an object library by using the New keyword, you can create an instance of an object library by using the CreateObject function. You use the CreateObject function to create instances of object libraries that do not support the New keyword. To use the CreateObject function, first declare a variable of the type equal to the type of object that you want to create. Then use the Set statement in conjunction with the CreateObject function to set the variable to a new instance of the object library.

For example, Microsoft Binder doesn't support the New keyword, but it does provide an object library, so you can reference it by using the References dialog box. To early bind the object library of Binder, use the CreateObject function, as shown in the following code:

```
Dim BinderObj As OfficeBinder.Binder
Set BinderObj = CreateObject("Office.Binder")
```

Note In the preceding example, the object library name for Binder is OfficeBinder.Binder, and the class instance is "Office.Binder." You can view the names of object libraries and their available classes by using the Object Browser.

You can create an object instance with the CreateObject function, which is late bound, by not declaring the object variable as a specific type. For example, the following code creates an instance of the Binder object by using late binding:

```
Dim BinderObj As Object
Set BinderObj = CreateObject("Office.Binder")
```

Note If you have different versions of the same Automation Server on your computer, you can specify the version to use by adding it to the end of the class information. For example, the following code uses Office as the Automation Server:

```
Dim BinderObj As Object
Set BinderObj = CreateObject("Word.Application.11")
```

Tip Word 97 was the first true Automation Server, and like its predecessor, Word 2003 doesn't require you to specify a version when creating instances of Word object libraries; Word is always used, regardless of the other versions of Word on the computer. In fact, you get an error if you try to specify a version number. Therefore, you can use the following syntax instead:

```
Set BinderObj = CreateObject("Word.Application.11")
```

Getting an existing object instance

As stated previously in this chapter, using the New keyword or the CreateObject function creates a new instance of the Automation Server. If you don't want a new instance of the server created each time you create an object, use the GetObject function. The format of the GetObject function is as follows:

```
Set objectvariable = GetObject([pathname][, class])
```

The pathname parameter is optional. To use this parameter, you specify a full path and file name to an existing file for use with the Automation Server.

Note   The specified document is then opened in the server application. Even if you omit the parameter, you must still include the comma (,).

The class parameter is the same parameter that's used with the CreateObject function. See Table 33-1 for a list of some class arguments used in Microsoft Office.

Table 33-1
Class Arguments for Common Office Components

Component	Class Argument	Object Returned
Access	Access.Application	Microsoft Access Application object
Excel	Excel.Application	Microsoft Excel Application object
	Excel.Sheet	Microsoft Excel Workbook object
	Excel.Chart	Microsoft Excel Chart object
Word	Word.Application	Microsoft Word Application object
	Word.Document	Microsoft Word Document object

For example, to work with an existing instance of Microsoft Word, but not a specific Word document, you can use the following code:

```
Dim WordObj as Word.Application
Set WordObj = GetObject(, "Word.Application")
```

To get an instance of an existing Word document called MyDoc.Doc, on your C: drive, you can use the following code:

```
Dim WordObj as Word.Application
Set WordObj = GetObject("c:\MyDoc.Doc", "Word.Application")
```

Of course, this code is always placed in a new function or sub that you declare in your module.

Working with Automation objects

After you have a valid instance of an Automation Server, you manipulate the object as though you were writing code within the application itself, using the exposed objects and their properties and methods.

For example, when developing directly in Word, you can use the following code to change the directory that Word uses when opening an existing file:

```
ChangeFileOpenDirectory "C:\My Documents\"
```

Note   Consult the development help for the Automation Server for specific information on the objects, properties, and methods available.

Just as in Access, Word is implicitly using its Application object; the command ChangeFileOpenDirectory is really a method of the Application object. Using the following code, you create an instance of Word's Application object and call the method of the object:

```
Dim WordObj As New Word.Application
WordObj.ChangeFileOpenDirectory "C:\My Documents\"
```

Tip   When using Automation, you should avoid setting properties or calling methods that cause the Automation Server to ask for input from the user via a dialog box. When a dialog box is displayed, the Automation code stops executing until the dialog box is closed. If the server application is minimized or behind other windows, the user may not even be aware that he or she needs to provide input, and therefore may assume that the application is locked up.

Closing an instance of an Automation object

Automation objects are closed when the Automation object variable goes out of scope. Such a closing, however, doesn't necessarily free up all resources that are used by the object, so you should explicitly close the instance of the Automation object. You can close an Automation object by doing either of the following:

✦ Using the Close or Quit method of the object (consult the specific Automation Server's documentation for information on which method it supports)

✦ Setting the object variable to nothing, as follows:

```
Set WordObj = Nothing
```

The best way to close an instance of an Automation object is to combine the two techniques, like this:

```
WordObj.Quit
Set WordObj = Nothing
```

An Automation Example Using Word

Perhaps the most common Office application that is used for Automation from a database application like Access is Word. Using Automation with Word, you can create letters that are tailored with information from databases. The following section demonstrates an example of merging information from an Access database to a letter in Word by using Automation and Word's Bookmarks. Ordinarily, you create a merge document in Word and bring field contents in from the records of an Access database. This method relies on using Word's MergeField, which is replaced by the contents of the Database field. It normally requires that you perform this action in Word — thus limiting the scope and capability of the function. For example, you will merge all records from the table that is being used rather than a single record.

The following example uses the Orders form, which calls a module named *WordIntegration*. The WordIntegration module contains a function named *MergetoWord()* that uses the Word Thanks.dot template file.

> **Note**   When you attempt to run this example, you must make sure that the path for the template in the Visual Basic code is the actual path in which the Thanks.dot template file resides. This path may vary from computer to computer.

The items that are discussed in this Word Automation example include the following:

✦ Creating an instance of a Word object

✦ Making the instance of Word visible

✦ Creating a new document based on an existing template

✦ Using bookmarks to insert data

✦ Activating the instance of Word

✦ Moving the cursor in Word

✦ Closing the instance of the Word object without closing Word

This example prints a thank-you letter for an order based on bookmarks in the thank you letter template (Thanks.dot). Figure 33-5 shows the data for customers; Figure 33-6 shows the data entry form for orders; Figure 33-7 shows the Thanks.dot template; and Figure 33-8 shows a completed merge letter.

The bookmarks in Figure 33-7 are shown as grayed large I-beams (text insert). The bookmarks are normally not visible, but you can make them visible by selecting Tools ➪ Options, selecting the View tab and going to the top section titled Show and then turning on the Bookmarks option by checking the option (third choice in the first column). The names won't be visible — only the bookmark holders (locations) will be visible, as shown in Figure 33-7. The names and arrows in Figure 33-7 were placed using text boxes to show where the bookmark names are assigned.

Figure 33-5: Customer data used in the following Automation example is entered on the Customers form.

Figure 33-6: Each customer can have an unlimited number of orders. Thank-you letters are printed from the Orders form.

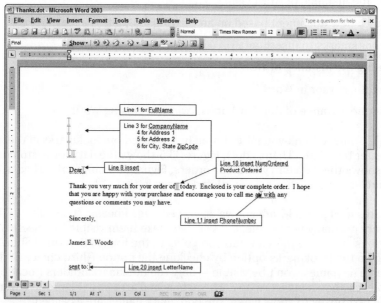

Figure 33-7: The Thanks.dot template contains bookmarks where the merged data is to be inserted.

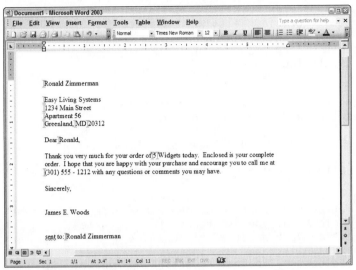

Figure 33-8: After a successful merge, all the bookmarks have been replaced with their respective data.

Caution If you click the Print Thank You Letter button in Access while Word is open with an existing document — which lacks the bookmark names specified in the code — the fields will simply be added to the text inside Word at the point where the cursor is currently sitting.

When the user clicks the Print Thank You Letter button on the Orders form, Word generates a thank-you letter with all the pertinent information. The following code shows the MergetoWord function in its entirety so you can see in-depth how it works.

```
Public Function MergetoWord()
' This method creates a new document in MS Word
' using Automation.
On Error Resume Next
Dim rsCust As Recordset, iTemp As Integer
Dim WordObj As Word.Application
Set rsCust =
DBEngine(0).Databases(0).OpenRecordset("Customers", _
dbOpenTable)
rsCust.Index = "PrimaryKey"
rsCust.Seek "=", Forms!Orders![CustomerNumber]
    If rsCust.NoMatch Then
        MsgBox "Invalid customer", vbOKOnly
        Exit Function
    End If
DoCmd.Hourglass True
Set WordObj = GetObject(, "Word.Application")
```

```
If Err.Number <> 0 Then
    Set WordObj = CreateObject("Word.Application")
End If
WordObj.Visible = True
WordObj.Documents.Add

' WARNING:
' Specify the correct drive and path to the
' file named thanks.dot in the line below.

  Template:="G:\Access 11 Book\thanks.dot",

' The above path and drive must be fixed

NewTemplate:=False
WordObj.Selection.Goto what:=wdGoToBookmark, Name:="FullName"
    WordObj.Selection.TypeText rsCust![ContactName]
WordObj.Selection.Goto what:=wdGoToBookmark,
Name:="CompanyName"
    WordObj.Selection.TypeText rsCust![CompanyName]
WordObj.Selection.Goto what:=wdGoToBookmark, Name:="Address1"
    WordObj.Selection.TypeText rsCust![Address1]
WordObj.Selection.Goto what:=wdGoToBookmark, Name:="Address2"
    If IsNull(rsCust![Address2]) Then
        WordObj.Selection.TypeText ""
    Else
        WordObj.Selection.TypeText rsCust![Address2]
    End If
WordObj.Selection.Goto what:=wdGoToBookmark, Name:="City"
    WordObj.Selection.TypeText rsCust![City]
WordObj.Selection.Goto what:=wdGoToBookmark, Name:="State"
    WordObj.Selection.TypeText rsCust![State]
WordObj.Selection.Goto what:=wdGoToBookmark, Name:="Zipcode"
    WordObj.Selection.TypeText rsCust![Zipcode]
WordObj.Selection.Goto what:=wdGoToBookmark,
Name:="PhoneNumber"
    WordObj.Selection.TypeText rsCust![PhoneNumber]
WordObj.Selection.Goto what:=wdGoToBookmark, Name:="NumOrdered"
    WordObj.Selection.TypeText Forms!Orders![Quantity]
WordObj.Selection.Goto what:=wdGoToBookmark,
Name:="ProductOrdered"
    If Forms!Orders![Quantity] > 1 Then
        WordObj.Selection.TypeText Forms!Orders![Item] & "s"
    Else
        WordObj.Selection.TypeText Forms!Orders![Item]
    End If
WordObj.Selection.Goto what:=wdGoToBookmark, Name:="FName"
    iTemp = InStr(rsCust![ContactName], " ")
    If iTemp > 0 Then
        WordObj.Selection.TypeText Left$(rsCust![ContactName],
iTemp _ - 1)
    End If
```

```
WordObj.Selection.Goto what:=wdGoToBookmark, Name:="LetterName"
    WordObj.Selection.TypeText rsCust![ContactName]
DoEvents
WordObj.Activate
WordObj.Selection.MoveUp wdLine, 6
' Set the Word Object to nothing to free resources
Set WordObj = Nothing
DoCmd.Hourglass False
Exit Function
TemplateError:
    Set WordObj = Nothing
    Exit Function
End Function
```

Creating an instance of a Word object

The first step in using Automation is to create an instance of an object. The sample creates an object instance with the following code:

```
On Error Resume Next
...
Set WordObj = GetObject(, "Word.Application")
If Err.Number <> 0 Then
    Set WordObj = CreateObject("Word.Application")
End If
```

Obviously, you don't want a new instance of Word created every time a thank-you letter is generated, so some special coding is required. This code snippet first attempts to create an instance by using an active instance (a running copy) of Word. If Word is not a running application, an error is generated. Because this function has On Error Resume Next for error trapping, the code doesn't fail, but instead proceeds to the next statement. If an error is detected (the Err.Number is not equal to 0), an instance is created by using CreateObject.

Making the instance of Word visible

When you first create a new instance of Word, it runs invisibly. This approach enables your application to exploit features of Word without the user even realizing that Word is running. In this case, however, it is desirable to let the user edit the merged letter, so Word needs to be made visible by setting the object's Visible property to True by using this line of code:

```
WordObj.Visible = True
```

Caution

If you don't set the object instance's Visible property to True, you may create hidden copies of Word that use system resources and never shut down. A hidden copy of Word doesn't show up in the Task tray or in the Task Switcher.

Creating a new document based on an existing template

After Word is running, a blank document needs to be created. The following code creates a new document by using the Thanks.dot template:

```
WordObj.Documents.Add Template:="G:\Access 11 Book\thanks.dot",
_ NewTemplate:=False
```

Note The path must be corrected in order to point to the Thanks.dot template on your computer.

The Thanks.dot template contains bookmarks (as shown in Figure 33-7) that tell this function where to insert data. You create bookmarks in Word by highlighting the text that you want to make a bookmark, selecting Insert ➪ Bookmark, and then entering the bookmark name and clicking Add.

Using Bookmarks to insert data

Using Automation, you can locate bookmarks in a Word document and replace them with the text of your choosing. To locate a bookmark, use the Goto method of the Selection object. After you have located the bookmark, the text comprising the bookmark is selected. By inserting text (which you can do by using Automation or simply by typing directly into the document), you replace the bookmark text. To insert text, use the TypeText method of the Selection object, as shown here:

```
WordObj.Selection.Goto what:=wdGoToBookmark, Name:="FullName"
WordObj.Selection.TypeText rsCust![ContactName]
```

Note You can't pass a null to the TypeText method. If the value may possibly be Null, you need to check ahead and make allowances. The preceding sample code checks the Address2 field for a Null value and acts accordingly. If you don't pass text to replace the bookmark — even just a zero length string (" ") — the bookmark text remains in the document.

Activating the instance of Word

To enable the user to enter data in the new document, you must make Word the active application. If you don't make Word the active application, the user has to switch to Word from Access. You make Word the active application by using the Activate method of the Word object, as follows:

```
WordObj.Activate
```

Tip   Depending on the processing that is occurring at the time, Access may take the focus back from Word. You can help to eliminate this annoyance by preceding the Activate method with a DoEvents statement. Note, however, that this doesn't always work.

Moving the cursor in Word

You can move the cursor in Word by using the MoveUp method of the Selection object. The following example moves the cursor up six lines in the document. The cursor is at the location of the last bookmark when this code is executed:

```
WordObj.Selection.MoveUp wdLine, 6
```

Closing the instance of the Word object

To free up resources that are taken by an instance of an Automation object, you should always close the instance. In this example, the following code is used to close the object instance:

```
Set WordObj = Nothing
```

This code closes the object instance, but not the instance of Word as a running application. In this example, the user needs access to the new document, so closing Word would defeat the purpose of this function. You can, however, automatically print the document and then close Word. If you do this, you may even choose to not make Word visible during this process. To close Word, use the Quit method of the Application object, as follows:

```
WordObj.Quit
```

Inserting pictures by using Bookmarks

It is possible to perform other unique operations by using Bookmarks. Basically, anything that you can do within Word, you can do by using Automation. The following code locates a bookmark that marks where a picture is to be placed and then inserts a .BMP file from disk. You can use the following code to insert scanned signatures into letters:

```
WordObj.Selection.Goto what:=wdGoToBookmark, Name:="Picture"
WordObj.ChangeFileOpenDirectory "D:\GRAPHICS\"
WordObj. ActiveDocument.Shapes.AddPicture
Anchor:=Selection.Range, _ FileName:= _
        "D:\GRAPHICS\PICTURE.BMP", LinkToFile:=False,
SaveWithDocument _
        :=True
```

Using Office's Macro Recorder

Using Automation is not a difficult process when you understand the fundamentals. Often, the toughest part of using Automation is knowing the proper objects, properties, and methods to use. Although the development help system of the Automation Server is a requirement for fully understanding the language, the easiest way to quickly create Automation for Office applications like Word is the Macro Recorder.

Most versions of Office applications have a Macro Recorder located on the Tools menu (see Figure 33-9). When activated, the Macro Recorder records all events, such as menu selections and button clicks, and creates Visual Basic code from them.

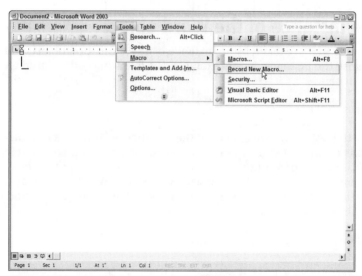

Figure 33-9: The Macro Recorder in Word is a powerful tool to help you create Automation code.

After selecting Tools ➪ Macro ➪ Record New Macro, you must give your new macro a name (see Figure 33-10). In addition to a name, you can assign the macro to a toolbar or keyboard combination and select the template in which to store the macro. If you are creating the macro simply to create the Visual Basic code, the only thing that you need to be concerned with is the macro name.

After you enter a macro name and click OK, the Macro Recorder begins recording events and displays a Stop Recording window, and the arrow changes to an open pointer attached to a cassette, as shown in Figure 33-11. You can stop recording events by clicking the Stop button (the button with a square on it). To pause recording events, click the other button, which is the Pause button.

Figure 33-10: Enter a macro name and click OK to begin recording the macro. In this example, the macro is named "MyMacro."

Figure 33-11: The Macro Recorder records all events until you click the Stop button.

After you have finished recording a macro, you can view the Visual Basic code created from your events. To view the code of a macro, select Tools ⇨ Macro ⇨ Macros to display a list of all saved macros. Then select the macro that you recorded and click the Edit button to display the Visual Basic editor with the macro's code. Figure 33-12 shows the Visual Basic editor with a macro that recorded the creation of a new document using the Normal template and the insertion of a picture using the Insert ⇨ Picture ⇨ From File menu item.

In the application for which a macro is created, the Application object is used explicitly. When you use the code for Automation, you must create an Application object accordingly. For example, the preceding macro uses the following code to create a new document:

```
Documents.Add Template:=" Normal.dot", NewTemplate:= False,
DocumentType:=0
```

This code implicitly uses the Application object. To use this code for Automation, copy the code from the Visual Basic editor, paste it into your procedure, and create an object that you use explicitly, as follows:

```
Dim WordObj as New Word.Application
WordObj.Documents.Add Template:=" Normal.dot", NewTemplate:=
False, DocumentType:=0
```

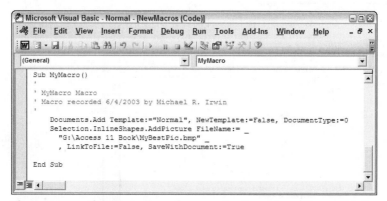

Figure 33-12: The Macro Recorder records all events until you click the Stop button.

The Macro Recorder enables you to effortlessly create long and complete Automation code without ever needing to read the Automation Server's documentation.

✦　　✦　　✦

Adding Security to Applications

Although Access provides the interface to maintain security options, it is Jet that actually performs security functions. The Jet security model has changed little since Access 95. Jet's security is still a workgroup-based security model; all users in a workgroup are bound to the same security rules. The rules enforced for individual users may vary from user to user, based on the permissions assigned to each user.

 On the CD-ROM In this chapter, you will use the database file Chap34 Start.mdb.

Understanding Jet Security

Jet security is defined at the object level for individuals or groups of users. The Jet security model is rather complex, but it isn't too difficult to understand when broken down into its core components, which are as follows:

- ✦ Workgroups
- ✦ Groups
- ✦ Users
- ✦ Object owners
- ✦ Object permissions

The two main reasons for employing user-level security are

- ✦ To protect sensitive data in the database.
- ✦ To prevent users from accidentally breaking an application by changing the objects (tables, queries, and so on) of the application.

By using passwords and permissions, you can allow or restrict access of an individual or groups of individuals to the objects (forms, tables, and so on) in your database. This information, known as a *workgroup,* is stored in a workgroup information file.

Understanding workgroup files

Jet stores security information for databases in workgroup information files, usually the default file is named "SYSTEM.MDW." This *workgroup information file* is a special Access database that contains a collection of user names and passwords, user group definitions, object owner assignments, and object permissions. The SYSTEM. MDW file is often located, by default, in the C:\Documents and Settings\<user name>\Application Data\Microsoft\Access\System.MDW folder. When Access opens a database, it reads the workgroup information file associated with the database. Access reads the file to determine who is allowed—and at what level— access to the objects in the database and what permissions they have to those objects.

You can use the same workgroup file for multiple databases. After you enable security for a database, however, users must use the workgroup information file containing the security information. If users use a workgroup other than the one used to define security, however, they are limited to logging into the database as the Admin user—with whatever permissions the database administrator left for the Admin user.

Tip

When securing a database, one of the first things that you need to do is to remove all permissions for the Admin user. Removing these permissions prevents other users from opening the database as the Admin user by using another Access workgroup file and obtaining the rights of the Admin user. Users can still open the database as the Admin user by using a different workgroup, but they won't have any object permissions. This measure is discussed later in this chapter in the section "Working with workgroups."

Understanding permissions

The permissions in Jet security are defined at the object level; each object, such as a form or report, has a specific set of permissions. The system administrator defines what permissions each user or group of users has for each object. Users may belong to multiple groups, and they always inherit the highest permission setting of any of the groups to which they belong.

For example, every table object has a set of permissions associated with it: Read Design, Modify Design, Read Data, Update Data, Insert Data, Delete Data, and Administrator. (See Table 34-1 later in this chapter for a complete list of permissions and their meanings.) The database administrator has the ability to assign or remove any or all of these permissions for each user or group of users in the workgroup. Because the permissions are set at the object level, the administrator may give a user the ability to read data from Table A, as well as read data from and write data to Table B, but prevent the user from even looking at Table C. In addition, this complexity allows for unique security situations, such as having numerous users sharing data on a network, each with a different set of rights for the database objects. All security maintenance functions are performed from the Tools ➪ Security menu item (see Figure 34-1).

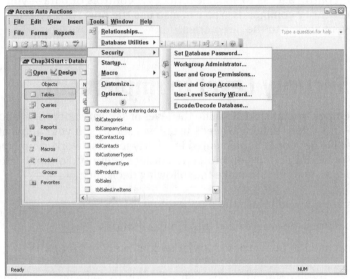

Figure 34-1: All Jet security functions are performed from the Tools ➪ Security menu.

Understanding security limitations

You need to be aware of the fact that you can't depend on the Jet security model to be foolproof. For example, security holes have been discovered and exposed in previous versions of Access — in effect, unprotecting every database distributed under the assumption that the code and objects were protected. The amount of resources involved in developing an application is often huge, and protecting that investment is essential. The most that you can do for protection is to fully and properly implement the Jet 4.0 security model and use legally binding licensing agreements for all of your distributed applications. Unfortunately, the security of your databases is at the mercy of software hackers.

As of the printing of this book, Microsoft has released the Microsoft Jet 4.0 Service Pack 7 update, which provides an updated sandbox mode. Sandbox mode allows Microsoft Office Access 2003 to block potentially unsafe expressions. In fact, if you do not install this service pack, some features in Office Access 2003 will not function properly.

Tip   You should monitor the Microsoft Update service on the Web at `http://office.microsoft.com/ProductUpdates/default.aspx` to keep your Windows operating system and Office programs up to date.

We recommend that you use Microsoft Access security to lock up your tables and prevent access to the design of your forms, reports, queries, and modules. However, if you want to control data at the form level — for example, suppose that you want to hide controls or control access to specific form-level controls or data — you have to write your own security commands. You can also use the operating system (Windows) to prevent access to the directories.

Choosing a Security Level to Implement

As an Access developer, you must determine the level of security appropriate for your application — not every database needs user-level security. If your application contains non-sensitive data or is implemented in a fairly low-risk workgroup, you may not need the powerful permission protection of Jet's security. For applications that need to be secure, you need to make the following decisions:

✦ Which users are allowed to use the database?

✦ Can individual users be categorized into similar groups?

✦ Which objects need to be restricted for individual users or groups?

After you have made these determinations, you are ready to begin implementing security in your application. Access includes a tool to help you implement security — the User-Level Security Wizard (available from the Tools ➪ Security menu choice). This chapter teaches you how you can implement security by using Access's interface; each security element is discussed in detail. A thorough understanding of the workings of the security model is essential in developing well-secured applications. (The wizard is discussed later in this chapter.)

On the CD-ROM   This chapter uses two example databases: Chap34Start.mdb and AAASecureWizard. Later in this chapter, you will see how the second database is created from the first database. You should copy the Chap34Start.mdb database from the CD, included with this book, into a subdirectory on your hard drive.

Creating a Database Password

You can use Jet security at its most basic level simply by controlling who can open the database. You control database access by creating a password for the databases that you want to protect. When you set a database password for a database, users are prompted to enter the password each time they attempt to access the database. If they don't know the database password, they are not allowed to open the database. When using this form of security, you are not controlling specific permissions for specific users; you are merely controlling who can and can't access the secured database.

To create a database password, follow these steps:

1. In Access, open the Chap34Start.mdb database exclusively.

Note   You *must* open the database exclusively in order to set the database password. To open the database exclusively, select the Open Exclusive button from the Open pull-down menu in the lower-right corner of the Open dialog box, as shown in Figure 34-2.

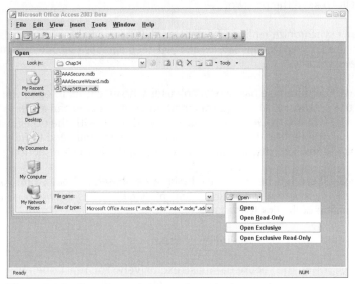

Figure 34-2: Opening a database in exclusive mode.

2. Select Tools ➪ Security ➪ Set Database Password (refer to Figure 34-1).

3. In the Password field, type the password that you want to use to secure the database (see Figure 34-3). For this example, use the password *bible*. Access does *not* display the password; rather, it shows an asterisk (*) for each letter.

Figure 34-3: Creating a database password is the simplest way to secure your database.

4. In the Verify field, type the password again. This security measure ensures that you don't mistype the password (because you can't see the characters that you type) and mistakenly prevent everyone, including you, from accessing the database.

Tip

For maximum security, when entering a password, you should follow standard password naming conventions. That is, you should make the password a combination of letters and numbers that won't represent any easily known or deduced combination. People often unwisely use a birthday, their name, their address number, or a loved one's name, which are all poor choices for passwords because another person could deduce them fairly easily. On the other hand, you shouldn't make the password so difficult to remember that you and others accessing the database will have to write it down to use it. A written password is a useless password.

5. Click OK to save the password.

Caution

You can't synchronize replicated databases that have database passwords. If you plan to use Jet's replication features and you need database security, you must use user-level security.

After you save the database password, any user who attempts to open the database must enter the password. Although this method controls *who* can access the database, it doesn't control *what* users are allowed to do with the objects and data after they have opened the database. To control objects, you need to fully implement Jet's user-level security, which is discussed in the following section.

Note

After a database has been protected with a database-level password, you must supply the password when linking to any of its tables. This password is stored in the definition of the link to the table.

To remove a database password, follow these steps:

1. In Access, open the secure database exclusively. You must open the database exclusively to be able to remove the database password.

2. Select Tools ⇨ Security ⇨ Unset Database Password. This menu option replaced the option labeled Set Database Password before the database password was set.

3. In the Password field, type the password of the database (see Figure 34-4).

4. Click OK to unset the password.

Figure 34-4: You can remove a database password by entering the password in the Unset Database Password dialog box.

Using Visual Basic to Set a Password

You also can set a database password using Visual Basic code. The following code changes the database password of the currently opened database:

```
Public Sub ChangeDatabasePassword()
  On Error GoTo ChangeDatabasePasswordErr
  Dim szOldPassword As String, szNewPassword As String
  Dim db As Database
  Set db = CurrentDb
  szOldPassword = ""
  szNewPassword = "shazam"
  db.NewPassword szOldPassword, szNewPassword
  Exit Sub
ChangeDatabasePasswordErr:
    MsgBox Err & ":  " & Err.Description
    Exit Sub
End Sub
```

If no database password is set, you pass a zero-length string ("") as the old password parameter. If a database password is assigned and you want to remove the password, pass the database password as the old password parameter and pass a zero-length string ("") as the new password.

If you remove a database password from an Access database, users are no longer required to enter a password to access the database unless you have enabled user-level security.

Note   Any user who knows the database password has the ability to change or remove the database password. You can prevent this situation by removing the Administer permissions from the database for all users except the database administrator. This is discussed in more detail later in this chapter.

Caution   Microsoft Access stores the database password in an unencrypted form. If you have sensitive data, this can compromise the security of the password-protected database. In situations where data security is critical, you should consider defining user-level security to control access to sensitive data. User-level security is covered in depth later in this chapter.

Using the /runtime Option

If you're not concerned with protecting your application but simply want to prevent users from mistakenly breaking your application by modifying or deleting objects, you can force your application to be run in Access's *runtime mode*. When a database is opened in Access' runtime mode, all the interface elements that allow changes to objects are hidden from the user. In fact, while in runtime mode, it is impossible for a user to access the Database window. When using the runtime option, you must ensure that your application has a startup form that gives users access to whatever objects that you want them to be able to access. Normally this is the main menu or main switchboard of your application.

Note You must purchase and install the Microsoft Visual Studio Tools for the Microsoft Office System to use the /runtime switch. This suite of tools includes a runtime version of Access that allows you to distribute a royalty-free licensed copy of your Access 2003 applications to users, whether they have Access on their machine or not.

Tip To assign a form as a startup form, open the database that you want to use, choose Tools ➪ Startup and select the form that you want to be the startup form from the Display Form/Page drop-down list. Startup forms are covered more in-depth in the following section.

To create a shortcut to start your application in Access's runtime mode, follow these steps, using the Chap34Start.mdb database:

   1. Go to the subdirectory that contains Microsoft Access (MSACCESS.exe).

Note On most computers, the MSACCESS.EXE file is located in the "C:\Program Files\Microsoft Office\OFFICE11\" folder.

   2. Highlight the Microsoft Access program and select File ➪ Create Shortcut, or right-click on the program file and select Create Shortcut from the menu-on-demand.

   Windows creates a shortcut in the same directory, naming it "Shortcut to Msaccess.exe."

   3. Right-click the newly created shortcut, select Properties from the menu, and then click the Shortcut tab when the Properties dialog box opens.

   4. In the Target: field, append the following parameters to the path of MSACCESS. EXE (program): A space, the full path name and filename of the database to open in runtime mode, another space, and then /runtime.

   For example, the following command line starts Access and opens the Chap34Start.mdb database in runtime mode on our computers:

```
"C:\Program Files\MicrosoftOffice\OFFICE11\MSAccess.exe" "C:
\Access 2003 Access Auto Auctions\Chap34Start.mdb" /runtime
```

Note The path to MSAcess.exe should have already been in the Target: field. Note that Windows automatically places the path and filename for MSAccess.exe in quotation marks. The /runtime switch should not be enclosed in quotes. If you enclose the /runtime switch in quotes, an error occurs when you attempt to execute the shortcut.

5. After you have specified the path and filename, placing the /runtime switch at the end of the Target: field, you can optionally remove the path name in the Start in: field.

Figure 34-5 shows how the Shortcut properties should look at this point.

Figure 34-5: Modifying the Target: and Start in: fields of the shortcut by using the /runtime switch of Access 2003.

6. After the fields have been updated, click the Apply button to process the changes and save the shortcut.

7. Finally, you can rename the shortcut icon to any name that you want and move it from the current directory to another directory, or even to the desktop. After you have created the shortcut, you can distribute or re-create the same shortcut for each user installation.

Tip If your database has a password associated with it, the user will still be prompted to enter the password prior to opening the database.

Cross-Reference Chapter 38 covers working with the Access runtime environment.

Using a Database's Startup Options

A slightly less secure alternative to using the /runtime option is to set a database's startup options. This alternative is not a complete solution for situations where tight security is paramount. Figure 34-6 shows the Startup options dialog box. To access the Startup options dialog box, select Tools ➪ Startup.

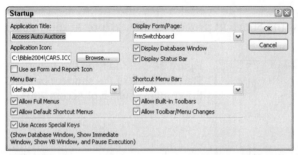

Figure 34-6: Using the Startup options dialog box provides another option for securing an application.

By making the appropriate specifications in the Startup options dialog box, you can do the following:

✦ Assign a title to the application.

✦ Assign an Application Icon to the application.

✦ Assign a form or data access page to immediately run when the database is open.

✦ Prevent the Database window (container) from being displayed.

✦ Prevent the status bar from being displayed.

✦ Designate a menu bar to be used on startup of your application.

✦ Designate a shortcut menu to be used on startup of your application.

✦ Prevent Access's built-in menus (full menus) from being displayed.

✦ Prevent Access's built-in shortcut menus from being displayed.

✦ Prevent Access's built-in toolbars from being displayed.

✦ Prevent users from modifying toolbars (toolbar/menu changes).

✦ Prevent users from using Access's special keys to display the Database window, display the immediate window, display the VB window, or pause execution.

To designate the frmSwitchboard form as the default form to open whenever the Chap34Start.mdb database opens, follow these steps:

1. Open the Chap34Start.mdb database and select Tools ➪ Startup to open the Startup dialog box.

2. Click in the Display Form/Page: field and select the frmSwitchboard form from the pull-down list (refer to Figure 34-6).

3. Click OK.

After you have assigned a form to open automatically, you can also specify that the Database window or status bar not be displayed to give even greater security to your application. By selecting these two items, when the user clicks the Close button on the startup form, the database window (container) will not display. By using a database password and the Startup options, you can assign minimum security to the database and your application.

Caution   The user can bypass the Startup options by simply holding down the Shift key while opening the database. However, if you assign a database password, users will still be required to enter the password in order to use the database.

Using the Jet User-Level Security Model

Most often when security is required, setting a database password and run-time options is simply not enough.

When you need more security, you can use Access user profiles that are implemented by the user-level/object permissions security of Jet 4.0. The Jet Database Engine offers additional levels of customization and security for your application. When using Jet level security, you need to complete the following series of functions:

1. Select or create a workgroup database.

2. Define the workgroup database's security groups.

3. Create the users of the workgroup database.

4. Define permissions for each user and security group.

5. Enable security by setting an Admin user password.

Enabling security

Jet database security is always on. Whenever a new workgroup database is created, an Admin user is automatically created within the workgroup. This Admin user has no password assigned to it. When the Admin password is blank, Access assumes that any user attempting to open the database is the Admin user, and that this user is automatically logged in to the database as the Admin user. To force Access (Jet) to ask for a valid user name and password to log in to the database (see Figure 34-7), you simply need to create a password for the Admin user. (Creating passwords is discussed later in this section.) To disable security, simply clear the Admin user's password. The security permissions that you have designed are still in effect, but Access doesn't ask for a user name and password — it logs on all users as the Admin user with whatever permissions were assigned to the Admin user. Be careful about clearing the Admin user's password when you have modified the permissions of your users.

Figure 34-7: When security is enabled, Jet forces all users to enter a valid user name and password to use the secured database.

Tip

Any changes that you make to security won't take effect until you restart Access. If you have cleared the Admin password only to find that some or all of the Admin user's permissions have been revoked, open the database and create a password for the Admin user. Then exit Access and restart Access (not the database). When you restart Access, you are prompted to enter a user name and password.

Working with workgroups

A *workgroup* is a collection of users, user groups, and object permissions. You can use a single workgroup file for all of your databases, or you can use different workgroups for different databases. The method that you use depends on the level of security that you need. If you give Administrative rights to users of some databases but not to users of other databases, you need to distribute separate workgroup files with each database. Access always uses a workgroup file when you open it. By default, this workgroup file is the SYSTEM.MDW workgroup file. This file comes with Access 2003.

Creating a new workgroup

You can create new workgroups or join existing workgroups by using the Workgroup Administrator program that comes with Access 2003 (see Figure 34-8). To begin creating a new workgroup, select Tools ➪ Security from the Access menu.

Note

You should completely close down Access after creating new workgroups or joining existing workgroups. When you use the Workgroup Administrator to join a workgroup, that workgroup is not actually used until the next time you start Access.

Figure 34-8: Using the Workgroup Administrator to create new workgroups and to join existing workgroups.

To create a new workgroup file, follow these steps:

1. Start Access (with or without a database), select Tools ➪ Security, and then select Workgroup Administrator.

2. Select the Create button in the Workgroup Administrator dialog box to display the Workgroup Owner Information dialog box.

   The workgroup that you create is identified by three components: Name, Organization, and Workgroup ID (see Figure 34-9).

Caution

In order to re-create the workgroup file in the event that it becomes corrupt or deleted, you need all three pieces of information. For this reason, to ensure that no other user can create your workgroup and access your secured database, you should supply a unique, random string for the Workgroup ID. Someone may possibly guess the name and organization used in your workgroup file if he or she knows who you are, but to guess all three items — especially if you create a random, unique ID — is almost impossible.

3. When you are satisfied with your entries, select OK to display the Workgroup Information File dialog box.

Figure 34-9: Workgroups are identified by these three key pieces of information. A workgroup can't be re-created without all three of these items.

4. Enter a name for the new workgroup file, and select OK to save it (see Figure 34-10). If you enter a filename that already exists, like SYSTEM.MDW, you will receive a confirmation box requesting that you confirm replacing the existing file.

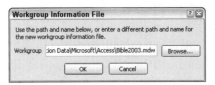

Figure 34-10: Assigning a filename for the new workgroup.

5. The Workgroup Administrator displays a confirmation dialog box (see Figure 34-11) containing the information that you entered for the new workgroup and explains the importance of writing down and storing the information. If you are satisfied with your entries, select OK to save your workgroup. If you want to change anything, click the Change button to return to Step 3.

Figure 34-11: Confirming the information for the new workgroup.

When you select the OK button in the Confirm Workgroup Information dialog box, a message displays to inform you that you have created the workgroup information file correctly.

Tip   In order to ensure that you can recover from the loss of your workgroup file, you should immediately make a copy of the workgroup file. In addition, you should write down the three pieces of information that you used to create the workgroup file, exactly as they were entered, in the event that you have to re-create the workgroup file from scratch. Store both the backup file copy and the written information in a secure place.

Joining an existing workgroup

When you create a new workgroup, Access automatically joins the new workgroup. If you don't want to use the new workgroup right away, or if at any time you need to use a workgroup other than the current workgroup, you can use the Workgroup Administrator to join another workgroup.

What Is Jet and a User Profile?

When you create a Microsoft Access database (.mdb or .mde), Access uses an internal program to create and work with the database and its objects. Microsoft calls this internal program the *Jet Database Engine*. Its purpose is to retrieve and store data in user and system databases. Some people refer to the Jet engine as a *data manager* that the database system is built upon. Jet only works with Access databases — it doesn't work with other ODBC databases, such as SQL Server, Oracle, and others. The current version of Jet is 4.0 (also in Access 2000 and 2002). When you installed Access, the installation program created several registry settings for the Jet engine. You can use the Registry Editor to examine and even change these settings for Access. However, we highly recommend that you do not change the setting in the Microsoft Windows registry.

Using Jet, you can build an Access user profile that is comprised of a special set of Window's registry keys, which will override the standard Access and Jet database engine settings.

To join an existing workgroup, follow these steps:

1. Activate the Workgroup Administrator program from the Tools ➪ Security menu.

2. The Workgroup Administrator dialog box displays the current workgroup (refer back to Figure 34-10). Click the Join button to select a workgroup file. If you aren't sure of the filename, click the Browse button to display a File dialog box in which to locate the workgroup file.

3. A prompt displays so that you can confirm or cancel joining the workgroup. Select OK and then select Exit to close the Workgroup Administrator.

Working with users

Every time a user opens an Access (Jet) database, Jet must identify the user opening the database. In Access, security is always enabled — regardless of whether or not you have explicitly created a workgroup for your database. If you have not defined a workgroup, Jet assumes that any user who opens the database is the Admin user. When a new workgroup is created, Access automatically creates a default user named Admin. The Admin user automatically receives full permissions to all objects in the database. Obviously, when you secure a database, you don't want everyone to be able to open the database with full permissions on all objects, so you must create additional users for the workgroup.

Adding and deleting user accounts

To add, delete, and edit user information, you use the User and Group Accounts dialog box (see Figure 34-12). To open the User and Group Accounts dialog box, select Tools ➪ Security ➪ User and Group Accounts ... from the Access menu. The Users tab of the User and Group Accounts dialog box consists of two sections: User and Group Membership. You use the User section to create and maintain user names and passwords. You use the Group Membership section to assign users to user groups. Assigning users to groups is discussed in detail later in this chapter.

To fully secure your database with users and groups, you should generally follow these steps:

1. Create a new user.

2. Add the new user to the Admins group.

3. Remove the Admin user from the Admins group.

4. Assign all object ownerships to the new user.

Figure 34-12: Creating and maintaining users in the User and Group Accounts dialog box.

When you create a user, you supply the user name and a personal identifier. Jet then combines these two items and processes them in a special algorithm, producing a unique security ID (SID). It is this SID that Jet uses to recognize users. In order to re-create a user in the workgroup, you need to know the user name and the personal ID (PID) that was used to create the user. Consequently, you should always write down and store all names and PIDs of users that you create in a safe place.

To create a new user in a workgroup, follow these steps:

1. Open the database Chap34Start.mdb.

2. Select Tools ➪ Security ➪ User and Group Accounts to display the User and Group Accounts dialog box.

3. Select the New button in the User section to display the New User/Group dialog box (see Figure 34-13).

Figure 34-13: Jet combines the User Name and Personal ID to create a unique SID for the user.

4. Enter the name **Student1** for the Name, and enter a unique Personal ID of **1234**. (You can enter any appropriate information into these two fields, if you don't want to use these example names.) Write this information down and store it in a safe place; you will need it if you have to re-create the user in the workgroup.

5. Select OK to save the new user.

After you have created the new user, Student1, you can assign Group Memberships and/or a password for the user. Notice that Student1 is automatically a member of the Users group. Any new member must at least belong to this group. You can make Student1 a member of the Admins group by simply selecting the Add button in the Group Membership section.

Caution To fully secure your database, you must remove all permissions for the Admin user, found under the Tools ⇨ Security ⇨ User and Group Permissions menu. (Defining Group Permissions is covered later in this chapter.) All Admin users share the same SID in all workgroups, on all machines. If you don't remove the permissions for the Admin user, an unauthorized user using a different workgroup can open the database as the Admin user with all permissions of the Admin user. The Admin user can't be deleted, so the Admin user account needs to be adjusted accordingly.

If you want to delete the user Student1 that you just created, follow these steps:

1. Select Tools ⇨ Security ⇨ User and Group Accounts to display the User and Group Accounts dialog box.

2. From the User Name drop-down list, select the User Student1.

3. Click the Delete button to delete the selected user.

Creating and changing user passwords

Any user who is a member of the Admins group can remove a password from any user account. A user who is a not a member of the Admins group can change his or her own password. However, a user who is not a member of the Admins group cannot change or create a password for any other user.

Caution

When Access opens and a password has been assigned to any user, the Logon Dialog box displays (refer back to Figure 34-7).

If no passwords are assigned to any of the users, however, Access will automatically open, using the Admin user. This means that any additional users that you create in Security will *not* be able to set a password. To correct this, you will need to create a password for the Admin user. Then exit from Access and restart Access, logging on as the user whose password you want to change.

To create or change the Admin password, follow these steps:

1. Open the database Chap34Start.mdb.

2. Select Tools ⇨ Security ⇨ User and Group Accounts.

Caution

Make sure that the user name selected is Admin (not Student1 that you created earlier).

3. Click the Change Logon Password tab (see Figure 34-14).

4. Because no password has been assigned to Admin, leave the Old Password field blank.

Figure 34-14: The Change Logon Password tab of the User and Group Accounts dialog box. Notice that the name is "Admin" and can't be changed.

Tip

If you are logging on as the Admin user after you have assigned a password, or if a password exists for the user that you logged on as, enter it in the Old Password field. If no password is assigned to the user, leave the Old Password field blank.

5. Move to the New Password field and enter the new password **Admin** (or any other password that you want to assign—remember that Access's security is case-sensitive) in the New Password field. Access *won't* show you the word that you are typing; rather, it shows an asterisk for each character that you type.

6. Move to the Verify field and enter the new password **Admin** again. (Again, remember that Access's security is case-sensitive.) Each character is replaced with an asterisk.

7. Click the Apply button to save the new password for the Admin user.

8. Click OK to close the User and Group Accounts dialog box.

Tip

After you have created a password for the user, you will have to exit from Access and restart Access for the changes to take effect. Simply closing the database and opening it again won't activate the security changes (such as assigning a password to Admin) that you made.

The Logon dialog box will not display if no passwords have been set for any users.

Users can't create or change passwords for other users, regardless of their permission settings.

Any user who is a member of Admins can clear the password of another user, so that user can log on if he or she has forgotten his or her password.

To change another person's password, you will have to start Access and open the database by logging on as the user whose password you want to change.

Working with groups

Groups are collections of users. A user may belong to one or more groups. You use groups to organize multiple users together who will be granted the same object permission privileges. You can then define object permissions to the group once, versus having to assign them individually for each user. When you create a new user, you simply add the user to the group that has the object permission privileges that the new user should have.

For example, you may have a number of users in a credit department and in a sales department. If you want to allow all of these users to look at a customer's credit history but restrict the sales staff to viewing only basic customer information, you have the following options:

✦ Create an individual user account for each user in each department and assign object permissions for each user.

✦ Allow all users in the credit department to log on as one user, and allow all users in the sales department to log on as a different user. You can then restrict the object permissions for each of these two users.

✦ Create an individual user account for each user in each department, and create a group account for each department. You can then make the permissions assignments for each of the two groups and place each user into his or her respective group to inherit the group's permissions.

Although creating a unique user account and assigning specific permissions to each user is a valid scenario, it is an administrator's nightmare. If policy dictates that one of the departments needs to have permissions added or revoked, the change has to be made to each of the users' accounts in that department.

The second method is straightforward and simple but presents many problems. If a user transfers from one department to another, he knows the user names and passwords for both departments and may be able to retrieve data that he is no longer authorized to view. In addition, if an employee leaves, the user name and password need to be changed, and each user of the workgroup has to be made aware of the change. In a multi-user environment, creating a unique user account for each user and then grouping them accordingly is a much better solution.

With the third option, the change can be made to the department group once, and all users inherit the new permission settings.

Adding and deleting groups

Just as Access automatically creates an Admin user in all new workgroups, it also automatically creates two groups: Users and Admins. Every user account in the system belongs to the Users group; you can't remove a user from the Users group. The Admins group is the all-powerful, super-user group. Users of the Admins group have the ability to add and delete user and group accounts, as well as to assign and remove permissions for any object for any user or group in the workgroup. In addition, a member of the Admins group has the ability to remove other user accounts from the Admins group. For this reason, you need to carefully consider which users you allow to be a member of the Admins group. The Admins group and the Users group are permanent groups; they can never be deleted.

Tip   Access doesn't enable you to remove all users from the Admins group; one user must belong to the Admins group at all times (the default is the user named Admin). If you were allowed to remove all users from the Admins group, you could set up security so tight that you would never be able to bypass it yourself! In general, when securing a database, you should place only one user and one backup user in the Admins group.

Note   Unlike the Admin user's SID, which is identical in every Access workgroup, the Admins group's SIDs are not identical from workgroup to workgroup, so unauthorized users using a workgroup other than the one that you used to define security can't access your database as a member of the Admins group. The Users group's SIDs are the same throughout all workgroups, however, so you need to remove all permissions for the Users group. If you don't remove permissions from the Users group, any user in any workgroup can open your database with the Users group's permissions.

To create a new group named *Sales,* follow these steps:

1. Open Access and then open the Chap34Start.mdb database and log in with the Admin user name and Admin password. Then select Tools ➪ Security ➪ User and Group Accounts to display the User and Group Accounts dialog box.

2. Select the Groups tab.

3. Select the New button to display the New User/Group dialog box (see Figure 34-15).

Figure 34-15: Jet uses the group name and personal identifier to create a unique SID for a group, just as it does for user accounts.

4. Just as you do to create users, enter the group name **Sales** and a personal ID of **Dept405**. (If you aren't following along with this example, you can enter your own group name and personal ID.) Also, just as before, write down this information and put it in a safe place because you will need it if you ever need to re-create the group.

5. Select OK to save the new group.

6. After this is complete, you can select OK in the User and Group Accounts dialog box to save your work.

If, at a later time, you want to delete the Sales group that you just created, follow these steps:

1. Select Tools ➪ Security ➪ User and Group Accounts ... to display the User and Group Accounts dialog box.

2. Select the Groups tab (refer to Figure 34-15).

3. From the drop-down list, select the Sales group to delete.

4. Select the Delete button to delete the selected group.

Assigning and removing group members

Assigning users to and removing users from groups is a simple process. You use the Users tab on the User and Group Accounts dialog box to add to and remove users from a group. You may place any user in any group, and a user may belong to more than one group. You cannot remove a user from the Users group nor can you remove all users from the Admins group — you must always have at least one user in the Admins group.

To add the user Student1 to the new group Sales, follow these steps:

1. Open Chap34Start. Select Tools ⇨ Security ⇨ User and Group Accounts to display the User and Group Accounts dialog box.

2. From the User Name drop-down list, select the user Student1 to modify her group assignments.

3. To assign the user Student1 to the group Sales, select the Sales group in the Available Groups list and select the Add button (see Figure 34-16). The Sales group displays in the Member Of list.

4. Select OK to save the new group assignments.

Figure 34-16: Assigning users to groups makes controlling object permissions much easier for the system administrator.

To remove the user Student1 from the group Sales, follow these steps:

1. Select Tools ⇨ Security ⇨ User and Group Accounts to display the User and Group Accounts dialog box.

Caution   Make sure that the user name selected is Student1 (not Admin).

2. Select the group Sales in the Member Of list and select the Remove button. The Sales group no longer displays in the Member Of list.

3. Select OK to save the new group assignments.

4. Because Jet uses the same SIDs for all Admin user accounts throughout all workgroups, you always need to remove the Admin user from the Admins group when securing a database. Figure 34-16 shows that the user Student1 has been added to the Sales group. Notice that Student1 is a member of two groups: Users and Sales. Before leaving this section, assign Student1 to the Admins group so that you can use this example later in this chapter.

The only remaining task is to set the appropriate object permissions for the Users and Sales groups.

Securing objects by using permissions

After you have defined your users and groups, you must determine the appropriate object permissions for each group. Permissions control who can view data, update data, add data, and work with objects in Design view. Permissions are the heart of the Jet security system and can be set only by a member of the Admins group, by the owner of the object (see the next section), or by any user who has Administrator permission for an object.

Setting an object's owner

Every object in the database has an owner. The *owner* is a user account in the workgroup that is designated to always have Administrator rights to the object. Administrator rights override the permissions defined for the logged-on user or defined for any of the user's groups. You can designate one user to be the owner of all the objects in a database, or you can assign an owner to individual objects.

Access queries require special consideration when assigning owners to objects. When creating a query, you can set the Run Permissions property of the query to either User's or Owner's (see Figure 34-17). When a password is defined for a workgroup, Run Permissions is automatically set to User's. Setting Run Permissions to User's limits the users of the query to viewing only the data that their security permissions permit. If you want to enable users to view or modify data for which they do not have permissions, you can set the Run Permissions property to Owner's. When the query is run with the Owner's permissions (WITH OWNERACCESS OPTION in an SQL statement), users inherit the permissions of the owner of the query. These permissions are applicable only to the query and not to the entire database.

Tip   When a query's Run Permissions property is set to Owner's, only the owner can make changes to the query. If this restriction poses a problem, you may want to set the owner of the query to a group rather than to a user account. Note that only the owner of an OwnerAccess query can change the query's owner.

Note   If you haven't assigned passwords to Admin or other users, the user is automatically assumed to be Admin and the query's Run Permissions property is set to Owner's.

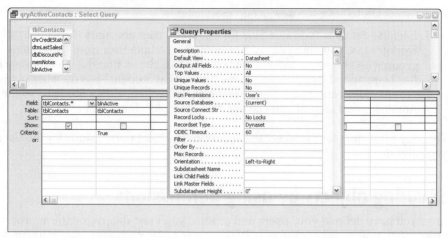

Figure 34-17: Setting a query's Run Permissions determines which users can run the query or modify the query.

To change the owner of any object in the database, follow these steps:

1. Select Tools ⇨ Security ⇨ User and Group Permissions to display the User and Group Permissions dialog box.

2. Select the Change Owner tab (see Figure 34-18).

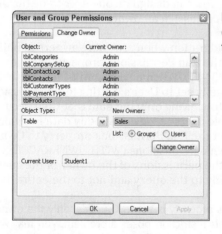

Figure 34-18: Transferring ownership of one or more tables from the Admin user to the Sales group.

3. Select the object (or objects) whose ownership you want to transfer. You can select the type of objects to display by changing the Object Type field.

4. Select the user or group that you want to make the owner of the selected object. To select a group name, first select the List: Groups radio button.

5. Select the Change Owner button to change the object's owner to the selected user or group.

Note Each object in a database has an owner. The database itself also has an owner. You can view the owner of the database by selecting Database from the Object Type drop-down list. You can't change an object's owner by using Access's interface. The only way to change a database's owner is to log on as the user that you want to make the owner of the database, create a new database, and then import the original database into the new database by using the File ➪ Get External Data ➪ Import menu option. When you import a database, the current user is assigned as the new owner of the database and all of its database objects. This is essentially what the Security Wizard (discussed later in this chapter) does for you.

Setting object permissions

Object permissions are the heart of Jet security. You can set one or more object permissions at a time for a user or group. When assigning permissions, you must keep in mind that some permissions automatically imply other permissions. For example, if you assign a user Read Data permission for a table, the Read Design permission is also granted because a table's design must be available to access the data. A more complex example is assigning permission for Insert Data — this automatically grants permission for Read Data and Read Design.

An object's permission assignments are persistent until one of the following conditions occurs:

✦ A member of the Admins group changes the object's permissions.

✦ The object is saved with a new name by using the Save As command from the File menu.

✦ The object is cut and pasted in the Database window.

✦ The object is imported or exported.

If any of the preceding actions occurs, all permissions for the manipulated object are lost and you will need to reassign them. When you perform any of these actions, you are actually creating a new object. Access assigns default permissions for each object type.

There are two ways that permissions can be granted to a user:

✦ **Explicit permissions** are permissions that are granted directly to a user. When you manually assign a permission to a user, no other user's permissions are affected.

✦ **Implicit permissions** are permissions that are granted to a group. All users belonging to a group inherit the permissions of that group.

Note Because permissions can be assigned implicitly and because some permissions grant other permissions (Insert Data, Read Data, and Read Design permissions), users may be able to grant themselves permissions that they do not currently have. Because of this possibility, you must plan carefully when assigning permissions to groups of users and to individual users.

To assign or revoke a user's permissions for an object, follow these steps:

1. Select Tools ➪ Security ➪ User and Group Permissions ... to display the User and Group Permissions dialog box. Select the Permissions tab.

2. In the Object Type drop-down list, select the type of object whose permissions you want to change.

3. In the User/Group Name list box, select the user or group account that you want to modify. To see a list of all Groups, click the List: radio button in the Name section.

4. In the Object Name list box, select the object (or objects) that you want to modify.

5. In the Permissions grouping section, select or unselect the permissions check boxes for the object(s).

6. Select Apply to save the permission assignments.

Remember that Admin user SIDs are identical throughout all workgroups. So after you assign Administer permissions to a specific user, you need to remove all permissions for the Admin user in order to secure your database. Figure 34-19 shows the Admin user's permissions being revoked for all tables in the database. Notice that all checkboxes have been cleared for all tables. Clearing the checkboxes prevents an Admin user from doing anything with table objects. You must repeat the process for each Object type until the Admin user has no permissions for any object.

Figure 34-19: Removing all permissions for the Admin user is critical to securing your database.

Setting default object permissions

You can create default permission assignments for each type of object in a database. These default permissions are assigned when you create new objects in the database. You set the default permissions just as you set them for any other object's permissions. You select the user or group to assign the default permissions, but you do not select a specific object name. Instead, select the first item in the Object Name list that is enclosed in <> and begins with "New." When you select the Object Type Table, for example, you select <New Tables/Queries> in the Object Name list. When you assign permissions for users and groups to these <New> items, the permissions are used as defaults for all new objects of that type.

Caution   When removing default permissions for table objects, make sure that users have the necessary permissions to create new tables. Otherwise, users will not be able to execute make-table queries.

Setting database permissions

Just as objects in a database have permissions, the database itself also has its own permissions. Selecting Database from the Object Type drop-down list will display the database permissions that can be modified (see Figure 34-20). The database permissions enable you to control who has administrative rights to the entire database, who can open the database exclusively (locking out other users), and who can open or run the database.

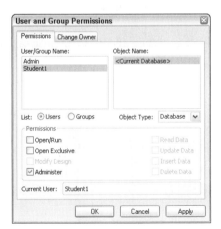

Figure 34-20: Assigning permissions for the entire database.

Securing your database for distribution: A basic approach

If you are securing a database for distribution, setting up detailed security for multiple users for all the objects in your database may not be important to you. Often, the only concern with shipping a secured database is protecting your development investment by securing the design of the application's objects and code. If you need this type of protection, you can distribute your application as an .MDE file (see the section "Protecting Visual Basic Code"). Another method is to follow these steps:

1. Create a workgroup to distribute with your database.

2. Remove the Admin user from the Admins group.

3. Remove all permissions for the Users group.

4. Remove all design permissions for the Admin user for all objects in the database.

5. Do not supply a password for the Admin user.

Remember that if you do not specify a password for the Admin user, Access will log on all users as the Admin user. Because the Admin user has no rights to the design of any object, users cannot access objects or code in Design view.

Table 34-1 summarizes the permissions that you can assign.

Table 34-1
Summary of Assignable Permissions

Permission	Permits a User To	Applies To
Open/Run	Open a database, form, report, or run a macro.	Databases, forms, reports, and or macros
Open Exclusive	Open a database with exclusive access.	Databases only
Read Design	View objects in Design view.	Tables, queries, forms, macros, and modules
Modify Design	View and change the design of objects, or delete them.	Tables, queries, forms, macros, and modules
Administer	For databases, set database password, replicate a database, and change start-up properties. For database objects, have full access to objects and data, including the ability to assign permissions.	Databases, tables, queries, forms, reports, macros, and modules
Read Data	View data.	Tables and queries
Update Data	View and modify but not insert or delete data.	Tables and queries
Insert Data	View and insert but not modify or delete data.	Tables and queries
Delete Data	View and delete but not modify or insert data.	Tables and queries

Using the Access Security Wizard

Access includes the Security Wizard tool to assist you in securing your database. The Security Wizard makes it easy for you to select the objects to secure. It then creates a new database containing secured versions of the selected objects. The Security Wizard assigns the currently logged-in user as the owner of the objects in the new database and removes all permissions from the Users group for those objects. The original database is not modified in any way. Only members of the Admins group and the user who ran the Security Wizard have access to the secured objects in the new database.

Tip
When you use the Security Wizard, make sure that you are logged in as the user that you want to become the new database's owner. You must already belong to the Admins group and you cannot log in as Admin. If you log in as Admin, Access will report an error when you attempt to run the Security Wizard. If you receive this error, simply log in as another Admins group user.

To start the Security Wizard, log into the database as a user who is a member of the Admins group. Then select Tools ➪ Security ➪ User-Level Security Wizard.

Follow these steps to create and open the AAASecureWizard database.

Note
These steps assume that you have created the user Student1 and assigned the user to the Admins group.

1. Exit Access and open the folder that contains Chap34Start.mdb. Copy this file and name the new copy AAA*SecureWizard.mdb*.

2. Start Access and open the AAASecureWizard database. When Access attempts to open the database, the Logon dialog box displays. The Logon dialog box displays automatically because the AAASecureWizard database inherited its permissions from the original database (Chap34Start).

3. Enter **Student1** in the Name field and select OK. (The user Student1 has no assigned password.) Access opens the AAASecureWizard database.

4. Select Tools ➪ Security ➪ User-Level Security Wizard from the menu to start the wizard.

The wizard displays a message advising you that you will need to use the existing workgroup information file, or it can create a new one for the current open database (see Figure 34-21). Select Create a new workgroup information file and click the Next button.

When you select Create a new workgroup information file, the next screen, shown in Figure 34-22, asks you for the filename for the new file, a Workgroup ID number (WID)—which you should write down and save, and optionally, your name and company.

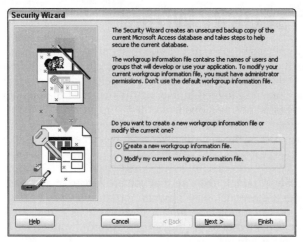

Figure 34-21: The Security Wizard helps jump-start your security implementation.

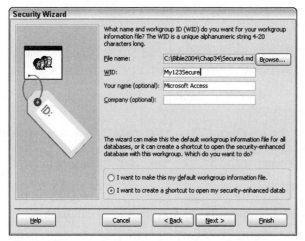

Figure 34-22: Assigning a unique WID and name to new workgroup information file.

When the new workgroup information file screen appears, it automatically assigns a random 20-character string of numbers and letters to the WID (Workgroup ID) field. You can change this WID to any value.

As Figure 34-22 shows, you can choose to make this the new default workgroup file for all databases (not recommended), or have Access create a shortcut to use this file only for this database (default). Selecting the option to create a shortcut associates this file with only one database. Click the Next button to display the next screen of the wizard.

The next screen of the wizard, shown in Figure 34-23, lets you select the objects to secure. By default, the wizard secures all objects in the database. If you deselect an object type (such as Tables or Forms), none of the objects of that type are exported to the secured database. If you do not want to restrict security permissions for a set of objects but still want those objects included in the new secured database, be sure to select the objects in the wizard. Later on, modify the user and group permissions for those objects in the new secured database. When you are satisfied with your object selections, select the Next button to continue.

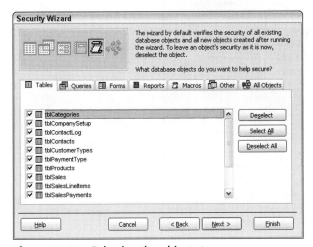

Figure 34-23: Selecting the objects to secure.

The next screen of the wizard, shown in Figure 34-24, asks you to create an optional security group account for a series of group actions. These include:

- ✦ **Backup Operators:** Can open the database exclusively for backing up and compacting.

- ✦ **Full Data Users:** Can edit data, but not alter design.

- ✦ **Full Permissions:** Has full permissions for all database objects, but can't assign permissions.

- ✦ **New Data Users:** Can read and insert data only (no edits or deletions).

- ✦ **Project Designers:** Can edit data and objects, and alter tables or relationships.

- ✦ **Read-Only Users:** Can read data only.

- ✦ **Update Data Users:** Can read and update, but can't insert or delete data or alter design of objects.

Check all of the optional security groups displayed in the wizard screen. After you have selected all groups, select the Next button to continue.

Notice that the next page of the wizard, shown in Figure 34-25, lets you choose to grant permissions to the Users group (the default is no permissions). By selecting Yes, you are able to assign rights to all object types in the database. Figure 34-25 shows this page with the Yes option selected. However, you should select the default choice: No — the Users group should not have any permissions. Select the Next button to continue to the next wizard screen.

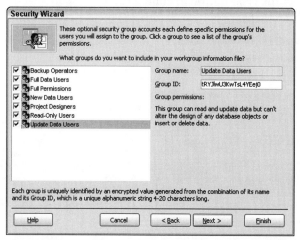

Figure 34-24: Additional optional security groups for the database.

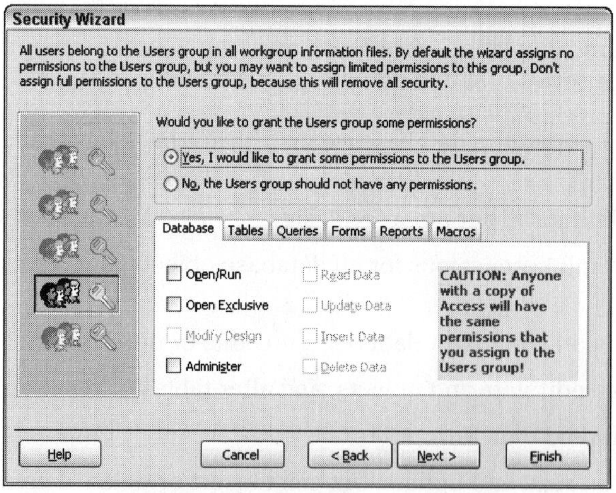

Figure 34-25: Choosing whether or not to assign permissions to the Users group.

Caution   If you decide to grant any permissions to the Users group, you should be aware that anyone with a copy of Access will have the same permissions that you assign to this group. Essentially, you are exposing the database to a security breach if you assign rights to this group.

The next page, shown in Figure 34-26, lets you add users to the workgroup information file. To add a user, enter the name and password information in the appropriate fields and select the Add a New User button.

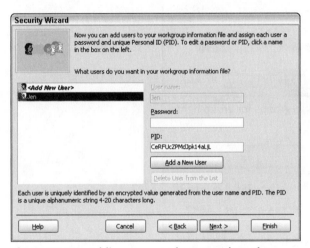

Figure 34-26: Adding users and passwords to the workgroup information file.

As Figure 34-26 shows, you can also remove users from the list by simply selecting their name from the list box on the left and selecting the Delete User from the List button. Select the Next button to continue.

The next wizard screen to display, shown in Figure 34-27, enables you to assign users to groups in your workgroup information file. If you added optional groups from the previous page (as shown in Figure 34-24), you can assign a user to any of these groups by checking the appropriate check box. To assign rights to a user, simply select the user from the drop-down list and then assign that user to groups using the check boxes. By default, all users, except the person creating the wizard, are assigned to new groups. Click the Next button to continue on to the next screen.

The last page of the wizard displays, as shown in Figure 34-28. In this screen, the Security Wizard asks you to provide a name for the old, and now unsecure, database. The default name is the same name as the current database with the extension .bak. Select the Finish button to finish creating the new secure database.

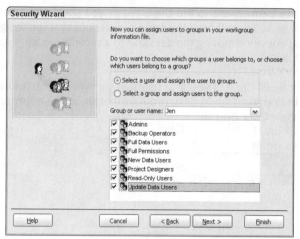

Figure 34-27: Adding users to groups for group rights.

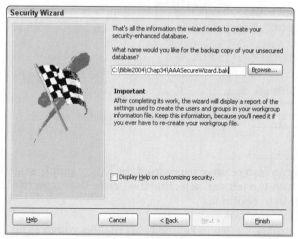

Figure 34-28: In the Final wizard screen, the Security Wizard asks you to assign a name for the old database.

Technically, the Security Wizard doesn't make any modifications to the current database; rather, it makes a backup copy by using the name that you specify and creates an *entirely new* database with secured objects. However, the new database is given the name of the original database.

Caution   When you distribute your secured application, be sure to distribute the database that the Security Wizard created for you.

When the Security Wizard has finished creating the new database, it generates a report called *One-Step Security Wizard Report*, as shown in Figure 34-29. The report contains all of the settings used to create the users and groups in the workgroup information file. You should keep this information. You will need it if you ever have the need to re-create the workgroup file.

Caution   If you click the Finish button and Access finds any problems, it won't create the security database or the backup that you requested. Generally, you will get this error if you have created the database and logged on as a user that secured the table and then re-logged on as another user to secure it. This wizard works best with databases that have not had any previously defined security.

Generally, making a copy of the original database and working with the secured database is a good idea. If you make changes to the original database, you will need to run the Security Wizard again to create a secured version of the database. In addition, making a copy of the original database and then removing it from development helps prevent accidentally distributing the unsecured database.

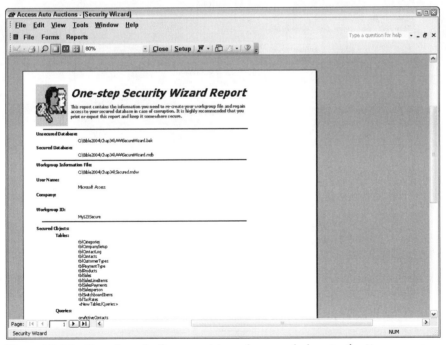

Figure 34-29: Choosing whether or not to assign permissions to the Users group.

Encrypting a Database

When security is of utmost importance, one final step that you need to take is to *encrypt* the database. Although it takes a great deal of skill (far more than the average computer user — or developer — possesses), it is possible to view the structure of an unencrypted database. A skilled hacker may use this information to reconstruct SIDs and gain full access to your secured database.

Encrypting a database makes using such tools to gain any useful information about the database virtually impossible. Only the database owner or a member of the Admins group (or a really good computer hacker) can encrypt or decrypt a database.

To encrypt a database, follow these steps:

1. Open Access, but do not open a database. Select Tools ➪ Security ➪ Encrypt/Decrypt Database (see Figure 34-30).

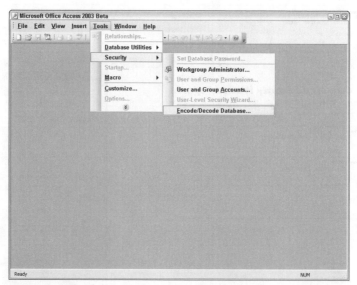

Figure 34-30: Encrypting a database helps secure it from highly skilled hackers.

2. Select the database to encrypt from the Encrypt/Decrypt dialog box.

3. Provide a name for the new encrypted database.

Access doesn't modify the original database when it encrypts it. Rather, Access creates a clone of the database and encrypts the clone. Just like when using the

Security Wizard, you should make a backup copy of the original database and store it somewhere safe to prevent accidentally distributing the unencrypted database. Remember that in a world of rapidly changing data, your backup will rapidly become out of date.

When encrypting a database, however, be aware of the following drawbacks:

✦ Encrypted databases don't compress from their original size when used with compression programs, such as WINZIP or the ODE Setup Wizard. Encryption modifies the way that the data is stored on the hard drive so compression utilities have no effect.

✦ Encrypted databases suffer some performance degradation (up to 15 percent). Depending on the size of your database and the speed of your computer, this degradation may be imperceptible.

Note   Encryption is performed in addition to securing a database. A secure database is one that is secured using users, groups, and permissions. Simply encrypting a database does nothing to secure the database for general Access users.

Decrypting a Database

You can decrypt a previously encrypted database. To decrypt a database, simply follow these steps (which are similar to the encrypting process):

1. Start Access but do not open a database. Select Tools ⇨ Security ⇨ Encrypt/Decrypt Database.

2. Select the database to decrypt from the Encrypt/Decrypt dialog box.

3. Provide a name for the new decrypted database.

Protecting Visual Basic Code

Although setting user-level security allows you to restrict access to tables, forms, and reports in your database, it does not prevent access to the Visual Basic code stored in modules. You control access to the Visual Basic code in your application by creating a password for the Visual Basic project that you want to protect. When you set a database password for a project, users are prompted to enter the password each time they attempt to view the Visual Basic code in the database.

Note   A Visual Basic project refers to the set of standard and class modules (the code behind forms and reports) that are part of your Access database (.mdb) or Access project (.adp).

1. Open any standard module in the database. For this example, open the basSalesFunctions modules in Chap34Start.mdb. When you open the basSalesFunctions module, the Visual Basic Editor displays.

2. In the Visual Basic Editor, select Tools ➪ Access Auto Auctions Properties. The Access Auto Auctions — Project Properties dialog box displays.

3. Select the Protection tab in the Project Properties dialog box. Check the option labeled "Lock project for viewing."

4. In the Password field, type the password that you want to use to secure the project (see Figure 34-31). For this example, use the password *bible*. Access does *not* display the password; rather, it shows an asterisk (*) for each letter.

Figure 34-31: Creating a project password restricts users from viewing the application's Visual Basic code.

5. In the Confirm Password field, type the password again. This security measure ensures that you don't mistype the password (because you can't see the characters that you type) and mistakenly prevent everyone, including you, from accessing the database.

6. Click OK to save the password.

After you save and close the project, any user who attempts to view the application's Visual Basic code must enter the password. Access prompts for the project password only once per session.

A more secure method of securing your application's code, forms, and reports is to distribute your database as an .MDE file. When you save your database as an .MDE file, Access compiles all code modules (including form modules), removes all editable source code, and compacts the database. The new .MDE file contains no source code but continues to work because it contains a compiled copy of all of your code. Not only is this a great way to secure your source code, it also enables you to distribute databases that are smaller (because they contain no source code) and always keep their modules in a compiled state.

Cross-Reference   See Chapter 36 to learn how to create an .MDE file.

Preventing Virus Infections

Implementing a good user-level security scheme will protect your database from unauthorized access to the information or objects in your database. User-level security does not, however, protect the physical database file from malicious macro virus attacks.

You probably have had experience at some point with a virus attack on your computer. Or most likely, you know someone who has. It goes without saying that it is imperative to install and run a virus scanning utility on your workstation. Even though you may be religious about keeping your virus scanner up to date, new viruses crop up all the time. Therefore, you have to be proactive about protecting your applications and sensitive data from exposure to these kinds of attacks.

When you run forms, reports, queries, macros, data access pages, and Visual Basic code in your application, Microsoft Office Access 2003 uses the Microsoft Jet Expression Service to scan the commands these objects execute to make sure that these commands are safe. Unsafe commands could allow a malicious user to hack into your hard drive or other resource in your environment. A malicious user could possibly delete files from your hard drive, alter the computer's configuration, or generally create all kinds of havoc in your workstation or even throughout your network environment.

The Microsoft Jet Expression Service checks its list of unsafe commands. When Access encounters one of the unsafe commands, it can block the command from execution. To tell Access to block these potentially unsafe commands, you must enable *sandbox mode*.

Tip   To review the list of unsafe commands, search Access help for "About Microsoft Jet Expression Service sandbox mode."

Enabling sandbox mode

Sandbox mode allows Access to block any of the commands in the unsafe list it encounters when running forms, reports, queries, macros, data access pages, and Visual Basic code. To enable sandbox mode, follow these steps:

1. Open Access, but do not open a database. Select Tools ➪ Macro ➪ Security. The Security dialog box displays, as shown in Figure 34-32.

2. In the Security dialog box, select the High or Medium option.

3. Select the OK button to close the Security dialog box.

4. Restart Access to apply the security change.

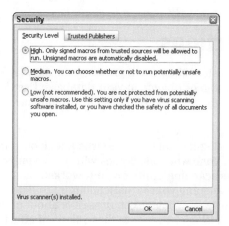

Figure 34-32: Enabling sandbox mode.

> **Note** When you enable sandbox mode, it applies to all Access users on the workstation.

The Security dialog box provides three levels of macro security:

✦ **High:** Macros must be digitally signed. Unsigned macros will not run. The status of the macro's digital signature is validated for digitally signed macros.

✦ **Medium:** The status of the macro's digital signature is validated for digitally signed macros. For unsigned macros, a prompt displays advising the user to enable the macro or to cancel opening the database.

✦ **Low:** Macros are not checked for digital signatures and no warning displays for unsigned macros.

A digital signature is an encrypted secure file that accompanies a macro or document. It confirms that the author is a trusted source for the macro or document. A digital signature is contained in a digital certificate. You, or your organization's IT department, can obtain a digital certificate through a commercial certification authority, like VeriSign, Inc. Search www.msdn.com for "Microsoft Root Certificate Program Members" to obtain information on how to obtain a digital certificate.

If you are sure of the integrity of your database, you can select the Low security setting. Digital signatures are generally implemented within large organizations that are willing to fund the added expense of purchasing and keeping digital signatures up to date. For most applications, however, you will probably use the Low setting.

If you or your organization has acquired a digital certificate, you can use it to digitally sign your Access project. To digitally sign your Access project, follow these steps:

1. Open the Access database to digitally sign. Select Tools ➪ Macro ➪ Visual Basic Editor from the Access menu. The Visual Basic Editor opens.

2. Select Tools ➪ Digital Signature from the Visual Basic Editor menu. The Digital Signature dialog box displays, as shown in Figure 34-33.

Figure 34-33: Digitally signing an Access project.

3. Select Choose. The Select Certificate dialog box displays, as shown in Figure 34-34.

4. Select the certificate to add to the Access project. Then select OK to close the Select Certificate dialog box.

5. Select OK to close the Digital Signature dialog box and save the security setting.

Figure 34-34: Choosing a digital certificate.

Note Do not sign your Access project until the application has been thoroughly tested and you do not expect to make any further changes to it. Modifying any of the code in the project will invalidate the digital signature.

Tip To prevent users from making unauthorized changes to the code in your project, be sure to lock the project and apply a project password.

With a full understanding of the Jet security model and how to manage it, you can create databases that protect your development investment and your users' data.

✦　　✦　　✦

Creating Help Systems

O ne item of an application that is often overlooked entirely is the inclusion of a comprehensive Help system. Creating a complete and useful Help system is a skill unto itself, and programmers often don't take the time to learn how to do it right. Understanding what makes a good Help system and how to create one can be a powerful tool in your development arsenal.

On the CD-ROM In this chapter, you will use the database file Chap35Start. mdb.

Understanding the Windows Help Structure

Great Help systems are more than just online documentation. A Help system needs to explain the how-to of your application in bits and pieces, and the user needs to be able to access a specific bit or piece of information related to the task at hand with minimum effort. In addition, these bits and pieces — called *topics* — need to be linked in a comprehensive web, enabling a user to easily travel from one related topic to another. Each topic can be linked to a form or control's Help Context Id property (see Figure 35-1) to provide instant access to the topic when the user presses F1 while the control or form has the focus.

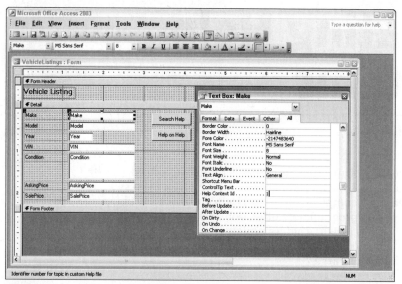

Figure 35-1: You can link Help topics to the form or control they relate to by using the Help Context Id property.

Help systems may consist of simple linked text topics, or they may contain graphics and multimedia to help educate the user. A good application of graphics in a Help system is the use of *hotspot graphics* to help explain an application's toolbars. Hotspot graphics, or *hypergraphics*, are graphic pictures that have links assigned to various regions of the graphic. These regions are often invisible; the user knows when the cursor is over a hotspot because the pointer turns into a pointing hand. When the user clicks the hotspot, the topic linked to the hotspot displays. When creating a hypergraphic of a toolbar, you can link a related topic to each tool button in the toolbar graphic. Then users can simply click the button that they want help on to display the appropriate Help topic, just as they would click the button on the toolbar.

The Help interface consists of numerous components, and understanding these components is key to mastering the task of designing great Help files, as well as getting the most out of using a Help file.

The Help Viewer

The Help Viewer is the application that displays the Help system. The Help Viewer contains three panes (see Figure 35-2):

> ✦ The Topic pane displays on the right side of the Help Viewer. This is where the topic information displays.

✦ The Navigation pane displays on the left side of the Help Viewer. You can customize this pane to display a table of contents, an index, a list of favorite Help topics, or a full-text search tab.

✦ The toolbar, which displays at the top of the viewer, allows users to display or hide the Navigation pane, or move forward to the next topic or back to the previous topic. Stop, Refresh, Locate, and Home buttons are also available.

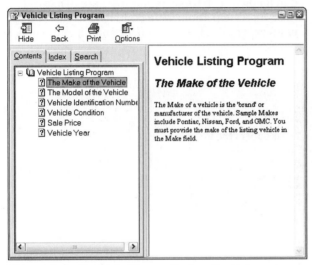

Figure 35-2: The Help Viewer displays the Help system.

You can customize the appearance of the Help Viewer to include or exclude the Index or Search tabs in the Navigation pane. However, every Help system must have a Contents tab. A Contents tab lists the topics that are available when a user clicks Help Topics in your application's Help menu, when a user clicks the Contents tab of any Help topic, or when he or she double-clicks your Help file in Windows Explorer. The Contents feature of a Help system is similar to the table of contents in a book.

The Contents tab

The Contents tab displays the Contents items in a collapsible outline format. Contents items that can be expanded are shown with a closed book icon. To expand a Contents item, select an item, and then select the Open button — or simply double-click the Contents item. When you expand a Contents item, the closed book icon changes to an open book icon, and the individual topics that can be viewed display. Each topic is preceded by a document icon. When users locate the items that they want help with, they can double-click the Help topic, or select it and click the

Display button to view the Help topic. To view a specific Help topic, select the Help Topic item, and then select the Display button — or just double-click the item. The Help Topic displays in the Help Topic pane.

The Topic pane

Help topics are the core element of a Help system. Each topic covered in your Help System should be contained in its own Help topic. Help topics are displayed in the Help Topic panes (see Figure 35-3). A Help Topic pane contains information specific to the topic, such as pertinent text, graphics, animation, or sound, and it may contain links to other topics.

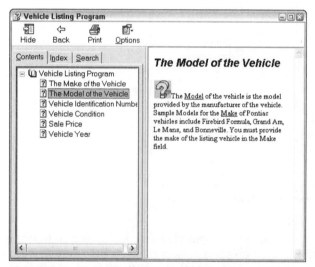

Figure 35-3: The Help Topic pane is where users of your Help system get the topical information that they need.

The Office 2003 Resource Kit includes Microsoft HTML Help Workshop. Microsoft HTML Help is an online Help authoring system based on Microsoft WinHelp 4.0. If you've used WinHelp or Help Workshop before, you will be familiar with many of the features of HTML Help and HTML Help Workshop.

Note   The Office 2003 Resource Kit is included in Microsoft Office Enterprise Edition 2003. Or, you can download it, free of charge, from the Microsoft Office Resource Kit Web site.

Like WinHelp, HTML Help uses a project file to combine topic, contents, index, image, and other source files into one compiled Help file. HTML Help also provides you with HTML Help Workshop, an authoring tool that makes it easy to view, manage, and edit your files in an enhanced user interface. Unlike WinHelp, HTML Help has no practical Help system limits. Help file size, topic size, contents entry limits, and keyword limits have all been (essentially) eliminated.

If you want even more control over how HTML Help is displayed and integrated into your solution, you can work directly with HTML Help Application Programming Interface (API) calls from your Visual Basic for Applications (VBA) code.

> **Tip** Implementing a Help button in Access requires that you use an API call to the HTML Help or WinHelp engine to display the Help topic.

Other Help tools included in the Office 2003 Resource Kit are

✦ The Answer Wizard Builder lets you add your own Help topics to the ones provided by the Microsoft Office Assistant.

✦ The HTML Help ActiveX control is used for creating Help pages on the Web.

These new tools greatly enhance the usability of the Help interface for the end user of your application.

Creating a Windows Help System

Creating Help systems for Windows involves the following:

✦ Write your Help topic files in HTML. You can use Microsoft Word or any authoring tool to create HTML files, as long as you create standard version 3.2 HTML source code.

✦ Create a Help project file (.hhp) to manage the interface objects that make up your Help system — topics, graphics, contents (.hhc), index (.hhk), and other source files — and to define the overall style of these objects.

✦ Create window definitions to define the style of window for displaying the Help information.

✦ Create a table of contents file for easy navigation to Help topics.

✦ Create an index file for indexing Help topics.

✦ Compile your Help file. (This is optional if you are using the HTML Help ActiveX control.)

✦ Test the Help system.

> **Tip** You don't need to include all of your Help topics in one Help file. The Help engine has the capability to use one index and one table of contents for multiple Help files, which is very useful when you have an application that consists of modular components. If the Help engine doesn't locate a referenced Help file on the end user's computer, that Help file's topics won't show up in the table of contents.

Creating Help topics

The most fundamental element in a Help file is the Help topic. The documents that you write are created by using a special formatting language known as *Hypertext Markup Language* (HTML). HTML topic files have an .htm or .html filename extension.

Although each Help topic or Web page that you write appears to be a document with text, graphics, or animated images on it, .htm files are actually text documents that have special HTML formatting codes. These codes, called *tags*, tell a browser how to display each page. Only the text that appears in a topic or Web page is actually in the .htm file. Any graphics, sounds, animated images, or other elements that appear are separate files that your HTML file points to. The browser copies or downloads the graphics, sounds, or other elements when it sees the tags telling it to do so.

Before you begin typing the descriptive text for your topics, you should define a list of all the topics that you want to include in your Help system. After you have created this list, organize it as best as possible (see Figure 35-4). This organization, in effect, creates a level 1 outline for your topics. After you have organized the topics, simply type the descriptive text below each topic. Creating your topics this way simplifies the effort in designing your topic structure.

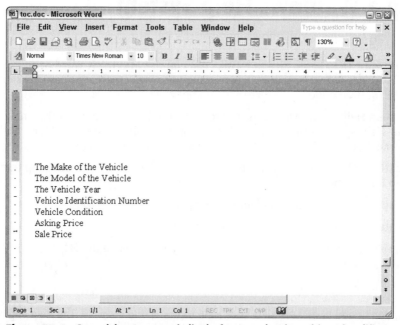

Figure 35-4: Organizing your topic list before you begin writing simplifies the design process.

The easiest way to write your Help system is to create a new HTML file for each Help topic. HTML Help is designed to work with multiple files, each containing a single topic. For larger Help systems, however, you may find it easier to develop one HTML file that contains all of the topics. By using the HTML Help Workshop, you can split the large file into individual HTML files later.

To create an HTML topic file, follow these steps:

1. Create a new document in Microsoft Word (or another product that supports HTML files).

2. Enter the text to be displayed for each topic.

3. Identify separate topic sections with a hard page break. You can create a hard page break in Microsoft Word by selecting Insert ➪ Break and then selecting Page Break.

4. Save the file as a Web page.

Tip
You can create a document template to use when creating your HTML files. A *template* is a file that contains all of the font, style, heading, and design elements that you use most frequently. You can distribute the template to all of the authors who will be creating the Help contents files.

Creating a Help project file

After you have written all of the Help contents files that you will use in your Help system, you can create an HTML Help Workshop project file. A Help project (.hhp) file contains information about the location of your HTML topic files, contents (.hhc) files, index (.hhk) files, image (.png, .jpg, .gif) files, and other files. Project files also contain Help window definitions and other options that customize the way that a Help system functions.

To create a Help project file, follow these steps:

1. Open the HTML Help Workshop.

2. Select File ➪ New ➪ Project. The New Project Wizard opens.

3. Follow the instructions on the wizard pages to begin creating the new project.

4. On the Existing Files page of the wizard, as shown in Figure 35-5, select the HTML files option to import your existing Help files into the project. The HTML Files page displays.

5. On the HTML Files page, shown in Figure 35-6, use the Add button to select the files to import. After you have selected all of the HTML files to include, select the Next button.

6. When the Finish page displays, select the Finish button to create the new project. The new project displays, as shown in Figure 35-7.

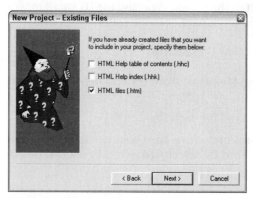

Figure 35-5: Using the New Project Wizard to import HTML files into a new project.

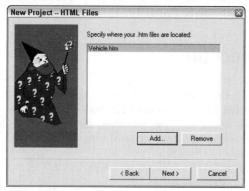

Figure 35-6: Selecting the HTML files to import into a new project.

When you create a new project, contents, or index file, the minimum necessary settings are added automatically. The project file is divided into sections; for example, [FILES] and [OPTIONS] are included in every Help project file. You can edit these sections by double-clicking the section title.

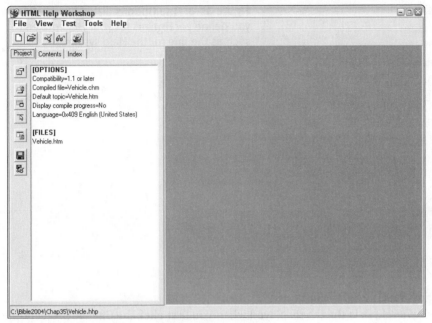

Figure 35-7: A new HTML Help Workshop project.

Adding graphics to a topic

Although most of your Help topics will consist primarily of text, it is often beneficial to include graphics in your Help topics. For example, if you use lots of buttons with images on them (such as toolbar images), you can display the picture with its Topic text to help the user associate the image with its function.

You can include the following types of graphics in your Help topics — .gif, .jpg, and .png. To insert a graphic in an HTML file using Microsoft Word, follow these steps:

1. Place the cursor where you want the graphic to appear in the topic.

2. Select Insert ➪ Picture ➪ From File from the menu.

3. Select the image file to insert.

Setting the Help project options

Your first task when creating a new Help project is to define the options for the project. Click the Change Project Options button on the HTML Help Workshop main screen to access the project Options dialog box (see Figure 35-8). The two main tabs that you need to be concerned with initially are the General and the Files tabs.

Figure 35-8: The Options dialog box is where you define parameters for your Help project, such as the title for the Help system.

Setting the General tab options

The General tab is the tab displayed when you first click the Change project options button. On the General tab, you can modify these settings:

✦ **Title.** This is the text string that appears in the title bar of your Help system. The words *Windows Help* are used if you leave this field blank and if the contents (.htm) file doesn't have a title specified. You should always provide a title specific to your Help program.

✦ **Default File.** This is the first HTML file to open in the Help system.

Setting the Files tab options

Clicking the Files tab on the HTML Help Workshop Options dialog box displays the page that you use to enter information about files associated with the current project (see Figure 35-9). The information that you supply on this tab is discussed in the following section, item by item. However, you need to be aware that you must specify the Contents file to use on this tab, or your Help system won't have Contents. Although you may not have created the Contents file yet, you may still specify the name of the Contents file that you plan to create (with full path), or you may create the Contents file first and then reopen the project and supply the name.

The information that you supply on the Files tab consists of the following:

✦ **Compiled file.** This is where you specify the name for your project when it compiles. You can name the file anything that you want, as long as it has the extension .chp. Prefixing the filename with a .\ causes the Help file to be created in the same directory as the HTML Help Workshop.

✦ **Log file.** You can create a text log file when your Help project is compiled by specifying a valid filename here. This log file contains the information printed to the screen during compilation. For small projects, you may not need a log file, so you can leave this box blank. For larger projects, however, you may want to create a log file so that you can review errors that you encounter when compiling the project.

✦ **Contents file.** You should always include a Contents for your Help project. Creating a Help Contents is discussed later in this chapter, but this is where you specify the full name and the path of the Contents file.

✦ **Index file.** You should also include an Index for your Help project. Creating a Help Index is discussed later in this chapter, but this is where you specify the full name and the path of the Index file. The specified Help Index must exist when you compile the Help file.

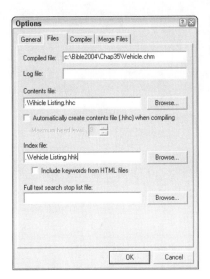

Figure 35-9: To include Contents in your Help file, you must specify the Contents filename here.

Defining windows

The Help Viewer is the three-paned window in which topics automatically appear. You never have to create a Help Viewer, but you can customize it. You can make changes to just one of the panes or to all of them. Window definitions change the size of the Help Viewer window, its position, its background color, and other attributes.

To specify the Help Viewer definition, follow these steps:

1. Select the Add/Modify Window Definitions button on the Project page. When you add the first window definition, a prompt displays, as shown in Figure 35-10, requesting the type of new window to define. Enter **Main** as the new type, and then click OK. The Window Types dialog box displays, as shown in Figure 35-11.

Figure 35-10: Adding the first window type to the Help project.

Figure 35-11: Defining the Main window type for the Help Viewer.

2. In the General tab, the Window Type field shows Main as the type that you specified in Step 1. In the Title bar text field, enter an appropriate title for the Main window.

3. In the Navigation Pane tab, select the check box labeled Window with Navigation Pane, Topic Pane, and Button.

4. Make sure that the Search Tab option and the Auto sync option are selected, as shown in Figure 35-12.

5. Click OK to save the window definition.

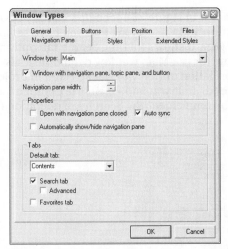

Figure 35-12: Selecting the display options for the window definition.

The HTML Help Workshop cross-checks the options that you selected for the new window definition with the Project Options. If the window definition contains any inconsistencies, the Resolve Window Definition Wizard displays, as shown in Figure 35-13.

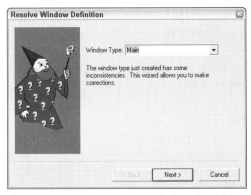

Figure 35-13: The Resolve Window Definition Wizard.

To use the wizard to resolve inconsistencies in your Help, follow these steps:

1. When the first screen in the Resolve Window Definition Wizard displays the name of the window definition that contains the inconsistencies, click the Next button to continue.

   The second wizard screen, shown in Figure 35-14, compares the options that you set for the window definition and the options that you have set in Project Options. In this example, the wizard shows that the Search tab option was selected in the Navigation pane for the Main window definition. It also shows that the Compile full-text Information option was not selected in Project Options. The wizard recommends that you implement the Compile full-text Information option in order to complement the Search tab definition for the Main window.

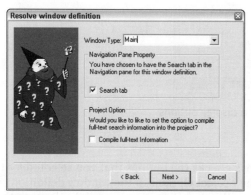

Figure 35-14: Resolving Search option inconsistencies.

2. If you agree with the wizard's recommendation, you can click the Compile full-text Information option in the wizard screen and then click the Next button to continue.

   The wizard then sets the option in Project Options so that additional new window definitions will include the full-text search feature.

Adding topic files to a project file

When you create a new project, you can automatically load existing files. If you create additional HTML files later, you can always add these to your project. You must supply at least one topic file in order to compile a Help project into a Help file. To add or remove topic files in a Help project, use the Add/Remove Topic Files button on the HTML Help Workshop main screen (see Figure 35-15).

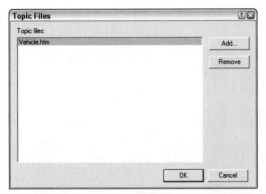

Figure 35-15: Use the Topic Files dialog box to add or remove topic files in your Help project.

To add topic files to your Help project, first select the Add/Remove Topic Files button to display the Topic Files dialog box. Then follow these steps:

1. Click the Add button.

2. Select the topic file that you want to add to the Help project.

3. Click the Open button to add the topic file to the project file. Files that you add to the project appear in the Help project definition script (see Figure 35-16).

To remove a topic file from your Help project, select the Add/Remove Topic Files button to display the Topic Files dialog box, and then follow these steps:

1. Select the filename that you want to remove from the Help project.

2. Click the Remove button.

Saving and compiling the project

In order to ensure that you are shipping a Help system without errors or broken links, you need to test your Help. In HTML Help Workshop, the Help project file compiles all of the necessary files into a compiled Help (.chm) file. When you compile a Help project, all of the included topic files, bitmap files, and Contents files are placed into one Help file with the .chm extension.

The compiled Help file can then be placed on your hard drive, a removable storage disk, a compact disc, a server location, an Internet location, or an intranet location.

During compilation, HTML Help Workshop uses the Help project (.hhp) file to determine how HTML topic files, contents (.hhc) files, index (.hhk) files, image (.jpg, .gif, .png) files, and any other elements that you have added to the project file will look in the single, compressed Help file. If any errors are found during the compilation, compiler messages are generated that point out the problems to the author.

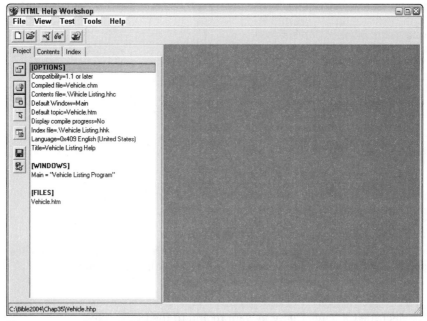

Figure 35-16: As you add files and change options, the text script that defines your Help project changes.

HTML Help Workshop performs these tasks during the compilation process:

- ✦ Reports missing topics or other errors in Contents and index files
- ✦ Reports broken links in topic, index, and Contents files
- ✦ Removes unnecessary white space or comments

To save and compile the project, select the Save all files and compile button on the Project page. As the project compiles, a progress report displays in the right pane of the HTML Help Workshop (see Figure 35-17).

Creating a table of contents

When you have finished adding all of the topic files that your Help project will use, you need to create a Contents file for your Help system. It is critical that you create a clear, concise, and comprehensive Contents file to make it easy for users to locate the topics that they need in order to get their job done.

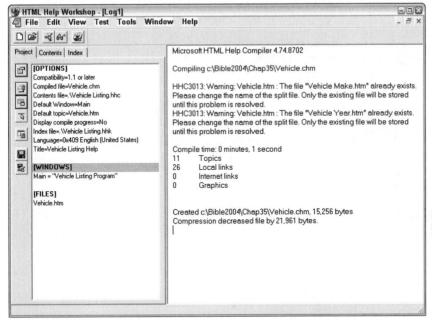

Figure 35-17: The right pane of the HTML Help Workshop displays the results of compilation.

Creating a new Help Contents file

Contents files are ASCII files saved with the .hhc extension. Contents files consist of specifications of three items:

✦ Headings

✦ Topics

✦ Commands

To create a new Contents file by using the HTML Help Workshop, follow these steps:

1. Select the Change Project Options button.

2. Select the Files tab.

3. Specify a filename for the new Contents file.

4. Select the Automatically Create Contents File (.hhc) When Compiling check box, as shown in Figure 35-18. In the Maximum Head Level field, click the maximum heading level for which you want entries generated in your Contents file. For example, if you select 3 for the maximum head level, entries are generated with <H1>, <H2>, and <H3> heading tags.

5. Save and compile the project. The new Contents items display on the Contents page, as shown in Figure 35-19.

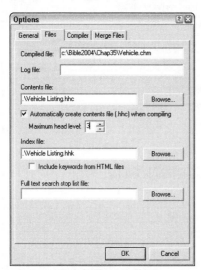

Figure 35-18: Automatically creating a Contents file.

Caution

If you make changes to a Contents file that has been automatically generated, you will lose those changes if you compile the project again. To prevent this, make sure that the Automatically Create Contents File When Compiling check box is cleared before you recompile.

Help Contents are just like tables of contents in books: They are essentially outlines. Headings appear with book pictures in the Help Contents. If the user clicks the book or the heading text, the Contents expands to show all items under the heading. When the HTML Help Workshop automatically creates the Contents file, it looks for text formatted as headings within the HTML files that you have included in the project. The hierarchy of the HTML file's styles becomes the hierarchy of the Contents items. For example, you have formatted your HTML file title as Heading 1, and you have formatted each topic under the title as Heading 2. When the HTML Help Workshop creates the Contents, it uses the Heading 1 items as Contents Headings, and the Heading 2 items as Page items under each respective heading.

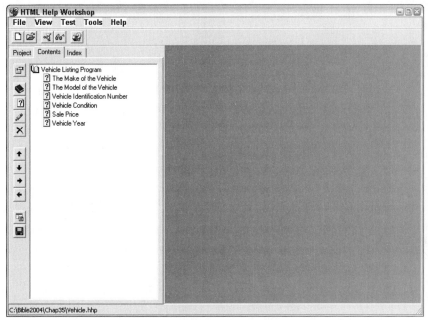

Figure 35-19: The Help system's Table of Contents.

Modifying the Contents items

You can add new Contents headings and pages to the ones that were automatically generated. To add another heading entry to the Contents, follow these instructions:

1. Position the cursor in the Contents page on the item immediately above the intended location for the new heading.

2. Select the Insert a heading button to add the heading above the selected item in the Contents page. The Table of Contents Entry dialog box displays (see Figure 35-20).

3. Enter a title for the new heading.

4. Select the Add button. The Path or URL dialog box displays, as shown in Figure 35-21.

5. Select the HTML file to use for the new heading, and then click OK. The filename displays in the Table of Contents Entry dialog box.

6. Click OK to create the heading.

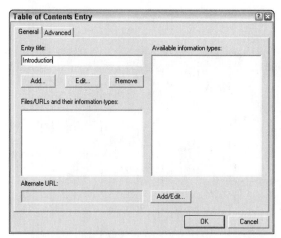

Figure 35-20: Defining a new Table of Contents heading.

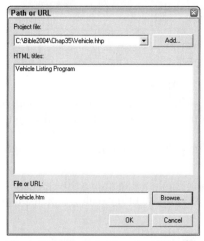

Figure 35-21: Selecting the HTML file for a new heading.

Creating a Help Index

Put yourself in the user's seat for a little while and ask yourself this question: If I needed to find this information, what keywords would I expect to find it under? In general, you should specify any and all keywords that a user may use to search for each topic.

Adding keywords to an index

Topic keywords are words that are listed in the index of a Help system. These keywords are used to quickly locate Topics; searching by keywords is faster than performing a full-text search. In addition, you can create keywords that don't even appear in the text of a topic, thereby allowing for many different ways to locate a topic of interest.

Consider using the following types of keywords:

✦ Nontechnical terms that are likely to occur to a beginning user.

✦ Technical terms that are likely to occur to an advanced user.

✦ Common synonyms for technical terms.

✦ Words that describe the topic in a general manner.

✦ Words that describe specific subjects within the topic.

✦ Inverted forms of keyword phrases, such as "combining Help files" and "Help files, combining."

To add a keyword to the Index, follow these steps:

1. Select the index tab. Select the Insert a Keyword button on the Index page. The Index Entry dialog box displays, as shown in Figure 35-22.

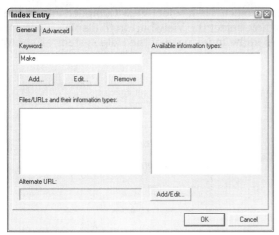

Figure 35-22: Adding a keyword to the Index.

2. Enter the keyword to include in the Keyword field, and then select the Add button. The Path or URL dialog box displays, as shown in Figure 35-23.

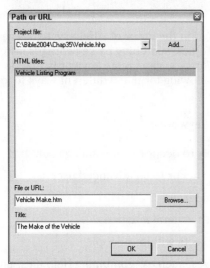

Figure 35-23: Selecting the HTML file source for the keyword.

3. Select the HTML file or files containing the information for the keyword. Then click OK. The Index Entry dialog box displays the selected filename.

4. Click OK to save the new keyword.

5. Compile and save the project. Then select View Compiled File. In the View Compiled File dialog box, select the View button to display the Help viewer. The keyword displays in the Index page of the Help system, as shown in Figure 35-24.

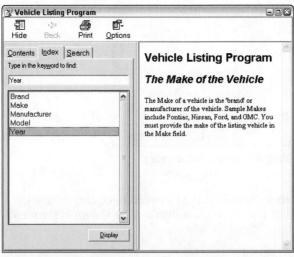

Figure 35-24: Using the Index to locate Help by a keyword.

Implementing a full-text search

Index keywords allow you to connect Help files to predefined search words. Users often want to locate information on a topic that doesn't appear in the predefined keyword list. A powerful feature of any Help system is the capability to perform full-text searches. The Search tab of the Help system allows the user to search by using any word or combination of words or letters.

Ordinarily, when a user runs your Help system and clicks the Search tab for the first time, the Find Setup Wizard appears. The wizard helps users set up a full-text search index on their computers. A full-text search index lists all of the unique words in the Help file.

You can create the full-text index for your users and ship it with your Help files. The disadvantage to this technique is that it can greatly add to the disk space needed to distribute your Help file. You can define your full-text search file by using the "Compile full-text search information" check box located on the Compiler tab in the Help project Options dialog box (see Figure 35-25).

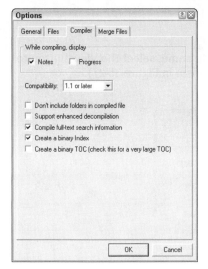

Figure 35-25: Using the Help project Options dialog box to define full-text search files.

When you compile your project with the Compile Full-Text Search Information option turned on, a full-text search (.fts) file is created for your Help system. You need to distribute this file with your Help file.

Caution   When using HTML Help Workshop, the number of topic files that you can view and add is limited to 5,000. Projects with more than 5,000 files will compile correctly, and links from entries in the index and Contents files will work, but you will need to use a text editor to view, add, or edit them.

Running your compiled Help file

To run your compiled Help file, click the View Compiled File button on the toolbar (the button with the eyeglasses on it). When you click this button, HTML Help Workshop displays the View compiled file dialog box (see Figure 35-26). In this dialog box, you tell HTML Help Workshop which Help file to run.

Caution   Remember to save and compile your Help system whenever you make any changes.

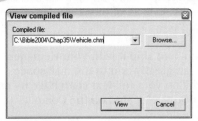

Figure 35-26: It's very important to thoroughly test your Help file before distributing it to users.

After you have selected the compiled Help file name, select the View button to run the Help file. The Help system displays (as shown in Figure 35-27).

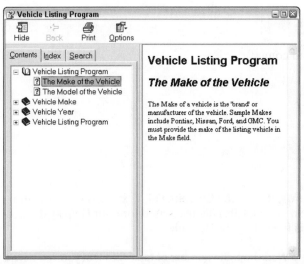

Figure 35-27: A finished Help file showing the Contents tab.

You can now test the contents and topic jumps in the Help file. If you click the Index tab of the Help file's main window, you see a searchable list of all the keyword index entries that you created for the topics (as shown in Figure 35-28).

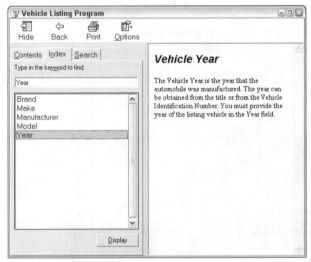

Figure 35-28: The keywords that you created for topics appear in the index for the Help file.

Integrating a Help File with Your Application

After you have created and compiled a working Help file, it's time to integrate it with your Access application. You can tie controls, forms, command buttons, and menu items to specific Help topics by using the techniques described in the following section.

Displaying form-level Help

The most common way to link an application to a Help file is to link forms or specific controls to topics in the Help file. You accomplish this task in two stages: first by specifying the Help File to use, and then by setting the Help Context ID property on the forms and controls. See Figure 35-29 for an example of setting the properties for the form.

You must specify the Help File name on each form in your application to prevent Access Help from displaying. If you are distributing your application with the Office Enterprise tools, and you don't supply a Help File name, an error occurs when the user attempts to access Help. If the Help file is located in a different folder than the running Access application, the Help File property on the form must include the full path to the Help file.

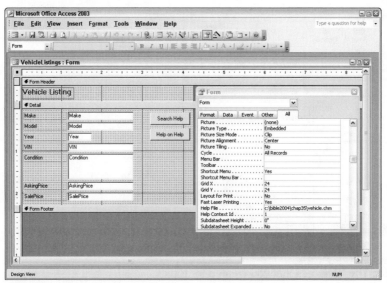

Figure 35-29: Setting up Help for a form.

After you have set the Help File property on each form, you need to set the Help Context ID for the form. This should be the ID of a topic that talks about the form in general.

Displaying control-level Help

After you have set the form's Help Context ID, you can set the Help Context IDs of all controls. Specify a unique number for each control that will display a different topic than the topic to which the form is linked. If you don't want a control to display a unique topic, leave its Help Context ID as 0. When the control's Help Context ID is 0, the form's topic displays when the user presses F1 while the control has the focus; otherwise, the topic whose ID matches the Help Context ID of the control with the focus is displayed when the user presses F1. See Figure 35-30 for an example of setting up Help for a control.

Make sure that you set Help Context IDs for the labels as well as the controls. Some users click the text box to get Help, while others click the label for the control. This way, the Help topic will display regardless of where the user attempts to locate Help.

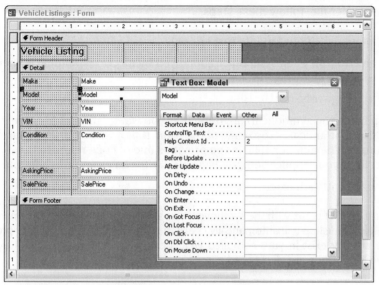

Figure 35-30: Setting up Help for a form control.

Tip

If the user presses F1 in a control that has its Help Context ID set to 0, and the form's Help Context ID is also set to 0, Access Help displays. If your application is distributed with the Office XP Developer Tools, Access's Help won't display and an error will occur. For this reason, you should always link each form's Help Context ID to a valid topic.

Mapping a Help Context ID to a Help topic

After you have established Help Context IDs for your forms and controls, you need to map each Help Context ID to its corresponding topic in the Help file. The HTML Help Workshop provides a tool for assigning a unique number to each of your Help file's topics.

The HTMLHelp API, included in HTML Help Workshop, provides information to applications about the Help file. This information enables an application to display a Help window.

Before you can use the HTMLHelp API to map your Help Context IDs, you must first create a header file. The header file establishes a link between the Help Context ID that you set in the application to a symbolic ID that can be used by the HTMLHelp API.

To create the header file, follow these steps:

1. Open Notepad (or your favorite text editor).

2. Create an entry for each symbolic ID, followed by its corresponding numeric ID, by using the following format:

```
#define IDH_symbolicID 1000
```

3. You can name the symbolic ID anything that you want. You should name it something that indicates the name of the topic that it refers to — VehMake, for example. The number 1000 in the previous line of code refers to the Help Context ID in your application. See Figure 35-31 for an example header file.

4. Save the file with a .h extension.

Tip   If you use an IDH prefix with the symbolic ID, as shown in the preceding example, HTML Help Workshop will automatically check that the topics mapped in your project file actually exist in your compiled Help (.chm) file, and that your context-sensitive Help topics are all mapped in your project file.

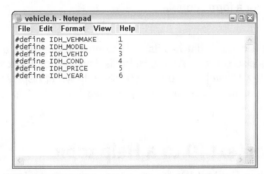

Figure 35-31: Creating a header file.

After you have created the header file, you can set up the HTMLHelp API to use the header file. To set up the HTMLHelp API, follow these steps:

1. Click the HTMLHelp API information button in the HTML Help Workshop. The HTMLHelp API information dialog box displays, as shown in Figure 35-32.

2. Click the Header file button in the Map page of the HTMLHelp API information dialog box. The Include File dialog box displays.

3. Enter the name of the header file that you created. Then click OK. The header filename displays in the Map page.

4. Select the Alias tab of the HtmlHelp API information dialog box. The Alias page displays (see Figure 35-33).

Figure 35-32: Setting up the HTMLHelp API information.

Figure 35-33: Mapping the symbolic IDs to Topics.

5. Select the Add button on the Alias page. The Alias dialog box displays, as shown in Figure 35-34.

6. Enter the first symbolic ID that you created in the header file.

7. Select the HTML file that contains the Topic that the symbolic ID refers to. Then click OK.

8. Repeat the Alias definitions for each of the symbolic IDs that you created in the header file.

Figure 35-34: Adding an HtmlHelp
API map definition.

9. After you have created all of the Alias definitions, click OK to save the
   HTMLHelp API information.

10. Save and compile the project.

The Map page of the HTMLHelp API allows you to include the header file information in your project. The Alias definitions establish the link between the symbolic
IDs and the individual Help topics in the Help system.

Testing the HTMLHelp API

After you have defined the HTMLHelp API information, you can use the HTML Help
Workshop to test the API connections. To test each API connection, follow these
steps:

1. Select the Test ➪ HTMLHelp API button in the HTML Help Workshop. The Test
   HTMLHelp API dialog box displays, as shown in Figure 35-35.

2. In the Compiled file field, make sure that the correct file displays. If not, select
   the current project to test. In the command field, select HH_HELP_CONTEXT.
   In the Map Number field, enter the Help Context ID that you want to test.

3. Select the Test button. The Help Viewer displays the Topic that you entered
   in the test dialog box.

If you encounter problems when testing the HTMLHelp API information, use the following checklist to locate and solve the problem:

✦ Have you included the numeric ID in the header file?

✦ Have you included the proper header file in the HTMLHelp API dialog box?

✦ Does each symbolic ID that you included in the header file match the alias?

✦ Is the alias mapped to the proper HTML file?

✦ Have you saved and recompiled the project?

Figure 35-35: Testing the HTMLHelp API definitions.

Testing Help in Access

After you have created the connections between your Access application and your Help system, you should be able to request Help directly from a form in your Access application. To try out your new Access Help system, run the Access form. Then press F1 on any field for which you have set a Help Context ID. The field's Help Topic displays in the Help Viewer, as shown in Figure 35-36.

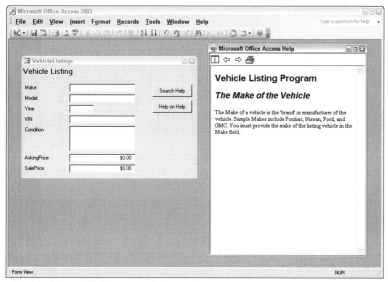

Figure 35-36: Displaying Help in an Access form.

Displaying the Table of Contents

When Help content displays for a field in an Access form, it displays in the Access Help window. Notice, in Figure 35-36, that the Help topic "The Make of the Vehicle" displays in the topic pane of the Help Viewer. But, the window title of the Help Viewer displays as Microsoft Office Access Help instead of "Vehicle Listing Program" as was defined in HTML Help Workshop. Notice also that no Table of Contents displays.

By default, Office Help displays an individual topic alone in the Office Help window. The Office Help window does not display a Navigation pane. This occurs even if you have defined a Table of Contents in HTML Help Workshop. This behavior is the default for all Help in Microsoft Office. You can verify this by pressing the F1 key for any property in an Access form. Figure 35-37 shows how Help displays when you press F1 for Help on a form's Record Source property.

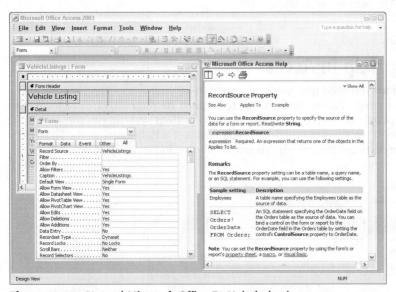

Figure 35-37: Normal Microsoft Office F1 Help behavior.

When the user requests Help on a specific topic, displaying the Help topic in its own window with no Navigation pane is a quick and efficient method to provide Help contents. In many situations, however, the user needs more guidance to obtain the help he needs. When the user is uncertain of the specific topic she needs help for, it is much more effective to provide a way to drill down through the available topics or to search by a keyword.

The Contents tab of the Help Viewer's Table of Contents pane provides the tools for drilling down through the Help system's available topics. The Index and Search tabs allow the user to search for a keyword. To display your Help system's Navigation pane, you must include Visual Basic code to call the HtmlHelp API.

To interface with the HtmlHelp API, you can use the mod_Help module included in this chapter's example file, Chap35Start.mdb. The mod_Help module includes the declarations for the API call to HtmlHelp. The module also includes the Show_Help procedure and the HelpEntry function. Figure 35-38 shows the mod_Help module in the Visual Basic Editor.

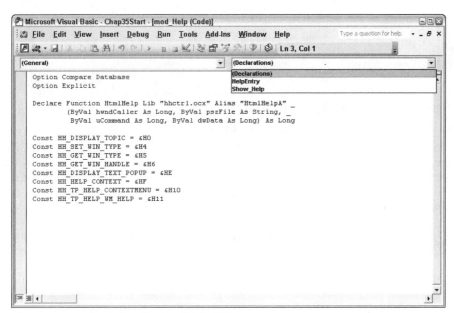

Figure 35-38: Declaring the HtmlHelp API.

The HelpEntry function instructs the HtmlHelp API to use the compiled Help file stored in the variable FormHelpFile. Figure 35-39 shows the Code window for the HelpEntry function. The FormHelpFile is initially set to a specific filename in a specific folder. For this example, the FormHelpFile is set to "C:\Bible2004 \Chap35\Vehicle.chm."

Tip   In your own applications, set FormHelpFile to the folder and filename for your application's Help system.

Figure 35-39: Defining the Help system's filename.

Next, the HelpEntry function assigns the default Help context ID for the topic to display in the HelpViewer's topic pane to the variable FormHelpId. The Help context ID refers to one of the Help Context IDs you created in the HtmlHelpWorkshop. For this example, the FormHelpId is set to "2" to display the topic "The Make of the Vehicle."

Note   To review assigning Help context IDs, refer to the section "Mapping a Help Context ID to a Help topic" earlier in this chapter.

The HelpEntry function calls the Show_Help procedure using the FormHelpFile and FormHelpId parameters. The Show_Help procedure uses the procedures to execute the HtmlHelp API call. The Code window for the Show_Help procedure is shown in Figure 35-40.

The mod_Help module provides the toolset for making the call to the HtmlHelp API. In order to execute the code in this module to display the complete Help Viewer, you need to include some Visual Basic code in your form.

You can include a command button on a form to display the Help Viewer with the Navigation pane. In this chapter's example file, the VehicleListings form includes the command button HelpSearch. When you select the HelpSearch button, the Help Viewer displays the Help Viewer showing the Navigation pane, the Topic pane, and the Help system title "Vehicle Listing Program" as was defined in HtmlHelp Workshop. Figure 35-41 shows the Help Viewer for the HelpSearch button.

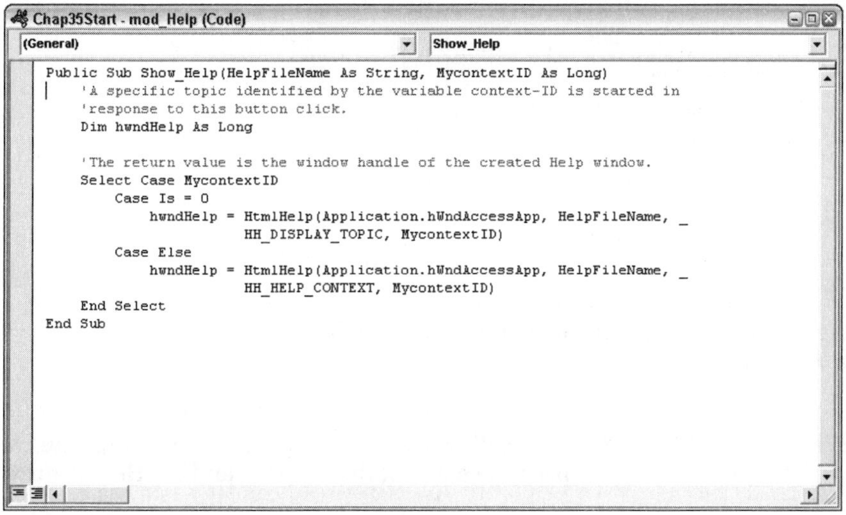

Chap35Start - mod_Help (Code)
(General)
Show_Help
Public Sub Show_Help(HelpFileName As String, MycontextID As Long)
'A specific topic identified by the variable context-ID is started in
'response to this button click.
Dim hwndHelp As Long
'The return value is the window handle of the created Help window.
Select Case MycontextID
Case Is = 0
hwndHelp = HtmlHelp(Application.hWndAccessApp, HelpFileName, _
HH_DISPLAY_TOPIC, MycontextID)
Case Else
hwndHelp = HtmlHelp(Application.hWndAccessApp, HelpFileName, _
HH_HELP_CONTEXT, MycontextID)
End Select
End Sub

Figure 35-40: Calling the HtmlHelp API.

Microsoft Office Access 2003
File Edit View Insert Format Records Tools Window Help
Type a question for help
VehicleListings
Vehicle Listing
Make
Model
Year
VIN
Condition
AskingPrice
SalePrice
$0.00
$0.00
Search Help
Help on Help
Vehicle Listing Program
Hide
Back
Print
Options
Contents
Index
Search
Vehicle Listing Program
The Make of the Vehicle
The Model of the Vehicle
Vehicle Make
Vehicle Year
Vehicle Listing Program
Vehicle Listing Program
The Make of the Vehicle
The Make of a vehicle is the 'brand' or manufacturer of the vehicle. Sample Makes include Pontiac, Nissan, Ford, and GMC. You must provide the make of the listing vehicle in the Make field.
Form View
NUM

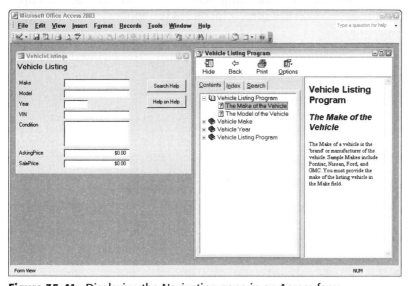

Figure 35-41: Displaying the Navigation pane in an Access form.

The HelpSearch command button's On Click event includes the Visual Basic code to call the HelpEntry function. Figure 35-42 shows the Code window for the HelpSearch_Click event procedure.

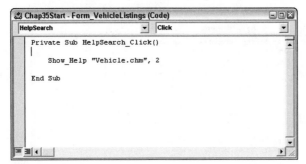

Figure 35-42: Using a command button to display the Help Viewer.

The HelpSearch_Click procedure calls the Show_Help procedure. When you call the Show_Help procedure , you pass the name of the Help file and the Help context ID to display.

By supplying complete, accurate Help that is fully linked with your application, you will be providing a professional program that lowers the amount of support required for the application and greatly increases the application's usability.

✦   ✦   ✦

Working with Advanced Select Queries and Other Query Topics

In this chapter, you work with more complex queries in greater detail than you did in earlier chapters. So far, you have worked with types of select queries and parameters. Earlier parts of this book (Chapters 5, 6, and 22) explained relatively simple select queries, in which you select specific records from one or more tables based on some criteria. Chapter 22 covered using parameters in queries so that you could pass information to the query at the time you run it. You have not, however, worked with all the options that can be used with these types of queries.

You work with advanced select queries and other query topics, such as using calculated fields and working with query properties and options. This chapter shows you how to create queries that display totals, create cross-tabulations, use calculated fields, find specific numbers of records in a query, and set properties and options of queries.

Select queries specify criteria for single or multiple fields (including calculated fields) using multiple tables. Select queries may also work with wildcard characters and fields not having a value (Is Null). Functions in queries can specify record criteria or create calculated fields. Finally, Access queries are a great tool for performing ad-hoc what-if scenarios.

This chapter focuses on four specialized types of advanced select queries:

✦ **Calculated Fields.** Using calculated fields in the query.

✦ **Number of records.** Finding a specific number of records in a query.

✦ **Total.** Calculates totals for records.

✦ **Crosstab.** Summarizes data in an easy-to-read, row-and-column format.

On the CD-ROM This chapter will use the database named CHAP36Start.mdb. If you have not already copied it onto your machine from the CD, you will need to do so now. After you have completed this chapter, your database should resemble the one in CHAP36End.mdb.

Using Calculated Fields

Queries are not limited to actual fields from tables; you can also use *calculated fields* (created by performing some calculation). A calculated field can be created in many different ways, including the following:

✦ Concatenating two Text type fields using the ampersand (&).

✦ Performing a mathematical calculation on two Number type fields.

✦ Using an Access function to create a field based on the function.

In the next example, you create a simple calculated field, DiscountPrice, from the curPrice and dblDiscountPercent fields in the tblSalesLineItems table by following these steps:

1. Create a new query by using the tblSalesLineItems table.

2. Select lngzInvoiceNumber, chrDescription, curPrice, and dblDiscountPercent from the tblSalesLineItems table.

3. Click an empty Field: cell of the QBE pane.

4. Press Shift+F2 to activate the Zoom box (or right-click and select Zoom).

5. Type DiscountPrice: tblSalesLineItems.CurPricetblSalesLineItems.CurPrice* tblSalesLineItems.dblDiscountPercent.

Your Zoom box should look similar to the one shown in Figure 36-1.

Note Because you are only using one table, you did not have to type in the name of the table before each field name. However, it is good practice to do so. You could have typed DiscountPrice: CurPrice-CurPrice*dblDiscountPercent.

6. Click the OK button in the Zoom box (or press Enter) to return to the Design Window.

7. Click the View button on the toolbar to see the resulting Calculated field.

Your screen should look similar to the one shown in Figure 36-2.

Figure 36-1 shows the expression from Step 5 being built in the Zoom window. DiscountPrice is the calculated field name for the expression. The field name and expression are separated by a colon.

At this point, you can save this query to use later, naming it qrySales Totals with Tax.

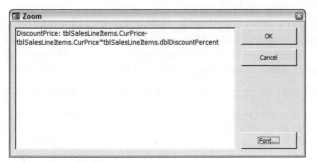

Figure 36-1: Creating a simple calculated field.

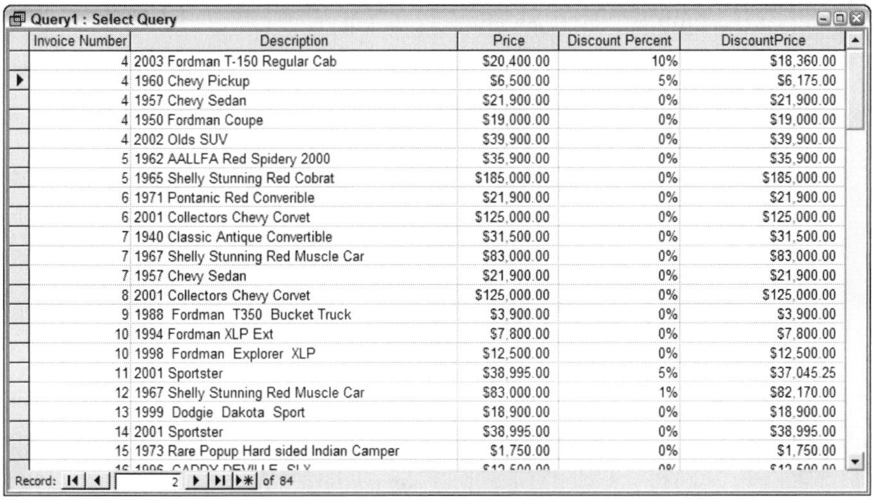

Invoice Number	Description	Price	Discount Percent	DiscountPrice
4	2003 Fordman T-150 Regular Cab	$20,400.00	10%	$18,360.00
4	1960 Chevy Pickup	$6,500.00	5%	$6,175.00
4	1957 Chevy Sedan	$21,900.00	0%	$21,900.00
4	1950 Fordman Coupe	$19,000.00	0%	$19,000.00
4	2002 Olds SUV	$39,900.00	0%	$39,900.00
5	1962 AALLFA Red Spidery 2000	$35,900.00	0%	$35,900.00
5	1965 Shelly Stunning Red Cobrat	$185,000.00	0%	$185,000.00
6	1971 Pontanic Red Converible	$21,900.00	0%	$21,900.00
6	2001 Collectors Chevy Corvet	$125,000.00	0%	$125,000.00
7	1940 Classic Antique Convertible	$31,500.00	0%	$31,500.00
7	1967 Shelly Stunning Red Muscle Car	$83,000.00	0%	$83,000.00
7	1957 Chevy Sedan	$21,900.00	0%	$21,900.00
8	2001 Collectors Chevy Corvet	$125,000.00	0%	$125,000.00
9	1988 Fordman T350 Bucket Truck	$3,900.00	0%	$3,900.00
10	1994 Fordman XLP Ext	$7,800.00	0%	$7,800.00
10	1998 Fordman Explorer XLP	$12,500.00	0%	$12,500.00
11	2001 Sportster	$38,995.00	5%	$37,045.25
12	1967 Shelly Stunning Red Muscle Car	$83,000.00	1%	$82,170.00
13	1999 Dodgie Dakota Sport	$18,900.00	0%	$18,900.00
14	2001 Sportster	$38,995.00	0%	$38,995.00
15	1973 Rare Popup Hard sided Indian Camper	$1,750.00	0%	$1,750.00
16	1996 CADDY DEVILLE SLX	$12,500.00	0%	$12,500.00

Record: 2 of 84

Figure 36-2: The resulting dynaset shown using calculated field DiscountPrice.

Calculated fields and the Expression Builder

Access has an *Expression Builder* that helps you create any expression, such as a complex calculated field for a query. In the next example, you create a calculated field named DueDate that displays a date 45 days in the future, based on an invoice date in tblSales table. You can use this date for a letter you plan to send to all buyers that have outstanding invoices; the date is based on the dtmInvoiceDate field in the table. To create this calculated field, follow these steps:

1. Create a new query using the tblSales table from the Chap36Start database.

2. Select the idsInvoiceNumber, dtmSaleDate, and dtmInvoiceDate fields from the tblSales table.

3. Click an empty Field: cell in the QBE pane.

4. Activate the Expression Builder by clicking the Build button on the toolbar (fourth from right side, the wand with three stars to the left and three dots across the bottom). Another method is to right-click to display the shortcut menu and select Build, while in an empty Field: cell of the QBE pane.

   Access displays the Expression Builder dialog box, as shown in Figure 36-3.

   In the next several steps, you will build the expression DateAdd ("d", 45, [tblSales]![dtmInvoiceDate]) for the calculated field. The DateAdd function adds a specified number of days, weeks, months, quarters, or years to another date. In this example, it is adding 45 days to the invoice date value.

5. Go to the bottom-left window of the Expression Builder dialog box and expand the Functions tree by double-clicking it.

6. Select the Built-In Functions choice (click it).

   Access places information in the two panes to the right of the one you're in (see Figure 36-4).

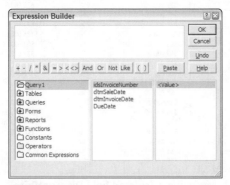

Figure 36-3: The Expression Builder dialog. This dialog box can be used to create any type of expression you want.

7. Go to the second window (which lists all the different categories of functions).

   You could skip this step and go immediately to the third column to find your function. If you do not select a category of functions, Access shows all the functions in the third window.

8. Go to the third window (which lists all the different types of date/time functions).

9. Move down through the column and select the DateAdd function (double-click it).

   Access places the function in the top-left window, with information about the three necessary parameters.

10. Go to the top-left window and click the parameter <interval>.

11. When the parameter is highlighted, simply type "d" (quotation mark, d, quotation mark).

12. Click <number> and replace it with 45.

13. Click <date> to highlight it.

    The function should look like the one shown in Figure 36-4.

14. Go back to the bottom-left window; double-click Tables.

15. Select the tblSales table (click it once).

    Access moves the parameter <Value> into the third, rightmost, column.

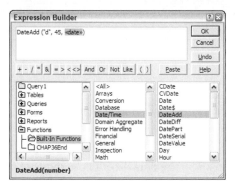

Figure 36-4: Expanding the Built-In Functions choice of the first window opens the other two, displaying a multitude of functions. It is being used to build a calculated field. The <date> parameter needs to be replaced with a field name.

16. Select dtmInvoiceDate from the middle window on the bottom (double-click it).

    Access places the table and field names (separated by an exclamation mark) in the last part of the DateAdd function.

17. Click OK in the Expression Builder.

Access returns you to the QBE pane and places the expression in the cell for you.

18. Access assigns a name for the expression automatically, labeling it Expr1. Should your field now show this name, change it from Expr1 to DueDate by overwriting it.

If you perform these steps correctly and widen the column to display the entire expression, the cell should look like the one shown in Figure 36-5. The DateAdd( ) function enables you to add 45 days to the field dtmInvoiceDate in the tblSales table. The d signifies that you are working with days rather than months, weeks, or years.

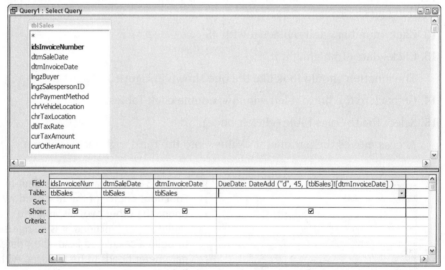

Figure 36-5: A query showing a calculated field built in the Expression builder and named DueDate.

Clicking on the View button, you can show the datasheet of the dynaset showing the new calculated field, DueDate, that will display a value 45 days from the invoice date.

Of course, you could type in the calculated field, but the Expression Builder is a valuable tool when you're creating complex, hard-to-remember expressions.

Creating complex calculated fields

In addition to creating calculated fields from fields in a single table, you can also create them using fields from multiple tables. You can even create calculated fields based on values in other calculated fields in the query.

For instance, you may want to create another calculated field based on fields in both the tblSales and tblSalesLineItems tables and the calculated field named DiscountAmount that you created earlier in the query qrySales Totals with Tax. This new calculated field, named Total Due with Discount/Tax, needs to use the previously created DiscountAmount calculated field and the dblTaxRate field from the tblSales table.

To create this calculated field, follow these steps:

1. Open the query qrySales Totals with Tax from earlier in Design mode.

2. Add the table tblSales to the query by clicking the Show Table button on the toolbar and adding the tblSales to the query.

   Resize the table and move it to the left of tblSalesLineItems.

3. Select the blnTaxable field from the tblSalesLineItems table and the dblTaxRate field from the tblSales table.

4. Click an empty Field: cell of the QBE pane.

5. Press Shift+F2 to activate the Zoom box (or right-click and select Zoom).

6. Type Total Due with Discount/Tax: IIf(tblSalesLineItems.blnTaxable, DiscountPrice + (DiscountPrice*tblSales.dblTaxRate), DiscountPrice).

   Your Zoom box should look similar to the one shown in Figure 36-6.

Figure 36-6: The Expression Builder dialog box. This dialog box can be used to create any type of expression you want.

7. Click the OK button in the Zoom box (or press Enter) to return to the Design Window.

8. Click the View button on the toolbar to see the resulting Calculated field.

Clicking on the view button, you should see a datasheet similar to the one shown in Figure 36-7. You will have to resize the fields to see the entire datasheet.

You can re-save your new query, with the new calculated field added.

Invoice Numb	Description	Price	Discount Percent	DiscountPrice	Taxable	Total Due with Discount/Tax
4	2003 Fordman T-150 Regular Cab	$20,400.00	10%	$18,360.00	☑	$19,278.00
4	1960 Chevy Pickup	$6,500.00	5%	$6,175.00	☑	$6,483.75
4	1957 Chevy Sedan	$21,900.00	0%	$21,900.00	☐	$21,900.00
4	1950 Fordman Coupe	$19,000.00	0%	$19,000.00	☑	$19,950.00
4	2002 Olds SUV	$39,900.00	0%	$39,900.00	☐	$39,900.00
5	1962 AALLFA Red Spidery 2000	$35,900.00	0%	$35,900.00	☑	$37,515.50
5	1965 Shelly Stunning Red Cobrat	$185,000.00	0%	$185,000.00	☑	$193,325.00
6	1971 Pontanic Red Converible	$21,900.00	0%	$21,900.00	☑	$23,323.50
6	2001 Collectors Chevy Corvet	$125,000.00	0%	$125,000.00	☐	$125,000.00
7	1940 Classic Antique Convertible	$31,500.00	0%	$31,500.00	☑	$33,468.75
7	1967 Shelly Stunning Red Muscle Car	$83,000.00	0%	$83,000.00	☑	$88,187.50
7	1957 Chevy Sedan	$21,900.00	0%	$21,900.00	☑	$23,268.75
8	2001 Collectors Chevy Corvet	$125,000.00	0%	$125,000.00	☑	$131,250.00
9	1988 Fordman T350 Bucket Truck	$3,900.00	0%	$3,900.00	☑	$4,143.75
10	1994 Fordman XLP Ext	$7,800.00	0%	$7,800.00	☐	$7,800.00
10	1998 Fordman Explorer XLP	$12,500.00	0%	$12,500.00	☐	$12,500.00
11	2001 Sportster	$38,995.00	5%	$37,045.25	☑	$38,527.06
12	1967 Shelly Stunning Red Muscle Car	$83,000.00	1%	$82,170.00	☑	$86,771.52
13	1999 Dodgie Dakota Sport	$18,900.00	0%	$18,900.00	☑	$20,034.00
14	2001 Sportster	$38,995.00	0%	$38,995.00	☑	$40,554.80
15	1973 Rare Popup Hard sided Indian Camper	$1,750.00	0%	$1,750.00	☑	$1,820.00
16	1996 CADDY DEVILLE SLX	$12,500.00	0%	$12,500.00	☑	$13,125.00

Figure 36-7: The datasheet containing two calculated fields.

The calculated field created in Step 6 is relatively complex. It uses the IIF() function, called the immediate if function, to check whether the blnTaxable field is checked in the tblSalesLineItems. It also uses the previously created calculated field named DiscountPrice.

The IIF function lets the calculated field perform two different calculations, based on the value of the blnTaxable field. If it is checked (or positive), the Total Due with Discount/Tax calculated field displays the resulting value of the DiscountPrice calculated field plus the correct amount of tax added, based on the tax rate field from the tblSales table. If the blnTaxable field is not checked (negative), it just displays the DiscountPrice field without performing a tax calculation.

This query now uses two calculated fields: DiscountPrice and Total Due with Discount/Tax. The second calculated field uses the values calculated in the first one and a field from the second table, tblSales.

This query demonstrates the power available in queries using calculated fields.

Finding the Number of Records in a Table or Query

To quickly determine the total number of records in an existing table or query, use the Count(*) function. This is a special parameter of the Count( ) function. For example, to determine the total number of records in the tblContacts table, follow these steps:

1. Start a new query using the tblContacts table.

2. Click the first empty Field: cell in the QBE pane.

3. Type Count(*) in the cell.

Access adds the calculated field name Expr1 to the cell in front of the Count(*) function. Your query's QBE pane should now look like the one shown in Figure 36-8. This query as created is pretty useless, because you can obtain the same information by simply selecting fields, setting no conditions in a query, and then looking at the bottom of the datasheet on the navigation line when you view it.

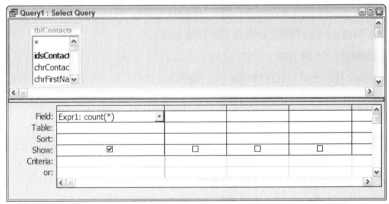

Figure 36-8: The QBE pane of a query using the Count(*) function.

The datasheet now has a single cell that shows the number of records for the Contacts table. The datasheet should look like the one shown in Figure 36-9.

If you use this function with the asterisk wildcard (*), this is the only field that can be shown in the datasheet, although you can use additional fields to set a criterion.

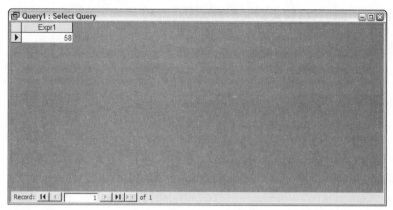

Figure 36-9: The datasheet of a Count(*) function for the tblContacts table.

The Count(*) function can also be used to determine the total number of records that match a specific criterion. For example, you may want to know how many contacts you have in the tblContacts table that are not sellers (buyers or both) and that live in Connecticut. Follow these steps to ascertain the number in the table:

1. Start a new query and select the tblContacts table.

2. Click the first empty Field: cell in the QBE pane.

3. Type **Count(*)** in the cell.

4. Double-click the chrContactType and chrState fields in the table to add them to the query.

5. Deselect the Show: cell for the chrContactType and chrState fields.

6. Type <> **seller** in the Criteria: cell for chrContactType.

7. Type **CT** in the Criteria: cell for chrState.

8. Go back to the first cell Expr1:Count(*).

9. Replace Expr1: with Total non Sellers in State of CT.

Figure 36-10 shows how the query should look. If you select the Datasheet option from the Query View button on the toolbar, Access again displays only one cell in the datasheet; it contains the number of non Sellers (Buyer and both) from the state of CT in the resulting dynaset (11). You could have left the default expression name of Expr1 if you wished. Renaming the default Expr1 to something more understandable makes the datasheet value more understandable.

Remember that only the field that contains the Count(*) function can be shown in the datasheet. If you try to display any additional fields, Access reports an error.

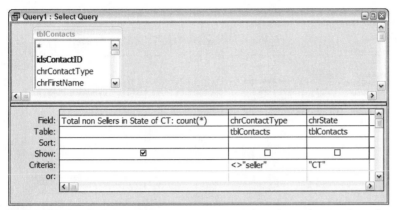

Figure 36-10: The query QBE pane that is used to show the number of no Sellers in state of CT.

Finding the Top (n) Records in a Query

Access not only enables you to find the number of records in an existing table or query, but it also provides the capability of finding the query's first (n) records (that is, a set number or percentage of its records).

Suppose that you want to identify the first 10 buyer records for the year 2003 — in other words, the first 10 sales of the year 2003. This is known as the Top (n) records. To determine the first (top) 10 sales for 2003 and their owners, follow these steps:

1. Create a new query using the tblContacts and tblSales tables.

2. Create a calculated field named Buyer Name using the chrFirstName and chrLastName fields from the tblContcts table.

   The calculation should be Buyer Name: chrFirstName &" "&chrLastName.

3. Select the chrContactType field from the tblContacts table and the dtmSaleDate field from the tblSales table.

4. Enter a criterion of <> **Seller** in the chrContactType field.

5. Enter a criterion of **Between 1/1/03 and 1/1/04** in the dtmSaleDate field.

6. Specify a sort order of Ascending in the dtmSaleDate field.

   At this point, you can click on the view button to see that there are 26 records in the resulting dynaset. Click on the view button to return to the Design surface.

7. Click the Top Values combo box next to the Totals button (_) on the toolbar.

8. Enter **10** in the Top Values property cell, as shown in Figure 36-11.

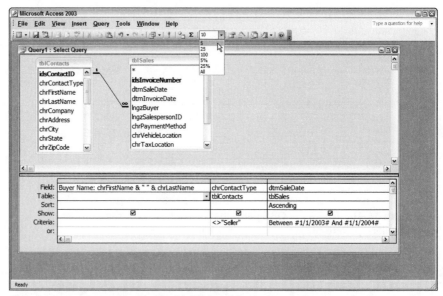

Figure 36-11: A query with five highlighted in the Top Values combo box on the toolbar open and showing a value of 10.

If you click the selection arrow of the Top Values combo box, you will see a series of default values — 5, 25, 100, 5%, 25%, and All. You can select one of these or type in your own value as was done here (10).

You are ready to run your query. When you click the Query View button on the toolbar, you should see the top 10 records in the dynaset, which should look like the one shown in Figure 36-12. This datasheet displays only the first 10 records in the dynaset.

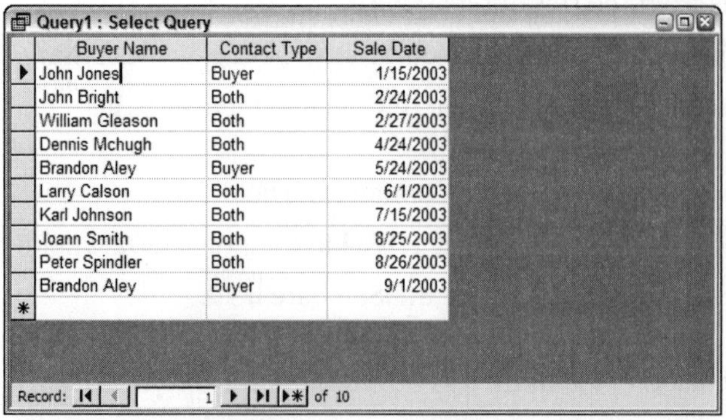

Figure 36-12: Datasheet view of the dynaset of the top (first) 10 records in a query.

You can specify any percent or real number for the Top (n) values of a query. This is very helpful for those times when you want to see only a specific number of records. It can be used with total queries, which you will create later in this chapter, showing the top 5%, 15%, or any other value you want to specify of records. Perhaps you may want to see the top 10% in value of buyers in the system.

How Queries Save Field Selections

When you open a query design, you may notice that the design has changed since you last saved the query. When you save a query, Access rearranges (even eliminates) fields on the basis of several rules:

✦ If a field does not have the Show: box checked but has criteria specified, Access moves it to the rightmost columns in the QBE pane.

✦ If a field does not have the Show: box checked, Access eliminates it from the QBE pane column unless it has sorting directives or criteria.

✦ If you create a totaling expression with the Sum operator in a total query, Access changes it to an expression using the Sum function.

Because of these rules, your query may look very different after you save and reopen it. In this section, you learn how this happens (and some ways to prevent it).

Hiding (not showing) fields

Sometimes you won't want certain fields in the QBE pane to show in the actual dynaset of the datasheet. For example, you may want to use a field such as chrContactType to specify a criterion or a sort without showing the actual field.

To *hide*, or exclude, a field from the dynaset, you simply click off the Show: box under the field you want to hide. Figure 36-13 demonstrates this procedure. Notice that the field chrContactType is used to specify a criterion of displaying only Buyers or Both (<> "Seller"). Because you don't want this field in the actual datasheet, you deselect the Show: cell for the chrContactType field.

Field:	chrContactType	chrFirstName	chrLastName	idsInvoiceNumber	dtmSaleDate	
Table:	tblContacts	tblContacts	tblContacts	tblSales	tblSales	
Sort:						
Show:	☐	☑	☑	☑	☑	☐
Criteria:	<>"Seller"					
or:						

Figure 36-13: The easiest way to hide a field is to uncheck the Show: check box of the field, as in chrContactType.

Any fields that have the Show: cell turned off (and for which you entered criteria) are placed at the end of the QBE pane when you save the query. Figure 36-14 shows the same query as Figure 36-13 after it is saved and redisplayed on the design screen. Notice that the chrContactType field has been moved to the end (extreme right) of the QBE pane. The location of a hidden field will not change the dynaset. Because the field is not displayed, its location in the QBE pane is unimportant. You always get the same results, even if you've placed a hidden field in the QBE pane.

Field:	chrFirstName	chrLastName	idsInvoiceNumber	dtmSaleDate	chrContactType	
Table:	tblContacts	tblContacts	tblSales	tblSales	tblContacts	
Sort:						
Show:	☑	☑	☑	☑	☐	☐
Criteria:					<>"Seller"	
or:						

Figure 36-14: A query that has been saved with a hidden field (shown unchecked); the field is moved to the end of the query. (Compare Figure 36-13.)

If you hide any fields in the QBE pane that are not used for sorts or criteria, Access eliminates them from the query automatically when you save it. If you want to use these fields and need to show them later, you'll have to add them back to the QBE pane.

Note   If you're creating a query to be used by a form or report, you must show any fields it will use, including any field to which you want to bind a control.

Renaming fields in queries

When working with queries, you can rename a field to describe the field's contents more clearly or accurately. This new name is the one that would be shown in the datasheet of the query. For example, you may want to rename the chrTaxLocation field of the tblContacts table to State for Tax Purposes. As you have already seen, renaming is useful for working with calculated fields or calculating totals; Access automatically assigns nondescript names such as *Expr1* or *AvgOfWeight*, but it's easy to rename fields in Access queries.

Note   If you specified a Caption name for the field in the table designer, this name will be used in the query.

To change the display name of the chtTaxLocation field, for example, follow these steps:

1. Create a new query and select the tblContacts table. Add the chrFirstname, chrLastName, and chrTaxLocation fields to the query.

2. Click in the chrTaxLocation field.

3. Place the cursor in front of the first letter of chrTaxLocation in the Field: cell.

4. Type State for Tax Purposes: (be sure to include the colon).

Figure 36-15 shows the query field renamed. The field has both the display name, which is State for Tax Purposes, and the actual field name, which is chrTaxLocation.

When you view this query, the new Column heading is State for Tax Purposes, instead of chrTaxLocation.

Field:	chrFirstName	chrLastName	State for Tax Purposes:chrTaxLocation	▾	
Table:	tblContacts	tblContacts	tblContacts		
Sort:					
Show:	☑	☑	☑	☐	
Criteria:					
or:					

Figure 36-15: A query field with the chrTaxLocation field renamed to State for Tax Purposes for display purposes.

Tip When naming a query field, delete any names assigned by Access (to the left of the colon). For example, remove the name Expr1 when you name the calculated field.

If you rename a field, Access uses only the new name for the heading of the query datasheet; it does the same with the control source in any form or report that uses the query. Any new forms or reports you create on the basis of the query will use the new field name. (Access does not change the actual field name in the underlying table.)

When working with renamed fields, you can use an *expression name* (the new name you specified) in another expression within the same query. For example, you may have a calculated field called Full Name that uses an Access function to join the first and last names fields. You created this type of field in an earlier query.

Note When you work with referenced expression names, you cannot have any criteria specified against the field you're referring to.

Hiding and unhiding columns in the QBE pane

Sometimes you may want to hide specific fields in the QBE pane. This is not the same as hiding a field by clicking the Show: box. Hiding a column in the QBE pane is similar to hiding a datasheet column, which is easy: You simply resize a column (from right to left) until it has no visible width. Figure 36-16 shows several fields in the QBE pane; in the next example, you hide one of its columns.

Field:	chrLastName	chrFirstName	idsInvoiceNumber	chrCategory	chrDescription	
Table:	tblContacts	tblContacts	tblSales	tblProducts	tblProducts	
Sort:						
Show:	☑	☑	☑	☑	☑	☐
Criteria:						
or:						

Figure 36-16: A typical QBE pane showing fields from several tables — tblContacts, tblSales, and tblProducts.

If you create the query shown in Figure 36-16, you can then hide the idsInvoiceNumber column. Follow these steps to hide the idsInvoiceNumber column:

1. Move the mouse pointer to the right side of the idsInvoiceNumber field on the *field selector*. The double-arrow sizing pointer displays.

2. Click the right side of the idsInvoiceNumber field and drag it toward the chrFirstName field until it totally disappears.

Figure 36-17 shows the QBE pane with the idsInvoiceNumber field being hidden. You can see the double-arrow mouse pointer as it is being moved to the left. In the picture, the field wasn't completely hidden so that you can see where the column has been moved to (next to chrFirstName) and see the double-arrow sizing pointer.

Field:	chrLastName	chrFirstName	dsInvoiceNumber	chrCategory	chrDescription	
Table:	tblContacts	tblContacts	tblSales	tblProducts	tblProducts	
Sort:						
Show:	☑	☑	☑	☑	☑	☐
Criteria:						
or:						

Figure 36-17: The QBE pane with a column being hidden by moving the double-arrow pointer.

Note   Although the idsInvoiceNumber field is hidden in the QBE panel of the design surface, it is still shown in the datasheet when you click the View button. Hiding a field in the query design *only* hides it in the query design.

After you hide a field, you can *unhide* it by reversing the process. If you want to unhide the idsInvoiceNumber column, follow these steps:

1. Move the mouse pointer to the left side of the field chrCategory on the selector bar (the bar with arrows appears). Make sure that you are to the right of the divider between chrFirstName and chrCategory fields.

2. Click the left side of chrCategory and drag it toward the chrDescription field until you size the column to the correct length.

3. Release the button; the field name *idsInvoiceNumber* will appear in the column you unhide.

Query Design Options

There are several specifiable default options when working with a query design. These options can be viewed and set by selecting Tools ➪ Options from the main menu and then selecting the Tables/Queries tab. Figure 36-18 shows this Options dialog box.

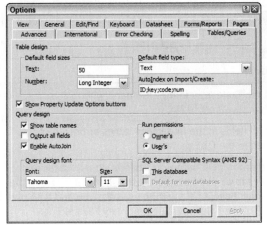

Figure 36-18: The Table/Queries page of the Options dialog box. The lower half concerns the fields for queries.

These six items can be set for queries:

- ✦ Show Table Names
- ✦ Output All Fields
- ✦ Enable AutoJoin
- ✦ Run Permissions
- ✦ Query Design Font
- ✦ SQL Server Compatibility Syntax (ANSI 92)

Generally, the default for Show Table Names is Yes, and the default for Output All Fields is No. Run Permissions offers a choice of either the Owner's permission or the User's (the default). Enable AutoJoin controls whether Access will use common field names to perform an automatic join between tables that have no relationships set; the default value is Yes. The Query Design Font is by default Tahoma and 10. The final section determines if the current database should use ANSI 92 SQL Server Syntax; the default is No.

Tip   When you set query design options, they specify default actions for new queries only; they do not affect the current query. To show table names in the current query, select View ⇨ Table Names from the main Query menu while designing the query.

Table 36-1 describes each Query design option and its purpose.

Table 36-1
Query Design Options

Option	Purpose
Show Table Names	Shows the Table: row in the QBE pane when set to Yes; hides the Table: row if set to No.
Output All Fields	Shows all fields in the underlying tables or only the fields displayed in the QBE pane.
Enable AutoJoin	Uses common field names to perform an automatic join between tables that have no relationships set to occur; the tables must have a field with the same name and type of data and one of the fields must be a primary key field.
Run Permissions	Restricts use in a multi-user environment; a user restricted from viewing the underlying tables can still view the data from the query. If set to Owner's, the user cannot view data returned from the query or run an action query.
Query Design Font	Used to set the Font type (name of font) and the size of the font used in queries.
SQL Server Compatible	Select this database to enable ANSI-92 SQL query mode so that you can create and run queries using ANSI 92 SQL Syntax. This is compatible with Microsoft SQL Server. Existing queries may not run correctly if you set this option after creating other queries.

Setting Query Properties

While creating a query, you can set query properties several ways: click the Properties button on the toolbar; right-click Properties and choose it from the shortcut menu; or select View ➪ Properties from the main Query menu. Access displays a Query Properties dialog box. Your options depend on the query type and on the table or field with which you're working.

You can use the *query-level properties* just as you would the properties in forms, reports, and tables. Query-level properties depend on the type of query being created and on the table or field with which you're working. Table 36-2 shows the query-level properties you can set.

	Table 36-2						
	Query-Level Properties						
Property	**Description**	**Query Select**		**Cross-tab**	**Update**	**Delete**	**Make-Table** **Append**

Property	**Description**	**Query**	**Select**	**Cross-tab**	**Update**	**Delete**	**Make-Table**	**Append**
Description	Text describing table or query	X	X	X	X	X	X	X
Default View	Values Datasheet, Pivot Table, or Pivot Chart	X	X	X				
Output All Fields	Show all fields from the underlying tables in the query	X					X	X
Top Values	Number of highest or lowest values to be returned	X					X	X
Unique Values	Return only unique field values in the dynaset	X					X	X
Unique Records	Return only unique records for the dynaset	X	X		X	X	X	X

Continued

Table 36-2 *(continued)*								
Property	*Description*	*Query*	*Select*	*Cross-tab*	*Update*	*Delete*	*Make-Table*	*Append*
Run Permissions	Establish permissions for specified user	X	X	X	X	X	X	X
Source Database	External database name for all tables/queries in the query	X	X	X	X	X	X	X
Source Connect Str	Name of application used to connect to external database	X	X	X	X	X	X	X
Record Locks	Records locked while query runs (usually action queries)	X	X	X	X	X	X	X
Recordset Type	Which records can be edited: Dynaset, Dynaset (inconsistent updates), or Snapshot	X	X	X				
ODBC Time-out	Number of seconds before reporting error for opening DB	X	X	X	X	X	X	X
Filter	Filter name loaded automatically with query	X	X					
Order By	Sort loaded automatically with query	X	X					
Max Records	Max number of records returned by ODBC database	X	X					
Orientation	Set view order for fields from left-to-right or right-to-left	X	X	X	X	X	X	X

Property	Description	Query	Select	Cross-tab	Update	Delete	Make-Table	Append
SubDatasheet Name	Identify subquery	X	X	X	X		X	X
Link Child Fields	Field name(s) in subquery	X	X	X	X		X	X
Link Master Fields	Field name(s) in main table	X	X	X	X		X	X
Subdatasheet Height	Maximum height of subdatasheet	X	X	X	X		X	X
Subdatasheet Expanded	Records initially in their expanded state?	X	X	X			X	X
Column Headings	Fixed-column headings			X				
Use Transaction	Run action query in transaction?				X	X	X	X
Fail on Error	Fail operation if errors occur				X	X		
Destination Table	Table name of destination						X	X
Destination DB	Name of database						X	X
Dest Connect Str	Database connection string						X	X

As you can see, working with queries offers many options for how the fields can be displayed and properties for each specific type of query.

The remainder of this chapter works with Advanced Select queries, and the next chapter works with all the action queries shown in Table 36-2.

Creating Queries That Calculate Totals

Many times, you want to find information in your tables based on data related to the total of a particular field or fields. For example, you may want to find the total number of contacts that are both buyers and sellers or the total amount of money each buyer has spent on vehicles last year. Access supplies the tools to accomplish these queries without the need for programming.

Access performs calculation totals by using nine aggregate functions that let you determine a specific value based on the contents of a field. For example, you can determine the average price for vehicles by type, the maximum and minimum price paid for a vehicle, or the total count of all records in which the type of contact is a buyer or both. Performing each of these examples as a query results in a dynaset of answer fields based on the mathematical calculations you requested.

Cross-Reference You have already worked with counts using the Count (*) function in the previous section.

To create a total query, you use a new row in the Query by Example (QBE) pane — the Total: row. The following section describes this handy tool in detail.

Showing and hiding the Total: row in the QBE pane

To create a query that performs a total calculation, create a select query and then activate the Total: row of the QBE pane. You can activate the Total: row by using either of these two selection methods (but, first, open a new query using the tblProducts table):

+ Select View ⇨ Totals from the Design menu.

+ Select the Totals button (the Greek sigma symbol button — Σ — which is to the right of the midway mark) on the toolbar (seventh from the right side).

Figure 36-19 shows the Total: row after it is added in the QBE pane. The Totals button is selected on the toolbar and the Total: row is placed in the QBE pane between the Table: and Sort: rows.

Note If the toolbar is not visible, select View ⇨ Toolbars from the Query menu. Then select Query Design and close the dialog box.

If the Table: row is not present on your screen, the Total: row appears below the Field: row and above the Sort: row. You can activate the Table: row by selecting View ⇨ Table Names from the Design menu.

To deactivate the Total row in the QBE pane, simply reselect either activation method (the Design menu or the Totals button). The Totals button is a toggle-type control that alternately turns the Total: row on and off.

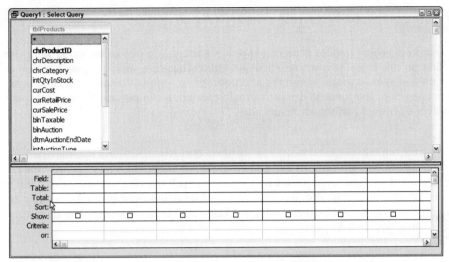

Figure 36-19: The Total row of the QBE pane is active in this figure. Notice the arrow pointing to the Total: row label, just below the Table: row.

The Total: row options

You can perform total calculations on all records or groups of records in one or more tables. To perform a calculation, you must select one of the options from the drop-down list in the Total: row for every field you include in the query, including any hidden fields (with the Show: option turned off). Figure 36-20 shows the drop-down list box active in the Total: row of the field.

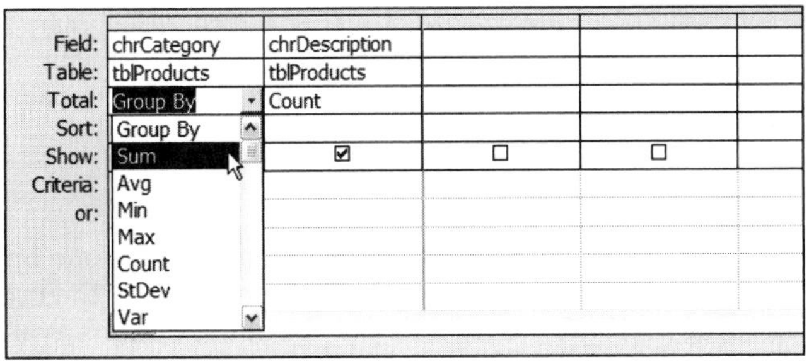

Figure 36-20: The drop-down list box of the Total: row activated. It has 12 choices in it. The Group By option is already selected, but the Sum option is highlighted as the cursor moves on it.

What Is an Aggregate Function?

The word *aggregate* implies gathering together a mass (a group or series) of things and working on this mass as a whole—a single entity. Therefore, an aggregate function is a function that takes a group of records and performs some mathematical function against the entire group. The function can be a simple count or a complex expression you specify, based on a series of mathematical functions.

Although only eight options are shown in Figure 36-20, you can choose from 12. You can view the remaining options by using the scroll bar on the right side of the box. The 12 options can be divided into four distinct categories: group by, aggregate, expression, and total field record limit. Table 36-3 lists each category, its number of Total options, and its purpose.

Table 36-3
Four Categories of Total Options

Category	Number of Options	Purpose of Operator
Group By	1	Groups common records together. Access performs aggregate calculations against the groups.
Aggregate	9	Specifies a mathematical or selection operation to perform against a field.
Expression	1	Groups several total operators together and performs the group totals.
Total Field Record Limit	1	Limits records before record limit performing a total calculation against a field.

The Group By, Expression, and Total Field Record Limit categories have one option each. The Aggregate category has nine options, all of which are used by the other three categories. The following sections provide details about the options available in each category.

Group By category

This category has one option, the *Group By* option. You use this option to specify that a certain field in the QBE pane will be used as a grouping field. For example, if you select the field chrCustomerType, the Group By option tells Access to group all

Dealer records together, all Wholesaler records together, and so on. This option is the default for all Total: cells. In other words, when you drag a field to the QBE pane, Access automatically selects this option. Figure 36-20 shows that this is also the first choice in the drop-down list box. These groups of records will be used for performing some aggregate calculation against another field in the query. We discuss this subject in more detail in the section titled "Specifying criteria for a Group By field," later in this chapter.

Expression category

Like the Group By category, the *Expression* category has only one option: Expression. This is the second-from-last choice in the drop-down list. You use this option to tell Access to create a calculated field by using one or more aggregate calculations in the Field: cell of the QBE pane. For example, you may want to create a query that shows each customer (buyer) and how much money the customer saved, based on the individual's discount rate. This query requires creating a calculated field that uses a sum aggregate against the curPrice field of the tblSalesLineItems table, which is then multiplied by the dblDiscountPercent field in the tblSalesLineItems table.

Cross-Reference We discuss this type of calculation in detail in the section titled "Creating expressions for totals," later in this chapter.

Total Field Record Limit category

The *Total Field Record Limit* category is the third category that has a single option: the Where option. This option is the last choice in the drop-down list. When you select this option, you tell Access that you want to specify limiting criteria against an aggregate type field, as opposed to a Group By or an Expression field. The limiting criteria are performed *before* the aggregate options are executed. For example, you may want to create a query that counts all vehicles by types of vehicles that are priced over $10,000 USD. Because the curSalePrice field is not to be used for a grouping (as is chrCategory) and won't be used to perform an aggregate calculation, you specify the Where option. By specifying the Where option, you are telling Access to use this field only as a limiting criteria field — before it performs the aggregate calculation (counting types of vehicles). This type of operation is also discussed in detail later in this chapter.

Aggregate category

The *Aggregate* category, unlike the others, has multiple options that you can choose from (a total of nine options): *Sum, Avg, Min, Max, Count, StDev, Var, First,* and *Last*. These options appear as the second through tenth options in the drop-down list. Each option performs an operation on your data (check out Table 36-2 for how you can use each option) and supplies the new data to a cell in the resulting dynaset. Aggregate options are what database designers think of when they hear the words *total query*. Each of the options performs a calculation against a field in the QBE pane of the query and returns a *single answer* in the dynaset.

For example, you may want to determine the maximum (Max), minimum (Min), and average (Avg) value of each type of vehicle in the tblProducts table. There can be only one maximum value for all vehicles. Several vehicles may have the same maximum value, but only one price is the largest. Another example of a total query would be if you wanted the total number (Count) of vehicles for each category in the tblProducts table (again, the query returns a single answer for each type). You can use these aggregate options to solve these types of queries.

You can also use it to find a single value in the table, without creating an aggregate grouping.

Whereas the Group By, Expression, and Total Field Record Limit categories of options (which we discuss in previous sections) can be used against any type of Access field (Text, Memo, or Yes/No, for example), some of the aggregate options can be performed against certain field types only. For example, you cannot perform a Sum option against Text type data; nor can you use a Max option against an OLE object.

Table 36-4 lists each option, what it does, and which field types you can use with the option.

Table 36-4
Aggregate Options of the Total: Row

Option	Finds	Field Type Support
Count	Number of non-Null values in a field	AutoNumber, Number, Currency, Date/Time, Yes/No, Text, Memo, OLE object
Sum	Total of values in a field	AutoNumber, Number, Currency, Date/Time, Yes/No
Avg	Average of values in a field	AutoNumber, Number, Currency, Date/Time, Yes/No
Max	Highest value in a field	AutoNumber, Number, Currency, Date/Time, Yes/No, Text
Min	Lowest value in a field	AutoNumber, Number, Currency, Date/Time, Yes/No, Text
StDev	Standard deviation of values in a field	AutoNumber, Number, Currency, Date/Time, Yes/No
Var	Population variance of values in a field	AutoNumber, Number, Currency, Date/Time, Yes/No
First	Field value from the first record in a number, table, or query	AutoNumber, Currency, Date/Time, Yes/No, Text, Memo, OLE object
Last	Field value from the last record in a number, table, or query	AutoNumber, Currency, Date/Time, Yes/No, Text, Memo, OLE object

Performing totals on all records

You can use total queries to perform calculations against all records in a table or query. For example, you can find the total number of vehicles in the tblProducts table, the average sale price, and the maximum and minimum sale price for each category. To create this query, follow these steps:

1. Select the tblProducts table.

2. Click the Totals button on the toolbar to turn it on.

3. Select the chrProductID and curSalePrice fields in the table.

4. Select the curSalePrice field two more times from the tblProducts table.

5. In the Total: cell of chrProductID, select Count.

6. In the Total: cell of the first curSalePrice, select Avg.

7. In the Total: cell of the second curSalePrice, select Min.

8. In the Total: cell of the third curSalePrice, select Max.

Your query should look similar to the one shown in Figure 36-21.

Field:	chrProductID	curSalePrice	curSalePrice	curSalePrice	
Table:	tblProducts	tblProducts	tblProducts	tblProducts	
Total:	Count	Avg	Min	Max	
Sort:					
Show:	☑	☑	☑	☑	☐
Criteria:					
or:					

Figure 36-21: A query against all records in the tblProducts table to show four calculated values — count, average price, min, and maximum price.

This query calculates the total number of records in the tblProducts table as well as the average, minimum, and maximum price for all vehicles.

You can save this query, naming it Calculations for Vehicles. You will use it again later.

Note The Count option of the Total: cell can be performed against any field in the table (or query). However, Count eliminates any records that have a Null value in the field you select. Therefore, you may want to select the primary key field on which to perform the Count total because this field cannot have any Null values, thus ensuring an accurate record count. That is why you selected chrProductID from tblProducts for the count operator.

If you select the Datasheet button on the toolbar, you should see a datasheet similar to the one shown in Figure 36-22. Notice that the dynaset has only one record.

This record specifies the count, average, minimum, and maximum value for all vehicles (regardless of type) in the tblProducts table.

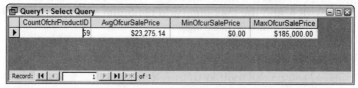

Figure 36-22: This datasheet of a dynaset was created from a total query against the tblProducts table. It only has one row, or record, in the dynaset.

Note Access creates default column headings for all total fields in a totals datasheet, such as those shown in Figure 36-22. The heading name is a product of the name of the total option and the field name. Thus, in Figure 36-22, the heading names are CountOfchrProductID, AvgOfcurSalePrice, MinIOfcurSalePrice and MaxOfcurSalePrice. You can change a column heading name to something more appropriate by renaming the field in the QBE pane of the Design window. As with any field that you want to rename, place the insertion point at the beginning of the field cell to be renamed (to the left of the field name) and type the name you want to display followed by a colon.

This query was performed against all records in a table or query, and the resulting dynaset has only one record.

Performing totals on groups of records

Most of the time, you need to perform totals on a group of records rather than on all records. For example, you may need to calculate the query for each type of vehicle (chrCategory). In other words, you want to create a group for each type of vehicle (car, minivan, truck, and so on) and then perform the total calculations against each of these groups. In database parlance, this is known as *control break totaling*.

Calculating totals for a single group

When you create your query, you specify which field or fields to use for grouping the totals and which fields to perform the totals against. Using the preceding example, to group the chrCategory field, you select the Group By option of the Total: cell. Follow these steps to create the query:

1. Open the Calculations for Vehicles query in design mode.

2. Add the chrCategory field to the beginning of the query.

3. Double-check to make sure the Total: cell for chrCategory says Group By.

The query in Figure 36-23 groups all like vehicles together and then performs the count total for each type of vehicle as well as the average price, min, and max price. Unlike performing totals against all records, this query produces a dynaset of many records — one record for each type of vehicle. Figure 36-24 shows how the datasheet looks.

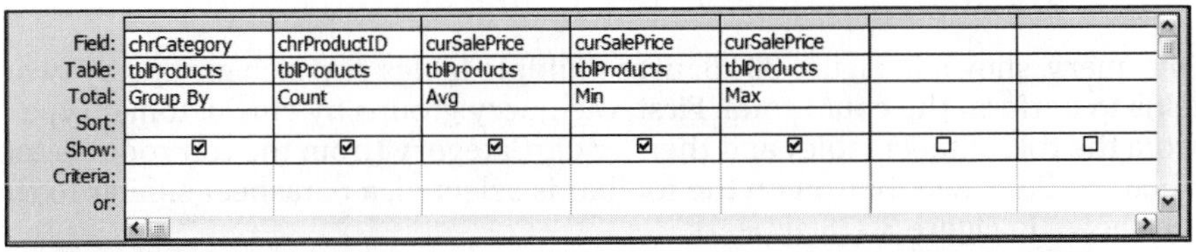

Figure 36-23: Totals against a group of records. First it groups all like vehicles together; then it counts the number of similar vehicles.

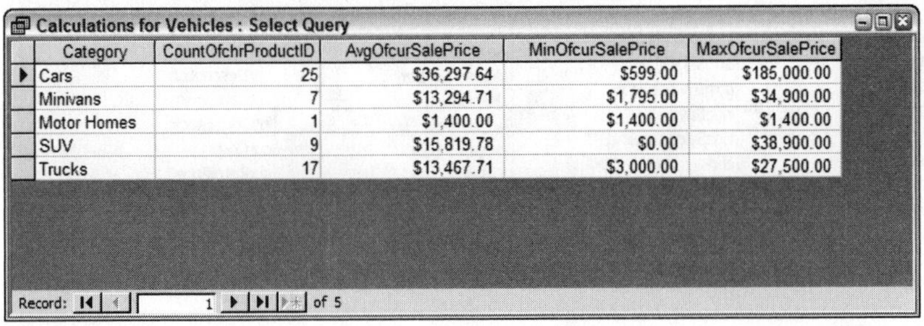

Figure 36-24: Datasheet of totals against the group chrCategory field, which shows the number of vehicles, average, minimum, and maximum price for each type.

The dynaset in Figure 36-24 has a single record for each type of vehicle. The count was performed against each type of vehicle; there are 25 cars, 7 Minivans, 1 Motor Homes, and so on. The Group By field displays one record for each unique value in that field. The chrCategory field is specified as the Group By field and displays a single record for each type of vehicle. Each of these records is shown as a row heading for the datasheet, indicating a unique record for each type of vehicle specified that begins with the Group By field content (cars, trucks , and so on). In this case, each unique record is easy to identify by the single-field row heading under Category.

Calculating totals for several groups

You can perform group totals against multiple fields and multiple tables as easily as with a single field in a single table. For example, you may want to group by both chrCustomerType from the tblContacts table and chrCategory to determine the number of vehicles each customer type (dealer, wholesaler, and so on) owns by vehicle type. To create a total query for this example, you specify Group By in both Total: fields (chrCustomerType and chrCategory).

Tip   The order in which you place the fields on the query will determine the order of grouping. For instance, selecting the chrCategory first will first sort by Vehicle Category type and then sort by Customer Type.

This query, shown in Figure 36-25, uses multiple tables and also groups by two fields to perform the count total. First, the query groups by chrCustomerType (from the tblContacts table) and then by chrCategory (from the tblProducts table). When the Datasheet button on the toolbar is selected, a datasheet similar to the one shown in Figure 36-26 appears.

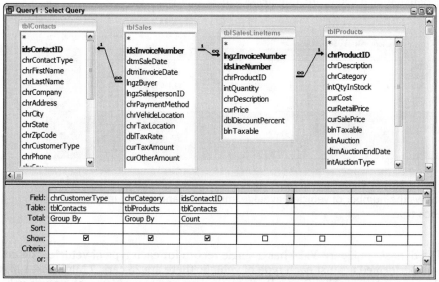

Figure 36-25: A multiple-table, multiple-field Group By total query to show all types of Customers and how many vehicles each owns, broken down by the type of vehicle.

The datasheet in Figure 36-26 shows several records for the customer type Dealer. This type of customer has 37 Cars, 4 Minivans, 1 Motor Home, 6 SUV and 7 Trucks. You can also see that the Auctioneer type has only 3 Cars, and Wholesalers have 7 Cars, 1 Minivans, 2 SUV and 3 Trucks. This datasheet has a unique record based on two Group By fields: chrCustomerType and chrCategory (as shown in Figure 36-25). Therefore, the unique row headings for this datasheet are created by ordering (Group By) both fields — first the chrCustomerType and then the chrCategory.

Tip   You can think of the Group By fields in a total query as fields that specify the row headings of the datasheet. The Group By option creates the rows of the resulting dynaset in sorted order within each column.

Query1 : Select Query

Customer Type	Category	CountOfidsContactID
Auctioneer	Cars	3
Dealer	Cars	37
Dealer	Minivans	4
Dealer	Motor Homes	1
Dealer	SUV	6
Dealer	Trucks	7
Other Retail	Cars	4
Other Retail	SUV	1
Other Retail	Trucks	1
Parts Store	Cars	3
Parts Store	Motor Homes	1
Parts Store	SUV	1
Parts Store	Trucks	2
Wholesaler	Cars	7
Wholesaler	Minivans	1
Wholesaler	SUV	2
Wholesaler	Trucks	3

Record: 1 of 17

Figure 36-26: Datasheet of a multiple-field Group By query.

Access groups records based on the order of the Group By fields in the QBE pane (from left to right). Therefore, you should pay attention to the order of the Group By fields. Although the order doesn't change the aggregate totals of the fields, the order of Group By fields does determine how the results are displayed in the datasheet. If you place the chrCategory field before the chrCustomerType field, the resulting datasheet shows the records in order by vehicle category first and then by type of customer. Figure 36-27 demonstrates this setup, showing the vehicle type records and the type of customers who bought them (with the total number).

Query1 : Select Query

Category	Customer Type	CountOfidsContactID
Cars	Auctioneer	3
Cars	Dealer	37
Cars	Other Retail	4
Cars	Parts Store	3
Cars	Wholesaler	7
Minivans	Dealer	4
Minivans	Wholesaler	1
Motor Homes	Dealer	1
Motor Homes	Parts Store	1
SUV	Dealer	6
SUV	Other Retail	1
SUV	Parts Store	1
SUV	Wholesaler	2
Trucks	Dealer	7
Trucks	Other Retail	1
Trucks	Parts Store	2
Trucks	Wholesaler	3

Record: 1 of 17

Figure 36-27: Changing the order of Group By fields. This datasheet has vehicle category before type of customer (versus the opposite in Figure 36-25).

By changing the order of the Group By fields in a totals query, you can look at your data in new and creative ways.

Specifying criteria for a total query

In addition to grouping records for total queries, criteria to limit the records that will be processed or displayed in a total calculation can be specified. When you're specifying record criteria in total queries, several options are available. A criterion against any of these three fields can be created:

✦ Group By

✦ Aggregate Total

✦ Non-Aggregate Total

Using any one, any two, or all three of these criteria types, you can easily limit the scope of your total query to finite criteria.

Specifying criteria for a Group By field

To limit the scope of the records used in a grouping, you can specify criteria in the Group By fields. For example, to calculate the total amount of money each customer paid for vehicles, the minimum and maximum value and where the customer last name is between "A" and "L" requires specifying criteria on the Group By calculated field: Full Name. Full Name is created by concatenating the last and full name together — Full Name: chrLastName & ", " & chrFirstName. Then it needs to sum, min, and max the values of the curPrice field of tblProducts. This type of query looks like the one shown in Figure 36-28. Notice that the Group By field, Full Name, has criteria of '>"A" And <"M". The other fields — lngzInvoiceNumber and three curPrice — specify the aggregate totals count, sum, min, and max.

By specifying criteria in the Full Name calculated field, you can ensure that Access performs the aggregate calculations on only those records that meet the Group By criteria. In this example, the count, sum, minimum and maximum value will be performed only for contacts whose last names are between A and L, inclusive. This query results in a 22 record dynaset, with one record each for each customer whose last name begins with A through L. Each record shows the total number of vehicles purchased, the total each customer has spent on vehicles they have bought, and the minimum and maximum price they have paid for a vehicle.

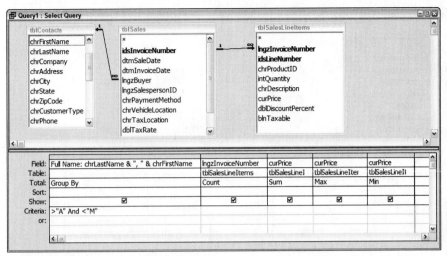

Figure 36-28: Specifying criteria in a Group By field. The calculated field Full Name specifies criteria.

Specifying criteria for an Aggregate Total field

At times, you may want a query to calculate aggregate totals first and then display only those totals from the aggregate calculations that meet a specified criterion. More specifically, you may want to perform aggregate calculations against *all* records and then add to the dynaset only those aggregate totals that meet a certain criterion. In effect, you're saying "I won't know which records I want to see until they're all totaled first. Then I want to see only those records that meet a particular criterion in my dynaset."

For example, you may want a query to find the average price for each type of vehicle, grouped by type of vehicles, where the average price of any vehicle is greater than $7,500 USD. This query should look like the one shown in Figure 36-29. Notice that the criterion >7500 is placed in the Aggregate Total field, curCost. This query calculates the average price of all vehicles grouped by type of vehicle. Then the query determines whether the calculated totals for each record are greater than 7500. Records greater than 7500 are added to the resulting dynaset, and records less than or equal to 7500 are discarded. The criterion is applied *after* the aggregate calculations are performed.

The resulting datasheet has only four of the five categories of vehicles; the Motor Homes average price is $1,200 USD, which is less than $7,500 USD and is not displayed.

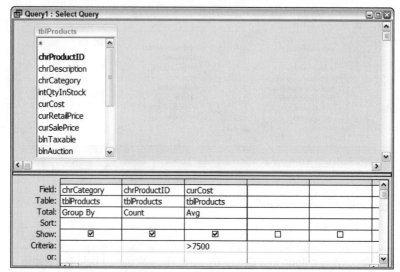

Figure 36-29: A query with a criterion set against an Aggregate Total field (Avg of the curCost field, greater than 7500).

Specifying criteria for a Non-Aggregate Total field

The preceding section showed you how to limit the records after performing the calculations against total fields. You also can specify that you want Access to limit the records based on a total field before performing total calculations. In other words, you can limit the range of records against which the calculation is performed. Doing so creates a criterion similar to the first type of criteria in the preceding example; the field you want to set a criterion against is *not* a Group By field.

The preceding section shows you how to limit the fields included in the dynaset by using the Group By criteria, which allows you to state specific criteria for which records you want to appear in the resulting dynaset. Suppose, however, that you want to filter the group of records based on criteria that you don't want in the resulting dynaset. Access allows you to do this as well. You can limit the range of records against which the calculation is performed, and you can make this limitation based on criteria that you don't want to appear in the resulting dynaset.

For example, you may want to display the total amount of money each customer has paid for vehicles during the first half of 2003 (through 30 Jun 2003), starting with February 4, 2003. You want to use the dtmSaleDate field of the tblSales table to specify criteria, but you don't want to perform any calculations against this field or use it to group by; you don't even want to show the field in the resulting datasheet.

Figure 36-30 shows how the query should look. Here you used the Where type of Total to limit the scope of records shown. Notice that Access automatically turned off the Show: cell in the dtmSaleDate field; when using a Where clause, this field cannot be used in the query. If you wanted to also see the dtmSaleDate field, simply add a second dtmSaleDate field to the QBE pane.

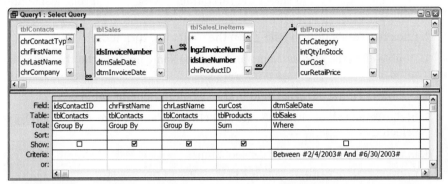

Figure 36-30: Specifying criteria for a Non-Aggregate field. Here you used the Where type of Total to limit the scope of the records shown.

 Note   In the query you just completed, Access displays only those records for customers that have purchased vehicles from February 4 to June 30, 2003, inclusive. All other records are discarded. Clicking the view button will show only five records.

Access automatically turns off the Show: cell whenever it encounters a Where option in the Total: cell of a field. Access understands that you are using the field only to specify criteria and that you don't want to see the actual field value displayed for the criteria field. The reason is that Access uses the field to evaluate the Where criteria before performing the calculation. Therefore, the contents are useful only for the limiting criteria. If you try to turn on the Show: cell, Access displays an error message. If you need to see the field contents in the datasheet, simply add a second copy of the field to the QBE pane. Only the field that has the Where condition in the Total: row is not shown.

Creating expressions for totals

In addition to choosing one of the Access totals from the drop-down list, you can create your own total expression based on several types of totals, such as using Avg and Sum or multiple Sums together. Or you can base your expression on a calculated field composed of several functions, or on a calculated field that is based on several fields from different tables.

Suppose that you want a query that shows the total amount of money each customer owed before discount. Then you want to see the amount of money these customers saved based on their discount (a calculated field you create named Total

Saved). You further want the information to be grouped by customer and sorted by highest amount owed. Finally, you want the Total Saved field to display dollar amounts (formatted like this $111.11). Follow these steps to create this query:

1. Start a new query and select the tblContacts, tblSales, and tblSalesLineItems tables.

2. Click the Totals button (the Σ) on the toolbar to turn it on.

3. Double-click the chrLastName and chrFirstName fields in the tblContacts table.

4. Double-click the curPrice field in the tblSalesLineItems table.

5. In the Total: cell of chrLastName and chrFirstName, make sure Group By is selected.

6. In the Total: cell of curPrice, select Sum.

7. In the curPrice column, select a Sort: order of Descending.

8. Click on an empty Field: cell in the QBE pane.

9. Type **Total Saved: Sum(tblSalesLineItems.curPrice * tblSalesLineItems.dblDiscountPercent)** in the cell.

10. In the Total: cell of the Total Saved expression, select Expression.

11. Making sure the cursor is still in the Total Saved field, click the Criteria: cell.

12. If the Property sheet is not opened, right-click to bring up the right-click menu and select Properties.

13. On the General tab, select a Format of Currency (for the Total Saved field).

Your query should be similar to the one shown in Figure 36-31. Notice that the query uses two fields from the tblProducts table to create the Total Saved: calculated field. You had to specify the table and the field name for the dblDiscoutPercent in the Sum function because the field exists in both the tblSalesLineItems and the tblContacts tables.

Note   You had to use the tblSales table, although you did not use any of its fields in the QBE pane for the query. It was necessary to use the tblSales table to maintain and build a link between the tblContacts table and the tblSalesLineItems table. In other words, if you had omitted the tblSales table, there would be no way to link the other two tables.

If you click the Datasheet button on the toolbar, your dynaset should be similar to the one shown in Figure 36-32. The Total Saved field is a calculated field that you created using the expression you built and specified as an Expression Total. Notice that the resulting display shows a currency format for the Total Saved field.

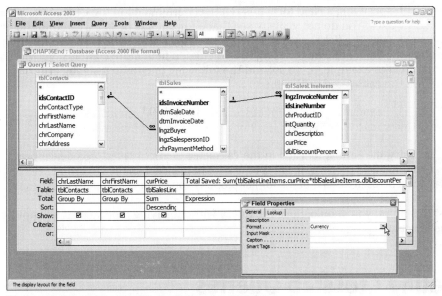

Figure 36-31: A query using an Expression Total.

Figure 36-32: A datasheet created by an Expression total.

Note   In the datasheet in Figure 36-32, the calculated field Total Saved shows the information in Currency format, using the Dollar sign and two decimal places. If you did
not specify a format for the field in the query design, you would see as many as 12
decimal places and no dollar sign. If all you want to do is limit the number of decimal places while using the thousands comma, you can specify a format of
Standard.

Although specifying a Field format is relatively easy to do in the QBE pane, it has one drawback: You do not visually see that a format has been assigned to the field. In lieu of using the field format property, you can also use the Format() function around the Sum() function making the Calculated field more complex, yet visibly accurate. For example, to do so, add the following line to the existing criteria formula in the calculated field cell:

```
Total Saved: Format(Sum(tblSalesLineItems.curPrice *
tblSalesLineItems.dblDiscountPercent),"Currency")
```

Tip   Using the Format function in the calculated field cell takes precedence over the format field property. If you specify a format function in the calculated field cell, it will be used instead of the format property you set in the property list.

At this point, you should close the query without saving it because it will not be used again.

Creating Crosstab Queries

Access permits use of a specialized type of total query — the crosstab — to display summarized data in a compact and readable format. A *crosstab query* summarizes the data in the fields from your tables and presents the resulting dynaset in a row-and-column format.

Understanding the crosstab query

Simply put, a crosstab query is a spreadsheet-like summary of the things specified by the row header and column header that is created from your tables. This query presents summary data in a spreadsheet-like format created from fields that you specify. In this specialized type of total query, the Total: row in the QBE pane is always active. The Total: row cannot be toggled off in a crosstab query!

In addition, the Total: row of the QBE pane is used for specifying a Group By total option for both the row and the column headings. Like other total queries, the Group By option specifies the row headings for the query datasheet and comes from the actual contents of the field. However, unlike other total queries, the crosstab query also obtains its column headings from the value in a field (table or calculated) rather than from the field names themselves.

Note   The fields used as rows and columns must always have Group By in the Total: row. Otherwise, Access reports an error when you attempt to display or run the query.

For example, you may want to create a query that displays the type of customer field (chrCustomerType) as the row heading and the category of vehicle (chrCategory) as the column heading, with each cell containing a total for each type of vehicle for each type of customer. Table 36-5 demonstrates how you want the query to look.

In Table 36-5, the row headings are specified by Type of Customer: Auctioneer, Dealer, Other Retail, and so on. The column headings are specified by the vehicle types: Cars, Minivans, Motor Homes, SUV, and Trucks. The cell content in the intersection of any row and column is a summary of records that meets both conditions. For example, the Dealer row that intersects the Minivans column shows that they bought four minivans. The Wholesaler row that intersects with the Trucks column shows that they purchased three trucks.

This table shows a simple crosstab query created from the fields chrCustomerType and chrCategory, with the intersecting cell contents determined by a Count total on any field in any of the tables.

Table 36-5 A Typical Crosstab Query Format					
Type of Customer	*Cars*	*Minivans*	*Motor Homes*	*SUV*	*Trucks*
Auctioneer	3				
Dealer	37	4	1	6	7
Other Retail	4			1	1
Parts Store	3		1	1	2
Wholesaler	7	1		2	3

Creating the crosstab query

Now that you have a conceptual understanding of a crosstab query, it is time to create one. To create a crosstab query like the one described in Table 36-5, follow these steps:

1. Start a new query and select the tblContacts, tblSales, tblSalesLineItems, and tblProducts tables.

2. Double-click the chrCustomerType field in the tblContacts table.

3. Double-click the chrCategory field in the tblProducts table.

4. Double-click the chrProductID field in the tblProducts table.

   You could select any field from any of the tables for this cell.

5. Select Query ➪ Crosstab Query in the Query menu or click the Query Type button on the toolbar (this method displays a drop-down list showing the types of queries), and select Crosstab Query.

6. In the Crosstab: cell of chrCustomerType, select Row Heading.

7. In the Crosstab: cell of chrCategory, select Column Heading.

8. In the Crosstab: cell of chrProductID, select Value.

9. In the Total: cell of chrProductID, select Count.

Your query should look similar to the one shown in Figure 36-33. Notice that Access inserted a new row named Crosstab: between the Total: and Sort: rows in the QBE pane.

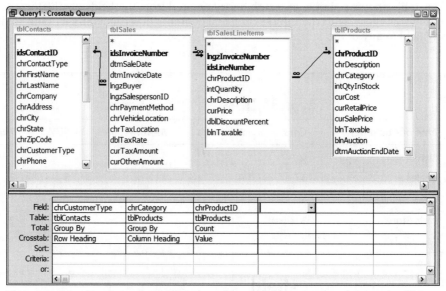

Figure 36-33: Creating a crosstab query of Type of Customers and Type of Vehicles.

As Figure 36-33 demonstrates, you must specify a minimum of three items for crosstab queries:

✦ The Row Heading field

✦ The Column Heading field

✦ The summary Value field

These three items are specified in the appropriate Crosstab: cells of the fields. After you specify the contents for the three Crosstab: cells, you specify Group By in the Total: cell of both the Row Heading and the Column Heading fields and an aggregate Total: cell operator (such as Count) for the Value field.

If you have done this procedure correctly, selecting the Datasheet button on the toolbar reveals a datasheet similar to the one shown in Figure 36-34.

Notice that the dynaset is composed of distinct (non-repeating) rows of customers, five columns (one for each type of vehicle), and summary cell contents for each type of customer and each type of vehicle. When no values are found, a null value is used rather than 0.

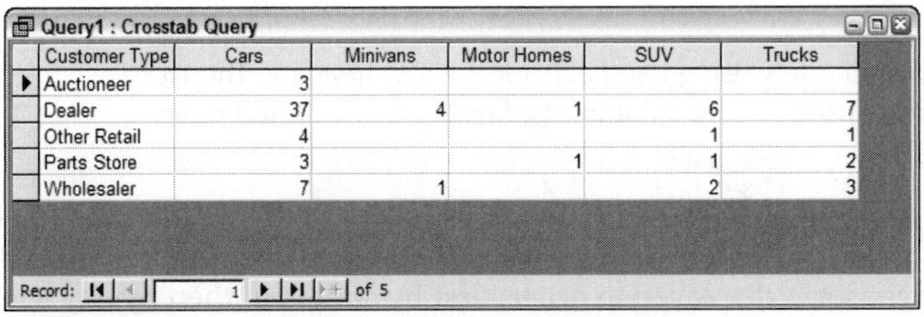

Customer Type	Cars	Minivans	Motor Homes	SUV	Trucks
▶ Auctioneer	3				
Dealer	37	4	1	6	7
Other Retail	4			1	1
Parts Store	3		1	1	2
Wholesaler	7	1		2	3

Query1 : Crosstab Query

Record: ◄ ◄ 1 ► ►► of 5

Figure 36-34: Datasheet of a crosstab query. Notice that the Headings for both the columns and rows are actual field values from the tables.

Tip

Figure 36-34 shows the default display value for null values — a blank cell. You can force Access to display a zero in these cells by simply entering a Format field property for the chrProductID field (Total Count, Crosstab Value field) by entering the format value of **0;;;0** (a zero, followed by three semicolons and another zero). This format tells Access to display all regular values as their actual value and the null values as a zero (fourth option in the custom format).

Entering multiple-field row headings

When working with crosstab queries, only one summary Value field and one Column Heading field can be specified. You can add more than one Row Heading field, however. By adding multiple Row Heading fields, you can refine the type of data to be presented in the crosstab query.

Suppose that you're interested in seeing the types of vehicles (columns) from the last crosstab query further refined to the level of state and city (instead of by type of customer). In other words, you want to see how many of each type of vehicle that you have from each city within each state. To accomplish this task, you will need to switch the type of headings being displayed — making the type of vehicle (chrCategory) the Column Headings and the State/City fields the Row Heading (chrState, chrCity). Such a query is shown in Figure 36-35. Notice that it has two Crosstab: cells that show Row Heading for the fields state and city. Access groups the Crosstab: rows first by the state and then by the city. Access specifies the group order from left to right.

Field:	chrState	chrCity	chrCategory	chrProductID	
Table:	tblContacts	tblContacts	tblProducts	tblProducts	
Total:	Group By	Group By	Group By	Count	
Crosstab:	Row Heading	Row Heading	Column Heading	Value	
Sort:					
Criteria:					
or:					

Figure 36-35: Crosstab query using two fields for the row heading. The type of vehicle field is now used for the column headings of this crosstab query.

Access presents a datasheet similar to the one shown in Figure 36-36 when the view button on the toolbar is selected. The row heading depends on both the State and City fields. The dynaset is displayed in order: first by state and then by city within the state.

Query1 : Crosstab Query

State	City	Cars	Minivans	Motor Homes	SUV	Trucks
AZ	Iron Springs	1				
CA	Montclair	1			1	
CO	Denver	1				
CT	Colchester	5	1		1	1
CT	Derby	2	1			
CT	Granby	3				
CT	Milford	4				
CT	Portland		1			
CT	Stratford				3	
GA	Sale Creek	1				
IL	Island Lake	2				
KS	Turon	2	2			
KY	Jackhorn					1
MA	Fairbanks	4				
MA	Springfield	3		1	1	2
MA	West Bridgewat	5			1	

Record: |◀ ◀| 1 |▶ ▶| ▶*| of 30

Figure 36-36: Datasheet with multiple-field row headings (State and then City) of a crosstab query.

A crosstab query can have several row headings but only one column heading. To achieve the same effect as a several-field column heading and a single-field row heading, simply reverse the heading types. Change the multiple-field column headings to multiple-field row headings and change the single-row heading to a single-column heading.

Tip   Although Access limits you to a single-field column heading, it is possible to create a multi-field column heading, as in a State and City, using a Calculated field. You can create a Calculated field of [state]+' '+[city] to create a Column Heading field and specify the type of vehicle as the Row Heading. The resulting datasheet will display all the combined Values of state and city as individual column heading.

Specifying criteria for a crosstab query

When working with crosstab queries, you may want to specify record criteria for the crosstab. Criteria can be specified in a crosstab query against any of these fields:

✦ A new field

✦ A Row Heading field

✦ A Column Heading field

Specifying criteria in a new field

You can add criteria based on a new field that will not be displayed in the crosstab query itself. For example, you may want to create the crosstab query you see in Figure 36-35, in which the two fields, chrState and chrCity, are used as the row heading. However, you want to see only records in which the type of customer (chrCustomerType) is a Dealer. To specify criteria, follow these additional steps:

1. Start with the crosstab query shown in Figure 36-35.

2. Double-click the chrCustomerType field in the tblContacts table to add it to the QBE pane.

3. Select the Criteria: cell of chrCustomerType.

4. Type **Dealer** in the cell.

Note   The Crosstab: cell of the chrCustomerType field should be blank. If it is not, select the check box (not shown) to blank the cell.

Your query should resemble the one shown in Figure 36-37. Notice that you added a criterion in a field that will not be displayed in the crosstab query. The chrCustomerType field is used as a grouping field, and because nothing appears in the Crosstab row, the field value is not displayed.

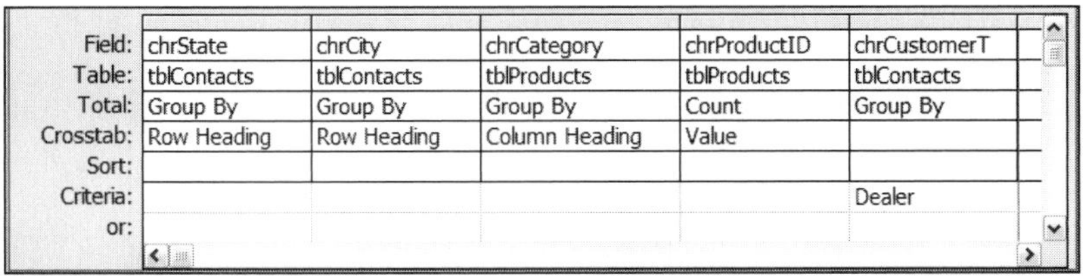

Field:	chrState	chrCity	chrCategory	chrProductID	chrCustomerT
Table:	tblContacts	tblContacts	tblProducts	tblProducts	tblContacts
Total:	Group By	Group By	Group By	Count	Group By
Crosstab:	Row Heading	Row Heading	Column Heading	Value	
Sort:					
Criteria:					Dealer
or:					

Figure 36-37: Specifying a criterion in a crosstab query on a new field. The chrCustomerType has a criterion of Dealer and the Crosstab: cell is left blank.

Now that the new criterion is specified, you can click on the Datasheet button of the toolbar to see a datasheet similar to the one shown in Figure 36-38.

Figure 36-38: The datasheet, after specifying a criterion on a new field. It shows a crosstab only for all customers who have a type of 'Dealer' (individual).

The datasheet in Figure 36-38 shows only columns and rows in which at least one of the intersecting row cells has a value. It only has 21 rows, instead of 30 in Figure 36-36 — nine were removed because there are no values in the columns of those rows. It also removes any columns that have no value in any of the cells.

Specifying criteria in a Row Heading field

You can also specify criteria for a field being used for a row heading. When you specify a criterion for a row heading, Access excludes any rows that do not meet the specified criteria.

For example, you may want to modify the crosstab query from Figure 36-35 to show only records for the states of New York, Massachusetts, and Connecticut. To create this query, start with the crosstab query shown in Figure 36-35. If you created the last query, remove the chrCustomerType column from the QBE pane. To create this query, make the QBE pane look like the one shown in Figure 36-39. When this query is viewed, only records from CT, NY, and MA are seen.

Figure 36-39: Criteria set against a Row Heading field — chrState for all NY, CT, and MA customers

You can specify criteria against any field used as a Row Heading field or for multiple Row Heading fields to create a finely focused crosstab query.

Specifying criteria in a Column Heading field

You can also specify criteria for the field you use as the column heading. When you specify the criteria for a column heading, Access excludes any columns that don't meet the specified criteria. For the next example, you want to modify the crosstab query to show only columns for Minivans, Motor Homes, and SUVs. To create this query, again start with the crosstab query shown in Figure 36-35. If you created the last query, remove the criteria for the chrState field from the QBE pane. Add the criteria of In ("Minivans","Motor Homes","SUV") to the chrCatetory field. The QBE pane should look similar to the one shown in Figure 36-40.

Field:	chrState	chrCity	chrCategory	chrProductID		
Table:	tblContacts	tblContacts	tblProducts	tblProducts		
Total:	Group By	Group By	Group By	Count		
Crosstab:	Row Heading	Row Heading	Column Heading	Value		
Sort:						
Criteria:			In ("Minivans","Motor Homes","SUV")			
or:						

Figure 36-40: A criterion specified against the Column Heading field – chrCategory. Here you want to see only three columns – Minivans, Motor Homes, and SUV.

The specified criterion is placed in the Criteria: cell of the Column Heading field chrCategory. If you now select the Datasheet button on the toolbar, you should see a datasheet that has only three column headings: Minivans, Motor Homes, and SUV. The other headings are eliminated.

Specifying criteria in multiple fields of a crosstab query

Now that you've worked with each type of criterion separately, you may want to specify criteria based on several fields. In the next example, you create a complex crosstab query with multi-field criteria from the previous examples.

You want to limit your records to only the states of NY, MA, and CT and only where the type of vehicle is a Minivan, Motor Home, or SUV. Finally, you want to see records where the only type of customer is a Dealer.

Starting with the query in Figure 36-40, add the chrCustomerType field and specify a criterion of "Dealer". Finally, specify criteria of In ("NY","CT","MA") for the chrState field. With these steps complete, your query should look similar to the one shown in Figure 36-41.

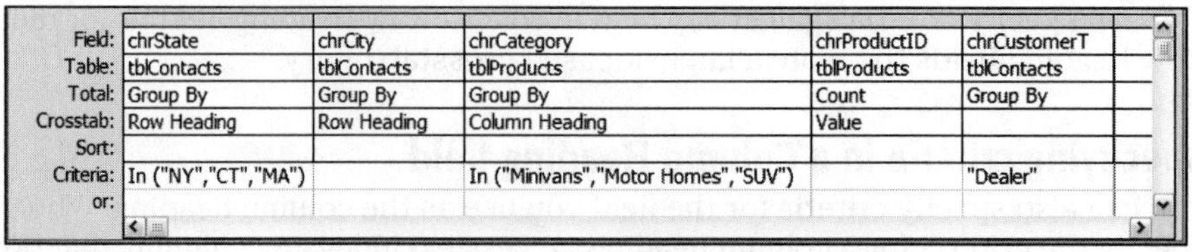

Field:	chrState	chrCity	chrCategory	chrProductID	chrCustomerT	
Table:	tblContacts	tblContacts	tblProducts	tblProducts	tblContacts	
Total:	Group By	Group By	Group By	Count	Group By	
Crosstab:	Row Heading	Row Heading	Column Heading	Value		
Sort:						
Criteria:	In ("NY","CT","MA")		In ("Minivans","Motor Homes","SUV")		"Dealer"	
or:						

Figure 36-41: A complex crosstab query with three field criteria.

When you select the View button on the toolbar, you see a datasheet similar to the one shown in Figure 36-42. The datasheet has three columns. The order of the rows and columns is alphabetical.

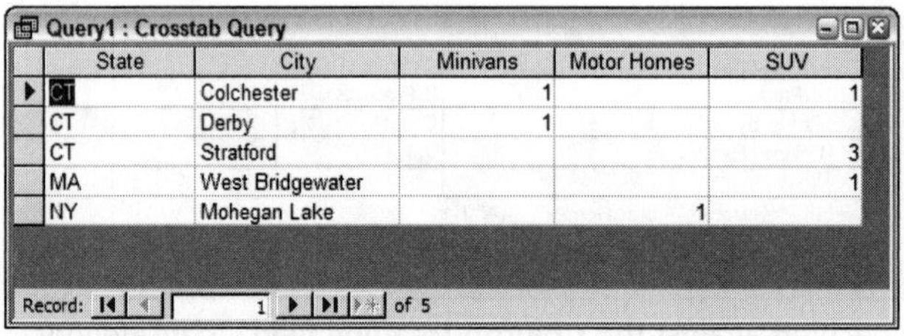

Query1 : Crosstab Query

State	City	Minivans	Motor Homes	SUV
CT	Colchester	1		1
CT	Derby	1		
CT	Stratford			3
MA	West Bridgewater			1
NY	Mohegan Lake		1	

Record: 14 ◄ 1 ► ►I ►* of 5

Figure 36-42: A datasheet of very complex crosstab criteria, with three criteria specified.

Specifying fixed column headings

At times, you will want more control over the appearance of the column headings. By default, Access sorts column headings alphabetically or numerically. This sort order can be a problem, especially when working with months or days of the week. In this case, your columns will be more readable if the columns are in chronological month order rather than alphabetical order.

Take the query in Figure 36-43 that shows vehicles by category. This crosstab query shows the number of cars sold for the first four months of date of sale. It doesn't differentiate between years — simply the months.

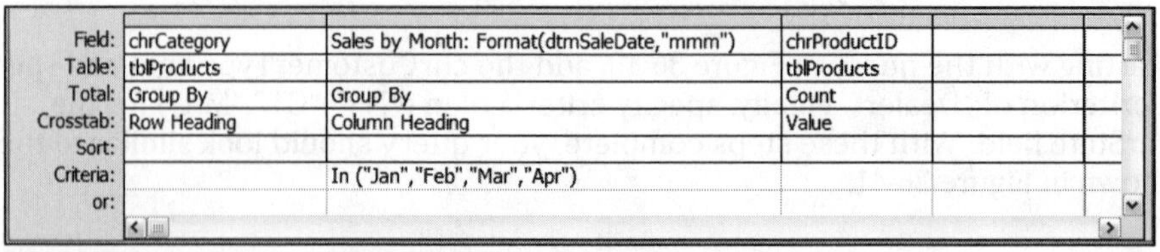

Field:	chrCategory	Sales by Month: Format(dtmSaleDate,"mmm")	chrProductID	
Table:	tblProducts		tblProducts	
Total:	Group By	Group By	Count	
Crosstab:	Row Heading	Column Heading	Value	
Sort:				
Criteria:		In ("Jan","Feb","Mar","Apr")		
or:				

Figure 36-43: A query with months specified as the column heading.

The resulting datasheet is shown in Figure 36-44. Notice that the months are in alphabetical order (April, February, January, March) instead of chronological order (Jan, Feb, Mar, Apr).

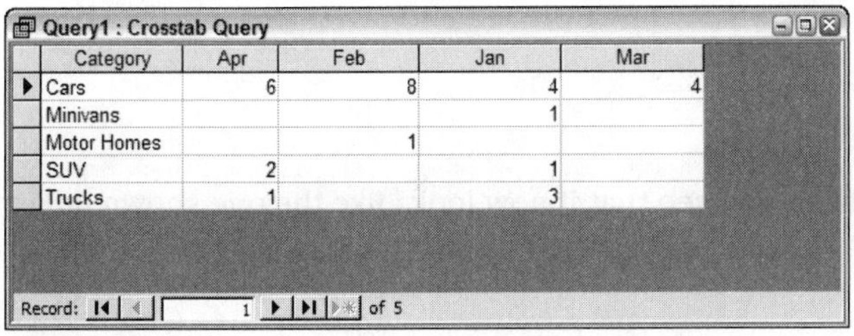

Category	Apr	Feb	Jan	Mar
Cars	6	8	4	4
Minivans			1	
Motor Homes		1		
SUV	2		1	
Trucks	1		3	

Figure 36-44: The datasheet of a query with months specified as the column heading.

To fix this problem, you can use the option Column Headings in the Query Properties box. This option lets you do the following:

✦ Specify an exact order for the appearance of the column headings.

✦ Specify fixed column headings for reports and forms that use crosstab queries.

To specify fixed column headings, follow these steps:

1. Begin with the crosstab query shown in Figure 36-43. Move the pointer to the top half of the query screen and click it once to make sure you are in the top pane.

2. If the Property window is not already open, click the Properties button (a hand holding a piece of paper) on the toolbar or select View ➪ Properties from the Query Design menu.

3. Select the Column Headings text box entry area (third choice).

4. Type **Jan, Feb, Mar, Apr** in the box.

The Query Properties dialog box should look like the one shown in Figure 36-45. When you move to another entry area, Access converts your text into "Jan," "Feb," "Mar," and "Apr," in the Query Properties dialog box.

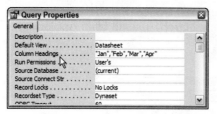

Figure 36-45: The Query Properties dialog box, specifying a display order for the Column Headings.

If you look at the datasheet, you see that it now looks like the one shown in Figure 36-46. The order for the column headings is now chronological Month order.

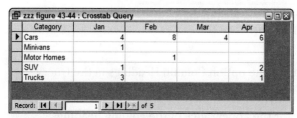

Figure 36-46: The datasheet with the column order specified in month chronological order.

The Crosstab Query Wizard

Access employs several Query Wizards, which are helpful additions to the query design surface. One such Wizard, the Crosstab Query Wizard, is an excellent tool to help you create a simple crosstab query quickly. To see the Crosstab choice, simply click on the New button, and the New Query selection window appears, as shown in Figure 36-47.

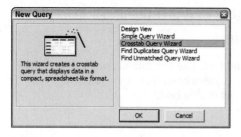

Figure 36-47: Selecting the Access Query Wizard from the New Query dialog box.

The Crosstab Query Wizard has some limitations, however:

✦ **Limitation:** To use more than one table for the crosstab query, you need to create a separate query that has the tables you need for the crosstab query. For example, you may have a Group By row heading from the tblContacts table (chrCustomerType) and a Group By column heading from the tblProducts table (chrCategory). The Crosstab Query Wizard allows you to select only one table or query for the row and column heading.

✦ **Workaround:** Create a query of the four tables, selecting the All Fields reference for each, and save this intermediate query. Then use this intermediate query as the record source for the Wizard.

✦ **Limitation:** The limiting criteria for the Wizard's query cannot be specified. **Workaround:** Make the Wizard do the query and then go in and set the limiting criteria.

✦ **Limitation:** You cannot use a calculated field for Row or Column headings. **Workaround:** Add the calculated field to an intermediate query and use the query for the Wizard.

✦ **Limitation:** Column headings or column orders cannot be specified. **Workaround:** Again, have the Wizard create the query and then modify it.

To use the crosstab query wizard, click the New button in the database window toolbar after clicking the Queries Object button and then select the Crosstab Wizard (third from the top, Figure 36-47) in the dialog box. Click OK and then follow the prompts. Access asks for the following:

✦ The table or query name for the source

✦ The fields for the row headings

✦ The fields for the column headings

✦ The field for the body

✦ The title

After you specify these things, Access creates your crosstab query and then runs it for you.

✦   ✦   ✦

Working with Action and SQL Queries

I n this chapter, you learn about a special type of query, called the *action query*, which enables you to change the field values in your records. For example, you can change a discount field to increase all discounts that are currently 0 to 5 percent or delete all information from the records of a contact that has not sold or bought anything in the past two years.

On the CD-ROM

This chapter will use the database named CHAP37Start.mdb. If you have not already copied it onto your machine from the CD, you will need to do so now. After you have completed this chapter, your database should resemble the one in CHAP37End.mdb.

About Action Queries

The term *action query* defines a query that does something more than simply select a specific group of records and then present it to you in a dynaset. The word "action" suggests performing some operation — doing, influencing, or affecting something. The word is synonymous with operation, performance, and work. This is exactly what an action query does — some specific operation or work.

An action query can be considered a select query that is given a *duty* to perform against a specified group of records in the dynaset.

Types of action queries

When you create any query, Access creates it as a select query automatically. You can specify a different type (such as action) from the Query Design menu. From this menu, you can choose from several types of action queries. The menu's selections are Make-Table, Update, Append, and Delete.

Like select queries, action queries create a dynaset that you can view in a datasheet. To see the dynaset, click the Datasheet button on the toolbar. Unlike select queries, action queries perform an action — specified in the Query by Example (QBE) pane of the query design — when you click the Run button (the button with the exclamation point) on the toolbar.

You can quickly identify action queries in the Database window by the special exclamation point icons that sit beside their names (to the right side). There are four different types of action queries (see Figure 37-1, which shows three of the four types); each has a different icon.

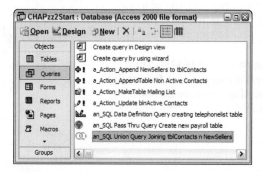

Figure 37-1: The query container of the Database window, showing the different types of queries and their icons — including Action, and SQL specific queries.

Looking at Figure 37-1, several types of action queries can be seen toward the top of the container. Notice that each has a unique icon associated with it. All have the exclamation point as part of the icon — the Append shows a Plus sign and the exclamation point, a Delete query (not shown) has a graphical X and the exclamation point, the Make-Table has a new table (starburst over top-right corner) and the exclamation point, and the Update has a pencil writing and the exclamation point.

Uses of action queries

Action queries can accomplish these tasks:

   ✦ Delete specified records from a table or group of tables.

   ✦ Append records from one table to another.

   ✦ Update information in a group of records.

   ✦ Create a new table from specified records in a query.

The following examples describe some practical uses for action queries:

✦ **Example:** You want to create history tables and then copy all inactive records to them. (You consider a record inactive if a customer hasn't bought anything in more than two years.) You decide to remove the inactive records from your active database tables.

What to do? Use a make-table query to create the history tables and a delete query to remove the unwanted records.

✦ **Example:** One of your former customers, whom you haven't heard from in more than four years, wants to make a purchase; you need to bring the old information back into the active file from the backup files.

What to do? Use an append query to add records from your backup tables to your active tables.

Caution

Unlike select queries, which display data in a specific manner, Action Queries perform actions against the data stored in the underlying tables. This action may be copying the information (data) to another table, modifying the contents of records within the current table, or even deleting records in the current table.

Because of the destructive nature of action queries, it is a good idea to observe the following rules: Always back up your table *before* performing the Action query, and always create and view the action query (use the Datasheet button on the toolbar) before *performing it.*

The process of action queries

Because action queries are *irreversible*, follow this four-step process when you're working with them:

1. Create the action query specifying the fields and the criteria.

2. View the records selected in the action query by clicking the Datasheet button on the toolbar.

3. Run the action query by clicking the Run button on the toolbar.

4. Check the changes in the tables by clicking the Datasheet button on the toolbar.

Caution

Consider backing up your table before creating and running action queries.

If you follow these steps, you can use action queries relatively safely.

Viewing the results of an action query

Action queries perform a specific task—many times a destructive task. Be very careful when using them. It's important to view the changes that they will make (by clicking the datasheet button) before you run the action query and to verify afterward that they made the changes that you anticipated. Before you learn how to create and run an action query, it's also important to review the process for seeing what your changes will look like *before* you change a table permanently.

Viewing a query before using update and delete queries

Before actually performing an action query, you can click the Datasheet View button to see which set of data the action query will work with. Meanwhile, when you're updating or deleting records with an action query, the actions take place on the underlying tables that the query is currently using. To view the results of an update or a delete query, click the Datasheet button to see whether the records will be updated or deleted before committing the action.

Note
If your update query made changes to the fields you used for selecting the records, you may have to look at the underlying table or change to a Select query to see the changes. For example, if you deleted a set of records with an action button, the resulting select dynaset of the same record criteria will show that no records exist — the condition specified has been performed. By removing the delete criteria, you can view the remaining table and verify that all the records specified have been deleted.

Switching to the result table of a make-table or append query

Unlike the Update or Delete queries, Make-Table and Append queries copy resultant records to another table. After specifying the fields and the criteria in the QBE pane of the Query Design window, the Make-Table and the Append queries copy the specified fields and records to another table. When you run the queries, the results take place in another table, not in the current table.

Clicking the Datasheet button shows you a dynaset of only the criteria and fields that were specified, not the actual table that contains the new or added records. To view the results of a Make-Table or Append query, open the new table and view the contents to verify that the Make-Table or Append query worked correctly. If you won't be using the action query again, do not save it. Delete it.

Reversing action queries

Action queries copy or change data in underlying tables. After an action query is executed, it cannot be reversed. Therefore, when you're working with action queries, create a select query first to make sure that the record criteria and selection are correct for the action query.

Caution
Action queries are destructive; before performing one, always make a backup of the underlying tables. You may also consider removing the Action query from your database after the action has been performed if the query will not be used again in the future.

Scoping Criteria

Action queries can use any expression composed of fields, functions, and operators to specify any limiting condition that you need to place on the query. Scoping criteria are one form of record criteria. Normally, the record criteria serve as a filter to tell Access which records to find and/or leave out of the dynaset. Because action queries do not create a dynaset, you use scoping criteria to specify a set of records for Access to operate on.

Creating Action Queries

Creating an action query is very similar to creating a select query. You specify the fields for the query and any *scoping criteria*. In addition to specifying the fields and criteria, you must tell Access to make this query an action-specific one — Append To, Table, Update To, or Delete.

Creating an update action query to change values

In this section, you learn to handle an event that requires changing many records. The type of query used is called an *update* action query.

Suppose that you have noticed that there are many more contact names in the tblContacts table (58) than in the tblSales table (53). This raises your curiosity, so you create a quick totals query to check the buyers who made sales and you find out that there were only 30 buyers based on that query. You then create a simple select query to check how many contacts were actual sellers or both (sellers and buyers) against the products table. To your surprise, there are only three records. Finally, you create another select query to check to see if you have any buyers that have no sales records, and you find two records. So if there are only 30 buyer contact records and only three seller/both contact records, why are the other contact records marked as active (blnActive)? You also know that there are at least two buyer records with no associated sales, and those records have the blnActive field set to yes (true).

Figure 37-2 shows all three of the queries you created to see how many buyers and sellers there were. Notice that Query2, top left corner, uses the Count aggregate function to determine how many sales each customer (contact) has. In contrast, Query3 simply creates a select query with a join between the tblProducts table and the tblContacts table, where the join includes only rows where both tables have the same value — thus, you see only the records that have associated sellers listed. In Query4, the type of link has been changed to show all contacts and only those records where the fields are equal from the sales table. It also has two criteria — only buyers where the idsInvoiceNumber field is Null.

At this time, you do not want to delete any contact records that have no apparent relationship to the system; however, you do want to mark those records as inactive, changing the value from true to false for the blnActive field in the tblContacts table.

> **Note**   If these contact records have no corresponding sales or products records, they are known as widowed records.

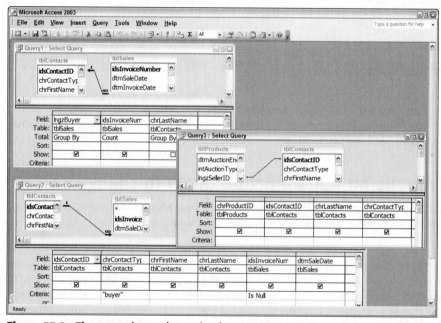

Figure 37-2: Three queries to determine how many contacts made purchases and how many were sellers.

It's possible to update each record in a table individually by using a form or even creating a select query dynaset to make these changes in the datasheet; however, this process can take a very long time if there are many records to change. The method is not only time-consuming but also inefficient. In addition, this method lends itself to typing errors as you enter new text into fields.

The best way to handle this type of event is to use an *update* action query to make many changes in just one operation. You save time and eliminate many of those typos that crop up in manually edited records.

To create an update query that performs these tasks, follow a four-step process:

1. Create a select query. View the data you want to update by clicking the Datasheet button.

2. Convert the select query to an update query; then re-check the query, by clicking on the view button to re-verify that only those records will be affected.

3. Run the update query after you're satisfied that it will affect only the records you want to affect.

4. Check your results.

Creating a select query before an update action

As outlined earlier, the first step in making an update query is to create a select query. In this particular case, the query is to find all contacts who have not made any purchases or are sellers and to change their active status from yes/true to no/false. Perform these steps to create this query:

1. Create a new query using tblContacts, tblSales, tblSalesLineItems, tblProducts, and a second copy of tblContacts from the CHAP37Start database.

2. Change the link from tblContacts to tblSales to include all records from tblContacts and only those from tblSales where the join fields are equal.

3. Link the tblProducts table to the second copy of tblContacts (named tblContacts_1) by linking the lnqzSellerId in tblProducts to idsContactID in tblContacts.

4. Select the idsContactID and chrContactType fields from the tblContacts table; the idsContactID field from the tblContacts_1 table; the idsInvoiceNumber and dtmSaleDate fields from the tblSales table; and the blnActive, chrLastName, and chrFirstName fields from the tblContacts table.

5. Specify a criterion of Is Null in the idsContactID field of the tblContacts_1 table.

6. Specify a criterion of Is Null in the idsInvoiceNumer field of the tblSales table.

7. Specify a criterion of Is Null in the dtmSaleDate field of the tblSales table.

   The Select Query Design window should now resemble the one shown in Figure 37-3.

   Add the sorting directives you see in the figure as well; the three fields are: idsContactID chrLastName, and chrFirstName of tblContacts tables,

   Notice that the QBE pane shows all the fields but shows criteria in only the three fields specified in Steps 5 through 7.

8. Click on the View button and examine the datasheet to make sure that it has only the records you want to change. Return to the design surface when you're finished.

The select query datasheet should resemble the one shown in Figure 37-4. Notice that only the records for contacts that have no sales or no contact ID as a seller appear in the dynaset — in other words, contacts with no associated records in the sales or products table. It shows a check box instead of yes, no, 0, or –1. This is done by specifying the field property Format as type Yes/No in the field blnActive in the table design.

Note Your example may show zeros instead — to see Yes/No, simply specify a field property of Yes/No as the Format type for the column.

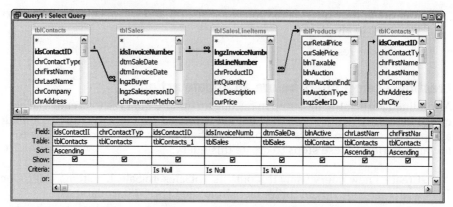

Figure 37-3: Creating a select query to be converted to an update query to change the value of the blnActive field.

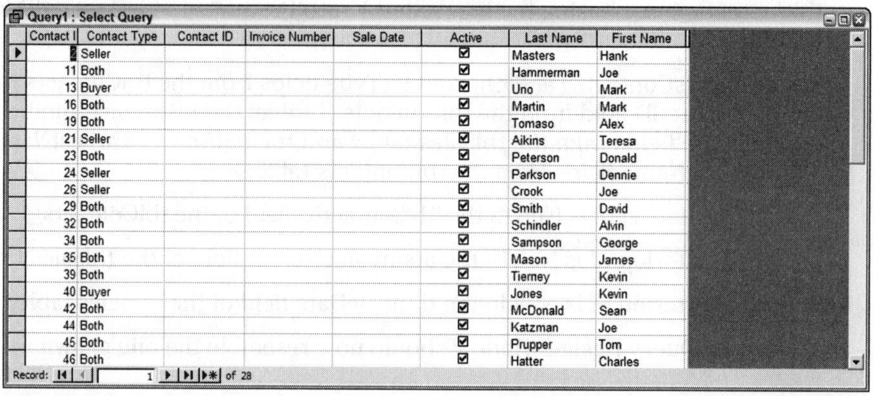

Figure 37-4: Dynaset showing only the records for contacts that have no associated records in products or sales.

As you see in Figure 37-4, in this case 28 records show no corresponding records, yet all these contacts are marked as active. You are now ready to convert the select query to an update query.

Converting a select query to an update query

After you create a select query and verify the selection of records, it's time to create the update query. To convert the select query to an update query, follow these steps:

1. Click on the View button to return to the design window.

2. Select Update Query from the Query Type button on the toolbar or select Query ➪ Update Query from the menu.

Access changes the title of the Query window from Query1: Select Query to Query1: Update Query. Access also adds the Update To: property row to the QBE pane, above the Criteria: row.

3. In the Update To: cell of blnActive, enter No as shown in Figure 37-5.

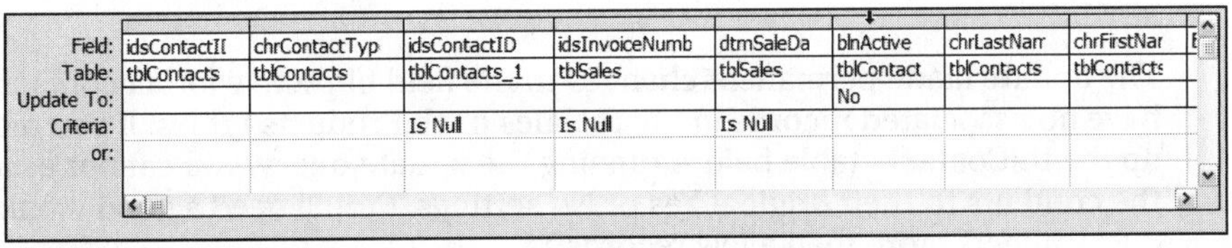

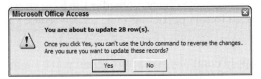

Field:	idsContactII	chrContactTyp	idsContactID	idsInvoiceNumb	dtmSaleDa	blnActive	chrLastNarr	chrFirstNar	E
Table:	tblContacts	tblContacts	tblContacts_1	tblSales	tblSales	tblContact	tblContacts	tblContacts	
Update To:						No			
Criteria:			Is Null	Is Null	Is Null				
or:									

Figure 37-5: The design pane for the update query. Notice that the blnActive Update To: cell has No in it.

4. Click the view button to re-verify that only those 28 records will be affected. After you verify that only those records are affected, return to the design window by clicking on the View button again.

5. Click the Run button on the toolbar (or select Query ⇨ Run from the menu).

Access displays the dialog box shown in Figure 37-6. This dialog box displays a message: "You are about to update x row(s). Once you click Yes, you can't use the Undo command to reverse the changes. Are you sure you want to update these records?" Two command buttons are presented: Yes and No.

Microsoft Office Access

You are about to update 28 row(s).

⚠ Once you click Yes, you can't use the Undo command to reverse the changes. Are you sure you want to update these records?

[Yes] [No]

Figure 37-6: The dialog box for updating records warns you that you are about to update x row(s) and that this action is irreversible.

6. Click the Yes button to complete the query and update the records. Selecting No stops the procedure (no records are updated).

Caution

If you're changing tables that are attached to another database, you cannot cancel the query after it is started.

Note

You can change more than one field at a time by filling in the Update To: cell of any field that you want to change. You can also change the field contents of fields that you used for limiting the records—that is, the criteria.

Checking your results

After completing the update query, check the results by clicking the datasheet button and examining the values in the datasheet. You could have converted back to a select query to be safe; however, the update query can be viewed more quickly by clicking the datasheet button — the update has already been performed at this stage.

The update made permanent changes to the field blnActive for all contacts that have no associated records in the tblSales or tblProducts tables. If you did not back up the tblContacts table before running the update query, you cannot easily restore the contents to their original Yes or No settings. (You'll need a good memory if your query affects more than a few records!)

Note   If you update a field that was used for a limiting criterion, you must change the criterion in the select query to the new value to verify the changes.

Although you will not use this query again, if you like, you can save this query by naming it a_Action_Update blnActive Contacts.

Cross-Reference   The results of this table will be used later in the section "Creating a simple append query."

Creating a new table using a make-table query

You can use an action query to create new tables based on scoping criteria. To make a new table, you create a make-table query. Consider the following situation as an example that might give rise to this particular task and for which you would create a make-table query.

Suppose a local automobile supply company has approached you for a mailing list of customers who have made car or truck purchases from you. This company wants to send these customers a coupon book for several cleaning products for each vehicle they have purchased. The supply company plans to create the mailing labels and send the form letters if you supply a table of customer information, sales dates, and vehicle information they purchased. The company also stipulates that, because this is a trial mailing, only those customers you've seen in the past six months should receive letters.

You have decided to send the company the requested table of information, so now you need to create a new table from the system tables. A make-table query will perform these actions.

Creating the make-table query

You decide to create a make-table query for all customers who purchased vehicles (cars and trucks only) and who have visited you in the past six months. Perform these steps to create this query:

1. Create a new query using the tblContacts, tblSales, tblSalesLineItems, and tblProducts tables.

2. Select chrFirstName, chrLastName, chrAddress, chrCity, chrState, and chrZipCode from the tblContacts table; dtmSaleDate from the tblSales table; chrDescription from the tblSalesLineItems table; and chrCategory from the tblProducts table.

3. Specify a criterion of Between Now() and Now()–182 in the dtmSaleDate field.

4. Specify a criterion of Cars or Trucks in the chrCategory field.

   The Query Design window should resemble the one shown in Figure 37-7. Some of the fields are missing from the left side of the query so that you can see the two fields (dtmSaleDate and chrCategory) that contain criteria.

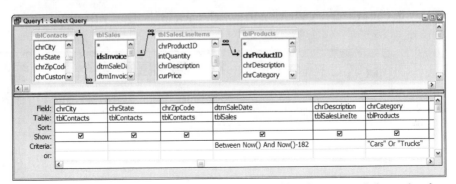

Figure 37-7: The select table for creating a make table of customer information for the past six months.

5. Click on the View button to verify that only the past six months of records are shown. Then re-click on the View button to return to query design mode.

6. Select Make-Table from the Query Type button on the toolbar.

   Access displays the Make Table dialog box, as shown in Figure 37-8.

Figure 37-8: The Make Table dialog box with a table name entered. Notice that the table can be saved in this database or another database.

7. Type **Mailing List for Coupons** in the Table Name: field; press Enter or click OK.

Notice that the name of the window changes from Query1: Select Query to Query1: Make Table Query. Other than the title, there is no other visual change to the query to tell you that it is a Make Table query.

8. Click the Datasheet View button on the toolbar to view the dynaset (re-verifying the fields and data that will be sent to the new table). See Figure 37-9.

9. Make sure that the dynaset has only the records you specified.

10. Click the Design button to switch back to the Query Design view.

First Name	Last Name	Address	City	State	Zip Code	Sale Date	Description	Category
John	Jones	11253 Main Stre	Springfield	MA	01111-1253	1/15/2003	2003 Fordman 1	Trucks
John	Jones	11253 Main Stre	Springfield	MA	01111-1253	1/15/2003	1960 Chevy Pic	Trucks
John	Jones	11253 Main Stre	Springfield	MA	01111-1253	1/15/2003	1957 Chevy Sec	Cars
John	Jones	11253 Main Stre	Springfield	MA	01111-1253	1/15/2003	1950 Fordman (	Cars
William	Gleason	196 East Street	Derby	CT	06418-	2/27/2003	1962 AALLFA F	Cars
William	Gleason	196 East Street	Derby	CT	06418-	2/27/2003	1965 Shelly Stu	Cars
John	Bright	46 Pleasantville	West Bridgewat	MA	02379-	2/24/2003	1971 Pontanic F	Cars
John	Bright	46 Pleasantville	West Bridgewat	MA	02379-	2/24/2003	2001 Collectors	Cars
Dennis	Mchugh	500 Ferret Lane	Jefferson	TX	75657-	4/24/2003	1940 Classic Ai	Cars
Dennis	Mchugh	500 Ferret Lane	Jefferson	TX	75657-	4/24/2003	1967 Shelly Stu	Cars
Dennis	Mchugh	500 Ferret Lane	Jefferson	TX	75657-	4/24/2003	1957 Chevy Sec	Cars
Brandon	Aley	1916 Erickson [	Fairbanks	MA	12333-	5/24/2003	2001 Collectors	Cars
Larry	Calson	60 Mexico Drive	Chicota	TX	75425-	6/1/2003	1988 Fordman	Trucks

Record: ◄◄ ◄ [1] ► ►I ►✳ of 13

Figure 37-9: The dynaset of contacts that have purchased cars or trucks from you in the past six months. In this example, the current date is before June 12, 2003. Your results will be different unless you use the same date.

11. Click the Run button on the toolbar or select Query ⇨ Run from the menu.

Access indicates how many records it will copy to the new table (see Figure 37-10).

12. Click the Yes button to complete the query and make the new table. Selecting No stops the procedure (no records are copied).

Figure 37-10: The dialog box for copying records.

Although you will not use this query again, if you like, you can save this query by naming it a_Action_MakeTable Mailing List.

When you're creating numerous make-table queries, you need to select Make-Table Query from the Query Type button on the toolbar or select Query ➪ Make-Table from the menu; either method renames the make-table query each time. Access assumes that you want to overwrite the existing table if you don't reselect the make-table option. Access warns you about overwriting before performing the new make-table query; as an alternative, you could change the Destination table name on the Property sheet.

Checking your results

After you complete the make-table query, check your results by opening the new table Mailing List for Coupons, which was added to the database container (see Figure 37-11).

chrFirstName	chrLastName	chrAddress	chrCity	chrState	chrZipCode	dtmSaleDate	chrDescription	chrCategory
John	Jones	11253 Main Street	Springfield	MA	01111-1253	1/15/2003	2003 Fordman T-150 Regular C	Trucks
John	Jones	11253 Main Street	Springfield	MA	01111-1253	1/15/2003	1960 Chevy Pickup	Trucks
John	Jones	11253 Main Street	Springfield	MA	01111-1253	1/15/2003	1957 Chevy Sedan	Cars
John	Jones	11253 Main Street	Springfield	MA	01111-1253	1/15/2003	1950 Fordman Coupe	Cars
William	Gleason	196 East Street	Derby	CT	06418-	2/27/2003	1962 AALLFA Red Spidery 20(	Cars
William	Gleason	196 East Street	Derby	CT	06418-	2/27/2003	1965 Shelly Stunning Red Cob	Cars
John	Bright	46 Pleasantville RD	West Bridge	MA	02379-	2/24/2003	1971 Pontanic Red Converible	Cars
John	Bright	46 Pleasantville RD	West Bridge	MA	02379-	2/24/2003	2001 Collectors Chevy Corvet	Cars
Dennis	Mchugh	500 Ferret Lane	Jefferson	TX	75657-	4/24/2003	1940 Classic Antique Convertil	Cars
Dennis	Mchugh	500 Ferret Lane	Jefferson	TX	75657-	4/24/2003	1967 Shelly Stunning Red Mus	Cars
Dennis	Mchugh	500 Ferret Lane	Jefferson	TX	75657-	4/24/2003	1957 Chevy Sedan	Cars
Brandon	Aley	1916 Erickson Drive	Fairbanks	MA	12333-	5/24/2003	2001 Collectors Chevy Corvet	Cars
Larry	Calson	60 Mexico Drive	Chicota	TX	75425-	6/1/2003	1988 Fordman T350 Bucket	Trucks

Record: 1 of 13

Figure 37-11: The new table Mailing List for Coupons created from a Make-Table query.

Note When you create a table from a make-table query, the fields in the new table inherit the data type and field size from the fields in the query's underlying tables; however, no other field or table properties are transferred. If you want to define a primary key or other properties, you need to edit the design of the new table.

Tip You can also use a make-table action query to create a backup of your tables before you create action queries that change the contents of the tables. Backing up a table using a make-table action query does not copy the table's properties or primary key to the new table.

Copying Any Database Object

To copy any database object (table, query, form, or other object) while you're in the Database window, follow these steps:

1. Highlight the object you need to copy.

2. Press Ctrl+C (or select Edit ➪ Copy) to copy the object to the Clipboard.

3. Press Ctrl+V (or select Edit ➪ Paste) to paste the object from the Clipboard.

4. Enter the new object name (table, form, and so forth) and click the OK button in the dialog box. If the object is a table, you also can specify Structure with or without the data or append it to an existing table.

Creating queries to append records

As the word *append* suggests, an append query attaches or adds records to a specified table. An append query adds records *from* the table you're using to another table. The table you want to add records to must already exist. You can append records to a table in the same database or in another Access database.

Append queries are very useful for adding information to another table on the basis of some scoping criteria. Even so, append queries are not always the fastest way of adding records to another database. For example, if you need to append all fields and all records from one table to a new table, the append query is not the best way to do it. Instead, use the Copy and Paste options on the Edit menu when you're working with the table in a datasheet or form.

Note   You can add records to an open table. You don't have to close the table before adding records. However, Access does not automatically refresh the view of the table that has records added to it. To refresh the table, press Shift+F9. This action requires the table so that you can see the appended records.

When you're working with append queries, be aware of these rules:

✦ If the table you're appending records to has a primary key field, the records you add cannot have Null values or duplicate primary key values. If they do, Access will not append the records and you will get no warning.

✦ If you add records to another database table, you must know the location and name of the database.

✦ If you use the asterisk (*) field in a QBE row, you cannot also use individual fields from the same table. Access assumes that you're trying to add field contents twice to the same record and will not append the records.

✦ If you append records with an AutoNumber field (an Access-specified primary key), do not include the AutoNumber field if the table you're appending to also has the field and record contents (this causes the problem specified in the first rule). Also, if you're adding to an empty table and you want the new table to have a new AutoNumber number (that is, order number) based on the criteria, do not use the AutoNumber field.

By following these simple rules, your append query will perform as expected and become a very useful tool.

Creating a simple append query

Here's an example that will help illustrate the use of append queries: You have found that you have many contacts records (from earlier in this chapter when you updated the blnActive field using the a_Action_Update blnActive Contacts query) that have no associated sales or products records related to them. You have decided to archive the records by appending them to an existing backup table named Non Active Contacts. This is a relatively simple process, because you have already identified the records by creating the query.

In this case, you want to add records to the backup table named tblNonActiveContacts for the nonrelated contacts in your active tables.

1. Create a new query using the tblContacts table.

2. Click on the title bar of the tblContacts table to select all the fields and drag them to the table grid.

3. Specify a criterion of No in the last field — blnActive.

4. Click the View button to verify that only those records where blnActive is No are displayed.

   Click the View button to return to the design window.

5. Select Append Query from the button or Query menu.

   Access opens the Append dialog box, as shown in Figure 37-12.

Figure 37-12: The Append dialog box for creating an Append Query.

6. Select **Non Active Contacts** in the Table Name: field; press Enter or click OK.

Notice that the name of the window changes from Query1: Select Query to Query1: Append Query. Access also adds the Append To: property row to the QBE pane, above the Criteria: row. It populates each cell with the name of the field in the Non Active Contacts table that the field contents will be moved to.

7. Click the Datasheet View button on the toolbar to view the dynaset (re-verifying the fields and data that will be sent to the new table).

8. Make sure that the dynaset has only the records you specified.

9. Click the Design button to switch back to the Query Design view.

10. Click the Run button on the toolbar or select Query ⇨ Run from the menu.

Access indicates how many records it will append to the new table (see Figure 37-13).

11. Click the Yes button to complete the query and make the new table. Selecting No stops the procedure (no records are copied).

Figure 37-13: The Append information box for appending records.

Although you will not use this query again, if you like, you can save this query by naming it a_Action_AppendTable Non Active Contacts.

Note   There is another query in your database named a_Action_Append NewSellers to tblContacts. This append query is used to append records from the table named NewSellers to the tblContacts table. It is put here so that you can see how you can append records from one system's tables into your tables. This could be when you obtain another company's list of sellers. Note that the NewSellers table does not have a idsContactID field. When you append the three records from the new table, Access will automatically assign a new idsContactID to each record.

At this point, you could create a delete query to remove these records from the table. You may want to read the next sections before moving on to the delete query.

Cross-Reference   You could jump ahead to the section "Creating a query to delete records" if you want to remove some records.

Backing up tables for a complex append query

Note The next several sections will demonstrate appending records from your four main tables into Inactive contacts and related records tables.

In addition to copying off nonrelated records, you may want to append records that are old in the system to backup tables. In other words, you may want to copy out-dated records from the three primary tables (tblSales, tblSalesLineItems, and tblProducts) to back up files. Perhaps, you will copy off any records where the customer (contact) has not made any purchases over the past two years. In this case, you need four backup files to perform this exercise. To create the backup files from the four tables, perform the following steps:

1. Press F11 or Alt+F1 to display the Database window.
2. Click the Tables object button to display the list of tables.
3. Click the tblSales table to highlight it.
4. Press Ctrl+C (or select Edit ⇨ Copy) to copy the object tblSales table to the Clipboard.
5. Press Ctrl+V (or select Edit ⇨ Paste) to display the Paste Table As dialog box.
6. Click Structure Only in the Paste Options section of the dialog box (or press Alt+S to select Structure Only).
7. Click the Table Name: box and type Inactive Sales Backup.
8. Click OK (or press Enter after typing the filename).
9. Open the Inactive Sales Backup table (which should be empty); then close the table.

Repeat this process for the remaining two tables (tblSalesLineItems and tblProducts tables), naming them Inactive SalesLineItems Backup and Inactive Products Backup, respectively.

To create an append query that copies the inactive contacts records, follow a four-step process:

1. Create a select query to verify that only the records that you want to append are copied.
2. Convert the select query to an append query and run it.
3. Check your results.

Note When you're using the append query, only fields with names that match in the two tables are copied. For example, you may have a small table with six fields and another with nine fields. The table with nine fields has only five of the six field names that match fields in the smaller table. If you append records from the smaller table to the larger table, only the five matching fields are appended; the other four fields remain blank.

Creating the select query for an append query

To create a select query for an append query, follow these steps:

1. Create a new query using the tblContacts, tblSales, tblSalesLineItems, and tblProducts tables from the database.

2. Select the dtmSaleDate field from the tblSales table.

3. Specify a criterion of < 1/1/2001 in the dtmSaleDate field.

   You may want to select some additional fields from each table, such as chrFirstName, chrLastName, chrDescription, chrCatetory, and so forth. The Select Query Design window should resemble the one shown in Figure 37-14. The only field and criterion that must be in this select query is the first field: dtmSaleDate. If you add any other fields, make sure that you remove them before converting this query to an append query.

4. Go to the datasheet and make sure that all the dtmSaleDate field contents are before January 1, 2001 (see Figure 37-15).

5. Return to design mode.

6. If you added additional fields to look at, remove all fields from the QBE pane except the dtmSaleDate field with the Criteria: of < #1/1/2001#.

With the select query created correctly, you are ready to convert the select query to an append query.

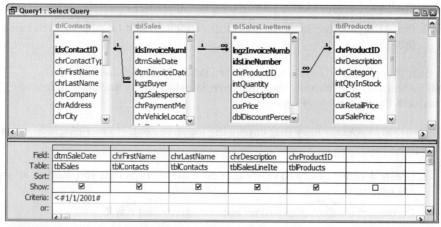

Figure 37-14: The tables tblContacts, tblSales, tblSalesLineItems, and tblProducts are in the top pane, and selected fields are in the QBE pane. Only the first field must be there for an append query.

Sale Date	First Name	Last Name	Description	Product ID
2/4/2000	Michael	Irwin	1908 Ford Model T Rumble I	CAR-202
2/4/2000	Michael	Irwin	1912 Ford Motel T Ice Truck	TRK-202

Record: 1 of 2

Figure 37-15: A dynaset of records for all sales before 1/1/2001. This will be converted to an append query.

Converting to an append query

After you create the select query and verify that it is correct, you need to create the append query (actually, three different append queries — one each for the tables tblProducts, tblSalesLineItems, and tblSales — because append queries work with only one table at a time). For this example, first copy all fields from the tblProducts table.

To convert the select query to an append query and run it, perform the following steps:

1. Make sure that only the dtmSaleDate field is present in the QBE pane.

2. Deselect the Show: property of the dtmSaleDate field.

3. Select Append Query from the Query Type button on the toolbar, or select Query ➪ Append Query from the Design menu.

   Access displays the Append dialog box, as shown in Figure 37-16.

Append

Append To

Table Name: Inactive Products Backup

○ Current Database
○ Another Database:
File Name:

OK
Cancel
Browse...

Figure 37-16: The Append dialog box. Use this box to select the table you want to append records into.

4. Type **Inactive Products Backup** in the Table Name: field or select it from the pull-down menu and press Enter or click OK.

5. Drag the asterisk (*) field from the tblProducts table to the QBE pane to select all fields.

   The QBE pane should look like the one shown in Figure 37-17. Access automatically fills in the Append To: field under the All field-selector column.

At this point, you can click the datasheet button to see what records Access will actually append to the new table. It should show you two records. After you view the records, you should then return to the design mode to continue with the action query.

6. Click the Run button on the toolbar (or select Query ➪ Run from the menu).

Access displays a dialog box that displays the message "You are about to append x row(s)." Then it presents two buttons (Yes and No). After you click Yes, the Undo command cannot be used to reverse the changes.

7. Click the Yes button to complete the query and copy (append) the records to the backup table. Selecting No stops the procedure (no records are copied).

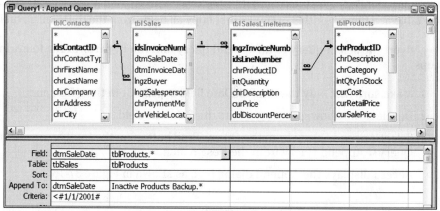

Figure 37-17: The QBE pane for an appended query. Append all older records from the tblProducts table into another table.

Tip   After you have run the Append query, you may want to open the Inactive Products Backup table to verify that it copied the records over—if you are following along with the example tables, it should have two records in the table.

After the tblProducts table's older records are backed up, you are ready to append records into the Inactive SalesLineItems Backup table and the Inactive Sales Backup table. Before you append fields from these other tables, however, you must remove the previous All selector field [tblProducts.*] from the QBE pane and the Visit Details table from the top pane.

To append the tblSalesLineItem records, follow these steps:

1. Continuing with the same query above, delete the tblProducts table from the top pane—this will automatically remove the tblProducts.* field from the grid.

Tip   Because you have already copied off the records from the tblProducts table, you no longer need it for the last two append queries.

2. Select Select Query from the Query menu or the toolbar.

3. Select the asterisk (*) field for the tblSalesLineItems table and drag it down to the QBE pane.

4. Click the View button to verify that the correct records have been selected. The datasheet should display two records. Click the View button again to return to the design window.

5. Reselect Query ⇨ Append Query to activate the Append dialog box.

6. Type, or select, **Inactive SalesLineItems Backup** for the name of the table to append to and click the OK button.

7. Click the Run button on the toolbar (or select Query ⇨ Run from the menu).

   Access displays a dialog box that displays the message "You are about to append x row(s)." Then it presents two buttons (Yes and No). After you click Yes, the Undo command cannot be used to reverse the changes.

8. Click the Yes button to complete the query and copy (append) the records to the backup table. Selecting No stops the procedure (no records are copied).

Tip   If you receive an error stating that there is an INSERT INTO error, check to see if you have a field name in the Append To: cell of the dtmSaleDate. If you do, remove it because this field should be blank.

With the tblSalesLineItems table records backed up, you should create an Append query for the tblSales table. To do so, follow these steps:

1. Remove the tblSalesLineItems table from the query (which will also remove the All selector field for the [tblSalesLineItems.*] QBE automatically). Leave the dtmSaleDate Field in the first row of the QBE pane with a criteria of < #1/1/2001#.

2. Repeat the preceding Steps 2 through 8 with the appropriate responses for the tblSales table.

3. After you have a select query active, select the asterisk (*) field for the tblSales table. Check your records: there should only be one.

4. Reselect Query ⇨ Append, and type or select **Inactive Sales Backup** for the name of the table to append to.

   Access will add the field name dtmSaleDate from the Append To: cell of the dtmSaleDate Field cell—and remove it from the Append To: cell, making the cell blank.

5. Click Run.

You do not have to save this query because it has already been run.

Caution   If you create an append query by using the asterisk (*) field and you also use a field from the same table as the All asterisk field to specify a criterion, you must take the criteria field name out of the Append To: row. If you don't, Access reports an error. Remember that the field for the criterion is already included in the asterisk field.

Checking your results

After you complete the three append table queries, re-check your results. To do so, follow these steps:

1. Go to the Database window and select each of the three tables to be appended to (Inactive Sales Backup: 1 record; Inactive SalesLineItems Backup: 2 records; and Inactive Products Backup: 2 records).

2. View the new records.

Note   At this point, you could see if Michael Irwin's record is now inactive; that is, it has no sales records associated with it. If it is, you could create another append query to move this record to another Inactive Backup database (perhaps named Inactive Contacts Backup).

Creating a query to delete records

Of all the action queries, the *delete query* is the most dangerous. Unlike the other types of queries you've worked with, delete queries remove records from tables permanently and *irreversibly*.

Like other action queries, delete queries act on a group of records on the basis of scoping criteria.

A delete action query can work with multiple tables to delete records. If you intend to delete related records from multiple tables, however, you must do the following:

✦ Define relationships between the tables in the Relationships Builder.

✦ Check the Enforce Referential Integrity option for the join between tables.

✦ Check the Cascade Delete Related Records option for the join between tables (for one-to-one or one-to-many relationships).

Figure 37-18 shows the Edit Relationships dialog box for the join line between the tblSales and tblSalesLineItems tables. Notice that the options Enforce Referential Integrity and Cascade Delete Related Records are both selected (as is Cascade update).

Notice that the relationship between the tblSalesLineItems and tblProducts tables is a many-to-one rather than a one-to-many. Therefore, cascade deletes from the tblSalesLineItems side will not work. To delete related records in the tblProducts table, you will need to create a separate Delete query first. However, the tblSales and tblSalesLineItems tables can have records deleted from both of them in one operation.

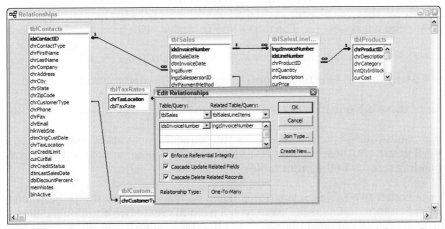

Figure 37-18: The Edit Relationships dialog box, showing that Referential Integrity is being Enforced and the Cascade Delete Related Records is active.

When working with one-to-many relationships without defining relationships and putting Cascade Delete on, Access deletes records from only one table at a time. Specifically, Access deletes the *many* side of the relationship first. Then you must remove the many table from the query and delete the records from the *one* side of the query.

This method is time-consuming and awkward. Therefore, when you're deleting related records from one-to-many relationship tables, make sure that you define relationships between the tables and check the Cascade Delete box in the Edit Relationships dialog box. By doing this, you can delete from all related tables by creating a single Delete query.

Caution Because of the permanently destructive action of a delete query, always make backup copies of your tables before working with them.

The following example illustrates the use of two Access action Delete queries. In this case, you have a couple of records to delete from the tlbSales and tblSalesLineItems tables. However, you also have two records to delete from the tblProducts table. This table will have to be worked with first.

Note Earlier, you copied records from tlbContacts to a non active contacts table. These records could also be deleted by separately deleting these records, based on the query that was used to append them to a new table.

Because the tblProducts records are dependent upon the tblSalesLineItems and tblSales tables, you will need to create a separate Delete query to get rid of these records.

You are going to delete all records of products that were sold before January 1, 2001. Recall that you already copied all old sales records to three backup tables in the append query section. The tables you're dealing with have these relationships:

✦ One tblSales record can have many tblSalesLineItems records.

✦ Many tblSalesLineItem records can have one related tblProduct record.

One of these is a one-to-many relationship; the other is a many-to-one relationship.

As a result, you will have to delete the tblProduct records separately from the other two. If you don't, these records may stay in the tblProducts table with no corresponding records in the other tables — widowed.

For the other two tables, if you don't define permanent relationships between the tables and turn on Cascade Delete, you'll need to create two additional delete queries. (You would need to delete from the tblSalesLineItems and tblSales tables — in that order.)

With relations set and Cascade Delete on, however, you have to delete only the records from the tblSales table; Access automatically deletes all related records in the tblSalesLineItems table. For this example, you have already appended the records to another table — or you have made a new table of the records that you're about to delete, set up permanent relationships among the three tables, and turned on Cascade Delete for relationships between tblSales and tblSalesLineItems.

Creating a dependent delete query

To create a *delete* query for all products that were used in sales older than 1/1/2001, perform these steps:

1. Make a backup copy of the tblProducts table, naming it "Copy tblProducts" using the Ctrl+C, Ctrl+V method.

2. Create a new query using the tblSales, tblSalesLineItems, and tblProducts tables.

3. Select dtmSaleDate from the tblSales table.

4. Specify a criterion of <1/1/2001 for the dtmSaleDate field.

5. Select the tblProducts.* field and drop it in the grid.

6. Click the View button to verify that it found the two records, appended to the Inactive Products Backup table earlier. Return to the Design window by clicking the View button again.

7. Select Query ⇨ Delete Query from the Design menu or the toolbar.

The name of the window changes from Query1: Select Query to Query1: Delete Query. A new row is added to the QBE pane—Delete:. This row is immediately above the Criteria field.

The Delete: cell of the dtmSaleDate field will say "Where" in it.

The Delete: cell of the tblProducts.* field will say "From" in it. The Delete Query Design window is shown in Figure 37-19. Notice that it has the criteria field, dtmSaleDate, in the first column with a criteria set of < #1/1/2001# and the tblSales.* field in the second column. The Delete: row shows a value of Where under the dtmSaleDate column and From under the tblSales.* column.

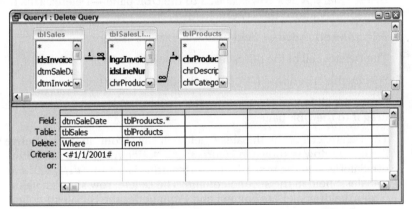

Figure 37-19: The delete query's QBE pane. The Delete: row has been added to the pane, and the where and from conditions are automatically set by Access.

8. Click the Run button on the toolbar (or select Query ➪ Run from the menu).

Access displays a dialog box with the message "You are about to delete x row(s) from the specified table (tblProducts). After you click Yes, you can't use the Undo command to reverse the changes. Are you sure that you want to delete the selected records?" In this case, it will report that you are about to delete 1 row(s) from the tblProducts table.

9. Click the Yes button to complete the query.

The records are removed from the tblProducts table. When you click Yes, Access deletes the records only in the tblProducts table. It does nothing with the records in the tblSalesLineItems or tblSales tables.

At this point, you could remove the tblProducts table, do the same delete procedure for the tblSalesLineItems table, and then follow up by doing the same to the tblSales table. However, there is a better way—cascade deleting from both tables at once.

Creating a cascading delete query

To create a *cascading delete* query for all sales older than 1/1/2001, along with their line items, perform these steps:

1. Make backup copies of both tables (tblSales and tblSalesLineItems), naming them "Copy of <name of file>" using the Ctrl+C, Ctrl+V method.

2. Create a new query using the tblSales table.

3. Select Query ⇨ Delete Query from the Design menu.

   The name of the window changes from Query1: Select Query to Query1: Delete Query. A new row is added to the QBE pane — Delete:. This row is immediately above the Criteria field.

4. Select the dtmSaledate field from the tblSales table.

   The Delete: cell of the dtmSaleDate field will say "Where" in it.

5. Specify the criterion < 1/1/2001 in the dtmSaleDate field.

6. Select the all fields selector from the tblSales table — asterisks (*) field and drag it to the QBE pane.

   The Delete: cell of the tblSales.* field will say "From" in it. The Delete Query Design window is shown in Figure 37-20. Notice that it has the criteria field, dtmSaleDate, in the first column with a criteria set of < #1/1/2001# and the tblSales.* field in the second column. The Delete: row shows a value of Where under the dtmSaleDate column and From under the tblSales.* column.

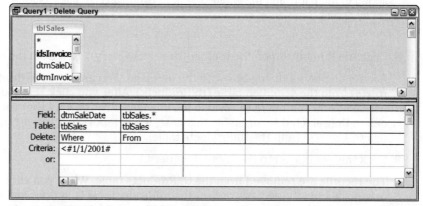

Figure 37-20: The delete query's QBE pane. The Delete: row has been added to the pane, and the where and from conditions are automatically set by Access.

7. Go to the datasheet and verify that only records that show a date less than January 1, 2001 (< 1/1/2001) are there.

8. Return to the Design window.

9. Click the Run button on the toolbar (or select Query ➪ Run from the menu).

   Access displays a dialog box with the message "You are about to delete x row(s) from the specified table (tblSasles). After you click Yes, you can't use the Undo command to reverse the changes. Are you sure that you want to delete the selected records?" In this case, it will report that you are about to delete 1 row(s) from the tblSales table. However, Access will also automatically delete the two rows from the tblSalesLineItems table. It will not report how many rows will be deleted from the other table that is linked to the table you selected.

10. Click the Yes button to complete the query.

   The records are removed from both tables. When you click Yes, Access deletes the records in the tblSales table and then automatically deletes the related records in the tblSalesLineItems table. Selecting No stops the procedure (no records are deleted).

Remember that a delete query permanently and irreversibly removes the records from the table(s). Therefore, it is important that the records to be deleted are backed up *before* they are deleted.

Checking your results

After completing the delete query, you can check your results by clicking the Datasheet button on the toolbar. If the delete query worked correctly, you will see no records in the datasheet.

You have now deleted all records of old sales (<1/1/2001) from the database tables tblProducts, tblSales, and tblSalesLineItems.

Tip

Delete queries remove entire records, not just the data in specific fields. If you need to delete only values in specific fields, use an update query to change the values to empty values.

Creating other queries using the Query Wizards

In the preceding chapter, you learned to use a Query Wizard to create a crosstab query. Access has two other Wizards that can help maintain your databases:

✦ **Find Duplicate Query Wizard:** Shows duplicate records in a single table on the basis of a field in the table.

✦ **Find Unmatched Query Wizard:** Shows all records that do not have a corresponding record in another table (for example, a sale with an invalid contact).

The Find Duplicate Query Wizard works on a single table. The Find Unmatched Query Wizard compares records from one table with another.

These Wizards (along with all the others, such as the Crosstab Wizard) are listed when you first start a new query.

Find Duplicate Query Wizard

This Wizard helps you create a query that reports which records in a table are duplicated using a field or fields in the table as a basis. Access asks which fields you want to use for checking duplication and then prompts you to enter some other fields that you may want to see in the query. Finally, Access asks for a title and then it creates and displays the query.

This type of Wizard query can help you find duplicate key violations, a valuable trick when you want to take an existing table and make a unique key field with existing data. If you try to create a unique key field and Access reports an error, you know that you have Nulls in the field or you have duplicate records. The query helps find the duplicates.

Find Unmatched Query Wizard

This Wizard helps you create a query that reports any orphan or widow records between two tables.

An *orphan* is a record in a *many*-side table that has no corresponding record in the one-side table. For example, you may have a sale tblSales table that does not have any corresponding contact it is related to (the sale is an orphan).

A *widow* is a record in the *one* side of a one-to-many or one-to-one table that does not have a corresponding record in the other table. For example, you may have a contact who has no sales in the tblSales table or product in the tblProducts table. The same situation exists if you have any products in the tblProducts table that have no corresponding sales related to them. We covered this situation in the update table section earlier in this chapter.

Access asks for the names of the two tables to compare; it also asks for the link field name between the tables. Access prompts you for the fields that you want to see in the first table and for a title. Then it creates the query.

This type of query can help find records that have no corresponding records in other tables. If you create a relationship between tables and try to set referential integrity but Access reports that it cannot activate the feature, some records are violating integrity. This query helps find them quickly.

To create an *unmatched record* from tblProducts to tblSalesLineItems (products in the system with no corresponding sales) query, using the Wizard, perform these steps:

1. Select the Queries button and click the New button of the Queries container of the Database window.

   Access displays the New Query window.

2. Select Find Unmatched Query Wizard from the choices and double-click it or click OK.

   The Find Unmatched Query Wizard's first screen appears, as shown in Figure 37-21.

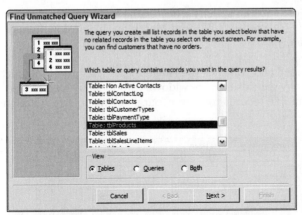

Figure 37-21: The first screen of the Unmatched Query Wizard. Here is where you select the tblProducts table.

3. Select the tblProducts table from the first screen of the Wizard by either high-lighting it and clicking the Next button or double-clicking the tblProducts table name.

You are moved to the second screen of the Wizard. Here you select the second table to match against.

4. Select the tblSalesLineItems table from the choices and click the Next button.

5. Make sure the chrProductID number field is highlighted in both tables on the third screen and click the Next button.

6. Select the fields you wish to see in the query — chrProductID, chrDescription, chrCategory, intQtyInStock, and curCost. Then click the Next button for the final screen, which is shown in Figure 37-22.

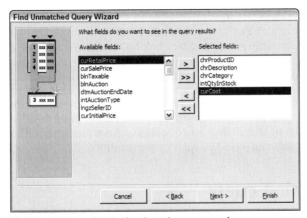

Figure 37-22: This is the fourth screen, where you select fields to see in the query.

7. In the final screen, you can specify a new name for the query. Simply accept the default name (tblProducts Without Matching tblSalesLineItems), and click the Finish button.

After the Query is created and you click the Finish button, Access automatically opens the query and shows any records that are widows (products with *no* related sales). Figure 37-23 shows multiple records that were found having no sales relationship.

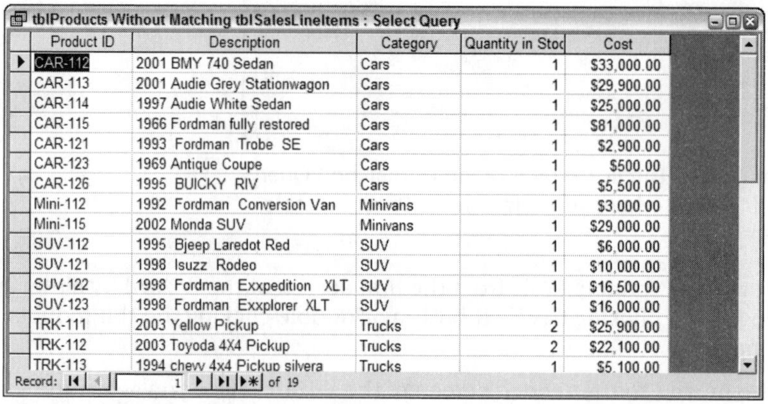

Product ID	Description	Category	Quantity in Stoc	Cost
▶ CAR-112	2001 BMY 740 Sedan	Cars	1	$33,000.00
CAR-113	2001 Audie Grey Stationwagon	Cars	1	$29,900.00
CAR-114	1997 Audie White Sedan	Cars	1	$25,000.00
CAR-115	1966 Fordman fully restored	Cars	1	$81,000.00
CAR-121	1993 Fordman Trobe SE	Cars	1	$2,900.00
CAR-123	1969 Antique Coupe	Cars	1	$500.00
CAR-126	1995 BUICKY RIV	Cars	1	$5,500.00
Mini-112	1992 Fordman Conversion Van	Minivans	1	$3,000.00
Mini-115	2002 Monda SUV	Minivans	1	$29,000.00
SUV-112	1995 Bjeep Laredot Red	SUV	1	$6,000.00
SUV-121	1998 Isuzz Rodeo	SUV	1	$10,000.00
SUV-122	1998 Fordman Exxpedition XLT	SUV	1	$16,500.00
SUV-123	1998 Fordman Exxplorer XLT	SUV	1	$16,000.00
TRK-111	2003 Yellow Pickup	Trucks	2	$25,900.00
TRK-112	2003 Toyoda 4X4 Pickup	Trucks	2	$22,100.00
TRK-113	1994 chevy 4x4 Pickup silvera	Trucks	1	$5,100.00

Figure 37-23: The datasheet shows the results of the Find Unmatched Query created with the Wizard.

After you have created the Wizard, you can easily delete these records by selecting them in the datasheet and pressing the Delete key. Then answer Yes to "are you sure you want to delete these records?" The unmatched record will be removed from the tblProducts table.

Saving an action query

Saving an action query is just like saving any other query. From design mode, you can save the query and continue working by clicking the Save button on the toolbar (or by selecting File ➪ Save from the Query menu). If this is the first time you're saving the query, Access prompts you for a name in the Save As dialog box.

You can also save the query and exit by selecting File ➪ Close from the menu or by double-clicking the Control menu button (in the top-left corner of the Query window) and answering Yes to this dialog box question: "Save changes to the design of '<query name>'?" You also can save the query by pressing F12.

Running an action query

After you save an action query, you can run it by double-clicking its name in the Query container (window). Access will warn you that an action query is about to be executed and ask for confirmation before it continues with the query.

Troubleshooting Action Queries

When you're working with action queries, you need to be aware of several potential problems. While you're running the query, any of several messages may appear, including messages that several records were lost because of *key violations* or that records were *locked* during the execution of the query. This section discusses some of these problems and how to avoid them.

Data-type errors in appending and updating

If you attempt to enter a value that is not appropriate for the specified field, Access doesn't enter the value; it simply ignores the incorrect values and converts the fields to Null values. When you're working with append queries, Access will append the records, but the fields may be blank!

Key violations in action queries

When you attempt to append records to another database that has a primary key, Access will not append records that contain the same primary key value.

Access does not enable you to update a record and change a primary key value to an existing value. You can change a primary key value to another value under these conditions:

✦ The new primary key value does not already exist.

✦ The field value you're attempting to change is not related to fields in other tables.

Access does not enable you to delete a field on the *one* side of a one-to-many relationship without first deleting the records from the *many* side.

Access does not enable you to append or update a field value that will duplicate a value in a *unique index field*—one that has the Index property set to Yes (No Duplicates).

Record-locked fields in multi-user environments

Access will not perform an action query on records locked by another user. When you're performing an update or append query, you can choose to continue and change all other values. But remember this: If you enable Access to continue with an action query, you won't be able to determine which records were left unchanged!

Text fields

When appending or updating to a Text field that is smaller than the current field, Access truncates any text data that doesn't fit in the new field. Access does not warn you that it has truncated the information.

SQL-Specific Queries

Access has three query types that cannot be created by using the QBE pane; instead, you type the appropriate SQL (Structured Query Language) statement directly in the SQL view window. These *SQL-specific* queries are as follows:

✦ **Union query:** Combines fields from more than one table or query into one recordset.

✦ **Pass-through query:** Enables you to send SQL commands directly to ODBC (Open Database Connectivity) databases using the ODBC database's SQL syntax.

✦ **Data definition query:** Enables you to create or alter database tables or create indexes in a database, such as Access databases, directly.

To create any of these queries, select from the Query ⇨ SQL Specific menu the type you want to create. (No applicable button is available on the toolbar.)

In addition to these three special SQL-specific queries, you can use SQL in a subquery (inside a standard Access query) to define a field or define criteria for a field.

Creating union queries

Union queries enable you to quickly combine fields from several tables or queries into one field. The resultant *snapshot* (like a dynaset) is not updateable.

For example, suppose a competing company retires and gives you all the client records from its business. You decide to create a union query to combine the data from both businesses and examine it. You will need to take your original tblContacts table and combine it with the records from the NewSellers table (3 records). Figure 37-24 shows a union query that returns the customer name, customer number, city, and state in order (by customer number). To create this query, follow these steps:

1. Create a new query using no tables (close the Show Table dialog box without adding tables).

2. Select Query ⇨ SQL Specific ⇨ Union from the Query Design menu bar.

   An SQL window is opened. This window is used to type in the Union Query that you wish to create.

3. Type **SELECT [chrLastName], [chrFirstName], [chrContactType], [chrCity] FROM tblContacts** on the first line.

4. Press Enter to move down a line in the SQL window.

5. Type **UNION SELECT [chrLastName], [chrFirstName], [chrContactType], [chrCity] FROM NewSellers** on the second line of the SQL window.

   The fields being specified for the union *must* be the same as those in the first table.

6. Press Enter to move down to another blank line in the SQL window.

7. Type **ORDER BY [chrLastName], [chrFirstName];** (ends with semi-colon) on the third line.

   Your query should look similar to the one shown in Figure 37-24. You do not have to have a blank line between each of the parts of the statement as in the one shown in Figure 37-24.

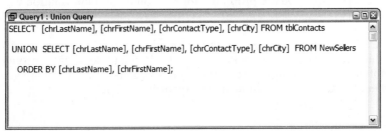

Figure 37-24: An SQL union query that combines the field contents of two different tables to be displayed as a single dynaset.

Notice that a union query has two or more SQL SELECT statements. Each SELECT statement requires the same number of fields, in the same order.

If you run this query, you will see the information requested in order by contact last name and first name.

> **Note** The dynaset created from a Union query is not updateable.

This union dynaset comprises 62 records (combining 59 from the tblContacts and 3 from the NewSellers tables).

When you use the Union command in the SQL SELECT statement, it copies only those records that are NOT duplicates when it joins the tables. The contents of all the fields being selected in the SQL Union query determine if duplication exists. If two records have the same contents in all the fields selected, they are considered duplicates and only one record will be displayed. If there are other fields, not used in the Union query, that have different values, they are not used to determine duplicity. If you want to see all records from the Union of two tables, simply use the keyword ALL after the UNION command — that is, UNION ALL SELECT.

Creating pass-through queries

A *pass-through query* sends SQL commands directly to an SQL database server (such as Microsoft SQL Server, Oracle, and so on). Often these database servers are known as the back-end of the system; with Access being the client tool or front-end. You send the command by using the syntax required by the particular server. Be sure to consult the documentation for the appropriate SQL database server.

You can use pass-through queries to retrieve records or change data, or to run a server-side stored procedure or trigger. They can even be used to create new tables at the SQL server database level (versus local tables).

After you create a pass-through query, you need to specify information about the database you want to connect to. You can type a connection string in the ODBCConnectStr property of the query property sheet directly or click Build and enter the information about the server you want to connect to. If you do not specify a connection string, you are prompted for the connection information when you run the query.

Figure 37-25 shows a pass-through query for a Microsoft SQL Server that creates a new table named Payroll and defines the fields in the table. A pass-through query is not limited to data definitions (creating a table or index); it can be any valid SQL statement to examine or manipulate the records in a back-end server.

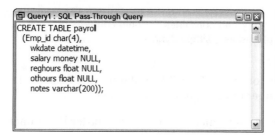

Figure 37-25: A pass-through query for SQL Server that will create a table named payroll in a database that resides on an SQL Server.

Caution Never attempt to convert a pass-through query to another type of query. If you do, Access erases the entire SQL statement you had typed in.

When working with pass-through queries, you should not perform operations that change the state of the connection. Halting a transaction in the middle, for example, may cause unexpected results.

Creating data definition queries

Of the three SQL-specific queries, the *data definition query* is the least useful against local tables. Everything that can be done with it also can be done by using the design tools in Access. The data definition query is, however, an efficient way to create or change database objects. With a data definition query, any of these SQL statements can be used:

✦ CREATE TABLE

✦ ALTER TABLE

✦ DROP TABLE

✦ CREATE INDEX

✦ DROP INDEX

For example, you could type the following code into the SQL query window (Data Definition Query) to create a local Access table named TelephoneList:

```
CREATE TABLE TelephoneList
( [TeleID] integer, [FullName] text, [Address1] text,
[Address2] text, [Address3] text, [Country] text, [Phone 1]
text, [Phone 2] text, [FaxPhn 1] text, [Notes] memo,
CONSTRAINT [Index1] PRIMARY KEY ([TeleID]) );
```

After it is created, this query could be run to create a new table named Telephone List. You could create a second Data-Definition Query to create an index for the table. For instance, you could create an index that would be in order by country and full name:

```
CREATE INDEX CountryName ON TelephoneList ([Country],
[FullName]);
```

Note You can have only one SQL statement in each Data-Definition Query.

Creating SQL subqueries in an Access query

Access 2002 enables you to create an SQL SELECT statement inside another select query or action query. You can use these SQL statements in the Field row to define a new field, or in the Criteria row to define criteria for a field. Using subqueries, you can do the following:

✦ Find values in the primary query that are equal to, greater than, or less than values returned by the subquery using the ANY, IN, or ALL reserved words.

✦ Test for the existence of a result from a subquery using the EXISTS or NOT EXISTS reserved words.

✦ Using the ANY, IN, or ALL reserve words in a subquery, you can compare values in the main query to the results of the subquery (not equal, equal, greater than, or less than).

✦ Create nested subqueries (subqueries within subqueries).

You can place an SQL statement in the Field: cell or in the Criteria: cell of the design grid. You would place it in the Field: cell to create a new field for the query. In contrast, you can use an SQL statement in the Criteria: cell of a field to define the criteria used for limiting the records of the cell.

✦　　✦　　✦

Increasing the Speed of an Application

When Microsoft introduced 32-bit Access, a number of new performance concerns came part and parcel with the new features and functions. Microsoft continues to make a conscious effort to improve the performance of Access 2003 with improvements in Jet as well as compilation techniques and features such as the formerly undocumented decompile command. The end result is that Microsoft has helped to ease your burden, but in no way has it completely taken it from you.

Tip   The published minimum RAM requirement for a computer to run Access 2003 on Windows XP or Windows 2000 is 128MB — with an emphasis on *minimum.* If you're going to do serious development with Access 2003, you should have at least 256MB of RAM or, preferably, 512MB or more. With today's computers and memory prices, this amount of memory is a valuable investment. In fact, simply adding more memory (128MB to 256MB) will increase speed much more than changing your processor (Pentium II to Pentium III or 4) or speed, due to the fact that Access 2003 must use the hard drive as a virtual memory area if it doesn't have enough memory. Hard drives are slow, and big hard drives are even slower — regardless of the processor speed.

Understanding Module Load on Demand

One of the great features of Visual Basic for Applications (the core language that replaced Access Basic in earlier versions of Microsoft Access) is the *load on demand* functionality of VBA. Using load on demand, Access loads code modules only as they are needed or referenced. In previous versions of Access, load on demand of modules wasn't fully realized because loading a module loaded the entire module's potential call tree. With Access 2003, the load on demand feature truly does help reduce the amount of RAM needed and helps your program run faster.

Tip Because Access doesn't unload code after it has been loaded into memory, you should periodically close your application while you develop. When developing, you have a tendency to open and work with many different procedures in many different modules. These modules stay in memory until you close Access.

Organizing your modules

You should be aware that when any procedure or variable is referenced in your application, the entire module that contains the procedure or variable is loaded into memory. To minimize the number of modules loaded into memory, you need to organize your procedures and variables into logical modules. For example, it's a good idea to place all Global variables in the same module. If only one Global variable is declared in a module, the entire module is loaded into memory. By the same token, you should put only procedures that are always used by your application (such as start-up procedures) into the module containing the Global variables.

Access 2003 prunes the call tree

The *call tree* for a procedure is any additional functions or procedures that the current procedure (or function) has referenced within it, as well as those referenced by the newly loaded functions and procedures, and so forth. Because a procedure may reference numerous additional functions/procedures (stored in different modules) based on the action taken by the procedure, this loading of all potentially called functions/procedures takes a lot of time and memory.

Remember that when a procedure or function is called, the entire module in which that function is stored is placed in memory.

Therefore, a potential call tree consists of all the procedures that *could* be called by the current procedure that you are calling. In addition, all the procedures that could be called from *those* procedures and so forth are also part of the potential call tree. For example:

1. If you call Procedure A, the entire module containing Procedure A is loaded.

2. Modules containing variable declarations used by Procedure A are loaded.

3. Procedure A has lines of code that call Procedures B and C — the modules containing Procedure B and Procedure C are loaded. (Even if the call statements are in conditional loops and are never executed, they are still loaded because *potentially* they could be called.)

4. Any procedures that could be called by Procedure B and Procedure C are loaded, as well as the entire modules containing those potential procedures.

5. And so on and so on and . . .

Fortunately for all Access developers, this complete loading of a potential call tree has been addressed in Access 2003. Access 2003 automatically compiles modules on demand, rather than the entire potential call tree. However, you can turn this feature off, thus making Access 2003 compile all modules at one time. Do this in the Visual Basic for Applications program rather than in Access. Access 2003 links directly to VBA's development environment for working with Visual Basic code. To check the status of the Compile on Demand option, follow these steps:

1. Select the Modules object type from the Object toolbar of the database.

2. Click the New object button to activate the Visual Basic Development Environment.

3. Select Tools ➪ Options. The Options dialog box appears.

4. Select the General tab.

5. Verify that the Compile on Demand check box, located on the bottom right side of the dialog box, is checked. If it's not, select it. Figure 38-1 shows the dialog box with the option selected.

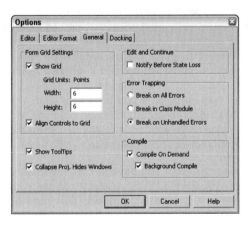

Figure 38-1: For maximum performance, leave the Compile on Demand check box selected.

6. Click OK.

7. Select File ➪ Close and Return to Microsoft Access (Alt + Q) or click the Access button (first button on toolbar) if you want to return to Access and leave the VBA window open.

Tip Unless you have a specific reason to do so, never deselect the Compile on Demand option. When you deselect this option, you can conceivably cause *all* of the modules in a database to load and compile, simply by calling just one procedure.

With the Compile on Demand option selected, Access 2003 won't load the entire call tree of a module, but it will load a portion of the call tree of the executed procedure. For example, if you call procedure A in module A, any modules that contain procedures referenced in procedure A are loaded and compiled. However, Access 2003 doesn't take into consideration procedures that may be called from other procedures in module A, and it doesn't look at the potential call tree of the modules loaded because one of their procedures is referenced in procedure A. Because Access 2003 loads modules one-deep from the executed procedure's immediate call tree only — and *not* the module's call tree — your applications should load and execute many times faster than they did in previous versions.

Even though Access 2003 has made a significant improvement in the way modules are loaded and compiled, you can still do a number of things to reduce the number of modules loaded and compiled. For example, you should never place infrequently called procedures in a module with procedures that are called often. At times, this may make your modules less logical and harder to conceptualize. For example, you may have a dozen functions that perform various manipulations to contact information in your application. Ordinarily, you may make one module called "modContacts" and place all the contact-related procedures and variables into this one module. Because Access loads the entire module when one procedure or variable in it is called, you may want to separate the contact-related procedures into separate modules (one for procedures that are commonly used and one for procedures that are rarely used and not referenced in commonly used procedures).

Tip

You need to be aware at all times that all modules having procedures referenced in a procedure of a different module are loaded when that procedure is called. In your application, if any of your common procedures reference a procedure that isn't commonly used, you will want to place the uncommon procedure in the same module with the common procedures to prevent a different module (containing the uncommon procedures) from being loaded and compiled. You may even decide to use more than two modules if you have very large amounts of code in multiple procedures that are rarely called. Although breaking related procedures into separate modules may make your code a little harder to understand, it can greatly improve the performance of your application.

To fully take advantage of Compile on Demand, you have to carefully plan your procedure placement. Third-party tools, such as *Total Access Analyzer* from FMS (www.fmsinc.com) print a complete module reference report. This can be invaluable for visualizing where all of the potential calls for various procedures are located.

Using the Access 2002-2003 Database File Format

Access 2003 supports several file formats including Access 2002, 2000, and 97. The new Access 2002-2003 file format exists (according to Microsoft literature) to ensure upward compatibility to future versions of Microsoft Access. Some Microsoft literature has claimed that the Access 2002-2003 file format enhanced performance for large database files. We have been unable to verify this on large data databases or large program files, but we do know that Access 2003 itself is slightly faster than Access 2002 and significantly faster than Access 2000 given the proper amount of memory.

You can open and even run Access 97 database files, but you can't make any design changes. You can open Access 2000 database files and make any desired changes to them. However, if you use features specific to Access 2002 or Access 2003, a user using Access 2000 won't be able to use those features and may have problems with compiling or running the application.

If you create a new database in Access 2003, the default new database file format is the Access 2000 file format. You can convert an Access 97 or Access 2000 database file to an Access 2002 database file format by using the menu selections Tools ⇨ Database Utilities ⇨ Convert Database ⇨ To Access 2002-2003 File Format.

Tip You can change the default file format for new files by using the Tools ⇨ Options ⇨ Advanced selection and selecting Access 2002-2003 from the combo box, as shown in Figure 38-2.

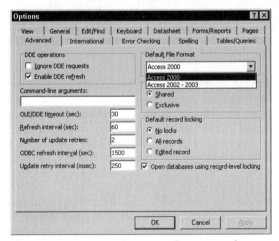

Figure 38-2: For maximum performance, change the default file format to Access 2002–2003.

The Access 2002-2003 file format should only be used in an Access 2002 or Access 2003 only environment where all users are using Access 2002 or Access 2003. Besides complete compatibility with all Access 2002 or Access 2003 features, you may experience some performance advantages when using the Access 2002-2003 file format with larger databases. However, in a mixed environment of Access 2000 and Access 2003 or Access 2003 users, you should stay with the Access 2000 file format for compatibility with Access 2000 users. An Access 2003 program can attach to Access 97 data files, but if you are trying to accommodate Access 97 users, you should simply stay with Access 97 data files.

Distributing .MDE Files

One way to ensure that your application's code is always compiled is to distribute your database as an .MDE file. When you save your database as an .MDE file, Access compiles all code modules (including form modules), removes all editable source code, and compacts the database. The new .MDE file contains no source code, but continues to work because it does contain a compiled copy of all of your code. Not only is this a great way to secure your source code, but it also allows you to distribute databases that are smaller (because they contain no source code) and always keep their modules in a compiled state. Because the code is always in a compiled state, less memory is used by the application, and you suffer no performance penalty for code being compiled at run time.

In addition to not being able to view existing code because it is all compiled, the following restrictions apply:

✦ You can't view, modify, or create forms, reports, or modules in Design view.

✦ You can't add, delete, or change references to object libraries or databases.

✦ You can't change your database's VBA project name by using the Options dialog box.

✦ You can't import or export forms, reports, or modules. Note, however, that tables, queries, and macros can be imported from or exported to non-MDE databases.

Tip   If you want to create a demo of your application — and if you don't want the users to be able to see your code or form and report designs — you should create an .MDE file. Because the designs of your forms, reports, and all code modules are simply not present (they are stored in a compiled version only), you don't have to worry about someone stealing your designs or code. An .MDE file is also good for distributing your work in environments where you don't want the user to change your designs.

Because of these restrictions, it may not be possible to distribute your application as an .MDE file. For example, if your application creates forms at run time, you would not be able to distribute the database as an .MDE file.

Caution   You have no way to convert an .MDE file into a normal database file. Therefore, always save and keep a copy of the original database! When you need to make changes to the application, you must open the normal database and then create a new .MDE file before distribution. If you delete your original database, you will be unable to access any of your objects in Design view.

Note   Some prerequisites must be met before a database can be saved as an .MDE file. First, if security is in use, the user creating the .MDE file must have all applicable rights to the database. In addition, if the database is replicated, you must remove all replication system tables and properties before saving the .MDE file. Finally, you must save all databases or add-ins in the chain of references as .MDE files or your database will be unable to use them.

To create an .MDE file, follow these steps:

1. Close the database if it's currently open. If you don't close the current database, Access will attempt to close it for you, prompting you to save changes where applicable. When working with a shared database, all users must close the database; Access needs exclusive rights to work with the database.

2. Select Tools ⇨ Database Utilities and then click Make MDE File (see Figure 38-3). The Database To Save as MDE dialog box displays unless you have a database open. See the next step for more information.

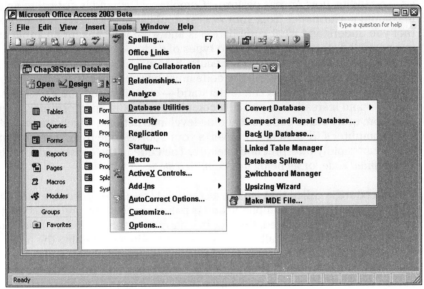

Figure 38-3: Access doesn't convert the existing database into an .MDE file; it creates a new .MDE file for the database.

3. In the Database To Save As MDE dialog box, specify the database that you want to save as an .MDE file, and click Make MDE.

   If you had a database open when you selected Make MDE File, this step is skipped and Access assumes that you want to use the previously opened database. If you want to use a different database, you need to stop creating the .MDE file, close the database, and select Make MDE File again. At that time, you will be asked for the database to save as an .MDE file.

4. In the Database to Save as MDE dialog box, specify a name, drive, and folder for the database. Don't attempt to save the .MDE file with the same filename as the original database.

Caution Don't delete or overwrite your original database! As stated previously, you have no way to convert an .MDE file to a normal database, and you can't edit any objects in an .MDE file. If you delete or otherwise lose your original database, you will never again be able to access any of the objects in the design environment.

Caution You can create an .MDE file only if you first convert the database into the Access 2002-2003 database format.

Understanding the Compiled State

Understanding how Access performs Compile on Demand is critical to achieving maximum performance from your Access application. However, it is also paramount that you understand what compilation is and what it means for an application to be in a compiled state. Access has two types of code — code that you write and code that Access can understand and execute. Before a procedure of VBA code that you have written can be executed, the code must be run through a compiler to generate code in a form that Access can understand — compiled code. Access lacks a true compiler and instead uses partially compiled code and an interpreter. A true compiler converts source code to machine-level instructions, which are executed by your computer's CPU. Access converts your source code to an intermediate state that it can rapidly interpret and execute. The code in the converted form is known as *compiled code*, or as being in a *compiled state*.

If a procedure is called that isn't in a compiled state, the procedure must first be compiled and then the compiled code is passed to the interpreter for execution. In reality, as previously stated, this doesn't happen at the procedure level, but at the module level; when you call a procedure, the module containing the procedure and all modules that have procedures referenced in the called procedure are loaded and compiled. You can manually compile your code, or you can let Access compile it for you on the fly. It takes time to compile the code, however, so the performance of your application will suffer if you let Access compile it on the fly.

In addition to the time required for Access to compile your code at run time, uncompiled programs use considerably more memory than compiled code. When your application is completely compiled, only the compiled code is loaded into memory when a procedure is called. If you run an application that is in a decompiled state, Access loads the decompiled code and generates the compiled code as needed (explained previously). Access does not unload the decompiled code as it compiles, so you are left with two versions of the same code in memory.

There is one drawback to compiled applications: They use more hard drive space than their decompiled versions. This is because both the compiled and decompiled versions of the code are stored on the hard drive.

Hard drive space shouldn't often become a problem, but if you have an application with an enormous amount of code, you can save hard drive space by keeping it in a decompiled state. Remember that a trade-off is made between hard drive space used and the performance of your database. Most often, when given the choice, a user would rather give up a few megabytes of hard drive space in exchange for faster applications.

Tip
You may use this space-saving technique to your advantage if you need to distribute a large application and your recipients have a full development version of Access. By distributing the uncompiled versions, you will need much less hard drive space to distribute the application, and the end users can compile it again at their location. If you are going to do this, you should put the entire application into a decompiled state. The topic of fully decompiling an application is discussed later in this chapter.

Putting your application's code into a compiled state

You have only one way to put your entire application into a compiled state: Use the Compile [mdb name] menu item from the Debug menu on the Modules toolbar in the Visual Basic for Applications development window (see Figure 38-4). To access the Debug menu, you must have a module open. Generally, you should always use the Compile [mdb name] command to ensure that all of the code is saved in a compiled state. Complex applications can take a long time to compile, and, in general, you should only perform a Compile [mdb name] before you distribute your application or before performing benchmark tests.

Figure 38-4: Compile [mdb name] (in this example, Ch38Start) is the only way to fully compile your application.

Note
When you use the Compile option in the Debug menu, you actually see the name of your project. This is the name that you used to save your database file the first time that it was created or saved. If you later rename the database file, the project name doesn't change. You can change it by using the Tools menu in the module window and selecting the current project name with the word *Properties* beside it.

Access 2003 has an option for compiling code to the Visual Basic for Applications program—Background Compile. Figure 38-1 shows this option under Compile on Demand; the default value for this option is True (selected). This option tells Access to compile code in the background rather than to compile it all at one time.

Tip   It is especially important to close your application after performing a Compile [mdb name]. To compile all of your modules, Access needs to load every single one of them into memory. All of this code stays in memory until you close down Access.

Losing the compiled state

One of the greatest roadblocks to increasing the performance of Access applications was the fact that an application could be uncompiled very easily. When the Access application was in an uncompiled state, Access had to constantly compile code as it was called. In fact, losing the compiled state was so easy to do in previous versions of Access that it would often happen without developers even realizing that they had done it.

In Access 2003, only portions of code affected by certain changes are put into an uncompiled state—not the entire application. By itself, this is a tremendous improvement over previous versions of Access.

The following actions will cause portions of your code to be uncompiled:

✦ Modifying a form, report, control, or module. (If you don't save the modified object, your application is preserved in its previous state.)

✦ Adding a new form, report, control, or module (this includes adding new code behind a form).

✦ Deleting or renaming a form, report, control, or module.

✦ Adding or removing a reference to an object library or database by using the References command on the Tools menu.

Okay, so you think that you have a handle on code that loses its compiled state? Well, here are a couple of "gotchas" that you need to consider:

✦ If you modify objects like reports or forms at run time through VBA code, portions of your application are put into an uncompiled state when the objects are modified. (Wizards often do this.)

✦ If your application creates objects like reports or forms on the fly, portions of your application are put into an uncompiled state when the objects are created. (Wizards often do this as well.)

Another serious flaw of Access was that an application's entire compiled state was tied to the filename of the database. This feature meant that your entire application would lose its compiled state, and all code would have to be compiled at the time that it was called if you renamed your database, compacted your database into a database of a different name, or copied your database to a database with a different name.

Fortunately, Access 97 fixed this serious problem, and it doesn't even exist in Access 2003. The compiled state of an application is still tied to its name, but now it is tied to its project name rather than to its filename.

Caution

When you change a project name (but not the filename), the entire application loses its compiled state. Because of this, you should change the project name only if absolutely necessary, and you should perform a Compile [mdb name] immediately after changing the project name.

Distributing applications in a compiled or uncompiled state

When distributing your Access application, you need to take into consideration a couple of issues concerning compilation.

Distributing source code for your application

First and foremost, if you distribute source code and allow your users access to modify or add objects, you must make them completely aware of the compilation issues. If your users don't fully comprehend what is happening with your application's compiled state, you can be sure that you will receive phone calls about how your program seems to be getting slower the more that users make changes to objects.

Putting an application in an uncompiled state

If your application is the type that will be constantly changing its compiled state (due to creating forms and reports dynamically), or if end users will be making modifications to the application's objects often, or if distributed file size is an issue, you may want to consider distributing the database in a fully uncompiled state.

To put your entire application into an uncompiled state, follow these steps:

1. Create a new database.

2. Import all of your application objects into the new database.

3. Compact the new database.

Cross-
Reference

Later in this chapter, you will also learn how to manually decompile the project. This has more benefits than simply letting the project become partially or completely uncompiled.

Organizing commonly used code that is never modified into a library

After your application is finished and ready for distribution, you may want to consider placing all commonly used code that will never be modified by an end user into a library database. A *library database* is an external database that your application database can reference and access. You will incur slight overhead by calling code from the library rather than by accessing it directly in the parent application, but the benefit is that the library code will never be put into a decompiled state — even if your application creates or modifies objects on the fly or if your users add new objects or modify existing objects. This technique can greatly increase an application's performance and keep the performance relatively consistent over time.

The first step for referencing procedures in an external database is to create the external database with all its modules, just as you would do in an ordinary Access database.

Caution

> Any procedures that you declare as "Private" are not made available to the calling application, so plan carefully what you want and don't want to expose to other databases.

After you have created the database and its modules, you must create a reference to that database in your application database (which is the database that your users will run). To create a reference, first open any module in your application database in Design view. When you have a module in Design view, a new command — References — is available from the Tools menu (see Figure 38-5). Select Tools ➪ References to access the References dialog box (see Figure 38-6).

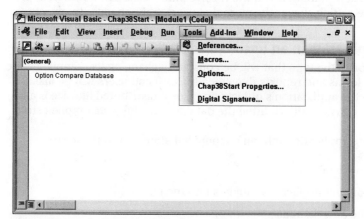

Figure 38-5: The References option appears on the Tools menu only when you have a module open and selected in Design view.

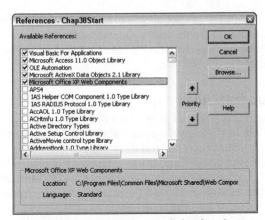

Figure 38-6: The References dialog box is where you resolve references to OLE automation servers and Access library databases.

In the References dialog box, you specify all the references that your application needs for using OLE automation or for using other Access databases as library databases. When making a reference to another Access database, as opposed to an OLE server created with another development tool like Visual Basic, you will probably need to browse for the database. Use the Browse dialog box as if you were going to open the external database. After you have selected the external Access database, it shows up in the References dialog box with a check mark to indicate that it is referenced.

To remove a reference, access the References dialog box again and deselect the referenced item by clicking its check box. After you have made all the references that you need to make, click OK.

After a database is referenced, you can call the procedures in the referenced database as if they existed in your application database. No matter what happens in your application database to cause code to decompile, the referenced database always stays in a compiled state unless it is opened and modified directly by using Access.

To reference an external Access database to call its procedures, follow these steps:

1. Create the library database and its modules.

2. Open the database in which you want to use the external procedures.

3. Open any module in Design view.

4. Select Tools ⇨ References.

5. Select the OLE server that you want to register. If it is an Access database, you will probably have to use the Browse feature to locate the database.

Tip   If your application uses *add-in databases* (a special type of library database), you should open the add-in database for read-only access. Opening add-ins for read-only access increases performance because Jet doesn't have to maintain locking information for the add-in database in an .LDB file.

Creating a library reference for distributed applications

If you are distributing your application, references stay intact only if the calling database and the library database are in the same or relative path. For example, if the main database is in C:\myapp on your machine, and if the library database is in C:\myapp\library, the reference remains intact if the library database is located in the same relative path, such as in C:\newdir for the main database and C:\newdir\library for the library database. If the relative path won't remain consistent upon distribution, your application's users must add the reference manually or you must create the reference by using VBA code.

The following procedure creates a reference to the file whose name is passed to it. For this function to work, the full filename with path must be passed:

```
bResult = CreateReference("c:\My Documents\MyLib.mdb").
```

The function is:

```
Public Function CreateReference(szFileName As String) As
Boolean
    On Error GoTo CreateReferenceError
    Dim ref As Reference
Set ref = References.AddFromFile(szFileName)
    CreateReference = True
Exit Function
CreateReferenceError:
    MsgBox Err & ": " & Err.Description
    CreateReference = False
    Exit Function
End Function
```

Tip   You can verify that a reference is set by using the `ReferenceFromFile` function. To verify a reference, pass the function, the full path, and the filename like this:

```
bResult =
ReferenceFromFile("C:\Windows\System\mscal.ocx").
```

The function returns True if the reference is valid and False if it isn't.

With the References collection, the primary concern of using and distributing libraries — losing references upon distribution — is now gone. However, library databases still have one major drawback: Access doesn't support circular references. This means that the code in your library databases can't reference variables or call procedures that exist in your parent database.

Whether you distribute your application as one database or as a primary database that uses library databases, if your applications are static (meaning that they don't allow modification of objects by end users or wizards, and don't perform object modifications on themselves), you should always distribute the databases in a fully compiled state so that your users experience the highest level of performance possible.

Improving Absolute Speed

When discussing an application's performance, the word *performance* is usually synonymous with speed. You will find two types of speed in software development — absolute and perceived. *Absolute speed* refers to the actual speed at which your application performs a function, such as how long it takes to run a certain query. *Perceived speed* is the phenomenon of an end user actually perceiving one application to be faster than another application, even though it may indeed be slower. This phenomenon of perceived speed is often a direct result of visual feedback provided to the user while the application is performing a task. Absolute speed items can be measured in units of time; perceived speed can't be measured in this manner.

Of course, some of the most important items for increasing actual speed are the following:

✦ Keeping your application in a compiled state

✦ Organizing your procedures into "smart" modules

✦ Opening databases exclusively

✦ Compacting your databases regularly

You should always open a database exclusively in a single-user environment. If your application is a standalone application (meaning that nothing is shared over a network), opening the database in exclusive mode can really boost performance. If your application is run on a network and shared by multiple users, you won't be able to open the database exclusively. (Actually, the first user can open it exclusively, but if he does, no other user can access the database until the first user closes it.) The preferred method for running an application in a network environment is to run Access and the main code .MDB file locally, and then link to a shared database containing the data on the server. If your application is used in this manner, you can open and run the code database exclusively, but you can't use exclusive links to the shared data.

To open a database exclusively in Access 2003, select the pull-down Open button and select Open Exclusive in the Open Database dialog box (see Figure 38-7).

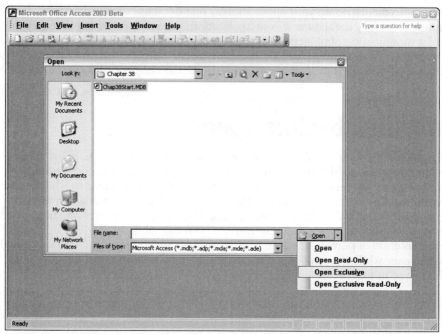

Figure 38-7: Select the Open Exclusive button on the pull-down Open button to open a database in a single-user environment to increase the performance of the database.

Tip   You can set the default open mode for a database on the Advanced tab of the Options dialog box to Exclusive. The default open mode is Shared.

Another often-overlooked way of maximizing your database's performance is to compact your database regularly. When records are deleted from a database, the hard drive space that held the deleted data is not recovered until a compact is performed. In addition, a database becomes fragmented as data is modified in the database. Compacting a database defragments the database and recovers used hard drive space.

All of the preceding methods are excellent (and necessary) ways to help keep your applications running at their optimum performance level, but these are not the only tasks that you can perform in order to increase the absolute speed of your application. Almost every area of development, from forms to modules, can be optimized to give your application maximum absolute speed.

If you use Jet as your data access engine, an Access application can run only so fast. With Jet, each time you open a table, run a query, or perform an operation on data, all the data referenced by the process or query must be moved from the data database (assuming that you have split your program and data database files) to the computer that's running the program. This means that you may be moving a lot of data across your network. This is simply not fast. An Access project that's using the

Microsoft Desktop Engine (MSDE or SQL Server 2000) can use stored procedures to minimize network traffic and can drastically speed up applications with large data databases. If you are working with large amounts of data, you should strongly consider writing the application using SQL Server as your back-end database file.

Tuning your system

One important aspect of performance has nothing to do with the actual application design—that is, the computer on which the application is running. Even though it's impossible to account for all the various configurations your clients may have, you can do some things for your computer and recommend that end users do them for theirs:

✦ Equip the computer with as much RAM as possible. This step often becomes an issue of dollars. However, RAM prices continue to decrease, and adding to a computer's RAM is one of the most effective methods that you can employ to increase the speed of Access.

✦ Don't use wallpaper. Removing a standard Windows wallpaper background can free up anywhere from 25K to 250K of RAM, and removing complicated bitmaps or high-color bitmaps can free up even more space.

✦ Close all applications that aren't being used. Windows makes it very handy to keep as many applications loaded as you want—in the odd chance that you may need to use one of them. Although Windows XP and Windows 2000 are pretty good at handling memory for multiple open applications, each running application still uses RAM. On machines with little RAM, unnecessary open applications can significantly degrade performance.

✦ Make sure that your Windows swap file is on a fast drive with plenty of free space. If possible, you should also set the minimum hard drive space available for virtual memory to at least 25MB of RAM and make it a permanent swap file.

✦ Defragment your hard drive often. Defragmenting a hard drive allows data to be retrieved from the drive in larger sections, thus causing fewer direct reads and less repositioning of the read heads.

Getting the most from your tables

In addition to reviewing all of the technical issues discussed in the preceding sections, it is advantageous to get back to the basics when designing your applications. Tools like Access enable novices to create relational databases quickly and easily, but they don't teach good database design techniques in the process. An exception to this statement is the Table Analyzer Wizard. However, even though the Table Analyzer Wizard offers suggestions that are often helpful in learning good design technique, its recommendations should *never* be taken as gospel. The Table Analyzer has proven to be wrong on many occasions.

Entire volumes of text have been devoted to the subject of database theory. Teaching database theory is certainly beyond the scope of this chapter (or even this book). However, you should be familiar with many basics of good database design.

Creating efficient indexes

Indexes help Access find and sort records faster and more efficiently. Think of these indexes as if they were book indexes. To find data, Access looks up the location of the data in the index and then retrieves the data from its location. You can create indexes based on a single field or based on multiple fields. Multiple-field indexes enable you to distinguish between records in which the first field may have the same value. If they are defined properly, multiple-field indexes can be used by Microsoft's Rushmore query optimization, which is the technology that Jet uses to optimize the speed at which queries execute, based on the search and sort fields of the queries and indexes of the tables included in the queries, in order to greatly speed queries.

Deciding which fields to index

People new to database development typically make two mistakes: First, not using indexes and, second, using too many indexes (usually putting them on every field in a table). Both of these mistakes are serious — sometimes a table with indexes on every field may give *slower* performance than a table with no indexes. Why? When a record is saved, Access must also save an index entry for each defined index. This can take time and use a considerable amount of hard drive space. The time used is usually unnoticed in the case of a few indexes, but many indexes can require a huge amount of time for record saves and updates. In addition, indexes can slow some action queries (such as append queries) when the indexes for many fields need to be updated while performing the query's operations. Figure 38-8 shows the index property sheet for a sample tblContacts table.

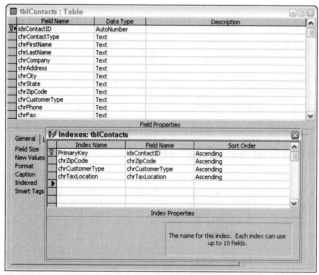

Figure 38-8: Note that common search fields like chrZip Code, chrCustomerType, and chrTaxLocation are indexed.

When you create a primary key for a table, the field (or fields) used to define the key is automatically indexed, and you can index any field unless the field's data type is Memo or OLE Object. You should consider indexing a field if all of the following factors apply:

✦ The field's data type is Text, Number, Currency, or Date/Time.

✦ You anticipate searching for values stored in the field.

✦ You anticipate sorting records based on the values in the field.

✦ You will join the field to fields in other tables in queries.

✦ You anticipate storing many different values in the field. (If many of the values in the field are the same, the index may not significantly speed up searches or sorting.)

When defining an index, you have the option of creating an ascending (the default) or a descending index.

> **Tip**
>
> Jet can use a descending index when optimizing queries only when the equal sign (=) operator is used. If you use an operator other than the equal sign, such as <, >, <=, or >=, Jet can't use the descending index. If you plan on using operators other than an equal sign on an index, you should define the index as an ascending index.

Using multiple-field indexes

If you often search or sort by two or more fields at the same time, you can create an index for that combination of fields. For example, if you often set criteria for LastName and FirstName fields in the same query, it makes sense to create a multiple-field index on both fields.

When you sort a table by a multiple-field index, Access first sorts by the first field defined for the index. If the first field contains records with duplicate values, Access then sorts by the second field defined for the index, and so on. This creates a drill-down effect. For a multiple-field index to work, a search criterion *must* be defined for the first field in the index, but not for additional fields in the index. In the preceding example, if you wanted to search for someone with the first name *Robert*, but you didn't specify a last name to use in the search, the second field in the index wouldn't be used. If you need to perform searches on the second field in a multiple-field index, but are not always specifying criteria for the first field in the index, you should create an index for the second field in addition to the multiple-field index.

Continuing with the LastName, FirstName index, if you wanted to search for the first name *John*, the multiple-field index wouldn't be used because you would be attempting to search only on the second field in the index.

Getting the most from your queries

The performance problems of many Access applications result from the design of their queries. Database applications are all about looking at and working with data, and queries are the heart of determining what data to look at or work with. Queries are used to bind forms and reports, fill list boxes and combo boxes, make new tables, and many other functions within an Access application. Because they are so widely used, it is extremely important to optimize your queries. A query that is properly designed can provide results minutes to hours faster than a poorly designed query that returns the same result set. Consider the following:

✦ When designing queries and tables, you should create indexes for all fields that are used in sorts, joins, and criteria fields. Indexes enable Jet to quickly sort and search through your database.

Tip   Sorting and searching is much faster if the indexes are unique rather than nonunique. Also, if you are using conditions in your queries, you will find that queries can run faster if the index is based on ascending order (as opposed to reverse, z to a, or descending order).

✦ When possible, use a primary key in place of a regular index when creating joins. Primary keys don't allow nulls and give the Rushmore query optimizer more ways to use the joins.

✦ Limit the columns of data returned in a select query to only those you need. If you don't need the information from a field, don't return it in the query. Queries run much faster when they must return less information.

Tip   If you need to use a field for a query condition *and* if it isn't necessary to display the field in the results table, deselect the view check box to suppress displaying the field and its contents.

✦ When you need to return a count of the records returned by an SQL statement, use Count(*) instead of Count([FieldName]) because Count(*) is considerably faster. Count(*) counts records that contain null fields; Count([FieldName]) checks for nulls and disqualifies them from being counted. If you specify a field name instead of using the asterisk, Count doesn't count records that have a null in the specified field.

Tip   You may also replace FieldName with an expression, but this slows down the function even further.

✦ Avoid using calculated fields in nested queries. A calculated field in a subordinate query considerably slows down the top-level query. You should use calculated fields only in top-level queries, and even then, only when necessary.

✦ When you need to group records by the values of a field used in a join, specify the Group By for the field that is in the same table that you are totaling. You can drag the joined field from either table, but using Group By on the field from the table that you are totaling yields faster results.

✦ Domain Aggregate functions, such as DLookup or DCount, that are used as expressions in queries slow down the queries considerably. Instead, you should add the table to the query or use a subquery to return the information that you need.

✦ As with VBA code modules, queries are compiled. To compile a query, Jet's Rushmore query optimizer evaluates the query to determine the fastest way to execute the query. If a query is saved in a compiled state, it runs at its fastest speed the first time that you execute it. If it isn't compiled, it takes longer the first time that it executes because it must be compiled, but it then runs faster in succeeding executions. To compile a query, run the query by opening it in Datasheet view and then close the query without saving it. If you make changes to the query definition, run the query again after saving your changes and then close it without saving it.

✦ If you really want to squeeze the most out of your queries, you should experiment by creating your queries in different ways (such as specifying different types of joins). You will be surprised at the varying results.

Getting the most from your forms and reports

Forms and reports can slow an application by taking a long time to load or process information. You can perform a number of tasks in order to increase the performance of forms and reports.

Minimizing form and report complexity and size

One of the key elements to achieving better performance from your forms and reports is reducing their complexity and size. Try these methods to reduce a form's or report's complexity and size:

✦ Minimize the number of objects on a form or report. The fewer objects used, the less resources needed to display and process the form or report.

✦ Reduce the use of subforms. When a subform is loaded, two forms are in memory — the parent form and the subform. Use a list box or a combo box in place of a subform whenever possible.

✦ Use labels instead of text boxes for hidden fields because text boxes use more resources than labels. Hidden fields are often used as an alternative to creating variables to store information.

Tip

You can't write a value directly to a label like you can to a text box, but you can write to the label's caption property like this: `Label1.Caption = "MyValue"`.

✦ Move some code from a form's module into a standard module. This enables the form to load faster because the code doesn't need to be loaded into memory. If the procedures that you move to a normal module are referenced by any procedures executed upon loading a form (such as in the form load event), moving the procedures won't help because they are loaded anyway as part of the potential call tree of the executed procedure.

✦ Don't overlap controls on a form or report.

✦ Place related groups of controls on form pages. If only one page is shown at a time, Access doesn't need to generate all of the controls at the same time.

✦ Use a query that returns a limited result set for a form's or report's RecordSource rather than using a table or underlying query that uses tables. The less data returned for the RecordSource, the faster the form or report loads. In addition, return only those fields actually used by the form or report. Don't use a query that gathers fields that won't be displayed on the form or report (except for a conditional check).

Using bitmaps on forms and reports

Bitmaps on forms and reports make an application look attractive and can also help convey the purpose of the form or report (as in a wizard). However, graphics are always resource-intensive, so you should use the fewest possible number of graphic objects on your forms and reports. This helps to minimize form and report load time, increase print speed, and reduce the resources used by your application.

Often you will display pictures that a user never changes and that are not bound to a database. Examples of such pictures include your company logo on a switchboard or static images in a wizard. When you want to display images like these, you have two choices:

✦ Use an Unbound Object Frame.

✦ Use an Image control.

If the image will never change and if you don't need to activate it in Form Design view, use an Image control. Image controls use fewer resources and display faster. If you need the image to be a linked or embedded OLE object that you can edit, use an Unbound Object Frame. You can convert OLE images in Unbound Object Frames.

Tip   If you have an image in an Unbound Object Frame that you no longer need to edit, you can convert the Unbound Object Frame to an Image control by selecting Change To Image from the Format menu.

Tip   When you have forms that contain unbound OLE objects, you should close the forms when they are not in use in order to free up resources. Also avoid using bitmaps with many colors — they take considerably more resources and are slower to paint than a bitmap of the same size with fewer colors.

If you want to display an Unbound OLE object but don't want the user to be able to activate it, set its Enabled property to False.

Speeding up list boxes and combo boxes

It's important to pay attention to the optimization of list boxes and combo boxes when optimizing your application. You can take a number of steps to make your combo boxes and list boxes run faster:

✦ When using multipage forms that have list boxes or combo boxes on more than one page, don't set the RowSource of the list boxes or combo boxes until the actual page containing the control is displayed.

✦ Index the first field displayed in a list box or combo box. This enables Access to find entries that match text entered by the user much faster.

✦ Although it's not always practical, try to refrain from hiding a combo box's bound column. Hiding the bound column causes the control's searching features to slow down considerably.

✦ If you don't need the search capabilities of AutoExpand, set the AutoExpand property of a combo box to No. Access is then relieved of the task of constantly searching the list for entries matching text entered in the text portion of the combo box.

✦ When possible, make the first nonhidden column in a combo or list box a text data type, and not a numeric one. To find a match in the list of a combo box or list box, Access must convert a numeric value to text in order to do the character-by-character match. If the data type is text, Access can skip the conversion step.

✦ Often overlooked is the performance gain achieved by using saved queries for RecordSource and RowSource properties of list boxes and combo boxes. A saved query gives much better performance than an SQL SELECT statement because an SQL query is optimized by Rushmore on the fly.

Tip

You will find one problem with combo boxes present in Access 2003, which poses a performance concern. Because Access 2003 supports hyperlinks, Access has to perform some additional work when first painting a combo box; it needs to determine the data type of the combo box.

The result is that the combo box takes a little longer to paint—up to a couple of seconds on some computers. If your combo box is a bound combo box, this isn't a problem because Access gets the data type from the ControlSource's data type. In addition, if you save a RowSource for the combo box when you save the form, Access determines the data type from the RowSource and doesn't need to determine the data type at run time. The only time that this paint delay is an issue is when you have an unbound combo box that has its RowSource set programmatically. When this is the case, the combo box will take slightly longer to paint the first time it is displayed.

Getting the most from your modules

Perhaps the area where you'll be able to use smart optimization techniques most frequently is in your modules. For example, in code behind forms, you should use the Me keyword when referencing controls. This approach takes advantage of the capabilities of Access 2003; using Me is faster than creating a form variable and referencing the form in the variable. Other optimization techniques are simply smart coding practices that have been around for many years. You should try to use the optimum coding technique at all times. When in doubt, try different methods to accomplish a task and see which one is fastest.

Tip   Consider reducing the number of modules and procedures in your application by consolidating them whenever possible. A small memory overhead is incurred for each module and procedure that you use, so consolidating them may free up some memory.

Using appropriate data types

You should always explicitly declare variables using the Dim function rather than arbitrarily assigning values to variables that haven't been dimmed. To make sure that all variables in your application are explicitly declared before they are used in a procedure, while in Visual Basic for Application's design surface, select Tools ⇨ Options, choose the Editor tab, and then set the Require Variable Declarations option on the tab (second from the top in the Code settings section).

Use integers and long integers rather than singles and doubles when possible. Integers and long integers use less memory, and they take less time to process than singles and doubles. Table 38-1 shows the relative speed of the different data types available in Access.

Table 38-1	
Data Types and Their Mathematical Processing Speed	
Data Type	**Relative Processing Speed**
Integer/Long	Fastest
Single/Double	Next to Fastest
Currency	Next to Slowest
Variant	Slowest

In addition to using integers and long integers whenever possible, you should also use integer math rather than precision math when applicable. For example, to divide one long integer by another long integer, you can use the following statement:

```
x = Long1 / Long2
```

This statement is a standard math function that uses floating-point math. You can perform the same function by using integer math (notice that the mathematical sign is the regular slash versus the backward slash) with the following statement:

```
x = Long1 \ Long2
```

Of course, integer math isn't always applicable. It is, however, commonly applied when returning a percentage. For example, you can return a percentage with the following precision math formula:

```
x = Total / Value
```

However, you can perform the same function using integer math by first multiplying the Total by 100 and then using integer math like this:

```
x = (Total * 100) \ Value
```

You should also use string functions ($) where applicable. When you are manipulating variables that are of type String, use the string functions (for example, Str$()) as opposed to their variant counterparts (Str()). If you are working with variants, use the non-$ functions. Using string functions when working with strings is faster because Access doesn't need to perform type conversions on the variables.

When you need to return a substring by using Mid$(), you can omit the third parameter to have the entire length of the string returned. For example, to return a substring that starts at the second character of a string and returns all remaining characters, use a statement like this:

```
szReturn = Mid$(szMyString, 2)
```

When using arrays, use dynamic arrays with the Erase and ReDim statements to reclaim memory. By dynamically adjusting the size of the arrays, you can ensure that only the amount of memory needed for the array is allocated.

Tip   In addition to using optimized variables, consider using constants when applicable. Constants can make your code much easier to read and won't slow your application if you compile your code before executing it.

Writing faster routines

You can make your procedures faster by optimizing the routines that they contain in a number of ways. If you keep performance issues in mind as you develop, you will be able to find and take advantage of situations like the ones discussed here.

Some Access functions perform similar processes but vary greatly in the time that they take to execute. You probably use one or more of these regularly, and knowing the most efficient way to perform these routines can greatly affect your application's speed:

✦ For/Next statements are normally faster than Select Case statements. They tend to process less logic.

✦ The IIF() function is much slower than a standard set of If/Then/Else statements.

✦ The With and For Each functions accelerate manipulating multiple objects and/or their properties.

✦ Change a variable with Not instead of using an If . . . Then statement. (For example, use x = Not(y) instead of If y = true then x= false.)

✦ Instead of comparing a variable to the value True, use the value of the variable. (For example, instead of saying If X = True then . . ., say If X then . . .)

✦ Use the Requery method instead of the Requery action. The method is significantly faster than the action.

✦ When using OLE automation, resolve references when your application is compiled rather than resolving them at run time by using the GetObject or CreateObject functions.

Using control variables

When referencing controls on a form in code, there are some very slow ways and some very fast ways to use references to form objects. The slowest possible way is to reference each control explicitly. This requires Access to sequentially search for the form name, starting with the first form name in the database and continuing until it finds the form name in the forms list (msysObjects table). If the form name starts with a z, this can take a long time if the database contains many forms. For example:

```
Forms![frmSales]![dtmSaleDate] = something
Forms![frmSales]![dtmInvoiceDate] = something
Forms![frmSales]![lngzSalespersonID] = something
```

If the code is in a class module behind the frmSales form, you can use the Me reference. The Me reference refers to the open object (forms or reports) and substitutes for Forms![formname]. This is a much faster method because it can go right to the form name. For example:

```
Me!dtmSaleDate] = something
Me![dtmInvoiceDate] = something
Me![frmSales]![lngzSalespersonID] = something
```

If your code is not stored behind the form but is in a module procedure, you can use a control variable like the following:

```
Dim frm as Form
set frm = Forms![frmSales]
frm![dtmSaleDate] = something
frm![dtmInvoiceDate] = something
frm!frmSales]![lngzSalespersonID] = something
```

This way, the form name is looked up only once. An even faster way is to use the With construct. For example:

```
With Forms![frmSales]
   ![dtmSaleDate] = something
   ![dtmInvoiceDate] = something
   !frmSales]![lngzSalespersonID] = something
End With
```

You can then reference the variable rather than reference the actual control. Of course, if you don't need to set values in the control but rather use values from a control, you should simply create a variable to contain the value rather than the reference to the control.

Using field variables

The preceding technique also applies to manipulating field data when working with a Recordset in VBA code. For example, you may ordinarily have a loop that does something like this:

```
. . .
Do Until tbl.EOF
MyTotal = MyTotal + tbl![OrderTotal]
Loop
```

If this routine loops through many records, you should use the following code snippet instead:

```
Dim MyField as Field
. . .
Set MyField = tbl![OrderTotal]
Do Until tbl.EOF
  MyTotal = MyTotal + MyField
Loop
```

The preceding code executes much faster than code that explicitly references the field in every iteration of the loop.

Increasing the speed of finding data in code

Use the FindRecord and FindNext methods on indexed fields. These methods are much more efficient when used on a field that is indexed. Also, take advantage of bookmarks when you can. Returning to a bookmark is much faster than performing a Find method to locate the data.

The procedure shown in Listing 38-1 is an example of using a bookmark. Bookmark variables must always be dimmed as variants, and you can create multiple bookmarks by dimming multiple variant variables. The following code opens the tblCustomers table, moves to the first record in the database, sets the bookmark for the current (first) record, moves to the last record, and finally repositions back to the bookmarked record. For each step, the debug.print command is used to show the relative position in the database as evidence that the current record changes from record to record.

Listing 38-1: **Using a Bookmark to Mark a Record**

```
Public Sub BookmarkExample()
Dim rs As Recordset, bk As Variant
Set rs =
Workspaces(0).Databases(0).OpenRecordset("tblContacts", _
dbOpenTable)
   ' Move to the first record in the database
      rs.MoveFirst
      ' Print the position in the database
      Debug.Print rs.PercentPosition
   ' Set the bookmark to the current record
      bk = rs.Bookmark
   ' Move to the last record in the database
      rs.MoveLast
      ' Print the position in the database
      Debug.Print rs.PercentPosition
   ' Move to the bookmarked record
      rs.Bookmark = bk
      ' Print the position in the database
      Debug.Print rs.PercentPosition
rs.Close
Set rs = Nothing
End Sub
```

Eliminating dead code and unused variables

Before distributing your application, remove any *dead code*—code that is not used at all—from your application. You will often find entire procedures, or even modules, that once served a purpose but are no longer called. In addition, it isn't uncommon to leave variable declarations in code after all code that actually uses the variables has been removed. By eliminating dead code and unused variables, you reduce the amount of memory your application uses and the amount of time required to compile code at run time.

 Tip   Although it isn't easy and is often impractical, removing large numbers of comments from your code can decrease the amount of memory used by your application.

Other things that you can do to increase the speed of your modules include opening any add-ins that your application uses for read-only access and replacing procedure calls within loops with in-line code. Also, don't forget one of the most important items: Deliver your applications with the modules compiled.

Increasing Network Performance

The single most important action that you can take to make sure that your networkable applications run at their peak performance is to run Access and the application database on the workstation and link to the shared network database. Running Access over the network is much slower than running it locally.

Improving Perceived Speed

Perceived speed is how fast your application appears to run to the end user. Many techniques can increase the perceived speed of your applications. Perceived speed usually involves supplying visual feedback to the user while the computer is busy performing some operation, such as constantly updating a percent meter when Access is busy processing data.

Using a splash screen

Most professional Windows programs employ a splash screen, as shown in Figure 38-9. Most people think that the splash screen is simply to show the product's name and copyright information as well as the registered user's information, but this isn't entirely correct. The splash screen greatly contributes to the perceived speed of an application. It shows the user that something is *happening*, and it gives users something to look at (and hence occupy their time) for a few seconds while the rest of the application loads.

 Note   In large applications, you may even display a series of splash screens with different information, such as helpful hints, instructions on how to use the product, or even advertisements. These are known as *billboards*.

To create a splash screen, create a basic form with appropriate data, such as your application information, logo, and registration information. Then set this form as the Display Form in the Start Up dialog box. Setting the form as the Display Form ensures that the splash screen is the first form to be loaded. You then want to call any initialization procedures from the On Open event of the splash form. A good splash screen should automatically disappear after a few seconds. To make this happen, use the timer event. Chap 38Start.MDB contains a simple splash screen named frmSplashScreen to help get you started and includes some simple code to initialize the timer and remove the form after a few seconds.

Figure 38-9: A Splash Screen to display product and version information.

You need to remember a few issues when using splash forms:

✦ Never use custom controls in a startup form. Custom controls take time to load and consume resources.

✦ Minimize code in startup forms. Use only code that is absolutely necessary to display your startup form and use a light form if possible.

✦ The startup form should call only initialization procedures. Be careful about call trees; you don't want your startup form to trigger the loading of many modules in your application.

Loading and keeping forms hidden

If you have forms that are displayed often, consider hiding them rather than closing them. To hide a form, set its Visible property to False. When you need to display the form again, set its Visible property back to True. Forms that remain loaded consume memory, but they display more quickly than forms that must be loaded each time they are viewed. In addition, if you are morphing a form or report (changing the way it looks by changing form and control properties), keep the form hidden until all changes are made so that the user doesn't have to watch the changes take place.

Using the hourglass

When your application needs to perform a task that may take a while, use the hourglass. The hourglass mouse pointer shows the user that the computer is not locked up but is merely busy. To turn on the hourglass cursor, use the Hourglass method like this:

```
DoCmd.Hourglass True
```

To turn the hourglass back to the default cursor, use the method like this:

```
DoCmd.Hourglass False
```

Using the built-in progress meter

In addition to using the hourglass, you should consider using the progress meter when performing looping routines in a procedure. The progress meter gives constant visual feedback that your application is busy, and it shows the user in no uncertain terms where it is in the current process.

Tip   Chap38Start.MDB includes two types of progress meters. Using the standard Microsoft Access progress meter that is displayed in the status bar creates the first type that is discussed in this chapter. The other meter is a pop-up form that uses a colored rectangle to show the progress of an activity.

The sample database file Ch38.mdb contains a number of progress meter samples. Each uses the progress meter a little differently but all run the same example. The example creates 50,000 records in a table named *SampleData*. Each of the examples uses a simple form with several text box controls and a button to start the process. The basic progress meter form in Design view is shown in the following figure. Each of the examples contains code to display either the built-in Access progress meter or one within the pop-up form. Each contains a button to start the process, as well as two text boxes to display the start time and end time of the process.

The following code demonstrates how to use the built-in progress meter in a loop to show the meter starting at 0 percent and expanding to 100 percent, 1 percent at a time. The first example is named *ProgressMeterUsingBuiltInAccessMeter*. This example doesn't actually use the text box in the sample progress meter form, but rather uses the progress meter built into Microsoft Access that displays as a series of little squares at the bottom left corner of the screen in the status bar.

Caution   If you don't display the status bar, you won't see the built-in progress meter when it runs.

The code to initialize, update, and remove the meter is shown in Figure 38-10.

Figure 38-10: Code to run the built-in progress meter.

The first step for using the percent meter is initializing the meter. You initialize the meter by calling the `SysCmd` function like this:

```
ReturnValue = SysCmd(acSysCmdInitMeter, "Creating Records", counter)
```

The acSysCmdInitMeter in this line is an Access constant that tells the function that you are initializing the meter. The second parameter is the text that you want to appear to the left of the meter. Finally, the last value is the maximum value of the meter (in this case, 100 percent). You can set this value to anything that you want. For example, if you were iterating through a loop of 50,000 records, you may set this value to 50,000. Then you can pass the record count at any given time to the SysCmd function; Access decides what percentage the meter shows as filled.

After the meter has been initialized, you can pass a value to it to update the meter. To update the meter, you call the SysCmd function again and pass it the acSysCmdUpdateMeter constant and the new update meter value. Remember, the value that you pass to the function is not necessarily the percent displayed by the meter. It can be the number of records processed or any number that when divided by the initial counter provides a percentage from 1 to 100. For example, if 50,000 records are being processed and the number 12,500 is passed to the meter, it will display 25 percent.

```
ReturnValue = SysCmd(acSysCmdUpdateMeter, i)
```

After all the records are processed, you will want to remove the meter from the status bar. To do this, use the following command. (There are no parameters to pass when you remove the meter.)

```
ReturnValue = SysCmd(acSysCmdRemoveMeter)
```

The progress meter displayed in the status bar is shown in Figure 38-11.

Figure 38-11: The progress meter displayed in the status bar.

Creating a progress meter with a pop-up form

To run the sample Progress Meter that uses the pop-up form, open the form ProgressMeterCallingEveryRecord and click the Search button. The progress meter form appears, and the bar grows from 0 to 100 percent. This should take about 30 seconds on a high-end Pentium machine, but a little longer on a slower machine.

The Progress Meter form in progress is shown in Figure 38-12.

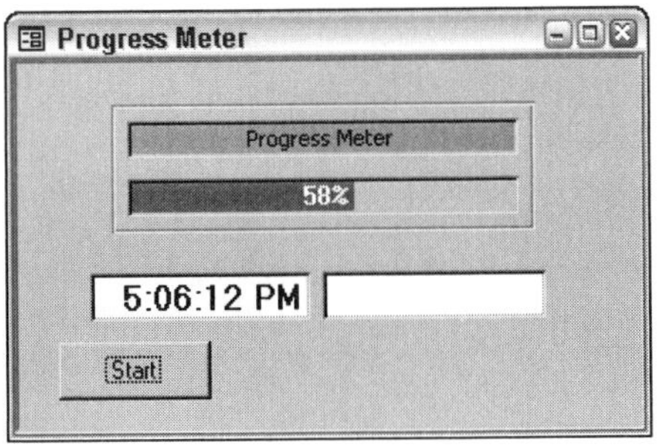

Figure 38-12: A graphical progress meter.

This progress meter has some advantages over the standard Microsoft Access progress meter. The progress meter that comes with Access uses the status bar to display the meter and isn't always as visible as you may want it to be. The pop-up progress meter pops up in the middle of the screen and is immediately visible to the user. The meter that comes with Access, however, usually displays faster because it requires less overhead to run, although with longer tasks the difference may not be noticeable. The speed of the pop-up meter can be controlled by updating the meter every *x* percent. Therefore, if the form meter is set for fast execution, it displays with comparable speed to that of the built-in meter.

The progress meter form is created from a few simple controls, as shown in Figure 38-9. It contains a rectangle control, two label controls, and option group controls. In Figure 38-12, you can see that the rectangle is shown 60 percent completed. In reality, the width of the rectangle is manipulated by the program that is used to display the meter's progress. The width is reset to 0 when the progress meter starts, and it is slowly built back to its original length.

The code for the progress meter is also simple and shown in its entirety, including the three-line function that is called in Figure 38-13.

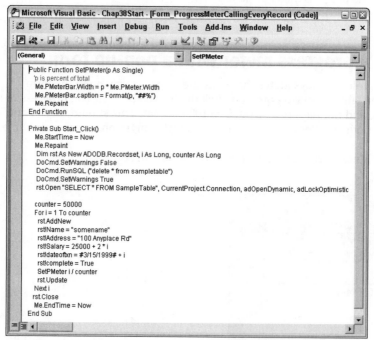

Figure 38-13: The Progress Meter form call to the pop-up progress meter.

The code that calls the meter is one simple line buried in the middle of the iteration loop. It calls the display function by passing it the iteration number and total number of iterations expected. In this example, *i* is the record number being processed and *counter* is the expected 50,000 records.

```
SetPMeter i / counter
```

The function SetPMeter consists of only three lines: one to display the rectangle and manipulate its width, one to display the caption on the bar as it grows inside the rectangle in the form, and one to repaint the screen each time so that the bar is animated.

```
Public Function SetPMeter(p As Single)
    'p is percent of total
    Me.PMeterBar.Width = p * Me.PMeter.Width
    Me.PMeterBar.caption = Format(p, "##%")
    Me.Repaint
End Function
```

Speeding up the progress meter display

This routine is called whenever you want to update the progress meter. You can decide when to do this. Generally, you should call the progress meter only when it is likely to be updated. If you know that you have 1000 records, you may call the meter every 10 records; if you have 10,000 records, you may call the meter every 100 records.

Although this code is simple, it is not the best. In fact, because this code calls the progress meter for every record, it is much slower than the built-in progress meter. Although the built-in progress meter processes this code in about 10 seconds, on our Pentium IV laptop with 256MB of memory, it takes over a minute to run this routine. A better approach is to call the progress meter only once in a while. The following code can replace the call in the code previously discussed:

```
If (i / counter) * 100 = Int((i / counter) * 100) Then
    SetPMeter i / counter
End If
```

The If statement checks to see if the calculation of the completion percentage is an integer (whole number). This calls the progress meter function (SetPMeter) that moves the progress meter rectangle and display the percentage completed. It is called only 100 times to move the rectangle; even though the IF statement is run 50,000 times, you may wonder why the If statement is faster. The reality is that the If statement takes very few resources to process, but a function that changes the width of a rectangle or control, writes to the screen, and then repaints the screen uses a lot of resources — as evidenced by the time to process falling by 90 percent.

Follow these steps to integrate the Progress Meter into your application:

1. Import the Form ProgressMeter into your application.

2. Change the code behind the form to interact with your application.

Working with Large Program Databases in Access 2003

When someone mentions large databases in Microsoft Access, they are generally thinking about a database with tables that contain hundreds of thousands of data records. Though this can be considered to be a large database, another definition is a database that contains hundreds of objects — tables, queries, forms, reports, and thousands of lines of VBA program code. Although you can sometimes solve data performance problems by changing the back end from Jet to SQL Server, you will probably have to deal with much more complex problems if you create applications with many queries, forms, reports, and lots of VBA module code.

If your database has hundreds of objects, especially forms and reports, you may have run into problems that cause your database to exhibit strange behavior. These include

✦ Not staying compiled or not compiling at all

✦ Growing and growing and growing in size, even after compiling and compacting

✦ Running slower and slower

✦ Displaying the wrong record in linked subforms

✦ Displaying compile errors when you know that the code is correct

✦ Corrupting constantly

Compacting your database doesn't always work as advertised. Compiling and Saving All Modules becomes a long wait with a seemingly perpetual hourglass. After you compact and open the database, it is uncompiled again. If you work with large databases, chances are good that these are well-known experiences. If you have one of these out-of-control databases, this section will show you how to solve these problems and get you up and running fast again.

How databases grow in size

Many things can cause a database to grow. Each time that you add an object to an Access 2003 database (.mdb) file, it gets larger. And why shouldn't it? You are certainly using more space to define the properties and methods of the object. Reports and forms take the most space because the number of properties associated with each form or report and each control on a form or report uses space. Table attachments (links) and queries take up very little space, but VBA code grows proportionally to the number of lines in both modules and code behind forms and reports. If you store data in your program database, this also takes up space proportionally to the number of records in the table. Many other reasons cause a database to grow.

When you first create a database using the Access 2002-2003 or Access 2000 database file formats, it uses about 60KB, depending on your hard drive type, size, and Access format (Access 2002 database format files are larger than Access 2000 database files). As you add objects, the database will start to grow. Adding a very simple form takes about 6K, whereas a simple report uses about 25K of hard drive space. Each time that you add another new form or report, more space is used. Each time that you add a new control and define some properties, even more space is used. When you define any event in a form or report that contains even a single line of VBA code, more overhead is used, because the form or report is no longer a lightweight object but one that is VBA-aware. This requires more space and resources than a lightweight form or report containing no VBA code. If you embed images into your forms and reports, these also will use space. Embedding bound OLE aware data, such as pictures, sound, video, or Word or Excel documents, uses more space than unbound objects or images.

Each time that you make a change to any object — even a simple one — a duplicate copy of the object is created until you compact the database. Within even a few hours of work, Access 2002 databases can begin to grow larger and larger. If the database contains thousands of lines of VBA code, the database can grow to two or three times its original size very quickly, especially when compiled and before it is compacted.

Simply compiling and compacting may not be enough

As you add, delete, and modify objects, Access doesn't always clean up after itself. You have probably learned that after you make changes to your objects, especially VBA code, you should open any module and select Debug ⇨ Compile and Save All Modules. After you do this, you should close the module, select the database container, and select Tools ⇨ Database Utilities ⇨ Compact and Repair Database... This action compacts the database to the same name and reopens the database running any startup commands or Autoexec macros that you may have. For the less aggressive, you may want to close the database first and compact the database to a different name, thus effectively creating a compacted backup. You can then use the new database or delete the old one and rename the new database to the original name.

Compiling and Compacting may not be enough to solve some of the problems mentioned at the beginning of the section. We worked with a large database that was originally converted from Access 97; we noticed it started at 15MB. After hundreds of minor changes, it was growing at a rate of 50K each time that we compiled and compacted it — even if we added no new objects, properties, methods, or VBA code. Out of necessity, this author has experimented with a variety of techniques to understand this phenomenon and solve our problems. More importantly, strange things started happening.

Even though we noticed that the database was growing larger, it took several compiles and compacts to get it to compile, and frequently after we compacted the database, it was no longer compiled. It also ran slower the first time we opened it. When the database displayed compile errors on perfectly written code, we knew that it was time to try new techniques.

Rebooting gives you a clean memory map

We have always noticed that strange behavior in any program gets better when you reboot your system. Access is particularly bad at *memory leaks*, especially if you're going in and out of form, report, and module design. If you don't want to reboot, at least close your database and exit Access before beginning the examination of your problem.

Repair does nothing if the database is not corrupt

We started by trying to repair the database. Though it was not corrupt, we thought maybe that would help. Although the repair utility ran fine and automatically compacted the database, it did nothing else, and the database was still growing.

You can fix a single corrupt form by removing the record source

Sometimes, you may have a single form that doesn't run properly. To fix this, try opening the form in Design view and removing any record source. Then, close and save the form. Reopen the form in Design view and reenter the original (or a new) record source. This may fix your problem. When the record source of an Access form or report is changed, it forces various pieces of internal code behind the form to be rebuilt. Sometimes, this simple process works.

Create a new database and import all of the objects

It's important to have your database as clean as possible. Although we're not sure if gremlins crawl into some obscure portion of the database file, we are sure that you can't import or export them. A technique that usually proves to be successful is to simply create a new database and then import all of the objects from the original database. Access 2003 makes it easy to import all of your objects by using the Select All button found in the Import Objects dialog box. You can get to this dialog box by first going to the database container of the new empty database file that you create and then selecting File ➪ Get External Data ➪ Import, selecting the original program database, and then clicking the Import button. You can then import all of your objects.

If you have any custom menus and toolbars, or if you have defined any Import/ Export specifications, you should remember to use the Options button and check off those options as shown in Figure 38-14. The default for these options is False. If you have created any startup properties in the database, you will have to create them again because they are not importable.

Caution   If you use externally referenced libraries or add-ins, you must manually reference these libraries in the new database. You can display a module and use the Tools ⟹ References menu to do this.

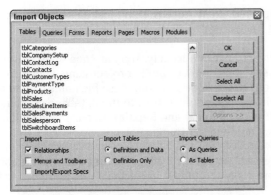

Figure 38-14: Importing Database Objects with the Options button pressed.

After working for some time in our large database, even creating a new database and importing all of the objects failed to help the database stay compiled or become smaller.

The decompile option in Access 2003

A little known startup command-line option is called "/decompile." You may have seen many of the command-line options, such as /nostartup, /cmd, and /compact. This option starts Access 2003 in a special way and, when a database is opened, saves all VBA modules as text. This works with module objects and all the code behind forms and reports.

To do this, go to the Windows Start menu Run command and type **msaccess /decompile** as shown in Figure 38-15. Hold down the Shift key before you launch Microsoft Access. This prevents any startup forms or autoexec macro processes from running. You don't want the database to run code that forces even a single module to be compiled. This prevents the decompile process from actually doing any good.

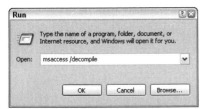

Figure 38-15: Starting Access 2003 with the decompile command-line option.

Access appears to start as usual. It takes about three minutes to open a database and decompile all of the objects in a 20MB database. At this point, the real question was if the database would get sufficiently smaller, run faster, and stay compiled after it was compiled and compacted.

After the database window is displayed, close Access. Don't just close the database window—actually exit Microsoft Access.

After you exit Access, you can restart Access normally. You can then open your database, open any module, and select Debug ➪ Compile projectname where projectname is simply the name of your project (original database file name). After the database compiles, you should close the module, return to the database container, and select Tools ➪ Database Utilities ➪ Compact and Repair Database. You will find that Access runs these procedures much faster than usual.

Caution   Make sure that you immediately exit Access 2003 after it finishes decompiling and then start Access again before running Compile projectname or Compact and Repair Database.

Using our test database, we then went to Windows Explorer and checked the size of the database. It had shrunk from 22MB to 15MB, a reduction of over 30 percent, and it has stayed compiled every time we compact it. The first time we ran the application, it seemed to run faster than ever. We aren't sure why it works faster or differently than manually opening and saving each VBA module as text—it simply does. Even more strangely, the database no longer seems to be growing each time we make a minor change, recompile, and compact the database. Although the decompile option may be a small miracle, it's always a good idea to follow the six steps to success (presented in the next section) before releasing any application to the ultimate users.

Summary—six steps to large database success

If you're ready to release your application for a real test by the users, you should follow the steps below to insure a clean-running system:

1. Reboot your computer to clean up memory.
2. Create a new Access database and import all the objects. Then close Access.
3. Restart Access by using the /decompile option while holding down the Shift key. Close Access after the database window is displayed.
4. Restart Access normally while holding down the Shift key.
5. Compile the database.
6. Compact and Repair the database.

By releasing a clean, fully compiled and compacted system, you will have fewer problems, your application will run faster, and you will have fewer technical or maintenance problems.

An interface for detecting an uncompiled database and automatically recompiling

It's very important that you make sure that a database is always in a compiled state. If you release your application as a modifiable .MDB file, your customers may make simple or even complex changes to your application and then complain because their system is running slowly. Although some of your customers may be serious developers, our experience is that many customers who make changes to Access databases don't know about compilation or compacting.

To see if your database is compiled, you can open the Visual Basic window for any module, display the Debug window, and type **? IsCompiled()**, as shown in Figure 38-16. If the database is compiled, it will display True. If it is in a decompiled state, it will display False, as shown in Figure 38-16.

Figure 38-16: Checking to see if an Access 2003 program is compiled.

To solve this problem, you can create an interface that automatically detects if the database is not in a compiled state and then gives the user the option of compiling the application. This automatic detection runs each time the database is opened. The user still has to compact the database, but the hard part is compiling. Figure 38-17 shows the message that is automatically displayed if the database is uncompiled. The code is shown in the following example.

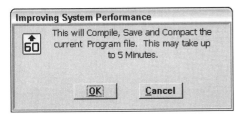

Figure 38-17: A dialog box to help the user compile your application.

One line of code can be added anywhere in your program to detect an uncompiled application and start the process.

```
If IsCompiled() = False Then DoCmd.OpenForm "MessageImprovingPerformance"
```

The code uses the Access 2003 built-in function IsCompiled to determine the compiled state of the application. If the application isn't compiled, the form is displayed, as shown in Figure 38-17. Users have two choices. If they are still testing, they may not want to compile yet. If they want to compile, they simply have to press the Yes button.

The compile and compact code is shown in Figure 38-18. The application is compiled first and then compacted. If the database is already compiled, the compile function is skipped and the database is only compacted. You can simply insert this module and the message box into any application and call the form.

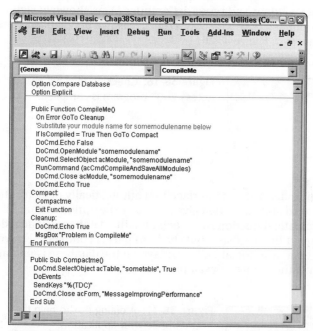

Figure 38-18: A module to automatically compile and compact your database.

Making small changes to large databases — *export*

One final tip for working with large databases: Always work with a copy of the program file and export the changed objects. When you are making lots of changes to a few objects to try a new technique or to get a stubborn algorithm to work, you are constantly opening and closing objects. This tends to negatively affect large databases. Work with a copy of the database, and then when you have the changes just the way you want, you can export the changed objects from the test database to the production database. Any object that you export with the same name as the production database will be exported with a 1 at the end of the name. You can then open the production database, delete the original objects, and rename the changed objects that have a 1 on the end of their name. New objects are obviously exported with their name intact.

Anything that you can do to make fewer changes to a large database, the better off you are. By following the tips and techniques in this section, you will have fewer problems and you will be more productive.

Through judicious use of the techniques discussed in this chapter, you will be able to increase the performance of your Access application to the highest level possible.

✦　　✦　　✦

Preparing Your Application for Distribution

You are indeed lucky if you have the luxury of developing only single-user, in-house applications and you never have to worry about distributing an application within a company or across the country. Most developers, in fact, have to worry about application distribution sooner or later. You don't even have to develop commercial software to be concerned with distribution; when you develop an application to be run on a dozen workstations in one organization, for example, you need to distribute your application.

This chapter covers all the preceding points to some degree. However, because some of the listed items, such as splitting tables and creating Help systems, are covered in detail in other chapters, this chapter focuses primarily on using the Package Wizard in Microsoft Office 2003 Developer.

You need to be concerned with many issues when preparing an Access application for distribution. Distributing your application properly not only makes installing and using the application easier for the end user, but it also makes updating and maintaining the application easier for you. In addition, you can decrease the support required for your application by including comprehensive online help.

On the CD-ROM   This chapter will use the database named CHAP39Start.mdb. If you have not already copied it onto your machine from the CD, you will need to do so now. The Package Wizard used later in this chapter will use the Access Auto Auctions.mdb. There is no CHAP39End.mdb for this chapter.

Defining the Startup Parameters of the Application

An Access database has a number of startup parameters that can greatly simplify the process of preparing your database for distribution (see Figure 39-1). You can access the startup parameters for a database by selecting Tools ➪ Startup or by right-clicking the database window and selecting Startup. You can still use an Autoexec macro to execute initialization code, but the Startup parameters dialog box enables you to set up certain aspects of your application, thus reducing the amount of startup code that you have to write. It is extremely important to correctly structure the startup parameters before distributing your Access application.

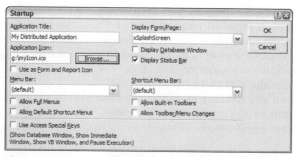

Figure 39-1: The Startup parameters dialog box enables you to take control of your application from the moment a user starts it.

Application Title

The text that you provide in the Application Title field displays on the main Access title bar. You should always specify an application title for your distributed applications. If you don't, the words Microsoft Access appears on the title bar of your application.

Application Icon

The icon that you specify in the Startup dialog box is displayed on the title bar of your application and in the task switcher (Alt+Tab) of Windows. Checking the box "Use as Form and Report Icon" also displays this icon when a form or report is minimized. If you don't specify your own icon, Access displays the default Access icon; therefore, you should always provide an application-specific icon for your application. You can create small bitmaps in Windows Paint and use available conversion tools to convert a .BMP file to an .ICO file format. You can also create icons or choose from tools such as IconMaker or the Command Bar Image Editor, which are available on many Internet sites.

Menu Bar

The Menu Bar box is used to specify a custom menu bar as the default menu bar. If you don't supply a custom menu bar, Access uses its own default menu bar, which may be inappropriate for your application.

Allow Full Menus

This setting determines whether Access displays its menus with all options available to the user or whether it disables items that can be used to create or modify objects. If you supply custom menus for all of your forms and reports and set the Menu Bar property to a custom menu bar, this setting has no effect.

Tip

> If you supply your own menu bars or use Access's menu bars but don't allow full menus, you must deselect Allow Built-in Toolbars or supply your own custom toolbars for each form. If you don't, the built-in toolbars may give users access to some features that you don't want to make available.

Allow Default Shortcut Menus

The Allow Default Shortcut Menus setting determines whether Access displays its own default shortcut menus when a user clicks an object.

Display Form/Page

The form that you select in this field displays automatically when your application is run. When the form loads, the Form Load event fires if it contains any code, thus eliminating the need to use an Autoexec macro. You should consider using a splash screen (which is discussed later in this chapter) as your startup Display Form.

Display Database Window

With most distributed applications, you may never want your users to have direct access to any of your forms or other database objects. Deselecting this option hides the Database window from the user at startup. But unless you also deselect the Use Access Special Keys option (which is discussed later in this chapter), users can press F11 or select Window ⟿ Unhide to unhide the Database window.

Display Status Bar

You can deselect the Display Status Bar option to completely remove the status bar from the screen. However, the status bar is an incredibly informative and easy-to-use tool; it automatically displays the various key-states, as well as the status bar text for the active control. Instead of hiding the status bar, you should make full use of it and disable only it if you have a very good reason to do so.

Shortcut Menu Bar

This setting is similar to the Menu Bar option (which was discussed previously), only it enables you to specify a menu bar to use as the default shortcut menu bar when a user right-clicks an object. Using custom shortcut menus that have functionality specific to your application is always preferable.

Allow Built-in Toolbars

Deselecting this option prevents Access from displaying any of its built-in toolbars. In general, you should always deselect this option and provide your own custom toolbars that you can display by using the Toolbar property for the form.

Allow Toolbar/Menu Changes

Deselecting this option prevents users from modifying either Access's built-in toolbars or your own toolbars, whichever you choose to use. Again, you almost always want to deselect this item to prevent your users from gaining access to features that you don't want them to have.

Use Access Special Keys

If you select this option, users of your application can use keys that are specific to the Access environment in order to circumvent some security measures, such as unhiding the Database window. If you deselect this option, the following keys are disabled:

✦ **F11 and Alt+F1:** Use these keys to show the database window (if hidden) and bring it to the front.

✦ **Ctrl+G:** Use this key to display the Immediate window.

✦ **Ctrl+Break:** In Access projects, use this key to stop Access from retrieving records from the server database.

✦ **Ctrl+F11:** Use this key to toggle between using a custom menu bar for a form and using a built-in menu bar.

✦ **Alt+F11:** Use this key to start the Microsoft Visual Basic Editor.

You should always deselect this option when distributing the application.

Using the Startup options saves you many lines of code that you would ordinarily need in order to perform the same functions and enables you to control your application's interface from the moment the user starts it. Always verify the Startup options before distributing your application.

Testing the application before distribution

After you finish adding features and have everything in place within your application, you need to take some time to thoroughly test the application. Testing may seem obvious, but this step is apparently overlooked by many developers, evidenced by the amount of buggy software appearing on the shelves of your local software stores. If you don't believe this to be true, check out the software support forums on the Internet; almost every major commercial software application has some patch available or known bugs that need to be addressed.

Distributing an application that is 100-percent bug-free is almost impossible. The nature of the beast in software development is that if you write a program, someone can — and will — find a way to break it. Specific individuals even seem to have a black cloud above their heads and can usually break an application (in other words, hit a critical bug) within minutes of using it. If you know of such people, hire them! They can be great assets to you when testing your application.

While working through the debugging process of an application, categorize your bugs into one of three categories:

✦ **Category 1: Major ship-sinking bug.** These bugs are absolutely unacceptable — for example, numbers in an accounting application that don't add up the way they should or a routine that consistently causes the application to terminate unexpectedly. If you ship an application with known Category 1 bugs, prepare yourself for a lynching party from your customers!

✦ **Category 2: Major bug that has a workaround.** Category 2 bugs are fairly major bugs, but they don't stop users from performing their tasks. For example, a toolbar button that doesn't call a procedure correctly is a bug. If the toolbar button is the only way to run the procedure, this bug is a Category 1 bug. If, however, a corresponding menu item calls the procedure correctly, the bug is a Category 2 bug. Shipping an application with a Category 2 bug is sometimes necessary. Although shipping a bug is officially a no-no, deadlines sometimes dictate that exceptions need to be made. Category 2 bugs will annoy your users but shouldn't send them into fits.

If you ship an application with known Category 2 bugs, document them! Some developers have a don't-say-anything-and-act-surprised attitude regarding Category 2 bugs. This attitude can frustrate users and waste considerable amounts of their time by forcing them to discover not only the problem, but also the solution. For example, if you were to ship an application with the Category 2 bug just described, you should include a statement in your application's README file that reads something like this:

> "The button on the XYZ form does not correctly call procedure suchand-such. Please use the corresponding menu item suchandsuch found on the Tools menu. A patch will be made available as soon as possible."

✦ **Category 3: Small bugs and minor nits.** Category 3 bugs are small issues that in no way affect the workings of your application. They may be misspellings of captions or incorrect colors of text boxes. Category 3 bugs should be fixed whenever possible but should never take precedence over Category 1 bugs. They should take precedence over Category 2 bugs only when they are so extreme that the application looks completely unacceptable.

By categorizing your bugs and approaching them systematically, you can create a program that looks and behaves the way its users think it should. Sometimes you may feel like you will never finish your Category 1 list, but you will. You will surely be smiling the day you check your bug sheet and realize that you're down to a few Category 2s and a dozen or so Category 3s! Although you may be tempted to skip this beta testing phase of development, don't. You will only pay for it in the long run.

Tip

Not all Access features are available when an application is run within the Access runtime environment (which is discussed with the Package Wizard, later in this chapter). You can operate in the runtime environment and use the full version of Access to test for problems with your code and with the runtime environment by using the /Runtime command line option when starting your Access application. Click Run on the Windows Start menu or create a shortcut. The following command line example starts Access and opens the Invoices database (if it is located at D:\MYAPPS\) in the runtime environment:

```
D:\OFFICE2003\ACCESS\MSACCESS.EXE /RUNTIME
D:\MYAPPS\INVOICES.MDB
```

You should always test and debug your application in the runtime environment if you plan to distribute the application with the Access 2003 Package Wizard.

Polishing Your Application

When your application has been thoroughly tested and appears ready for distribution, spend some time polishing your application. Polishing your application consists of the following:

✦ Giving your application a consistent look and feel.

✦ Adding common, professional components.

✦ Adding clear and concise pictures to buttons.

✦ Using common, understandable field labels and button captions.

Giving your application a consistent look and feel

First and foremost, you should decide on some design standards and apply them to your application. This is incredibly important if you want your application to look professionally produced. Figure 39-2 shows a form with samples of different styles of controls.

Your design decisions may include the following:

✦ Will text boxes be sunken, flat with a border, flat without a border, chiseled, or raised?

✦ What backcolor will the text boxes be?

✦ What color will the forms be?

✦ Will you use chiseled borders to separate related items or opt for a sunken or raised border?

✦ What size will buttons on forms be?

✦ For forms that have similar buttons, such as Close and Help, in what order will the buttons appear?

✦ Which accelerator keys will you use on commonly used buttons, such as Close and Help?

Making your application look and work in a consistent manner is the single most important way to make it appear professional. For ideas on design standards to implement in your applications, spend some time working with some of your favorite programs and see what standards they use. In the area of look and feel, copying from another developer is generally not considered plagiarism but is rather often looked upon as a compliment. Copying does *not* extend, however, to making use of another application's icons or directly copying the look and feel of a competitor's product; this is a very bad practice. For an example of a good look-and-feel environment, see the Microsoft Office Compatible program.

An application may be certified Office Compatible by meeting certain user-interface requirements as laid out by Microsoft. An Office-Compatible application uses the same menu structures as all the Office applications, such as Word, Access, Excel, and so on. In addition, toolbars are also similar and, where applicable, have the same button image that Microsoft uses. Making an application look like an Office application saves the developer time by giving clear and concise guidelines for interface features, and it helps end users by lowering the learning curve of the application.

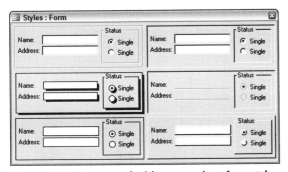

Figure 39-2: You can decide on any interface style that you like for your application. However, after you decide on a style, use it consistently.

Although you may not want to have your application independently tested and certified Office Compatible, you may want to check out the specifications and use some of the ideas presented to help you get started designing your own consistent application interfaces.

Adding common professional components

Most commercial/professional applications have some similar components. The most common components are the splash screen, About box, and switchboard. Be aware that the splash screen (see Figure 39-3 for a good example) not only aids in increasing perceived speed of an application but also gives the application a polished, professional appearance from the moment a user runs the program. Figure 39-4 shows a skeleton splash screen that can be used with any system. You simply change the content to what you want.

Figure 39-3: A splash screen not only increases perceived speed of your application, but it also gives your application a professional appearance.

 Note   Figure 39-4 shows the design window for a splash screen template that you can use when building your own applications. This form is included in the CHAP39Start. mdb database. It is named SplashScreenTemplateSimple. Import this form into your application and use it as a template for creating your own splash screen.

Figure 39-4: Use this form as a template to create your own splash screens for your applications.

Your splash screen should contain the following items:

✦ The application's title

✦ The application's version number

✦ Your company information

✦ A copyright notice ((c) Copyright)

In addition, you may want to include the licensee information and/or a picture on the splash screen. If you use a picture on your splash screen, make it relevant to your application's function. For example, some coins and an image of a check could be used for a check writing application. If you like, you can also use clip art for your splash screen; just be sure that the picture is clear and concise and doesn't interfere with the text information presented on your splash screen.

To implement the splash screen, have your application load the splash form before it does anything else (consider making your splash screen the Startup Display Form). When your application finishes all of its initialization procedures, close the form. Make the splash form a light form and be sure to convert any bitmaps that you place on your splash screen to pictures in order to decrease the splash form's load time.

The second component that you should implement is an application switchboard. The switchboard is essentially a steering wheel for users to find their way throughout the functions and forms that are available in the application. You can use the switchboard itself as a data-entry form, as shown in the switchboard example in Figure 39-5. You can also use a command button to display another form. This is the switchboard named frmSwitchboard created for the Access Auto Auctions systems in this book.

Make sure that the switchboard redisplays whenever the user closes a form. The switchboard provides a familiar place where users can be assured that they won't get lost in the application.

Figure 39-5: The switchboard provides a handy way to navigate throughout the application.

The third component that you should implement is an About box (see Figure 39-6). The About box should contain your company and copyright information, as well as the application name and current version. Including your application's licensee information (if you keep such information) in the About box is also a good idea. The About box serves as legal notice of your ownership and makes your application easier to support by giving your users easy access to the version information. Some advanced About boxes call other forms that display system information (Figure 39-6 has an additional button — System Info). You can make the About box as fancy as you want, but usually a simple one works just fine.

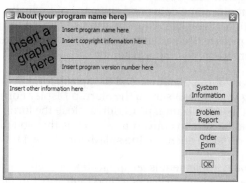

Figure 39-6: The implementation of an About box is a polishing technique that also provides useful information to the user and protects your legal interests.

Note Figure 39-6 shows the an About box template form that you can use when building your own applications. This form is included in the CHAP39Start.mdb database. It is named AboutTemplateA. Import this form into your application and use it as a template for creating your own About box.

Tip Most users love pictures, and most developers love to use pictures on buttons. Studies have shown that clear and concise pictures are more intuitive and are more easily recognized than textual captions. Most developers, however, are not graphic artists and usually slap together buttons made from any clipart images that are handy. These ugly buttons make an application look clumsy and unprofessional. In addition, pictures that don't clearly show the function of the button make the application harder to use.

Select or create pictures that end users will easily recognize. Avoid abstract pictures or pictures that require specific knowledge to understand them, such as wiring symbology. If your budget permits, consider hiring a professional design firm to create your button pictures. A number of professional image galleries and tools to create and edit buttons are available.

Picture buttons that are well thought out can really make your application look outstanding, as well as make it easier to use.

The About box should be accessible from a Help menu on all menu bars. The submenu title should be About My Application. Of course, substitute *Your program name here* with your application's actual name.

The splash screen, About box, and switchboard may seem like trivial features, but they can greatly enhance your application's appeal. They take little time to implement and should be included in all of your distributed applications.

Creating comprehensive and intuitive menus and toolbars

Before you even consider distributing an application, you need to make the application as intuitive as possible. Menus and toolbars are absolutely vital for usability with any Windows application.

Bulletproofing an Application

Bulletproofing an application is the process of making the application idiot-proof. It involves trapping errors that can be caused by users, such as invalid data entry, attempting to run a function when the application is not ready to run the function, and allowing users to click a Calculate button before all necessary data has been entered. Bulletproofing your application is an additional stage that should be completed in parallel with debugging, and should be performed again after the application is working and debugged.

Using error trapping on all Visual Basic procedures

An error-handling routine gives you a chance to display a friendly message to the user, rather than some unintuitive default message box; Figure 39-7 shows a message box with a Run-Time error '2102' which is unintuitive; however, it also shows a more detailed message of a form missing or misspelled. The user, will not know the name of the form or if it is misspelled or missing. Thus an error trap routine is needed.

Figure 39-7: An error message resulting from a procedure with no error-handling routine.

One of the most important elements of bulletproofing an application is making sure that the application never *crashes*—that is, never ceases operation completely and unexpectedly. Although Access provides built-in error processing for most data-entry errors (for example, characters entered into a currency field), automatic processing doesn't exist for Visual Basic code errors. You should include error-handling routines in every Visual Basic procedure, even if you use just the following error line in your code:

```
On Error Resume Next
```

When running an application distributed with the Office 2003 Developer Package Wizard, any untrapped error encountered in your code causes the program to terminate completely. Your users can't recover from such a crash, and serious data loss may occur. Your users have to restart the application after such an application error.

Separating the code objects from the tables in the application

You should separate your code objects (forms, reports, queries, modules, and macros) from your table objects. Many benefits are gained from distributing these objects in separate .MDB files:

✦ Network users benefit from speed increases by running the code .MDB (the database containing the queries, forms, macros, reports, and modules) locally and accessing only the shared data on the network.

✦ Updates can easily be distributed to users.

✦ Data can be backed up more efficiently because only one file is needed, and disk space and time aren't used to continuously back up the code objects.

All professionally distributed applications—especially those intended for network use—should have separate code and data database (.MDB) files.

Documenting the application

Most developers don't like to write documentation; it's simply no fun and can be quite frustrating and time-consuming. Taking the time and effort now to prepare thorough documentation, however, can save hours of technical support time down the road. Even if you don't plan to distribute a full user's manual, take time to document how to perform the most common functions in your application. If you have created shortcuts, make sure to share them with the users.

Creating a help system

Although documentation is extremely important for getting users started on your application, a Help system that is well-written, thorough, and context-sensitive is just as important. A Help system puts pertinent information at users' disposal with just a click of the mouse or a push of a button.

Implementing a security structure

The final item that you need to consider before distributing your application is the level at which you want to secure your application. You can secure specific individual objects, or you can secure your entire application. If it's important to you to secure design permissions for all of your objects in order to protect your source code, you need to be aware that you can't rely solely on Microsoft's word that the security in Access works. Microsoft touted the security model of Access 2.0 as being the most secure available. It was discovered, however, that an average Access developer can unsecure an Access 2.0 database in about five minutes, with only minimum coding! Although no method for unsecuring a secured Access 97, Access 2000, Access 2002, or Access 2003 application has yet been discovered, a method may be uncovered in the future. You must understand and accept this risk when you distribute a secured Access application.

The Access 2003 Developer Extensions

After you finish your application, you need to find a way to distribute it to your customers. Distribution includes delivering all files necessary to run your application on some form of media, such as floppy disk or CD-ROM, or via electronic distribution channels, such as the Internet. The media should include some sort of setup program that automates copying the files to the user's computer, sets up any shortcut items, registers necessary controls, and sets values in the system registry. The Access 2003 Developer Extensions Package Wizard is just the tool. It is one of the tools included in the Access 2003 Developer Extensions (ADE). These are part of the new Visual Studio Tools for the Microsoft Office System software package. The tools provide the resources needed by developers to quickly and easily test, create, and deploy their Access solutions to their clients. They consist of the following components:

Access Runtime	Provides a standalone, redistributable Runtime Solution. The ADE gives you a license to install unlimited copies of the Access Runtime.
Package Wizard	Used to bundle and deploy Access database systems you build. The wizard guides you through configuring and redistributing your product. It outputs a Microsoft Windows Installer (*.msi) setup file.

| Custom Startup Wizard | Used to create MDE files with custom startup properties. |
| Property Scanner | Used to search all collections, objects, and properties of a database for a specific value or term. It lets you search any or all objects in the database. |

Using the Package Wizard

The Package Wizard lets you package and deploy Access database solutions. The wizard guides you through the steps necessary to bundle standalone Access applications, with options to also bundle the Access Runtime as well as create shortcuts that start the correct Access binary. The resulting output of the Package Wizard is a Microsoft Windows Installer (.msi) setup file that guides end users step-by-step in deploying your Access solution files, based on your specifications.

The wizard is an Access database add-in and is included in and installed, by default, with the Microsoft Office Access 2003 Developer Edition.

You may be asking yourself, "What if my users don't own Access?" When you distribute your application with the Package Wizard, end users can run your application by using the Access runtime environment without needing to purchase a full version of Access. The Package Wizard makes it easy to package and distribute all the necessary runtime files. This is (mostly) transparent to users; they don't realize that Access is running in the background. Certain design interfaces are hidden from users to prevent them from creating Access applications with the runtime executable. Purchasing Microsoft Office Access 2003 Developer Edition gives you the licensing rights to distribute your application with the runtime environment to an unlimited number of users — with no royalty fees! So, even if you plan to create your setup program with a third-party tool, you need to purchase at least one copy of Microsoft Office Access 2003 Developer Edition to obtain the legal rights to distribute your application with the runtime files.

Tip   Note that the runtime version of Access can't be used to open .adp or .ade files; however, you can use the Package Wizard to create a setup program to distribute .adp or .ade files to users who already have the full version of Access installed.

When you distribute your application using the Package Wizard, you can configure your custom setup program to do the following:

✦ Specify a product name for your install package and install language you want to use.

✦ Copy your application's files to specified root and subfolder locations on a user's hard drive.

✦ Create Windows shortcuts that start your application or program files in the Start Menu and Desktop.

✦ Include Access Runtime files.

✦ Embed a EULA (End User License Agreement) file, banner image, and background image.

✦ Specify runtime parameters at startup (/ro Open Read Only, /user UserName, /pwd Password, and so on).

✦ Add Windows Registry keys and entries for your application.

✦ Group files, shortcuts, and registry keys and entries into components that users can select to install or uninstall.

✦ Install other Access files, such as drivers for accessing various data sources and any .OCX custom controls that are used by your application.

✦ Run an application or open a file after the setup program is finished installing your application.

Restrictions of the Package Wizard

The Access runtime environment is an excellent way (and currently the only way) to distribute your applications to users who don't own a licensed copy of Microsoft Access. As previously stated, the Access runtime is almost transparent to the user. Unfortunately, some limitations do exist with the release version of the ADE. Some of these issues affect the behavior of your application, and some are problems inherent in the Package Wizard itself. You need to be aware of the limitations, and you probably want to make your end users aware of some of them as well.

Some key points and pitfalls to be aware of when designing your setup routine include the following:

✦ Runtime applications that don't include custom help files generate errors when referring to the Access Help file. As stated previously, you should always attempt to distribute applications with Help systems. Even a rudimentary Help system is better than no online help at all.

Tip

If you elect against shipping a Help file with your application, you can prevent Access from generating an error by not providing a Help menu item on any of your custom menus and by creating an Autokeys Macro that traps the F1 key. The F1 key doesn't have to do anything in the macro. Simply including it in the Autokeys macro causes the macro to trap the F1 key when it is pressed. This prevents it from being passed to the Access runtime, thus calling up the Help file.

✦ Attempting to close a runtime application with the CloseCurrentDatabase method generates an error. The runtime version of Access doesn't run without an application loaded and therefore generates the error if you attempt to close the current database. To terminate your application, use the Quit method of the DoCmd object.

✦ Uninstalling Microsoft Access 2003 breaks applications installed with a custom setup program. Unfortunately, the uninstall program in Access doesn't know when a runtime Access application is installed on the computer, and it changes registry settings that are crucial to running your runtime Access application.

✦ The Package Wizard doesn't support Administrative (setup /a) and Run From Network Server installations. Performing a network installation places all the setup files onto a server drive so that all workstations on the network can run the setup program from the server rather than from floppy disk. If you distribute your application to run in a network environment, instruct your users to copy all files from each disk in the distribution set to the same directory on the network and then run the setup program in this directory from each workstation.

✦ Reinstalling your application with the custom setup program fails if the user has performed a Maintenance Removal of Workgroup Administrator. A user can do this by rerunning the setup program and deselecting the Workgroup Administrator component (which is discussed later in this chapter). If a user removes the Workgroup Administrator component and attempts to reinstall your Access runtime application, the installation fails. Attempting to run the setup program again after the failure results in a successful installation.

Tip   You can prevent end users from removing the Workgroup Administrator component by setting the component to Hidden on the Components page of the Setup Wizard. This setting is discussed later in this chapter.

The Package Wizard is unable to use exclusively locked files. If you try to add a file in the wizard that is exclusively locked by another user or another application, the wizard responds with an application-defined or object-defined error. When users trigger this error, Access cancels the creation of your custom setup program disk images. When creating disk images with the Package Wizard, you should close all possible applications in order to avoid potential lock conflicts.

Using the Package Wizard to create distribution disks

The Package Wizard makes it easy for you to create the necessary .cab and .msi files and setup programs for your application. Like other wizards, the Package Wizard prompts you for information so that it can create the exact configuration that you want.

To start the Package Wizard, simply select Start ➪ All Programs ➪ Microsoft Office ➪ Microsoft Office Access 2003 Developer Extensions ➪ Package Wizard from Windows. You may have placed your Developer Extensions in another location and may have to find where they are. Figure 39-8 shows how to start the Package Wizard.

On the CD-ROM   The Package Wizard will be used to package the Access Auto Auctions.mdb. You will need to have it available for doing this part of the chapter.

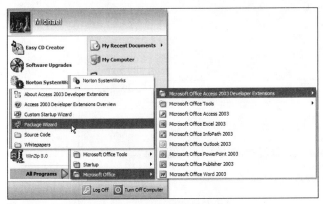

Figure 39-8: Starting the Package Wizard.

After you have loaded the Package Wizard, you are ready to begin the process of creating a setup routine for your application. Follow these steps to package the Access Auto Auctions database:

1. Start the Package Wizard from the Start button in Windows.

   The first time you run it, the Welcome screen is displayed. You can check the Skip the welcome screen check box to stop it from displaying in the future.

2. Click the Next button in the Welcome Screen to go to Step 1 of 7.

3. Accept the Create a new template radio button choice and click the Next button to move to Step 2 of 7.

4. On this screen (2 of 7), under the Installation Options section (top half of screen), select the File to package field and find the Access Auto Auctions.mdb file by clicking on the Browse ... button to the right of the field. After you find and select the Access Auto Auctions.mdb, you will be returned to this screen.

5. In the Installation Options section, accept the default Root installation folder: of Program Files and type in AccessAutoAuctions in the Installation subfolder: field.

   If you want to include the Runtime files, check the check box for this option.

6. Drop to the Output Options section, and specify a Destination for files generated by this wizard: *.

7. Make sure both of the check boxes are checked: Compress install files into a cab file and Embed the cab file in the setup msi.

   At this point, your screen should look similar to the one shown in Figure 39-9.

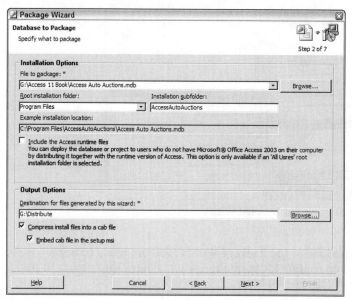

Figure 39-9: The second of seven screens for the Package Wizard.

8. Click the Next button.

9. On the Step 3 of 7 screen, select the Icon named MtnScene.ico or another icon to be used in the package.

10. Click the Next button.

This takes you to the fourth screen. Here, you can specify any other files or registry keys that you would like to install.

11. Click the Next button again to skip this screen.

12. On Step 5 of 7, you must enter a value for the following fields: [General Properties] Product Name: and Install Language:. [Featured Information] Feature Title: and Feature Description:. You can use the values shown in Figure 39-10.

Notice that you can also specify an EULA and two image files.

13. Click on the Next button.

14. You are now on the Step 6 of 7 screen and must fill in the following fields: Publisher, Product Version, and Title [Windows Explorer "Properties" Information]. Figure 39-11 shows the sixth screen with values added. You can add these values or the values you want to add.

15. Click the Next button to move to the final screen.

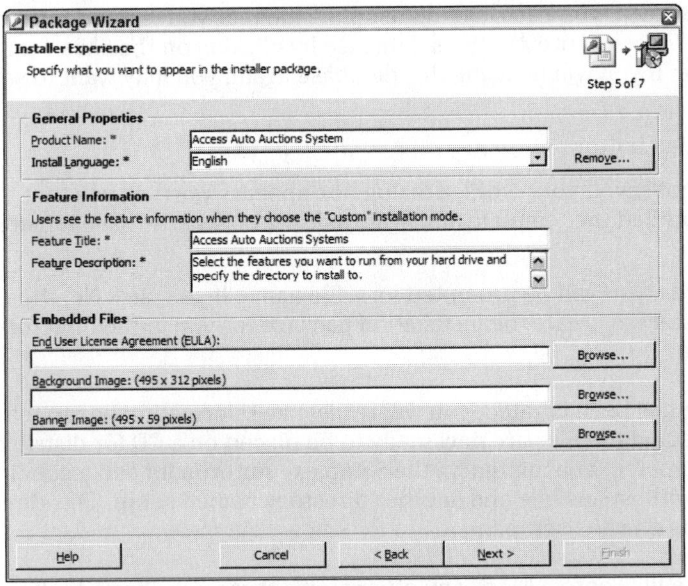

Figure 39-10: The fifth of seven screens for the Package Wizard.

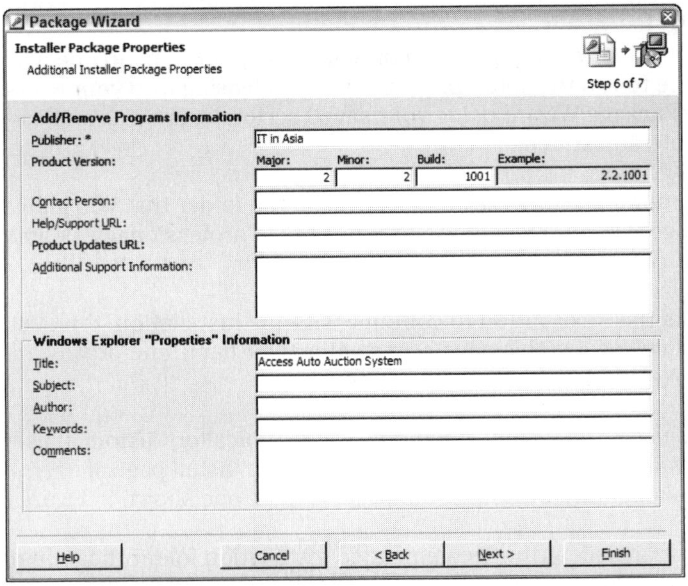

Figure 39-11: The sixth of seven screens for the Package Wizard.

16. On this last screen, you can save the template file that you created for distributing the Access Auto Auctions database by clicking on the Save Template As . . . button. If you will be using this database again, you may want to save your work.

17. Click the Finish button.

If you have not saved your work, a dialog box appears warning you that you have modified the template and again asks if you want to save it before continuing.

If you click Yes, you will be prompted for a file name. If you click No, the system will start to create the installation package for you in the directory you specified.

When the package has been created, you will receive an information box to tell you that it has finished and the files are now ready to be placed on a CD for distribution. The package has created, at a minimum, the Setup.exe Autorun.inf and a subdirectory named Files with an .msi file and another directory named setup. This directory setup contains one file: setup.ini.

You can copy these files onto a CD or any other media that you will use to distribute your application system.

Testing the setup program

Whenever you create a new setup program or make changes to an old one, you should take the time to run the setup program before releasing it to your users. When you run the Package Wizard using your saved scripts, it is quick and easy to make any last minute adjustments.

To run the setup program, locate the Setup.exe file in the folder that you indicated to use in the Package Wizard. When you run Setup.exe, a professional welcome screen displays, as shown in Figure 39-12.

After the user clicks the Next button to continue with the installation, the Customer Information page displays. On this page, users enter their name and organization and then click the Next button to move to the next page.

The next page asks users the type of setup they want: Typical or Custom. If users select Typical, they are immediately taken to the Ready to Install page. If users select Custom, they are taken to the Custom Setup page, like the one shown in Figure 39-13.

On this page, users can accept the recommended installation folder that you designated in the Package Wizard, or they can select Browse to choose another folder.

When ready, users select the Next button to move to the Ready to Install page. Then, users click the Install button to install the application.

The setup program confirms that the installation has been successfully completed.

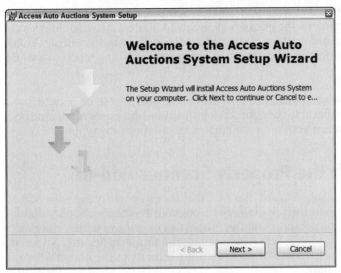

Figure 39-12: The setup program starts with a welcome and a warning about shared files.

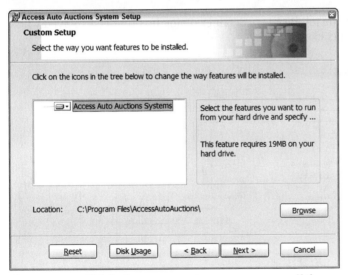

Figure 39-13: This is the custom setup page users see if they request Custom setup.

The Package Wizard makes it easy to create a setup routine for any Access application. It virtually eliminates the guesswork involved in identifying all the files that an application needs in order to run correctly. Additionally, it automatically builds a professional installation interface that adds that final finishing touch to a well-built application.

Although deciding what to distribute to your users and how to distribute it requires some time and considerable thought, taking this time and energy to learn the Package Wizard enables you to create perfect installations every time!

Working with the Property Scanner Add-In

In addition to the Package Wizard, the ADE includes a Property Scanner Add-In tool. This tool lets developers search globally throughout the Access application for a custom string. The tool searches all the properties or code in tables, queries, forms, reports, and modules. When completed, the Property Scanner Add-In displays a search results list and lets the user jump directly to the object where the custom string was found.

You access the Property Scanner Add-In by selecting Tools ➪ Add-Ins ➪ Property Scanner from the menu.

Figure 39-14 shows the full Property Scanner dialog box that is displayed when the Advanced button is clicked.

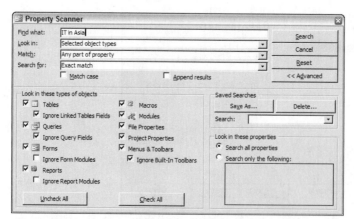

Figure 39-14: The Property Scanner dialog box is activated.

Notice that it is being used to find the value IT in Asia. To find all instances of this value, the user clicks the Search button and Access finds all occurrences, activating a display window showing a record for each value found.

✦   ✦   ✦

Appendixes and Reference Material

Access 2003 Specifications

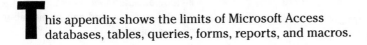

This appendix shows the limits of Microsoft Access databases, tables, queries, forms, reports, and macros.

Microsoft Access Database Specifications

Databases

Attribute	Maximum
MDB file size	2GB, minus space needed for system objects (because your database can include attached tables in multiple files, its total size is limited only by available storage capacity)
Number of objects in a database	32,768
Number of Modules	1,000
Number of characters in object names	64
Number of characters in a password	14
Number of characters in a user name or group name	20
Number of concurrent users	255

Tables

Attribute	Maximum
Number of characters in a table name	64
Number of characters in a field name	64
Number of fields in a record or table	255
Number of open tables	2,048, including tables opened by Microsoft Access internally
Table size	2GB (minus space needed for system objects)
Number of characters in a Text field	255

Attribute	Maximum
Number of characters in a Memo field	65,535 when entering data through the user interface; 1GB when entering data programmatically
Size of OLE object field	1GB
Number of indexes in a record or table	32
Number of fields in an index	10
Number of characters in a validation message	255
Number of characters in a validation rule	2048
Number of characters in a table or field description	255
Number of characters in a record	2,000 (excludes Memo and OLE Object fields)
Number of characters in a field property setting	255

Queries

Attribute	Maximum
Number of tables in a query	32
Number of enforced relationships	32 per table, minus indexes that are on the table for the fields or combinations of fields that are not involved in the relationship
Number of fields in a recordset	255
Dynaset size	1GB
Sort limit	255 characters in one or more fields
Number of sorted fields in a query	10
Number of levels of nested queries	50
Number of characters in a cell of the design grid	1,024
Number of ANDs in a WHERE or HAVING clause	99
Number of characters in a SQL statement	64,000 (approximately)

Forms and Reports

Attribute	Maximum
Number of characters in a label	2,048
Number of characters in a text box	65,535
Form or report width	22 inches (55.87 cm)
Section height	22 inches (55.87 cm)
Height of all sections plus section	200 inches (508 cm) headers in design view
Number of levels of nested forms or reports	7 (form-subform-subform)
Number of fields/expressions you can sort or group on (reports only)	10
Number of headers and footers in a report	1 report header/footer; 1 page header/footer; 10 group headers/footers
Number of printed pages in a report	65,536
Number of characters in an SQL statement that is the Recordsource or Rowsource property of a form, Report, or control (both .mdb and .adp)	32,750
Number of controls or sections you can add over the lifetime of the form or report	754

Macros

Attribute	Maximum
Number of actions in a macro	999
Number of characters in a condition	255
Number of characters in a comment	255
Number of characters in an action argument	255

Access Projects Specifications

Access Project	
Attribute	*Maximum*
Number of objects in a Microsoft Access project (.adp)	32,768
Modules (including forms and report modules)	1,000
Number of characters in an object name	64
Number of columns in a table	250 (MS SQL Server 6.5) 1,024 (MS SQL Server 7.0 and 2000)

Forms and Reports	
Attribute	*Maximum*
Number of characters in a label	2,048
Number of characters in a text box	65,535
Form or report width	22 inches (55.87 cm)
Section height	22 inches (55.87 cm)
Height of all sections plus section headers in design view	200 inches (508 cm)
Number of levels of nested forms or reports	7 (form-subform-subform)
Number of fields/expressions you can sort or group on	10 (reports only)
Number of headers and footers in a report	1 report header/footer; 1 page header/footer; 10 group headers/footers
Number of printed pages in a report	65,536
Number of characters in an SQL statement that is the Recordsource or Rowsource property of a form, Report, or control (both .mdb and .adp)	32,750
Number of controls or sections you can add over the lifetime of the form or report	754

Macros	
Attribute	*Maximum*
Number of actions in a macro	999
Number of characters in a condition	255
Number of characters in a comment	255
Number of characters in an action argument	255

Microsoft SQL Server database

Maximum capacity specifications can be found in the SQL Server documentation.

Access Auto Auction Tables

The Access Auto Auctions database file is made up of 13 tables. There are six primary data tables, five lookup tables, and two support tables.

The primary data tables contain data that is used and updated daily by users of the system, such as sales and inventory information. The lookup tables also contain data that is updated on a less regular basis, such as contact types, product categories, and tax rates. Support tables are used by the system itself to display menus or preference items used to set up the company.

The primary data tables are as follows:

- ✦ tblSales
- ✦ tblSalesLineItems
- ✦ tblSalesPayments
- ✦ tblContacts
- ✦ tblContactLog
- ✦ tblProducts

The lookup tables are as follows:

- ✦ tblCustomerTypes
- ✦ tblTaxRates
- ✦ tblPaymentType
- ✦ tblSalesperson
- ✦ tblCategories

The support tables are as follows:

- ✦ tblCompanySetup
- ✦ tblSwitchboardItems

This appendix displays a database diagram of the 11 primary and lookup tables and the relations between them. Figures of each of the tables are shown in the Table Design window.

Table Structures

Figure B-1 diagrams the Access Auto Auctions tables in the database container.

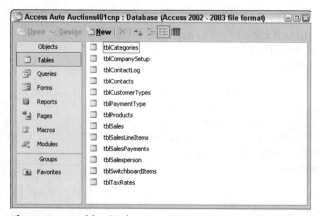

Figure B-1: Tables in the Access Auto Auctions database container.

Figure B-2 diagrams the Access Auto Auctions database relationships.

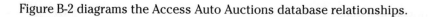
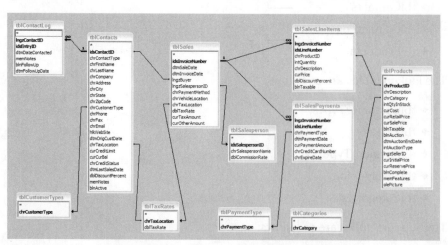

Figure B-2: The database diagram showing tables and relationships.

Figures B-3 through B-14 show the structures of the primary tables in the AccessAutoAuctions.mdb database file.

tblSales : Table	
Field Name	Data Type
🔑▶ idsInvoiceNumber	AutoNumber
dtmSaleDate	Date/Time
dtmInvoiceDate	Date/Time
lngzBuyer	Number
lngzSalespersonID	Number
chrPaymentMethod	Text
chrVehicleLocation	Text
chrTaxLocation	Text
dblTaxRate	Number
curTaxAmount	Currency
curOtherAmount	Currency

Figure B-3: The tblSales table.

tblSalesLineItems : Table	
Field Name	Data Type
🔑▶ lngzInvoiceNumber	Number
🔑 idsLineNumber	AutoNumber
chrProductID	Text
intQuantity	Number
chrDescription	Text
curPrice	Currency
dblDiscountPercent	Number
blnTaxable	Yes/No

Figure B-4: The tblSalesLineItems table.

tblSalesPayments : Table	
Field Name	Data Type
🔑▶ lngzInvoiceNumber	Number
🔑 idsLineNumber	AutoNumber
chrPaymentType	Text
dtmPaymentDate	Date/Time
curPaymentAmount	Currency
chrCreditCardNumber	Text
chrExpireDate	Text

Figure B-5: The tblSalesPayments table.

tblContacts : Table	
Field Name	Data Type
🔑▶ idsContactID	AutoNumber
chrContactType	Text
chrFirstName	Text
chrLastName	Text
chrCompany	Text
chrAddress	Text
chrCity	Text
chrState	Text
chrZipCode	Text
chrCustomerType	Text
chrPhone	Text
chrFax	Text
chrEmail	Text
hlkWebSite	Text
dtmOrigCustDate	Date/Time
chrTaxLocation	Text
curCreditLimit	Currency
curCurBal	Currency
chrCreditStatus	Text
dtmLastSalesDate	Date/Time
dblDiscountPercent	Number
memNotes	Memo
blnActive	Yes/No

Figure B-6: The tblContacts table.

tblContactLog : Table	
Field Name	Data Type
lngzContactID	Number
idsEntryID	AutoNumber
dtmDateContacted	Date/Time
memNotes	Memo
blnFollowUp	Yes/No
dtmFollowUpDate	Date/Time

Figure B-7: The tblContactLog table.

tblProducts : Table	
Field Name	Data Type
chrProductID	Text
chrDescription	Text
chrCategory	Text
intQtyInStock	Number
curCost	Currency
curRetailPrice	Currency
curSalePrice	Currency
blnTaxable	Yes/No
blnAuction	Yes/No
dtmAuctionEndDate	Date/Time
intAuctionType	Number
lngzSellerID	Number
curInitialPrice	Currency
curReservePrice	Currency
blnComplete	Yes/No
memFeatures	Memo
olePicture	OLE Object

Figure B-8: The tblProducts table.

tblCustomerTypes : Table	
Field Name	Data Type
chrCustomerType	Text

Figure B-9: The tblCustomerTypes table.

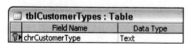

tblTaxRates : Table	
Field Name	Data Type
chrTaxLocation	Text
dblTaxRate	Number

Figure B-10: The tblTaxRates table.

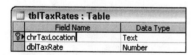

tblPaymentType : Table	
Field Name	Data Type
chrPaymentType	Text

Figure B-11: The tblPaymentType table.

tblSalesperson : Table	
Field Name	Data Type
idsSalespersonID	AutoNumber
chrSalespersonName	Text
dblCommissionRate	Number

Figure B-12: The tblSalesperson table.

tblCategories : Table

Field Name	Data Type
🔑▶ chrCategory	Text

Figure B-13: The tblCategories table.

tblCompanySetup : Table

Field Name	Data Type
🔑▶ OptionName	Text
Value	Text
Category	Text
User	Text
Description	Text

Figure B-14: The tblCompanySetup table.

✦　　✦　　✦

Using the CD-ROM Included with the Book

This appendix provides you with information on the contents of the CD that accompanies this book. For the latest and greatest information, please refer to the ReadMe file located at the root of the CD.

This appendix provides information on the following topics:

+ System Requirements
+ Using the CD
+ Files and software on the CD
+ Troubleshooting

System Requirements

Make sure that your computer meets the minimum system requirements listed in this section. If your computer doesn't match up to most of these requirements, you may have a problem using the contents of the CD.

You must have Windows XP or Windows 2000 or later. Microsoft Office 2003 only works with these operating systems.

✦ PC with a Pentium processor running at 120 Mhz or faster

✦ At least 128MB of total RAM installed on your computer; for best performance, we recommend at least 256MB or more

✦ A CD-ROM drive

Office 2003 Specific Requirements:

✦ PC with Pentium III, IV or Pentinum M recommended

✦ Microsoft Windows 2000 with Service Pack 3 or Windows XP or later operating system

Using the CD

To install the items from the CD to your hard drive, follow these steps:

1. Insert the CD into your computer's CD-ROM drive.

2. A window appears displaying the License Agreement. Press Accept to continue. Another window appears with the following buttons (which are explained in greater detail in the next section):

   Access 2003 Bible: Click this button for options to install all of the example files specific to the book and to view an eBook version of the book.

   Super Bible: Click this button to view an electronic version of the *Office 2003 Super Bible*, along with any author-created materials from the Super Bible, such as templates and sample files.

   Bonus Software: Click this button to view the list and install the supplied third-party software.

   Related Links: Click this button to open a hyperlinked page of Web sites.

   Other Resources: Click this button to access other Office-related products that you might find useful.

Files and Software on the CD

The following sections provide more details about the software and other materials available on the CD.

Example files for *Access 2003 Bible*

These files will be installed into a directory named Access 2003 Bible or you can choose any directory to install these files. Below this directory will be 39 subdirectories named Chapter 01, Chapter 02 ... through Chapter 39. Each subdirectory will contain all of the files necessary to follow the examples in each chapter. Some chapter directories in the beginning of the book contain no files. Most chapters contains a start file to begin the chapter with such as CHAP03Start.mdb while some have both a start and end file so you can follow the examples or see the completed examples in files such as CHAP04End.mdb. Many chapters also use additional database files, graphics, document files or help files as found in each chapter subdirectory and explained at the beginning of each chapter. You will also find links on the CD to a Wiley web site to download any later corrections to the material. You can also go to www.databasecreations.com which is maintained by the authors where you can also download corrected files, demos and free software specifically related to Microsoft Access.

eBook version of *Access 2003 Bible*

The complete text of the book you hold in your hands is provided on the CD in Adobe's Portable Document Format (PDF). You can read and quickly search the content of this PDF file by using Adobe's Acrobat Reader, also included on the CD.

eBook version of *Office 2003 Super Bible*

The *Super Bible* is an eBook PDF file made up of select chapters pulled from the individual Office 2003 *Bible* titles. This eBook also includes some original and exclusive content found only in this *Super Bible*. The products that make up the Microsoft Office 2003 suite have been created to work hand-in-hand. Consequently, Wiley has created this *Super Bible* to help you master some of the most common features of each of the component products and to learn about some of their interoperability features as well. This *Super Bible* consists of over 500 pages of content to showcase how Microsoft Office 2003 components work together.

Bonus software

The CD contains software distributed in various forms: shareware, freeware, GNU software, trials, demos, and evaluation versions. The following list explains how these software versions differ:

✦ **Shareware programs:** Fully functional, trial versions of copyrighted programs. If you like particular programs, you can register with their authors for a nominal fee and receive licenses, enhanced versions, and technical support.

✦ **Freeware programs:** Copyrighted games, applications, and utilities that are free for personal use. Unlike shareware, these programs do not require a fee or provide technical support.

✦ **GNU software:** Software governed by its own license, which is included inside the folder of the GNU product. See the GNU license for more details.

✦ **Trial, demo, or evaluation versions:** Software usually limited either by time or functionality, such as not permitting you to save projects. Some trial versions are very sensitive to system date changes. If you alter your computer's date, the programs may "time out" and will no longer be functional.

Software highlights

Here are descriptions of just a few of the programs available on the CD:

Database Creations, Inc. — Business!, POSitively Business, EZ Access Developer Tools Suite, appBuilder, Access Project Security Manager(APSM), Inventory Manager with Barcoding, Report Manager Professional, appWatcher, and Search Manager Professional.

Business! Accounting Demo — **Database Creations** — www.databasecreations. com: Business! is the most popular accounting software available for Microsoft Access users today. The product is fully customizable and includes all source code. It includes all typical accounting functions including sales, customers, A/R, purchases, suppliers, A/P, inventory, banking, general ledger, fixed assets, and features multi-company accounting for any size business. Priced under $1,000 for a multi-user LAN version, it is one of the best values for small businesses. For developers, a version is available with inexpensive distribution rights for around $2,500. Business received 4 stars from *CPA Software News* for best mid-range accounting software. It also won the Microsoft Access Advisor reader's choice award for best accounting system. View more information on this product at www.databasecreations.com.

POSitively Business Demo — **Database Creations** — www.databasecreations. com: POSitively Business is an add-on system for Business!. It adds point of sale functionality and includes all source code. The product includes a mouse-less point of sale interface, security, administrative and setup options, cashiers, cash counter, sales analyzer, barcoding and much more. The software works with standard point of sale hardware including cash drawers, light poles, hand-held scanners, receipt printers and credit card scanning keyboards. Pricing is currently $795 for one register and discounts are available for multi registers. You can also purchase a point of sale hardware bundle which includes a cash drawer, receipt printer, credit card scanning keyboard, laser scanner, light pole and bar code font. Call for latest pricing. Developer versions of POSitively Business with royalty free distribution rights are also available. We also have a reseller program for resellers and VAR's. Call us or visit www.positivelybusiness.com to learn more.

EZ Access Developer Tools Suite — Database Creations — www.database creations.com: The EZ Access Developer Tools is specifically designed for Access developers to help them create great Access applications. The suite consists of eight separate products. Each can be easily integrated into your application to provide new functions in a fraction of the time it would take you to create them yourself. These products will save you hundreds of hours of development time. Think of them as a library of over 100 pre-designed, pre-programmed interfaces you can legally steal and use with your applications royalty free!

Read each of the embedded reviewers guides in the demo for a complete overview of each product. Currently, you can purchase the entire EZ Access Developer Tools Suite for only $395. View additional information on this product from www.databasecreations.com.

The eight EZ Access Developer Tools that comprise the Suite include:

- ✦ EZ Report Manager
- ✦ EZ Search Manager
- ✦ EZ Support Manager
- ✦ EZ Extensions
- ✦ EZ Security Manager
- ✦ EZ File Manager
- ✦ EZ Application Manager
- ✦ EZ Controls

appBuilder — Database Creations — www.databasecreations.com: The appBuilder provides a way for Access developers to create an application shell when building custom applications. There are two ways to use the appBuilder. Start with our application shell and add your objects (tables, queries, reports, forms, modules, etc..) or use our Application Generator Wizard to choose, configure and automatically add the components to your Access application. The Wizard guides you through the process of selecting over 40 different features and lets you add your own custom text and graphics. Then, add your tables, queries, forms and reports to the application switchboard you have selected. We even include a second wizard to help you build flexible menu systems for your application.

With the appBuilder you receive:

- ✦ appBuilder including 40 components from the EZ Access Developer Tools Suite
- ✦ Application Generator Wizard

✦ Menu Editor Wizard

✦ On-line Help

✦ FREE Check Writer Application with Source Code

✦ Five additional Switchboards not found in the Suite

✦ Source code included

✦ Use Royalty Free in your applications

Purchase the appBuilder for only $495 or for $595, purchase both the appBuilder and EZ Access Developer Tools Suite.

Access Project Security Manager — Database Creations — www.database creations.com: If you use Access 2003 or Access 2003 Projects with the new MSDE or SQL Server 2000, there is no security provided for forms or reports. You only have the limited data security provided by MSDE and SQL Server 7 and no user security. With the Access Project Security Manager, you can easily add your own security. This avoids having to create separate application front ends for each group of users.

Purchase the Access Project Security Manager for $299 for a single developer/single application. Multi developer/applications and site licenses are also available. Visit www.databasecreations.com for more information and pricing.

Inventory Manager 4 with Barcode Modules — Database Creations — www. databasecreations.com: The Inventory Manager is an open source code, fully customizable stand-alone inventory management program for Microsoft Access. This product allows you to enter inventory items, enter suppliers and warehouses and includes a simple chart of accounts and general ledger. Use the Inventory Manager stand-alone or integrated with existing purchasing or sales applications you may have developed. The demo also includes a demo version of the optional barcode modules, which allow you to print barcodes and adjust inventory quantities in stock or transfer goods between warehouses.

Purchase Inventory Manager 4 for $595 for a multi-user version or for $995 with the bar code modules. A royalty free developer version is also available. Please visit www.databasecreations.com for more information and current pricing.

PenSoft Payroll — Pensoft Corporation — www.pensoft.com: PenSoft Payroll from PenSoft Corp. is a stand-alone payroll package for small to medium businesses. It interfaces with Yes! I Can Run My Business to provide complete employee, hour, tax, deduction, and benefit processing. The software contains all tax tables for the United States. For more information and pricing, please visit www.databasecreations.com.

Report Manager Professional — Database Creations — www.databasecreations. com: The Report Manager Professional is a tool for managing and printing reports you create in Microsoft Access. All source code is included and you can use the interfaces royalty free in your applications.

Search Manager Professional — Database Creations — www.databasecreations. com: The Search Manager Professional is a collection of powerful search interfaces and search engines for Microsoft Access applications. All source code is included and you can use the interfaces and search engines royalty free in your applications.

Comprehensive list of software

Here is a list of all the products available on the CD. For more information and a description of each product, see the CD Interface Bonus Software section of the CD.

Acc Compact	Access Form Resizer	Access Image Albums
Access Property Editor	Access to VB Object Converter	AccessBooks
AccessBooks Updater	AccessViewer	Acrobat Reader
Advanced Office Password Recovery	All-in-1 Personal Organizer	appBuilder
Application Builder/ Application Generator	appWatcher	Business Forms Library Sampler
c:JAM	Camtasia Studio	Capture Express
Change Management System	Check Writer	ClipMate
Code 128 Fonts demo with VBA	COM Explorer	CompareDataWiz 2002
CompareWiz 2002	CONTACT Sage	Cool Combo Box Techniques
Data Analysis	Data Flow Manager, Adv Ed	Data Flow Manager, Stnd Ed
Data Wiz	Database	Database Browser Plus
Database Password Sniffer	DataDict	Datahouse
DataMoxie	DataWiz 2002	DB Companion
DBSync	DeskTop.VBA	Document Management
Drag-N-Dropper	DynaZIP MAX	Excel Import Assistant
Excel Link	EZ Access Developer's Tool Suite	EZ File Manager Sampler

Filter Builder	Fort Knox	Fundraising Mentor
Gantt Chart Builder (Access)	GuruNet	InspireApps.com Manager
Inventory Manager with Barcoding	Jeff-Net Access Utility	Judy's TenKey
Keyboard Express	King James Access Bible	LASsie
Mach5 Mailer	Macro Express	Macro Magic
Mdb2txt	Mouse Over Effects	OfficeRecovery Enterprise
OfficeSpy	Outcome XP	Pendragon Forms
Picture Builder Wizard	Positively Business	PrettyCode.Print
Procedure Creator	Project Security Manager	PROMODAG StoreLog
Recover My Files	Registry Crawler	ReplaceWiz 2002
Responsive Time Logger	RFFlow	Rovoscape ActiveCandy
Schedule XP	Screen Capture	Search Manager Pro
Secrets Keeper	Selector	ShortKeys
ShrinkerStretcher	SimpleRegistry Control	Smart Login
SmartBoardXP	SmartList To Go	SnagIt
SPEED Ferret	Splitter for Access	Spreadsheet Assistant
Summary Wizard	Surgical Strike	Table Lynx
TeeChart Pro ActiveX Control	Turbo Browser	UnTools
User Manager	VBToolBox	V-Tools
WBS Chart Pro	WebMerge	WinACE
WinRAR	WinZIP	Word Link
X2Net WebCompiler	Xbooks	Yes I Can Run My Business
Zip Code Companion	ZipCode Lookup	

Related Links

Check out this page for links to all the third-party software vendors included on the CD, plus links to other vendors and resources that can help you work more productively with Office 2003.

Other Resources

This page provides you with some additional handy Office-related products.

ReadMe file

The ReadMe contains the complete descriptions of every piece of bonus software on the CD, as well as other important information about the CD.

Troubleshooting

If you have difficulty installing or using any of the materials on the companion CD, try the following solutions:

✦ **Turn off any anti-virus software that you may have running.** Installers sometimes mimic virus activity and can make your computer incorrectly believe that it is being infected by a virus. (Be sure to turn the anti-virus software back on later.)

✦ **Close all running programs.** The more programs you're running, the less memory is available to other programs. Installers also typically update files and programs; if you keep other programs running, installation may not work properly.

✦ **Reference the ReadMe:** Please refer to the ReadMe file located at the root of the CD-ROM for the latest product information at the time of publication.

If you still have trouble with the CD, please call the Customer Care phone number: (800) 762-2974. Outside the United States, call 1 (317) 572-3994. You can also contact Customer Service via the web at www.wiley.com/techsupport. Wiley Publishing, Inc. will provide technical support only for installation and other general quality control items; for technical support on the applications themselves, consult the program's vendor.

✦ ✦ ✦

Using Standard Naming Conventions

As you can imagine, you can use quite a few variables in a program. This can make it difficult to remember what all of your variables are used for. The same is true of objects in your Access databases, such as tables, forms, and reports. As the number of objects and variables increases, so does the inherent complexity of the programs that use those objects and variables.

Part of the solution to this problem is to use descriptive names for both objects and variables. This is only part of the solution, however. The other part involves using some sort of standard naming convention so you can immediately understand the type of data referred to by a variable or object name.

For professional developers, adhering to a standard makes it easier to maintain other developer's programs. In development projects with multiple programmers, naming conventions can make it easier to understand what each object or variable is used for, the data type of variables or other critical information needed to properly code and debug a program efficiently

However, for a casual or power user or even the novice developer, adhering to naming conventions can be a less than productive experience. Where naming conventions are supposed to make programs easier to read and maintain because they instantly tell the VBA developer, they can do the exact opposite.

Figure D-1 shows two Microsoft Access database containers. The database container on top uses a standard naming convention prefix. The database container on the bottom uses no special naming convention for the table objects. Which do you think is easier to read?

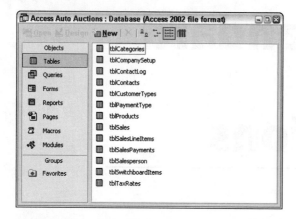

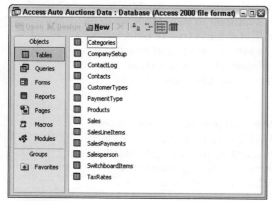

Figure D-1: Object naming conventions

Tip

There are several competing naming conventions used for Microsoft Access. One is the *Leszynski Naming Conventions* (LNC) developed by Stan Leszynski (www.kwery.com) and the other is the *Reddick Naming Conventions* developed by Greg Reddick. The tables in the remaining portion of this chapter provide an overview of these standards. If you wish to see the entire detailed naming conventions, you can view the file ReddickNamingConventions.pdf on the example CD in this book.

Both of these naming conventions suggest using prefixes for several different types of Microsoft Access items – objects (tables, queries, forms, reports, data access pages, macros, modules), table fields, form and report controls, ADO and DAO recordset objects, and variables.

Microsoft Access database object naming conventions

These naming conventions suggest using leading tags also known as prefixes. This means that the naming convention precedes the standard business name such as tblProducts.

The standard Microsoft Access object names are shown in Table D-1.

Table D-1 Object Naming Conventions		
Prefix	*Object*	*Example*
tbl	Table	tblProducts
qry	Query	qryActiveProducts
frm	Form	frmProducts
rpt	Report	rptProducts
mcr	Macro	mcrAutoexec
mod	Module	modSalesFunctions
cls	Class Module	clsSetup
fsub	Subform	fsubProductsDisplayAll
rsub	Subreport	rsubSalesLineItems

Microsoft Access table field naming conventions

Another portion of the naming conventions covers fields in tables. Figure D-2 shows the tblSales table with and without these prefixes. Table D-2 shows these table-field naming conventions.

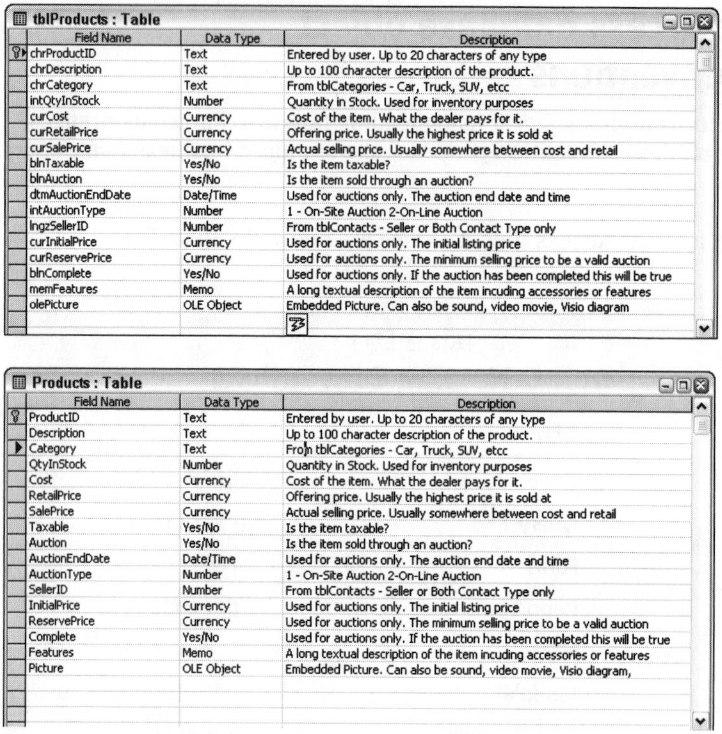

tblProducts : Table

Field Name	Data Type	Description
chrProductID	Text	Entered by user. Up to 20 characters of any type
chrDescription	Text	Up to 100 character description of the product.
chrCategory	Text	From tblCategories - Car, Truck, SUV, etcc
intQtyInStock	Number	Quantity in Stock. Used for inventory purposes
curCost	Currency	Cost of the item. What the dealer pays for it.
curRetailPrice	Currency	Offering price. Usually the highest price it is sold at
curSalePrice	Currency	Actual selling price. Usually somewhere between cost and retail
blnTaxable	Yes/No	Is the item taxable?
blnAuction	Yes/No	Is the item sold through an auction?
dtmAuctionEndDate	Date/Time	Used for auctions only. The auction end date and time
intAuctionType	Number	1 - On-Site Auction 2-On-Line Auction
lngzSellerID	Number	From tblContacts - Seller or Both Contact Type only
curInitialPrice	Currency	Used for auctions only. The initial listing price
curReservePrice	Currency	Used for auctions only. The minimum selling price to be a valid auction
blnComplete	Yes/No	Used for auctions only. If the auction has been completed this will be true
memFeatures	Memo	A long textual description of the item incuding accessories or features
olePicture	OLE Object	Embedded Picture. Can also be sound, video movie, Visio diagram

Products : Table

Field Name	Data Type	Description
ProductID	Text	Entered by user. Up to 20 characters of any type
Description	Text	Up to 100 character description of the product.
Category	Text	From tblCategories - Car, Truck, SUV, etcc
QtyInStock	Number	Quantity in Stock. Used for inventory purposes
Cost	Currency	Cost of the item. What the dealer pays for it.
RetailPrice	Currency	Offering price. Usually the highest price it is sold at
SalePrice	Currency	Actual selling price. Usually somewhere between cost and retail
Taxable	Yes/No	Is the item taxable?
Auction	Yes/No	Is the item sold through an auction?
AuctionEndDate	Date/Time	Used for auctions only. The auction end date and time
AuctionType	Number	1 - On-Site Auction 2-On-Line Auction
SellerID	Number	From tblContacts - Seller or Both Contact Type only
InitialPrice	Currency	Used for auctions only. The initial listing price
ReservePrice	Currency	Used for auctions only. The minimum selling price to be a valid auction
Complete	Yes/No	Used for auctions only. If the auction has been completed this will be true
Features	Memo	A long textual description of the item incuding accessories or features
Picture	OLE Object	Embedded Picture. Can also be sound, video movie, Visio diagram,

Figure D-2: Table field naming conventions

Table D-2
Table Field Naming Conventions

Prefix	*Object*
`idn`	Autonumber (Random)
`idr`	Autonumber (Replication ID)
`ids`	Autonumber (Sequential)
`bin`	Number (Binary)
`byt`	Number (Byte)
`cur`	Currency
`dtm`	Date/Time

Prefix	Object
dbl	Number (dbl)
hlk	Hyperlink
int	Number (Integer)
lngz	Number (Long)
mem	Memo
ole	OLE Object
sng	Number (Single)
chr	Text (Character)
bln	Yes/No (Boolean)

Microsoft Access form/report control naming conventions

Another area covered by naming conventions are control names on forms on reports. These are used whenever you are naming a control on a form or report. Table D-3 shows these conventions.

Table D-3
Form/Report Control Naming Conventions

Prefix	Object
frb	Bound Object frame
cht	Chart (Graph)
chk	Check Box
cbo	Combo Box
cmd	Command Button
ocx	ActiveX Custom Control
det	Detail (section)
gft[*n*]	Footer (group section)
fft	Form footer section

Continued

Table D-3 *(continued)*	
Prefix	**Object**
fhd	Form header section
ghd[*n*]	Header (group section)
hlk	Hyperlink
img	Image
lbl	Label
lin	Line
lst	List Box
opt	Option Button
grp	Option Group
pge	Page (tab)
brk	Page break
pft	Page Footer (section)
phd	Page Header (section)
shp	Rectangle
rft	Report Footer (section)
rhd	Report Header (section)
sec	Section
sub	Subform/Subreport
tab	Tab Control
txt	Text Box
tgl	Toggle Button
fru	Unbound Object Frame

Microsoft Access Visual Basic variable naming conventions

The final major area covered by the standard Access naming conventions are Visual Basic data variables. Table D-4 shows these conventions.

Table D-4
Visual Basic Data Variable Naming Conventions

Prefix	Object
bln	Boolean
byt	Byte
ccc	Conditional Compilation Constant (#xxx)
Cur	Currency
dtm	Date
dbl	Double
err	Error
int	Integer
lng	Long
obj	Object
sng	Single
str	String
typ	User-Defined Type
var	Variant

There are many more tags that are defined by the standard naming conventions. In fact, there are close to one thousand different tags. Professional developers use these standards to varying degrees. Some ignore them for anything but data variables while others ignore them completely. Others try their best to follow them religiously. You will have to make your own decisions.

Are naming conventions really necessary in Access?

The human mind is a wonderful thing. It can provide wondrous creative solutions to problems. It can turn manual nightmares into automated algorithmic processes. But give the human mind something just a little foreign and processing slows to a crawl as the brain's disruptive subroutine circuitry is invoked with a nearly endless loop. Having to filter out the characters that precede the business names makes it much more difficult to read and understand the purpose of the application.

The same could be true for variable and field naming in tables. Imagine if written English words required naming conventions. Perhaps all predicates could be prefixed with `pre`, verbs with `vrb`, nouns with `nou`, adverbs with `adv`, adjectives with `adj`, and so on. The sentence below:

```
The Quick Brown Fox Jumps Over The Big Computer
```

would become:

```
preThe adjQuick adjBrown nouFox vrbJumps advOver preThe adjBig
nouComputer
```

Though it can be read, it makes it much harder to understand the words as you first must filter out the prefixes. Only in rare instances would a word be questionable as to its meaning or content. Our experience is far more important than our need to explicitly understand sentence structure or grammar.

How does a professional developer know that zip codes, phone numbers, and Social Security numbers are almost always defined as text strings? Fields like Salary, Total Expense, or Amount Paid are obviously currency or numeric data types, while Date of Birth or the Last Sale Date is probably always stored as a date data type. This simply takes experience and common sense. This same experience or training lets us all know how to read a sentence with the correct understanding of words, intonation, or grammar.

The bottom line is that sometimes less is more. You have to program in a style that suits you and your environment. While naming conventions can be good, consistency is always better. If you are investing in a set of naming conventions, check a few simple things:

1. Do they make sense? Do they seem like common sense dictated them rather than some committee whose sole purpose was to get something on paper through compromises, endless debate, and finally exhaustion and frustration?

2. Are they endorsed by an international board such as ISO or even Microsoft? Notice the main Microsoft Access sample file named Northwinds.mdb does not use any naming conventions.

✦   ✦   ✦

Index

Continued

Wiley Publishing, Inc.
End-User License Agreement

READ THIS. You should carefully read these terms and conditions before opening the software packet(s) included with this book "Book". This is a license agreement "Agreement" between you and Wiley Publishing, Inc. "WPI". By opening the accompanying software packet(s), you acknowledge that you have read and accept the following terms and conditions. If you do not agree and do not want to be bound by such terms and conditions, promptly return the Book and the unopened software packet(s) to the place you obtained them for a full refund.

1. **License Grant.** WPI grants to you (either an individual or entity) a nonexclusive license to use one copy of the enclosed software program(s) (collectively, the "Software," solely for your own personal or business purposes on a single computer (whether a standard computer or a workstation component of a multi-user network). The Software is in use on a computer when it is loaded into temporary memory (RAM) or installed into permanent memory (hard disk, CD-ROM, or other storage device). WPI reserves all rights not expressly granted herein.

2. **Ownership.** WPI is the owner of all right, title, and interest, including copyright, in and to the compilation of the Software recorded on the disk(s) or CD-ROM "Software Media". Copyright to the individual programs recorded on the Software Media is owned by the author or other authorized copyright owner of each program. Ownership of the Software and all proprietary rights relating thereto remain with WPI and its licensers.

3. **Restrictions On Use and Transfer.**

   (a) You may only (i) make one copy of the Software for backup or archival purposes, or (ii) transfer the Software to a single hard disk, provided that you keep the original for backup or archival purposes. You may not (i) rent or lease the Software, (ii) copy or reproduce the Software through a LAN or other network system or through any computer subscriber system or bulletin-board system, or (iii) modify, adapt, or create derivative works based on the Software.

   (b) You may not reverse engineer, decompile, or disassemble the Software. You may transfer the Software and user documentation on a permanent basis, provided that the transferee agrees to accept the terms and conditions of this Agreement and you retain no copies. If the Software is an update or has been updated, any transfer must include the most recent update and all prior versions.

4. **Restrictions on Use of Individual Programs.** You must follow the individual requirements and restrictions detailed for each individual program in the About the CD-ROM appendix of this Book. These limitations are also contained in the individual license agreements recorded on the Software Media. These limitations may include a requirement that after using the program for a specified period of time, the user must pay a registration fee or discontinue use. By opening the Software packet(s), you will be agreeing to abide by the licenses and restrictions for these individual programs that are detailed in the About the CD-ROM appendix and on the Software Media. None of the material on this Software Media or listed in this Book may ever be redistributed, in original or modified form, for commercial purposes.

5. Limited Warranty.

(a) WPI warrants that the Software and Software Media are free from defects in materials and workmanship under normal use for a period of sixty (60) days from the date of purchase of this Book. If WPI receives notification within the warranty period of defects in materials or workmanship, WPI will replace the defective Software Media.

(b) WPI AND THE AUTHOR(S) OF THE BOOK DISCLAIM ALL OTHER WARRANTIES, EXPRESS OR IMPLIED, INCLUDING WITHOUT LIMITATION IMPLIED WARRANTIES OF MERCHANTABILITY AND FITNESS FOR A PARTICULAR PURPOSE, WITH RESPECT TO THE SOFTWARE, THE PROGRAMS, THE SOURCE CODE CONTAINED THEREIN, AND/OR THE TECHNIQUES DESCRIBED IN THIS BOOK. WPI DOES NOT WARRANT THAT THE FUNCTIONS CONTAINED IN THE SOFTWARE WILL MEET YOUR REQUIREMENTS OR THAT THE OPERATION OF THE SOFTWARE WILL BE ERROR FREE.

(c) This limited warranty gives you specific legal rights, and you may have other rights that vary from jurisdiction to jurisdiction.

6. Remedies.

(a) WPI's entire liability and your exclusive remedy for defects in materials and workmanship shall be limited to replacement of the Software Media, which may be returned to WPI with a copy of your receipt at the following address: Software Media Fulfillment Department, Attn.: Access 2003 Bible, Wiley Publishing, Inc., 10475 Crosspoint Blvd., Indianapolis, IN 46256, or call 1-800-762-2974. Please allow four to six weeks for delivery. This Limited Warranty is void if failure of the Software Media has resulted from accident, abuse, or misapplication. Any replacement Software Media will be warranted for the remainder of the original warranty period or thirty (30) days, whichever is longer.

(b) In no event shall WPI or the author be liable for any damages whatsoever (including without limitation damages for loss of business profits, business interruption, loss of business information, or any other pecuniary loss) arising from the use of or inability to use the Book or the Software, even if WPI has been advised of the possibility of such damages.

(c) Because some jurisdictions do not allow the exclusion or limitation of liability for consequential or incidental damages, the above limitation or exclusion may not apply to you.

7. U.S. Government Restricted Rights.
Use, duplication, or disclosure of the Software for or on behalf of the United States of America, its agencies and/or instrumentalities "U.S. Government" is subject to restrictions as stated in paragraph (c)(1)(ii) of the Rights in Technical Data and Computer Software clause of DFARS 252.227-7013, or subparagraphs (c) (1) and (2) of the Commercial Computer Software - Restricted Rights clause at FAR 52.227-19, and in similar clauses in the NASA FAR supplement, as applicable.

8. General.
This Agreement constitutes the entire understanding of the parties and revokes and supersedes all prior agreements, oral or written, between them and may not be modified or amended except in a writing signed by both parties hereto that specifically refers to this Agreement. This Agreement shall take precedence over any other documents that may be in conflict herewith. If any one or more provisions contained in this Agreement are held by any court or tribunal to be invalid, illegal, or otherwise unenforceable, each and every other provision shall remain in full force and effect.

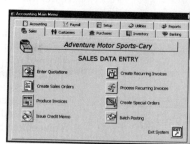
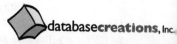